MW00804017

African Folklore

Board of Editorial Consultants

African Folklore

An Encyclopedia

Philip M. Peek and Kwesi Yankah, Editors

Routledge
New York London

Editorial Staff
Development Editor: Kristen Holt
Production Editor: Jeanne Shu
Editorial Assistant: Mary Funchion

Published in 2004 by
Routledge
29 West 35th Street
New York, NY 10001–2299
www.routledge-ny.com

Published in Great Britain by
Routledge
11 New Fetter Lane
London EC4P 4EE
www.routledge.co.uk

Routledge is an imprint of Taylor & Francis Books, Inc.

10 9 8 7 6 5 4 3 2 1

Printed on acid-free, 250-year-life paper.
Manufactured in the United States of America

Library of Congress Cataloging-in-Publication Data

African folklore: an encyclopedia/Philip M. Peek and Kwesi Yankah, editors.
    p. cm.
Includes bibliographical references and index.
  ISBN 0–415–93933-X (HB: alk.paper)
   1. Folklore—Africa—Encyclopedias.   2. Africa—Social life and customs—Encyclopedias.
I. Peek, Philip M. II. Yankah, Kwesi.
  GR350.A33 2003
  398'.096'03—dc21

                                2003007200

To Our Teachers:

William Bascom, Richard Bauman, Alan Dundes, Henry Glassie,

John McDowell, Alan Merriam, John C. Messenger, and Roy Sieber

TABLE OF CONTENTS

INTRODUCTION

The Continent of Africa

Most Africanists, and most Africans, consider the continent of Africa and its peoples as a whole and comprehensive entity. There are thousands of different ethnic groups living on this extraordinarily diverse continent, many of which have been affected by the same issues and have thus developed overlapping cultural practices.

A consideration of sub-Saharan Africa and North Africa together does not necessarily ignore their individual traits. Rather, such a scholarly treatment simply acknowledges geographical and historical realities. North Africa has long been part of Saharan and sub-Saharan Africa. Commerce and conflict marked ancient Egypt's relations with peoples to the south for centuries. Since the seventh century, scholars, traders, and administrators have disseminated the Arabic language and the Islamic religion across North Africa and the Sahara and down the East African coast. Today, the Organization of African Unity (OAU) recognizes the common concerns shared by African nations.

To non-Africans, the continent can appear impenetrable. Yet for those living on the continent, movement across regions has always been relatively easy. Many peoples have maintained close contact for centuries; consequently, most Africans are multilingual. Coastal, trans-Saharan, and interior trade and travel have ensured that African peoples share and exchange not only language but material goods, intellectual concepts, and cultural traditions.

Earlier studies of African peoples exaggerated both their similarities *and* their differences. Current scholarship does not presume a cohesive, unproblematic "Africanaity," but it does recognize that African cultures share significant historical and cultural experiences. One can accept a degree of commonality while acknowledging the existence of internal differences. Earlier scholarship made too many broad generalizations about African cultures, but that does not mean that the existence of shared transnational or transethnic traits should be ignored today.

Another aspect of this issue is that, periodically, one must submit specific cultures to comparison. One can never know what is or is not unique, or even meaningful, in cultural studies if one never compares among cultures. For example, research has confirmed that many African peoples tell dilemma tales (stories that end with questions, not answers). But the question remains, why are there more dilemma tales told in Africa than anywhere else in the world?

The Study of African Folklore

For these reasons, we welcome the opportunity to present material that spans the whole African continent and hundreds of cultures in a single volume, thereby emphasizing both the singularities and commonalities of African folklore traditions.

The discipline of folklore has been shadowed for too many years by debates over terminology and the scope of the field. Initially, in Europe, the term *folklore* referred literally to the "lore" of the "folk," that is, the illiterate members of a literate society; for some, that definition still holds. Folklore studies were essential to the European nationalist movements of the nineteenth century. Folklore scholarship, although perhaps not specifically named as such, is present in the earliest developmental stages of anthropology in Europe and the United States; even the earliest psychoanalytic research of Freud and Jung relied heavily on the study of folktales and other forms of folklore.

The scope of folklore study has continued to expand in the United States. In the nineteenth century, European-based scholarship developed the discipline, but since the middle of the twentieth century, research based in the United States has continued to expand the boundaries of folklore study. The editors' concept of folklore scholarship in Africa is broad, in keeping with current thought in the United States, and this expansive position is reflected by *African Folklore: An Encyclopedia*. The relevance and impact of contexts such the electronic media, urban settings, and contemporary life in general are considered repeatedly in the entries.

The question of who exactly constitute the "folk" is no longer of concern to contemporary folklorists. Although it may be simplistic to respond that "we are all folk," most scholars do, essentially, assume that position. Nevertheless, folklore study's traditionally narrow scope when applied to a European context needs some clarification and contextualization when applied to an African setting. Most folklorists presumably consider their position as less comprehensive than the classic anthropologists' study of "whole" cultures (which even they shy away from today); they focus instead on subgroups within a cultural whole, or, as is perhaps more apt today, on groups within the larger nation state. The traditional focus on rural peoples has given way to an acknowledgement of the necessity of studying folklore in urban contexts as well.

Tradition generally signified an uncritical adherence to ancient cultural ways and tended to be considered in opposition to "contemporary" or "modern" practices. Current scholarship appreciates that all human groups are guided by traditions that may have ancient or recent origins. Equally, tradition in contemporary Africa need no longer depend exclusively on oral transmission but may be carried by any and all media, as demonstrated in papers compiled from the 1998 conference on African oral literature, held in South Africa. The conference focused on oral literature within contemporary African contexts (Kaschula 2001).

It is generally recognized today that any accepted pattern of behavior, way of speaking, or complex of ideas that shape action can be called a "tradition," regardless of the length of time it has been in existence.

In the late nineteenth and early twentieth centuries, the "lore" of folklore generally referred to folktales. What little folklore scholarship there was in Africa was largely limited to ancient myths and animal tales. These genres are significant, but their continued appearance in collections far exceeds their relative importance among all the forms of folklore in African cultures. Today, most folklorists view their subject matter along the lines of European folklife studies and anthropologists' "expressive behavior" studies. The spoken arts are but one among many forms of cultural expression of interest to folklorists.

Nevertheless, even with this much broader scope, one must be continually aware of the problem of considering African genres in European terms. There are considerable—and intriguing—differences between the typologies of different peoples. For example, the Isoko of the Niger Delta have no myths, but they have three different types of proverbs. The Edo of Benin City, also in southern Nigeria, transform a factual prose narrative into a fictional one by adding songs. The fieldworker has to be continually alert to defining features of the many spoken arts genres, as well as to the fascinating overlaps of various media. Among the peoples of West Africa, we often find proverbs illustrated on cloth and carved on "linguist's staffs." The graphic writing of *nsibidi* (of southeastern Nigeria) can be represented in gestures, tattoos, costumes, cloth, and two-dimensional inscriptions. Proverbs can be drummed or carved as well as spoken. Myths of origin and legends of migration may not be told verbally but are acted out in masquerades. Cloth "speaks" by depicting a proverb in its pattern, or demonstrating social status by the wearer's style of wrapping.

The editors accept the term *verbal arts* as encompassing the vast range of arts based around verbal performance. *Verbal arts* avoids placing the derivative form in the primary position. *Oral literature*, therefore, presents a bit of a reversal (whereas *literary orature* might be the most accurate representation of what folklorists refer to and study). Nevertheless, many folklorists have grown quite accustomed to such terminology and present cogent arguments in its favor; several such arguments are present in this volume. Therefore, we have encouraged our contributors to use the terms they prefer. We recommend readers refer to entries by Ruth Finnegan, Isidore Okpewho, Harold Scheub, and Kwesi Yankah for further discussion of terminology. Readers may find entries on the histories of folklore scholarship in France, Germany, Japan, and Portugal helpful and informative as well, as they too address terminological debates. Several topical entries, such as "Typology and Performance in the Study of Prose Narratives in Africa," and "Performance Studies and African Folklore Research" further develop these academic issues, as do numerous entries treating oral narratives and oral traditions.

The large number of entries on various verbal art forms (such as epics, riddles, political oratory, and children's songs) also reminds us not only of the creativity and diversity of human speech forms (in relation to other cultural expressions) but to the primacy of the heard, as opposed to the seen, world. Sound, not sight, seems most essential in many African societies. Several folklorists have attempted to reorient their scholarship in recognition of this by referring to *auditory arts* (Peek 1994), *orature* (Haring 1994), or *auriture* (Coplan 1994). These terms attempt to overcome the limitations of our overwhelmingly visually oriented language.

In addition, we must note that silence, the absence of human speech and sound, is emphatically "learned" behavior, as opposed to being natural. In other words, speech and sound are so important that their absence can be felt (Peek 2000; Yankah 1998).

One reality in the scholarship of the spoken word is that we have never resolved the dilemma of how best to represent speech on paper, how to precisely transcribe orality. We cannot enter that debate fully here, but we do wish to observe that there have been attempts, though few, to at least provide original African texts with their translations in European languages.

Outdated reliance on an older definition of folklore, which equates the field with the study of spoken arts only, ignores the range of other expressive genres, such as material forms and ritual behavior. Most would accept Bascom's classification of myths, legends, and folktales as constituting prose narratives, a grouping that is then encompassed by the term *verbal art*, which in turn is encapsulated by *folklore* (as discussed above), with *culture* forming the outermost category.

The other issue related to definitions is scope of topics. As the editors of *African Folklore: An Encyclopedia,* we are far more concerned with process than isolated product. The most emphatic demonstration of that emphasis here is the large number of entries on aspects of performance. Many folklorists have adopted a a dramatalurgical approach to all forms of verbal arts, from formal oratory to personal narratives, from puppet play scripts to children's riddling sessions. Lists of proverbs severed from their meaning, removed from a context of use, no longer suffice.

We conclude this part of our introduction with a definition of folklore that we believe reflects the breadth and depth of current folklore scholarship: Folklore is those esoteric traditions (oral, customary, or material) expressed in the form of artistic communication used as operational culture by a group within the larger society (primarily to provide group identity and homogeneity).

This definition accommodates the appropriate scope of folklore studies without becoming universalist. The emphasis is on artistic communication (for many, the most apt minimal definition of folklore) and on the "usefulness" of these esoteric traditions. Thus, we must understand the emic (culture-specific) aspects first, before moving to the etic (comparative "universal") dimensions. Although not available to, or understood by, the whole cultural group (thus we speak of esoteric vs. exoteric levels), these traditions serve critical purposes of group identification for some within that group. This introduces, intentionally, a functional dimension; but it is functional for the group itself. This must be emphasized because much attention paid folklore is by those outside a group seeking to use the group's traditions for their purposes, be it academic, governmental, or commercial. Entries that address folklore and education, government attitudes towards dancing troupes, theater for development, and tourist arts reveal the use—and abuse—of folklore by outsiders.

One of the major strengths of this volume is the breadth of accomplished contributors. Nearly one-third of the scholars represented in *African Folklore: An Encyclopedia* are African, and over one-half of them currently teach in Africa. Approximately one-half of the contributors are from the United States, but a large number also hail from Europe, the Americas, and the Middle East. In addition to geographical breadth, we have scholars of many different disciplines and backgrounds. The contributors to *African Folklore: An Encyclopedia* include both those senior scholars who defined the field and the younger scholars who are shaping it today.

"In the beginning was the Word . . ."

The importance of human speech in African cultures cannot be overemphasized. This primacy of the human voice and of the exchange of life through words is demonstrated over and over again in Africa. Although we did not set out to focus on orality, creative speech, verbal arts, and so on, the importance of speech was continually apparent. Just skimming our list of entries, the reader will immediately notice how many entries address speech and the spoken arts. African life starts with naming traditions and prayers and continues through greetings and songs, libations and lullabies, praise names and insults, and funeral orations and spirit possession. Informal gossip and formal oratory, individual speech and epics of empires—the scope of artful speech is endless. One must even consider speech about speech (metafolklore), surrogate languages (drum languages and gestures), and the absence of speech in culturally constructed silences. Electronic media has simply expanded the realm of performed speech and song even further.

A problem continuing to face African folklore scholars is that of how best to represent speech on paper, that is, how to move from orality to the literary. Space does not permit a full discussion of that issue here, but we do wish to observe that there have been attempts, though few, to at least provide translations of original texts in European languages. Several series of publications have tried, such as *Classiques Africaines*, some of the Oxford Library of African Literature, and the ILCAA series from Japan. Unfortunately, the harsh realities of publishing costs seem to have weighed too heavily against such worthy efforts. Nevertheless, local writers and scholars throughout Africa publish in local languages, and continued pressure by academics does ensure some representation of African languages in illustrative texts, though perhaps only as appendices. We can never have enough records in Africa's many complex languages and dialects.

An important component of this complex of the primacy of speech and the power of the word in Africa is the fact that most Africans are multilingual. Without getting into debates about how (and whether) language determines thought and worldview, we simply wish to acknowledge a relationship of some kind between speech, language, and thought; thus, one who speaks several languages necessarily possesses, or has access to, several viewpoints.

The African Diaspora

For centuries the significance of the African heritage of the countries and peoples of the Americas has been ignored. Indeed, one could say that even the existence of this heritage has been challenged. At one time many assumed that Africans in the Americas had lost virtually all of their traditional culture during the horrors of the Middle Passage and enslavement in the Americas. This same argument then maintained that African American culture was only comprised of imitations of European traditions. Although one can well understand how that might have happened, we now know that many African traditions did survive. Fortunately, we are well beyond this perspective today, but the breadth and depth of the debt of the Americas to Africa should be more widely recognized. Some of our African American entries are cited under "Diaspora," while others are listed by genre, such as musical instruments, basketry, or religions. We find ancient African roots in the Gullah dialect of the Georgia Sea Islands and the hinterland villages of Suriname. There are also the modern revitalization movements of communities such as Oyo Tunji Village in South Carolina. Even the recent "invention" of Kwanzaa must be considered. The majority of examples are from the Americas, but Africans elsewhere, such as the United Kingdom, are included for discussion as well.

Again, we can only provide a representative sampling in covering the vast and vital heritage of African folklore. In this work we can only suggest the variety of arts, beliefs, and cultural practices that continue to act as vital forms of expression for millions of Americans (we use the term *Americans* in its full meaning). The African heritage is primarily voiced and lived by African American peoples, from Brazil to Jamaica, from Guyana to Nova Scotia, but it is not exclusively theirs. As the reader will find, there are many aspects of the African heritage that are shared by the whole of the Americas, no matter the ethnic origins of the practitioners in question. Many African American traditions have important European components, such as the Catholic elements of Haitian Vodou, but in most cases the essential parts are clearly African in origin. And many forms of cultural expression in the Americas have now, in turn, affected African cultures: perhaps music provides the clearest examples, such as Ghanaian reggae and Liberian rap groups.

Black Atlantic English has been accepted by linguists as an appropriate label for the English spoken by Africans and African descendants in the United States, England, West Africa, and the Caribbean. This presents yet another means by which to link peoples of Africa and the diaspora.

The variety of forms of African American folklore is striking, as is the continuing elaboration of these African elements. As with African traditions, we are struck by the creativity displayed in the continued adherence to aspects of the African heritage. Carnival, for example, has become virtually a worldwide phenomenon, after developing among Africans in the Caribbean and Brazil. It now forms the base of Europe's largest festival, the Notting Hill Carnival in London; it is also celebrated in Brooklyn, New York, and Toronto, Canada, among other places. Body arts and front yards, foods and folktales, quilts and religions, music and clothing—virtually every aspect of life now has its rightly recognized African elements. Some may be recent "traditions," such as the popularity of Ghanaian kente cloth or Malian *bogolan* cloth, but more often than not we find centuries of practice behind these customs.

It should also be noted that some elements of "American" culture that some hold close to "our" image are, at root, African. Surely "American" music, from the banjo to hip-hop, owes its essence to Africa. So too are we indebted to Africa for that wonderful institution, the front porch!

It is amazing to think that it was not until the late 1960s that the African heritage of the Americas was recognized even by the scholarly community. It is a very recent scholarship, and its direction of development is noteworthy. All of the major early scholars of African folklore studied in both Africa and the Americas. All recognized that they had to turn to Africa to understand their American subjects. Melville J. Herskovits in Haiti, William Bascom in Cuba, Daniel Crowley in Trinidad: each of these turned to Africa in order to complement and deepen his research in the Americas. In fact, many contemporary Africanists and African Americanists continue to "cross-over" from Africa to the Americas, and vice versa, today.

We are fortunate to have exemplary essays from major scholars of the African American heritage in this volume, and yet, as all would admit, there is so much more to be said. We need to distinguish that the African heritage of the Americas is not simply an historical matter, it is an ongoing, ever-changing phenomenon. From the seventeenth century until today, Africa influenced, and continues to influence, the Americas, in subtle matters such as voice inflection, and in total complexes such as Vodou and Santeria. There are African communities in the Americas, such as Oyo Tunji, as well as those in places such as Brazil and Surinam that have been in existence for centuries, initiated by escaped slave kingdoms.

There are myriad instances of continuity and creativity, retentions of the old alongside invention of the new. The African heritage of the Americas, especially in the arts, is one of deep roots and startling freshness. It is irrepressible and undeniable.

Distribution

As editors of a volume spanning the vast topic of African folklore, we have come to realize that, while we could not address every single African culture, we could present a representative, and still detailed, sample of African folklore culture. *African Folklore: An Encyclopedia* contains entries on urban and rural folklore, on pastoralists and farmers, on women and men, on visual and verbal arts, and much more. Only those who have tried to create an encyclopedia know that one can never be truly encyclopedic. Especially if one is seeking to represent a whole continent, one seems doomed to failure. But we are confident that we have succeeded in our effort to provide representation of the peoples of Africa and their forms of folklore that gives an accurate and extensive sense of the variety of forms and traditions active in Africa.

Organization of the Book

There are over three hundred entries in *African Folklore: An Encyclopedia*. Given the range and scope of these entries, several tools have been employed to ensure easy navigation of the volume, and access to essential information. These include:

- An alphabetical list of all entries.
- A comprehensive index.
- The following appendixes:
  - A detailed filmography of documentary films on Africa.
  - The complete holdings of the Archives of Traditional Music at Indiana University.
  - A list of early M.A.s and Ph.D.s in African folklore.
  - A survey of African Studies Centers and Libraries in the United States and Africa.
- Eight different regional surveys on the major folklore forms of those areas, along with comment on the study of those forms.
- Accompanying maps highlighting major ethnic groups.
- Brief surveys of African countries providing basic statistics, historical notes, references to major ethnic groups and cultural issues, and commentary on current problems in those countries. Population numbers are United Nations estimates for the year 2000.
- Extensive use of cross-references at the end of nearly every entry, and over seventy blind entries.
- There are approximately one hundred black and white photos accompanying various entries. The majority of these were taken by the contributors themselves during periods of field research. They enrich the writing and provide visual examples of the concepts, practices, art forms, and objects discussed.

African Folklore: An Encyclopedia contains regional surveys and thematic groupings, as well as many individual entries on various peoples. Thus, it represents much of Africa and gives the uninitiated a good introduction to African folklore.

Although we have a number of survey essays (e.g., on epics, medicine, performance, and religion), most are culture-specific entries with a focus on some aspect of folklore, such as visual arts, healing, or cultural identity. While many forms of folklore are found in most cultures, not all peoples elaborate the same expressive forms to the same extent; thus, joking relationships, beadwork, or praise poetry are not found universally. There are large subgroupings that treat women's folklore, dynamics of performance, theater, and musical expression. Although we cannot say something about every group, we have included information on rural and urban peoples, forest and grasslands, hunters and pastoralists, and farmers and fisherfolk, from the Ethiopian Highlands to the Zanzibar coast, from the Sahara to the Niger Delta. Thus, the volume is not absolutely comprehensive, but it is representative of African peoples. While we could not present full surveys of all folklore forms among all major ethnic groups, most peoples are represented somehow and can be traced through the index and cross-referencing.

Conclusion

Tragically, we cannot end without observing the horrible impact on African peoples' lives of the seemingly unending series of droughts, dictators, and disasters, of the staggering loss of life to AIDS, and of continuing political and military disruptions. In many cases, one must acknowledge the very real loss of culture as well as lives. Although there are many cases where traditions have continued to serve the people, such as Iteso children using traditional folktales to sort out their disrupted lives, there are other cases where ceremonies have not been performed in so long that most have forgotten them.

In the midst of chaos in Liberia, Rwanda, Ethiopia, and Angola, people persevere. They may even develop new forms of folklore. This should not surprise us, as folklore is comprised of creative expressions of life and meaning and is essential to purposeful existence; thus it persists in even the most dire situations.

We invite the reader to use this volume to find answers to specific questions, as well as to formulate new questions and then seek their answers, too. We hope that, in your use of this volume, you are as excited by this material as we have been in bringing it together in this volume.

We give special thanks to our Advisory Board members Dan Ben-Amos, Daniel Crowley, Gerald Davis, Ruth Finnegan, Rachel Fretz, Micheline Galley, Veronika Görög-Karady, Lee Haring, Harold Schueb, and Ruth Stone.

Creating an encyclopedia is an exhilarating yet exasperating project that involves many people. We have first acknowledged those teachers who originally guided us and those colleagues who aided us in the current endeavor. In a very real sense, we thank all of our contributors not only for their excellent entries but for their support and patience as we developed the project. Several colleagues, notably Frances Harding and David Samper, led us to other contributors. We must next acknowledge those colleagues who tragically passed away during the course of this project: Kofi Agovi, T. K. Biaya, Daniel Crowley, and Gerald Davis.

Over the years, many students from Drew University aided with manuscript preparation. Our sincere thanks to Jennifer Joyce for preparing most of the country entries. We must also acknowledge those who toiled with manuscript in various states of repair: Katie Boswell, Megan McBride, Tara Ondra, Janet Wong, Sandra Yoshida, and Andrea Zaia. Another area of critical aid was that of translation—sincere thanks to Kristine Aurbakken and Jerry Vogel.

We also thank the many editors who encouraged us over the years, first with Garland, then with Routledge Reference. Most especially we thank those who helped us complete this project: Laura Smid, Kate Aker, Kristen Holt, Mary Funchion, and Jeanne Shu.

Much needed time and facilities for final manuscript preparation were provided by a fellowship at the Sainsbury Research Unit for the Arts of Africa, Oceania, and the Americas, University of East Anglia, Norwich, England. Sincerest thanks as well to those who provided shelter during the final stages: Lee and Sylvia Pollock, Beverly Ben-Salem, the Folklore and Folklife Department at the University of Pennsylvania, and the University of Ghana.

And, as always, our appreciation for our long-suffering spouses, Pat and Victoria, must be acknowledged.

PHILIP M. PEEK AND KWESI YANKAH

References

Coplan, David B. 1994. *In the Time of Cannibals: The Word Music of South Africa's Basotho Migrants.* Johannesburg: Witwaterstand University Press.

Haring, Lee, ed. 1994. African Oral Traditions. *Oral Tradition* (special issue), 9:1.

Kaschula, Russell. 2001. *African Oral Literature: Functions in Contemporary Contexts.* Claremont, South Africa: New Africa Books.

Peek, Philip M. 1981. The Power of Words in African Verbal Arts. *Journal of American Folklore* 94: 371.

Peek, Philip M. 1994. The Sounds of Silence: Cross-World Communication and the Auditory Arts in African Societies. *American Ethnologist* 21: 3.

Peek, Philip M. 2000. Re-Sounding Silences. In *Sound,* ed. P. Kruth and H. Stobart. Cambridge: Cambridge University Press.

Yankah, Kwesi. 1986. Beyond the Spoken Word: Aural Literature in Africa. In *Cross Rhythms* 2. ed. Daniel Avorgbedor and Kwesi Yankah. Papers in African Folklore. Bloomington: Trickster Press.

Yankah, Kwesi 1995. *Speaking for the Chief: Okyeame and the Politics of Akan Royal Oratory.* Bloomington: Indiana University Press.

Yankah, Kwesi. 1998. *Free Speech in Traditional Society: The Cultural Foundations of Communication in Contemporary Ghana.* Accra: Ghana Universities Press.

LIST OF CONTRIBUTORS

David Adu-Amankwah
Department of Folklore and Ethnomusicology
Indiana University

Kofi Agawu
Department of Music
Princeton University

† **Kofi Agovi**

Ali Jimale Ahmed
Department of Comparative Literature
Queens College and the City University of New York Graduate Center

Akinsola Akiwowo
Sociology and Anthropology (Emeritas) University of Ife (Nigeria)

E. J. Alagoa
Department of History
University of Port Harcourt

Ali B. Ali-Dinar
African Studies Center
University of Pennsylvania

Joe Amoako
Department of English
Delaware State University

Alfred Anangwe
Department of Sociology and Anthropology (Emeritus)
University of Ife (Nigeria)

Martha G. Anderson
Division of Art History, School of Art and Design
Alfred University

Akosua Anyidoho
Department of Linguistics
University of Ghana

Mary Jo Arnoldi
Department of Anthropology, National Museum of Natural History
Smithsonian Institution

Lisa Aronson
Department of Art and Art History
Skidmore College

Daniel K. Avorgbedor
School of Music
Ohio State University

Senait Bahta
Department of Anthropology
University of Asmara (Eritrea)

Karin Barber
Centre for West African Studies
University of Birmingham (UK)

Robert Baron
Folk Arts
New York State Council on the Arts

Philippe Beaujard
Centre National de la Recherche Scientifique (France)
Centre d'Études Africaines, École des Hautes Etudes en Sciences Sociales

Stephen Belcher
Independent Scholar

Marla C. Berns
Fowler Museum of Cultural History
University of California, Los Angeles

Rima Berns-McGown
Independent Scholar

Judith Bettelheim
Department of Art
San Francisco State University

† **T. K. Biaya**

Daniel P. Biebuyck
Anthropology and Humanities (Emeritus)
University of Delaware

David A. Brinkley
National Museum of African Art
Smithsonian Institution

Ulrich Braukämper
Institute of Ethnology
University of Göttingen (Germany)

David H. Brown
W. E. B. Du Bois Institute for Afro-American Research
Harvard University

Karen McCarthy Brown
Religion and Society, Graduate School
Drew University

Richard Allen Burns
Department of English and Philosophy
Arkansas State University

John W. Burton
Department of Anthropology
Connecticut College

Mohamed El-Mahdi Bushra
Department of Folklore
University of Khartoum (Sudan)

Geneviève Calame-Griaule
Centre National de la Recherche Scientifique (France)

Elizabeth L. Cameron
Department of Art History
University of California, Santa Cruz

Robert Cancel
Department of Literature
University of California, San Diego

Margret Carey
Bead Study Trust Newsletter
Museum Ethnographers Group

Amanda Carlson
Department of Visual Arts
University of Dayton

S. Terry Childs
Archaeology and Cultural Resources
National Park Service

Cati Coe
Department of Sociology, Anthropology, and Criminal Justice
Rutgers University

Jean-Paul Colleyn
Centre d'Études Africaines
École des Hautes Études en Sciences Sociales (France)

John Collins
Music Department, School of Performing Arts
University of Ghana

Cecelia Conway
Department of English
Appalachian State University

Donald Cosentino
World Arts Program
University of California, Los Angeles

† Daniel Crowley

† Gerald Davis

Jo de Berry
Save the Children

Alex de Voogt
School of Asian, African, and Amerindian Studies
Leiden University (The Netherlands)

Jean Derive
LLACAN / UFR Lettres, Langues, Sciences Humaines
Université de Savoie (France)

Boureima Tiekoroni Diamitani
West African Museums Program (Senegal)

Esi Dogbe
Department of Pan-African Studies
University of Louisville

Christiano Henrique Ribeiro dos Santos
Universidade do Estado do Rio de Janiero
Centro de Ciencias Sociais, Program de Estudos e Debates dos Povos
  Africanos e Afro-Americanos

Elom Dovlo
Department for the Study of Religions
University of Ghana

Margaret Thompson Drewal
Department of Theater and Performance Studies
Northwestern University

Caleb Dube
Department of Sociology
DePaul University

Ennis B. Edmonds
Pan-African Studies Program
Barnard College, Columbia University

Lillie Johnson Edwards
Department of History
Drew University

Joanne B. Eicher
Department of Design, Housing, and Apparel
University of Minnesota

Hasan M. El-Shamy
Folklore Institute
Indiana University

Paul Faber
KIT Tropenmuseum (The Netherlands)

Kayode Fanilola
Foreign Language Department
Morgan State University

Ruth Finnegan
Faculty of Social Sciences
The Open University (UK)

Barbara Frank
Department of Art
State University of New York at Stony Brook

Marion Frank-Wilson
Librarian for African Studies
Indiana University

Rachel I. Fretz
Writing Program
University of California, Los Angeles

Graham Furniss
School of Oriental and African Studies (SOAS)
University of London

Paulette Galand-Pernet
Centre Nationale la Recherche Scientifique
Unité de Recherche Littérature Orale Arabo-Berbère (France)

John G. Galaty
Department of Anthropology
McGill University

Micheline Galley
Centre National de la Recherche Scientifique (France)

Michelle Gilbert
Department of Fine Arts and International Studies Program
Trinity College

Veronika Görög-Karady
Centre National de la Recherche Scientifique (France)

George P. Hagan
Institute of African Studies
University of Ghana

Thomas A. Hale
Department of Comparative Literature
Pennsylvania State University

Paul W. Hanson
Ursuline College

Frances Harding
School of Oriental and African Studies (SOAS)
University of London

Lee Haring
Department of English (Emeritus)
Brooklyn College of the City University of New York

Dunja Hersak
Department of Art History
Université Libre de Bruxelles (Belgium)

Isabel Hofmeyr
Department of African Literature
University of Witwatersrand (South Africa)

Jarita C. Holbrook
Bureau of Applied Research in Anthropology
University of Arizona

Linda Hunter
Department of African Languages and Literature
University of Wisconsin

Abdullahi Ali Ibrahim
Department of History
University of Missouri

dele jegede
Art Department
Indiana State University

Jennifer Joyce
Columbia University

Egara Kabaji
Department of Literature
Moi University (Kenya)

Russell H. Kaschula
Bureau for African Research and Documentation
University of Transkei (South Africa)

David Kerr
Department of English
University of Botswana

E. Kezilahabi
Department of African Languages and Literature
University of Botswana

Doreen Helen Klassen
Department of Social Science
Sir Wilfred Grenfell College
Memorial University of Newfoundland

Corinne A. Kratz
Center for the Study of Public Scholarship
Emory University

Alisa LaGamma
Arts of Africa, Oceania, and the Americas
Museum of Metropolitan Art

Jérôme Lentin
Department of Arabic
Institut National des Langues et Civilisations Orientales (France)

Edward Lifschitz
National Museum of African Art
Smithsonian Institution

Petros Mafika Lubisi
Department of African Languages
University of Zululand (South Africa)

Elísio Macamo
Department of Sociology
University of Bayreuth (Germany)

Yousif Hasan Mandani
Department of Folklore
Institute of African and Asian Studies
University of Khartoum (Sudan)

Minette Mans
Performing Arts Department
University of Namibia

Adeline Masquelier
Department of Anthropology
Tulane University

Daniel Mato
Department of Art History
University of Calgary

Joseph L. Mbele
Department of English
St. Olaf College

Michael McGovern
African Studies
Emory University

Patrick McNaughton
Department of Art
Indiana University

John C. Messenger
Department of Anthropology, College of Social and Behavioral Sciences
   (Emeritus)
Ohio State University

John Middleton
Department of Anthropology (Emeritus)
Yale University

Mustafa Kemel Mirzeler
Africana Studies
Western Michigan University

Farah Eisa Mohamed
Institute of African and Asian Studies
University of Khartoum (Sudan)

Makali I. Mokitimi
Department of African Languages
University of South Africa

Benson A. Mulemi
Department of Anthropology
The Catholic University of Eastern Africa

Diana Baird N'Diaye
Center for Folklife and Cultural Heritage
Smithsonian Institution

Adrien N. Ngudiankama
Institute of Education
University of London

Isak Niehaus
Department of Anthropology and Archaeology
University of Pretoria (South Africa)

Imeyan A. Noah
Department of Languages and Linguistics
University of Calabar (Nigeria)

Andrew J. Noss
Wildlife Conservation Society (Bolivia)

Kathleen Jenabu Noss
Department of Ethnomusicology
University of California, Los Angeles

Philip A. Noss
United Bible Societies (UK)

Samuel Gyasi Obeng
Department of Linguistics
Indiana University

Ernest Okello Ogwang
Department of Literature
Makere University (Uganda)

Isidore Okpewho
Department of Afro-American and African Studies
State University of New York at Binghamton

Mikelle Smith Omari-Tunkara
School of Art and Art History
University of Arizona

Jeff Opland
Brooke Hall
Charter House School

Kofi A. Opoku
Department of Religion
LaFayette College

Simon Ottenberg
Anthropology Department (Emeritus)
University of Washington

Oyekan Owomoyela
Department of English
University of Nebraska

B. Okíntúndé Oyàtádé
School of Oriental and African Studies (SOAS)
University of London

Wade Patterson
Program Officer
New Mexico Enlowment for the Humanities

Barry Lee Pearson
English Department
University of Maryland

E. A. Péri
Department for International Development (UK)

Philip M. Peek
Department of Anthropology
Drew University

Alec J. C. Pongweni
Department of English
University of Botswana

Susan J. Rasmussen
Department of Anthropology
University of Houston

Daniel B. Reed
Archives of Traditional Music
Indiana University

Allen F. Roberts
African Studies Center
University of California, Los Angeles

Katherine Roberts
Folklore Institute
Indiana University

Mary Nooter Roberts
Fowler Museum
University of California, Los Angeles

Hagar Salamon
Department of Jewish and Comparative Folklore
The Hebrew University (Israel)

David A. Samper
Department of Folklore and Folklife
University of Pennsylvania

Harold Scheub
Department of African Languages and Literature
University of Wisconsin

Dorothea E. Schulz
Institute of Ethnology
Free University (Germany)

Gerhard Seibert
Centro de Estudos Africanos e Asiáticos (Portugal)

Christiane Seydou
Centre National de la Recherche Scientifique (France)

Amnon Shiloah
Department of Musicology
The Hebrew University (Israel)

Sónia Silva
Independent Scholar

Arthur K. Spears
Anthropology Department
City College, City University of New York

Debra Spitulnik
Department of Anthropology
Emory University

Christopher B. Steiner
Department of Art History
Connecticut College

Phillips Stevens Jr.
Department of Anthropology
State University of New York at Buffalo

Bradford Strickland
Postdoctoral fellow
American Association for the Advancement of Science

Beverly J. Stoeltje
Department of Anthropology
Indiana University

Esi Sutherland-Addy
Institute of African Studies
University of Ghana

Tonya Taylor
Department of Folklore and Folklife
University of Pennsylvania

Hayley S. Thomas
Assistant Dean, Undergraduate College
Bryn Mawr College

Farouk Topan
School of Oriental and African Studies
University of London

Mary Arnold Twining
English Department
Clark Atlanta University

John Michael Vlach
American Studies Department
George Washington University

Jerome Vogel
Drew University and the Museum for African Art

Mbugua wa-Mungai
Institute of Jewish Studies, Faculty of Humanities
Hebrew University of Jerusalem (Israel)

Richard M. Wafula
Folklore Institute
Indiana University

Maude Southwell Wahlman
Department of Art and Art History
University of Missouri-Kansas City

Michael Wainaina
Literature Department
Kenyatta University (Kenya)

Maureen Warner-Lewis
Department of Literatures in English
University of the West Indies (Jamaica)

Yael Warshel
Department of Communication
University of California, San Diego

Richard Westmacott
School of Enviromental Design
University of Georgia

Robert W. White
Department of Anthropology
University of Montreal

Kwesi Yankah
Dean, Faculty of Arts
University of Ghana

Mourad Yelles
Institut Maghreb-Europe
Université Paris 8

LIST OF ENTRIES

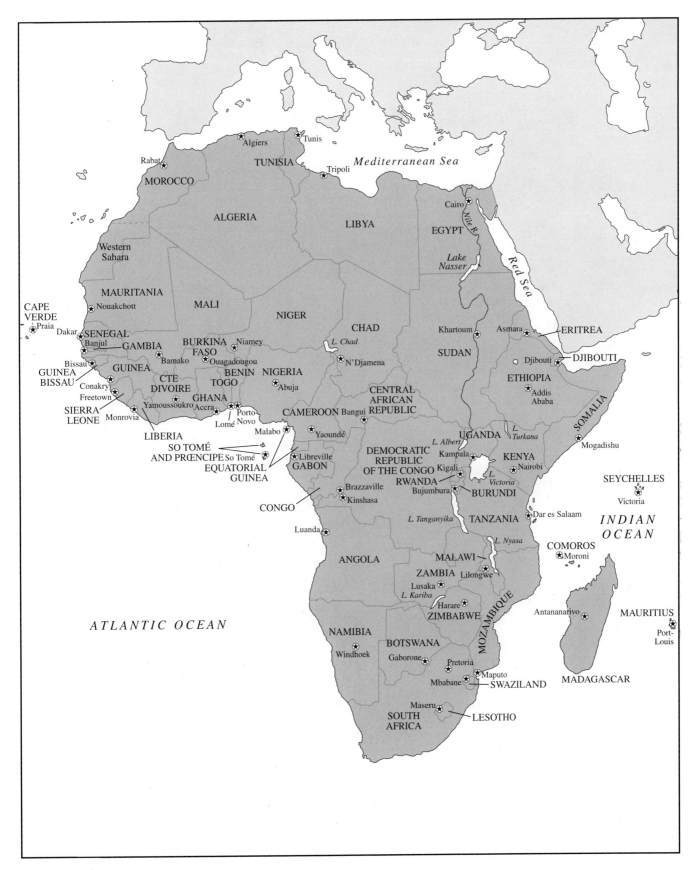

Africa

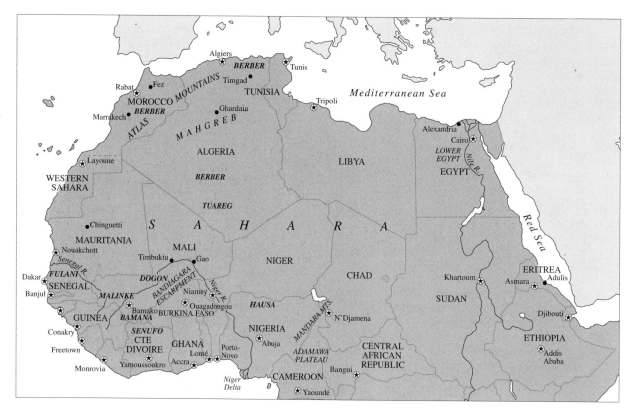

North Africa

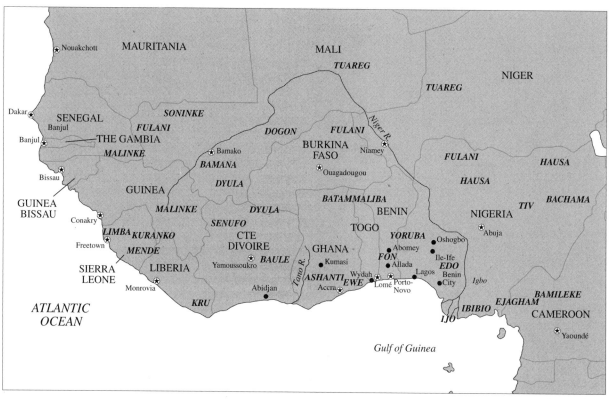

West Africa

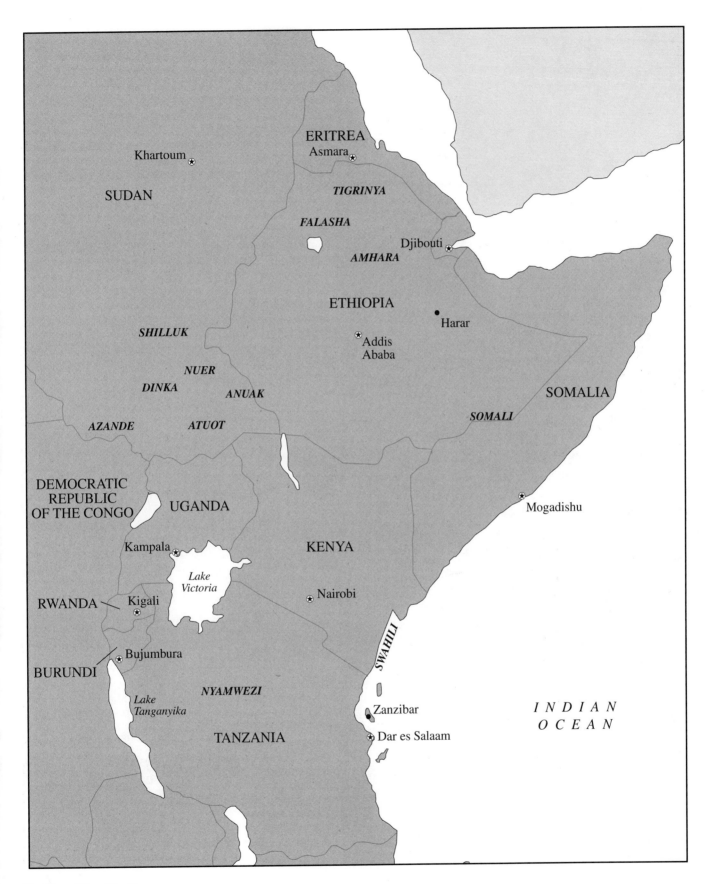

Northeast Africa: The Horn

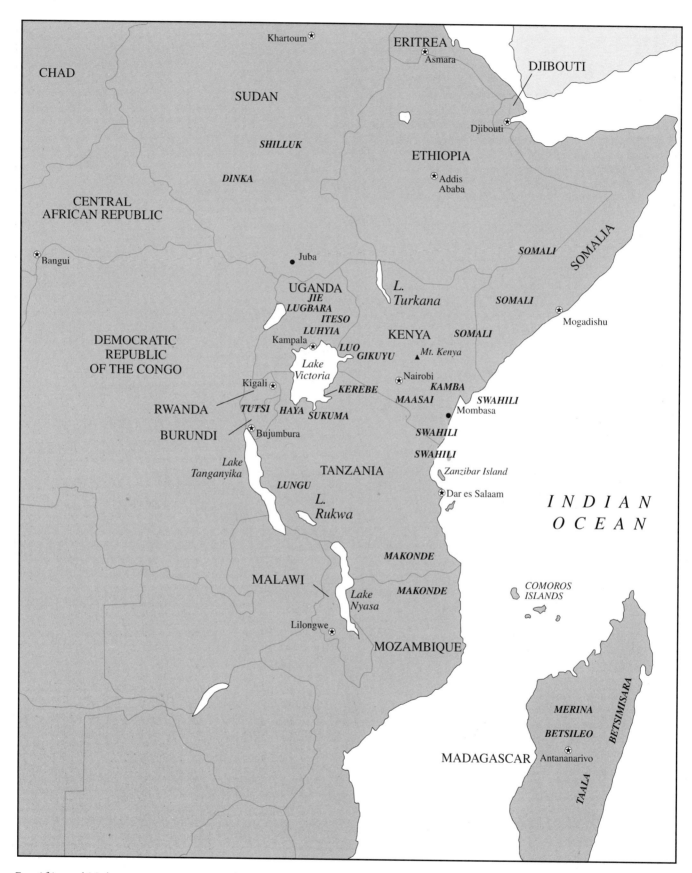

East Africa and Madagascar

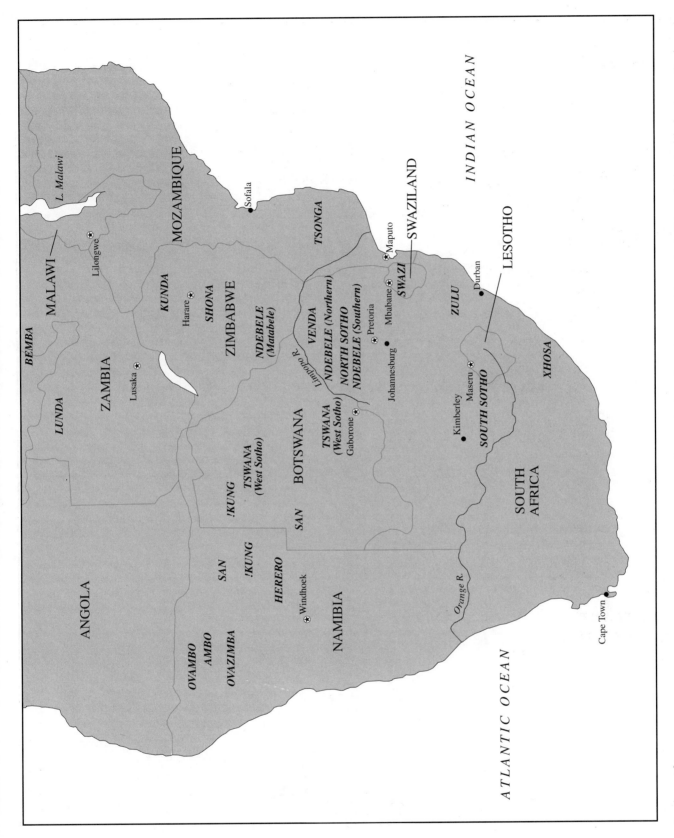

Southern Africa

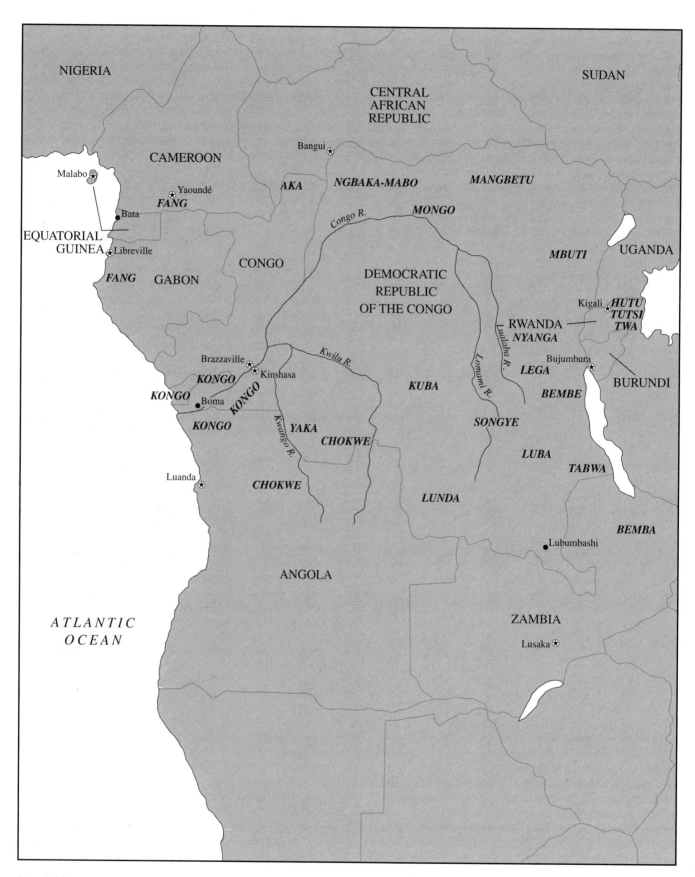

Central Africa

AFRICAN AMERICANS

See **Diaspora**

AKAN/ASHANTI

See **Beadwork; Chief; Color Symbolism: The Akan of Ghana; Concert Parties; Gender Representation in African Folklore; Jokes and Humor; Queen Mothers; Rattray; Tricksters in African Folklore**

ALGERIA

One of Africa's largest countries, Algeria is bordered by the Mediterranean to the north, Tunisia and Libya to the east, Niger and Mali to the south, Mauritania, Western Sahara, and Morocco to the west. Since the late twentieth century, Algeria has suffered from much politically motivated violence. As early as 1830, when the French first invaded, there was fierce opposition to foreign control. Algeria remained a province of France until the liberation movement arose in the 1950s. Independence was finally granted in 1962. Within several years, there was another revolution led by the Algerian military, which ruled for ten years until elections in 1976. Then, Colonel Houari Boumedienne, who had led the military government, was formally elected president. With his death in 1978, the Revolutionary Council took over once again until the 1990 elections, when the gains made by the Islamic fundamentalist movement were nullified by the military, which seized power in 1992. Virtual civil war has continued ever since, with thousands of Algerians being killed. Fortunately, a majority of the population accepted the elections of 2001 and a relative peace has been maintained.

The new constitution officially recognizes those of Arab and of Berber identity, the latter being the original inhabitants of the country. The Berber language is also officially recognized, although Arabic continues as the general language, and French is used in business and government. The current population is approximately 31 million. Islam is the major religion, with 98 percent of the population being Sunni Muslims. There are over

a dozen institutions of higher learning, and an adult literacy rate of over 62 percent.

Petroleum is Algeria's main export. In 1991, foreign oil companies were permitted to acquire up to 49 percent of the oil and gas reserves. Oil and gas constitute nearly one-third of the country's GNP. A variety of other mineral wealth is also exported including iron, lead, phospates, and zinc as well as marble, salt, and coal. Although little of Algeria is suitable for agriculture, it is known for its citrus fruits and wine. Industrial production is growing but increased urbanization and agricultural decline have led to increased migration to Europe.

Our best evidence of the ancient Saharan civilization, established as early as 6,000 BCE, is in the fabulous rock art at Tassili and other sites far into Algeria's Saharan territory. These rock paintings and engravings, depicting elephants, giraffes, even cattle, prove that the Sahara was once fertile and supported an extraordinary civilization that must have had ties to North African cities, such as Carthage and ancient Egypt. Some scholars even speculate on links to other African civilizations to the south on the basis of these detailed paintings.

PHILIP M. PEEK

ANCESTORS

An important part of the cosmology of West African peoples, the belief in ancestors affirms that life continues after death, that the spirit realm is not an alien world inaccessible to humans, and that even after death, relationships are not eternally severed between the deceased and their living descendants. Among the major ethnic groups in West Africa such as the Akan (in Ghana and the Ivory Coast), the Ga (in Ghana), the Ewe (in Ghana and Togo), the Fon (in Benin), the Yoruba and Igbo (in Nigeria), those who have attained the status of ancestors are given honorific titles such as Nananom Nsamanfo (Akan), and Togbi Togbuiwo (Ewe). These titles literally mean "grandparents."

To be an ancestor, a person must be a progenitor because the cult of ancestors is composed of one's descendants. But there can be rare exceptions where a person who did not have biological children, but who cared for the extended family, is accorded the honor. Apart from having descendants, one must lead a moral life worthy of emulation and one of community service. Traditionally it is believed that an upright life is normally rewarded with old age. Such a person who is endowed with experience and wisdom then becomes an elder within the community. The person must die of natural causes. Some types of death are considered to be a curse in West African communities and negate the prospects of becoming an ancestor (Assimeng 1989, 60). At death the proper funeral rites must be performed for the deceased person to ensure passage into the spirit world of the ancestors. The invocation of such a person by name in ritual signals recognition as an ancestor by living descendants.

Ancestors form the spiritual segment of their families and are the most intimate spiritual link between their living descendants and the spiritual world of God, the gods, and other spirit powers. They serve as intermediaries and mediators between their descendants and the spirit world, promoting the welfare of their descendants. A wide range of requests are therefore put to them by their living descendants, including requests for children, prosperity, a good harvest, and general well-being. They mediate these boons for their descendants from God and the gods. The ancestors are particularly seen as transmitters of life who enable their descendants to procreate. As Dzobo (1992, 232) points out, their concern with sexuality reflects a desire to increase the size of the family, ensuring the continuity of the family line. The ancestors are believed to reincarnate in their own families; thus, an emphasis on procreation benefits past, present, and future family generations.

The ancestors also offer protection to their descendants from inimical powers. A good illustration of this belief is manifested in a special sacrifice known as the *Sane* (debt) sacrifice among the Naga of northern Ghana. In this sacrifice a person is made to replace through divination the items supposedly used spiritually by ancestors to divert a spiritual attack on the person. Ancestors are also concerned with healing and may reveal healing remedies to descendants through dreams, and so forth.

The ancestral roles have an ethical basis. The ancestors are regarded as the guides and guards of the moral conduct of their descendants. Although they reward the good with boons, they punish or ignore belligerent and negligent descendants. They are also believed to provide spiritual sanctions to various traditional taboos, especially sexual taboos. Such taboos when broken destroy the moral fabric of the communities that they helped to establish. The filial bonds with their descendants also oblige the latter to act in a manner that does not tarnish their ancestral name.

Often the ethical role of the ancestors takes on a judicial aspect. This is implied in the belief that they reward or punish good and bad descendants respectively. They also serve as symbols of justice. Elders who adjudicate cases pray to the ancestors for wisdom and discernment and invite them to witness the proceedings. Anthony Emphirim-Donkor (1997, 125) notes, "This is to ensure that everything said and done is carried out in spirit and in truth." The Egungun ancestral mask cult of the Yoruba of Nigeria also judges cases while the elders are masked as ancestors. Their decisions are regarded as those of the ancestors.

In performing all these roles the ancestors serve as important religious foci of social order and continuity. Among the Ewe, as Fiawoo (1967, 266) points out, "the values set on kinship find expression in the ancestral cult." Filial piety as expressed in the ancestors and shared by others leads to a recognition of the social foundations of one's life and fosters social cohesion, solidarity, and corporate identity. Ancestral links also engender the resolution to maintain the traditions of the ancestors for others yet to be born. This entrusts responsibility for the future in the hands of the living. The ancestors are therefore the key element connecting the symbiotic religious and social lives of the people.

The ancestral beliefs partially account for the way religion is intertwined with various aspects of West African life. The links of the ancestor cult with economic and political life gives a sense of continuity and security to living descendants. As founders of communities, the ancestors are linked with land, a traditional symbol of identity for their descendants. The ancestral traditions of land use also affect economic life. The legitimacy of political authority is also vested in the ancestors. In most West African communities those who hold political authority do so in proxy for the ancestors. They are responsible to the latter and regularly function in priestly roles, communicating and maintaining communion with the ancestors on behalf of themselves and those whom they lead.

The ultimate role of the ancestors is to serve as symbols of an ideal after-life, and of the possibility of salvation for those still living (Dovlo 1993). Most West African peoples hold that after death one must cross a river between the world of the living and the world of the ancestors, so as to be integrated into ancestral spiritual segments of their families. This is the ideal after-life scenario, in which one finds peace in being reunited with the family. It reaffirms the sense of community that forms the basis for the entire cult of the ancestors. Those who do not cross this river become "wandering ghosts." They remain restless in the world of the living and are considered hostile to the living.

The roles that ancestors play generate a mixture of respect, filial love, fear, and reliance in their descendents. The latter perform various rituals of communication, communion, appreciation, remembrance, and consultation so as to be in harmonious relationship with the ancestors. The rituals involve libation prayers, offerings, animal sacrifices and festivals, as illustrated by, for example, the *Adae* Festival of the Akan of Ghana.

The rituals performed for the ancestors have led to a debate as to whether they are simply venerated, or actually worshipped. Peter Sarpong (1970) and Fashole-Luke (1980) argue that they are only venerated and not worshiped. Others (Sawyer 1966, Pobee 1979, 66) argue that though pietistic adoration may not be strong in rituals directed at the ancestors, many of the elements of ancestral rites are not different from those accorded to the gods or God. Bolaji Idowu (1973, 180) has also argued that the notions of veneration and worship are psychologically too close for a distinction to be made in the case of the ancestors. Moreover, some ancestors are apotheosized into gods, as is particularly the case among the Yoruba of Nigeria. Among the Mende of Sierra Leone, the Supreme Being is regarded as the great ancestor. It is therefore difficult to rule out the fact that the ancestors enjoy a level of worship and rituals pertaining to them that go beyond veneration.

It seems that insistence that the ancestors are venerated and not worshipped involves a level of apologetics that seeks to make them comparable to saints, so as to make them acceptable in a Christian context. This, however, involves imposing a Christian and Western template which insists that "only God deserves worship." The position of West African traditional religions would be that "only God deserves ultimate worship." In that case, the ancestors may be accurately seen as receiving veneration and a degree of worship in traditional West African religion.

References

Dovlo, Elom. 1993. Ancestors and Soteriology in African and Japanese Religions. *Studies in Interreligious Dialogue* 3, no. 1:48–57.

Dzobo, N. Values in a Changing Society: Man, Ancestors, and God. In *Person and Community*, eds. Kwasi Wiredu and Kwame Gyekye. Washington, D.C.: The Council for Research into Values and Philosophy.

Ephirim-Donkor, Anthony. 1997. *African Spirituality. On Becoming Ancestors.* Trenton, N.J.: African World Press.

Fashole-Luke, E. W. 1980. The Ancestors: Worship or Veneration—Introduction. *Sierra Leone Bulletin of Religion.* n.s. 1 (December): 37–50.

Fiawood, D. K. 1976. Characteristic Features of Ewe Ancestor Worship. In *Ancestors,* ed. William H. Newell. The Hague: Mouton.

Idowu, Bolaji. 1973. *African Traditional Religion. A Definition.* London: SCM Press.

Pobee, J. S. 1979. *Towards an African Theology.* Abingdon/Nashville: Parthenon Press.

Sarpong, Peter. 1970. A Theology of Ancestors. *Insight and Opinion.* 6, no. 2:1–9.

Sawyer, Harry. 1964. Ancestor Worship I—The Mechanics. *Sierra Leone Bulletin of Religion* 6, no. 2 (December):25–33.

———. 1966. Ancestor Worship II—The Rationale. *Sierra Leone Bulletin of Religion.* 8, no. 2 (December):33–37.

ELOM DOVLO

See also **Cosmology; Divination; Religion: African Traditional Religion**

ANGOLA (REPUBLIC OF ANGOLA)

Located on southern Africa's west coast, Angola (including to the north the small former Portuguese enclave of Cabinda) is a large country of approximately 13 million people with a climate that ranges from tropical to subtropical. Angola's capital and largest city is Luanda, which has a population of over 2 million. Thirty-seven percent of Angola's ethnic population is Ovimbundu, 25 percent is Kimbundu, 13 percent is Bakongo, while one-quarter of the population consists of other unidentified groups. There is also a small population of mixed Portuguese and African heritage called *mestiço*. The major languages spoken throughout the country are Portuguese, Ovimbundu, Kimbundu, and Kongo. Nearly half of Angola's people (47%) still practice their traditional indigenous religions, while 37 percent are Roman Catholic, and 15 percent are Protestant.

After centuries of Portuguese rule and years of unrest due to its Fascist government, a national war of liberation began in 1961. Angola finally won its independence from Portugal on November 11, 1975. Following the rapid process of decolonization, major conflicts arose between the three major parties that were vying for postcolonial power. The situation was further complicated by interference by countries such as apartheid-era South Africa and the United States, who supported UNITA, and the former Soviet Union and Cuba, who supported the MPLA during the Cold War period. Since 1975, more than 1,500,000 people have died and 2 million people have been either displaced or have fled the country. The situation has slightly improved since the end of the Cold War in 1991, but when UNITA lost the 1998 elections, their leader, Jonas Savimbi, continued the civil war allegedly funding his efforts with "blood diamonds"—illegally mined and sold diamonds. With Savimbi's death in 2002 and the incorporation of many UNITA fighters into the government, reconciliation and peace now seem possible.

Although the economy of Angola has greatly suffered because of the war, early twenty-first century yearly oil revenues are 3.5 billion; nevertheless, since the end of the civil war corruption continues and currently 2 million people face starvation. Part of the problem is the thousands of remaining landmines, preventing the return to normal life and to the farming of the country's fertile soil. (One in 415 Angolans has had a landmine injury.) In addition to crude oil, diamonds and minerals are important exports.

Angola's years of turmoil have prevented many cultural rites and celebrations. In addition to the historically important Kongo peoples, the Chokwe are perhaps the best-known group, recognized for their extraordinary verbal and visual arts.

JENNIFER JOYCE

ANIMALS IN AFRICAN FOLKLORE

Animals are frequent protagonists and subjects of African folklore. There are several principal reasons why people are so likely to think about animals via narrative. As James Fernandez (1995) suggests, it is difficult to know how we would understand our own identity as human beings, were it not for "the 'other animals' that serve so conveniently and appropriately as a frame for [his] own activity and reflectivity." In other words, what it means to be human is often understood by recognizing contrasts to, and similarities with, animals.

When people tell stories about animals, they are usually talking about themselves, or at least about animal/human relations. An important effect of this parallel thinking is that through animal proverbs, tales, songs, epithets, and other narrative forms, we humans can discuss ourselves and each other indirectly. Such an expressive device is an example of allegory—a term derived from two Greek particles: *allos,* "other," or something next to or beside a point of reference, and *gory,* from the verb *agoreuein,* which is "to speak publicly," but with specific reference to the *agora* or marketplace. "Speaking publicly" in a market implies bargaining, debate, and negotiation: in other words, politics. Such a sense is carried through to the word *allegory,* for as is illustrated by the well-known allegory *Animal Farm* by George Orwell (1945), the political messages conveyed by seemingly innocent little stories can be very trenchant indeed. Here is the point, then: Using animals as the heroes and subjects of folktales allows indirection because the foibles or vices of some person or faction can be contemplated and discussed without outright confrontation. In the small, face-to-face communities that characterize much of Africa, avoiding conflict, while bringing attention to disharmonious behavior through narratives, is of critical importance.

Cosmogonic Myths

The protagonists or auxiliary characters of cosmogonic myths are often animals. In some such accounts, animal or animal-like beings trod the earth before humans did, and it was they who established the first parameters of social life as humans would come to know it. The Dogon people of Mali speak of primordial, proto–human beings called Nommo, who shared attributes with mudfish and snakes—animals often considered "amorphous and virtual" and "everything that has not yet acquired form," as Mircea Eliade (1959, 148) put it. According to the famous Dogon sage Ogotemmeli (Griaule 1970), Nommo had unarticulated serpentine members, undifferentiated gender, and other traits embodying all that is potential and not yet formalized. One Nommo decided to defy God by stealing a piece of the sun to bring fire to earth as the basis of human culture. The Nommo fitted out a granary (or silo) as an ark for his descent, with all categories of plant, animal, and human ethnicity necessary to the world that humans would come to know. As he began his trip downward along the rainbow, God discovered the Nommo's betrayal and furiously hurled lightning bolts that so accelerated the ark's trajectory that it crashed to earth. As it did, the plants, animals, and people it bore were dispersed to their present locations, and the snakelike arms and legs of the Nommo were broken at what would become the shoulders, elbows, wrists, hips, knees, and ankles: body parts and appendages necessary for the Dogon agricultural lifestyle.

Tricksters

Animals often serve as tricksters in African folklore. Hares, small antelopes, and several other animals engage in hilarious adventures through which they grossly exceed and often subvert expectation by outwitting beasts ostensibly far more powerful and important than they. Paradoxically, by reversing all that is ordinary, they teach what is ordinary to rapt audiences. Through trickster tales, children learn and adults reaffirm social norms and proper behavior.

Most famous of all African tricksters is Anansi, the spider of Ashanti lore that has found a place in the hearts of people far from its native Ghana (Pelton 1989). Indeed, Anansi came to the Americas via the trans-Atlantic slave trade, and he is alive and well in Jamaica and many other places. Spiders, including some quite big ones in semitropical parts of Africa, inhabit interstices: their webs stretch across paths or between one structure and another in such a way that they seem neither here nor there, and yet are both here and there at the same time. Anansi is "Mr. In-Between" himself, able to be all things and none, simultaneously. As such, Anansi personifies possibility, and his preposterous misadventures are the stuff of humor with a didactic edge.

Not all spider tricksters are web-spinners. Su, the trickster of the Sara peoples of southern Chad (Fortier 1967), is a large, red, hairy, hunting spider that is always rushing from one place to another as it seeks its prey, never being anyplace at any given time. One of Su's adventures exemplifies the creative hypotheses that all African animal tricksters achieve. A chief had a beautiful daughter who was physically able to speak, but refused to do so; her silence meant that she could not marry, thus thwarting her father's wishes to create a political alliance through her wedding. The chief promised his daughter's hand to whomever could

oblige her to talk, but handsome suitor after handsome suitor failed. When Su offered to try, everyone laughed that such an insignificant creature would have such grand pretensions. Su entered the daughter's house carrying a large bundle of straw with which he tried to thatch her roof—from the inside, rather than the outside. Su's defiance of gravity meant that the straw fell all over him in a most comical way. The young woman could not contain her laughter, and when she called Su a fool, her father was so overjoyed to hear her first word that he gave her to Su to wed. Such a seemingly simple story underscores the essential need for communication, with an added message that often the least important soul has the best ideas.

Proverbs and Praises

Animals are the subject of a great many African proverbs and praises. The Tabwa people of Congo-Kinshasa have many sayings about lions, for instance, such as "to see a lion is to escape from it" (Roberts 1995). The first refers to the fact that lions are supremely gifted hunters, whose prowess and powers are such that they need hunt only an hour a day, even during seasons when game is most dispersed and difficult to find. The other twenty-three hours, they lay about like "honey poured out in the sun," as one writer had it (Anne Morrow Lindbergh, cited in George Schaller 1972, 120–2). When lions are not hunting, they are not hungry, and their erstwhile prey often graze surprisingly close to where a pride is relaxing. "To see a lion is to escape from it" refers to such easygoing times, for it is when one does not see the lion, that it may be sneaking up behind some unsuspecting victim. Political use of such a phrase is obvious: the most powerful people may be benign most of the time, but all should beware their ruthlessness as they clandestinely pursue their own interests.

African rural peoples, such as the Nuer of the Sudan (Evans-Pritchard 1977) may live so interdependently with their cattle and other livestock that the relationship bears the intimacy of psychological identification. Nuer take their own names from the colors and patterns, horn shape and size, and other attributes of favorite cows and oxen. A Nuer youth chants his ox-name as he dances before young women or engages in dueling with clubs or other sports; and in the old days, he would shout the name as he hurled a spear at an enemy or a game animal. Songs and poems are composed praising one's cattle, and it is never quite clear—to an outsider, at least—whether the subject of these narratives is an ox or a person.

Invectives

Animals are often invoked as invective, in playful insults as well as hurtful words meant to instigate a fight. Among the Yoruba and related peoples of southeastern Bénin Republic, for instance, young men in rival Gelede masquerade societies may taunt each other through songs, provocative choreography, and the iconography of masks made for the occasion. A mask seen in the town of Cové depicts a dog standing on its back legs, trying to bite a bat hanging from a tree; a bird atop the tree tries to attack the bat from above (Roberts 1995). The song accompanying the masked performance mocks the members of a rival Gelede society as being like the bat, neither birds nor beasts, but a little of both in such a precarious position that they have no particular status whatsoever.

Insults can be taken much farther than this innocent play. We all know what can happen in the United States if someone calls an adversary a "pig," an "old goat," a "fox," or the colloquial term for "female dog." Among Tabwa people of Congo-Kinshasa, the quickest way to make someone furious is to call the person an animal—not any particular beast, just "Animal!" The message is that you, fool that you are, are not even human, and thus hardly worth contempt.

References

Eliade, Mircea. 1957. *The Sacred and the Profane.* New York: Harcourt Brace.

Evans-Pritchard, E. 1977. *Nuer Religion* (1956). New York: Oxford University Press.

Fernandez, James. 1995. Meditating on Animals, Figuring Out Humans! In *Animals in African Art: From the Familiar to the Marvelous,* by Allen Roberts. Munich: Prestel for the Museum for African Art, New York.

Fortier, Joseph. 1967. *Le mythe et les contes de Sou en pays Mbaï-Moissala.* Paris: Juillard.

Griaule, Marcel. 1970. *Conversations with Ogotemmeli.* New York: Oxford University Press.

Orwell, George. 1996. *Animal Farm.* New York: Signet Classic.

Pelton, Robert. 1989. *The Trickster in West Africa.* Berkeley: University of California Press.

Roberts, Allen. 1995 *Animals in African Art: From the Familiar to the Marvelous.* Munich: Presented for the Museum for African Art. New York.

Schaller, George. 1972. *The Serengeti Lion: A Study in Predator-Prey Relations.* Chicago: University of Chicago Press.

ALLEN F. ROBERTS

See also **Divination; Tricksters in African Folklore.**

ARABIC FOLK LITERATURE OF NORTH AFRICA

The language (or more precisely the linguistic layers) of North African Arabic folk literature has not yet been paid the attention it deserves. This is due to the emphasis generally placed on literary or anthropological aspects of the texts, the reluctance to grant legitimacy to colloquial or colloquializing speech, and the difficulties of performing a suitable analysis. The following considerations should thus be considered programmatic, rather than based on extensive research.

Since the late twentieth century, a number of studies have showed that it is more fruitful to look at linguistic productions in Arabic as taking place on a linguistic continuum and ranging between colloquial (*ʾâmmiyya, därija*) and literary (*fusʾhʾâ*) Arabic, rather than in terms of diglossia (with a high and a low variety). This type of analysis should be applied to literary productions as well, be they learned or popular because phenomena observed are basically the same, even if the properly literary character brings along some additional specific characteristics.

Variation

Contrary to what is usually assumed, Arabic folk literature (folk tales, epics, proverbs, songs (about women, children, wedding, or work), poetry (whether religious, gnomic, satirical, love, or elegiac), riddles and other verbal art forms are indeed composed in a multiplicity of linguistic varieties that can be described as neither daily colloquial, nor standard literary, Arabic. Phrased more positively, these forms are expressed as a set of mixed varieties in which the two polar types mingle and interfere in various ways. The basic ingredients (phonological, morphological, syntactical and lexical) are not necessarily used as they would be in the two original varieties, and they contribute in shaping a new, multiform variety of a third type. Sometimes this form is colloquializing, sometimes more classicizing; but in any case it has its own distinctive linguistic characteristics. This applies to oral as well to written folk literature, which shows that, from this point of view also, no clear dividing line can be drawn between the spoken and the written.

Other facts make the complex nature of this linguistic system even more complicated, and its description and analysis more difficult. On one hand, the colloquial background may add its mark. This holds especially true for the lexicon: "local" material may spread over larger areas and enrich the common cumulative lexicon of folk literature. The result can be temporary or long-lasting misunderstandings; the latter case explains certain semantic or stylistic transformations.

Beyond local variation, literature is produced within sociologically or geographically distinct communities (although often living in close contact): For example, Bedouin, rural, urban or regional. This literature developed (through processes hardly studied in the early twenty-first century) traditions and true literary lingua francas, the most strongly established of which became transregional. It should be noted here that Jewish folk literature is not, linguistically speaking, to be set apart from its Muslim counterpart, notwithstanding the occurrence of specific features of North African Judeo-Arabic dialects and, obviously, of Jewish religious or community themes. These regional linguistic commonalities also often cross the borders of literary genres: "many rural songs [. . .] are also performed in the manner and to the tune of urban songs" and "conversely, many urban songs are also performed in the bedouin way" (Belhalfaoui 1973, 24, 25).

On the other hand, folk literature, being well established as such, constitutes a large cumulative corpus with its own archives. The diachronic variation of the dialects as well as the one of its genuine linguistic usage is incorporated into it, and supplies it with successive contributions that do not stop interacting. Some texts, especially those belonging to the most fixed genres, can thus be rather difficult to understand properly. They are, for this very reason, invaluable to the historian of language.

Finally, one has to take into account that folk literature, as any literature, uses language for the purpose of artistic expression; thus the language is played with, as new linguistic constructions are developed, and submitted to new formal constraints (with specific modifications or distortions, especially in the case of sung poetry). Such creativity also brings about conscious meditations on the literature itself as a cohesive illustration of a culture, and an awareness of intentional or traditionally preserved archaisms, clichés and, on the contrary, of creative innovations. In short, folk literature uses language metalinguistically and, at the same time, lets it conform with respect to the codes and conventions it shapes to itself (reserving some of them for specific genres).

Intrinsic variation due to the creative mixing of colloquial and standard Arabic combines with other types of variation, due to dialectal variety (which has itself to be set within the sociolinguistic distinction between urban, rural, and Bedouin dialects), to diachronic depth, and to phenomena proper to the literary use of language.

Typology

In order to set up a typology of intermediate language varieties used in North African Arabic folk literature, one should probably start with distinguishing between prose and poetry, although the forms act upon each other. This distinction only partly coincides with the one that can be drawn between literary genres with low-specialized transmission (e.g., folk tales) and with high-specialized transmission (e.g., sung poetry). In this respect, epics might be considered closer to poetry: they actually include poems, the prose sequences being most often transitions between or comments on them. Folk tales, which allow a greater commitment of the storyteller, are more open to the evolution of the dialects, even if archaisms and formulas are normally scrupulously preserved. More fixed genres, like proverbs or ritual songs (of which the language can be very mixed), are less exposed to variation; more exactly, the variants observed in them often show evidence of sequences having been replaced because they were no longer intelligible. Poetry is many sided: it can be either very colloquializing, or composed in a much more mixed and codified variety (e.g., *melh'ûn*)—even in late-twentieth-century pieces (as betrayed by words referring to modern objects or concepts, or by French borrowings), or very classicizing works (as in many songs in praise of the Prophet). But it has to be emphasized that no one-to-one correspondence can be established between language variety and literary genre. One comes across religious or even didactic poems in colloquial as well as across classicizing rural songs (Norris 1968, 92ff).

A very general classification is given for Algerian poetry of the beginning of this century by Jean Desparmet (1907, 444), and is reiterated by Jacques Grand'Henry (1981, 652) who, extending it to "the linguistic levels in Arabic Maghrebine folk poetry," makes a distinction between "Andalusian and archaic urban colloquial Arabic," "West-Algerian Bedouin [colloquial] Arabic," and "Neoarabic of Koranic inspiration." If such a classification rightly draws attention to three of the main trends which historically contributed to shaping Maghrebine folk poetry, and if it is also to its credit to show that linguistic levels cross the frontiers between literary genres, it can only be considered indicative from the point of view of the linguistic typology of texts. Indicative also are the useful remarks made by authors like Pierre Cachia (1989, 59–62) on the language of Egyptian *mawwâl* or by Sibylle Vocke (1990, 58–74) on the language of Moroccan *melh'ûn*-poetry; al-Fâsî (1991) is invaluable but restricted to the lexicon of this last genre. Concerning prose folk literature, descriptive remarks made by scholars will have to be collated, but even a quick glance at the texts reveals wide discrepancies between the linguistic varieties they use.

An accurate linguistic typology would have to take into account the different literary "dialects" (and their complex interactions) and to be founded on a thorough comparative inventory of precise linguistic features. Below are short descriptions of such features. One will notice that they are not different, as a whole, from the features characteristic of those intermediate varieties, usually referred to as Middle Arabic, which have been used for

centuries, all over the Arabic-speaking world, in other nonstandard types of (written) literature.

Phonetics (consonants, vowels, syllabic structure) is largely colloquial, but allows itself borrowings from standard Arabic, and uses interdialectal variants. The best example is the one of the *qâf* (uvular stop), of which the Bedouin (in both the dialectal and common meanings) realization *gâf* (postpalatal voiced stop) is widely used and is even the rule in some lexemes. In poetry, an *-i* can always (and an *a-* sometimes) be added to a word ending with a consonant; a final vowel can always be dropped. For the purpose of rhyme, an *-n* (and sometimes other consonants like *-d*) can be added to a word ending with a vowel. *Aw* and *u / û* often alternate. Written documents—which are not rare—show that an orthographic norm (with local variants) has been set up to transcribe colloquialisms or colloquializing pronunciations. Largely dependent on the classical norm, it also uses genuine notations (mostly generalizations of existing classical orthographic peculiarities) like alif before an initial cluster of two consonants to indicate that it has to be pronounced *CC-* (and not *CVC-*), or alif after a final vocalic *wâw* even in nonverbal forms.

Nominal morphology, although rather colloquial (thus *CV* syllables with unstressed vowel are usually not found) is more mixed. It does not refrain from playing with vowel length (and with consonantal gemination), and from switching—for the same root—from a noun form to another (and sometimes new) one. Some noun forms, which are of infrequent use in both colloquial and standard varieties, are particularly valued and sought after, like *teCCâC* (verbal noun of the second derived verbal stem) or *CaCCân* (verbal noun or adjective). The range of plural forms is wide and includes some unprecedented (analogical) ones.

Verbal morphology is basically colloquial (with e.g., *n-* . . . [*u*] for the first person of the imperfective), although preverbal particles (like Moroccan *ka-*) are rather rare in poetry. The active participle is readily used with its colloquial constructions and aspectual values. The use of the verbal derived stems is more complex: proper colloquial stems like *CCâC* are found, but the so-called passive stem with prefixed *n-* occurs more frequently than in the colloquials (where the *t-* prefix stem is predominant); apophonic (standard) passives are not excluded. As is the case with nouns, short vowels can be lengthened, and vice-versa. Switching from some derived stems to some others, considered of a higher expressive and/or stylistic value, can be observed. Colloquial auxiliary verbs are of constant use; among them, originally motion or posture verbs are very important narrative devices.

Pronouns are often colloquial: personal pronouns (whether independent or bound), demonstrative (and, maybe to a lesser degree, interrogative) pronouns and adjectives. The relative adjective usually appears in its (invariable) colloquial form (*illi, ildi,* etc.) but the relative pronouns seem to occur more frequently in their standard forms. *Dû* and *dâ* have special uses. Predominantly colloquial are also quantifiers and adverbs. For genuine standard prepositions, colloquial counterparts are often substituted (like *l(V)* for *'ilâ*).

With syntax, classical nominal desinential inflexion (declension) is normally absent, and occurs only in classicisms or pseudo-classicisms. The use of a final (often conjunctive) element *n* is probably historically related to *tanwîn* (the mark of indefiniteness) but has a quite different function. The use of colloquial genitive particles (*ntâ*, *dyâl* etc.) is not rare. The pseudo-verbal presentative particle *ra-* is frequent. The negation system is extremely mixed; the second element <u>*sh(i)*</u> of the dimorphematic colloquial negative particles is not infrequent. The concord (agreement) system is also mixed and complex. Regarding the syntax of subordinate clauses, syndetic as well as asyndetic constructions abound; the subjunctive particles are often colloquial. The conjunctive particle, used in its colloquial (*u*, *w*[*V*]) as well as in its standard (*wa*) shape, is an easily identifiable stylistic device. Word order, as can be expected, is less constrained than in both the standard and colloquial varieties.

Finally, the lexicon is particularly rich and complex. The most usual words (referring to the most fundamental objects and operations), for example, nouns meaning "things," "letter," "man," "poor"; verbs meaning "to take," "to show," "to want," "to jump"; adverbs meaning "much," "quickly," as well as particularly descriptive and expressive words (e.g., a verb meaning "to wiggle") are most often colloquial. But the lexical resources of all the linguistic registers are mobilized: words and locutions can thus be ancient or archaic (and this raises the issue of the possible survival of an old preclassical literary tradition; see Pellat 1987, 239), classical, colloquial, borrowed from European languages, original creations (for instance by playing with forms and stems as already mentioned). A real technical lexicon has thus been constituted (especially in poetry), made up of numerous words of various origins, which have undergone complex semantic evolutions and have been finally sanctioned by tradition. These terms—sometimes occurring in the texts next to synonyms then functioning as glosses—are often unintelligible to the layman, who nevertheless remains receptive to their stylistic effect.

References

Belhalfaoui, Mohamed. 1973. *La poésie arabe maghrébine d'expression populaire*. Paris: François Maspéro.

Cachia, Pierre. 1989. *Popular Narrative Ballads of Modern Egypt*. Oxford: Clarendon Press.

Desparmet, Jean. 1907. La poésie arabe actuelle à Blida et sa métrique. In *Actes du XIVème Congrès International des Orientalistes* (Alger 1905). Paris: Leroux.

Fâsî, Muhʾammad al-. 1991. *Maʾlamat al-Malhʾûn, II, 1: Muʾjam lughat al-malhʾûn*. Rabat: Al-Hilâl al-ʾarabiyya (Matʾbûʾât Akadîmiyyat al-mamlaka al-maghribiyya, Silsilat ʾal-Turâthʾ).

Grand'Henry, Jacques. Les niveaux de langue dans la poésie populaire arabe du Maghreb. In Bono Homini Donum: *Essays in Historical Linguistics in Memory of J. Alexander Kerns*, eds. Yoel, L. Arbeitman and Allan R. Bombhard. Amsterdam: *Studies in the Theory of Linguistic Science*. Vol. 4, *Current Issues in Linguistic Theory*, Vol 2. 1981. Amsterdam: Benjamins.

Norris, H. T. 1968. *Shinqîtî Folk Literature and Song*. Oxford: Clarendon Press (The Oxford Library of African Literature).

Pellat, Charles. 1987. Malhʾûn. In *Encyclopédie de l'Islam*, (2d ed.). Leiden: Brill.

Vocke, Sibylle. 1990. *Die marokkanische Malhʾûnpoesie*. Wiesbaden: Harrassowitz.

JÉRÔME LENTIN

See also **Languages; Maghrib, Music: Arab and Jewish Music of North Africa**

ARCHITECTURE

Traditional African architecture is frequently described as nothing more than an assortment of small mud huts, an evaluation meant to dismiss the topic from further consideration. Although some Africans do indeed build their houses with clay, these dwellings are not the simple structures that they might outwardly seem. Earthen-walled structures can vary significantly in size, configuration, or decoration even within a single ethnic group, a circumstance that points toward the complexity of building designs across the African landscape. Further, even the most cursory survey of indigenous African architecture will reveal a number of monumental buildings, including palaces, shrines, fortresses, and mosques, that are certainly comparable to European structures built during the same periods. The faulty characterizations that portray African architecture as marginal and minimal demand revision. For centuries Africans have crafted buildings that signal and embody the cultural richness of the continent. Because the building traditions of Africa are as numerous and as different as its peoples, one should speak of African architecture*s*.

The basic environmental patterns within the continent provide one of the reasons for the diversity of African architectural traditions. Building practices that were developed, for example, to cope with the conditions of the equatorial rain forests would not be used in the desert regions. Those peoples living in the arid grasslands of northern Ghana often build houses topped with flat roof terraces that would certainly erode into huge lumps of mud if constructed just 200 miles to the south where seasonal rains are prolonged and intense. Housing types will vary as well with differing economic activities and social customs. Nomadic cattle herders, who must constantly move their livestock onward to new pastures, build temporary shelters with readily available materials. By contrast, long-settled groups of farming peoples who claim ownership over particular patches of ground construct residences that are fixed, permanent, and substantial; their houses are as rooted as the crops they raise. Further, there is a direct connection between house form and the pattern of family organization. An ethnic group that sanctions monogamous marital unions will generally require only a single freestanding dwelling to shelter a couple and their children, while societies that practice polygyny will build compound houses where a man will live with his several wives in a cluster of small buildings gathered around a common yard. Other determinants affecting building and design decisions might include location (rural or urban), religion (Christianity, Islam, or traditionalist), status of the owner (royalty, commoner, or slave), personal wealth, historical period, and the degree of contact with foreign influences.

The following profiles provide a quick tour of traditional architecture in the major geographical regions of Africa. They not only furnish examples of representative building types and technologies, but also suggest some of the historical and cultural forces at work in the construction of houses.

Zimbabwe

On a nearly mile-high plateau in southern Zimbabwe there stand a set of impressive granite ruins, abandoned by their Shona builders sometime in middle of the fifteenth century. This place called Zimbabwe (venerated houses), has provided the country previously known as Rhodesia with its new name. The entire site contains twelve sets of house foundations along with the remains of their enclosing walls. The largest and most intact of these is the so-called Elliptical Building, which has an outer wall 32 feet tall and 17 feet thick at its base tapering to a width of about 4 feet at the top. Forming an 800 foot-long encircling perimeter, this wall was laid up without mortar in smooth, regular courses and topped off with decorative frieze in a chevron pattern. At regular intervals along the top of the wall stand stone monoliths, some of them as much as 14 feet tall. Visitors entered the enclosure of the Elliptical Building by means of a narrow pathway formed by the outer wall and an equally impressive inner wall. Curving about halfway around of the enclosure, the path led to a 30-foot-tall conical tower that was 18 feet in diameter at its base, thought to have previously served as some sort of altar. Other features suggest the presence of at least eight dwelling houses.

All the attention given to visual symbolism at Zimbabwe, when coupled with evidence that perhaps only twenty-five people lived within the walls of the Elliptical Building, suggests that the structure was meant primarily to serve ritual rather than residential functions. It is believed that a small group of elites, the ancestral leaders of the Shona, consolidated their authority over the other peoples of region some time round 1400 CE and extracted tribute in the form of gold, ivory, iron, copper, salt, and cloth, which was presented to them at Zimbabwe. The elements of courtly ornament and sculpture recovered by archaeologists, when viewed within the architectural contexts of Zimbabwe's stone walls, suggest a high degree of luxury and confidence among this ruling group. Clearly they understood that built form could effectively reinforce their claims to authority and respect.

Fulani

The Fulani are widely dispersed across the West African savannah, from eastern Senegal to northern Cameroon. Divided into three subgroups—nomads, farmers, and urban dwellers—each is distinguished by a different set of building forms. Among the nomadic Fulani, who live principally as cattle herders, entire families occupy temporary shelters consisting of light frames covered with woven mats or with a thatch made of long grass. These structures may be either dome shaped, approximately 18 feet in diameter and 8 feet high, or oblong in plan, roughly 24 feet long and 9 feet wide. Those Fulani who converted to Islam and then took up the routines of fixed cultivation have adopted a more permanent form of architecture, erecting round houses with adobe walls topped by a conical roofs. Several of these cone-on-cylinder forms are loosely grouped to form family compounds, with men and women each living in their own separate buildings. The earliest compound houses of urban Fulani were similar to those of farming families but their construction was more substantial. Encircled with high perimeter walls made with thick adobe bricks, admission into a compound was gained through a special entry lobby. Visitors were allowed no further into the household than this room. Over time the various round houses in the compound, often built as two interlinked cylinders topped with flat roofs, were replaced with square and rectangular units. These changes are indications of the growing influence of the so-called Sudanic style of architecture, a material sign of the expanding influence of Islamic culture in West Africa after 1300 CE. Given the well-known commitment to Islam among the urban Fulani, it is not surprising that they would, in due course, also adopt Islamic architectural traditions.

Tuareg

The Tuareg are a nomadic people who raise camels, which they trade throughout the eastern Saharan desert ranging from the Niger River all the way to Algeria. Given the necessary mobility of their lives, they live in tents. They use two types: one consists of a large piece of cloth, roughly 15 by 20 feet, that is stretched over a set of poles; the second is fixed frame tent employing a dome-shaped armature draped with mats or pieces of cloth. Seeming to be nothing more than minimal, temporary shelters, these tents actually demonstrate a sophisticated understanding of materials. Often called *black tents*, their coffee-colored cloth coverings are made from goat hair. The open weave of this fiber tightens under the sun's rays providing both a dense shade against radiant heat. In the coolness of the desert evening, when temperatures can drop as low as 45 degrees Fahrenheit, the cloth usefully retains the heat generated during the day. The mats covering the fixed frame tents can be easily adjusted to enhance the comfort of the occupants. Rolled up along the sides of the tent during the day to promote ventilation, they can be quickly dropped back down to provide protection from a sudden sand storm. Although Tuareg tents have drab exteriors, inside they can be decorated with colorful blankets displaying all manner of geometric designs. Even the much plainer palm mats may be woven with bands of alternating color. Some Tuareg, particularly those living in the southern portions of the Sahara, have taken up a more sedentary farming life and in the process they have begun to build permanent houses following closely the examples provided by their Mande- or Hausa-speaking neighbors. Such a move may ultimately signal the end of the Tuareg tent-making tradition.

Iraqw

Today the Iraqw, a farming group living in the hills of northern Tanzania, build round mud-walled houses topped with conical thatched roofs. Providing shelter for livestock as well as people, the human occupants sleep on a platform about 8 feet above the house floor, while most of the ground level is used as a stable where cows and goats are penned during the evening. Although the Iraqw house is small, usually not more than 16 feet in diameter, the space immediately in front of the door is also claimed as part of the building and is treated as an all-purpose living room. Called an *afeni*, this courtyard is dug out about a foot lower than the threshold of the doorway. It is plastered repeatedly with dung to make it smooth and hard.

In earlier times (but even as recently as 1976) Maasai warriors would raid the Iraqw in order to steal their cattle. The Iraqw responded by retreating to highlands where they constructed underground houses. These buildings were formed by digging rectangular pits roughly 36 by 30 feet. They were entered by means of an excavated passage or, if the house was dug into the slope of hill, through a door located in the downhill wall. Their flat roofs made of woven branches plastered with clay were supported by as many as seventy poles. In these low, windowless buildings that were not more than 6 feet tall, the Iraqw hid with their livestock, hoping that the earthen camouflage would provide sufficient protection.

Zulu

One of the major ethnic groups of South Africa, the traditional Zulu build distinctive dome-shaped houses covered in grass. Although other neighboring groups erect similar domed dwellings, the Zulu *indulu* is thought to be more sophisticated in its construction. First, a circle approximately 16 feet across is marked out and a foundation trench is dug around its circumference. Next hundreds of small rods of varying lengths are planted in the foundation and bent to form interlacing arches of increasing height. Inclining inward as they rise, the uppermost of these arches eventually touch at the apex of the dome about 8 feet above the ground where they are lashed together. Thatch is then applied on top of this dense framework and firmly secured in place by a net made of rope. The more elaborate *indulu* are finished with decorative patterns, criss-cross designs and swags, which are woven into the rope netting.

In past times, when the Zulu were known for their vast herds of cattle, they grouped their houses into a large circles surrounding a livestock pen called a kraal. The houses were in turn enclosed by a sturdy timber stockade. The Zulu homestead was then actually a fortified camp and it served as the pattern for the "war towns" that they developed during the nineteenth century. These towns could be as much as a half a mile in diameter and might contain as many as fourteen hundred houses. But with the collapse of Zulu military power, their subsequent shift to mixed farming, and the decline of the practice of polygamous marriage, the size of the kraal homestead was diminished as well. Today a kraal might consist of only a small goat pen and by accompanied be three domed houses.

Bamileke

The Bamileke inhabit the lush forests of western Cameroon and thus have access to large quantities of bamboo with which to construct their houses. Opting for a square floor plan, they begin with a stone foundation measuring about 15 feet on each side. A bamboo frame, standing as much as 20 feet high, is then raised and lashed in place. The roof, which is conical in shape, is truly a tour de force of carpentry. Rising at least 15 feet above the ceiling and extending about 3 feet beyond the walls of the house, it is stiffened by a pyramidal frame and supported by a series of posts standing around the building. The walls may be plastered with clay or sided with bamboo poles tied vertically to the frame. The houses of chiefs follow the same pattern but are larger in every dimension and may feature doorways decorated with carved wooden frames.

The rectilinear quality of Bamileke space is seen throughout the typical homestead. All its courtyards, gardens, and fields are either square or rectangular in shape and its various buildings—the owner's house, those of his wives and servants, and his granaries—are all square in plan and are placed at the corners of fenced yards. All these structures are similar in size except for the owner's house, which is slightly larger and taller, a physical indication of his superior social status.

Yoruba

One of the largest ethnic groups in West Africa, millions of Yoruba are found in southwestern Nigeria where their homeland extends from the Gulf of Guinea through the adjacent rain forest to the southern portions of the savannah. This environmental diversity, as might be expected, is reflected in the range of methods which the Yoruba employ in constructing their houses. Near the coast wood-framed dwellings are covered with palm leaves, while further inland house wickerwork walls are coated with mud plaster. In the rain forest and savannah regions, building walls are formed by layers of mud each about a foot thick and 2 feet high.

Despite the differences in construction technique, all Yoruba houses follow a set of common plans. The basic house form is a free-standing rectangular building, 10 by 20 feet divided into two rooms of equal size that is covered by a gabled roof. If larger dwellings are required, several of these units can be linked end to end thus forming a building with up to eight rooms. Because the Yoruba, at least since the sixteenth century, have been an urban people, they maintain a primary family residence in town and use smaller rectangular buildings for shelter when working their farm plots, which can be located as much as twenty miles away. The Yoruba name for an urban compound is *agbo ile* (a flock of houses), a name which suggests that compounds are conceived as clusters of smaller buildings. The Yoruba compound house is best seen as a gathering of farm houses on an urban site. In the savannah region a traditional compound might be arranged around a broad, open courtyard more than 70 feet across, while in the rain forest area the compound was formed around a smaller courtyard sheltered by the extended roofs of its surrounding building units. The edges of these roofs are joined together around the edges of an impluvium, or shallow pool built to catch rain water. Some of the old palaces of Yoruba chiefs were also built in the impluvial style but they might include up to thirty courtyards; the vast scale of such a building immediately signaled the ruler's eminence.

Batammaliba

Occupying a territory that straddles the border between northern Togo and the Republic of Benin, the Batammaliba (also known as the Tamberma or Somba) are an agricultural people who practice mixed farming. Their houses, often described as miniature castles, are visually quite striking. The rooms in a Batammaliba house are located in the bases of towerlike units that stand about 14 feet high. Both round and oval in section, these towers are linked by short connecting walls to form an enclosure about 30 feet in diameter. The sleeping rooms are placed in a tower standing at the center of the enclosure; those for the males are on the ground level and for the females, above them in a separate chamber. The space between this tower and its encircling walls is spanned by heavy rafters and covered by a two-foot-thick roof. Set at height of 8 feet, the roof provides both a protected shelter for livestock and a second-floor terrace where the women tend to their domestic duties. Two granaries, actually large clay jars with holding capacities of hundreds of bushels, stand atop the forward towers on either side of the entry chamber. Topped with tall conical grass roofs, their profiles do recall visually the turrets seen on European fortresses.

Fang

Deep in the rain forests of northern Gabon, the Fang carve out clearings for their villages. These neatly organized farming settlements consist of two long rows of houses arranged in straight lines on either side of a broad plaza. At both ends of this grassless commons stands an *aba* or council house, a structure reserved as the gathering and eating place for men. Women and children reside in the collective buildings flanking the central plaza. The women's abodes, called *kisin*, contain both a kitchen and sleeping space. Fang men may sleep either in a portion of his wife's house, which is partitioned for his use or in a separate adjoining house. Lacking windows, these houses are lit only by the front door that opens toward the center of the village and the rear door that leads to the household garden.

To build a house, the Fang first assemble a frame made with over one hundred wooden poles and then cover it with prefabricated panels made of palm leaves and bamboo strips. The Fang describe this process not as carpentry but as "weaving a house." As of the early twenty-first century, a new building type inspired by European influences has begun to appear in their forest villages. Featuring concrete floors and walls and metal roofs, they are called *cold houses* because they contain no cooking fires. Used only on ritual occasions, this kind of house functions chiefly as a sign of monetary success since the cost for its construction is ten times that of a traditional house.

Attempts to identify regional patterns for African architecture have provided mainly deterministic descriptions aimed at linking certain building types with particular environmental causes. Yet the ethnographic record clearly shows that Africans will react to similar environmental conditions in different ways. In the savannah region of northern Ghana, for example, the Dagomba who build round houses live next to the Gonja who live in rectangular dwellings. Several of the architectural profiles given here show the marked variation in building forms, construction techniques, and spatial organization even within a single group. Further, over time some peoples—the Fulani would be a good example—will change their ideas about what constitutes an acceptable building and thus develop or borrow new plans, technical means, and modes of decoration. Because buildings are basically a material reflection of the dynamic forces of culture and history, they are best understood as expressions of biography rather than geography. Although traditional African architecture has yet to be thoroughly documented, it offers a potent means for understanding the daily lives and concerns of African people.

References

Blier, Suzanne Preston. 1987. *The Anatomy of Architecture: Ontology and Metaphor in Batammaliba Architectural Expression.* Cambridge: Cambridge University Press.

Bourdier, Jean-Paul, and Trinh T. Minh-Ha. 1996. *Drawn from African Dwellings.* Bloomington: Indiana University Press.

Denyer, Susan. 1978. *African Traditional Architecture: An Historical and Geographical Perspective.* New York: Africana Publishing.

Fernandez, James W. 1977. *Fang Architectonics.* Working Papers in the Traditional Arts, No. 1, Philadelphia: Institute for the Study of Human Issues.

Oliver, Paul, ed. 1971. Shelter in Africa. London, Barrie and Jenkins.

———. 1987. *Dwellings: The House across the World.* Austin: University of Texas Press.

Prussin, Labelle. 1969. *Architecture in Northern Ghana: A Study in Forms and Functions.* Berkeley: University of California Press.

———. 1986. *Hatumere: Islamic Design in West Africa.* Berkeley: University of California Press.

Thornton, Robert J. 1980. *Space, Time, and Culture among the Iraqw of Tanzania.* New York: Academic Press.

Vlach, John Michael. 1976. Affecting Architecture of the Yoruba. *African Arts* 10, no. 1:48–53.

JOHN MICHAEL VLACH

See also **Batammaliba; Housing, African American Traditions**

ARCHIVES OF TRADITIONAL MUSIC (INDIANA UNIVERSITY)

The Archives of Traditional Music (ATM) fosters the educational and cultural role of Indiana University through the preservation and dissemination of the world's music and oral traditions. Archives holdings document the history of ethnographic sound recording, from wax cylinders made during museum expeditions in the 1890s to recent commercial releases on compact disc. The ATM has particularly strong holdings of African music and oral data. Included in ATM African materials are tapes collected by major scholars in their respective disciplines, some of the earliest recordings ever made in Africa, as well as some of the largest collections of African country-specific recordings in existence.

Highlights of the African materials at ATM include the BBC Somali Collection, which consists of over 400 hours of recordings of speech and music collected by the Somali Services of the BBC World Service. The BBC Somali Collection, together with other Somali holdings in the ATM, represents almost certainly the largest sound collection of Somali materials in the world. The ATM also holds the large and growing Liberia Collections Project, which includes not only recordings but also photographs and paper documents, including Liberian government documents that no longer can be found in Liberia itself. (This appendix refers only to sound recordings, and does not include other media formats held by the ATM. Check the website *www.onliberia.com* for a complete listing of Liberia Collections Project materials.) The world's largest collection of Egyptian Coptic music, collected by Martha Roy from 1932 to 1977, is also held at the ATM. In addition to these and other ethnographic field collections from all parts of the African continent, the ATM holds broadcast collections as well as hundreds of commercial releases of African music. Although they are not included in the appendix that follows, ATM's commercial collections are extensive, and include many commercial releases of field recordings. Particularly noteworthy among the commercial holdings is the complete International Library of African Music's *Sound of Africa* series, comprising over two hundred commercial releases of field recordings made in southern Africa by Hugh Tracey.

Many major figures in their respective academic disciplines have deposited collections at the ATM. These include ethnomusicologists George Herzog (Liberia, 1930–1931), Alan Merriam (Zaire, Rwanda, and Burundi, 1951–1952, 1959–1960), John Blacking (South Africa, Uganda, and Zambia, 1957–1965), Roderic Knight (The Gambia and Senegal, 1970) and Ruth

Stone (1970–1976), linguist Charles Bird (Mali, 1968–1978), art historians Hans Himmelheber (Ivory Coast, Liberia, and Mali, 1950–1960) and Henry Drewal (Dahomey and Nigeria, 1970–1973), folklorists Phil Peek (Nigeria, 1970–1971) and John Johnson (Mali and Somalia, 1966–1989), anthropologists Melville and Frances Herskovitz (Dahomey, Ghana, and Nigeria, 1931) and Jean Rouch (Niger, 1960), and historian David Robinson (Senegal, 1968–1969). The ATM also holds copies of the Erich von Hornbostel Demonstration Collection from the Berlin Phonogram-Archiv, which includes forty-three recordings made in Africa between 1900 and 1913, the Laura Boulton Collection, including hundreds of recordings of music made on nine expeditions to Africa between 1929 and 1969, and the Dennis Duerden Collection of music and oral data recorded in the 1960s in Cameroon, Ghana, Guinea, South Africa, Sierra Leone, the Gambia, Kenya, Malawi, and Nigeria. These specific references represent merely a sampling of the rich and extensive holdings of African music and oral data at the ATM.

DANIEL B. REED

See also **Appendix: Field and Broadcast Sound Recording Collections at the Indiana University Archives of Traditional Music.**

ASTRONOMY

African astronomy encompasses all the ways that Africans conceptualize celestial bodies. Though little studied, there is a large corpus of writings in English, French, German, and Portuguese that describes various aspects of African astronomy and spans five centuries and the entire continent. Usually, documentary evidence of various types of African astronomy is embedded in larger ethnographic studies or within travel accounts. Scholars of African astronomy today scour these records for fragments of information which nevertheless can lead to new ethnographic fieldwork.

This introduction provides an overview of the types of things one finds in African astronomy, giving specific examples. The topics presented are celestial names, astrology and healing, architecture, calendars, and celestial navigation. The ethnic groups represented are drawn from both North and sub-Saharan Africa.

Celestial Names

Because the sky and its motions are mapped and well understood, it is known exactly what people were seeing on any night given good weather conditions, thus, in theory, any differences that are seen in names should reflect cultural and environmental differences.

South Africa contains around a dozen different ethnic and cultural groups. In 1997, Keith Snedegar published a work on the starlore of four South African groups: the Sotho, the Tswana, the Xhosa, and the Zulu people. The Sotho, Tswana, Xhosa, and Zulu people of South Africa are all part of the Niger-Congo linguistic group. Snedegar identified the names of various celestial bodies in each of the four groups and provided an analysis of his findings. He found that some of the local names reflected the physical appearance of the celestial body, such as the name for Canopus, (Sotho-Twana / Xhosa / Zulu) Naka / U-Canzibe / uCwazibe, meaning "brilliant," and the Milky Way, Mo-lalatladi, / Um-nyele / umTala, being called a hairy stripe. Canopus is the second brightest star in the night sky and is not visible from the United States. Most of the names are significant for the local calendar, including agricultural activities such as the time for planting, the time that animals are observed to mate or give birth, and the weather. One clear example is the now no longer practiced traditions of having initiations when Canopus is sighted just before sunrise. The person who sighted the star first was given a cow by the chief.

Other celestial bodies are named for local animals, with no correlation between the appearance of the celestial body and the mating or birthing season of the animal. The South Africans seem to have many celestial bodies named for nondomesticated animals, a practice which probably reflects their local environment. Further research may reveal what role these undomesticated animals traditionally played in South African life. The name for Sirius—the drawer up of the night—Kgogamashego / Imbal'ubusuku / inDosa, specifically refers to the time to go home after partying all night, which implies an active nightlife for the locals.

None of the names or activities directly refer to women although it is not clear if women are doing the planting and hoeing when the Pleiades, known as Selemela / Selemela / isiLimela, rose, an occurrence which marks the beginning of the planting season. The four South African groups have celestial objects that reflect seasonal events, but it is not clear that the sightings themselves were used to determine part of the local calendar.

The study of celestial names can provide insight into local flora and fauna and tidbits of cultural practice as shown here. The African voice along with myths and folklore could provide far more parallels between cultural norms and celestial names. Thus far, Snedegar's work is the most comprehensive in this regard.

Astrology and Healing

Contemporary astronomers take great care to distinguish their field from astrology; yet historically many "astronomers" made their living as astrologers. Thus, the definition between astrology and astronomy has not always been as rigid as it now stands. The study of astrologers in Africa can be useful because they often kept detailed records of the positions of the sun, moon, and planets over extended periods of time. They differ from astronomers in that the astrologers then utilized this information for purposes of divination and prediction.

Tunisia shares borders with Algeria and Libya. Sicily lays to the northeast, a few hours by boat from the capital of Tunisia, Tunis. Gabes is an oasis town along the eastern coast of Tunisia. The Tunisians are a mixture of Europeans, Berbers, Turks, Egyptians and Africans. Tunis is near the famous port of Carthage, which was founded by the Phoenicians (from what is now Lebanon); since then Tunisia has been conquered by Rome and the Vandals, incorporated into the Ottoman Empire, and colonized by France. Most Tunisians are Muslim though there are minority Christian and Jewish populations.

The following is drawn from an interview in 1999 with an occultist healer, who lived in one of the suburbs outside of Gabes, Tunisia. As part of his healing diagnosis, the healer requested the client's time and date of birth, mother's name, and a description of the ailment. He then did a series of calculations before giving a treatment plan. When asked to explain the calculations, he drew several diagrams and, utilizing a translator carefully, explained that there are the twelve signs of the Zodiac and each sign is associated with one of the elements: air, water, earth, and fire. Each sign rules the heaven for 30 days, which he broke down into three 10-day periods. The daylight hours he divided into twelve equal divisions of time, and the same was done for the night hours, thus, the "hours" have to vary in length over the course of the year. Each resulting hour is associated with a color, a symbol, a planet, and can represent one or two signs of the Zodiac. Similarly, each planet is associated with a color, a metal, and a precious stone. Thus, for each birth date and time he assigned a color, a symbol, a planet, a sign of the Zodiac (or two), a metal, and a precious stone. Knowing how each of these related to each other was important. He utilized all this information in his diagnoses and treatments, along with the description of the ailment.

Interestingly, he traced his occultist intellectual heritage to Egypt, and the Egyptian calendar is based on a ten-day week. The healer was conscious of the fact that astrology is not sanctioned in Islam, however, he felt that what he did, whether right or wrong, was between himself and God, and no one else's business. In his community and among his extended family, he had always been known as a strange child who was not interested in playing with other children. His father noticed his attraction to the occult books in his family's library, so in an effort to dissuade him, threw them in a bonfire. However, the healer simply wrote to occultists in Europe and other places around the world to identify books and share techniques, eventually building his own library on occult matters. He does not accept payment for his work as a healer, yet the community manages to support him with gifts.

In many Muslim societies in Africa, there are traditional healers who utilize astrological information for diagnosis and treatment. The details of how the calculations are done are hard to locate, although the number of such astrologer/healers seems to be quite high. Thus far, this type of traditional healer appears to be limited to Muslim African societies.

Architecture

The Tamberma Batammaliba of Togo are part of the Niger-Congo linguistic group. They reside in Togo east of the town of Kante. The study of Suzanne Preston Blier, now of Harvard University, focuses on the architecture of the Batammaliba. The Batammaliba build two-story houses containing ten "rooms" on each level with mud walls. The name Batammaliba, which means "those who are the real architects of the earth" (Blier 1987, 2) reflects the importance of architecture within their culture.

The ceremonial calendar of the Batammaliba is a stellar calendar. Certain stars and constellations, which are associated with deities, rule certain times of the year. When a star or constellation is observed to set at sunset, that deity is said to have descended to Earth and begins walking from west to east. The deity rules until it reappears in the east at sunset. In addition to observing the stars to determine the ceremonial calendar, the Batammaliba observe the winter solstice. Since the stellar observations determine the true year, the observation of the solstice is not necessary in terms of creating an accurate calendar. However, the Sun is

important as it represents the deity Kuiye, who is said to reenter peoples' homes at midwinter.

Kuiye, the sun god, presides over the month of December. The doors of the Batammaliba houses are aligned to the midwinter sunset, the sunset of the winter solstice. The house of Kuiye is thought to lie in the west, and when the sunlight enters the house at midwinter, it symbolizes the return of Kuiye/the Sun. In addition to the door alignment, a hole is put in the roof of the bedroom on the second floor, which allows Kuiye to enter the bedroom when the Sun transits the zenith (directly overhead). There is a hole in the roof in the middle of the house, which stays covered most of the time, but it is the place that women go to give birth regardless of the time of day. They position themselves under the hole and face the door, thus symbolically gaining the protection of Kuiye during their labor. The bottom floor of the house often contains shrines to various deities which are aligned to get bathed in sunlight during certain times of the year. When there is a death, the body is positioned in the same manner as the women giving birth, under the central hole and facing the door to receive Kuiye's blessings. The funerals are timed to take place in December and January, the time of Kuiye. Certain rites take place at sunrise, in the morning, at midday, in the afternoon, and at sunset symbolically recreating the cycle of the life of the deceased, while also incorporating ideals of regeneration and rebirth, like the Sun's returning each morning.

One of the most important people in the Batammaliba village is the architect, whose main duty is to build houses. However, as Blier emphasizes, the construction of the house is filled with ritual. The architect, therefore, is much like a priest in his own right, and is treated accordingly by the local population, being given gifts and free meals. It is the architect who actually sets the alignment of the door to the midwinter sunset. Though the architect oversees all the rituals associated with building, the aligning the house and setting of the door are the only items of celestial importance assigned to him that are mentioned.

There are many archaeological sites in Africa in which astronomical alignments have been recorded. However, most studies are of unoccupied sites and therefore cultural connections are often only hypothetical but are occasionally supported by local practice. Blier's study is important because it is both a study of an occupied site and a record of the significance attributed to the alignments by present-day inhabitants.

Calendars

The determination of the calendar year was of vital importance to people all over the world. Times for migration, planting, harvesting, and hunting needed to be accurately determined and thus an exact calendar was needed. Since few cultures understood or practiced the mathematics necessary to calculate the parameters of the Earth's orbit around the Sun, all calendars must have been based on years and sometimes generations of observations. Thus, the determination of the calendar relied upon recognizing and recording celestial events; however, the method of preserving the knowledge varies.

There are three types of African calendars—lunar, solar, and stellar calendars—with the combination calendar being the fourth. Lunar calendars are based upon observations of the moon. One lunar cycle is 29.5 days. The Islamic and Jewish calendars are both lunar calendars. The problem is that combinations of lunar cycles do not add up to a calendar year. Twelve lunar cycles is equal to 354 days; while thirteen lunar cycles is 383.5 days. Two examples of African ethnic groups that rely primarily on lunar calendars are the Ngas of Nigeria and the Mursi of Ethiopia. The Ngas have a system in which the new year is determined by the last new moon before harvest. The last new moon is marked by a complicated ceremony referred to as "shooting the moon" (LaPin 1984). The ceremony has to take place the day before the new moon is sighted, and symbolizes the high priest (Gwolong Kum) and the Ngas people capturing and killing the moon, which is deified, for it to be reborn in the new year (the next day). Ideas of rebirth, renewal, and cleansing by killing the past are all incorporated into the changing of the year for the Ngas. The Mursi primarily follow a lunar calendar, but use agricultural activities and celestial markers to determine which is the current month. As such, the month names are not fixed and are debated until these secondary markers are seen (Turton and Ruggles 1978).

The solar calendars involve observing the position of the sun over the course of the year. The solstices mark the northern and southern extremes of the Sun's position. Measuring the year from winter solstice to winter solstice is 365.24 days. This is called the tropical year and is 20 minutes short of the calendar year. Stellar calendars involve observing the position of stars. The ancient Egyptian calendar is a stellar calendar. Marking the time from seeing a star, for example Aldebaran, at sunset on the horizon, until the next time Aldebaran appears on the horizon at sunset is 365.25 days. This measures the true year or the calendar year.

The Akan of Ghana are part of the Niger-Congo linguistic group, and dominate Ghana north of Accra. They migrated into this region, displacing the Guan people several centuries ago. The Guan had a 6-day week, while the trading week from the south was 7 days. What the Akan have done is use all possible combinations of the two weekly methods which amounts to 42 days. They combine nine of these cycles to make up their year which add up to 378 days. Every three years they drop an entire cycle making 1092 days total. Not including a leap year, our calendar adds up to 1095 days, thus the Akan calendar is accurate to within three days. Lunar cycles are only observed along the coast of Ghana where marine activity is important (especially tides).

The Akan calendar has a definite history, marking the encounter between two cultures: the Akan and the Guan. It is clear that someone, or a group of people, mathematically calculated the best method for determining the year while maintaining their 42-day cycle, a process which must have also involved observations of the solar cycle. This raises questions such as, What does the calendar imply in a diplomatic sense? And, Why were the calendars combined, instead of simply designating one the dominant calendar, as in many other parts of Africa?

Celestial Navigation

The Kerkennah Islands lie 12 miles east of the city of Sfax in Tunisia, North Africa; there are two islands named Gharbi and Chergui which are translated as "west" and "east," respectively. The islands can be reached by passenger ferries run by the Tunisian government, there are three ferries to fill the eight roundtrips

a day schedule. The cost of the ferry trip is free for locals and about 30 cents for tourists including Tunisian tourists. The two islands are joined by a causeway, which was originally built by the Romans. Fourteen villages span the two islands. Three cultures of origin are acknowledged by the islanders: Berber, Turkish/Islamic, and Greek/Roman. The Tunisian Arabic spoken throughout the country is part of the Afro-Asiatic linguistic group. The following is taken from four field seasons on the Kerkennah Islands, focusing on how and why the local fishermen continue to use the stars for navigation.

The navigation techniques of the Kerkennah fisherman include bathymetric navigation, an intimate knowledge of the flora and fauna, celestial navigation, an understanding of the wind, weather, and current patterns, and the memorization of routes.

Bathymetric navigation uses the features of the sea floor to determine location. The fishermen fish throughout the Gulf of Gabes. A map of the seafloor surrounding Kerkennah shows depths up to 85 feet in the area between the island and the mainland, but on average a depth of about 32 feet. The seafloor drops off to the southeast but remains shallow for some miles to the north. There are very few places deeper than 13 feet to the north of the islands for about a mile. Since the seas around Kerkennah are shallow, the fishermen use long poles to probe features when they cannot easily see the bottom. Many of the villages are located at the mouths of sea floor features called *loueds*. These features are channels that lead from the villages to deep water. The *loueds* are said to be natural features and some say that Allah put them there for the fishermen. Thus, the sea around Kerkennah is shallow with distinctive topographical features, but also flora and fauna congregate in particular ocean regions. The fishermen know which regions sport certain sea grasses and where schools of fish are found and also use this knowledge for navigation.

The fishermen understand the wind, weather, and current patterns associated with Kerkennah. The weather must be noted to avoid storms and high winds. Knowing the direction and strength of the currents allows the fishermen to adjust their course to account for drift. Both sailing boats and motorized boats are used on Kerkennah. The sailing boats directly use the wind, but those fisherman using motorized boats use the wind for finding direction. Thus, in terms of knowledge of the wind, current, and weather patterns there did not appear to be an obvious distinction between the fishermen using motorized boats and those who sailed.

The fishermen use visual markers, wind and current patterns, and their knowledge of the sea floor for navigation, at night they also use the stars. As the sky darkens, the fishermen first look for Ursa Major and use the leading edge of the scoop to find Polaris. They know that five times the distance between the two leading stars is the distance to Polaris. Once they have located Polaris, they get their bearings using Polaris as a marker for the north. They have memorized the locations of their fish farms relative to the position of Polaris and their village. The most common name used for Ursa Major was *le sept* (the seven), which refers to the number of bright stars in Ursa Major. It was also referred to as "la cassarel" (the saucepan). Polaris is called *Smiya* which is Arabic for north. In English, these are the Big Dipper and the North Star, respectively. The fishermen of the village of Mellita used other constellations to keep track of time. They mentioned *le fleur de balance* which was identified by Captain Ali, one of the current ferry captains, as the belt of Orion. They estimate that each night *le fleur de balance* rose 3–5 minutes earlier each night. This figure is about correct for their latitude of 34 degrees north where it rises 4 minutes earlier each night. The moon was said to rise 1 hour 1/7 minutes later each night. This is roughly true between third quarter and first quarter but is not accurate for most of the month during most of the year. They use their understanding of these times to estimate the distances they had traveled. In El-Attaya, a young fisherman called Orion *le bras de balance* (Fr., *bras* arm), rather than *le fleur de balance*.

The role of celestial navigation is not one of special significance, but rather one of many effective techniques used by the fishermen. The fishermen of Kerkennah say that they learned how to navigate from their fathers and grandfathers. They readily acknowledge their complex heritage when discussing the origins of villages and the physical characteristics of their fellow islanders, however no one suggested an origin for their navigation traditions.

The celestial navigation of Kerkennah shows links to the navigation of the ancient Phoenician, Islamic, and Mediterranean seafarers. The Phoenicians are noted to have based their navigation system on Ursa Major, Ursa Minor, and Polaris. The fishermen of Kerkennah use Ursa Major and Polaris, however, other than the use of Polaris, the rest of the constellation of Ursa Minor is not used. The accounts of Marco Polo and Nicolas de Conti state that by the sixteenth century, the Islamic seafarers of the Mediterranean used only Ursa Major and Polaris as the base of their celestial navigation system. This is true for Kerkennah today since the only other constellation, *le fleur de balance*, is used for timekeeping, not for finding direction.

Interestingly, the navigation system of the Kerkennah Islands is changing. The celestial navigation component is no longer being widely taught to young navigators. The reason for the change has nothing to do with new technology but is due to education demands on the young navigators. The Kerkennah Islanders take great pride in the performance of their children in all aspects of education. Parents wish their children to become medical doctors, lawyers, and other such professions. They do not want them to become fishermen. However, fish is an important part of their diet and the fishing needs to be done. Therefore, the children are taught a scaled-down version of their traditional navigation to enable them to travel safely to nearby fishing areas and return, only. They are not taught night navigation.

Navigation practices of Africa have received little study. However, the National Science Foundation has recently provided funds to do a study of the navigation practices in East Africa. Hopefully, the results of this study will lead to more scholarship on African celestial navigation methods.

References

Bartle, Philip F.W. 1978. Forty Days: The Akan Calendar *Africa* 48, no. 1:80–84.

Blier, Suzanne Preston. 1987. *The Anatomy of Architecture: Ontology and Metaphor in Batammaliba Architectural Expression.* New York: Cambridge University Press.

Frampton, J. 1929. *The Travels of Marco Polo.* London: Argonaut Press.

Holbrook, J. C. 1998. Unpublished interview with Suzanne Preston Blier.

———. 1999. Unpublished interview in Gabes, Tunisia.

———. 2002. Celestial Navigation, Charfia, and the Blind Navigator. Berlin: The Max Planck Institute for the History of Science, in press.

LaPin, Dierdre, and Francis Speed. 1984. *Sons of the moon: A Film.* Berkeley: University of California Extension Media Center.

Snedegar, K. 1997. Ikhwezi. *Mercury* 26:12–15.

Turton, D., and C. Ruggles. 1978. Agreeing to Disagree: The Measurement of Duration in a Southwestern Ethiopian Community, *Current Anthropology* 19, no. 3, 585–600.

JARITA C. HOLBROOK

See also **Architecture; Cardinal Directions; Cosmology; Divination**

AZANDE

See **Tricksters: Ture of the Azande**

B

BACHAMA

See **Joking Relationships**

BANJO: AFRICAN ROOTS

African musicians, forcibly brought to the New World as slaves, brought with them from West Africa a plucked lute with a hide-covered-gourd sound chamber and several strings including a short thumb drone string. Interaction with Scottish and Irish musicians resulted, by the 1830s, in the invention of the five-string wooden rim banjo, which retained the African short thumb string drone and radically influenced American music.

History

Today the banjo is heard around the world, from the Blue Ridge Mountains to the Amazon River basin. The twentieth-century banjo tradition rests upon a much older African heritage. West African griots (storyteller/musicians) and other nomadic musicians brought the forerunner of the banjo from their homeland to the New World over the course of the seventeenth century. This early instrument appears in West Africa by 1621, and in the West Indies (Martinique) by 1678. Today, Wolof *jeles* from the Savannah grasslands of Senegal, Mande *jillikea* of Mali, and other praise singers and storytellers of various African regions still play plucked lutes with a short thumb drone string and a long pole neck attached to a gourd in a knocking or beating style.

The lute was already present in West Africa by the seventh century; another version of the instrument arrived, with Islam, in the eleventh century. Thus, well before the slave trade was fully developed—at least by the fourteenth century—two strong traditions flourished. For example, for the *halam*-like *tidinet* (known since at least 1824), Braknas musicians prefer the black tuning that allows for spectacular effects rather than the white Arabic tuning favored by educated people. The Wolof tunings, like mountain banjo tunings, are called high tuning and low tuning, and other specialized tunings are used for only one or two tunes. Wolof "middle tuning" is related to the way that the *tidinet* was played by their enemies for 150 years; thus the practice is a testament to cultural exchange.

African Songs

In 1789, the African Equiano said, "We are a nation of dancers, musicians, and poets. Thus every great event . . . is celebrated in public dances which are accompanied with songs and music suited to the occasion." The Ashanti, for example, thought it "absurd" to worship in any way other than with chanting or singing. The dances might last for half an hour, and some individual did special dances in the center of the group circle. Sometimes the Ashanti celebrated a successful hunt or a special seasonal festival, such as the "Yam Customs."

African music is especially improvisational, conversational, and interactive. The aesthetic is more rhythmically complex and diverse, and less melodically intricate, than Scottish or Irish music. Music of Africa especially emphasizes singing. Nevertheless, in 1623, Captain Richard Jobson wrote in his *The Golden Trade or a Discovery of the River Gamba [Gambia] and the Golden Trade of the Aethiopians* that he observed during his travels that the griot offered a "perfect resemblance to the Irish Rimer." Before 1800, the Scottish surgeon Mungo Park recited the duties of the singing men (Jillikea) encountered in the land of the Mandingos and the Minkes. By improvising texts and tunes to earn money, the griots create "extempore songs" to honor kings, to "divert the fatigue" of the traveling group, or to obtain "welcome from strangers" (Southern).

Enslaved West African griots arrived in the Carribean in the seventeenth century, and the American South in the eighteenth century. African gourd seeds had preceded the musicians across the waters to the New World. These memory keepers, praise singers, and healers played the creole *bania* in Dutch Guiana with a short thumb string tuned as a low bass drone. Before 1701, the songsters invented the strum strump in Jamaica, and by 1744 decorated their similar calibash merrywang with carving and rib-bands. Perhaps inspired by the English cittern or Spanish guitar, the tuning pegs and flat neck of the strum strump easily permitted the sliding and bending of notes. Another account from Jamaica written before the end of the eighteenth century describes slaves arriving with African instruments actually in their hands en route to Savannah, Georgia: They "were made to exercise, and encouraged, by the music ['of their beloved banjar,'] to sing and dance." For "this purpose, such rude instruments are collected before their departure" from Guinea.

Written records express few of the thoughts of Africans upon being forcibly removed from their homeland, undergoing the treacherous Middle Passage, and being put to work as slaves in the Caribbean and the American colonies. Folksongs, however express and preserve these crucial memories. Enslaved songsters and musicians sang improvisational, sometimes satirical songs. Signifying songs offer clues as to what Africans thought of being forced to submit to, and adopt the ways of, the predominant white culture. "The Guinea Negro Song" about Virginia was also sung in North Carolina by former slaves:

The Engeley man he {s}teal-a me,
And give me pretty red coat-ee.
The 'Melican [American] man he ta-kee me
And make me fence rail to-tee.

The Eng-lie man he 'teal me,
A lack ta lou-li-la-na,
A lack ta lou-la-lay,
And carry me to Ber-gi-my [Virginia].

By the mid-eighteenth century, an African-American cultural tradition was well established in the colonies of Maryland and Virginia (the invention of the cotton gin had increased the need for slaves, and thus the slave labor force). Many of the early arrivals to the colonies were Wolof griots or other musicians. Their musical influence was felt early on. In his "1744 Eclogues in Imitation of Virgil's," Reverend Cradock dramatizes the singing and enamored courtship of Pompey for his slave companion Daphen:

I sing as well as evern Negro sung/
Nor Sambo has a Banjar better strung.

According to other eighteenth-century accounts, blacks improvised lyric songs and music for dancing. Storytellers and musicians made and played a three- or four-string "large gourd, or pumpion" instrument covered with a bladder or skin and "with a long neck attached," strung with horsehair, hemp, or catgut. The instrument had tuning pegs and sometimes a flat fingerboard. For almost one hundred years, only African American musicians played the *banjar* in a thumping style now called clawhammer.

The Banjo in North America

The banjo plays both rhythm and melody and has traditionally interacted with percussion; in an African context, percussion would be represented by the so-called talking drums. But after the Stono insurrection (1740) in South Carolina, the authorities made drumming (and brass horns) illegal in the English colonies. Fortunately, the banjo, and the echoes of African traditions and memories it carries, survived.

A banjo player in Virginia in 1838 suggests the vitality of the African American playing tradition. Wearing a "long white cowtail, queued with red ribbon" and a hat "with peacock feathers" and "pods of red pepper," he played for a dance. For his "tumming," this honored musician was served a "huge loaf of larded persimmon bread with a gourd of beer" even before the

men clapped "Juber up and Juber down, Juber all around the town." This scene shows how the banjo and "patting" Juba, for example, began to replace drumming. This shift was brought about by the marked influence of the West African griots.

African Americans, perhaps exclusively, played the gourd banjo in North America from at least 1740 to about 1830. In *Narrative of the Life of an American Slave* (1845), Frederick Douglass says: "The slaves selected to go to the great Farm . . . would make the dense old woods, for miles around, reverberate with their wild songs, revealing at once the highest joy and the deepest sadness."

African American banjo players lived on the mountain frontier by 1800; they often worked as rounders and roustabouts on the Mississippi river and its tributaries. The two major areas of early black banjo playing, still influential today, were the region covered by Maryland, Virginia, and North Carolina and, later, the New Orleans and Mississippi River region. In the Deep South region, especially at Congo Square, the banjo and drum flourished as well.

The call and response musical exchange of shanties, field hollers, group corn-shucking songs, spirituals, and the banjo songs and dance music grew as different African peoples met and mixed as slaves. Sea shanties, rowing song, and long shore and river roustabout songs also influenced the old banjo tradition. Black songster and banjo traditions were strongly influencing each other, while also gaining exposure to European and American forms of music.

Musical Innovators

Most early African American musical innovators remain unidentified, but a few specific names are available to us today. The banjo player Picayune Butler (d. 1864) became famous from New Orleans to New York: In approximately 1830, the entertainer George Nichols "first sang 'Jim Crow' as a clown, afterwards as a Negro. He first conceived the idea from . . . a banjo player, known [along the river route] from New Orleans to Cincinnati as Picayune Butler." At least one banjo song—"Picayune Butler's Come To Town"—suggests the excitement created by this musician's arrival. Butler sang on the street for money, accompanied himself "on his four stringed banjo," and provided minstrel Nichols with the song "Picayune Butler is Going Away." He prefigured the traveling country bluesman.

Butler did not take up the five-string wooden-rim banjo invented around 1842, but over the more than thirty years of his career that is documented, he was apparently influenced enough by European approaches to melody to add a fourth string to his banjo. In 1857, Picayune Butler played in a New York banjo contest. According to eyewitnesses, he would have won if he had "not been indisposed. Even though he broke two of his four banjo strings, he still plucked through the required waltz, reel, schottische, polka, and jig with artistry."

African American banjo players exchanged musical ideas and created a new, distinct, complex, and little recognized genre of banjo songs. Banjo players also contributed to the emergence of fiddle songs in their exchanges with white Scottish and Irish fiddlers, who had arrived in North America in the eighteenth century. Both the banjo and the African American playing style, characterized by knocking, beating, and thumping, began to take hold among whites by the 1830s.

Southern musicians, who became crucial teachers and performers, often remained close to home. But some, like Sweeney of Appomattox and his brothers, carried banjo music to diverse musicians and the American public through fairs, circuses, and later the enormously popular minstrel shows. No early white banjo player was more influential than Joel Sweeney. By the early 1840s, he was credited (perhaps over enthusiastically) with the creation of a new banjo which had five strings and an open back made, originally, from a cheese hoop. What has confused many scholars and music historians is that the fifth string he added was not the short thumb string which arrived from Africa that we now call the fifth string, but the bass (fourth) string. These radical changes led folklorists John and Alan Lomax to declare that the five-string banjo is "America's only original folk instrument." This instrument created by blacks and whites together was, by 1843, widely heard across the country.

Eventually rural blacks, such as the fieldhand Jim Crow and the boatman Gumbo Chaff, became stage types and figures for the greater white population, well known in the urban cultural arena. Minstrelsy initially celebrated African American traditions, but increasingly grew commercialized and began to dismiss, satirize, and caricature blacks.

William Henry "Master Juba" Lane (1825–1853) was probably the only African American actively involved in minstrelsy before 1858. A noted banjo player and dancer, he learned jigs and reels from "Uncle" Jim Lowe in the saloons and dance halls of New York's Five Points and Harlem neighborhoods. Lane is immortalized by Charles Dickens in his *Notes on America* (1842). Eventually, Lane left the United States to pursue a career in England; he performed on stage at the Vauxhall Gardens in London in 1848.

Minstrel tradition eventually resulted in the flourishing of classical parlor, orchestra, and ragtime picking styles. Sturdy manufactured instruments began to be made for the minstrels and resulted in the commercial production and popularization of numerous attractive instruments during the late nineteenth century; a later result was the invention of the tenor banjo (played in quartets and jazz bands) and the bluegrass banjo, and their accompanying plectrum and finger picking styles.

Cross-cultural Music Exchange

Steamboat travel took off in 1850, and cultural exchange increased. Blacks (often leased out by their Southern masters) sometimes worked side by side in the flourishing water transport industry with Irish and German laborers. One amusing anecdote is that of an unnamed old man who worked on the Mississippi. He said that many of the packet boat songs, such as "Natchez Under the Hill," were "reels an' jigs," not spirituals, and that once he became a Christian he should not sing these "sinful songs," which were "often brought in by and caught from the Irish." Fortunately the musicians, in keeping with much in African American tradition, did not separate the sacred and the secular, and thus did not "disremember" all the "devilment songs." Many continued to play the old lonesome "breakdowns" and "jump up" songs. On some steamboats, like the Joe Fowler, every "evening after dinner [instrumental] music was provided by some of the colored/'cabin boys,'" and for a few thrilling moments, one was allowed to occupy the center of the floor and "do the cakewalk."

Cultural and regional exchange on the frontier and the rivers expanded even more when blacks and whites traveled and mixed during the Civil War, particularly on board ships. In 1876, a journalist spent many evenings with black longshoremen in Cincinnati waterfront dance halls. He printed texts of twelve social and work songs accompanied by the banjo and fiddle. Eventually their interaction created the string band, which initially emerged from the pairing of the banjo and fiddle.

When banjo playing was still strongly shared by traditional black and white players, this cross-cultural musical exchange gave rise to at least three types of banjo songs, identified on the basis of the relationship between the instrumental and vocal melodies. Built upon brief repeated riffing melodic or rhythmic figures, banjo songs tend to be rhythmically complex, creating a conversational, call and response relationship between the vocal and the instrumental melodies, which often bear little resemblance to each other.

The banjo played a significant role in the working and social lives of African Americans on board ships, in the fields, on the railroad, in the mines, and at home. The African American banjo tradition charts a pathway from unaccompanied field hollers and group work songs to the emergence of guitar-accompanied country and blues songs. The banjo songs of longing and joy comprise an unbroken tradition that expresses a shift in social roles, from enslaved African to American citizen.

About 1900, during the era of increasingly restrictive and racist Jim Crow laws, black banjo players began to put down their banjos, setting their songs, comprised of increasingly assertive commentary, to the now readily available guitar, and set about creating the genre known as the blues. Nonetheless, the roots of the old-time banjo tradition live in the memories and hands of a few musicians who play in a style that was popular at the turn of the twentieth century. The instrument still echoes at the crossroads between West African griots, African slaves in the North American colonies, traveling country bluesmen, and the mountain and minstrel banjo players who eventually formed old-time string bands and banjo orchestras. Their descendants in the twentieth century created country music, bluegrass, and revival bands, as well as New Orleans marching music, ragtime, swing, Dixieland jazz, and big band jazz. The banjo—America's first musical invention—has made an invaluable contribution to the American indigenous music heritage.

References

Coolen, Michael Theodore. 1984. Senegambia Archetypes for the American Folk Banjo. *Western Folklore* 43:146–61.

Conway, Cecelia. 1995. *African Banjo Echoes in Appalachia.* Knoxville: University of Tennessee Press.

Conway, Cecelia and Scott Odell. 1998. *Black Banjo Songsters of North Carolina and Virginia.* Washington, D.C.: Smithsonian Folkways.

Epstein, Dena J. 1977. *Sinful Tunes and Spirituals: Black Folk Music to the Civil War.* Urbana: Univeristy of Illinois Press.

Kubik, Gerhard. 1989. South Africa: The Southern African periphery: Babnjo Traditions in Zambia and Malawii. *The World of Music*, 31, no. 1:3–39.

Hugill, Stan. 1961. *Shanties from the Seven Seas.* Mystic, Conn.: Mystic Seaport Museum.

Levine, Lawrence W. 1977. *Black Culture and Consciousness: Afro-American Folk Thought from Slavery to Freedom.* New York: Oxford University Press.

Nathans, Hans. 1962. *Dan Emmett and the Rise of Early Negro Minstrelsy*. Norman: University of Oklahoma Press.

Oliver, Paul. 1970. *Savannah Syncopators: African Retentions in the Blues*. The Blues Series, ed. Paul Oliver. New York: Stein and Day.

Webb, Robert Lloyd. 1984. *Ring the Banjar: The Banjo in America from Folklore to Factory*. Cambridge: The MIT Museum, 1984.

Wheeler, Mary. 1944. *Steamboatin' Days*. Baton Rouge: Louisiana State University Press.

CECELIA CONWAY

See also **Diaspora; Musical Instruments: Focus on Namibia; Music in Africa: Overview**

BAO

Bao, which means "board" in Swahili, is an East African board game. This game is a variation of Mancala, a group of board games particularly popular in Africa, but are also played in Asia and the Americas. It is played by two players who commonly use a wooden board with four rows of eight holes and sixty-four counters. The rules are the most complex of all Mancala variations. They allow counters to be distributed in both clockwise and counter-clockwise directions and the direction may change during a move. Two enlarged or square holes in the center of the board allow counters to accumulate during the game to facilitate multiple captures. Contrary to most Mancala variations, the counters are not all on the board at the start of play. Forty-four of them enter the game one by one with each turn and when all are entered they will remain on the board. Captured counters are not taken from the board but are distributed in the rows of the player who captured them. This arrangement also allows for multiple captures. The captures in Bao create the highest turnover of counters between two players in a game compared to those in any other Mancala variation or board game. Capturing is obligatory and Bao rules dictate the outcome of a move once it has started. The possible length or complexity of a move may require complex mental calculations. This has provided Bao with the status of most difficult Mancala variation and made it an object of psychological investigation.

Bao is played in East Africa and its presence follows the Swahili trade routes and the spread of Islam in that region. Players can be found mostly in Kenya and Tanzania but also in, for instance, Malawi, Mozambique, Madagascar, Somalia and Zambia. The oldest boards in museum collections with the characteristic enlarged holes in the center of the board were acquired in the 1890s. The first description of Bao was given by Flacourt in 1658 and concerned players in Madagascar. His description does not mention the two enlarged holes in the center of the board but otherwise clearly refers to Bao as it is known today. Detailed rules of Bao (which have taken two to fifteen pages to describe in the Bao literature!), have not appeared in print until the second half of the twentieth century. Today the rules found in Kenya, Tanzania and, for instance, Madagascar are practically identical. The distribution of Bao rules and the strong similarities that still exist suggests that the rules of Bao have remained similar throughout the Swahili-speaking region since their distribution occurred at least two centuries ago or as early as the 1600s. The history of master players of Bao in Zanzibar confirms that the same Bao rules were played in Zanzibar for more than

one hundred years. It also shows that championship play has been in place for this period of time.

Since the game was distributed in the Swahili-speaking regions of East Africa, there is a specific Swahili vocabulary in use describing moves and rules in the game. Championship play also created a vocabulary for strategic moves. *Takata* and *mtaji* are common words in most regions. *Takata* or *takasa* means "to cleanse" and refers to a move that does not make a capture. Although *takata* is sometimes used in other Mancala variations in the area, *mtaji* appears limited to Bao. It refers to a possible capture move in the second part of the game, the part in which all counters are on the board. The counters, commonly seeds from the caesalpinia bonduc, are known as komwe, although kete and soo are also used. *Kitakomwe* is then a strategic term which is only used in Bao and, among other meanings, refers to the battle for the capture of the enlarged hole. The enlarged hole is often known as *kuu*, meaning "big," or *nyumba* meaning "house." The penultimate holes on the inner two rows, are known as *kumbi*, and *kitakimbi* refers to the attacks on this particular position. This idiom for positions and move sequences in Bao is another indication of the central role of championship play in Bao history.

Bao is played mostly by men in Bao clubs. Similar to other Mancala variations, the scene of play may involve a crowd of players commenting on a single game and frequent exchanges of challenges and judgments by players and spectators. Speed appears an important element reflected in often short thinking times and the almost universal dexterity in the execution of complex moves. Distributing a number of seeds in consecutive holes in one throw has become a common skill among players. Children sometimes play in Bao clubs before the arrival of the men while both women and children may play at home in the sand, but are known to use different or simplified rules.

The islands of Pemba and Zanzibar as well as the mainland of Tanzania, particularly the coastal cities, are best known for championship Bao. A psychological study of Bao in Zanzibar reveals that Bao experts possess cognitive abilities that are not known for other board games and are beyond the capabilities of other humans. The complex captures and high turnover of seeds require intricate calculations of moves. Masters of Bao excel in making such calculations, have strategic foresight and often specialize in characteristic parts of the game.

The 1994 Bao tournament in Zanzibar. Photo © Alex de Voogt.

At least three Bao masters have reached legendary status and became regarded as the best players of their time. Ibrahimi Said Mkiwa (1916–2000), known as Mkiwa, was born on mainland Tanzania, but moved to Zanzibar where he learned Bao and became a master of the game. He toured both Zanzibar, Pemba and Dar Es Salaam to become the most illustrious player of the 1940s and 1950s. Shaame Kondo Khamisi (1938–1984?), known as Nahodha ("Captain"), was born in Tumbatu, off the coast of Zanzibar. He did not start playing until he frequented Zanzibar town in his early twenties. He soon rivaled Mkiwa in the 1960s and 1970s. He was frequently invited to tournaments on Tanzania mainland, sometimes by President Nyerere who himself was an enthusiastic player. The 1990s showed a shift to Dar Es Salaam for excellence in Bao where Juma Ali Njowine (1956–), known as Njowine, has gained fame. In 1995 and 1997, Abdulrahim Muhiddin Foum (1971–) from Zanzibar, known as Abdu, became the first to play Bao blindfolded. This involved playing a game of Bao without assistance of a board or other aid and in which moves are only communicated verbally with a player who does have access to a board with counters. Only the starting point and direction of a move needed to be communicated.

The intricate rules of Bao have not facilitated the introduction of Bao to Europe or the Americas, or encouraged programming of the rules by computer scientists. Apart from most complex and volatile, Bao also remains the most popular African Mancala variation next to Wari.

References

Flacourt, E. de. 1658. *Histoire de la Grande Isle Madagascar*. Paris.
Townshend, P. 1982. Bao (Mankala): The Swahili Ethic in African Idiom. *Paideuma* 28:175–191.
Townshend, P. 1986. Games in Culture: A Contextual Analysis of the Swahili Board Game and Its Relevance to Variation in African Mankala. Ph.D. dissertation, University of Cambridge.
Voogt, A. J. de. 1995. *Limits of the Mind: Towards a Characterisation of Bao Mastership*. Leiden: CNWS Publications.
ALEX DE VOOGT

See also **Mancala, Wari**

BASCOM, WILLIAM R. (1912–1981)

A quiet, patient man, William Bascom's scholarship continues to grow in importance over the years—not only his monumental work on divination, but his careful documentation of the continuity of African traditions in the Americas. Bascom was Melville Herskovits's first graduate student and remained Herskovits's colleague at Northwestern for many years. A generation of major Africanists studied with this extraordinary pair of scholars at Northwestern University. Although they taught together for many years and they coedited *Continuity and Change in African Cultures* (1959), Bascom was not just a shadow of Herskovits. He became director of the Lowie (now Hearst) Museum in 1957 and stayed at University of California, Berkeley, for the rest of his life.

Bascom first went to study the Yoruba of Nigeria in 1938, basing his work in Ife where, as a mark of his rapport with the people, he was given two of the extraordinary bronze heads by the Oni of Ife. These were returned to Ife a few years later. He also carried out field research in Ghana, and in the Americas he worked with Yoruba descendents in Cuba (where he met his wife Berta) and with Gullah speakers on the Georgia Sea Islands.

Although Bascom was initiated into the Yoruba Ogboni society, he honored their pledge of secrecy and never published anything he learned of this organization. But he did publish other basic material on the Yoruba, such as his ethnography, *The Yoruba of Southwestern Nigeria*, and numerous articles. Among his most important works, one must note his magnificent study of Yoruba divination, *Ifa Divination: Communication Between Men and God* (1969) and the no less important monograph on the related system of divination, *Sixteen Cowries* (1980).

In addition to his major research on Yoruba divination in Africa and the Americas, he also produced significant publications in social anthropology, the visual arts, and culture change. Bascom's essays on the study of folklore are among the most important defining statements of the discipline. A majority of these major publications appeared in the *Journal of American Folklore* and include Folklore and Anthropology (1953), Four Functions of Folklore (1954), Verbal Art (1955), The Myth-Ritual Theory (1957), Folklore Research in Africa (1964), The Forms of Folklore: Prose Narratives (1965). In addition to these seminal articles, he published more broadly on Africa. Of special importance is *African Dilemma Tales* (1975), which surveyed this narrative form so representative of African interest in debate and puzzlement.

After his appointment to the Lowie Museum directorship, he became more involved in African visual arts, although he had published a small volume with Paul Gebauer in 1953 for the Milwaukee Public Museum. *African Arts* was a fine catalog of an 1967 exhibition and in 1973 Bascom published *African Art in Cultural Perspective: An Introduction*.

It is in his final series of publications that we find his exemplary scholarship and lasting contribution to African and African American studies. Bascom and Richard Dorson, the then dean of American folklorists, engaged in a debate over the origins of African American tales, with Dorson claiming these tales were derived from Europe, Asia, and the Americas. Although many disputed these claims, it was William Bascom who carefully documented the obvious African roots of many African American narratives in a series of articles in *Research in African Literatures* (later published posthumously as *African Folktales in America*). Intriguingly, Bascom and Dorson died on the same day: September 11, 1981.

William Bascom was the epitome of the unassuming, careful scholar whose research continues to guide us through significant publications in folklore and anthropology as well as African and African American studies.

References

Bascom, William R. 1944. *The Sociological Role of the Yoruba Cult-Group*. Memoirs of the American Anthropological Association, No. 63. Menasha, Wis: American Anthropological Association.
———. 1967. *African Arts: An Exhibition at the Lowie Museum*. Berkeley: University of California Press.
———. 1969a. *The Yoruba of Southwestern Nigeria*. New York: Holt, Rinehart and Winston.

———. 1969b. *Ifa Divination: Communication Between Gods and Men in West Africa.* Bloomington: Indiana University Press.

———. 1972. *Shango in the New World.* Occasional Publications of the African and Afro-American Research Institute, No.4. Austin: Univ. of Texas Press.

———. 1973. *African Arts in Cultural Perspective: An Introduction.* New York: Norton.

———. 1975. *African Dilemma Tales.* Paris: Mouton.

———. 1980. *Sixteen Cowries: Yoruba Divination from Africa to the New World.* Bloomington: Indiana University Press.

Bascom, William R., and Melville Herskovits, eds. 1959. *Continuity and Change in African Cultures.*

Ottenberg, Simon, ed., 1982. *African Religious Groups and Beliefs: Papers in Honor of William R. Bascom.* Meerut, India: Folklore Institute.

PHILIP M. PEEK

See also **Diaspora; Dilemma Tales; Divination: Overview; Ifa**

BASKETRY: AFRICA

Men and women in Africa have produced a breathtaking array of basketry objects from time immemorial. Unlike ceramics, baskets deteriorate easily, but the ancient archaeological specimens unburied from the dry sands and tombs of Egypt, and the paintings in these tombs, suggest that basketry in Africa, as elsewhere, is simultaneously a very versatile and conservative art. Centuries-old techniques are still employed to produce similarly shaped objects. Many objects have fallen into disuse, being replaced by modern, mass-produced equivalents. Others have been invented, which sometimes draw upon non-African traditions.

Uses

Grass, palm, wood, reed, sisal, bamboo, less often animal and synthetic fibers; a knife, an awl, some container for soaking the fibers in water—these are common ingredients in African basket making. Unlike the textile arts, basketry dispenses everywhere with frames, bobbins, and shuttles. Its technological simplicity is the source of both its limitations and possibilities. In the African continent, different kinds of interwoven objects, from simple ropes, slings, handles, and wrappers to more complex formats not always in the shape of containers—as the word *basketry* might suggest—have been put to a wide variety of uses over time. Dresses, rain capes, sandals, belts, hats, bracelets and anklets, necklaces, headdresses, purses, sacks, and combs have been used to cover and adorn the body; boxes and cases, to enclose personal possessions; hampers and baskets of different sizes and shapes, to carry and store provisions; trays, to winnow grain, and loosely woven objects, to sieve flour and strain liquids; bowls and plates, to serve dried foods, and some impermeable bowls with tightly woven and often coated walls, to serve and store beverages. There have been houses whose walls, doors, and roofs are basketry objects, and woven mats and furniture inside them. Fences, enclosures, large granaries, beehives, poultry carriers and coops have also been interwoven. Quivers have been used for carrying spears, and sheaths, knives; different traps, for catching birds, rodents, and fish; helmets and shields, for protecting the warrior in battle; canoes and ship sails, for transportation. All manner of receptacles, including such fancy shapes as the nested wedding baskets from Upper Volta, have functioned as trade measures. In the musical domain, one finds rattles and less often harps, and in the ritual domain, basketry masks—such as those of the Chewa of Malawi and the Salampasu of the Democratic Republic of the Congo—and more often containers: the Chokwe and related peoples have divined with a basket filled with odds and ends, and the Sango of Gabon have placed the potent reliquary figures, bones, and so forth, of their Bwiti cult inside baskets.

Equally important, baskets have been instrumental in exploitative contexts imposed by forces and actors outside Africa. In Angola, during the precolonial caravan trade, porters often carried provisions and goods inside interwoven hampers. The carrying receptacles that workers used at the Congolese mine pits in the early twentieth century, and at the coffee plantations in colonial Angola were baskets.

Convenient as any classification of basketry items by domain and function may be, it should not be forgotten that many baskets in Africa are multifunctional within and across domains. A bowl that serves for storing flour may also serve for covering it. A hamper that functions as a carrying receptacle may also function as a trade measure. A mat that is used for sitting may also be used for wrapping the dead. Utility and ceremony are not qualities intrinsic to different interwoven objects. A basket may simultaneously or sequentially serve different utilitarian and ceremonial or ritual functions. Any classification that rigidly distinguishes baskets according to their function, and opposes ritual to utility is likely to omit, if not misunderstand, the sociocultural diversity of Africa.

Decoration

For decoration purposes, the African basket maker may simply choose to play with different stitches and techniques; or incorporate dyed fibers into the work, creating various designs; or add other materials onto the basket surface, such as beads, cowries, metal, feathers, leather, animal hairs, cloth, and buttons. The Ibo of Nigeria, for example, cover the entire outer surface of some of their baskets with shells. Less often, the African basket maker allows the added material to play a structural—instead of merely decorative—role. Some bowls from the Democratic Republic of the Congo and *ifu* lidded baskets from the Aghem-Fungom area of the Cameroon Grassfields have wooden feet. The interlaced decorations engraved on the wooden surface of the Kuba bowls' feet are characteristic of Kuba matting. It is not uncommon across the continent to see basketry motifs reproduced in other artistic mediums, such as wood, metal, and clay. The converse is also true. Basketry designs are sometimes transposed from other mediums. The Zulu women in South Africa draw inspiration from their beadwork.

Profusely decorated baskets are often associated with political leadership and ritual. A case in point is the impressive pagoda-style hat ornamented with brass plates, which some Mongo chiefs in the Democratic Republic of the Congo wore in the past. Chiefs and other prominent figures, however, do not hold a monopoly over embellishment, or at least, not over all types of embellishment. Many utilitarian basketry objects used by common people are impressively decorated. Prior to their forced displacement, the Angolan Hambukushu refugees residing in Ngamiland, northwestern Botswana, used to ornate their everyday vase-shaped baskets with beads. The *ifu* basket from Camer-

Woman making basket. Photo © Sónia Silva.

oon, decorated though it is with beads and cowries, is a powerful symbol of womanhood. It is not only chiefs and kings who appreciate adornment and elaborate textures. Usefulness and decoration are not always incompatible. In any case, art does not per force require decoration. Is a plain, unadorned basket necessarily lacking in artistry and sophistication?

Two opposite views recur: some claim that the objects created prior to colonialism are artistically superior to the ones manufactured today for local use or sale to outsiders, the first being authentic and the second, artistically valueless. Others hold that the so-called authentic baskets are (or were) mostly utilitarian, hardly displaying any artistry, especially if compared with the ones being produced today for the international market, which reveal a greater emphasis on design and technical expertise. Art, the latter claim, can only emerge when the basket maker is set free from the heavy burden of functionality.

Artistry, however, requires neither authenticity nor uselessness. Functional, authentic baskets and tourist ones may or may not meet the requirements, whatever they are. Though basketry is ubiquitous in Africa, today, as yesterday, different peoples accord different degrees of importance to this art in their material culture, and exhibit different degrees of excellence and creativity in the baskets they make. The same holds true, needless to say, for the individual basket makers within each people.

Techniques

Evidence of all main basketry techniques is found in Africa: the coil (mainly the sewn type), the plait (mainly the twill), the twine, and the stake-and-strand, sometimes termed *wickerwork*. It is possible to roughly distinguish areas where certain techniques predominate: for example, the area of Ethiopia, Burundi, and Rwanda, and the vast region of Southern Africa are best known for their exquisite sewed coiling. The Ethiopians coil food-tables with lustrous colors that may change up to ten times in a linear inch of stitches; the Hutu and Tutsi of Burundi and Rwanda are renowned for their delicate and gracious bowls with conical lids and spiral motifs; the Zulu, for their colorful, geometrically decorated flared baskets; and the Hambukushu and Bayei, for the named motifs on their jars and bowls. Inspired by the local environment, mainly the animal world, these motifs are known by highly distinctive names: "Tail of the Swallow," "Knees of the Tortoise," "Urine of the Bull."

In the Democratic Republic of the Congo, central and eastern Zambia, northern Mozambique, and along the coast of East Africa, the twill predominates. The Congolese Tetela, the Zambian Ambo and Ngoni, and the Mozambican Makonde produce most of their basket ware using this technique. The ones with the most impressive and complex patterns, some of them figurative, are found in the lower Congo and Madagascar. Throughout the continent the presence of the open twine and stake-and-strand is ubiquitous. Twined openwork is used in the manufacture of fishing and/or hunting traps, and stake-and-strand is the technique employed in the making of all manner of fences, enclosures, and walls. Weaving by means of twine and wickerwork is the most widespread basketry technique in Africa.

Specialization

The art of basketry in Africa is structured and perceived along gender lines. It is generally correct to say that women coil while men weave, but cases disproving this rule exist. The Tsonga who lived in southern Mozambique in the early twentieth century stored their prized possessions in a coiled box, made by men, and men in the Cameroon Grassfields once coiled small, hand-held battle shields. If men may coil, women may weave. Women in Cabinda twill exquisite mats celebrated for their proverbial designs. In Kenya they twine the world-famous *kiondo* bag. The Tonga women twine the multifunctional *cisuo* basket.

Where both men and women create baskets, it has been suggested that each gender specializes in the kind of objects it needs to carry out its daily tasks: women might make household items and men nets, for example. However, among the Ambo, Ngoni, Makonde, and Tsonga, women's baskets are the work of men, for only they weave. The only instance across Africa in which one category of basketry objects is time after time manufactured and utilized by the same gender, the male, is the traps used for fishing and hunting. It is also true that baskets often symbolize the gender of their users, especially in the case of women. In Aghem-Fungom a woman's big farming basket symbolizes her role as a cultivator and nurturer; when she dies, the basket is smashed and buried with her.

Boy with hat. Photo © Sónia Silva.

The Tonga of southern Zambia say that their basket makers are chosen and inspired by ancestral spirits. In most African contexts, however, the art is open to all, provided one is of the appropriate sex. All it takes to learn is to observe an older relative or neighbor at work, and practice a great deal. Typically, most accomplished basket makers are late middle-age to elderly persons who rarely if ever become full-time specialists. They devote most of their time to other economic activities, such as farming, fishing, and hunting, and basketry is an activity they squeeze in between others, or carry out during the less busy periods of the yearly economic cycles. As they see it, basketry yields an additional income, providing enough money to buy paraffin, soap, oil, or sugar. When promoters of handicrafts or other individuals either assure the purchasing of baskets or otherwise fund the basket makers, these tend to be younger, and the time they spend making baskets longer.

Regional and International Markets

Many baskets are produced for use in the artist's household or on commission. Hawkers selling the baskets that they make are also frequent, as is bulk sale at regional markets. In Cote d'Ivoire, several men sell their twined, lidded baskets at the Korhogo market. Loads of baskets have also been directly sold to missionaries, traders, explorers, researchers, development workers, and tourists. The Botswana motif baskets and the Kenyan sisal bags have for decades been sold to marketing agents, who place them on the international market. Middlepersons inform the basket makers of the tastes and expectations of their distant clients: new, neat, and brightly decorated bowls, jars, platters, table mats, and bags are in high demand. Granaries and fishing baskets have no place in the Western home, and an old, used look is only welcome in other African artistic expressions, mainly wood carvings, which are highly valued as fine art in the West. In order to adapt to these expectations, basket makers have successfully employed different strategies. Some have relied entirely on traditional techniques and materials. Others have relied on old techniques but used new materials, such as artificial dyes and synthetic fibers, from plastic to telephone wire. Others still have adopted new techniques. In the 1960s the Bala (Songye) men in the Democratic Republic of the Congo used a new wrapping and assembling technique to produce raffia objects, from baskets to porte-verres, which they sold to Europeans in the cities. To this date, the Luvale living in northwestern Zambia use a somewhat equivalent technique to make shopping and laundry baskets, tea trays, and nested boxes, which they sell to well-to-do locals, government staff, and missionaries.

Basketry in Africa is very much alive. Both traditional and modern models can be seen. It is sometimes assumed that the drastic historical changes that Africa has undergone during the last century have slowly but surely eradicated most traditional basketry. Baskets fell into disuse one after the other. Innumerable baskets: however, were abandoned long before. As early as the second millennium CE wooden boxes were replaced the coiled toiletry baskets in Thebes, Egypt. In the first decade of the twentieth century the Tsonga *nhlaba* basket was already a rare sight. The adoption of styles and techniques from neighboring groups and even non-Africans precedes colonialism. The old, indeed traditional matting technique of sewing together individual plaited strips, recurrent along the east coast of Africa, most prob-

ably originates in the Arab world. The finest mats are woven in Madagascar, but examples are found as far west as the Democratic Republic of the Congo. The changes of the last century have not irremediably devastated the making and use of all baskets. Next to plastic buckets and enamel basins, baskets will be part of the African arts for a long time to come.

References

The African-American Institute. 1978. *African Grass and Fiber Arts. June–October 1978*. New York: The African-American Institute.

Dias, Margot. 1968. Contribuição para o Estudo da Cestaria em Gaza—Moçambique. *Ethnographica* 4, no. 13:4–19.

Ebert, Melinda C. 1977. Patterns of Manufacture and Use of Baskets among Basarwa of the Nata River Region. *Botwana Notes and Records* 9:69–83.

Geary, Christraud. 1987. Basketry in the Aghem-Fungom Area of the Cameroon Grassfields. *African Arts* 20, no. 3:42–53,89–90.

Instituto de Antropologia. 1988. *Cestaria Tradicional em África*. Coimbra, Portugal: Instituto de Antropologia, Universidade de Coimbra.

Levinsohn, Rhoda. 1984. *Art and Craft of Southern Africa: Treasures in Transition*. Craighall: Delta Books.

Merriam, Alan P. 1968. Art and Economics in Basongye Raffia Basketry. *African Arts* 2, no. 1:14–17, 73.

Newman, Thelma R. 1974. *Contemporary Africa Arts and Crafts: On-Site Working with Art Forms and Processes*. New York: Crown.

Sieber, Roy. 1980. *Furniture and Household Objects*. New York: The American Federation of Arts.

Trowell, Margaret. 1960. *African Design*. London: Faber and Faber.

SÓNIA SILVA

See also **Basketry, African American**

BASKETRY, AFRICAN AMERICAN

Clearly related to African basketry, African American baskets reflect some values of African world cultures, both continental and diasporic. For example, the coiled basketry styles have come across the Atlantic Ocean from West Africa to the Caribbean islands to the southeast coast of the United States. In traditional African societies, the textile and fiber arts are used in matting for building walls, floor coverings and decorative household items. Natural fibers are found in the environment, either harvested from the wild or remaining to be gleaned from crop harvest. Although some of the uses differed between the African and African American situations, the harvested and gleaned fibers are utilized in culture-specific items such as chair bottoms, mats, hats, and carrying and storage baskets of all types.

Varieties of basket styles which date from plantation times include: split oak or ash, coiled grass, twilled and twined fibers, and pine straw. These styles have been derived from the African heritage of African Americans and, in some instances, from the Native American people to whom the Africans escaped in pre-emancipation times. Some of the cultural influences among the Native, African, and European American groups have not yet been pinpointed, so that precise attributions may be made as to the actual provenience of each element in material and non-material culture traits.

Treatments of the various natural fibers include drying them in sun or air, and wetting those once dried to render them pliable. The sweet grass used for the coiled baskets is a single strand grass (*Muhlenbergia filipes*) which grows in the southern marshlands. It is dried after harvesting from the wild by hanging in the sun or spreading on a flat roof. The rushels or bulrushes (*Juncus roemerianus*) are dried away from direct sunlight as they have a heavier stalk. The white oak split materials must be harvested at a certain time in the spring when the wood is just right for the splitting and drying. It can be stored in the earth to keep the moisture content stable until it can be processed and used. The pine straw (*Pinus pilustris*) is picked up from the ground in the region from about 100 miles inland to the coast where the longleaf pine grows with needles 8–9 inches long.

The materials are, for the most part, worked by hand. Often the basket makers wear aprons or some other covering over their clothing for protection against the pricking of the cut straw and other materials. Tools usually include an awl, a draw shave, a knife, and scissors among others. The draw shave and mallet are used to split the oak, ash or other wood, which may be woven into various shapes. The awl, originally made from animal bone (hence called the "bone"), is now made by cutting off and smoothing down the bowl end of a spoon handle so that it may be thrust into the bundled sweetgrass. As the opening is accomplished by this method, the palmetto strip, cut on the end to form a point, is pulled through the aperture and drawn through very tightly so as to secure the preceding round of bundled straw to the following one. The basketmakers call this activity "sewing" the baskets, not weaving as it would be with the wood split or other baskets.

Origins of these baskets are in African cultures that were chiefly devoted to hunting, gathering, and agriculture in the past. Dwellings, containers, clothing, and ceremonial items among others were formed of natural substances that were found in the environment. Africans in the Americas adapted to the new surroundings in reaffirming their basketry styles, shapes, forms and uses. Nevertheless, the coiled baskets of the southeast coastal United States have definitely been linked with the coiled basketry of the Senegambian region in West Africa as well as other areas. The baskets from both sides of the Atlantic have been shown to be congruent in their outlines and construction.

References

Arnow, Jan. 1987. *By Southern Hands*. Birmingham: Oxmoor House.

Chase, Judith Wragg. 1971. *Afro-American Art and Craft*. New York: Van Nostrand Reinhold.

Davis, Gerald. 1973. Afro-American Coil Basketry in Charleston County, South Carolina. In American Folklife, ed. Don Yoder. Austin: University of Texas Press.

Perdue, Robert, E. Jr. 1968. African Baskets in South Carolina. *Economic Botany* 22:289–92.

Rosengarten, Dale. 1986. *Row Upon Row: Seagrass Baskets of the South Carolina Lowcountry*. Columbia: McKissick Museum, University of South Carolina.

Teleki, Gloria Roth. 1975. *The Baskets of Rural America*. New York: Dutton.

Twining, Mary Arnold. 1978. Harvesting and Heritage: A Comparison of Afro-American and African Basketry. *Southern Folklore Quarterly* 42:159–74.

MARY ARNOLD TWINING

See also **Basketry, Africa; Diaspora**

BATAMMALIBA

See **Architecture; Astronomy**

BEADWORK

In its simplest form, beadwork is just a string of beads, which may be organized in any number of ways, although some beadwork can be extremely elaborate. Some of the evidence for early beadwork is indirect, that is, from its representation on figures: for instance, terra-cottas from Nok, (first century BCE), and from Djenne-Jeno in Mali (sixth century); or on bronzes from Ife (early fourteenth century) and Benin City (from the fifteenth century onwards). The beads depicted on these pieces could have been made locally from metal, terra-cotta, wood, or even sun-dried clay. Multiple strings of beads are shown as worn around the neck as chokers, or in longer strands to cover the chest; others are worn round ankles or wrists; there are also some elaborately beaded headdresses. Sometimes, archaeological excavations reveal actual ancient beadwork *in situ*, which gives a clearer sense of beadwork was actually made and worn. In southern Africa, there were burials with imported glass beads at fifteenth-century Ingombe Ilede, in the Zambezi valley; and other early burials in a cave at Klasies River Mouth, South Africa, with numerous shell and ostrich eggshell beads that indicated the body areas around which these were worn. At Igbo-Ukwu, in southern Nigeria, the ninth-century burial chamber of a dignitary showed that the corpse was buried wearing long armlets of blue beads threaded on copper wire, which survived in their original form; beads around the skull and the lower legs indicated a beaded headdress and beaded anklets. Many other beads were found lying in rows, which suggested that they were sewn onto a cloth in that order. Over 63,000 beads were found on that site.

Beginning in the nineteenth century, imported beads became valued as prestige markers, and were reserved for important people simply because of their distant, even "exotic," place of origin. Glass beads were brought into Africa from outside the continent. Starting from the early first millennium, traders exported beads into western Africa from the Near East (this is the type of bead so abundant at Igbo-Ukwu); other traders brought beads of the Indo-Pacific type into the coastal areas of eastern Africa. From the late fifteenth century onward, Portuguese and other Europeans exported Venetian glass beads, which eventually superseded the glass beads of Indian origin. Traders and explorers (both Arab and European) had to pay a fee in beads and other goods in order to pass through the land of the king or chief concerned. This setup meant that he had a virtual monopoly of any beads that arrived. It also meant that beads, which were relatively scarce before the 1800s, became increasingly common, and those kings and notables who had previously used elephant ivory, lion and leopard skins, and feathers as regalia came to replace them with beads, whether distinctive beads, or beads in enormous quantity. An example is the Zulu king Dingane, who, in the early nineteenth century, reserved most of the glass beads that came into the country for himself and his wives; a contemporary account describes Dingane and his wives as extensively covered with fringed bead garments. In another extreme example, the king of the Kuba, in Zaire, in the late twentieth century wears beadwork regalia weighing 185 lbs.

Craft Specialization

There was no strict rule dictating that beads and beadwork were made or worn by men or by women; it depended on the culture of the ethnic group concerned. In making stone beads, men did the main part of the work, leaving the finishing touches of polishing and threading to the women; likewise, with metal beads. In contrast, the ostrich eggshell beads made by the San (Bushmen) were made by women. Bead working tends to be carried out according to the complexity and the prestige value of the work involved. In Yorubaland, Nigeria, professional male bead workers were employed to make the beaded crowns, robes, and other regalia worn by the city kings. This skill was the virtual monopoly of one extended family, whose members traveled about the country to carry out their commissions. Men also made ritual beadwork such as diviner's bags and necklaces, since things to do with royalty and religion were generally a male preserve. In Cameroon, also, professional men beaded thrones, stools, calabashes, and masks.

Beadwork for more ordinary "civilian" wear was strung by women, who mostly used imported Venetian seed beads. Beads were and are worn as ornament, and might include a charm against illness or misfortune. Typically, this beadwork would start with a simple string of beads round a baby's neck or waist, which was added to as the child grew. Girl babies graduated to a small fringe on a belt, and as she grew to marriageable age, she would accumulate more bead ornaments. Married women would modify their beadwork as they progressed from being a newly married bride, to one who had her first child, to one whose son had been initiated, and so on. Beadworking was usually a social activity, during which designs were shared and taught to the younger beaders.

Symbolism

Beads played an important part in marking the stages in a woman's life. When a girl reached puberty, it was an occasion for celebration, as she was now of an age to marry and bear children, her most important role. The maidens of the Iraqw of Tanzania, during their seclusion in the bush, while learning a woman's duties, made back skirts of beaded leather, which are among the most spectacular examples of beadwork from eastern Africa. Among the Kalabari, girls attend a "coming out" ceremony at which they wear numerous massive coral beads, which may have to be borrowed from members of the extended family. Something similar still happens in Ghana, where, at the Dipo coming-of-age ceremony, girls of the Krobo and Ga ethnic groups wear almost nothing but a mass of beads. This is designed to enhance the girl's charms and to improve her chances of finding a good husband. If the family does not have enough beads, extra ones will be rented from another family that has the beads, but not a girl of the right age. Even after a woman has married, she may wear a string of beads round her waist; such beads are private between her and her husband, and she may rattle these beads as a "come on" signal. Prostitutes in parts of western Africa could use the same signal as an advertisement, while in Zambia, a woman who wore her string of waist beads

visibly round her neck was regarded as a loose woman. In eastern Africa, men wore relatively little beadwork, while women would wear beaded ornaments on their heads and round their necks; their leather garments were usually embellished with beadwork. In southern Africa, on the other hand, both men and women wore beadwork, sometimes in great quantity. The beadwork of the Ndebele, Xhosa, and Zulu is perhaps the best known, and the Zulu "love letters" the best known of them all.

Almost everything written about the Zulu includes a mention of Zulu love letters. These were first written about in 1907; subsequent studies of the subject appeared in 1951, 1963 and 1994. There is quite a body of misconception about them, based perhaps on cursory reading; and in some ways the term *Zulu love tokens* is preferable. Certain colors are associated with meanings; and if the colors are assembled in a sequence, they can then be "read off" and the message conveyed. Such messages are not to be thought of as letters written with words, and to be read in private; their context is in a nonliterate society, where the women and girls do their beading together, and where everybody knows how things are within the community. In this way, a girl can indicate that she admires a particular young man, and regrets that he has not asked to marry her; or a woman can make a formalized declaration about her relationships or her position within the community. One source of information, a Zulu princess Magogo Buthelezi said, "to appreciate and understand these letters it is necessary to have a sound knowledge of the people's mode of living, their psychology, traditions, folklore etc." She also said, "The modern illiterate miss will also use her own designs and colors to mislead her parents and rivals." Beadwork messages of this sort were very specific to one particular area; outside that area, they would have a different meaning, or even none at all. As literacy becomes more widespread in KwaZulu, the use of beadwork to convey messages is dying out. It seems that to "read" one of those pieces of beadwork, one has to take the center as the starting point; this produces symmetry in the color arrangements, which is important in any interpretation, and also has a pleasing aesthetic effect.

In a contemporary bead production factory the beads are still made by hand. Kazuri Beads Company, Nairobi, Kenya. Photo © Hal Noss, www.halnoss.com

Sorting beads for sale and export at Kazuri Beads Company, Nairobi, Kenya. Photo © Hal Noss, www.halnoss.com

Manufacture

There are two primary methods of making glass beads. They may be wound: here a small amount of glass is wound onto a wire mandrel or rod to form the desired bead, which is allowed to cool before being slipped off the wire. These may be recognized by minute air bubbles, which go horizontally to the perforation. The other, commoner sorts of beads are drawn beads; where a gather of glass is drawn out to form a long tube, which is then cut up into the required lengths and finished off. The small seed beads are all made in this way, as well as beads with longitudinal stripes; the layered chevron beads are a spectacular type of drawn bead. With drawn beads, the air bubbles run vertically, parallel to the perforation.

There are several distinct types of beads. Chevron beads, which range in size from 0.3 to 2 inches, are made of layers of white, red, and blue glass in a star-shaped mould; the ends are ground so that a chevron design appears. There are usually five layers, but the oldest have seven. Aggrey beads, first mentioned in the early sixteenth century, which seem to have come from the Guinea Coast, were highly prized for their rarity, and have

been the subject of fierce academic argument. Indeed, almost any valuable bead has been called an aggrey bead and are now thought to be tubular translucent dichroic beads, blue in reflected light, but greenish-yellow when seen with the light behind them. They may originally have been a rare blue coral, found in the Gulf of Guinea, but nobody really knows. Red coral from the Mediterranean was imported into Benin City, Nigeria, by the Portuguese from the late fifteenth century and made into beads reserved for the king and his court. These became important enough to warrant a yearly festival of their own, in which all the beads were assembled and fortified by a blood sacrifice, which re-empowered them and augmented the strength of the royal relics and the king's power. There are perhaps more powder-glass beads found in Africa than anywhere else, particularly in Ghana. There is one sort, called Bodom, which is the most highly valued of them all, reserved for the most important people. Their origin is forgotten: they are "dug out of the ground." Furthermore, folklore has it that if one of those beads were put in a pot with a charm and some mashed plantains, another bead would appear after one year. There are many other recipes for the propagation of these beads.

Trade

Beads are used to indicate status, for adornment, and as currency. The trade in beads became a major industry, employing bead makers in Venice, Bohemia, Germany, and France, to name a few centers. Shipping handlers operated from the United Kingdom and the Netherlands. In Ghana (the former Gold Coast) alone, an average of thirty-four metric tons of glass beads were imported annually between 1827 and 1841; the value of this trade amounted to 15.7 percent of the total in 1846. The volume of beads that flowed into the whole of Africa must have been staggering. Now the flow of trade goes the other way, with fashion designers successfully using African beads and beadwork to enhance their creations.

References

Carey, M. 1986. *Beads and Beadwork of East and South Africa.* Aylesbury, U.K.: Shire Books.

———. 1991. *Beads and Beadwork of West and Central Africa.* Aylesbury, U.K.: Shire Books.

Drewal, H. J., and J. Mason. 1998. *Beads, Body and Soul: Art and Light in the Yoruba Universe.* Los Angeles: UCLA Fowler Museum.

Evocations of the Child: Fertility Figures of the Southern African Region. 1998. South Africa: Human and Rousseau.

Fagg, W. B. 1980. *Yoruba Beadwork: Art of Nigeria.* Lund Humphries.

Francis, Jr., Peter. 1993. *Where Beads are Loved (Ghana, West Africa).* New York: Lapis Route Books, The Center for Bead Research.

Magogo (Ka Dinuzulu Ka Cetshwayo Ka Mpande) Buthelezi, Princess. 1963. Interview by Killie Campbell. Killie Campbell African Library, Campbell Collection, University of Natal, Durban, South Africa.

Morris, J., and E. Preston-Whyte. 1994. *Speaking with Beads.* London: Thames and Hudson.

Stevenson, M., and M. Graham-Stewart. 2000. *South East African Beadwork 1850–1910: From Adornment to Artefact to Art.* South Africa: Fernwood Press.

Wood, M. 1996. *Chapter on Zulu Beadwork in Zulu Treasures: of Kings and Commoners.* South Africa: KwaZulu Cultural Museum.
MARGRET CAREY

See also **Body Arts**

BEMBA

See **History and Religious Rituals: Bemba Traditions**

BENIN (PEOPLE'S REPUBLIC OF BENIN)

Located on the coast of West Africa and neighbored by Togo, Burkina Faso, Niger, and Nigeria, Benin is a tropical country of nearly 6,220,000 people. The city of Porto-Novo is the country's capital and home to 330,000 people. Cotonou is the second most important city where the university and Supreme Court are located. Ninety-nine percent of the population is African, mostly consisting of the Fon, Adja, Yoruba, and Bariba peoples. The remaining 1 percent of the population is of European descent. Most Beninois practice traditional indigenous religions such as Voodoo (70%), while 15 percent are Muslim and 15 percent are Christian.

On August 1, 1960, Benin (called Dahomey until an official name change in 1975) gained its independence from France after sixty-eight years of colonization. After twenty-two years of a one-party dictatorship, a multiparty democracy was restored in 1990. Benin remains one of the least developed countries in world, a fact that can be partially attributed to limited economic growth, which has worsened in recent years. Benin has no significant natural resources, although the agricultural sector grows palm products, cassava, corn, coffee, yams, cotton, cocoa, and groundnuts. The country's small industries produce shoes, beer, cement, palm oil, and textiles.

In 1625, the Fon people established the notorious Dahomey kingdom. It was a highly organized bureaucratic empire that had an army that included both women and men. The former military units gave rise to exaggerated European stories about "Amazon women." The kingdom also produced sophisticated arts such as Fon applique cloths, which were made for and used by the kings. The art form is still practiced today, although it is made primarily for tourists. The palace and its exceptional bas reliefs were restored in the 1990s.

JENNIFER JOYCE

BENIN KINGDOM

See **Body Arts: Body Decoration in Africa; Queen Mothers**

BERBERS

See **Maghrib: Berber Peoples: Their Language and Folklore**

BIRTH AND DEATH RITUALS AMONG THE GIKUYU

Due to social changes—principally, the predominance of Christian and Western practices felt to be markers of "modernity," and new economic realities—Gikuyu birth and death rituals are no longer performed with the frequency of the past. Individual choice and financial ability largely determine what rituals, or their aspects, are performed. For instance, the actual birth of a child is no longer a communally celebrated ritual event; such a celebration seems to have been replaced by the annual birthday party, a ritual dominant all over Kenya. Whereas the slaughter of sheep or goats was, in the past, connected to religious or quasi-religious occasions, now Kenyans generally stage "goat-eating" parties to celebrate just about any milestone in a family member's life: circumcision, passing an exam, negotiations for a marriage proposal, a promotion at work, or college graduation. Furthermore, most Gikuyu death rituals have been substituted by Christian-like funeral rites.

Numbering about six million, the Gikuyu are a Bantu group whose mythical point of origin is Mūkūrūe wa Gathanga, in what is the contemporary Murang'a District of Central Kenya. Four mountains that hem the land (and had a central place within the tribe's religious practices) roughly mark off the area the Gikuyu have traditionally occupied: Mount Kenya, Ol-Donyo Sabuk, the Aberdare Ranges, and the Ngong Hills. Gikuyu prayers traditionally began with an invocation to these four mountains. In terms of contemporary administrative units, the Gikuyu live in the Nyeri, Murang'a, Thika and Kiambu districts of Kenya's Central province, while the Ndia and Gicugu peoples, "cousins" of the Gikuyu, occupy the Kirinyaga district of the same province. The Nyandarua district within the province was established as a squatter settlement scheme after the attainment of Kenyan independence. Its population is predominantly Gikuyu, but since they are "returnees" from all over Kenya, their brethren living within the traditional lands regard them as a diaspora community. An even bigger diaspora lives in the Rift Valley and Nairobi provinces, engaged in agriculture and business. The Meru, Embu and Kamba are neighbors of the Gikuyu in the Eastern province while the Maasai are generally found to the south and southwest in the Rift Valley province. Intermarriage occurs regularly with neighboring nations, as well as others, but by far the most historically conspicuous are Gikuyu-Maasai marriages (Muriuki 1974, 29; Sankan 1971, ix-xi; 19–20).

Preparations for Birth

Spread out over a vast territory, the Gikuyu traditionally emphasized different elements of the birth and death practices, depending on the dominant practices within their regions, but the broad parameters of such customs are the same. Preparations for birth began during a woman's pregnancy, when she must eat certain foods, and avoid others, for the welfare of both herself and the fetus. The actual birth took place in the woman's hut under the supervision of another woman beyond childbearing age (kīheti). The midwife's age was important, since it was believed that as long as a woman was still sexually active, she was unclean and therefore could not perform a midwife's role. A sheep sacrifice was offered to Ngai in order to ease a difficult birth. Great care was taken to prevent the newborn baby from falling to the ground, for this was seen as an ominous beginning; if it happened, a sheep sacrifice was required to cleanse the baby. The father would then be invited to the hut's porch from where he inquired cryptically from the attending women as to "whom" they had "seen." They then announced the baby's identity based on its rank in relation to its siblings within a fixed patrilineal naming system, but this was varied in exceptional circumstances, such as matrilocal households. The women ululated five times for a boy's birth and four times for that of a girl. Once the baby had been bathed, the afterbirth and the severed bit of the umbilical cord were wrapped with leaves from a *mūthakwa* tree and placed under a bush for consumption by scavengers. The afterbirth was never buried; doing so was considered tantamount to burying a woman's fertility.

Traditional Practices after Birth

During the four or five days after giving birth that a new mother traditionally spent in seclusion (the exact number of days depending on the child's sex), the dirt in the hut was piled up in a corner; only after the seclusion was over would the mother sweep it out to the garbage pit. During this period, her head hair, alongside every woman who had shared a meal with her, was shaved on this day. Her head hair was shaved on days that anyone had shared a meal with her. She did not bathe until she had been shaved. Sweeping, shaving, and bathing were meant to take away the uncleanness associated with the biological process of birth. The mother's purification was finally achieved through the slaughter of a ram.

After the clean-up on the fourth or fifth day, the baby's father fetched food from the fields in order to symbolically give the baby a bountiful start in life. The collective eating of the food by the baby's siblings was meant to welcome the new member into the family. It was customary to call upon the spirit of Ngai (the Gikuyu deity), as well as ancestral spirits, *ngoma* (the sleeping ones), during birth ceremonies.

Special circumstances could lead to variation in the ritual procedure outlined above. These might be difficult births, the birth of twins as a firstborn (always counted in the singular) or the death of mother, child, or both during birth. Severely handicapped babies were suffocated to death, while firstborn twins were thrown into the bush. Purification rituals took place immediately after the disposal of bodies. A month from the day of the mother's shaving, her husband had sexual intercourse twice with her to ceremonially cleanse the baby from the contagion arising from its contact with the mother's amniotic fluids. The "clean" husband contracted the uncleanness and thus neutralized it, according to traditional belief.

The Second Birth

The second birth, also known as returning the child to the womb, took place at varied ages between two and a half to ten years, but it had to be before the actual circumcision. It centered upon the awareness that the child had attained an age at which it could be sent off to live more independently of the mother, in preparation for the transition to maturity. Generally, though, it was done when the child was considered knowledgeable enough to warrant "expulsion" from the mother's bed, so that the husband could pay conjugal visits without inhibition.

Under an elder's guidance, a ram whose fur was uniform in color was used to purify any uncleanness (*thahu*) the child may have acquired from its kins(wo)men. Specifics of this ritual vary, but it generally involved mixing soil (taken from under the ram's hooves), clean river water and the ram's *taatha* (undigested contents of sheep's intestines) in the calabash used to bathe the child after its birth. The child had to be the first to eat the meat during this ceremony. The mother's head was then shaved by a midwife after which she shaved her child. A boy and girl who had already gone through the second birth ritual would fetch four leaves or branches from the *mūkenia* and *mūtei* trees; these were used to splash the contents of the calabash upon first the child and then the mother from head to toe. The mother repeated the process upon herself. This process was done four times on both of them regardless of the child's sex. The men present continuously chanted "May you be rid of any defilement that may have come to you" as the splashing was done. Seated on a stool, the mother would hold the child in her lap as a midwife bound them together with a cord made of of the sheep's intestines. Acting as if to cut the cord with a razor, the midwife would declare, "I sever" upon which the mother would reply, "sever [the ram's cord], but not that between parent and child" (Gathigira 1986, 24; Leakey 1977 vol. 2, 554). After the fourth or fifth such chant (depending on the child's gender), the cord was severed as the women ululated the appropriate number of times. A girl child then accompanied her mother to the field to collect either food or firewood, while a boy, having received a bow and a set of arrows, accompanied his father on a hunt. The child was thus inducted into its future adult roles. After the family members left, the neighbors finished up the food and beer and then departed. Thereafter, a boy slept in his father's hut and a girl in the girls' bedroom (*kĩrĩrĩ*) of her mother's hut. That night the parents marked the ceremony's end by having ceremonial sexual intercourse twice.

Adoption into Another Clan

Adoption into another clan was also regarded as a symbolic birth. This was done, for instance, to a man (never a woman) who had been cast out of his clan. This type of "birth" involved the slaughter of a ram, the swearing of an oath and the "binding" of a newcomer to his new family by a strip of the ram's skin. Symbolic birth also took place when Gikuyu Karĩng'a ("authentic" Gikuyu) married individuals from Gikuyu clans deemed to be "impure" (Gikũyũ kĩa Ukabi) because of their mixed Gikuyu-Maasai blood. The bride's hands were bound with strips of sheepskin as a medicine man used *taatha* to cleanse her of impurities arising from her mixed heritage. A similar ceremony would be performed upon a woman marrying into a Gikuyu-Maasai clan. Finally, since the blacksmiths' (Atũri) clan specialized in the vital iron-working trade, Gikuyu from "outsider" clans had first to be symbolically reborn if they wished to marry into it. A goat was slaughtered for the cleansing ceremony, a strip of its skin would "bind" the newcomer to the clan and a metal wrist coil, or a ring for a male entrant, was given as a mark of membership in the blacksmiths' clan.

Purification Following Death

A popular Gikuyu tale holds that long ago Ngai's messenger, Chameleon, had been sent to relay the very simply phrased but extremely important message that man would never die. However, Chameleon was too slow and Ngai, perhaps eager that the people should receive quickly the good tidings, dispatched a second messenger, the bird Nyamĭndigi. For unknown reasons, the bird corrupted the original message; man would die and perish forever, like the roots of the mythical *mŭkongoe* plant. (This may help to explain why Chameleon is not a very popular Gikuyu folktale character!) A common death superstition relates to an owl hooting near a homestead or perching anywhere within its compound. This is taken as an omen of imminent death within that homestead. In the past this required purification, but in contemporary times it is enough to just hurl objects at the bird to drive it away.

The Gikuyu interred only elders and the rich, since the burial of young people was symbolically seen as burying the nation's future. Corpses of the poor and those that had not attained eldership were normally abandoned in bushes and scavengers, mainly hyenas, determined their fate. Because of his legendary greed, and for his role in consuming corpses, Hyena in Gikuyu folktales is "rewarded" with the most contemptible roles. Barring special circumstances, such as deaths occurring within the compound where circumcision initiates were being hosted, entering a deceased person's hut or physical contact with a corpse was deemed to be contaminating and required cleansing by a medicine man. In the case of a child who died before its second birth, the mother carried the corpse from the homestead and the father carried a flaming torch. The torch and the child's possessions, such as the bathing calabash, were placed alongside the corpse, which was set on the ground with the head facing towards the homestead. This positioning indicated a connection with the home even in death. Other than cases of this nature, women never handled corpses. However, if the child had gone through the second birth, the father carried the corpse; only in regard to such a child was he allowed to display his grief. As a sign of sorrow, a bereaved woman shaved her husband's head and she was in turn shaved by a similarly grieving female neighbor or, in her absence, a woman beyond childbearing age. This process was repeated upon the child's mother after three days. Application of castor oil on her body and the breaking of all earthenware pots used in cooking the oil were further marks of such a mother's grief. A second shaving, a bathing session in the river and the anointing of her body with newly cooked castor oil marked the end of the woman's grief phase. A ram was then slaughtered and a medicine man used its *taatha* to cleanse the woman before she conceived again.

Near-death adults, other than male elders and elderly widows who had been co-wives, were evacuated from the homestead and secluded in shelters in bushes near the village set aside for this purpose (Leakey 1977, vol. 2, 938–986). The aim was to ward off the contagion that their dying within the homestead would have wrought. Close relatives tended them until they died but if they recovered, a ceremony to purify and welcome them back was held. Before relatives who had been sent to the bushes could return to their homestead, they had their heads shaved by an old woman and were cleansed by a medicine man. A poor person without relatives to attend to him or her in the bush was left to die in his or her hut. Thorn bushes were used to bar the hut's door and a hole was dug out in the rear to enable entry for scavengers. Afterwards, either a clansman or someone who had benefited in some way from the deceased would provide a sheep with which to pay a volunteer, usually a stranger, to raze the hut. Such purging served to drive the deceased's spirit away from the homestead. An obscure practice said to have been performed on childless spinsters and bachelors involved the former's genitalia being stuffed with a long maize cob while the latter's buttocks were smeared with ash before their corpses were abandoned in the bush. This was a symbolic way of expunging such individuals from social records; having produced no progeny who could name their children after them, they were seen as having led unproductive lives that were best forgotten.

Only sons who had undergone their second birth, under supervision of respected elders, could prepare their father's body for interment, if he had been admitted to eldership, or have any physical contact with it. The rest of the family was expected to play other ceremonial roles like cooking, keeping the fires in the homestead burning, and feeding the stock since they could not be taken to pasture until the man had been buried. In principle, daughters were not allowed near their dead father's body, and even in the case of a senior widow who qualified for an elder's interment, only unmarried daughters could be present before the sons took out her corpse. All hair was shaved off the body before the corpse was anointed with oil derived from a ram's fat. Standing at its back, a first-born son held the torso by the head while last-born sons held the lower part as they carried the corpse to the grave. It would be placed over a goatskin in a sleeping position, with the head pointing toward the gate of the homestead to indicate continued connectedness to it. If the deceased was either wealthy or a respected elder, his body was wrapped in a fresh ox-hide, instead of a sheepskin, and the ox's meat given to the supervising elders as payment for their services. The body was stripped of any ornaments, which were put in the grave. A ram's skin was used to cover the body before the grave was filled up with soil and a tree planted on top. A medicine man then cleansed the deceased's sons before they could return home for their shaving. After the shaving, another sheep was slaughtered to cleanse the homestead. Beer was brewed for the deceased's peers who, before drinking, poured libation to the departed spirit. These rituals having been completed, the homestead had to be relocated; this practice required the slaughter of another sheep to mark the relocation. On the morning of the actual shift, the sheep's skin was left in the sun to dry and only a poor man was allowed to take it away later.

The most significant death ritual was the *hukŭra* (unburying) ceremony, which was held approximately four weeks from the day of death. Lasting eight days and nights, it involved the slaughter of a sheep and the performance of ceremonial sexual intercourse twice during four of those nights to cleanse the surviving spouse(s) and children from the contagion of death. If a husband had died, widows identified male partners with whom to perform the sex rites. Only after the successful completion of the *hukŭra,* under strict supervision by elders from the council, could participants continue with their normal sex lives. From the day of death to the completion of the *hukŭra* it was taboo to let the fire go out completely within a man's homestead, for that would not bode well for the arrival of his spirit in the world of the *ngoma* (the sleeping spirits).

Modern Practices

Early Christian missionaries' condemnation of many aspects of Gikuyu rituals and general traditional practices as pagan led to their gradual abandonment. Other than Christianity's being presented as the route to "progress," the steady colonial-era assault of Kenyan customs generally meant that few Gikuyu could resist joining the "modernity" bandwagon. Arguably, the Gikuyu, more than many other Kenyan peoples, have shown greater dynamism in abandoning, or refashioning, most of their traditional ways. This may be partly because of their relatively early contact with missionaries and traders, their proximity to Nairobi, and their own desire to embrace a different lifestyle. Among contemporary Gikuyu, there has been profound transformation, and sometimes outright discontinuity, of most of the practices discussed above. For example, with regard to births, it is logistically impossible to dispose of the afterbirth according to customary ritual, since most births now take place in hospitals. At another level, for the Gikuyu it is still vital that a family lineage, and therefore the future, be secured through many (legitimate) children, traditionally seen as a man's "wealth" alongside a multitude of wives and a large herd of cattle. Nevertheless, economic constraints and the general effects of "modernity" mean that polygamy (the customary vehicle for achieving such goals) is now practiced only minimally. This, however, only changes the general Gikuyu perception of "wealth" and does not diminish the joy with which they greet the arrival of new children. It is common among "modernized" Gikuyu, in Nairobi and Kiambu particularly, to throw lavish birthday parties for friends and relatives to "hold/greet the baby" (kũnyita/kũgeithia mwana), as the practice is called. Such parents, depending on their economic fortune, may set a specific day for this, and organize for the slaughter and roasting of a goat. However, since this is costly, visitors are expected to bring cash as well as material gifts for the baby, often turning the party into an opportunity for fund-raising and display.

In the Central province, there are pockets of two atavistic minority groups that have become visible particularly over the last ten or so years with a "return to the roots" call, viz. Mũngiki ("a multitude") and Hama ya Ngai Mũtũũra Muoyo (Tent of the Living God). Adherents are also found in other parts of the country following patterns of Gikuyu settlement. However, the two quasi-religious groups are most conspicuous in Nairobi because of their magnetic attraction of poor urban Gikuyu and other youth and the political limelight they enjoy when they often dabble in politics. They hold severe positions on prohibitions related to women, advocate clitoridectomy and the snuffing of tobacco, sport dreadlocks, and sometimes don sheepskin wrappers and headgear. Beyond this, their "roots" agenda does not include the practice of traditional birth and death rituals and is silent on almost all other areas of Gikuyu cultural practices and, as such, the two groups would merit full research.

With regard to deaths, a contemporary nonuniversal Gikuyu practice is to raze only the nonpermanent houses of deceased persons. During the wake that begins the day a death occurs, Christian hymns are sung as burial arrangements —often involving the raising of funds for funeral expenses and making property settlements—are made. Whereas a tree would have been planted on an elder's grave, the practice is to plant flowers on all graves and to erect headstones and crosses. It is no longer possible to abandon corpses either in bushes or huts/house, since the law calls for the "hygienic" disposal of all deceased persons, age, sex, or social status notwithstanding. The hukũra ceremony, or any other involving ceremonial sex, is no longer practiced. Further,

due to shrinkage in land ownership, homesteads cannot be moved at will. Sheep are often unavailable for use in the numerous cleansing ceremonies due to harsh economic realities. In fact, these traditional customs remain largely unknown to most contemporary Gikuyu people.

References

Finnegan, R. 1970. *Oral Literature in Africa*. London: Oxford University Press.
Gathigira, S. K. 1933. *Mĩikarire ya Agĩkũyũ* (Translations of the Gikuyu). Karatina: Scholar's Publications.
Kabetu, M. N. 1966. *Kĩrĩra Kĩa Ugĩkũyũ* (About Gikuyu Customs). Nairobi: Kenya Literature Bureau.
Kenyatta, Jomo. 1938. *Facing Mount Kenya*. London: Secker and Warbug.
———. 1966. My People of Kikuyu. Nairobi: Oxford University Press.
Leakey, L. S. B. 1977. *The Southern Kikuyu before 1903*. Vols. 1–3. London, New York and San Francisco: Academic Press.
Mugo, E. N. 1982. *Kikuyu People: a Brief Outline of their Customs and Traditions*. Nairobi: K.L.B.
Muriuki, G. 1974. *A History of the Kikuyu People 1500–1900*. Nairobi, Oxford & New York: Oxford University Press.
———. 1990. The Kikuyu in the Pre-Colonial Period. In *Kenya Before 1900*, ed. B. A. Ogot, Nairobi: E.A.E.P.
Mwangi, R. 1974. *Kikuyu Folktales Their Nature and Value*. Nairobi: Kenya Literature Bureau.
Sankan, S. S. 1971. *The Maasai*. Nairobi. E.A.L.B.

MBUGUA WA-MUNGAI

See also **Cosmology; Songs for Ceremonies**

BLACKSMITHS: DAR ZAGHAWA OF THE SUDAN

The Zaghawa occupy the northern part of the Darfur province in western Sudan, along the Sudanese-Chadian borders. The Zaghawa's homeland is called Dar Zaghawa ("the Land of Zaghawa," Tubiana and Tubiana 1977, 1). In Dar Zaghawa, iron working, hunting, drumming, and pottery making are entrusted to a specific endogamous social group called the Hadaheed. Today, the Hadaheed identify themselves as Zaghawa, and there is much interaction between the two groups.

Although in some places of eastern, northern, and western parts of the Sudan, iron working is regarded as an ordinary job, among the Dinka and the Bari of southern Sudan, iron working is entrusted to a separate servile group (Whitehead 1953, 271). In Darfur province to the west, iron working is considered an inferior occupation, especially when the female members are involved in pottery making. In all parts of Africa blacksmiths are either regarded in extreme terms, either with respect or with contempt (McNutt 1991, 81).

Within the Zaghawa society, the Hadaheed occupy an inferior social position. The Hadaheed are traditionally identified as practitioners of iron working, they also practice drumming, hunting, and pottery making. The very name Hadaheed (i.e., iron workers) indicates the prevalence of iron working over other trades.

Among every section of the Zaghawa, there is a blacksmith chief, or "Sheikh." The Sheikh has to supply the ruler annually with iron tools, leather robes, water skins, and game meat, without recompense. The Hadaheed ascribed the causes of their social position to their present small number, and for their uncleanness, in the past (Dinar 1986, 42). The Zaghawa consider the Hadaheed to be dirty and illiterate drunkards and pagans. The Hadaheed's defense strategy against such accusation is based upon Islamic principles. They claim that knowledge of iron working is a gift from God, and not a hereditary practice. In both Chad and Dar Zaghawa, the dominant group justified the servile status of blacksmith in relation to Islamic traditions (Palmer 1967, 74). Thus, blacksmiths were regarded as descendants of the Jews of Arabia, and were later cursed by Prophet Mohammed (Nachtigal 1971, 402). Thus, blacksmiths are accused of being "different" and hence vulnerable to hostile treatment. Such an attitude became fixed in tradition and was passed from one generation to another.

For the Hadaheed, iron working is to a great extent a ritualized trade. Iron smelting was only carried out on Mondays, Wednesdays, and Fridays, when a ram or a goat is sacrificed (Dinar 1986, 48). During the smelting process, the blacksmiths dress in worn-out clothes, and sing for the whole period. This situation is comparable to other African traditions where blacksmiths were excluded at shelters, anoint themselves, and have certain offerings and ceremonies (Haaland 1985, 56). Such rituals extend further to the blacksmith tools: for example, hammers, anvils, tuyueres, and even the iron furnaces were personalized and portrayed as sexual organs (Marret 1985, 77). Such relationship between human procreation and parturition indicates that smelting was regarded as a symbol for generating cultural continuity (Lemelle 1992, 169).

Hunting, like iron working, is ritualized (Herbert 1993, 165). Among the Hadaheed, hunting is not carried out on Wednesday or at the end of lunar months. In these trips, bathing and sexual intercourse are prohibited, so as to guarantee a successful hunt. Within the Zaghawa's society the Hadaheed are also despised for being drummers, pottery makers, tanners, and butchers. The contempt for these trades is mainly due to their uncleanness, and thus exends to the person/s who perform them. Thus, the Hadaheed are despised not simply for practicing these trades, but instead for the beliefs held by the rest of Zaghawa society that are associated with them, which consequently affect the social status of the Hadaheed.

One of the most obvious causes of prejudice is the fact that it creates advantages and material benefits for the dominant group (Cruz 1970, 16). In the past, within the barter system, the Hadaheed had to trade iron tools, game meat, and pottery vessels, all time-consuming and laborious tasks, in return for money, cloths, and grains from the Zaghawa. Due to their political and economic hegemony, the Zaghawa have manipulated the prejudice against the Hadaheed as a means of economic exploitation and political domination.

Folklore plays a great role in denoting the social status of the blacksmith, which is a context within which the blacksmiths became a part of the group's history, culture, and traditions. The interdependence between the rest of the Zaghawa and the Hadaheed guarantees a continuous supply of artisans and specialists, and hence provides a division of labor based upon traditional beliefs. Although more contemporary forms of iron making and food procurement are now prevalent, the social status of the Hadaheed in Dar Zaghawa remains unchanged.

References

Dinar, Ali B. 1986. Folkloric Analysis of the Social Status of the Blacksmith and Iron Working among the Zaghawa Hadahid of Northern Darfur-Sudan. M.A. thesis, University of Khartoum-Sudan.

Haaland, R. 1985. Iron Production, Its Socio-Cultural Contexts and Ecological Implications. In *African Iron Working—Ancient and Traditional*, eds. R. Haaland and P. Shinnie. Norway.

Herbert, Eugenia W. 1993. *Iron, Gender, and Power—Rituals of Transformation in African Societies*. Bloomington: Indiana University Press.

Lemelle, Sidney J. 1992. Ritual, Resistance, and Social Reproduction: A Cultural Economy of Iron Smelting in Colonial Tanzania 1890–1975. *Journal of Historical Sociology*, 5 no. 2: 161–182.

Marret, P. 1985. The Smiths Myth and the Origin of Leadership in Central Africa. In *African Iron Working—Ancient and Traditional*, eds. R. Haaland and P. Shinnie. Norway.

McNutt, Paula M. 1991. The African Ironsmith as Marginal Mediator: A Symbolic Analysis. *Journal of Ritual Studies*, 5 no. 2: 75–98.

Nachtigal, Gustav. 1971. *Sahara and Sudan—Wadaai and Darfur*, trans. A. G. B. Fisher and H. J. Fisher. New York: Barnes and Noble.

Palmer, H. R. 1928. *Sudanese Memoir—Being Mainly Translations of a Number of Arabic Manuscripts Relating to the Central and Western Sudan*. London: Cass.

Tubiana, Marie-Jose, and J. Tubiana. 1977. *The Zaghawa from An Ecological Perspective*. Rotterdam: Balkema.

Vaughn, J. H. 1970. Caste System in the Western Sudan. In *Social Stratification in Africa*, eds. A. Tuden and L. Plotinov. New York: Free Press.

Whitehead, T. A. 1953. Suppressed Classes Among the Bari-Speaking Tribes. *Sudan Notes and Records* 34:271.

ALI B. ALI-DINAR

See also **Metallurgy and Folklore; Northeastern Africa ("the Horn"): Overview**

BLACKSMITHS: MANDE OF WESTERN AFRICA

Blacksmiths affect a large part of the life experiences and folklore of Mande peoples, who inhabit the great plains and wide river basins from the western edge of Burkino Faso to Gambia and the Atlantic Ocean. These peoples include the Bamana (Bambara), Maninka (Malinke), Wasuluka, Dyula, Somono, Bozo, Marka, and several other ethnic groups, such as the Soninke to the north, the Khassonke to the west, and the Kuranko and Susu (or Soso) to the south. This entry focuses for the most part on the Bamana, Maninka, Wasuluka, who along with the Dyula are considered by many scholars to constitute the historical core of Mande culture.

Even in the twenty-first century, the blacksmith provides vital products and services to the Mande. Male members of Mande blacksmith families work in wood and iron, while female members are the potters. As such, the women possess stature and prominence, both as object makers and sorcerers, which parallels that of their male counterparts. Smiths' products surround the Mande at home and abroad. They include stools, doors to private quarters, the delightful sculptures that lock those doors, the kitchen's stirring sticks and butcher knives, and the courtyard's mortars and pestles. The women in blacksmith families make all the clayware that the Mande use. In the fields, farmers use many types of hoes and knives, each designed for a specific type of work. In the bush, hunters still carry the knives, light axes, and guns that smiths have made for decades, if not centuries, and even their ammunition is provided by blacksmiths (McNaughton 1979a, 1988). Finally, other specialists such as the boat builders of Bozo and Sorko society, use tools that smiths make for them.

In addition, the blacksmiths are also sculptors. Thus, when the Mande attend mask festivals, tend to their altars, participate in initiation association ceremonies, or honor deceased twins with sculpted portraits, they are reminded of the smiths, who provide the sculptures and ritual works used in these ceremonies.

The Blacksmith at Work

This plethora of visible objects is supported by the keenly felt presence of the blacksmiths themselves, who work day in and day out at their forges. Even the smallest towns have three or four practicing blacksmiths. When they are not visible, the blacksmiths are generally easily heard, as their hammers ring out in high pitched patterns throughout the village.

Often people stop to watch the blacksmith at work, indulging in light conversation just to pass the time or while waiting for an item. Watching reveals the marvel of expertise, but not necessarily the inherent hard work and technical organization. An adze moves effortlessly around a piece of wood, as chips fly and in short order a recognizable form emerges. With expert smiths it is uncanny how quickly and precisely this happens. By design, but as if by miracle, an implement or mask grows by reduction into the world of tangible objects (McNaughton 1979b).

Mande smiths carve by conceiving the finished product before beginning, then roughing it out with a large adze, and finally working it into degrees of refinement with lighter adzes and a finishing knife. Much skill is required to make exact shapes, because wood does not always give way to an adze predictably. Experts, however, can carve the most subtle shapes with ease. Iron forging demands control; blacksmiths must carefully control heat and hammer blows to direct a semiviscous metal into shapes. Repeated submerging in hot charcoal causes carbon to be absorbed into the metal's surface, tendering it a hard carbon steel, while the core remains more supple, as iron.

Thus, through the sights, sounds, and products that frame people's lives, blacksmiths occupy a phenomenological foreground, which helps to explain the prominent place of the blacksmith in traditional Mande folklore.

Iron Working and the Supernatural

Working with iron is believed to demand large quantities of supernatural energy (*nyama*); the earliest Mande oral lore describes blacksmiths as possessing (and using) extraordinary levels of it. They also traditionally possessed numerous special skills that enabled them to harness that power and play additional roles in society: from sorcerer and herbal doctor to divination expert and initiation association leader (McNaughton 1987). Generation after generation of smiths have played these roles effectively enough to garner an awesome reputation for their

profession—although in every generation there have certainly been plenty of mediocre blacksmiths, whose rudimentary skills are recognized as such by other Mande. Plus, so many smiths work in these "extra-smithing" enterprises that the profession as a whole is seen as conflict mediators and advisor to leaders, along with others. In fact, the smiths lead Komo (for men) and Nya Gwan (for women), two of the most supernaturally potent spiritual associations in the Mande. And many Mande say that smiths have at one time or another been in charge of many or all the spiritual associations (of which there are about ten). Thus, the typical Mande everyday life experience of smiths includes constant contact with their products, constant use of their extra-smithing services, and constant awareness of their seemingly supernatural powers and skills.

The prominence and importance of Mande blacksmiths extends deep into history. Research by archaeologists Susan and Roderick McIntosh has shown that locally made iron played an important commercial role in early complex society before and after the time of Christ (1983). The historian George Brooks has suggested that, especially during the period between 700 and 1100 CE, the smiths had very likely maneuvered themselves into positions of great importance through their iron working, their vast ken of secret and supernaturally charged expertise and the activities of their influential spiritual associations.

People's living experiences and imaginations always merge and feed each other, and in the Mande psyche they converge forcefully around blacksmiths. Lore takes many forms, much of which is simply part of daily life realities. Smiths, for example, are said to be so charged with the energy called *nyama* that it spills out into their tools and forge, and can either be dangerous for ordinary people if they are not cautious, or beneficial if smiths manipulate it in particular ways. Smiths can use it to cure certain illness, and people come to them for the cure. In fact, blacksmiths are believed to possess so much of this energy, and can become so adept at using it to do extraordinary things, that an aura of power surrounds the profession. Thus people say smiths can develop the ability to turn into animals, or become invisible. They can also create special relationships with wilderness spirits, by which they gain additional extraordinary abilities. They can control the location of rain. And some can simply look at you and understand your problems and your needs. Other members of society, such as sorcerers and cult priests, can learn such things too, but smiths have a ready disposition to learn them, and many are believed to become formidably expert at it (McNaughton 1988).

Blacksmiths in Folklore

Smiths are very prominently featured in traditions called *ladaw*, which are vignettes, anecdotes, and little bits of information that give people pleasure, but are also taken seriously as explanations for things in the world. Smiths also appear frequently in the narrative "stories that explain things" (*manaw*) and praise songs that glorify heroes (*fasaw*), which together compose the lengthy and well-known oral epics performed by professional bards. Finally, smiths are frequently featured in the songs (*donkili*) performed at public festivals and masquerade performances, and are characters in Mande rural theater.

In all of these contexts, blacksmiths take on a variety of guises. They can appear as the highly skilled and hard-working providers of community material needs and as the powerful professional manipulators of the energy (*nyama*) that runs the world. They can appear as heroes who undertake grand military or supernatural activities to make the world better, and as warmongering empire-builders who do not let scruples or people stand in their way.

Here is a sampling of some of the blacksmith characters that appear in Mande lore. Domajiri is said to have been the world's first human, and while he was born of extremely powerful, dangerous, and chaotic deities, he became one of humankind's great benefactors. He invented the young men's initiation association called Ntomo, which offers years of important social and spiritual education, and some traditions say he invented the whole complex system of Mande spiritual associations (the *jow*). He also invented the mask that Ntomo members use in their ceremonies, and from one of the wood shavings he invented the lion (Imperato 1983; Zahan 1960).

Three generations later came N'Fajigi, whose control of the energy called *nyama* was so pronounced that he introduced the men's Komo and the women's Nya Gwan associations, both of which are considered by many Mande to possess the ultimate in supernatural power (McNaughton 1979a). He also introduced one of the most powerful of spiritual devices, the Komo headdress, and many say he introduced the Mande to the concept of amulets and other material instruments of tremendous supernatural power.

The Sunjata Epic features two famous Mande smiths, Sumanguru Kante and Fakoli. Sumanguru was a famous sorcerer-leader who tried to build a huge empire through fearsome military and supernatural activity. He killed the leaders of nine local states and wore pants, a shirt, and a hat all made from human skin. He is said to have owned great numbers of charged occult devices, and kept an enormous magical serpent in a secret palace chamber. In oral tradition he is likened to a huge bird of prey that can pierce rock with its talons while flying high in the sky (Bird and Kendall 1980; Diabate 1970; Johnson 1986; Niane 1965).

Sumanguru's great protagonist was Sunjata Keita, who had a blacksmith ally named Fakoli Dunbia, nephew of Sumanguru Kante. Fakoli's wife, also a great sorcerer, had been stolen by Sumanguru, and to avenge the theft, Fakoli switched allegiances. He was a supreme military strategist, statesman, and master of public speaking, and he possessed a strangely large head, full of the capacity for supernatural actions (Bird and Kendall 1980; Diabate 1970; Niana 1965). Those actions help defeat Sumanguru.

The great drama in the Sunjata Epic involves horrendous supernatural duels that are situated amid tremendous military battles. In the end Sunjata uses his sorcery to overpower Sumanguru, who then vanishes into a mountain at Kulukoro, a Niger River town near Mali's capital, Bamako. The spot has a modest shrine and a priest, and some people visit it from all over the western Sudan, in hopes of acquiring some of Sumanguru's ancient power (Niane 1965).

Occasionally in Mande lore, there is an ambiguous relationship between the blacksmiths and the supernatural objects that they use. Nerikoro provides a good example. In the oral traditions it is sometimes hard to tell if Nerikoro is a powerful sorcerer-smith or an equally powerful Komo association headdress. The best interpretation is probably both. Some stories

describe it as the ancient Komo mask of N'Fajigi, who introduced the occult to the Mande. Others assign it to the time of Samory in the late 1800s, calling it the most famous Komo mask of the recent past. And sometimes it seems to be neither mask nor person, but rather a wilderness spirit associated with the mask and its owner. But no matter what it seems to be it always possesses uncanny abilities, as in an interesting oral tradition where a man named Bankisi Sediba tries to kill Nerikoro to aggrandize his own power. During the course of that story, Nerikoro neutralizes deadly mystical poisons buried secretly in the earth, renders harmless a group of armed men set to ambush him, and predicts the coming of the Europeans as it destroys Bankisi.

References

Bird, Charles S., and Martha Kendall. 1980. The Mande Hero. In *Explorations in African Systems of Thought*, eds. Ivan Karp and Charles S. Bird. Bloomington: Indiana University Press.

Diabate, Massa M. 1970. *Janjon et autres chants populaires du Mali.* Paris: Presence Africaine.

Imperato, Pascal James. 1983. *Buffoons, Queens, and Wooden Horsemen: The Dyo and Gouan Societies of the Bambara of Mali.* New York: Kilima House.

Johnson, John W. 1986. *The Epic of Son-Jafa: A West African Tradition.* Bloomington: Indiana University Press.

McIntosh, Roderick J., and Susan Keech McIntosh. 1983. Forgotten Tells of Mali, *Expedition* 25, no. 3:35–46.

McNaughton, Patrick R. 1979a. *Secret Sculptures of Komo: Art and Power in Bamana (Bamabara) Initiation Associations.* Philadelphia: Institute for the Study of Human Issues.

———. 1979b. Bamana Blacksmiths. *African Arts* 12, no. 2:65–71, 92.

———. 1987. Nyamakalaw: The Mande Bards and Blacksmiths. *Word and Image* 3, no. 3:271–88.

———. 1988. *The Mande Blacksmiths: Knowledge, Power, and Art in West Africa.* Bloomington: Indiana University Press.

Niane, Djibril Tamsir. 1965. *Sundiata: An Epic of Old Mali.* Trans. G. D. Pickett. London: Longmans.

Zahan, Dominique. 1960. *Societes d'initiation Bambara: Le N'Domo, Le Kore.* Paris: Mouton.

PATRICK MCNAUGHTON

See also **Epics: West African; Metallurgy**

BOARD GAMES

See **Bao; Draughts; Mancala; Wari**

BODY ARTS: BODY DECORATION IN AFRICA

Throughout human history, members of all societies have developed unique forms for enhancing the human body through adornment. Within Africa, such aesthetic practices vary enormously from culture to culture, as do the precious materials harnessed to this end. The earliest observations of African forms of adornment by Europeans emphasized their exotic and timeless nature. The same fascination with the decorated body in Africa, especially that of women, continues to be reflected in the visual collages produced by contemporary photographers Angela Fisher and Carol Beckwith (Fisher 1984; Beckwith and Fisher 1990, 2000). The panoramic vistas they afford the viewer at once expand the geographic parameters of what is perceived to be African, while providing a celebratory look at the continent's immense diversity. Nevertheless, they perpetuate an Africa which is only rural, exotic, and timeless.

Regional traditions of adornment provide visual systems that may be creatively drawn upon by individuals to express a personalized aesthetic. While such traditions reflect important local sensibilities, they also document historical exchanges across cultures. In Africa, physical refinement of the body with jewelry may be complemented by lavish clothing and hairstyles. Actually, the decoration of the human body involves even more than these obvious alterations. Some people might use nakedness, the complete absence of adornment of the body, as a stage in an initiation ceremony. Others may completely cover the body as in masquerades. There can be temporary decoration such as hair decoration or cutting, or there can be permanent decorations as with scarification. Body decoration is used throughout Africa by various cultures to mark stages of growth and rites of passage. From birth, through initiation and marriage, to death, changes in the appearance and decoration of the human body serve to communicate the status of the individual. Although much body decoration is significant, it is also possible that the decoration exists only for the enjoyment of esthetic expression.

Over the centuries and across the vast geographical expanse of the continent, different African societies have variously measured wealth in gold, silver, brass, ivory, and beadwork. Refined by highly talented specialists, these materials were translated into forms of adornment in order to enhance their owner's power and prestige. In Africa, as in other world cultures, jewelry constitutes an important emblem of its wearer's status and identity.

Goldwork and Gold as Currency

For over fifteen hundred years, West African gold has been part of the world economy. Its trade across the Sahara by Berber nomads became part of the international financial market, beginning in the third and fourth centuries. By the eighth century, exportation of gold to North African and Egypt gave rise to the most important of the early West African Iron Age states. The kingdom of ancient Ghana dominated the southern border area of modern Mauretania and Mali until the thirteenth century. During the height of its power in the fourteenth century, the ruler of the neighboring empire of Mali, Mansa Musa, made a famous pilgrimage to Mecca. In doing so he brought Mali's affluence and sophistication to the notice of the rest of the Muslim world. Upon his arrival in Cairo he so lavishly spent the one hundred camel-loads of gold that accompanied him that the value of gold plummeted and did not recover for a number of years.

Beginning in the fifteenth century, European merchants began to visit various centers along the West African coast and observed local forms of adornment firsthand. A Portuguese expedition arriving in 1482 was met by an Akan chief whose arms, legs, and neck were "covered with chains and trinkets of gold in many shapes, and countless bells and large beads of gold were hanging from the hair of his beard and his head." For the next four hundred years the trade in gold was concentrated along

what was known as the Gold Coast until Ghana's independence in 1957.

Although an ancient artistic tradition, most African goldwork that survives today dates only as far back as the nineteenth century. Because it functioned as wealth, it was continually traded and recycled. The king mandated that all ornaments be melted down and redesigned annually on the occasion of the Yam Festival and imposed a tax on their recasting. It is important to consider, however, that leaders along the Gold Coast appreciated gold not only as a raw material denoting wealth, but for the symbolic significance it took on when refined. According to Asante history, the formation of its confederation in 1701 was ushered in with an official decree that all objects and symbols of the past be destroyed.

Gold dust circulated as a form of general currency throughout the region until the end of the nineteenth century. Unlike Ghana, southeastern Cote d'Ivoire had no comparable system of chiefs or related tradition of regalia. There was no particular restriction on the ownership of goldwork, which principally took the form of personal adornments that could be commissioned by wealthy individuals. Worn by men and women as signs of beauty and prestige, they were attached to the hair or suspended from a necklace on special festive occasions. Today such works are regarded as part of a family's legacy, and as heirlooms, are passed from one generation to the next. In the Lagoons region, adding to this family treasury allowed an individual to enhance his social status. This accomplishment was recognized through a ceremonial exhibition that publicly displayed his wealth.

Baule beads and pendants, which can be discs, rectangles, tubes, or bicones inspired by Akan designs, are cast of impure gold mixed with a high percentage of silver or copper. In addition to these abstract forms, a classic design is that of a human face or head. Although most examples depict a male face with beard, moustache, elaborate hairstyle, and facial scarification, an enormous range of interpretations of this standardized motif exist. The mask's meaning also varies and while in some areas it is regarded as a "portrait" of a friend or lover, in others it depicts ancestors or former leaders. Beyond their aesthetic beauty, such works appear to have had the power to alleviate conflict by contributing to the resolution of disputes and shielding the wearer from physical attack.

Silverwork

In the kingdom of Dahomey (now present-day Benin), royal arts were cast from imported metals such as the foreign currency obtained through trade with Brazilian, Spanish, and American trading partners. Here human beings were the resource exchanged for silver dollars converted into courtly adornment by West Africa's premier silversmiths, a family known as Hontondji. Their patrons, the kings of Dahomey, controlled a precolonial inland state, founded in the early seventeenth century. Until the mid-nineteenth century, the kings of Dahomey prospered through their involvement as intermediaries in the Atlantic slave trade.

The prestige of enhancing one's person with what is literally wealth is reflected in the fact that armlets made of silver dollars were skillfully beaten out so that they retained the impressions of the iron lion of England and heads of George III and his queen. Not only was the material used to fashion Dahomean jewelry a foreign import, but so were a range of the motifs emphasized including automobiles, airplanes, crucifixes, and chameleons, among others. Others emphasize indigenous images associated with power, such as the calabash and animal horn containers used for mystically powerful materials.

Brass

Benin is a living kingdom in the contemporary nation of Nigeria that traces its origins back six hundred years. Since its founding in 1300, individual leaders have used lavish adornment as a means of defining their place within a dynasty of divine kingship. Benin emerged as a regional power through control of local trade networks. In 1485, these were expanded to include a series of European trading partners. In the late fifteenth century, the principal form of currency introduced by the Portuguese was a unit of brass, known as the *manilla*. This wealth was melted down to fashion the works of art for which Benin is celebrated.

Coral

At the court of Benin, worldly wealth accrued through trade was transformed into ornaments commissioned by the king for himself and members of the court. Meticulous attention was given to details of costume and ornament. These in turn clarified the role and status of the figures depicted. In one such example, the identity of the central figure of a warrior chief is indicated by the leopard-tooth necklace he wears and his high-ranking status by a coral-bead collar, a lavishly woven wrap, and brass ornament at his left hip.

From the fifteenth century on, coral beads from the western Mediterranean constituted one of the principal commodities imported to Benin through trade. So integral were they to the aesthetic of the court, however, that oral traditions relate them to the origins of the dynasty. The choice of coral as an emblem of leadership reflects the fact that the well-being of the kingdom, both spiritual and economic, is attributed to the beneficence of the sea god, Olokun. Consequently, the king alone owns all coral and stone beads and may envelope his person with a complete beadwork costume that includes a crown, collar, robe, ornaments, and even shoes. Although he may distribute beadwork to chiefs, titleholders, and members of palace associations, this merely constitutes a loan to the wearer.

Ivory

Ivory was Benin's most precious resource and the king controlled its trade to the outside world. Because of its physical power and scale the elephant was considered an important emblem of leadership and use of its ivory also drew upon these associations. Although oval pectoral masks cast in brass were often distributed by the king to vassal rulers, ivory ornaments were generally commissioned for the king himself.

In present-day Zaire, ivory was the material of choice used to create personal adornment in various central African societies. Among the central Pende, mask forms were replicated in miniature to be worn suspended around the neck. Although wooden versions were carved by healing specialists as remedies prescribed by diviners, ivory pendants were made by professional sculptors to be worn decoratively. Because bodily contact altered the material's aesthetically preferred whiteness, owners scrubbed ivory daily with water and abrasive sand, which also had the effect of blurring the carved features over time.

Luba ivory pendants likewise reflect their close association with the body and are among the most intimate and personal of all works produced by Luba sculptors. Carved from bone, horn, and ivory, they are suspended diagonally across the chest or attached to the arm from cords together with other objects including amulets, beads, and horns. The female figures represented are portraits or at least likenesses named in memory of important individuals. Although each is unique in its detail, all share a minimalist conception of the human form emphasizing the head and torso adorned with references to nineteenth-century Luba female coiffures and scarifications. In homage to the memory of certain revered ancestors, such works were anointed with oil, a practice that together with regular handling and bodily contact has given them a smooth lustrous surface and a rich caramel color.

Beadwork

In eastern and southern Africa, complex styles of adornment have historically made use of the monochrome seed bead as a unit of design. Tens of thousands of these may be strung or sewn to compose elaborate multicolored ornaments that drape the body, a practice that blurs the boundaries between jewelry and dress. Among the earliest known examples of African jewelry are beads made from ostrich eggshell. Beads manufactured in Egypt and Iran were imported during Roman times. By the ninth century, Arab traders had established settlements along the East African coast where glass beads, fabrics, and porcelain from as far away as China were exchanged for African ivory, slaves, and gold. In 1498, this Indian Ocean trade was taken over by the Portuguese who found that local consumers had developed preferences for beads manufactured in India. Between the sixteenth and eighteenth centuries, massive quantities of glass beads were imported from Austria, the Netherlands, and Czechoslovakia.

Within the Republic of South Africa, a series of culturally distinct beadwork traditions have developed. In the land whose mineral wealth of diamonds and gold would later be exploited by European colonizers, imported glass beads constituted a precious resource and form of wealth. Archaeologists suggest that trade in beads and other imported goods were an important factor leading to the development of large chiefdoms and ethnic identities during the eighteenth and nineteenth centuries. Regional leaders controlled access to beads and had them woven into articles of finery as signifiers of power and influence. Like Akan gold which was continually recast, it is difficult to find extant examples of beadwork that predate the nineteenth century because bead works were often restrung. Among the features that distinguishes these forms of artistry is that their makers are female.

Beadworks from the Transvaal region, and a related tradition of mural painting, have provided several generations of Ndebele women with an important means of visual expression. Fashioned into a hierarchical series of adornments, Ndebele beadwork is primarily designed to identify its wearer's stage of life. As children, young girls wear a small beaded band with tassels, or *ligabi*. At puberty, this is substituted for a stiff, rectangular-shaped apron, the *isiphephethu*. On the occasion of her wedding cere-monies, an Ndebele bride usually wears, among other items, a beaded veil and a long beaded train. Her subsequent status as a married woman is denoted by different kinds of beaded aprons (*liphoto* and *ijogolo*), a beaded blanket *irari*, and metal neck, arm, and leg rings, *idzila*. The idea that beadwork serves to situate individuals within the Ndebele social framework and de-marcate their progression through life is also extended to male members at the conclusion of their initiation into adulthood. That event marks a boy's passage from a feminine sphere of influence to a male one and constitutes one of the rare instances in which Ndebele men wear beadwork.

The oldest known articles of Ndebele beadwork are com-posed of mainly small, white beads with minimal linear color designs. Although the types of beaded works designed during the twentieth century have generally remained consistent, significant stylistic changes are reflected in the colors, patterns, and materi-als used over time. The availability of a wider range of colored beads during the 1940s and 1950s led to more complex designs and color schemes. Since the late twentieth century, Ndebele beaded works have incorporated figurative images drawn from women's experience of everyday life and their environment. These motifs include lettering, telephone poles, light fittings, airplanes, and houses.

By the end of the eighteenth century, imported beads had reached northern Natal where the foundations of the Zulu em-pire were being laid under the leadership of King Dingiswayo. Until that time the region had been organized into small chief-doms whose members were farmers. An emerging Zulu kingdom absorbed many of these Nguni chiefdoms and displaced others. The power of the Zulu kings became entrenched through a combination of military superiority and their control of foreign goods. The increasingly active role played by Portuguese traders settled at Delgoa Bay probably intensified both regional conflict and the centralizing mandate of the Zulu kings to command authority over this artery of trade. Dingiswayo decreed com-merce in foreign goods to be his personal privilege and ordered that any of his subjects engaging in their barter be put to death. By 1819 his successor and nephew, Shaka, had established him-self as the all-powerful ruler of a single kingdom and continued to expand the Zulu Kingdom's influence over the next decade. Among his strategies for centralizing regional power, all new bead varieties were brought to his capital and reserved for his own use and distribution.

When the first British traders settled at Port Natal in 1825, they found that glass beads had been incorporated into a cohesive Zulu culture and played an important role in many of the rituals, customs, and ceremonies of the Zulu nation. The varieties and colors of the beads that people were permitted to wear reflected both their social position and personal achievements. In men's ceremonial dress beads were combined with feathers, animal skins, and large copper and bronze arm rings. Strings of metal beads were often the reward for feats of valor.

The decline and fragmentation of the Zulu monarchy during the reign of King Cetshwayo (1872–1879) may be seen reflected in a diversification of Zulu beadwork styles. Although Cets-whayo prevailed over the British at the famous battle of Isandl-hlwana, his subsequent capture was followed by the disintegra-tion of Zulu unity. The ensuing lack of centralized control, greater access to beads through trade, and desire by various groups to build independent identities for themselves led to a proliferation of new forms of beadwork.

In contrast to the official statement made by the regalia of royalty, personal forms of Zulu adornment designed according to a codified system of pattern and color have been described as a language able to communicate on a number of different levels. As in Ndebele society, Zulu beadwork commented on the wearer's age group, marital status, economic level, and region of origin. Beyond this, however, rectangular bead panels made by young women for their lovers publicly acknowledged their courtship. Referred to as "love letters," their compositions fur-thermore convey specific messages across color and linear con-figurations. In such instances, colored beads did not act as an alphabet but rather as ideograms. A particular bead or combina-tion of beads, triggered a series of associations. In some instances these referred to universally recognizable phrases used during courting, while in others, they were of a more intimate and idiosyncratic nature, not overtly legible to outsiders.

Since the 1920s, a sense of Zulu ethnic, cultural, and national consciousness has been revived under traditional leadership. Each spring young women come to the capital from all over the kingdom to perform a national dance before their monarch and his assembled guests. The king uses this occasion of the Umh-langa or Reed dance to speak directly to the youth of the nation and as a platform from which he can make larger political state-ments. As many as four thousand girls dressed in the finest dancing costumes are matched and complemented by the regalia of older men and women, speakers from the royal house, and the KwaZulu government.

In the 1820s, an influx of newcomers converged upon resi-dents of the eastern Cape's Xhosa-speaking chiefdoms. These included both northern Nguni-speaking refugees from the Zulu campaigns of expansion and British settlers. Although the more recent African arrivals became incorporated into Xhosa society, they continued to be identified as members of immigrant chief-doms, such as the Thembu and Mfengu. In the nineteenth cen-tury, Thembu and Mfengu ceremonial dress adopted wide collar necklaces composed of beads and buttons woven into a solid fabric. When compared to Zulu beadwork, Xhosa designs appear relatively subdued and do not reflect overt symbolic meaning. The simple configuration of the beaded collar, however, at once distinguishes the wearer from his neighbors and associates him with a specific ancestral place of origin.

Because of its association with African culture and identity during the rise of African nationalism in the later half of the twentieth century, traditional dress incorporating beadwork came to be associated with anticolonialism. On the day Nelson Mandela was sentenced, he stunned the entire court by appear-ing at his trial wearing full "traditional" dress with blankets, thick skins, and beads around his neck and arms, as well as his knees and ankles. This powerful visual statement served to symbolically underscore the message of his speech from the dock in which he rejected the legitimacy of the entire trial and justice system. Although the African National Congress (ANC) released a photograph of Mandela wearing beadwork from the eastern Cape, images of him and other ANC leaders could not be pub-lished locally following his conviction and the banning of the organization. It was therefore not until 1990 that this thirty-year-old photograph was seen in South Africa.

Although some ancient traditions are changing due to increased contact with different aesthetics and clothing traditions, many traditional body art markers of individual status continue to be used. In fact, now new traditions can be seen, especially in the cities. Young men in West Africa now wear earrings, a practice due as much to contemporary European and American custom as to local customs.

References

Biebuyck, Daniel. 1973. *Lega Culture.* Berkeley: University of California Press.

Blier, Suzanne. 1998. *Royal Arts of Africa.* London: Calmann and King.

Cole, Herbert M., and Doran H. Ross. 1977. *The Arts of Ghana.* Los Angeles: Museum of Cultural History, University of California.

Hammond-Tooke, David, and Anitra Nettleton, eds. 1989. Ten Years of Collecting 1979–1989. Johannesburg, University of the Witwatersrand.

Ezra, Kate. 1992. *The Royal Art of Benin.* New York: Metropolitan Museum of Art.

Fisher, Angela. 1984. *Africa Adorned.* New York: Abrams.

Fisher, Angela, and Carol Beckwith. 1990. *African Ark: People and Ancient Cultures of Ethiopia and the Horn of Africa.* New York: Abrams.

Garrard, Timothy F. *Gold of Africa.* 1989. Geneva: Barbier-Mueller Museum.

Roberts, Mary Nooter, and Allen F. Roberts, eds. 1996. *Memory: Luba Art and the Making of History.* New York: Museum for African Art.

Rubin, Arnold, ed. 1988. *Marks of Civilization.* Los Angeles: Museum of Cultural History, University of California.

ALISA LAGAMMA

See also **Beadwork; Body Arts: Hair Sculpture; Metallurgy; Textiles Arts and Communication**

BODY ARTS: AFRICAN AMERICAN ARTS OF THE BODY

Arts of the body are among the most prolific and accessible traditions of African American expressive culture. Like African American speech, oral literature, dance and music, the arts of dress and personal adornment reflect continuities of artistic ideas, values, skills, and knowledge, rooted on the African continent, which are constantly innovated and adapted as expressions of uniquely African American cultural identities.

Diversity of Genre

African American body arts traditions incorporate many elements or genres. These genres include knowledge, skills, and artistry in the construction, reshaping, and embellishment of clothing, hairstyling and barbering, and cosmetic and other arts applied to the body by artisan specialists skilled in these traditions. African American body arts also include the arts of self-presentation, that is, the way that individuals put together elements of dress, and modify and embellish their bodies as statements of cultural identity.

Continuity of Traditions

African American traditions of the body are expressive of a wide range and diversity of beliefs, skills, performances, values, and artistic communications that reflect the many-faceted African diasporic experience and that of the African continent itself. The expressive culture of New African diaspora communities bears both similarities and differences to the older communities of African descendants in North America. In both instances, there are cultural continuities in traditions rooted in the continent of Africa and traditions practiced in the Americas.

Hairstyling

The decoration and embellishment of the hair is one of the clearest and most widespread examples of African continuities in the body arts of the African diaspora. The textures of African hair lend themselves to a rich variety of options for styling. These options which include cutting, dreading (felting), braiding, coiling, twisting with thread have gone in and out of fashion and have a wide geographical distribution. Some of these hairdressing arts, skills, and aesthetic values have survived the Middle Passage and have passed from one generation to the next. The expertise and artistry of cornrow hair braiding, so called in the United States because of the resemblance of the completed braids to rows of maize, has been as historically familiar in African American communities of the southern United States as it is in the Guyanas and in the islands of the Caribbean. However, cornrow braiding is only one of many traditions of dress and personal adornment that connect African Americans to their African cultural roots.

Other dress and adornment traditions, such as the wearing of headwraps, were restricted for many decades, confined to children and older women in public, due to the association, in this case, of head wrapping with forced dress codes of captivity. For hundreds of years, braiding in the United States African American communities were worn only by very young girls and very old women. In the 1970s, the braiding tradition in the United States was revitalized and even augmented as an art form within the corpus of African American hairstyling by West African women, coming from Senegal, the Gambia, and Mali, who brought a high level of artistry, skills, and specialized knowledge of braiding to the United States. The context of practice changed (or was augmented) from an activity practiced almost exclusively in the home, to a major source of immigrant African wealth and as a highly elaborated part of African American body arts. Ways of tying and wearing decorative head scarfs are widespread among people of the African diaspora, are commonly identified as a communication of African identity. However the style of wrap, techniques of tying, the configuration of the silhouette, the signaling power of the wrap and the identity or message indicated may be quite different for the Ivorian woman at a *soirée dansante* in Philadelphia and the African American college student at Spelman University in Atlanta, although each one may see the wrap as connected to her African identity. Within one pan-African tradition, specific features may signal affiliation to ethnic group, to a religious group, to indicate status within a group or honor a patron divinity.

Decorative Scarring

Decorative scarring had long been abandoned in the United States only to be reclaimed in the 1970s as part of the assertion of pride in African heritage by African American Greek-letter fraternities on academic campuses. As in West African societies, the purpose of the marks burned into the skin of African-American "Greek-letter" pledges were applied to indicate status or affiliation as part of the ordeals of initiation into lifelong brotherhoods.

Dress

Graham White and Shane White have remarked that soon after captivity, Africans were issued clothing which conformed to European codes of appropriate dress as they applied to servile roles. Nevertheless, the Africans working as captive labor on American plantations were still able to wrest out of the materials and technologies available to them a distinct and African-rooted expressive culture of dress. After the events leading up to the American revolution in the late 1770s stopped the flow of imported clothing from Europe, it fell to African American women to produce much of the textiles and the clothing for the captives. Thus, the expertise and agency of African American seamstresses ensured the continuity of African-influenced clothing traditions within captive communities. They applied ideas of beauty and appropriate dress that were passed down from African-born forebears in the juxtaposition of pattern and color. They patched old clothes in manners analogous to the decoration of quilts and remade secondhand clothes into new items of dress. Their knowledge of natural dyeing from barks and from the indigo plants applied to producing different colored threads allowed them to determine the color palette from which to choose (White and White, 1998).

In subsequent years, the modification of store-bought items of dress and the persistent vitality of tailoring, dressmaking, and millinery traditions in African American communities continued to create a distinctive expressive culture of African American dress through much of the nineteenth and twentieth centuries.

The adoption of African textiles, and other visual symbols of belonging to a larger pan-African world community along with access to African clothing from the 1970s led to an intensification and revitalization of African influences on social dress traditions among African Americans in the United States and in the Caribbean. At the same time, reinterpreted African aesthetics of dress returned to the African continent via the influence of African American dress on continental African young people reveling in the new independence from colonialism.

Aesthetics

African influences on the choices of African American textile artists in the south and in the Caribbean, as documented by Thompson (1969), Twining (1977), Wahlman (1983), Frye (1980), and others, have been observed as well in the arts of dress both in construction of clothing and in social dress. Improvisation and originality in African American arts of the body, like quilting and jazz, have have always been central aesthetic values. The skills of "taking trick making luck," as the Caribbean expression goes—creating something spectacular with very limited resources—are values born out only partially out of the limited access to resources which historically too often characterized the situation of African American artists of bodily adornment and dress.

African American Dress and African Identity

Since the late twentieth century, increased contact between Africa, the United States, and the Caribbean, including the presence of people from more recent African diasporas, have brought aesthetic ideas that have revitalized African American dress as well as renewed access to African items of dress, skilled traditional African tailors, and hairstylists. African immigrants have also brought their regional and ethnic traditions of dress and values. The wearing of kente cloth is deeply significant to African American wearers and to Africans of the Ghanaian diaspora in the United States. Although kente is valued as a cloth of status by both groups, the traditions of Ghanaians related to the wearing of kente as a marker of high status, and of their ethnic and national identity is perceived by many Ghanaians as qualitatively different from the African American use of kente (and its often imitated patterns) as a generalized marker of identification with Africa, and as empowerment and entitlement (Kreamer, 1999).

African body arts include both material culture and arts of performance. They can be understood as part of the visual vocabularies of community and individual self-naming. From the occupational arts of African American beauty salons to the highly solemn traditions of dressing the dead, these arts incorporate both everyday social and ritual dress; however, little formal folklore research has been done on these traditions.

Historically, and up to the present day, African Americans have taken advantage of the possibilities afforded by the genre and the means available to adorn the body. African American body arts reflect the continuity of traditions, skills, knowledge, and aesthetic values that have been adapted and readapted, shaped and reshaped on the American continent into several expressive traditions which are all uniquely African American, but which have influenced and inspired contemporary body arts all over the world.

From knowledge and practice of cornrow hair braiding throughout the diaspora, to the symbolic communications conveyed in the aesthetics and symbolism of social and ritual dress of religious practitioners of Santería in New York, Puerto Rico, and Cuba, African diasporic arts of dress and body decoration reflect continuities with traditions rooted on the African continent.

The acceptance of African body aesthetics has broadened the range of what is considered beautiful by African Americans. This reaffirmation of values has led to a period of renaissance of African American body arts that has taken advantage of the wider options and resources available to both specialized artists-hair stylists, braiders, dressmakers, and tailors and to ordinary people who excel at the arts of dress.

References

Griebel, Helen Bradley. 1990. The African American Woman's Headwrap: Unwinding the Symbols. In *Dress and Identity*, eds. Mary Ellen Roach-Higgins, Joanne B. Eicher, and Kim K. P. Johnson.
Holloman, Lillian O. 1990. Clothing Symbolism in African Greek Letter Organizations. In *African American Dress and Adornment:*

A Cultural Perspective, eds. B. Starke, L. Holloman, and B. Nordquist. New York: Kendall Hunt.

Kreamer, Kristin Mullen. 1995. Transatlantic Influences in Headwear. In *Crowning Achievements: African Arts of Dressing the Head*. Berkeley: University of California.

Price, Richard, and Sally Price. 1980. *Afro American Arts of the Suriname Rain Forest*. Berkeley: University of California Press.

Ross, Doran, Raymond Aaron Silverman, and Agbenyega Adedze. 1999. *Wrapped in Pride: Ghanaian Kente and African American Identity*. Los Angeles: UCLA Fowler Museum of Cultural History Textile Series, no. 2.

Thompson, Robert Farris. 1969. African Influences on the Art of the United States. Reprinted in *Afro American Folk Arts and Crafts*, ed. William Ferris. 1983, Jackson: University of Mississippi Press.

White, Shane, and Graham White. 1998. *Stylin': African American Expressive Culture from Its Beginnings to the Zoot Suit*. Ithaca: Cornell University Press.

DIANA BAIRD N'DIAYE

See also **Body Arts: Hair Sculpture; Textile Arts and Communication**

BODY ARTS: HAIR SCULPTURE

All over the continent of Africa, hair art forms a vital part of body adornment for both men and women. The human head has historically functioned as a portable three-dimensional canvas for creatively expressing individual, as well as communal, aesthetic, and social values. The head may be adorned in intricately designed headdresses, wigs, jeweled crowns, or hair sculpture. Due to the variety in thickness and texture—from the tightly curled to the wavy and natural—African hair easily lends itself to several hair-sculpting techniques. In various African societies, hair art also developed in relation to the type of emphasis placed on other forms of body ornamentation. Thus, where elaborate jewelry, body painting, or cicatrices were intended to serve as the focal point, hair was cut and shaved to frame the visage accordingly. For example, married Swahili and Maasai women of East Africa traditionally shaved their heads completely to highlight large earrings, while Akan queen mothers in West Africa partly shaved the hair around the nape and forehead to distinguish their regal stature. Sometimes several techniques, including threading, braiding, twisting, cutting, and shaving, were combined to create unusual coiffures for special occasions.

In some African cultures, the head itself was coaxed into specially defined shapes from its bearer's infancy into adulthood. These shapes were not only desired for their aesthetic effect, but often were considered to distinguish social standing, enhance a person's gait, and express the spiritual values that the community deemed important. Perhaps the most outstanding example, is the Mangbetu of Central Africa who prized cone-shaped heads as signs of increased intelligence. An infant's cranium was molded with tight bands of hide and tree bark, a process repeated at regular intervals until the child reached adulthood (Sagay 1983, 25). Mangbetu women designed special hairstyles to complement the conical shape. They braided the hair in a spiral around the scalp to the apex, attached hair extensions, and wove these into disc-shaped crowns.

Influence of Slavery

Africa's sustained contact with Europe during the transatlantic slave trade, and later in the colonial era (nineteenth and twentieth centuries), affected the trajectory of African hair art. African slaves sent to the plantations of the New World retained some knowledge of hair sculpting techniques, which they passed on to their descendants. Nevertheless, the new environment in the African diaspora induced significant modifications to the practice of African hair art. Under the harsh conditions of slavery, time-consuming designs had to be stripped down to their bare essentials. Furthermore, the rise of eighteenth-century racial ideologies about African inferiority had the most negative impact on cultivating mixed attitudes toward natural African hair and so-called Negroid features. African hair was denigrated in such terms as "kinky," "nappy," "woolly," or "frizzled," in contrast to more desirable "silky," "straight" Caucasian hair types. Thus, the trend in styling natural African hair with hot irons and chemical straighteners began in the late nineteenth century.

Political and Sociocultural Influences

Global political and sociocultural currents of the late twentieth century revived interest in African coiffures, especially among a new generation of Africans on the continent, and in the diaspora. The Negritude political and literary movement of the 1940s, the anticolonial struggle of the 1950s and 1960s, as well as the rise of black consciousness among African Americans, sought to affirm "black pride" in the cultural achievements of African people. The popular slogans "black is beautiful," "African personality," or "L'Africanité" were born in the wake of that political fervor. Also in the 1960s and 1970s, popular cultural icons like South African singer Miriam Makeba, Jamaican reggae musician Bob Marley, and African American political activist Angela Davis ushered in a resurgence in plaits, dreadlocks, braids, natural afros, and African-inspired haircuts. Fashion's drive towards new experiences variously labeled "mysterious," "exotic," "primitive," and "earthy" also increased the currency of African hair art, textiles, fine art, and black fashion models.

Techniques and Designs

In Africa, skills and techniques of natural hairdressing are acquired mostly by informal apprenticeships, and infrequently by formal vocational training. The former process remains the most prevalent. The novice gleans the skills by observing an expert hair artist, perhaps a family member. African hair art has been slow to appear on the curricula of vocational schools on the African continent. The problem may be attributed to lingering colonial prejudice within some African educational institutions against the worthiness of indigenous African art. Limited facilities and resources have also hampered the expansion of formal training opportunities in the art. The situation is slightly different outside the continent, where institutions in some European and North American metropolises now offer programs in African hair art on professional courses in hair care and cosmetology. An industry is also growing in trade journal publication, marketing programs, exhibitions, and in the manufacture of a variety of hair care products specifically designed for natural or processed African hair.

In many African societies, the creation of hair designs is often a collaborative process between the artist and the client, with the enthusiastic participation of onlookers. The execution of the design; however, ultimately depends on the shape of the client's head, the structure of the face, and the occasion for which the design is intended. Hairstyling sessions often last several hours, even days, for the execution of more elaborate coiffures. New hair designs have sometimes been created to chronicle particular historical and political events in sculptural form. For example, Walantu Walansa, a thread-sculpted hairstyle, was created to reflect the government's new green revolution policy in Ghana in 1974 (Dogbe 1991, 15). In Nigeria, Eko Bridge heralded the constitution of a famous bridge by the same name. Other designs are visual renditions of proverbs and folktale heroes like the monkey and Ananse (spider).

Many of the ancient styles reveal the rich history of inter-ethnic trade, such as the trans-Saharan caravan trade, where jewelry from distant lands became prized ornaments for embellishing various coiffures. Elsewhere, nature and man-made technological feats have inspired magnificent styles, such as those created by Fulani women of the western Sahel region, that replicate the architecture of these phenomena. Southern African and West African women wove beads, purchased from European merchants and slave traders, into hair ornaments to match complete body ensembles. It is possible to trace the nature of European-African contact through a careful examination of trade goods, and industrial castoffs, that became resources for body adornment.

Traditionally, the most basic tools required, besides the artist's skill, to create African hair art included a comb, some grease, a razor (if needed), and the desired accessories for decoration. For more elaborate coiffures, thread, hair extensions, dyes, and special ornaments may be used.

The most widespread hairdressing technique is braiding. This involves weaving three sections of hair into strands, which may be left to cascade individually down the client's head, or massed up into buns, knots, or other desired styles. The woven locks can further be cropped into short bangs, rebraided, meshed, coiled, or sculpted into magnificent three-dimensional patterns that simulate an infinite variety of shapes such as stars, bridges, snakes, baskets, topiaries, and brimmed hats.

Twisting achieves an effect similar to the three-strand braid, except the hair is sectioned into single or two-fold strands that are twisted into ropelike locks. Often, braid designs feature a combination of both the woven and twisted techniques. Many contemporary cascading braid designs, like silky twists, dreadlocks, and kinky locks have been greatly influenced by techniques mastered by Maasai male warriors (known as morans), whose long history of twisting delicate braids using red ochre, animal fat, and clay is legendary (Sagay 1983, 31).

Another variation on the twisted or three-strand braid is the technique of cornrowing, in which hair is parted into simple or intricately shaped sections (with equal attention paid to detail in the design created by the parted lines on the scalp), and braided in a creeping fashion along the scalp, with or without artificial hair extensions. Braid patterns differ significantly, depending on whether an overhand, underhand, or twisting motion is used. The loose strands at the end of each braided section are usually decorated with beads and ornaments, or molded into a variety of coiled, threaded, or wrapped designs.

Hair threading traditionally involves wrapping wool yarn, extra-strong mercerized cotton, metallic, or nylon thread, tightly and evenly (or unevenly for a specific effect) around small sections of hair. The hair becomes stiff but pliable and easily coiled or coaxed into bold geometric shapes perched atop the crown. A late-twentieth-century variation on threading involves wrapping shiny synthetic hair, instead of thread, around the natural hair (also called silky locks).

Beyond their use in men's basic grooming routines, shaving and cutting play an important role in accentuating symmetry, definition, and intricate detail in the execution of some sculpted hair styles for both men and women. When combined with other techniques, varying degrees of shaving (from total hair removal to fades) focus attention on only the highlighted parts of the cranial canvas, or on jewelry.

The increasing virtual and actual traffic of people, commerce, popular music, art, and artists across borders continues to fuel the appeal of African hair sculpture among a wider global audience. People of all ethnic backgrounds frequently wear African-inspired hairstyles as a fashion statement, to mimic the styles of entertainment icons, or as a form of cultural identification.

References

Dogbe, Esi. 1991. African Hair Sculpture—Part 2. Uhuru 2, no. 2: 13–15.

Fisher, Angela. 1984. Africa Adorned. New York: Abrams.

Rooks, Noliwe M. 1996. Hair Raising: Beauty, Culture, and African American Women. New Brunswick, N.J.: Rutgers University Press.

Sagay, Esi. 1983. African Hairstyles. Oxford and Ibadan: Heinemann.

ESI DOGBE

See also **Body Arts: African American Arts of the Body; Body Arts: Body Decoration in Africa; Dress**

BOTSWANA

Botswana is a country of 1,620,000 located in the center of southern Africa. Hot and dry, it is landlocked and bordered by South Africa, Zimbabwe, and Namibia. Most of Botswana's people live in the eastern part of the country, as the rest of the country is predominantly made up of the Kalahari Desert. Gaborone, a city of 133,000 people, is the capital.

Botswana was first colonized by the English in 1895, and formally called the British Protectorate of Bechuanaland. It became independent in 1966 as the Republic of Botswana. The government is parliamentary republic and, as of 1998, President Festus Mogae serves as head of state. Historically, Botswana had strained relations with apartheid South Africa and Rhodesia.

Most of Botswana's population resides in the rural areas of the country. The two major ethnic groups are the Tswana and the Kalanga. Major languages are (Se)Tswana, English, Khoisan dialects, Kalanga, and Herero. Approximately three-quarters of the population is Christian and 70 percent of the adult population is literate.

In 1990, the Kuru Art and Cultural Project was formed by speakers of Khoisan who were inspired by their community's ancient rock paintings. The group not only received international recognition, but also encouraged and expanded Botswana's art scene.

In the thirty years since its independence, Botswana has achieved one of the world's highest economic growth rates after having been among the ten poorest countries in the world. Such remarkable prosperity is due, in part, to rapid expansion of mining of nickel, copper, and cobalt. It is also one of the world's leading producers of diamonds. Botswana has fostered its tourism industry, as it is renowned for its beautiful scenery and abundant wildlife. Chobe National Park is one of the country's game parks and home to the world's largest elephant herds. This growing tourism industry, as well as a successful commercial agriculture industry (dominated by livestock), have also aided the economic success of the country.

JENNIFER JOYCE

BRAZIL

See **Diaspora; Religions: Afro-Brazilian Religions**

BURKINA FASO

Located in western Africa, Burkina Faso is a landlocked country of approximately 12,060,000 people who are of the Mossi, Gurunsi, Senufo, Lobi, Bobo, Mande, and Fulani ethnic groups. Burkina Faso, neighbored by Mali, Niger, Benin, Togo, Ghana, and Cote D'Ivoire, has a climate that ranges from tropical to arid. Nearly 50 percent of the people speak Mossi, with Senufo, Fula, Bobo, Mande, Gurunsi, and Lobi being the nation's other most commonly spoken languages; French is the official language. Half of the population is Muslim, 40 percent practice traditional indigenous religions, and 10 percent are Christian. Ouagadougou, the nation's capital, is also its largest city, with 442,000 inhabitants.

In the early fourteenth century, the first Mossi kingdom was established in the area of what is now Burkina Faso. This kingdom survived for almost six hundred years when, in 1896, the French withstood Mossi resistance and claimed the territory as the "Republic of Upper Volta." When French colonial rule finally ended on August 5, 1960, the nation's name was changed to Burkina Faso. After leading a coup in 1983, Captain Thomas Sankara became head of state and was widely respected throughout West Africa; however, he was assassinated during another coup in 1987.

Unfortunately, in the years since independence, the country has suffered from severe drought, which has damaged the largely agricultural economy. In the 1990s, however, the nation's economy has benefited from a slight annual growth rate. Burkina Faso's natural resources include manganese, limestone, marble, gold, uranium, bauxite, and copper, while agricultural production revolves around millet, sorghum, corn, rice, livestock, peanuts, shea nuts, sugarcane, cotton, and sesame. The country's principle industries and sources of revenue are agricultural processing, brewing, and light industry. Tragically, adult literacy in Burkina Faso is only 19 percent, which is the second lowest in the world.

Burkina Faso has produced many of Africa's filmmakers. The government has nationalized its movie theaters and strongly encourages the showing of films by African directors. Ouagadougou is the home to the biannual Pan-African Film Festival, which has been a strong force in the development of the African film industry for several decades.

JENNIFER JOYCE

BURUNDI

Burundi is one of the smallest and most crowded countries in Africa, with a population of nearly 7 million peoples living in 27,834 square miles. Bujumbura is the country's capital and largest city. Burundi lies just south of the equator in east central Africa. It is neighbored by Rwanda, Tanzania, and the Democratic Republic of Congo. Its climate is cool and pleasant, as it is a rather mountainous country. Burundi's population is predominantly Hutu (83%), while 15 percent is Tutsi. The remaining 2 percent is made up of the Twa and other groups. The major languages spoken are Kirundi, French, and Kiswahili. Over half of Burundi's people are Christian, while 32 percent are practice traditional indigenous religions. Approximately 1 percent are Muslim.

After many years of colonization, Burundi won its independence on July 1, 1962, and formed its own republic state. The history of Burundi is one of a people deeply divided. In 1993, the murder of the only democratically elected president Melchior Ndadye, killed only a few months after taking office, sparked vast interethnic violence. In 1994, the presidents of both Burundi and Rwanda were killed. Another period of violence followed and more than 150,000 were killed as a result.

In addition to the country's cycles of violence, the nation's development has been further hampered by population pressure and geographical isolation. Burundi consequently remains one of the poorest countries in the world. Burundi's natural resources consist of nickel, uranium, cobalt, copper, platinum, coffee, tea, and cotton. Its economy is primarily agricultural.

JENNIFER JOYCE

C

CALL-AND-RESPONSE

See **Dialogic Performances: Call-and-Response in African Narrating**

CALLAWAY, BISHOP HENRY H. (1817–1890)

Edward Tylor, the "father of anthropology," personally supported his research and Paul Radin once asserted that he had "laid the foundations for the scientific study of native African religion and folklore" (1970, 1). Nevertheless, one hardly encounters the name of this extraordinary Anglican missionary, Bishop Henry Callaway, at all any longer.

Born in Lymington, England, in 1817, Henry Callaway always wanted to be a minister in the Church of England; but spiritual doubts led him to the Quakers. By 1844 he had become qualified to practice medicine and he married in a Quaker ceremony the next year. The loss of his first two children to illness surely increased his questioning of organized religion. In 1853 he left the Quakers and rejoined the Church of England. The following year he departed for Durban to began his missionary work.

Callaway immediately began recording Zulu customs and language with his primary translator and informat, Umpengula (Benham 1896, 77). He soon had amassed hundreds of pages of data and published *A Kaffir's Autobiography* in 1861. Callaway's first major academic contribution was *Nursery Tales, Traditions, and Histories of the Zulus* (1868). In his introduction, Callaway observed that these tales were a means of "discovering what was the character of the mind of the people."

In addition to noting the importance of the Zulu narratives themselves, Callaway also contributed the rigor of his fieldwork, the recognition of the indigenous perspective, and the value of original language texts. Although any collection of texts made over one hundred years ago has intrinsic value, Callaway's research techniques are especially impressive. His initial motivation in learning Zulu may have been to translate Christian prayers and psalms, but his work took him far beyond this. Callaway's insistence on publishing parallel Zulu and English texts provides an invaluable record for today's scholars. In fact, it is still a struggle to get indigenous texts published today. He anticipated recognition of the value of studying personal narratives.

Another noteworthy contribution by Callaway was the recognition of the importance of good informants and his care in authenticating the recorded accounts. In his journal of 1860, he wrote, "It is very important whilst tracing out their [Zulu] traditions to be careful not to mingle with them suggestions of our own, or thoughts which they have already had suggested to them by others" (Benham 1896, 225). From the preface to his collection of Zulu narratives:

> A native is requested to tell a tale; and to tell it exactly as he would tell it to a child or a friend; and what he says is faithfully written down . . . What has been thus written can be read to the native who dictated it; corrections be made; explanations be obtained; doubtful points be submitted to other natives; and it can be subjected to any amount of analysis the writer may think fit to make.

It is at this analytical stage that Callaway loses contemporary scholars because he sought to establish universal associations for these tales, a goal which fit the cultural evolutionist paradigm of the time. His few footnotes always present assumed parallels with European and Asian "fairy tales." Nevertheless, the rigor and consideration he advised remain as excellent guides for fieldworkers today. In fact, his commentary never reveals the disparaging observations characteristic of his contemporary, the missionary Henri Junod.

Callaway's most important work, *The Religious System of the Amazulu*, was published in 1870. Surely his assertion that the people had "a well-defined religious system" was a unique position, especially for an Anglican missionary at the end of the nineteenth century. This work was to include four sections covering traditions of creation, ancestor worship, divination, and "medical magic," and witchcraft. As with his folklore volume, Callaway presents his informants' accounts verbatim in Zulu with parallel English translations and only occasional footnotes.

A year later, Callaway offered an analysis of divination in which, as a nineteenth-century religious "man of science," he sought to understand human spirituality in its broadest sense. Callaway asserted that "there is a power of clairvoyance, naturally belonging to the human mind, or, in the words of a native

[Zulu] speaking on this subject, 'There is something which is divination within man' " (1871–1872, 165, 168–69). This perspective was not well received at the Royal Anthropological Institute and, despite Edward Tylor's support, Callaway never received funds to complete publication of the fourth section of his *Religious System of the Amazulu*. He returned to South Africa and became the Bishop of Kaffraria, but he conducted no further folklore research. Ill health forced his retirement to Devon, England, in 1887, where he died in 1890.

Clearly, Callaway struggled with his personal religious beliefs and scientific training throughout his life, but his goals were always humanitarian. While he may not have achieved personal peace, in the end he left a priceless record of Zulu personal narratives, tales, and historical records in their own language.

References

Benham, Marian S. 1896. *Henry Callaway, MD, DD, First Bishop for Karrraria, His Life-History and Work, A Memoir*, ed. Rev. Canon Benham. London: Macmillan.

Callaway, Bishop Henry. 1868. *Nursery Tales, Traditions, and Histories of the Zulus.*

———. 1871–1872. On Divination and Analogous Phenomena Among the Natives of Natal. *Journal of the Royal Anthropological Institute* 1:163–85.

———. 1970. *The Religious System of the Amazulu* (1870). Cape Town: C. Struik.

Radin, Paul. 1970. *African Folktales* (1952). New York: Pantheon Books.

PHILIP M. PEEK

See also **Divination; Southern African Oral Traditions**

CAMEROON (UNITED REPUBLIC OF CAMEROON)

Cameroon is a country on the western coast of central Africa, neighboring Nigeria, Chad, Central African Republic, Congo, Gabon, and Equatorial Guinea. The country's climate ranges from tropical to semiarid. Slightly larger than California, Cameroon has a population of around 15 million. Its capital and largest city is Yaounde. Thirty-one percent of the country's population is Cameroonian Highlander, 19 percent is Equatorial Bantu, 11 percent is Kirdi, 10 percent is Fulani, and the remaining 29 percent is made up of various smaller groups. The major indigenous languages are Fulani, Ewondo, Duala, Bamelike, Bassa, and Bali, with English and French being the official languages of the state. Over half of the population practice traditional indigenous religions, 33 percent are Christian (mostly Roman Catholic), and 16 percent are Muslim.

During its long history of colonization, Cameroon was ruled by Germans (who lost their territory after World War I), British, and French until the nation finally won its independence on January 1, 1960. Actually, British Southern Cameroon gained its independence a year later and joined the former French Cameroon, while British Northern Cameroon joined Nigeria. Unfortunately, the country has been plagued by political turmoil since its independence. In 1992, however, the country held its first multiparty elections after twenty-five years of a single-party rule, but there has been little change in the government policies of President Biya. Tragically, Cameroon is ranked as one of the most corrupt nations in the world and has a poor human rights record. Further troubles exist in ongoing border dispute with Nigeria about their shared coastal areas.

Cameroon's major industries and sources of revenue are timber, oil, coffee, cocoa, cotton, bananas, peanuts, and tea. It does seem to be recovering from the economic problems of the 1990s. Cameroon used to have a literacy rate of 76 percent, the highest in Africa, until the World Bank forced the country to abandon its free primary education program; the rate has now dropped to 63 percent. Nevertheless, the country is trying to maintain its extensive educational system with seven universities, thirty-three teacher's training colleges, and a dozen different institutes for specialist training. Another bright spot is its successful national soccer team, which won the gold medal at the 2000 Olympics, and has competed in the World Cup in 1982, 1990, 1994, 1998, and 2002. Cameroon's Korup rain forest is soon to be a national park, as it was recently discovered to contain more than 42,000 trees, including seventeen tree species than had never before been described.

The ancient kingdoms of the highlands, such as the Bamileke and Bamum, have long been recognized for their spectacular royal architecture and arts such as elaborate beaded masks, sculptures and thrones. Coastal peoples have large canoes with carved decorations.

JENNIFER JOYCE

CAPE VERDE (REPUBLIC OF CAPE VERDE)

Located off the west coast of Africa, Cape Verde is a temperate archipelago of ten islands inhabited by some 437,000 people. Praia, a city of 37,670 is the nation's capital. Seventy-one percent of Cape Verde's population is Creole, 28 percent is African, and 1 percent is European. The two major languages spoken on the islands are Portuguese and Kriolu (Crioulo or Creole). The majority of Cape Verdeans are Catholic (80 percent), while the remaining population practice traditional indigenous religions. Most of the islanders are descendants of the Portuguese settlers and African slaves. The blending of these two cultural groups formed the basis for the Cape Verdean Kriolu language.

Portugal ruled these islands for nearly five hundred years but after a fierce liberation struggle for many years, Cape Verde gained its independence on July 5, 1975. After fifteen years of single-party rule, Cape Verde adopted a new constitution and reimplemented a multiparty system. Unfortunately, such changes have not solved the country's economic woes. Environmental erosion, drought, and an underdeveloped economy have plagued Cape Verde since independence. Only 15 percent of the land is suitable for cultivation and the country is consequently unable to become self-sufficient in food production. What little agriculture there is produces corn, beans, manioc, sweet potatoes, and bananas. Textiles have been a successful industry, while fishing has potential to become a great source of revenue for the country.

The Cape Verdean Kriolu culture has a vibrant literary and musical tradition and Cape Verdean bands have become relatively popular on an international level. Local drama, poetry, and music are also broadcast on the national television service. Their spectacular festivals and Cesária Évora, one of their most popular singers, have become known throughout the world.

JENNIFER JOYCE

CARDINAL DIRECTIONS

A cardinal direction is a pivotal line or course along which persons or things move. An object is pivotal if a related part rotates around it or if it determines an effect. A direction, for its part, is an act of management and guidance or a line leading to a place or point. Cardinal directions, as the meanings of the term's constituent parts suggest, are at once among the products and the producers of culture. Cultural forms and practices from across Africa and the African diaspora help clarify the nature of this dialectic.

Historical Developments

In cultures around the world, cardinal directions have figured prominently in navigating the oceans and land routes, locating objects in referential practice, and addressing ancestors, gods, and spirits. It is widely assumed that relatively early in human history, cardinal directions were determined through such means as the rising and setting of the sun and moon, seaward and landward paths, the course of rivers, and the movement of the stars. Tied to many of these movements and positions, flora also signified direction. In regions of North America, for example, bark grows thicker and its folds run deeper on the north and west side of numerous tree species. Also, the branches of these same trees tend to be thicker on the south and east side while their roots grow vertically to the east of the tree.

Over time, key directions were given material form: crosses, circles, diamonds, and an array of intersecting lines were chiseled into rock, cut into skin, carved into wood, and woven into a host of oral cultural forms. Early Asian and Middle Eastern societies were highly sophisticated with regard to this inscription process. Near 2500 BCE, Babylonian astrologers charting star movements sketched a 360-degree circle in the sky, giving 30 degrees to each of their twelve constellations. At around the same time, Chinese inventors constructed the first magnetic compass. It was discovered that magnetite (or, lodestone), placed on wood and floated in water, reliably pointed due south (actually, the earth's magnetic north and a point halfway between sunrise and sunset).

It was around 1000 CE that the Chinese compass was introduced to Europeans, initiating a process that would have profound import for world history. In the fourteenth century, the Portuguese map maker Pedro Reinel drew the first thirty-two point compass rose. Originally called a wind rose, this diagram was typically inscribed on maps and nautical charts and depicted the eight major winds, the eight half winds, and the sixteen quarter winds. In contemporary terms, these thirty-two directions map the cardinal points along with the primary, secondary, and "tertiary" intercardinal points. Today's standardized cardinal points include north (0/360 degrees), east (90 degrees), south (180 degrees), and west (270 degrees). Of significance is the fact that Reinel first drew his compass rose on a map of West Africa. Suffice it to say here that advances in navigation were intimately linked to the context of trade expansion and a host of colonial ambitions.

Cartographic Perspectives

Cartography has been usefully described as a key facet of any "general history of communication about space" (Harley 1987 I, 1). David Woodward and G. Malcolm Lewis (1998) distinguish three broad foci of cartography: material cartography, performance cartography, and cognitive cartography. It is the intersection of each of these categories that will be the focus of much of the present essay.

Mental maps, a term widely used in much cognitive cartography, can be employed to designate mental representations of key human spatial ideas. Consider the example of the "cardinal direction cross" (two intersecting lines with terminal points marked N, S, E, W). How might such a mental representation form? For centuries now, material signs such as the cardinal direction cross have been an important part of human "surrogate reasoning," that is, problem solving employing "external" aids such as the calculator, pen, compass, or diagram. Over time, the cross was constructed as a "mental surrogate" (Barwise and Shimojima 1995) which, throughout the process of its construction, invested place with novel meanings (performance), while being invested itself and articulated with other meaning systems such as corporeal schemata, language, and a host of material objects.

This dialectic between cognitive, performative, and material representations is, of course, at work in many African cultural forms and practices. Consider the example of the *aduno kine* (life of the world), a Dogon rock painting found on the Bandiagara escarpment in Mali. In this painting, the cardinal directions cross forms the arms and torso of the universal order while two ellipses at the head and legs signify celestial and terrestrial placentae. Marcel Griaule (1949) demonstrates that this generative image became the architectural basis for "village" layout, individual residences, hearth spaces, the organization of agricultural fields, weaving designs, and even gendered sleep patterns. Similarly, in rock paintings of a Dogon creation myth, the cardinal direction cross—this time with a circle at its center—represents the god Amma, who, in creating the earth, threw a ball of clay which expanded in four directions—the top being north and the bottom being south. The same representation of the cardinal directions is also found in the *kanaga* mask and sanctuary wall drawings (Griaule and Dieterien 1951).

Cardinal directions also figure prominently in the Bakongo *tendwa kia nza-n'kongo* (the four moments of the sun). Here, the corner points of diamond and cross shapes signify the sun's travel through four stations— dawn, noon, sunset, and midnight. Variations on the Bakongo design are also found in Kongo funerary art from the Democratic Republic of the Congo (DRC) and rock paintings from Angola (Thompson and Cornet 1981). The Tabwa people of the DRC have a variety of aids for the telling and remembering of myths and oral histories. One example is the incisions on the skin of initiates to the Butwa society that tell of the migration of mythic and ancestral figures. A V-shaped line on a society member's back intersected by a second line running up the spine distinguish east from west and mirrors the path of the Milky Way and Orion's Belt (Woodward and Lewis 1998). Finally, Tabwa "villages" are generally plotted in a north-south orientation (Roberts 1988). Each of the cultures mentioned above worked with the skies in imagining the cardinal directions.

Little has been said thus far about the semiotic dimension of the cardinal direction cross. The cross is what Charles Saunders Peirce defined as a diagram. Peirce's threefold division of signs includes signs related to their object by convention (symbol), by existential connection (index), or by resemblance (icon). Hypo-icons are signs based on iconicity but that also exhibit indexical and/or symbolic features. There are three types of hypo-icons: images, metaphors, and diagrams (for an important discussion of the primary components of the diagram see Blackwell and Engelhardt 2001). In most definitions, the diagram is noted for the efficiency of information processing it enables.

Language is a particularly useful place to look at the dialectic between cognitive frameworks and performance. Consider a long-term project being carried out by the Language and Cognition section of the Max Planck Institute for Psycholinguistics. The project engages ethnographic work in some twelve cultures and spans at least ten years. One of the major contentions of the group is the existence and importance of covariation between categories of spatial reference and nonlinguistic conceptualizations—a contention in dialogue with the Sapir-Whorf hypothesis (see Lucy 1992). Stephen Levinson and his colleagues (2002), drawing from the Institute's work with an array of cultures, argues that there are at least three broad spatial coordinate systems used in languages: (1) the "relative" frame in which objects are located via subject-centered points of the corporeal field (left/right, back/front)—example: The tomato is to the left of the apple (subject's view); (2) the "intrinsic" frame wherein object-centered coordinates focus on the object's intrinsic facets—example: The tomato is at the apple's side; and (3) the "absolute" frame in which objects are referred to with regard to their position in relation to fixed cardinal directions—example: The tomato is to the south of the apple. Lucy (1998) and Haviland (1998) provide important refinements of these distinctions. Working with the distinctions, it stands to reason that Bantu Kgalagadi speakers, who operate with a mixture of relative and absolute frames (Levinson et. al. 2002), maintain a substantively different orientation to the world than English speakers who rely on a mixture of intrinsic and relative frames (the latter being dominant).

Bodily Center, Social Body

Necessary to any discussion of cardinal directions is the notion of a center. Many cultures consider the center to be an invariant "cardinal place" (Hanks 1990). Also widespread is the idea of a "moving center" (or a "bodily space" Hank 1990, 90) based on the corporeal field. Examples of this "moving center" include the *fitula* or ceremonial candelabra from Mali. The *fitula* is placed in the ground at the center of ceremonial performances. Diverted from the central axis of the candelabra are four stems reaching toward the four cardinal directions and supporting a total of twenty-eight oil cups (Prussin 2002, image 2004). Among the Fulbe of Mali there exists a woman's hairstyle that features five sets of beads arranged in concentric circles around a center point (the "axis of personal space" Prussin 2002, image 1994). The Taureg *tamakeit* from Mauritania also illustrates the bodily center. This central pole and primary wooden supports of the

Taureg tent serves to establish a gendered locale (Prussin 2002, image 1993A).

The cultural forms and practices of the Ga people of Ghana make frequent reference to a center cardinal place. *Dzeng kodzii enumo* is the phrase used to refer to the four cardinal directions while *dzeng teng* refers to the middle of the world (Kilson 1971: 74). The ritual hair style of Ga mediums known as the *kukuru* consists of five braided "cones" whose positioning reproduces Ga conceptions of the four cardinal directions and a center. The ritual brooms of Ga priests are also fashioned after the same conceptions.

While individual bodily space is often at the core of the notion of the "moving center," the social body is of equal import in African cultures. In southern and northern central Africa, concern with life, death, afterlife, and community inform many burial practices. Some 20,000 years ago, ancestors of the San residing in what is now Botswana and in the Kalahari Desert of Southern Africa buried their dead facing east with knees tied close to the chest (fetal position). From around 1700 BCE, Nubian cultures in what is now Sudan buried their dead in round graves, set in a fetal position with the head facing east. Further south, near the site of Ancient Kerma (2400–2050 BCE), bodies were laid in narrow, circular graves, covered with leather sheets, and contracted into the fetal position—again with the head facing east. Charles Bonnet suggests that such an eastward-facing positioning of the head was a "rule obeyed in all the necropolises right to the end of the kingdom's [Kerma] history" (1997, 90). Finally, King Piy (747–716), who was buried with his ancestors beneath a pyramid at Kurru, provided burial accommodations for four of his horses. The animals were entered standing and facing east. In many of the ancient upper and lower Nile river valley cultures, the east represented the place from which emerged newly forged creation. The passage from death to life was a process of remolding or reformulation. Like Khoprer ("the Becoming One") from the mythology of the Egyptian Old Kingdom, whose representation is that of the scarab beetle pushing its eggs encased in a ball of its own dung, the rising of the sun in the east is one of the ultimate acts of creation. Death and loss in the social body is balanced by an anticipated generation of novel forms.

Hybrid Cartographies

The very flexible cognitive structures and cultural practices around the world are the result of long-standing streams of human exchanges (Gupta and Ferguson 1992). These exchanges also cross temporal boundaries. African cultural forms and practices, for example, have made their way off the continent and combined with non-African religious practices to form unique hybrids. For example, Yoruba beliefs and ritual practices have combined with biblical texts and Christian liturgy in the Celestial Church of Christ. Founded in 1947 by the Nigerian-born Samuel Oschoffa, the church boasts some 3 million members who are scattered from the United States and Canada to Europe and from Togo and Cote d'Ivoire to Senegal (Adogame 1998). The actual site of worship for church members is considered to be sacred ritual space. The Holy Spirit is believed to manifest itself in the four archangels positioned at the four cardinal directions. Church members pray while facing the cardinal directions. The Archangel Michael, located at the east, holds the *ida*, or spiritual sword and is the dominant of the four angels. Gabriel, at the west, is the angel of blessing. Raphael, the angel of health, is located at the south, while Uriel presides over the north and oversees gift giving and receiving.

Haitian vodou is a complex "agglomeration" involving: (1) Kongo symbolism, Fon and Yoruba beliefs, and Yoruba alters (all these brought to the island by coastal, northwestern and central African slaves in the early 1500s); (2) beliefs of indigenous South American Indians; and (3) Catholicism—originally introduced by colonizing Spanish and French forces (Barris 2000). The notion of vodou itself is often interpreted to name intermediary powers, unexplained natural forces, and gods. In this conception, voodoo are associated with ancestral objects and they wield total control of the cardinal directions on earth.

Finally, uncovered in New York City (lower Manhattan) in 1991, is a site now called the New York City African Burial Ground. Throughout much of the eighteenth century, the site was occupied by freed and enslaved African peoples. Thought to be buried in the area (stacked three deep in some locations), are 10,000 to 20,000 people—most of them laid to rest facing east (Frohne 2000). Artists Houston Conwill, Joseph DePace, and Estella Conwill Majozo recently collaborated on an instillation entitled *The New Ring Shout*. A 40-foot diagram constructed of brass and terrazzo, the work is built into the floor of the central rotunda of the 290 Broadway Building (the "290 Building" was erected virtually atop the burial ground). In a series of bold acts of insensitivity, planners and laborers on the thirty-four-story building poured concrete on graves, damaged grave sites, and destroyed collected remains. The commemorative work, *The New Ring Shout*, draws heavily upon BaKongo cosmology and the *yowa* cross, a representation of, among other things, the movement of the sun through its four stations (see MacGaffey 1983).

Emerging from bodily orientation and celestial movements, then represented in a host of material forms, cardinal directions solidify into cognitive schemata. At the same time, cardinal direction image-schemata, when put into practice via various forms of navigation, spatial reference, and object formation, themselves reconfigure the corporeal field, semantic relations, locales and pathways, and social relations.

References

Adogame, Afe. 1998. Building Bridges and Barricades. *Framed: Marburg Journal of Religion* 3, no. 1:1–9.

Barris, Roann. 2000. Calling on the Gods: The Embodied Aesthetic of Haitian Vodou. *Eastern Illinois University Aesthetics*. Available from ⟨http://www.ux1.eiu.edu/~dfrb/haitianvodou.htm⟩; accessed 22 December 2002.

Barwise, Jon, and Atsushi Shimojima. 1995. Surrogate Reasoning. *Cognitive Studies: Bulletin of Japanese Cognitive Science Society* 4, no. 2:7–27.

Blackwell, Alan, and Yuri Engelhardt. 2001. A Meta-Taxonomy for Diagram Research. In *Diagrammatic Representation and Reasoning*, eds. P. Olivier, M. Anderson, and B. Myers, Springer-Verlag.

Bonnet, Charles. 1997. The Kingdom of Kerma. In *Sudan: Ancient Kingdoms of the Nile*, ed. Dietrich Wildung, Paris: Flammarion.

De Maret, Pierre. 1994. Archaeological and Other Prehistoric Evidence of Traditional African Religious Expression. In *Religion in Africa: Experience and Expression*, eds. Blakely Thomas, Walter van Beek, and Dennis Thomson. London: James Currey.

Frohne, Andre. Commemorating the African Burial Ground in New York City: Spirituality of Space in Contemporary Art Works. *Ijele: Art-e Journal of the African World*. 1. Available from http://www.ijele.com/ijele/vol1.1/frohne.html; accessed 15 December 2002.

Griaule, Marcel. 1949. L'image du monde au Soudan. *Journal de la Societe des Africanistes* 19:81–87.

Griaule, Marcel, and Germaine Dieterlen. 1951. *Signes graphiques soudanais*. L'Homme, Cahiers d'Ethnologie, de Geographie et de Linguistique 3. Paris: Hermann.

Gupta, Akhil, and James Ferguson. 1992. Beyond "Culture": Space, Identity, and the Politics of Difference. *Cultural Anthropology* 7, no. 1:6–23.

Hanks, William. 1990. *Referential Practice: Language and Lived Space among the Maya*. Chicago: The University of Chicago Press.

Harley, J. B. 1987. The Map and the Development of the History of Cartography. In *The History of Cartography*, vol. 1. eds. J. B. Harley and David Woodward. Chicago: The University of Chicago Press.

Haviland, John. 1998. Guugu Yimithirr Cardinal Directions. *Ethnos* 26, no. 1:25–47.

Kilson, Marion. 1971. *Kpele Lala: Ga Religious Songs and Symbols*. Cambridge, Mass.: Harvard University Press.

Levinson, Stephen, et al. 2002. Returning the Tables: Language Affects Spatial Reasoning. *Cognition* 84, no. 2:155–188.

Lucy, John. 1992. *Language Diversity and Thought*. Cambridge, Mass.: Cambridge University Press.

———. 1998. Space in Language and Thought: Commentary and Discussion. *Ethnos* 26, no. 1:105–111.

MacGaffey, Wyatt. 1983. *Modern Kongo Prophets: Religion in a Plural Society*. Bloomington: Indiana University Press.

Prussin, Labelle. 2002. Harvard Divinity School, Center for the Study of World Religion: Image Bank, 2002. Available from ⟨http://www.hds.harvard.edu cswr/imagbank/annc-ann.htm⟩; accessed 20 December 2002

Roberts, Allen F. 1988. Tabwa Tegumentary Inscription. In *Marks of Civilization: Artistic Transformations of the Human Body*, ed. Arnold Rubin. Los Angeles: Museum of Cultural History.

Thompson, Robert Farris, and Joseph Cornet. 1981. *The Four Moments of the Sun: Kongo Art in Two Worlds*. Washington, D.C.: National Gallery of Art.

Woodward, David, and G. Malcolm Lewis, eds. 1998. *The History of Cartography*. Vol. 2, Book 3, *Cartography in the Traditional African, American, Arctic, Australian, and Pacific Societies*. Chicago: The University of Chicago Press.

PAUL W. HANSON

See also **Astronomy; Cosmology; Housing: African American Traditions**

CARIBBEAN VERBAL ARTS

Between 1519 and 1867, approximately 5 million African slaves arrived in the Caribbean and the Guyanas. European observers of Caribbean life during this period commented on the constant chatter of the enslaved and their love for formal speech. These behaviors stemmed from African cultural sources: the reliance on orality rather than literacy; the grounding of community in constant acknowledgment of the presence of other humans; and the high incidence of formality in social interaction within markedly hierarchical societies.

Far less hierarchical social relations have since evolved in the Caribbean, primary hierarchical principles in the Caribbean having historically been bound up with skin-color differentials. The inclination to formality in speech has, therefore, not survived the social leveling produced by the demographic preponderance of dark-skinned peoples in the region, the ongoing collapse of color and class rigidities, and the democratization engineered by educational access and communication technology. In Caribbean discourse, little privilege is given to considerations of age or ethnicity, while persistence and volume assure the speaker a listenership. Residual formal speech has, in the twentieth century, been confined to masquerade styles, such as in the Grenada and Trinidad Pierrot Grenade, or to peasant weddings and festivals in the Anglophone territories of St. Vincent, St. Kitts, Jamaica, Guyana, Trinidad, and Barbados. The hallmark of such speech was the use of polysyllabic words and Latin phrases, some of them neologisms, some contextually misapplied. Another genre of masquerade speechifying is *robber talk*, grandiloquent boasts performed by the "robber" at the traditional Trinidad carnival.

Another traditional verbal skill, particularly among males, has been the composition of rhymed couplets. Although this practice seems currently confined to popular lyrics in Jamaican dancehall music, it was previously a verbal game at which males in barbershops and other leisure locations competed for supremacy. In a similarly competitive vein, parallel or opposing proverbs are traded at wakes in Guyana villages during sessions. Proverbs have been a dominant device incorporated into the narrative and analytic commentaries of Caribbean peoples. Proverbs derive from the Bible, and from Europe by way of education, but the majority are African derived in sentiment, their reliance on animal references, and their metaphoric format.

Hostile Verbal Exchanges

Hostile verbal exchanges may win an appreciative audience response because the exchanges constitute an exhibition of appropriate proverbs. Another memorable device in verbal abuse is the outlandish simile. The formulaic themes of these heated exchanges include accusations of ugliness, unhygienic personal habits, and poverty. Many relate to sexual promiscuity, deviance, ineffectiveness, and infertility. Quarreling or telling off is a more issue-focused type of verbal aggression, for which an audience may not be an essential element. In either of these confrontations, the "setup" or "suck-teeth" may occur. This is an indrawn fricative through clenched teeth and slightly parted lips either pouted or laterally lengthened. It is a provocative sign of scorn and disrespect. The body language of confrontation involves placing the hand akimbo, thumping of the outthrust chest, pointing of the index finger into the face of the interlocutor, raising of the dress and exposure of the behind, and the exaggerated flinging of one hand away from the body. The female embellishment to this last gesture may include walking away from the interlocutor with a slow, exaggerated swing of the hips and buttocks.

Another hostile verbal device is called a drop word or throw word. This employs indirection, but while its meaning is not shrouded as in a proverb, the addressee is not the obvious interlocutor. The latter is merely the medium to whom the remark is addressed, but within the earshot of the intended recipient. Then there are the direct remarks meant to embarrass the addressee, to tease as in a joking relationship, or to flatter. Each island has

a slate of terms for these speech forms, with Trinidad being noteworthy in this regard. There, the term *picong* refers to a coded remark which is said in jest, but which contains the germ of a deprecating truth.

Folktales

Wakes continue to be occasions for the narration of folktales in rural areas of the Caribbean. Folktales were also traditionally recounted on moonlight nights on house verandahs and steps. In Jamaica, Grenada, St. Lucia, and Dominica, riddle sessions may precede the recounting of tales, and riddles can be posed in casual adult gatherings and among schoolchildren. In the francophone-influenced Eastern Caribbean, riddles are known as *tim-tim*, based on the exclamatory announcement of a riddle session: "Tim, tim," the riddle-giver cries, to which the listeners shout, "Bwa shess!" (Dry wood).

The tales which follow the riddle warm-up session derive from Europe, and in large part from Africa; dilemma tales, *duppy* (ghost) stories, wonder-child and monster stories form part of the repertoire, but trickster tales predominate. The trickster may be the Akan spider Anansi, after whom the folktales are generically named, the Senegambian rabbit-sized antelope variously called Rabbit or Hare, or the Yoruba tortoise. The trickster is called Malice in Haiti, his dupe being Bouki, the Wolof term for hyena. Among other dupes are Tiger, Elephant, Alligator, Dog, and Monkey. The Jamaican Big Boy character in tales called after him is a combination of trickster, dunce, and word-magician. Some folktales still contain songs, sometimes cryptic, in which the audience participates, while narrative devices include the use of onomatopoeia and ideophones, hand and facial gestures, and opening and/or closing devices. Among closing formulae is Jamaica's: "Jack Mandora, me no choose none," an apparent disclaimer on the part of the narrator for having told the fiction, and the Eastern Caribbean's: "The wire ben', the story en'" or "Crick crack, Monkey break he back." In fact, "crick crack" is one of the main opening formulae in the eastern Caribbean, the *r/conteur* throwing out the first word and the audience replying with the second. This call-and-response device is repeated at intervals throughout the narrative.

It is only among the declining group of Amerindians that creation narratives are to be found, and only among Maroons, descendants of runaway slaves in Surinam and Jamaica, that the germs of potential epic narrative can be discerned in the recall of community founders, migration treks, and mythically stated rationalizations of their special relationships with other groups. In Indian communities within Guyana and Trinidad, there is a storytelling tradition centered around royal personages, public officials, and Hindu deities. Indeed, the main dramatic production of Hindu communities there is the staging of the Ramleela, based on the holy text, the Ramayana, in which Lord Ram liberates the cosmos from the forces of chaos by rescuing his wife Sita from her abductor, the demon king Ravana, with the aid of the monkey god, Hanuman. The African parallels to this sacred lore lie in the tradition of religious narratives about Yoruba *orisha* or divinities worshiped in religions such as Cuba's *regla de ocha* or *santeria*, and Bahia's *candomble* in Brazil. The *orisha* religion is practiced in Trinidad, but the corpus of divine narratives has been lost, although a large number of chants in the Yoruba language is still in use, the meanings of which are unclear to their singers, but which, when decoded, in large part relate to the submerged narrative corpus. These chants function to call the deities into religious ceremonies and to accompany the dances that form an integral part of the ceremonial. Given the social and religious restrictions historically imposed on non-Christian religions in the Caribbean, a number of residual Yoruba secular songs, like dirges and marriage songs, have been absorbed into this corpus of chants in both Cuba and Trinidad. Some chants form part of liturgical antiphonies and are unaccompanied by the drum, which is integral to the performance of the majority of the sacred songs.

Call-and-Response Mechanisms

Traditional folk melodies are short and repetitive, with call-and-response patterning being basic to many Caribbean song, instrumental, and performance styles. Even in conversation, it is normal for the listener to underline the speaker's discourse by uttering "ok," "yes," or vocables to signal that the hearer is comprehending, and that the personal interaction is taking place. Apart from the structural principle of antiphony, whether of lead-singer and chorus, or alternating pitch sequences, another structural device is rhyme, either of consecutive or alternating lines. In addition, even or near-even syllable quantity appears to be one of the structural properties of blocks of lines or breath-groups in calypso and dancehall songs.

It is still possible to detect the melodic and rhythmic legacies of Akan, Fon, Yoruba, and Central African musical traditions in Caribbean folksongs, along with those from France, Spain, Portugal, and England.

Although call-and-response mechanisms and choruses make for regularity, stock melodic phrases and rhythmic patterns may also constitute formulaic structures that allow new songs to be formed. This was the manner in which the stock of traditional folksongs was replenished. The methodology is still revived in extempore calypso composition in Trinidad where performers utilize a narrow range of melodies, and in the reggae and dancehall song genres in Jamaica where various rhythmic sequences become attractive to other singers, who exploit the effectiveness of these established rhythms in creating new songs.

Popular Songs

Thematically, Caribbean popular song has focused on social commentary and complaint, exaltation of the song genre itself, incitement to dance and sexual activity, boasts, and celebration of spiritual forces. Under the influence of European and North American song traditions, some singers also treat romantic love, but the treatment of love in the indigenous tradition has been male centered in its predatory and misogynist inclinations. On the other hand, the sentimental Arabic treatment of love as passed through the Spanish tradition, together with the high demographic presence of whites in Spanish Caribbean populations, have meant that the theme of romantic love has continued to be vigorous in the Hispanophone Caribbean.

With the increase in quality and variety of audiovisual technologies, contemporary Caribbean song genres enjoy strong local, regional, and in some cases, international popularity. Song types such as Haitian *kompa*, St. Lucian *kadance*, Guadeloupean and Martinican *zouk*, Jamaican reggae, and Trinidadian soca are outgrowths of traditional song types, both sacred and secular, now blended with musical influences from contemporary India, Africa, Europe, North and Latin America. Meanwhile, the spread of rural electrification and easy access to radio, television and cable, the wide diffusion of CDs, VCRs, and DVDs, have made formidable inroads into the popularity of traditional genres such as storytelling and proverbs. On the other hand, storytellers are reviving the art of live narrative, creating new tales based on contemporary experiences, utilizing older tales and themes, and performing in new settings such as libraries, fairs, and indoor concerts. For their part, poets, dramatists, and novelists are turning to the language styles of the speech culture to derive events, tropes, and structures for their contemporary artistic work.

References

Abrahams, Roger. 1983. *The Man-of-Words in the West Indies: Performance and the Emergence of Creole Culture*. Baltimore and London: The Johns Hopkins University Press.
Crowley, Danel. 1954. Form and Style in a Bahamian Folktale. *Caribbean Quarterly* 3, no. 4:218–34.
———. 1956. The Midnight Robbers. *Caribbean Quarterly* 4, nos. 3 and 4:263–74.
Dance, Daryl C. 1985. *Folklore from Contemporary Jamaicans*. Knoxville: The University of Tennessee Press.
Edwards, Walter. 1978. Tantalisin and Busin in Guyana. *Anthropological Linguistics* 20, no. 5:194–213.
Reisman, Karl. 1974. Contrapuntal Conversations in an Antiguan Village. In *Explorations in the Ethnography of Speaking*, ed. R. B. A. J. Sherzer. London: Cambridge University Press.
Tanna, Laura. 1984. *Jamaican Folk Tales and Oral Histories*. Kingston: Institute of Jamaica Publications.
Warner-Lewis, Maureen. 1994. *Yoruba Songs of Trinidad*. London: Karnak House.
———. forthcoming. The Oral Tradition in the African Diaspora. In *Cambridge History of African and Caribbean Literature*, edited by A. Irele. London and New York: Cambridge University Press.

MAUREEN WARNER-LEWIS

See also **Diaspora; Performance in Africa; Verbal Arts**

CARNIVALS AND AFRICAN AMERICAN CULTURES

In the late twentieth century, carnivals in the Americas are characterized by an organized procession of costumed participants, music, a limited time span, a beginning and an end, an organized program of activity, a set of performers, an audience, and a place and occasion for the performance. National governments, cultural agencies, and private industry most often are the sponsors of carnival activities and prizes. The timing of carnival as well as the specific names of each country's celebrations fluctuate with national interests and religious heritage. In Trinidad and New Orleans, historically influenced by French Catholic colonization, carnival is celebrated during the week before Ash Wednesday. So as not to conflict with other celebrations in the New York metropolitan area, the parade is held on Labor Day weekend in Brooklyn. In Jamaica and the Bahamas, as a result of British colonial calendric festivities, carnival occurs during the Christmas-New Year holiday. In Santiago de Cuba and Loiza,

Puerto Rico, carnival corresponds with the day honoring Saint Santiago, the patron of those cities, July 26.

African Heritage

The thousands of people who participate in carnival are as varied as the celebrations themselves. Yet at the core of most of these celebrations is a presence and aesthetic formed by the African heritage in the Americas. This African heritage is manifested in different ways. In addition to the obvious continuity of specific masquerading forms and styles, there is the broad tradition of parading in large groups, comprised of musicians, masqueraders, and singers. There are also organizational features that demonstrate African traditions. Some participants have inherited the right to perform, such as members of Afro-Cuban *cabildos* (mutual aid/religious societies). Others belong to neighborhood associations like the black Mardi Gras Indian tribes of New Orleans. Still others join carnival groups that are open to the public based on a payment of fees, like the *mas* (masquerade) bands of Trinidad. Many of these cultural organizations are predicated on ethnic identity and thus the public display of identity during carnival often counters and moves toward the nationalization of culture, which most carnivals today represent.

For example, membership in the Cabildo Carabali Isuama of Santiago de Cubas initially was determined by African nation of origin. Historically, the *cabildo* functioned as a condensed monarchy, which exerted authority over the membership and the community. In Santiago some more famous *cabildo* members were also freedom fighters during the Ten Years War and the War of Independence, ending in 1898. In public performance today, the authority of the *cabildo* hierarchy is comprehensible to all members of the society. There is no hidden subtext here; *cabildo* royalty is authority. Even though *cabildo* costumes imitate European courtly dress, rank, and authority are not being imitated per se, but rather the Afro-Cubans have appropriated a form or style in an attempt to dominate it. By retaining the regalia of the courtly entourage and performing in carnival, *cabildo* members assert their continued presence and perhaps subversive authority in Cuban society today, for *cabildo* authority may challenge government authority. In fact, these carnival performances may provide one means for the survival of Afro-Cuban heritage in contemporary Cuba. In a parallel carnival tradition, the courtly entourage in Jamaican Jonkonnu may seem to be an evocation of a superficially British style, but the underlying aesthetic and performance rules appear to be African-Jamaican, the result of a complex interwoven history. The form is British, but the assemblage aesthetic and the dance patterns are profoundly African derived.

Modern Elements

At the other end of the performance spectrum are new elements which are continually incorporated into carnival performances. In Cuba, it is assumed that carnival will include floats with dancing women, but in 1989 the crowd was quietly spellbound at 2 A.M. when fifteen Afro-Cuban boys performed a moonwalk. Both the break dancing and the moonwalk were performed by males between the ages of twelve and eighteen. Through aesthetic competition they were expressing publicly their participation in a broader world culture of young black youth and their competency in a non-indigenous cultural expression.

Costumes

Carnivals in the African Americas exhibit an enormous variety of traditions, yet individual eclecticism fits into a relatively standardized norm for each national carnival tradition. One of the best ways to understand this twentieth-century hybridity is by a small case study of carnival costumes. In many cases there are rather strict rules governing costume design. For instance, in the Bahamas, all costumes are made from cut and fringed crepe paper molded with wire and pasted onto a cardboard frame. In Trinidad band leaders and designers meet well in advance of the pre-Lenten celebration to hold "*mas* launchings," when themes and designs are presented. Each band supports a King and Queen who compete in distinct categories. Trinidad is best known for its King and Queen costumes which are designed larger and larger in recent years. Poles are attached to the body to support the costume superstructure. Carnival regulations allow wheels on the costume base, as long as the performers' feet and torso are free enough to "dance" across the Savannah stage during the competitions.

A participant in Brooklyn Carnival, Labor Day weekend, 1990. A majority of carnival-players are Trinidadian, or of Trinidadian descent, and the costumes are designed in the Trinidadian *Mas* style. Photo © Judith Bettelheim.

Junkanoo Festival, Nassau, Bahamas, 1960s. All Bahamian costumes are made from cut and sheared colored paper. Photo reprinted courtesy of the Bahamas Tourist Association.

Trinidad Sailors are one of the many traditional characters of "Ole Time Mas" and are predominantly Afro-Trinidadian. Within the confines of traditional Sailor masques there is a broad area for experimentation. Costume by costume a good deal of individual ingenuity is apparent. In 1984 Extra-Terrestrial Voyage included Stray Sailors, Flying Saucer Sailors, and Launch Pad Columbia spaceship costumes. The 1988 Mystical and Legendary Voyages of Old Fashioned Sailors included headdresses based on royal regalia and costume decorations derived from military dress.

Other important Trinidad costumes related to the "Ole Time Mas" tradition include the African-derived Moco Jumbie, or stilt dancer and the Midnight Robber with his fringed cowboy-like pants, long-sleeved shirt, decorated cape, dark glasses, and fringed wide-brimmed hat or fancy headdress. Another character, the Pierrot, wears a costume decorated with cloth strips and a heart-shaped breast plate. Although the name is French, Pierrot is based on a famous Afro-Trinidadian character, the stick fighter. Today the Pierrot carries a staff in recognition of his former role as the competitive and sometimes dangerous stick fighter, who is no longer allowed in carnival.

Both the cloth-strip costume and costumes based on the Amerindian model are ubiquitous in Caribbean festivals. The Amerindian costumed character unites most Caribbean carnivals and is portrayed by men of African descent. In Trinidad there are two types of Amerindians: the bare-chested Red Indian who wears a loin cloth and miscellaneous feathers, and the male or female Fancy Indian whose costume consists of elaborate variations on a vague Plains Indian model.

Parading in Haiti, in Jamaica, in the Virgin Islands, in the Dominican Republic, in Bermuda, in the Bahamas, in St. Kitts-Nevis, and especially in Caribbean New Orleans, the Afro-Amerindian is aggressive, proud, and defiant. After all, there is a lot of unity between the African American and the Native American, both spiritually and politically. A specific Indian type originating on Nevis spread to other islands along with emigrant laborers. Playing Wild Indian, or the Wild Mas Dance, in Nevis has been popular since the turn of the twentieth century and their prototypical Amerindian costume consists of fringed pants, short skirtlike aprons, long-sleeved tops, and tall peacock-feathered headdresses. The circular headdress is made from cardboard covered with tissue paper and mirrors, and surmounted by tall, upright feathers. All band members dress this way, and the costumes worn by Bermuda Gombey bands and the Dominican Republic Masquerade (or *cocola*) bands are identical versions of the Nevis Afro-Amerindian.

In Jamaica the Amerindian costumed character is part of a *Roots*-style Afro-Jonkonnu band. The Jonkonnu street festival is characterized by an entourage of wire screen masked and costumed male dancers, performing mimed variations on an established repertoire of dance steps. Roots Jonkonnu includes not only the Amerindian, but the Cowhead, Horsehead, Pitchy Patchy (the cloth-strip costume), Devil, and Warrior. Roots bands encapsulate a "Fierce" aesthetic, rural and aggressive. Fancy Dress bands demonstrate strong European influence, but in their imitation of courtly costumes they incorporate a strong Afro-Caribbean aesthetic flavor, a true "Creolization." Their costumes are characterized by wildly colored prints juxtaposed with strips or checks. Each character wears the courtly attire appropriate to her/his rank: King, Queen, Flower Girl (Princess), and Courtier.

Cuban carnival includes some uniquely marvelous costume types. Carnival in Santiago is regarded by Cubans as the most "Cuban" of all celebrations, after all Santiago is on the Caribbean side of the island and has the largest Afro-Cuban population. Three types of carnival groups, the *conga*, the *comparsa*, and the *paseo*, are distinguished by their music and costumes. The *conga*, led by the *corneta china* (a double-reed horn), consists of a small group of musicians playing drums and metal percussion instruments. Accompanied by neighborhood residents who may act out a narrative in period costume—such as the 1989 performance of Columbus's landing—the *conga* musicians wear matching pants and shirts, and perhaps a special cap. In the 1989 carnival, the Conga Los Hoyos wore gold lame baseball caps. Individual *conga* dancers can be dressed according to group preference. They may perform as ninja dancers, clowns, feather men, or cigar smoking old wise men.

Comparsas are distinguished by choreographed paired dancers and the famous Santiago bands of *caperos*, men who wear elaborately decorated capes and hats. Caperos run in an undulating line while forming intricate figure-eight patterns. Each *comparsa capero* group is distinguished by a special style of cape with painted scenes outlined in sequins. The *comparsa* dancers' costumes are determined by the danced theme, be it a Mexican "hat dance," or a tribute to Hungarian folk culture, or a Cuban version of a Jamaican Rastafarian dance. These are danced narratives in costume.

The newest type of Cuban carnival group is the *paseo*. Larger and more elaborately choreographed than other groups, the paseo seems to have more flexibility in its costuming and routines. Paseos boast between 300 and 1,000 male and female costumed dancers. Some may perform tributes to the *orichas* (gods) of the Yoruba-derived Santeria religion, each wearing a costume specific to the *oricha's* own colors: blue and white for Yemaya; red and white for Chango; black and red for Elegua, etc. Often the *paseo* also incorporates Tropicana-style nightclub routines with scantily clad sequined dancers.

There is an enormous variety in carnival costumes. The list goes on: Haitian Rara bands with their sequined capes and baton-twirling drum majors, Santo Domingo horned *diablos* (devils), Puerto Rican *caballeros* (horsemen) and *vejigantes* (large-headed figures), and Belizian John Canoe dancers. Many carnivals in the North American cities of Toronto, Brooklyn (New York), and San Francisco, for example, are the result of Caribbean migrations and these celebrations are as hybrid as their populations. Yet at the core of the carnival are reflections of the African heritage in the Americas. In San Francisco, the largest carnival groups are costumed in homage to Brazilian or Trinidadian groups. In Brooklyn, Trinidadian-style bands and Haitian-style Rara bands parade together. All these carnivals are linked by a common heritage produced by European colonialism and African-derived cultural forces. No matter how innovative new carnival performances may be, the African heritage in the Americas continues to underscore many traditions.

References

Bettelheim, Judith, ed. 2000. *Cuban Festivals: A Century of Celebration.* Kingston, Jamaica: Ian Randle Publishers.
Hill, Errol. 1972. *The Trinidad Carnival: Mandate for a National Theatre.* Austin and London: University of Texas Press.
Kinser, Samuel. 1990. *Carnival American Style: Mardi Gras at New Orleans and Mobile.* Chicago and London: The University of Chicago Press.
Nicholas, Robert W. 1998. *Old-Time Masquerading in the U. S. Virgin Islands.* St. Thomas: The Virgin Islands Humanities Council.
Nunley, John, and Judith Bettelheim. 1988. *Caribbean Festival Arts.* Seattle and London: University of Washington Press.
Plantation Society in the Americas—Carnival in Perspective. 1990. New York: Athens Printing Company.
Riggio, Milla, ed. 1998. "Trinidad and Tobago Carnival," *TDR: The Drama Review*, 42, no. 3:(T159).

JUDITH BETTELHEIM

See also **Caribbean Verbal Arts; Masks and Masquerades**

CARTOONS

In Africa, as elsewhere, cartoons are driven primarily by the political and socioeconomic environment. The principles that sustain their creation and enjoyment—exaggeration, robust witticism and humor, and the simple and effective mode of graphic presentation—are the same in Africa as they are in other parts of the world. Cartooning in Africa is a relatively recent phenomenon. Its development was a predictable component of the print

media that missionaries set up in the second half of the nineteenth century as part of their proselytizing agenda.

Two examples serve to illustrate this pattern. In 1859 a weekly newspaper, *Iwe Irohin*, was established in Abeokuta, southwestern Nigeria. In 1883, the Christian community in Ghana successfully established the Presbyterian Press. As a result of educational, economic, cultural, and political factors, media organizations in colonial Africa had a fledgling and remarkably difficult beginning. In colonial and postcolonial Africa, newspapers were established by various interest groups: inspired African nationalists and political activists; expatriate entrepreneurs; and newly independent nation-states desirous of projecting the voice and views of government. But sustaining the print media in Africa where a low literacy rate combines with other operational difficulties remains a daunting mission. Literacy, cultural, and economic predicaments translate to a high mortality rate for print media in Africa. The current media efflorescence in many parts of Africa is a phenomenon that became noticeable only in the last two decades of the twentieth century. Although in pre-independent Africa, there were a few newspapers like Nigeria's *West African Pilot* that bravely employed cartoons to advance anticolonial views and lambaste political lackeys, cartoons produced by African cartoonists did not become a regular staple of the print media until the third-quarter of the twentieth century.

Range and Diversity

In the twenty-first century, a variety of comic books, some in African languages, appear on the market, their subject matter extracted from the cultural milieu of their intended readerships. Two examples, both of them comic books extolling African folktales, demonstrate the versatility of African cartoonists in adapting the medium to suit their specific objectives. Abunuwasi, a thirty-two-page comic book written in Swahili and published in 1996 by Gado, the Kenya-based Tanzanian artist whose real name is Godfrey Mwampembwa, plumbs African fables and comes up with the exploits of Abu Nuwasi, a popular, clever trickster character in Swahili folktales. Gado, an award-winning editorial cartoonist for the *Kenyan Daily Nation*, is one of Africa's most spectacular manipulators of the medium. In terms of adaptation and mastery of techniques, both verbal and visual, Gado, whose work has been exhibited locally and internationally, combines elements from his African traditions with modernist inclinations.

The other cartoonist whose work is equally remarkable is the Nigerian Dokun Abioye who, in 1992, published the first edition of his monthly comic book, *Folktales*. He ascribed his inspiration for the project to his uncle, whose knowledge of Yoruba folktales left a strong impression on the cartoonist during his adolescent years. Written in English, the tale is centered on the exploits of the tortoise: a wily, beguiling animal who, in spite of the physical limitations, is often portrayed as the smartest animal in the wilderness. The tortoise usually outwits humans. But, on occasions, his cleverness also creates its own impediments. In Abioye's 1992 edition, the tortoise commits a social transgression and the Oba (ruler) sends him on an impossible task: to bring the flower of wisdom from the other world. In the end, he outwits two villages and the ruler who had sent him on the initial errand. The way Abioye's animal characters were created and the ease and deftness with which he handled the visual language radiate dazzling brilliance uncommon among cartoonists. Unfortunately, Abioye died before his project could fully take off.

Gado and Abioye share one passion: using cartoons to instill morals in the citizenry. Using folktales and creating enchanting characters that animate popular fables, Gado and Abioye are able to inspire and empower their readers, while drawing attention to the morals in each episode. For every published Gado and Abioye, dozens of other comic books exist in Africa. Political cartoons differ from comic books in terms of subject matter, audience, and intent. Comic books can afford to be heroic, moralistic, inspirational, entertaining, or didactic. Political cartoons, on the other hand, are driven by the immediacy of topic, and the frugality with which darts are shot at political actors. The emphasis is often not on aesthetic elegance, but the message conveyed by the medium.

Political Cartooning

Political cartoonists in Africa strike a delicate balance; they are easy targets for intolerant political leaders or overzealous security agents. In countries where the rule of law is observed more on paper than in practice, where lifelong presidencies are not rare and some rulers often act as if the state was their personal estate, political cartoonists run the risk of being placed under state surveillance should they become so foolhardy as to think that "press freedom" applies to individuals. Cartoons convey different meanings to different audiences. To the overwhelmed editor who is concerned with steering his establishment clear of any litigation, political cartoons are libelous until proven otherwise. This is why self-censorship is normative in many newspaper organizations. Unlike scripts that can be edited easily, cartoons require the cooperation of the cartoonist should the need for editing arise. To the underprivileged and the downtrodden, political cartoons are effective where government inadequacies are parodied and politicians satirized. But most aggrieved politicians, in spite of a tendency to feign altruism, harbor residual resentment for political cartoonists, whom they would rather run out of town. To the brash, bigoted military dictator, political cartoons, especially those that express divergent views, are unquestionably subversive. Editorial cartoonists are quick to realize the precariousness of their situation. They recognize that their relationship with the government is like the proverbial chicken perched on a line: Neither the chicken nor the line will be at ease.

Text, Context, and Sources

The context within which African cartoonists operate is a major contributory factor to the form and substance of their cartoons. Cartoonists employ various stylistic devices to present their gags. Some thrive on narratives while others are reticent, employing economy of visual and textual power. Some cartoonists revel in septic humor: a mixture of raunchy social jokes and tantalizing gender-oriented insinuations. Other cartoons derive their power from sheer intellectual elegance, a robust play on text that challenges the readers to look beneath the facade in unraveling the conundrum. In almost all instances, the format of a cartoon is dictated by its message.

In one single-panel cartoon published in the May/June 1994 edition of *Africaman* by the London-based Nigerian cartoonist,

Bisi Ogunbadejo, five schoolgirls are presented. One of them throws a challenge to another: "Come on then, say it—are you a virgin?" To which the other student replies, "Not yet." In yet another cartoon that Ogunbadejo once did for *The Guardian*, a Lagos-based newspaper, a student comes home and tells his father that he skipped school because he had an accident: he fell into the river. When his father points out that his school uniform is not wet, the boy replies that he took them off before he fell into the river.

Subjects vary: from spousal banters to office romance, traffic humor to epileptic public utilities. In a single-panel cartoon published in the *Herald of Zimbabwe*, a man and a woman are seen walking down the street. A sign displayed in the foreground reads: "20 months for stealing skirt to please woman." The clearly disturbed man can be "heard" commenting on the situation: "Now, whilst he's in jail somebody else will steal the woman's heart." Although the mode in which cartoons are presented is equally important, cartoons stand the chance of becoming bland and trite, mere illustrations, where there is no punch line, either visually or verbally. Indeed, the verbal domain is an important fountain for the generation of ideas that are translated into two-dimensional images in the hand of a competent cartoonist. African cartoonists feast on verbal puns that they pick up on regular basis: at the bust stop, at social events, at political rallies, during casual discussions in public vehicles, at the beach, or at the drawing table. Political cartoonists in Africa are swamped by a cascade of ideas issuing almost interminably from political actors. In a continent where, at least from the perspective of the political cartoonist, a sizeable number of rulers, civilian but especially military, appear to be intellectually challenged, political gaffes seem to tumble from the mouth of politicians by the hour.

Perhaps the best-known example in this regard is that of a general who, in the 1970s, terrorized his country and regaled the international community with equal brutality and buffoonery. His name: Idi Amin Dada, the larger-than-life field marshal of Uganda. Idi Amin's reign has been immortalized through his brutality and the creative imagination of humorists. In the thick political air that enveloped Nigeria during the infamous regimes of military dictators, published cartoons, beer parlor jokes and bus stop snickers became an essential commodity that and lifted the spirit of many Nigerians. From 1984, when Generals Buhari and Idiagbon sacked the civilian administration of Shagari in Nigeria, to 1998, when General Abacha's sudden death brought relief to Nigerians, cartoonists developed the art of double-speak and managed to avoid imprisonment.

In considering humor and satire, particularly in the media, the cartoonist is aware of the tremendous leverage that he or she has in regard to the subject at hand. In most instances, the point is not about truth or objectivity. That, from the perspective of the cartoonist, belongs to the editorial department, or to the newsroom. Just as cartoonists have drawn from oral traditions, folk tales, gossips and rumors, they also draw from social and political innuendoes. Through the manipulation of images, the inversion of text and the subversion of meanings among other tricks, the cartoonists in the print media have come to understand that in getting the message across, truth may, and often is, sacrificed. But in this vein, they succeeded in questioning the truth. Indeed, the closest thing to truth as far as cartoonists are concerned is perception. Cartoonists who function within an environment where cajolement, subtle intimidation, or blatant exercise of power are normative and recourse to civil discourse is discouraged or even prohibited, are at liberty to employ any sleight of the hand tricks. The primary goal of cartoonists is to communicate with their audience, to entertain them to the best of their ability, while employing all manner of tricks that will facilitate the achievement of this objective. This calls for restraint and freedom, creativity and responsibility. Editorial cartoonists function in a pressure zone as a result of the constraints and limitations that their medium imposes on them. There is the constraint of space. Regular editorial cartoonists who work in newspaper organizations where there is commitment to daily cartoons, usually in the Op-Ed pages, are constantly on the edge as they strive to produce pungent cartoons that respond to ongoing developments in the political arena.

Cartoonists and Their Tricks

Nigerian cartoonists could not have wished for better supply of material during General Abacha's tenure as self-appointed president. In cartoon after cartoon, they poured ridicule on Abacha, couching their venom in a variety of guises that at once flatter and scathe. The print media in Nigeria found ways to satirize Abacha during the years that he terrorized the nation. In the Punch newspaper, Kaycee and Ebong are two of the cartoonists whose cartoons graphically said what many Nigerians knew but dared not say. In "Once Upon a Time", Kaycee shows the usurpation of power and the emasculation of justice. Moses Ebong depicts the gluttonousness of the military in his cartoon, "The Note We Missed". By imposing Abacha's portrait on the Nigerian currency, and by depicting two sensuous ladies on the watermark, the brutality of Abacha's regime and the personalization of the nation's wealth are encoded. The travesty that Abacha's regime signified in the history of Nigeria is fully underscored with the dialogue, framed with the text, "I Love Viagra," an obvious reference to the manner in which the general was said to have died. Kaycee and Ebong are from the *Punch*, the newspaper that almost single-handedly popularized cartoons in Nigeria in the 1970s. Despite the severe limitations that many African media houses contend with, cartooning continues to flourish on the continent. Nigeria has perhaps the largest number of cartoonists in Africa although, unlike in Kenya, Nigerian cartoonists do not have an association. After the epic of Lash (Akinola Lasekan), the country's first cartoonist who worked for the *West African Pilot* from 1939 until the first military coup d'etat in 1966, a new group of cartoonists—Oke Hortons, Ore Gab Okpao, Ayo Ajayi, Josy Ajiboye, Cliff Ogiugo, Kenny Adamson, and dele jegede among others, emerged. Today, cartoonists are considered as a critical core of the print media personnel. A similar situation exists on the East African coast. In Kenya alone, there are about fifteen editorial cartoonists working for the five dailies and about seven weeklies. The number of cartoonists in Uganda is about the same while, in Tanzania, the number jumps to more than twenty. On the East African coast, according to Gado, there is an association of cartoonists, called Katuni that caters to the interests of its members through workshops, seminars and exhibits. Some of these cartoonists—Gado (Godfrey Mwampembwa), Madd (Paul Kelemba), Fran (Fran Odoi), Stano (Stanislous Olonde), Kingo (James Gayo) and Kham (James Kamawira)—represent the first generation of cartoonists

in a new dispensation that offers them the advantage of shaping the future.

A rich example of the range of these cartoonists can be seen in Kenya's *Daily Nation* in which cartoonists inveigh against numerous local, national and international issues. Most frequently visited themes concern the role of the World Bank (WB) and the International Monetary Fund (IMF), often considered inimical to national pride and economic development. In one poetically pungent example published in the *Daily Nation* (January 3, 2000, 6), the WB and IMF, personified by a white benefactor with a gushing moustache and what appears to be a demonic smile, dispenses the organizations' largesse to an African government, represented by a hand in tattered suit holding a pan. But a second look at the cartoon, which has not a single word, reveals the pathetic poignancy of the situation. The pan is perforated.

But it is to Gado that one returns for the creation of some of the most graphically refreshing and visually stimulating pieces. Still on the same topic (IMF), Gado chooses to play on words. The Kenyan nation, apparently delusional about its physical (and fiscal) wellness, is portrayed as a machismo, an athletically buoyant "Mr. Kenya". Of course, a glance at this image shows a wimpy, effeminate man in a pathetic show of muscle flexing before a bemused white man, IMF, whose responsibility it is to emphasize the havoc that has been wreaked through an apparent communication problem: "Wow, wow! I said I'm coming to see your fiscal progress not physical progress!!" Elsewhere, in Zimbabwe, the presence of the IMF is also regularly invoked in cartoons. The *Herald* in its April 16, 1999, edition carried a cartoon by I, Mpofu which, in a few lines, portrays an embattled the Zimbabwean president Robert Mugabe attempting to scale a hurdle that is comprised of land distribution, new constitution, and IMF. But the right to speak truth to power is not native to Zimbabwe, and Gado proves this in one of his sterling cartoons in the *Daily Nation* (February 12, 2000). In it, a grim-looking Mugabe metamorphoses into a gas pump: an empty one! Gado's cartoons exemplify the visual-verbal technique that oscillates between (re)presentation, unsparing critique and transformation. As with many others, this cartoon is rich in symbolism. In a way that recalls the employment of social hierarchy, Mugabe looms large as a fuel pump. But what is the essence of a gargantuan dispenser that contains nothing? Is Gado implying that to Zimbabwe, the stupefied man at the pump, the credibility of Mugabe, rather than fuel, constitutes the real crisis? Is Mugabe thus the proverbial empty barrel that makes the most noise? But you ask: does Mugabe hear the yearnings of his subjects? Does he even care?

Effect on Population

In conclusion, cartoons offer perhaps the most solid index by which the success and relevance of popular art in Africa may be measured. Because they have an unmatchable capacity to transcend barriers and boundaries—racial, social, educational, political, and aesthetic among many others—cartoons encapsulate the two radically oppositional principles of force and innocuousness. They are at once formidable and dispensable: provoking as they cajole; entertaining as they castigate. The cartoonist in Africa straddles the two worlds of then and now, of the traditional and the modern, the ruler and the ruled. As in many other departments of visual culture, the African cartoonist has imbued this genre with a uniquely African flavor without which it will become yet another lackluster, highbrow idiom.

DELE JEGEDE

See also **Electronic Media and Oral Traditions; Oratory; Popular Culture**

CENTRAL AFRICAN FOLKLORE: OVERVIEW

The oral literature of the diverse ethnic groups established in Central Africa is well documented. European, Gabonese, and Congolese professional anthropologists and linguists author some of the most comprehensive studies, although numerous missionaries and colonial officers with extensive and sympathetic experiences among particular ethnic groups also provide first-rate accounts, at least in part, of the literary output of Central Africa. Much of this rich literary creativity and patrimony is unknown to the world at large, however, because of language barriers (for example, significant works have been published in Flemish, French, and Portuguese), and the limited availability of key sources. What follows is a guide to some of the formal types and organizing concepts of the oral literature of the Bantu-speaking peoples of Central Africa; specific references for further examination are offered, in the absence of major syntheses and comparative studies.

Bantu-speaking peoples constitute the principal population of the vast Central African region. Additionally, in northern Congo, the Central African Republic and southern Sudan, ethnic groups like the Zande, Nzakara, Gbaya, Ngbaka, and Ngbandi belong to non-Bantu linguistic stock, some of whose literature is well studied. The region is also sparsely populated by various Pygmy and archaic Pygmy-related or Pygmy-influenced groups. Their hunting and gathering activities, their mysterious forest experiences, and their folklore expressed in orally transmitted traditions and texts have left a lasting imprint on Bantu institutions and ideology in Central Africa. Very little is known about the literature of these Pygmy groups.

The widespread recurrence of certain genres and types of literature, of particular characters acting and interacting in specific situations, the contextual settings in which the orally transmitted texts operate, and their functions and meanings are all suggestive of fundamental formal, functional and semantic similarities within an extraordinary framework of individual, local, and ethnic creativity and diversity. Essential to the establishment of these fundamentals are ethnic classifications of oral literature and, concomitantly, their form of expression, their content and ideas, their basic purpose, function and sociopolitical, and ritual context. Unfortunately, few complete ethnic studies of oral texts exist in the scientific literature for comparison and classification. One such example however, for the Nyanga, a Bantu people of the eastern Congo rain forest, provides a useful point of reference for a general overview of different genres of literary expression.

The Different Forms of Orally Transmitted Texts

Several major categories of orally transmitted text are explicitly recognized by the Nyanga people. These different genres are respectively called *karisi, uano, mushumo, inondo, mubikiriro, ihamuriro, mushenjo,* and *rwimbo.* Other stylized forms of expression among the Nyanga are referred to as *nganuriro, mwanikiro, kishambaro,* and *ihano.*

The *karisi* category of texts includes long, sung and recited epic narratives that center on the feats of an anthropomorphic hero. The miraculously born Nyanga hero, called Mwindo, is similar in character and action to protagonists in poetically structured epic narratives among the Lega (Kiguma, Wabugila, Museme, Mubila, etc.), the Mongo of west-central Congo (Lianja), the Tetela and Mbole of east-central Congo (Lofokefoke), the Dwala (Djeki-la-Njambe) of southern Cameroon, the Fang and other populations in Gabon and Congo. Since the late twentieth century, these fascinating, complex texts were sung and recited on various secular occasions for a general audience although study suggests that, among some populations at earlier times, these texts were intimately linked with the Pygmies from Gabon and Congo and performed only on special politico-ritual occasions. The performance of epics can be viewed as multimedia events in which numerous other forms of artistic expression mingle with everyday gestures: it involves dancing, singing, chanting, costuming (among the Mongo, for example, the bard wears Lianja's paraphernalia and acts out his deeds), playing musical instruments, mimicry, screaming, praise giving, gift giving, and food and beverage distributions. In contrast to tales, epics are distinguished by the large number of actors (human, animal, supernatural, fictive creations) interacting in various situations with the central hero, the atmosphere of grandiose and exceptional events, the rhythmic flow of the narrative, the cataloguelike enumerations and the rich vocabulary. These epics are not just extremely important poetic creations characterized by the wealth of their oral expression, loftiness of tone, recurring stylistic devises (formulaic expressions, repetitions, onomatopoeia, prosodic rules), but also serve as extraordinarily revealing and authentic insider documents on the cultures of these diverse populations. Epics like Mwindo and Lianja shed light on material culture, technology, sociopolitical organization, religious belief and practice, cosmology and value systems of the Nyanga and Mongo peoples. Although centering on the fictive feats achieved by a heroic personage, the epics directly or indirectly contain historical references, making overt and cryptic statements about migrations, encounters with diverse peoples, feuds and warfare, and changing institutions and values.

In addition to the heroic epics, there also exist sophisticated accounts of large-scale clan and ethnic migrations (classified by the Bembe as *mse'eleco*), of encounters between populations, of the emergence of royal dynasties and the achievements of succeeding generations of chiefs, as they occur among the Kuba, Luba, Lunda and Cokwe. These texts can be identified as "historical epics," albeit embellished by fictional events and lacking the stylistic grandeur of the heroic recitations.

The individuals who perform these epics are not professional itinerant bards, nor do they hold any special status, clan or caste affiliation, as they do in other regions of Africa. They are simple farmers, hunters and/or craftsmen who learned the craft from a close kinsman (father, grandfather, maternal uncle, or in-law) or a friend with whom they had established a blood brotherhood pact. The reasons why they learned are not merely conditioned by personal preferences and aptitudes. Some, like the Mongo bards, maintain their calling was inspired in a dream. Nyanga bards also refer to some sickness that was caused by the spirit of Karisi. These bards are well known and admired in the areas where they live, and cared for lavishly when they perform. In some regions, such as the Lega, female bards are acceptable. In all cases, these bards are exceptionally gifted individuals.

Among the populations where the epics flourish in Central Africa, the bards are few; however, numerous persons who are avid listeners of the epics love to tell episodes, fragments and abstracts about the patterned lives of heroic figures. Among the Nyanga, for example, these heroic tales are much longer and less frequent than any other tale types, and they are similar to their epic counterparts in both style and content. In fact, these tales sometimes expand on heroic feats, situations, and events in which known heroes are involved. Do these heroic tales predate the epics per se? Were some epics developed by gifted narrators who assembled and synthesized a number of tales revolving around a particular heroic being? The questions remain open.

The second Nyanga oral category called *uano* includes innumerable folktales whose major characters are animals, anthropomorphized animals, and humans in diverse roles, abstract characters and/or divinities, specters, monsters, and ogres. Frequently, in these types of tales there occurs an extraordinary mix of human, animal and supernatural actors all performing in a distinctly human setting (the village, the hunting camp, the fields) and engaging in the most diverse human activities (gathering, hunting, fishing, cultivating, courtship, marriage, friendship pacts, judicial procedures, rituals, and cults). In many Bantu societies, cycles of tales revolve around particular animal characters like *nteta*, *kabuluku*, and *mboloko* (terms for dwarf antelopes) among the Nyanga, Luba and Tetela: *kabundi* (a mixture of squirrel and marten) of the western Luba or chameleon (*kou*), turtle (*nkulu*) and spider (*sangba ture*) among different populations. Some of the central characters in these epiclike tale cycles are trickster-heroes. The tales cover an incredible range of topics that are social, political, religious and/or philosophical in nature, but invariably have a strong bearing on the system of values, etiquette, savoir-faire, general behavior, social organization, kinship, and marriage. One frequent type of tale treats the situation of a father or mother willing to marry their daughter only to a person able to perform a prescribed, seemingly impossible, task. Invariably this task leads to the failure of many suitors and culminates in the ultimate success of a weak and supposedly insignificant actor. The folktales, commonly known to most male and female individuals in a given society, certainly function as elements of entertainment and communal interaction. They also provide deeper moral and philosophical lessons and often contain many etiological, didactic, and explanatory elements. Interesting examples are the dilemma tales found among the Mongo and other peoples. These tales expose a problem, develop it, and end on a question that generates a debate among members of the audience. The tales and ensuing deliberations often point to the ambiguities and paradoxes that govern social relations. Since folktales allow for improvisation and are told by many individuals having diverse backgrounds, personal experiences, and narrative skills, variations in style, content, length, and detail are the norm. Frequently, oral performance lends a special flavor to these tales, even to those that appear rather dull and uninspired in writing. Audience participation and the narrator's skill in mimicry, gestural emphasis, voice and sound imitation, intonation, and singing add a dimension that is lost in most publications.

The third Nyanga category of texts, *mushumo*, covers a large range of succinct aphoristic or sententious statements that are identified in Western literature as proverbs or maxims. This genre of universal occurrence is the least studied and the most difficult to interpret because of its inherent conciseness, the complexity of its symbolic references and its reflection of the deepest societal assumptions and values. In some areas, the structure of these proverbs closely follows a stylistic and prosodic pattern so that most of what are labeled as songs are simple proverbial statements or concatenations of these aphorisms. Recitation of proverbs occurs in many different situational contexts like teaching, general discussions and judicial procedures in the men's meeting-houses, and in prescribed or optional initiations, which are linked with life cycle or membership in voluntary associations. Some of the finest aphorisms, demanding specialized exegesis by preceptors and other experts and linked with high-level initiations, stand out from the bulk of proverbs not by their wording or overt meaning. Instead, these aphorisms evoke something of a higher intellectual order by covert references, statements and their multivocal interpretations. Thus, the aphorisms used in the *bwami* initiations of the Bembe and Lega, and the *bukota* and lilwa initiations of the Mitoko and Mbole, are known as *bitondo bya kisi*, literally "words of the land," expressing the deepest economic, social, political, religious, moral and philosophical values of a people. Because they concentrate a maximum of meaning in a minimum of words, proverbs are also powerful rhetorical devices used in solving difficult family issues and judicial cases.

Closely related to proverbs are two other types of concise formulations. Among the Nyanga, the principal examples are riddles (*inondo*). These stereotyped, frequently epigrammatic, expressions occur at dances, riddling sessions, and gatherings, usually of women and adolescents. Riddles focus on pleasure, communal interaction and entertainment, but they are also pedagogical tools teaching the youth about the world around them. The other form occurs in populations like the Lega, the Tetela and ethnic groups along the Congo River, where slit-drums and other musical instruments transmit messages to distant persons and villages. Intricate periphrastic expressions underlie this system of sonorous communication. Called *lukumbu* by the Lega, these stereotyped formulae, which may occur in concatenations, are proverblike statements that are concise and impossible to interpret out of context. Among the Lega, all men receive their own drum-name when reaching social adulthood. Since the number of such periphrastic expressions is limited, the drum-names of one's father, even one's grandfather, are frequently added. For women there exists only a single standard formula that is differentiated by the addition of the father's or husband's drum names. Animals (e.g., eagle, pangolin, elephant), activities (e.g., hunt) and other events of vital importance (e.g., death) are also the subject of periphrastic name giving.

Praise prose and poetry (the *musenjo* category among the Nyanga) are prevalent in societies having centralized political systems like the Shi and Hunde of eastern Congo. In Rwanda and Burundi, these elaborate, poetic, and repetitive praises entail much improvisation and address not just kings and chiefs but even highly prized cattle. The *kasàlà* of the western Luba are also a form of panegyrics often of clan groups. They feature lofty, sometimes even hyperbolic, imagery.

Divination, healing, oath-taking systems, cults, and blood-brotherhood pacts are widespread throughout Central Africa. These institutions are crucial to the activities of the society and feature specialized texts, sung and/or recited. The texts include standardized, sometimes rigidly formulated, invocations and prayers (the *mubikiriro* category among the Nyanga), exhortations, imprecations, incantations, and spells (*ihamuriro* among the Nyanga). These difficult, formulaic genres, well documented for the Kongo, Yaka, Songye, Mongo, are often ignored in discussions of African oral literature.

Many of the preceding texts are sung, if only in part. Nevertheless it is necessary to distinguish a category of songs per se (the *nyimbo* category among the Nyanga) that involve special, often heavily improvised, texts and are appropriately produced only on special occasions. First, these song texts relate to the celebration of events in the life cycle of individuals and families, like the births of children in general and those of twins in particular. Other examples comprise lullabies, matrimonial and mortuary songs, hypocoristic and love songs, dirges, elegies, and lamentations. The Nyanga and others sometimes talk about "day songs" and "night songs," referring to joyful performances of song at these times involving young people. These are songs of few words with largely improvised short texts that include personal reflections, remembrances, and succinct anecdotes.

The sung texts that accompany masked dances in areas like the Pende deserve special attention. There, a parade of masks engage in elaborate performances, which in their totality of text, music, gesture, dance, costume, and paraphernalia, constitute a pantomime or character drama involving fun, mockery, critique, praise, authority, awe, and "terror religiosus."

Among the Nyanga (who developed specialized terminology around these forms of speech), other forms of standardized discourse exist that probably could not be classified as literary, although the population concerned considers them distinct from ordinary verbal communication. An example is what the Nyanga call *nganuriro*, literally "true stories": men tend to sit together in the men's house to listen to accounts of what happened, what was seen, experienced, or achieved after hunting or trapping, or after a visit to a remote place. Recounting dreams also falls in this category. The style in which these events are narrated is generally concise, sometimes hyperbolic and unconstrained. The mood is facetious or melodramatic. Reality and fiction are intimately intermingled.

The Performance Context

The settings, the occasions, and the composition of the audience differ from case to case and from genre to genre. Familiar settings for oral performances of diverse type are the family home and compound, the men's meeting house, the smithy, the central village plaza or dance floor, or the hunting or fishing camp. More specialized settings are the men's or women's initiation houses, cult houses, the lodges where men and/or women of a certain status gather, the sites of enthronement of chiefs and other status holders, or the shacks or special enclosures where maskers dress or expert healers and diviners discharge their functions. The performances may be allowed any time of the day, others are strictly prescribed to be sung or narrated either during the day or in the evening and at night. Many texts are performed as part of the daily routine of living; others are reserved for special occasions and particular events. In these and many other situations the participant audience varies greatly, from the general public to privileged listeners-participants. The composition of the audience may be determined by gender, age-sets and age grades, cult affiliations, political and ritual statuses, and levels of initiatory experience. Concomitantly, the frequency with which texts are produced, the degree of exclusivity and secrecy of the oral performances, and the levels of meaning associated with the texts vary greatly.

In one way or another, the presentation of oral texts almost always involves a combination of actions that imply many constitutive elements and possible variations. Group participation is one of these elements. Texts are produced in a milieu of listeners who become active participants as apprentices, initiates, clients, patients, and even as part of the broader audience. The interaction between the narrator-singer and the persons present takes many forms, from encouragements formulated as simple ejectives, exclamations, and handclapping to praises, repetitions, questions, and comments on the narrated text. On numerous occasions one or more persons in the audience are intimately involved with the narrator-singer as apprentices. The apprenticeship may be formal, as is the case for the performances of epics, where one or more persons may sit closely to the bard and, depending on the degree of knowledge already acquired, may help him out when his memory fails or encourage him with stereotyped exclamations. The apprenticeship status may be less obvious when a young person—a narrator's favorite companion (a child or grandchild, a nephew)—simply acts as an attentive and responsive listener.

The Interrelation of the Arts

Music, as singing or handclapping, invariably accompanies oral performances. Epics, typically sung in their entirety, feature support from special musical instruments like harps, rattles, or percussive sticks; the music sustains the harmonious flow of the narrative and forms a continuum when the bard hesitates for words. Parts or entire tales may be sung, supported by choruslike responses from their audience; when mainly narrated or recited the tales can be interspersed with song to create dialogues of response from the listeners. Aphorisms sung by soloists and choruses during initiations are accompanied by drums, rattles, harps, zithers, and xylophones. The musicians do not merely sustain the rhythmic flow of the words and of the corresponding dances but also intersperse the performance with drum beats that contain praises for the excellence of individual dancers or singers. An especially intriguing case is found in certain ultra-secret rites where aphoristic and periphrastic texts are not spoken but suggested, reproduced as "songs without words" on mirlitons (rattles), slit-drums, horns, or whistles. As with the drum communications discussed above, this language of suggestiveness works particularly well because the tonal character of Bantu languages allows for the reproduction of units of sound that have semantic import.

The display of visual art, like sculpture or decorative design, is virtually inconceivable without its intensive association with texts of different types. These texts can either explain the essence of the exhibited patterns in symbolic ways or convey explanations on their use and function. This intimate link between text and object escapes us in most cases: texts have typically been recorded for their own sake, and art examined without sufficient knowledge of the languages in which the pertinent texts occur. Sadly, the art may simply have been collected without any knowledge of the relevant texts or texts may have been added ex posteriori, at best by guessing. Every *nkisi* power figurine among the Kongo or Songye peoples, for example, has its own set of praise and exhortative formulae, its own invocations, eulogies, incantations, and imprecations. Each Pende mask has its own songs; every pot lid among the Woyo is a sculptural condensation of one or more proverbs and/or riddles. Wooden or ivory anthropomorphic figurines among the Lega and Bembe people are intimately linked with aphorisms that imbue them with a range of meaning. The aphorisms explain the sculptures in context, but they also serve as sources of inspiration for the artists. Groups of masks among the Lega have their own sets of identifying and explanatory texts all key to their use and function. Decorative designs engraved, incised, or painted on art objects (masks, figurines, staffs, etc.), painted on the body, on panels, lintels or house walls, or drawn in the sand are not just associated with special terminologies. Here context is key. Explanations occur, particularly for initiations and cults, in specialized settings with elaborate standardized texts and aphoristic statements. Sophisticated examples of this are found in the decorative designs on Cokwe drums and in sand drawings among the same people, in body paintings among the Pende, Bembe and Tetela, and on houses among the Mangbetu.

Gesture, facial expression, rhythmic movement, and dance, as well as pitch and distortion of voice, are fundamental to the transmission of oral texts. Not only do they function in emphatic ways, providing texture and ton, they also convey meaning that is not transmitted by the words. The majority of texts collected have been transcribed without these features, leaving the reader with the unadorned framework of a performative act.

Preservation

There is no doubt that much remains to be learned from and about Central African oral literature. The great vanished cultures of the West and the East are best known through their visual arts and their literatures. Without their literatures little would be known about the philosophical, cosmological, ethical, and value systems of these cultures, let alone their history or social life. In anthropology as well as in folklore and comparative literature, only limited attention has been given to collecting, translating, annotating, and interpreting the orally transmitted texts of Central Africa. Scholars in various disciplines and of many nationalities, including a considerable number of Africans, have involved themselves with this type of study, but funds, programs, and broad academic and public interest are still lacking. An enormous field of knowledge remains stored in the minds of Central African singers and narrators. There are enough older and younger bards, narrators and singers left in Central Africa, who have a perfect knowledge of the most diverse textual genres to warrant accelerated efforts to collect the oral masterpieces. African scholars, who have deep knowledge of their mother tongues, should play a major role in this endeavor, the results of which would further testify to the amplitude and depth of African thought. The need is not merely for linguistically and anthropologically justified scholarly text, but also for readable, well-annotated translations that address themselves to the wider public, so as to increase knowledge and appreciation of the literary output of Central Africa. Special efforts should be made to connect texts and visual arts through field research, so as to transcend the guesswork that often obfuscates the interpretation of the African visual arts.

References

Biebuyck, Daniel P., and Kahombo Mateene. 1969. *The Mwindo Epic from the Banyanga*. Berkeley and Los Angeles: University of California Press.

———. 1970. *Anthologie de la littérature orale Nyanga*. Brussels: Académie Royale des Sciences d'Outre-Mer.

Boelaert, E. 1957, 1958. *Lianja Verhalen, I: Ekofo-Versie, II: De Voorouders van Lianja*. Tervuren: Musée Royal de l'Afrique Centrale.

de Dampierre, Eric. 1963. *Poètes nzakara*. Paris: Classiques Africains 1.

de Rop, A. *De gesproken woordkunst van de Nkundo*. 1956. Tervuren: Musée Royal de l'Afrique Centrale.

Evans-Pritchard, E. E. 1967. *The Zande Trickster*. Oxford: The Clarendon Press.

Jacobs, John. 1959. *Tetela-Teksten*. Tervuren: Musée Royal de l'Afrique Centrale.

Manga Bekombo Priso. 1994. *Défis et Prodiges. La fantastique histoire de Djèki-la-Njambé*. Paris: Classiques Africains 25.

Mufuta, Patrice. 1968. *Le chant Kasàlà des Luba*. Paris: Classiques Africains.

———. 1992. *N'Sanda Wamenka. Récits épiques des Lega du Zaire*, 2 vols. Tervuren: Musée Royal de l'Afrique Centrale.

Pepper, H., and P. De Wolf. 1972. *Un mvet de Zwè Nguéma*. Paris: Classiques Africains 9.

Thomas, J. M. C. (in collaboration with Arom, S., and Mavode, M.). 1970. *Contes, proverbes, devinettes ou énigmes, chants et prières ngbaka ma'bo*, (Lacito 6). Paris: Klincksieck.

Van Caeneghem, R. 1938. *Kabundi Sprookjes*. Brussels: Vromant.

Van Wing J., and Cl. Schöller. 1940. *Légendes des Bakongo Orientaux*. Louvain: Aucan.

DANIEL P. BIEBUYCK

See also **Gesture in African Oral Narrative; Griots and Griottes; Oral Traditions and Oral Historiography; Oral Literature: Issues of Definition and Terminology; Oral Narrative; Oral Traditions; Southern Africa: Contemporary Forms of Folklore; FolkTales**

CENTRAL AFRICAN REPUBLIC (C.A.R.)

The Central African Republic is a thinly populated country of 3.6 million located in the center of Africa, bordering Chad, Sudan, Democratic Republic of Congo, Congo, and Cameroon. Most of the country is a broken plateau interspersed with deep river valleys. The southwestern area of the country has rain forests, while a desert region is found in the extreme northeast. Bangui, a coastal river port, is the capital and largest city. The Central African Republic is composed of four major ethnic groups: the Banda, Baya (a pygmy group), Mandja, and Sara. French is used as the principal language in business and government, but Sango is the national language used by the various ethnic groups; there is some Arabic spoken as well. Half of the population is equally divided between Protestants and Roman Catholics, 24 percent practice traditional indigenous religions, 15 percent are Muslim while 11 percent are unclassified.

The Central African Republic was formally a territory in French Equatorial Africa called Ubangi-Shari. It gained its independence from France in 1960. Its name in French, the official language, is Republique Centrafricaine. Unfortunately, the Central African Republic became known throughout the world for its infamous president, later self-proclaimed emperor, Jean Bedel Bokassa, an army sergeant who led the 1966 coup. His brutal rule and eccentric excesses cost many lives and wasted much of the country's wealth. Although he was overthrown in 1979, the country is still struggling for stability. The government is now a republic under the military rule, led by the Head of State and President Ange-Felix Patasse.

Principle exports are agricultural products (coffee, cotton, and peanuts). Timber, textiles, and diamond mining are its largest industries and sources of revenue. Despite many episodes of drought and poor infrastructure, and despite its land-locked situation, the Central African Republic has been able to adequately meet most of the nation's basic food needs, as well as remain relatively prosperous in comparison to neighboring countries because of its relatively successful diamond and timber industries. Nevertheless, it has one of the world's lowest life expectancies at 45 years.

JENNIFER JOYCE

CERAMICS

There is little doubt that ceramics are among the earliest and most ubiquitous forms of material culture produced in Africa. Fired clay objects from Africa take both nonfigurative and figurative forms. The term *terra-cotta* is frequently used to distinguish figurative sculpture from functional vessels, or to distinguish art from craft. This distinction corresponds to the predominance of men as sculptors and women as potters; however, across the continent, there are men who produce utilitarian wares and women who produce figurative ceramics.

Objects made of fired clay found in the Sahara Desert have been dated from 8000 BCE, suggesting the indigenous invention of ceramics in Africa. The essential permanence of ceramics (also called pottery or earthenware) means that evidence of its early production survives in the archaeological record, providing a means for reconstructing historical sequences that predate European contact. The versatility of the medium of clay has long been acknowledged, as have its sculptural possibilities. Yet clay's essential malleability contrasts dramatically with the fundamental conservatism recognized as a feature of most utilitarian vessel styles. Indeed, many archaeologists use pottery styles for reading culture history precisely because of the assumption that a specific combination of clay body, technique, form, and decoration characterizes the ceramics of any one ethnic group. When changes occur in a pottery style, they are usually (but not always) attributed to changes in social, historical, or cultural circumstances. The archaeological and ethnographic records prove this premise to be generally true; however, the variables governing continuity or change in ceramic forms and functions are contextually specific and need to be investigated against such particularities.

Utilitarian Pottery

Although economic circumstances tend to govern the quantity, type, and decoration of vessels a group produces, function is a key determinant of size, shape, and ornamentation. The majority of nonfigurative ceramics in Africa serve the domestic purposes of settled agriculturalists. They are used for storing, transporting, cooking, and eating a range of foodstuffs and liquids. As many as forty named vessel types, each with a specific form and function, may be produced by a single ethnic group. Pots hold water, beer, palm wine, grains, oils, butter, cosmetics, medicines, ink, or dye solutions. Pots with perforations are sieves or drying chambers for meat or fish; bowls with heavily incised interiors are grinders; and shallow bowls raised on stands are serving dishes or oil lamps. Pots for storing and cooling water often are large with little or no necks for easy access and for maximum surface area for evaporation; vessels for transporting water often have an elongated neck and/or an everted rim to minimize spillage; and pots that are small and round will distribute heat more effectively when on a cooking fire.

The low-fire unglazed pottery typical of Africa is particularly suited to the uses described above—its porosity allows for natural evaporation of liquids through the vessel walls and the open texture of the clay and low-firing temperature (rarely above 650 degrees Centigrade and often much lower) are highly resistant to thermal shock associated with open flame cooking.

Other utilitarian objects found within African households are also produced of fired clay. Ceramic finials secure the thatching of roofs and prevent rain from entering at the top. Ceramic pipe bowls are produced across Africa, usually by men. Pipes dating to the seventeenth century have been found in Ghana and nineteenth to twentieth century ceremonial pipes are common to the Cameroon Grasslands. The resonating chambers of drums, tuyeres for iron-smelting furnaces, weights for fishing nets, spindle whorls, lamps for burning oil, burners for incense, and certain types of furniture, including stools and bed stands, are also made of fired clay.

African utilitarian ceramics are distinguished by a striking range of decoration. Before firing, the surface may be modified by various types of impressed ornamentation, achieved by rouletting, grooving, incising, and comb stamping. Surfaces also may be modified before firing by burnishing or applying pigments, and during the firing, by blackening the entire vessel in a reduction atmosphere or by achieving a mottled effect with the application of a vegetal solution while the vessel is still hot. Like vessel size and profile, decoration is controlled in part by function. Cooking pots tend to have the least ornamentation because the soot of a cooking fire quickly turns them black. By contrast, water-carrying pots are the most highly decorated because they are the most often seen, frequently becoming extensions of a woman's program of self-decoration. Such vessels leave the private, often restricted domain of a woman's kitchen and enter the more public, social domain of the compound, village or beyond. Additionally, among certain peoples (e.g., the Bole of northern Nigeria and the Gbaya of the Central African Republic), highly ornamented pots are stacked around the interior perimeter of a woman's sleeping room where they may reflect her, or her household's, economic and social standing.

Pottery Used in Rituals

A range of decorated ceramic containers appears in ritual or sacred contexts, used for making offerings, for marking points of contact with the supernatural, or for containing spirits themselves. Such pots often have a design vocabulary distinctive from that of a group's domestic wares. Common across Africa, for example, is the application of small clay pellets to a pot's surface to distinguish it as a spirit vessel. More elaborate are vessels with applied figurative elements (either in low or high relief), such as pots used by the Bini of southwestern Nigeria in shrines dedicated to Olokun, the god of the seas and rivers; Igbo vessels made for the cult of the yam spirit, Ifijioku; and Yoruba bowls used in cults dedicated to the thunder god, Shango. Among the Akan-speaking peoples of Ghana, ritual grave vessels are covered in relief images of human beings or heads, snakes, lizards, frogs, and crocodiles, often referring to Akan proverbs.

Figurative Ceramics

The most sculpturally complex ceramic vessels are those where a human head surmounts the neck of the vessel. These largely date to the last two millennia, and certain examples have been found in archaeological contexts. Pots made in this style in the twentieth century have been produced by various groups living in West and Central Africa, such as the Akye of the southern Ivory Coast, the Yoruba of southwestern Nigeria, the Yungur, Tula, Longuda, Cham/Mwona, and Jen of northeastern Nigeria, the Mangbetu, Azande and related groups of northeastern Zaire, the Lunda, Lwena and Chokwe of Zaire, Angola, and Zambia, and the Woyo of the Cabinda-Zaire borderlands. The style of modeling the heads and bodies of these figurative vessels varies considerably from group to group, often reflecting actual modes of permanent and ephemeral self-decoration. Yungur women artists of northeastern Nigeria exploit the creative possibilities of the clay, producing highly expressionistic portrait pots whose faces carry the details of scarification and tooth-chipping distinctive to the Yungur.

Abatan is among the best-known female Yoruba potters (b. ?1885); she produced lids in the form of a half-figure of a woman used in the veneration of the river deity, Erinle. As with the Yungur vessels, these lids were modeled according to Yoruba concepts of female beauty. Among the most famous examples of cephalomorphic vessels are those made from the end of the nineteenth century to the early 1930s by Mangbetu men as prestige objects for local Mangbetu chiefs and for Europeans. With their elongated foreheads and elaborate halo-shaped coiffures, the heads on these vessels are idealized representations of Mangbetu women.

A number of examples of figurative ceramic sculpture come from archaeological sites in Nigeria. Those with the earliest dates are associated with the Nok culture of northern Nigeria (500 BCE–200 CE). They include nearly life-size hollow-built heads, many once attached to full figures up to 1.2 meters high, and small solid figurines. How they were used remains unknown. Nevertheless, their level of technical accomplishment and formal variation is all the more remarkable given their early dates. Other somewhat later figurative ceramic traditions, dating after the twelfth century, are associated with the towns of Ife, Benin, and Owo. All these examples, though distinctively stylized, represent relatively naturalistic heads largely associated with royalty. The celebrated Ife examples have faces bearing all-over delicate vertical lines and elaborately sculpted coiffures/crests, whose iconographic meanings are unclear.

Recovered from mound sites south of Lake Chad are figurative ceramics associated with an ancient, largely mythical people called the Sao. Produced between the eleventh and thirteenth centuries, the Sao corpus includes small solid heads, human figurines, and zoomorphic figurines mostly used as grave goods. Other sculptural figurines have been found in a series of mound sites around the modern town of Jenne in the Middle Niger region of Mali. Their strikingly complex postures and iconographical details have raised as yet unanswered questions about who produced them and how they were used. The flourescence of terra-cotta production in this area has been dated from 1000 to 1200 CE.

The figurative ceramics found in northern Ghana and attributed to the Koma provide evidence of trade links between this region and towns in the Middle Niger, like Jenne. Koma ceramics include human heads, full figures and animals, recovered mostly in burial contexts. The Akan peoples of southern Ghana, most of whom likewise produced commemorative ceramic heads set up, in groups, on grave sites, also were involved in the trans-Saharan trade network. Although there are certain stylistic consistencies in the sculpting of their faces, these ceramic portraits of state chiefs carry features distinctive to their derivations in specific Akan city-states (e.g., Adanse-Fomena, Twifo-Heman, Fante, Kwahu, Anyi, and Aowin). Evidence of this funerary tradition dates to the seventeenth century, and among certain Akan groups women still make these ceramic portraits.

Ceramics in Mortuary Contexts

It is notable that like these Akan, Koma, Sao, and Jenne examples, many African figurative and nonfigurative ceramics were, and continue to be, used in mortuary or funeral contexts. Large clay pots are used as burial urns and have been found archaeologically in Mali, Niger, Chad, Cameroon, and elsewhere. Across northern Nigeria and northern Cameroon figurative ceramic finials identify the houses of important men, and then, when they die, are moved to their graves. Dakakari women of northern Nigeria make tomb sculptures with complex anthropomorphic and zoomorphic tableaux. In Zaire, the Kongo ba Boma erect cylindrical ceramic burial monuments made by men, often with an upper platform surmounted by figures representing the deceased. The relationship between ceramics and burials may have to do with the relative permanence of clay and its ability to withstand the ravages of time, particularly within the African environment. The symbolic connection between the transformative process of firing clay and the passage from living to ancestral status may also make ceramic objects appropriate to pre- and postburial ritual contexts.

Despite the flood of modern replacement containers entering the African marketplace by the late twentieth century, the production of ceramics persists, often quite vigorously. The practicality of pottery containers has not yet been fully superseded by mass-produced equivalents. Women and some men continue to work in clay, producing not only utilitarian, but also figurative vessels and sculpture still used in ritual or sacred contexts, despite the fact that social, economic, political, and religious changes have rendered many such objects obsolete.

References

Barley, Nigel. 1994. *Smashing Pots: Feats of Clay from Africa*. London: British Museum Press.

Berns, Marla C. 1989. Ceramic Arts in Africa. *African Arts*. 22, no. 2:32–36; 101–102.

Drost, Dietrich. 1968. Topferei in Afrika: Okonomie und Soziologie. *Jahrbuch des Museums fur Volkerkunde zu Leipzig* 24: 131–270.

Fagg, William and John Picton. 1970. *The Potter's Art in Africa*. London: British Museum Press.

Roy, Christopher D. 2000. *Clay and Fire: Pottery in Africa*. Iowa Studies in African Art: The Stanley Conferences at The University of Iowa, volume IV. Iowa City: School of Art and Art History, The University of Iowa.

Stossel, Arnulf. 1984. *Afrikanische Keramik: traditionelle Handwekskunst sudlich der Sahara*. Munich: Hirmer Verlag.

MARLA C. BERNS

See also **Cosmology; Gender Representation in African Folklore**

CERAMICS AND GENDER

Ceramic arts are generally recognized throughout West Africa as a woman's art form. Women potters produce a wide range of containers, cooking pots, braziers, and incense burners for domestic use. In some regions, they provide architectural ceramics such as rainspouts and roof finials. Women also produce vessels for ritual contexts, such as burial jars and offering plates. They also make pots in which herbal remedies and other sacred materials are prepared, stored, and protected. Women were probably responsible for most of the ceramic wares that have come from archaeological contexts throughout west Africa, and they may have had a role in creating the terra-cotta figurative sculpture often presumed to be the work of male artists (see Berns).

Female potters across the Sudanic region of West Africa are often wives and mothers of blacksmiths, from the Mande heartland to the mountains of Cameroon. Blacksmiths and potters maintain near monopolies on the artistic domains of pottery production and iron working, in part by keeping knowledge of these specialized technologies within their families through endogamous marriage practices. Thus, among the various Mande peoples (e.g., Bamana, Maninka, and Soninke), certain family names, such as Kante, Fane, and Sumaworo, are recognizable as blacksmith-potter patronyms, even when not all members of the family practice the trades that are their birthright. Similarly, most Senufo potters are the wives of metalworkers, either blacksmiths or brass casters, even though many of the men have given up the trade and have turned to the more profitable craft of weaving.

Potters from metalsmithing families are respected for wielding spiritual powers beyond those of ordinary women. They often serve their communities as midwives, healers, and diviners. Among the Bamana and Maninka, certain blacksmith families have the right to perform the circumcision and excision that are believed to be essential to a child becoming an adult.

A potter from such a family with the strength of character and the courage may apprentice herself to an elder for many years before becoming a "master-of-the-knife." Potters also share with their blacksmith husbands specialized knowledge of medicinal plants and herbal remedies. They may be called upon to create protective amulets and to divine the future.

It is not surprising that these two crafts would be interrelated in both practical and ideological ways. For both trades, the busiest time of year is the end of the dry season, a time when those who rely on farming for livelihood are spending long days preparing the fields. Equally important, they share parallel technologies of using fire to transform materials from the earth (iron ore and clay) into useful cultural objects. The materials with which they work are often considered to be spiritually charged and therefore dangerous to those without the sacred knowledge essential for protection. Members of the larger society often harbor ambivalent feelings of fear, respect, and disdain toward the social category of blacksmiths and potters. However, individuals still are valued for their creative abilities and for the critical roles they play in society.

Exceptions to the blacksmith-potter paradigm are significant because they signal the presence of traditions of different origins or at least different histories. Dyula potters of the Kadiolo region of southern Mali are the wives of griots who have left behind the practice of praise singing and now earn a modest income farming, trading, and occasionally, leatherworking. Among Fula populations of the Inland Niger Delta and Fouta Djallon regions, potters are more often the wives of griots, weavers, or leatherworkers than of blacksmiths or jewelers. Elsewhere in West Africa, pottery production is not associated with any particular endogamous occupational craft group. Potters throughout the coastal regions are often the wives of farmers or traders and there is greater freedom for a woman to choose to become a potter.

Although women dominate pottery production in West Africa, exceptions exist among the Dogon of Mali, the Mossi of Burkina Faso, and among the Fula (Peul) and Maninka (Malinké) populations of the Fouta Djallon region, where both men and women work with clay. Among the Hausa of northern Nigeria, pottery production is dominated by male craftsmen. Among the Moba of northern Togo, male and female potters are distinguished by the use of different technologies and by the gender-specific categories of activities for which their products will be used. Thus Moba male potters corner the market on beer pots, while female potters produce a greater variety and quantity of vessels essential to the domestic tasks of women. Similarly, in western Cameroon, men carve clay pipes and make special prestige vessels. In each of these settings where men work with clay, pottery production is not their exclusive domain, nor do male potters provide the full range of pots for the needs of society. Their roles as ceramic artists seem to be more specialized than those of their female counterparts.

References

Barley, N. 1994. *Smashing Pots. Works of Clay from Africa*. London: British Museum Press.

Berns, M. 1993. Art, History, and Gender: Women and Clay in West Africa. *African Archaeological Review* 11:133–53.

Frank, B. 1998. *Mande Potters and Leatherworkers. Art and Heritage in West Africa*. Washington, D.C.: Smithsonian Institution Press.

Herbert, E. 1993. *Iron, Gender, and Power. Rituals of Transformation in African Societies.* Bloomington: Indiana University Press.

Kreamer, C. M. 2000. Money, Power and Gender: Some Social and Economic Factors in Moba Male and Female Pottery Traditions (Northern Togo). In *Clay and Fire: Pottery in Africa.* Iowa Studies in African Art: The Stanley Conferences at the University of Iowa, IV. Iowa City: School of Art and Art History, The University of Iowa.

LaViolette, A. 1995. Women Craft Specialists in Jenne: The Manipulation of Mande Social Categories. In *Status and Identity in West Africa: Nyamakalaw of Mali*, eds. D. C. Conrad and B. E. Frank. Bloomington: Indiana University Press.

Picton, J. ed. 1984. *Earthenware in Asia and Africa.* Colloquies on Art and Archaeology in Asia, no. 12. London: University of London Percival David Foundation of Chinese Art.

Roy, C. D. 1987. *Art of the Upper Volta Rivers.* Meudon, France: Chaffin.

———, ed. 2000. *Clay and Fire: Pottery in Africa.* Iowa Studies in African Art: The Stanley Conferences at the University of Iowa, IV. Iowa City: School of Art and Art History, The University of Iowa.

Spindel, C. 1989. Kpeenbele Senufo Potters. *African Arts* 22, no. 2: 66–73, 103.

Sterner, J., and N. David. 1991. Gender and Caste in the Mandara Highlands: Northeastern Nigeria and Northern Cameroon. *Ethnology* 30, no. 4:355–69.

BARBARA FRANK

See also **Blacksmiths: Mande Western Africa; Gender Representation in African Folklore; Women's Expressive Culture in Africa**

CHAD (REPUBLIQUE DU TCHAD)

Chad is an arid to semiarid country of nearly 7,270,000 located in the heart of northern central Africa. Its neighboring countries are Sudan, Libya, Niger, Nigeria, Cameroon, and Central African Republic. N'Djamena, with a population of 531,000, is the capital and the largest city in the nation. The ethnic makeup of Chad consists of two hundred distinct groups, 78 percent of whom live in rural areas. Over a hundred different languages are spoken in Chad, but the major languages are French (the official language), Arabic, Fulde, Hausa, Kotoko, Kanembou, and Sara Maba. Half of the population is Muslim, one-quarter is Christian, and one-quarter practices traditional indigenous religions.

Since the ninth century CE, Chad has prospered under the usually united ruler-states of Kanem and Bornu. The sultans of these states established successful trading empires which created trade and commerce between North Africa's Mediterranean coast and the Central African interior. Chad has been controlled by the French since 1900 as part of French Equatorial Africa and became independent in 1960. There has been sporadic civil war since 1965, an ongoing conflict in which the French have periodically intervened and even Libya became involved in 1983.

The natural resources in the region are petroleum, salt, uranium, and kaolin, while the agricultural resources include cotton, cattle, fish, and sugar. The nation's strongest industries are livestock products, beer, and textiles. Unfortunately, due to the country's geography, the exportation of such products has been difficult and unprofitable because Chad has no direct access to the sea. The great lake of the same name is shrinking.

Throughout the years Chad has suffered turmoil among its various ethnicities and religions. The country's three main geographical regions of the northern Sahara, middle Sahel region, and southern savanna have played a role in dividing the peoples of these disparate regions, who speak different languages and have different lifestyles and economies.

JENNIFER JOYCE

CHECKERS

See **Draughts**

CHIEF

Chief refers to a person of eminence or high office, a community leader or overlord. In Africa, the British used *chief* (the French *chef*) as a common term of reference for a variety of traditional leaders. This was done to facilitate the study, codification, and promulgation of customary laws, rules, and regulations to support the framework of, and in some cases, create and impose (Mamdani 1996, 41) "native authorities" as an instrument of power in colonial territories. Though in some African societies (e.g., Asante, Dahomey, Botswana, and Buganda) women held positions of power parallel or even superior to male titleholders, women were addressed not as chiefs but as queen-mothers or princesses (Bryden 1998; Manuh 1988; Herskovits 1967; Rattray 1923).

In the most sophisticated and hierarchical traditional systems, the holder of the chiefly position received recognition as king or queen, and their unique traditional titles were respected, for example, The Alafin of Oyo, the Kabaka of Buganda, the Shilluk Reth, the Asantehene, and so forth. Some historical documents, referred to traditional rulers or leaders as cabooseers before chief came into vogue.

Traditionally, African kings and chiefs invariably combined secular and ritual powers. Some had more mystical than secular functions, making the ruler a priest-king or a divine-king. In Asante, however, the priest-king was taboo (*Ohene komfo, yekyiri*), thus clearly defining the chief as a secular functionary, a rational politico-jural ruler.

In many societies long led by religious and divining leaders, contact with European traders in the nineteenth century began a process of secularization. In some cultures the accumulation by religious leaders of secular functions led eventually to the loss of their sacred functions. In others, the process led to a separation of religious and secular functions and the emergence of secular rulers—chiefs—side by side with ritual leaders (as among the Ga people of Ghana).

In the past, chiefs played many roles. They were judges and maintained the rule of law. They served as military leaders and led in wars. They were custodians of communal ideals and enacted rites and customs that sustained the moral and cultural values of society. For the survival of the community, they organized food production and ensured food security. In many cultures, the traditional worldview postulated a bond between a ruler and the health of the environment, which made the ruler directly responsible for the observance of regulations about exploitation of nature and the resources of the land. Having lost their military functions under colonialism, chiefs still retain many of these functions especially in rural communities.

In some cultures (e.g., the Igbo), chief is a mere honorific title that one takes as a mark of personal achievement and outstanding generosity. The title must be "constantly validated to be retained" (Uchendu 1965, 20), and no family has exclusive claim to any title. In many cultures, appointive and hereditary titles exist side by side. Slaves and commoners acquire the title through service appointments. Hereditary chiefs are selected from royal lineages and ceremonially installed. Succession disputes and conflicts, frequent in chiefly polities, were and are still the indication of the value a people place on the institution. Yet succession conflicts represent the single most serious threat to the survival of chieftaincy.

In several cultures, social anthropologists designated as chiefs the ritual officials prominent in the settlement of disputes or the sustenance of community well-being. For example, the Leopard Skin Chief among the Nuer of the southern Sudan has only ritual power (Evans-Pritchard 1940). However, he plays a key role in the settlement of blood feuds, an obviously political function.

Whether ritual, symbolic, or secular, chiefly status evokes and goes with special praise names, honorific titles and, more importantly, physical symbols, costumes, and other signals of distinction. Most prominent among such symbols are Drums, Spears, Masks, Shields, Stools, Skins, Maces, Robes, and Headgears. Standing for mystical power, or the spirit of the community, most of these symbols are the focus of special ancestral rituals that people believe sustain the life of the corporate group. These sacred symbols are often at the center of succession conflicts in Africa.

In many of the former French colonies, chiefs have virtually disappeared. In the former British colonies, chiefs, having played a very prominent part in the system of indirect rule, became the victims of the rising tide of African nationalism and the struggle for independence. The institution, however, has recovered its prestige. Chiefs have become at once both the symbol of the dignity and identity of African cultures and, as natural leaders, kingpins of national stability and progress. As Africans struggle to establish the basis of democratic governance in their own traditional modes of governance, some states (e.g., Swaziland and Ghana) are giving a pivotal role to their traditional rulers. In multiethnic states, this gives prospects for the establishment of new chiefly councils. Beyond the Regional and National Houses of chiefs the there is envisioned, for example, a West African subcontinental House of Chiefs. The rise of such cross-cultural councils of chiefs is largely attributable to not only the large numbers of highly educated persons holding traditional titled positions in ethnic communities, but also of the perception of common values that support communitarian life and the culture of leadership in Africa.

Yet education, a major factor of change in Africa, is constantly eroding the social basis and communal support for chieftaincy. Educated subjects no longer offer assured labor, financial support, and services in token of traditional allegiance to their communities and chiefs. Conversely, on account of their education, professional occupations, and conversion to non-African religions, many chiefs are not able to perform the traditional rites, and judicial and social services traditionally due to their subjects.

The title chief now generally goes to people of wealth and political influence and seems destined to lose its mystic aura.

References

Arhin, Kwame. 1985. *Traditional Rules in Ghana: Past and Present.* Accra: Sedco Publications.
Beattie, John. 1998. *Bunyoro: An African Kingdom.* New York: Holt, Rinehard and Winston.
Bryden, Lynne. 1998. Women Chiefs and Power in the Volta Region of Ghana. *Journal of Legal Pluralism and Unofficial Law.* 37/38: 227–48.
Busia, K. A. 1951. *The Position of the Chief in Modern Asante.* Oxford: Clarendon Press.
Evans-Pritchard, E. E. 1940. *The Nuer.* Oxford: Clarendon Press.
Herskovits, M. J. 1967. *Dahomey: An Ancient West African Kingdom.* Evanston: Northwest University Press.
Mamdani, M. 1996. *Citizen and Subject.* Princeton: Princeton University Press.
Manuh, T. 1988. The Asantehemaa's Court and its Jurisdiction over Women: A Study in Legal Pluralism. *Research Review* 4, no. 2: 50–66.
Rattray, R.S. 1963. *Ashanti.* Oxford: Clarendon Press.
Uchendu, V.C. 1965. *The Igbo of Southern Nigeria.* New York, Holt, Rinehart, and Winston.

GEORGE P. HAGAN

See also **Okyeame; Queen Mothers**

CHILDREN'S FOLKLORE: ITESO SONGS OF WAR TIME

In the mid-1990s, the people of Teso, northeastern Uganda, emerged from a protracted civil conflict, in which they were very much the losers. Between 1986 and 1992, the Itseo people had supported and participated in a rebel movement against the government forces of Uganda. Government forces quelled this rebellion through a strategy of moving the Iteso people off their land and into heavily guarded settlement camps. This allowed them to create a free-fire zone, in which anyone outside the camps was assumed to be hostile to the government and was captured or killed. Being in the camps, however, also placed the Iteso at the mercy of the cattle raids of the neighboring Karamojong people. Raiding by Karamojong, involving groups of armed men sweeping in and taking livestock, has a long history in Teso. But with the majority of Iteso in camps and unable to enact traditional defenses such as moving or selling their cattle, the raiding reached devastating proportions.

By 1992, with the rebellion defeated by government forces, the Itseo were once again free to move out of the camps and return to their villages. Yet the economy and culture of the region, which had previously relied so heavily upon cattle resources, was all but destroyed. The loss of cattle in Karamojong raiding meant that households could not restore traditional agricultural practices using ox-ploughs and were rendered extremely vulnerable economically. The loss of cattle also meant that traditional marriage practices involving bridewealth exchange could not be fulfilled. But perhaps most important about the loss of cattle was the damage done to the Iteso's sense of self-identity, which is built upon a love of, and pride in, cattle.

In the intervening years since the end of the conflict, the Iteso have faced the triple challenge of economic, social, and emotional recovery. Despite the constraints and additional threats such as drought, the impact of HIV/AIDS, and continuing Karamojong raiding, it is a challenge they have met with a high degree of cultural resilience and innovation.

The Karamojong Outmaneuvered

One outcome of this recovery process has been a proliferation of Iteso folklore regarding the relationship between Karamojong and Iteso. Children in particular are highly praised if they can narrate stories concerning the relationship between the two peoples. The first set of stories that children are encouraged to narrate are those that dwell on the early history of the Iteso people. Iteso folklore has it that the Teso are related to the Karamojong but emerged as a separate group of people when the cleverest individuals from the Karamojong decided to move on, break away, and set up a new kind of society based on principles of development and progress (Webster et al. 1973, 29). Children are encouraged to learn and recite this history.

However, the stories of children and young people that earn particular commendation around the nighttime fire are those stories whose subject is an event in the recent conflict in which Iteso managed to defeat and outwit Karamojong raiders. Despite the overall losses sustained by the Itseo from the Karamojong, it is acknowledged that there were times when the Iteso managed to maintain the upper hand and to prevent a certain herd of cattle being stolen, or to escape a certain death. These stories are much enjoyed and take on a very stylized form. The Iteso character is always in danger of losing cattle in a raid and even losing his or her own life until by some act of cunning and cleverness they manage to outmaneuver the Karamojong. So, for example, in tales of the Iteso being caught in a home by approaching raiders, the Itseo person quickly dons a sheep or cattle hide, managing to escape with the herd. A plethora of other tales involve Iteso who hide in the rafters when Karamojong raiders enter their home. The Iteso characters jump down behind the entering Karamojong, lock the door and run away. When another group of Karamogong reach the home, they shoot through the door thus killing all the Karamojong inside. At the end of all these stories the children and young people conclude by saying, "The Karamojong left with their tails behind them."

Obviously, these are tales of Iteso resistance, the stories are told to affirm that although the Iteso lost almost everything to the Karamojong they did not lose the ability to trick and outwit the Karamojong when they could and defend themselves as much as possible. But more than this, these tales follow long established patterns of storytelling in Iteso culture. Lawrence notes that telling fables or stories (*awaragasia*), is an ancient Teso practice (1957, 179). As in other East African societies, such narratives are suffused with moral imagination and act as a forum for resolving, articulating, and assessing the ambiguities of social life (Beidelman 1993). In Teso the particular moral principle stressed in such narratives is that of "knowledge," "outwitting," and "cleverness" (*acoa*). There are many tales in Teso that exemplify the value of this sort of knowledge (Akello 1995, 4).

Grace Akello (1981) has studied the thought patterns in Iteso *awaragasia*. There is a wide range of tales with animal characters. She notes (1981, 129) that the Hare figure, Opooi, is often the hero of *awaragasia*. The Hare is valued for characteristics of *acoa*, of cunning and trickery, of wit and intelligence. She states that the trickery of Hare is not despised by Iteso audiences but condoned even though it might involve cruelty. In the tales, the Hare often outwits the Leopard, Erisa, who is portrayed as stealthy and cruel, over confident, vengeful and unpredictable, and the Lion, Engatuny, who is seen as cruel, merciless, ferocious, a senseless killer, and without intelligence.

The modern-day Iteso tales of Iteso versus Karamojong exactly follow this logic. In them the Iteso display cunning and cleverness as compared to the ruthless stupidity of the Karamojong. The Iteso are the tricky heroes and the Karamojong, the cruel adversaries. It is no coincidence that the Karamojong are said to have their "tails behind them." The word for tail here is *ekori*, indicating the tail of a wild animal, rather than the word used for the stunted tail of sheep, goats, and hares, *aikunet*. An explicit parallel is being made between Karamojong and the fierce Leopard and Lion of *awaragasia*, who were so often outwitted by the Hare. These tales confirm an important Iteso principle of self-identity, that which is manifest in the creation stories of the Iteso where the Iteso separated from the Karamojong because they were more intelligent and progressive.

Folklore as Healing Therapy

The proliferation of Iteso folklore concerning relations between them and the Karamojong is part of a process of postwar reconstruction. In this process therapeutic emotional healing and the restoring of a sense of self is as important as renewed economic viability. The stories are just one example of a process of emotional healing; there are many more. The tales retell the conflict to stress that, despite the circumstances, Itseo people were able to act with *acoa* in the conflict, which led to their survival and development as a people. The tales affirm Iteso principles of cleverness and ability through which the Iteso emerge victorious. They are tales that reverse the actual history of weakness and powerlessness that the Iteso felt at the hands of the Karmojong. They are stories in which the listeners, victims themselves, remember in stylized ways that make them feel good and not humiliated.

This phenomenon is typical of many of the ways the Iteso have come to terms with their past suffering, recreating it into folk history and subduing the pain that the events entailed. In the creation of a new genre of tales in present-day Teso there is evidence of a living purpose of folklore in healing and binding together a community after rupture as well as passing on history and morality. It is especially important that children, a new postwar generation, are key participants in this process. The children are acclaimed when they tell and elaborate on the stories. They are thus innovators, creators, and receivers of folklore, which is an important cultural resource after a time of immense pain and suffering. In Teso, folklore has thus become a resource through which the Iteso strengthen themselves and their children to face a difficult present and uncertain future with renewed identity and self-belief.

References

Akello, G. 1981. *Iteso Thought Patterns in Tales*. Dar Es Salaam: Dar Es Salaam University Press.

—————. 1995. *Self Twice Removed: Ugandan Women.* London: International Reports, Women and Society, CHANGE.

Beidelman, T. 1993. *Moral Imagination in Kaguru Modes of Thought.* Bloomington: Indiana University Press.

Lawrence, J. C. D. 1957. *The Iteso: Fifty Years of Change in a Nilo-Hamitic Tribe of Uganda.* London: Oxford University Press.

Webster, J. B., et al. 1973. *The Iteso During the Asonya.* Nairobi: East Africa Publishing House.

JO DE BERRY

See also **Cosmology; East African Folklore: Overview**

CHILDREN'S FOLKLORE: KUNDA SONGS

The Kunda of Zambia are a societal group that has assimilated many people from other regional societies. The Kunda generally are matrilineal, but because some of the people they have assimilated follow patrilineal kinship patterns there is occasionally competition between maternal and paternal kin for the loyalties of children. Still, *visimi*, the songs which children sing, are usually taught to them by their mothers or their maternal kin in the various regional dialects of their mothers. The lessons these songs teach tend to be about ways to build and manage alliances for survival. The Kunda explain that these songs teach children to follow the "ways of staying" (*makhalidwe*, or traditional knowledge) of their mothers and maternal kin.

Kunda country is characterized by a harsh environment that periodically has very scarce resources. The unpredictability of the climate and movement of herds of buffalo, antelope, or elephant, and sometimes even attacks by wild animals such as lions, means that children must learn to stay alert and watchful at all times. In the face of such difficult circumstances, the Kunda must learn to live with unpredictability, and to rely on personal cunning and strength. Animal behavior or climate swings often serve in folk songs as metaphors for the unpredictability of human politics.

For instance, many songs are about Kalulu, a very clever scrub hare who manages to come out ahead in nearly any difficult situation. In one song Kalulu makes an exchange with another animal for some food, which leaves the other animal hungry. This instigates a lengthy series of other exchanges between other animals for food, and in every case the exchange leaves the other animals feeling shortchanged. In a reverse series of exchanges to amend the situation, all the animals still find they have ended up with a poor deal, but feel that at least an attempt at recompense has been made. All except Kalulu, that is, who manages to make the gesture of recompense but only after eating heartily.

Another genre of folk songs illustrates ways to cooperate with distant people so as to survive in the most difficult of circumstances. A song describes a girl or boy returning to the village, only to find that all the inhabitants have died. The boy or girl is forced to wander among other villages, sleeping in chicken coops and scavenging for food. The song continues:

> Go! Go quickly little child! To the village of your extended relatives! Find out what they need, and start doing some jobs for them, do some chores. They will see that you are useful to them, and they will feed you. They will take care of you. This is what we tell you—your mother, your fa-ther, your aunties, your uncles—don't sleep in the chicken coop any longer.

Thus, song is employed to impart lessons that may prove valuable to the child as he or she navigates his or her way to adulthood in the unforgiving landscape the Kunda call home.

References

Mwanalushi, Muyuda. 1990. *Youth and Society in Zambia.* Lusaka: Multimedia Publications.

Ngulube, Naboth M. J. 1989. *Some Aspects of Growing Up in Zambia.* Lusaka: Nalinga Consultancy Publishing.

Sumbwa, Nyambe. 1993. *Zambian Proverbs.* Lusaka: Zambia Printing Co. Publications.

BRADFORD STRICKLAND

See also **Tricksters in African Folklore**

CHILDREN'S FOLKLORE: NDEBELE

Not to be confused with the Ndebele of South Africa, who are well known for their decorative arts, the Ndebele people of Zimbabwe are cousins with, or descendants of, the Zulu of South Africa. The Ndebele are located in the southwestern part of Zimbabwe. Their founding ruler was uMzilikazi and the last Ndebele king was uLobegula.

As a primarily oral people the Ndebele possess oral art forms that serve a variety of functions. African scholars have suggested the term *orature* to label these oral art forms. In Ndebele society orature is used as a medium for socializing children. Consequently, children's orature is a reflection of the society's culture and history. Today most of the traditional oral forms have changed particularly in terms of the media and forms of existence. This entry focuses on lullabies, folktales (*inganekwane*), jokes (*amaphoxo*), riddles, tongue twisters, material forms, and games, and adopts a chronological presentation of the oral forms, that is, it presents them in a manner that corresponds to the developmental stages of children, from birth through early adolescence. The infant forms take a primarily poetic structure, and as the children grow older the forms become more narrative except for songs.

Lullabies

Lullabies are children's poetry composed with the understanding and appreciation of the child's needs. They are among the earliest oral forms to which infants are exposed. They do not have a fixed performance location. Although they are usually performed to entertain or soothe a crying baby, lullabies also serve as media for socializing children. Mothers or any other adult performs them. A lullaby can either be slow, rhythmic, or sleep-inducing, depending on what the intention for it is. As a socialization tool, lullabies are used to introduce infants and babies primarily to the language of the society. The following example illustrates this:

Ola ola	Ola, ola
Nank'amabhecezana	I see some pumpkin pieces
Enhla kwembiz'enkulu	At the corner of a big pot
Udle mabili	Eat two of them

Utshiye mathathu	And leave three
Utshiyel'umntwana	For the baby
Ol ola	Ola, ola
Nant'ubhec'es'levini	I see a small piece of a pumpkin on your chin

Parents usually use this kind of rhyme when they play with a child or are putting them to sleep. Some of the words in a lullaby are built around vowel sounds (*Ola, ola; Udle*), click sounds (*amabhecezana*, the click sound is the *c* in the word, its sound is similar to the sound made by a mechanical watch), and rhymes. Lullabies also expose infants to the language and the tradition of singing.

Nursery Rhymes and Games

As they grow older, children are introduced to nursery rhymes and games that carry lessons on language, and morals. In addition to their use within families, rhymes are now used in the classroom as a learning aid in math and language. The following example illustrates some of these. It is about a child called Yeye taking a walk with her father. In addition to language exposure, the children who hear the nursery rhyme are given a lesson: the need to wash one's hands before one eats a meal. Whereas only adults or older children perform lullabies, both adults and children perform rhymes and games.

Ngubani lo	Who is this
NguYeye	It is Yeye
Uhamba lobani	Who is with her
Loyise	Her father
Wamphathelani	What did he bring her
Amasi	Some milk
Ngendleb'enjani	In what kind of a container
Ebomvu	A red one
Wayifaka ngaphi	Where did he place it
Esibayeni	In the kraal
Es'khulu, es'khulu	The big kraal
Nguye lo umadla engagezanga	She is the one who eats with unclean hands

Today, some teachers use game rhymes to motivate children to learn the letters of the alphabet. Children are challenged to create rhymes that enhance their learning, for instance, in counting games or spelling rhymes.

Folktales

One of the earliest folklore forms that children are exposed to is the folktale. Like lullabies, adults perform these to children in their earliest years, but some older children, under the supervision of an elder, perform the stories too. They are performed during the winter, and in the early hours of the evening. There is a taboo that if one performs them outside the stipulated restrictions, the performer will grow horns. Folktales are an important medium for socializing children in that they incorporate various other folklore forms such as songs, jokes, and riddles. They are also constructed in a manner that allows audience participation. Most of the tales targeted at children carry important moral messages, such as good behavior, kindness, respect, cooperation, and love. Some of the messages are contained in the titles of the tales, for example as in "The Greedy Dog" or "A Kind Woman."

Many of the characters in the tales are animals, as children usually like animal characters, finding them entertaining and humorous.

A Ndebele tale has an introduction, a conflict, and a conclusion. It also uses stock phrases that, over time, children are expected to know. Another important aspect of the tale is the performer, who is expected to be a dramatic narrator of the story. Thus, most of the performers in Ndebele society are grandmothers or mothers of the family, usually those that can vocalize, act, and dramatize action, and sing. Schoolteachers also play the part of the performer, or sometimes they read written folktales to students. Singing is required as many tales contain a song that plays an important dramatic part in the story, especially in audience participation. A song's emotional content is used to dramatize the high points of the story, and highlight secret messages. In order to prepare an audience, especially children, to appreciate a character's feelings or problems, the performer has to charge them emotionally through song. Some songs contain mysterious, borrowed, or difficult words for children. So, this gives them the opportunity to expand their vocabulary. Other things that are used to capture children's interest are the food served and the fire around which a tale is built. Since folktaling occurs in the winter months, the harvesting period, children are treated to corn kernels roasted on the fire. Sometimes riddling is also used as a means to attract them. Another folklore form that is part of folktaling is a game called *imfumba*, in which an opponent has to guess the hand in which the other person is hiding something. Traditionally the adult performing tales for the children supervised the game.

Riddles

In traditional Ndebele society, riddling did not exist as a separate oral form. Riddles were always an adjunct of folktaling under the supervision of an adult. However, today riddles are performed separately from tales, usually by children, mostly at school. There are different types of riddles: traditional ones, puzzle riddles, and joke riddles. Traditional riddles depict traditional Ndebele culture, while contemporary ones depict the experiences of contemporary society. The following riddles testify to these observations. The first pair is drawn from traditional society, and the second pair from contemporary society. Here is an example of a traditional riddle: "Ngikulibha ngentaba ephahlwe ngabafana ababili—likhanda lendlebe" (I riddle you with a mountain that stands between two boys). The answer is, the human head and two ears. The imagery and the language are reflective of traditional society. The language is based on natural phenomena such as mountain. Another traditional riddle is "Ngikulibha ngenkunzi ebomvu esesibayeni esakhiwe ngezigodo ezimhlophe" (I riddle you with a bull in a kraal made out of white poles). The answer is, the tongue and teeth. Like in the previous riddle, the language used is derived from rural and agricultural life and experiences. Cattle played an important economic and symbolic role in Ndebele society. They were used for farming, as a measure of wealth, and as a medium of religious practices. Ndebele society has a high concentration of vocabulary built around cattle. This is evident from the riddle, in the words *bull* and *kraal*. While riddles are meant to sharpen children's observational skills, they also teach them language.

More recent riddles reflect the technological and literacy changes that have been experienced in Ndebele society. For example, one contemporary riddle goes, "Ngikulibha ngomfana ohamba ngekhanda—yipenseli" (I riddle you with a boy who walks on his head). The answer is, a pen or a pencil. This riddle records the introduction of Western writing via colonialism to the Ndebele society. Another riddle reflecting more contemporary experiences via colonialism and greater exposure to nontraditional cultures is, "What dog cannot bite?" The answer is "a hot dog."

Songs

Besides lullabies and songs in folktales, there are traditional songs that are used to socialize children. Important events in a person's life are celebrated with music (ceremonies) that children may participate in. These songs exploit the musical and poetic quality of language. However, most children, especially in their earlier years, engage more in game songs that are sung in the evenings soon after meals. In traditional society children formed themselves into a circle and joined their hands, and sung a song while dancing to it. This was a symbol of communal solidarity. Children created songs and games primarily from their natural surroundings. Some of these traditional performances were discontinued as a result of the war of liberation.

Jokes (Amaphoxo)

Jokes are very popular with contemporary Ndebele children, especially those attending elementary school. Most of the jokes that they tell reflect the changes that the society has experienced since colonization. There are various categories of jokes: those concerned with elders' ignorance about contemporary technology and experiences, the English language, the clash between rural and urban life, and simple joke contests between children. In the jokes, rural children are described by their urban counterparts as being ignorant. Rural children sometimes turn the tables against their urban friends. The following self-explanatory jokes illustrate these categories:

Kuthiwa kwakukhona omunye umuntu owagebhela iradio phansi esithi ufuna ukuzwa iunderground news.

(There was an individual who is said to have dug his radio into the ground so that he could listen to underground news, he said.)

Wenziwa yikuthi wezwa kuthiwa uJune uyeza wahamba wayamkhansila kukhalenda.

(When you heard people say that the month of June was approaching, you ran to your calendar and drew a line across the month.)

Ngabuya lawe koBulawayo wathi, "Khangelanini amakhiwa afake imbawula phezulu," usitsho amalayithi.

(I took you to the city for a visit, and after you saw streetlights you commented, "Look, white people put heaters up in the sky.")

Umfana wedolobheni wathi uchago luvela embodleleni.

(A boy from the city commented that milk came from a bottle.)

Waphupha usidla isinkwa wavuka uqede umqamelo.

(One night you dreamt about eating a loaf of bread, and the next morning when you woke up you realized that in your sleep you had been eating up your pillow.)

Tongue Twisters

Some of the distinctive features of the Ndebele language are click sounds, notably those represented by c, q, and x. Most tongue twisters of the language are built around these clicks. Verbal dexterity and a rich vocabulary are considered important and vital skills in Ndebele society. Such dexterity is primarily built around the different articulations and combinations of the clicks and the high speed at which they are to be said without a slip of the tongue. At this stage of their development, children are supposed to have mastered the subtleties of the language. Here are two examples that play on the click sounds: "Ngihlangane lexhegu ligax' iqhele liqag' iqhaga ngomlomo" (I met an old man with a piece of cloth on his back, and he was holding a gourd on his lips). X and Q are the core sounds of the tongue twister. They become more complicated; however, when combined with H. The H helps to create an aspirated Q or X sound. Children are pitted against each other in a contest to demonstrate their mastery of the click sounds. The second example, "Iqhele likaMqhele liqunywe liqhalaqhala" (Mqhele's piece of cloth was cut by the ill-behaved girl) is a play on the Q sound and its combinations with H.

Material Art Forms and Games

Besides contemporary toys, Ndebele children have always used available materials to create their own toys, and they also engage in games to bond with other children. Mud and vegetable materials, especially grass and wood, have been used in the past to make miniature animals, human beings, baskets, and clothes. Nowadays, some children use wire and scrap metal to create artistic pieces. One of the popular games they play is hide and seek.

Nicknaming and Nicknames

Almost every child has a nickname at one time in its lives. Children use these to ridicule one another, their parents, grandparents or teachers, or to joke with each other. Sometimes the nicknames simply describe an innocent appearance of an individual. One's appearance and behavior may be a source of a nickname. If one has a big forehead, stomach, or feet, they are likely to be called "Big Forehead," "Stomach," or "Big Feet."

References

Dube, Caleb. 1990. Children's Orature (Oral Art) in Matebeleland in Zimbabwe: Tradition and Innovation as Revealed by its Use. In *Proceedings of the Workshop and Conference on Regional Audio-Visual Archives, AVA-90*, Falun, Sweden, July 5–11, 1990. Falun/Oslo: Dalarna Research Council and Norwegian Collection of Folk Music, Department of Music and Theater Studies, University of Oslo.

———. 1989. *Ndebele Oral Art: Its Development within the Historic-Socio-Economic Context.* Master of Philosophy thesis, African Languages and Literature, University of Zimbabwe.

CALEB DUBE

See also **Folktales; Riddles; Songs for Ceremonies; Tongue Twisters, East Africa**

CHOKWE

See **Central African Folklore; History and Cultural Identity: The Chowke**

CLASSIQUES AFRICAINS

In 1964, a group of French Africanists—Eric de Dampierre, Michel Leiris, Gilbert Rouget, and Claude Tardits—founded the Association of Classiques Africains, whose object was two-fold: first, to contribute to a better knowledge of African literature outside of its country of origin; and second, to increase the number of literary documents available for research on the civilizations of Africa. As anthropologists, linguists, and musicologists, they had the opportunity to attend and appreciate, among the local audiences, performances of poets, singers, musicians, and storytellers. Therefore, they decided to collect these orally told or sung texts, which in their original forms already were "open air classics." As well, they gathered a certain number of manuscripts belonging to the traditional local heritage. In the meantime, other researchers doing fieldwork in various parts of Africa joined the initial founders of the association, and have since then taken an active part in developing the Classiques Africains collection.

Twenty-eight volumes have been published by Classiques Africains. Each is provided with an introduction on the sociocultural setting in which the texts were recorded. Twenty-seven are bilingual, presenting the original language in transcripts with a French (sometimes also English) translation supplied with linguistic and ethnographical comments. Several volumes contain a record or cassette that demonstrates some of the oral and musical elements of the performances.

The list of present publications below should give an idea of the variety of the genres concerned, among which epics play an outstanding part. The distributor for all the volumes is Servédit, Paris.

References

Bâ, Âmadou-Hampâté. 1974. *L'éclat de la grande étoile*, suivi du *Bain rituel*, récits initiatiques peuls.

Bâ, Amadou-Hampâté, and Lilyan Kesteloot. 1968. *Kaïdara, récit initiatique peul.*

de Dampierre, Éric. 1963. *Poètes nzakara.*

———. 1987. *Satires de Lamadani.* 2 vols. and cassette.

de Wolf, P. and P. 1972. *Un mvet de Zwè Nguéma*, chant épique fang recueilli par H. Pepper (with record).

Derive, Jean, and Gerard Dumestre. 1999. *Des hommes et des bêtes. Chants de chasseurs mandingues.*

Dumestre, Gérard. 1979. *La geste de Ségou, racontée par des griots bambara* (with record).

Dumestre, Gérard, and Lilyan Kesteloot. 1975. *La prise de Dionkoloni.*

Fortier, Joseph. 1967. *Le mythe et les contes de Sou.*

———. 1974. *Dragons et sorcières, contes et moralités du pays Mbaï-Moïsaala.*

Galley, Micheline. 1971. *Badr as-zîn et six contes algériens.* (2d. ed. 1993).

Galley, Micheline, and Abderrahman Ayoub. 1983. *Histoire des Beni Hilal et de ce qui leur advint dans leur Marche vers l'ouest, versions tunisiennes de la Geste hilalienne.*

Galley, Micheline, and Zakia Iraqui Sinaceur. 1994. *Dyab, Jha, La "âba . . . Le triomphe de la ruse. Contes morocains du fonds Colin.*

Goody, Jack, and S.W.D.K. Gandah. 1980. *Une récitation du Bagré* (including English version).

Lacroix, Pierre-Francis. 1965. *Poésie peule de l'Adamawa* (2 vols.).

Mufuta, Patrice. 1968. *Le chant kasàla des Luba.*

Platiel, Suzanne. 1984. *La fille volage et autres contes du pays san.*

Priso, Manga Bekombo. 1993. *Défis et prodiges. La fantastique histoire de Djéki-la-Njambé* (with record).

Rodegem, F.M. 1973. *Anthologie rundi.*

Seydou, Christiane. 1972. *Silâmaka et Poullôri*, récit épique peul (with record).

———. 1976. *La geste de Ham-Bodêdio ou Hama le Rouge* (with record).

———. 1991. *Bergers des mots*, poésie peule du Mâssina.

Seydou, Christiane, Brunehilde Biebuyck, and Manga Bekombo Priso. 1997. *Voix d'Afrique*, Anthologie Vol. 3, Poésie.

Smith, Pierre. 1975. *Le récit populaire au Rwanda.*

Sow, Alfâ Ibrâhîm. 1966. *La femme, la vache, la foi.*

———. 1971. *Le filon du bonheur éternel.*

MICHELINE GALLEY

See also **French Study of African Folklore; Oxford Library of African Literature**

COLOR SYMBOLISM: THE AKAN OF GHANA

The Akan of central Ghana incorporate an active and complex system of symbolic display in their ceremonial, ritual, and everyday life. Their intricate goldwork, cast bronze, and carved wooden figures are well known, as are the complexly woven kente and stamped *adinkra* cloths. Color plays a prominent role as a visual symbolic form in establishing a subtext for ceremony or ritual occasions, establishing identities of individuals and participants, defining relationships, and by contextualizing the appearance of ceremonial regalia and ritual objects. It enhances royal regalia either as a complimentary embellishment of objects to identify them to the specific occasion or as symbol of rank and status. Color gives religious ritual a sacred presence, reflecting the temper and meaning of the moment as well as the cycle of the ceremony. Visually prominent and ritually significant during funerals, color serves to indicate the complex relationships of extended families during this period of mourning and transition.

Though many hues are today found in use among the Akan, there remain three primary groupings of color commonly identified with symbolic or ritual usage. Defined in broad inclusive categories they include white (*fufu*) and various shades of red or russet (*kokoo* or *kobene*) or dark tones (*tuntum*). Each cluster of colors embodies associations that reflect spiritual and cultural values and symbolic references that are shared by the larger Akan population and contextually defined to circumstance and ritual appearance. Cloths (*ntoma*) of different colors are often the most visible element during ceremonies and their color will reflect the event and define an individual's participation in the ceremony.

White

White (*fufu*) among Akans represents spirituality, sacredness of place, purity, virtuousness, joyousness, and victory. After recovery from a long illness, an individual and their family wear white cloths for a period of time to reflect their joy at the recovery of their family member. A woman who has recently delivered a baby dresses in a white cloth to recognize a successful delivery and to celebrate her new child. *Fufu* serves to portray the purity of souls, as individuals who have been absolved of guilt in a court case mark their shoulders and heads with white clay, known as *hyire*, to demonstrate their innocence and happiness. White also serves to establish ceremonial, ritual, and spiritual identity. Shrines are painted white and their priests solemnly sprinkle *hyire* on the ground and themselves to sanctify rituals and establish contact with the spirit of the shrine. Priests dedicated to Nyame (the chief deity among the Akan) are known by the manner in which their hair is shaved and by the use of white clay markings on their bodies. Three parallel lines of white clay are drawn from the crown of the head extending down the forehead and continuing down each cheek. Similar lines are drawn on each shoulder and upper arm and across the chest. As the lines are drawn with three fingers, the priest recites a dedication that equates the divinity to the white clay. Therefore, white in this usage serves as a badge of office reflecting priestly devotion, as well as acknowledging the spirituality of God.

Funerals of priests are celebrated by their family who wear white cloth and dust white powder on themselves to acknowledge the priest's spirituality. Shrines and chief's houses have white walls and red foundations and men who help the king repair the floors have three bands of red clay (*ntuwma*) wiped across their foreheads by the king as a sign of appreciation and honor. During the repair of royal tombs, a dark russet cloth known as *kuntunkuni* is worn to indicate the sorrow of those working when they think of the great deeds of their kings and in honor of the dead. Women who whitewash the local shrine house, where the spirit (*obosom*) lives, spread some of the white wash across their breasts to show their participation during the repairing of the spirit's house.

Stools belonging to royals and family elders are cleaned and whitened with clay on festive days to acknowledge the purity of the owner's soul (*kra*). Newly named chiefs and their followers wear white and brightly colored cloths to demonstrate their happiness and celebrate the installation of the new chief. During funerals for an elderly relative, family members reverse tradition and wear white to celebrate the new ancestor rather than the dark cloths normally worn. The cycle of grieving for widows or widower's ends when dark cloths are cast off and a white cloth is put on during the Kunyae ceremony, which ends the yearlong period of mourning.

Retainers at court, known as *akyerefo*, are responsible for ensuring the ongoing purity of the king's soul; they often wear white cloths or mark their bodies with *hyire* during state ceremonies such as the Odwira and Adae. Other court attendants (*akonuasoafo*) who carry the royal stools are dressed in white cloth, and the state sword bearers (*afenasoafo*) spread white clay on their arms and necks or draw patterns on their foreheads and temples to indicate their ceremonial office and spiritual duties. Stoolbearers also whiten their left hand and put white clay on their eyelids. The left hand, which is normally associated with body functions, is used to hold the stool on the stoolbearer's neck and needs to be symbolically cleansed to hold the king's stool. The white clay on their eyelids reflects their bedazzlement by the king's glory.

During the Odwira ceremony, an annual festival of renewal and ritual cleansing, when shrines would be freshened, earlier kings remembered, and the nation cleansed, the Asantehene would first wear a barkcloth (*kyenkyen*) that was naturally white-gray reflecting the archaic nature of the ceremony as well as its spiritual function. Later when addressing the blackened stools of his predecessors, the king is dressed in old dark cloths, reflecting the presence of the royal dead and the seriousness of ritual offerings made to them. Afterwards the king wears rich and brightly colored cloths to celebrate and complete the Odwira ceremony. By these acts, ceremonial sequence is symbolically marked by chiefs wearing different colored cloths and changing them as new cycles were initiated.

Red, Russet, and Orange

Today the colors most often seen among the Akan are red, russet or orange hues. Collectively identified as *kobene* or *kokoo*, they also include purple, violet or pink and others within this range of color. Red-russet colors are themselves ambiguous in symbolic association being defined through a number of ceremonial, social, and personal contexts. *Kobene* is broadly identified with danger and warfare, blood, anger, heat (emotion), unrest, melancholy, bereavement and death. It reflects the seriousness of an occasion and can define a personal state of being or mark a national catastrophe.

Men wear red cloth and smear red clay (*ntowma*) across their shoulders, arms, and forehead to indicate defiance and anger. A well-known saying describes this frame of mind: "*M'ani abere*" (My eyes are red). This indicates sorrow and anger at the loss of a family member or the individual's spirit during a national crisis, such as a call to war. In the past, combatants in a battle would wear red to reflect the fierceness of the struggle and their anger. Members of the Akan army's rear guard (*kyidom*) were conspicuous by wearing vermilion or red cloths as they protected the state stools and chiefs who themselves were dressed in dark brown cloths sometimes stamped with *adinkra* symbols (abstract stamped symbols with proverbial cognates).

Funerals

Funerals play an important role in Akan society and life. They are conspicuous in part due to the prominent play of color of different hued cloths, headdresses, or the markings found on arms, shoulders, and face displayed by family and lineage relations during funerary ceremonies. It is in this context that color serves to define kinship and the various temporal segments of funerary rituals that can extend over a year. Through the different colored cloths worn at funerals a visual code of relationship to the deceased is given. Family relations are signified through the red cloths worn identifying members of the matrilineage (*abusua*), with black (*tuntum*) being worn by nonmatrilineal family and friends. The symbolic appearance of red (*kobene*) in this usage extends the bond of blood to both living and dead members of the matrilineage and to distinguish nonblood relations and other mourners. This is seen in the cloths worn by the *matrikin* of red or russet-brown for men, and with women wearing a red upper garment and a black skirt. Contemporary women's clothing may be stylish and up-to-date, but it continues to conform to customary color usage. Funerary cloths worn by men and women may be also stamped with dark brown *adinkra* symbols. They will be stamped upon various hued cloths ranging from blue-black to bright colors depending upon the period of the mourning ritual and the relation of the mourner to the deceased.

Bands of red cloth worn around the head known as *abotiri* often have red peppers placed in them so that both the color and hot taste of the pepper serve to remind the wearer of their loss. In addition to the red cloths and headdresses, designs known as *kotobirigya* are worn by women of the matrilineage and daughters of the deceased. Painted in a red dye (*esono*), triangles, semicircles, or simple parallel lines will be applied on temples, cheeks, and foreheads. Blood relations will also mark their upper bodies with red clay (*ntwuma*) in broad wipes of color, known as *asafie*, placed on the arms, shoulders, and chest. This use of color symbolically confirms membership in a common bloodline, the *abusua*. Another form of cosmetic symbolism is used by women of the *matrikin* to indicate their grief, as they will draw a band of shiny black soot encircling the head at the base of the hair. Known as *densikram*, it is worn by mature women only. Lips and eyes are also be blackened in sorrow.

In the past the head of the deceased might be shaved and three lines of color, red, black, and white would be drawn on it. Similar lines or daubs of color are found on clay pots made for the deceased that would be ultimately deposited in a place sacred to the matrilineage known as *esense* or the "place of the pots." These pots, called *abusua kuruwa* (clan pots), were venerated representing the individual as a member of the lineage. This symbolic unity of the matrilineage through the use of color continues through the various ceremonies of remembrance for the dead throughout the year held at the *esense*.

Dark Colors

As noted, the dark colors, black, or brown or a deep blue (*birisi*) characterized night, death, sorrow, sadness, bereavement, depression, and seriousness of purpose. Symbolic transformation through color takes place when a king's white stool is blackened at the time of his death. It then is placed in the royal stool house joining those of preceding kings and where it is also venerated. The stools of previous kings are blackened as a sign of respect and age and as recognition that they belong to the "other world" of ancestors. Among the Akan, issues of history and articles of great age are conceived of as being black. In addition objects taken as spoils of war are blackened and placed in the stool house near the stool of the king who captured them to honor that king and the nation. The personal possessions and badges of office of important elders or notables are blackened and kept in the matrilineage house as objects identified with their office and good works.

Color plays an active symbolic role in Akan political statecraft. As a nonverbal statement of power relationships, color can symbolically address issues of polity between states through colors worn by the king or displayed on state umbrellas. When issues of grave national concern, such as war are to be discussed, the king and other chiefs sitting in council wear dark brown cloths known as *kuntunkuni*, a cloth normally worn at funeral to reflect the solemnity of the occasion. The dark cloth also symbolizes the ultimate power and authority of the king to act decisively for the state. Correspondingly, a combination of color and the cognate proverb of an *adinkra* symbol stamped on the cloth expresses the position of the state upon an issue. When sitting at court hearing cases, the king dresses in dark cloth to indicate the seriousness of the issues addressed and his responsibility to render justice and where necessary assign penalties as judged.

Gold

Gold (*sika*) as color and material was reserved to the king and those he honored. It had no absolute value but had great symbolic value indicating richness, royalty, high social status, wealth, and financial rank. Gold jewelry is never worn at funerals; instead, wooden carved bracelets are painted with black enamel to reflect the seriousness of the funeral. Spiritual and symbolic significance is attributed to gold as the king wears round gold disks (*kra sika*) that symbolized the purity associated to his soul (*kra*) with the subsequent well-being of the nation. Gold was reserved to the Asantehene and only his wooden stool (*dwa*) was permitted to have gold medallions or panels attached to it. Among the Akan, stools of the queen mother or other lesser kings were limited to silver attachments; to do otherwise and apply gold without permission was to challenge the king and the state. Perhaps the most prominent symbolic motif among the Akan is the Golden Stool of the Akan. Cast in gold, the Golden Stool (*Sika Dwa*) serves as symbol of the collective soul of the people, and functions as a locus of political union of those states that make up the Akan nation.

References

Antubam, K. 1963. Ghana's Heritage of Culture. Leipzig.

Bellis, J. O. 1982. The "Place of the Pots" in Akan Funerary Custom. Bloomington: African Studies Program, Indiana University.

Hagan, G. P. 1970. A Note on Akan Color Symbolism. *Research Review*, 7, no. 1.

Rattray, R. S. 1927. *Religion and Art in Ashanti*. London.

Reindorf, C. C. 1895. *A History of the Gold Coast and Asante*. Basel.

Mato, D. 1988, 1991, 1992, 1994. Interviews and Personal Communications collected in Ghana.

DANIEL MATO

See also **Beadwork; Body Arts; Cosmology**

COMOROS (COMOROS FEDERAL ISLAMIC REPUBLIC)

Comoros, a tropical country of 714,000 people, consists of four islands located off of Africa's southeast coast. Its capital city is Moroni, which has a population of 30,000. Comoros' ethnic population consists of Arabs, Africans, and Indians. The major languages spoken are Shaafi-Islam, Swahili, French, and Arabic. The country is predominantly Sunni Muslim (86 percent), while the remaining 14 percent are Roman Catholic.

In 1843, the French laid claim to the Comoran islands. Three of the islands voted for independence in 1970, but Mayotte chose to stay French. After a coup led by European mercenaries, Comoros gained its independence from France on July 6, 1975, and subsequently formed its own Islamic republic. After eight years under one-party rule, the government returned to a multi-party system in 1990.

Unfortunately, despite such recent reforms, there is still no political stability. At the time of independence, the United Nations listed Comoros as one of the world's least developed nations. Today the islands are still impoverished and 80 percent of the population is underemployed as subsistence farmers. Adult literacy is approximately 57 percent. Ninety-five percent of the country's revenue comes from the exportation of vanilla, cloves, and ylang-ylang, a perfume essence. Tourism and perfume distillation are also major sources of revenue for Comoros.

JENNIFER JOYCE

CONCERT PARTIES

Concerts or concert parties are open-air popular theater events performed throughout rural and urban Ghana by traveling bands of actors and musicians. Concerts creatively fuse morality play, slapstick comedy, and popular band music; in the 1990s some attempted at to convert the audience to new forms of Christian faith. The plays, dance, music, and roadside paintings (that advertise the performance) have a hybrid message that reflects rapid change and modernity, yet remain rooted in local and traditional culture. Early influences include Akan tales about the spider trickster hero Ananse, nativity plays performed at Christian missions, silent films of Charlie Chaplin and Al Jolson, tap dancing, ragtime, and stand-up comedians of American vaudeville and "blackface" minstrel shows. The genre reaches back to the early decades of the twentieth century in the Gold Coast (now Ghana) towns that first acted as a buffer between Europe and the powerful inland kingdoms and that have a long history of breakaway Christian churches.

Teacher Yalley is generally said to have performed the first Ghanaian concert in 1918 in English for a small urban educated wealthy elite in Sekondi and Accra. At about the same time, Bob Ishmael Johnson began to perform at Empire Day celebrations. First as the "Versatile Eight," and later in 1930 as the "Two Bobs and the Carolina Girl," his program included a short introduction with dance, jokes, and ragtime songs followed by an hour-long play. The three main characters were the Gentleman, the Lady Impersonator, and the Joker or "Bob" (named after Bob Johnson), the latter being a fusion of the mischievous Ananse of Akan folklore, a hero/antihero full of ambition and folly, and the "blackface" actor of American minstrel shows. They toured rural areas, added highlife songs in pidgin English and Fanti and attracted a more popular, less wealthy audience. The plays (only partially scripted) became longer, the number of actors increased, and by the 1940s they included social and political themes such as the "Coronation of King George VI"

and the "Downfall of Adolf Hitler." Plays in the 1950s supported the independence struggle, and some addressed corruption and inefficiency in high places. By this time the Akan language was used throughout and guitar band highlife music embellished the play, so that play and music were inseparable. By the 1960s and 1970s concerts were at their height and there were fifty to sixty groups touring the country (and neighboring countries as well). In the late 1970s and early 1980s, they dwindled in popularity due largely to economic hardship, government curfew, and competition from lower-cost video screenings and from "spinners" (traveling high-tech light shows with recorded rather than live music). Performances in the 1990s appealed to a young, unsophisticated, semiliterate, working-class constituency of generally rural individuals, or first generation city dwellers. References to national politics were virtually absent. Audiences became smaller. Charismatic Christianity had gained in popularity and opposed dancing and the portrayal of "devils" in the paintings and plays. Because youngsters liked to dance, concerts that formerly started their play at 11 P.M. and finished at 3 A.M., now performed music until 1 A.M. and, following an irreverent comedy interlude, the play itself continued until dawn.

Today, the cast size has increased, but the actors still portray conventional stereotypes of men and women and the narratives are still framed by the Joker or "Bob." The comedy skit that introduces the play separates it from everyday life, and is broad and coarse with robustly farcical and antifeminine elements. Much of the humor derives from incongruities in the use of words or behavior. As the bands tour from one part of Ghana to another, they adapt the jokes so as to be ethnically specific, but the message is rarely politically or sexually subversive. There is much audience participation: the audience cries jeers, applauds, and climbs on stage to give money or candy to the actors.

The plays, paintings, and music give insight into the local reworking of transnational media. They depict a world of fantastic experience that is also firmly set in the everyday life of contemporary (generally rural) Ghana. Fragmented references to Christian, Islamic, and traditional religious practices coexist, as

Concert party painting for City Boys Band, Int. by Mark Anthony, Ghana, 1994. Play being advertised is "Nea Onyame Ahyirano No." 8 × 8 feet, on plywood. Photo © Michelle Gilbert.

Concert party painting by Mark Anthony for City Boys Band play called "Nea Onyame Ahyirano No," Ghana, 1994. 8 × 8 feet, on plywood. Photo © Michelle Gilbert.

in everyday life. The plots are linear but formulaic, with repetitive themes and sometimes as many as twenty scenes. Scenic breaks are signaled by highlife interludes: the lyrics may or may not comment on the plot. Although the younger concert bands sing mostly about love and orphans, most concert plays in the 1990s carried a strong moral message. Common themes include jealousy and envy, wealth and poverty, co-wife rivalry, orphans, inheritance disputes, chieftaincy affairs, tensions between good and evil, witchcraft, ancestors, contests between Satan and traditional deities, and conflict between traditional religions and Christianity. Violence dramatizes the moral lesson and repetition of themes within a play reinforces the moral tale. The endings generally offer neat solutions; the evil perpetrator dies and the intended victim is saved. Concert plays draw on folktale personages such as dwarves, giants, and gods, as well as stock characters from everyday life such as the lineage elder, queen mother, chief, spirit medium, Islamic mullah, and Christian priest. Plays in the 1990s often drew on material from Christian prayer groups, and focused on the competition and challenge between Christian and traditional religious beliefs and practices.

Since the 1980s, some concert bands have begun to perform regularly on television in Akan, Ga, and Ewe. The short plays include a few songs, and are far more realistic: they use female as well as male performers, never use black and white minstrel makeup, and rarely show local gods. Those performed at the National Theatre in Accra appeal to a young, middle-class audience. Television audiences include middle-class, middle-aged Christians who would never go to see a live performance. In the 1990s, some charismatic churches, such as Kristo Asafo and Power Light, began to do concerts to advertise their churches. The hour-long church plays, usually included a scene where Satan was defeated by an angel. By 2000 they were no longer attracting large crowds and ceased to tour Ghana.

Although concert parties started out as entertainment for the elite, they quickly became adapted to suit the preferences of poorer rural dwellers. They brought urban attractions and fashions to remote villagers, and allowed the newly urban audience to reflect on their previous rural lives and personal morality. By the year 2000, due to competition from low cost video, television, and spiritualist Churches, only six concert groups groups toured Ghana.

Concert parties were also performed throughout the 1960s and 1970s in Ewe-speaking Togo. Borrowed from Ghana, they were a smaller and solely urban phenomena centered in Lome, and had ceased by the 1980s.

References

Barber, Karen, and John Collins, Alain Ricard, eds. 1997. *West African Popular Theatre*. Bloomington: Indiana University Press.

Collins, John. 1994. *Highlife Time*. Accra: Anansesem Pubs.

Gilbert, Michelle. 1998. Concert Parties: Paintings and Performance. *Journal of Religion in Africa* 28, no. 1:62–69.

———. 2000. *Hollywood Icons, Local Demons: Ghanaian Popular Paintings by Mark Anthony*. Hartford: Trinity College.

———. 2003. Images choc: peintures-affiches du Ghana/Shocking Images: Ghanaian Painted Posters. In *Ghana hier et aujourd hui/ Ghana Yesterday und Today*, eds. Christiane Falgayrettes-Leveau and Christiane Owusu-Sarpong. Paris: Musee Dapper.

MICHELLE GILBERT

See also **Music: West African Highlife; Performance in Africa**

CONGO (REPUBLIC OF THE CONGO)

Located in central Africa, Congo is a tropical country neighbored by Angola, Democratic Republic of Congo, Central African Republic, Cameroon, Gabon, and the Atlantic Ocean. For some the country is better known as Congo-Brazzaville, named after its capital and largest city of a million people. Of the nation's approximately 3 million people, nearly half are Kongo (48 percent), 20 percent are Sangha, 17 percent are Teke, and 14 percent are composed of other smaller groups. The major languages spoken are French, Lingala, Kikongo, Teke, Sangha, and M'Bochi. Half of the nation's people are Christian, 48 percent practice traditional indigenous religions, and 2 percent are Muslim.

The French established their control over the Congo in 1882, but did not create a formal colony until 1910. Due to the colony's allegiance to General Charles deGaulle, it was declared capital of the empire and of liberated France from 1940–1944. On August 15, 1960, Congo gained its independence from France after fifty years of colonial rule. Since 1968, the nation had been ruled as a one-party state by the Marxist-Leninist–inspired style of the Congolese Workers Party (PCT). In 1990, however, the PCT agreed to give up its Marxist ideology and one-party system. In 1995, the Government of National Unity was formed and brought an end to the politically motivated fighting that had blighted the nation during the late twentieth century. Only 30 years old, Joseph Kabila became president in January 2001, after his father, Laurent Kabila, was assasinated. Although a peace agreement was signed in December 2002, there is still very little peace in the Congo.

Wood, potash, petroleum, and natural gas are Congo's natural resources. Agricultural production centers around cocoa, coffee, tobacco, palm kernels, sugarcane, rice and peanuts, while the industrial sector manufactures cement, textiles, and processed agricultural and forestry goods. Though Congo's manufacturing sector is small, it has great potential for growth and should benefit the economy in years to come.

The metropolitan region of Congo's capital Brazzaville and the nearby former Zaire's capital of Kinshasha has long been a great cultural center in central Africa. This region has produced *soukous*, a Congolese musical style that has been popularized throughout Africa, as well as in Tokyo and Paris. Congolese writers have been recognized for their contributions to public service, as many have used their creativity and knowledge to educate the public. The renowned Congolese poet and novelist Tchicaya U'Tam'si worked for UNESCO for many years before his death in 1988.

JENNIFER JOYCE

CONTEMPORARY BARDS: HAUSA VERBAL ARTISTS

The Hausa are known throughout much of West Africa as traders and artisans. They have settled in Ghana, Nigeria, Niger, and Chad, but are usually associated with the Hausa city-states, such as Kano, in Nigeria. In the earth nineteenth century, the Fulani jihad (holy war) brought all the Hausa together under Islam and merged the two people in the cities. Today, the Hausa-Fulani form one of the largest ethnic groups in Nigeria and they continue to cherish their ancient arts, including music and the verbal arts.

A number of prose forms are usually distinguished in Hausa terminology. The prose narratives *labari* and *tatsuniya* are contrasted as "presumed real" and "fictive" narratives respectively. While the term *tatsuniya* predominantly means "traditional tale," it is sometimes also used to denote a conundrum or riddle, more often referred to as *ka cinci ka cinci*, or "pick up, pick up" which acts both as name conveying the interactive nature of the genre and as introductory formula. *Tatsuniyoyi* (pl.) as "tales" refer to animal/trickster tales, to narratives of "human to human" interaction, and of "human to supernatural being" interaction. Heroes and villains, larger than life stereotypes, inhabit the center of each story, predictable in their heroism or their villainy. Conflict or contest between protagonists is an important characteristic as the tale develops the encounters and interactions between characters. Discussion of personal emotion or psychological state is unusual; such dimensions are conveyed primarily through the acting out of dialogue and action of the characters. The storyteller's art of "acting out" is focused on the use of voice and facial expression. Although the character stereotypes may allow the audience to very quickly grasp the potentials of any particular situation established by the storyteller, the direction of the interactions of two stereotypes is less predictable. Outcomes are more in the gift of the tale-teller's skills. The stereotyped characters of tales are both human (such as the ill-treated but faithful daughter, the corrupt judge, the pious cleric, the country bumpkin, the city slicker, the disobedient child, or the arrogant prince) and animal (such as the hare, jackal, lion, or hyena) as well as liminal characters such as Dodo (evil spirit/monster) and Gizo (trickster). Each one among this cast of characters has an accompanying package of features ranging from aspects of personality, such as cunning, to manner of speech, such as a lisp in the case of Gizo.

Within short-form verbal arts, *karin magana* distinguishes proverbs/sayings. The Hausa term implies folded speech, thereby allusive diction, which requires, on the part of the listener, interpretation of imagery or secondary reference. A functional distinction among short-form expressions identifies *kirari* as epithet, often used in praise, and *habaici* as innuendo depending upon the presumed intent of the speaker. Allusive diction is an integral part of many communicative contexts and while *karin magana* are recognized as a distinct form, they constitute the building blocks of other discrete genres within Hausa folklore.

Rhythmic or nonprose language is generally represented by the term *waka* which is, in common parlance, a single term covering both instrumentally accompanied, solo or "lead and chorus," oral song, and also another genre: written poetry intoned without accompaniment. In drawing the distinction in normal Hausa parlance, they would be distinguished as *waka baka* (oral waka) and *rubutacciyar waka* (written waka.) Song has been closely associated with praise-singing in traditional aristocratic courts.

"Tied" singers in patron–client relationships with nobles have both sung the praises and vilified the rivals of their patrons; among the most famous have been Dankwairo, Jankidi, and Sarkin Tabshi. In the latter half of the twentieth century, the popularity of singers and their financial independence through the sale of records and tapes and through TV appearances have allowed them to work as freelance artists, among the most famous being Mamman Shata and Dan Maraya Jos. The poetry-writing tradition derives from the Islamic religious jihad of the early nineteenth century when poetry became a favored vehicle for the reformists' battle for the hearts and minds of the people. The poets of that era included a woman scholar and organizer, Nana Asma'u, daughter of the leader of the jihad, Usman dan Fodio. In the late twentieth century, secular writing has expanded the range of topics addressed beyond the strictly religious concerns of earlier years. Well-known modern poets include Akilu Aliyu and Mudi Spikin.

There is a further range of labels for creators of such genres and for other performers. *Mai tatsuniya* simply implies *storyteller*, but the term *maroki*, literally "one who begs," specifically suggests a praise-singer in search of reward for his services; *mawaki* (one who sings), on the other hand, could be applied to a singer or a poet. There are further terms for public entertainers of various kinds, such as *yan kama* (burlesque players), *yan gambara* (rap artists), and *yan bori* (musicians and performers associated with the spirit-possession cult). Popular culture in Hausa at the beginning of the twenty-first century presents a dynamic mix covering a variety of oral performances ranging from the earthy, irreverent rap dialogues of *yan gambara* as they work the markets of northern Nigeria to the public manifestation in the modern media—radio and television—of the tied praise-singer perceived as representing cultural "tradition." At the same time, an explosion of popular fiction writing during the 1990s has led to an even greater explosion of commercial Hausa-language video film production, another medium in which notions of traditional oral culture and its practitioners are embedded. For an introduction to Hausa folklore, see Ames (1973), Furniss (1996), and Skinner (1969).

References

Ames, D. W. 1973. A Sociocultural View of Hausa Musical Activity. In *The Traditional Artist in African Societies*, ed. W. L. D'Azevedo. Bloomington and London: Indiana University Press.

Furniss, G. 1996. *Poetry, Prose and Popular Culture in Hausa.* Washington, D.C.: Smithsonian Institution Press.

Skinner, A. N., ed. 1969. *Hausa Tales and Traditions: An English Translation of* "Tatsuniyoyi Na Hausa," *originally compiled by Frank Edgar.* Vol. 1 (1969), London: Frank Cass; Vols. 2 and 3 (1977), Madison: University of Wisconsin Press.

GRAHAM FURNISS

See also **Folktales; Medicine: Folk Medicine of the Hausa; West Africa: Overview**

COSMOLOGY

The foundation of traditional African cosmologies is a spiritual view and experience of life. This view undergirds traditional understanding of being, existence, and the phenomenal world. This spirit world consists of the Supreme Being, the deities or divinities, ancestors, various spirit powers, the human being and nature. This is particularly the case in West Africa, which forms the focus of this article, especially the Akan and Ewe ethnic groups of Ghana.

Supreme Being

In Africa, there is belief in a Supreme Being (God), who is the ultimate eternal source and ground of being. Each ethnic group has a variety of names and appellations for the Supreme Being. Some of these are Onyame (Akan), Mawu (Ewe), Chukwu (Igbo), and Olodumare (Yoruba) (Mbiti, 1970). The Supreme Being is creator and sustainer of the world and is believed to be essentially spirit in nature, absolutely potent, and morally pure. Various attributes, names, proverbs, symbols, and greetings reveal how Africans conceive this being as a spiritual reality that not only gives life but also influences it in diverse ways. The Akan proverb "No one points out Onyame to a child" underscores the fact that the knowledge of God is believed to be innate to the African.

Though all beings derive their existence from the Supreme Being, they vary in terms of degrees of spiritual essence, potency, and morality. The deities and ancestors occupy an important position between humans and the Supreme Being. In traditional belief, they also activate and influence the phenomenal world in various ways. Thus to ignore their influence will amount to operating in the world at only one level of reality, that is, the material and ignoring the real essence that underpins the world which is the spiritual.

Dieties

The deities constitute a group of spirit beings known by various traditional names such as Obosom (Akan), Trowo (Ewe), Vodu (Ewe/Fon), Orisha (Yoruba), and so on. They are also referred to in various writings on African traditional religions as the lesser gods or divinities. They are believed to possess various powers delegated to them by the Supreme Being for the purpose of sustaining the world and human community. There are multitudes of such deities varying in number and function from society to society across Africa. Some key deities are believed to inhabit nature and control its functions. For example, most African peoples believe that the earth, bodies of water, thunder, and so forth operate under the aegis of deity. The earth spirit (known as Asase Yaa or Asase Afua among the Akan), normally female, is responsible for fertility and the maintenance of moral order. Acts such as homicide and immorality are considered to be particularly abhorrent to her.

Some deities are worshiped by various units of traditional social structure such as the family, clan, ethnic group, and communities such as villages and towns. These deities guide, guard, and protect the life of the members of the community. An example of such deities is the titular deities of the Akan. They are the deities of the major bodies of water that are within the geographical area occupied by the Akan such as the rivers Tano, Bea, and Lake Bosomtwe. They also serve as the patron deities of the patrilineal clans of the Akan (Busia, 1976, 197ff). Among the Yoruba some of the most important deities, known as Orisha, are apotheosis of primeval ancestors and are linked with the ethnic group as well as nature. For example, Shango, the deity of thunder and lightning, is believed to be an ancestral ruler of the Yoruba Kingdom of Oyo. Some of their deities are also patrons of occupational and professional guilds. For example, Ogun, the ancestral ruler of life in Nigeria who is the god of war, is also the patron of metallurgy (Awolalu, 1979, 33ff).

Allegiance to a deity, especially one of the minor ones, is however dependent on consistency in role performance. A deity that is unable to serve its adherents puts its potency in doubt. African people often neglect to serve a deity who no longer serves their needs effectively. Similarly new deities are adopted if found to be more potent and benign. Also though conceived as spirit, the deities are conceived in more anthropomorphic terms than the Supreme Being. They marry, have children, travel, eat, sleep, and so forth. Often representative images are made of these deities, however, this is not normally the case with the Supreme Being.

Ancestors

Though the deities mediate between the Supreme Being and humans, the ancestors occupy a more intimate position as mediators between their descendants and all other spirit beings. They are closer to humans than the deities because of their filial bonds with descendants. Ancestors are normally deceased progenitors who led exemplary lives and distinguished themselves as elders within the community. At death they are believed to assume a special spiritual potency that enables them to serve as intermediaries between their living descendants and the spiritual world. Some call them the living dead (Mbiti 1990). Ancestral beliefs indicate a strong belief in the continuance of life after death, and the ancestral status itself symbolizes the ideal afterlife attainment.

Ancestors wield influence on their living descendants as guides and guards of moral conduct who seek their welfare and protect them. The latter role of protection is important because of the strong belief in a range of spirit powers (ranging from moral through amoral to evil spirit powers) that adversely influence the lives of the humans. Powers such as Ekwensu and Akologeli of the Igbo of Nigeria and Sasabonsa of Ghanaian lore, and the power of witchcraft are normally acquired and used by humans mainly to hurt fellow human beings. For humans have the power of asserting their spiritual potency destructively against fellow humans through such powers as witchcraft and sorcery. These negative powers often act capriciously, though they find immoral persons easy prey.

Achieving Personhood

The human being, therefore, encounters positive and negative spiritual powers within the world. These powers influence human life because the human being is a unique being created out of physical and spiritual elements. Apart from sharing the general spiritual power that activates the universe known as Sunsum (Akan) and Gbogbo (Ewe), each person has a special and direct spiritual source in the Creator who is the soul (OkraAkan; Kla [Ga], Luvo [Ewe], Ori [Yoruba], Chi [Igbo]). The importance of this belief that an individual derives his being from the Supreme Being is summed up in the Akan proverb: "Every person is a child of Onyame, no one is a child of the earth!" Thus though the earth symbolizes motherhood and fertility, she is not the ultimate source of life.

A person's phenomenal existence begins when the Supreme Being blesses the sexual union of a man and woman with the life force or soul. Life is the greatest gift of the Supreme Being and to live it to its fullness is the goal of African peoples. Traditional prayer requests are normally summed up in the wish to have abundant life known as Dagbe (Ewe) and Sunkwa (Akan) (Gaba 1997, 99). This implies a life endowed with good health, children, wealth and material prosperity, and peace and success in all one's endeavors.

Though these goals may appear mundane, there is a subtler level of attaining fullness of life. Material success is normally seen as a reflection of subtler spiritual attainment. This subtler level involves attainment of personhood. To be born human does not mean to be born a person. Maturation into personhood is a moral journey in African cosmology. The individual's growth is judged by the virtues he inculcates and exhibits in life. Virtues such as humility, hospitality, piety, patience, hard work, and honesty among others are highly appreciated. When a person matures along this line the Ewe say of such a person, "Ame Nutoe," and the Akan, "Oye Nipa," meaning he or she is human, that is, a real person. Otherwise the opposite would be said, and the person in question may even be called an animal (Gyekye 1992, 109).

The Ewe also call such persons Bometsila. Bome, in Ewe cosmology, is a pre-earth spirit dwelling place. Bometsila literally means one who has remained in this prenatal spirit realm. To call someone Bometsila is to imply that the person, although born into this physical world (*kodzogbed*), shows no growth or development in conduct. It means that the person has not matured or realized his human potentials on earth, that the person leads a dehumanized way of life, a life not rooted in the ethics of the community.

Concern about life, however, is not restricted to the ethics of interhuman relationships. Traditional cosmology is incomplete without the realms of nature that constitute the theater of human life and existence. Nature originates from the Supreme Being and is activated by spirit force from the Supreme Being. Its elements are therefore avenues for the manifestation of a variety of spiritual forces. Nature is also seen as a means of understanding and conceptualizing the Supreme Being (Mbiti 1990, 48ff). It is traditionally conceived as an indicator of the state of human relationship to the Him. When nature becomes destructive to humans through epidemics or floods, then it indicates His displeasure. Otherwise nature sustains life, nourishing it with food and water. It is also a source of healing and cures as traditional pharmacopoeia draws mainly on herbs, roots, and animal life. Various taboos relating to nature serve as a source of moral enforcement contributing to social cohesion. Elements of nature are also symbols of social groupings. Animals serve as Totems for the Akan matrilineal groups for instance while as stated earlier water bodies associated with deity serve as patrons of the patrilineal groups.

Various aspects of nature, especially the animal world is the source of proverbs that form the traditional font of wisdom that guide sound and proper conduct. Nature is therefore a religious universe, an experiential educator that people must be related to in reverence, kinship, affinity, and in symbiotic relationship.

Thus the human journey in life is a journey of moral and spiritual maturation. The Akan refer to it as Obra and the Ewe as Kodzogbe. The latter literally means "the place or day of judgment." Eventually, when death comes, the soul goes to the Supreme Being, so that it may be held accountable for its life on earth; the spirit finds rest with its ancestors if it is deemed worthy of a place among them.

References

Awolalu, J. O. 1979. *Yoruba Beliefs and Sacrificial Rites*. London: Longman.

Busia, K. A. 1976. The Ashanti. In *African Worlds: Studies in the Cosmological Ideas and Social Values of African Peoples*, ed. Daryll Forde. Oxford: Oxford University Press.

Ephirim-Donkor, Anthony. 1997. *African Spirituality. On Becoming Ancestors*. Trenton, N.J.: African World Press.

Gaba, C. R. 1997. The Religious Life of the People. In *A Handbook on Eweland. Vol. 1, The Ewes of Southeastern Ghana*. Accra, Ghana: Woeli.

Gyekye, Kwame. 1992. Person and Community in African Thought. In *Person and Community: Ghanaian Philosophical Studies I*, eds. Kwasi Wiredu and Kwame Gyekye. Washington, D.C.: The Council for Research in Values and Philosophy.

———. 1996. *African Cultural Values. An Introduction*. Philadelphia Pa. and Accra, Ghana: Sankofa.

Idowu, Bolaji. 1973. *African Traditional Religion. A Definition*. London: SCM Press.

Mbiti, J. S. 1970. *Concepts of God in Africa*. London: SPCK.

———. 1990. *African Religions and Philosophy*, 2d ed. London: Heinemann.

Opoku, Kofi Asare. 1978. *West African Traditional Religion*. Singapore: FEP International Private.

ELOM DOVLO

See also **Astronomy; Cardinal Directions; Religion: African Traditional Religion**

COTE D'IVOIRE (REPUBLIC OF COTE D'IVOIRE)

Cote d'Ivoire (Ivory Coast) is a tropical country that lies along the Gulf of Guinea on the west coast of Africa. It lies east of Liberia and Guinea, south of Mali and Burkina Faso, and west of Ghana. Abidjan, a main port and Cote d'Ivoire's largest city, is also the country's capital and once known as "the Paris of West Africa." Cote d'Ivoire's 16 million people comprise four major ethnic groups: the Baule, Bete, Senufo, and Malinke. More than sixty languages are spoken, however, the major languages are French, Dyula, Agni, Kru, Senufo, and Malinke. The majority of the population is Muslim (60 percent), while 28 percent practice traditional indigenous religions. The remaining population is Christian (12 percent).

After sixty-seven years of French colonization, Cote d'Ivoire won its independence on April 7, 1960, founding a republic with a president and a legislature called the National Assembly. Cote d'Ivoire's first president, Felix Houphouet-Boigny, died in 1993 and was succeeded in 1995 by Henri Konan Bedie. This administration quickly became known for its corruption and for the concept of "Ivoirianity," by which Bedie tried to prevent political opposition. After decades of being Africa's most open nation, encouraging thousands of workers from other countries, this policy demanded both parents be Ivoirian for one to participate in elections. Bedie was overthrown in a military coup in 1999. The elections of 2000 were strongly contested and the subsequent period of unrest finally deteriorated into a full-blown civil war pitting, in very general terms, northern peoples against those in the south.

During its first twenty years of independence, Cote d'Ivoire had one of the highest economic growth rates in the world, as the nation was the world's leading producer of cocoa and a major producer of coffee. Yamoussoukro, the home village of Houphouet-Boigny and what is to become the country's new capitol, is the site of the largest Christian basilica in the world. The structure, modeled after Saint Peter's in Rome, was built during more prosperous economic times and was a gift to the pope from Houphouet-Boigny. In the late twentieth century years Cote d'Ivoire has suffered an economic downturn, primarily due to decreased revenue from cocoa and coffee, however, the country is still one of the most prosperous in Africa.

Cote d'Ivoire is renowned for its traditional arts, as well as contemporary Western-influenced artists. The woodcarvings of the Baule, Senufo, and Dan peoples are treasured in the world's museums. Music and dance, woven textiles, and ceramics are other important artistic traditions that have thrived in Cote d'Ivoire. Among the many popular Ivoirian singers, Alpha Blondy is the best known internationally.

JENNIFER JOYCE

CROWLEY, DANIEL J. (1921–1998)

Daniel J. Crowley received his doctorate in anthropology from Northwestern University in 1956, where he was mentored by pioneering Africanist scholars Melville J. Herskovits and William R. Bascom. Focusing at first on the cultures of the Caribbean, Crowley undertook a study of the oral traditions that he encountered on New Providence Island in the Bahamas and eventually presented his findings in *I Could Talk Old Story Good: Creativity in Bahamian Folklore* (1966), a volume still hailed as a pioneering work of folktale scholarship. Like many of the Northwestern graduates of his era, Crowly was keenly interested in the processes of cultural change and the impact of contemporary conditions on the received patterns of tradition. Consequently, in his research, the dynamic behaviors of narrators as they attempted to keep their stories fresh and exciting for their audiences were highlighted.

Crowley's studies in the West Indies earned him a brief teaching appointment at the University College of the West Indies in Port of Spain, Trinidad. During his tenure, he experienced a transformative encounter with the famous Trinidadian celebration of carnival. This annual celebration, an exciting fusion of music, song, dance, theater, costume, and parades, so fascinated Crowley that for the rest of his life he investigated the event not only on various islands in the West Indies but also in Brazil, Bolivia, Senegal, Guinea-Bissau, and Goa. The "carnival volume" of the *Caribbean Quarterly*, which was edited by Crowley in 1956, is still acknowledged as the foundational work for all students of this traditional festival.

Crowley turned his attention to Africa in 1960, when he traveled to what is now Democratic Republic of the Congo to analyze the art of the Chokwe people in the Katanga (now shaba) province. Although a civil war would cut short his planned research, he was still able to conduct many in-depth interviews with a wide range of artisans including potters, carvers, and weavers, and to collect more than eight hundred examples of their work. His field investigations on artists' lives would later be complimented by a long series of studies on contemporary marketing practices for indigenous art in various African countries. Appearing regularly in the magazine *African Arts* from 1970 through 1985, his reports would eventually expand beyond Africa to include the native arts of the Pacific, Southeast Asia, South America, and the circumpolar regions.

Because he was eager to embrace all the world's cultures as his topic of study, Crowley was an energetic traveler whose collective journeys would encircle the globe at least nine times. But within the broad scope of his scholarship, the peoples of Africa and the African diaspora were his foremost concern. He never forgot Herskovits's assertion that racist thinking in the United States and Europe had denied Africans and their descendants recognition for their impressive history of cultural achievements. Crowley set as his chief goal the investigation of African and African American art, in both its visual and verbal modes, to help ensure that their history would not become merely a past denied.

References

Crowley, Daniel J. 1956 *Caribbean Quarterly* (carnival issue), 4, nos. 3 and 4.
——. 1961. Folklore Research in the Congo, *Journal of American Folklore*, 60, no. 294:457–60.
——. 1962. Negro Folklore: An Africanist's View. *Texas Quarterly*, 5:65–71.
——. 1966. *I Could Talk Old Story Good: Creativity in Bahamian Folklore.* Folklore Series, No. 17. Berkeley: University of California Press.

———. 1970. The Contemporary-Traditional Art Market in Africa. *African Arts*, 4:43–9, 80.

———. 1973. Aesthetic Value and Professionalism in African Art: Three Cases from the Katanga Chokwe. In *The Traditional Artist in African Societies*, ed. Warren L. d'Azevedo. Bloomington: Indiana University Press.

———. 1999. The Sacred and the Profane in African and African-Derived Carnivals. *Western Folklore* 58:223–28.

———, ed. 1977. *African Folklore in the New World*. Austin: University of Texas Press.

Tokofsy, Peter, ed. 1999. Studies of Carnival in Memory of Daniel J. Crowley. *Western Folklore*, 58, nos. 3 and 4.

JOHN MICHAL VLACH

See also **Caribbean Verbal Arts; Carnivals and African American Cultures; Central African Folklore: Overview**

D

DANCE: OVERVIEW WITH A FOCUS ON NAMIBIA

Dance in Africa is a social activity, something performed in a specific environment and having purpose and meaning. Both overt and covert meanings and messages are conveyed and confirmed by means of dance performances. Within the immense diversity of dancing in Africa, it is important to remember that much of the continent follows global contemporary dance styles, although some of these are also regional and peculiar to clubs and night spots of Africa. The dances discussed in this entry will, however, focus on dance traditions that form part of the African heritage, but are still contemporary in that they are constantly evolving and adapting to changing circumstances through performance.

The complexity and ephemeral character of dance demands a holistic approach. Looking only at the movements, actions, and style of the dance would convey an impoverished image, as the environment, in combination with the actions and reactions of dancers as well as onlookers, tells us what is important and gives an inkling why.

In much of Africa there are multiple words for dance, but these often have several meanings and associations. Typically, there might be one word that denotes a complete event, including music, texts, meaning, purpose, and the movements. In most of Africa, the dance is not conceptualized separately from the music. The rhythms of the dance dictate the musical rhythm, and the social context provides the need and function. Song, dance, and the playing of musical instruments together form an integrated whole in most African dances. This connectiveness is strengthened and supported by the accessible nature of participation for members of the community, except in the case of dances limited to specific societies or genders. It is common that dances relate to specific events important to the particular society, including rituals such as celebrations, seasonal events, *rites de passage*, and also recreation. For this reason, dance is filled with meaning. Dances are sometimes the public face of rituals or activities that are otherwise private or secret, for example, circumcision (*mukanda* of Mbwela in Angola, *onyando* of Ovazimba in Namibia), initiation, healing, or transformation ceremonies.

Dances reflect and respond to societal structures relating to status, gender, age, clan, and class. Within the dance, individuals negotiate their social place in a bodily statement of performance quality and by applying the societal rules for the dance. Hence, the order in which people may perform, and exclusions from the dance are two of the indications of societal structure. Certain dances, such as *ekofo* dances in the Congo, are limited to those who have been initiated into the *ekofo* society and might involve payments to elders of that society. But dances also provide an important means of communication between people and their ancestral spirits and/or god. For this reason there are a great variety of dances that involve trance or spiritual possession, for example, *n/om* (healing) dances of Ju/hoansi, the *arub* (healing) dance of Damara, and *malombo* of Vhavenda.

Dances in most parts of West, Central, and East Africa are integrally related, if not dictated to by the drum, and might be danced either by all ordinary people who know them, or by "specialists," such as shaman or elite societies, for example, the Masques de Sagesse (Cote d'Ivoire) or Nyau (Malawi). Many of these dances are performed as masks, some of which are quite spectacular, such as the Dogon Great Masks (Mali), the body-concealing masks of Senufo (Cote d'Ivoire), or Nkongela (Zambia), or Mgbula (Nigeria) dancers. Recreational dances are less formal and might also involve large groups of people performing simultaneously. In Namibia, Botswana, and southern Angola, it is more common that individuals, or two or three persons, enter the dance, play, and return to their positions in the circle so that the next might enter and play.

Set choreographic patterns, around which variations are possible, appear everywhere. Other dances, and especially individual dances, allow more space for improvisation, but always within a given cultural framework. This framework dictates the "rules" for the dance in terms of modality (lines, circles, singles, groups, etc.), participation and exclusions, event, place and time, components, and relation to music.

Dances in Africa are often recognized by the body stance from which movements commence and return. This is referred to as "basic earth" position (Mans 1997), the "natural bends" (Dagan 1997), or "dooplé" (Tiérou, 1992). Dancers place their feet flat, about hip-width apart, knees slightly bent, torso inclined forwards (in varying degrees); the head might incline towards the ground or upwards or sideways. This stance promotes balance, allows free movement of shoulders, hips, and pelvis, as well as forward and backward movements on the feet. It also provides a good starting position from which to propel elevations. A further common body element is the inclination to a free articulation of the various parts of the body in relation to one another—whether it involves rotation of the shoulders, hip and pelvic contractions or vibrations, or leg and arm articulations.

Movement components vary diversely across the continent, but again, one of common factors that emerges is the generally close connection between feet and ground and the often downwards (into the earth) motion, described in stamps, swishes, hops, heel and toe thumps, accentuated with downward head and arm motions. These components are closely related to the aesthetics of the culture and often provide a focal point for dancers and onlookers. For example, certain dances involve mainly shoulder movements, with very little foot or arm work. All attention is aimed at these shoulder movements, and a good dancer is judged by the correctness, subtlety, and control displayed in this small area of the body.

Within most African cultures, custom dictates that circles are preferred to straight lines. Thus, the modalities of dance organization also involve circles, even circles within circles. This is confirmed by Tiérou (1992). In some dances, for example, Namibian /gais (Damara), the dancers form a long, snaking line that performs s-shapes around the seated singers. However, lines are not unknown and are seen, for example, in the Namibian harvest dance epera (Kwangali) or Tanzanian mganda military dances.

Meanings and Messages in Namibian Dances

Namibia is a large, arid, and lightly populated country on the southwestern side of Africa, north of South Africa, and south of Angola. It has been at different times a German and British colony, and was later occupied by South Africa. The population is made up of Khoekhoe-speaking people (e.g., Nama, Damara, and Haiom), different San (Bushman) language groups (e.g., Ju/'hoansi, !Kung, Kxoe, Nharo, and Khomani), different Bantu-speaking groups (e.g., Ovaherero, Owambo, Vakwangali, Valozi, Batswana, Hambukushu, Vasambyu, Vagciriku, and Ovazimba), and European-based language groups (e.g., German, Afrikaans, English, and Portuguese). The country is, therefore, linguistically, culturally, and musically diverse. It has only been politically independent since 1990. Because of its occupation by South Africa until the end of twentieth century, very little research was undertaken on Namibian folklore, particularly dance. Four broad categories of Namibian dance are discussed here:

Namibian Dances of Nonritual, Playing Character.
This is the most common genre of dance in the country. Movements and music differ, greatly, however, from area to area. These dances are played for mainly for entertainment, but some are specific to events. For example, okuzana pokati—literally, to play between upper and lower torso—is only performed by Ovazimba mothers during girls' first menstruation ceremony, and uudhano wopankondjelo (Owambo) always contains liberation texts. But the basic dance structure, the rules for playing, and the musical structure remain true to the form in that culture. Some dance-play is gender-specific. While there are several rea-

sons for this, one influence has been the migrant labor practice, taking men away from their communities for extended periods. This has influenced the participation and occurrence of dances and the character of movements. It is only in affected areas that women play the drums and dance with the same "horn"—shaped arms as men (see discussion of meanings below).

Dances with Ritual Connections.
Much of Namibia's dance heritage is based on ritual dances and ritualized movements. Over time, many of these have declined in importance, for example, initiation, circumcision, and healing dances. Where dances have been retained, they have taken on a different character, namely, that of social entertainment. Therefore, many of the dances that were originally ritual dance are now entertainment dance or play. Most of the rituals that involved dance were life-stage transformations, such as the girls' traditional wedding or coming-out ceremony (ohango, efundula) and boys' circumcision (onyando, tcoqma). As these events have become quite rare, some of the songs and dances have been transformed in terms of meaning (not structure) and are now danced on less serious occasions or re-created at cultural festivals.

A more commonly practiced category of ritual dance is a healing, trance, and possession dance. These dances are part of the heritage throughout the country, but take place mainly in the northern and eastern regions. In Bantu-speaking cultures, healings are conducted by one or more specialist healers who are often also known for their dancing skills. In the Caprivi region, such healing dances are performed throughout the night, and include a nondancing period of divination, followed by a curing, which again involves dance. Further south, Ju'hoansi, !Kung, and Kxoe people dance their communal healings very regularly, even fortnightly. In these societies, healers are those who are able to feel and control the rising and boiling of the n/om (the supernatural energy that rises within the body of the healer as s/he enters trance). Several might dance, and, in trance, communicate with the spirit world. This experience can be very painful and dangerous for the shaman, should he or she get lost and not find a way back. For this reason, they are carefully observed in their dance by the singers and assisted where necessary. In the Damara arub healing dance, shamans are given the ability to communicate with spirits in a dream. Each shaman in the dance sings his/her own song for this purpose. A shaman might heap hot ash and burning coals onto his or her lap and head when the pain of possession strikes.

Formalized Movements with Ritual Connections.
Many rituals involve movement actions that are named as a genre, yet are not considered dance by the people. On the birth of a male baby or twins, when a brave deed has been done, when a lion has been killed, or when a daughter has undergone ritual transformation, men might perform high, stylized leaps, dodges, and poses with the waving or throwing of a spear. This is performed with much excitement, and although women may not perform these movements, they ululate in encouragement. In other cases, men perform movements with a military quality. They follow the instructions and movements of a leader, moving forwards or backwards as a group, while responding to his shouted instructions with loud, concerted shouts. They might even wear a military uniform and perform marching movements, but with many African additions that add flavor and humor to the performance.

Formalized Nonritual Movements.

This category includes movements that might or might not be performed with song, but are usually considered work, not music nor dance. When the fields are tilled or the harvest is winnowed in a communal effort, there are songs and synchronized rhythmic movements that ease the task. This is also the case with the shaking of the milk calabash, the pounding of millet in the mortar, or the grinding of ochre or maize on a rock (although the latter would be an individual effort). Songs might have encouraging texts along the lines of, "Let's work together and finish this task," or they might praise family lineage or cattle.

Because of the prevalence of pastoral cultures in Namibia, it is not surprising to find that this occupation is so prominently displayed in dances. In dance-play such as *ondjongo* (Ovahimba), *omutjopa* and *onkankula* (Ovazimba), and *outjina* (Ovaherero), ownership of cattle is celebrated. The songs praise not only family lineage, but also the cattle of one's ancestors, even the place where cattle stay and grow fat. This is concretized in dance movements, where arms are raised to resemble large-horned animals. In certain cases, a man may crouch on all fours, stamping his feet to raise dust, while the woman dances around him with a light touch on his head to "control" him. In *onkankula* (a sitting dance for men), the main aim of the dance is cattle praise. Individual male animals are danced in the owner's arm movements. Its characteristics—herd leadership, a limp, or strangely shaped horns—are imitated in the arm and torso movements, while the feet of the performer stamp and lift high in a regular rhythmic pattern. Everybody claps their hands in the same rhythmic pattern until a new player begins, or somebody interjects with a praise song.

In other dances, song texts do not necessarily talk about cattle, but the messages remain implicit in arm movements. This is the case in *ekoteko* a Ngandjera dance for mothers of girls entering the "traditional wedding" transformation (*ohango*). In days past, it was possible for several hundred girls of marriageable age to participate in this week-long event. The girls completed preliminary rituals, such as being presented to the king or chief of the area, being anointed at the place where they stayed in daytime isolation under supervision of the "master of ceremonies." At night, however, there were gatherings in front of their living area, and here dancing took place in the company of relatives, friends, and prospective husbands. It was here that mothers would perform *ekoteko*, while brides performed other dances. In *ekoteko* two dancers usually take turns, while other participants stand in a circle surrounding them, singing and clapping their hands. Dancers' arms are raised in two horns, and they move around one another in small circles while performing rapid stamping sequences with their feet. These dances are still played today even though *ohango* is now a very rare occurrence.

By contrast, in *epera* (Vakwangali) it is the male dancer's arms that are raised in a metaphor of the bull, symbolizing virility and protection of the women with whom he is dancing. Interestingly, these horn-shaped arm positions are rarely seen in the dances of people whose main economic activity is the raising of goats or pure agriculture.

Among the Ju/'hoansi, animals are danced in a different way. Animals and their spirits form an important part of the Ju/'hoan cosmology, each having a different spirit and power. The eland, in particular, is an animal with immense spiritual meaning, so too *djxàní tcxáí* (the eland dance). It is not surprising, therefore, that Ju/'hoan dances (and their musical repertoires) are assigned animal names, with a few exceptions. Hence there are Eland, Giraffe, Elephant and Springbok musical repertoires among others. These may only be performed in certain groupings, and custom prescribes the repertoires to be performed to ensure a successful hunt or to celebrate a successful hunt. Some are performed for healing purposes (*n/om tzisi*) and others for important life stage events (see Olivier 1997 for musical analyses). In this way, it can also be said that Ju/'hoansi are dancing their animals.

At times, societies transmit educative messages to members. These are captured within the dance itself in the form of mimed actions and explained in the texts of songs. For example, in Namibia's northwest, along the edge of the Namib desert, there is an area with several good fountains surrounded by high mountains. This isolated community embraces several cultures. One of these, the Nama people, performs dances accompanied by music played by a flute ensemble. One of the songs tells the story of a goat thief in the community. The dancers "capture" a flautist, tie a scarf around his neck, and graphically demonstrate how the thief is hanged. There is no doubt about the warning in this portrayal!

On a lighter note, yet strangely disturbing, is the enactment of a leopard in the /gais dance. The dancer leaves the line of dancing men and turns into a leopard, moving on all fours with stealth among the singers. The "hunters" stalk and eventually corner the leopard, sending in a dog (also a dancer) and men with sticks and spears. The killing is explicitly portrayed, yet the rhythm and flow of the dance are never disturbed. Today, a leopard hunt would be fairly uncommon, and children watch this dance with large eyes and nervous excitement.

Conclusion

The above discussion has not covered all Namibian dances. Often, Namibian dances are also meant to convey messages about themes such as family relations, societal mores, praise and thanks, militancy and battle readiness, courtship, and peace and reconciliation. All of these are found in instances of Namibian dance. Clearly, the medium is considered a potent form of communication and an appropriate vehicle for expressing serious themes. In this context, dance is far more than mere entertainment.

References

Asante, K. W., ed. 1996. *African Dance. An Artistic, Historical and Philosophical Inquiry.* Trenton, N.J.: Africa World Press.

Dagan, E. A., ed. 1997. *The Spirit's Dance in Africa. Evolution, Transformation and Continuity in Sub-Sahara.* Montreal: Galerie Amrad African Arts Publications.

Hanna, J. L. 1987. *To Dance is Human: A Theory of Nonverbal Communication.* Chicago: Chicago University Press.

Katz, R., M. Biesele, and V. St. Denis. 1997. *Healing Makes Our Hearts Happy. Spirituality & Cultural Transformation among the Kalahari Ju/'hoansi.* Rochester, Vt.: Inner Traditions.

Mans, M. E. 1997. Namibian Music and Dance as Ngoma in Arts Education. Ph.D. dissertation, University of Natal.

Olivier, E. 1994. Musical Repertoires of the Ju/'hoansi: Identification and Classification. *Proceedings of the Meeting Khoisan Studies: Multidisciplinary Perspectives.* Cologne: Rüdiger Köppe Verlag.

Tiérou, A. 1992. *Dooplé. The Eternal Law of African Dance.*
Choreography and Dance Studies Vol. 2. Switzerland: Harwood
Academic Publishers.

MINETTE MANS

See also **Masks and Masquerades; Music; Southern African Folklore: Overview**

DECORATED VEHICLES (FOCUS ON WESTERN NIGERIA)

Public transport vehicles in Nigeria are frequently decorated with vividly painted designs and written messages. This art form seemed to emerge along with sign painting and popular literature, often referred to as "Onitsha market literature" (cheaply printed novels and chap books offering advice on all aspects of life). While these forms demonstrate an attraction to printed words, they still rely largely on oral tradition and local folklore. These vehicle inscriptions are derived from every conceivable source, from traditional proverbs and adages to advertising slogans and religious phrases. Most of the following were recorded from "mamy wagons" in Lagos in the 1940s and 1950s. Mamy wagons are trucks that have been converted into roofed, but open-sided, buses. The decorative tradition is also employed on minivans and taxis. The sayings are painted on the front board above the cab, along the sides, or on the rear gate.

The themes developed on the sides of trucks, minivans, and taxis—sometimes in large mobile murals, but also in small scenes—are derived from a wide variety of popular culture sources. Films provide familiar heroes and scenes (Chinese "Kung Fu" movies are favorites in Nigeria). Animals are usually ferocious, seldom comical, and never "cute," although sometimes creatures of beauty are used, such as birds. While most of the examples cited here reflect Christian Yoruba traditions, very similar adages citing Allah and seeking his protection (usually written in Arabic) are also seen.

Truck and taxi drivers are engaged in a difficult business and always seek spiritual protection, guidance, and aid. In addition to the prayers and blessings written on the outside of their vehicles, protective amulets and medicines are often hung or hidden in vehicles in order to protect passengers, avoid accidents, prevent police bribery, and reward hard work. The adages and images decorating the outside of the vehicles continue this function. Ogun is honored by many Yoruba drivers; he is the *orisha* of iron.

Decorated vehicles are found worldwide, and include everything from elaborately embellished bicycles to animal carts, skate boards to motorcycles, sixteen-wheel trucks to wheelchairs. The traditions introduced in this entry find intriguing correspondence in Haiti, which has a strong Yoruba heritage; thus, decorated vehicles join other African American artistic expressions.

Here are a few Yoruba examples, grouped loosely by topic:

Religious Instructions and Inspirational Messages

1. Oba Bi Olorun Kosi
   (There is no King like God)
2. Anu Oluwa Po
   (The Compassion of the Lord is Plenty)
3. Oluwa ni oluso-agutan mi
   (The Lord is my Shepherd)
4. Olorunsogo Transport Service
   (God's Created Glory Transport Service)
5. Bami gberu mi, Oluwa
   (Help me to carry my load, oh Lord)
6. Gba oro mi ro, Oluwa Transport
   (Accept my problem and consider it, Oh Lord)
7. Fi mi lokan Ba le.
   (Give me peace of mind)

Metaphorical Inscriptions

1. Leke leke
   (White Egret)
2. Adaba Konko
   (Tiny Dove)
3. Things Fall Apart [title of Chinua Achebe's first novel]
4. Aiyekoto
   (The World Dislikes Truth)

Compliments to Family Members

1. Ola-Iya
   (Success Due to Mother)
2. Ola Egbon
   (Success due to senior brother)
3. Agborondun Bi Iya Kosi
   (No one cares like Mother)

Humorous Expressions

1. Olobe Lo Loko
   (The woman who owns the soup pot owns the husband)
2. Man Must Whack!
   (We humans must strive to eat) [pidgin English expression]
3. To Be a Man Is Not Easy [a popular Igbo saying]

References

Cosentino, Donald. 1988. Divine Horsepower. *African Arts* 21:3.
Lawunyi, Olatunde Bayo. 1977. The World of the Yoruba Taxi Driver. In *Readings in African Popular Culture*, ed. Karin Barber, pp. 146–51. Bloomington: Indiana University Press.
Pritchett, Jack. 1979. Nigerian Truck Art. *African Arts* 12, no. 2: 27–31.
Thompson, Robert Farris. 1996. Tap-Tap, Fula-Fula, Kia-Kia: The Haitian Bus in Atlantic Perspective. *African Arts* 29:2.

AKINSOLA AKIWOWO

See also **Popular Culture**

DEMOCRATIC REPUBLIC OF CONGO (FORMERLY REPUBLIC OF ZAIRE)

Located in Central Africa, Democratic Republic of Congo is an equatorial country bordered by Angola, Zambia, Tanzania, Burundi, Rwanda, Uganda, Sudan, Central African Republic, and Congo. One of the largest nations in Africa at 905,365 square miles, it encompasses most of the huge Congo River basin, along with a small stretch of land on the Atlantic Ocean at the mouth of the Congo River. Of the nation's approximately 51.7 million people, most are of the Bantu ethnic group, although there are more than two hundred other African groups in the country. There are also at least 200,000 refugees from neighboring countries. The major languages spoken are French (the official language) and four national languages: Kiswahili, Tshiluba, Kikongo, and Lingala. Seventy percent of the population is Christian (with 22 million Roman Catholics and 13 million Protestants), 20 percent practice traditional indigenous religions, and 10 percent are Muslim. Kinshasha, the country's capital, is also its largest city with 4.7 million inhabitants.

On June 30, 1960, the former Zaire (named Congo until 1971, then Zaire until 1997, when it was renamed the Democratic Republic of Congo) gained its independence from Belgium after fifty-four years of colonial rule. In the late nineteenth century, the territory of the former Zaire was dominated by the Belgian King Leopold. During Leopold's reign in the area, thousands of Africans were killed, as he demolished entire villages in his quests for wealth. When the area was colonized by Belgium in 1908, the social situation improved from that of Leopold's time, but abuse of the indigenous population did not entirely cease. After mounting unrest, Belgium gave the former Zaire its independence in 1960. The years following independence were unstable, and civil war, economic decline, and social strife have afflicted the nation. The country never seemed to recover from the murder of its first real leader, Patrice Lamumba, who is still remembered throughout Africa. In 1965 Joseph Desire Mobutu seized power of the nation and changed it to a one-party state. Among the most corrupt of African leaders, Mobutu's vast personal wealth was greater than his country's debt. Amidst economic and social turmoil, Mobutu's power lasted until 1997 when he was forced into exile, where he died of cancer within four months. Laurent-Desire Kabila, the new head of state, was killed and his son became president in 2001. As of 1997, the government has promised its nation a new constitution, but this had yet to be accomplished in the early years of the new century. The Democratic Republic of Congo's future remained uncertain as civil strife continued.

Democratic Republic of Congo's natural resources include copper, cobalt, zinc, diamonds, manganese, tin, gold, bauxite, rare metals, iron, coal, hydroelectric potential, and timber. Agricultural production revolves around coffee, palm oil, rubber, tea, cotton, cocoa, manioc, bananas, plantains, corn, rice, and sugar. Principle industries and sources of revenue include mineral mining, consumer products, food processing, and cement. Adult literacy is 77 percent.

Kinshasha, the nation's capital, has been described as the dance and music capital of Africa. Musicians such as Rochereau Tabu Ley, Papa Wemba, Pablo Lubidika, and Sandoka have popularized *souskous*, or the "Congo rumba" style of music, which has become internationally renowned. In terms of traditional African arts, the Congo is the source of some of the most spectacular sculptures and masks in the world's museums.

JENNIFER JOYCE

DIALOGIC PERFORMANCES: CALL-AND-RESPONSE IN AFRICAN NARRATING

In African performances, the actors and audience are co-performers (Fretz 1994; Brenneis 1986). Many types of performers—dancers and diviners, storytellers, and singers—depend on an actively responsive audience to excel. In fact, many performances cannot begin without an appreciative group of responders. Kapchan, in her study of spectacles occurring in Moroccan markets, points out that the audience defines the *halqa*, the "space of play and leisure." The performer must "draw out and elaborate the introduction to his spiel until a large enough audience has been lured to constitute a circle" (1996, 38). The encircling audience and the performer together create the dialogic performance. In many African narrative performances, the audience creates the performance as much as the narrator does. Indeed, the Chokwe say that without the periodic "answering" (*kutahziya*) from an active audience, a performance cannot be fully realized and certainly cannot excel.

Audience participation has been noted from the earliest scholarship, though listener comments have not always been acknowledged in the documentation of narratives texts. Only the more formalized exchanges between narrator and listeners, which appeared to be intrinsic to the narrative composition, were included. Africanists call these interactive patterns of songs and chants, "call-and-response." Ruth Finnegan, in her classic study, *Oral Literature in Africa*, writes:

> These songs fulfill various functions in the narrative. They often mark the structure of the story in a clear and attractive way. Thus, if the hero is presented as going through a series of tests or adventures, the parallel presentation of episode after episode is often cut into by the singing of a song by the narrator and audience. . . . The songs also provide a formalized means for audience participation. The common pattern is for the words of the song, whether familiar or new, to be introduced by the narrator, who then acts as leader and soloist while the audience provide the chorus. (1977, 386)

The singing thus creates a pleasing antiphonal sound which often builds in intensity and volume as the performance progresses (Fretz 1995).

Though dialogues between narrator and listeners distinctively enhance most African performances, they have only come into the limelight of scholarship since the 1970s. Whereas earlier researchers tended to view oral narratives as entities transmitted by rote from person to person, more recent scholars view storytelling as a creative act, as collaboration between a narrator and audience. Such a shift in the model of storytelling, from storytelling as object transmission to narrating as a creative process, has been accompanied by a shift in research concerns (Georges 1969, 1976). In other words, performance studies moved research on

African narration away from collections of translated tales, often depicting the stories as simple, flat, didactic renditions (Okpewho 1992; Finnegan 1970) to more fully realized documentations of lively performances. Isidore Okpewho, a Nigerian scholar noted for his writings about African oral literature, claims that "the study of performance has become one of the most exciting and rewarding developments in the study of oral literature in recent years" (1992, 42). He explains that seminal studies in the 1970s, such as research by J. P. Clark (1977) and Harold Scheub (1975), initiated attention not only to the performer's dramatization of events, but also to audience comments and questions and to the narrator's reactions to listeners' participation. In fact, Okpewho highlights "the warm presence of an audience" as the distinctive mark of African oral literature:

> It is therefore in the study of performance that we are able to see the essential character of oral literature as distinct from written literature, that is, as an art form created in the warm presence of an audience as against the cold privacy of the written work. (1992, 42)

It is not surprising, then, that interactions between performer and audience characterize African narration. However, if one scans the printed works on African tales from the 1900s to the 1970s, and even some publications since then, one hardly could find this key hallmark—audience presence and participation. Too often, the audience is absent or marginalized to introductory headnotes or explanatory footnotes. When present, the audience is remarkably wise, voicing only on-topic remarks appropriate to the narrative and interjecting no interruptive or distractive comments! One wonders if these are real audiences or if, perhaps, the researcher edited with a heavy hand. Unfortunately, the deletion of audience participation also undercuts the reader's appreciation for the artistry of the narrator. For, if one cannot hear the comments made by the restless audience, one cannot admire the skillful wordplay when the performer weaves a listener's comment into the story. Sometimes the interaction between narrator, as one character, and audience member, as another, might be critical to the reader's interpretation of ensuing actions (Fretz 1987). Indeed, when listener comments disappear from the published text, the performance loses some of its dynamic artistry and seems flat and pale. As Ruth Finnegan so aptly explains,

> In all this the participation of the audience is essential. It is common for members of it to be expected to make verbal contributions—spontaneous exclamation, actual questions, echoing of the speaker's words, emotional reaction to the development of yet another parallel and repetitious episode. Further, the audience contributes the choruses of the songs so often introduced into the narration, and without which, in many cases, the stories would be only a bare framework of words. (1976/1970, 385)

The excision of audience participation, in performances distinctive for their dialogic nature, can be attributed to several sources. Some scholars admit, off the record, to editing out irrelevant audience comments and rationalize that participants mentally do the same. Others point out that the Western print-dominated conceptions of narrative, superimposed on oral storytelling, keep researchers from hearing and seeing the full performance. Usually, such critiques pinpoint the errors of earlier, biased scholarship and of previous, poorly translated documents (Okpewho 1992; Finnegan 1970), but rarely assess the minimal presence of audience in some current publications. In addition, writers are influenced by disciplinary agendas, and thus, they foreground certain features and circumscribe or overlook others. Finally, all too often, the researchers' language skills and recording equipment limit what they can perceive, translate, and present in print (Finnegan 1970; Okpewho 1992). Fortunately, many African scholars, including African poets, novelists, and playwrights, study their own oral traditions and contribute to the growing body of knowledge about oral performances (J. P. Clark 1977; K. Yankah 1995).

Recent research across the disciplines, however, more clearly and consistently displays the dialogic nature of oral performances. Not only do more researchers intensively study indigenous languages as well as work with local assistants, but they often include both languages in the final texts (when editors permit). The advances of technological equipment (tape recorders, video and movie cameras) enable scholars to document and analyze more features of performance, such as the performance situation and the nonverbal communication of facial expression, tone of voice, and gesture. Though perhaps inadvertently, the scrutiny of technologically advanced cameras or stereo recordings makes artificially staged audiences awkwardly visible and muted or silenced listeners easily heard. Clearly, the ever-increasing attention to performances in context (cf., Duranti and Goodwin 1992) has contributed to a better understanding of performer–audience interaction. Thus, the discussion, once restricted to easily recognized, formulaic, call-and-response patterns in songs and chants, has expanded to a more comprehensive exploration of dialogic performance.

An analysis of specific narrative moments, among various ethnic groups in Africa, reveals the types of narrator–listener exchanges and allows us to envision (and hear) the wide range of narrator–audience exchanges. Such dialogues vary extensively in three fundamental ways:

First, formal patterns of generic shape, which are the expectations for performances in a particular genre, prefigure the extent and type of audience response. Many African narrative performances open with a lively exchange between narrator and audience that immediately draws the listeners into the story world. For example, among the Haya in Tanzania, narrators say, "*Nkaiaj nabona*" ("I came and I saw"), and the audience responds, "*Bona tulole*" ("See so that we may see"). Peter Seitel explains that "the expression appears as 'See so that we may see' . . . to indicate the active role members of the audience play in a successful performance" (1980, 28).

Second, informal patterns of a narrator–audience's interactive style, which, though they develop at the outset of narrating, tend to shape the patterns emerging throughout the performance. These patterns include metanarrative commentary such as—praise, blame, or inattention—which the listeners offer, based on their aesthetic expectations for performance quality; of course, these critiques vary according to occasion and identity of the narrator. For example, Donald Cosentino compares two renditions of a similar story. When the listeners hear the second version, they are dissatisfied because they had certain expectations for how the images should unfold. Thus, the audience joins in and helps to create the tale.

Both performers employed the same set of surface elements and the same technique of narrative construction.

But Sally was hastier than Kalilu. She obviously kept the picture of the death's head in her mind, but failed to objectify it sufficiently for her audience. She did not re-create with her words and gestures a picture equivalent to the one etched in their minds, and so, in exasperation, they undertook that re-creation themselves:

SALLY: So too for her now that grave sounded: *jen, jen, jen, jen, jen, jen*. Now she saw only the head of that child of hers, and *kpu*, she grabbed the head tightly. However, they had said: a person must not touch their heads. When she grabbed her child's head, then a plain skull was all that remained in her hands.
AUDIENCE: Yes. Then she went and she stood . . .
SALLY: I saw the inside of those things long ago. That was a plain skull with which she frightened the children.
AUDIENCE: What did they do then?
SALLY: She said, "Eat my daughter's skull!"
AUDIENCE 1: Is it finished?
AUDIENCE 2: Don't wait any more.
AUDIENCE 3: She said that what little she had heard long ago, she had spoken.

Sally's performance plainly frustrated her audience. She left incomplete the verbal reconstruction of the picture of the mother's death's head which conjured in their minds the polar image she was trying to develop. (Cosentino 1982, 53–4)

Not only do audiences spontaneously correct and contribute to the performance, they also might praise or criticize the narrator's singing and storytelling. In one instance among the Chokwe of Congo, someone in the audience—thrilled by the narrator's performance—called out: "Mama! What a joy! What a story! Listen to that song!" (Fretz 1987, 172). However, during another moment that same evening, an audience member, bored with a performance, tells the narrator to end quickly: "Really. This story isn't very good. Speak up [hurry], so you can finish it" (Fretz 1987, 189).

Finally, contextual asides and interruptions include those exchanges between narrator and audience that respond to a situational feature such as the sound of a dog barking, the call of a bird, or someone's footsteps. Isidore Okpewho discusses the narrator's response to such moments and notes that performers often weave such contextual features into their stories; he calls such inclusions "ring asides" (Okpewho 1992). But audience members also might draw the group's attention toward external stimuli, either distracting them from the performance or, through a comment, intertwining the immediate present into the story's action.

In conclusion, audiences in many parts of Africa respond throughout storytelling performances. Actively engaged listeners participate with commentary, questions, and interjections. They even directly address the characters in the story and, as it were, enter into a dramatic dialogue with them. Audiences especially enjoy those performances that engage them and that directly invite, even depend on, their participation. In turn, performers feel gratified by an audience that answers. The call-and-response patterns between narrator and audience, whether formal or informal, are intrinsic to African performances throughout Africa.

Not only narrating but also many other types of African performances depend on the dialogic back-and-forth between performer and audience. Increasingly, scholars document the exchanges between all participants in a performance and, thus, recognize the centrality of the audience to the spectacle. For example, Chernoff highlights the interplay not only of drummers but also of drummers with the audience (Chernoff 1979). Masqueraders running through a village certainly expect a responsive audience—some who cheer and others who run away. Even diviners depend on the responses of clients and often play to a wider circle of participants who watch and comment on the proceedings (Peek 1991). In fact, the formal patterns of call-and-response sets, though more easily documented by early scholars, should be seen as a part of persvasive dialogic pattern. Perhaps the term *coperformance* best characterizes the dialogic relationship between participants in most African performances.

References

Clark, J. P. 1977. *The Ozidi Saga*. Ibadan: Ibadan University Press.
Chernoff, John Miller. 1979. *African Rhythm and African Sensibility: Aesthetics and Social Action in African Musical Idioms*. Chicago: University of Chicago Press.
Cosentino, Donald. 1982. *Defiant Maids and Stubborn Farmers: Tradition and Invention in Mende Story Performance*. Cambridge: Cambridge University Press.
Ben-Amos, Dan. 1976. Analytical Categories and Ethnic Genres. In *Folklore Genres*, ed. Dan Ben-Amos. Austin: University of Texas Press.
Bauman, Richard. 1986. *Story, Performances, and Event: Contextual Studies of Oral Narrative*. Cambridge: Cambridge University Press.
Drewal, Margaret Thompson. 1991. The State of Research on Performance in Africa. *African Studies Review* 34, no. 3:1–64.
Finnegan, Ruth. 1970. *Oral Literature in Africa*. Oxford: Clarendon Press.
Fretz, Rachel. 1987. Storytelling Among the Chokwe of Zaire: Narrating Skill and Listener Responses. Ph.D. dissertation, UCLA.
———. 1994. Through Ambiguous Tales: Women's Voices in Chokwe Storytelling. *Oral Tradition* 9:230–50.
———. 1995. Answering in Song: Listeners' Responses in *Yishima* Performances. *Western Folklore*.
Georges, Robert A. 1969. Toward an Understanding of Storytelling Events. *Journal of American Folklore* 82:313–28.
———. 1976. From Folktale Research to the Study of Narrating. *Folk Narrative Research: Some Papers Presented at the VI Conference of the International Society of Folk Narrative Research, Studia Fennica* 20:159–68.
Haring, Lee. 1994. Introduction. *Oral Tradition* 9.
Kapchan, Deborah. 1996. *Gender on the Market: Moroccan Women and the Revoicing of Tradition*. Philadelphia: University of Pennsylvania Press.
Okpewho, Isidore. 1992. *African Oral Literature: Backgrounds, Character, and Continuity*. Bloomington: Indiana University Press.
Scheub, Harold. 1975. *The Xhosa Ntsomi*. Oxford: Clarendon Press.
Seitel, Peter. 1980. *See So That We May See: Performances and Interpretations of Traditional Tales from Tanzania*. Bloomington: Indiana University Press.
Yankah, Kwesi. 1995. *Speaking for the Chief: Okyeame and the Politics of Akan Royal Oratory*. Bloomington: Indiana University Press.

RACHEL I. FRETZ

See also **Central African Folklore; Gesture in African Oral Narrative; Performance in Africa**

DIASPORA: AFRICAN COMMUNITIES IN THE UNITED KINGDOM

It has been rightly claimed that there is evidence, both archaeological and literary, to support the theory that Africans were present in Roman-era Britain. Edwards (1990, 2), writes, "It will be a nice irony against racist opinion if it could be demonstrated that African communities were settled in England before the English invaders arrived from Europe centuries later." Killingray (1994, 2–3) has demonstrated that, as far back as the Middle Ages, a small number of Africans from North Africa traveled the British sea routes. From about the sixteenth century onward, Europe's engagement in the trans-Atlantic slave trade brought a number of Africans to Britain. Many of the adults were engaged in servile roles as manual laborers or seamen. The children were often exotic, aristocratic "pets." At this time, although the majority of the people of African origin lived in the major slaving ports of London, Liverpool, and Bristol, they were to be found all over the country.

There are two major groups of people of African descent living in the United Kingdom at the beginning of the twenty-first century. Although it is difficult to distinguish one group from the other simply by appearance, the difference becomes more evident with closer observation. The first group is that of the African people from the continent of Africa and their descendants, and the second is African-Caribbean people and their descendants. The ancestors of the vast majority of African-Caribbean people were originally from Africa, forcefully separated from the continent for over four hundred years during the trans-Atlantic slave trade. The African people in this group came to live in the United Kingdom from the Caribbean Islands.

Many African people came to the United Kingdom to study. From the sixteenth century onward, European traders recognized that some formal education improved the service provided by the African slaves to their European masters. By the eighteenth century, a number of African chiefs and traders recognized the value of literacy and numeracy and began to entrust their European trading partners with the education of their children in the United Kingdom. It has been reported that between fifty and seventy African children were at school in Liverpool in 1794 (Killingray 1994, 7). From the nineteenth century onward, education was to be a major impetus for Africans to go to the United Kingdom.

In the nineteenth century, and the earlier part of the twentieth century, Africans arrived in the United Kingdom with the goal of obtaining their academic and/or professional qualifications, after which they would eturn to their countries of origin. They had to leave friends and families behind and endure years of separation and isolation while studying in Britain. Many who studied in the Uninted Kingdom later became active in the independence movements of their respective countries. Many organizations that later became political African parties were formed in United Kingdom before the 1960s. Two examples of such political organizations are the British Somali Society, formed in the mid-1930s, and the Somali Youth League, formed in the 1940s. There was also the Egbe Omo Oduduwa, a Yoruba cultural organization, formed by Chief Obafemi Awolowo and fellow students in London in 1946, which, two years later, became a political party in Nigeria. Prominent African political figures such as Jomo Kenyatta, Kwame Nkrumah, Julius Nyerere, and many lesser-known medical, intellectual, military, and administrative leaders received their education in the United Kingdom.

Until about the 1980s, when the economic situations in many African countries were turning from bad to worse, and the Structural Adjustment Programme was put in place, the general tendency for the majority of African people who came to study in the United Kingdom was to complete their studies and then return to Africa. Most Africans who took up permanent residency in the United Kingdom before the 1980s had various reasons apart from political and economic instabilities in their home countries. Within the Yoruba community, and among many Nigerian communities in London, for example, it was generally believed that only those who failed to succeed in their chosen academic and/or professional pursuits, and were, as a result, ashamed of their failure, would choose to remain in the United Kingdom. The type of employment and the quality of life awaiting them in Nigeria was superior to that which they could secure in the United Kingdom.

Since the 1980s, the situation has been changing, and the number of Africans seeking permanent residence in the United Kingdom has increased tremendously. Many Africans who qualified as British citizens in the 1960s, but had returned to Africa when economic and political instabilities erupted there, came back to live in the United Kingdom. For similar reasons, the vast majority of children born in the United Kingdom before January 1983, while their parents were studying, returned to live in the United Kingdom. These children, born at a time when British citizenship was easily acquired by a child at birth, are now adults in their twenties and thirties They had returned with their parents to live and receive their education in Africa, but as a result of emerging economic and political crises in many African countries, found their way back to the United Kingdom. This situation is particularly true of Nigerians and Ghanaians, but similar cases may be found within the Gambian, South African, Somalian, Ugandan, Kenyan, Tanzanian, and Ethiopian communities.

This situation has given rise to vibrant African communities, where people are no longer in a hurry to complete their studies and return to Africa. The people of the African communities are developing a "settler mentality." This is evident in the number of African people owning, rather than renting, their properties. There has also been a considerable increase in the number of Africans owning their own businesses in the larger cities of London, Manchester, Liverpool, and Birmingham. In London, for example, the "corner shop" business selling African food was once dominated by Indian and Pakistani businessmen. However, in many parts of London, Nigerians and Ghanaians have entered the field. This is clearly observable in Finsbury Park (North London), Hackney (East London), Peckham (Southeast London), and Brixton (Southwest London).

The fact that those who are permanently resident have developed a "settler mentality" has started to make an impact on other aspects of their lives. For example, since the late 1980s, it has been relatively easy to find Africans who are employed as security officers, taxi cab drivers, and cleaners, but are highly qualified, often holding advanced degrees. Those once employed as attendants or till operators in the supermarkets, have established businesses of their own in the food industry, importing food items from their countries of origin and distributing to a network of small businesses throughout the United Kingdom. Those who were once employed as security officers established their own security companies. Some who had been employed by the local councils to manage council estates started their own estate management businesses. They bought flats and houses, rented them out, and managed other people's properties for them. Pharmacists, exploited for years in Indian and Pakistani privately owned pharmacy businesses, freed themselves from such ill treatment by establishing their own pharmacies. These are some of the success stories.

One kind of business where Somalis became very prominent in London in the 1990s was the cybercafe, especially in North London. African businesses were usually situated where a large concentration of African resided, because they are seen as the first and most powerful market for the businesses of African business people. This explains why the majority of African businesses are concentrated in North London, East London, and South East London. A similar trend was observable in areas where there was a concentration of Africans in Liverpool, Birmingham, and Manchester. Significantly among Nigerians and Ghanaians, and less prominently among Kenyans and Sierra Leoneans, there has been the establishment of vibrant, African-led Pentecostal and Evangelical churches in the United Kingdom. One such church is the Kingsway International Christian Centre (KICC) based in Hackney, East London. It was founded by Pastor Matthew Ashimolowo, a Nigerian, and said to be one of the fastest growing churches in the United Kingdom, at the turn of the century, with a membership of about 6,000.

African communities in Britain are easily identified by their clothing. One can easily identify Nigerians from the different parts of that country by their manner of dress on Sundays (for Christians) and on Fridays (for Muslims). Ghanaians, Somalis, Ethiopians, Kenyans, Tanzanians, and Ethiopians can all be identified by the way they choose to present themselves on special occasions, such as the birth of a baby, marked in some communities by a naming ceremony, and in others by a party. Weddings are elaborate ceremonies in African communities and are occasions for presenting oneself in the best, most colorful dress. There are also housewarming and birthday parties. Depending on the means of the host, these parties are often lavish, with invitations extended to many people and generous provisions of food and drink for all who attend.

As a result of economic and political crises in many African countries, an increasing number of Africans want to work and to live in the United Kingdom, partly because of an inaccurate impression that it is easy to make money there. The devaluation of many national currencies in African nations makes the situation worse. At the same time as people are experiencing hardship in Africa, and becoming more and more desperate to emigrate to the United Kingdom, the borders in Europe are becoming harder to penetrate. Apart from people fleeing the trauma of war in Angola, the Democratic Republic of Congo, and Sierra Leone, the general belief is that people seeking entry into the United Kingdom are economic refugees. There is now a large number of asylum seekers in many British detention centers, and many cases involving Africans are pending in British courts,

as an increasing number of young Africans seek opportunities to work and live in the United Kingdom. Unless the political and economic living conditions in African countries improve, it is likely that the number of Africans seeking a better life in the United Kingdom will continue to increase.

References

Adi, Hakim. 1998. *West Africans in Britain 1900–1960: Nationalism, Pan-Africanism and Communism*. London: Lawrence & Wishart.

Edwards, Paul. 1990. *The Early African Presence in the British Isles*. Occasional Papers, No. 26. Edinburgh: Centre of African Studies, University of Edinburgh.

Killingray, David, ed. 1994. *Africans in Britain*. Ilford, Essex, UK: Franck Cass and Company Limited.

Oyètádé, B. Akíntúndé. 1993. The Yoruba Community in London. *African Languages and Cultures* 6, no. 1:69–92.

B. AKÍNTÚNDÉ OYÈTÁDÉ

DIASPORA: AFRICAN COMMUNITIES IN THE UNITED STATES

The decades since 1960 (marking the beginning of the postcolonial era in Africa) have seen the acceleration of African immigrant populations settling in Europe and in the United States and the emergence of new African diaspora communities and transnational expressive culture.

African Transnational Migration

The diasporas of the seventeenth to the nineteenth centuries were forcibly created by the slave trade, when Africans were separated from their communities of origin and settled throughout the American continents, against their wills, as a captive labor force. In more recent times, impelled by the forces of globalization, Africans have been the agents of their own migration to Europe and North America. The formation of newer diasporas has taken place as people born on the African continent have arrived in the United States in search of political asylum, economic survival, and educational opportunities. In the year 2000, there were over 881,300 immigrants from the African continent living in the United States. Immigration of Africans to the United States is part of a larger and more complex contemporary global phenomenon. Older diasporic communities tended to be characterized by more or less permanent settlement and ever-diminished contact with home communities, accompanied by a paradoxical longing for return to an idealized homeland. Newer patterns of economic and educational immigration are facilitated by the availability of low-cost, high-quality information exchange through the Internet, as well as more accessible travel options.

Established and Emerging Diaspora Communities

The expressive culture of new African diasporic communities bears both similarities and differences to the older communities of African descendants in North America. In both instances, there are cultural continuities in traditions rooted in the continent of Africa and traditions practiced in the the United States.

For example, West African traditions related to masking and festival were continued wherever possible, from the period of captivity through the present, in African diasporic communities from Brazil, to Trinidad, to New Orleans. The aesthetics of carnival and festival have permutated into diverse expressions, but some of the core vocabularies of dance, the visual aesthetics of dress and movement, and the relationship of masking to social and sacred expressions have remained close to their African roots. Traditions in the preparation of akara, or black-eye peas fritters, were passed down with and revitalized. For several generations, braids were worn only by very young girls and very old women in African American communities. In the 1970s, the braiding tradition in the United States was revitalized and even augmented as an art form within the corpus of African American hairstyling by West African women coming from Senegal, the Gambia, and Mali, who brought a high level of artistry, skills, and specialized knowledge of braiding to the United States. The context of practice changed, or was augmented, from an activity practiced almost exclusively in the home, to a major source of wealth and as a highly elaborated part of African American body arts.

There is significant regional diversity within older diaspora African American populations of the United States, for example, zydeco music in New Orleans and go-go music in Washington, D.C. But the cultural traditions of Africans of the new diasporas are differentiated much more by the home communities they come from and remain in contact with on the African continent. Examples are rites-of-passage celebrations of the All Ngwa society of Igbo-speaking Nigerians and naming ceremonies among Yoruba-speaking Nigerians, both of which take place in cities throughout the United States.

African Immigrant Cultural Diversity and Geographical Distribution

African-born immigrants in the United States are a diverse group and cannot be construed as one community. Arriving, as they do, with widely diverse linguistic, regional, religious, ethnic, and political affiliations, they also migrate under different circumstances. These influences on the course of individual lives and fortunes also shape the cultural and ethnic communities immigrants create. With such a wide range of cultural communities and references on which to draw, the scope of new African diaspora culture is equally broad. Nigerians, Ethiopians, Somalis, and Egyptians constitute the largest documented immigrant populations in the United States. The Cape Verdean communities, based mainly in New England, are the oldest post-slavery/new diaspora communities. The expressive culture of African immigrants is equally broad. African community enclaves have emerged in large cities with substantial, already established populations of African descent. New York, Washington, D.C., Oakland, California, the twin cities of Minneapolis and St. Paul, Houston, Atlanta, and Chicago have been primary sites of settlement.

Forms of African Immigrant Expressive Culture

First-generation, new diaspora immigrants often choose to draw on the community expressive culture of their homelands to shape their group identities in the host country. Through actively cre-

ating and re-creating practicing and performing traditions from home, both among community members and in public settings, they use tradition as a tool to build community. They emphasize aspects of culture that serve them in this effort while choosing to discard other aspects that do not fit the context of the host country. For example, in Somalia, women within a clan take responsibility for preparing young kinswomen for marriage. The preparations include composing poetry called *buranbur* that they recite and dance at all female gatherings. Many of the women have come to the United States as refugees in the wake of the civil wars between clans in Somalia. In several U.S. cities, women have taken the initiative to use the structure of this poetry to sing about their lives in exile, and the social form of the *buranbur* wedding celebrations serves to bring the clans together so that women representing several clans (that may be antagonists in the home country) work together to plan and participate in wedding festivities for each of their daughters.

The types of expressive culture that are more likely to prove resilient and adaptable are often, but not exclusively, those that are portable (fit in a suitcase), for which materials or satisfactory substitutions are readily available. These traditions may be easily reproducible in a new environment. Equally important criteria for the continuity of expressive culture are the presence of skilled practitioners and the iconic value and meaning of traditions to the lives and the needs of immigrants. Such culture is hardly ever carried over unchanged, but is newly created according to a culturally hybrid aesthetic.

First-generation African immigrants actively and consciously attempt to re-create culture in a new place with the goal of maintaining cultural connections between their relatives in Africa, themselves, and their American-born children. Traditional foodways are prepared for family meals and for any number of group events (such as independence celebrations). Parents initiate and fund cultural weekend schools and camps and send their children home for school vacations or even to attend school and live with relatives.

As a Nigerian student, Adesola Adeola, notes, the current American emphasis on cultural diversity and ethnic self-assertion may have encouraged the proliferation of ethnic, as opposed to national, community cultural organizations. The practice of body arts, from the artful application of henna, to traditional tailoring, to social dressing, are used as colorful signifiers of ethnic identity. In addition to pan-Nigerian organizations in the United States, there are many ethnic Nigerian community organizations. Examples with branches throughout the United States are the Egbe Isokan Yoruba organization promoting Yoruba culture; Zumunta, a Hausa organization; and Akwa-Ibom, one of several regional Nigerian organizations. The establishment of these organizations, patterned after town associations on the continent, is part of the creative agency of recent African émigrés and provides an incubator for African new diaspora cultural creativity.

New diasporic culture does not merely consist of recontextualized versions of homeland culture. It is a hybrid, regenerated, phoenix-like, from the traditional culture that preceded it. Expressive traditions, as articulated in the host country, affect and transform the culture back home. They affect creative processes, products, and available technologies. Traditions and cultural processes now travel across the Atlantic and back home again, leaving their influence felt in the cities in which African immigrants settle. Ideas, processes, and expressions are in constant contemporary circulation and are simultaneously rooted in traditions that are centuries old.

References

Apraku, Kofi. 1994. *African Émigrés in the United States: A Missing Link in Africa's Social and Economic Development.* New York: Praeger.

Arthur, John A. 2001. *Invisible Sojourners: African Immigrant Diaspora in the United States.* New York: Praeger.

Ashabranner, Brent, and Jennifer Ashabranner. 1999. *The New African Americans.* Linnet.

N'Diaye, Diana Baird. 1997. Community Building and Bridging: African Immigrant Folklife in Washington, D.C.

Stoller, Paul. 1999. *Jaguar: A Story of Africans in America.* Chicago: University of Chicago Press.

Swigart, Leigh. 2001. *Extended Lives: The African Immigrant Experience in Philadelphia.* Philadelphia: The Balch Institute.

Wamba, Phillipe E. 2000. *Kinship: A Family's Journey in Africa and America.* New York: Plume.

DIANA BAIRD N'DIAYE

See also **Women's Expressive Culture in Africa**

DIASPORA: AFRICAN TRADITIONS IN BRAZIL

Brazilian folklore and culture is permeated by African influences. Afro-Brazilian populations were imported as slaves from a diversity of African regions, from the sixteenth century through the first half of the nineteenth century. The violence of slavery, the absorption of white Portuguese cultural values, and the Afro-Brazilian population's ability for adaptation all supported the formation of a unique culture. Afro-Brazilian folklore is the expression of the resistance and the survival of a culture oppressed by centuries of slavery and social exclusion. What may be defined as cultural resistance is also felt as amalgam, syncretism, compromise, acculturation. Therefore, we may say that this culture can no longer be called African, but Afro-Brazilian. Such a phenomenon also means that the Afro-Brazilian culture is also rich with Portuguese, European, and Native Brazilian expressions.

Language

The Afro-Brazilian influence on Brazilian Portuguese linguistics is very intense. This aspect is not so evident in the formal language, but it is fundamental in the popular language. The people's speech is full of African traces. It occurs in the transformation of words with difficult elocution, such as consonant groups (e.g., *negro* becomes *nego*) and in stronger aphereses (tá = estar, ôce = vôce, cabá = acabar, Bastião = Sebastião). There is also the loss of final sounds in words ending in "l" and "r" (general = genera, cafezal = cafezá, esquecer = esquecê). Also very common are the reduction of "ei" and "ou" diphthong in popular speech (cheiro = chêro, peixe = pêxe, lavoura = lavôra, couve = côve). In addition to these aspects, there is the expressive insertion of African vocabulary in Brazilian Portuguese. Words such as *anau* (dough made with corn meal), *atabaque* (drum cylinder), *babalorixa* (medicine man / priest), *banguela* (person without teeth), *banze* (noise / disorder), *batuque* (percussion), *bengala* (stick), *bunda* (derriere), *cachaça* (alcoholic beverage), *caçula* (the youngest son), *camundonpo* (mouse), *fulo* (angry person), and *mulambo* (rag / a tattered suit), are extremely common in the Brazilian vocabulary. The singing and soft speech of the people from Bahia is deeply African; the sonority is very characteristic of the Yoruba idiom.

In the area of religion, a great number of African words were preserved. This phenomenon is largely restricted to the Candomblé communities, in which the African languages were preserved in a very impressive way. Thus, in Candomblé houses, one can find multiple re-creations regarding the lexicon and semantics, a result of its formation from many distinct linguistic variants and from many unique semiological aspects. These linguistic levels appear as follows: 1) in the popular Portuguese spoken in the Candomblé houses, with recurrent references to regional terms, to popular words, and to vulgar terms, mainly used in profane situations; 2) in the Portuguese language with strong semantic presence of expressions in Yoruba, Ewe-Fon, and Kimbundu—especially used in conversations among neophytes, as an introduction to a ritual language and in the community's daily life (either in profane activities or in the preparation of more complex rituals); 3) in the Portuguese language spoken by experienced members, in which Yoruba, Ewe-Fon, and Kimbundu terms are predominant. The use of more African ways of speaking is seen as the reaffirmation of ancient people and as a way of excluding the neophytes from the conversations, since they do not yet have access to the rituals' deeper details; 4) in the exclusive use of Yoruba, Ewe-Fon, and Kimbundu as something restricted to the cult's more complex moments, in which the gods are evoked (Orixas, Voduns, and Inquices) through singing, prayers, and evocations.

Within this cultural universe, there is the coexistence of expressions of the people's status as linguistic outcasts from the official language, in which "pedir a bênçâo" ("asking the blessing") is translated in the common Candomblé communities as "Motumbá" in places of Yoruba origin, as "Kolofé" in places of Jeje origin, or as "Mucuiu" in places of Bantu origin. In these three words, with different origins but equivalent significance, is summed up the meaning of the reverence paid by the more experienced members to gods and their beliefs.

Dance and Theater

One of the most popular Afro-Brazilian dance and theatrical manifestations—the Congada—clearly shows the blend of cultures. The Congada is an adaptation of the medieval French epic *Le chanson de Roland* (The Song of Roland), appropriated by the Jesuits priests as an Afro-Brazilian catechism instrument. The festivity's patron saint is Sao Benedito, the great saint of Afro-Brazilian population. The Congada is a staging of the holy war, in which two Afro-Brazilian groups stand for good and evil. The group representing good wears blue, is Christian, and is headed by the emperor Carlos Magno ("The King of Congo"). The group representing evil, on the other hand, wears red outfits, is Moorish, and is headed by Ferrabras (seen as the Devil). The battle's climax is reached with the Christian victory over the Moors. Eventually, the Moors are converted to the Christian faith, and both groups are united in songs and dances of praise for Sao Benedito. The name *Congada* is very characteristic of this dramatic dance in Brazil's Northeastern region; however, it is also known as *Cavalhada* in the state of Minas Gerais and as *Ticumbi* in the state of Espirito Santo.

Samba and Carnival

The festive profile of Afro-Brazilian folkloric manifestations, consisting of hymns, dances, and percussion, is one of its most well-known aspects. Despite its European roots, Brazil's Carnival is an essentially Afro-Brazilian cultural product. The groups that formed the great samba schools of Rio de Janeiro were originally from the city's slums and its central areas in the first decades of the twentieth century. The samba was born in these same areas and is, likewise, a typically urban manifestation. The samba usually took place at the houses of respectable members of the Afro-Brazilian community, mostly in the back part of the house. As a form of Afro-Brazilian sociability, the samba is a musical, rhythmical expression of dance and percussion. In Rio de Janeiro the cradle of the samba was at the home of "Aunt Ciata," a famous *mulata* ("of mixed blood"), married to João Batista da Silva (a successful Afro-Brazilian who attended medical school and eventually held an important position at the police ministry during the government of the President Wenceslau Bras).

Capoeira

Capoeira, a blend of fighting and dancing, is one of the most representative forms of Afro-Brazilian body expression. It appeared in Brazil (mainly in Salvador, and eventually reaching the states of Pernambuco and Rio de Janeiro) among African slaves and served as a self-defense technique as well as entertainment. Thus, it became a popular practice among Afro-Brazilian and half-blooded classes. During the nineteenth century, up to the beginning of the twentieth century, the capoeiristas (persons who could do the capoeira) were greatly feared, mainly for the deadly power of their blows. For decades, the capoeiristas were the target of police repression. By the end of the twentieth century, capoeira had lost its outcast profile and had been absorbed by the urban middle classes. Lacking its fighting character, capoeira became solely a form of entertainment, primarily, an expression of physical performance, similar to a dance executed with singing and African musical instruments. The musical dimension is mainly highlighted by a musical instrument called the *berimbau*. Berimbau is composed of a 5-foot-long woolen arch, a metal string (wire), and a soundbox, a small cut gourd, all tied up by a cotton string in the fore part of the arch. The player uses a slender wooden stick to strike the string or a heavy coin to pluck the musical notes. There is also a small woven basket full of seeds (*caxixi*), which helps to set the rhythm. These performances are called capoeira circles, in which the capoeiristas form pairs and perform leg and arm movements in fast and rhythmic strokes. It is common to find "capoeira gym centers" in great urban centers such as Salvador, Rio de Janeiro, and Sao Paulo, where the former slaves' fighting form is seen as a sport or as a healthy body exercise practice.

Culinary Arts

African cuisine combines a profusion of flavors, scents, and colors. This gastronomy's main seasonings are *azeite de dendê* (oil extracted from the fruits of the *dendezeiro*, or African oil palm) and pepper. The city of Salvador, in the state of Bahia, is the center of this very unique cuisine. The dishes from Bahia are famous: acarajé (beans rolls fried on azeite de dendê), abará (boiled beans rolls), caruru (okra with shrimp and azeite de dendê), cocada (coconut sweet pastry), and so on.

These dishes are also offered to African deities worshiped in the Candomblé services. As such, these foods take on a votive meaning. Each divinity has a preferred food. For instance: acarajé is offered to Lansa (deity of lightning, wind, and tempest), abará belongs to Oxum (beauty and rivers goddess), and caruru is one of the most appreciated dishes by Xangô (deity of justice and thunder). Besides the ritual context, the trade in these foods has represented since slavery an important source of economic activity for Afro-Brazilian women (the so-called *baianas de tabuleiro*).

Afro-Brazilian Medical Practices

Afro-Brazilian medical practice is very important in the Brazilian history context. Since slavery times, these African-rooted therapeutic practices have been current in urban centers. In a prejudiced way, Afro-Brazilian practitioners, *erveiros* or *raizeiro*, were called witch doctors and charlatans by the upper classes. However, their background involves a great wealth of knowledge regarding plants, infusions, unguents, teas, and cataplasms. For centuries, this popular medical practice in Brazil has been the only resource for the less-favored classes, given the difficult access to the Brazilian public health system. These healing practices are strongly connected to religious expressions, which blend African, Native Brazilian, and Portuguese traditions. Within this context, there are devotions to Catholic saints, Native Brazilian rites, and African practices.

The main principle is to assure healing through the intervention of supernatural forces. Afro-Brazilian therapeutic practices were extremely important during the cholera and smallpox epidemic in Rio de Janeiro at the turn of the twentieth century. In this period, Afro-Brazilian doctors were found in the streets of Rio de Janeiro, applying leeches as a healing method, as were herbalists selling their preparations. The use of plants as part of magical healing practices has a strong African cultural heritage (and also Native Brazilian) and is still widely used in Brazil today. Old women healers can be found practicing the healing arts through prayers and blessings and by using some mystical plants. In general, they are sought out by mothers of small children suffering from some kind of illness. These practices are very common throughout Brazil, including the country's great metropolises. They are more frequently found in the outskirts and in the slums of cities, where there is a lack of regular and official medical treatment.

Folklore Characters

In Afro-Brazilian folklore there are two very interesting characters: Curupira and Saci. Curupira is a small jungle genii whose feet are turned backwards (a feature found in many West African stories). This is his way of deceiving whoever wants to follow him, by going to the opposite direction. Curupira is a jungle protector who deceives, misguides, and scares hunters. Saci, on the other hand, may be called a dwarf or a primordial character. He is a one-legged Afro-Brazilian boy who wears a red hood and smokes a pipe. In some descriptions, he has holes in his hands. Saci has magic powers; therefore, he may disappear or start whirlwinds. From many studies regarding Brazilian folklore, there remains some doubt concerning the Saci character, and there is no precise record of his origin. One thesis of Saci's origin retraces one of the jungle's spirits known among the Yorubas (Nigeria / Benin) and among the Jejes (from the ancient kingdom of Dahomey, now Benin). This divinity is called Aroni among the Yorubas and Aziza among the Jejes. He is described as a small, one-legged man who smokes a pipe made out of spiral shell. In a certain way, he is the African Prometheus, since in one of his myths, he appears as the one who gives fire to men, having stolen it from heaven. He is also very artful with medical techniques and with healing herbs; therefore, he is able to teach men this power. The whirlwinds, which made the dead leaves fly, are considered manifestations of Aroni. This divinity is connected to Ossaim (who is one of the most important divinities in the Candomblé religion). Such descriptions, collected in Africa by Pierre Verger, lead us to conclude that Saci is a continuation of Aroni in Brazil.

For centuries, Brazil's African heritage was neglected as a legitimate folklore expression. Such a phenomenon is one of many ways of racial discrimination. The Afro-Brazilian festive meetings—the samba—were repressed by the police until the beginning of the twentieth century. In one way or another, there has been a considerable advance regarding Afro-Brazilian cultural heritage, starting in the 1950s, with the Campanha Nacional em Defesa do Folclore (National Campaign for Folklore Preservation). One of the great consequences of this campaign was the creation of Museu do Folclore Edison Carneiro (Edison Carneiro Folklore Museum) located in Rio de Janeiro. In recent years, studies of the old Candomblé meeting places carried out by Instituto do Patrimonio Historico e Artistico Nacional (IPHAN—National Artistic and Historical Heritage Institute) have been another crucial step. There is no longer room for neglecting the strength and value of African heritage in the Brazilian cultural formation.

References

Bastide, Roger. 1959. *Sociologia do Folclore Brasileiro*. São Paulo: Anhambi.

Cascudo, Luis da Camara. *Made in Africa*. 1965. Rio de Janeiro: Civilização Brasileira.

Chalhoub, Sidney. 1996. *Cidade Febril. Cortiços e Epidemias na Corte Imperial*. Sao Paulo: Companhia das Letras.

Mendonca, Renato. 1973. *A Influência Africana no Português do Brasil*. Rio de Janeiro: Civilização Brasileira.

Ramos, Arthur. 1935. *Folclore Negro do Brasil*. Rio de Janeiro: CEB.

Santos, Cristiano H. R. 2001. Candomblé. In *Concise Encyclopedia of Language and Religion*. Oxford: Elsevier.

———. 2001. Macumba. In *Concise Encyclopedia of Language and Religion*. Oxford: Elsevier.

CRISTIANO HENRIQUE RIBEIRO DOS SANTOS

See also **Caribbean Verbal Arts; Diaspora; Religions: Afro-Brazilian Religions Vodou**

DIASPORA: SEA ISLANDS OF THE UNITED STATES

The area known as the Sea Islands, or the Low Country, may be defined as the southeastern coastal and island region extending from southern North Carolina to northern Florida. The islands consist of brackish and salt marshes, beaches and wooded tracts apart from the inhabited and arable lands. Some of the better known islands are Johns, James, and Wadmalaw near Charleston, South Carolina; Edisto, where there is a palm-lined beach; and Ladies and St. Helena Islands near Beaufort, S.C., where Penn Center, founded as a school for the islanders after Emancipation (1863) and before the end of the Civil War (1865) is located. Daufuskie, known through the photographic work of Jean Moutassamy-Ashe and the film *Conrack*, Sapelo, and St. Mary's in Georgia are three islands still reached by boat. Jekyll has been developed into a conference center; Ossabaw is a privately owned writers' colony. St. Simon, the site for Lydia Parrish's *Slave Songs of the Georgia Sea Islands*, has been suburbanized since the 1950s and Sea Island has been developed as a luxury resort. Hilton Head has also been developed, as have Dataw and other smaller islands.

Until the 1930s, the Sea Islands were accessible only by boat. Causeways and bridges, which now connect some of the islands to the mainland, have made a major impact on the life of the islanders. Historically, there have been three main ethnic groups: African American, European American, and Amerindian. The latter have been subsumed into a triethnic group, locally known as "Brass Ankles." Inhabited originally by Yamassee and other Native Americans, the area was invaded, explored, marched through, settled on, and written about successively by the Spanish, English, and French. Captive Africans were brought to work the land after the Amerindians were killed or forced out, making possible large single-crop economies, such as the British-supported prerevolutionary indigo cultivation, as well as rice, cotton, and, in later years, potatoes, tomatoes, soybeans, and cabbage.

During the mosquito season in the summer, the islands' European American residents moved away to escape malaria, leaving behind the enslaved Africans, many of whom had the sickle-cell gene that protected them from the ravages of insect-borne diseases of the malarial swamps. As a result of this geographic, economic, and social isolation, these residents succeeded in preserving many of their African customs in their material folk culture and life. This continuity and reaffirmation of their ancestral cultures is evident in the distinctive patterning of their quilts, which reflect Ashanti and Ewe strip-weaving designs in silk and cotton, respectively; the construction of baskets through the use of natural materials and methods of manufacture; women's modes of hair tying; cookery; the "knitting" of fishnets; and the practice of fishing, in which the nets are cast, dropped, and dragged. African influence persists, too, in the Sea Islanders' insurance and burial societies, praying bands, and community social groups, called "lodges," for which the African secret societies are the analogues. The Sea Island Creole language (also known as Gullah or Geechee) is part of an African-English Creole continuum (called Afrish by Baird), which includes the Creole languages of the Caribbean, such as Jamaican and Barbadian. The Africanity of Gullah has been demonstrated by Lorenzo Dow Turner in an epochal study of folklore and naming customs, some of which are still practiced today.

Children's games of the Sea Islands often involve English language game songs such as "Little Sally Walker (or Waters)," but the accompanying movement, dance, and game interaction is typically African in social emphasis. Children's toys are put together from used cans, wire hangers, and natural substances (sand, wood, etc.). Joint grass dolls are a popular toy. Women also make "dollbabies" out of salvaged scraps from quilt making or other domestic sewing. These dolls may can be dressed in plantation-era costumes or in the typical, layered look of the independent African Sea Island working woman.

Several books, mostly by outsiders, have been written about the area and include travel accounts, novels, folklore collections, explorers' journals, educational and religious missionaries' diaries, military records, and studies in history, language, and sociology. Charlotte Forten Grimke, W. F. Allen, Lucy McKim Garrison, Thomas Wentworth Higginson, William Gilmore Simms, Abigail Christensen, Charles Colcock Jones, Elsie Clews Parsons, Julia Peterkin, Guy B. and Guion Griffis Johnson, and Guy and Candie Carawan were all European Americans who wrote about the island people. Many others, including recent arrivals such as Tina McElroy Ansa and Eugenia Price, who produced books from African American and European American perspectives, respectively, have written with fascination about the area and its people, whose traditional life has commanded attention and respect.

The formerly high population concentration of African American residents has changed in recent years for two main reasons: northward migration of the African American islanders in search of better economic opportunity and the influx of European Americans through suburban, resort, and commercial developments. Unconscionable taking of African American-owned land for back taxes and seemingly large premiums paid for shore land on Kiawah, Hilton Head, and Daufuskie Islands (S.C.) have benefitted the developers and threatened the serene beauty, cultural integrity, sacred burial places, and general access to some of these islands.

References

Carawan, Guy, and Candie Carawan. 1989. *Ain't you Got a Right to the Tree of Life?* Athens: University of Georgia Press.

Creel, Margaret Washington. 1988. *A Peculiar People*. New York: New York University Press.

Dabbs, Edith McBride. 1971. *Face of an Island*. New York: Grossman Publishers.

———. 1985. *Sea Island Diary*. Spartanburg, S.C.: The Reprint Company.

Jones, Bessie, and Bess Lomax Hawes. 1986. *Step it Down*. Athens: University of Georgia Press.

Jones-Jackson, Patricia. 1987. *When Roots Die*. Athens: University of Georgia Press.

Moutoussamy-Ashe, Jeanne. 1982. *Daufuskie Island*. Columbia: University of South Carolina Press.

Parrish, Lydia. 1965. *Slave Songs of the Georgia Sea Islands*. Hatboro, P: Folklore Associates.

Parsons, Elsie Clews. 1923. *Folk-Lore of the Sea Islands, South Carolina*. Cambridge, Mass.: American Folklore Society.

Rose, Willie Lee. 1967. *Rehearsal for Reconstruction*. New York: Vintage.

Turner, Lorenzo Dow. 1974. *Africanisms in the Gullah Dialect*. Ann Arbor: University of Michigan Press.

Twining, Mary Arnold, and Keith E. Baird. 1991. *Sea Island Roots: African Presence in the Sea Islands of South Carolina and Georgia*. Trenton, N.J.: Africa World Press.

Wood, Peter. 1975. *Black Majority*. New York: Norton.

MARY ARNOLD TWINING

DIASPORA

See **Basketry, African American; Caribbean Verbal Arts; Carnivals and African American Cultures; Divination: Ifá Divination in Cuba; Housing: African American Traditions; Indian Ocean Islands; Languages; Music; Religions: Afro-Brazilian Religions; Santeria in Cuba; Spirit Possession: Comfa of Guyana; Textiles: African American Quilts Vodou; Yards and Gardens: African American Traditions**

DILEMMA TALES

A dilemma tale is defined as a story that leaves audiences "with a choice among alternatives, such as which of several characters has done the best, deserves a reward, or should win an argument or a case in court. ... The narrator ends his story with the dilemma," which the listeners must then debate (Bascom 1975, 1).

The dilemma tale is defined by its mode of performance. It differs from what Europeans call myth, the narrative that answers questions about how human beings and their culture have developed. It also differs from legend, the oral history of a well-known person or place. Myth and legend are answers; they are accepted by the populace as truthful accounts of what happened in the past. The dilemma tale, however, is a question, a fictional problem, posed to the populace. In contrast to the etiological marker of myth or legend, or the closure provided by the formulaic endings common to many folktales, the dilemma tale encourages controversy and contention, thus deferring closure indefinitely. Therefore, the dilemma genre forms a performance code of its own; its rules distinguish it from other genres and determine when and for whom it may be performed. Especially in West Africa, where palaver is the means towards action and cohesion, the dilemma tale flourishes. But it is a favored genre all over Africa, hardly found elsewhere in such profusion.

A Luba (Congo) example: Four brothers—Karasai the shooter, Kabomi the keensighted, Karengerezi the hearer, and Kaibrizi the driver—go in quest of a remedy for their father's foot ailment. They find it and lose it. By applying their several skills, they recover the remedy, take it home, and heal their father. Which of the four did most for his father (Rehse 1910, 366)?

A Limba (Sierra Leone) example: Unbeknownst to one other, three brothers are courting the same young woman. One acquires a magic glass, the second a magic animal tail, and the third a magic skin. Surprised to find each other on the road home, they look in the glass; the young woman has died. Carried on the magic skin, they are transported back to her, where they revive her with the magic tail. "Which is the one of those three who owns the love?" The ethnographer present at the telling of this dilemma tale notes that, when they tried to solve the dilemma, the audience could not avoid arguing (Finnegan 1967, 218–19).

Once written down and published as a text, the dilemma tale invites disparate approaches. Should it be understood as a sequence of incidents, like a folktale, or as an elaborated riddle, or is it an entirely distinct, essentially African, genre, which cannot be contextualized in terms of other, more familiar (to

European/ American scholars) genres? For Bascom, the greatest authority on the genre, African dilemma tales are an interesting oddity among prose narratives. They have some relation, not clear, with formal courts of law (Bascom 1975, 14). Whatever their meaning, they are narrated, as are other tales. Their cognitive function is to attest to difference and the impossibility of resolution. Another approach would be overtly to connect the dilemma tale to other genres as a means of determining its meanings and functions. The riddle, for instance, with its insistence on a correct answer, is a playful form of the acquisition of knowledge and acceptance into a circle of knowers. Perhaps the dilemma tale is a riddle for grownups, played in a similar theatre as the riddle, but one where debate is expected, disagreement is welcomed, and a correct answer will never be more than provisional. A more promising approach sees it as a kind of interactional theater, in which the printed texts are scripts. No other text in African folklore insists so urgently on performance. The scripts achieve their realization in the performance situation; every event is unique. If written scripts only imply possibilities for performances, the literal meaning of each dilemma tale is inherently variable, and only performance can reveal its meaning. Thus the dilemma tale provides folklore scholarship, oriented to texts for so long, with an opportunity to explore the contrasting consequences of text and performance orientations.

References

Bascom, William R. 1975. *African Dilemma Tales*. The Hague: Mouton.
Finnegan, Ruth. 1967. *Limba Stories and Story-Telling*. Oxford: Clarendon Press.
Haring, Lee. 1982. *Malagasy Tale Index*. FFC no. 231. Helsinki: Suomalainen Tiedeakatemia.
Rehse, Hermann. 1910. *Kiziba land und leute*. Stuttgart: Verlag von Strecker und Schroeder.

LEE HARING

See also **Bascom, William; Caribbean Verbal Arts; Folktales**

DINKA

See **Northeastern Africa**

DIVINATION: OVERVIEW

In a constantly changing world, it is difficult to have sufficient knowledge to act wisely. Nevertheless, answers to the mundane as well as extraordinary questions that arise daily are available. One has only to ask the correct question of the appropriate source and then be able to interpret the answer accurately. A diviner can perform these acts.

African diviners manage standardized procedures by which otherwise inaccessible information is revealed. Usually, this process is governed by an extensive body of esoteric knowledge, available only to the diviner. Occult communication is revealed through a mechanism, such as a diviner's basket of symbolic objects or cast cowrie shells, or directly through the diviner, acting as a spirit medium. Divination sessions are central to the expression and enactment of cultural truths as they are reviewed in the context of contemporary realities (Peek 1991).

All African societies, urban and rural, use divination (perhaps even more than in the past) to aid in problem solving and decision making; divination continues to serve as the primary institutional means of articulating the epistemology of a people. While one primary divinatory form often characterizes a culture, such as the Ifa system of the Yoruba (Bascom 1969), all cultures, and even individual diviners, will employ several different types of divination. For example, the Baule of Cote d'Ivoire use cast leather thongs, mouse divination, and spirit possession to resolve problems. Some divination forms are restricted to private sessions, while other forms are employed in public rituals. No matter the format, whether through sortilege or spirit mediumship, the cryptic oracular message is normally debated within the divinatory congregation of diviner and clients and before specific plans of action are formulated.

As managers of such critical processes, diviners are a carefully selected group in most African societies. Only those who are "called" may serve, as among the Zulu, where ancestral spirits possess future diviners; most diviners must go through extensive training and initiation periods, with a final public demonstration of their abilities. Not only the integrity of diviners and their extensive training but the skeptical attitudes of clients who often travel far distances for consultation argue against facile attacks on the veracity of divination sessions. Diviners are not charlatans manipulating a fearful clientele but sensitive, learned specialists who are very respectful of the roles they have been granted as communicators between worlds.

For many years, serious research on African divination systems was hampered by prejudice and ignorance. Inappropriately developed and analyzed typologies have further confused matters. Many studies simply generated contextless lists of divinatory mechanisms and omens that became endless catalogues because virtually anything that registers change can be interpreted for meaningful messages. Equally problematic are studies that rigidly attempt to separate divination systems as intuitive or logical, mediumistic or mechanical (see discussions in Devisch 1985 and Zuesse 1987). All forms of divination participate in cross-world communication (Peek 1994) and intentionally meld different cognitive processes. The temporal and spacial situating of a divination session, the symbols employed, and the behavior of the diviner all serve to emphasize the liminality of the divinatory process. No matter how extraordinary the divination session is, the enigmatic oracular message will be debated in terms of present reality before a plan or action is decided. Thus, the divination enterprise involves a nonordinary, nonnormal cognitive process, which is then reviewed in terms of contemporary reality.

Despite earlier problems with divination research, there have nevertheless been several informative and insightful studies, such as those by Evans-Pritchard (1968), Middleton (1971), Werbner (1973), and Turner (1975). Analyses focusing on social dynamics have been further developed in work by Mendosa (1982) and Rasmussen (1991).

Africanist scholars have begun to use divination systems as valuable resources for a variety of research goals. Divination sessions serve to revise and review individual and group histories and thereby become sources for historical studies and personality research (Blier 1990). Regional studies (Peek 1982; Pemberton 2000) provide valuable comparative and historical data. All divination sessions are ritual encounters, whose dramaturgical dimensions are highly informative of various cultural dynamics

(Roberts 1988). Divination systems are often closely related to medical (Ngubane 1977; Morris 1986) and judicial practices.

As the embodiment of culture, divination systems comment on all aspects of a culture. Virtually every expressive and artistic form of behavior is involved. Divinatory verbal arts range from esoteric and archaic languages to major prose narrative forms such as myth, legend, and folk tale. Ifa divination of the Yoruba (which was carried to the Americas with slaves) generates long verses full of mythical references, historical details, and prescriptions for proper sacrifices. Visual arts serve to focus both diviner and client on their serious enterprise. From the diviner's often complex regalia to the divination mechanisms themselves, major cultural symbols are carefully presented and elaborated (Pemberton 2000; La Gamma 2001).

Because of divination's centrality, future studies of African peoples should make better use of diviners and divination systems. Effective responses to life's problems demand both established tradition and creative innovation and sensitive intuition and careful reasoning; such combinations are artfully orchestrated by African diviners.

References

Bascom, William R. 1969. *Ifa Divination: Communication Betwen Gods and Men in West Africa*. Bloomington: Indiana University Press.

Blier, Suzanne Preston. 1990. King Glele of Danhome. Part One: Divination Portraits of a Lion King. *African Arts* 23, no. 4:42–53, 93–4.

Devisch, Rene. 1985. Perspectives on Divination in Centemporary sub-Saharan Africa. In *Theoretical Explorations in African Relgions*, eds. W. Van Binsbergen and M. Schoffeleers. London: KPI/Routledge and Kegan Paul.

Evans-Pritchard, E. E. 1968. *Witchcraft, Oracles, and Magic Among the Azande* (1937). Oxford: Clarendon Press.

LaGamma, Alisa. 2001. *Art and Oracle*. New York: Metropolitan Museum of Art.

Mendonsa, Eugene L. 1982. *The Politics of Divination*. Berkeley: University of California Press.

Middleton, John. 1971. Oracles and Divination among the Lugbara. In *Man in Africa*, eds. M. Douglas and P. M. Kaberry. New York: Doubleday Anchor.

Morris, Brian. 1986. Herbalism and Divination in Southern Malawi. *Social Science and Medicine* 23:367–77.

Ngubane, Harriet. 1977. *Body and Mind in Zulu Medicine*. London: Academic Press.

Peek, Philip M. 1982. The Divining Chain in Southern Nigeria. In *African Religious Groups and Beliefs*, ed. S. Ottenberg. Meerut, India: Folklore Institute.

———. 1991. The Study of Divination, Present and Past and African Divination Systems: Non-normal Modes of Cognition. In *African Divination Systems: Ways of Knowing*, ed. P. M. Peek. Bloomington: Indiana University Press.

———. 1994. The Sounds of Silence: Cross-World Communication and the Auditory Arts in African Societies. *American Ethnologist* 21, no. 3:474–94.

Pemberton, John, III, ed. 2000. Insight and Artistry in African Divination. Washington, D.C.: Smithsonian Institution Press.

Rasmussen, Susan J. 1991. Modes of Persuasion: Gossip, Song, and Divination in Tuareg Conflict Resolution. *Anthropological Quarterly* 64:30–46.

Roberts, Allen F. 1988. Through the Bamboo Thicket: The Social Process of Tabwa Ritual Performance. *The Drama Review* 32: 123–38.

Turner, Victor. 1975. *Revelation and Divination in Ndembu Ritual*. Ithaca, N.Y.: Cornell University Press.

Werbner, Richard P. 1973. The Superabundance of Understanding: Kalanga Rhetoric and Domestic Divination. *American Anthropologist* 75:1414–40.

Zuesse, Evan M. 1987. Divination. In *The Encyclopedia of Religion*, ed. M. Eliade. New York: Macmillan.

PHILIP M. PEEK

See also **Animals in African Folklore; Cosmology; Divination: Household Divination among the Kongo; Religion, Silence in Expressive Behavior**

DIVINATION: HOUSEHOLD DIVINATION AMONG THE KONGO

For the Kongo peoples of the Democratic Republic of Congo, life is a continuous experience of uncovering truths. Truths about the past, the present, and the future, related to a variety of ecological, social, physical, and spiritual issues, can be apprehended through the appropriate means and methods. Divination makes such truths available to humankind. The two main places where divination is practiced are the private home and in the diviner's home, known as *nzo za bangaanga/nzo za Ngombo*.

The Kongo term *mpeve* means "spirit possession," that is, going into ecstatic communion with spirits. It is one of several words (such as *bikula*, "to prophecy" or "to foretell") that comprises the Kongo's extensive religious vocabulary. The state of ecstasy is described by the Kongo as a special gift, during which one is possessed by unseen dead relatives in order to uncover that which is unknown in this world. Divination has therapeutic and revelatory functions. In its therapeutic function, it provides diagnoses and therapies relevant for particular predicaments and diseases. In its visionary function, known as *luengisa* (to enlighten or to reveal), it digs into the past, the present, and the future on various questions. Thus, a family with someone with the gift of divination is said to be well protected.

In its household context, divination is primarily a female experience. Only women can enter the trance states necessary for divination. People with the gift for divination traditionally include mothers of twins (*ngudi a mapasa*), twins (*mapasa*), the child born after the the twins (*nlandu*), and others believed to be special children in the Kongo cosmology. Women are believed to have a paramount protective role in the household; therefore, they retain the privilege of being intermediaries for messages from the spiritual realm relating to the welfare of the family. Although a person might enter into a state of ecstasy during the day, night is the preferred time for divination rites. In Kongo cosmology, night is when that the dead are awake and nearer to the physical universe, that is, to the world of the living.

Divination takes place in the conjugal chamber. This room, which, in the Kongo tradition, is not to be entered by any other person but parents, is opened up to become the forum where people enter into dialogue with deceased relatives and friends. The sudden onset of possession is characterized by shouts, songs, or special words that indicate that the process of communication with the spirit world has begun. These cries and songs are part of the rich liturgy of Kongo divination. The diviner's spirit speech is multilingual; several languages may be spoken in the course of one manifestation. Some are recognized as spoken (earthly) languages, whereas others fall in the category of *Ndinga za zulu* (heavenly languages) or *Ndinga za Mpinda* (mysterious languages). Even when they are recognized as languages spoken among the Kongo, they are distinguished by an unprecedented linguistic elegance. Despite the presence of various languages, dialogue is carried on in a language and in metaphors that are grasped by the human interlocutors present, who must ask the invisible visitor to use an intelligible linguistic medium. This constitutes the first phase of the liturgy.

The second liturgical phase is establishing the identity of the spiritual entity (or visitant). This is important for conveying the authenticity of the spirit. The visitation is unwelcome whenever the identity is not revealed. Thus, after demanding, "Vova ndinga yoyo tufueti bakisa" ("Speak the language which we can understand"), the spirit is asked, "Ngeye I nani?" ("Who are you?"). Once the language barrier is broken and the visitant's identity is revealed, the dialogue starts to flow. The next standard question is, "Nki wizidi?" ("What is the reason for your visit?"). Normally, there are three possible answers: courtesy, a report on the family's welfare, or the imparting of information. Whatever the nature of the visit, the welfare of the family is most important because, as is believed among the Kongo and elsewhere in Africa, the ancestors' primary function is to care for the physical and social health of their living kin. It is in its curative and informative dimensions that divination works as the art of disclosing truth. If it is understanding a disease, for example, the visitant reveals its nature and causes and the traditional medicines that have to be used or the healer who has to be consulted. Whenever the family has not followed these instructions, the visitant will return and blame them for the worsening course of the illness.

The informative or predictive dimension of divination (*luengisa*) is twofold: the visitant may warn of a coming danger (social, physical, or ecological) or illuminate an unclear situation (such as familial misfortune, past or present). In the case of a warning of impending danger, the visiting spirit might engage, through the possessed person, in a struggle with the invisible enemies or vicious spirits that wish to harm the household. In response, the possessed person stands up and walks in the directions that the enemies are said to come from in order to argue with them and cast them out. She can use salt, kola nuts, water, and other traditional objects for defeating the vicious forces.

The third and last liturgical phase of Kongo divination are the concluding words, a recapitulation of recommendations ("Vanga mayilutelele": "Do what I have told you") and promises ("Si Ngiza kiuvilakene ko": "I will come back, I have not forgotten you"), to which the hearers can respond "Never forget us and pass on our love to other members of the family." The medium waves good-bye with her hands, indicating the departure of the visitant and the end of the session She does not regain consciousness immediately, but rather falls into a deep sleep. When she wakes up, the other members of the family tell her what has transpired.

The rituals and symbols that accompany most of the divination session have liturgical significance and therapeutic effect. Songs and special verbal expressions constitute the rituals through which either the visitation is celebrated (*kembila wizi kututala*) or a special feeling of unhappiness (*kiadi*) and suffering (*mpasi*) is expressed. Critical elements include palm wine, kola

nuts, salt, saliva of either the person in ecstasy or those witnessing. These are always found in the house where somebody with the divination gift lives. They have a sacredotal connotation, since the possessed person is also thought to have a sacred or priestly function.

Palm wine is poured on the person in ecstasy as a sign of richness, fertility and honor. Kola nuts, which symbolize power, are ground up and thrown on the medium. The saliva of the medium becomes the saliva of the visitant. When she spits on people, it indicates blessing and power. Salt is thrown in the indicated part of the house and appropriate locations as medicine against evil spirits and people with bad intentions.

ADRIEN N. NGUDIANKAMA

See also **Central African Folklore: Overview**

DIVINATION: IFÁ DIVINATION IN CUBA

The Afro-Cuban Ifá divination system closely follows its Yoruba source in philosophy, format, equipment, and personnel (Bascom 1952, 1969; Abiodun 1975). Introduced to the island by a handful of Africans who arrived in Cuba as early as the 1830s, Ifá is widely practiced in contemporary Cuba as well as in the United States, Puerto Rico, Mexico, Venezuela, Panama, and Spain. It has recently been reintroduced into Brazil by Cuban-initiated Brazilians. Five Africans—Adechina Ño Remigio Herrera, No Carlos Adé Bí, Oluguere Ko Ko, Ifá Omí Joaquin Cadiz, and Ifá Bí Francisco Villalonga—were the founders of Ifá's five principal Cuban lineages (*ramas*).

Babalawos are priests of Orunmila (also, Orula), the interpreter-*orisha* who divines Ifá—understood as "total knowledge." Orula's oracular equipment includes the divining chain (*okuelé*), used by one *babalawo* in day-to-day sessions, and the circular wood tray (*tablero de Ifá*), along with the sixteen sacred palm nuts (*ikín*, used in high-level sessions in which Orula's secrets are "brought to the floor" (*bajón de orula*), and which requires at least three diviners as witnesses and speakers. As in the Yoruba system, Ifá's wisdom is contained and distributed within a grid of 256 compound figures (*odu* in Yoruba, *letras* in Spanish), which are the permutations of sixteen ranked principal figures, called *meyi* ("double"). The *babalawo's* interpretation emerges from his reading of these *odu*, octagrams produced as the eight-lobed *okuelé* (*opele* in Yoruba) chain is cast to a surface or as sequentially marked in Orula's divination dust (*aché* or *yefá*), which is spread over the surface of the tray. Three principal *odu* are extracted, two of which serve as "witnesses". Then, the positive or negative valence (*iré* or *osobo*) of the *odu*, and the type and spiritual source of the valence (e.g., witchcraft via the intervention of the dead) are defined through further inquiry. Both the *ikín* system and the *okuelé* chain require the aid of pairs of *ibos* (e.g., a stone, piece of white chalk, shell, or doll's head), spiritual "messengers" between the oracle and the client's "destiny" (*ori*) that are held in the client's fists. In the more momentous *bajón*, Orula's equipment and regalia are formally arrayed around the *tablero*, which is placed on a white sheet covering a straw floor mat: Orula's *sopera* (lidded wood or porcelain tureen for the *ikín*), *irofá* (deer antler tapper, which replaced the Yoruba Orunmila's ivory one), *iruke* (beaded horsetail flywhisk). The *babalawo*, barefoot and dressed in white, wears Orula's yellow-and-green beadstrands (*eleke* or *collar de mazo*) and pillbox cap (*gorro*). The annual Reading of the Opening of the Year on January 1 is a public *bajón* attended by many hundreds of *babalawos*; the youngest (often around ten years old) manipulates the *ikín* to produce the three *odu*, whose interpretation lasts all night as each participant "speaks" in ascending order of seniority. Until the 1960s, this reading gathered all of the Ifá "families" in the house of Bernardo Rojas in Marianao, a mansion called the "Vatican" because of Rojas's great influence. Today, a major collective of four to eight hundred Havana *babalawos* led by Lazaro Cuesta, called "The Organizing Commission of the Sign of the Year," as well numerous individual groups around the island, perform this annual reading.

The Afro-Cuban Ifá corpus, comprehensively recorded in privately circulated notebooks (*libretas*) since the first decades of the twentieth century, has become highly standardized. The Spanish and Canary Island descended Creole *babalawos* Ramon Febles Molina (c. 1842–1936) and Bernardo Rojas Torres (1881–1959), respectively, were among the first to transcribe the oral Ifá corpus, based upon interviews with their African masters, such as Rojas's "godfather," Adechina (c. 1811–1905) and Ño José Akón Kón. The most widely circulated published "manuals" were compiled by a non-*babalawo*, the shrewd and mysterious figure Pedro Arango, at mid-century. Interpretive manuals, called *Dice Ifá* ("Ifá says"), emphasize the oracular advice and mythical narratives of each of the 256 *odu*, while practical manuals, *Tratódos de Odduns*, emphasize the ritual solutions to each *odu*. The latter details the fabrication of particular Eshús and *inshe osains* ("protective charms") appropriate to each *odu*.

The Dice Ifá and the Tratódos de Odduns elaborate what *babalawo*s in the oral tradition had to spin out verbally in their interpretations: 1) a laconic epithet or proverb (*refrán*), which encapsulates the *odu*. The *refrán* of Otura Di, nicknamed Otura Diablo says, "Here was where the Jimaguas [Ibeji twins] defeated the Devil" (Castillo n.d., 313). "Here was where" marks the *odu* as a set of spiritual coordinates in which a particular issue originated—was "born"; 2) Lucumí invocational prayers (*súyeres*) addressing the *odu's* forces; 3) which principal *orishas* are to be praised ("*maferefún Obatalá y Changó*"); 4) list-like narrations of advice (*consejos*), which delineate the range of experiences, events, prescriptions, and proscriptions relevant to the client's position vis-a-vis the *odu* ("Ifá says: that you have many children and that you have blisters or sores on your body; you must make *ebó*; you cannot attend drum dances because, as a result, you could go to jail . . . give thanks to Baba [Obatalá] and Changó . . . you have a debt with Yemayá . . . you have a struggle, and if you want to win it, you must put a little spread of fruit [*placita*] and two little drums before the Twins . . . don't eat salty or hot food . . .") (Castillo n.d., 313); 5) prescriptions for *ebó* (sacrifices), which clean away the problems of the *odu*; and 6) *historias*, mythical story precedents that reveal situations and their resolution through proper *ebó*. In Otura Dí, for example, the Twins blackmail the devil into removing an insidious trap he has set on the crossroads for all passers-by (a dangerous "hole" in the ground); the devil is driven to fatigue when tricked into dancing to the drum they borrow from him; he agrees to remove the trap if they cease drumming.

To clean away the evils of Otura Dí, *babalawo*s may kill, ignite with kerosene, and burn a chicken over the chalk drawing of the *odu*. Though the Ifá corpus is undoubtedly of Yoruba provenance, Otura Dí's figure of the "Devil," its references to the Afro-Cuban social mix of drumming, dancing, drinking, and gossip, as well as the elaborate blackmail plot, suggest that Ifá's *consejos* and *historias* are saturated with the Cuban historical experience and may have borrowed from non-African popular narrative forms (see Lopez Valdes 1985, 87–8).

Babalawos study and memorize their Dice Ifá's, but authoritative performances depend upon cogent face-to-face verbal interpretations of the *odu* and its *historias*. Officially, diviners gain reputation through their knowledge, seniority, deeds, and knowledge (*mayoribád, historia,* and *conocimiento*), as well as their moral character and "manliness." Women, homosexual men, and even mildly effeminate men are rigorously excluded from access to Ifá's secrets. Individual *babalawos* rise to prominence through patronage relations as they acquire the socially invested spiritual capital to initiate others and found a "branch" (*rama*) of Ifá radition. The foundation of this spiritual capital is the enabling token of Ifá's reproduction, the secrets of Olofin—the acquisition of which has been the defining issue of Ifá politics in the twentieth century. Exiled Cuban *babalawos* in 1970s Miami, unable to procure Olofin from Havana's reigning authority, Miguel Febles Padrón (1910–1986), traveled to Oshogbo, Nigeria, to learn from the Yoruba *babalawo* Ifá Yemi, thereby completing a circuit of transatlantic cultural transmission that began during the late colonial period.

References

Abiodun, Rowland. 1975. Ifá Art Objects: An Interpretation Based on Oral Traditions. In *Yoruba Oral Tradition*, ed. Wande Abimbola. Ile-Ife: University of Ife.

Anonymous. n.d. *Tratado de Odduns de Ifá*. n.p.

Bascom, William. 1952. Two Forms of Afro-Cuban Divination. In *Acculturation in the Americas*, ed. Sol Tax. Chicago: University of Chicago Press.

———. 1969. *Ifá Divination: Communication between Gods and Men in West Africa*. Bloomington: Indiana University Press.

Castillo, Jose M. n.d. *Ifá en la tierra de Ifá*. N.p.

Fatunmbi, Fa'Lokun. 1992. *Awo: Ifá and the Theology of Orisha Divination*. Bronx N.Y.: Original Publications.

Hewitt, Julia Cuervo. 1983. Ifá : Oraculo Yoruba y Lucumi. *Cuban Studies/Estudios Cubanos* Winter: 25–40.

Lopez Valdes, Rafael L. 1985. El lenguaje de los sgnos de Ifá y sus antecedentes transculturales en Cuba. In *Componentes Africanos en el etnos Cubano*, by Rafael L. Lopez Valdes. Havana: Editorial de Ciencias Sociales.

Lopez, Lourdes. 1975. *Estudio de un bablao*. Habana: Departamento de Actividades Culturales, Universidad de la Habana.

Matibag, Eugenio. 1997. Ifá and Interpretation: An Afro-Caribbean Literacy Practice. In *Sacred Possessions: Vodou, Santeria, Obeah, and the Caribbean*, eds. Margarite Fernández Olmos and Lizabeth Paravisini-Gebert. New Brunswick, N.J.: Rutgers University Press.

DAVID H. BROWN

See also **Diaspora; Divination; Santeria in Caba**

DJIBOUTI (REPUBLIC OF DJIBOUTI)

Djibouti is a small country of nearly 690,000, located on Africa's eastern coast between Somalia, Ethiopia, and Eritrea. Its climate ranges from arid to semiarid. Djibouti is the country's capital and largest city, with a population of 383,000. The country's ethnic composition is mostly split between Somali and Afar peoples. The major languages spoken are French, Arabic, Somali, and Saho-Afar. The country is predominantly Muslim (94 percent), while 6 percent of the population is Christian.

On June 27, 1977, Djibouti gained its independence from France and formed its own one-party republic. Opposition to the government's autocratic rule and restrictions on freedoms of speech and association have been factors in underground political movements. Nonetheless, the country remained relatively stable until 1992, when peace was disrupted by civil war stemming from a power struggle between Afar- and Somali-speaking groups. Since that time, the government has made strides in implementing greater democracy. Although a multiparty republic has been created, continuing conflicts have overshadowed such advances. At the end of the twentieth century, refugees fleeing famine and conflict in Somalia, Ethiopia, and Sudan increased the population of Djibouti by up to one-third.

Djibouti's major resource is its harbor, which has attracted Arab and European powers for centuries. Until recently, it housed France's largest overseas military force (in 1989, 950 ships were in the harbor, including 177 warships). The United States has also placed a large force there.

Djibouti has few natural resources, although the discovery of gas reserves could create revenue from potential exportation. The maritime and construction industries have been Djibouti's main industries and sources of revenue.

PHILIP M. PEEK

DOGON

See **Animals; Words and the Dogon**

DOLLS AND TOYS

"What the year will bring is found in the games of children."
Songay proverb

Children play with toys to cope with the present, practice skills for the future, and simply have fun. Although toys and play are important components in a child's development, their entertainment value can never be discounted. Toys help create an alternative reality in which learning and experimenting can safely take place. It is a completely absorbing existence in which time and the mundane world recedes while the child's consciousness becomes completely absorbed in the play world. Most African toys temporarily replicate the adult world and give girls and boys, through playing with these toys and exploring alternatives in the play world, the opportunity to process events the child sees occurring around him or her. This rehearsal also allows a child to enact upcoming adult roles and to invent new ways of dealing with the future.

African toys are often made by the children who play with them or by their mothers, rather than being purchased items or gifts. Exceptions occur when adult canoe makers, for example, make miniature canoes for young boys or Mossi blacksmiths or

Igbo sculptors carve dolls for young girls. Plastic dolls and other manufactured toys have made appearances with the rise of colonial and postcolonial consumer markets and are popular with urban families who live in a Westernized cash economy.

Children use natural, found, or discarded materials to create toys that show their astute observations of the world around them. In rural areas where herding is a way of life, boys might create and play with clay figures of cows. Cars, airplanes, radios, or any object a child might find attractive, but usually unattainable, can be constructed by pegging together soft woods or by twisting discarded wire into fantastic shapes. New models of cars or airplanes that a child might observe influence his or her creations—although the toy often improves on the original. In the 1960s, in the Democratic Republic of the Congo, for example, boys' toy airplanes echoed the UN's transport planes and helicopters.

Girls' dolls present a slightly more complicated case because of the confusion of children's playthings with dolls for adults, or ritual figures. Many scholars do not use the term "doll" for the ritual figures used by adult women, due to a belief that this association with children's toys trivializes the ritual figures. In a recent publication on southern African dolls, including dolls for both play and ritual, authors termed the ritual objects "fertility figures" and "child figures." However, it can be argued that children's dolls are not trivial, and that both types of object, whether used for play or in ritual, function in the same way and are called by the same name in the vernacular. Here, the English term "doll" is used to refer to both types of figure.

Colonial authorities, merchants, missionaries, curious explorers, adventurers, and other Europeans and Americans who traveled and lived in Africa established the broad category of African dolls. Working within a European American framework and handicapped by using men as translators when talking to the women, they called the anthropomorphic figures that older, mature women treated like living children, "dolls." The created category of "African doll" contains figures, both children's toys and ritual figures, that depict human beings—usually a child—that are treated as living children (see Cameron 1996, 21–7 for a discussion of where play and ritual overlap).

Little girls play with dolls. This seemingly universal truth holds throughout Africa. Girls treat the dolls as infants, feeding, bathing, and dressing them, putting them to bed, getting them up, cuddling and singing to them. The primary purpose of this role playing is not to teach child-care, for a girl learns this by taking care of her younger siblings. Rather, as the girls imitate the women they observe in daily life, they try out their future adult roles and their culturally sanctioned desire to become mothers is reinforced.

Like the boys making wire cars, girls or family members make most play dolls out of ephemeral or readily available materials. Many sources note that mothers help young girls construct their dolls. As the maker grows older and more adept, the dolls become more sophisticated. Mothers and grandmothers, it is noted, make the best dolls.

Girls imaginatively transform anything available into pretend babies. Young girls tie mangos and corncobs into their wrappers like infants. Cow or sheep bones with drilled holes for earrings are sometimes adapted. A common material for dolls is clay. After the girls mold dolls and allow them to dry, the images are placed in cooking fires. Then they are decorated with found or donated bits of cloth and beads. This practice has been documented among the Zulu, Tabwa, and Kuba, and appears to be widespread throughout Africa.

In some parts of southern Africa, a perceived link exists between a girl's behavior towards her doll and her future as wife and mother. If in play, Nguni girls stage fights between their dolls, adults will reprimand the girls and tell them that they will not be good wives. Adults instructed Ambo and Nyaneka girls to handle their dolls gently as they represented the promise of future children.

At puberty, in women's initiations, and in engagement and marriage ceremonies, small ritual figures may symbolize a young woman's ability to bear children and the first child itself. Family members might give an initiate a small figure that the novice must treat as an infant. Among the Zaramo, this figure is called *mwana hiti* (child of wood) and, after being secluded with the initiate, is displayed to the public at the initiate's coming-out ceremonies.

Although not toys, doll-like figures will be a part of many women's adult lives. Small ritual figures also may be part of engagement and marriage arrangements. Among the Fali of Cameroon, a young man made a doll called *ham pilu* as a betrothal present for his bride. He would decorate it with beads, bells, coins, and other additive materials and designate its sex as that desired of their first born. The bride cared for the doll until her own child was born, at which time she discarded the figure. Other dolls encourage fertility, such as the Nguni woman who carries a doll, treating it as a real child, until she herself becomes pregnant. Dolls among the Yoruba, Malinke, Bamana, and Luba might also be surrogates for children who have died.

These doll-like figures have historically been placed in the same category as children's toys and dolls. Ethnographers, colonial administrators, missionaries, explorers, and other Europeans and Americans observed women manipulating these miniature figures as if they were babies—feeding, bathing, clothing, and cuddling them. These early expatriates had been taught that African cultures and societies were "primitive" and that Africans themselves were "childlike." Based on these assumptions, they described the ritual figures as dolls, and this categorization has survived. To further complicate these issues, Europeans and Americans often consider toys and dolls as trivial. Many African peoples, however, see children's dolls as important objects and look to how a girl treats a doll to indicate her future success as a mother. Also, small human figures might move from one category to another. An Asante *akua ma*, a figure used by women when they are unable to conceive, is sometimes given to the child, conceived through its intervention, as a plaything.

The diverse Westerners who began to collect information on dolls had contradictory experiences. One early museum-collecting expedition found that girls and mothers eagerly sold their dolls, even making new ones within sight of expedition members. In contrast, most collectors and scholars comment on the difficulty of gathering either information about or the "dolls" associated with adult ritual. The psychological, religious, and personal meanings the figures have in women's lives are usually listed as the reason women will not abandon them.

For toys, dolls, and ritual figures, a tourist market has flourished that accommodates objects to an outsider market. Asante *akua ba*, for example, have been adopted by African Americans as symbols of an African heritage, and carvers have responded by carving thousands for export. African artists, based on the tastes of American audience, have adapted the figures, making the schematic bodies more figural. The figures might become larger, expanding from the normal 6 inches to sometimes as much as 2 feet in height, or smaller, as when the form becomes a golden pin. Americans and Europeans "discovered" wire toys made by young boys and began to buy them. As a result, an industry now exists in which grown men create elaborate toys for sale.

Many African toys only last for a few hours. Others are guarded for a lifetime. Some are produced for sale, as opposed to personal play. Whatever the life-span or final destination, African toys and dolls play an essential part in the life of the children who create and play with them.

References

Cameron, Elisabeth L. 1996. *Isn't S/He a Doll? Play and Ritual in African Sculpture.* Los Angeles: UCLA Fowler Museum of Cultural History.

Davison, Patricia. 1983. Wireworks: Toys from Southern Africa. *African Arts* 16, no. 3:50–2.

Delarozière, Marie-Françoise, and Michel Massal. 199 *Jouets des enfants d'Afrique: Regards sur des merveilles d'ingéniosité.* Éditions UNESCO.

Dell, Elizabeth, ed. 1998. *Evocations of the Child: Fertility Figures of the Southern African Region.* Cape Town: Johannesburg Art Gallery and Human & Rousseau.

Lutton, Eric. 1933. "Poupées d'Afrique occidentale. *Bulletin de Musée d'Ethnographie du Trocadéro* 5:8–19.

Makoena, Napho. 1990. "Wire Toys from Katlehong Township. In *Art from South Africa.* London: Thames and Hudson.

ELISABETH L. CAMERON

See also **Children's Folklore; Initiation; Tourism and Tourist Arts**

DRAMA: ANANG IBIBIO TRADITIONAL DRAMA

Anthony Graham-White (1974) distinguishes three types of drama in sub-Saharan Africa: traditional drama, drama of the colonial period, and literary drama. Traditional drama is that which was performed prior to the colonial period and, in some cases, is still performed today. It is expressed in the vernacular, is not written down, is typically based on the social organization of the village, and is performed by members of a special society or age-set. Traditional drama is to be distinguished from ritual and storytelling performances, although both may, on occasion, display dramatic elements. Most traditional dramas are satiric comedies, reenactments of historical events, and mimetic representations of hunting. The most common forms are comic skits that rely on action rather than words and alternate with songs and dances.

Traditional performances of drama are in the open air, and actors are not separated from the audience by sets, lighting, or a raised stage. Sometimes the lines of actors are memorized, but often performers are permitted to improvise. There is no strict separation of actors and spectators; actors may move freely among the audience, and spectators may get up to dance with performers. Because they have seen other performances and thus have acquired standards of comparison, spectators watch as critics, and their responses to performances prompt competition among troupes. Masks and costumes are commonly worn and voice-disguisers used to shield the identity of actors in certain dramas, especially from women, from whom identities and other "secrets" of the society are carefully hidden.

Among some peoples, particularly in West Africa, traditional drama is well developed. Most of it, however, has gone unstudied. This is so because most observers of such performances have had little or no interest in drama or have confused it with ritual and storytelling events, which may have a dramatic flavor but are not traditional drama as defined here. Few good accounts of performances exist in the literature, and of these, the description of traditional drama among the Anang of southeastern Nigeria is one of the most complete. It was recorded by a colonial administrator with a degree in anthropology (Jeffreys 1951) and later by an anthropologist with a strong interest in folklore (Messenger 1962, 1971).

The Anang, one of the six Ibibio-speaking peoples, are not centrally organized politically, but are composed of twenty-eight village groups, or *iman*. Before contact with the British in 1901 and the establishment of colonial government in 1914, most of the villages in each group possessed drama societies, called *ekon*, but a half-century later, one of the largest of the *iman* boasted but two village troupes. One of these numbered over a hundred male members of age fourteen to thirty, half of them actors and half musicians, dancers, prop men, equipment carriers, and guards. Once formed and sponsored by one or several patrilineages, a troupe devised a seven-hour performance and practiced it one day of an eight-day week for six years before presenting it during the dry season of the seventh year (seven being the Anang sacred number) in most villages of the *iman* and sometimes in villages of contiguous groups. At the end of the dry season, the troupe disbanded and a new one was formed under the guidance of senior members of the previous company.

The origin of a troupe is often chronicled in a legend. One of these recounts how an apprentice diviner wandered into a forest where he observed ghosts of former diviners performing *ekon* and was commanded by them to found the society and taught how to "play" *ekon* and how to build a shrine and call into it the guardian spirit. It was customary for two priests to aid the guardian spirit, one to control rain at performances and the other to ward off attacks of evil ghosts, witches, and sorcerers and to prevent masks from splitting, dancers from falling, and actors and singers from forgetting their lines. Also hired was a carver to produce masks, puppets, and other paraphernalia. The priests and carver were paid from funds donated by the sponsoring kin groups and from fees collected from incoming members as the company was formed and later from villages in which performances were given.

Ekon was played in a village square, surrounded on three sides by the audience. The open side of the square was occupied by a puppet stage, the orchestra, and a hut that served actors donning their garb. The performance focused on a series of often bawdy satiric plays acted by men, some of whom played women's roles, and by puppets manipulated from behind a stage of blankets and palm branches hung from a bamboo frame. Between each skit, music was played, satiric songs were sung by the orchestra, and songs were voiced by a chorus of dancers. Mummers, wearing both masks and costumes, ran about the square, while singing acrobats displayed their skills, which included tight-rope walking, or magicians exhibited sleight-of-hand deceptions.

During a performance, there was much interaction between players and the audience. Some members of the troupe dressed as women and circulated in the audience, selling soap, while others accosted men with simulated sexual advances. Occasionally, a spectator would enter the square and dance with the chorus, and when widely known songs were sung by players, the audience would join in. Some of the plays involved actors chasing members of the audience or inviting them to participate in segments of a skit. *Ekon* guards were posted about the square to prevent any violence, since the satire often was directed toward a spectator or a group of them. Even though there was seldom legal redress against defamation, and the guardian spirit would punish a person assaulting a performer, spectators, at times, became so incensed at barbs directed their way that they took action and had to be subdued by guards. The usual response of maligned spectators, however, was to flee the square amid derisive laughter from the audience. Such responses to satire point to the social control function of *ekon*, which was profound.

It was customary for another village in the *iman* to be singled out for the lion's share of satiric attacks on its groups (for instance, patrilineages, age-sets, societies, or women) and individuals (especially important ones). The satire was based on information collected over six years by "spies," who might include women married to men of that village, who were willing to divulge scandals, carvers who spent prolonged periods carving pieces for the societies of the village, or women traders from the village, whose gossip in the markets might reveal the misbehavior of neighbors at home. When a troupe performed in the seventh year, it played first in its own village and last in the village thus targeted. The last performance always drew the largest crowds and demanded extra guards to cope with violence.

An analysis of the satire expressed in drama and song reveals that it was directed against groups, individual misbehavior, and conditions such as poverty, mental illness, and ugly physical appearance. The groups most often attacked were the hated Igbo, Hausa traders who cheated customers, overly warlike villages, traditional courts, native courts introduced by the British, and the colonial administration and its taxation policies, Christian missions, as well as nativist church denominations, modern large towns, and Europeans generally. The behavior of individuals chosen for satire focused on the resentment of men against domineering and sexually demanding women, the corruption of indigenous shamans and court judges, stupidity and drunkenness, lack of skill, disrespect shown parents and elders, and the imitation of European ways. Much of Anang culture and personality were writ large in the satire of *ekon*.

Skits in a performance could last from a quarter to three-quarters of an hour, and depending on their length, could number from four to a dozen during the course of seven hours. An example of a skit was one that satirized a nativist church, the dogma and rituals of which combined Christian and Anang religions. Actors in it were church dignitaries, dressed in exaggerated European attire, who performed healing services for several parishioners by inducting possession, just as indigenous shamans might do, through manipulation of a huge wooden Bible. A sterile woman was impregnated by the Holy Spirit in the priest who simulated coitus with her; a hunter with a wooden dog who was unable to flush game had the Bible passed several times over the animal's head to improve his skills in the forest; and a humpbacked man was surrounded by the dignitaries, all of whom became possessed, with the result that the hump was transformed into a gigantic wooden penis. Both the hunter with his hinge-jawed dog and the former humpback rushed into the audience, the former to bite spectators, and the latter to attempt coitus with women, who retreated screaming at his approach. During the skit, there was much singing, praying, and dancing by the actors.

Many of the songs rendered by the orchestra, dancers, mummers, and actors dealt with mistreatment of kin, especially elders, and breaking taboos, two of the most serious offences among the Anang. Singers told of a man who sold certain of his grandchildren and in-laws into slavery to Igbo traders. Since he "talked out of the side of his mouth to people," the deity punished him by giving him "a twitch at the mouth." In another song, a man fell from an oil palm tree and suffered grave injury as punishment for delaying his father's funeral beyond three years. Each *iman* forbids its members to eat the meat of a particular animal; this creature, according to legend, aided the founder of the village group in some manner and was thus honored. One song alleged that a man killed and ate a squirrel, sacred to the Anang, which, in the past, would have led to his trial and execution if found guilty. Although the songs alluded to here were brief, some contained over a hundred words.

A final word must be said about the dialogues of actors, which are characterized by the use of archaic words and punning. Many of the puns were based on the tonal nature of the Ibibio language. One such pun in a play centers on an aggressive demand for a gift of a uniform (a soldier's or conductor's coat) made by a domineering wife to her husband, a chief. She wielded a machete which she frequently shook in his face; he wore a mask carved and painted to portray anguish. "So you want an *enyen ket*?" was his response, which prompted an even more vehement demand on her part. With this, he chased her about the square, trying to gouge out her eye with a long wooden thumb attached to his own: Depending on how "*enyen ket*" is uttered tonally, it can mean "uniform" or "one eye"!

References

Graham-White, Anthony. 1974. *The Drama of Black Africa*. New York: Samuel French, Inc.

Jeffreys, M. D. W. 1951. The Ekon Players. *Eastern Anthropologist* V: 41–7.

Messenger, John C. 1962. Anang Art, Drama, and Social Control. In *Arts, Human Behavior, and Africa*, ed. Alan P. Merriam. New York: African Studies Association.

———. 1971. Ibibio Drama. *Africa* XLI: 208–22.

JOHN C. MESSENGER

See also **Performance; Puppetry; Theater**

DRAUGHTS (JEU DE DAMES; CHECKERS)

The first variation of the game draughts dates from around 1500 CE and became popular in Great Britain, France, and central Europe. The British continued to play this variation into the twentieth century. Their game is now referred to as Anglo-Saxon draughts, or checkers, as it is known in the United States. The game is characterized by its sixty-four black and white squares with twelve white and twelve black draughtsmen, or checkers, on the board. In France, the Anglo-Saxon game was replaced by "Polish" draughts in the eighteenth century, a game that had developed in the Netherlands in the seventeenth century. The playing board counted one hundred black and white squares with twenty pieces on each side. This game of Polish (or continental) draughts would compete with Anglo-Saxon draughts as the European powers gained colonies throughout the world.

The French and British colonization of Africa and the Caribbean brought the game of draughts overseas. With the landing of the French in Haiti, for instance, the game of draughts became popular on the island. The French conquest of West Africa did the same for areas now known as Senegal, Cote d'Ivoire, and Mali. The British game found its greatest stronghold in the United States, where the popularity of checkers was to outdo that in the British Isles themselves. In Africa and the Caribbean, the Anglo-Saxon version conquered the British territories, while the continental game became popular in those of the French and Dutch. The Italians, who had their own version, which was also played on sixty-four squares, took their game to Ethiopia and Eritrea, where it can still be found.

The game of draughts gained considerable prestige in western Europe, although it remained a children's game in countries such as Germany and even the United States, despite the serious competition that existed in American checkers clubs. In other countries, it rivals the status of chess, or at least its popularity. Much of the African and Caribbean history of the game would have been lost if later draughts champions had not come from former French and British colonies. France was the first to invite talented players from Africa to its championships as early as the 1890s.

From the 1890s onwards, the history of African draughts becomes a history of African draughts players reaching the European continent. After the introduction of draughts to Africa and the Caribbean, the game had become so popular that in Senegal, for instance, it became the number one sports activity. Senegalese players were the first to visit the European continent in the 1890s as competitors. At that time, Senegal was a part of France, and French players dominated the championships of the game. In 1910, the first African player won a tournament in Europe. Woldouby, champion of Senegal, took Paris by storm and beat the strongest players of France in the Paris Tournament of 1911. Still remembered by the "Woldouby-position" that was named after him, he was only a prelude to the talented players who would later visit Europe.

Although draughts remained popular in the colonies, players would not reach Europe in significant numbers until after World War II. After the war, France lost its superiority in the game, and Dutch players took over, soon to be joined by Russian stars. In 1947, the Federation Mondiale du Jeu de Dames (the World Draughts Federation) was set up to organize a world championship and develop ranking and rating systems. The many, but subtle, differences in rules of play frustrated unity, and a new set of rules was agreed upon to allow for an international standard. These rules of international draughts were accepted and used by all Russian, Dutch, and French, as well as African and other international players. The Anglo-Saxon game maintained its separate world championship events, although its organization intensified the links with the new international federation.

In 1956, the champion of Haiti was invited to the world championships in the Netherlands and gained the title of master, and in 1959, another Senegalese took the Paris championship, entered the world championships, and took the title of grand master. Grandmaster Baba Sy became a legend in the Netherlands, where he spent most of his career. He set the world record for simultaneous draughts matches at 150 games and became challenger for the world title in 1963. For unknown reasons, the world title match between Baba Sy and the Russian Kouperman was never played. For about five years, Baba Sy reigned in the international draughts championships, until he was joined by stronger talents from Russia and the Netherlands. In the 1980s, some time after his untimely death, Baba Sy was proclaimed world champion of 1963, with the agreement of the Russian federation.

The evident talent pool in West Africa, and also in Haiti and Surinam, became the center of attention in the 1980s. The Confederation Africaine du Jeu de Dames was set up, and the 1980 world championships were held in Bamako, Mali. In 1984, Dakar, Senegal, and in 1988, Paramaribo, Surinam, took their turns as host city for the world championship event, recognizing and supporting the local players organizations. By now, a steady stream of draughts talents was entering the international tournaments, and these players were establishing themselves as masters or grand masters. Although the accomplishments of Baba Sy were never equaled in the twentieth century, Senegalese players took third place in world championships, and grand masters are now found in Mali, Ivory Coast, Senegal, and Surinam.

International draughts is played on a checkered board with one hundred squares. One player owns twenty white pieces and the other, twenty black ones. White opens the game. Pieces move diagonally, one square at a time, and may capture by jumping over an adjacent opponent's piece. A king is made upon reaching the other end of the board. A king may move more than one square at a time and capture likewise. Capturing is obligatory, and if there is a choice of capture, the player is obliged to choose the move that takes the maximum number of pieces. This last rule differs from continental draughts and is frequently omitted in West Africa.

Apart from the obligatory multiple capture, international draughts is strategically similar to what is played in West Africa. Small differences, such as playing on the white instead of the black fields, or a different position of the board between the players, may also be present. In tournaments, players seem to play faster than average and show particular resilience in tactical combinations. The playing style of West Africans has often been characterized as that of the classic school, with defensive play making them difficult opponents to beat. Their fast play and love for combinations in the game have made them popular with the audience. Frequent contact with the international draughts scene has increased their access to the draughts literature and exposure to clocks and notation forms. They also participate in (mainly Dutch) draughts clubs, tournaments, and exhibition games. Senegal is seen as the third most important country, after the former Soviet Union and the Netherlands, in terms of playing strength and players numbers.

The Anglo-Saxon game, checkers, has traditionally been dominated by Scottish, English, and, later, American players. In 1991, a Barbados player, Ronald King—better known as Suki—took one of two available world titles. The frequent draws in the game had developed a variation in which the first two—and later, the first three—moves of the game were dictated to the players in order to avoid repetitive openings and subsequent draws. Later, the "go-as-you-please" variation was reinstated, and two world championship titles became available: three-move and go-as-you-please. Since 1991, Ronald King has been world champion in go-as-you-please, the dominant version in Barbados, and after 1994, he also held the three-move title, the first player to hold both titles simultaneously.

The Anglo-Saxon-derived game differs from international draughts in the size of the board and the number of pieces. The checkers are commonly referred to as red and white, and red will start the game. The pieces can only move and capture forward, and a player is not forced to choose the move with the most captures. The king may move and capture forward and backward but not more than one square, in international draughts.

Continental and Anglo-Saxon draughts were the only European board games that were introduced to Africa and the Caribbean with considerable success. The number of African countries joining the world championships of draughts is still increasing, and the successes of African and Caribbean players has fueled the popularity the game already enjoys. Together with mancala, draughts and checkers are the most important gaming pastimes in Africa and the Caribbean islands.

References

Beek, W. E. A. 1997. *The Fascinating world of Draughts: 50 Years of the World Draughts Federation.* Maastricht: Shaker Publishing B.V.

Kruijswijk, K. W. 1966. *Algemene historie en bibliografie van het damspel.* The Hague.

Oldbury, D. 1978. *The Complete Encyclopaedia of Draughts.* Torquay.

Stoep, A van der. 1984. *A History of Draughts.* Rockanje.

ALEX DE VOOGT

See also **Mancala**

DREAMS

The paradigms of early European missionaries and ethnologists have contributed a great deal towards the misunderstanding of dreams in Africa. Central to the evolutionist paradigm was the distinction between scientific and rational "Western thought," and mystical "primitive thought." European scholars speculated that Africans confused dreaming and waking realities, or valued dreams more than waking perceptions. For example, a Zulu man would treat a friend as an enemy because of a dream in which the latter intended to harm him.

One of the most interesting interventions was Tylor's (1871) theory of animism. He suggested that it was from the attempts of primitives to come to terms with dream experiences that the ideas of the spirit and soul arose. The appearance of the dream self that wanders about at night gave humans an idea of their own duality. Moreover, the appearance of the dead in dreams suggests that the soul had an after-life. For Tylor, a belief in spiritual beings was the central idea of religion.

Psychoanalysts, such as Freud and Jung, continued to use dreams as a means of constructing Africa as "the other." They perceived the dreams of Westerners as analogous to the waking realities of Africans: dreams were an indication of the "savage world" within the Western person that had to be subdued and civilised. Jung visited East Africa in 1925 and perceived African society as equivalent to an inner region of the mind.

Today this binary distinction between "scientific" and "primitive" mentalities is seen as a Western fiction with little relevance to any other contexts. The most decisive break with evolutionism occurred with the application of Freud's psychoanalytic theory to dreams in Africa. Psychologically minded anthropologists have sought to demonstrate the universality of deep psychoanalytic processes and to investigate how these were modified by local social structure and symbolic meanings. Lee (1958) examined the social influences on the manifest content of dreams as reported by some six hundred subjects at a hospital in Zululand, South Africa. He recorded significant differences between the dreams reported by men and by women and found that dreams were stereotyped in terms of central themes and imagery. His evidence seems to confirm Freud's hypothesis that dreams are a form of wish fulfillment and that dream experiences express unresolved conflicts in the dreamer. Men's dreams of owning large herds of superb cattle and of lovemaking were pleasant wish-fulfillment dreams. Men also dreamt of beer drinking, feasts, and fighting. In contrast, women dreamt of babies, snakes, still water, flooded rivers, and of a small, muscular, and hairy witch-familiar with an exceedingly large penis known as the *tikoloshe*. Newly married brides and women with a record of marital infertility tended to dream of babies, and these dreams were of a wish-fulfilling nature. Dreams of water were also associated with childbirth. Indeed, the Zulu word *isiZalo* refers to both the uterus and the river-mouth. Single women, widows, and married women who had borne few children dreamed of still water. For them, the wish for offspring was still present, but not as strong as for the baby-dreamers. Dreams of flooded waters were nightmares that produced great anxiety. These dreams tended to occur among married women with considerable experience of childbirth and indicated a fear of the economic pressure of further childbearing. Yet, in the face of cultural pressure to continue bearing children for as long as possible, this fear could not be overtly expressed. Dreams of sexual attack by the *tikoloshe* and snakes, Lee maintains, expressed the fears and frustrations of sexual relations within marriage.

Nevertheless, the value of the psychoanalytic approach to the study of dreams in Africa was seldom realized. Dreams were still perceived as personal phenomena and were largely ignored in social research. They were, however, occasionally referred to in anthropological studies of religion and cosmology. Students were compelled to recognize how dreams were treated as one-way channels of information between spiritual beings and certain individuals.

Evans-Pritchard (1958) included a chapter on dreams in his well-known study of witchcraft amongst the Azande of Anglo-Egyptian Sudan. He contends that Azande not only perceived bad dreams as signs of witchcraft, but also as a direct experience thereof. Berglund (1989) emphasized the cosmological impor-

tance of dreams amongst Zulu-speakers. Zulu believed that the shades (or ancestors) revealed themselves to their descendants through dreams. At night, the shades entered through the mouths of dreamers, brought them good news, and showed the dreamers where to locate lost cattle. During the first months of pregnancy, the shades could also announce the sex of an expected child. Dreams of green and black snakes, and of buffaloes, indicated a boy; those of puff adders and of crossing rivers showed that the child would be a girl. The absence of dreams brought about great anxiety because it indicated a lack of interest on the part of the shades. As servants of the shades, diviners were called to their profession by frightening and incomprehensible dreams, such as vomiting snakes. Hereafter, dreams taught diviners about their practice and about herbs. Diviners often placed *imphepho* plants underneath their pillows, so that their dreams would be clear. Although they include the topic of dreams in their studies, Evans-Pritchard and Berglund's comments are fragmentary and fall short of systematic theoretical treatment.

Perhaps the most expansive consideration of dreams within anthropological studies of Africa has focused on independent church movements. Some authors explicitly seek to develop a sociological approach to the study of dreams. Although Curley (1983) concedes that dream experiences arise in the individual psyche, he insists "the anthropologist must study them in their capacity as social facts rather than as clues to the workings of the mind." The primary data of students of African churches has not been the subjective reconstruction of "dreams as dreamt," but rather "dreams as told to others." Curley (1993, 135) argues that, "individual experiences such as dreams become proper grist for the anthropological mill when they are communicated to others, acted upon, and interpreted in a given social context." Scholars of the churches have viewed the narrations of dreams as purposeful public performances with definite effects on social action. Through their studies, they show how church members tactically manipulate dreams in social encounters and how dream narrations feature in the collective life and social organization of churches.

Charsley (1973) found that the narration and interpretation of dreams was at the heart of services of a Pentecostal-type church in Uganda. Dreams were perceived as "messages from God" about what had happened and what should happen. He describes dream telling as "a channel through which members can bid for status within the group, by attempting to contribute valuably to its life" (Charsley 1973, 252). It provided secondary church leaders, such as clerks and the rank and file of women members, with an opportunity to exert an active influence on events of the church. Prominent male members generally told of dreams of the church as an organized group and of instructions to read particular Biblical passages and to sing particular hymns. Thereby, they were accorded recognition for contributing a "message from God," regarded as significant for the group. Women were more inclined to tell dreams that displayed fellow church members in an unfavorable light (such as wearing dirty church uniforms). Since these dreams often led to confessions and to ritual forgivings, the women dream tellers were able to determine the course of events in the church. These were ambitious bids for status by women, but were tolerated by the church leadership.

Curley (1983) adopts a similar perspective, but highlights differences between the social roles of "conversion" and "reconfirming" dreams in a fundamentalist church in Cameroon. Conversion dreams contained explicit religious images such as the cross and showed vulnerability prior to the conversion, as opposed to physical strength thereafter. Such dreams were told upon occasions such as baptism and were used as personal charters to claim full membership status in the congregation. They were signs of communion with God and became a fund of the common knowledge of the church. As a "repository of striking images," the dreams helped to establish religious truth and to confer legitimacy upon the church as a select group of worshippers. Reconfirming dreams were narrated during church services and testified that the dreamer still had an active spiritual life. Their themes were generally the spiritual power that came with religious faith (e.g., to heal the sick). They often had a competitive aspect and expressed rivalry between title-holders in the church. Through the narration of confirming dreams, men expressed a desire for recognition and for advancement within the ranks of the church. The narrations attested to religious fervor, the ability to derive meaning from experience, and also to verbal skills that were necessary for the assumption of positions of leadership and authority. However, such rivalry was softened when expressed in the form of a dream, since the narrator was not held responsible for what he dreamt.

Over the past two decades, there has been renewed interest in dreams as sites of cultural meaning. Jedrej and Shaw's collection *Dreaming Religion and Society in Africa* (1992) has laid an excellent foundation for the elaboration of fresh perspectives. Many of the essays contained in this edited volume seek to overcome the separation of the "subjective" from the "social," and of "meaning" from "power." Their research explores how the meanings of individual dreams, as well as the meanings of dreams in general, are negotiated and defined in different social and cultural contexts, rather than how their meanings fit into external explanatory frameworks.

One example from this volume is Holy's (1992) work on the role of dreams among the Berti of Dafur, in the Sudan. For the Berti, dreams did not indicate the innermost desire of the dreamer, as Freudian analysis would suggest, but rather, tapped into something completely outside the dreamer. Dreams did not indicate what the dreamers wanted, but rather, what the dreamers would get. The Berti perceived of dreams as intensely personal and rarely shared them with anyone else. Each dreamer interpreted his or her own dreams. There were, nonetheless, complex frameworks for interpreting dreams that were culturally shared and used in everyday life. Dreams were believed to be in code, and they had to be decoded in terms of the indices and symbols they contained. Indices were signs that showed only one form of a general class. For example, owning a goat is one way of getting rich. Therefore, to dream of a goat indicates wealth and prosperity, although it may not actually be acquired through ownership of goats. Dream symbols were recognizable because they were used in everyday waking life. They could be colors, animals, or various kinds of objects. Dream symbols could be interpreted literally or in terms of a reversal of content: they could have either a positive or negative value, or they could carry a general or specific message. Therefore, one had to consider the context of the symbol within the dream. For example, falling into a dry well and not being rescued might indicate death (a specific event), but falling into a dry well and being rescued from it might indicate a good future (a general omen).

Although Holy provides a detailed description of the rules that the Berti use to interpret dreams, he does not show whether these rules operate consciously or unconsciously.

Hence, there is no single, all-encompassing framework that has characterized the study of dreams in Africa in recent years. Instead, the study of dreams has been marked by a variety of concerns. These include the social contexts of dreams, their symbolism, the hermeneutics of dream interpretation, and the uses of dreams as sources of ideas that structure identities and experiences in the everyday world. Most important has been the recognition that the images provided by dreams are filtered through the prisms of local cultural traditions. For this reason, culture may well be a key word in future studies of dreams and dreaming in Africa.

References

Berglund, A. 1989. *Zulu Thought Patterns and Symbolism.* London: Hurst and Company.

Charsley, S. R. 1973. Dreams in an Independent African Church. *Africa* 43, no. 3:244–57.

Curley, R. 1983. Dreams of Power: Social Process in a West African Religious Movement. *Africa* 53, no. 3:20–38.

Evans-Pritchard, E. E. 1958 (1937). *Witchcraft, Oracles and Magic Among the Azande.* London: Oxford University Press.

Holy, L. 1992. Berti Dream Interpretation. In *Dreaming, Religion and Society in Africa*, eds. M. C. Jedrej and Rosalind Shaw. Leiden: E.J. Brill,

Jedrej, M. C., and Rosalind Shaw eds. 1992. *Dreaming, Religion and Society in Africa.* Leiden: E.J. Brill,

Lee, S. G. 1958. Social Influence in Zulu Dreaming. *Journal of Social Psychology* 47:265–83.

Tylor, Edward Burnett. 1958 (1871). *Primitive Culture. Vol. 2. The Origin of Religion.* New York: Harper Torchbooks.

ISAK NIEHAUS

See also **Divination; Gender; Religion**

DRESS

African dress, a system of nonverbal communication, aids in personal and sociocultural identification of African people in their daily lives. Dress involves both modifying and supplementing the body with the involvement of all five senses. The visual aspects of dress (such as shape, silhouette, and color) appear primary, but the other senses are also involved, such as touching skin, textiles, or leather, smelling scents applied to or associated with body or fabric, hearing the rustle of textiles or jangle of jewelry, and tasting pomades or lipstick.

"Dress" is a more comprehensive concept than either clothing or fashion. Dress encompasses more than clothing, for it includes covering and modifying the body. In addition, although ritual and ceremonial dress may change, they are usually not fashionable, for their rate of change ordinarily occurs more slowly than the concept of fashion implies. Regalia of chiefs and rulers, such as those of the kings of Benin and Yoruba people and the Asantehene of the Asante are one example.

Common patterns of dress differentiate groups and individuals from one another in Africa, but idiosyncratic and personal styles are also frequent. Urban Africans in cities like Dakar, Abidjan, Lagos, Johannesburg, and Nairobi wear styles in apparel, hairstyles, and accessories current in the fashion centers of Paris, London, New York, and Tokyo, because television, cinema, newspapers, and magazines, along with travel or study abroad, influence them. However, Africans also display coiffure, body painting, clothing, and jewelry that are identified not only as African but often as a marker of a specific ethnic group. Such examples stem from community traditions that demonstrate a continuity with the past, even when undergoing change. Many African men and women wear cosmopolitan fashions daily, but choose ritual and ceremonial ensembles from their ethnic heritage for special occasions and events like puberty rituals, funerals, and marriage ceremonies.

A common African tradition of dress involves variations of wrapping cloth around the body, fully or partially covering the torso. The toga-style associated with the political figure in Ghana of the late Kwame Nkrumah and the Asante people exemplifies fully wrapping the body, whereas the wrapped cloth of Masaai warriors primarily covers the torso. Another style for both men and women involves wrapping cloth (called *pagne* in French-speaking countries) around the lower body, usually from the waist to mid-calf or ankles, and combining it with a tailored garment such as a blouse, shirt, or jacket on the upper body (or sometimes, leaving it bare).

Women may vary the wrapper style by wearing two layers on the lower body (the top one from the waist to the knees and the lower from the waist to the ankles), combined with a blouse on their upper body. The two wrappers are called "up and down" by the Igbo of Nigeria to designate the top and bottom layers, respectively. Ghanaian women are known for an ensemble with a blouse that has a peplum covering the top of the wrapper at the waist. Women in many parts of Africa wrap cloth around their bodies from the top of their breasts to their ankles. Women, as among the Yoruba and Kalabari, may also wrap their cloth (sometimes even adding a layer) to suggest a fulsome body, not a slim-waisted one, hinting at pregnancy and fertility.

Veils and head coverings are wrapped, as seen in Tuareg men's veils, Hausa men's turbans, and Yoruba women's headties. Veils are often associated with women, but among the Tuareg, veils relate to men's status and allow privacy and social separation. Muslim men's turbans signify their successful trip to Mecca. The changing shapes of Yoruba women's headties from year to year demonstrate only one example of swiftly changing fashion in Africa.

Preshaping is used for textiles and skins to make garments and other items (such as hats and gloves) by cutting and stitching. Fabrics are cut and sewn to make short and full-length garments for both men and women. Short garments include the Mande hunter's tunic enhanced with attached packets that carry sacred messages inside. Full-length garments include the women's boubou of Senegal, the full-length gowns of Herrero and Efik women, and the men's garment called caftan throughout several West African countries and djellaba in North Africa. Skins are preshaped for fashioning shoes and boots and often trimmed with beads, feathers, or fur as found in the slippers of rulers, such as the Asantehene of the Asante people of Ghana.

Preshaping is also used to make many kinds of jewelry by molding metal or clay or carving wood or ivory. Beads, made of various materials, both natural and hand-crafted, may adorn the neck, wrists, upper arm, waist, knees, and ankles, and many are preshaped. Bedecking with beads is common among many

Africans, such as Masaai men and Zulu women. Some beads of metal or seed pods produce sounds when the wearer walks or dances and are often used in masquerade ensembles.

Dress marks an individual's many identities, such as gender, age, occupation, religion, community, and ethnicity. For example, wrapping a woman's cloth to the left or a man's to the right designates gender, as does the use of several styles of caps for Yoruba men in contrast to the headties worn by Yoruba women. In some groups, boys and girls before puberty may go without clothes and wear only beads; at adolescence or when entering school, they wear trousers and shirts or frocks. Schoolchildren often wear uniforms, a practice encouraged during colonial times and continued since then.

Wearing a similar or identical textile for a wrapper outfit, shirt, or blouse commonly identifies group affiliation in many parts of Africa. Members belonging to Herero organizations called "flags" wear colored cloth to show their national political affiliation and use the English word "uniform" to indicate their dress. Many ethnic groups throughout Africa order identical cloth to wear for critical life events, such as honoring the individual on a significant birthday, when attending a wedding as identification with the bride and groom, or showing support for a political party. Members of Kalabari women's organizations in Nigeria wear specified textiles for special events, or both male and female extended family members wear the same textile to display their kinship affiliation at masquerade festivals or other celebrations.

Rituals that mark puberty, either socially or biologically, underscore gender difference and separate rituals are generally held for boys and girls. Types of body marking or apparel that accompany the ritual wearer emphasize the adult roles of male or female in the society. The ritual may include permanent marking like scarification and cicatrization, or temporary colorings. Before the late 1970s, Ga'anda girls of northeastern Nigeria were cut with a designated system of patterns over a specified time period. Such temporary colorings as ashes, or white and red chalks may also be used during time.

Dress distinctions in coiffure and ornaments show the transition from boy to man in the case of East Africans like the Maasai, Samburu, Turkana, and Pokot. Dress for puberty rites distinguishes preinitiates from initiates, and boys from girls, among the Pedi of Sekhukhuneland in South Africa. The smocked shirt and string or leather apron is still worn by female initiates, but continual transformations have developed a new Sotho dress, consisting of a length of cloth wrapped around the waist, a headscarf, and bangles.

Some traditions in dress relate to traditions of handwork in cloth production, spinning, weaving, and dyeing. Although both men and women weave, women apparently spin more frequently than men. Some hand-woven wrappers are worn in rituals or indigo dyes that fade on the skin are painted on both men and women. Factory-made (often imported) cloth for wrappers, however, is more commonly found than hand-woven. Both men and women hand-dye textiles, sometimes using hand-woven cloth or, more often, commercially manufactured and, sometimes, imported cloth. Cloth for hand-dyeing is also produced in indigenous textile mills. Textiles dyed with excess indigo that color the body blue are also prized. Other handwork processes are found, such as beating indigo cloth with mallets to make it shiny for Tuareg men's turbans and embroidering Hausa and

Yoruba men's gowns and hats. Both men and women practice the arts of tailoring and dressmaking; generally, men practice embroidery.

A wealth of fabrics for dress abound, as Africa has been a strategic world market for many centuries. Textiles from around the globe are imported throughout the continent, such as posh velvets (some embroidered with gold or silver threads) and the cotton plaid fabrics from India known as madras, embroidered eyelet cloth from Switzerland, woolens and worsteds from Britain, and printed cotton cloth from Europe, Japan, and Indonesia. Indigenous African resources for textiles include cotton, silk from the anaphe caterpillar, raffia from the raffia palm tree, and pounded bark cloth. Other apparel and accessory items also result from trade: derby hats, boaters, top hats, canes, and walking sticks came from Europe, coral, and glass beads from Italy, the Nehru suit in the 1960s from India, and handbags and platform shoes from Europe and America.

Ensembles that cover a masquerade dancer are more properly called costume since dress provides information about an individual's personal identity, whereas costume conceals individual identity by portraying the identity of a character in a dance, a play, or a masquerade. Personal characteristics of a dancer are not of importance and may require being hidden from the audience by covering the hands and feet along with the rest of the body and head. Indeed, a masked dancer often assumes the persona of a spirit from another world, just as costume in a theater or dance performance highlights the identity of the character being performed. One example is the ensemble of red gown, red bonnet, and red sash of a spirit worn by a spirit medium in the Hausa *bori* ceremony in southern Niger.

Africans contribute inspiration for dress to the rest of the world, as in the case of intricate and plaited coiffures, the shirt known as *dansiki*, and the headtie known as *gele*, transported by American Peace Corps volunteers from their association with Yoruba, and the ubiquitous African trade beads originally made in Venice, Italy. Kente cloth, associated with Ghana, and the mud-cloth of Mali (known as *bogolonfino*) have influenced the contemporary American fashion scene. African Americans select these fabrics in order to identify with their African heritage.

References

Adepegba, Cornelius, and Joanne B. Eicher. 1996. Body Arts (Africa). In *The Dictionary of Art*, Vol. 1, ed. Jane Turner. London: Macmillan Publishers.

Arnoldi, Mary Jo. 1996. Ritual (Africa). In *The Dictionary of Art*, Vol. 1, ed. Jane Turner. London: Macmillan Publishers.

Eicher, Joanne B. 1969. *African Dress: A Selected and Annotated Bibliography of Sub-Saharan Countries.* Lansing, Mich.: African Studies Center, Michigan State University.

———. 1996. Dress (Africa). *The Dictionary of Art*, Vol. 1, ed. Jane Turner. London: Macmillan Publishers.

Eicher, Joanne B., and Mary Ellen Roach-Higgins. 1992. Describing and Classifying Dress: Implications for the Study of Gender. In *Dress and Gender: Marking and Meaning*, eds. Ruth Barnes and Joanne B. Eicher. New York: St. Martin's Press. Paperback, 1993.

Hendrickson, Hildi, ed. 1996. *Clothing and Difference: Embodied Identities in Colonial and Post-Colonial Africa.* Durham, N.C.: Duke University Press.

Pokornowski, Ila M., et al. 1985. *African Dress IL A Select and Annotated Bibliography.* Lansing, Mich.: African Studies Center, Michigan State University.

Sieber, Roy, and F. Herreman, eds. 2000. *Hair in African Art and Culture.* New York/Munich: Museum for African Art/Prestel.

JOANNE B. EICHER

See also **Body Arts; Color Symbolism; Gender; Textile Arts and Communication**

E

EAST AFRICAN FOLKLORE: OVERVIEW

Research in East African folklore started around the middle of the nineteenth century. European travelers, missionaries, linguists, and anthropologists recorded narratives, songs, proverbs, and other genres. These collectors had different aims, ranging from the desire to understand East African cultures for the sake of advancing missionary and colonial goals, to the need to enhance the comparative study of languages and cultures.

Initially, the material collected was published in Europe. Later, the missionaries and the colonial governments created publishing and printing facilities in East Africa. Their presses published the materials either in the original language only, or with accompanying translation in German, French or English. Sometimes they published only the translations. Over the years, these efforts resulted in the accumulation of much folklore material from different ethnic groups.

As the collectors were foreigners, their access to the folklore was much more limited than it would have been for indigenous collectors. Apart from the language barrier, the foreigners tended to be seen as agents of the colonial power structure. They were not able, for example, to hear and record anticolonial and antimissionary folklore. That they could only record certain types of folklore, such as folktales, helped shape the perceptions of what African folklore was like, such as the notion that African folklore consists mostly of "fireside" tales. The truth, however, is that through their experiences under colonialism, the East African people created, and expressed themselves in, various forms of anticolonial folklore, such as songs, jokes, and rumors. Vampire stories, for example, and urban legends, which were often connected to the experience of colonialism, were common in those days, but were rarely recorded and published.

The struggle for, and attainment of, independence inspired the East Africans to examine their traditional cultures more seriously than they might have done before, under the impact of colonial education. Writers and scholars like Mathias Mnyampala (Tanganyika), Okot p'Bitek and Taban lo Liyong (Uganda) and Henry Anyumba (Kenya), pioneered this effort. Educational institutions, government departments, and ministries of culture promoted the recording of folklore as part of the effort to document national cultures and foster national pride. Under colonialism, learned societies had been formed, which established such journals as *Uganda Journal*, *Kenya Past and Present*, and *Tanganyika Notes and Records*, which later became *Tanzania Notes and Records*. These journals established a tradition of publishing folklore materials.

As institutions of higher learning were established, especially after independence of their respective countries, they created opportunities for teaching folklore and for creating an indigenous cadre of folklore researchers and scholars. Universities such as Makerere, Nairobi, Dar es Salaam, and a number of later ones, introduced programs in oral literature. These universities accumulate collections of folklore materials gathered by students and faculty. Many undergraduate and graduate projects continue to be done in this area, resulting in a rich source of folklore-related dissertations held at these institutions. In all the East African countries, there are also museums, archives, and research centers with folklore holdings. The main research centers include the Institute of Swahili Research at the University of Dar es Salaam, the East African Center for Research in Oral Traditions and African National Languages (EACROTANAL) in Zanzibar, and the Institute of African Studies at the University of Nairobi. Radio stations also have folklore holdings, even though these are not gathered according to the methods of professional folklorists.

There are also amateur recordings of folklore, available on cassette and videotape. These are likely to be sold on the streets, in kiosks, and marketplaces. For example, several of the famous epics of the Haya of Tanzania are available on cassette tape from street vendors. They are a valuable record, even though they do not come with field notes or information on the performers. What impact these recordings might have on the oral tradition is a subject of much debate among the scholars of African folklore.

With new technology, therefore, the dissemination of folklore has taken new forms: newspapers, cassettes, television, and the Internet have all become media for disseminating folklore. The traditional boundaries within which ethnic groups define themselves are increasingly being undermined by such processes as urbanization and easy communication. Folklore of the various ethnic groups is now carried to all corners of East Africa and the world with great ease. The dynamics and consequences of this contact, and the intermingling of various forms of folklore, require further investigation and study.

Although there is not, as of yet, an association of East African folklorists; however, the Kenya Oral Literature Association is a notable starting point; it sponsors conferences, research projects, and a growing list of publications. Equally significant is that East African folklorists are enhancing their international contacts with membership and participation in such bodies as the International Society for Folk Narrative Research (ISFNR) and the International Society for Oral Literature. A major landmark in this respect is that the ISFNR held a meeting in Africa for the first time in Nairobi in 2001. A selection of papers from that conference, published in *Fabula* (2002), attests to the vigor and skill of East African folklorists.

There are, however, certain problems and issues worth noting. Research in East African folklore has always been subject to various constraints. At the beginning, as mentioned, such constraints included language barriers. Europeans struggled to record folklore in languages they either did not speak or which they did not know very well, which forced them to use local translators. The collectors did not have the kind of recording equipment that is available today, or the kinds of roads and vehicles that make modern travel so much easier. There are also political constraints; no research can be done without research clearance. The politics of research clearance can be complex and problematic, both facilitating and complicating the work of researchers. The political instability that affects many African countries can negatively impact folklore research, as collectors cannot do field work due to governmental restrictions, or concerns for their physical safety. Years of political upheavals in Uganda, for example, have slowed down research work.

Despite all the work that has been done since the mid-nineteenth century, there are still many areas of East Africa that have not been well served by the researchers. East Africa is a vast region, with hundreds of languages and cultural traditions. Most of the languages are not written, and the folklore research that might have been done in most of these societies is rudimentary and less than professional. The emphasis on folktales, proverbs, and songs has obscured the complexity of the folklore. New paradigms must be explored in the study of East African folklore. There is a need to uncover and use indigenous nomenclature and classification systems in recording and interpreting folklore. Categorizations such as folktale, proverb, and prose narrative are problematic, given that they are imposed upon African genres, but derived from non-African contexts; they are perhaps even inimical to the proper understanding of the East African material in question.

There is also the problem of access to the recorded material. Though much folklore material has been recorded, it is scattered in various places across the world. Another problem is that the material is available in many languages: Portuguese, German, French, English, and the many local languages. Translations of all these materials into several languages would be ideal, so that people speaking different languages could all have access to them. But this is a complex problem, given the multiplicity of languages involved. What is needed, at least, are comprehensive bibliographies and other finding aids for all the material that is available in various publications, archives, and research centers.

East African folklore reflects the complex historical dynamics of the societies of the region, which continue to be affected by such phenomena such as migrations, refugees, and tourism. The spread of new media, such as radio, television, audio and video-cassettes, CDs, and the Internet encourages the preservation and dissemination of forms of folklore. Popular performances are now made available by such means, and these same media, in turn, encourage the rapid spread of foreign influences on East African folklore. The folklorists, indigenous and foreign, are increasingly becoming aware of these dynamics and their implications. They have begun to take up the challenge of recording and studying the transformations of folklore in the context of all these processes.

References

2000. *Fabula* 43, nos. 1 and 2.
Haring, Lee. 1972. East African Oral Narrative: Progress Report of a Survey. *Research in African Literatures* 3, no. 2:190–95.
Mbele, Joseph L. 1997. Folklore Research in East Africa. *American Folklore Society Newsletter* 26, no. 3:4–6.

JOSEPH L. MBELE

EDUCATION: FOLKLORE IN SCHOOLS

Folklore, in the sense of vernacular cultural practices, is involved in African education in at least three ways. One is its role in the traditional education or socialization of children, as elders pass on their knowledge to the next generation. A second is the contradictory ways in which missionaries and colonial officials conceived of "tradition" and enshrined their policies not only in colonial administration, but also in school curricula. A third is the attempt by independent African nations to recuperate tradition in order to create a national culture; often, these state-sponsored efforts involve schools as a mode of intervention.

Child Socialization and Traditional Forms of Education

Up until the 1960s and 1970s, scholars of traditional forms of child socialization in Africa generally saw education as the way African societies reproduced themselves from generation to generation, autonomous and unchanging, a process disrupted by colonialism and Westernization. These scholars argued that these educational processes were primarily informal, situational, and practical in contrast to Western-style schools, which concentrated on formal and abstract knowledge and served as gateways to jobs in the colonial administration. Although scholars of socialization stressed the importance of generational continuity for the reproduction of society and the status of elders in their theoretical discussions, their ethnographic data pointed to the importance of peer groups (or age-groups) in the socialization of children and youth.

Within the analytic framework of cultural continuity, these studies gave functional explanations for folklore, especially children's games and play, in which creative and aesthetic practices maintained order and hierarchy, relieved social tension, and expressed social ideals and values. In play, children prepared for their future roles in society by imitating adult activities. Songs, dances, proverbs, riddles, and insults all served to educate children about the ideals and values of a group and to maintain the status quo. Through artistry, folklore served as an especially memorable and heightened form of socialization.

Functional explanations for African socialization may also have been prompted by local notions about the importance of folklore. Some African scholars and promoters of tradition, especially in anglophone West Africa during the 1960s and 1970s, also stressed the educative value of local traditions in teaching children social and moral behavior; however, their functional arguments were primarily used to bolster the importance of folklore, rather than serving as the basis for a study of child socialization. In other words, they used some of the same language and concepts as those studying child socialization in Africa, but for different purposes.

Some formal educational practices, such as crafts apprenticeship and Quranic schools, have been present in Africa prior to and alongside Western forms of education, but these have generally not been the subject of much study regarding socialization, because they are considered more formal. Initiation ceremonies are also important formal sites for socialization in some areas of Africa.

Western anthropologists have since undermined the paradigms of modernization and tradition that served as the basis of studies of socialization in Africa: rather than seeing colonialism and "modernity" as forces that transform African societies, anthropologists now examine how Africans transform and localize "modernity" and other globalizing forces. Their studies focus on how Western schools have been incorporated into African understandings of education, systems of knowledge, and social hierarchies, rather than posing a threat to their order, and argue that tradition is generated through contestation and in everyday, situated practices. African scholars of folklore, especially in anglophone West Africa, are more concerned with the aesthetic and artistic elements of music, drama, and oral literature, rather than with traditional forms of socialization and functional explanations. Therefore, although no doubt vernacular traditions continue to play a role in children's education and socialization in Africa, academics, both in Africa and the West, are no longer focused on this topic. Yet there is much that could be done in this area with looking at how learning happens in situations of differential power; as a result of power structures in which some people have more status than others, not everyone gains access to tradition.

Western Education and Tradition

It is a commonplace to say that schools in Africa are Western imports, with the corollary that they alienate African students from their languages, cultures, and religions. First established by missionaries, especially in anglophone Africa, schools aimed to convert Africans to Christianity and to divorce them from traditional practices the missionaries saw as uncivilized. During struggles for independence, African nationalists critiqued schools for alienating them from their own languages and cultural practices.

However, the story is more complex than this. The missionaries were selective, according to their own criteria, about which cultural practices were antithetical to Christianity and which could be appropriated or replaced. Conservative Protestant German missionaries in Africa, specifically in the Gold Coast (now Ghana), Cameroon, and Tanganyika (now Tanzania), were influenced by Romantic nationalism, especially by neo-Romantic movements after the 1880s in Europe, and sought to preserve selected indigenous traditions, particulary language and history. Bruno Gutmann, a missionary in Tanganyika, integrated Chagga dances into church on Sunday afternoons for the youth,

"rediscovered" a fertility dance performed at maize harvests, and Christianized the texts of the accompanying songs. In 1933, another missionary organized a folk festival with the theme: "What Can Be Done to Save Bena Folkhood from Destruction?" Basel missionaries in Cameroon struggled with the contradiction of being carriers of a different national culture at the same time as they wished to preserve local culture, which they felt had its own national spirit and soul.

In the Gold Coast, Basel missionaries were interested in creating a nation unified by language. This idea formed the basis of Basel mission school policies, especially concerning the promotion of local languages for the purposes of schooling. Through local language study, selected items of folklore were taught in schools, in order to strengthen moral and Christian teachings. Folktales and proverbs, along with Biblical stories and hymns, were included in local language readers used in Basel Mission schools (from the first edition in 1891 to the later edition of 1950) in the Gold Coast. Through their codification of local languages, missionaries solidified and increased consciousness of the connection between ethnicity (as the nation), culture, and language, an association that continues to reverberate in African countries today.

Colonial practices also served to codify vernacular traditions, especially after World War I, when colonial administrations in Africa began to take a greater interest in education. Although colonial policy in francophone West Africa was based on the principle of assimilation, rather than accommodation to local culture, this was never particularly consistently carried out. Education was oriented towards the manpower needs of French West-Africa and emphasized agriculture and other vocations. During the 1930s and 1940s, at the École Normale de William Ponty in Dakar, Senegal, which was a training college for students aged eighteen to twenty-nine from all over francophone West Africa, students were encouraged to record folk plays and sociological data during their holiday vacations, and students presented imitations of traditional customs at annual school celebrations. Their plays were characterized by cross-cultural elements and the absence of any ritual—which was primarily the domain of adults and religious specialists and not appropriate for youth. In colonial Algeria, and perhaps elsewhere in French colonies, schools sought to create mediators, citizens who were neither too Westernized nor too indigenous.

In British colonies, the policy of Indirect Rule heightened colonial interest in local vernacular traditions. Contemptuous of local intellectuals, colonial officials sought to create a new elite from the sons of chiefs who would embody the "best" of the local traditions that they considered worthy of preservation when combined with Western civilization. In the tradition of Romantic nationalism, British colonial teachers felt that development of the nation could not take place unless it was built on local culture, which would form a foundation for the selective assimilation of Western ideas and practices. One example of the kind of school these ideas created was Malangali school in Tanganyika, founded by W. B. Mumford in 1928. The school was based on tribal tradition: boys wore traditional dress, were taught by village elders, and twice a week practiced spear throwing, dancing, and other recreational activities. Also founded were Garkida school in northern Nigeria, where folklore formed the basis of lessons, and Achimota College in Ghana, which incorporated local music and dance into extracurricular activities within a anglicized frame. These schools also promoted industrial and agricultural education, as well as local languages and history. Therefore, colonial schools promoted a simplified, desacralized, and reified vision of vernacular traditions, an approach that focused on performing arts.

These experiments in "Africanized" education did not last very long, because Africans sought modernity under their control, rather than a type of education that they felt was inferior. When Africans in villages in anglophone Africa began building schools under their own initiative, they generally started schools that were academic and focused on English, and these were the kinds of schools promoted by independent African governments. After 1945 in francophone West Africa, Africans advocated for schools that resembled those found in urban areas.

Education and Folklore after Independence

Inheriting contradictory notions of vernacular culture, independent African governments have had ambivalent feelings toward folklore; while it is a symbol of the nation and a rich heritage, it also seems to contradict the goal of progress and modernity. African academics have often been at the forefront of persuading their governments of the importance of tradition. Government and academic interests in vernacular culture converge in the field of education. State promotion of folklore has often used education as a site of intervention, not only because schools are nominally under government control and a way to reach the nation's children, but also because academics focus on their domain of education. Government and academic efforts to recuperate vernacular traditions have also revived functionalist reasons to justify their promotion, with the argument that folklore educates and integrates society and thus is valuable to the nation's development.

The data for this section is sporadic and full of gaps, dependent on if, and where, documents and articles that spoke to cultural policies and school policies in various countries could be found. The postcolonial intersection of folklore and education in Africa is a literature that needs to be developed.

In West and southern Africa (and perhaps throughout Africa), cultural traditions are often showcased as performing arts (dance, music, drama, and drumming) to create national art forms. The showcasing of different ethnic traditions on one stage represents the national polity, at the same time as it heightens the connection between a particular style and an ethnic group. State-sponsored national, regional, and provincial level arts festivals took place in Nigeria and Ghana in the 1960s and 1970s, and in Namibia in the 1990s, some of which were organized for schoolchildren. Some of the national cultural competitions for artists and students were driven by international level festivals, such as the Second World Black Festival of Arts and Culture, held in Lagos in 1975, or South African Development Community regional arts festivals in the 1990s. Performing arts festivals in these countries have became a way of representing the nation and a way of speaking across many linguistic boundaries. Teachers and students are more subject to political pressure and sometimes easier to organize, through school cultural troupes and clubs, than community level or Western-trained artists.

When folklore has been included in school curricula in African primary and secondary schools, it has been incorporated into academic subjects and national school examinations, as a different kind of content within a Westernized frame of knowledge. In Kenya, the teaching of oral literature in the schools is explicitly marked by the goal of nation building: folktales are chosen for their ability to show the similarity or unity of Kenya's many ethnic groups and for their moral purpose which can help the nation develop. Oral literature is included in English literature classes and is part of the national examinations. Verbal art seems to be most easily integrated into African schools, both ideologically and practically, and is generally done so through vernacular language classes. Yet because of the ambivalence of governments, as well as students and teachers, the presence of "folklore," as either performing arts or systematized school knowledge, may be sporadic or uneven in schools, despite official promotion and policies. In some countries, especially in francophone Africa, schools may not be involved at all in local language or cultural instruction. Africanization may not appear through folkloric dances or lessons on folklore, but through a focus on modern arts, such as modern African literature.

Academics have persuaded governments to support folklore by institutionalizing programs of study in universities. The teaching of vernacular traditions in universities is important symbolically for primary and secondary levels of education, since university education represents the pinnacle of schooling and thus determines what is important knowledge. Whereas in universities in Cote d'Ivoire and South Africa the goal of these courses or programs (in drum language and oral literature) is research and documentation of vernacular traditions, in Nigeria and Ghana the goal is to create practitioners and artists: these academic programs explicitly aim to preserve tradition by rejuvenating and transforming it through new artistic creations.

International bodies, such as UNESCO, have contributed to the promotion and preservation of local traditions by African governments and academics, through its attempt to set worldwide cultural policy, protecting and documenting indigenous traditions (such as the Inter-Governmental Conference on Cultural Policies in Africa held in Accra in 1975). In localizing these global discourses and institutions, Ghana's government focused on cultural education in its 1987 education reforms, sponsored by the World Bank, which was concerned with administrative and financial issues in education and not with making the schools more in touch with local cultural traditions.

Often, parents, teachers, and students conceive of local traditions as antithetical to the goal of schooling, which is to create "modern" people. Evangelical Christianity, growing stronger in Africa, also emphasizes that cultural traditions are antithetical to Christianity and may make Christians uncomfortable with the teaching of folklore in schools. Furthermore, older people remember a time when tradition was considered abhorrent by their teachers and students were punished for attending community festivals and rituals. The teaching of folklore in African schools is thus driven by various pressures, both local and international, by academics, governments, Christians, and international agencies, as they redefine and negotiate historically complex (and sometimes contradictory) concepts like *tradition*, *nation*, and *progress*.

References

Clignet, Remi P., and Philip J. Foster. 1964. French and British Colonial Education in Africa. *Comparative Education Review* 8, no. 2:191–98.

Coe, Cati. 2000. "Not Just Drumming and Dancing": The Production of National Culture in Ghana's Schools. Ph.D. dissertation, University of Pennsylvania.

Colonna, Fanny. 1997. Educating Conformity in French Colonial Algeria. Trans. Barbara Harshaw. In *Tensions of Empire: Colonial Culture in a Bourgeois World*, eds. Frederick Cooper and Ann Laura Stoler. Berkeley: University of California Press.

Fiedler, Klaus. 1996. *Christianity and African Culture: Conservative German Protestant Missions in Tanzania, 1900–1940*. Leiden: E. J. Brill.

Hallden, Erik. 1968. *The Culture Policy of the Basel Mission in the Cameroons. 1886–1905*. Lund: Berlingska Boktryckeriet.

Kalabash: A Biannual Magazine on Namibian Culture. Ministry of Education and Culture, Government of Namibia.

Mumford, W. Bryant. 1930. Malangali School. *Africa* 3:265–92.

Niangoran-Bouah, Georges. 1981. *Introduction a la Drummologie*. Abidjan: Sankofa.

Osofisan, Babefemi Adeyemi. 1974. The Origins of Drama in West Africa: A Study of the Development of Drama from the Traditional Forms to the Modern Theatre in English and French. Ph.D. dissertation, University of lbadan.

Read, Margaret. 1987. Children of Their Fathers: Growing Up Among the Ngoni of Malawi. [1968]. Prospect Heights: Waveland Press.

Samper, David. 1997. "Love, Peace, and Unity": Romantic Nationalism and the Role of Oral Literature in Kenya's Secondary Schools. *Folklore Forum* 28:29–47.

Sienaert, E. R., and A. N. Bell, eds. 1988. *Catching Winged Words: Oral Tradition and Education*. Durban: Natal University Oral Documentation and Research Centre.

CATI COE

See also **Children's Folklore; Government Policies toward Folklore**

EGYPT

Occupying the extreme northeast corner of the African continent, the modern nation state of Egypt must be distinguished from its namesake, "Ancient Egypt" which occupied virtually the same territory. Egypt, still centered on the famous Nile river, is bordered by the Mediterranean to the north, Israel and Palestine to the east, with Sudan to the south and Libya on the West. Egypt first, and soon the rest of North Africa, would change forever as Islamic Arabs swept across the area in the seventh century. Although Napoleon attacked Egypt in 1798, the modern history of Egypt is usually traced from 1882, when the English occupied the territory after domination by the Ottoman Empire since the sixteenth century. Modern Egypt's importance to Europe was no longer its romantic past but the Suez Canal, which opened in 1869. In 1922, Egypt attained some degree of independence with a British-controlled monarchy. This government was overthrown in 1952 by General Gamal Abdel Nasser, who became a strong voice for African independence elsewhere on the continent until his death in 1970. Subsequent Egyptian leaders have grown close to the United States, and Egypt is one of the largest recipients of foreign aid from the United States. Recently, there has been an increase in domestic turmoil as Islamic fundamentalists and government agencies have clashed.

Although Egypt is a predominantly Islamic country, with over 50 million Sunni Moslems, there has always been an important and ancient Coptic Christian community numbering about 7 percent of the country's population. There is also a notable urban Jewish population as one finds throughout the cities of North Africa, as well as a large number of Christians of various denominations. The total population is approximately 67 million people. Life expectancy is relatively high for African countries at sixty-three years. The adult literacy rate is around 51 percent.

In the past, Egypt's major exports were cotton and agricultural products, such as dates, from the rich lands along the Nile river. Now Egypt has a developed industrial sector, which exports pharmaceuticals, automobiles, and kitchen appliances. There are also sizeable mineral and oil exports. And tourism remains a major source of income as many come to visit both contemporary and ancient Egypt.

In some ways, through trade and travel it might be said that Ancient Egypt was more involved in the rest of Africa than modern Egypt, although the nation has played a strong role in the Organization of African Unity. The major point remains that Egypt was and always will be part of the African continent.

PHILIP M. PEEK

ELECTRONIC MEDIA AND ORAL TRADITIONS

African oral traditions have been a very important inspiration for broadcasting content and style, from the first days of radio in Africa up through the twenty-first century. Locally produced radio and television programs feature traditional genres of communication such as storytelling, advising, drama, political oratory and song. In addition, national media produce live coverage of cultural festivals and ceremonies, which include oratory, songs and dance performances.

The broadcasting of oral traditions has several important implications for African nation-states as well as for specific ethnic cultures. Transmitting folklore via new media can contribute to cultural and linguistic preservation and revival. It can also function in projects of national integration and public education. In some cases, broadcasting oral traditions is problematic and even controversial. Since mass media introduce new possibilities for both production and reception, they can dramatically transform the structures and social functions of oral traditions.

Across Africa, there is evidence of two-way influence between oral traditions and electronic media. Stylistic elements of oral traditions appear in the speech styles of broadcasters and conversely, the speech styles of broadcasters are having a long-term effect on language use in face-to-face contexts.

Background and Examples from Zambia

Hundreds of radio stations and scores of televisions stations exist in contemporary Africa. Virtually every nation has its own state-run radio and television operation, and many nations have independent broadcasting as well. Africa's earliest official radio station was established in South Africa in 1924. Two years later broadcasting was inaugurated in Algeria, to be followed in 1927 by Kenya. In 1959, the first television station south of the Sahara was set up in Ibadan, Nigeria. These early broadcasting efforts were designed mainly for European settlers and they offered very little programming for Africans.

The Central African Broadcasting Station (CABS) in Lusaka was one of the first radio stations to develop programs for African listeners during the colonial period. At the time, Lusaka was the capital of the British colony of Northern Rhodesia (now Zambia). By the late 1940s, CABS was world famous for its impromptu plays in indigenous languages and its unique methods for acquiring original sound material via rural recording tours. The CABS served Northern Rhodesia, Southern Rhodesia (now Zimbabwe), and Nyasaland (now Malawi). Seven languages were used: Bemba, Lozi, Ndebele, Nyanja, Shona, Tonga, and English. Early radio programs included morality plays ("The Lame Man and the Blind Man"), folk stories ("The Ingratitude of Mr. Lion") and talk shows ("Your Questions Answered"). In addition, traditional storytelling genres were adapted for contemporary tales about the pressures of social change and the conflicts between older and younger generations.

Present-day Radio Zambia, part of the Zambia National Broadcasting Corporation (ZNBC), follows directly in the footsteps of the pioneering CABS. Radio is the most widely consumed medium in Zambia, reaching nearly 60 percent of all national households. Radio Zambia has three channels, each of which is devoted to different kinds of programming. Radio 2 and Radio 4 broadcast exclusively in English. Most folklore-related programming occurs on Radio 1, which broadcasts in the seven official Zambian languages: Bemba, Kaonde, Lozi, Lunda, Luvale, Nyanja and Tonga. Examples of translated titles include "Traditional Songs," "Our Culture," "By the Fireside," "Stories and Legends," "Poets Corner," "Your Questions Answered," "Points of View" and "Advisors." Elements of traditional oratorical styles and narrative structures pervade even the more Western-derived media formats, such as programs on current events, farming techniques and children's healthcare.

Two popular Bemba talk shows on Radio Zambia, *Baanacimbuusa* and *Kabuusha Takolelwe Boowa* are inspired directly by indigenous modes of advising. *Baanacimbuusa* (Women Advisors) is a half-hour discussion program that airs every Saturday morning. The program's title, format and message are drawn considerably from oral traditions. In Bemba culture, *baanacimbuusa* is the name for the leaders of the girls' initiation ceremony

known as *cisungu*. During the *cisungu* ceremony, the *baanacimbuusa* lead the initiants through a number of rites which demand great agility, endurance, and obedience. Other elder women perform songs and dances, which teach the girls how to behave in marriage. Besides their specific ritual roles, the *baanacimbuusa* are viewed as experts in matters of marriage, family, and childbirth. The "Baanacimbuusa" radio show reflects Bemba ways of imparting knowledge about socially appropriate conduct. A well-known *cisungu* song about the teaching role of *baanacimbuusa* plays as the opening theme song. On each program, the host introduces a topic which a panel of elder women then discuss. Topics center on family and marriage problems such as infertility, widows' rights, troublesome relatives, teenage pregnancy, and adultery. Using traditional oratorical styles, panelists elaborate on the issues and offer suggestions for listeners who have such problems in their own lives.

Another advice program, *Kabuusha Taakolelwe Boowa*, takes its name from a well-known Bemba proverb meaning "the inquirer was not poisoned by a mushroom." It airs for one hour every Sunday morning, and has been running on Radio Zambia for nearly forty years. The program features an expert advisor who answers listeners' letters on a variety of subjects including corrupt politicians, adulterous spouses, in-laws who demand more marriage payments, and employers who exploit their workers. The program stresses the survival value of consultation, as indicated in its title proverb. Kabuusha advisors frequently use proverbs and various forms of imperatives to exhort listeners and to prescribe appropriate conduct. They also draw heavily on other oral traditions such as Christian sermonizing and nationalist discourse.

Functions of Oral Traditions in Electronic Media

Broadcasting oral traditions is important in Africa as people look to the media "to provide explanations, give advice and act as an arbiter of social morality" (Mytton 1983, 85). The *Baanacimbuusa* and *Kabuusha* programs in Zambia are prime examples of this. In Uganda, radio songs which build on traditional storytelling genres are used to comment on gender identities and contemporary national politics. Thematic elements of the Kiganda founding myth and formulaic elements of trickster stories recur throughout these radio songs and lend authority to the songs' messages.

Transmitting folklore via new media can also assist in cultural and linguistic preservation and revival. In contexts where languages are in danger of losing speakers or where traditional lore is known by only a few elder members of culture, mass media can help document and promote indigenous traditions. They can also function in projects of national integration and public education. In multiethnic nations, mass media can be used to promote awareness and pride in a rich and diverse cultural heritage. For example, for many years, evening television in Cote d'Ivoire featured a program of folktales told in different national languages followed by dance performances filmed in a village of the featured ethnic group.

The broadcast of oral traditions has also been a subject of intense debate in many African nations. Critics have argued that it fosters heightened ethnic factionalism and leads to the corruption of traditional cultures that were never meant for electronic

Electronic media have become part of traditional ceremonies, as in this celebration of the *Ngoni nc'wala* (annual first fruits ceremony) in eastern Zambia. Photo © Debra Spitulnik.

Music and other genres of communication on radios and cassette players draw in customers and provide a focus for socializing at the marketplace. Kasama town center market, Zambia. Photo © Debra Spitulnik.

formats. In Zambia, where there are seventy-three officially recognized tribes, the Zambia National Broadcasting Corporation (ZNBC) has struggled to develop a policy about the coverage of traditional ceremonies. Roughly twenty different ethnic groups annually celebrate a cultural heritage event, such as a first fruits ceremony, a seasonal migration ceremony, or an event of historic conquest. It is too costly for the ZNBC to provide regular coverage of all cultural ceremonies. At the same time, media producers are worried that selecting only a few will offend the ethnic groups who do not get covered. In this context, some Zambians have argued that national media contribute to the commercialization of traditional ceremonies. The Ngoni people have an annual ceremony which is regularly covered by state media, and in many years the ritual's master of ceremonies has been a famous radio broadcaster. Local elites often use the media coverage for their own purposes and ritual participants sometimes ignore the central activities and instead mug up to the television cameras. Although oral traditions can be incorporated and transformed within electronic media, this shows how the presence of electronic media can alter the performance of traditions in their original contexts.

In countries where mass media are highly censored, oral traditions may used in broadcasting to give greater exposure to suppressed political groups and opinions. Because oral traditions often use indirection and allegory to express political critique, their messages may not be immediately obvious to media censors. Broadcasting oral traditions for such purposes can have both positive and negative effects. As an avenue for expressing political views, it could help foster a more vibrant civil society. Alternatively, it may be socially disruptive and lead to further political repression.

Challenges in Adapting and Promoting Oral Traditions in the Electronic Media

One hotly debated issue concerns the dominance of imported Western programs in both African radio and television. Roughly 80 percent of Television Zambia programs are imported, with the majority being American action and drama series. There are also several American children's programs, such as *Sesame Street*. Similarly, very high percentages of imported programs air on state television in Uganda, Kenya, Cote d'Ivoire, and many other African nations. European and American music is pervasive on radio. Policymakers, cultural analysts, and national citizens alike are concerned about whether the dominance of such Western media content is an example of media imperialism. The fear is that foreign media may erode traditional culture and traditional values, and that they may create a more homogeneous global culture.

In the 1970s and early 1980s, UNESCO hosted extensive deliberations about these imbalances in the global flow of media products and produced detailed policy recommendations. Since that time, several international organizations have worked to foster the production and exchange of indigenous broadcast material in Africa. Much of this involves programming that is inspired by indigenous oral traditions. The Union of National Radio and Television Organizations of Africa (URTNA), based in Senegal, promotes the exchange of locally produced programming among African nations. Satellite and videocassette are used to transfer media products from one nation to another. Two other UN organizations, WHO (World Health Organization) and FAO (Food and Agricultural Organization), provide support to produce local radio dramas for health and farming education.

Bringing oral traditions into mass media is sometimes problematic. For example, the *Baanacimbuusa* radio program in Zambia cannot broadcast exactly the same kinds of advice that is given in face-to-face contexts, because the radio audience extends beyond the ritual audience of women and mature girls. The public nature of radio forces the women advisors to use euphemisms and withhold some information that may not be appropriate for all listeners.

Similarly, it is difficult to adapt many traditional song and dance performances to television formats because they are so embedded in rituals and communities. Media producers need to be sensitive when they remove material from their original performance contexts. Media audiences may have completely different reactions to mass-mediated cultural traditions than they would if they were direct participants in an ongoing event.

One problem is that rituals have different functions and different temporal structures than broadcasting typically does. This creates a challenge in adapting a song that lasts thirty minutes or a dance that lasts one hour. In addition, some traditions are forms of praying and they involve entire communities. They are not meant to be entertainment for isolated groups of viewers and listeners. It may be difficult to retain the same sense of the sacred in mass communication. Furthermore, the dialogic nature of face-to-face communication is very important for most oral traditions. Storytellers often ask rhetorical questions to their audiences. Proverbs are often stated as riddles, or in call-and-response formats. The most successful media adaptations of oral traditions preserve these dialogic features.

The Ghana Broadcasting Corporation (GBC) has been very successful in developing culturally oriented children's television. In one of its first efforts, the GBC asked the National Theatre Company to collect folktales and adapt them for television. Characters in the folktales were represented as masked figures on television. The programs were not well received because audiences could not relate to the masked characters. Young children were confused and frightened by the masks, while older children and adults argued that the characters were not realistic. A new format was later developed for a program entitled *By the Fireside*, using school children as actors and participants. Each show opens with children dancing and singing traditional songs that foreshadow the moral message of the story of the day. The program uses Akan, which is understood by roughly 60 percent of the population, and English, which is the national language. The studio set represents a rural village. Two storytellers occupy center stage and the children are gathered around as the audience. Stories are based on traditional tales, but they often interweave contemporary themes about urban life and national politics. Like traditional oral forms of education, most of the programs are very didactic, with moralistic messages such as do not be greedy, work together, tell the truth, and respect your elders. After a tale is told, individual children are asked to say what they have learned, and the correct answer is then repeated.

In Nigeria, the regional broadcasting service of Kano State (CTV) produces numerous television dramas that build on oral traditions. One very popular situation comedy, *Kuliya*, is named after the Hausa legal court. The program is in the Hausa language and it features the conniving activities of a man named Buguzum, his wife Hajiya, and the loyal servants who try help them out of their dilemmas. The plot structure resembles that of trickster stories and episodes always have a clear-cut moral message. Following the folklore tradition in which character names are metaphors that reveal personality traits, the name Buguzum symbolizes an overbearing person who beats or thrashes others. As with the Ghanaian television adaptations, the Kano TV dramas are not just reenactments of traditional stories. They address contemporary problems, for example, dealers who sell fraudulent tour packages for pilgrimage trips to Mecca or thieves who numb their victims with drugged kola nuts.

Reciprocal Influences Between Oral Traditions and Electronic Media

The preceding examples illustrate the two-way influence between oral traditions and the electronic media in Africa. Both the content and the style of numerous mass media genres are greatly influenced by indigenous traditions. At the same time many indigenous communication genres have been transformed by the presence of electronic media. In Mali, for example, the popular broadcast of griot music on national radio has resulted in a gradual alteration of song messages, text structures, harmonic patterns and even social functions. Mass media introduce new possibilities for both production and reception, and they are also caught up in different political and economic arenas. In the traditional context, there is a hereditary bond between patron and musician, and the patron is the central addressee of the song's message. Radio, television, and the recording industry have created a whole new set of commercial opportunities, however. Many griot artists are more interested in building careers through electronic media than through historical social relationships. They produce praise songs about people whom they do not know well. In the process, the textual features of historical chronicle are diminished and replaced by excessive flattery and ordinary conversation.

Even everyday language use is influenced by the mass media. Radio Zambia has inspired a range of linguistic innovations in popular speech. For example, the name of the *Chongololo* radio program, a show about wildlife preservation, has become a derogatory term for Zambians who try to act like Europeans. Other program titles, such as "Over to You," are used in conversations to joke and to create a friendly rapport. This is analogous to the way that media discourse such as the Star Trek phrase "beam me up" circulates in American culture. Because of their high visibility and mass reach, radio and television can be important catalysts for language learning and language change, They contribute to the circulation and valorization of a set of standard phrases and key words in public culture.

One can conclude from these many cases that the rise of electronic media does not pose a strong threat to oral traditions in Africa. From its beginnings, African broadcasting has drawn extensively from a rich array of oral traditions such as drama, storytelling and oratory. The postcolonial period has seen an even greater experimentation with indigenous genres in mass media. African nations and international agencies alike are discovering how indigenous communication forms can be integrated into mass media for health education, farming campaigns, and cross-cultural exchange. Discussion forums that take place in face-to-face village settings can also occur on a mass scale with talk radio programs. The dynamic interaction between oral traditions and mass media poses a challenge for simplistic dichotomies between "tradition" and "modernity," and it highlights the very vibrant nature of communication in African societies.

References

Barber, Karin, ed. 1997. *Readings in African Popular Culture*. Bloomington: Indiana University Press.

Bourgault, Louise Manon. 1995. *Mass Media in Sub-Saharan Africa*. Bloomington: Indiana University Press.

Cancel, Robert. 1986. Broadcasting Oral Traditions: The "Logic" of Narrative Variants—The Problem of "Message." *African Studies Review* 29, no. 1:60–70.

Fardon, Richard, and Graham Furniss, eds. 2000. *African Broadcast Cultures: Radio in Transition*. London: James Currey.

Gerbner, George, Hamid Mowlana, and Kaarle Nordenstreng, eds. 1993. *The Global Media Debate: Its Rise, Fall, and Renewal*. Norwood: Ablex.

Ginsburg, Faye. 1994. Culture/Media: A (Mild) Polemic. *Anthropology Today* 10, no. 2:5–15.

Heath, Carla W. 1997. Children's Television in Ghana: A Discourse About Modernity. *African Affairs* 96, no. 383:261–75.

Mugambi, Helen Nabasuta. 1994. Intersections: Gender, Orality, Text, and Female Space in Contemporary Kiganda Radio Songs. *Research in African Literatures* 25, no. 3:47–70.

———. 1997. From Story to Song: Gender, Nationhood, and the Migratory Text. *Gendered Encounters: Challenging Cultural Boundaries and Social Hierarchies in Africa*, eds. Maria Grosz-Ngate and Omari H. Kokole. New York: Routledge.

Mytton, Graham. 1983. *Mass Communication in Africa*. London: Edward Arnold.

Schulz, Dorothea. 1997. Praise without Enchantment: "Griots," Broadcast Media, and the Politics of Tradition in Mali. *Africa Today* 44, no. 4:443–64.

Spitulnik, Debra. 1993. Anthropology and Mass Media. *Annual Review of Anthropology* 22:293–315.

———. 1996. The Social Circulation of Media Discourse and the Mediation of Communities. *Journal of Linguistic Anthropology* 6, no. 2:161–87.

———. Forthcoming. *Media Connections and Disconnections: Radio Culture and the Public Sphere in Zambia.* Durham: Duke University Press.

Ugboajah, Frank Okwu, ed. 1985. *Mass Communication, Culture and Society in West Africa.* München: Zell.

DEBRA SPITULNIK

See also **Government Policies toward Folklore; Radio and Television Dramas; Women Pop Singers of Mali**

EPICS: OVERVIEW

In Africa, the term *epic* is applied to a wide range of lengthy oral poetic narratives, usually performed by a specialist, often with musical accompaniment. The subject of the narrative is usually seen as historical, although the nature of the history involved will vary from myths and legends of origin to recent historical anecdote, and the characters are considered heroic in local terms. Performances will often incorporate songs, as a part of the action or as praise of characters within the story (and their descendents among the audience), and in some cases may include dancing. Recorded lengths of performances range from half hour to a continuous seven-night narrative.

Traditions of oral epic performance are found across Africa, and for convenience may be divided into three groups on the basis of geography, content, and performance features. One group, probably the smallest, represents African adaptations of Arabic epic traditions: this includes the cycle of the Bani Hilal through northern Africa, especially in Egypt and Tunisia, whose hero, Abu Zayd, is a black poet (Connelly 1986), and along the east coast a number of Swahili epics known generically as *utenzi* (Knappert 1983). Some Swahili epics are translations of Arabic texts (*Herakili, Ras al-Ghul*); at least one, *Liyongo Fumo*, represents an adaptation of local material to this imported form. Liyongo was a prince and a poet, and his preserved songs seem to provide the core of his narrative. Performance of these epics has not been exhaustively documented, but appears to be principally a recitation of a memorized text, and manuscripts play an important role in the diffusion of stories. The texts employ an adapted Arabic metrical scheme.

Throughout central Africa, and extending west and south, there is an epic tradition that is the vehicle for traditions of origin centered on a culture hero such as Mwindo of the BaNyanga, Lianja of the Mongo, or Ozidi of the Ijo. Myth overpowers history in these epics, and the biography of the hero provides the matrix in which the numerous (and variable) episodes of the cycle may fit. The Swahili Liyongo and the Malagasy Ibonia may be connected to this tradition, as also might southern African trickster figures such as the Zulu Hlakanyaka. The hero is typically a precocious, almost monstrous, child who is born to avenge his father or to struggle with him. The hero also engages in a number of adventures that may carry him into the heavens, below the earth or the waters, and to the land of the dead. The hero is typically accompanied by a female relative who serves as protector, inspiration, and manager. Performances typically feature a master-singer (who has been initiated into the practice through occult means) accompanied by an ensemble, and take place in a relatively public space. The master-performer narrates, sings, and mimes the action with a considerable degree of audience participation. The verbal element consists of a mix of prose and songs.

A subgroup of these central African traditions is found among the Fang peoples of Gabon and Cameroon, and is known as the *mvett*. The term designates the instrument (a bamboo chordophone) and the genre. The *mvett* centers not on a given hero, but on an entire world (of times gone by) in which the immortals of the clan of Engong confront the mortals of the clan of Oku in a never-ending series of conflicts. The performer is thus free to plot the story and to embellish it in any effective way. Warriors struggle through magical obstacles rather than against weapons, and the magic is clearly a counterpart to modern technology. The *mvett* plays somewhat more than do the hero-centered cycles with romantic complications; the women who often accompany the men on their adventures are lovers rather than siblings.

Throughout West Africa, in a region centered in the Sahel and bounded roughly by Niger and Senegal, is the third and largest group of epics, unified by the social position of the performer, internationally known as the griot and at home by a variety of local terms: *jeli* or *jali, gawlo, mabo, gesere, gewel*. The performers are members of an endogamous status group, and this institution is shared among a number of neighboring peoples: various Mande groups such as the Soninke, the Mandinka, and the Bamana, as well as the Fula, the Wolof, and the Songhay. The practice of singing epics also seems to have spread among the groups, although each shows a distinct repertoire of stories and an idiomatic style of narration. Political history provides the narrative foundation for these epics, although in many cases the historical element is purely a veneer. The action, however, is human centered and takes place in something close to the immediate past: Mwindo's visits to other planes do not recur here. Magic serves to protect or destroy warriors, and to bring victory, and where magic does bring victory it is almost always associated also with treachery.

The best-known epic of this region is certainly the epic of Sundiata, founder of the empire of Mali. An influential prose version was published by D. T. Niane in 1960 (English translation in 1965) and has inspired further work. There are dozens of published accounts of his life and a growing body of recordings from Mali, Guinea, and the Gambia. This story is centered on a hero, although a "full" epic will usually begin well before his birth with a migration from Mecca or some account of the creation of the world. In childhood, Sunjata is crippled by hostile sorcery, and the high point of the epic may be the moment when, impelled by his fury at an insult to his mother, he rises to his feet and takes his first steps to uproot a baobab. He later goes into exile to avoid conflict with a brother, and, while he is absent, Sumanguru the sorcerer-blacksmith invades the Mande and oppresses the people. Sunjata is summoned back to defeat him, which he does with the help of his sister. After her brother has been defeated a number of times, she seduces Sumanguru to learn the secret of his power, and so Sunjata is able to overcome him.

The traditions of Segou provide another corpus whose wealth is of a different order. The epics of Segou constitute a rough cycle, which is based on a selective king-list (Wolof epics offer the same organization) and recount the history of the kingdom from the early eighteenth century to the early 19th century.

Many of the most popular pieces deal with the conquests of the last king, Da son of Monzon, and establish an almost conventional pattern: a vassal or neighbor insults Segou, and after initial setbacks a way is found (often through seduction) to defeat him. The Bamana traditions of Segou interact very closely with the Fula epics from the adjacent region of Massina, and there seems some evidence for Soninke contribution as well. In this polyglot environment, epics lose much of their historical weight and develop along purely narrative and artistic lines. A number of other groups in this broad region also offer documented epic traditions: the Songhay, the Mandinka of the Gambia, and the Wolof. Many of these focus upon nineteenth-century heroes upon one side or another of the Islamic movements of the period.

Performance practice varies somewhat from group to group and over time, but is centered upon a male master-narrator who in the Mande is accompanied at the least by his *naamu*-sayer, an apprentice who responds at each line with encouraging words, and possibly by accompanists. Women often participate for lyric passages and clan-praises, which in some sense are their special domain. Musical instruments include the *balafon*, the wooden xylophone, and various sorts of harp-lutes: the *kora*, the *ngoni* (a widespread four-stringed instrument also known as the *molo* or the *hoddu*) and now also guitars.

This region also offers a nonhistorical corpus of epics best documented among the Mande peoples: that of the hunters. The late Malian hunters' bard Seydou Camara has bequeathed a considerable body of recorded material, which is now being increased by others. Hunters' epics focus on the condition of the hunter, as defined in terms of society rather than natural history. While a staple plot element involves a monstrous beast that a hunter must slay, the resolution often turns on the hunter's relations with his wife, and she is the key to his success. Many of these narratives occur as folktales rather than epics among neighboring peoples.

Although the earliest attempt to convey an African epic in print goes back at least to 1856, and the collector Leo Frobenius devoted a volume to the "minstrelsy of the Sahel" (1921), doubts have persisted until relatively recently about the existence of African epic. The growing mass of collected and published material dispels those doubts, and the challenge now is one of analysis and appreciation. A valuable early survey is that of Daniel Biebuyck (1976), somewhat amplified with additional Swahili material by Knappert (1983). In his dissertation (1978) and in his published edition of the *Epic of Son-Jara*, John W. Johnson has attempted to define the criteria of African oral epic, while Isidore Okpewho has approached epic traditions from the perspective of the Parry-Lord school of oral composition. Working in French, at first with Bamana traditions, Lilyan Kesteloot has produced a number of valuable analytic essays and editions, and in collaboration with Bassirou Dieng has produced a study and anthology (1997).

References

Belcher, Stephen. 1998. *Epic Traditions in Africa*. Bloomington: Indiana University Press.

Biebuyck, Daniel. 1976. The African Heroic Epic. In *Heroic Epic and Saga*, ed., Felix Oinas. Bloomington: Indiana University Press. 336–367.

Connelly, Bridget. 1986. *Arabic Folk Epic and Identity*. Berkeley: University of California Press.

Frobenius, Leo. 1921. *Spielmannsgeschichten der Sahel. Atlantis VI.* Iena: Eugen Diederichs. Rpr., Martin Sändig.

Johnson, John W. 1978. *The Epic of Son-Jara: An Attempt To Define the Model for African Epic Poetry.* 3 vols. Ph.D. Dissertation, Indiana University.

———. 1986. *The Epic of Son-Jara according to Fa-Digi Sisoko: A West African Tradition.* Bloomington: Indiana University Press.

Johnson, John W., Thomas Hale, and Stephen Belcher. 1997. *Oral Epics from Africa: Voices from a Vast Continent.* Bloomington: Indiana University Press.

Kesteloot, Lilyan, and Bassirou Dieng. 1997. *Epopées d'Afrique noire.* Paris: Karthala.

Knappert, Jan. 1983. *Epic Poetry in Swahili and Other African Languages.* Leiden: E. J. Brill.

Niane, D. T. 1965. *Sundiata: An Epic of Old Mali.* Trans. G. D. Pickett. New York: Longman.

Okpewho, Isidore. 1979. *The Epic in Africa: Toward a Poetics of the Oral Performance.* New York. Columbia University Press.

Seydou, Christiane, ed. and trans. 1976. *La geste de Hambodedio ou Hama le rouge.* Classiques africains. Paris: Armand Colin.

Thoyer, Annik, ed. and trans. 1995. *Récits épiques des chasseurs bamanan du Mali.* Paris: L'Harmattan.

STEPHEN BELCHER

See also **Central African Folklore; Myths; West Africa: Overview**

EPICS: LIONGO EPIC OF THE SWAHILI

The Swahili inhabit the East African coast and adjacent islands. They are also scattered in different parts of the East African interior and in the Persian Gulf. They had become a distinct culture by the ninth century CE on the coast of southern Somalia and northern Kenya. It is impossible to determine precisely when a distinctly Swahili culture emerged, for the East African coast seems to have been settled by precursors of the Swahili as early as the first century CE. These were agricultural and maritime people.

Swahili folklore incorporates indigenous African elements and imported ones. The indigenous creations include songs, folktales, and local legends. Many of these are shared by the people who populate the interior of the continent, with whom the Swahili had been in contact for centuries. Long-distance trade, whereby people of the interior came to the coast and the Swahili went inland, was the major reason for these contacts. This process, naturally, led to the sharing of folklore. Elements of the folklore of central and southern Africa became integrated into Swahili folklore. Early collectors of Swahili folklore on the East African coast were able to record tales from freed slaves who came from such distant places as Malawi.

Among the most notable forms of indigenous folklore is the the Liongo epic tradition, which consists mainly of narratives and songs about the hero, Liongo Fumo, a great warrior, dancer, and composer and singer of songs. Liongo was so popular that he incurred the envy of the ruling king, who feared that Liongo might usurp the throne. The epic is essentially about attempts by the king to kill Liongo, which succeed only after Liongo's son is sent to find out the secret about Liongo's vulnerability, and then kill him. All the events of this epic take place on the Kenya coast.

The external elements in Swahili folklore are mostly from Arabic, Iranian, and Indian traditions. From its beginnings, Swahili culture was influenced by sea-faring outsiders from the Persian Gulf area, who brought Islam to the Swahili. In time, Islam became a major characteristic of Swahili culture. These outsiders many of whom settled on the East African coast and became Swahili, made significant contributions to Swahili folklore. These include many epic tales based on the Islamic tradition about the activities of Prophet Muhammad and his followers, not to mention the *Tales of a Thousand and One Nights*. Such figures as emperor Haroun Al-Rashid, as well as Abu Nuwas, a trickster who is celebrated throughout the Middle East and Gulf area, are celebrated in Swahili folklore.

Swahili folklore reflects the agricultural and maritime base of Swahili culture. Tales, songs, beliefs, proverbs and other forms abound, dealing with the sea and its creatures, real or imagined. Agricultural songs coexist alongside sailors' songs, tales about fishermen, and stories of the sea and the mythical forces and creatures in it holds.

As in other African folklore traditions, the various forms of Swahili folklore are not isolated entities, but interact among themselves in various ways and constitute a dynamic system. Proverbs, for example, might be based on folktales; they appear in the form of songs and are also projected in tales. There are tales that elaborate on the messages of proverbs, songs, and proverbs, which allude to tales, and so forth.

Unlike most African folklore traditions, Swahili folklore has developed in a culture with a long history of literacy and urbanization. Writing has existed in Swahili culture for about a thousand years, resulting in written records of much Swahili folklore. The oral folklore and the written versions influenced have influenced each other through the ages.

Towns have been a part of Swahili cultural experience for over a millennium. Swahili has much folklore dealing with or based on the urban experience. Urban legends and tales dealing with the divide between town and country are a key feature of Swahili folklore.

The Liongo epic embodies and illustrates the complex history of orality, literacy, and urbanization in Swahili culture. Swahili folklore was originally an oral tradition, consisting mainly of songs and narratives. Later some of these forms were written down; oral folklore also inspired written compositions, especially in poetry. It is thus impossible to draw a distinct line between oral and written dimensions of the Liongo epic. On a general level, there has been a complex interaction between the oral and written tradition in Swahili culture, which complicates the situation of Swahili folklore. The Liongo epic is also largely an urban phenomenon, in the sense that most of its events have an urban setting.

References

Steere, Edward. 1870. *Swahili Tales, As Told by Natives of Zanzibar.* London: Society for Promoting Christian Knowledge.

Taylor, W. E. 1924. *African Aphorisms, or Saws From Swahililand.* London: The Sheldon Press.

JOSEPH L. MBELE

See also **East African Folklore: Overview**

EPICS: WEST AFRICAN EPICS

In Africa, even in societies that have a system of writing (borrowed or invented), the goal of every text emanating from the corpus of traditional literature, and intended for verbal performance, is to enter into the global sociocultural context. The epic, more so than any other form of discourse, has conserved this quality of oral production destined to be received by a public. Its semantic message is inseparable from its pragmatic scope, and its delivery is experienced as a sort of ritual. The tradition is thus perpetuated through ideological representations and specific values that are illustrated by heroes and their deeds, and through a sense of communion experienced in exaltation induced by the particular form of this type of text and the status and role of its performer. In this ritualistic aspect, the feeling of identity on which a community is grounded and which assures cohesion and solidarity is constantly revived.

In order to elicit exaltation—a key notion in the ethics and aesthetics of the epic narratives—every textual and extratextual resource is brought into play. In addition to the storyline in which the action and the actors are always characterized by absolutism and paroxysm (universal signs of heroism), the epic combines the power of the word with that of music which plays a fundamental role as much by its themes (i.e., melodies supporting and rhyming the words, and musical phrases identifying a certain hero or a particular action) as by the specific instruments indispensable for the recitation. The bards (or griots) insist that these instruments "speak" and that they even "communicate the words of the ancestors" to their listeners. If the narrative is not accompanied by music and narrated by a designated performer, it loses its status as epic and merely functions as an informative piece on such and such a character or an event.

The identifying and mobilizing nature of the epic in Africa explains in and of itself the extremely diverse production of epic narratives, insofar as the specific focal points of the self-identity of each group are conditioned by its ecological and historical background, social and political organization, ethical and religious values, or general worldview. In this respect, Africa offers a rich range of situations: the texts published to date allow us to recognize several types of orientations that can be qualified as mythological, historical, "*corporative,*" and religious epics.

Whereas the epic of a mythological type is found essentially in Central Africa, the three other types are common in West Africa.

Historical Epics

Even though the epics of West Africa have legendary features, they draw upon a historical base and celebrate characters who have had an impact on their times. In effect, the history of the entire area is marked by the building of great centralized empires whose internal organization was based on a hierarchical class system in which each saw his place assigned by his birthright, status, and social function; this is particularly true of the griot who, through his inherited status, plays a predominant role as a verbal artist, caretaker of the historical and epic "literary" heritage, and privileged mediator in all the workings of the society. The bards, categorized as genealogists and historiographers, have the prerogative of narrating the epics and of reciting the mottoes that identify the important figures.

The dialogue between history, legend, and myth varies from group to group. One may thus find epics that are metaphorical and apologetic interpretations of historical chronicles, such as the numerous narratives concerning the reign of Jaara reported by the traditional Soninke griots or the long "frescoes" covering the reign of the Damels of Cayor over four centuries, developed by Wolof griots during enthronement or funeral ceremonies. Others resemble the "Geste" recounting significant episodes around the individual who, as historical as he might be, still dons the archetypal image of the epic hero: gifted child, of extraordinary birth, who achieves his destiny after a long itinerary punctuated by challenges, trials, and struggles where magic helps him vanquish tyrants or djinns ("genies"). *Maren Jagu* of the Soninke and *Zarbakaan* of the Zarma also conform to this heroic pattern.

Malinke Epics

The most celebrated Malinke epic is *Sunjata*, named after the hero. This well-known historical figure succeeded in establishing the glorious Mali Empire after defeating the king of Sosso, Sumanguru (or Sumawuro), thus influencing African history from the thirteenth to the sixteenth centuries. Profoundly implicated in the country's history as liberator, unifier, and administrator of the Mande, Sunjata Keyta nonetheless appears in the symbolic world of the epic that, combining real, mythical, and magical elements, transforms his historical destiny by placing him in the creation myth of the first Mande village founded by the three master-hunters of the celestial ark. Sunjata has become an emblematic figure who, to this day, reaffirms the unity of the Manding world even beyond national borders. This epic, which chronicles an entire historical and social heritage, has become the symbol of the destiny of a vast group of people. It is thus the object of a kind of institutionalization: the bards only produce the public version of the official version of the "true history of the Mande," which is preserved by a cenacle of "the Masters of the Words" and transmitted, in a ritualized and confidential manner, during the restoration of the sacred dwelling, Kama Blon of Kangaba, site of the septennial cult of Mande everlastingness.

Through the emblematic character of Sunjata, this epic integrates the contours of Malinke identity in the history of the Mande, from its mythical origins to its emergence and territorial expansion and to its sociopolitical organization. For other peoples, such as the Bamana and the Fulani (Peul), the epic is merely a pretext composed of facts and historical figures, for fueling the ideology which governs their community, an ideology of power for the first and liberty for the second.

However close they are to their subjects, textual form, and modes of expression (rhythmical declamation and lute accompaniment), the Bamana and Fulani epics depart one from the other by the values they transmit and by the performer's attitude toward the text.

Bamana Epics

The Bamana epic, which centers around four great sovereigns, Biton Koulibali, Ngolo, Monzon, and Da Diara (eighteenth through nineteenth centuries) is in fact based upon the history of "The Force of Segou," a title designating imperial power as well as the sovereign himself, conferring to the latter an allegorical rather than a personal character on the ruler. As for the epic action, it is essentially expressed in the "game of men," for example war, the principal occupation of a power base relying on its armed force and not on its indigenous sociopolitical system capable of cementing Bamana unity. By presenting Segou's expansionist politics as involving territorial conquest by a mercenary army only motivated by the appropriation of bounty, the Bamana epic seems to exalt a quasi-feudal ideology of violence and power. By punctuating the narration with digressions, commentaries, comparisons between past and present, the griot readjusts an outdated story and a bygone ideology with present-day realities and values. This procedure also allows the bard to exhibit his personal talents in order to capture the admiration of the audience that is sensitive to his art of telling as to the epic's contents.

Fulani Epics

In Senegal, the Geste of Samba Gueladio Diegui is the most renowned. This figure belongs to the Denyanke dynasty founded by Koli Tenguella in the middle of the sixteenth century, but history is completely transmuted by epic interpretation that embroiders the story of this Samba on a stereotyped epic scheme. The victim of his uncle who usurps the power owed to him, he regains power with the help of a magic weapon (the gift of a water djinn) and an army of Moorish allies. An invincible hero, he nevertheless encounters death because of a woman's betrayal. This narravite, well stocked with adventures, evokes that of Sunjata in the Malinke epic.

In Mali, the Fulani epic, which centers on figures of the eighteenth and nineteenth centuries, falls under two categories: the legendary epic, where heroes of the pre-Islamic times are extolled—Silamaka, Boubou Ardo, Ham-Bodedio are some of the most famous who represent the *pulaaku*, traditional ideal of the Fulani; the other epic form that could be considered close to historical chronicles relates events and deeds of heroes of the Dina, the Fulani Empire of Massina, founded by Sekou Amadou in the beginning of the nineteenth century.

Furthermore, the Fulani bard's interpretation is austerely discreet and his performance is sober. The implicit nature of his delivery reinforces the complicity between listener and speaker. The narrator prefers including griots in the actual text alongside the hero who incarnates the cardinal virtues and the socioethical code. This set of values constitutes the essential, albeit ideal, expression of identity of the Fulani people whose orientation lies in stressing total independence, not only from others but also toward the constraints inherent in the human condition. The emphasis is thus placed on the hero himself and on the events he is involved in, however minute they may be, which are but pretexts to illustrate his character and his behavior. The more lackluster the pretext, the more glorious the exploit, and the more representative of the hero.

The epic action can generally be summarized as a transgression motivated by a challenge and resulting in an agonistic situation involving two characters who are so valorous that recourse to a magical weapon is necessary in order to declare a winner. Here, features of Fulani identity are internalized, which can be explained by their background. They are a pastoral people, who because of their diaspora, could only maintain their identity at the most profound and inalienable level, that is, an ideology of the self. This same personalization of the hero is found among other nomadic peoples such as the Tuareg "Cycle of Aligurran," a paragon of wisdom and perspicacity. Another example comes from North Africa, the "Geste hilalienne," which, through the characters of Dyab and Zazya, glorifies the primordial virtues of a traditional nomadic world.

Corporate Epics

In addition to those inspired by true historical figures, there are epic narratives that can be defined as *corporate* because they reflect an inherent professional specificity on which a group bases the most pertinent sense of its identity and the reasons for its cohesion. Whether found among entire populations, or in associations or confraternities within a larger group, these narratives recount heroic struggles between djinns and the ancestral master-hunters and master-fisherman who incarnate the representative virtues of the profession but who, above all, have established the primordial pacts with the animal and supernatural worlds on which rests the harmony between man and the natural world. As guarantors of these pacts, the confraternities of the Bamana and the Malinke hunters perpetuate the apprenticeship of practices that are as much technical as they are ritual. The epics are performed with a musical accompaniment on the harp-lute at ceremonies during which a community that is both professional and initiatory sees the models and traits of its identity thus reaffirmed. The narrators of these texts, who are often healers or diviners, are not statutory or hereditary bards. Their narratives, however, are constructed, formulated, and performed along the same lines as the historical epic. The epic of Sunjata, for example, begins with an episode linking it directly to certain hunting narratives.

Other narratives of this type exist among the fishing populations such as the Fanta Maa of the Bozo of Mali and the Pekane of the Subalb'e of Senegal, which is performed without musical accompaniment during a magic ritual associated with the collective hunt of the crocodile. This ceremony ostensibly is designed to placate the supernatural forces in order to obtain control over the game and, above all, to rekindle the unity, cohesion, and identity of this population.

One could also classify in this category of epic the *daari* of the Fulani (Peul) of Ferlo in Senegal who, like the Subalb'e (fishermen) and the Seb'b'e (warriors), also focus their narratives on their activities as cattle herdsmen. The scenes mainly center around the cattle raids led by the Fulani from different clans, as a means of mutually affirming their equal value with respect to their common ideology. Another text that passes as the "cattle's motto" is performed like an epic even though it recounts no other exploit than that of the perpetuation of the tradition of cattle raising. Called the Fantang, it is a sort of mythical narrative, a kind of foundation text comparable to the corporate narratives, since it justifies attribution of cattle raising to the Fulani, the establishment of such "caste people" as coopers and bards, and special relationship among these three statutory groups.

Religious Epics

Lastly, coming from the areas of Africa where Islam was implanted, there is a type of written verse-epic, drawing on Arabic models such as the Fulani and Hausa *qacida* that relate the jihad led by the great historical figures of past centuries in order to impose their hegemony and ideology. These texts, one of the best known of which is the *qacida* in Pulaar (the Fulani language of Senegal) based on the life of El Hadj Omar, are the work of lettered "clercs" whose evident religious militancy does not lessen their poetic talent. They are long poems destined to be memorized and sung in the mosques by the *talibe* (students) or from door to door by blind beggars, for an illiterate public. A concern for historical accuracy is complemented by a glorifying and hagiographic intention; however, the exaltation of the heroes' victories and deeds always involves a broader project that of the victory of the soldiers of God over the world of infidels and the subsequent establishment of divine law.

A Social Institution

The robust vitality of the epic genre in Africa (how many of these texts remain to be yet discovered?) appears to be linked to the prevailing importance of the spoken word in the cultures of this continent where oral communication has retained a status and an efficiency which, in other cultures, has been greatly modified by writing. By its very orientation, the epic cannot be dissociated from its public expression, both oral and musical. Because of its identity and mobilizing functions, the epic is as much a literary genre as it is a social institution. In effect, it is evident that what classifies these texts as epics is their modality and their performance context, as well as their inclusion in a social system to whose dynamics they significantly contribute, which only the power and the resources of the spoken word can ensure.

References

Cisse, Youssouf Tata, et Wa Kamissoko. 1988. *La grande Geste du Mali*. Paris: Karthala-Arsan.

———. 1991. *Soundjata, la gloire du Mandé*. Paris: Karthala-Arsan.

Correra, Issagha. 1992. *Samba Guéladio, épopée peule du Fuuta Tooro*. Dakar: Initiations et Études africaines 36. Université de Dakar-IFAN.

Coulibaly, Dosseh Joseph. 1985. *Récit des chasseurs du Mali, Dingo Kanbili, une épopée des chasseurs malinké*. Paris: EDICEF, CILF.

Dumestre, Gérard et Kesteloot, Lilyan. 1975. *La prise de Dionkoloni, épisode de l'épopée bambara*. Classiques africains 15. Paris: Les Belles Lettres.

Dumestre, Gérard. 1979. *La geste de Ségou*. Classiques africains 19. Paris: Les Belles Lettres.

Galley, Micheline & Ayoub, Abderrahman. 1983. *Histoire des Beni Hilal et de ce qui leur advint dans leur marche vers l'ouest*. Classiques africains 22. Paris: Les Belles Lettres.

Hale, Thomas A., ed. and trans. 1996. *The Epic of Askia Mohammed* (recounted by N. Malio). Bloomington: Indiana University Press.

Hayidara, Sh. T. 1987. *La geste de Fanta Maa, archétype du chasseur dans la culture des Bozo*. Niamey: CELHTO.

Innes, Gordon 1974. *Sunjata: Three Mandinka Versions*. London: SOAS.

———. 1976. *Kaabu and Fulaadu: Historical Narratives of the Gambian Mandinka*. London: SOAS.

Johnson, John W. 1979. *The Epic of Sunjata According to Magan Sisoko*. Bloomington: Folklore Pulications Group.

———. 1986. *The Epic of Son-Jara*. Bloomington: Indiana University Press.

Johnson, John W., T. Hale, and S. Belcher, eds. 1997. *Oral Epics from Africa*. Bloomington: Indiana University Press.

Kesteloot, Lilyan et al. 1993. *Da Monzo de Ségou, épopée bambara* (1972), 4 fasc. Paris: L'Harmattan.

Kesteloot, Lilyan, and D. Bassirou. 1997. *Les épopées d'Afrique noire.* Karthala Éditions UNESCO.

Meillassoux, Claude, L. Doucoure, and D. Simagha. 1967. *Légende de la dispersion des Kusa. épopée soninké.* Dakar: IFAN.

Meyer, Gérard. 1991. *Récits épiques toucouleurs. La vache, le livre, la lance.* Paris: Karthala-ACCT.

Mounkaila, Fatimata. 1988. *Mythe et histoire dans la geste de Zarbakane.* Niamey: CELHTO.

Ndongo, S. M. 1986. *Le Fantang. poèmes mythiques des bergers peuls.* Paris: Karthala-IFAN-UNESCO.

Ngaide, Mamadou Lamine. 1983. *Le vent de la razzia, deux récits épiques des Peuls du Jolof.* Dakar: IFAN.

Niane, Djibril Tamsir. 1960. *Soundjata ou l'épopée mandinque.* Paris: Présence africaine.

Saada, Lucienne. 1985. *La Geste hilalienne.* Paris: Gallimard.

Seydou, Christiane. 1972. *Silâmaka et Poullôri, récit épique peul raconté par Tinguidji.* Classiques africains 13. Paris: Les Belles Lettres.

———. 1976. *La geste de Ham-Bodêdio ou Hama le Rouge.* Classiques africains 18. Paris: les Belles Lettres.

Sy, Amadou Abel. 1978. *Seul contre tous, deux récits épiques des pêcheurs du Fouta Toro.* Dakar-Abidjan: NEA, Traditions orales.

Thoyer, Annik. 1995. *Récits épiques des chasseurs bamanan du Mali.* Paris: l'Harmattan.

CHRISTIANE SEYDOU

See also **French Study of African Folklore; West Africa: Overview**

EQUATORIAL GUINEA (REPUBLIC OF EQUATORIAL GUINEA)

Located on and off of central Africa's western coast, Equatorial Guinea is a country of 452,000 living on two small islands (Bioko, formerly known as Fernando Po, and Annobon) and a mainland territory that is called Rio Muni. Bordered by Cameroon to the north and Gabon to the south, the country has an equatorial climate. Equatorial Guinea's capital and largest city is Malabo, which has a population of 58,000. Most of the country's population is of the Fang group (80 percent), while 15 percent are Bubi, and 5 percent consist of various smaller groups. Spanish, Fang, Benge, Combe, Bujeba, Balengue, Fernandino, and Bubi are the most widely spoken languages. Sixty percent of the population is Catholic, while the remaining 40 percent are either Protestant or practice traditional indigenous religions.

Until 1778, Portugal controlled this area, but then ceded it to Spain. On October 12, 1968, Equatorial Guinea gained its independence from Spain, only to form its own repressive one-party republic. From independence until 1979, Equatorial Guinea was ruled by the very sadistic Macias Nguema who led the country to a massive chaotic state whereby tens of thousands of people were either murdered or died of disease and starvation. During his reign, an additional one-third of the nation's people went into exile. The years following Nguema's rule have not seen many great improvements, as the economic situation is largely corrupt and environmental decay due to uncontrolled logging has plagued the nation.

Though the country grows cocoa, coffee, timber, rice, yams, and bananas, most food is still imported and malnutrition is rampant. Fishing, sawmilling, and palm oil processing have been Equatorial Guinea's main industries and sources of revenue. Bioko was dominated by cocoa plantations worked primarily by migrant Nigerians. Unfortunately, 70 percent of the economy comes from foreign aid, mostly from Spain and France, who compete for influence. Current exploitation of gas and oil by United States, France, and Spain, however, may soon increase government revenues.

JENNIFER JOYCE

ERITREA (STATE OF ERITREA)

Located in the northeast corner of Africa, Eritrea is bordered by Sudan, Ethiopia, Djibouti, and the Red Sea. The climate ranges from a hot and dry desert on the sea coast, to cool and wet conditions in the central highlands. Eritrea has a population of nearly 4 million, with a large overseas immigrant population. Its capital and largest city is Asmara, which is home to 400,000 people. Half of all Eritreans are ethnic Tigrays, 40 percent are Tigre and Kunama, 4 percent are Afar, 3 percent are Saho (Red Sea coast dwellers), and 3 percent are made up of various smaller groups. Although there are many languages spoken throughout the country, Tigrinya and Amharic are the predominant ones. Although Arabic is accepted as an official language, English is used in higher education settings. Muslims, Coptic Christians, Roman Catholics, and Protestant compose the majority of the religious community.

Eritrea has a long colonial history that began in 1868 when it was first settled by Italians. From 1941 to 1952 the British occupied the land until it became federated with and later annexed by Ethiopia. After a three-decade long struggle led by the Eritrean Liberation Front (ELF) and the Eritrean Popular Liberation Front (EPLF), Eritrea gained its independence from Ethiopia on May 24, 1993, and became Africa's newest nation. During the long battle for liberation, between 60,000 and 70,000 people lost their lives. An additional 700,000 people were forced into exile from the country. In 1998, a border conflict grew into a full-fledged war between Ethiopia and Eritrea with thousands more being killed. Fortunately, a ceasefire was negotiated and UN peacekeepers moved in by 2001.

The status of women is among the best in Africa due to the war of liberation war. The intensity of the struggle grew in the 1970s when the EPLF split from the ELF. A more radical group, the EPLF had many women among its active members. In addition, the EPLF discouraged female circumcision and granted women the right to own land and choose their husbands in the areas that they liberated. Women are now assured of at least 30 percent representation in the legislative body.

Gold, copper, iron ore, and potash are Eritrea's natural resources. The country's agricultural sector also produces sorghum, fish, lentils, tobacco, coffee, and sisal. Eritrea's main industries and sources of revenue are food processing, beverages, and textiles. Since the end of the war the government has begun to restore agricultural and communications infrastructure, and crop production has since increased. Medical services and educational institutions are improving greatly.

JENNIFER JOYCE

ESTHETICS: BAULE VISUAL ARTS

The Baule now number about one million people. They traditionally lived in what is called the Baule V, a region of wooded savannah that extends into the forest area of south central Cote d'Ivoire. This was one of the last areas of West Africa to be penetrated by Europeans, as heavy forest, a lack of navigable rivers, and the martial reputation of the inhabitants protected it. The first French explorers entered the Baule area in the second half of the nineteenth century, and the Baule were still actively resisting the colonial regime in the first decade of the twentieth century. The first studies of the Baule were done by French colonial administrators, in particular, Maurice Delafosse. There is no single work which presents a basic ethnography of the Baule, although the combined articles of Mona and Pierre Etienne give extensive information. Jean-Pierre Chauveau studied many aspects of Baule culture in the 1970s and 1980s. Cyprien Arbelbide studied Baule proverbs in 1973. Baule history has been studied by Jean-Noel Loucou and Timothy Weiskel. Philip Ravenhill has written on Baule figures. The principal source on Baule art is Susan Vogel's catalogue for the recent exhibition *Baule Art Western Eyes*, which has a bibliography of works in both English and French.

Our knowledge of Baule history makes it clear that the people have been in the process of constant migration for at least several hundred years. Baule oral history states that they were originally from the Ashanti area of Ghana, and that after losing the region in an eighteenth-century dynastic struggle, they fled westward under the authority of their queen, Aura Pokou, pursued by an Ashanti army. Arriving at the Comoe river in eastern Cote d'Ivoire, they found it flooded and impassable. The queen consulted a diviner and was told that she needed to sacrifice her most precious possession in order to lead her people to safety. She threw her newborn child into the river, and the waters parted, allowing the people to escape. They traveled to what is now the town of Sakassou, where she settled and from there the various Baule subgroups spread out.

Recent scholars (Garrard, Loucou, Vogel, Weiskel) tend to believe that the actual process of Baule settlement and the formation of their culture must have taken place over a millennium rather than over a couple hundred of years. Their language, political organization, and their material culture are too changed from the original Ashanti prototypes for the process to have been completed so quickly.

Baule culture combines some elements that remain almost indistinguishable from their Akan originals (gold and bronze work, the forms and uses of stools and chairs, and the use of prestige objects made of gold-covered wood) with others (carved wooden statues and masks, systems of divination, and social organization) that do not seem to have originated in Ghana, but are more similar to the practices of Ivorian groups. Unlike major Ghanaian groups, they do not have a centralized state or institutions that extend beyond the village level. Some current French historians posit that the Baule were a creation of the colonial period, like many other African groups. There is, however, no question that the people we call Baule speak one language and are culturally extremely similar.

Like the Ashanti, the Baule make extensive use of proverbs and proverbial expressions. Speaking well is a very important part of personal prestige, and speaking Baule well means expressing oneself indirectly through allusive expressions and proverbs. These same proverbs are illustrated in bronze and gold objects and in the decorative motifs on pottery and textiles. Like the Ghanian Akan, the Baule had a currency based on the exchange of gold dust, and used bronze weights illustrating proverbs to establish the value of gold. They also made (and continue to make) prestige objects like staffs and flywhisks of gold covered wood, carved into forms that illustrated proverbs. Although paper money has replaced gold dust as currency, gold and gold-covered objects are still displayed at funerals, and are considered part of a family treasure that may never be sold.

The great importance of masks and masquerades in Baule culture is one of the elements that distinguish them sharply from the Ghanaian Akan, who use almost no masks, and even from the Akan groups in Cote d'Ivoire such as the Agni and the Akye, who have only a few masks of which we are aware. The peoples now living to the west and north of the Baule (the Guro and Yaure, the Wan and the Senufo) use many masks which seem closely related in style and function to those of the Baule. It seems likely that Baule masking traditions are strongly influenced by their Ivorian neighbors, in contrast to their metalworking and ceramics, which are startlingly similar to those of their Akan relatives to the East.

Essentially, the Baule have two kinds of masks. The first are small face masks carved in a naturalistic style, worn with cloth costumes, and which can be seen by men, women, and children. These are kept in the village, and portray women, men, and domestic animals. Stylistically, they resemble the masks of the Guro and Yaure peoples.

Then there are the sacred men's masks, which are kept in bush shelters, incarnate bush spirits, are worn with raphia costumes, and are never seen by women, on pain of death. These are large helmet masks, which portray ferocious-looking composite animals. They resemble some masks of the Senufo and the Mande of Mali.

Despite the likelihood that Baule masks originated with other groups, they have, to a remarkable extent, been "Baule-ized" in style. Whatever their diverse origins, Baule works in all media display a consistent set of esthetic preferences. Surfaces are carefully worked to produce a smooth, shiny finish. Cloth, pottery, wood, and metal masks are all covered with finely detailed decoration, frequently displaying design elements that refer to proverbs.

The Baule express an esthetic preference for full, round, voluminous shapes and closed forms in both their pots and statues. They seem to prefer things that seem to us elegant and refined, and restrained rather than extroverted. Even the style of dancing preferred by Baule women displays this esthetic, with its emphasis on subtle, restrained movement.

A comparison with the esthetics of the neighboring Senufo people shows that the Baule make rounded, finished objects, while the Senufo create taller, rougher, slightly concave forms. While there are naturally some exceptions, the research done on Baule esthetics, as displayed in their sculpture, by Susan Vogel shows a remarkably consistent set of standards.

The Baule clearly enjoy looking at, talking about, and evaluating objects. An early writer, Hans Himmelheber, used the Baule as an example of the existence of the "art for art's sake" esthetic in Africa. Perhaps it would be more accurate to say that the

Baule simply take a connoisseur's pleasure in objects that are well made and finely decorated.

References

Arbelbide, Cyprien. 1975. *Les Bauole d'apres leurs dictons et proverbes.* Abdijan: Ceda.

Chauveau, J. P., and J. P. Dozon. 1987. Au coeur des ethnics ivoiriennes . . . l'etat. *L'etat contemporain en Afrique.* Paris: Harmattan.

Etienne, Pierre, and Mona Etienne. 1962–1964. L'organisation sociale des baoule. *Étude Regionale de Bouake.* Abdijan: Ministere du Plan.

Ravenhill, Philip. 1980. Baule Statuary Art: Meaning and Modernization. Working Papers in the Traditional Arts, No. 5. Philadelphia: ISHI.

———. 1996. *Dreams and Reveries: Images of Otherworld Mates among the Baule of West Africa.* Washington, D.C.: Smithsonian Press.

Vogel, Susan Mullin. 1997. *Baule: African Art Western Eyes.* New Haven: Yale University Press.

JEROME VOGEL

ESTHETICS

See **Body Arts; Dress**

ETHIOPIA (PEOPLE'S DEMOCRATIC REPUBLIC OF ETHIOPIA)

Located in northeastern Africa, Ethiopia is a landlocked country surrounded by Sudan, Eritrea, Djibouti, Somalia, and Kenya. The country's climate ranges from temperate in the highlands, to arid in the lowlands. Of Ethiopia's some 66,180,000 people, 40 percent are Oromo, 32 percent Amhara and Tigre, 9 percent Sidamo, and 19 percent consist of various other groups. The most widely spoken languages in the country are Amharic, Tigrinya, Oromo, Somali, Arabic, Italian, and English. Between 45 percent and 50 percent of the population is Muslim, 35 percent to 40 percent is Ethiopian Orthodox Christian, while the remaining population practices animist and various other religious traditions. Addis Ababa, the nation's capital, is also its largest city, with 2,220,000 inhabitants.

Ethiopia is the oldest independent country in Africa. The nation has one of Africa's oldest histories, which reaches back to the Axum empire of the first century CE. The beginning of modern Ethiopia, however, was developed by Emperor Tewodros in 1885. Unlike the rest of the continent's nations, Ethiopia successfully defeated attempts made to colonize the land. In 1936, however, Fascist Italy invaded Ethiopia and, while it did not colonize, it ruled the land until 1941. Emperor Haile Selassie was known as Ras Tafari before being crowned emperor; the name is still in use among the Rastafarians of Jamaica, who consider him a sacred figure. Although widely recognized outside of Africa as great leader, Selassie's somewhat dictatorial rule was finally overthrown by a military coup in 1974.

The next period of Ethiopian history was marked by the violent rule of the Dirgue, a military council headed by Megistu Haile Miriam. He was overthrown in 1991.

In the past forty years, Ethiopia has suffered from periodic famine, drought, and interethnic political tensions. In 1961, the Eritrean liberation movement began. This battle lasted until 1993, when Ethiopia finally granted Eritrea its independence. In 1998, another border dispute erupted into warfare but a ceasefire was accepted a few years later, with UN peacekeepers as monitors. An unstable government, famine, and continuing interethnic violence have marred the nation and the economy has subsequently suffered.

Ethiopia's natural resources include potash, salt, gold, copper, and platinum, while agricultural production revolves around primarily coffee, hides and skins, and agricultural products. Principle industries are processed foods, textiles, cement, building materials, and hydroelectric power.

Ethiopia's history dates back two thousand years and the nation's cultural achievements are likewise extensive. Addis Ababa, the nation's capital, is the Organization of African Unity's headquarters. The most spectacular arts are found in the Christian Coptic churches and monasteries. In addition to the buildings themselves, the clergy's regalia and the accompanying sacred manuscripts demonstrate a vibrant artistic tradition.

JENNIFER JOYCE

EVANS-PRITCHARD, SIR EDWARD EVAN (1902–1973)

The late Sir Edward Evan Evans-Pritchard, professor of social anthropology at Oxford University from 1947 to 1970, was one of the first and most dedicated individuals in the field of African studies to encourage the collection and study of indigenous folklore. As a student of Malinowski at the London School of Economics in the 1920s, Evans-Pritchard was deeply influenced by his mentor's insistence that a primary goal of fieldwork was to amass "native" texts verbatim and record them in the vernacular.

For Evans-Pritchard the task was twofold. First, he was well aware, in the 1920s and 1930s, that African peoples were in the throes of massive and unstoppable pressures of social change, a direct consequence of European colonial policies. Thus, he saw the collection of folklore and oral tradition as paramount to providing a record of social and cultural worlds as they might have existed in precolonial Africa. This general effort might well be called an effort at salvage ethnography. In North America, this tradition had been initiated by Franz Boas, and by the 1920s many anthropologists working with indigenous peoples in North America could only record "memory cultures," oral traditions that were relics of societies long transformed by European colonization.

A second major goal of Evans-Pritchard, also via the inspiration of Malinowski, was to record local texts, legends, and folklore as a means to understand and interpret the ethos of a people, or characteristic features of their mode of thinking and classification. Thus, a local text might be regarded as a "pure" form of ethnographic representation when recorded in the vernacular, unblemished by secondary translation and exegesis.

With these critical points of method in mind one can turn to a brief assessment of Evans-Pritchard's achievements in the field of African folklore. It may be said that in the modern era no anthropologist published a greater volume of folklore and texts than Evans-Pritchard. Most of this material focused on Azande traditions, a people he lived with in the Sudan for some twenty months in the middle 1920s. The publication of Azande texts and folklore was indeed a consistent theme throughout his career amid his other published work, voluminous in its own right. A considerable portion of his work on the Azande was collected and written by Azande field assistants he hired, a practice following that of Boas and George Hunt in their early American anthropological research among Northwestern coastal peoples. All told, he published some twenty articles on Azande custom and tradition, which included extensive vernacular texts. In addition, at his own expense, he published a series of short monographs, as well as three larger works solely concerned with Zande folklore, most notably, *The Zande Trickster* (1967) and *Man and Woman among the Azande* (1974).

Beyond his concern for publishing all the Zande texts and folklore he collected from his own fieldwork (he claimed to have published only a fraction of what he collected), Evans-Pritchard played a key role in initiating and promoting African folk traditions on a par with established literary traditions. This is most notable in his founding, with Godfrey Leinhardt, Ruth Finnegan, and W. H. Whiteley, the Oxford Library of African Literature (Oxford University Press).

In retrospect, one can argue that Evans-Pritchard played a leading role in the study of African folklore, transforming it from a preprofessional antiquarian hobby, typical of early European travelers, into a respected and important sub-field of African studies.

References

Beidelman, T. O. 1974. *A Bibliography of the Writings of E. E. Evans-Pritchard*. London: Travistock Publications.
Burton, John W. 1992. *An Introduction to Evans-Pritchard*. Fribourg: University Press of Switzerland.

JOHN W. BURTON

See also **Divination; Tricksters in African Folklore; Tricksters: Ture of the Azande**

EVIL EYE

The belief complex referred to as Evil Eye (often capitalized) exists in Africa only in North African societies; reports of it south of the Sahara should be reexamined. It designates a complex system of beliefs and behaviors, protection and cure, centering on the belief in a harmful power that is projected through the direct gaze of a person. Some people have the power and some do not; who might have it is not always known, and its projection may be willful or involuntary. The power is stimulated by envy, anger, or malice. Children, the elderly, and sick people are especially vulnerable, but Evil Eye can inflict any manner of harm upon anyone's person, household, or property. Apotropaic amulets, often representations of horns, eyes, open hands, mirrors, or blue gemstones, are worn or fixed to possessions, and the walls and doorways of houses. People may make verbal disclaimers after a flattering remark about another person, or that person's family or property (i.e., "What a beautiful child! Oh, but it seems fussy, is it well?").

If divination reveals Evil Eye as the cause of some misfortune, a specific ritual is available to exorcize or neutralize it. Tension and suspicion are inherent in society; like witchcraft, Evil Eye offers a credible explanation for misfortune, and sociologically it has been seen to have "social control" functions, making people mindful of their social manners lest they be suspected. Evil Eye belief complex is a variant of classical witchcraft beliefs, but in many areas it coexists with witches, or beliefs in various beings of the night who do all the evil things attributed to witches elsewhere.

Influenced by Freud's speculations in his essay, "Das Unheimlich" (1917–1920), Evil Eye was long generally held to be a "universal superstition" (Schoeck 1955). Careful cross-cultural research by John M. Roberts in 1976, and contributors to the two most comprehensive volumes on the subject, by Maloney (1976) and Dundes (1981), showed that the phenomenon is localized in Indo-European and Semitic areas of the Near East and circum-Mediterranean, from India to Spain, and the North African Maghreb. It diffused into northern Europe, the British Isles, and specific areas of Spanish influence in the Americas, notably Mexico. In nearly all areas it is closely associated with envy; indeed, in much scholarship it has come to be regarded as synonymous with that emotion.

In these areas, concepts of Evil Eye are complex and institutionalized, reaching their most elaborate form in late medieval Italy, where the power was used by the classic supernatural witch, the *strega*, who flew by night, poisoned wells, inflicted disease, kidnapped and ate children, and committed various other horrible and obscene acts, and who, in the Christian context, was the earthly agent of Satan; it was also used by a suspected agent who persists in the modern world, the *jettatore*, who, when inflamed by envy (*invidia*) or other negative human emotions will cast *mal'occhio*, Evil Eye. It is counteracted by *gratia*, (divine grace), bestowed by God, expressed as a blessing.

Evil Eye is coincident with Arab culture throughout the Maghreb; it predates the spread of Islam. It is also reported in Ethiopia and Sudan. Generalizations about the phenomenon are problematic, however, as cultural conceptions of the phenomenon may vary. In Algeria, Evil Eye (*ain*) is a mystical power inherent in some individuals, clearly a variant of witchcraft beliefs, distinct from *sahir*, sorcery is learned evil magic (see Jansen 1987); it is counteracted by *baraka*, blessing invoking God's holy power. Among the Arab Rubatab in Sudan, the power of Evil Eye is classified as *sahir*, and it may be cast through words (Ibrahim 1994).

Some general and specific attributes are similar to those in the Middle East. A cure among the Shilluk of Sudan is accomplished by blinding the eye of a sheep; dried sheep's eyes are protective amulets in Iran. And as in some areas of the Middle East, in some Sudanic areas it may be conceived as the province of special, low-class people. Among the Amhara of Ethiopia (Reminick 1974), it is attributed to a castelike group of landless craftspeople, referred to as *buda*, "evil eye people." Among Amhara social mechanisms to avoid suspicion, and methods of protection and cure, are perhaps simpler than but otherwise similar to those employed in the Middle East or southern Europe; but the fear of Evil Eye is pervasive and serves social functions valuable among subsistence-level people. By identifying a potentially evil outsider, it strengthens social solidarity, but it negates a sense of superiority, as it encourages people to extend social propriety to all, and not to boast of their own good fortune, lest they arouse the envy of the evil "eye people."

Reports of "Evil Eye" elsewhere, especially in sub-Saharan societies, should be reexamined. They certainly indicate specific cultural elaborations on the widespread, probably universal, unease people feel at the direct stare of another, especially a competitor, potential adversary, or stranger; they may indicate beliefs in dangerous power transferable through the eyes. Such reports may also indicate that someone has looked upon something he or she was forbidden to see: as in the Elizabethan, and biblical, sense, "seeing" can mean "knowing." The eyes are one of several means through which witches and sorcerers are widely believed able to project malign influence, and envy or anger can trigger it. Beliefs in witches and/or sorcerers are found in all sub-Saharan African societies, and references to "Evil Eye" among any of them are probably attributes of these agents of supernatural evil. In several societies persons with red eyes, or with eye disorders, may be suspected of being witches. Attributes of witches in tropical Africa are similar to those in medieval Europe without their Christian trappings.

Thus, the occasional use of the term "evil eye" in the hundreds of ethnographic reports of sub-Saharan African societies may be the ethnographer's choice of label for a common method of identification of, or attack by witches, such as J. G. Peristiany's (1939) use of the term for the Kipsigis. Robert and Barbara Levine (1966, 119–120) describe a named malevolent power (*okobiriria*) transmitted through the eyes of some light-skinned Gusii, usually women, which causes small objects to cling to and burrow into the skin of light-skinned infants, killing them if not rubbed off quickly with clarified butter. Gusii consider lightly pigmented skin to be delicate, thin and easily permeable by supernatural influence; darker-skinned people are less likely to project and to be affected by the power. The belief, which Gusii say came from the Kipsigis, seems a peculiar variant on the general sub-Saharan African belief in the witchcraft power, which is the corrupted form of a personal power, usually named, that exists in everyone. Or the term *evil eye* may be used as equivalent of concepts of "envy" or other negative emotions

which activate witches, and hence it may become a synonym for witchcraft itself; this seems to explain Helmut Schoeck's erroneous attribution of *Evil Eye* to Azande, and other societies, in a widely reprinted article (1955).

It is interesting to note that among the Amhara, the *buda* have attributes identical to those of witches in societies below the Sahara. The verb "to eat" most often describes the *buda*'s attack; the *buda* can turn themselves into hyenas, or seduce their victims through sexual suggestion. Reported also among the Shilluk, the evil-eye people can animate and enslave corpses of the dead. It might be suggested that Evil Eye in the areas immediately north of the Sahara is transitional between the forms in Arab areas, and the elaborate witchcraft beliefs of societies to the south.

References

Dundes, Alan, ed. 1981. *The Evil Eye: A Folklore Casebook*. New York: Garland.

Ibrahim, Abdullahi A. 1994. *Assaulting with Words: Popular Discourse and the Bridle of Shari'ah*. Evanston: Northwestern University Press.

Jansen, Willy. 1987. *Women Without Men: Gender and Marginality in an Algerian Town*. Leiden: Brill.

Levine, Robert, and Barbara B. Levine. 1966. *Nyansongo: A Gusii Community in Kenya*. New York: Wiley.

Maloney, Clarence, ed. 1976. *The Evil Eye*. New York: Columbia University Press.

Peristiany, J. G. 1939. *The Social Institutions of the Kipsigis*. London: Routledge and Kegan Paul.

Reminick, Ronald A. 1974. The Evil Eye Belief Among the Amhara of Ethiopia. *Ethnology* 13:279–91.

Schoeck, Helmut. 1955. The Evil Eye: Forms and Dynamics of a Universal Superstition. *Emory University Quarterly* 11:153–61.

PHILLIPS STEVENS JR.

See also **Sahir**

EWE

See **Music**

F

FALASHA

See **Jews of Ethiopia; Music: Arab and Jewish Music of North Africa; Northeastern Africa**

FANG

See **Architecture; Central Africa**

FESTIVALS: MUTOMBOKO FESTIVAL OF THE LUNDA

> You are the one who has assumed leadership.
> Great One, you are the remnant of the ancient
>   Royal Highness.
> The sovereign ruler who is as firmly planted
>   as a banana tree.
> The strong one, you walk over the weak ones
>   and subdue even the those who resist
>   your firm control.

(praise for Kazembe sung by Chipolobwe Mwadya
                                            Misenga, 1989)

Mwata Kazembe is the traditional ruler of the Lunda people living in Zambia's Luapula Province. He is the center of an annual festival called the Mutomboko that is held every year in the town that houses his capital, Mwansabombwe. The festival usually lasts two days, with at least a third day, preceding the main events, dedicated to more informal celebratory activities, such as dancing, music, drinking, and general revelry. There are usually several ceremonial events, some involving ritual activities that characterize each Mutomboko festival. The gathering is marked by a high level of celebratory license, knit together by the music, dance, and song of Lunda and visiting performers.

One of the objects of the festival is to celebrate the position of "perpetual" kingship among the Lunda, and there is an emphasis on retellings and celebrations of seminal events in Lunda history. These include accounts of the original migrations of Lunda royalty and their soldiers into the area from the west, from what is now called the Democratic Republic of the Congo. There is a much larger group of people who call themselves Lunda, with links to the larger Luba group in the Congo. In fact, several migrations have led to at least one more group of Lunda people settling in the northwestern Province of Zambia. This latter group is closely associated with the Ndembu and speak a language different from that spoken by the Luapula Lunda. Nevertheless, both groups recognize their common ancestral ties by maintaining formal cordial relationships, with their chiefs often attending each other's festivals and installments. They also readily acknowledge the Lunda king in the Congo, Mwata Yamvwa, as their progenitor and traditional overlord.

The Mutomboko usually takes place on the last weekend in July, the date roughly corresponding to the installment of Mwata Kazembe XVII, Paul Kanyembo Lutaba, in 1961. This Kazembe is credited with reviving and formalizing a set of older rites and activities that have become the current festival. In its current form, the Mutomboko ceremonies are preceded by a day or two of celebration and the bringing of gifts to Mwansabombwe, the home or palace of Mwata Kazembe. The gifts come from all parts of the Lunda area, consisting mostly of foodstuffs and locally brewed beer (made of maize or finger-millet) and, occasionally, cash. Formal activities begin in the afternoon of the day before the major rites and ceremonies. On this afternoon, there is a gathering of elders and notables to conduct important business and the performance of dances meant to celebrate the occasion and honor Kazembe. The elders and officials sit in a large section just outside the wall of the palace, facing a small courtyard, ringed and partly shaded by miyombo trees. A large crowd attends the ceremony, celebrating the events, applauding the skills of the dancers and musicians, and praising the Mwata himself. This ceremony is called the *Mutentamo*, and its specific purposes, as noted by several Lunda scholars, are the:

1. Investiture of Lundahood on a non-Lunda citizen for gallantry or other achievements.
2. Installation of a member of the royal family, or an important councillor, to a hereditary office, *umwanso*.
3. Removal of insignia of office from the holder for disloyalty to the Mwata and gross misconduct.

4. Welcoming of an important visiting chief or dignitary from outside the Mwata's jurisdiction. (Chinyanta and Chiwale 1989, 35)

After the various ceremonies and addresses, mostly conducted by the Mwata's spokesman, Kazembe closes the ceremony by dancing an abbreviated version of the Mutomboko, translated as "the dance of conquest," to the cheers of the gathered crowd.

On the morning of the second and final day, Mwata Kazembe, dressed in a plain, white, short-sleeved shirt, a white head scarf, and white pajama-like trousers, moves from his home to a small shrine within the palace compound called the *nakabutula*. There, the keeper of the shrine smears the Mwata's face and arms with an ochre-colored powder called *inkula*. He then moves outside the western gate of the compound, near the site of the previous day's gathering, and visits the miyombo trees, where the royal grave keepers give him permission to travel outside the boundaries of the palace for the ceremonial activities he is about to conduct. He is further smeared with a white powder called *ulupemba*. From that point, Kazembe is carried on an uncovered palanquin, called the *umuselo*, sitting in what the Mwata calls his "coffin," made of zebra skin and supported by two thick poles, manned by eight carriers. They proceed to the banks of the Ng'ona River, followed by dignitaries and the large crowd of people. When he is set down, Kazembe must walk to a ritual barrier, a gate consisting of a spear held by several acolytes, and ask permission of the keepers of the shrine to pass to the point where, historically, his "brother" Chinyanta was drowned for revealing the secret that salt was to be found in this place. The actual location of this event is given in oral traditions as the Mukelezi River in the Lualaba area of the Congo. Kazembe then moves to the river and offers a number of items in sacrifice to the spirit of Chinyanta: *ulupemba* powder, cooked fish, chicken, groundnuts, and cassava, all of which are commonly consumed by the Lunda. As people cheer each toss of food into the river, functionaries fire old muzzle-loaders or *mazo* guns, in celebration. The Mwata then moves to another location downstream, to offer a similar sacrifice to Kasombola, Chinyanta's brother, who was drowned with him. Kazembe then returns to the *umuselo* and is carried back to his palace.

Although many dignitaries and commoners mill around the Mwata's compound, Kazembe and his associates rest, eat, and prepare for the afternoon activities. These periods between activities are also important opportunities for visitors to seek an audience with the Mwata and for him to greet visiting dignitaries. Somewhere around 2 P.M., Kazembe emerges from his palace and is carried on the *umuselo* toward the compound's gate. At that point, while stationed at the gateway, Kazembe's retainer, known as Katamatwi, uses a ceremonial sword to cut the head off a young goat, just as the carriers run past carrying the Mwata. Hundreds of people surround, follow, and precede the *umuselo* as it speeds Kazembe towards the dancing arena. A few thousand people are already gathered at the arena prior to the Mwata's arrival. On the western side, there is a covered area where the Lunda aristocracy, invited guests, visiting dignitaries, and Kazembe himself sit in the shade. Most of the spectators sit on bleacher-type benches along the northern side of the arena, while others surround the raised dancing area. After some introductory remarks by government officials and Lunda dignitaries, a series of dances are performed by local women. There are three age

groups that dance separately. Approximately six very young girls (around eight to ten years old) perform a dance called *chiwaza*. They begin at the eastern end of the arena, near the orchestra comprised of various types of drums and a xylophone, walk to the other end where the dignitaries sit, kneel down, and clap three times in praise of the Mwata. They then perform the chiwaza as they move across to the orchestra then back to Kazembe. They kneel again, honor Kazembe, and depart. Another group of young women, of adolescent age, use the same pattern, but dance a different step called *chilumwalumwa*. Finally, mature women, ranging from their twenties to their forties, perform the dance called *wakubasha*. The women then give way to a number of Lunda dignitaries who dance the Mutomboko.

The Mutomboko is performed by Lunda notables dressed in the traditional garb of the court. This means they wear long-sleeved Western-style shirts, under dark, solid-color sport coats. Around their hips, they wear a *mukonzo* wrap or skirt, usually navy blue or black, with a broad, lighter-color stripe near the bottom seam. The cloth is gathered and drawn together at the waist and overlaps a leather belt, *inshipo*, that is worn underneath. Many of the dignitaries have several strings of beads around their necks. Most of the men also wear calf-length argyle socks, held up with garters. The various dancers are chosen spontaneously by the Mwata, each rises from his place, kneels before Kazembe, claps three times, and then moves to the arena. On the way, he must wrest a weapon, either a sword or an axe, from an attendant. This is done in a stylized manner, with the dancer grasping the weapon and the attendant resisting once or twice. The dancer then strides toward the orchestra in time to the music, brandishes the weapon to salute the musicians, and then turns to begin the Mutomboko. The dance is said to have origins in antiquity, having been performed after victorious battles and momentous occasions. Although there are many stylistic variations of the dance, the core consists of moving forward while also shifting laterally, one step to the left and two to the right, with legs swerving high, then coming down hard. The same pace is kept when the dancers charge two steps forward, then one back. The weapons are rhythmically brandished, and at times there is a mime of attacking an enemy with sword or axe. Most performers maintain a disdainful facial expression, at once detached and arrogant. All this is danced to the specific Mutomboko music and beat, as played by Kazembe's court musicians. The dancers come from a group of chiefs, headmen, traditional councillors, ritual specialists, and heirs. The heirs are usually young boys, dressed in a similar manner to the adults, but acknowledged by the audience in an enthusiastic way that celebrates the youthful promise of the royal princes. As each dancer performs, members of the audience, depending on the perceived quality of the dance, rush to press coins or bills into the dancers' hands or pockets or onto a cloth laid down on the ground near the dancers. The youngest dancers are especially recognized in this way. When each dancer finishes, he kneels again before the Mwata, claps three times, and then takes his seat.

Finally, the Mwata's bard, of late, the aristocrat Chipolobwe, comes to the microphone in the covered area where the dignitaries sit and recites several praise epithets, requiring the audience to respond to each. He then introduces Mwata Kazembe, who slowly strolls towards the raised dance area. As the crowd cheers wildly, the Mwata moves about in rhythm to the drumming, then selects both a sword, *mpok*, and battle axe, *mbafi*, again meeting with ceremonial resistance from an attendant. As he moves towards the orchestra, another attendant called the *masumba*, who also makes the Mwata's garments, holds a two-stranded, red cloth "tail," which he struggles with in restraining Kazembe from unleashing his weapons at the nearest onlookers during the Mutomboko performance. After saluting the orchestra with his weapons, Kazembe then settles into the most regal-looking style of the Mutomboko, drawing loud cheers and muzzle-loader shots as he moves in, at times, frenzied forms of attack and then settles back into a smoother, though always threatening, rhythm of dance. It is quite evident that the perception of the gathered Lunda people is focused on the importance and centrality of the mwata, and the dance is the focal point of their praises and celebration. After a time, Kazembe finishes the dance by brandishing the sword, then driving it into the ground. As people swarm onto the dance area, the mwata returns to the *umuselo* and is carried once around the arena before departing to return to his palace. In the evening, there is a feast in the palace grounds for local and visiting dignitaries.

The annual festival serves many purposes. First, the Mutomboko is a celebration of Lunda ethnic identity as it is represented in the person of Kazembe and the various rituals that draw on history and mythology. Although numerically a small group, the Lunda exercise a good deal of influence in both the Luapula Province and, at times, even in national politics. Second, the festival is a powerful economic entity, providing many gifts for Kazembe to distribute as he sees fit, but also filling the rest houses and small inns of Mwansabombwe's business community. Further, small restaurants and many bars are simply filled to capacity during the three or four days of Mutomboko. It is not uncommon for some business people to open otherwise dormant establishments only for the festival and earn enough money to sustain them for months thereafter.

Though Mwansabombwe, located on the main north-south route in the province, is a relatively thriving community during most of the year, it is clear that the height of the economic year is the festival. The Mutomboko draws an increasing number of visitors who come by bus, automobile, and even air to attend the ceremony. This combination of cultural affirmation and economic opportunity seems to be a growing practice in both Zambia and some neighboring countries. Although the only nationally and internationally known festival in the country in the late 1960s was the annual Kuomboka of the Lozi people, by 2001, the Zambian tourist bureau listed no fewer than fifty annual traditional festivals.

References

Cancel, Robert. Unpublished interview with the late Mwata Kazembe XVIII Chinyanta Munona, July 1997; praise poetry recorded from royal bard Mr. Chipolobwe Mwadya Misenga, May 1989.
Chinyanta, M., and Chileya J. Chiwale. 1989. *Mutomboko Ceremony and the Lunda-Kazembe Dynasty*. Lusaka, Zambia: Kenneth Kaunda Foundation.
Cunnison, Ian G. 1959. *The Luapula Peoples of Northern Rhodesia: Customs and History in Tribal Politics*. Manchester, U.K.: Manchester University Press.
———. 1951. History on the Luapula. *The Rhodes-Livingstone Papers* number 21. Manchester: Manchester University Press.
Gordon, David. 2001. Owners of the Land and Lunda Lords: Colonial Chiefs in the Borderlands of Northern Rhodesia and the Belgian Congo. *International Journal of African Historical Studies* 34, no. 2:315–38.
Matongo, Albert K. 1992. Popular Culture in a Colonial Society: Another Look at Mbeni and Kalela Dances on the Copperbelt, 1930–64. In *Guardians in Their Time: Experiences of Zambians Under Colonial Rule, 1890–1964*, ed. Samuel N. Chjipungu. London: Macmillan Press.
Mwata Kazembe XIV. 1951. *Ifikolwe Fyandi na Bantu (My Ancestors and My Peoples)*. Macmillan and Co. In Central Bantu Historical Texts II: Historical Traditions of the Eastern Lunda, trans. and annotated by Ian Cunnison *Rhodes-Livingstone Communication, Number Twenty-Three*. Lusaka, Zambia: The Rhodes-Livingston Institute.
Pritchett, James A. 2001. *The Lunda-Ndembu: Style, Change and Social Transformation in South Central Africa*. Madison: University of Wisconsin Press.
Turner, Victor W. 1969. *The Ritual Process*. Ithaca, N.Y.: Cornell University Press.

ROBERT CANCEL

See also **Government Policies toward Folklore; History; Performance in Africa**

FILMS ON AFRICAN FOLKLORE

Folklore is not made of timeless archaisms, but is being reshaped and recreated constantly (Dundes 1980). One can speak of folklore every time one is confronted by a culturally codified behavior. It means that the members of a group immediately understand a behavior and its context while it remains obscure to people coming from another cultural background. History and change is an important dimension of this codification; today, cultures are not viewed as essentialized organic wholes.

Historically, the term *folklore* was first used only to refer to archaic parts and regional cultural specificities of "civilized countries." Due to racial prejudices and ethnocentric biases, African cultures were for a long time excluded from folklore studies, as they were perceived to represent an earlier stage of evolution. Although the term *folklore* was already central in texts by Tylor and Boas at the end of the nineteenth century, it was used only for film subjects in Africa by the German ethnographers of the 1920s and the 1930s, as they shaped ethnographic subjects into *Kulturfilme*.

Films, like books, were often based on a double paradox: the ethnographers were going into the field, but they were trying to describe what had just disappeared (Owusu 1978). In a brilliant essay, Johannes Fabian criticized the use of literary devices by mainstream anthropology to inscribe exotic cultures in a remote and frozen time (Fabian 1983). The same critique can certainly be addressed to many ethnographic films. The basic assumption was that cultural patterns had remained unchanged until the clash with Western civilization and their consequent destruction. The urgent agenda of ethnographic documentary filmmakers was then defined in terms of a salvage agenda.

Under the catalogue heading of "folklore," most of the ethnographic films that were filed were those that tried to gather raw material. This corresponds to a tradition of collecting, identifying, and classifying data. As late as 1959, the *Rules for Film Documentation in Ethnology and Folklore* proposed what we can call a "natural science" treatment for ethnographic film. That is, the films should conform themselves to a descriptive mode, recording rituals and technical processes, as they would have occurred without the presence of an observer. The fundamental question of interpretation was considered to come only secondarily. We know now that the two moments—of collection and interpretation—cannot be totally separated and that we cannot observe anything without, at least unconsciously, interpreting it. The observer, as Marcel Mauss noted, is always part of the subject (Mauss 2001). "The belief that film can be unmediated record of the real world," writes Jay Ruby, "is based on the idea that cameras, not people, take pictures and the naïve empiricist notion that the world is as it appears to be" (Ruby 1982, 124–5).

Films have often been produced by explorers and individual fieldworkers, but museums and universities have sometimes invested money in audiovisual projects as well. In the 1920s, museums were well suited to produce ethnographic films; they could send cameramen on their expeditions and then attract audiences to their programs. The American Museum of Natural History's library has some videorecordings reflecting this time of exploration. Later, museums contributed to film production with the aim of counterbalancing the lifelessness of artifact displays. Notable recent productions include *African Religions and Ritual Dances* (1971), co-produced by the University Museum (Philadelphia) and the Nigerian Olatunji Center of African Culture; *Spirits of Defiance* (1989), shot by Jeremy Marre in Zaire (currently, Congo), for the BBC and the American Museum of Natural History; and *Togu na & Cheko* (1989), produced by the National Museum of African Art and the Smithsonian Institute. Universities have also co-produced some major works. In France, the audiovisual unit of the National Center for Scientific Research, the film committee of Musée de l'Homme, and the Ministry of Cooperation have financed many films on African folklore. Since the late 1960s, television channels (PBS in the United States, BBC, Granada TV, and Channel 4 in the United Kingdom, La Sept-Arte in France and Germany, STSR in Switzerland, and RTBF in Belgium) and, later, independent producers working for those channels have been a major source of funding for documentary films.

The films were at first silent, then accompanied by a didactic expository narration. Until the 1960s, as Eric Barnouw has noted, ethnographic films tended to be illustrated lectures (Barnouw 1974; 1993, 251). They then became became more and more "dialogic," allowing for several distinct voices. With light cameras equipped with synchronized sound, the so-called informants could speak for themselves directly in the film and ensure what David MacDougall calls an "internal" commentary (MacDougall, 1988). Progressively, information came more from social interactions captured in the field, but external commentary is still employed, notably, to explain complex realities such as possession and shamanism, which cannot be deduced from the "reading" of the visuals.

New Forms of Folklore

After the excesses of nineteenth-century evolutionism, major trends in anthropology, such as Boasian particularism, cultural relativism, and functionalism, encouraged the study of human cultures as synchronic systems. Since the mid-1970s, time and change have been ultimately recognized as a major dimension of culture. For example, Ogun, the Iron God of the Yoruba people, is worshipped today by truck and taxi drivers (*In Un dieu au bord de la route, 1993*). As Manthia Diawara argues, mythological figures persist in West African politics (as, for instance, the series Sunjata–Samory–Seku Ture attests) and in the music of Salif Keita and Mory Kante (Diawara 1998). After the fall of Portuguese colonialism, citizens of Bissau reinvented their carnival, which had been forbidden for a long time. In *Yangba Bolo* (1985), women and men perform a modern popular dance to celebrate the exploits of Central African basket players. In *Bikutsi, Water Blues* (1988), a rather imaginative staged documentary made by the Cameroonese director Jean-Marie Teno to support a public health campaign, music, radio, and schools are all used to convince people to drink purified water. The title is after a traditional rhythm from the forest in South Cameroon. *Masters of the Streets* (1989), by the Belgian Dirk Dumon, shows how popular painters, the most famous being Cheri Samba, evoke in their work social and political themes. These painters are altogether artists, advertisers, educators and public health officers. The gifted Congolese director Ngangura Mweze also used Cheri Samba to comment on his portrait of Kinshasa and its new forms of folk expressions (*Kin Kiesse*, 1982). *Six Pence a Door* (1983), by Mbele Sibiuso, deals with Contemporary Black Art in South Africa. *Future Remembrance* documents, in a fresh and respectful way, the art of popular photographers in Ghana. Through his own imagination and that of his client, the photographer helps present and define the person as a distinct individual.

A retrospective look reveals that change and movement is only a contemporary phenomenon. Mamy Wata is an interesting figure; its representation all over West Africa is based on ancient mythology as well as Indian images introduced on the West African coast by European traders in the early time of contact (*Mammy Water; Mamy Water: In Search of the Water Spirits in Nigeria*, 1989; *Mami Wata, The Spirit of the White Woman*, 1988). Another fascinating and curious mixed product of history is shown in the film *An Immortal Story*, which tells how, for centuries, the inhabitants of São Tomé Island transmitted, through theatrical performances, a story about the Frankish king Charles the Great. The popular theater play, played with music, masks, and dances, raises the question of transgression of the law by princes and kings.

No filmmaker has stressed the importance of cultural creativity more than Jean Rouch when, forty years ago with his African friends, he improvised wonderful "performative" films, such as *La Chasse au lion à l'arc* (1970), *Jaguar* (1954/1967), *Moi un Noir* (1957), *La Goumbé des jeunes noceurs* (1965), *Cocorico*, and *M. Poulet* (1974). [The term *performative* is used here to indicate that what the film depicts did not exist before the shooting of the film itself.] If we consider that in 1999, J. Fabian proposed the performance as a method of ethnography "with" the people described (Fabian 1990), Rouch, with his camera, was remarkably prescient. He was also well aware of the mixed nature of tradition and paid attention to new forms of popular cultures such as the ritual and theatrical satire of colonial regimes (*Les Maîtres Fous*, 1955) or the humorous identification to sports and cinema stars by modest people of Accra or Abidjan. And wonderful characters named Ray Sugar Robinson in *Moi un Noir* and Dorothy Lamour in *La Goumbé des Jeunes Noceurs* (1965) showed up in Rouch's films.

The city, like any other context or milieu, produces its own folklore. At least one-third of the African population now lives in cities, and the rural exodus continues. In 1960, only two African cities had more than one million inhabitants; forty years later, more than thirty exceed that number. *A Nous la Rue* (1986), by the Burkinabe Mustapha Dao, shows how, at the end of the school day, streets are the stage of children's little crimes, loves, football games, dances, cooking, games, and music. *Adama, the Fula Magician* (1981), by the American Jim Rosselini, follows a deaf street performer in Ouagadougou. *The Dodos* (1980), portrays a festival that Mossi have borrowed from the Hausa that takes place in the streets of Ouagadougou; teams of young people compete, inventing animal masks and special dance steps.

We can speak of the folklore of the *sapeurs* (elegant young people) in Libreville (*Papa Wemba*, 1986) or of the street kids in Burundi (*Bichoraï*, 1994). Filmmakers have paid attention to new forms of business: *God Gave Her a Mercedes* (1992), *Asante Market* (1982), and *Profession revendeuse* all portray woman who fall into the category of "Mama Benz," businesswomen, so named for the chauffeured car they own. In the market of Lome or Kumasi, they control diverse trades and earn a great deal of money. In the first film, an interesting sequence shows pieces of cloth called "dynasty" (after the American TV series), "Mandela," or "democracy." (It is a pity, however, that in this film, repeated shots of a vodou performance are shown in a rather sensationalist way.)

African filmmakers such as Mariama Hima (*Baabu Banza*, 1984) and Felix Samba N'diaye (*Les malles*, 1989) show the work of craftspeople recycling old cans in Niamey or Dakar. Some productions are "unidentified audiovisual objects" rather than real films, but are nonetheless interesting. The ethnomusicologist Benoit Quersin recorded an astonishing "tradition" with a tiny camcorder: in a mission girls' school in Zaire, run by Bavarian sisters, "Snow White" has been, since 1935, the subject of the year-end show. The film mixes Lomongo songs, tunes from German folklore, Tyrolian costumes, and the young Zairian girls' sense of acting (*Snow White in Congo*, 1993).

Many African people today have a mixed religious heritage and try to reconcile traditional religion with Islam or Christianity (*Akum*, 1978; *Day of Rest*, 1957; *Heal the Whole Man*, 1995; *Mary Akatsa*, 1990; *Les Mille et une églises, Spite*, 1986; *The Land of the Prophets*, 1988). In a way, any African religion is syncretic, because it has to respond to new problems. Sometimes, historical changes favor a revival of old customs. The Mursi of Ethiopia, who had suffered several years from drought, starvation, cattle disease, and attacks by their neighbors, decided to perform a *Nitha*, a ceremony that had not taken place in thirty years. Many films consider with nostalgia the loss of traditions, but some African intellectuals talk about "the tyranny of fetishes" (*Bois sacré*, 1975). Although African Sufism does not really enter into the category of new forms of religious expression, *Mouridism*, a movement founded by Sheik Amadu Bamba and predicting progress for Africa, has a prophetic dimension (*Grand Magal à Touba*, 1962; *Baraka*, 1999).

The Myth and Other Narratives

The true recording of an African "myth" on film, as a fixed, complete, and coherent text, is so rare that one could reasonably doubt the very existence of the genre. Very often, myths, tales, proverbs were considered independently of social contexts. Sometimes, ethnographers have constructed a systematic text from heterogeneous fragments resulting from "maieutic" dialogues with their "informants." Actually, many films hide this preliminary work behind a "divine" commentary telling the myth or a cultural chart, out of any context of enunciation. Ever since the invention of synchronized sound cameras, if the "meaning" of many oral productions doesnot seem obvious or consistent, it is synthesized by an external commentary.

Jean Rouch's impressive series dedicated to the Dogon ritual cycle of the *Sigui*, shot between 1966 and 1973, was no exception, although Rouch is also the groundbreaking filmmaker who made many films as a shared creation with the subjects. The *Sigui* series pays tribute to Marcel Griaule's and Germaine Dieterlen's writing on the Dogon creation myth. These authors postulate a highly developed religious pantheon of pre-Islamic deities, surviving in fragments and protected by secrets. The ultimate aim of their ethnography is to reconstitute the entire mythic system, with the help of "privileged" informants. The *Sigui* is a ceremony that takes place every sixty years among the Dogon of the Bandiagara cliffs in Republic of Mali. Before the series began shooting, foreigners had never witnessed it, although Marcel Griaule and his team had done intensive research on the subject since 1931. In 1966, Germaine Dieterlen and Jean Rouch decided to make a complete film of this important ritual. They followed, year after year, this fascinating itinerant ceremony, which goes from the Tiogou village to the Songo shelter, along the cliff. Rouch's camera reconstitutes a ritual itinerary in which different villages play their part but that nobody in the field is supposed to witness entirely. The seventh film is a representation of a symbolic ceremony ending the cycle; the region was devastated by a severe drought, and it was impossible to go there with a camera. Since then, the region has almost completely converted to Islam; thus the *Sigui* series footage remains a unique visual archive. *The Pale Fox* (1984), by Luc de Heusch and *The Dogon, Chronicle of a Passion* (1997), by Guy Seligman propose another look at this cosmogonic myth and ethnography. Other films, like *God Is Reborn Every Year*, shot among the Bobo of Upper Volta share the assumption that the key to ritual interpretation resides in creation myth. In *Koumen* (1977), astutely visualized by Luovic Segarra, the Muslim scholar Amadou Hampaté Ba tells the initiatic *Fula* legend.

In this symbolic ethnographic trend, the mythological narrative is a patient and endless reconstruction, dialogically produced by the foreigner "students" and Dogon elders. The resulting writing of a myth is fascinating but also highly questionable, because researches in communication, sociolinguistics and anthropology have illustrated that the presence of interlocutors generally influences the manner in which the storyteller presents the story. Some films track performances by popular storytellers. In *The Soro*, by Inoussa Ousseini (Niger), we see oral competition between the participants to a festival. In the *Nelisita* (1982), the imaginative Angolan filmmaker and anthropologist Rui Duarte cuts from feature sequences to the story telling. Another film by the same author, *Une seule pierre ne cale pas le chaudron* (1978), shows how a cultural heritage can shift and blend with outside influences. In *Angano, Angano* (1989), people from Madagascar tell their stories directly to the camera David MacDougall's film. *Under the Men's Tree* (MacDougall 1974) shows Jié people of Uganda talking about traditional as well as modern themes. Oral transmission trains people in eloquence, charm, and public performance. The verbal talents of ordinary people is striking in films like *Angano . . . Angano, Hamar Trilogy* (1990), *Turkana Conversations* (1976), and *Memories and Dreams* (1992). In *To Live with Herds* (1972), David and Judith Mac-Dougall explain that one of their characters often liked to give them small lectures on things they ought to know. In *Un Dieu au bord de la route*, it is not Western intellectuals who synthesize African folktales, but famous Nigerian writers such as Sole Soyinka, Amos Tutuola, and Bode Sowande, who are, in a way, blurring the boundaries between tradition and international reception.

Films are particularly useful for transmitting the less tangible, unwritten aspects of texts. Meaning is conveyed not only by what is written, but by tune, inflection, gestures, silences, hesitations, and laughing. African specialists of oral narratives might be less the guardians of an intangible memory than theoreticians in charge of criticizing the present time. Their function is often to adapt to new contexts elements they have inherited from their ancestors, as Andrew Apter has shown among the Yoruba of Nigeria (1992). When films and writing deny this historical dimension by shaping everything into canonic texts, they freeze a culture in an eternal present. As the film *The Gods-Objects* (1989) shows, a Togolese diviner may refer to mythological events in a particular context, for instance, to diagnose and cure a sick person. Time is, in any case, a constitutive dimension of social reality. Diachronic shootings with repeated fieldwork in the same region with the same persons do not show static systems, but social realities enduring contradictions and change. This is one important conclusion of the remarkable work of John Marshall in Southern Africa, Melissa Llewelijn-Davies in Kenya, and of the teams of Leslie Woodhead and David Turton and Johanna Head and Jean Lydall in Ethiopia.

For a filmmaker from the West, recording and editing tales and other oral narratives is a critical problem. One of the striking characteristics of folklore narratives is the occurrence of repetition. It is very common that in the same tale, the same episode is told several times. These repetitions have a function—they lead to progressive change in the story—but they belong to conventions that contradict the treatment of time and narrativity in Western documentary cinema. The difficulty is to attain a form that can be acceptable by both standards, but if for aesthetic and production reasons, the filmmaker has to cut, at least he or she should keep a copy of the uncut material.

In the Mande cultural area in West Africa, speech is the essence of the special art of the griots, a group of people who were once at the service of an aristocracy. *Les Gens de la par*ole, by Jean-Francois Schiano (1980) explains the role and functions of the griots in Mali: ensuring that famous people and their genealogy are remembered and entertaining at public events with music, songs, praises, and tales. These functions historically related to the powers of Mande kingdoms to evolve rapidly, even if major ceremonies keep the ancient majesty (*The Griots Today; The Griot in the Circle; Born Musicians: Traditional Music from the Gambia*). The short film *Griottes of the Sahel: Female Keepers of the Songhay Oral Tradition in Niger* captures the meanings of this ambiguous status from the female perspective. In the same culture, *Sassale* give voice to the griots, who evoke the events that led to their status. Oral narratives often occur in musical contexts, the griots being musicians and singers as well as storytellers.

Music

Many films focus directly on musical performances, others give them a prominent place and many, simply, cannot avoid music when considering African culture and folklore. Special mention should be made of *Bangusa Timbila* (1982); *Batteries Dogon* (1966); *Batteurs de calebasses* (1967); *Baule* (1970); *Bitter Melons* (1966); *Black Music in South Africa; Music; The Chopi Timbila Dance* (1980); *Chuck Davis, Dancing through West Africa* (1986); Djembefolla (1991); *Discovering the Music of Africa* (1967); *Hamar Herdsman and His Song* (1987); *Have You Seen DRUM Recently?; Horendi* (1972); *Konkombe* (1988); *Mbira dza Vadzimu* (1978); *Music of Guinea* (1987); *N/um Tchai* (1966); *Pangols* (1995); *Songs of the Adventurers* (1987); *Songs of the Badius* (1986); *A Spirit Here Today* (1994); *Turu and Bitti* (1971); *Under the African Skies* (1989), and *The Voice of the Spirits—Lobi Music from Burkina* (1992). The short piece *The Griot Badye* (1977), by Jean Rouch and Inoussa Ousseini shows how a Nigerian traditionalist draws his inspiration from birds to compose his music.

Many of these works are excellent, but strangely enough, some films on music spoil the music and the songs themselves through the addition of an intrusive informative voiced narration; in one film, the audience is told that the xylophone player is an outstanding artist, but the narration obliterates his music. It can only hoped that the raw footage still exists, with the actual sound as it was before the "fatal" mixing, and that one day, it will be restored.

Some films focus on dance and its relation to music. The work of Allan Lomax was especially pioneering and ambitious. Lomax proposed two theoretical approaches—choreometrics and cantometrics—to show that the patterns of movement and of song vary in orderly ways by culture area and that these expressive systems are correlated with important aspects of social organization (*Choreometrics*, 1974; *Dance and Human History*, 1976). Other films are more conventionally centered on single locations: *Dance like a River* (1985); *The Dance of the Bella; Studies of Nigerian Dance* (1966); *The Left-Handed Man of Madagascar* (1990); *Nande Dances; Tribal Dances of West Africa* (1969). *The Dance of the Queens in Porto Novo* (1969) is particularly interesting. This film was been shot in the courtyard of the royal palace and shows the preparation of the ritual dance and then the performance itself, when the queens, accompanied by a female orchestra, dance and sing in front of the king. A synchronous half-speed recording has been made to study more closely the movements. In Cote d'Ivoire, a Yacuba folk festival, popularized by spectacular postcards, is made up of acrobatic dances by men and small girls (*Images from Yacuba Country*, 1963).

More and more frequently, films focus on new types of destiny, the life of many artists in Africa now being composed from different heritages and shaped by new influences. In Senegal, a man, who has studied music, sings opera in the streets of Dakar while earning a living doing odd jobs (*Abraham and the Odd Jobs*, 1996). Musicians sometimes perform to praise nationalists or freedom movements (*Bangusa Timbila*, 1982; *Rhythms of Resistance*, 1988; *We Jive Like This*, 1992). African musicians living in Europe go back to their home country after years of exile (*Djembefolla*, 1991); a famous female singer from Congo (Zaire) learns polyphonic songs from her mother in Brussels (*Mizike Mama*, 1992), and in the large cities of Nigeria, music finds new forms (*The Memory of Black People*, 1979).

Games

John Marshall's films, always of outstanding observational quality, cover every aspect of !Kung and G'wi social life. Particularly interesting are the short films on games of children and adults: *Baobab Play* (1957); *Playing with the Scorpions* (1957); *The Melon Tossing Game* (1966); *The Tug of War* (1957); *N!owa T'ama, A Joking Relationship* (1957). In this last film, women and girls from three separate tribes gather at a mango grove to play a long and intense game in which undertones of social and personal tension become apparent.

Masks

Masks have often been associated with the field of documentary film and African folklore, but it is a complex relationship. The mask attracts the eye of the camera, but the image can easily lead to misconceptions. The mask is never what it seems to be: it is not a representation of a God, it is not the God itself, it cannot be defined by the sum of what is said about it, and its power is always invested in different objects and locations. Commentary, interviews as well as written analysis, appears to be unable to convey the complex meaning of mask performances.

Nevertheless, films remain the best medium for conveying an idea of those spectacular performances. The American art historian and anthropologist Christopher Roy could witness and film danced performances with masks we used to see only in glass cases: *Yaaba Soore: The Path of the Ancestors* (1986); *The Dance of the Spirits: Mask Styles and Performances in the Upper Volta* (1988). Guy Le Moal's films on Bobo masks are also excellent. The most popular, *The Great Molo Mask* (1968), reveals the ritual making of a mask, from the cutting down of the tree, through the carving and decoration, including the offerings that have to be made during the process. *Dwo Has Killed* (1971) shows the social and political functions of the Molo mask. The "mask" as a character seems to be God's instrument to repress antisocial conducts. *Masks Made with Leaves* stresses the role of children in Bobo Fing religious life. In *Hivernage at Kouroumani*, the masks bid farewell to the villagers, to let them farm during the rainy season until the next harvests. More recently, the films *Ouagadougou, Portraits of Gods* (1992), by the Belgian filmmaker Benoit Lamy and Sakoma Kuye (1997) and Alphonse Kodini Sanou from Burkina Faso, adopts a more narrative form; a young man who has spent years in Europe returns to Africa to learn more about the masks.

The carving of sacred masks and ritual objects being secret, it has been rarely filmed. *Cameroon Brass Casting*, by Paul Gebauer, showing mask brass molding by the Bamun of Cameroon in 1950, is an interesting document. Mali has a rich tradition of masks, the most famous abroad probably being those of the Dogon. *The School of the Masks in Dogon Country*, shot by François de Dieu in black and white in 1959, shows young boys carving masks under an elder's supervision. *African Carving. A Dogon Kanaga Mask* (1975), by Eliot Elisofon, reveals, as did

The Great Molo Mask, that the carving is itself an important ritual. The carver works in a secluded cave outside of the village; his gestures repeat the movements of the dancers who wear the mask. Dogon masks play an important role during funeral rituals, as shown in a film by Marcel Griaule, as well as in several films made by Jean Rouch and Germaine Dieterlen: *Under the Black Masks* (1938); *Ambara Dama* (1974); *Funerals in Bongo—Anaï Dolo 1848–1970* (1972) and the *Sigui* series. In 1966, D. Luz made several short films on Dogon customs for the IWF of Göttingen, documenting, notably, in *Mask Dances in Sanga* the Kanaga and Sirige masks' performances. *Togu na and cheko* (1989), produced by the National Museum of African Art in Washington, studies change and continuity in the art in Mali. The worldly famous Tyi-wara masks of the Bamana feature in two films: *The Bambara of Mali* (1970) and *Diary of a Dry Season: Tyi-wara* (1987). Finally, mention should be made of *The Bend in the Niger* (1971), a journey along the river by Eliot Elisofon, in which we meet Songhaï, Fula, Bamana, and Dogon cultures. Among the Senufo, the coming of age of boys requires an initiation to the Poro. Blacksmiths, who have a special status based on a magic power, are the only ones qualified to carve the masks (*The Senufo*, 1969).

Shot in Cote d'Ivoire, the Stephane Kurc series *Dialogue avec le sacré* (1982) analyzes different types of masks and sculptures and their metaphysical meanings. The anthropologist Ariane Deluz made for Swiss television a film on a Guro female secret society, the *Kné*. The main object, called "mask" in Ivoirian French, is covered and never seen by anybody, female or male (*From the Village of the Dead to the Village of Living People*, 1983). The short film *The Children of the River* (1963), shot by Monique and Robert Gessain in Senegal, shows Bassari masks brought out during farming rites. Women dance with masks called Gwangwuran and Odener. The same anthropologists also filmed rituals of Bassari initiation, including a dance that had already been filmed by Dittmer for the IWF of Göttingen (*The Children of the Chameleon*, 1969; *The Time of the Chameleon*, 1969).

The famous antiwitch Gelede festival of the Yoruba in Nigeria is shown in a film by Peggy Harper (*Gelede: a Yorulea Masquerade*, 1970). The festival culminates in the midnight appearance of the Efe mask in the market place of Ijio, near the Benin border. The film *Owu: Chidi Joins the Okoroshi Secret Society* (1994), by the German anthropologist Sabine Jell-Bahlsen, focuses on the initiation of a young boy into a men's secret society. Several masks (notably Owu, Icharra, and Nono) appear along the ritual process. The aforementioned black-and-white *Disumba* (1969), made by the ethnomusicologist Pierre Salée in Gabon, reconstitutes the initiation ceremonies of the Bwiti, the Mitsogho male brotherhood. During the ritual, the initiates take a hallucinogenic substance called *iboga*, so as to encourage seeing the deities appearing under the form of masked dancers. A Japanese filmmaker, Susumo Noro, has shot a film called *Jungle Gods* (1973) on the same subject for the NAV Man TV series. Sequences with dance and masks may also be shown in films dealing with other topics, as *Maama Tseembu* (1992).

For fifty years, the treasures of African folklore and art have been acquired, sometimes by force, sometimes with the consent of African peoples in question, and sold in Western markets. The process has been documented in *The Statues Also Die* (1953); *The African King* (1991); and *In and Out of Africa* (1992).

Spirit Possession

Cults in which divinities express themselves through the voices of the dancers they have chosen and "taken" flourish all over Africa. Spirit possession has found some cinematic coverage, although in less detail and abundance than in literature. In books, the emotional aspect of the experience has often been undermined, but in films, this dimension is better expressed. Many films dealing with trance and possession, such as Rouch's *Les maîtres fous* (1955), conform to the psychoanalytical position that fantasy life translates an attempt to gain psychic mastery over traumatic experiences. However, in other contexts (in Togo, Mali, Bijago Islands) those possessed appear to be very quiet persons, fulfilling their duty as officials of a cult. Filming a rainmaking ceremony that Rouch has also filmed several times, Olivier de Sardan focuses on relations between Islam and possession dances and on the way religious attitudes face vital problems affecting the community (*The Old Woman and the Rain*, 1972). The moving pictures convincingly restitute the different attitudes—not only of the possessed people, but also of the filmmakers—implied by such an abstract phrase as "possession crisis." Jean Rouch dedicated many films to this topic as it occurs among the Zerma-Songhaï in Niger. *Initiation to the Dance of Possession*, shot in Tillabery in 1948, was probably the first film on the subject to be shown in a movie theater (during the Biarritz Festival). Rouch's material is especially interesting because he filmed the same ritual several times over the course of many years, including the rain ceremony called Yenendi (*Yenendi: The Men Who Make Rain*, 1950; *Yenendi in Bukoki*, 1973).

Hampi (1965), a film named after a sacred vase, was shot during a ceremony in which the sacred vase was placed in the open-air Museum of Nyamey in 1960. *Turu and Bitti* (1967) is a one-shot-sequence film, in which Rouch's camera seems to add another instrument to the band that induces the possession dances. *Wanzerbe* (1968), named after a village, shows a dance of possession, organized to designate the next head magician. (As is often the case when politics is at stake, things are not going smoothly.) In *Tanda Singui* (1972), the people of Yantalla, a Nyamey district, build a shed for Dongo, the thunder divinity. Several deities possess their "horses": Zakao, Dongo's slave; Harakoy, Dongo's mother and Dongo himself. *Horendi* (1972) is a visual analysis—with some shots in slow motion—of the relationships between dance and music during the initiation to the dance of possession. *Initiation* (1975) is about the same deity. When an old possession cult priest dies, his followers ritually break his sacred vases and weep for the deceased (*Pam Kuso Kar*, 1974). Nigeria welcomes at least two forms of possession cults that may be called the Bori complex, among the Hausa, and the Orisha cults, among the Yoruba tribe.

In the north of Nigeria, each year before the rains, the people call the spirits of the possession cult (Bori), in order to propitiate the next harvests (*Shan Kubewa* 1971). *African Religious and Ritual Dances* (1971), shot by Babatunde Olantunji in the Yoruba area, shows a ritual fire dance to Shango, the god of thunder, who possesses the dancer. Set in an area of Togo and Benin marked by a shared traditional culture, several films show how a person's life depends on the gods' good will: *The Voodoo's Daughters* (1990); *Sakpata* (1963). *Voudouns—Die Kunst mit den geisten zu leben* (1995). These films explains how the Voodoo have been sent on earth by the supreme God to oversee and dictate mankind's condition. Senegal is well represented regarding spirit possession rituals: curing ceremonies based on trance and possession and dealing with mentally troubled people are so important that the doctors of the Psychiatric Hospital of Dakar tried to combine them with Western medicine (*Réalité*, 1969; *The N'doep*, 1972; *Borom xam xam*, 1975; *Seven Nights and Seven Days*, 1982). In Mali, curing possession cults exist as other cults that do not have any therapeutic dimension (*The Ways of Nya Are Many*, 1983; *The Diary of a Dry Season II and IV*, 1987).

One film, at least, deals with possession in Cote d'Ivoire: *Dipri Festival in Gomon* 1960, shot among the Abidji. In Cameroon, as a film made by Bernard Juillerat shows, an evil spirit can penetrate into the body of a person and must be extracted through an exorcism (*Matsam*, 1969). The Zar cult, well known in East Africa thanks to the work of Michel Leiris, has been filmed (*The Zar*, 1982). Igor de Garine has shot several films on possession trance among the Massa and the Mussey of Chad (*The Moon of Bogodi*, 1965). In Central Africa, trance and possession exist among the Tshokwe (*Dances of the Tshokwe*, 1930), the Mitsogho, and the Nyaneka. A splendid black-and-white film by John Marshall, *N'um Tchai: The Ceremonial Dance of the !Kung Bushmen* (1966) deals with shamanism. Several films have been shot on spirit possession by Lombard and Fieloux in Madagascar (*Biro; Le prince charmant*, 1981).

Medicine

Many of these possession cults attempt to find solutions for affliction and, therefore, have a therapeutic dimension. Some films deal with folk medicine and with clashes between traditional forms of curing rituals and Western medicine. *Bono Medicines* (1981), produced under the guidance of the anthropologist Michael Warren, describes healing ceremonies in Ghana. Explanations, centered on spiritual forces, are given by traditional healers, while Western and Ghanaian doctors and a Peace Corps volunteer prefer explanations that draw on Western medicine. *Alter Ego* (1986) is a reflexive film made by a Dutch ethnopsychiatrist working in Africa. *In Africa for a Spell* (1986) films a meeting between a psychiatrist and a traditional healer, both from Cameroon, who discuss and debate their differing methods. In *Kambla, the Healer* (1978), a traditional doctor introduces himself to the audience and explains his work. After having shot a curing ceremony with Kambla, the director, accompanied by a doctor, comes back several months later and confronts the two specialists. *Makumukas*, already quoted, shows an impressive curing ceremony among the Nyaneka (a Herrero group) of Angola. In *Iel-solma* (1986, Burkina Faso) traditional healers talk about their secret knowledge. *Spite* (1984) shows a Cote d'Ivoire prophet-healer who attracts a large number of patients and followers. *Vimbuza chilopa* (1991) deals with folk medicine in Malawi. In several films not specifically about medicine, curing sessions are nonetheless presented (*The Nuer*, 1970; *Mukissi* 1974; *Maama Tseembu Oracle*).

Divination

The theme of divination is very much related to that of possession and medicine, as is illustrated in the film *Maama Tseembu Oracle*, which is centered on the person of a female diviner. In the course of the film, we see her initiating a young colleague, who goes through a spectacular possession crisis and a symbolic death. Possession is a modality of divination and sickness, as any suffering has to be diagnosed and conjured. The pattern "suffering (sickness) . . . divination . . . curing initiation" is a classic one. There is always a danger in a film—in which the cultural context can only be briefly explained—to freeze alien conceptions in closed systems. Anthropology has to react against synchronic and ideal portraits or "given" cultures as they have many times been presented in documentary films. *Biotope et geste de travail vezo* (1975) proposes a visual study of Vezo divination practices and of possession crises (from ancient forms to the modern ones). The life of the Hamar, in Ethiopia, depends on cattle. When a problem occurs, the "master of the goats" sacrifices some animals and reads the future in their entrails (*Sacrifice and Divination in Hamar*, 1984). This film is particularly interesting because it shows the personal strategies of a single character rather than relying on broad cultural stereotypes. In *The Prophet Family*, the first part of her *Diary of a Maasai Village* (1984), Melissa Llewelijn-Davies presents a prominent prophet's activities, as a group of men from another district brings twenty-five cows as a present in exchange for prophecies and protection rituals. In *Sigui 70* (1970) by Jean Rouch, we can see a famous divination device among the Dogon of Mali. In 1966, D. Luz documented the same divination process for the IWF in Göttingen (*Dogon–Oracle*). Among the Kabiye of North Togo, soothsayers are consulted at the market or, more privately, in homes (*Divination and Justice among the Kabiye*, 1979). In Chad, when the Massa, who live near the Logone river, were preparing the collective fishing, they first used to perform a complex divination session (*The Massa, People of the Logone River*, 1958). Divination is also the main activity of prophetic cults (films on this topic are mentioned in the section dedicated to new religious movements). Divination, or even inspiration, can play an important role in resolving conflicts.

Justice

In *The Maama Tseembu Oracle*, a film that shows fascinating spirit possession experiences, the audience witnesses an extraordinary scene in which a soothsayer accuses a man of having committed witchcraft. Azande people from Sudan also depend upon oracles to explain events and predict the future. The outcome of an adultery trial can be decided by a ritual ordeal (*Witchcraft among the Azande*, 1981). *The Cows of Dolo: Resolving Conflict among the Kpelle*, filmed in Liberia in 1968, analyzes the conflict resulting from the wounding of a crop-eating cow by a Kpelle farmer. The conflict is resolved through a hot-knife trial-by-ordeal. Additional information can be gained by reading the work of James L. Gibbs, who worked as anthropologist on the film. The work of the Dutch anthropologist and filmmaker Emile Rouveroy van Nieuwaal must be mentioned, too. He has made very detailed filmed case studies, documenting traditional justice in Togo; topics of his films include an adultery trial among the Anufo of Northern Togo and the crisis resulting from a succession to office among the Tyokossi (*Sherea—Dispute Settlement at the Paramount Chief in N'zara* (*North Togo*, 1975). The late Anne Retel-Laurentin showed the same complexities of the trials among the Nzakara and gave the same respect to the concept and practice of the ordeal.

Shaping the Human Body

In Africa, coming-of-age rituals and rites of passage generally require forms of inscription on the body of the initiates. The rituals often involve attendance at a "bush school," in which the initiates receive instruction and endure physical ordeals, hazing, and harsh punishments. The uninitiated person has died, and a new person, who receives a new name, is born. Separate initiation schools for girls and boys intensify the solidarity between members the same sex and of the same age-set. Sexual ritual mutilation is often part of the initiation. Most of the time, unfortunately, these rituals have been filmed, with a lack of contextualization and in a manner that promotes exoticism.

H. Baumann shot some precious footage, which became the film *Dances of the Newly Circumcised*, in Angola in 1930. *Circumcision* (1949), filmed by Jean Rouch in Niger, concerns a class of thirty Songhá boys from a village in the Hombori Mountains. In *Goumbou in Sahel* (1965), in a Sarakole village in Northern Mali, the young male initiates sing "the song of the fear" and the blacksmiths, who are also surgeons, dance with circumcision knives.

The French anthropologists Monique and Robert Gessain have filmed the ceremonies that mark the end of the Bendele initiates' retreat in Central African Republic. Those rituals include body decoration, manipulation of sacred objects, songs, dances, and pantomime (*The Children of the Dance*, 1966). *Imbalu*, the film about a rite of passage among the Gisu of Uganda, by R. Howkins Richard and S. Heald, and *Initiation*, (1973) filmed among the Musey in Chad, should also be mentioned. The Nuba of Sudan emblematically incarnate African folklore with their dances, body painting, and spectacular wrestling matches. This martial group has been popularized in Western countries through the photographs of Leni Riefenstahl, a former official propaganda filmmaker for the Nazis. Chris Curling has created a metadocumentary of sorts for the BBC (The South Eastern Nuba, 1982), which discusses Riefenstahl's work on the Nuba.

Female excision has been documented in a film by G. Lartizien (*Banda—Excision Ceremonies*), in *Garçons et filles* (1962) and in *Cbaya—Cliterodectomy*. This important subject is also discussed in films dealing with women's issues in general (*Women with Open Eyes*, 1996). *Becoming a Woman in Okrika* (1990), by Judith Gleason and Elisa Mereghetti, documents a rite called *Iria* in Nigeria. In this film, where the interviews are obviously livelier and more interesting than the didactic narration, the young women's bodies are painted by the elder women, who fatten them and teach them the "ethos" of womanhood. After an elaborate celebration, the young women run a race pursued by young men and their leader, incarnating a mythological personage armed with sticks. By passing through this rite, the women abandon girlish fantasies and prepare for childbearing.

Scarification is another way to formalize changing of status or of identity (*Djonkor: Scarifications of the Maidens*, 1965; *Scarifications of Maids*, 1955–63). Hair dressing (like "savage" speaking into a phonograph) is a classic of colonial imagery in film as well as in photography and postcards (*Arts and Crafts in Northeastern Angola*, 1930; *Zulu, "Shloko" Hair Dressing*, 1964; *!Ko Bushmen, Making and Applying of Women's Headdresses*, 1972; *Tattooing of Forehead and Temples*, 1972; *Sara Madjinngai, Dressing the Hair of a Boy by Shaving*, 1968). The famous festival called *gereol*, performed by the Fula Wodaabe in Niger and Nigeria, continually attracted the camera. In this tribe of the West African Sahel, the young men, fully dressed and in full makeup, perform a beauty contest, and the young ladies choose their favorite (*Nomads of the Sun*, 1954; *The Wodaabe, the Herders of the Sun*, 1992). In the second title, the famous German director Werner Herzog presents an idealized version of this institution and uses Gounod's, Handel's, Mozart's, and Verdi's music to magnify dance figures and cattle movement filmed in slow motion.

Initiation and Collective Rituals

Rituals and folklore are often regarded as mutually exclusive categories, as the second implies discursive practices that are not supposed to exist in the first. But as Victor Turner, Richard Schechner, and others have shown, stories may exist within the ritual process. Communication with gods or other spiritual entities is often embedded in other problems such as illness, drought, witchcraft, misfortunes, and conflicts. Rituals are performances that give meaning and suggest solutions to those problems; therefore, they adopt a dramatic frame.

Sometimes, rituals rest on stories that belong to other forms of folk narratives. *Autour du Baw-Naan Lebu* (1984), for instance, by the Senegalese filmmaker Gaï Ramaka, shows how the symbolic finality of a ceremony among the Lebu is meant to make the God laugh in order to bring about rainfall. The *yenendi* rituals, filmed several times by Jean Rouch in Niger, do not involve the same symbolism, but have the same function. The religious life of the Kabre of northern Togo involves great festivals of purification, in praise of life forces, and to banish hostile powers (*Rhythms and Sacred Pomp in the Life of the Kabre of Northern Togo*, 1966). Initiation, purification of the village, and propitiatory sacrifices are interrelated also among the Bobo and the Bolon (*Yele Danga*, 1966). Among the Diola of Casamance, in southern Senegal, the rite of manhood is a keystone of resistance to Islamic or Christian proselytism (*Sikambano*, 1991). In *The "Unbound" Mouth* (1970), the bridegroom must fast, and his mouth is "bound" until the wedding day, when he breaks the fast. Some customs have lost or never had a sacred dimension. Among the Samo of Burkina, for example, the New Year, which arrives after the harvest, is acknowledged by wrestling between brave young men (*Premier mil*, 1975).

Gender

Marriage is, of course, a major rite of passage and has inspired many films, especially interesting for gender studies. Mention must be made of *Akuren and Loditmwe* (1976), *Zaghawa Dances* (1957), and *Una Corte Pittoresca*, filmed among the Ndebele of South Africa. A generation of female anthropologists and filmmakers have befriended their African female subjects and thus produced especially sensitive and illuminating films on women in Africa in the early 1990s. For more than twenty years, Melissa Llewelyn-Davis had been working and living with the Maasai of the Loita Hills in Kenya, near the Tanzanian border. *Memories and Dreams* (1994) is a follow-up to her previous works *A Maasai Diary* (1984) and *The Women's Olamal* (1984). The latter documents a political struggle in which the Loita Maasai women force the men to perform a fertility ritual. *Memories and*

Dreams is an exemplary work on long-term relationships and a unique exploration of an African community's changing attitudes towards women's roles, sex, love, and marriage during the past twenty years. *The Hamar Trilogy* (1990, Southern Ethiopia), by Joanna Head and Jean Lydall, invites several women from different generations to reflect on marriage and sex in their culture. We follow two girls through the rituals of marriage, and revisit one of them a few years later. *Contes et Comptes de la Cour* (1992), by Eliane de Latour, documents the life of four wives of a local chief, obliged to stay confined to their courtyard. They are not totally powerless—using go-betweens, they control a small trade network—but they are confronted with the jealousy inherent to polygamous marriage. These films are outstanding due to the quality of the relations between the filmmakers and the subjects (the degree of intimacy, the discrete reflexivity), the complexity of information and the sometimes conflicting values within the same culture. John Marhall's life story of a !Kung woman in the Kalahari desert is also fascinating. In this extraordinary film, Marshall accumulated footage over a thirty-year period and focused on the life of !Nai, a wonderful character, who analyzes in the film the dramatic change in the life of the !Kung after they were removed from their nomadic life and relocated on a government settlement. The film acknowledges reflexivity, as it documents the impact of film shooting in an "exotic" environment.

Funeral Rituals

As funerals are a major public event and, most of the time, spectacular feasts (at least when the defunct is an elder), they have often been filmed. Jean Rouch, sometimes with the help of Germaine Dieterlen, has made many films on Dogon funerals. *Cemetery in the Cliff*, filmed in 1951, follows the Dogon funeral ritual of a man who died in the village of Ireli. *Funerals in Bongo—Anai Dolo 1848–1970*, chronicles the funeral of an elder of the masks society, who was reputed to be 122 years old. *The Burial of the Hogon* (1972) describes the funeral rites as the Hogon, the paramount religious leader of the Sanga region dies and is buried. The hunter-warriors gather near the deceased priest's house and simulate a battle, using guns, spears, or millet stalks, while the body is placed in a sacred cave. The shooting of *Ambara Dama* (1974), is a remarkable story: Ambara had given the information on the funeral rituals (*Dama*) to Marcel Griaule, the initiator of a huge ethnographic project on the Dogon. Years later, and years after Griaule's death, his former student, Jean Rouch, uses the book to film the funeral of Ambara. Interestingly enough, in 1956, François de Dieu had filmed the *Dogon Funerals of Professor Marcel Griaule*, as the Dogon celebrated the memory of the man who studied their customs for so many years. Rouch also made some films on funeral rituals (*Pam Kuso Kar*, 1974; *Souna Kuma*, 1975; *Simiri Siddo Kuma*, 1978). He eventually filmed *Moro Naba* (1957), the funeral ceremony of the traditional leader of the Mossi of the Ouagadougou region in Upper Volta (now Burkina Faso). The film contains the election ceremonies for the successor, the feast for the end of mourning, and the ceremony in the palace, with warriors in traditional dress. The procession is extraordinary, with the elder daughter and elder son incarnating the defunct chief in different parts of the ritual, as does a wood statue carried by the dancers.

In Voubira, among the Lobi of Burkina Faso, Fiéloux and Lombard have filmed the mourning for Bindouté Da, a prominent, "traditional" chief and a colonial agent. His nineteen wives prepare a huge quantity of millet beer to welcome the guests. A diviner transmits the ultimate will of the defunct chief. His children mime his life history, and the filmmakers evoke his life too, using archives and family photographs (*Bindouté Da's Bobur*, 1988). *Minyanka Funerals*, from the *Diary of a Dry Season* (1987) series, shows the funerals of an old woman who had an important function in a possession cult. At midnight, a possessed man, incarnating the deity of that particular cult, weeps and laments over the corpse

Two years after his father's death, the Cameroonese director François Woukoache filmed the ceremonies that take place at the end of the traditional mourning period, which provided him with an opportunity to examine the Bamileke legacy and the Christian identity of many young people in Cameroon today (*Melina*, 1992). Among the Massa in North Cameroon, young men, called *guru*, or sacred herders, perform a special ritual during funerals (*Guruna, Sacred Herders*, 1958). The same director, the anthropologist Igor de Garine, shot *Réjouissances sénégalaises* (1967) in the Serer village of Khombole in Senegal, where an old dancer had died. *On the Grave of a Chief* (1965), filmed in Chad, documents the funerals of the village's headman. Here, too, the friends of the deceased evoke his personality through performance. *Les Somba, hommes des chateaux* (1956), by Henry Brandt, describing the life of highlanders in North Benin, shows part of a funeral dance. The same type of sequence, as performed by the Fali of North Cameroon, can be seen in *The Fali* (1972) by Jean Gauthier. In the south of Madagascar, among the Mahafay, Raymond Arnaud filmed the two last days of an old woman's funeral (*Funerals in Mahafaly Country*, 1980). Jacques Lombard shot two films on funeral ritual in the same region, *Funerals of a Mahafale Herder* (1988) and a short film describing the carving of a "funeral staff", *aloalo*, by a sculptor from the same region. In 1962, Aimé Fournel filmed *Exhumation*, showing the last tribute paid to recent ancestors when they are given a new grave.

Professions

Some films produced by the IWF of Göttingen minutely describe the technological process of iron making, but we are only interested here in the symbolic apparatus associated to this process. In West Africa, in the Mande region and surrounding areas, blacksmiths belong to an endogamous social class. In many other places, such as among the Senufo, they have a special status, too. The very act of iron making is often metaphorically compared—in songs, prayers, and incantations—to breeding. Blacksmiths are very often magicians, surgeons, and weapons makers. Nicole Echard has made two excellent films on the subject in 1967 among the Hausa of Niger: *Blacksmiths, Sons of Women*, showing the functions and activities of the blacksmiths, including songs, dances, and bewitching ritual, and *Wedding of Fire*, an accurate reconstitution of the fusion of iron in a blast. In *Inagina, the Ultimate House of Iron* (1997), a documentary with a poetic narration, eleven Dogon blacksmiths meet to build a traditional furnace. Several films document ironmaking in northern Cameroon (*Kirdi*, 1963; *Ironmaking among the Matakam*, 1953; *Dokwaza*, 1988).

Other professional groups may have cultural specificities, rules, and obligations. They may also be the official leaders of particular rituals. Among the Hausa of Niger, the butchers form a despised, but feared, corporation. Each Wednesday in Bagagi, in the Mawri region, they are the principal participants in one of the chief community rituals (*Mahauta, The Butchers from Mawri*, 1965). *Three celebrations* (1987), shot near Koutiala in Mali, follow folkloric festivals performed by blacksmiths, clowns, and hunters. Similarly, *Les rites de chasse en pays minyanka* (1990), by the Malian writer Urbain N'Dembélé, emphasizes the relation between expertise and secret knowledge.

Conclusion

The status of the other is never totally objective. Projection or fabrication always creates and shapes, to a certain degree, exoticizing imagery, because it functions within a "system of opposition and identity" (see Nichols, 191, 205). Trinh T. Minh-Ha has called the tradition of certain knowledge into question in her films *Reassemblage* (1982) and *Naked Spaces* (1985). In that sense, films pasting together images of African folklore may also be analyzed as reflecting the filmmaker's personal folklore. These biases are obvious in travel films such as *In the Country of the Black Sultans* (1925), with its images of stone eaters, snake charmers, clowns, and wrestling, and its condescending narration, or *Black Majesty* (1930), in which American millionaires explore the "wild" continent. As already mentioned, wildness is often exploited in the portrait of the Nuba of Sudan (*In the Search of the Nuba Warriors*). Such a folklorization is also obvious in films tribalizing the geographic map (*Black African Heritage: The Congo*, 1973; *Simba, the King of Beasts*). Folkloric stereotypes are indeed still very common in television reportage, but more and more frequently, filmmakers make a special effort to avoid such bias. To present accurate descriptions is the main goal and difficulty for anthropologists and filmmakers in the field. They can never be totally satisfied with the result, but they can work to improve their ethnography.

The moving picture seems to be the perfect tool to depict ceremonies as well as the performances of artists such as griots, clowns, and storytellers, who offer a pleasant diversion from the harsher aspects of life. But documentary cinema can also confront intrinsic complexities of African ways of life. In African performances, one can observe public events that are organized to attract audiences or please high-ranking individuals, and events that fulfill an educational and initiatory function. Nearly everywhere in Africa, culture used to be transmitted through apprenticeship and initiation. In this case, transmission was strictly codified by ritual protocols, interdictions, and secrecy (Bellman 1984). Even entertaining activities may convey messages related to more secret forms of knowledge. As cinema belongs to mass communication, it has dealt mainly with performances of the first category and has treated in a more elusive way the initiatory contexts. There is, in fact, a striking contradiction in the attempt to show what is precisely forbidden, because if the filmmaker succeeds, he or she only proves that the rule regarding secrecy is not firmly enforced, and thus it loses its power.

Night creates different meaning than day; this represents a major difficulty for filmmakers. Good or threatening spirits are supposed to be active, or more active, during the night, and many rituals occur in the darkness. A significant amount of messages, gestures, and rituals are therefore out of reach of the camera. In many rituals, daylight images can only give a reductionist view of African folklore, and artificial light inevitably transforms the situation. Many filmic sequences, as we see them today, result from a compromise and have to be understood as such. Do such films succeed or fail in their goal to accurately report upon a context? Anthropologists and filmmakers, as well as the filmed African subjects themselves, continue to ponder this question, but to observe, one needs an observer.

References

Note: This paper would not be written without a grant from the AMNH (American Museum of Natural History) received in 1998 to study the relations between documentary film and anthropology.

Apter, A. 1992. *Black Critics and Kings. The Hermeneutics of Power in Yoruba Society*. Chicago: University of Chicago Press.

Barnouw, Erik. 1974. *Documentary, A History of Non-Fiction Film*. Oxford: Oxford University Press. Rev. ed. 1984, 1993.

Bascom, William. 1965. Folklore and Anthropology. In Dundes, ed.

———. 1984. The Forms of Folklore. In Dundes, ed.

Bellman, B. L. 1984. *The Language of Secrecy: Symbols and Metaphors in Poro Ritual*. New Brunswick: Rutgers University Press.

Bendix, Regina, and Rosemary Lévy Zumwalt, eds. 1995. *Folklore Interpreted: Essays in Honor of Alan Dundes*. New York : Garland Publishing.

Diawara, Manthia. 1998. *In Search of Africa*. Harvard University Press.

Dundes, Alan, ed. 1965. *The Study of Folklore*. Englewood Cliffs, N.J.: Prentice Hall.

———. 1984. *Sacred Narrative: Readings in the Theory of Myth*. Berkeley: University of California Press.

———. 1980. *Interpreting Folklore*. Bloomington and London: Indiana University Press.

Fabian, Johannes. 1990. *Power and Performance: Ethnographic Explorations through Proverbial Wisdom and Theater in Shaba, Zaire*. Madison: University of Wisconsin Press.

Hockings, Paul, ed. 1975, 1995. *Principles of Visual Anthropology*. Series title: World Anthropology. The Hague: Mouton.

Lems-Dworkin, Carol. 1996. *Video of African and African-Related Performance: An Annoted Bibliography*. Evanston, Ill: Lems-Dworkin.

MacDougall, David. 1975. Beyond Observational Cinema. In *Principles of Visual Anthropology*, ed. Paul Hockings. The Hague: Mouton.

———. 1998. *Transcultural Cinema*. With an introduction by Lucien Taylor. Princeton, N.J.: Princeton Universoty Press.

Mauss, Marcel. 2001. *Sociologie et anthropologie,* 9th ed. Paris: PUF, Quadrige. Pref. by Cl. Lévi-Strauss.

Owusu. 1978. Ethnography of Africa: The Usefulness of the Useless. *American Anthropologist* 80, no. 2:310–34.

Ruby, Jay, ed. 1982. *A Crack in the Mirror. Reflexive Perpective in Anthropology*. Philadelphia.

See the Filmography to "Documentary Films and African Folklore" at back of book, for a detailed listing of African-themed documentaries.

JEAN-PAUL COLLEYN

FOLKTALES

The folktale is perhaps the quintessential expression of verbal art in Africa, often attracting the community's most sensitive narrators, particularly those with a keen sense of observation and imaginative description. Although its significance may have decreased with the spread of literacy and urbanization in Africa, the folktale is still vividly narrated in rural domestic settings. In parts of rural Ghana, narrators have moved beyond casual telling, and have formed professional storytelling associations in the last thirty years; these organizations entertain communities at wakes and other important events. Storytelling has also moved to the mass media in recent times and may be heard or seen on radio and television.

Even though the tale is told largely for artistic reasons, performers and audiences hardly lose sight of its moral or meaning, whether it advocates patience, punishes greed and selfishness or merely explains the source of the crab's fatty shell. In any case, themes in the folktale may be conveyed by a set of characters with stereotypical traits belonging to the human, animal, and metaphysical realms. Human characters range from infant protagonists, to maidens, young suitors, kings, and old ladies.

Tricksters

Tales involving animals and tricksters are the most prevalent. Such stories may juxtapose the brute strength of big and ferocious beasts like the leopard, elephant, and wolf, with the fragility of small but wily animals, known for their intrigues and enormous capacity to outwit bigger opponents, including supernatural beings. Such wily creatures are often heroes, tricksters, and culture bearers.

Characterized by Radin as "creator and destroyer, giver and negator, he who dupes others and who is always duped himself" (Radin 1952, xxiii), the trickster appears in multiple forms in Africa, mostly as an animal, but occasionally as a human being, or a deity. In contemporary Egyptian culture, there are two trickster figures, both humans, who are believed to have existed in the past (El-Shamy 1980, 219–21). In Yoruba and Fon cultures, the tricksters are deities. In several other parts of Africa, the tricksters are animals. Among the Bantu, it is the little hare. The tortoise is the trickster in some parts of West Africa. Among the Ila of Zambia, hare and tortoise co-exist as tricksters. The antelope, squirrel, weasel, and wren also occur as tricksters in other parts of Africa.

The spider, the best-known trickster in Africa, exists among the Limba of Sierra Leone, the Hausa of Nigeria, Gbaya of Cameroon, Sara of Chad, Luo and Azande of Sudan, and Ngbandi of Congo (Finnegan 1970, 315 et seq.). Among the Akan of Ghana and in parts of Cote d'Ivoire, the spider is Ananse. The eminence of Ananse as a character in Akan and Ghanaian folktales in general, as is evident in the label *anansesem*, "matters of Ananse," which designates the folktale based on whether or not it features Ananse. Ananse indeed embodies the quintessence of esthetic pleasure. This delight is achieved through cunning, trickery, humor, and the outwitting of physically superior adversaries.

Significantly, Ananse was transported in the African diaspora during the transatlantic slave trade to the Caribbean. Besides the presence of Ananse in Caribbean tales, the name evokes associations of farce, fiction, and entertainment. In the St. Vincent Islands, "Anansi story" stands for all amusements displayed during wakes, whether these are tales of the spider, riddles, or games.

The artistic merits of the folktale are only partly realized in text. While the literary ingredients of irony, metaphor, hyperbole, personification, and so forth can be discerned in a tale text, it takes a good performer to portray optimally the folktale as an art form. Thus, even though the trickster in Africa is considered the best embodiment of esthetic pleasure, delight, trickery, humor, and fantasy, this can be realized only through the agency of performance. In the case of Ananse, for example, he cannot be effectively depicted outside the culture's perception of his stereotypical trait as an anomalous speaker: he whines. In the West Indies, he also lisps and stutters and often speaks poor English.

Performance

The fact that the folktale is considered a source of aesthetic pleasure is illustrated in the formulas that frame a performance. The opening and closing formulae invariably depict the absence of truth in the tale. The opening formula used by Haya of Tanzania, "See so that we may see" (Seitel 1980), chanted by the audience, places a responsibility on the teller to portray vividly an imaginative experience that fulfills the society's aesthetic canons. The Ashanti-Akan of Ghana use the introductory formula, "We don't really mean it, we don't really mean it" (that the impending narration is true). Among the Fanti-Akan, the narrator's formula, "The tale is not meant to believed," elicits the audience's response, "It is meant to be kept," once again emphasizing imaginative fantasy as the dominant aesthetic. Indeed, among the Agni of Cote d'Ivoire, the expression for telling a tale means, "to lie" (Galli 1983, 22).

In certain cultures, the performance is further boosted by the presence of an auxiliary performer, or intermediary, who receives the tale and passes it on to the wider audience. As in royal oratory and epic singing, the respondent receives the narration in bits as it is told and either repeats it literally it or adjoins a phrase of assent. Such institutionalized mediations in tale telling are found among several cultures in West Africa. They also exist in certain traditions of storytelling among African Americans (Jones-Jackson 1987, 44).

Histrionics

In enacting the tale itself, the narrator relies on dramatic, literary, and linguistic devices, and, indeed, deploys every technique within his artistic reach. Even though he is instructing his audience about moral values, the aesthetic factor is dominant as the tale's ploc may already be known. The story is appreciated, tasted, even eaten, if it is aesthetically pleasing. So the storyteller mimes, growls like a leopard, whines like Ananse, and tiptoes his way as Ananse sneaks to the kitchen of God's in-laws. The narrator stretches every sinew to enact all roles in the plot single-handedly and vividly portray a multisensory experience in words.

Descriptive skills are inevitable here, and one important device African narrators have used to good effect are descriptive adverbials—ideophones (Noss, 1972)—which vividly depict multisensory experience: sound, smell, sensation, touch, and color. Other devices are descriptive details, dialogue, personalization, and song.

Song

Song, dance, and music are indispensable in storytelling, and performances without these elements are considered drab. But one should distinguish here between the intranarrative song, which is an integral part of a tale's plot, sung by a character in the tale, and song spasmodically injected by the audience to arrest boredom.

The intranarrative song may be performed by a character in dramatic moments, either as a dialogue device, to delay action, achieve a magical feat, highlight agony, or mark relief. Owing to the importance of song in narration, a performer among the Gbaya may apologize in advance if his tale has no song (Noss 1977, 138).

Even when there is no song in a tale's plot, any member of the audience, in certain cultures, may petition the narrator and lead a song to arrest boredom. The song interjected may have no thematic relevance to the tale at hand, but like the intranarrative lyric, it enlists total participation by petitioner, narrator, and the rest of the audience.

Songs in folktales have simple choruses and lend themselves easily to communal involvement, drumming, and dancing. This compels total immersion by the entire congregation, who may provide background rhythm by clapping or beating on improvised instruments.

Closing Formula

As the tale ends, the closing formula once again underscores the supremacy of the communal aesthetic. The Akan say, "If my tale is sweet, if it is not sweet, take it back and forth." This is indeed a formulaic acknowledgment of the inherent hazards in exposing oneself to the evaluation of a critical audience, whose high expectations may have been upheld or disappointed.

It is not surprising that tale telling is depicted as a burden in parts of Africa; for after his turn, the narrator among the Gbaya of Cameroon sets the "burden" under a tree (Noss 1977, 136) and among the Akan transfers the "burden" onto the head of a chosen performer (Yankah 1983, 12), who is challenged to equal or surpass the previous effort.

The folktale in Africa is a burden, but it is a burden gracefully borne by narrators and diffused to embrace the audience at large.

References

Agovi, J. K. 1973. Preliminary Observations on the Modern Short Story and African Folktale Tradition. *Research Review* 9:123–9.

Dundes, A. 1980. The Making and Breaking of Friendship as a Structural Frame in African Folktales. In *Structural Analysis of Oral Tradition*, ed. Pierre Maranda and Eli El. Chicago: University of Chicago Press.

El Shamy, Hassan. 1980. *Folktales of Egypt.* University of Chicago Press.

Evans-Pritchard, E. E. 1967. *The Zande Trickster.* Oxford: Clarendon Press.

Finnegan, R. 1967. *Limba Stories and Storytelling.* Oxford: Clarendon Press.

———. 1970. *Oral Literature in Africa.* Oxford: Clarendon Press.

Galli, S. 1972. Storytelling among the Agni-Bona. In *Cross Rhythms*, ed. Kofi Anyidoho et al. Bloomington: Trickster Press. 1983.

Jones-Jackson, P. 1987. *When Roots Die: Endangered Traditions on the Sea Islands.* Athens: University of Georgia Press.

Noss, P. 1970. Description in Gbaya Literary Art. *In African Folklore*, ed. Richard Dorson, Bloomington: Indiana University Press.

———. The Performance of the Gbaya Tale. In *Forms of Folklore in Africa*, ed. Bernth Lindfors. Austin: University of Texas Press. 1997. 135–143.

Okpeuho, Isidore. 1972. *African Oral Literature: Background, Character, and Continuity*. Bloomington: Indiana University Press.

Pelton, R. D. 1980. *The Trickster in West Africa: A Study of Mythical Irony and Sacred Delight*. Berkeley: University of California Press.

Radin, P. 1952. *The Trickster*. New York: Schoken Books.

Scheub, H. 1975. *The Xhosa Ntsomi*. Oxford: Clarendon Press.

Seitel, P. 1980. *See So That We May See: Performances and Interpretations of Traditional Tales from Tanzania*. Bloomington: Indiana University Press.

Yankah, K. 1983. *The Akan Trickster Cycle: Myth or Folktale?* Bloomington, Indiana: African Studies Program.

———. 1989. From Africa to the New World: The Dynamics of the Anansi Cycle. In *Literature of Africa and the African Continuum*, ed. Jonathan Peters et al. Washington, D.C.: The Three Continents Press and African Literature Association.

KWESI YANKAH

See also **Dilemma Tales; Prose Narratives; Tricksters**

FOLKTALES OF THE BAMANA

The Bamana (or Bambara) language, spoken mostly in Mali and in eastern Senegal, is part of the Mande language family. From both a linguistic and a cultural point of view it belongs to the Manding group that covers much of Mali, part of eastern Senegal, northern Guinea, northern Cote d'Ivoire, and southwestern Burkina Faso. The two Mande languages that are the most similar are Mandinka and Dyula.

Bamana tales comprise a rich and varied cultural-literary heritage, and a wide selection of Bamana folk tales has been collected and studied by Western scholars, particularly since the 1970s. Earlier, especially during the colonial period, only soldiers, missionaries, and colonial administrators were interested in this material. The major earlier collectors were Lieutenant Lanrezac, author of a book on Sudanese folklore, Maurice Delafosse, and especially F. V. Equilbecq. After them, linguists, ethnographers, and anthropologists, each with his or her own agenda, entered this field of study.

The first collection of tales published in Bamana with a French translation was done by an African interpreter, Moussa Travele, who published seventy-one folk tales and twenty-two proverbs in 1923. Soon afterwards came the ethnographic work of Charles Monteil (1924), but it was not until nearly fifty years later that further bilingual collections were published. In 1971, Charles Ballieul published eighteen texts in Bamana. Veronika Görög-Karady and Gérard Meyer published forty-four texts in 1974 and twelve in 1985. Other collections were published by Pierre Deglaire and G. Meyer (1976), V. Görög-Karady and Abdoulaye Diarra (1979), G. Meyer (1988), Gérard Dumestre (1989), and Annik Thoyer (1997). Görög-Karady and Meyer also published twenty-four Bamana tales in French translation in 1984, and twenty more in 1988. In Mali, Popular Editions of Mali has published several collections in French of which those by Isa Traore (1970) and Bokar N'Diaye (1970) contain Bamana tales.

Performance

Well-recorded and carefully transcribed texts record performance contexts. Men, women, and young people can recite tales in turn in the evening; it is not considered suitable for one person to monopolize the word. The performer uses the introductory formula "Here is the tale I have chosen" and the ending formula "I return the tale to where I found it." Songs are inserted in the tales to make the audience participate. In order to recite the narrative, the storyteller regularly calls up a person, the respondent, who, in the name of the audience, punctuates every phrase with a word of approbation. The storyteller as well as the respondent may offer their explanatory and moralizing commentary at the end of the story. Often the final sequences of a tale will vary according to the version being narrated.

Themes

Bamana tales emphasize themes that are important for collective survival, such as the opposition between the strength of blood ties and the fragility of marriage ties, male–female antagonisms, tensions within polygynous families, the often difficult relations between parents and children, and relations between the human world and the supernatural world, and between the human and animal realms. Classified as fiction, the Bamana tale allows the expression of true feelings, even those that are violent or antisocial, and also allows for different forms of tension silenced or denied by official social discourse.

Among the female personages in Bamana stories is the demanding young girl who rebels against the customary marriage process and wishes to choose her husband for herself, and the young animal seductress who is disguised as a human in order to destroy the man who wants to marry her. These threatening female figures are opposed to the devoted mothers who guard their children against perilous male or female alliances. Another negatively portrayed female character is the evil mother, the sorceress who threatens the life of her son or her daughter-in-law. This sorceress mother character is absent from the repertoire of most neighboring peoples, for example, the Fulani. Another common female character is the old woman who takes the role of mediator, counselor, or bearer of news. This function is never filled by an old man, although it is occasionally attributed to a hunter.

A unique feature of Bambara tales is the presence of the incest desire, which occurs more frequently and more overtly than in the tales of other peoples in Africa or in the West. In Mali, the theme of incest is absent among the Fulani and the Dogon, populations that have much contact with the Bamana. Many stories present amorous attractions between brothers and sisters; many others depict a father who declares a strong desire to marry his own daughter. However, this plan is put to a stop by the intervention of a supernatural being. Also present are stories, rare or nonexistent among neighboring peoples, which demonstrate the father's hostility toward his sons and his aspiration to prevent their access to sexuality and to marriage.

Bamana tales propose models of behavior both positive (the protagonist does what should be done), or, more often, negative (the protagonist does not act honorably and is punished as a result). Thus, the rules of the genre are regulated by the dialectics of good and evil, and by the final imposition of respect for social law. (For ethnosociological and ethnopsychological interpretations of Bamana tales refer to the studies of Veronika Gorog-Karady [1987, 1992, 1994] and to the introductions of the previously cited works).

References

Dumestre, Gerard. 1989. *La pierre barbue Contes du Mali.* Angers: Bibliotheque Municipale.

Görög-Karady, Veronika. 1992a. Tales and Ideology: The Revolt of Sons in Bambara-Malinke Tales. In *Power, Marginality, and Oral Literature.* Cambridge: Cambridge University Press.

———. 1992b. The Law of the Father. Paternal Authority and Marriage Test in Bambara Malinke Tales. In *Interpreting Folktales, Marriage Tests, and Marriage Quests in African Oral Literature, Marvels and Tales,* vol. 6, no. 2.

———. 1994. Social Speech and Speech of the Imagination: Female Identity and Ambivalence in Bambara Malinke Oral Literature, *Oral Tradition* 9, no. 1:60–82.

———. 1997. *L'univers familials dans les contes africains, Liens de sang, liens d'alliance.* Paris: L'Harmattan.

Görög-Karady, Veronika, and Diarra Abdoulaie. 1979. *Contes bambara du Mali.* 2 vols. Paris: Presses orientaliste de France. (Bambara and French.)

Görög-Karady, Veronika, and Gerard Meyer. 1985. *Contes bambara.* Paris: Conseil International de la Langue francaise. (Bambara and French.)

Thoyer, Annick. 1997. *Le riche et le pauvre et autres contes bamanan du Mali.* Paris: L'Harmattan.

Travele, Moussa. 1977. *Proverbes et contes bambara* (1923). Paris: Maisonneuve et Larose. (Bambara and French.)

VERONIKA GÖRÖG-KARADY

See also **Dilemma Tales; Folktales; Linguistics and African Verbal Arts; Old Man and Old Woman; Oral Literature: Issues of Definition and Terminology; Oral Narrative; Oral Traditions, African; Performance in Africa; Prose Narratives**

FOLKLORE

See **Maqalat**

FOODWAYS: CATTLE AND SORGHUM GRAIN IN JIE COSMOLOGY

The Jie people, who live on the central Karamoja Plateau in northern Uganda, have a mixed economy of agriculture and animal husbandry, with a strong emphasis placed upon the latter. In 1996, the Jie population numbered about 50,000, and they lived within the borders of Najie, a flat land of approximately 1,300 square miles, situated in a dry and warm high plateau zone. As a distinct ecological zone, Najie has thin wild vegetation and a dry climate. Sorghum is cultivated as the most important crop in the Jie peoples' diet and economy. Varieties of sorghum grow well in the cotton soil of Najie, as do numerous varieties of fruits, bushes, and thorny plants that are all important to the economy of the Jie people.

The historical dependence of the Jie on sorghum and cattle for their livelihood plays a special role in creating a dual and complementary cosmology, which informs social and political relations. While cattle signifies male food, sorghum signifies female food. In the Jie culture in general, cattle are the primary source of conflict and resentment within the family as well as between communities. When conflict over cattle occurs, women offer their sorghum grain and sorghum beer as a sign of peace. While the cattle brand (*amachar*) regulates relationships between fathers and sons and between older and younger brothers, sorghum regulates relationships between mothers and daughters, and between older and younger sisters.

The Jie Deities

This dual and complementary nature of cattle and sorghum grain can perhaps be better understood by learning about the Jie cosmology. A predominant interpretation of the Jie deities is characterized by the dual and complementary nature of cattle and grain metaphors. According to the Jie storytellers Rianoro, Logwee, and Lodoch (interviewed by the author in the village of Jimos in 1996), the Jie people have two deities: Akuj, a male deity, and his counterpart Ekipe, a female deity, who live in the sacred hills in the wilderness. While Akuj is associated with the sun, Ekipe is associated with the moon. Akuj and Ekipe periodically visit the villages from the world that is located behind the clouds in the deep sky, where there is no death, hunger, or aging.

When Akuj visits the people in the villages, he burns the land and causes the crops to fail and the cattle to die, thus creating prolonged drought and famine. When Ekipe visits the people, incessant winds blow and the rains pour, causing people to suffer from the cold. The Jie world is harmonious when Akuj and Ekipe achieve a balanced relationship. According to most Jie storytellers' interpretation, Akuj and Ekipe are the projection of the sun and the moon, respectively. The dual and complementary qualities of the Jie deities are attributed to their dual ancestors Orwakol (the male ancestor) and Losilang (the female ancestor), who gave cattle and grain to the Jie people as gifts.

The dual qualities of the Jie deities are also projected in their staple foods of cattle and sorghum. It is in this sense that cattle and sorghum occupy a special place in the Jie people's diet. Cattle products such as milk, blood, and meat, and sorghum products, such as sorghum bread, and sorghum beer, are not only staple food in a practical sense, they are also the food used on ceremonial occasions when ritual performances require their consumption.

The Jie historical traditions show a gradual development of the symbolic powers of cattle and sorghum. The development of the supremacy of cattle and sorghum are closely associated with their symbolic equation with the Jie ancestors and their relationships with the ancient Jie politico-religious system. In a number of traditions, cattle and sorghum are assigned special significance, which reveals how cattle and sorghum gained supremacy over other food staples.

Various traditions demonstrate a gradual process whereby agricultural-pastoral cosmology and its ritual performance became the bulwark of the ancient Jie politico-religious system. According to the Jie storytellers, the politico-religious leadership was founded on cattle keeping and a sorghum-based agriculture, which gradually developed during the preceding centuries. The early agricultural leaders were also political leaders, whose power stemmed from their ability to solicit powers from the ancestors in order to ensure good sorghum crops and green pastures. Thus, the annual agriculturally oriented ritual served, and continues to serve, to legitimize and rejuvenate the politico-religious leaders and their power. For this reason, many Jie storytellers consider the *ekeworon*, or fire maker, to be the original leadership figure; he and his eldest wife serve as the first and foremost officials of agricultural ceremonies, which are performed to ensure the blessings of the ancestors for new crops and the safe return of the cattle from the grazing lands.

The dominant ritual that marks the appropriation of symbolic power by the cattle is a male initiation ritual known as the *asapan*, which is performed approximately every forty years. The appropriation of power by sorghum, however, takes place through the performance of the harvest ritual called *ngitalio a ngimomwa* (customs of sorghum), and it is based on the annual movement of the sorghum grains from the granary of the fire maker's eldest wife to the Jie gardens and back to her granary, ritually. These rituals embody the most important social roles of cattle and sorghum grains. The performance of both the *asapan* and the harvest ritual is an enactment of myths, and it constitutes a cosmic gift exchange. These rituals represent a cosmological gift exchange between the deities and humankind. The symbolic power of cattle and grain is derived from the everyday sharing of cattle and grain among the people and from their practical use in the discourses of everyday life. In both the male initiation and in the harvest rituals, eating is the dominant metaphorical act in appropriating symbolic power.

MUSTAFA KEMAL MIRZELER

See also **East African Folklore**

FOODWAYS: YORUBA FOOD VENDORS

Street vendors are found everywhere in Africa : at bus and train stations, taxi stands, and city street corners. Competition is fierce, so one has to work hard to attract buyers. Amounts are small—a box of matches, a few oranges, fried cakes—so one must sell as much as possible to earn a decent wage. The following examples of food vendors' sales songs were recorded in Lagos, Nigeria. Yoruba food vendors, usually women and small children, are known for their creativity in attracting people to buy their wares. Their sales cries depend on catchy melodies as well as lyrics which identify their wares in some humorous or striking fashion. The following are a few examples.

For Pounded Yam (*iyan*)

Iyan re!	Good Pounded Yam!
Obe re!	Good Stew!
E woju obe	Look at the color of the stew

For Corn Starch (*ogi*)

Ologi dida re, toro o!	I'm the seller of ogi, three penny measure!
Ologi dida re, kobo kakan	I'm the seller of ogi, one penny measure!
Toro, kobo	Penny, one penny measure.
Ni mobu ogi yio	That's how I have portioned my ogi!

For Fried Plantains (*dodo*):

Omu agba	Shaped like a full woman's breast
Omu ewe	Shaped like a teenager's breast

For Bean Pudding (*ole*) and Corn Flour Pudding (*eko*):

Ole re!	This is ole!
Eko re o!	This is eko!

For Kerosene (*epo*):

Epo oyinbo	Whiteman's oil
Epo anti	Aunty's oil
Epo buroda	Brother's oil
Mogbepo de	I bring oil
Toro	In three penny measure
Kobo	In one penny measure
Lepo oyinbo	Is whiteman's oil

AKINSOLA AKIWOWO

FRENCH STUDY OF AFRICAN FOLKLORE

The first Europeans to be seriously interested in African cultures and in the spiritual life of indigenous peoples were Catholic and Protestant missionaries. The main objective of their presence in Africa, as elsewhere in the non-Christian world, was evangelical work. Such a task required language training, as well as knowledge of institutions, mores, customs, and local belief systems. From this perspective, the discovery of indigenous verbal arts offered valuable access to the mental world of the people in question. Certain genres such as proverbs, sayings, and fables could be used directly in sermons; the words of the Christian Scriptures could be adapted to the melodies of native songs. Knowing the tales with their relatively simple vocabulary facilitated learning the language concerned. Furthermore, people were often favorably impressed by the missionaries' efforts in gathering texts, and this contributed in creating relationships of trust between the missionaries and their flocks.

The Forerunners: Missionaries and Administrators

The French Catholic missionaries and the Francophone Swiss Protestant missionaries settled in areas that extended beyond the current borders of Francophone Africa into certain British and Portuguese colonies. A forerunner was Eugène Casalis, who spent close to twenty-five years in Sotholand (now Lesotho in southern Africa) and whose ethnological and linguistic works (1841, 1859) contain a rich sampling of Tswana poetry, songs, proverbs, enigmas, and stories in French. As early as the second half of the nineteenth century, among the French missionary congregations, the White Fathers, the congregation of the Holy Spirit and of the African Missionaries of Lyons, France, were notable. They settled on the coast of Dahomey (now Benin) and Nigeria. One of their members, Father Pierre-Bertrand Bouche, published an anthology of Nago (Yoruba) proverbs and riddles in 1883 and, in 1885, an ethnological monograph, two chapters of which are devoted to stories and maxims. Several other church people also prepared language manuals, dictionaries, and linguistic studies containing texts of narratives in the original language. These included translations, as well as occasional commentaries. The Songay manual published in 1897, which presents sixteen tales and is the result of the collaborative work of Father Hacquard and A. A. Dupuis, is one example.

It was not until the end of the nineteenth century that the missionaries were joined in these endeavors by colonial administrators (although the first governor of Senegal, Baron Roger, published Wolof tales much earlier in 1828), doctors, and military staff. For the training of the staff of the French overseas territories, a specialized school (the Colonial School) was created in 1889. Subsequently, several governors and administrators of the colonies in West Africa—including Maurice Delafosse, Henri Gaden, and René Basset—authored ethnographic, historical, and linguistic works containing, on a regular basis, texts of oral literature. The pioneering work by François-Victor Equilbecq, published in three volumes in 1913–1916, must be granted a special place because the author undertook the collection of texts on a very large scale. His published corpus contains 117 texts in the first edition, to which 50 others were added in a posthumous edition in 1972. He gathered these texts between 1904 and 1912 during his successive stays in Senegal, Guinea, and Mali, as well as in Gourma country (currently a part of today's Burkina Faso). Like the approach of a folklorist today, he gives the name, the ethnic origin, and brief information about the storytellers as well as about the conditions of the gathering effort. For example, he notes that the propitious time for tale telling is the evening, the half-light. He is conscious of the problems of translation and the difficulties raised by the passage from the oral form to the written text, hoping that "neither the content nor the details have had to suffer from his concern for improvement" (1972, 23). He is not only respectful toward the social groups he explores but also familiar with contemporary studies dealing with folklore in Europe and elsewhere. His scholarly knowledge allows him to identify the recurrent themes, characters, motifs, and procedures used by the African storytellers that are also found elsewhere, and at the same time, to point out the specific features of the narrative world peculiar to West Africa.

The interest taken by the colonial administration in the scholarly works of these agents is demonstrated by the creation in 1916 of the Committee for the Historical and Scientific Study of French West Africa in Dakar. The purpose of this committee was to coordinate and centralize the research undertaken under the patronage of the general government. The publications of the Committee (issued as a quarterly beginning in 1918) changed names several times. Beginning in 1938, the review appeared under the title *Bulletin de l'Institut Français d'Afrique Noire* (Bulletin of the French Institute of Black Africa); then, after independence in 1958, as *Bulletin de l'Institut Fondamental d'Afrique Noire* (Bulletin of the Fundamental Institute of Black Africa). This periodical often offers important samples of texts and studies on oral narratives. During the period between the two world wars, the administrators and officials of public and religious education continued to promote ethnographic and linguistic scholarship. Several monographs appeared with an appendix or an independent chapter devoted to the texts of oral literature. Volumes devoted exclusively to verbal arts also appeared, thanks in particular to René Trautmann, a medical practitioner, and to the administrators mentioned earlier, such as Maurice Delafosse and Henri Gaden.

The Beginning of Professional Ethnology

Modern ethnography began in France with Marcel Griaule who, with several other scholars, undertook field work (Mission Dakar-Djibouti in 1932, followed in 1935 by research in Dogon country, in present day Mali). During the latter mission, Griaule's investigation was primarily focused on Dogon cosmogony and thought system. He gathered numerous myths on the world's creation and on the origins of cultural objects including masks. His followers and younger colleagues—Germaine Dieterlen, Solange de Ganay, Michel Leiris, Deborah Lifchitz, and Denise Paulme (who, beginning in 1960, was to specialize in the study of African tales)—also gathered and studied oral traditions. Leiris did remarkable work on the Dogon's secret language used on specific occasions and connected to various religious events (initiation, funerals, etc.). In his work, songs, formulas, and invocations are always given in Dogon and include an in-depth analysis. Solange de Ganay in 1941 published more than 200 *proiretoumules* ("mottoes"), studying their functions and the various circumstances of their usage. Deborah Lifchitz, who died very young in a Nazi concentration camp, had time to publish only three topical articles, among which was a study in 1940 that focused on the identification of Dogon oral genres.

The Post-War Period

If France's participation in the study of African oral tradition has always been important, her contribution constituted almost 25 percent of all the topical production from 1960 onward. The general recourse to increasingly perfected tape recorders revolutionized the collection of texts and the technique of oral investigation; this acceleration can be measured particularly in the field of publishing. The number of collections of monolingual and bilingual texts increased spectacularly (see, in this regard, the bibliographies published by Görög-Karady in 1981 and 1992). French publishing distinguished itself by the high number of bilingual works, especially the prestigious collection *Classiques Africains* (twenty-six volumes since 1963). The carefully translated texts are usually accompanied by a substantial study as well as extensive ethnographic and linguistic annotations. The collections *Bibliothèque* and *Tradition Orale*—created respectively, in 1967 and 1972 by the Société d'Etudes Linguistiques et Anthropologiques de France (SELAF) (The French Society for Linguistic and Anthropological Study)—also contain several volumes of excellent quality bilingual texts, as well as essays on African oral narratives. Finally, beginning in the 1970s, the Conseil International de la Language Française (The International Council of the French Language) also published paperback collections (*Fleuve et Flamme* ["River and Fire"]; *Textes et Civilisations* ["Texts and Civilizations"]) devoted to monolingual and bilingual texts and to topical studies. The publishing houses Karthala and Harmattan also put out a great number of works in that field.

The academic institutionalization of African studies in France in the 1960s also played a role in promoting the development of studies on spoken arts. However, this development remains limited, for there is still no Chair of African Oral Literature in French universities. Courses and seminars, along with the defense of doctoral dissertations, rather numerous between 1970 and 1990 in this field, always take place within the framework of other disciplines, such as comparative literature, Francophone literatures, ethnology, anthropology, linguistics, and African studies.

But interest in the verbal arts also intensified beginning in the 1960s as a result of the impact made by the work of scholars of the formalist and structuralist schools (in particular, Vladimir Propp and Claude Lévi-Strauss) on oral cultures, especially in the field of narrative genres, that is, myths and tales. Furthermore, most of the collections of oral texts included a majority of folk tales, while scholarly analysis tended to focus on the narrative genres, at least in the case of African studies. In the Africanist field, the first well-known scholars, like Denise Paulme and Geneviève Calame-Griaule, were also mainly involved in the study of tales.

Having done field work in several African societies, Denise Paulme (1976, 7–17) tells how she discovered that although the tales she had gathered in different groups were often very close to each other and had a common basic structure, they differed from each other, sometimes quite extensively. This observation led her to a research method, which consisted of collecting within a given geographic area—in her case, West Africa—the greatest possible number of versions of the same tale-type. Noting the similarities and especially the differences in the structure and elements of the story, she raised questions regarding the departures among the versions. Could they be explained by differences in economic, political, and familial organization or by differences in behavior models and in the ideal values each society offered its members? The answers she arrived at varied from case to case. Using an ethnologist's approach (she does not consider herself a folklorist), she set herself the task of uncovering through stories the problems social groups pose for themselves. A second part of her work consisted of an effort at classification and typology of the African tales, an endeavor inspired by the work of Propp and Alan Dundes, along with the development—in collaboration with Claude Bremond—of an index of ruses in the trickster stories.

The work of Geneviève Calame-Griaule is deeply influenced by the work of her father, Marcel Griaule. Her special interest has been in language and in the role of the different "words" in Dogon society, and more particularly in "literary words," (words about words), that is, the system of genres. In a 1970 article—a milestone in the field—she insisted on the relevance of the study of verbal arts in an ethnolinguistic perspective based on the intimate knowledge of the culture and the language, as well as on a global approach to literary phenomena. At her initiative, several collective ethnolinguistic works were produced (1977, 1987), which, among other topics, dealt with the relationships of the producers of texts to their audience and the local classifications of the genres, as well as the concrete social function of oral literature in African societies. She also wrote numerous studies (gathered into a single volume in 1987) on tales and, more particularly, on the symbolic content of the Dogon and Isawaghen tales. Her comparative analyses also reflected the influence of structuralism and Freudian psychoanalysis.

Since the late 1960s, the study of African orality has been a permanent item on the program of two research groups of the Centre National de la Recherche Scientifique (CNRS) (The National Center of Scientific Research), which exist outside of the university structure proper.

The first group, Languages and Civilizations with Oral Traditions (LACITO) has a wide geographic specialization. Ethnolinguistic researchers from this group have produced remarkable works. Three notable studies appeared in the same year, 1970. The first one was the book by Jacqueline Thomas who presented in one thousand pages the various Ngbaka oral genres (Central African Republic). The texts are given in their original language and also in literal and literary translation. Abundant ethnobotanical, ethnological, and linguistic comments and notes allow the reader to place the texts in their cultural context. Other important works from the team working in Central Africa were those by Jean Derive (1970) [?], who focused on the problems of written transposition and translation of the oral texts. The ethnomusicologist Simha Arom (1970) has published Ngbaka *chantefables*. He also gives the characteristics of the genre and provides the musical notation of all the songs. Suzy Ruelland completed a comparative study of nineteen Fon versions of "The Girl with No Hands" (AT706). Another scholar, Luc Bouquiaux (1970), offers a broad sampling of the Birom narrative genres from northern Nigeria.

The second ethnolinguistic research group of the Centre National de la Recherche Scientifique (CNRS) "Language and Culture in West Africa" (founded in 1970), has operated for twenty-six years. Its exclusive focus has been on the languages and cultures of West Africa. From the beginning, several of its members specialized in the study of traditional literatures and created a subgroup to this end. Informed mainly by the comparative method, their research is based on bodies of stories gathered by the members of the group in their respective fields, thanks to their knowledge of one or several languages of Africa. Among the founding members are Genevieve Calame-Griaule (Dogon, Iswaghen), Veronika Görög-Karady (Bambara), Suzy Platiel (San), Christiane Seydou (Peul or Fulani), Diana Rey-Hulman (Tyokosi). Other researchers—Ursula Baumgardt (Peul or Fulani), Jean Derive (Jula or Dyula), Paulette Roulon-Doko (Ngbaya), Suzy Ruelland (Tupuri) it joined the group later on. In addition, Brunhilde Biebuyck (Mongo), Dominique Casajus (Tuareg), and Denise Paulme (Dogon) were associates for a relatively longer period of time.

With the joining in 1995 of CNRS with the Africanist section of LACITO, a new enlarged research group was created under the name Language, Languages and Cultures of Black Africa (LLACAN) (Langage, Langues et Cultures d'Afrique Noire), extending its field of operation to the whole of sub-Saharan Africa. The research group on oral traditions is pursuing its work within this new institutional framework.

The close collaboration of these scholars, each one with his or her linguistic and ethnological speciality, enables, under very favorable conditions, a comparative approach, based on the exploration of the mechanisms of variability. Indeed, this type of ethnosociological and ethnolinguistic analysis adopts the pragmatic assumption that the body of texts forms a system and that only the systematic confrontation of the texts can release the meanings of which the tale is the bearer. In this regard, research on the tale of the "Enfant Terrible" (V. Görög-Karady, et al.,

1980), a character defying all laws and authority could be considered exemplary to the extent that, in each ethnic body of texts being studied (Bambara, Dogon, Samo, Tyokossi), multiple versions and variants of the tale were available and that, one after the other, intracultural and intercultural comparisons could be done. Some other collective works prepared over the years include the studies devoted to the African versions of the two tale-types "Magical Objects" (AT 563) and "Animal Allies" (AT 554) (cf. *Cahiers d'Études Africaines* 1972, vol 12, no. 45), widespread throughout the world, underscore the profound originality of the African corpus. Studies gathered by Geneviève Calame-Griaule on the theme of the tree were published in three volumes in 1969, 1970, and 1974 and are very different from each other. Some focus on the various functions of the trees (nurturing, legal, etc.); others offer the inventory of plants that appear in the tales; still others still deal with a plantlike motif. More recent research on the representation of kinship relations in six ethnic corpora led to the publication in 1992 of a book on marriage, edited by Veronika Görög-Karady. (The English text is published in *Marvels and Tales* VI, 2, December 1992.)

To better coordinate French research on African oral tradition with similar international efforts, several colloquia with British and German scholars were organized (in France, in Germany, and in England) and two international conferences were held in Paris in 1982 (*Analyse des coules—Problemes de méthods*) and 1987 (*La recherche du sens*). The collected papers were published in 1984 and 1989. Another work, the result of a Franco-British symposium, which allowed the research directions of specialists of orality from both countries to interface, was published as *Genres, Forms, Meaning* (1982).

Along with these collective activities, the members of the research group are also involved in personal research on a vast array of subjects. On a regular basis, they publish collections of new sets of texts they have gathered themselves. Ursula Baumgardt has studied the repertory of a Peul (Fulani) woman storyteller along with the image of woman and child belonging to this corpus. Dominique Casajus has published Tuareg poetry and stories and also several studies on these genres. Jean Derive has done very original research on the system of genres in the Jula (Dyula) society. Among other topics, he is interested in the contribution of orality to the general theory of literature and the problems of the written transposition of the oral literature. Veronika Görög-Karady focuses on the analysis of the literary representation of the relations of domination within the familial framework and in the global society among the Bamana-Malinke. She is also interested in the functioning of stereotypes (ethnic, social, racial, and sexual) in the various oral genres and in various cultures. She also studies the development of the discipline of oral literature and the documentary aspects of the research. The main interest of Suzy Platiel is in the role of the tales in linguistic training of the children in Samo society and in the representation of the children in the stories. Diana Rey-Hulman, who has been working since 1982 in Guadeloupe, focuses more particularly on the dynamics of communication, along with the evolution and the changes of the status of oral genres. Christiane Seydou has become the specialist of Peul (Fulani) orality. She has published important collections of texts (epics, poetry, and stories) and, more specifically, studies the African epic genres so as to draw out the constituent features.

She has also written numerous articles on the stories, the epics, and the poetry of the Fulani of Mali.

Outside of these organized efforts, many other scholars have made considerable contributions to the field. Among them are Pascal Boyer, who has studied the epic genres in several cultures; Jean Cauvin, who has produced a dense work on the articulation of the image of language and thought in the proverbs (Mali); Jacques Chevrie, who has done much to introduce African verbal arts to a broader audience; Gerard Dumestre, a specialist in the Bambara (Bamana) language, who has published beautiful epic texts; Maurice Houis, who has written on the problems of the oral style; Lilyane Kestellot, who, teaching both in Africa and in France, has published numerous epic and narrative texts and has studied various oral genres; Suzanne Lallemand, who has done work on sexual education in tales from all over Africa; Alain Ricard, who positions himself between the written and the oral and writes on the new oral genres of the "concert party" and popular theater; Pierre Smith, who has done work on various Rwandan narrative genres; and Dominique Zahan, who is well versed in the spiritual universe of the Bambara and published a book in 1963 on their different literary words.

VERONIKA GÖRÖG-KARADY

See also **Classiques Africaines; Epics: Overview; Folktales of the Bamana; Prose and Poetry of the Fulanji; Words and the Dogon**

FROBENIUS, LEO VIKTOR (1873–1938)

Leo Viktor Frobenius was born in Berlin, Germany, on June 29, 1873. With an autodidactic background, Frobenius became an ethnologist and culture historian and one of the most famous researchers on Africa during the first half of the twentieth century. Between 1904 and 1935, he carried out twelve expeditions to various African countries to collect ethnographic data, oral traditions, material objects, and folklore. As a theoretician, he developed the idea of "cultural morphology," which conceives of cultures as living organisms, that is, they are born, and progress through "infancy," "youth," "adulthood," "old age," and finally, "death." They are dominated by *Paideuma*, a kind of cultural soul that is considered to act more or less independently of men. Irrationalist ideas of this type have always met with skepticism, and have been mostly discarded by modern research. However, much of the data from Frobenius's field research, and particularly his immense collections of fairy tales, legends, fables, sagas, and myths, proved to be of lasting value.

In 1910, Frobenius compiled his *Black Decameron*, a collection of love stories and tales of eroticism. From 1921 to 1928, he published a series of twelve volumes entitled *Atlantis: Volksmärchen und Volksdichtungen Afrikas* (Atlantis: Fairy Tales and Popular Poetry of Africa). They mainly focused on western Africa between Senegal and Cameroon, the Kasai region of the Congo, the Maghrib, Kordofan, and areas of central-southern Africa such as present-day Zimbabwe and Zambia, they were partly translated into English, French, Spanish, and Italian. In 1938, Frobenius put forth the idea of establishing a universal folkloristic archive, which, because of his death in the same year in Italy, and then the outbreak of World War II, could not be realized.

References

Major works of Leo Frobenius on folklore

Frobenius, Leo. 1910. *Der schwarze Dekameron. Liebe, Witz und Heldentum in Innerafrika*, Berlin: Vita-Verlagshaus.

———. 1921–28. *Atlantis. Volksmärchen und Volksdichtungen Afrikas.* 12 vols. Jena: Eugen Diederichs.

———. 1938. Das Archiv für Folkloristik. *Paideuma* 1, no. 1:1–18.

Selected works on Leo Frobenius

Braukämper, Ulrich. 1986. Frobenius, Leo. *Enzyklopädie des Märchens* 5, nos. 2–3:378–83. Berlin, New York: Walter de Gruyter.

Haberland, Eike, ed. 1973. *Leo Frobenius, 873–1973. An Anthology.* Wiesbaden: Steiner.

Niggemeyer, Hermann. 1950. Das wissenschaftliche Schrifttum von Leo Frobenius. *Paideuma* 4:377–418.

ULRICH BRAUKÄMPER

FULANI

See **Epics; Prose and Poetry of the Fulani**

G

GABON (GABONESE REPUBLIC)

Located on central Africa's west coast, Gabon is a tropical country of nearly 1,240,000 and is neighbored by Equatorial Guinea, Cameroon, and Congo. Gabon's capital and largest city is Libreville, which has a population of 419,000. Twenty-five percent of the country's population is Fang, 10 percent is Bapounon, and 65 percent is made up of various other groups. The major languages spoken are French, Fang, Eshira, Bopounou, Bateke, and Okande. Between 55 percent and 75 percent of the population is Christian, while less than 1 percent are Muslim. The remaining population practices traditional indigenous religions.

In 1888, the territory was linked to the French Congo, but in 1910 became a separate colony and part of French Equatorial Africa. Gabon gained its independence from France on August 17, 1960, and subsequently formed its own republic. As a result of strong opposition to one-party rule, the country established a multiparty system with a president in 1990 after twenty-two years under one-party rule. Gabon's principle industries are petroleum, lumber, and minerals such as manganese, uranium, gold, zinc, and iron ore. Because of such rich natural resources, Gabon has one of the highest gross domestic products per capita in Africa. Despite such apparent success, there remains a vast gap between the statistics of wealth and actual poverty that many Gabonese live with. Nevertheless, there is 63 percent adult literacy. The exquisite reliquary carvings of the Fang and others in Gabon are among the most highly prized of African arts.

Gabon is known for its town of Lambarene where Albert Schweitzer set up his mission hospital. Schweitzer, who won the Nobel Peace Prize for his efforts on behalf of the "Brotherhood of Nations," modeled his hospital after an African village, consisting of numerous simple dwellings. Alhough he held a distorted image of African society as being unable to advance in Western ways, he nevertheless saved many lives and cured thousands at his missionary hospital.

JENNIFER JOYCE

GAMBIA, THE (REPUBLIC OF THE GAMBIA)

The Gambia is a subtropical country with a population of over 1 million people, which is located in western Africa. Except for a small coastal strip, The Gambia frames the Gambia river and is completely surrounded by Senegal. Banjul, a city of 49,200 is the country's capital and largest city. Nearly three-quarters of the population is rural. Forty-two percent of the population is Mandinka, 18 percent is Fula, 16 percent is Wolof, and 24 percent is composed of various smaller groups. English, Mandinka, Wolof, Fula, Sarakola, Dyula are the most widely spoken languages. The country is mostly Muslim (90 percent), while 9 percent are Christian and 1 percent practice traditional indigenous religions.

On February 18, 1965, The Gambia gained its independence from the British, who ruled over the country through Sierra Leone since 1807. Until the country's armed forces overthrew the government in July of 1994, The Gambia had been West Africa's only postcolonial country with an uninterrupted multiparty system. The Gambia's main industries and sources of revenue are tourism, brewing, peanuts, fish, and woodworking and metalworking. Unfortunately, the weak economy and political unrest of the later twentieth century years has resulted in reduced revenue from tourism, a major industry since independence.

Gambians share many cultural and political similarities with their Senegalese neighbors. Both nations share Islam as the dominant religion, as well as the major ethnolinguistic groups of Mandinka, Wolof, and Fula. The countries also share similar economies that are heavily reliant on the cultivation of cash crops such as groundnuts. Popular throughout West Africa are griots, hereditary Gambian bards and musicians who have maintained their traditional musical art throughout the ages. Once related to ruling families, Gambian griots now perform on Radio Gambia and have attained widespread popularity.

JENNIFER JOYCE

GENDER REPRESENTATIONS IN AFRICAN FOLKLORE

A discussion of gender representation in African folklore requires mention of representation as a communicative activity involving the selective and purposive use of language or images to obtain attention or consent. However, the subjects of representations may not hesitate to contest its forms, contents, or outcomes.

Such a discussion must remember, too, that Africa is a vast continent of more than fifty nation-states, and thousands of ethnic groups, languages, and folklore traditions. With regard to gender specifically, the discussion also needs to take stock of women's roles as composers, sponsors, and audience. Despite the negative representations so often portrayed, women have not been absent in African folklore since the eighteenth and nineteenth centuries, when its collection and study was first undertaken by European travelers, missionaries, linguists and administrators (see Finnegan 1970, Dorson 1972, Klipple 1992, Okpewho 1992). Although the initial focus was on collection and analyses of folklore texts taken out of their cultural and performance settings (see Haring 1994), this changed from the second half of the twentieth century, when studies began emphasizing folklore as performances in context (see Albert 1964; Finnegan 1992; Stoeltje, Fox, and Olbrys 1997).

The growing awareness of gender in the mid-twentieth century galvanized the emergence of women as subjects in folklore, and redirected attention to women's experiences. Their role in the labor process, in reproduction, in ritual, and their representation in oral and written literatures, gradually came to be recognized as legitimate, rather than merely as an appendage to the work and visibility of men (see Farrer 1975, Stoeltje 1988, 141). This awareness directed scholars to the investigation of how folklore texts encode and legitimate gender ideologies under the rubrics of tradition, identity, culture, or custom, and to map out the intersections between gender representations and women's social lives. African folklore scholars have begun to investigate the links between folklore and asymmetrical gender representations that are often legitimized in the name of national identity or tradition. In one respect, this association reflects the bias of Johann Gottfried Herder's influential eighteenth-century model of society, which integrated folklore with patriarchy and nationalism and elevated the masculine as the authority figure, while devaluing the female as "the first failing stone in the human edifice" (see Fox 1987, 72). Herder's model was transmitted directly to Africa through the Basel Missionaries in Ghana who, in their writing of history, incorporated Herder's concern with cultural meaning and with the relationship between society and state (McCaskie 1986).

The bias toward the male subject was maintained throughout the twentieth century; nevertheless, the critique of earlier scholarly discourse on African folklore, with its focus on women's experience, was successfully established. It is in this regard that two of Ruth Finnegan's (1970, 108) observations deserve critical attention. First, she argues that men more than women were the "bearers of tradition" in many cultures of Africa. Second, she claims that most Limba storytellers and storytelling activities were performed by men (Finnegan 1967, 69–70). Of importance for the continued study of African folklore is the view that men, more than women, tend to be bearers of tradition. Even if this was the case for a specific society, it raises the questions of Why? How so? What do the women, in fact, do? and, not the least, Are such specific cases cross-culturally applicable? Here we stand to learn from Elizabeth Gunner's (1979) analysis and reevaluation of the Zulu (South Africa) izibongo praise poetry, and the concomitant and pervasive assumption that it was mainly a male preserve or that it paid attention only to Zulu women of high status (see Cope 1968, Dhlomo, 1947, 1948, Lestrade 1935). By showing that neither the ordinary women nor the izibongo traditions were strangers to each other, Gunner has debunked the patriarchal hegemony and its lenses that constructed the izibongo as a male preserve in the popular imaginary. Using empirical evidence, she has shown that lower-class women have always had an active presence in the izibongo tradition at the levels of performance, composition, repertoires, voices, and identities.

A study that illustrates women's creations of folklore texts and outlines the contexts of performance is Harold Scheub's work with Nongenile Mazithathu Zenani, a female Xhosa ntsomi or traditional storyteller (1970, 1972). Zenani's technique and repertoires draw the attention of even her detractors, who identify and empathize with her story line and development, often in spite of themselves. Zenani occupies a powerful position in the oral tradition of her culture, demonstrating that although women have encountered restricted access to social, economic, and expressive in cultures throughout Africa, these conditions have not stopped them from exploring alternative means of expression. Zainab Mohamed Jama (1994) has illustrated how Somali tradition restricts women's access to gabay and geerar poetry genres and therefore denies them the opportunity to become active spokespersons for their society; however, the Somali women were able to reverse their expressive fortunes by circulating their poetry using cassette tapes and radio broadcast, resulting in an unprecedented expansion of their audience.

The actual or potential roles of African folklore in reinforcing or subverting normative gender ideologies have been variously noted by scholars. Florence Abena Dolphyne (1991), for one, has noted this in an Asante (Ghana) folktale in which a man wants to take a second wife on the claim that the first wife cannot alone do all the domestic chores and meet his needs in time. The woman objects saying that everything seems to be going on well between them. To prove his point, he asks her to prepare the Asante kenkey meal. The laboriousness of the preparation left her exhausted and her hands blistered. She gives up, begs the elders of her family to apologize on her behalf to the husband for having been so stubborn, and to tell him that she has no further objections to his marrying a second wife. Dolphyne argues that the telling of this kind of tale shapes the definition of gender roles, conditioning members of a society to accept them as something natural and inevitable.

This capacity to instruct an audience with regard to gender ideologies can be observed in Rattray's (1930) collection of Akan Asante folktales, and in Okot p'Bitek's (1978, 11–14) collection of Acholi (Uganda) folktales. Both of these examples teach that a woman should not choose her husband, but should defer to the authorities designated by society to choose for her. In the Akan tale, the maiden Kwaboso refuses the man chosen for her to marry, claiming that his body crawls with ticks. When Kwaboso refuses the selected suitor, fairies attack her while she is harvesting plantains, telling her, "You are the one whom, when they take to give to anyone, you shake your head pusu pusu." Luckily, at that moment the rejected suitor chances on them and brings them down with his gun, thus saving Kwaboso who thereafter sends word that she is now ready to marry him. A similar tale is found in one of Okot p'Bitek's collections of Acholi folktales. A beautiful maiden called Awili rejects all suitors in preference for the handsome Onguka, who turns out to be an ogre. Onguka's plans to kill and eat Awili's flesh are foiled in the last minute, thanks to her crippled sister who tricks the ogre into fetching water for her in a basket. This gives them time to escape back home, where the ogre who tries to follow them is killed.

Michael Jackson (1977) has observed the pervasive power of language in Kuranko (Sierra Leone) social life and thought, especially the ability to make the distinction between male and female seem so "natural" or divinely sanctioned. Extending this perspective to Karin Barber's (1995) comprehensive study of Yoruba (Nigeria) *oriki*, we observe how traditional poetry reinforces gender ideologies. Barber's analysis not only illuminates the praise poetry but points to the encoding of male and female behavior celebrated in these poems performed by women. Daring actions by males are admired while similar acts by women are interpreted as the overstepping of boundaries, as "going too far."

Peter Seitel (1980) has noted how Haya (Tanzania) tales encode worldview, categorize the landscape along gender lines, and place men and women in their respective domains. In a tale titled "She Killed One. We've All of Us Come," a gluttonous wife prepares food and eats from the field, alienating herself from her husband, the domestic and the human spheres. When she kills an animal which is stealing her food, other animals team up to avenge, overwhelming the husband and the chief to whom she runs for protection. In the end the bees rescue her by stinging and dispersing the animals. In seeking to chastise the woman for her gluttony, which caused her alienation from her family and the human domain, the tale defines her responsibility to her husband and the family and locates her in the domestic sphere, censoring any alternative perception. Seitel (1980: 228) concludes that the tale has immense potential for the regulation of female behavior.

On the contrary, however, other examples of women's performance of folklore interrogate or openly subvert prevalent gender ideologies. Judith T. Irvine (1992, 1996) shows how Wolof (Senegal) co-wives perform, or, sponsor the performance of *xarxar* ritual insult poetry during the wedding ceremony of an incoming co-wife, to satirize or even to ruin her honor and that of her family. The collusive and collective composition of *xarxar* poetry by the co-wives who sponsor it, and the lower-class women who perform it, allow each group to tactfully disclaim responsibility for the poem's insults.

Examples of women's use of folklore forms to express their views and explore their experiences are abundant in Lila Abu-Lughod's (1986, 233) study of Awad ʿAli Bedouin (Egypt) women's folk poetry. Through their performances Awad ʿAli women make defiant statements about their unhappiness and the difficulties that their society places on them. They can also express sentiments of romantic love which otherwise violate their expected traditional honor code. Rachel I. Fretz's (1994) analysis of Chokwe (Congo, formerly Zaire) women's storytelling demonstrates that they express their aspirations and explore grave matters that affect them as women, such as their inability to bear children or conflicts with a co-wife, through narrative performance. The ambiguous tales do not easily conform to conventional narrative patterns, and therefore Chokwe women are able to create new perceptions of themselves and their gendered environments. Aware that they are narrating from within male domains, they subvert this world view by recourse to ambiguity, posing the story as a dilemma in which both the narrator and audience grapple for answers.

In Madagascar, women's and men's speech forms are distinctive and even have labels. Elinor Keenan (1974) has identified the Malagasy (Madagascar) use of *resaka* and *kabray* speech forms by women and men, and notes how the men's mastery of formal, ceremonial and highly stylized *kabray* speech forms contrasts with women's mastery and use of blunt, pointed and direct *resaka* speech, used to handle business that calls for fast responses. This marks women as norm-breakers and labels them as having a *lavalela* (long tongue). However, Keenan points out that the men call upon the women to express what they feel but are reluctant to state bluntly.

Kwesi Yankah's (1995) study of Akan oratory points to examples of institutionalized channels and gender-specific genres through which Akan women assert their verbal artistry such as the *nsuie* (dirge), and the *adenkun, nnwnkoro,* and *mmombe* songs. He notes that these forms contrast with the *apae* royal panegyric, a male performance domain. Yankah emphasizes that the relative male domination of communication channels and modes cannot be divorced from the general restrictions and taboos that govern speaking. For example, he points to an expression regarded as the quintessence of traditional wisdom or eloquence: *aberawa*, or "the old lady." The term identifies woman with wisdom and has a bearing on the key role of women in Akan society insofar as the position of *aberawa*, an older woman, or *obaapanin*, a female functionary responsible for women, exists in the official counseling body to the chief. Equally important is the fact that the position of chief would be meaningless without that of the *ohemmaa*, the queen mother, the only one among the chief's counselors who can reprimand him publicly. The queen mother's power lies in her responsibilities for settling disputes, for advising the chief, and in her public ritual and ceremonial functions such as funerals (see Stoeltje 1994, 1997).

Oral tradition elucidates Asante queen mothers' powers and responsibilities in a folktale featuring the unparalleled trickster of Akan folklore, Ananse. In a volume edited by Christiane Owusu-Sarpong (1998, 31–7) the spider Ananse lures, traps, and kills almost all the animals in the land except Amoakua, who observes him and then lures him into his own trap. Faced with the prospect of death at the hands of Amoakua, Ananse makes a cry of appeal to the Crocodile queen mother; at her intercession Amoakua grudgingly spares Ananse. Later, when Ananse tries to trick and kill none other than the Crocodile queen mother herself, she puts him in his place by crushing him with her all-powerful tail. The significance of the tale is its focus on the centrality of the queen mother in Akan social life. Not only does she intercede on behalf of Ananse (one of her important functions in human society is intercession on behalf of those in trouble), but in the act of smashing Ananse she demonstrates that no one, except perhaps the most foolhardy like Ananse, should attempt to challenge or outwit the queen mother. The tale illustrates that the queen mother not only possesses wisdom and administers justice, but also that she embodies power in Akan social and political affairs (see Stoeltje 1995, 15, 21).

The representations of women in African folklore vary widely, depending on a complex set of variables. These include gender ideologies embedded in the social and political organization of each society, and, most importantly, whether the researcher who collected and analyzed the oral traditions of a particular society attended to gender differences; this involved investigating the experience and performance of women as well as men, and taking note of whether tales and songs are performed by men or women, and the effects of gender differences on the repertoires of individuals.

References

Abu-Lughod, Lila. 1986. *Veiled Sentiments. Honor and Poetry in a Bedouin Society*. Berkeley and Los Angeles: University of California Press.

Albert, Ethel. 1964. "Rhetoric," "Logic," and "Poetics" in Burundi: Culture Patterning of Speech Behavior. *The Ethnography of Communication*. American Anthropologist Special Publication, eds. John Gumperz and Dell Hymes. 66, no. 6:35–54.

Barber, Karin. 1995. Going Too Far in Okuku: Some ideas about Gender, Excess, and Political Power. In *Gender Identity in Africa*, eds. Mechthild Reh and Gurdun Ludwar-Ene. Munster: Lit Verlag.

Cope, Trevor, ed. 1968. *Izibongo, Zulu Praise Poetry*. Oxford: Clarendon Press.

Dhlomo, H. I. E. 1947. Zulu Folk Poetry. *Native Teachers Journal*, 5–7.

———. 1948. Zulu Folk Poetry. Continued *Native Teachers Journal* 28:46–50.

Dolphyne, Florence Abena. 1991. *The Emancipation of Women*. Accra: Ghana Universities Press.

Dorson, Richard, M. 1972. Africa and the Folklorist. In *African Folklore*, ed. Richard Dorson. Garden City, New York: Anchor Books.

Farrer, Claire. 1975. Introduction. *Women and Folklore*, ed. Claire Farrer. Prospect Heights: Waveland Press.

Finnegan, Ruth. 1967. *Limba Stories and Story-telling*. Oxford: Clarendon Press.

———. 1970. *Oral Literature in Africa*. Oxford: Clarendon Press.

———. 1992. *Oral Traditions and the Verbal Arts*. New York: Routledge.

Fox, Jennifer. 1987. The Creator Gods: Romantic Nationalism and the Engenderment of Women in Folklore. *Journal of American Folklore* 100:563–72.

Fretz, Rachel I. 1994. Through Ambiguous Tales: Women's Voices in Chokwe Storytelling. *Oral Tradition* 9, no. 1:230–50.

Gunner, Elizabeth. 1979. Songs of Innocence and Experience: Women as Composers and Performers of Izibongo, Zulu Praise Poetry. *Research in African Literatures* 10, no. 2:239–67.

Haring, Lee. 1994. Introduction: the Search for Ground in African Oral Tradition. *Oral Tradition* 1, no. 9:3–22.

Irvine, Judith, T. 1992. Insult and Responsibility: Verbal Abuse in a Wolof Village. In *Responsibility and Evidence in Oral Discourse*, eds. Jane E. Hill and Judith T. Irvine. Cambridge: Cambridge University Press.

———. 1996. *In Natural Histories of Discourse*, eds. Michael Silverstein and Greg Urban. Chicago: University of Chicago Press.

Jackson, Michael. 1977. *The Kuranko. Dimensions of Social Reality in a West African Society*. London: Hurst.

Jama, Zainab Mohamed. 1994. Silent Voices: The Role of Somali Women's Poetry in Social and Political Life. *Oral Tradition* 9, no. 1:185–202.

Keenan, Elinor. 1974. Norm-Markers, Norm-Breakers: Uses of Speech by Men and Women in a Malagasy Community. *Explorations in the Ethnography of Speaking*, ed. Richard Bauman and Joel Sherzer. London and New York: Cambridge University Press.

Klipple, May Augusta. 1992. *African Folk-tales with Foreign Analogues*. New York: Garland Press.

Lestrade, G. P. 1935. Bantu Praise Poetry. *The Critic* 4:1–10.

McCaskie, T. C. 1986. Komfo Anokye of Asante: Meaning, History and Philosophy in an African Society. *Journal of African History* 27:315–39.

Okpewho, Isidore. 1992. *African Oral Literature*. Bloomington: Indiana University Press.

Owusu-Sarpong, Christiane, ed. 1998. *Trilingual Anthology of Akan Folktales*. Kumasi: Department of Book Industry, College of Arts, University of Science and Technology.

p'Bitek, Okot. 1978. *Hare and Hornbill*. London: Heinemann.

Rattray, R. S. 1930. *Akan-Ashanti Folk Tales*. Oxford: The Clarendon Press.

Scheub, Harold. 1970. The Technique of the Expressive Images in Xhosa Ntsomi Performance. *Research in African Literatures* 1, no. 2:119–40.

———. 1972. The Art of Nongenile Mazithathu Zenani, A Glaceka Ntsomi Performer. In *African Folklore*, ed. Richard M. Dorson. Garden City, New York: Anchor Books.

Seitel, Peter. 1980. *See So That We May See: Performances and Interpretations of Traditional Tales from Tanzania*. Bloomington and London: Indiana University Press.

Stoeltje, Beverly J. 1988. Introduction: Feminist Perspectives. *Journal of Folklore Research* 25, no. 3.

———. 1995. Asante Queen Mothers: A Study in Identity of . . . In *Gender and Identity in Africa*, eds. Meththild Reh and Gudrun Ludwar-Ene. Munster: Lit.

———. 1997. Asante Queen Mothers. *Queens, Queen Mothers, Priestesses, and Power*, ed. Flora Kaplan. New York: The New York Academy of Sciences.

Stoeltje, Beverly J., Christie Fox, and Stephen Olbrys. 1999. The Self in Fieldwork. *Journal of American Folklore* 112, no. 444: 158–82.

Yankah, Kwesi. 1995. *Speaking for the Chief: Okyeame and the Politics of Akan Royal Oratory*. Bloomington: Indiana University Press.

ERNEST OKELLO OGWANG

BEVERLY J. STOELTJE

See also **Queen Mothers; Women's Folklore**

GERMAN STUDY OF AFRICAN FOLKLORE

A journal or a series of monographs specializing in African folklore does not exist in the German-speaking countries. Materials on this topic have mostly been published in periodicals of African linguistics, oriental studies, and ethnology (cultural anthropology), such as *Afrika und Übersee, Zeitschrift der Deutschen Morgenländischen Gesellschaft, Zeitschrift für Ethnologie*, and *Paideuma*, or in separate works and in chapters of books. A lexicon for research on folktales, narratives, and oral traditions in Africa, initiated by Wilhelm Möhlig and Herrmann Jungraithmayr was, however, completed in 1998. A number of entries relevant to the African continent are also to be found in the *Encyklopädie des Märchens* (Encyclopedia of Folktales), which is being edited in a special program at Göttingen University. A limited number of articles on African oral literature are published in the periodical *Fabula: Zeitschrift für Erzählforschung* (*Fabula:* Journal of Research on Folktales).

History of Research

Materials to some extent relevant to folklore are already to be found in the works of missionaries and travelers of the mid-nineteenth century, for example, Johann L. Krapf, Heinrich Barth, and Gustav Nachtigal. However, a scholarly focus on African folklore does not predate the late nineteenth century, and it can roughly be divided into three major periods: (1) from about 1900 to the end of World War I, when Germany was a colonial power, (2) the period to the end of World War II, and (3) the phase from the 1950s to the present. Due to the considerable number of noteworthy works on folklore that have appeared in print from the beginning of the twentieth century, it is beyond the scope of an overview such as this to mention them all.

Rudolf Prietze (1904; 1914), who specialized in folktales mainly on the Hausa and the Kanuri in modern northern Nigeria, was one of the first German Africanist folklore scholars. (English translations of his works are currently being done by G. Seidensticker-Brikay in Maiduguri, Nigeria). The Hausa became the focus of folklore studies also for Julius Lippert (1905) and Adam Mischlich (1929/1911). In the German colony of Cameroon, the missionary J. Sieber documented fairy tales and fables of the Vute, while the ethnologist Günter Tessmann focused on the folklore of the Baya and Fang. One of the first anthologies of Swahili poetry was composed by Carl Velten during his employment in the colonial government of German East Africa. In the same colony, the missionary Bruno Gutmann contributed a monograph about poetry and systems of thought of the Chagga in 1909. In 1911 (2d ed., 1921) Carl Meinhof, one of the founders of African linguistics, published a collection of fairy tales from different parts of Africa. Numerous contributions on folklore are implicitly to be found in the works of another authority in the field of African languages, Diedrich Westermann. The participation of the orientalist Enno Littmann in expeditions to Eritrea and northern Ethiopia between 1905 and 1913 provided a voluminous corpus of folklore research from this area, particularly of the Semitic-speaking Tigray.

In 1904, Leo Frobenius departed for his first African journey to the Kasai region of the Belgian Congo, which was followed by eleven further expeditions to various parts of the continent until 1933. His research resulted in one of the most comprehensive collections of African fairy tales, legends, fables, myths, and sagas, which were published in a series of twelve volumes labeled *Atlantis. Volksmärchen und Volksdichtungen Afrikas* (*Atlantis*: Fairy Tales and Popular Poetry of Africa) (1921–1928). These books appeared in a special series of fairy tales from all over the world, which was produced by Eugen Diederichs publishers and were partly translated into English, French, Spanish, and Italian. Geographically, they mainly focused on western Africa between Senegal and Cameroon, on the Kasai region, on the Maghrib, on Kordofan, and areas of central-southern Africa, such as present Zimbabwe and Zambia. Love stories and tales of eroticism were published in the *Black Decameron* (1910). Shortly before his death in 1938, Frobenius announced the idea of establishing a project entitled *Archiv für Folkloristik* (Archive of Folklore), which, because of the outbreak of World War II, was not systematically implemented.

Frobenius, who had started his folkloristic collections before World War I, continued this work until the 1930s. Adolf Jensen, one of his disciples, carried out field research in southern Ethiopia in 1934 and 1935, and, in cooperation with his travel companion Hellmut Wohlenberg, published a chapter on folklore in his book *Im Lande des Gada* (1936). During the late 1930s,

Ludwig Kohl-Larsen documented fairy tales and legends in Tanzania. Some of his material, including his stories on giants, were, however, not published until 1963. In western Africa, studies on folklore were carried out during the 1930s by the missionary Eugen Ludwig Rapp (with special focus in the Akan area) and by the linguist Johannes Lukas (mainly in the region around Lake Chad). An important compilation, entitled *Schöpfung und Urzeit des Menschen im Mythus der afrikanischen Völker* (Creation and Primeval Times of Man in the Myth of African Peoples) by Hermann Baumann appeared in 1936. In the same year Hans Alexander Winkler's *Ägyptische Volkskunde* (Egyptian Folklore) was published.

The third period of folklore studies started with the first German ethnological expedition to Africa after World War II, carried out by the Frobenius Institute in Frankfurt on Main to southern Ethiopia from 1950–1952. Like another journey to these regions, which followed in 1954–1956, it was headed by Adolf Jensen. His companions Eike Haberland and Helmut Straube included chapters on folklore (*Erzahlgut*) in their ethnological monographs on the Oromo and the Omotic-speaking peoples respectively. The tradition of the Frobenius Institute to carry out field studies in northeastern Africa continued, and a monograph entitled *Praise and Teasing: Narrative Songs of the Hadiyya in Southern Ethiopia*, based on research of the mid-1970s, is being composed by Ulrich Braukämper in cooperation with Tilahun Mishago. A thesaurus on the base of index files labeled *Afrikanisches Märchen- und Mythenarchiv* (Archive of African Myths and Fairy Tales), which was initiated by Hermann Baumann in Munich, was donated to the Frobenius Institute in the early 1970s.

Ernst Dammann, a missionary and linguist, published materials on Bantu folktales, particularly of the Swahili coast and of Southwest Africa, from the 1940s to the 1960s. New anthologies of fairy tales were published in the Eugen Diederichs series: by Ulla Schild on West Africa (1975) and by Andreas and Waltraud Kronenberg on Nubia (1978). Jürgen Zwernemann, a Hamburg museum ethnologist, compiled a study on folktales of four savanna peoples, the Moba, Kassena, Gurma und Nuna in the borderlands of northern Togo and Ghana with Burkina Faso (1985).

Since the 1970s, the major contributions to African folklore in Germany have been made by the Institute of Ethnology at Münster and the two institutes of African languages, at Cologne and at Marburg/Frankfurt am Main. Starting with his first field study among the Bulsa of northern Ghana in 1966–1967, the Münster ethnologist Rüdiger Schott focused on the collection of folkloristic data. His monograph on this people, which appeared in 1970, dealt with poetry and folktales as a central element of their live patterns. These genres were also evaluated as particularly relevant source materials for the anthropology of religion (1990). The emphasis on *Erzählforschung* (research on folktales) has remained his particular interest ever since his further field studies in Burkina Faso, and it was transferred to some of his disciples working in the same regions of West Africa. Franz Kröger completed the collection of folklore among the Bulsa, while Sabine Steinbrich and Sabine Dinslage carried out their field research among the Lyela of Burkina Faso in the early 1980s. Research on folklore by these scholars are continuously published.

As professor of African languages at Marburg and since 1985 at Frankfurt, Herrmann Jungraithmayr wrote and initiated works on African folklore with a regional concentration on Chadic-speaking groups in Nigeria, Cameroon and Chad (e.g., 1981). His colleague Rudolf Leger dealt with proverbs as an educational and integrational factor in the society of the Piya and other groups of the Nigerian Middle Belt. Although focused on linguistic research, most German Africanists at the universities of Hamburg, Cologne, Frankfurt, Mainz, Bayreuth, and Leipzig contribute to topics of folklore. This particularly applies to Wilhelm Möhlig (Cologne), who initiated editions of articles on African oral literature (e.g., 1988) with contributions by scholars worldwide, and completed a lexicon on folklore research. Möhlig's colleague Thomas Geider specializes in the documentation and scientific analysis of African folktales. In 1990, he published a study on the position of the ogre, an outrageous giant monster in the beliefs of the Kenyan Pokomo. He then joined an interdisciplinary project in northeastern Nigeria and started new studies on aspects of Kanuri folklore.

Theory and Methodology

The question of whether any defining traits or trends regarding the choice of topics, methodology, and theories can be traced in German studies of African folklore deserves mention. Some pioneer works on the folkloristic genre in general had already been carried out since the end of the eighteenth century in Germany by scholars such as Johann Gottfried Herder and the brothers Jakob and Wilhelm Grimm. The methodological break through of the Finnish School in comparative folklore (especially Aarne 1908), mostly published in German, became remarkably popular in central Europe. It can be assumed that these conditions stimulated the interest of professional scholars in ethnology, philology and linguistics, as well as autodidacts among missionaries and colonial administrators, in drawing special attention to folkloristic documentation in Africa.

German scholars seemed to have been eager to know how, for example, Reineke, the clever fox, looked in the African context. However, most of the early collections by Frobenius, Meinhof, Prietze, and so on predominantly remained merely descriptive and rarely aimed at explicit methodological considerations or the construction of comprehensive theories. Frobenius categorization of African cultures on the base of certain *Weltbildern*, such as the Aethiopic and Hamitic concepts of the world, largely derived from folktales and myths, definitely failed to become an acceptable approach. Regarding the works of the first two phases of German research on African folklore, only Baumann's book on myths of creation has remained a useful analytical compilation of the respective phenomena.

Since the beginning of the twentieth century, German scholarship in ethnology and folklore studies has been dominated by a historically oriented focus. Functionalist interpretations have consequently never gained a noteworthy foothold in works on folktales and myths. Although the founders of psychoanalysis, Sigmund Freud and Carl Gustav Jung, established their theories in German-speaking countries, their impact on folklore studies in general remained limited and it can hardly be traced in works on Africa.

Early-twenty-first-century trends in the methodology and theory of German folklore research are more influenced by con-temporary English and American approaches, such as Ruth Finnegan's works or Stith Thompson's "Motif-Index of Folk-Literature," than by a critical reflection of these historically oriented above-mentioned functionalist and psychological works. French structuralism, mainly represented by Claude Lévi-Strauss and Luc de Heusch, has never influenced German folklorists working on Africa. Myths, for example, are predominantly interpreted according to the euhemeristic approach as reflections of historical facts, however remote in the past. This means that any mythologem, defined as a mythical narrative, a basic or recurrent theme of a myth, is conceived as a kind of historical source that can be subjected to a rationalistic interpretation. Consequently, the position of structuralist researchers, who tend to classify myths as patterns of imaginative concepts, cannot be of much relevance. Because of the dominating use of oral traditions, folktales, and myths as historical source materials, the anthropological school of symbolism of the 1970s did not gain an important position in German folkloristic studies either.

In critical analysis of African folktales, the studies of Thomas Geider (1990) on the Pokomo in Kenya and Sabine Steinbrich (1997) on the Lyela in Burkina Faso are presently the most substantial and comprehensive in German language. Geider, a linguist, places particular emphasis on problems of translation, aspects of linguistic analysis, and an extended and well-documented corpus of case studies. In Geider's discussions about various approaches of methodology, it is clear that he favors a view of folklore as a kind of ethnographic method, much like those employed by Michael Jackson, Thomas Beidelman, and Ruth Finnegan. For Steinbrich, a central goal of her analysis was to investigate the relations and borderlines of imagination and reality in folktales. She questions how far the folktales can be considered as a reflection of the real patterns of life, and thus authentic sources for the ethnohistorical reconstruction of a given culture. She refers to the epistemological problems involved and rightly advocates a thorough awareness of all cognitive aspects in anthropological fieldwork.

References

Aarne, Antti A. 1908. *Vergleichende Märchenforschungen.* Helsingfors: Druckereiderfinnischen Literaturgesellschaft.

Baumann, Hermann. 1936. *Schöpfung und Urzeit des Menschen im Mythus der afrikanischen Völker.* Berlin: Reimer (2nd ed. 1965).

Braukämper, Ulrich, and Tilahun Mishago. 1999. *Praise and Teasing: Narrative Songs of the Hadiyya in Southern Ethiopia.* Frankfurt on Main: Froebinius Institute.

Dammann, Ernst. 1942. Die Quellen der Swahili-Dichtung. *Der Islam* 26:250–68.

Frobenius, Leo. 1910. *Der schwarze Dekameron. Liebe, Witz und Heldentum in Inner-Afrika.* Berlin: Vita-Verlagshaus.

———. 1921–1928. *Atlantis. Volksmärchen und Volksdichtungen Afrikas.* 12 vols. Jena: Eugen Diederichs.

———. 1938. Das Archiv für Folkloristik. *Paideuma* 1, no. 1:1–18.

Geider, Thomas. 1990. *Die Figur des Oger in der traditionellen Literatur und Lebenswelt der Pokomo in Ost-Kenya.* 2 vols. Köln: Rüdiger Köppe Verlag.

Gutmann, Bruno. 1909. *Dichten und Denken der Dschagga-Neger. Beiträge zur ostafrikanischen Volkskunde.* Leipzig: Verlag der Evang. -Luth. Mission.

Jensen, Adolf, and Hellmut Wohlenberg. 1936. *Im Lande des Gada.* Stuttgart: Strecker und Schröder.

Jungraithmayr, Herrmann. 1981. *Märchen aus dem Tschad.* Düsseldorf, Köln: Eugen Diederichs.

Kohl-Larsen, Ludwig. 1963. *Das Kürbisungeheuer und die Ama'irmi Ostafrikanische Riesengeschichten*. Kassel: Erich Röth.

Kronenberg, Andreas and Waltraud. 1978. *Nubische Märchen*. Düsseldorf, Köln: Eugen Diederichs.

Leger, Rudolf. (in press). The Unity between World and Reality. In *Proverbs as an Educational and Integrational Factor in Piya Society (Northern Nigeria)*, ed. Yusuf Fadl Hasan. Proceedings of the 6th International Congress of African Studies, Khartoum, December 11–14, 1991. Khartoum: University Press.

Lippert, Julius. 1905. Haussa-Märchen. *Mitteilungen des Seminars für Orientalische Sprachen* 8, no. 33: 223–50.

Littmann, Enno et al. 1913. *Deutsche Aksum-Expedition (1905–1910)*. 4 vols. Berlin: Reimer.

Meinhof, Carl. 1921. *Afrikanische Märchen* (1911). Jena: Eugen Diederichs.

Mischlich, Adam. 1929. *Neue Märchen aus Afrika* (1911). Leipzig: R. Voigtländers.

Möhlig, Wilhelm J.G., Herrmann Jungraithmayr, and Josef F. Thiel, eds. 1988. *Die Oralliteratur in Afrika als Quelle zur Erforschung traditioneller Kulturen*. Berlin: Reimer.

Möhlig, Wilhelm J.G., and Herrmann Jungraithmayr, eds. 1998. *Lexikon der Erzählforschung in Afrika*. Köln: Rüdiger Köppe Verlag.

Prietze, Rudolf. 1904. *Haussa-Sprichwörter und Haussa-Lieder*. Kirchhain N.L.: Max Schmersow.

———. 1914. Bornulieder. *Mitteilungen des Seminars für Orientalische Sprachen* 17, no. 3:134–260.

Schild, Ulla. 1975. *Afrikanische Märchen*. Düsseldorf, Köln: Eugen Diedrichs.

Schott, Rüdiger. 1970. *Aus Leben und Dichtung eines westafrikanischen Bauernvolkes. Ergebnisse völkerkundlicher Forschungen bei den Bulsa in Nord-Ghana 1966/67*. Köln, Opladen: Westdeutscher Verlag.

———. 1990. *Afrikanische-Erzählungen als religionsethnologische Quellen—dargestellt am Beispiel der Bulsa in Nord-Ghana*. Köln, Opladen: Westdeutscher Verlag.

Sieber, J. 1921. *Märchen und Fabeln der Wute. Zeitschrift für Eingeborenen-Sprachen* 12:53–72:162–239.

Steinbrich, Sabine. 1982. *Gazelle und Büffelkuh. Frauen in den Erzählungen der Haussa und Fulbe*. Hohenschäftlarn: Renner.

———. 1997. *Imagination und Realität in westafrikanischen Erzählungen*. Köln: Rüdiger Köppe Verlag.

Velten, Carl. 1898. *Märchen und Erzählungen der Suaheli*. Stuttgart, Berlin: Spermann.

———. 1907. *Prosa und Poesie der Swahili*. Berlin: Selbstverlag.

Winkler, Hans Alexander. 1936. *Ägyptische Volkskunde*. Stuttgart: Kohlhammer.

Zwernemann, Jürgen. 1985. *Erzählungen aus der westafrikanischen Savanne*. Stuttgart: Franz Steiner.

ULRICH BRAUKÄMPER

See also **Frobenius**

GESTURES IN AFRICAN ORAL NARRATIVE

African oral narratives, such as folktales, urban myths, and personal experience stories, often come to life through a storyteller's vivid facial expressions, colorful reenactment, and dynamic gestures. These aspects of performance are generally included in the study of gesture, defined as any movement of the body that is part of the communication process. Although scholars of African oral narrative invariably comment on the dramatic nature of African storytelling, only a handful have studied the types and functions of gesture, let alone gesture terminology. Yet, even these few studies on hand gestures, as well as on bodily movement and posturing, provide valuable insight into what makes much African storytelling so appealing to listen to, or more aptly stated, to watch.

Hand Gestures

Hand gestures have a wide variety of functions in relation to oral communication, particularly to storytelling. Although they are often regarded as primarily mimed versions of spoken communication, gestures can imitate, amplify, substitute for, and even contradict speech. These functions are categorized by scholars of gesture in various ways. In their study of Swahili-language gestures in Kenya, Carol Eastman and Yaha Ali Omar distinguish gestures that are verbal-dependent from those that are independent of speech and those that are mimetic. Doreen Klassen's study of Shona storytelling in Zimbabwe, however, goes further in that it examines the varied ways in which gesture can be mimetic or imitative of an oral narrative.

Eastman and Omar's classification of gestures makes several significant distinctions. In separating those gestures that are verbal-dependent from those that are verbal-independent, they differentiate gestures that clarify the meaning of ambiguous words from gestures that are readily understood as a shorthand expression within a specific social or cultural context. Consequently, a gesture may help clarify a local idiom or a verbal expressive such as an ideophone. However, speakers may also use a commonly understood gesture, sometimes called an emblem, in place of an expression such as "Alright," "yes," "Nothing," or even, "How should I know?" Some scholars dismiss these gestures as agreed-upon by the culture as a whole, while others probe the significance of using a particular gesture within a specific social situation.

Klassen, like Eastman and Omar, considers gesture to have a mimetic dimension, but finds at least four ways in which gestures in Shona storytelling are imitative. Firstly, she separates those gestures that reenact an action from those that diagram it. Secondly, she examines those gestures that have an indirect relationship to whatever they are describing. Next, she discusses those aspects of gesture that reveal the space and time dimension of a narrative. And lastly, she reveals how gestures, and particularly bodily movements, make transparent the form and moral dimensions of a narrative.

Body Gestures

Gestures that reenact an action make visible a narrative in various ways. At times a narrator uses her body to portray the action of a character in a narrative, seemingly becoming the character. Consequently, the listener sees how a large animal ambles, how a hawk swoops down on its prey, how a thief disappears from sight, or how a tiny animal gives a threatening pursuer a beady-eyed look. At other times, a storyteller uses part of her body to diagram or map an object or action. Again, the listener sees an imaginary path through the woods, the outline of a woven basket, an arm serving as a tree trunk, or the shape of a straw protruding from a hidden drinking gourd. Rarely a storyteller offers an anthropomorphic gesture, one that appears to give human attributes to the action of an animal, and so the audience

Ambuya (Grandmother) Majuru (right) explains the use of gesture in Shona language storytelling to Nenite Zhakata at her home near Sadza, Zimbabwe. Photo © Doreen Helen Klassen.

observes how a woman would catch flies with her hand, although she is describing a crocodile snapping at them with his snout.

As an Illustration of Complex Concepts

However, gesture in storytelling is more complex than these forms of imitative and diagrammatic behavior. Gesture often has a less obvious way of relating to its narrative counterpart. Shona speakers, for example, may even gesture abstract concepts like *silence* or *darkness*. In the sentence, "Kunze kusviba kuti svii," (outside it is dark), the ideophone for *doing* and the word for *pitch black* may be accompanied by flattened palms moving in acircular motion at waist level and the speaker, when queried, may explain that the darkness of the sky is like the blackness one sees at the bottom of a deep, deep pool. This gesture, then, is metaphoric, well beyond the notion of mere imitation.

Gestures may also place a story in space in a visible, pictorial manner. As a storyteller begins to tell a story, she may divide up the gesture space in front of her to represent various settings, characters, and attitudes within the narrative. Home and likeable characters, for example, are often enacted near the body. Distant places and morally reprobate characters, on the other hand, may be restricted to a gesture space at arm's length from the storyteller, as well as more spatially separated from the audience. Additionally, attitudes and emotions may be enacted in contrasting spaces. Gestures enacted at shoulder level may express a different emotion, such as surprise, than those enacted at waist level.

Gestures help locate the story in space and time in other ways as well. Some gestures are deictic, that is, pointing or showing direction. Even these gestures convey the quality of movement in a particular direction. They may illustrate not only where a character is coming from or going to, but also the mood, the pacing, and sometimes the attitude or intent of the individual. Moreover, the form of pointing, whether using the lip, index finger, or full handlike the social and cultural context, also conveys the meaning of a deictic gesture (Creider 1986, 157). Time-related gestures, known as beats and enacted as a chopping motion, may be used in enumerating lists or suggesting the passing of time. Creider refers to these as "book-keeping" gestures

and notes than in East African languages, "usually the fingers of one hand are hooked over successively greater numbers of fingers on the other hand" (1986, 158). Storytellers may appear to freeze a motion in space, sometimes called a Butterworth, when they stumble over a word, resuming the motion only when the verbal portion of the story appears to catch up with the gestural aspect.

The foregoing discussion assumes that a gesture represents only the character whose actions are being narrated at the moment, but that is not always the case. Sometimes a gesture expresses the reaction of one character within the narrative to another character whose action is being described at the time. For example, when a grandmother, who has been using a motion low in the gesture-space to diagram the motion of a crocodile rustling through sand, suddenly raises her vocal pitch and her hand, we cannot assume that the crocodile has learned how to fly. Instead, the careful listener knows that the rising hand expresses the surprise of an onlooker in the story at seeing a crocodile coming toward her, perhaps at a socially inappropriate moment.

Timing of Gestures

Gestures, however, do not appear randomly in a well-told narrative. Gestures and other bodily movements are distributed in such a way that an observer can often sense the shape of sentences, paragraphs, and the rising action of a story simply by observing these movements. In African women's storytelling, as in many other cultures, gestures generally correspond with the most emphatic point of a phrase, sentence, or even a paragraph, though the nature of emphasis may vary from language to language (Creider 1978; 1986). And just as tone of voice and expressive language may become more intense as a story nears its climax, so do gestures often become more frequent and more dynamic. In fact, at times gestures replace spoken communication at the height of a conversation or dramatically told story (Eastman 1992; Klassen 1999).

When a gesture accompanies a verbal expressive, or ideophone, it differs from a gesture accompanying a sentence. This is not surprising as ideophones, sometimes referred to as *ideas in sound*, may convey the equivalent of a whole sentence or paragraph within a single word. Yet, the gesture will occur on the ideophone and reveal both the quality and the length of the action. Because ideophones use sound symbolism to express qualities such as relative speed, length of time, magnitude, and even expectedness versus surprise, gestures accompanying them also reflect these characteristics. For example, the Shona ideophone *mhi* (to swoop up) is monosyllabic and spoken with a high pitch, so its corresponding gesture entails a single swift upward movement enacted high in the gesture space. Creider too notes the co-occurrence of high tone and high-gestures among the Luo of Kenya (1986, 336). Similarly, the Shona ideophone *kanganda* (to walk like an important person) with its three syllables is gestured as a repeated motion. Because ideophones are idiomatic, and are often given relatively local interpretations, Shona grandmothers insist that gesture is essential to communicating their explicit meaning. In addition, according to linguist Daniel Kunene, among Sotho speakers, gestures not only accompany or replace ideophones, they may even lead to the coining of a new word (Kunene 1965, 37).

Bodily Posturing

It is not only hand gestures, but also bodily posturing, which is important in African storytelling. The seasoned storyteller knows how and whether or not to sit like a grandfather relating clan history, a grandmother retelling a folktale, or a young person testing his friends' gullibility with yet another contemporary legend. Bodily posturing often cues the listener concerning the type of story being told, its believability, and the level of artistry of the teller. However, one is seated not only physically, but also morally in many African cultures. Among the Shona of Zimbabwe, for example, being seated is an important metaphor for social relations. Consequently, when the Shona speak of people being seated *chechetere*, or all at one level, they are saying that there is social harmony, since no individual is seated above others.

As with the terms for being seated, those related to walking or standing also have both cultural and moral expectations. On the one hand, there are cultural expectations of how one walks, whether like a respected old man or a respectful young woman. On the other hand, how one walks, is also considered to be a moral issue, so it is not surprising that Shona speakers use numerous terms for walking which may describe the physical size, mood, social intentions, and moral integrity of a walker. In fact, the Shona have over 250 ideophones, to describe a walker. When these ideophones, which are invariably gestured, are used within a story, the listener sees not only a physical picture, but also a foreshadowing of the intentions and trustworthiness of the walker. Father Michael Hannan's *Standard Shona Dictionary* includes ideophones for walking such as *go go go* (wearing hobnailed boots), *mhemha mhemha* (slowly, with stoop, in search of lost object), and *pezhu pezhu* (girl or woman in short dress).

Unlike bodily posturing, other bodily movement, such as crossing one's legs while telling a story, could easily be dismissed as a storyteller making herself more comfortable, but analysis of videotaped storytelling performances suggests otherwise. Klassen's study of Shona women's *ngano* (storysong) performance describes how storytelling grandmothers cross and uncross their legs at the paragraph junctures within a story. This change of body positions also corresponds with a change of scene within a story, or with a shift of genre such as from narrating to singing. Consequently, these movements provide the audience with insight into how the narrator sees the form and the events of the story.

Terminology

A study of gesture, however, is not complete without an understanding of the language-specific terminology used for gestures. Scholars like Eastman and Omar, as well as Creider, refer to indigenous terminology, while Harold Olofson provides a detailed description of Nigerian Hausa language about facial expressions, gaze, and hand gestures, based on theatrical stage directions, as well as interviews. Similarly, J. H. Farquhar's mid-twentieth-century study of the African hand provides insight into Zimbabwean symbolism concerning the hand and its movements. These studies, while helpful, begin to explore gesture in just a few of Africa's many languages.

Gesture has traditionally been considered to be integral to effective communication in African oral narrative. Yet, in more formal contexts, particularly those influenced by Western education, gesture use is often more restrained. By comparison, informal storytelling sessions, whether in rural or urban contexts, are still saturated with gestures. However, more systematic study of gestures in African oral narrative is needed, particularly to supplement those studies that focus essentially on gesture in greeting and leave taking (Creider 1977). These studies should address more fully how gesture relates to gender, age, social class, social context, and the genre performed. And, as Creider notes, there is also a need for studies which compare how gesture use varies with the grammatical structures of various language groups (1986). It is hoped that recent interest in the anthropology of the body will foster further research on gesture in African narrative.

References

Creider, Chet A. 1997. Towards a Description of East African Gestures. *Sign Language Studies* 14:1–20.

———. 1978. Intonation, Tone Groups and Body Motion in Luo Conversation. *Anthropological Linguistics* 20:327–39

———. 1986. Interlanguage Comparisons in the Study of the Interactional Use of Gesture: Progress and Prospects. *Semiotica* 62, no. 1 and 2:147–63.

Eastman, Carol M. 1992. Swahili Interjections: Blurring Language-Use/Gesture-Use Boundaries. *Journal of Pragmatics: An Interdisciplinary Monthly of Language Studies* 18, no. 2 and 3: 273–87.

Eastman, Carol M., and Yahya Ali Omar. 1985. Swahili gestures: Comments (*vielezi*) and exclamations (*viingizi*). *Studies in African Linguistics* 48, no. 2:321–32.

Farquhar, J. H. 1948. The African Hand. *NADA: The Southern Rhodesia Native Affairs Department Annual* 25:25–8.

Klassen, Doreen Helen. 1999. "You Can't Have Silence with Your Palms Up": Ideophones, Gesture, and Iconicity in Zimbabwean Shona Women's *ngano* (Storysong) Performance. Ph.D. dissertation, Indiana University.

Kunene, Daniel P. 1965. The Ideophone in Southern Sotho. *Journal of African Languages* 4, no. 1:19–39.

Olofson, Harold. 1974. Hausa Language about Gestures. *Anthropological Linguistics* 16:25–39.

DOREEN HELEN KLASSEN

See also **Call-and-Response in African Narrating; Dialogic Performances; Ideophones; Performance in Africa**

GHANA (REPUBLIC OF GHANA)

Located on the coast of West Africa, Ghana is a country of nearly 20 million people. The nation, neighbored by Cote D'Ivoire, Burkina Faso, and Togo, has a climate that ranges from tropical on the coast to semiarid in the north. Forty-four percent of Ghana's people are Akan, 16 percent Moshi-Dagomba, 13 percent Ewe, 8 percent Ga, and 19 percent are of various other ethnic groups. The major languages spoken in the country are English, Akan (including Fanti, Asante, and Twi), Ewe, Ga, and Hausa. Thirty-eight percent of the people practice traditional indigenous religions, 30 percent are Muslim, 24 percent are Christian, and 8 percent practice various other religions. Accra, a city of over 965,000, is the nation's capital.

The Ashanti Federation, centered in Kumasi, became increasingly powerful in the nineteenth century, but after several hard fought battles was subdued by the English in 1874. Reflecting its ancient source of wealth, this English colony was known as the Gold Coast; after independence it was renamed Ghana after the first of the ancient Western Sudanese kingdoms. On March 6, 1957, Ghana gained its independence from Britain after fifty-six years of colonial rule. Kwame Nkrumah not only led the country to independence, but became an important spokesperson for all Africans as he campaigned against European colonialism and exploitation. In the years following independence, Ghana suffered severe economic and political decline. After several decades of military coups and problematic civil governments, both the nation's government and economy steadily improved in the late twentieth century.

The country's natural resources include gold, diamonds, bauxite, manganese, fish, timber, and oil. Agricultural production revolves around cocoa (one of the world's largest producers), coconuts, coffee, subsistence crops, and rubber, while principle industries include mining, lumber, light manufacturing, fishing, and aluminum. Ghana's Akosombo Dam on the Volta river was one of the first major development schemes in Africa, but has proved ineffective in the long run. Located just outside Accra is the University of Ghana, one of the finest universities in Africa. With women constituting 51 percent of the labor force, Ghana has one of the highest ratios of gender parity in the workforce in the world.

The territory now called Ghana was the site of much of the European's West African slave trade. Of the old slave forts, Cape Coast and Elmina have become important historical sites and especially visitors of African ancestry from the United States visit the forts and their historical displays. In fact, tourism has become an increasingly important source of income.

E. T. Mensah, a Ghanaian musician, is responsible for creating the musical tradition of Highlife. In the 1930s, Mensah's band, The Tempos, blended the musical style of big-band jazz with indigenous musical traditions and created the popular music of Highlife, which was quickly popularized throughout Africa and the world. The University of Legon's School of the Performing Arts has also contributed to the world of music, dance, and drama through educating students in the Ghanaian artistic tradition since 1943.

JENNIFER JOYCE

GIKUYU

See **Birth and Death Rituals among the Gikuyu**

GOSSIP AND RUMOR

As "discreet indiscretion" (Bergmann 1993), gossip is a moral discourse about the behavior, social situation, and character of absent others; it is talk about someone with someone else. Gossip is a "form of sociable interaction which depends upon the strategic management of information through the creation of others as 'moral characters' in talk" (Yerkovich 1977). As a speech act, gossip allows people the possibility to express their community's values and beliefs on ideal, proper, and moral behavior and also, with considerable force and intention, to influence proper behavior without risking direct confrontation. Thus, as scandal, gossip

functions as a system that asserts collective norms as well as creating and maintaining strong, communal bonds because the process of gossiping creates and strengthens social ties of intimacy (see Gluckman 1963). For an individual, knowing the latest gossip increases their status, reputation, and social standing within a social network since they claim special access to knowledge and the privilege to speak it. Groups and individuals can use gossip as a political strategy to advance their own interests and also to persuade others. Therefore, as text and as a social activity, there are three relationships at play when people gossip: between the gossips and the subject of the gossip, between the gossips and their community; and the personal relationship between the gossips.

Rasmussen's (1991) study of gossip among the Tuareg of Niger points to the important role of gossip in conflict management. Gossip allows for the expression of familial, social, and political discord indirectly and euphemistically. For the Tuareg, gossip articulates alternative and contradictory interpretations of social experience and social ties. The different viewpoints expressed in gossip provides an effective discourse between individual strategy and collective rules (Rasmussen 1991).

Like gossip, rumor allows people to speak to power indirectly and anonymously. Rumor is an expression of belief that arises in ambiguous situations where there is little or no reliable information on events that are important to a community. Sociologist Tamotsu Shibutani (1966, 32) argues that rumors are "the cooperative improvisation of interpretations." He further proposes that rumor is "a recurrent form of communication though which [people] caught together in an ambiguous situation attempt to construct a meaningful interpretation of it by pooling their intellectual resources." This definition highlights several key factors. First, rumor is recurrent and when rumors are told and retold, people make alterations—they embellish, exaggerate, or distort. Second, rumor is not a product of individual creation which then spreads; it is a collaborative process without a defined author. And third, the fewer the facts or reliable or trustworthy information available, the greater the role of the group's unconscious, fears, and anxieties in their interpretation of events.

This process of oral transmission allows for elements from myth, folklore, oral history, witchcraft, sorcery, and worldview to become part of the rumor text. For example, the work of Peter Geschiere (1997) in Cameroon suggests that rumors of the occult are often intertwined with local and national politics. Rumors of witchcraft and sorcery often signal political and economic change or turmoil and are often attempts of people to gain control over the disruption such changes bring. When people's insecurities and apprehension over local and national politics grow, so do rumors claiming that politicians use sorcery and witchcraft to accumulate power and wealth. Geschiere argues that there is a thin line between discourses of power and discourses of the occult.

In another example, Luise White (2000) documents rumors of bloodsuckers in colonial East and Central Africa. These persistent and powerful rumors talk of colonial employees (firemen, police, surveyors, game wardens) who captured Africans, killed them and took their blood. In colonial Tanzania, rumors described how government agents seized people, hung them upside down, and drained their blood. Similarly, Kampala police were accused of kidnapping residents and throwing them into pits until their blood was drained. And in Nairobi and Mombasa, members of fire brigades were rumored to capture Africans and draw their blood. These "vampire men" used Western technology and tools, including automobiles, fire stations, black overalls, buckets, and syringes, to accomplish their nefarious deeds. White argues that these rumors represent symbolically the conflicts and problems that are associated with the new economic order imposed by colonial administrations. No other idea could articulate the magnitude of the conflict and complications that such changes brought to personal definitions of work and of the self.

Brad Weiss' ethnography of the Haya of Tanzania shows that rumors of blood-stealing and selling continue in contemporary East Africa. The Haya use these rumors to explain rapid accumulation of wealth; for example, when a member of the community builds a new house, it is rumored that he acquired the money by selling stolen blood. These rumors suggest that the pursuit of wealth and power is always socially problematic. Furthermore, these rumors express "connections between bodies and commodities, semantic value and economic transactions, rural livelihoods and urban travels, as well as local 'experience' and global 'events' " (Weiss 1996, 219). However, the presence of fantastical creatures and situations, such as blood-sucking vampires or genital-stealing sorcerers in Nigeria, should not obscure the fact that rumors are shaped by the real, lived experiences of people caught in social, political, and economic events that are often beyond their control. Rumor is one tactic people use to try to gain some sense of control over these events.

In Africa, news, rumor, and gossip circulate through unofficial oral channels of communication that have been labeled *radio trottoir* or "pavement radio" (Ellis 1989): the modern, urban version of the "bush telegraph." Stephen Ellis defines pavement radio as "the popular and unofficial discussion of current affairs in Africa, particularly in towns. . . . [it] thrives on scandal in the sense of malicious news, and rarely has anything good to say about any prominent persons or politician" (1989, 321–22). Pavement radio also reports alternative news to the often censored, ignored, and uninformative national television, print, and radio media. According to Ellis (1989), pavement radio operates in an oral culture where the spoken word carries equal, if not more, weight than the written word. Pavement radio is a democratic media—it is anonymous and it carries information only as long the people find the content interesting and relevant. Therefore, over time and space, pavement radio helps to form a popular consciousness. Spreading malicious gossip and rumors about unscrupulous politicians through pavement radio, Ellis suggests is a tactic of self-defense for the poor and the powerless because it helps people to contain the behavior of politicians who are often unconstrained by law.

The study of gossip and rumor is essential to an understanding of the intimate lives, fears, experiences, and concerns of Africans trying to make sense of their world.

References

Bergmann, Jorg. 1993. *Discreet Indiscretions: The Social Organization of Gossip.* New York: Aldine.

Ellis, Stephen. 1989. Tuning in to Pavement Radio. *African Affairs* 88:321–30.

Geschiere, Peter. 1997. *The Modernity of Witchcraft: Politics and the Occult in Postcolonial Africa.* Charlottesville and London: University of Virginia Press.

Gluckman, Max. 1963. Gossip and Scandal. *Current Anthropology* 4, no. 3:307–16.

Rasmussen, Susan J. 1991. Modes of Persuasion: Gossip, Song, and Divination in Tuareg Conflict Resolution. *Anthropological Quarterly* 64, no. 1:30–47.

Shibutani, Tamotsu. 1966. *Improvised News: A Sociological Study of Rumor.* Indianapolis, Ind: Bobbs-Merrill.

Weiss, Brad. 1996. *The Making and Unmaking of the Haya Lived World.* Durham and London: Duke University Press.

White, Luise. 2000. *Speaking with Vampires: Rumor and History in Colonial Africa.* Berkeley and London: University of California Press.

Yerkovich, Sally. 1977. Gossiping as a Way of Speaking. *Journal of Communication* 27:192–96.

DAVID A. SAMPER

See also **Insults and Ribald Language, Personal Narratives**

GOURDS: THEIR USES AND DECORATION

The hollowed-out gourd is used as a container throughout sub-Saharan Africa. As the fruit of one of the continent's earliest cultivated plants, the gourd or calabash, as it is commonly if imprecisely called, has long been exploited and selectively adapted by both nomadic and sedentary peoples. It should be noted that *gourd* is the botanically correct term for the fruit of the flowering plant (*Lagenaria siceraria*) widely cultivated in Africa. *Calabash*, on the other hand, is the proper name for the fruit of a tropical American tree (*Crescentia cujete*). Because the latter is recognized in common usage, it will still be used interchangeably with *gourd*.

The remarkable number of shapes and sizes in which it grows has made it suitable for a host of purposes ranging from the obvious to the ingenious. Simply opened and cleaned, gourds are used for storage or for serving food and drink. In combination with other materials, they become musical instruments, smoking pipes, fishing floats, or ritual regalia. The gourd's high versatility is essentially due to its inherent properties: it is light, durable, portable, tractable, and watertight. The medium also lends itself to a rich and varied array of decorative enhancements—ranging from surface dyes and patinas and complex patterns of incised or burned designs to the addition of elements as basic as fiber or as precious as beads and cowries.

Decoration

The most elaborate traditions of gourd decoration are confined to particular areas of the African continent. Of them, northeastern Nigeria can be singled out as a zone of outstanding achievement, diversity, and inventiveness. Some peoples of this region who decorate calabash containers, such as the Fulani, Kanuri, and Hausa, are well known. Other groups are less familiar, yet their work has received some attention in the literature—the Ga'anda, Tera, and Yungur, among others (see Berns 1985, 1986). In this region, gourds, both decorated and undecorated, are the focus of a remarkable range of domestic, social, and ritual activities.

Gourds, along with other major food crops, are usually cultivated on farms during the rainy season or they may be planted directly within the compound where they are encouraged to trail over fences and the thatched roofs of houses. The gourd plant, a climbing annual with very rapid growth, ripens its fruit between four and six months after planting.

Gourds are grown in four basic shapes in northeastern Nigeria and elsewhere: globular, flattened-globular, tubular, and bottle shaped. Within these categories, gourds of many sizes and contours have been developed, and their degree of diversification is a credit to the skills of the African cultivator. The Hausa, for example, cultivate at least four spherical gourds of varying diameters—the smallest ones are made into ink wells (*kurtun tawada*) while the largest ones (*gora*) are fitted with handles and used as fishing floats. Contours reflect similar botanical adaptations, particularly in bottle gourds, whose profiles vary considerably.

Usually picked when they reach full maturity, gourds may be harvested when unripe if a particular size or shape is desired. The spongy, fibrous contents are first removed either by leaving the gourd in the sun until the pulp dries and shrivels or by soaking the fruit in water until the pith rots. It is then cut open, depitted, and scraped clean. Where the gourd is opened

Yungur men playing *dimkedims* during Wora, Dirma, November 1981. Photo © Marla C. Berns.

determines the shape of the resulting container and the ways it can be used. The shell is left to dry until it has thoroughly hardened, which may take from one to two months. Then it is ready for decoration or for use.

Regardless of shape, all gourds are amenable to decoration, having a hard yellow shell a few millimeters thick, protected by a green outer skin usually removed before decoration and a softer white underlayer that varies in thickness. The contrasting color and porosity of the gourd surface have influenced the evolution of its decoration. The options for artistic embellishment are many. Beyond the imposition of design and pattern, the gourd lends itself well to changes in color, texture, and relief. Even if no ornamentation is applied, the surface changes with time.

As is true over most of Africa, northeastern Nigerian peoples decorate gourds in six different ways: pyro-engraving, pressure-engraving, carving (scraping), painting, dyeing, and addition of decorative materials. Within the advantages and limitations of particular processes, a remarkably wide range of variations has developed. It should also be understood that choices made by individual groups are based on more than just aesthetic criteria. Choices of technique and design have been conditioned by various sociohistorical realities. Although gourd decoration is primarily a woman's occupation, men also do this work, as is true among the Hausa.

Pyro-engraving, which involves burning lines into the surface of the gourd with a hot metal blade, is the most widely used and versatile technique. In pressure-engraving, the second most common, a sharp point is dragged across the gourd surface with considerable force. Because so little surface material is removed, the engraved design is filled with a blackening agent to allow it to stand out crisply against the unmarked ground.

Although carving and painting are less frequently used, a large variety of decorative materials can be added to the surface of the gourd, like leather, beads, basketry, or plaited raffia. Prestigious materials like glass beads (especially in the Cameroon grasslands), cowrie shells, and metal wire (including brass, copper, and steel, especially in South Africa) are also applied.

Utility

Gourd containers are essential items of household equipment. Although they are used primarily by women as utensils and

Waja women using gourd bonnets to shield their babies from the sun when going to a well to fetch water, Talasse, February 1982. Photo © Marla C. Berns.

receptacles for food and drink, men also own bottle gourds carried as canteens. Moslem men carry gourd flasks for religious ablutions. Although not seen often in northern Nigeria, smoking pipes made from bottle-shaped gourds are popular across the continent, particularly in the eastern and central regions.

The gourd's many domestic uses, and the care with which the gourd is decorated, enhance its ability to communicate about social as well as economic values. Among many groups in northeastern Nigeria, collections of decorated gourds are an essential part of bridewealth payments or dowries. Marriage customs often dictate that a bride take to her new husband as many as (and often more than) a hundred decorated gourd containers, ranging in size from large bowls to small cups.

The importance of a woman's gourd collection in establishing social and economic status is nowhere clearer than among the pastoral Fulani. A young girl sets up an independent household and gains full marital status two or two and a half years after the birth of her first child. Her formal entry into her husband's homestead is marked by two complementary ceremonies, both called *bangtal*, that publicly establish the economic positions of each partner. At the first, the man is given a herd, symbol of his economic independence. At the second, the girl is raised to the status of wife and mother through the formal presentation of household items as gifts, including gourds, mats, cloth, and a bed, which are then exhibited. The large number of milk gourds in her dowry mark a woman's right to milk her husband's herds. Whenever a new camp is made in the transhumant cycle, the Fulani wife displays her gourd collection; the size of her gourd collection increases with each addition to her household. It is clear that among the pastoral Fulani a woman's prestige is intimately tied to her reproductive powers, that is, her ability to add to the workforce.

The visual and symbolic associations of women with gourd containers also extend to festival contexts. Many groups in this region organize elaborate communal gatherings to celebrate life cycle transitions. As already noted, a new bride's collection of gourds is often exhibited once she makes the final transition to the status of married woman. Additionally, young women who participate in marriage festivities often carry a decorated gourd in one hand as a part of the costume that distinguishes the occasion.

The significance of women as food preparers is probably pivotal to the gourd decoration complex, and it may be that the ornamented container, which presents the end product of this effort, is a meaningful emblem of this role. Men depend on women for their meals and for the beer that households must contribute to various social and ceremonial activities. Communal beer drinking is another context, ranging from the purely social to the highly sacred, where gourd containers figure prominently. In most areas, beer made from guinea corn or millet is always imbibed in a plain or a decorated calabash bowl, often sealed on the inside with a red or black pigment. Like palm wine in southern Nigeria, beer is an important social lubricant, and has also long served as a crucial nutritional supplement.

Although decorated gourds usually appear in secular contexts where beer is consumed, there is a strong prohibition against their use during ritual activities or sacrificial libations, when sharing beer is a primary means of cementing ties with powerful spirit forces. This may be because the exclusion of women from such sacred contexts is extended to the objects made by their

hands and with which they are so intimately associated. In fact, among the Ga'anda of northeast Nigeria, the same proscription applies to the food bowls used regularly by ritual priests: they may never eat from the decorated containers a wife typically uses for serving her husband's meals.

There is another context in which gourds play a crucial ancillary role: divination. A number of groups in the region use calabash bowls as divining instruments. Among the Yungur, the diviner (*sife*) uses a plain gourd sealed with red ochre for holding water (into which various activating ingredients have been introduced) as a means of calling forth spirits. Essentially the *sife* asks a series of yes or no questions that are answered by the position of a small gazelle horn dropped into the water. A vertical position is affirmative, and a horizontal position is negative.

The use of gourds in divination may relate to the symbolic meanings that have been associated with these containers. For example, among the Yungur, a plain gourd "has the power to restore the status quo whenever the social situation has been, or is about to be, dangerously disturbed" (Chappel 1977, 18). Illness or accusations of "witchcraft" certainly represent such disturbances and thus make gourds appropriate symbolic as well as instrumental components of divination. Yungur informants claim that two disputing villages could arrange a truce if a "white" (i.e., plain) gourd was overturned at the crossroads between them. Placing a gourd between two disputants "cools" them so that their anger will be dispelled.

Not surprisingly, gourds are prominent vehicles for symbolic verbal expression. The Hausa identify the universe as a spherical gourd, its halves representing the sky and the earth, and the rims, where they join being the horizon. The Fulani compare a gourd filled with smaller gourds to "the sky filled with stars" or even "Allah and the stars" (Chappel 1977, 22). In addition to these cosmological analogies, gourds commonly figure in proverbs and riddles. Some Hausa examples include "A rarrabe da d'an duma da d'an kabewa" (One will distinguish between the bitter gourd and the sweet), that is, "We shall be able to distinguish between true men and false" (C. E. J. Whitting 1940, 12); "Kowace k'warya tan da murfinsa" (Every gourd has its lid [matching half]) or "Everyone has the chance to decide what suits him and what does not"; "K'warya ta bi k'warya, in ta bi akushi, sai ta fashe" (A gourd follows a gourd; if it follows a wooden food bowl, then it will break) or "Don't tackle what is beyond you" (R. C. Abraham 1962, 593–94). For the Hausa, spicing one's speech with aphorisms, parables, and idioms, classified together as proverbs (*karin magana*), is a popular way to project mastery of language (Skinner 1968, 79).

Gourds, both decorated and undecorated, figure in various public festival contexts not only as ornaments and symbolic attributes but also as musical instruments. During sacred or ceremonial events, gourd instruments can create distinctive tonal voices that link the community to the forces regulating its survival. A striking example is the large drum (*dimkedim*) played during the Wora funeral celebration held by the Yungur. Two large globular gourds, joined together with rope covered in dung, create a lower resonating chamber and are attached to a hollow wooden cylinder that is fitted with a head of antelope (duiker) skin. Only at such funerals are three of these spectacular drums played together by male members of one royal lineage.

The preceding examples emphasize the importance of gourd instruments in specific ritual contexts, where their ownership and performance are often the exclusive prerogative of special families. Calabashes also are used to make a variety of instruments played by professional musicians in northern Nigeria, as well as across the continent. The gourd has long been adapted to this purpose because of its versatility as a resonating chamber that can be struck, blown into, or scraped. The Hausa, who consider musicianship a traditional craft, make a great variety of instruments from calabashes of different shapes and sizes. For example, hemispherical bowls can be overturned and struck with the fingers (with or without rings thereon) or with sticks; bottle gourds can be filled with stones and used as rattles; globular gourds, which are 30 to 70 centimeters in diameter, are made into kettle drums; and five varieties of spike-bowl lutes, with one or two strings plucked or played with a bow, are made with calabash sound boxes over which skin has been stretched. Perhaps the most famous gourd instrument is the Kora, a fretless harp-lute instrument played mostly by Mande-speaking peoples of West Africa (in Gambia, Mali, and Guinea). The sound box is a large hemispherical gourd and twenty-one strings are attached to a long wooden neck.

The wide range of uses to which gourds have been put help explain why the gourd has become the object of such intense artistic elaboration, both in northeastern Nigeria and virtually across the continent. The time and labor invested in its decoration enhance the economic and social implications of its cultivation and use. Because their appearance is enhanced, decorated gourds also may be regarded as better to use. Moreover, it may be because they satisfy an essential material need that their decoration is socially valued. The ability to decorate them well gives women, and some men, a special avenue for achieving recognition and prestige.

References

Ames, D. W., and A. V. King. 1971. *Glossary of Hausa Music and Its Social Contexts*. Evanston: Northwestern University Press.

Beckwith, C., and M. van Offelen. 1983. *Nomads of Niger*. New York: Abrams.

Berns, M. C. 1985. Decorated Gourds of Northeastern Nigeria. *African Arts* 19, no. 1:28–45.

Berns, M., and B. Rubin Hudson. 1986. *The Essential Gourd: Art and History in Northeastern Nigeria*. Museum of Cultural History, Los Angeles.

Chappel, T. J. H. 1977. *Decorated Gourds in Northeastern Nigeria*. London: Ethnographica.

Rubin, B. 1970. Calabash Decoration in North East State, Nigeria. *African Arts* 4, no. 1:20–5.

Sieber, R. 1980. *African Furniture and Household Objects*. Bloomington: Indiana University Press.

MARLA C. BERNS

See also **Ceramics; Musical Instruments: Focus on Nambia; West Africa: Overview**

GOVERNMENT POLICIES TOWARD FOLKLORE

Official government attitudes toward folklore in Africa have been complex and often contradictory. African state officials and intellectuals have discussed and argued the meanings of terms like *authenticity, tradition, progress, folklore,* and *culture* from the moment of their respective nation's independence. In order to understand African states' policies toward folklore and culture, it must be remembered that such policies have almost always been linked to larger political goals.

In many African states, the term *folklore* immediately signals a particular understanding of the relation between history and culture. In this idealized model, African history is split into three stages. The first is a precolonial period, during which African peoples practiced their religions, livelihoods, musics, and arts autonomously. The second is the colonial period, culminating with the political domination of the continent from the late nineteenth century through the second half of the twentieth century. During this period, African culture is presented as being in decline, suppressed by colonial regimes that also lured urbanized and European-educated African elites with a tainted and inauthentic (European) set of aesthetic ideals in music, theater, and art. In the third and final stage, independent African nations needed to organize folkloric and cultural policies to recuperate the vitality of precolonial artistic expression that could aid in the process of economic and cultural development. There are a number of paradoxes implicit in this paradigm that become clearer through examination of some examples.

The Republic of Guinea gained independence from France in October of 1958, while France's other West African colonies chose to remain affiliated with the European nation. Embarking on an ambitious program of pan-Africanist Marxism, Guinea rejected any kind of economic, military, or cultural aid that had political strings attached. In this way Guinea distanced itself from communist and capitalist countries, while promoting a policy of economic, cultural, and psychological self-sufficiency. A great part of this policy relied on the support of two resources: the "inexhaustible" strength of "authentic" African tradition, and the equally infinite enthusiasm and energy of Guinean youth. This, however, presented a contradiction because all the ethnicities that populated Guinea gave great power and privilege to elders. This was true in precolonial- as well as colonial-era social organizations.

The government responded to this paradox by effectively siding with the younger generation, but rhetorically honoring the ideal of tradition. Thus traditional culture was forcibly stripped of the secrecy and exclusivity that conferred power upon the elders who controlled it, but was simultaneously turned into popular folklore. During the 1959–1962 "Demystification Program," soldiers and ethnologists moved from village to village, especially in the coastal and southeastern forest regions of the country. Finding progressive (usually young and Western educated) people to help them, they uncovered each village's cache of ritual objects, including masks and carved figures. They exposed them to noninitiates (which was supposed to bring infertility, death, and other disasters down on the community), and often burned the objects in a bonfire in the center of the village. Their goal was to show that life would go on, and thus "demystify" these groups of supposedly backward and superstitious people, and throw them into the progressive, socialist new order.

Ironically, the cultural experts who accompanied the soldiers and bureaucrats had another goal. They saved the most accomplished and well-made masks and brought them to the National Museum for display. They announced to villages that their "superstitious" religious practices were now prohibited, but asked them to perform religious dances and music in the village one last time so that the best performers could be recruited into the national ballet (*Les Ballets Africains*) or orchestra. Soon people found numerous aspects of their "traditional" life—many of which had been of little interest to the colonial regime—simultaneously outlawed and represented to them as folklore.

Another aspect of the uses of folklore was epitomized by Mobutu Sese Seko's regime in 1970s Zaire. Here, the emphasis was on authenticity. In the early 1970s, as Mobutu changed the names of the country, the cities, the streets, and even the citizens from inauthentic European to authentically African ones, he also supported the development of "*spectacles d'animation politique*" (political mobilization spectacles) throughout the country. Although his government was receiving billions of dollars from European and American governments to stand as an anticommunist bulwark against such socialist neighbors as Angola, Tanzania, and Zambia, Mobutu borrowed the revolutionary and anti-imperialist rhetoric of socialist nations, using large-scale cultural manifestations to raise popular morale and consciousness. As in Guinea, the message transmitted was ambiguous. Clearly, state support of popular theater, dance, and music worked to counteract the effects of the denigrating and condescending attitude that had been expressed toward many of these genres by colonial governments and officials. It was clear, however, to most people that these folkloric manifestations had a "bread and circus" aspect temporarily distracting the populace from political and economic problems that Mobutu's government was doing little to solve.

A further aspect of such state-sponsored folkloric culture is the phenomenon of the invention of tradition. A case in point is Mobutu's "authenticity" period costume. A European-style hat made of leopard skin (a traditional symbol of chiefly power throughout much of Africa) and a wooden cane (typical of airport tourist art, but again referring to the staffs indicating chiefly or ritual power common to much of Central Africa) became the key symbols of Mobutu's traditionlike claim to sovereignty. Some have characterized such folkloric regalia and performances as *Afrokitsch*, while others have embraced them because of their reference to a glorious precolonial African past. In either case, the judgments, like various African states' choices to support these forms of culture, have been more often based on political than aesthetic considerations.

References:

Botombele, Bokonaa Ekanua. 1975. *Politique culturellel en Republique du Zaire*. Paris: UNESCO.

Cosentino, Donald, 1991. Afrokitsch. In *Africa Explores: 20th Century African Art*, ed. Susan Vogel. New York: Prestel.

Duvignaud, Jean. 1976. Festivals: A Sociological Approach. *Culture*. 3, no. 1:13–25.

Kapalanga, Gazungil Sang'Amin. 1989. *Les spectacles d'animation politique en Republique du Zaire*. Louvain: édition des Cahiers théâtre Louvain.

Ministry of Culture, People's Revolutionary Republic of Guinea. 1979. *Cultural Policies*. Paris: UNESCO.

Morrisseau, Leroy. 1964. Le theatre dans la revolution africaine, *Presence Africaine* 52.

MICHAEL MCGOVERN

See also **Tourism and Tourist Arts**

GREETINGS: A CASE STUDY FROM THE KEREBE

The Abakerebe live on a small island called Bukerebe in Lake Victoria, not far from the northern Tanzanian town of Mwanza. The Kerebe are basically agriculturalists and fishermen. Their staple foods are cassava meal, sweet potatoes, and bananas; their cash crops are cotton and rice. The island is very fertile and many kinds of fruits grow on it, such as oranges, bananas, pineapples, mangoes and papayas. Every homestead has at least ten to fifteen orange trees. The harvesting season gives some people a considerable and dependable income. The fishing industry has also made a number of people reasonably rich from sales of Nile perch and *dagaa*. The island is the breadbasket of Mwanza town. Small as it is, the island has nevertheless produced a significant percentage of Tanzania's intellectuals and literary artists. The Kerebe are also well known for their traditions, especially in the area of dances, oral traditions and epic narrations.

The inhabitants of this island and other islands surrounding it have a complex system of formal greetings which is a bit perplexing to those who do not speak the language. Like in other Bantu-speaking people, greetings among the Kerebe define kinship and good neighborliness. They also delineate character and draw lines of relationships. Greetings are a manifestation of humanness and respect for other people, friends, and strangers. *To visit* and *to greet* are words represented by the same word, *kubwacha*. A visit (greeting) shows how much a relative values a relationship and the way he or she wants it to continue. It is the highest manifestation of love and solidarity amid fears of life and the struggle for survival.

Greetings as a Definition of Being

Greeting among the Kerebe is greatly phenomenological—this is perhaps what is unique and interesting about it. The whole formality of greeting places emphasis on being. A greeting is an existential affirmation of being in time. It is an assurance that one still has another day to live or at least a minute. A greeting is therefore always a plodding into the nuances of the temporality of being. The Kerebe form of greeting also reveals that their concept of life is child centered; a phenomenon that presupposes that the horizon of the future is what defines the present. Greetings among the Kerebe take four variables into consideration: time, gender, age and relationship. All four variables must be considered before a greeting is uttered. To the Kerebe it comes naturally, though contemplation may take place a few meters before meeting the approaching person.

The general word for the infinitive *to greet* is *kubwacha*; but when the variables of time and age are considered, other verbs in causative form come into the picture. The verb "*to greet*" can therefore be defined as follows:

Kubwachaa: This word is used as *to greet* from 5 A.M. to 6 P.M. It means to see someone after darkness has evaporated. It can be used without considering the variable of age. As a general word it can also cross the boundaries of time.

Kulyaguzy: The word is used as *to greet* from 6 P.M. to 5 A.M. It means to see someone after sunset. It can also be used without considering age, but only during the time specified above. The two verbs above are derived from other verbs: *kucha* (to appear), which means "the appearance of light and the end of the night" (*obwire*) or darkness, and *kugwa*, which means "to fall."

Kusuzya: The word means to great someone of equal age (within one year). It is derived from another verb, *kusula*, which means "to see someone," usually with a purpose of determining the person's health.

Kulolosya: This word means "to greet someone who is younger by at least two years"—a period which seems to have been the normal spacing time between births among the Kerebe. The word is derived from the verb *kulola*, which means "to see," usually "to see first;" but in this case there is an element of keeping watch over someone or something. The word implies that the older person was told by parents to watch over the younger regardless of gender because the older saw the world first.

Kuchatatya: This means to great someone who is very young, usually a person who, age-wise, one could have fathered, regardless of gender. The word is a combination of two words: *Kucha* (verb) and *tata* (noun). The word *tata* means "father," but due to the belief that the "child is the father of man" (Soyinka 1976; Tempels, 1956) the word *tata* also means "son."

Kulamya: This is a special verb which is only used as *to greet* with reference to a chief (*omukama*). Kulamya means "to greet a chief." The word is derived from the verb Kulama! which means "to live long. Kulamya therefore means to wish a chief long life.

In Chart 1 are simplified charts of greetings according to age, time and gender. The charts given show greetings between man and man, woman and woman, and between man and woman, depending on who starts the greeting formality.

The response "Lelota" comes from the verb *lala* (to sleep). The greeting "Lelota" is a short form of "Olele ota," which means "How have you slept?" The response, "Shibilota!" is derived from the verb *kusiba*, meaning "to spend the afternoon." It also means "to fast." A person can also say "Sibilota!" a short form of "Osi-bile ota," which translates "How have you spent the afternoon?" The word *lyagwasugu* means "Yes, the sun has fallen (set)." The word *sugu* is a polite word for "yes" with the connotation of "yes, your honor." The word *kampile* is an initial word prefixed before giving thanks. It comes from the verb *kuha* (to give). It is possibly a short form of "akompele" which means "that which you have given to me!" *Kampile* is also a word which connotes

high respect. "Bwachatata" means "it (the sun) has risen, my son."

"*Lyagwatata*" means "it has fallen (set), my son." The word *sula* is a short form of the greeting "Nkusula," which means "I am visiting you to know your health," the connotation being "how is your health?" It must be emphasized at this point that although some people use the long form to retrieve the original meaning, the words have become formulaic and serve as greetings. In this respect if a person says "*Sula!*", he means "I am greeting you as a younger person in the morning," and if he says "*Sibilota*" he means "I am greeting you as an elder person in the morning."

Some people prefer to use the evening greeting from 4 P.M., others start using it around 6 P.M. when the sun is actually beginning to set. The morning greeting usually begins after the second cockcrow which in Bukerebe Island is around 4 A.M. Normally the younger one starts the greeting formality.

The greeting "Bwachaasugu" and its response "Bwachaa-mawe" is a modern phenomenon (Chart 2). Traditionally, only the queen mother could greet other women with "Bwachaa-mawe," which is a man's greeting to a woman. Today it has become a general greeting to women who are of a grandmother's status. The reason, in my view, for vulgarizing the greeting is the decline of respect to chieftainship after President Nyerere abolished it immediately after independence to reduce ethnic antagonisms and conflicts. The word *mawe*, which is attached to *bwacha*, means "mother," but like *tata* it also means "daughter." It is also worth noting that it is the vowel length and tone that differentiates the women's greeting "Suula" from the men's "Sula."

One thing that can be noted from Chart 3 is that in case a man and woman of same age meet, the woman has to give

Chart 1: Man to man

Time	Relative to Your Age	Your Greeting	His Response
5 A.M.–Noon	Older	Sula	Lelota
5 A.M.–Noon	Same Age	Sula	Sula
5 A.M.–Noon	Much younger	Kampilebwachasugu	Bwachatata
Noon–5 A.M.	Older	Lyagwasugu	Sibilota
Noon–5 A.M.	Same Age	Lyagwasugu	Lyagwasugu
Noon–5 A.M.	Much younger	Kapile–Lyagwasugu	Lyagwatata

Chart 2: Woman to Woman

Time	Relative to Your Age	Your Greeting	Her Response
5 A.M.–Noon	Older	Suula	Lelota
5 A.M.–Noon	Same Age	Suula	Suula
5 A.M.–Noon	Much Younger	Suula or Bwachaasugu	Suula or Bwachaamawe
Noon–5 A.M.	Older	Lyagwasugu	Sibilota
Noon–5 A.M.	Same Age	Lyagwasugu	Lyagwasugu
Noon–5 A.M.	Much Younger	Lyagwasugu or Bwachaasugu	Sibilota or Bwachaamawe

Chart 3: Man to Woman

Time	Relative to Your Age	Your Greeting	Her Response
5 A.M.–Noon	Older	Bwachamawe	Bwachaatata
5 A.M.–Noon	Same Age	Bwachamawe	Bwachaasugu
5 A.M.–Noon	Much Younger	Bwachamawe	Bwachaatata
Noon–5 A.M.	Older	Lyagwamawe	Lyagwaatata
Noon–5 A.M.	Same Age	Lyangwamawe	Lyagwaasugu
Noon–5 A.M.	Much Younger	Lyagwamawe	Lyagwaatata

Chart 4:   Special Greeting of Time, Man to Man

Age	Greeting	Response
Older	Kampile-sumalama	Tangunu
Same Age	Sumalama	Sumalama
Much Younger	Kampile-sumalama	Tangunu

the man a respectable greeting normally given to older persons. Younger women nowadays refuse to deliver this greeting. When this happens, both the man and woman simply smile and continue with other procedures of the greeting formality. Also notice that women lengthen the vowels to differentiate if from the men's. The greeting does not change when the woman starts and the man responds.

When a woman meets a man or a man meets woman the exchange of greetings is as woman to woman (Charts 4 and 5). This special greeting of time is used between people who have not met for a long time, usually a lapse of one year and above. In this greeting the normal division of a day's time does not apply. There is only immeasurable time.

Greetings According to Relationship

Among In-laws (*Ensanzi*)

In-laws regard themselves as equals. Parents of both sides greet each other with "Sula" from 5 A.M. to noon and with "Sibilota" from 1 P.M. to 4 P.M., and with "Iyagwasugu" from 4 P.M. to 5 A.M. This greeting cuts across gender. The same greeting is used between children of the two families and sometimes it spreads into the two clans. The son-in-law and daughter-in-law use the same greeting to other members of the opposite side, but not to the parents and their brothers and sisters. In greeting a father-in-law or mother-in-law, the normal greeting is used but with more respect than that given to one's real parents. Extreme humility in delivery or greetings to the parents of the wife's or husband's parents is how society judges the character of the son-in-law or daughter-in-law. Fathers-in-law and mothers are not supposed to look directly into the face of their daughters-in-law and son-in-law. The couple is required to do the same and must kneel during the entire greeting formality, on one knee for man, and on both knees for women. When greeting a mother-in-law, the son-in-law does not use the normal greeting. He is required to take a squatting posture and say "Mwanagilamo mayo" (Have you slept well, mother-in-law?), if the greeting takes place at home. But when meeting her on the path, he will say "Mwanagilayo moyo." The affix -*mo*- is for

Chart 5:   Special Greeting of Time, Woman to Woman

Age	Greeting	Response
Older	Malama	Mangunu
Same Age	Malama	Malama
Much Younger	Malama	Mangunu

inside the home and -*yo*- is for "there in the home." It is taboo for the son-in-law to mention or call his mother-in-law by her name.

There is a special kind of greeting between brother and brother's wife. A brother's wife is greeted with special and carefully selected praise names. Below is an example:

Greeting (brother)	Response (sister-in-law)
— sula	Suula
— sula chombeka	Suula
— sula niwe wena	Suula
— sula manchwanta galunga omugobe, etc.	Suula
— sula	Suula
— sula, you are the foundation of home	Suula
— sula, you are the beginning and the end	Suula
— sula, to you whose saliva seasons vegetables, etc.	Suula

The whole process is a play on metaphors and symbols which often cause a smile from the sister-in-law and laughter from the listeners. There is normally a special kind of joking relationship between in-laws. This kind of greeting extends to all the sisters of brother's wife and to all the daughters of her brothers. Her husband extends the same greeting to them.

Woman Greeting a Brother

A woman, however much older she is than her brother, must greet him with "Bwachaasugu," as she normally greets older men; she must greet him with great respect, usually with both knees on the ground. This is done because of the high status of male children in Kerebe patrilineal culture. The male children were traditionally the inheritors of their father's property. Modern women have come to question this ideology and no longer kneel to younger brothers as they consider it demeaning.

Greeting an Uncle

Uncles are highly respected and have to be greeted with "Kampile bwachasugu," regardless of age. An uncle, however young, is always considered elder. This greeting is given to the whole family. This kind of respect may stretch for an entire generation with grandchildren continuing to respect their grandfather's uncles. Very often a joking relationship develops between uncles and children of their sisters especially when the age difference is great. Uncles are the ones to run to in times of difficulties, and the ones to whom people feel free to reveal their innermost secrets and feelings. They also have special privileges in marriage procedures.

Greeting a Husband

A husband is always regarded as an elder and greeted with great respect by his wife. She greets him with "Suula" and the husband replies with "Lelota," with an air of respectable pride. The way the couple greet each other often reveals what is happening in their home and the nature of their relationship. Today, educated women are not comfortable with this gender inequality, especially when the marriage has produced children. Society is always keen to hear how couples greet each other. A wife who does not greet her husband as being younger to him is regarded rude, uncompromising and ill-mannered, a behavior usually associated with the way her parents brought her up. It is likely that Kerebe wives were traditionally often much younger than their husbands; the age difference was significant enough to warrant the greeting, in which respect is afforded based on age difference.

Royal Greetings

The chief is normally greeted with praise names. Praises start from a distance before reaching the chief. The normal formulaic greeting is "Kasinge Lugaba Kamele Wetu" (Hail! The giver and ruler of us all). The chief only nods his head in appreciation. The person delivering the greeting puts the palms together and makes a low clap as the greeting is uttered. Men make a slight bend, while women kneel on both knees. The chief may wish to ask further questions in a greeting pattern to the person especially to those he knows and his relatives. But to the general public a nod is good enough.

Those seeking favors from the chief sometimes exaggerate the performance with much praise and extreme humility. Traditionally those who held positions in the chiefdom had to pay homage to the chief with gifts collected from their area.

The mother of the chief is greeted with the normal greeting but she replies "Bwachaatata" and "Bwachaamawe," to men and women respectively. As pointed out earlier, women greet her as if greeting a man. The wife of the chief may also use the same greeting if she wants to assume authority over other women.

Modes of Delivery

When an elderly person meets a female relative, the woman will step out of the path and kneel down to deliver the greeting without looking at him straight into the face. The normal greeting is "Bwachaasugu," and the old man will reply "Bwachamawe." The first question from him is always "Akwaonka?" (Is the child suckling?). The woman answers "Akwonga sugu" (the child is suckling, your honor). The old man will then ask "Mwanagilayo kuzima?" (Did you sleep well there in your home?). The emphasis is always on "Obuzima" (being well), which is a basic element in the Bantu concepts of life (Tempels 1959; Mbiti 1969; Nkurunziza 1989). She will then narrate the health of the whole family while still kneeling. When she is through, it is then her turn to ask the old man the formulaic question "Newe abomwawe bata?" (And how are the ones who reside in your homestead?). The old man will then diligently narrate his side of the health story. The dialogue is often punctuated with exclamations, and words encouraging the speaker to continue and answer follow-up questions.

When the old man is through, the first part of the greeting formality is over. The woman will then stand up and explain where she is going, and the persons she is going to see and for what reason. The old man will also explain his destination. But the well-being of the persons to be visited is always at the center of the greeting conversation. This is the second part of the greeting. The third part is the end of the greeting, consisting mainly of messages, greetings to the family at home and to the homes of her destination and the final farewell.

Traditionally this is what is means to greet someone. A greeting normally lasts five to ten minutes. But when two old men meet, a greeting may last for fifteen minutes or more. Sometimes they may look for shade, sit and continue with the conversation if something has befallen to one of the two families. Another reason for their greeting taking a longer time is that both of them have long lists of people staying in their homesteads. The list includes grandchildren and may be great-grandchildren. It is rare for the whole family to be in good health taking into account malaria bouts which often strike the islanders. Apart from the long lists, old people have a lot to tell about their ailing body parts, where they feel pain, and their deteriorating body strength. These are often narrated in forms of complaints with explanations resembling a doctor–patient dialogue. Sometimes changes of behavior among youths of the new generation become part of the greeting. One could hear an old man saying, "We are well, but your son! Since he came back from town with his talking box, we have never known peaceful sleep."

As it can be observed from this mode of delivery the question of being is at the center of the greeting formality. Even in the same homestead, those who get up first in the morning are obliged to greet those who are still sleeping before going to the field or on any other errand. Being is connected with good health and the well being of the entire family and the clan. A person who is in good health is one who can work. It is for this reason that if one meets a person or people who are working, the first word that is uttered is "Milimo" (work), or "How is work?" The person who is passing may even help the workers before continuing with the journey. The response to "Milimo?" is "Milimo nizyo" (Yes, this is work!), which emphasizes the idea that to work is to survive.

There are two more words which need a bit of an explanation since they are part of the greeting formality. The two responses are "Goodbye" and "Thank you." The concept of goodbye among the Kerebe follows the variables of time and context or circumstance. During the day, the one leaving will say "Msibemo" (Have a good stay during the day), and the one being left will answer "Yee sugu msibeyo" (Yes your honour, have a nice stay too where you are going). In the evening and at night, it is "Mmagilemo/mnagileyo" (sleep well in/sleep well there). But when saying goodbye to people working or doing something the one passing will say "Mzikolega" (Continue working as I go). Sometimes the nature of the work is mentioned. The passer by can say "Lyombeka?" when greeting people building a house (kwombeka, "to build") and say "Mwombekehoga" or "Mwombekega" (Continue building as I go). Even when people are sitting down talking, the introductory greeting is "Mhoile?" (Are you resting talking?) and when bidding farewell, the saying is "Mheyohoga" or "Mhoyega" (Stay well talking). When greeting the bereaved, the saying is "Mwanagilamo mumabeho" (Did you sleep well in the cold). When leaving, the saying is "Mnagilemo mumabeho" (Sleep well in the cold). Coldness is mentioned because people sleep outside the house for three days after the burial.

The saying for "Thank you" reflects the centrality of hospitality among beings hence the Kerebe say "Wkola kuzima!" (You have done well) or "Wasemazya" (You have caused things to go well or to happen). Doing good to others is to cause something good to happen. "Wasemezya" is, therefore, phenomenological expression of causality of goodness which is associated with being.

In the two sayings "Goodbye" and "Thank you" as conceived by the Kerebe, we notice the concept of *wellness*. Good sleep is the basis of good health and wellness. A person who does not wake up well is sick and one who does not wake up at all is dead. In the word *wasemezya* we see the idea that doing good to others is a cause of continuity and the well being of others.

Phenomena of Time and Change

The phenomena of time and change occupy the center of the greeting formality especially where two people have not met for a long time. This is why the normal greeting is abandoned in favor of the special greeting of time. In this greeting, people ask questions about the physical aspects which have markedly changed over time on a person. Questions move carefully into elements of causality. Questions will be asked about where the person was, and what he was doing, what happened. If the greeting act takes place at home, observable changes at the home's environment will be explained, beginning with people who have passed away and newly constructed houses due to heavy rains and disasters. Children will be called from where they are so that the visitor may observe how they have grown and a proper introduction made. These detailed explanations of phenomena are the ones that make a greeting and a visit one and the same thing.

The phenomena of change and time make the art of greeting a person one does not know a very tricky one. People who change fast, for example, being gray-haired before their time, usually smile without responding when given respectable greetings they do not deserve. Time and change is normally observable through the following: gray hair, baldness, loss of teeth, wrinkles on face and hands, bending of the spinal cord and knees, and control of foot steps and voice. Properties like a walking stick and a hat add to the phenomena of change. These are some of the signs one must look at before delivering a greeting. When two young men or women who do not know each other meet, the greeting formality is even trickier. Sometimes the face, height, and body may help in sizing each other in terms of age, but youths often go for a respectable greeting as a result it is normal to hear people arguing for a greeting, the young and the old alike. If such arguments take place at home, it is usually the mothers that are called to clear the matter. A mother may simply say, "When I was pregnant, this one was already walking." Once solved the younger one has to accept it and start the greeting formality with respect. Old people come to the rescue when a relationship is not clear.

If someone is not satisfied with the greeting accorded to him/her, the person may simply refuse to response and keep quiet. It is up to the person who uttered the greeting to demand an explanation. Another way of refusing to accept a greeting politely is to reply in the same greeting accorded to you. The other person will realize that you are dissatisfied with the greeting. For instance, a person may think that he/she is older and say "Lelota." The person being greeted would reply "Lelota" to express dissatisfaction. The greeting "Lelota" by "Lelota" does not exist. One of the two has to yield or else greet each other as equals "Sula, sula."

Greeting among the Kerebe is not something that is fixed once and for all and for everyone. Although a general structure is there, it is time, change, age, sex, and relationship that finally determine the kind of greeting to be accorded to a person. Greeting is a phenomenological project that is carried out on a daily basis. The person one greets as a younger person today can be older tomorrow if he marries or is married into the family, or when a relationship one was not previously aware of becomes known. In Kerebe greetings, ontological and temporal issues occupy the center of being. To be or not to be is daily question in Kerebe culture.

References

Hartwig, Gerald. 1976. *The Art of Survival in East Africa: The Kerebe and Long Distance Trade, 1800–1895.* New York: Africana Publishing Company.

Mbiti, J. S. 1969. *African Religions and Philosophy.* London: Heinimann Educational Books.

Nkurunziza, Deudedit. 1989. *Bantu Philosophy of Life in the Light of the Christian Message: A Basis for an African Vitalistic Theology.* Frankfurt on Main: Peter Verlag.

Tempels, Placide. 1959. *Bantu Philosophy.* Paris: Presence Africaine.

E. KEZILAHABI

See also **Cosmology; East African Folklore: Overview; Gender Representations in African Folklore**

GRIAULE, MARCEL (1898–1956)

A French pioneer in ethnographic field research in Africa, Marcel Griaule, a disciple of Marcel Mauss, undertook his first African sojourn to Ethiopia in 1928. He gave a literary account of this experience in *Les Flambeurs d'hommes* (The Burners of Men). He then organized the famous Dakar-Djibouti mission (1931–1933) that traversed Africa from east to west, from Senegal on the Atlantic Ocean to Ethiopia and the Red Sea. The team he led conducted field research in fifteen countries, bringing back a great quantity of information as well as one of the most important collections of objects currently housed at the Musée de l'homme in Paris. During this expedition, Griaule discovered Dogon country in Mali (previously, the French Sudan), which would remain his favorite research area until his untimely death.

His work is important and diversified, especially in the field of the anthropology of religion. *Masques dogons* (Dogon Masks), a model monograph on an institution, demonstrate his early interest in language and the verbal and kinetic arts. In his youth, he had been himself attracted to literature and had contributed to the Surrealist journal *Documents* (1929). *Masques dogons* contains notations of songs and myths transmitted in a secret language as well as a delineation (unusual at the time) of the dance movements. He was also a pioneer in visual anthropology and in the application of aerial photography to social sciences.

In 1946, Griaule's meeting with the old hunter, Ogotemmêli, led him to focus his interest on the mythology and cosmogony of the Dogon and the neighboring peoples, which he took pleasure in comparing with those of the great ancient civilizations. Griaule related his conversations in *Dieu d'eau* ("God of Water," but the English translation was published as *Conversations with Ogotemmeli*), an important book whose relevance continues today. He was then initiated by the Dogon to an even higher level of esoteric knowledge and began an account of their myth of creation, the first volume of which (*Le Renard Pale* [1965], *The Pale Fox* [1986]) was published by Germaine Dieterlen after Griaule's death.

Marcel Griaule was a politically committed ethnologist. He defended Ethiopia against Fascist Italy in 1936 (*La Peau de l'Ours, The Bearskin*). Concerned with the economic development of the people he was studying, he had a dam built in Dogon country. Recipient of the first chair in ethnology at the Sorbonne, he championed African cultures in the face of Western prejudice.

References:

Griaule, Marcel. 1929 Mauvais oeil, Totemisme abyssin, and Jeux abyssins, *Documents* 6:218, 316–19, 332–33.

———. 1991. *Les Fambeurs d'hommes* (1934), Paris, Berg International. English translations: *Abyssinian Journey* (1935), London: John Miles; *Burners of Men* (1936), Philadelphia: Lippincott.

———. 1936. *La Peau de l'Ours*. Paris, Gallimard.

———. 1994. *Masques dogons* (1938). Paris: Institut d'ethnologie.

———. 1938. *Jeux dogons*, Paris, Institut d'ethnologie.

———. 1966. *Dieu d'eau. Entretiens avec Ogotemmêli* (1948). Paris: Fayard. English translation: *Conversations with Ogotemmeli, An Introduction to Dogon religious ideas* (1965), Published for the International African Institute by the Oxford University Press.

Griaule, Marcel, and Dieterlen, Germaine 1991. *Le Renard Pâle* (1965). Paris, Institut d'ethnologie. English translation: *The Pale Fox* (1986), Chino Valley, Arizona: Continuum Foundation.

GENEVIÈVE CALAME-GRIAULE

See also **French Study of African Folklore; Words and the Dogon**

GRIOTS AND GRIOTTES

Griots and their female counterparts, griottes, are masters of words and music for many societies in the Sahel and Savanna regions of West Africa. Too often described simply as storytellers or praise-singers, griots actually perform so many other functions that no single term in English adequately conveys the nature of what they do. Bard, wordsmith, or artisan of the word partially describe these individuals.

Griots recount genealogies, narrate epics, compose songs to mark important events, sing the praises of others, serve as intermediaries in delicate family, clan, and community negotiations, entertain at, preside over or otherwise participate in weddings, naming ceremonies, and installations of chiefs, teach people of all ages about the past, exhort troops about to go into battle as well as athletes entering competition, serve as spokespersons, interpret speeches, announce news, maintain the legal, family, and historical records of a people, and give advice to their patrons.

Male griots play a variety of instruments, ranging from the twenty-one-stringed kora, a kind of harp-lute, to the 3-to-5 stringed ngoni, also known as the *koni, xhalam,* or *molo,* an instrument closer to the guitar, the xylophone-like *balafon,* and different kinds of drums. Griottes in the vast Mande world play the *newo, nege,* or *karinyan,* a small piece of slit metal pipe with a striker, while Moor women play the *ardin,* a 14-to-17 stringed harp-lute.

Today, the instrumental and vocal music of griots and griottes has had an audible impact on contemporary Afro-pop musicians, many of whom are descended from a griot ancestor, for example Youssou N'Dour of Senegal. Some griots have performed on the *kora* with symphony orchestras in the United States. Many of them, both men and women, have produced CD recordings of their music.

It is quite likely that griots have been practicing their profession for at least a thousand years, and probably longer. The earliest written references date to the mid-fourteenth century. The modern term *griot* stems from an early seventeenth-century French word, *guiriot.* Although *guiriot* does not appear in any African language, there is some evidence pointing in the direction of an African root. According to this theory, *griot* would have come from the word Ghana, from the empire by the same name. Slaves imported from Ghana to Morocco from the tenth century on were called *agenaou,* or people from Ghana. Sold into Spain as early as the fourteenth century, the *agenaou* became known as *guineos,* the Spanish word for Africans. The Spanish traveled to West Africa in the fifteenth century, ahead of their French neighbors. French captains arriving in West Africa in the early sixteenth century, probably with mixed French-Spanish crews, may have created the term *guiriot* when told by Spanish crewmen that the griots who announced the arrival of local chiefs were simply *guineos.* Further historical and linguistic research is needed to confirm this theory.

Although *griot* serves as a regional term across the Sahel and Savanna today, it remains controversial not only because of the ambiguity surrounding its roots, African, European, or both, but also for two other reasons. The first is that every society that supports griots has its own term. Mandinka *jali* in The Gambia, Bamana *jeli* in Mali, Wolof *gewel* in Senegal, Moor *iggio* in Mauretania, Soninké *geseré* in Mauritania and Mali, Songhay *jeseré* in Mali and Niger, Hausa *marok'i* in Niger and Nigeria, and Fulani *mabo* and *jawando* are just some of the many words that are used today. The second is that griots and griottes have a seemingly ambiguous social status in society.

To outsiders, especially early European travelers, griots appeared as clowns and paid flatterers. In some societies, griots were not buried in the ground but in the hollows of trees, a tradition followed from the sixteenth up through the twentieth century. Finally, the very distinctiveness of griots within the local social structure, reinforced by descriptions of them offered by other members of society, gave the impression that they were so different that one could not even marry a griot. Even today, people of griot origin often encounter obstacles to marriage to people who are not griots.

But these negative views do not match other evidence suggesting that griots were key members of society: a ruler always kept his griot by his side for advice, for service as a spokesperson, and for negotiations; griots are given great rewards for their services, even today; finally, some of the most famous of them appear on postage stamps after they die.

The explanation for this apparent paradox comes from the power of the words of griots over other people. Griots and their patrons form a symbiotic couple. The dynamics of that relationship are marked by words and rewards. It is clear that griots are not of low class or captive origin. They are instead skilled artisans of the word whose talents are normally appreciated by all members of society, but sometimes feared by those whom they believe deserve criticism.

Although the origin of the profession remains unknown, the African societies that support griots and the griots themselves

Installation of regional chief Bakari Sanya in Faraba Banta, The Gambia, Oct. 2, 1991. On left: Adama Suso, Mandinka, *jalimuso*, or *griotte*, playing the *karinya* or *newo*, a small metal pipe with striker. On right: Ma Lamini Jobarteh, Mandinka, *jali*, or *griot*, playing the 21-stringed *kora*, a type of bridge harp. Photo © Thomas A. Hale.

have their own versions of how the first griot appeared. The earliest and most widespread etiological tale about griots tells of two brothers who go hunting, become lost, and run out of food. When one brother weakens, the other goes off some distance, cuts a piece of flesh from his thigh, returns, cooks it, and serves it to his sibling, thus saving his life. When the reviving brother learns how his benefactor has managed to find food, he decides to devote the rest of his life to singing the praises of his brother. After Islam arrives in West Africa, the origin tale becomes linked to Muhammad. The griot becomes a man named Surakata who, for a variety of reasons, ends up singing the praises of the Prophet.

Traditionally, the profession of griot was passed down from father to son and mother to daughter. In fact, griots and griottes learn from a variety of sources, such as other parents, friends, other griots encountered during travels, and even music heard on the radio. A typical career itinerary might include the absorption of the sounds and activities of griot life from childhood on, participation as a backup singer or musician at ceremonies during youth, apprenticeship with a master during the late teen years, travel across West Africa while in their twenties and thirties, and then a return home to perform in their forties for wealthy patrons and sometimes even heads of state. By this time, the griot or griotte may be called a master griot, *ngaara* or *jeliba* in the Mande world or *jeseredunka* in the Songhay world.

Not all those who come from griot families take up the profession. Many become farmers, business people, or civil servants. They may become patrons of griots themselves, as in the case of Babani Cissoko, a wealthy Malian businessman who once gave a small airplane to a griotte he admired, and $250,000 to a high school marching band in Florida that was raising money to go to the Macy's Thanksgiving Day parade. Some have become ministers in African governments.

Although one might expect the profession to disappear in the face of literacy, Westernization, and the growing influence of the electronic age, for many reasons the opposite is happening. First, thanks to Alex Haley's *Roots*, griots have become known around the world and the term *griot* has spread throughout the African diaspora. Second, inexpensive air travel has enabled griots to shift their performance context from the courtyards of the nobility to the global village. In addition to performing for expatriate communities of Africans outside the continent, they also appear in the concert halls, university auditoriums, schoolrooms, churches, and community centers of Paris, London, New York, Chicago, San Francisco, and Tokyo, as well as in small cities and towns around the world. Third, in many cases griots have embraced contemporary communications technology in order to reach these audiences. Satellites, television, radio, cassettes, CDs, and amplifiers are familiar to those who travel widely. Finally, the high rewards available to the most talented or most enterprising griots today has encouraged younger generations to learn the profession and strike out on their own.

Griots practice both verbal and musical art. Their verbal art lies at the heart of the profession, but their music is often an essential component of the entire picture. The verbal art of griots ranges from brief praise-songs to epics that may take many evenings to recount and add up to as many as eight thousand lines when transcribed. The epics tell about heroes that go back as far as the Ghana empire a millennium ago. The most widely read epic available to readers around the world is the story of the thirteenth century ruler of Mali, Sundiata, or Son-Jara. It now appears in a wide range of formats, from an illustrated children's story to a reconstructed prose version for junior high school and high school students, and a three thousand-line linear transcription and translation. More recent leaders such as the Senegalese national hero, Lat Dior, who died fighting the French in 1886, are also the subjects of epics. These epics, recorded during the last few decades, reveal how people today interpret the stories of heroes from the past. From a Western perspective, they are examples of fiction. But from an African viewpoint, these texts constitute the history and cultural heritage of a people. Nineteen of the twenty five epics excerpted in *Oral Epics from Africa*, the first collection of its kind to appear in the world, are narrated by griots and griottes.

References

Camara, Sory. 1976. *Gens de la parole Essai sur le rôle et condition des griots dans la société malinké*. Paris: Mouton.

Dramé, Adama, and Arlette Senn-Borloz. 1992. *Jeliya: être griot et musicien aujourd'hui.* Paris: Harmattan.

Hale, Thomas A. 1990. *Scribe, Griot and Novelist: Narrative Interpreters of the Songhay Empire.* Gainesville: University Press of Florida.

———. 1994. Griottes of the Sahel: Female Voices from West Africa. *Research in African Literatures* 25, no. 3:71–91.

———. 1997. From the Griot of Roots to the Roots of Griot: A New Look at the Origins of a Controversial African Term for Bard. *Oral Tradition* 12, no. 2:249–78.

———. 1998. *Griots and Griottes: Masters of Words and Music.* Bloomington: Indiana University Press.

Johnson, John Willam, Thomas A. Hale, and Stephen Belcher. 1997. *Oral Epics from Africa: Vibrant Voices from a Vast Continent.* Bloomington: Indiana University Press.

THOMAS A. HALE

See also **Epics; Myths; West Africa: Overview; Women Singers of Mali**

GUINEA (REPUBLIC OF GUINEA)

Guinea is a tropical country of 7,860,000 people located on Africa's west coast. Its neighboring countries are Guinea Bissau, Senegal, Mali, Cote D'Ivoire, Liberia, and Sierra Leone. Guinea's capital is Conakry, a costal city with a population of 705,000. Thirty-five percent of Guinea's people are Fulani, 30 percent are Malinke, and 20 percent are Soussou. The remaining 15 percent of the population is made up of various ethnic groups. The major languages spoken are French, Fula, Mandinka, Susu, and Malinke. The country is overwhelmingly Muslim (85 percent). Of the remaining population, 8 percent are Christian and 7 percent practice traditional indigenous religions.

The area became a French protectorate in 1888. Sekou Toure, a militant descendent of nineteenth-century Malinke leader Samori Toure, led Guinea to its independence from France on October 2, 1958. Guinea chose not to maintain its economic ties to France and it has suffered for this decision ever since. Until his death in 1984, Toure dictated Guinea's one-party republic. With the end of Toure's regime, many political reforms have been made, and many of the previous government's socialist structures have since been dismantled. Although Guinea has yet to achieve a stable and tolerant political scene, a multiparty republic with a new constitution has been implemented.

Much of Guinea is rich in natural resources such as bauxite, diamonds, and gold. The economy has not benefited, however, due to underdevelopment under Toure's state-controlled marketing and distribution of products. Governmental reforms since 1987 have tried to improve Guinea's economic situation and bauxite and diamond exportation has become a main source of revenue for the country.

JENNIFER JOYCE

GUINEA-BISSAU (REPUBLIC OF GUINEA-BISSAU)

Guinea-Bissau is a small tropical country of over 1 million peoples, and is located on West Africa's coast between Senegal and Guinea. Bissau is the country's capital and largest city with a population of 200,000. Thirty percent of the population is Balante, 20 percent Fulani, 14 percent Manjaca, 13 percent Mandinka, and 23 percent are composed of various smaller groups. Portuguese is the official language and Kriolo (or Crioulo) is the lingua franca. Fula, Mandinka, Manjanka, and Balanta are the most widely spoken indigenous languages. Over half of all Guinea-Bissauans still practice traditional indigenous religions (65 percent). Thirty percent of the remaining population is Muslim and 5 percent are Christian.

On September 10, 1974, Guinea-Bissau gained its independence from Portugal after a long struggle for independence that began in 1962. The successful liberation struggle played a major role in the liberation of other African colonies. A Marxist governmental model was followed for a number of years. After ten years of one-party rule, Guinea-Bissau shifted to a multiparty system in 1991. The political system, however, is still unstable and there was a military coup in 1999.

Guinea-Bissau is one of the poorest countries in the world. The recent discovery of oil, bauxite, and phosphates could potentially create revenue from foreign exploitation. Eighty percent of the population is engaged in agriculture, such as the production of peanuts, rice, palm kernels, and groundnuts. Fish is one of the major exports. Despite this fact, much of the country's food must still be imported because of poor infrastructure and a lack of governmental incentives to produce surplus.

JENNIFER JOYCE

H

HAUSA

See **Contemporary Bards: Hausa Visual Artists**

HAYA

See **Gender**

HEALING AND SPIRIT POSSESSION IN SÃO TOMÉ AND PRÍNCIPE

Introduction

After five hundred years of Portuguese colonial rule, São Tomé and Príncipe gained independence in 1975. A flourishing local Creole society and culture is the outcome of the encounter of the dominant Catholic Portuguese culture and African cultures. The majority of the population belongs to the group known as the Forros—native Creoles who are descended from the early white colonists and African slaves. The descendents of a small, marooned community formed in the sixteenth century in the south of São Tomé island are known as Angolares. The offspring of contract workers from Angola, Mozambique, and Cape Verde, recruited for the local plantation economy from 1875 to 1960, who were born in the archipelago are locally called Tongas.

African beliefs in witchcraft (*feitiço*) and divination are common among Forros, Angolares, and Tongas, existing side by side with Christian beliefs; the two are frequently fused into new syncretic forms. Old women are frequently beaten after they are accused of being a *feiticeira* (witch). The belief in *uê bluku*, or the Evil Eye, which is associated with envy and functions psychosocially as a leveler of socioeconomic differences, is of European origin. In São Tomé, protection against the Evil Eye includes use of the *ulua*, the fruit of a palm tree (*Borassus aethiopum*), a pulpous plant called *babosa* (*Aloés humilis*), a wooden cross, a horseshoe, an old chamberpot, rotten eggs, or a bottle filled with stale urine, placed close to the entrance of the house.

Traditional healers and ritual specialists, known as *curandeiros*, oversee the local spirit-possession cult, *djambí*. The term stems from the word *nzambí* or *njambí*, meaning "the Almighty" and "God" in *kímbundu* and *kíkongo*, respectively. The term *chinguilar* (to invoke the spirits of the dead) has the same linguistic origin. The *curandeiro* is initiated and trained by an elder master of the cult in the wisdom and the practices of the *djambí*. He enacts the cult either to treat a particular case or to commemorate the annual feast day of his own principal spirit. In the latter case, preceding the *djambí*, he may lead a procession accompanied by drums from a nearby Catholic church to his own compound.

During the ceremony, which lasts from sunset to sunrise, a fire illuminates the scene, while the drummers summon the spirits of the ancestors who have returned to afflict the living. One *puíta* (large drum), three drums, and three *sucalos* (rattles) provide for the *batuque* (drumming). The sound of the drums varies according to the ethnic origin of the spirit called. Women stamp cassava leaves in a big mortar to the rhythms of the drums. Tables with dishes and drinks are laid out for the spirits and decorated with leaves and flowers collected in the graveyard. The *curandeiro* presiding over the ceremony is the spirit medium determining the identity of the spirits who have caused the disease or misfortune of an individual, a family, or a whole community. Besides the family and friends of the patient, hundreds of outsiders attend the events. The spectators eat and drink, and they may come and go during the ceremony. Attendants are often suddenly possessed by a spirit, thereafter falling into a trance and dancing to the rhythms of the drums.

The possessed speak in tongues of the spirit that only the *curandeiro* can understand. The language varies, for the spirits belong to Forros, Angolares, Angolans, Cape Verdians, Mozambicans, and Tongas who died on the island. The possessed may walk over the red-hot wood without being burnt. The afflicted person and his or her relatives provide for the food, drinks, and the chicken, goats, or pigs that are ritually killed during the nightly drama.

The Christian cross and human bones belong to the essential paraphernalia of the cult. Together with wooden figures, candles, palm oil lamps, eggs, and other food put on an altar, they are also present in the chapel in the *curandeiro's* compound. Here he receives the patients for individual treatment by other methods. To fight the devil and misfortunes, *curandeiros* also use formulas, charms, spells, and devotions from old magic books like *Breviário de Rezas e Mandingas, Confortadora Cruz de Caravaca*, and the book of *São Cipriano*. (The latter's author is not the famous bishop of Carthago with the same name, but a powerful sorcerer from ancient Phoenicia.)

When a child or adolescent suffers from illness or problems such as nightmares or bed-wetting, the blame is often ascribed to a double who has remained in the extraterrestrial realm, causing these misfortunes by constantly calling to the child on earth. The double claims his or her presence, considering the flight to earth as treason. To cure the child, the parents ask a *curandeiro* to perform a sacrifice called *pagá-dêvê*, literally meaning "to pay the debt." The ritual is done at night, preferably on a Thursday or Saturday, in the presence of the patient, either along a stream, at a waterfall, at the beach, or on a crossroads. Neither father nor mother may be present during the *pagá-dêvê*. To reconcile the double, a wooden dish with a variety of food, sweets, flowers, and small flags is usually put on the ground to pay the unsettled debt of a former life. In addition, two small, simply carved human figures of both sexes made from the wood of the *ocá* (silk-cotton tree, Ceiba petandra) may also be used. The patient is cured if the double's spirit accepts the offering.

Unlike the *curandeiro,* other traditional healers and specialists can be either man or woman, usually an elderly person within the local community. A local healer who diagnoses diseases by the examination of urine is called *pia-dô-záua*. According to his diagnosis, he prescribes infusions that the patient must drink and then monitors the effect of the treatment through further examination of the patient's urine. The herbalist, known as *stli-jon mátu*, uses natural products to grind mixtures that the patient takes according his prescriptions. The herbalists' knowledge of the properties of local medical plants is remarkable, and they are even sought after in neighboring countries and in Lisbon. They treat all types of diseases, including venereal and intestinal diseases, fevers, parasite infections, and tuberculosis. Another type of local therapist, the *tchiladô ventoso*, makes small cuts with a sharp knife in the swollen or painful parts of the skin to let out the bad blood that has caused the pain. He also uses an ox horn, cut through the middle and equipped with a small opening at the conic end to suck with his mouth. Since he takes into account the dominating lunar constellations, he cures only on certain days.

References

Espírito Santo, Calos. 1998. *A Coroa do Mar.* Lisbon: Editorial Caminho.

Eyzaguirre, Pablo B. 1986. *Small Farmers and Estates in São Tomé, West Africa.* Unpublished Ph.D. thesis. Yale University.

Valverde, Paulo. 2000. *Máscara, Matro e Morte em São Tomé.* Oeiras: Celta Editora.

GERHARD SEIBERT

See also **Diaspora; Medicine; Spirit Possession**

HERO

The term *hero* is used mostly in relation to heroic and epic traditions; it designates a person who, after accomplishing great things, is celebrated in song, narrative, and various other genres. The distinguishing characteristics of a given hero may be bravery, intelligence, perseverance, supernatural powers, or a combination of any of these factors. Generally, the hero embodies and exemplifies social values, ideals, and aspirations.

It seems prudent, however, to view the hero also as complex, contradictory, and dynamic. Heroes may embody and exemplify social ideals and values, but they also tend to possess the ability and willingness to transgress those ideals and values. They may be admired, but they may also be feared. Though celebrated, heroes tend to be problematic, often troublesome, and even antisocial. Restlessness and a desire for adventure, rather than conformity and a wish for stability, seem to be the hallmarks of heroism.

The ambiguity and contradictoriness of the hero's personality make it possible for the hero to be viewed differently by different people, especially since apprehending the hero, like reading a text, is a form of interpretation and appropriation that depends on the viewers' position, perspective, and interests. A character may be celebrated as a hero in one place, but be seen differently elsewhere. The boundaries between the hero, the villain, and the trickster, for example, may be more tenuous than we conventionally imagine. With time, also, people's perception of a hero may change; a hero of a certain time may not be a hero in another era. There are, thus, diachronic and asynchronic factors that render the image of the hero complex and dynamic.

Due mostly to the kind of research that has been done and the perspective of the researchers, we generally think of the hero as a male figure. The existence of female heroes, however, should be recognized. There are female figures who are alter egos of male heroes. There are others, such as the mother, the sister, or the aunt, who play crucial, even determining, roles in the careers of male heroes, and who can thus be seen as heroes in their own right. These factors challenge the traditional view of the hero as male. The role or status of hero in a given epic may not necessarily belong exclusively to an individual, but may be shared by more than one individual.

A rethinking of the heroic and epic traditions and ongoing research on other traditions demonstrate considerable diversity in the manifestations of the hero figure. There are different concepts of heroism, ranging from the militaristic to the shamanistic. Nevertheless, the hero is the focal point of discourses about social values and aspirations, whether the hero embodies, exemplifies, or transgresses those values and aspirations. The image of the hero is an ideological construct and vehicle; it is a projection of the concerns and outlook of a specific society or social group. Often, the image of the hero is used to stake claims of certain kinds. To enhance their social status, for example, people typically claim connection to the hero.

Ultimately, it must be determined whether the term *hero* is adequate, appropriate, or applicable to the traditions of different parts of the world. Just as terms such as *epic* or *folktale* are not necessarily congruent with African nomenclature, the term *hero* may not have equivalents in certain African languages. It carries meanings and associations that may not apply to the African realities. Researchers ought, perhaps, to pay attention to indigenous categories and concepts and study the African traditions on their own terms. Comparative studies can follow, based on a deep understanding of each specific tradition.

References

Bird, Charles S., and Mary Kendall. 1980. The Mande Hero: Texts and Context. In *Explorations in African Systems of Thought*, ed. Ivan Karp and Charles S. Bird, pp. 131–49. Bloomington: Indiana University Press.

Mbele, Joseph L., 1982. The Hero in the African Epic. *Africana Journal*, 13, no. 1–4:124–41.

JOSEPH L. MBELE

See also **Epics, Myths**

HERO IN SUKUMA PROSE NARRATIVES

The Sukuma live on the southern side of Lake Victoria in northwestern Tanzania. The first inhabitants of Sukumaland appear to have been hunters and gatherers, the remnants of whose culture are visible in such forms as rock paintings. Sukuma oral traditions mention these ancestors.

Sukuma folklore incorporates a wide diversity of forms, including narratives, songs, and other discursive forms. Among the most pervasive narratives are those concerning *shing'weng'we*, a monster figure. In these narratives, *shing'weng'we* may appear either alone or with other *shing'weng'we*. There are, among the Sukuma, different conceptions of what *shing'weng'we* really is, in appearance and attributes.

Typically, this monster is confronted by a young hero, Masala Kulangwa. The adventures of Masala Kulangwa and *shing'weng'we* are told everywhere in Sukumaland. In some *shing'weng'we* tales, *shing'weng'we* does not interact with Masala Kulangwa, but with other human characters, male or female.

Masala Kulangwa is a trickster hero, perhaps the most well-known in Sukuma folklore. There are, however, other trickster heroes, such as Ibambangulu, who is said to have had the ability to expand his body until he filled a room. He also had the ability to leave his and his dog's footprints on rocks.

There is virtually no mention of epic in the literature on Sukuma folklore. However, it is logical to view the cycle of tales around Masala Kulangwa as the prototype of an epic tradition. Subsequently, epics were created around such heroes as Ng'wanamalundi. Ngw'anamalundi is a historical as well as a cult figure. He had many heroic achievements, such as defeating Maasai cattle raiders and outwitting the colonialists who imprisoned him. He also had great magic powers. His grave in Seke, in the Shinyanga region, is an important shrine.

There are also other heroes, both male and female, who are celebrated in song and narrative. These figures tend to be shamanistic; their medicines or magic powers are a hallmark of their prowess.

The historic experience and interactions of the Sukuma with their neighbors is a key theme in the folklore. Most notable in this regard is the experience of raids by the Maasai. This is a constant theme in folk tales, epics, and other forms of folklore. The hero Ngwanamalundi, for example, confronts the Maasai cattle raiders and retrieves the cattle they have stolen.

Various songs of the Sukuma have been published, including hunting songs, work songs, and political songs. Dances and singing are central in Sukuma culture. These activities are often organized as competition between two rival sects, the Giika and the Gaalu. Members of these sects exist in every Sukuma village and community. The contestants strive to win through a variety of means, including not only singing skills but magic, medicines, spectacular attire, and antics. The group that ends up attracting the most spectators wins the contest.

Because of the competitive tradition between Giika and Gaalu, the character of the songs is polemical and satirical. When they comment on social and political issues, the singers tend to use the same strategies. The language and imagery are rather earthy and hard hitting. Over the years, from the days of colonialism to the present, this has sometimes caused the singers to be harassed by the authorities.

There are, however, other kinds of dances for which the Sukuma are well known, such as the snake dance and the bugobogobo, an agricultural dance. It appears that the snake dance evolved from a hunters' dance. The bugobogobo is an efficient mechanism for harmonizing the rhythm of hoeing the fields and keeping the farmers entertained.

References

Millroth, Berta. 1965. *Lyuba: Traditional Religion of the Sukuma*. Uppsala: Almqvist and Wiksells Boktryckeri AB.

Welch, Elvie Adams. 1974. Life and Literature of the Sukuma in Tanzania, East Africa. Dissertation. Howard University.

JOSEPH L. MBELE

See also **East African Folklore; Epics; Tricksters in African Folklore**

HERSKOVITS, MELVILLE J. (1895–1963)

The founder of African studies in the United States, Melville J. Herskovits collected and analyzed African folklore in the course of ethnographic research in West Africa and as part of a long-term project to examine the retention and transformation of African cultural elements in the Americas. Many of the "Africanisms" he identified in the Caribbean, Latin America, and the United States consisted of folklore traced to African sources. Since he studied African folklore found on both sides of the Atlantic, Herskovits was able to observe how it changed as he developed his theories of acculturation and culture change. Drawing from his broad comparative perspective, he described such common features found in sub-Saharan Africa as the performance of narratives as dramatic expression, delight in double entendre, improvisation, the presence of multiple narrative forms, the uses of folklore for moral education, and the artful use of indirection in speech and folklore.

Folklore, for Herskovits, meant verbal creative expression. He also counted other aesthetic forms among his extraordinarily broad research interests of music, dance, games, and material culture. Like other folklorists of the early and mid-twentieth century, Herskovits classified texts and analyzed their origins and distribution. He challenged the Eurocentric biases of the comparative folklorists of his time through identifying multiple sources from Africa, as well as Europe, for the folktales of Africans in the New World. In *Suriname Folk-Lore* (1969)—co-authored, like many of his works on folklore, with his wife and close collaborator Frances S. Herskovits—he found, for example, that the The Good Child and the Bad story among Suriname Creoles contains "correspondences" with the Frau Holle,

Cinderella and Magic Whip tales of Europe, as well as the motif of the orphaned child from the *notchievi* cycle of Dahomean tales. Commonalities among the folklore of Africa, Europe, and Asia were ascribed to historical contacts among the peoples of the "Old World cultural province" that encompassed these three continents.

A trip to West Africa in 1931 resulted in the collection of folktales in pidgin English in the Gold Coast (now Ghana) and extensive collecting of folktales, riddles, proverbs, and verse forms in Dahomey (now Benin). After revisiting Dahomey in 1957, the Herskovitses published their only book about African folklore, *Dahomean Narrative: A Cross-Cultural Analysis* (1959). When collecting folktales on these field trips, they closely observed the performance of narratives and recorded full texts in interviews with informants, departing from the predominant approach of folklorists whose collections consisted of the abstracts of texts. Through observing folklore as it was performed, in context, Herskovits achieved fresh insights about the nature of folklore and how it functioned in African culture and society. While other folklorists of his day viewed folklore as consisting of texts, Herskovits saw it also as performance, contending that the telling of folk tales among "Negroes everywhere" involved a "dramatic presentation with a principle impersonator and a chorus" (1969 [1936], 142): that is, a performance with participation by an audience.

Narratives collected by Herskovits and his wife were transcribed from the translations of interpreters as they were being told. In Dahomey, rather than relying solely upon "men of reputation as storytellers," informants were chosen so as to represent a broad range of social ranks and ages. Through their choices of informants, Herskovits and his wife were able to study variations in particular tales, tale types, regions, and styles of narration.

Oral narrative was viewed as a kind of literature, to be analyzed on the same plane as a "short story or novel . . . taking into account . . . plot construction, character development or other points that a literary critic or student of comparative literature would consider" (1961, 452). Herskovits also asserted that the literary analysis of oral narratives should include unities of time, place, and action, devices to heighten emotion and create suspense, imagery, content, values and style.

The master storyteller in Dahomey commands multiple stylistic devices. He manipulates tense to convey how incidents happen at different times, uses multiple verbs in an active voice, and creates emphasis, all contributing to the effect of "descriptive images filled in with a few rapid strokes, to leave uncluttered for the foreground for dramatizing the thematic progressions" (1958, 67).

Improvisation was seen by Herskovits as a fundamental pattern in African creative expression, used with particular potency for praise or ridicule. The professional verse makers of Dahomey composed new songs within traditional structures to praise ancestors of important families and the accomplishments of prominent men. Songs of derision were improvised and sung to the Herskovitses when they unsuccessfully tried to persuade some Ashanti to sing into a phonograph. Singers of songs that accompanied the *avogan* social dance in Abomey satirized the people of different neighborhoods with new songs, and women improvised new verses to the rhythm of their pestle in pounding millet to indirectly reproach, protest against, or threaten an un-

named co-wife. Herskovits was intrigued by the pervasive, artful use of indirection among peoples of African descent, that he described as "the tendency to speak in terms of circumlocution and innuendo, the habit of the constant use of inference" (1935, 120).

Proverbs in Africa employ indirection to vent anger, reproach, or instruct. In a pioneering work of proverb scholarship based on field research with a Kru informant from Liberia living in Chicago, Herskovits examined the situations in which proverbs are used and tied their meaning to context. Among the Kru, proverbs are used to correct children and warn them of proscribed behavior, rebuke wrongdoing adults, comment on "current happenings," insult a non–family member, "settle disputes," and "commiserate a relative or friend on ill-fortune" (1930, 228).

Writing in general terms about proverbs throughout Africa, Herskovits observed that in native courts they are cited in a similar way as legal precedents in European courts (1935, 230). He viewed proverbs as primary vehicles for the moral education of African young people, teaching what is right and wrong and pointing to basic values (1961, 453). Animal tales are likewise used for moral education. The trickster character teaches that "wisdom and perspicacity are better than strength, that the old are wiser than the young, that malice often brings about destruction, that impetuousness is dangerous, that obedience is rewarded, and other moral precepts of like character" (1935, 228).

Riddles in Africa have different meanings for the young and older people. Double entendre, also used extensively in narrative forms, is especially prevalent in riddles, where the "skilled use of the hidden obscenities" are not understood by children. In Dahomey the Herskovitses found the double entendre was especially important when riddling was practiced during rites for the dead, since it gave the deceased so much pleasure when they were alive. *Dahomean Narrative* also described the distinctive stylistic characteristics of riddles: their use of exaggeration and their references to the grotesque, and the forbidden. While some riddles are metrical and in couplets, others are told in everyday speech.

Dahomean Narrative contained an unusually comprehensive account of the variety of forms found in Dahomey. Through the treatment of a wide range of narratives, *Dahomean Narrative* departed from most previous works on African folklore, which had concentrated upon animal tales. The Herskovitses described in detail the system of naming and classifying narratives used by the Dahomeans themselves. The two broad categories of narratives include the *hwenoho*, "time-old story . . . translated variously as history, as traditional history, or as ancient history" and the *heho*, or "tale" (1958, 14–15).

In planning his first trip to West Africa, Herskovits expected that Dahomean culture would represent a baseline for his studies of the retention of African traditions in the Americas. He was drawn to its relatively unacculturated character, due to its having been "almost less affected than any other by the circumstances of European control" (1967 [1937]: vol. 1, i), and its significance as a primary source culture for Africans in the Americas who retained Africanisms. Herskovits recognized, however, that the cultures of Africans in the Americas varied greatly in their extent of African retention. For example, centuries of isolation among the Maroons of Suriname resulted in a "culture that is more African than the West African cultures of today," (NUHP,

MJH/Elsie Clews Parsons, 11/11/29), on one extreme of what he would later call a "scale of intensity of Africanisms" (1966 [1945], 51). West Africans, shown photographs of Maroon material culture, were startled that traditions preserved in the New World were forgotten in Africa (SCHP, West Africa Diary, 3/21/21).

In Dahomey, the Herskovitses saw how folklore incorporated cultural change brought about by colonization. *Dahomey: An Ancient African Kingdom*, published in 1937, discussed narratives that referred to the automobile and experiences in a European war. In his consideration of such narratives, Herskovits departed from conventional representations of African traditional folklore as embedded in an ethnographic present frozen in time, immune from outside influences. Three decades later, in *Dahomean Narrative*, the Herskovitses discussed the impact of colonization upon narratives in their analysis of "narrative and the changing culture," where the "amalgamation of the new with the old" (1958, 72) included reference to the French franc, trains, European tools, and writing.

While Herskovits considered the impact of cultural change upon African folklore in writings that were explicitly about Africa, his works about Africans in the Americas rendered the sources of Africanisms as fixed reference points that had not been subject to cultural change. His writings on the cultures of African descendents in the New World, were deeply concerned with the transformations of African traditions that occurred in the Americas, analyzed through the conceptual approaches he developed concerning the cultural processes of acculturation, syncretism, and reinterpretation.

The legacy of Herskovits in African folklore studies has been perpetuated by the students he trained at Northwestern University. He taught there for most of his career, beginning four years after he received his Ph.D. in anthropology in 1923 from Columbia University, where he had studied with Franz Boas. In 1948, Herskovits established the African Studies Program at Northwestern, the first of its kind in the world. Students of Herskovits who have studied the folklore and traditional arts of Africans and New World blacks include Robert Plant Armstrong, Warren D'Azevedo, William R. Bascom, Justine Cordwell, Daniel J. Crowley, James W. Fernandez, John C. Messenger, Jr., Alan P. Merriam, and Richard Waterman.

References

Baron, Robert. 1994. Africa in the Americas: Melville J. Herskovits' Folkloristic and Anthropological Scholarship, 1923–1941. Ph.D. dissertation, University of Pennsylvania.

Herskovits, Melville J. 1935. Social History of the Negro. In *Handbook of Social Psychology*, ed. Carl Murchison, p. 207–67. Worcester, MA: Clark University Press.

———. 1967. *Dahomey, an Ancient African Kingdom*. (1937). Evanston, IL: Northwestern University Press.

———. 1966. Problem, Method and Theory in Afroamerican Studies. *Afroamerica*, 1 (1945): 5–24. Reprinted in *The New World Negro*. Ed. Frances S. Herskovits, p. 43–61. Bloomington, IN: Minerva Press.

———. 1961. The Study of African Oral Art. *Journal of American Folklore*, 74: 451–56.

Herskovits, Melville J., and Frances S. Herskovits. 1969 *Suriname Folk-Lore*. (1936). New York: AMS Press.

———. Tales in Pidgin English from Ashanti. *Journal of American Folklore*, 50:52–101.

———. 1958. *Dahomean Narrative, A Cross-Cultural Analysis*. Evanston: Northwestern University Press.

Herskovits, Melville J. and Sie Ta'gbwe. 1930. Kru Proverbs. *Journal of American Folklore*, 43:225–93.

Archival Sources

Northwestern University Library: Melville J. Herskovits Papers
Schomburg Center for Research in Black Culture Archives, New York Public Library (NY): Melville J. Herskovits Papers (SCHP).

ROBERT BARON

See also **Bascom, William R.; Diaspora; West African Folklore: Overview**

HISTORY AND CULTURAL IDENTITY: THE ASHANTI

The Ashanti are one of approximately six major ethnic groups constituting the Akan of Ghana. Other Akan-speaking people are the Fanti, Akwapim, Kwahu, Akim, Bono, and Agona.

Ashanti, formerly composed of eleven chiefdoms, was unified over three hundred years ago, and became the most powerful among the Akan states. It reached its peak of prominence in the seventeenth century during the reign of King Osei Tutu, who died at the beginning of the eighteenth century. An Ashanti confederacy that was established in 1701 was dissolved by the British in 1900. The British finally colonized the Ashanti in 1901 after several unsuccessful attempts.

The Ashanti region, dubbed the cradle of Ghana's cultural heritage, is the most populous of all the ten administrative regions of Ghana. Kumasi, its administrative capital, is also the seat of Asantehene, the king of the Ashanti. As of 2003, the king of Ashanti is Otumfuor Osei Tutu II, who ascended to the Golden Stool in 1999, after his predecessor Otumfuor Opoku Ware II. The official residence of the king is the Manhyia Palace. Kumasi also houses the Ghana National Cultural Center, where all the cultural artifacts of the surrounding villages are assembled. Obuasi, 36 miles southwest of Kumasi is one of the richest gold mines in the world. Bonwire, northwest of Kumasi, is the home of kente, the gorgeous and intricately woven cloth, a sample of which decorates the foyer of the United Nations headquarters in New York. Ntonso, 11 miles north of Kumasi, is the home of the Adinkra cloth, a special tie-and-dyed fabric used for funerals. Approximately nine miles north of Kumasi is Ahwia, where the world-famous fertility doll called Akuaba and other woodcarvings are made.

The Ashanti kingdom is composed of a number of different chieftaincies (*oman*). Each *aman* is governed by a chief, *omanhene*, and a queen mother, *ohemmaa*, who is generally the chief's biological sister or mother. She is expected to advise the chief, and reprimand him in ways his councelors cannot. When a chief's stool is vacant, the queen mother proposes his successor, advising on the successor's eligibility from the viewpoint of kinship and character. The queen mother is consulted on matrimonial affairs within the royal lineage. She has her own stool, elders, and spokesmen, and she has her own court, which hears domestic cases and disputes between members of the royal household.

The king is the head of the national council comprising the *amanhene*. The king, chiefs, and queen mothers are chosen from particular matrilineages in their towns, which have the right to provide the ruler. It is from the Ashanti that several ethnic groups in Ghana borrowed the institution of chieftaincy.

The Ashanti are largely farmers; they occupy mostly equatorial forest land. Their staple crops are yams, plantains, bananas, yams, cassava, and maize. Other specialist occupations include woodcarving, metalwork, pottery making, weaving, hunting, and trading.

The Ashanti believe that a human being is formed from the blood of the mother and the spirit of the father. This belief reflects the social organization, for two sets of bonds derive from the conception of procreation, and determine two sets of groupings and relationships. These are the mother-child bond, and the father-child bond.

The Ashanti have several verbal art forms, including story telling, riddles, praise poetry, dirges, and proverbs (which are sometimes told competitively). Women's verbal art forms include *mmobome* (sung by women when their men have gone to war), and *nnwonkoro*. The Ashanti cherish their history and heritage. They have some of the most pristine folklore forms, which have not been influenced by modernity.

KWESI YANKAH

HISTORY AND CULTURAL IDENTITY: THE CHOKWE

On a contemporary map of Central Africa, three national, colonial-drawn borders artificially cut through the savannahs where the Chokwe (also Cokwe, Tshokwe, Tutshokwe, Quioco, Bajok) people live in southern Zaire, northeastern Angola, and northwestern Zambia. Every year, many families, traveling along footpaths to visit relatives on the other side, cross back and forth across these often invisible boundaries. Approximately 600,000 Chokwe live in Angola, another 300,000 in Congo (formerly, Zaire), and 100,000 in Zambia. (See Bastin, 1966). All of these present-day Thuchokwe (singular Kachokwe) trace their origins to Lunda nobles once living in the Nkalaany Valley of western Shaba, in today's Republic of the Congo.

Origin Myth

According to oral history as recounted by Lunda and Chokwe peoples alike, the Lunda nobles began moving out from the Nkalaany Valley in the sixteenth century when Chibinda Ilunga, a Muluba hunter from the East, arrived in the Lunda court and married the Lunda queen, Lweji (Lima 1971, 41–65; de Heusch 1982, 180–82). Discontented with his rule, the queen's brothers decided to emigrate. The Lunda diaspora includes the following peoples, who all trace their ancestors to these emigrating chiefs: Chokwe, Minungu, Lwena (also known as Luvale), Luchazi, Songo, Lunda Ndembu, and Lunda of Kazembe. One of the brothers, Ndumba wa Tembo, settled in Saurimo, Angola, and it was his maternal nephew, Mwachisenge, who was given the title of supreme chief of the Chokwe. This same title, "Mwachisenge," together with a special bracelet (*lukano*), has been passed down through the generations from maternal uncle to maternal

nephew, as a sign of the highest chief among the Chokwe. The present-day bearer of the bracelet and Mwachisenge title lives in Samutoma village, of Shaba province in Congo.

Historical Expansion

The Chokwe have been known throughout history as independent, indomitable warriors, hunters, and traders. By the eighteenth century, the Angolan Chokwe had established power over the matrilineal peoples around them and had claimed rights to the farming and hunting. During the eighteenth and early nineteenth centuries, the Chokwe were known as excellent hunters and traders all along the trade route from Central Africa to the Angolan coast, where they traded with Europeans. They exchanged ivory, wax, and male slaves for European weapons, mostly guns. In raids on other peoples en route, they captured the men as slaves and integrated the women and children into Chokwe society through marriage. Thus they assimilated other peoples and expanded throughout the area. Not until the 1880s did the Chokwe return to the Congo, when a group of Lunda hired Chokwe warriors to fight for them in Shaba province. For a brief time, these warriors gained victories over the Lunda (1880–1887) and thus facilitated the Chokwe expansion into Shaba as well. The Chokwe continued to expand north and west out of Angola until the late 1930s (See Miller 1970, 175–201 for Chokwe history).

Village Life and Social Organization

Chokwe independence and ease of assimilating other peoples can be attributed in part to their political and social organization. Chokwe political power is decentralized. Though all chiefs recognize the title Mwachisenge as a sign of supreme chieftanship, Chief Mwachisenge of Samutoma is a ritual chief who has little practical influence over the lives of Chokwe people beyond his own village.

Chokwe villages are insular, socially cohesive units. Though matrilineal, the women move to the homes of their spouses after marriage. A group of brothers and maternal uncles, along with their wives and children, build a village together. Often small, ranging from forty to eighty people, these villages frequently move their locations in search of better fishing, hunting, gathering, or farming areas or to escape sorcery accusations or conflicts with relatives. As subsistence farmers and roaming hunters, the Chokwe are extremely mobile and thus, of necessity, live in very small villages. This kind of self-sufficiency enables the Chokwe to maintain their language and customs as they move from one locale to another and from one country to the next. As a consequence, their way of life survives times of great upheaval and change.

Folklore and Fame

The Chokwe's reputation among neighboring groups in Central Africa differs somewhat from their reputation in the West. Their neighbors know them as great hunters, sorcerers, diviners, and healers; they both fear their sorcerers and visit their healers. In a similar vein, Africanist scholars remember the Chokwe for their history as expansionists, for their assimilation of other peoples along the trade routes of Central Africa. In contrast, many

Westerners, especially art connoisseurs, recognize the Chokwe for their artistic traditions. They admire the remarkable masks, ancestor figurines, carved chairs, and divining baskets, which can be viewed in museum displays on African life and art throughout the world.

Travelers and researchers, from the early 1900s on, have collected and/or documented Chokwe arts, that is, the more visible, striking features of Chokwe life: the ancestor figurines (*mahamba*), carved chairs (*yitwamo*), and masks (*akishi*) from the *mukanda* initiations (Bastin 1961; Crowley 1975). Early twenty-first-century researchers study Chokwe life in greater detail, paying attention to local concerns and daily routines; they document and analyze artistic expression and ritual performances in the contexts of Chokwe daily life. For example, such studies concern the practices of healers (*mbuki*), diviners (*tahi*), and sorcerers (*nganga*), and the lives of women and women's initiation rites (*mwadi*) (See Bastin 1982, 1988; Fretz 1987; Jordan 1993; Kubik 1988, 1993; Sesembe 1981; Yoder 1988).

Unlike these more easily observed and transported objects, the verbal arts have been minimally described until recent times. For instance, the documents of Chokwe tales (*yishima*) from the early 1900s, translated into Western languages such as Portuguese, lack the vitality and aesthetic qualities of Chokwe storytelling as performed for local audiences (See Barbosa 1973; Havenstein 1976). Current studies focus on the teller's interactions with the audience and record both verbal and nonverbal features of the performance. Such research includes documentation of both artistic and everyday forms of speech: for example, narrating and telling proverbs (*kuta yishima*), indirect speaking and telling parables (*kubwa nyi misende*), recounting historical events or recent news (*kulweza sanoo*), and "just talking" (*kuta pande*) (Fretz 1987; 1994; 1995).

Historically, whenever the Chokwe relocated, they carried with them their knowledge of healing, divining, and sorcery, their renowned abilities in mask making and carving of ancestral figurines, and their oral tradition as represented by myths, tales, and proverbs. Thus, they created a web of interconnected traditions that still transcends the colonially imposed national boundaries. Today, they continue to traverse the borders that separate their families and clans. However, as the political situations in the Republic of the Congo, in Angola, and in Zambia shift, the alliances between these neighboring countries change, often making their journeys more difficult and urgent. Not only do they cross the border for family visits and for the lucrative diamond trade, but they also escape as refugees from war-torn areas. In addition, these erstwhile hunters and traders now cross more intangible, intellectual frontiers through radio broadcasts, education abroad, and leadership positions in international organizations. As communication with the rest of the world accelerates, the opportunity for travel beyond their homelands increases for the more educated and well-connected. Having learned throughout their history to be resilient, to assimilate other cultures, and to create syncronistic arts, the Chokwe, no doubt, will continue to improvise on new experiences and, thereby, both retain and revitalize their traditions.

References

Barbosa, A. 1973. *Folclore angolano, ciquenta cantos quicos, texto bilinque*. Luanda: I.I.C.A.

Bastin, Marie-Louise. 1982. *La sculpture tshokwe*. Translated by J. B. Donne. Arcueil, France: Offset Arcueil.

———. 1988. "*Entites Spirituelles des Tshokwe* (Angola)." *Cuanderni Poro* 5:9–59.

Crowley, Daniel J. 1975. Aesthetic Value and Professionalism in African Art: Three Cases from the Katanga Chokwe. In *The Traditional Artist in African Societies*, ed. Warren L. d'Azevedo. Bloomington: Indiana University Press.

De Heusch, Luke. 1982. *The Drunken King or The Origin of the State*, trans. Roy Willis. Bloomington: Indiana University Press.

Fretz, Rachel I. 1995. Answering in Song: Listener Responses in Yishima Performances. *Western Folklore* 9(2):95–112.

———. 1994. Through Ambiguous Tales: Women's Voices in Chokwe Storytelling. *Oral Tradition*, 9, no. 1:230–50.

———. 1987. Storytelling among the Chokwe of Zaire: Narrating Skill and Listener Responses. Ph.D. Dissertation, Folklore and Mythology, UCLA.

Havenstein, A. 1976. *Fables et contes anaolais*. St Augustin bei Bonn: Verlag des Anthropos-Institus.

Holdredge, Claire Parker, and Kimball Young. 1927. Circumcision Rites among the Bajok. *American Anthropologist* n.s. 29:661–9.

Jordan, Manuel. 1993. *Le Masque comme processus ironique: Les makishi du Nord-Ouest de la Zambie. Anthrooolosie et Societe* 17, no, 3: 41–61.

Kubik, Gerhard. 1981. *Mukanda na makishi—Circumcision school and masks—Bescheidunasschule und Masken*. Berlin: Museum fur Volkerkunde, Musikethnologischen Abteilung.

———. 1993. *Makisi Nvau Mawiko: Maskentraditionen im bantu-sorachiaen Afrika*. Munich: Trckster Verlag.

Lima, Mesquitela. 1971. *Fonctions sociolosiaues des fiaurines de culte "hamba" dans la societe et dans la culture tshokwe*. Luanda: Instituto de Investicacao Cientifica de Angola.

McCulloh, Merran. 1951. *The Southern Lunda and Related Peoples (Northern Rhodesia, Ancrola. Belgian Conao)*. Ethnographic Survey of Africa, West Central Africa, Part I. London: International African Institute.

Miller, Joseph C. 1970. Cokwe Trade and Conquest in the 19th Century. In *Pre-Colonial African Trade*, ed. Richard Gray and David Birmingham. London: Oxford University Press.

———. 1988. *Wav of Death: Merchant Capitalism and the Angolan Slave Trade* 1730–1830. Madison: University of Wisconsin Press.

Sesembe, Nange Kudita wa. 1974. Tshikumbi, Tshiwila et Mungonge: Trois rites d'initiation chex les Tutshokwe du Kasai Occidental. *Cultures au Zaire et en Afriaue* 5:111–35.

———. 1981. L'homme et la femme dans la society et la culture Chokwe: de l'anthropologie et la philosophie. Unpublished dissertation. Universite Catholique de Louvain, Louvain-la-Neuve, Belgium.

Yoder, P. Stanley, 1981. Disease and Illness Among Cokwe: An Ethnomedical Perspective. Ph.D. Dissertation, Anthropology, UCLA.

RACHEL I. FRETZ

See also **Central African Folklore; Myths**

HISTORY

See **History and Folklore: The Luba**

HISTORY AND FOLKLORE: THE LUBA

The Luba, and neighboring peoples of the southeastern part of the Democratic Republic of the Congo (formerly Zaire), have a rich heritage of folklore and related oral history, including epic poetry, proverbs, maxims, king lists, genealogies, migration accounts, and religious songs. These Luba artistic forms do not exist in isolation, but rather in tandem with visual arts and performances. The symbiosis of the verbal and the visual deserves to be better understood because it places African art on the threshold between art history and literature. Just as stories evoke images, so do objects evoke stories, and creativity flourishes in this multimedia ferment.

Luba oral literature hinges on an epic that details the origins of Luba sacred kingship. The epic relates the heroic exploits of the Luba culture hero Moidi Kiluwe, who brought civilization to Luba people in the form of sacred kingship as well as advanced technologies of hunting and blacksmithing. His son, Kalala Ilunga, became the first Luba king after overcoming his tyrannical maternal uncle, Nkongolo Mwamba. Primary transcriptions of the Luba epic can be found in de Heusch (1982), Mudimbe (1991), and Reefe (1981), and related stories have been recorded and transcribed by foreigners (Womersley 1984).

More interesting, however, are the ways that the Luba themselves record and transmit their histories. So central is the epic to Luba cultural identity that an ingenious mnemonic device was devised by Luba historians in the last several centuries to safeguard and transmit the teachings of the past. Called a *lukasa*, (memory board), it is studded with beads, shells, and metal pins that serve as reminders to court historians, called "men of memory," as they verbally recite the histories of the kingdom on occasions such as kings' investiture rites, initiations, funerals, and voyages when they accompany rulers (Reefe 1981). Each prominent chieftaincy possesses its own *lukasa*, and historians from each region recite the "official" history of the kingdom in a slightly different fashion to reflect local interests and claims and to accommodate perpetually changing circumstances (Roberts and Roberts, 1996).

Lukasa memory boards share much in common with a Luba musical instrument called a *kasanji*, which looks like a *luksasa* with keys. Luba titleholders, chiefs, and historians play tone poems on *kasanji*; plucked ideophones recall the past and praise the king. The singing also triggers nostalgia. As one Luba titleholder states, *kasanji* is like a historical memorandum, "a whole history can be recounted" (Roberts and Roberts 1996, 144–5; Gansemans 1980).

Closely related to *kasanji*, tone poems are clan songs, panegyrics, and eulogies that laud the deeds and accomplishments of kings, chiefs, and lineage heads, called *numbi*. One particular category of praise poems is called *kasala*, which are sung to encourage bravery, express joy, and lead ceremonies to honor the dead (Mufuta 1969). While the songs are composed of well known verses, there is also considerable improvisation, and the singer of *kasanji* "feels . . . the sentiments of an entire social group" and is "the mirror of society" (Falk-Nzuji 1974, 48–50).

Many Luba chiefly emblems are used in performative contexts as reminders of royal history, for they are considered to be sacred replicas of the insignia carried by the protagonists of the epic. Sculpted wooden spears, staffs, ceremonial axes and knives, bowstands, stools, and cups were the emblems of the original hunter-blacksmith culture hero Mbidi Kiluwe, who left them to Kalala Ilunga when the latter acceded to the throne. During royal investiture rites of the last two hundred years, Luba kings, chiefs, and dignitaries have incarnated the culture heroes: gripping the emblems of their forebears, contemporary rulers enact the sacred origins of kingship (Roberts and Roberts 1999).

Certain types of Luba sculpture are made to evoke particular events and personages in the Luba epic during dance and other mnemonic performances. A double ended spear, for example, is a signifier for a historical episode when Nkongolo, the cruel despot, nefariously invited his nephew, Kalala, to perform a dance for him on a mat that secretly concealed a pit filled with doubletipped spears. Through a diviner's prescience, Kalala was forewarned, and during the dance, a drummer's tonal beats guided his footsteps safely across the dance floor to prevent his demise. Today, Luba rulers own such spears, and Mbudye dancers perform skits that dramatize this episode at public ceremonial occasions as an iconic reminder of the double-edged nature of authority and the dynamics, tensions, and paradoxes inherent to power. Through objects and actions, history is narrated and relived (Roberts and Roberts 1996).

Other kinds of emblems encode local family histories, legitimize descent, and validate clientele to the kingdom. Many chiefs and dignitaries possess staffs of office that serve not merely as status emblems but also as sculpted historical narratives. Staffs are used widely throughout Africa and serve various purposes, from healing to litigation (Nooter 1990; Roberts 1994). A Luba chief will recite the history encoded by his staff whenever his legitimacy is challenged, or simply as a way to familiarize descendants with their ancestral past. An historical narrative of such an object can take days or even weeks to recite, reflecting the depth of historical knowledge that such an object imparts. The staff, "read" from top to bottom, serves as a kind of three-dimensional map as well as a repository of spiritual authority (Roberts and Roberts 1996, 162–74).

In addition to oral and sculpted narratives, proverbs are central to Luba life, in both secular and sacred contexts. They are elicited on many occasions and are prompted by many visual stimuli. During initiation rites into the Mbudye association, which guards the precepts and prohibitions of Luba royalty, proverbs are the primary vehicle for transmission of knowledge. Often a proverb is linked with a visual sign, such as a natural object, a sculpted figure, or painted wall murals. As the initiate moves down the symbolic path of knowledge, signs mark the way and stimulate proverbs relating to the importance of maintaining secrets, for example, by holding on to the rules of Mbudye "as tightly as if they were flies, without ever letting go" (Nooter 1991).

Luba proverbs also figure in contexts of daily life and quotidian conversation, as well as during initiation rites for adolescents when boys and girls, respectively, undergo transformations to mark passage into adulthood. Body arts obtained during such rites, such as women's scarification patterns and male accoutrements and articles of dress that incorporate beadwork and incised geometric patterns, are mnemonic forms that trigger proverbs, with attendant commentary, discussion, and debate. Many proverbs express leadership qualities or assist with gender dynamics and express ideas too political for direct speech. A common proverb about the dually gendered nature of power states, "Men are chiefs in the daytime, but women are chiefs at night."

Finally, "songs for twins" form a critical body of esoteric wisdom among Luba, who sing on all religious occasions, ranging from funerals, initiations, and investitures to the night of the new moon each month when villagers rejoice and make offering to their ancestors (Roberts 1985). The songs for twins, usually sung by groups, are arcane verse whose references are so powerful that the songs alone can induce a trance. Songs for twins are sung when diviners or association members enter a state of spirit possession and personify the spirits of culture heroes past.

References

Faïk Nzuji, Clémentine. 1974. *Kasala: Chant héroïque Luba.* Lubumbashi: Presses Universitaire du Zaire.

Gansemans, Jos. 1980. Les Instruments de Musique Luba (Shaba, Zaire). *Annales du Musée Royal de l'Afrique Centrale.* 103:3–49.

Heusch, Luc de. 1982. *The Drunken King, or, The Origin of the State.* Bloomington, Indiana University Press.

Mudimbe, V.Y. 1991 *Parables and Fables: Exegesis, Textuality, and Politics in Central Africa.* Madison: University of Wisconsin Press.

Mufuta, Pierre. 1969. *Le Chant kasala des Luba.* Paris: Juillard, Collection Classiques Africaines.

Nooter, Mary H. 1990. Secret Signs in Luba Sculptural Narrative: A Discourse on Power. *Iowa Studies in African Art,* 3:35–60. Iowa City: Project for the Advanced Study of Art and Life in Africa.

———. 1991. *Luba Art and Polity: Creating Power in a Cental African Kingdom.* Ph.D. Dissertation, Columbia University, University Microfilms, Ann Arbor.

Reefe, Thomas Q. 1981. *The Rainbow and the Kings: A History of the Luba Empire to 1891.* Berkeley: University of California Press.

Roberts, Allen F. 1985. The Social and Historical Contexts of Tabwa Art. In *The Rising of a New Moon: A Century of Tabwa Art,* ed. Allen F. Roberts and Evan Maurer, Seattle: The University of Washington Press for the University of Michigan Museum of Art.

———. 1994. *Staffs of Life: Rods, Staffs, Scepters, and Wands from the Coudron Collection of African Art.* Iowa City: Project for the Advanced Study of Art and Life in Africa and the University of Iowa Museum of Art.

Roberts, Mary Nooter, and Allen F. Roberts. 1996. *Memory: Luba Art and the Making of History.* New York: The Museum for African Art and Prestel.

———. 1999. Anticipation and Longing: Congolese Culture Heroes Past, Present, and Future. In *Tshibumba: Painter of a Cultural Hero Lumumba,* ed. Bogumil Jewisewicki. New York and Munic: Museum for African Art.

Womersley, Harold. 1984. *Legends and History of the Luba.* Los Angeles: Crossroads Press, University of California.

MARY NOOTER ROBERTS

HISTORY AND RELIGIOUS RITUALS: BEMBA TRADITIONS

The Bemba people live in the great plateau region of northern Zambia. Bemba is one of six national languages recognized by the government for the production of school texts, radio and television programming, and literary translations. Because of their language and historical presence as a power in the region, the Bemba are a major ethnic group in the country.

Oral traditions locate the origin of the Bemba in the area of present-day Congo (formerly Zaire), where the Luba live. Their origin myth claims that a chief named Mukulumpe, who ruled in the land of Luba or Kola, married a magical woman named Mumbi Mukasa, a member of the crocodile (*Ngandu*) clan. They

had three sons, Katongo, Chiti, and Nkole, and one daughter, Chilufya. The sons angered Mukulumpe when they built a large tower that eventually collapsed and killed many people. He had Katongo's eyes put out and exiled the other two. Chiti and Nkole took along Chilufya and three half-brothers named Chimba, Kapasa, and Kazembe. The details of the journey vary between versions, but the group moved east, crossing the Luapula River, leaving members of the party in various areas to rule the local people. At the deaths of Chiti and Nkole, the children of Chilufya became the rightful heirs to the chiefship, thereby introducing the matrilineal inheritance pattern that exists today. They eventually reached the places that would become seats of Bemba traditional hegemony, such as the royal burial grounds at Mwalule and the site of the first paramount chief at *Ngwena* (Roberts 1973).

Archeological and linguistic research suggests that the Bemba people probably predated the arrival of the Bena Ngandu chiefs to the area they now rule. Numerous related ethnic groups do, in fact, have ruling clans that trace themselves back to the original Bena Ngandu lineage. Evidence from various sources estimates the establishment of this chiefship among the Bemba some time in the seventeenth century. The Bemba spread their influence and expanded their polity mainly by military force, regularly raiding their neighbors' livestock and fields. Records document nineteenth-century battles between the Bemba and Fipa, Ngoni, Mambwe, Lungu, Bisa, and Tabwa, among others.

By the late nineteenth century, several important Bemba chiefs had become involved in the region's slave trade. At around the same time, Roman Catholic missionaries of the White Fathers order tried to extend their influence to the northern Bemba area. At first rejected by the local chiefs, the Catholic priests were able to take advantage of a complex and, for the Bemba, deteriorating situation. Pressure from the colonial government, the British South Africa Company, hostile neighbors such as the Ngoni, and slavetraders seeking to increase their influence inspired some Bemba chiefs to meet with and test the intentions of the missionaries.

After the European priests were allowed access to some villages, the formative event of Bemba-Catholic relations took place upon the death of Chief Mwamba in October 1898. Mwamba actually left the custodianship of his people to Father Dupont, of the Kayambi mission. While the French priest "ruled" for a fairly short period, his presence and negotiations allowed the Bemba to form alliances and pacts that kept their various chiefdoms from some of the feared social and political upheavals of the period. Although other Christian missions arrived and made some headway, there remains a particularly strong tie between the Bemba of chiefs Mwamba, Chitimukulu, and Nkula, and the Catholic Church.

Religious practices among the Bemba are focused on several common areas. The first is that ancestors, in particular the spirits of dead chiefs, are regularly venerated and propitiated. These spirits, known as *imipashi* (*umupashi*, s.), are honored during rites linked to key economic activities such as preparing fields for planting, harvest, fishing, and hunting. The chief of each Bemba constituency is the ritual leader and plays the key role on these occasions. At times he has ritual experts (*bakabilo*) to aid him in these activities, and, when the rites are more localized for smaller groups or villages, headmen (*bene mushi*) also carry out similar tasks.

Throughout the Bemba region, there are locations where powerful nature spirits (*ngulu*) reside. These places are generally unusual geological formations or natural phenomena, such as waterfalls, caves, or large rock outcroppings. These spirits are also propitiated in conjunction with specific seasonal activities. Here too, the chiefs or their ritual experts conduct the ceremonies for the welfare of the community. The term *ngulu* is also used to label the practice of spirit possession, whereby certain individuals, sometimes in ceremonies and sometimes spontaneously, become conduits of particular nature or ancestral spirits.

The intersection of these older forms of worship and control of the spirit world with imported Christian practices is rather complex. It is common for Christians to participate in certain localized seasonal practices of communal rites carried out by chiefs and their surrogates. Christian services regularly employ traditional Bemba musical forms in the creation and performance of hymns. However, the more that Christianity is combined with older rites, the more likely it is that these rites will be the practice of syncretic or apostolic churches rather than that of mainstream Catholic or Protestant congregations. There is also the tacit recognition of the Bemba spirit called Lesa as the equivalent of the Christian "God." While evidence suggests that pre-Christian views of Lesa relegated him to a relatively ordinary status as one of many spirit beings, over time, Lesa has been accepted as the creator spirit among Bemba Christians (Maxwell 1983).

A key ritual that is both communal and highly personal is the initiation of girls into adulthood. There is no comparable rite for Bemba males. The ceremony of female initiation is called *cisungu*. In times past, the ceremonies took several months and required the girls to spend most of that time in rural isolation from the rest of the village or town. Today, the ceremonies are much shorter and adapted to the needs of contemporary young women; for example, convenient times are found so that formal schooling will not be interrupted. Essentially, the initiation is conducted by older, experienced women (*banacimbusa*), who are usually also midwives. The ritual employs the use of symbolic icons or emblems (*mbusa*) to instruct the candidates in the many skills and knowledge required of women in Bemba society. Although physical hardship is a part of the ritual, no form of excision or female circumcision is practiced among the Bemba (Richards 1988; Corbeil 1982).

References

Corbeil, J. J. 1982. *Mbusa: Sacred Emblems of the Bemba*. Mbala, Zambia: Moto-Moto Museum, and London: Ethnographica, Ltd..

Maxwell, Kevin B. 1983. *Bemba Myth and Ritual: The Impact of Literacy on an Oral Culture*. New York: Peter Lang.

Richards, Audrey I. 1956/1988. *Chisungu: A Girl's Initiation Ceremony Among the Bemba of Zambia*. London: Faber and Faber Ltd.; 3rd ed., London: Routledge.

Roberts, Andrew D. 1973. *A History of the Bemba: Political Growth and Change in North-eastern Zambia Before 1900*. Madison: University of Wisconsin Press.

ROBERT CANCEL

HOUSING: AFRICAN AMERICAN TRADITIONS

Between 1505 and 1870, when millions of Africans were captured and transported to the Americas to toil their lives away as plantation slaves, their cultural habits made the voyage to the New World along with their bodies. While these people faced oppressive and exploitive conditions, they nevertheless managed to carry on a wide variety of expressive forms rooted in African habits. Aspects of language, religious practices, foodways, and the performing arts, especially in distinctive modes of music, song, dance, and narration, were widely reported as evidence of the enduring African character of the enslaved population. But tangible expressions of African tradition such as art, household objects, clothing, technology, and architecture—indeed, almost any vestiges of material culture—were rarely mentioned in period descriptions of slave life. This absence can best be understood in the light of the general policy among slaveholders that held that any visual reminder of the African homelands constituted a direct threat to their authority and thus had to be quickly eradicated. An episode at Hopeton Plantation on the Georgia coast is instructive. There, sometime around 1850, an African man called Okra built a small house. Mud walled and topped with a thatched roof, it was immediately torn down. According to former slave Ben Sullivan, plantation owner James Couper "ain't want no African hut on he place."

By the middle decades of the nineteenth century, slave housing was not significantly different from buildings inhabited by working-class whites. However, during the formative period of the plantation economy, the presence of African-inspired architecture was more evident. The retention of African housing was linked ultimately to demographic dominance. In South Carolina in 1720, for example, Africans outnumbered white people by a ratio of ten to one. Thus, when a visitor to the colony during that period remarked that the place "looked more like a negro country than a country settled by white people," his assessment probably reflected not only the numbers of Africans that he saw but the houses that they had necessarily been compelled to build for themselves. Archaeological investigations at some of those house sites have uncovered the foundations of the mud walls that outlined rectangular plans measuring not more than 10 × 21 feet. Assuming that these houses once had thatched roofs, they would resemble not only the dwelling destroyed by James Couper but buildings that can still be found all along the Atlantic rim of Africa from Guinea to Angola.

When they were confronted with the pressures of turning a profit from the undeveloped American wilderness, planters, it seems, allowed their slaves a certain amount of leeway in their domestic conduct as long as the required tasks were completed. Expedience on the part of the planters thus provided the slaves with an opportunity to utilize their African traditions and thus the chance to build what their descendents would call "ground houses," that is, dwellings with clay or earthen walls. But once the plantations were fully operational, say after 1750, planters routinely asserted more direct control over the daily lives of the slave population. Consequently, from the mid-eighteenth century onward, African plans and building techniques (as well as other African customs) were systematically suppressed, and African American houses became nothing more than variants of the most typical kinds of Euro-American houses.

While the continuity of African architectural traditions was ultimately disrupted in the United States, the saga of the ubiquitous houses known as "shotguns" offers an instance of a subtle, but ultimately profound, African influence on American vernacular architecture. The shotgun house type, which developed in Haiti as an amalgam of Native American, European, and African influences and then entered the United States through New Orleans in the early nineteenth century, has had a lasting impact on the American South. Today, thousands of shotgun houses can be found throughout the region. The basic shotgun house is a one-story building that is long and narrow; it is one-room wide and three or more deep. Unlike most American folk houses, the shotgun is oriented with its gable to the front and has its entrance in the gable end rather than on the longer side. This formal difference should be read as a sign of the building's alternative history.

Shotgun houses in the United States are descended from small rural Haitian houses called *cailles*. Known on the island of Hispaniola since the early sixteenth century, they were generally constructed with walls of woven lath that were plastered with mud; their roofs were made either of thatched grass or palm leaves. In plan, the house consisted of two rooms and had its front door located at the narrow gable end of the building. The gable entrance of this dwelling is a feature that finds its precedent in the houses of the Arawaks, the indigenous people of Haiti, while its construction techniques show clear linkages to northern France, the homeland of the colonial class (although parallels can be found in Africa as well). The aspect of this house that connects most deeply with African architectural practices are its dimensions; rooms are small, containing, generally, slightly more than 80 square feet of floor space. This average size compares closely with the average room sizes in West and Central African houses, which commonly range between 8 × 8 feet and 12 × 12 feet. Since the room units in Euro-American folk houses are generally 250 square feet or larger, the Haitian shotgun prototype aligns most closely with the African size spectrum.

The consistent use of particular dimensions indicates that a discrete proxemic code, the most central element of any architectural tradition, had made the voyage across the Atlantic from Africa intact. What we see in the intimate spaces of Haitian houses is that African architectural influences flow directly to Haiti with the trade in slaves. Then, after a period of encounter with other equivalent traditions, a new house form evolves and becomes commonplace. One could say that a core concept for an African building is provided with a new exterior. The resulting building, a Creolized architectural form, is then carried on to North America in yet another migration and eventually becomes a distinctive marker of southern identity. While the African attributes of the shotgun house are no longer widely acknowledged, it is, nonetheless, a building with African roots, and its history reveals much about the tenacity of African traditional culture.

References

Ferguson, Leland. 1992. *Uncommon Ground: Archaeology and Early African America, 1665–1800*. Washington D.C.: Smithsonian Press.

Georgia Writer's Project. 1940. *Drums and Shadows: Survival Studies Among the Georgia Coastal Negroes*. Athens: University of Georgia Press.

Vlach, John Michael. 1976. The Shotgun House: An African Architectural Legacy. *Pioneer America* 8, no. 1:47–56; 8, no. 2: 57–70.

Wood, Peter H. 1974. *Black Majority: Negroes in Colonial South Carolina from 1670 through the Stono Rebellion*. New York: W. W. Norton.

JOHN MICHAEL VLACH

HUNTING: AKA NET HUNTING

Community net hunting was traditionally practiced by a variety of ethnic groups across the central African forests and savannas. Few agriculturalists continue to net hunt today, and the practice is associated principally with ethnic groups such as the Mbuti in the Democratic Republic of the Congo (Ichikawa 1983; Turnbull 1961) and the Aka in the Central African Republic and the Democratic Republic of the Congo (Bahuchet, 1985).

Techniques vary somewhat among ethnic groups, but, in general, net hunting is a community activity involving people of all ages and both sexes. Among the Aka in southwestern Central African Republic, infants are carried by their mothers, and children begin to actively contribute as young as five years of age. The number of participants ranges from less than ten to over one hundred.

Women generally outnumber men, and occasionally, a net hunting group comprises only women. Among the Aka both women and men beat and guard nets, whereas sex roles are more strict in Mbuti net hunts where the women beat while the men carry and guard the nets.

The number of nets ranges from five to more than twenty. Aka nets measure 3.2 by 4.9 feet in height and 16 to 131 feet in length. Mbuti nets are up to 320 feet long. Net twine is made from the cambium fiber of the woody vine *kosa* (*Manniophyton fulvum*). Wooden hooks at each end fix the net to small trees or vines, the top of the net is hooked on other vegetation, and the bottom is pegged to the ground.

The Aka generally form a closed circle of nets (*dibouka*) around a promising patch of forest, with a circumference of only 984 feet. The hunters communicate by means of hiqh-pitched calls and whistles as they set the nets, consistently accomplishing the remarkable feat of closing a circle of nets in dense forest vegetation without being able to see the other members of the hunting party. Immediately upon finishing, the net carriers begin searching the enclosed area, beating leaves, and shouting to drive animals from their hiding places. The other participants remain near the nets to spot flushed animals, to frighten them into the nets, and then to seize them before they can escape. Each round of setting the nets, driving, and moving to the next

Ba Aka net hunting, Dzanga Sangha Special Dense Forest Preserve, Central African Republic. Photo © Hal Noss, www.halnoss.com.

site takes only 10 to 15 minutes. In contrast, Mbuti net hunters generally set the nets describing an arc up to 0.93 miles long, begin the drive up to 0.6 miles away, and a day's hunting comprises four to eight casts.

In Aka *mulongo* net hunting, the participants depart from their village in the morning and return in the evening. These hunts usually begin 2 to 2.5 miles, or one hour's walk, from the community and cover several kilometers during the ten to thirty casts of the nets. Hunters frequently leave their nets in the forest where the day's hunt ends in order to resume the following day's hunt at that point. The nets are rolled and tied to the top of a pole, with a covering of leaves to shed rain. Net hunting also takes place from seasonal and mobile forest camps (*kumbi*) that can last from several days to several months.

Aka nets are owned by both women and men. A captured animal is the property of the net owner (*konja*), even if that person is not present. However, the head of the animal belongs to the person who sets the net, while the ribs and belly belong to the person who first seizes the animal. These sharing rules reinforce cooperation during net hunting and reflect the cooperative nature of Aka society, providing meat to participants who are not net owners.

The leader of the net hunt is always a man, unless only women are participating. This person is one of the first to leave the settlement, choosing the starting and ending points for the day's hunt. Once the hunt begins, the leader may determine the general direction of the hunt and may identify likely places to set the nets, but other hunters frequently take over these responsibilities as the hunt flows quickly through the forest.

The leader may call for a rest during the day, particularly in order to attribute blame if the hunt is unsuccessful. The group then identifies a man who has slept with his wife the previous day, or whose wife is pregnant, or a women in the early stages of pregnancy. This person must remain behind the hunting group until something is captured. The death of a person from the community also is a cause for poor hunting success, and net hunting is suspended for several days. A forest camp where someone dies is abandoned, and hunters avoid areas where people are buried.

Rituals

Rituals associated with net hunts are no longer commonly practiced, particularly during *mulongo* (day) hunts. However, on occasion before the hunt, hunters will rub leaves and spit on their nets while imitating the cry of a captured duiker in order that their net will kill "meat." The blood of a captured animal will also be spilt on a net that has not captured anything for some time. Also for luck, hunters will make a loud popping noise by clapping one hand down on a leaf placed over their other fist before taking down nets left in the forest overnight.

Before a *kumbi* net hunt, the camp leader may arise before dawn and, from the edge of camp, call out the names of the animals of the forest while the other camp members echo him from their huts. Then, before the hunt, the leader will take each net, rub leaves and spit on it, while again calling the names of the animals. The hunters may also conduct a small dance before the hunt, following one hunter, who is holding a hoop decorated with leaves as he dances and weaves and imitates the calls of the hunt.

Ba Aka net hunting, Dzanga Sangha Special Dense Forest Preserve, Central African Republic. Photo © Hal Noss, www.halnoss.com.

The *jengi* dance is performed in Aka communities to bring good luck to net hunters (Bahuchet 1985; Sarno 1993). The *jengi* is a forest spirit in a large raffia mask. Only men may touch him, and they form a protective circle between the *jengi* and the dancing women, circling the drummers. The *jengi* periodically runs off into the forest and then returns as the dance continues through the night, every night for several weeks or more.

Prey

Net hunts are selective in capturing small terrestrial mammals such as duikers and porcupines. Aka net hunts capture, on average, eight animals per day, whose total body weight averages 101 pounds. Larger animals are rarely encountered, as the noise of the hunting group warns them away, and in any case, they can tear through or jump over the nets to escape. Whether or not animals are killed, most participants return with some forest products for consumption or sale: several kinds of edible nuts such as payo, caterpillars, at least thirty species of edible mushrooms, numerous fruits, wild yams, honey from six species of bees, edible koko leaves, and ngongo leaves for wrapping or roofing.

The net hunters' prey species are the most abundant terrestrial mammals and generally the most resilient to hunting pressure. Combined with settlement mobility throughout extensive hunting ranges, traditional net hunting has been, therefore, ecologically sustainable. Thus, protected areas such as the Dzanga-Sangha Special Reserve in southwestern Central African Republic permit net hunting as a traditional hunting method practiced for subsistence purposes.

Growth of urban centers and the development of transportation links, however has reinforced the importance of commercial meat production through net hunting among the Mbuti (Hart 1978) as well as the Aka. Initially, market hunting may reinforce community structure as cooperation among large numbers of participants is essential for successful net hunting. But in the long run, bush-meat markets are in many ways detrimental to net-hunter societies. The demand for meat in large urban centers far surpasses the relatively small resident population's consumption needs, and net hunters have intensified their hunting efforts. In recent years, hunting ranges have been reduced by logging and agricultural colonization of African forest regions, by permanent settlement of previously mobile populations, by population growth of resident populations, and even by the creation of national parks. Game populations decline in the face of increased hunting pressure.

Other hunting methods that are more effective in producing meat for commercial ends and in areas with less abundant game are replacing nets. For example, cable snares capture larger animals, and captures belong to the individual hunter, resulting in considerably higher returns (in meat or cash) per hunter. For these reasons, agriculturalist ethnic groups in the Central African Republic like the Banda (whose name means "net"), Ngando, and Ngbaka abandoned net hunting decades ago. As Aka men are presently switching from nets to cable snares, Aka women today hunt more often than men, and net hunts include more women than men. In this form, net hunting remains an effective hunting method that provides a variety of subsistence and commercial resources, including meat, and that serves to maintain Aka society and identity as people of the forest.

References

Bahuchet, S. 1985. Les pygmees Aka et la foret Centrafricaine: ethnologie ecologique. Paris: Societe d'Etudes Linguistiques et Anthropologiques de France.

Hart, J.A. 1978. From Subsistence to Market: a Case Study of the Mbuti Net Hunters. Human Ecology 6:325–53.

Ichikawa, M. 1983. An Examination of the Hunting-dependent Life of the Mbuti Pygmies, Eastern Zaire. African Study Monographs 4:55–76.

Sarno, L. 1993. Song from the Forest: My Life among the Ba-Benjelle Pygmies. Boston: Houghton Mifflin.

Turnbull, C. M. 1961. *The Forest People*. London: Chatto and Windus.

ANDREW J. NOSS

See also **Central African Folklore**

HUTU

See **Folktales; Rwanda**

I

IBIBIO

See **Drama: Anang Ibibio Traditional Drama; Puppetry; Verbal Arts: The Ibibio of Southeastern Nigeria; West Africa: Overview**

IDENTITY AND FOLKLORE: KUNDA

The Kunda of Zambia are a polity of approximately 35,000 Bantu-speaking people in the central Luangwa River valley. They are a group distinct from the Chikunda of the Zambezi River valley. The Kunda of Zambia claim some ancestral relation with the Kunda polities of the Congo basin, but they have no practical affiliation with those peoples within historical memory.

Kunda lore, or "folk knowledge," is best characterized by the idiomatic term, *makhalidwe wa Akunda*, which translates as "Kunda ways of staying." *Makhalidwe wa Akunda* refers to the widest variety of knowledge-based practices among Kunda people by which they survive politically, maintaining the identity and integrity of the polity, and survive as people in a biological sense. Kunda folk teaching collapses biology and politics so that a person who survives biologically in Kunda country, or is born of Kunda parents, necessarily has a Kunda political identity. Many Kunda people will even say that the real objective of knowing these "Kunda ways of staying" is *mphamvu kukhoka wanthu*, or the "power to gather people": that is, the power to increase the polity and its family lineages. In the Kunda idiomatic universe, political power and the physical power of bodies are constituent products of practices of knowing.

There is no noun for *knowledge* in Kunda language. There is only the verb "to know" (*kudziwa*), and its affiliate wisdom or intelligence (*nzeru*). By Kunda idiomatic practice a Kunda person cannot know an abstract thing called knowledge. Kunda knowing is always active. Kunda people always know how to do some action (*ncito*, or a "job"), which is enacted for the results it has. Kunda knowing also always is "owned" by its practitioner, and the ones who taught it to him/her. All ways of staying that Kunda people know, they know because those ways of staying make survival possible, and because an elder who practiced that knowledge before told it to them. That action is told only to

members of one's own lineage because it enhances the chances of survival for their lineage. It is usually guarded knowledge, kept from other lineages who may be in direct competition with one's own lineage for survival. The dynamic interrelations between group identity and the management of knowledge is crystallized in a proverb well known to most Kunda people: "Chikumo chimodzi sichitola sabwe," which translates as "One thumb cannot pick a louse."

Kunda people describe the very real sense in which all acts of knowing accumulate people and power to the owners of practical knowledge. There is nothing known to Kunda people which falls outside of Kunda ways of staying, except the ways of staying of other people—actions which build alliances with and substantiate non-Kunda political entities. Kunda elders advise young people that the most important thing about staying well is to follow ones' lineage elders with respect (*kukhonka mokolo*), following the things that they know to do and for the results they produce for their lineage. No two family lineages know the exact same variety of "jobs," but there are a few things that most all Kunda lineages do know: Kunda etiquette, proverbs (*miyambo*), some folk songs (*visimi*), some stories (*mbili*), which illustrate or enact the primary importance of Kunda lineages and the need to substantiate the power of elders and chiefs in order to maintain control of Kunda country.

References

Boone, Olga. 1961. *Carte Ethnique du Congo: Quart Sud-est.* Tervuren, Belgium: Musée Royal de l'Afrique Centrale.

Kumakanga, Stevenson L. 1975. *Nzeru za Kale* (Wisdom from Long Ago)(1949). Blantyre, Malawi: Dzuka.

Mwale, E. G. 1952. *ZaAchewa*. London: Macmillan.

Poole, E. H. Lane. 1949. *Native Tribes of the Eastern Province of Northern Rhodesia: Notes on their Migrations and History*, 3rd ed. Government of Northern Rhodesia.

Strickland, Bradford. 1995. *Knowledge, Agency, and Power among the Kunda of Eastern Zambia*, Ph.D. Dissertation, Chapel Hill, North Carolina.

Sumbwa, Nyambe. 1993. *Zambian Proverbs*. Lusaka: Zambia Printing.

BRADFORD STRICKLAND

See also **History and Cultural Identity: The Chokwe; Central African Folklore: Overview**

IDEOPHONE

The ideophone (idea-phone), first defined in C.M. Doke's *Bantu Linguistic Terminology* as "a vivid representation of an idea in sound" (1935, 118), is a form of expressive vocabulary that is very prominent in African language usage. Lists of several thousand ideophones in a given language may readily be compiled and they may comprise a quarter or more of the words in a dictionary. They are used with great frequency and effectiveness both in the ordinary language of daily conversation and in the dramatic style of oral art (Samarin 1965, 117).

Ideophones are a class of words that represent the full range of sensual experience including sound, sight, smell, taste, and feeling. Not only do they imitate noises (onomatopoeia), they also express action and motion; they portray color, odor and texture; and they reveal manner, intensity and emotion.

In the speech of the Gbaya people of Cameroon and the Central African Republic, *bababa* depicts the determined tread of an old man, *títítítí** reveals someone running on tiptoes, *volok-volok* is the bounding gait of a hungry hyena, *hóng-hong-hóng* is the distant baying of dogs, *béréng* is the color of the reddish horizon as the sun sets, *wékéké* is the emptiness of an abandoned village, *sélélé* is the silence of a peaceful night, *pirrr* is the fluttering of a little bird's wings, and *faa-faa* are the measured wing-beats of a great bird of prey.

Speakers may use ideophones to reveal their attitude toward what they are describing. A tall lissome maiden may be presented *goyɛɛ* in all her beauty, the delicate mouth of an infant may be admired by comparing it to the little round mouth *búδúk* of a certain small white and highly esteemed fish. The speaker may also use ideophones pejoratively and for making insults: a person's disheveled hair is *wasa-wuzu*, someone's bloodshot eyes might be likened to the eyes of the weaverbird that are bright red, *kéréré*.

Ideophones may sometimes be identified as a distinct class of words by their phonemes. Sounds that are not otherwise found in the lexicon of a language often feature as part of ideophone patterns. Many ideophones have simple syllable structure that lends itself to lengthening or repetition. In doubled and tripled forms there may be alternation of consonants or of vowels. In some languages ideophones are set apart by special markers; in other languages they take very minimal grammatical marking. Their function in a sentence is usually to describe action or objects, and sometimes in elliptical manner they may replace a noun or a verb. Not infrequently there is a derivational relationship between ideophones and nouns and verbs (Cameroon Pidgin English: *chuk* "to pierce, to stab"; *chuku-chuku* "thorn"; *chuku-chuku beef* "porcupine").

The most distinguishing feature of ideophones is their especially close relationship of sound and meaning (Okpewho 1992, 92–96). For example, the lengthening of a final vowel or nasal sound reflects duration while repetition denotes repeated action (Sango: *ngbiii* "for a while"; *ngbi ngbi ngbi* "again and again"). Repetition may also indicate intensity (Fula: *cúb* "early"; *cúb-cúb* "very early"). Tone variation often distinguishes size and weight: a high tone identifies something small and light in weight and

the same form in low tone depicts something that is big and heavy. By extension what is small and light may appear to be insignificant while the big and heavy is important and even dangerous.

However, associations of sound with meaning vary across language and culture. Thus, to be snow-white is rendered in Gbaya as *ndáká-ndáká* and in Xhosa and Zulu as *qhwa*; in Hausa whiteness is qualified as *fat* or *kal* and in Swahili as *pe*. A rooster crows *ghukughúkúu!* in Gikuyu of Kenya, in Kinyarwanda of Rwanda it crows *kokoyíkúu!* and in Gã of Ghana it crows *kokotsíokóo!*

Ideophones are an important feature of aesthetic expression for the artist (Finnegan 1970, 64–65). Indeed, the eloquence of oral performers may be judged by their creative manipulation of ideophones. In a short lyric, the Cameroonian poet Dogobadomo Beloko adopts ideophones to sing the praises of Hare, a favorite Gbaya folktale character who often represents the cleverness of the underdog:

Lémté	*Lémté*
Guwang guwang	*Guwang guwang*
Gu guwang	*Gu guwang*
Máá-yi kó Domo,	The running of Rabbit,
Domo ãã sí-i!	There goes Rabbit!

Lénné depicts Hare's long ears laid back on his head as he bursts into sudden flight. *Guwang guwang gu guwang* is his loping gait as he runs off in the distance confident that he is out of the reach of his pursuers. When *guwang* is used singly, it may describe a gentle fall of something like a young sapling when it is cut down or when the wind blows it over.

An ideophone may be a key word in riddles and proverbs. In southern Cameroon *Haaa!* is a one-word riddle. It is an ideophone that represents the satisfied exclamation of a drinker after taking a large swig of strong liquor. The answer to the riddle is therefore "local home brew."

Ideophones are often considered to be a feature of oral language. Some people suggest that they can be coined at the whim of the speaker. Perhaps it would be more accurate to say that there is a reservoir of sound symbolic shapes from which the artist can draw to create new ideophones. Nevertheless, the precision of meaning that is given to ideophones in usage is evidence for their stability in each language community. Like any other words, they may be borrowed and transmitted from language to language through the vicissitudes of history and culture. They are found even in the newly developing forms of pidgin and creole languages of Africa's rapidly growing cities (e.g., in Sheng of the Streets of Nairobi: "mos-mos" is slowly and "chap-chap" is quickly). A streetwise young man is called a "san-san boy" in the Pidjin English of Cameroon.

For the linguist and literary scholar the semantics of ideophones may appear to be ambiguous and elusive. For the translator they present a quandary. Can their meanings be transferred into languages that make little use of ideophones, or should they simply be transcribed and retained in translation? Extensive recording and analysis of ideophones and ideophone usage is needed before their semantics and aesthetics will be fully understood.

References

Doke, C. M. 1935. *Bantu Linguistic Terminology*. London: Longmans Green.

*Acute accent mark indicates high tone.

Finnegan, Ruth. 1970. *Oral Literature in Africa*. Oxford: Clarendon Press.

Noss, Philip A. 1972. "Gbaya Tales," in *African Folklore*, ed. R. M. Larson. Bloomington, Ind. Indiana University Press.

Okpewho, Isidore. 1992. *African Oral Literature*. Bloomington: Indiana University Press.

Samarin, W. J. 1965. "Perspective on African Ideophones." *African Studies* 24: 117–121.

Voeltz, F. K. Erhard and Christa Kilian-Hatz, eds. *Ideophones*. Amsterdam: John Benjamins, 2001.

PHILIP A. NOSS

See also **Folktales; Gestures in African Oral Narratives; Oral Performance Dynamics**

IGBO

See **Visual Arts: Uli Painting of the Igbo; West African Folklore: Overview**

IJO

See **Oral Tradition and Oral Historiography; Water Ethos: The Ijo of the Niger Delta; West Africa: Overview**

INDEXES: MOTIF AND TALE-TYPE

See **Typology and Performance in the Study of Prose Narratives in Africa**

INDIAN OCEAN ISLANDS: THE PROCESS OF CREOLIZATION

There are several islands and island groups in the Indian Ocean that share an intriguing history of settlement, bringing together African, Asian, and European peoples and traditions. Embodying the very definition of creolization, the folklore and arts of these settlers reflect, in varying combinations, their diverse roots stemming from different countries, ethnic groups, and periods of migration. Each has its own signature history and cultural configuration, so they will be discussed serially, beginning with the Comoros Islands, then moving to Seychelles, Mauritius, Réunion, and finally "the big island," Madagascar.

Four green volcanic islands, lying between Mozambique and Madagascar, make up the Comoros archipelago: Anjouan (Nzwani), Grande Comore (Ngazidja), Mohéli (Mwali), and Mayotte (Maoré, a "territorial collectivity" of France). The population numbers about half a million people of African extraction, whose forebears intermarried with Malagasy, Arabs, and Persians. The culture is a unique combination of African and Islamic traditions, which are transmitted to the young by grandparents and Quranic teachers. In this archipelago, to which repeated coups d'état and uprisings (1989, 1992, 1995, and 1997) have failed to bring prosperity, unemployment is high, and prices of staples continually rise. Tourism is negligible despite an agreeable climate, beautiful beaches, and robust dance traditions. All the islands, especially the underpopulated Mohéli, have breathtaking agricultural potential.

The folklore of the Comoros blends African traditions with an ideological stress on Islam. It includes heroic recitations by royal reciters, legends of Quranic figures and *djinns* (spirits), and oral history connecting the islands to King Solomon. Place legends feature the active volcano Karthala on Grande Comore, whose 1977 eruption buried most of the village of Singani. One major narrative genre is the *hadisi* (from Arabic *hadith*, "the words of and about the Prophet"), which includes historical legends and sacred narratives secularized. The subgenre *wana hadisi*, "anecdote," combines humor with an initiatory function, for instance, to impart sexual education to a woman about to be married. The other major narrative genre, sometimes scorned as childish, is *hale*, a lie or fiction told at evening. In purportedly historical stories, the two genres overlap, paralleling similar genres in East Africa and Madagascar. Proverbs have much force; riddles show more influence of modern times than the other genres.

Folktales have been extensively collected on Mayotte by Noël Gueunier and Sophie Blanchy. Michael Lambek has analyzed spirit narratives in Mayotte. Mohéli and Anjouan await careful research, particularly on the practices surrounding the central Comoran custom of *grand mariage* (the big marriage).

The Seychelles archipelago is located north-northeast of Madagascar in the Indian Ocean. Settlement and creolization began in the late eighteenth century, with the importation by European planters of African slaves to work their cotton plantations. A century later, nearly all of the 20,000 Seychellois were of African descent. Around that time, Indian merchants immigrated from Bombay, Gujarat, and Kutch, and a few Chinese also settled there. Today the 68,932 people of Seychelles, a mixture of Asians, Africans, and Europeans who speak both English and *kreol*, recognize no ethnic division and constitute a true creole society. Their African and Malagasy cultural patterns give their islands a cultural profile quite distinct from that of Réunion or Mauritius. Tourism is a key source of revenue.

As in East Africa, separate spheres for men and women harbor separate kinds of the folklore. Women's activities are concentrated in the household, men's, at places of work and recreation. "Thus, from an early stage, men's recreational and social activities take place away from the household, on the football field, at a dance, at the toddy seller's on the road. They come home to eat and sleep but not to socialize" (Benedict 1982, 263). Weddings and dances are both occasions for communication and subjects for folklore. Traditional music exists side by side with imported "world music" on cassette. In dance, the traditional *moutia* coexists with the Mauritian *séga* and other regional forms.

Proverbs, riddles, games, and folktales show the African origin of many Seychellois. Pirate legends reflect the island's history and attract treasure hunters. As well as practicing Christian religion, many people maintain beliefs in witchcraft or sorcery: *grigri*, *malfezans*, or *pti talber*. With her cards or fortune-telling book, a *bonnfamm dibwa* can find out who is responsible for misfortune or illness. Government policy encourages the preservation and presentation of material culture and ethnobotany, as well as collecting and publishing of folklore and literature in creole and sponsoring a "Festival Kreol." The Institi Kreol incites Seychellois to elaborate and improve their oral tales in writing.

Mauritius, a long-uninhabited island of 2,040 square kilometers located 559 miles east of Madagascar in the Indian Ocean, houses strands of population reflecting successive colonization by Holland, France, and Britain. From about 1735, France imported slaves from Portuguese East Africa and Madagascar to work its sugar plantations. After Britain took over in 1815 and abolished slavery in 1835, the planters were obliged to import indentured laborers from India to succeed the slaves. Thousands of freed slaves went east to the island of Rodgrigues; most remained to make up the "creole" strand of the population. Other ethnicities include the Indo-Mauritian descendents of indentured laborers (much subdivided), Hakka-speaking Chinese, and a few Franco-Mauritians. Independent since 1968, Mauritius is proud of this "rainbow" of cultures, a diversity that fosters a capacity for crossing cultural boundaries and participating in other people's traditions.

Paradoxically Mauritius acquires its folkloric image through the preromantic novel *Paul et Virginie* (1787) by the Frenchman Bernardin de St. Pierre. Meanwhile, the diverse populations nurture distinct traditions. Well-known African tales were collected by Charles Baissac, a Creole who recognized his people's ability for cultural convergence.

Mauritian folk religion is a unique amalgam. Tamils and Telugus, though speaking different languages from North Indians, share Hinduism with them. At home, Telugus practice pan-Hindu festivals yet maintain their distance from other groups. Tamil temples house black stone images identified as the Catholic Saint Theresa and Virgin Mary. Creole Catholics of African extraction practice Indian rites; self-identified Hindus and Muslims go as pilgrims to the grave of Père Laval, a nineteenth-century French Catholic missionary. Religious symbols in the home, women's clothes, ornaments, ritual costume, and special foods remind people of their ethnic affiliations. Today the rapid pace of modernization and the prosperity of the country offer still more choices and pose the question of how traditions shall be evaluated.

The spectacular volcanic island of La Réunion lies 497 miles east of Madagascar, part of the archipelago of the Mascareignes (including Mauritius), a French possession since 1638. At that time it was named Ile Bourbon and had a mixed population of Europeans and Malagasy slaves. With the cultivation of coffee in 1725 it became a plantation society that engendered slave escapes; with the introduction of sugar (1815), numbers increased, notably the region's only population of poor whites; with the abolition of slavery in 1848, the island acquired Indian indentured laborers. Because so many were Muslims, these acquired the creole name Zarab. The island suffered poverty and neglect until becoming an overseas department of France in 1946.

As would be expected in a Creole society, folklore in La Réunion is created out of the convergence of Africans, Malagasy, French, and Indians. The importance of proverbs there seems to be a Malagasy contribution. A university project in the 1970s collected dozens of tales. It revealed virtuosic performers among the poor whites, the most condemned of the island's groups, who preserve French tales. Réunionnais of African and Malagasy background know African animal stories and trickster tales pitting the clever hero Ti Zan against the ogre Gran Dyab. Indian religious narratives are performed in creole during festivals.

Folk religion in this nominally Catholic island nourishes werewolf and Evil Eye beliefs, traditional cults like Saint Expédit (known also in the Caribbean), and practices like the *promès*, a vow made in exchange for a hoped-for cure or success. At the *kavadi* festival, Indo-Réunionnais undergo ordeals to thank the deity for granting such favors. The Afro-Malagasy strand of Réunion's Creole tradition awaits systematic study.

Madagascar, the world's fourth-largest island (227–208 square miles), was settled by waves of Malayo-Polynesian migrants. Malagasy culture results from a fusion of Indonesian and Swahili (East African) traditions. One result is a broad ethnic division between highlanders of predominantly Malayo-Indonesian origin (Merina with a population of 1,643,000; Betsileo, 760,000) and coastal people of mixed African, Malayo-Indonesian, and Arab ancestry (Betsimisaraka 941,000; Tsimihety 442,000; Antaisaka 415,000; Sakalava 374,000). The eighteen ethnic groups speak dialects of a common language. Another result, enhanced by the isolation of a huge island, is a unique folk culture linked to the Comoros Islands to the north but quite distinct from Africa only 249 miles to the west.

The earliest narrative to be recorded is a myth of the origin of social classes, published by the French colonist Flacourt in 1658. As the British began to impose themselves on Madagascar from 1820 and their Protestant missionaries started schools, examples of the haunting *hainteny* (art of speech) of the highland Merina were published. One newly literate Merina wrote an epic version of the popular hero tale, "Ibonia" about 1830. Systematic collecting began only after missionaries had been expelled in 1836 and then readmitted in 1869. In their *Antananarivo Annual* (1875–1900) they published tales, legends, proverbs, riddles, customs, and ethnographic observations. The classic Merina collection is Lars Dahle's *Specimens of Malagasy Folklore* (1877); other collections followed, notably among the Sakalava and Bara. Proverbs impart values such as the prestige of the dead and a fear of isolation: "Even the dead like to be many." Thousands of Malagasy proverbs have been collected and translated, leading to the conclusion that eloquence is prized here as much as in West Africa. After French conquest of Madagascar in 1896, Jean Paulhan's translations of Merina *hainteny* in 1913 drew attention to folk poetry. This genre uses riddlelike form and metaphor in a stylized verbal duel. Other observers recorded samples of oratory at weddings and funerals, which confirmed the high place of verbal eloquence and raising questions of gender attribution.

Madagascar's folk culture is both diverse and unified. The African influence is discernible in cotton spinning, millet cultivation, musical instruments like the scraper, the rattle, and the earth bow, social patterns like the all-important reverence for ancestors, and tales of African origin. Islam introduced writing. European influence, intensifying as Britain and France vied for control of the island through the nineteenth century, brought the Roman alphabet and literacy as well as firearms and provoked an ironic legend in which the presence of colonists is inflicted on Malagasy because a taboo was broken. The Indonesian heritage persists, as P. Beaujard has shown in his studies of folk narrative among the Tanala (Forest People). The uniqueness of the mix is offered by P. Ottino as a stimulus to cultural research. Assessment of published folktales revealed some four hundred independent plots not known outside of Madagascar and at least sixty-five versions of internationally known folktale types.

References

Allaoui, Masséande Chami. 1997. Genres of Comoran Folklore, trans. Lee Haring. *Journal of Folklore Research* 34:45–57.

Beaujard, Philippe. 1991. *Mythe et société à Madagascar (Tanala de l'Ikongo): Le chasseur d'oiseaux et la princesse du ciel*. Paris: L'Harmattan.

Blanchy, Sophie, and Zaharia Soilihi. 1991. *Furukombe et autres contres de Mayotte = Furukombe na hadisi za hale zangina za Maore*. Paris: Éditions Caribéennes.

Carayol, Michel. 1980. La littérature orale réunionnaise. In *Encyclopédie de la Réunion*, vol. 7. Saint-Denis.

Carayol, Michel, and Robert Chaudenson. 1979. *Contes créoles de l'Océan Indien*. Fleuve et Flamme. Paris: Conseil International de la Langue Française.

Gueunier, Noël J., ed. and trans. 1994. *L'oiseau chagrin: contes comoriens en dialecte malgache de l'île de Mayotte*. Compilers Noël J. Gueunier and Madjidhoubi Said. Paris: Peeters.

Haring, Lee. 1991. Prospects for Folklore in Mauritius. *International Folklore Review* pp. 83–95.

Haring, Lee. 1992. *Verbal Arts in Madagascar*. Philadelphia: University of Pennsylvania Press.

———. 1994. *Ibonia, Epic of Madagascar*. Lewisburg: Bucknell University Press.

Koechlin, B., ed. 1984. *Les Seychelles et l'Océan Indien*. Paris: Presses Universitaires d'Aix-Marseille/Éditions l'Harmattan.

Sussman, Linda K. 1980. Herbal Medicine on Mauritius. *Ethnopharmacology* 2:259–78.

Zistwar ek sedmo sesel. Contes, devinettes, et jeux de mots des Seychelles. 1983. Paris: Éditions Akpagnon.

LEE HARING

See also **French Study of African Folklore; Madagascar**

INITIATION

The term *initiation* evokes rites of passage, especially those that frame the passage from childhood to adulthood, leading to the integration of the young individuals into the social group. These rituals still play an important role in many traditional African societies. They deal with a specific age-group and take place at a critical time in the development of the individual who undergoes a process of psychological, intellectual, and physical transformation. Adolescents tends to challenge, indeed to reject, the models that society tries to impose upon them. They aspire to take the place of the elders, while the latter fear being dispossessed of their privileges. The initiation rites are intended both to promote the transformation of the young into adults and to resolve latent conflicts among generations.

A relatively universal process, the scenario of initiation in its broad outline is made up of three main stages. First, there is the symbolic death of the young person, figured by a separation (experienced as mourning) from the family and the group. The second stage involves the gestation of the new individual, corresponding to a period of seclusion of the initiates in a site (such as sacred woods, cave, and so on) located outside the limits of the normal social space of the community. Third, initiation is marked by the rebirth and integration of the individual, who returns to the family and the village; this return is generally celebrated by a feast.

During the reclusion-gestation period, the initiates undergo various intellectual, moral, and physical tests, culminating in a ritual of symbolic death and renaissance. They receive secret teachings, including learning a special language, religious knowledge, and information on the group's system of cultural and social values. During this period, the transformation of the person is not only moral, but also physical because operations such as circumcision, excision, and/or scarifications symbolically mark accession to the fullness of adult sexuality. For if initiation implies acquiring knowledge and social virtues, at a deeper level it also means fertility, an essential value in traditional societies.

Other collective or individual forms of initiation exist, the extreme form being mystical (or shamanic) initiation in which the individual accomplishes his "voyage" alone. The different stages of life can be underlined by rites of passage, such as changing age groups in certain societies. Marriage constitutes an important passage for the woman, since, traditionally, it marks the greatest change in her physical and social status. Death constitutes the ultimate and last transformation of the individual in this world; the rites surrounding it are aimed at easing this passage into the "other world."

The initiatory training includes the teaching of oral traditions and verbal arts (enigmas, proverbs, mythical texts in a secret language, sacred songs, and so on) that are specific to this contest and help to acquire knowledge. In addition, the esoteric meaning of everyday forms of verbal art are explained and commented upon. In the preparation of the future initiates, the tale especially plays an essential role.

Indeed, in their structures, many tales, stemming from the most varied cultures, reproduce the initiation scenario outlined above. The necessity of the "passage" seems to be a universal concern, and every society prepares their children very early to overcome conflicts and to succeed in the tests and transformations involved in this "passage." The tales, whose pedagogic function is very important and which transmit the system of traditional values and cultural models, teach the behaviors needed to pass the initiation and, conversely, those that lead to failure or improper integration into the group.

These ideas are expressed indirectly through the language of imagery and symbols. Among the stories that can be interpreted as initiatory, one can include types from Aarne-Thompson's international classification that exist in African folklore; for example, there are "The Dragon-Slayer" (AT300), "The Kind and Unkind Girls" (AT480), "The Two Travelers (Truth and Falsehood)" (AT613), "Snow-White" (AT709), and so on. These types bring into play one or two heroes or heroines. When there are two central characters, the most frequent occurrence, the tale is structured in two opposing sections. The second reproduces mirrorlike the inverted image of the first: the "positive" hero behaves according to the norms and succeeds in his quest whereas the "negative" character is immature and fails.

In these stories, there is a transposition in symbolic form of the different stages of real initiation. First, there is the Departure. The hero leaves his family and village, either for a "natural" reason (state of lack provoked by poverty or famine), or as a result of a conflict with an individual belonging to an older generation (a role often held by the stepmother). This conflict can be organized around an object symbolically linked to the parents' fertility. For example, in "The Kind and Unkind Girls" type, the heroine breaks or loses the stepmother's calabash or gourd, which she must then go seek or repair. The tale thus emphasizes the necessary renewal of the generations.

Second, there is the "Voyage and Quest" type. After crossing a symbolic boundary, the hero finds himself in another world (bush or forest), a wild space as opposed to the cultural space of the village, the habitat of genies, ogres, and the dead. He has various encounters and undergoes ordeals in which he must display social qualities (patience, politeness, discretion, sobriety, obedience, intelligence, and respect for the elderly). At the end of the voyage, he meets the main initiator who subjects him to the ultimate test symbolizing initiatory death and resurrection. This episode often corresponds to a descent into the depths of water, an image of a return to the mother's womb.

Third, there is the "Return and Reintegration" type. The central character returns to the village bringing riches as symbols of knowledge and adult fertility won during the quest. The negative hero who behaved badly in the tests is punished, sometimes by death.

Initiation is a triumph over the self. In their figurative and symbolic form, the tales prepare the young individuals for this symbolic "death" from which they will be reborn as new and fertile beings, ready to play their roles as adults in society. Thus, we see that forms of folklore are used in initiation ceremonies, and themselves use the initiation sequence in their narrative structure.

References

Aarne, Anti, and Stith Thompson. 1961. *The Types of the Folktale, A Classification and Bibliography*. Helsinki: Academia Scietiarum Fennica.

Calame-Griaule, Genevieve. 1984. The Father's Bowl: Analysis of a Dogon Version of AT 480. *Research in African Literatures* 15:2: 168–84.

———. 1987. *Des cauris au marche, Essais sur des contes africains*. Paris: Societe des africanistes.

———. 1992. Mohammed Ag-Agar or Oedipus in the Sahel. *Marvels and Tales* VI:2 (Special Issue: "Interpreting Folktales," guest editor, V. Görög-Karady): 187–218. .

———. 1996. Les chemins de l'autre monde, Contes initiatiques africains. *Cahiers de Litterature Orale* 39/40:29–59.

Van Gennep, Arnold. 1981. *Les rites de passage* (1909). Picard: Nourry.

Vidal, Pierre. 1976. *Garcons et filles. Le passage a l'age d'homme chez les Gbaya Kara*. Paris: Labethno Paris X (Nanterre).

Zahan, Dominique. 1960. *Societes d'initiation bambara. Le n'domo, le kore*. Paris-La Haye: Mouton.

GENEVIÉVE CALAME-GRIAULE

See also **Folktales; Gender Representation in African Folklore; Myth; Southern African Oral Traditions; Typology and Performance in the Study of Prose Narratives**

INSTITUTIONAL STUDY OF AFRICAN FOLKLORE

Africa has been a battleground in the folklorist's attempt to assert the autonomy of folklore. As a result, there has been much interdisciplinary debate surrounding the concept of African folklore between the late eminent folklorist Richard Dorson and literary scholars and anthropologists. The first debate arose in 1965, when Dorson was invited to conduct a folklore seminar in London by the Department of Africa of the School of Oriental and African Studies (SOAS) at the University of London. He used the opportunity to speak out against W. H. Whiteley's handling of African prose material in Whiteley's book *A Selection of African Prose; 1: Traditional Oral Texts*, calling attention to the lack of comparative notes and motif references, which a folklorist would normally look for, and the imbalance of genres represented. Whiteley's book was a lesson in "How not to publish folklore texts," according to Dorson.

A repeat of this confrontation took place in 1967, at the Oral Data Conference in Wisconsin, cosponsored by the African Studies Programs of the University of Wisconsin and Northwestern University. There, while literary scholars expressed disappointment at the folklorist's neglect of esthetics, Dorson drew attention to the lack of comparative perspectives in the approach of the literary scholar, linguist, and anthropologist.

Simply put, in the attempt to assert the autonomy of folklore as a discipline, folklorists have prescribed a host of mutually exclusive criteria or rules. Besides more recent definitions of *folk* and *folklore* offered by Dundes and Ben-Amos, the issue of what, exactly, constitutes folklore has been based on the nature of the material under study, as well as the evolutionary status of the people to which the material belongs. While Dorson adopts these two criteria in his book *African Folklore*, he also advocates a third, which unwittingly repudiates the previous two: Folklore is what folklorists have studied by their methods.

Applying all three criteria simultaneously, the problematic outcome is evident in the contradictions in the following propositions in Dorson's book: (1) Chatelain's book *Folktales of Angola* (1894) is folklore because it contains comparative notes; but (2) anthropologists studying Africa in the past were wrong to not label the material as folklore; but (3) what was in Africa before the arrival of an elite in "recent" decades is not folklore.

Besides the muddling of criteria in the assessment of African folklore material, the attempt to trace elitism or shades of "traditions" in Africa to recent decades overlooks centuries of "elitism," written poetry, and religious pluralism that existed long before the African contact with Western civilization.

Despite the folklorist's ambivalent signals in appraising African materials, the continued study of African folklore throughout the world has not been hampered by definition games. To put this in perspective, highlighted below are some of the significant landmarks in the institutional study of African folklore in the United States, Europe, and on the African continent, placing particular emphasis on the study of oral literature. We have here used oral literature, verbal art, and folklore interchangeably.

United States

Perhaps the single most significant event in the history of African folklore in the United States is the African folklore conference organized at Indiana University in July 1970, under the direction of Richard Dorson. This brought together folklorists, anthropologists, linguists, and literary scholars who had done fieldwork on African folklore. The conference was the culmination of a series of events that had reinforced the visibility of African folklore among American scholars. These included an informal seminar on African folklore in London in 1965 (which was attended by Richard Dorson and other American folklorists), an oral data conference in 1967 at Wisconsin, and a trip to Africa in early 1970 by Dorson.

The study of African folklore in the United States has been based at two major institutions of learning: Indiana University and the University of Wisconsin–Madison, the two institutions that offer doctoral programs in African folklore or oral literature. There are also several other universities where doctoral dissertations on African folklore have been written. The University of California, Berkeley, for example, is responsible for two out of four early doctoral dissertations that classified African tales. These are Ojo Arewa's classification of tales in the northern East African cattle area, and Winifred Lambrecht's tale type index for Central Africa.

Two other early dissertations on tale classification come from Indiana University. Klipple's *African Folklore with Foreign Analogues* (1938) was the earliest African folklore doctoral dissertation, written even before the Indiana University Folklore Institute (and later department) was established. This was followed nineteen years later by Kenneth Clarke's *Motif Index of the Folktales of West Africa* (1957). The bulk of African folklore dissertations written at Indiana emerged after 1964, when the Folklore department achieved autonomy. Since then, dissertations have been written on a wide range of genres (such as folktale, myth, dirge, proverb, epic, legend, and folk music), and specific courses on African folklore have been taught. Graduate courses offered at Indiana include "Seminar in African Folklore," "African Epic and Praise Poetry," and "Middle-Eastern and Sub-Saharan African Narratives," taught, respectively, by John Johnson, Hasan el-Shamy, and Ruth Stone.

The University of Wisconsin–Madison covers African folklore studies within the Department of African Languages and Literatures. Renowned scholars there include Harold Scheub and Daniel Kunene. The department is devoted to the combined study of language and oral and written literatures in Africa. This is a cardinal example of the medley of perspectives from which verbal art in Africa has been examined. The earliest dissertation on African oral literature from this department (established in 1963), Harold Scheub's *The Ntsomi: A Xhosa Performing Art* (1969), has influenced several Wisconsin dissertations on African folklore. Wisconsin has produced a number of doctoral dissertations on African oral literature and related topics. A majority of these explore the African narrative, and aspects including structure, performance, and rhythm.

Courses offered at Wisconsin include "The African Storyteller," "Structures of African Narratives," "Seminar in Traditional African Literature," and "Seminar in Southern African Oral Tradition and Written Literature."

Another important place for the study of African folklore has been the University of Pennsylvania, where the Folklore and Folklife department taught undergraduate and graduate courses in African folklore, until the department metamorphosed into the Center for Ethnography and Folklore. Scholars in African folklore at Pennsylvania include Dan Ben Amos. Pennsylvania has been responsible for several important dissertations on African folklore, including Peter Seitel's landmark research on *Proverb and the Structure of Metaphor among the Haya of Tanzania* (1972).

Interest in African folklore or oral literature within the United States is also exemplified in the number of journals that have devoted some of their pages to the subject. These include *Research in African Literatures, Journal of Folklore Research* (formerly *Journal of the Folklore Institute), Journal of American Folklore, Ba Shiru, The Conch,* and *Folklore Forum.*

Of these journals, *Research in African Literatures* (R.A.L) has devoted the most attention to African folklore. Established in

1970 as the publication of the African Literature Committee of the African Studies Association and the African Literature Seminar of the Modern Languages Association, R.A.L. (now published by the African Literature Association) has allotted more than a third of its volumes to oral literature in Africa. By the end of 1984, eight special issues on African oral literature had been published by R.A.L., with the following subtitles: "African Folklore in the New World" (7:2, 1976), "African Folklore," (8:2, 1977); "African Song" containing discussion on praise poetry (11:3, 1979), "Genre and Classification in African Folklore" (11:3, 1980), "Oral Tradition" dealing with the epic, proverb, and folktale (12:3, 1981), "Epic and Panegyric Poetry" (14:3, 1983), "African Oral Narrative" (15:2, 1984), and "African Poetry and Song" (15:4, 1984).

The *Journal of American Folklore* (*JAF*) is the oldest of the journals publishing African folklore material in the United States. Established in 1888 by the American Folklore Society, *JAF* was originally meant to support the collection of the rapidly vanishing remains of folklore in America, including relics and lore of the English, African Americans, and Native Americans. Its interest in cultures lying outside the Euro-American world has been secondary; even so, until 1958, it had published eighteen notes and brief expositions. Over the past century, *JAF* has carried about fifty major essays on African folklore. The American Folklore Society was responsible for the publication of Lord Chatelain's *Folktales of Angola.*

Contrary to the editorial policy of *JAF*, the *Journal of the Folklore Institute* (now *Journal of Folklore Research*) has a primarily international outlook. It is published by the Indiana University Folklore Institute; the faculty constitutes a collective editorial board. With increased emphasis on the international scene and comparative studies at the time, *JFI* (founded in 1964) saw the need "for a periodical in English which will bring into focus the folklore research now being vigorously prosecuted by dedicated scholars around the world." To this end, special issues devoted to different geographical areas have been published. *JFI* has carried over forty essays on African folklore. Special issues on Africa include (4:2/3, 1967) published proceedings of the informal seminar on theories and concepts of folklore held in London in 1965, and the special issue (6:2/3, 1969) on Africa based on the African oral data conference held in Wisconsin–Madison in 1967. This contains contributions on data collecting in Africa, the uses of African verbal art, African music, and archiving. Another *JFI* issue which is Africa-oriented (1983) was based on a conference in Paris, organized by the Paris-based African oral literature research group.

The *Folklore Forum,* published by students of Indiana University, has also carried material on African folklore. Since it started in 1968, *FF* has published several articles on African folklore. In 1973, *Folklore Forum* (Bibliographical and Special Series, 11) published a special issue on Yoruba folklore, the outcome of papers presented to Professor Abimbola by Africanist students while he was a visiting professor at the Folklore Department. Students of Indiana University also started a series of publications on African folklore in 1981, entitled *Cross Rhythms: Papers in African Folklore,* published by the Trickster Press. Three volumes have appeared thus far.

Another significant publication is *Ba Shiru,* published by the Department of African Languages and Literatures of the University of Wisconsin. The journal began in 1970 and publishes material on linguistics and oral and written literatures. Though irregularly produced, *Ba Shiru* has published several articles on African folklore, devoting an issue in 1975 (6:2) to African oral narratives. Significantly, this journal intersperses its articles with oral narratives collected from the field with informant data.

Finally, mention should be made of the *Conch*, subtitled "Sociological Journal of African Cultures and Literatures," which has a wider scope and deals with various aspects of African life, including oral and written literatures. This journal began in 1969 and has published special issues on African culture and oral traditions.

Apart from journal publications on African folklore, annual meetings and conferences organized by the African Literature Association, African Studies Association, and the American Folklore Society have provided outlets for the discussion of topics in African folklore in the United States. Of particular significance here is the African Literature Association; its selected papers, published annually, have included several essays on African folklore/oral literature.

Europe

The contribution of Europe to the study of African folklore and oral literature dates much earlier than the United States, partly due to its long colonial history in Africa. These contributions range from early nineteenth century folklore collections by missionaries, explorers, linguists, and anthropologists, to rigorous analytical perspectives brought to bear on data by trained folklorists, scholars of oral literature, ethnolinguists, and anthropologists of French and British schools. In recent years, Hungary and other central and eastern European countries have become particularly visible in African folklore research, through the institution of specific programs on Africa and the sponsoring of international conferences on African folklore.

In Britain, Ruth Finnegan's book *Oral Literature in Africa* (1970) has been compulsory reading material in all courses on African folklore. African oral literature is offered in institutions such as the School of Oriental and African Studies (SOAS) of the University of London, as well at the Center for West African Studies at the University of Birmingham.

In France, the research team Langage et Culture en Afrique de l'Oues is the most visible in the study of oral literature in Africa. It started in 1968, when fifteen Africanists in cultural anthropology and linguistics began studies on West Africa. In 1970, the group was recognized by the Centre National de la Recherche Scientifique (CNRS) and renamed the Equipe de Recherche Associee (ERA). Its membership consists of such prominent linguists, oral literary scholars, ethnolinguists, and anthropologists as Genevieve Calame-Griaule, Gerard Dumestre, Veronika Gorog-Karady, Christiane Seydou, and Brunhilde Biebuyck, who trained as a folklorist at Indiana University.

Having conducted fieldwork among several ethnic groups in West Africa (such as the Bambara, Fulani, Dogon, Shanga, Kru, Bete, Zarma, etc.), the group is subdivided into several sections, including a section on oral literature. The French school, which concentrates on the study of folktales, has in recent years fallen in step with methodological approaches adopted by American folklorists, mainly the use of motif and tale type indexes for comparative purposes, and the study of the folktale as a communicative event. Significantly, the group uses motif and the tale type indexes not as a means of projecting a tale's historical source or ur-form, but as part of the process of exploring meaning.

In 1981 and 1982, the French school organized two conferences on oral literature in Britain and France, respectively. The first, held at Wolfson College at Oxford, brought together graduate and faculty members SOAS, members of the Institute of Social Anthropology, and the French scholars. Proceedings of the symposium appear in a book, *Forms and Meanings: Essays in African Oral Literature*, edited by Veronica Gorog-Karady. This consists of ten essays on African oral narratives using comparative, literary, and anthropological approaches.

The second conference, held in 1982, was in Paris. Among the papers presented here was one jointly done by the French scholars on *The Meaning of Variability and the Variability of Meaning*. In this essay, the French group outline and exemplify their newly fashioned agenda: that of searching for culture-specific meanings through the study of variants, "versions," themes, motifs, sociocultural contexts, textual context of elements in the tale, and communicative strategies used during performance. Theirs is not a univalent approach, but an amalgamation of all perspectives that are relevant in exploring the nuances of cultural meaning.

Such a synthesis of approach in the exploration of meaning is the distinctive mark of the French school, and could influence the course of folklore research. Significantly, the Organizing Committee for the Eighth Congress of the International Society for Folk Narrative Research (after the French School) made "Folk Narrative and the Quest for Meaning" one of its central themes in a meeting in Bergen. Today, courses on African oral literature are taught in the Institut National de Langues et des Civilisations Orientales (INALCO), Sorbonne Nouvelle, and Nanterre Université. There is, however, no autonomous oral literature or folklore department in France.

While this survey of the study of African folklore is not exhaustive, this section concludes with a reference to the Hungarian contribution to African folklore studies. It is possible to extend as far back as the nineteenth century and trace the beginnings of individual research on Africa by Hungarians. Scholars like Lazzlo Magyar, Emil Torday, and Bela Bartok all made expeditions to Africa and collected artifacts and music.

Generally, however, Hungary was little exposed to overseas cultures, due to its lack of colonial activities. This has changed, however, over the course of the last half century. Institutions in Hungary have recently shown interest in Africa. In the past thirty years, for example, the Department of Folklore at Eotvos University has had lectures on African folklore. In 1981 a specific research program on "Folklore Today—Africa" was launched; thanks to the efforts of Wilmos Voigt, the prominent Hungarian folklorist and Director of the Folklore Department. The African folklore research program is state supported, and has sent Hungarians to do fieldwork in places like Libya, Angola and Mozambique.

The Hungarian contribution is especially marked by the organization of international conferences on African folklore in 1982. Another conference was held in 1984. The participants in both conferences came from all over the world, including eastern Europe, the United States, and Africa.

The most significant event of the 1984 conference was the official founding of the International Association for the Study of Oral Traditions in Africa (IASOTA). This had been proposed in the 1982 conference under the working name, International Association of Oral Literature of Africa.

In 1991, an International Society for Oral Literature in Africa (ISOLA) started taking shape, and held its first conference at SOAS. This was followed in 1995 with another conference at the University of Ghana. In 1998, the University of Cape Town in South Africa held the third international conference of ISOLA. It was at this third international conference that ISOLA was officially inaugurated. Its sole aim has been to promote and coordinate the study of oral literature as a legitimate and recognized discipline within secondary and tertiary institutions. Papers presented at the Cape Town conference appear in *African Oral Literature*, edited by Russell Kaschula. In 2002, a follow-up conference was held by ISOLA in Chamberly, France.

Africa

The part being played by Africans themselves in today's study of African oral literature or folklore is made more evident in the following brief account.

It begins with the informants, research assistants, and private collectors, and extends up to scholars, authors, co-authors, educational institutions, and professional associations in Africa. Assistance from informants and research assistants was largely unacknowledged, however, until recent decades. Today, not only are informants acknowledged, but scholars like Peter Seitel test the validity of analytical statements they have made on fieldwork material through extended correspondence with field informants and subsequent visits to the field. Furthermore, book and monograph titles such as John Johnson's *The Epic of Sunjata according to Magan Sisoko* and Charles Bird's *The Songs of Seydou Camara* proclaim the names of informants. Coauthors are also named, such as is the case with George Herzong and C. Blooah's *Jabo Proverbs from Liberia* and Daniel Biebuyck and C. Mateene's *Mwindo Epics*.

Well-cited books on African folklore written by Africans have appeared in the last fifty years. In such works, African scholars trained in European, American, and African universities have combined intuitions, fieldwork, and ethnic models, as well as the analytical perspectives of Western scholars, to examine folklore and oral literature within their own localities. Some of the better-cited work in this category include J. H. K. Nketia's *Funeral Dirges of the Akan Peoples* (1955), S. A. Babalola's *The Content and Form of Yoruba Ijala*, and John Mbiti's *Akamba Stories*; the last two were both published in 1966 as part of the Oxford Library of African Literature series. Of late, Isidore Okpewho's *African Oral Literature* has made a major mark in the study of the subject.

In the United States, African students at such institutions as Indiana University, the University of Wisconsin–Madison, the University of Pennsylvania, and the University of California at Berkeley have contributed to the corpus of doctoral dissertations on African folklore. At Indiana University, Kwesi Yankah's 1985 dissertation (The Proverb in the Context of Akan Rhetoric) won the Esther Kingsley Award for outstanding doctoral dissertation, the first folklore dissertation to win the prestigious award.

On the African continent itself, a sustained study of African folklore (oral literature in particular) began in the 1960s under the patronage of institutes of African studies, and later in autonomous departments of Linguistics, African Languages and Litera-

ture, and English. In Sudan, there is now a Department of Folklore at the University of Khartoum. In most of these departments, trained folklorists who are Africans teach courses in oral literature or folklore.

Established in 1972, the Department of Folklore at the University of Khartoum, Sudan collects and documents traditional genres and artifacts from different parts of Sudan, and trains graduate students in Sudanese, African, and Middle Eastern folklore. It offers graduate diplomas, and masters and doctoral degrees in folklore. Courses offered cover topics including folklore theory, fieldwork methodology, applied folklore, introduction to African and Middle Eastern folklore, and the structural analysis of myth. The faculty includes Sayyid Hammid Hurreiz and Sharafeldin Abdel-salam, both of whom obtained their doctoral degrees at Indiana University. Ahmed Abdal Rahim Nasr, a third faculty member, obtained his doctorate at the University of Wisconsin–Madison.

Besides the Department of Folklore, other institutions in Sudan that collect and analyze folklore materials include the College of Fine and Applied Arts and the Center for Folklore Studies, which is a wing of the Ministry of Culture.

Sudan has hosted international conferences on folklore, the first of which was in 1968, and the second in 1970. Proceedings of the first conference have been published as *Sudan in Africa*, edited by Yusuf Fadl. The second proceedings were published under the title *Directions in Sudanese Folklore and Linguistics*. In 1981, Khartoum again hosted a conference on Folklore and National Development. Folklore monographs and journals in Sudan include *Sudanese Heritage Series, Sudan Notes and Records, Journal of Sudanese Studies, Journal of Culture*, and *Al-Waza*. There is also an archive in the Folklore department, which currently holds over three thousand tapes.

In Nigeria, the academic study of African folklore was initiated in the latter part of the 1960s, when oral literature courses were taught at the University of Ibadan, the University of Lagos, and the University of Nigeria. These universities offered a B.A. in Yoruba within the institutes of African Studies. From 1970 onwards the study of oral literature in Nigeria shifted from African Studies institutes to departments of Linguistics and Nigerian Languages or African Languages and Literatures, in Lagos, Ife, Ibadan and Illorin universities. Degrees offered in oral literature have been upgraded from bachelors through masters in the mid-seventies, to Ph.Ds in the 1980s. Other institutions offering oral literature courses in Nigeria include Bayero University's Center for the Study of Nigerian Languages and Oral Documentation, the University of Calabar, the University of Jos, Ahmadu Bello University, and the University of Port Harcourt.

The increased interest in African folklore studies in Nigeria also led to the formation of the Nigerian Folklore Society in 1980. The society is assisted by the government, and has held annual conferences since 1980. The proceedings of the first conference appeared as *Oral Poetry in Nigeria*.

Nigeria was also the seat of the now defunct Africa-based African Literature Association. The annual meetings of this organization attracted scholars from Europe, the United States, and other parts of Africa. Papers presented at such meetings covered both oral and written literatures. In 1981, the theme of the ALA conference was "Oral Performance in Africa," which has now been published. Journals in Nigeria publishing African folklore material include *African Notes, Odu*, and *Yoruba*.

In Ghana, courses in oral literature are taught at the Institute of African Studies, as well as in the Linguistics and English departments of the University of Ghana. Trained folklorists and scholars of oral literature teaching in oral literature programs in Ghana include Kofi Anyidoho, Kwesi Yankah, Esi Sutherland–Arday, and Kwaku Owusu Brempong.

The Institute of African Studies was established by Dr. Kwame Nkrumah, the first president of Ghana, as a semiautonomous institution within the University of Ghana. It was intended to play a dominant role in the intellectual effort to uncover, through interdisciplinary research, the rich culture and history of the African peoples. The institute carries out research and teaches in a wide range of fields including history and politics, religion and philosophy, societies and cultures, language, drama and literature, music and dance, visual arts, gender, culture and development, family studies, and cultural aspects of population issues.

The institute offers courses at undergraduate and graduate levels. Courses taught include appropriate technology for rural development, culture and development, African heritage through literature, oral literature of Africa and the diaspora, African popular culture, African music, African dance, and drama, as well as Ghanaian languages. The institute publishes monographs and the journal *Research Review*, as well as the Occasional Research Paper series.

The Institute of African Studies is also the home of the Ghana Dance Ensemble, made up of thirty-five drummers and dancers drawn from all the regions of Ghana. The group features as a resource and outreach program of the institute. It runs workshops and seminars and has a rich repertoire of traditional dances and music, which it performs for audiences in Ghana and abroad.

The University of Ghana is also the seat of the International Centre for African Music and Dance (ICAMD), founded by world-renowned ethnomusicologist J. H. Kwabena Nketia in 1993. The center serves the following functions:

A focus for the development of materials and programs in African music and dance that meet the needs of scholars, research students, and creative artists

A clearinghouse for information on events, artists, scholars, and institutions concerned with the study and promotion of African music and dance; and

A forum for international meetings, conferences, seminars, workshops, and special events in music and dance.

The center has a library and audiovisual archive. The library stocks important books on African culture, African music and dance, and books on other cultures. It has copies of dissertations, theses, long essays and very rare documents that cannot be found in Europe and America. The audiovisual center holds over fifteen hundred audiocassettes, of which six hundred are field recordings by researchers, staff of the center, and graduate students, as well as recordings of conferences, seminars, and workshops organized by the center. Ghana also has a National Folklore Board, operating under the National Commission on Culture.

In Malawi, folklore and oral literature is taught to undergraduates in the second and fourth year of university education in the departments of English, Chichewa, and Linguistics at Chancellor College, Zomba. As part of the course requirements, students work on long papers based on folklore research done in their respective ethnic groups. *Kalulu*, a bulletin of oral literature, first published in 1976 and edited by Jack Mapanje and Enoch Mvula, is a forum for the publication of such research materials.

In East Africa, African oral literature is taught in several universities, including Kenyatta University in Kenya and Makerere University in Uganda. In southern Africa, universities that teach oral literature include the University of Zimbabwe, where it is offered in the African Languages and Literature Department, the University of Botswana, where it is taken at the English Department, the National University of Lesotho, and the University of Cape Town, South Africa, where it is taught in the Department of Linguistics and Southern African Languages.

The above survey, while not exhaustive, demonstrates the transcontinental interest that the study of African folklore and oral literature has aroused in recent decades. Heli Chatelain once said, "African folklore is not a tree by itself, but a branch of one universal tree." While the comparative potential of African folklore material demonstrates this, the progress of African folklore studies must not be measured in terms of how many universal categories, principles, or theoretical frames encompass Africa; the yardstick of progress lies in the quality of perspectives harnessed in study and research. The search for such a goal begins at the end of interdisciplinary feuds and advances along the path of a stable diversity of scholars and tools.

References

Arewa, E. Ojo. 1966. *A Classification of Folktales of the Northern East Africa Cattle Area by Types.* University of California, Berkeley.

Ben-Amos, Dan. 1972. "Toward a Definition of Folklore in Context. In *Toward New Perspectives in Folklore*, eds. Americo Paredes & Richard Bauman. Austin: University of Texas Press.

Biebuyck, Brunhilde. 1984. The Many Faces of the French Research team 246: Langage et Culture en Afrique de l'Ouest. *Research in African Literatures* 15:262–88.

Biebuyck, Daniel, and Kahombo Mateene. 1969. *The Mwindo Epic.* Berkeley and Los Angeles: University of California Press.

Bird, Charles with Mamadu Keita and Bourama Soumaouro. 1974. *The Songs of Seydou Camara.* Bloomington: Indiana University–African Studies Program.

Calame-Griaule, Genevieve, et al. The Meaning of Variability and the Variability of Meaning. *Journal of Folklore Research* 20, nos. 2/3:153–70.

Chatelain, Heli. 1894. Folktales of Angola. *American Folklore Society Memoirs* 1.

Degh, Linda. Foreword: A Quest for Meaning. *Journal of Folklore Research* 20, nos. 2/3:145.

Dorson, Richard. 1972. Africa and the Folklorist. In *African Folklore*, ed. Richard Dorson. New York: Doubleday.

Dorson, Richard. Introduction. *Journal of the Folklore Institute* 1 no. 1:3.

Dundes, Alan. 1965. What is Folklore? In *The Study of Folklore*, ed. Alan Dundes Englewood Cliffs, N.J.: Prentice-Hall.

Gerard, Albert S. 1981. *African Language Literatures: An Introduction to the Literary History of Sub-Saharan Africa.* Washington: The Three Continents Press.

Hale, Thomas. Report on the International Colloquium on Folklore in Africa Today, August 27–31, 1984, at the University of Budapest, Hungary. *African Literature Assoc. Bulletin* 10, no. 4: 4–6.

Harris, Marjorie, comp. *African-Related Doctoral Dissertations and Masters Theses Completed at the University of Wisconsin Madison through 1980.* University of Wisconsin, Madison, African Studies Program.

Hasan, Salah M. 1984. Folklore Studies and Research in the Sudan. *The Middle East and South Asia Folklore Newsletter* 2–4.

Hasan, Yusuf Fadl, 1975. ed. *Sudan in Africa.* Khartoum: University of Khartoum Press. *Directions in Sudanese Folklore and Linguistics,* eds. Sayyid Hurreiz Bell, Khartoum: University of Khartoum Press.

Herzog, George, and C. G. Blooah. 1936. *Jabo Proverbs from Liberia.* London: Oxford University Press.

Kaschula, Russell, ed. 2001. *African Oral Literature: Functions in Contemporary Contexts.* Claremont, South Africa: New African Books, 2001.

Johnson, John W. 1979. *The Epic of Sunjata 1 according to Magan Sisoko.* Bloomington: Folklore Institute, Folklore Publications Group.

Lambrecht, Winifred. 1967. *A Tale Type Index for Central Africa.* University of California, Berkeley.

Okpewho, Isidore. 1992. *African Oral Literature: Background, Character and Continuity.* Bloomington: Indiana University Press.

Seitel, Peter. 1980. *See So that We May See.* Bloomington: Indiana University Press.

Bea Vidas, 1984. Outline History of Hungarian African Studies. *Artes Populares* 10/11:119–30.

Voigt, Vilmos. 1984. Welcoming African Folklorists *Artes Populares* 10/11:xxv–viii.

KWESI YANKAH

See also **Maqalat: Concepts of Folklore in the Sudan; Oral Literary Research in Africa; Oral Literature: Issues of Definition and Terminology; Performance in Africa**

INSULTS AND RIBALD LANGUAGE

They are not inclined to talk of Procreation in obscene or too expressive Terms; they believe it to be designed by Nature for obscure Retreats; and therefore very improper to be talked of in broad terms: But he that can cleanly express this Subject in well meaning Hints, passes for a Wit. Hence each of them aims at diverting Fables or Similitudes tending this way.
(Bosman: 1907 [1705]: 443–44).

Nearly three hundred years ago, William Bosman made this observation, and we would do well to acknowledge the aptness of his insight about language behavior in Africa. Certainly more research is needed in this area of "taboo" behavior, but what data there is on insulting and ribald language demonstrates the validity of Bosman's comment. Although sexual and excretory terms are proscribed in African cultures, they carry none of the emotional power of insult and obscenity which they do in European languages. "Bad words" based on bodily functions are available, and in some cultures young boys use them to insult others, but it is clear that adults consider such language suitably employed only by uneducated youth. On the other hand, great interest and delight is taken in the creative use of imagery, some of it sexual, in effective speech and entertaining narratives and songs.

In southern Nigeria, restricted terms for body parts and functions are recognized; they can be employed as insults, but only in the vaguest way, and are generally regarded more as ignorant or uneducated speech than as truly painful slurs. Throughout Africa, one hears minor insults as a speaker refers to another's alleged animal-like appearance or in appropriate behavior—monkeys, hyenas, and goats are the most frequent references. Indicative of the differences between southern Nigerian and European insulting speech is the fact that a powerful insult among Nigerians is to claim to be another's father. However, any association with the classic European insult about sexual relations with another's mother quickly disappears when one learns that it is also insulting to claim to be another's mother, no matter what the sexes of the protagonists may be. In actual fact, the insult revolves around the assertion of seniority of age over the individual being insulted. Although this can lead to physical violence, the worst possible insult for southern Nigerians is to wish death upon another's family, thus wreaking havoc upon that individual's lineage. Other studies reveal culturally specific creativity in insulting language (Warren and Bremprong 1977; Peek 1996).

Further insight into the significantly differing criteria of insults may be gained when ribald language is investigated in tales and other verbal art forms. Even in "sanitized" collections of folktales from Africa, there are accounts of bizarre and extreme behaviors, with some stories containing startlingly violent and graphic imagery. But closer examination of such narratives as "The Whore Meets Her Match," in which the "Peripatetic Penis" finally conquers the misbehaving woman (Cosentino 1982), quickly reveals that lewd thoughts are in no way brought forth. Instead, even outsiders can recognize that the extraordinary imagery is serving other purposes, which are generally pointed social commentaries in which the vividness of the imagery serves to highlight the behavioral transgressions. Thus, for example, an instance of swollen testicles, usually described in excruciating detail, is in no way "obscene," but does demonstrate the appropriate punishment of inappropriate sexual behavior.

Work by African folklorists and linguists further supports such interpretations. Boadi (1972) noted that elders have access to a level of explicit language which younger speakers do not, and thus their proverbs are far more affective. We know most African languages recognize such restricted speech, which can include elaborate sexual metaphors only available to elders. The Isoko of the Niger Delta call such speech *emedidi*, or "deep words."

Other evidence of the artful use of sexual imagery comes from rituals that occur throughout Africa, in which men and women will "compete" against each other with insulting songs, usually characterized by gross descriptions of each other's sexual organs. During such ceremonies of ritual reversal and sexual license, the atmosphere is decidedly convivial, as all respond with laughter, never insult.

Culture-specific and performance-specific interpretations of meaning and functions must be continually sought, but in general, the sexual references in African verbal arts have more to do with the aesthetic and entertainment value of the bizarreness of the metaphor, the exaggeration of the action, and the vividness of the imagery, than with any real concern with vulgarity or desire to be obscene. As a vehicle for social commentary, such references are made no less serious by the laughter evoked. Mary Douglas has observed, "In any culture insulting terms are the most illuminating indication of accepted values" (1984, 12). These values are not just reflected in the content but in the performative dynamics of exchange and the creative production of vivid, startling images. Although it must be left to others to explain the sexual basis of European and European-American obscene insults, compared to the common denominator of creative wit in African abusive language, they appear relatively "witless."

References

Boadi, Lawrence. 1972. The Language of the Proverb in Akan. In *African Folklore* ed. Richard Dorson. New York: Doubleday.

Bosman, William. 1907. *A New and Accurate Description of the Coast of Guinea* (1705). London: Ballantyne.

Cosentino, Donald J. 1982. Mende Ribaldry. *African Arts* 15, no. 2: 64–67, 88.

Douglas, Mary. 1984. Social and Religious Symbolism of the Lele. In *Implicit Meanings*. London: Routledge and Kegan Paul.

Olajuba, Chief Oludare. 1972. References to Sex in Yoruba Oral Literature. *Journal of American Folklore* 85:152–66.

Peek, Philip M. 1982. Sexual References in Southern Nigerian Verbal Art Forms. *African Arts* 15, no. 2:62–63, 88.

———. 1996. The Roles of Sexual Expressions in African Insulting Language and Verbal Arts. In *Folklore Interpreted: Essays in Honor of Alan Dundes*, ed. R. Bendix and R. L. Zumwalt. New York: Garland Press.

Warren, Dennis M., and K. Owusu Bremprong. 1977. Attacking Deviations from the Norm: Poetic Insults in Bono (Ghana). *Maledicta*, no. 1: 141–66.

PHILIP M. PEEK

See also **Gossip and Rumor; Jokes and Humor; Language; Performance in Africa**

ISLAMIC BROTHERHOODS: BAYE FALL AND YENGU, A MOURIDE SPIRITUALITY

Islam has existed in Senegal since the eleventh century. In the 1880s, the collaboration between Sheikh Amadou Bamba (1853–1927) and Sheikh Ibrahima Fall (1858–1930) gave it a new momentum through the Mouridiyya, the Sufi brotherhood of Mourides. Today the latter coexists with the Tidjaniyya, Layeniyya, and other local Muslim brotherhoods. Bamba, a scholar from a family of learned people and Quranic schoolmasters, attended Quranic school in Senegal and Mauritania. As soon as it was founded, the Mourides recruited and integrated different ethnic groups from diverse sociopolitical levels and families (noble men, free men, dependents, slaves and people of caste) from the Wolof and Serer territories colonized by the French.

This religious revival also involved the work of social and political reorganization, as well as economic integration. The holy man and his followers expressed this new order in the sanctification of labor, which defined the real Mouride person and his/her religious identity. In this context, Bamba restructured the religious order by establishing the Baye Fall Daara in 1896, a working and spiritual school different from that of the usual Quranic instruction and characteristics in a *daara tarbiyya*. A year later, he raised the Baye Fall Daara to the rank of a congregation by consecrating Ibrahima Fall as Sheikh, whom he sent to settle in Saint-Louis, then the capital of Senegal, on the behalf of the Brotherhood. This act completed the dual work of mod-

ernizing the brotherhood and conceptualizing a different spiritual path. This not only allowed mystical union with the supreme creator, but also permitted followers to acquire more knowledge and power than the usual Koranic disciple.

The second and last movement of the brotherhood began with Bamba's retreat, in 1887, with Ibrahima Fall. During this seclusion, he reported that he received a visit from the angel Gabriel who announced to him the divine mission to raise Touba, a holy city and tree leading to paradise, "Chajaratoul Muntaa," which would be the center from which "Africanized Islam" would spread throughout the world (Ross 1995, 223–24). That revelation extended this work of sociopolitical revitalization and religious revival beyond the limits of Senegal, and it confirmed Ibrahima Fall as Bamba's disciple.

The material expression of its founders' prophetic vision is reflected in the architecture of the huge Touba mosque (1925–1963), which incarnates for the follower the forms of the master and his disciple. Sheikh Amadou Bamba and Sheikh Ibrahima Fall are, in the eyes of the faithful, the two holiest men of Mouridism. These revered icons are represented by the white and black iconography and clothing (derived from the famously mysterious

The drummer is shown in the midst of the Yengu ceremony. He goes into an ecstatic trance, which he likewise conveys to the audience. Photo © T.K. Biaya.

black and white photography of Bamba, his only portrait) and the colorful light and dark patchwork clothing of Baye Fall's followers, which is linked to their "work" as beggars. Bamba and Fall were able to develop a movement that was simultaneously a local Senegambian Islamic revitalization movement, and an increasingly international brotherhood.

The growing influence of Mouridism beyond Senegal demonstrated that the French colonial administration could scarcely contain Bamba. His actions led to accusations by the French, condemnations, and successive deportation to Gabon (1895–1902) and Mauritania (1903–1907). When he finally returned to the country, he was placed under house arrest at Thieyenne before he got back to Diourbel in 1912. During this return to the cradle of Mouridism, he was continually greeted by ecstatic crowds shouting "God is back." To this Bamba only answered, "I am but a humble servant of God and of the prophet and cursed be those who will not consider me as such." This epithet henceforth served to paradoxically mark him by his humility, and his greatness within the faith. But this ambiguity did not prevent a confusion in the minds of his followers, who saw him as a political rebel, triumphant over colonization.

Today Touba—a holy city founded by Bamba and Fall in 1886, with its huge mosque inaugurated in 1963—is the lighthouse of world Mouridism. This religious metropolis is also the annual pilgrimage destination of the black Muslim world (Thiam 1990, 17). With a population of nearly one million in 1997, it competes with Mecca in importance. In fact, the mapping of its expansion shows that it could be perceived as the center of an architectural style whose influence is felt in Rome, New York, Melbourne, and Soweto, where religious Mouride holidays are celebrated. International respect for Touba, and submission to the General Kalif who resides there as practiced by followers of Mouridism worldwide, illustrates the truly global nature of this Islamic brotherhood.

Being Baye Fall, An Act of Spirituality

The substantive phrase "Baye Fall," meaning "Father Fall," establishes a relationship stronger than that of Mouride disciple obtained through birth and Quranic education. The action of conversion and its declaration are done in ritual submission and extreme humility. The subject kneels down at his marabout's feet and solemnly declares: "I am submitting myself to you, body and soul, on earth and to the hereafter. What you will tell me to do, I will do. What you will forbid, I will never do." This conversion doubles again the Mouride's imbuing with spirituality, and erases any other ethnic and social identity through the chain of symbolic relationships to the congregation founder Mane (grand-father) Sheikh I. Fall. The subject becomes his symbolic grandson or granddaughter. Upon entering the working *daara* (group), the converted person discovers the institutionalization of physical labor as a condition sine quanon and as a means of acceding to God (Wade 1967:197–198). He or she also experiences spirituality in its ultimate expression through self-sacrifice. The Baye Fall follower will spend the rest of his or her life in the marabout's service, who, he believes, will lead his soul, when he dies, to a place next to Ibrahima Fall. They will enter paradise together with Amadou Bamba, also called *serigne* (master) Touba.

Female Baye Fall dancing in a circle. Photo © T.K. Biaya.

Within the urban or rural *daara*, submission (*ndjebbel*) shows the first stage of the quest for mystical unity. Like the Khane-Gah (the Sufis from Iran), the Baye Fall people sit in a circle, motionless, heads bent down, singing Sheikh Bamba and Ibrahima Fall's praises all night long, eventually achieving a state of ecstasy (Sy 1969, 288). Next, there are the acts of apprenticeship and/or feats of strength. Yengu, literally meaning "performed movement in action," the action of making the soul move, constitutes the highest spiritual expression of Baye Fall. It is the display and the exhibition of physical strength, from motionlessness through trance to ecstasy, and to the spiritual experience of the energetic void. The Baye Fall stand as an antithesis of standard Islam, for they do not abide by the common practices of Islam and orthodox Mouridism (i.e., nonrespect of the five principles of Islam, use of amulets, alcohol drink and drug use, violence around sacred places). Followers of Ibrahima Fall are very unique Muslims, and their practices are considered extreme by outsiders.

Yengu, Spiritual Performance

Apart from the annual pilgrimage to Touba and other major Mouride religious events, the Baye Fall congregation organizes its own rituals, evening memorial prayers, and other gatherings. The presentation of gifts to the marabout, the opening of a new school, baptism of a new born, and other ceremonies are symbolic acts intended to honor the memory of Ibrahima Fall.

During the private performance, which takes place in the house or inner yard of the host, the marabout (who is also the master of ceremony) is sumptuously dressed and sits in an armchair surrounded by knowledgeable disciples on the carpet next to him. His guests take up seats from which they can watch the mystic performance. During the public sequence, onlookers and spectators attracted by the songs and the sounds of the drums augment the audience. This public session takes place under a big tent that is erected to shelter the ceremony. The marabout occupies the front row which allows him, while he follows the spectacle, to receive the homage rendered by disciples and visitors in quest of blessing.

The private performance is brief. Once everybody is seated, the marabout's griot, holding an adze and a calabash, or his female griot, wearing a hat, stands up, shouts the master's names and utters a praise song for the *serigne* (master). Disciples assigned to the master's protection stand up and walk about the room with their hands on the handles of their sabers. They put on leather belts decorated with metallic nails in which they place their daggers. All of a sudden a *talibe* brandishing a sharp saber appears, cries aloud praises to the marabou, while the griot whom he relieved is singing under his breath, yielding his central voice and position to the Baye Fall's warrior. Continuing his praise, the latter slides the blade of his weapon over his neck from top to bottom, beating his body with the sharpened blade like strong butcher's strokes. He vainly attempts to cut off his neck and to lacerate his body. Finally, with repeated strong stabs he strikes on his rounded chest, uttering the panegyric story of his marabout's life and devotion to the congregation: his name of power, his maraboutic lineage, his good deeds and merits, the blessings that he received from General Kalifs and their families and those from Baye Fall marabout and his families, extending back to Ibrahima Fall and Amadou Bamba. To show that this is not a hoax, the performer cuts off the strings in leather holding the rosary and the marabout's picture he wears at his neck. This private performance is done without music.

After the meal, the public performance begins with a Mouride choir singing orthodox religious songs combining Quranic verses in Arabic and Wolof religious poetry. This initial stage precedes the *yengu* (the spiritual performance). After a first entrance made of songs and dances, the marabout and his learned guest introduce the night conference. Soon after the conference, the second round of songs, music, and dances starts and only stops very early in the morning with the Baye Fall's anthem, which has also accompanied their entrance on stage:

Laa ilaha illa'llah fall, laa ilaha illa'llaahaa
Laa Haha illa'llah fall, laa Haha ifla'Hah fall
Laa 1laha illa'llah fall, laa Raha illa'Haahaa
(repeated 15 times).

Immediately, the demonstration of spiritual devotion starts. On the esplanade the atmosphere is one of excitement generated by the "spiritual movement" of the Baye Fall such as their superhuman gestures of self-flagellation, with their symbolic destruction of human pride. Men and women appear at every corner running on the esplanade where a corridor used for the spectacle has been arranged. This "no man's land" separates the dancing group from the audience; it also puts the latter out of reach of the performers' dangerous movements. Devotees, male or female, may quickly whirl a club, sometimes weighing 11 pounds, above their heads, then strike their backs. The impact of the contact between the two bodies produces a muffled sound followed with a "ahan" sound, stirring up a murmur of satisfaction among the other Baye Fall. Some seize heavy cement blocks which they break on their foreheads, while others might drive awls into their eye, slash themselves with a saber, or cut themselves with a knife, arousing fear and admiration within the crowd. These spiritual demonstrations of power and physical strength, culminating in trance and energetic void experience, are done with the help of special medicines.

Meaning of the Performance

None of the other Islamic brotherhoods practice this type of ecstatic religious expression. These manifestations of the *yengu* spirituality are in no way meant to entertain; rather, they aim to religiously celebrate an event and enrich the audience with a spiritual and mystical perspective, encompassing Sufism and showing at the same time the function and central position of the Baye Fall congregation in the Mouride movement. The Baye Fall is preeminently the Mouride who had been able to complete the divine work of submission. In the context of the devotees' work on behalf of their marabout, the marabout, in return, like Ibrahima Fall toward Bamba, cares for of the disciple's soul in life and death. In establishing this chain of meanings and hierarchy of spiritual contacts, the *yengu* seeks to evoke and reenact both Amadou Bamba's humility (as with the initial submission of the prophet Rasul to Allah) and Ibrahima Fall's conversion and submission to Bamba. It preordains the divine promise of the angel on earth and the Mourid repentance. In this way, these spiritual manifestations symbolically display the intense Sufi faith (Lings 1975) visibly expressed through paradigmatic submission and the institutionalization of work as a religious act par excellence (Cruise O'Brian 1970, 145). They also magnify the whole contribution of the Baye Fall congregation to the realization of the divine work. Finally, this manifestation of the Mouride way stands as a unique expression of Africanized Islam.

References

Babou, C. A. M. 1997. Autour de la genese du mouridisme, *Islam et Societe au Sud du Sahara* 11:5–38.

Coulon, C. 1983. *Les musulmans et le pouvoir en Afrique noire*. Paris: Kharthala.

Cruise O'Brian, D. B. 1971. *The Mourides of Senegal. The Political and Economic Organization of an Islamic Brotherhood*. Oxford: Clarendon Press.

Diop, A. -B. 1981. *La Societe Wolof. Tradition et changement*. Paris: Karthala.

Lings, M. 1975. *What is Sufism?* London: G. Allen & Unwin.

Lo, M. 1993. Un aspect de la poesie "Wolofal" mouride. Traduction et analyse de quelques titres de serign Mbay Jaxate. Memoire de maitrise, Dept. de Lettres Modernes, Universite C.A. Diop, Dakar.

Roberts, Allen F., and Mary Nooter Roberts. 2003. *A Saint in the City: Sufi Arts of Urban Senegal*. Fowler Museum of Cultural History, UCLA. Seattle: University of Washington Press.

Ross, E. 1995. Touba, A Spiritual Metropolis in the Modern World. *Canadian Journal of African Studies* vol. 29, no. 2:222–59.

Sy, C. T. 1970. *La confrerie senegalaise des mourides*. Paris: Presence africaine.

Thiam, M. 1990. Introduction. *Ahmadou Bamba face aux autorites coloniales. (1889–1927)*, 0. Ba. Dakar, Imprimeries SIPS.

T. K. BIAYA

See also **Religion: African Traditional Religion; Ritual Performance; Spirit Possession**

ITESO

See **Children's Folklore: Iteso Songs of War Time; East African Folklore: Overview**

J

JAPANESE STUDY OF AFRICAN FOLKLORE

The development of folklore studies in Japan as well as the development of African studies there demonstrates the changing concepts of the focus for such scholarship. The study of "others" (in this case, Africans) was only slightly more problematic than the study of the "folk" because of the hierarchical nature of Japanese society. Thus, today's assumptions about folkloristics being the study of the "folk" (whoever they may be) in their own terms was as "foreign" to Japanese scholars as it was for so long to Europeans. Although much influenced by European academic traditions, Japanese Africanist scholarship is different than that of European and American scholars in that the Japanese continue to use research teams in which a number of scholars from different disciplines work together in the field.

Perhaps most striking to one not familiar with Japanese academic history is the similarity of founding dates for their academic associations with those in Europe. The Anthropological Society of Tokyo (now the Anthropological Society of Japan) was founded in 1884 and has remained focused on physical anthropology. The Linguistic Society of Japan was founded in 1896, but only later was ethnology formally recognized, with the founding of the Japanese Society of Ethnology in 1934. The Folklore Society was founded the next year. Initial folklore studies in Japan were conducted in Okinawa and Hokkaido, not among the Japanese per se; therefore the discipline of folklore has remained somewhat marginalized (as has African studies) due to the perceived differences from Japanese culture.

Although the formal recognition of folklore as a discipline occurred later in Japan than in Europe and the United States, the establishment of African studies occurred at much the same time. The Japanese Association for African Studies was founded in 1963, and interest in the study of Africa and its peoples has grown steadily since then. Major research projects in Africa actually began several years earlier, when Kinji Imanishi and Junichiro Itani went to central Africa to study the mountain gorilla in 1958. Building on this early work by primatologists, anthropologists continue to constitute the largest professional group in Japanese African studies. The dominant theme in anthropological research today is ecological anthropology, which reflects a consistent interest among Japanese scholars in human interaction with the environment, an interaction that includes other species (not just other primates) as well. Typically, multidisciplinary teams of scholars engage in long-term, localized projects. This diversity of research topics may be augmented by more developmental studies in the future.

There are several productive centers of African studies in Japan. One of the oldest (established in 1964) is the Institute for the Study of Languages and Cultures of Asia and Africa (ILCAA) at the Tokyo University of Foreign Studies, which promotes wide-ranging study of the languages and verbal arts of African peoples in their cultural and historical contexts. The Center for African Area Studies maintains Kyoto University's prominence in Japanese African studies through diverse research projects and publications. The third major center of Africanist research is the National Museum of Ethnology in Osaka, where scholars carry out a vigorous research and publications program while presenting art and material culture displays from throughout Africa. Africanist scholars are scattered throughout Japan at various universities and museums, such as Nagoya University and the Little World Museum of Man near Inuyama, which has many African exhibitions.

The various series published by the Institute for the Study of Languages and Cultures of Asia and Africa (ILCAA) constitute the single most impressive body of African folklore scholarship in Japan. Monographs in the ILCAA's series, often the results of team research projects, cover a variety of African cultures and present folk tale collections in original languages as well as English or French translations, detailed language studies, archival information, and historical texts. ILCAA's various monograph series demonstrate a keen interest in languages and linguistic analyses, with publication of numerous language lists, questionnaires, texts, and manuals. Studies of taxonomies and typologies dominate, with the folkloristic interest in ethnobotany and ethnozoology reflecting links to ecological anthropology, an orientation that remains central in Japan. Kyoto African Study Monographs continue to be another source of material in English by Japanese Africanist folklorists. Although there are very few studies of visual arts or performance, there is an increasing interest in urbanization and culture change.

It must be noted that these few words on the Japanese study of African folklore are limited by the author's lack of familiarity with the Japanese language. Far more research has been published in Japanese. Nevertheless, there is an extraordinary amount of excellent research published by Japanese scholars in English and French on African folklore. It is hoped that more exchanges will take place, so that those outside of Japan can benefit from the vast amount of research on African folklore by Japanese Africanists, that adjustments will be made within Japanese universities so that courses on African topics are more accessible, and that Japanese scholars will continue to make their valuable researches available in European languages.

References

Peek, Philip M. 1990. Japanese Anthropological Research on Africa. *African Studies Review* 33:93–131.

Philips, John E. 1994. *African Studies in Japan*, paper presented at St. Antony's College, Oxford University, February 24.

Posnansky, Merrick, ed. 1992. *Proceedings Japanese/American Workshop for Cooperation in Africa*. September 18–21. James S. Coleman African Studies Center, UCLA.

Sofue, Takao. 1961. Anthropology in Japan: Historical Review and Modern Trends. In *Biennial Review of Anthropology 1961*, ed. B. J. Siegel, pp. 57–72. Stanford, Calif.: Stanford University Press.

Tanno, Yasuko. 1989. *African Studies in Japan*. *African Research and Documentation* (University of Birmingham UK): 28–31.

Tomikawa, Morimichi. 1971. Present Situation of African Anthropology in Japan. *KBS Bulletin on Japanese Culture* 110:1–15.

PHILIP M. PEEK

JEWS OF ETHIOPIA

Today, the Beta Israel (or Falasha) of Ethiopia no longer live in Ethiopia, because most of the community, numbering close to 65,000, had been airlifted to Israel, in two operations in 1984 and 1991. When considering the folklore of this community, it is essential to bear in mind that seldom has any community undergone so dramatic, complete, and irreversible a change in so short a period of time.

In their homeland, the Beta Israel lived in northwestern Ethiopia, in approximately five hundred small villages scattered across a vast, predominantly Christian and Muslim territory. Although similar in appearance to their non-Jewish Amhara and Tigrinia Ethiopian neighbors, the Beta Israel were an occupational as well as a religious minority. Various oral traditions addressed the separate identity of the group. Some of these traditions, incorporating legends of King Solomon and the Queen of Sheba, placed them within the larger stream of Ethiopian history, while others posited them as a distinct ethnic group that had come to Ethiopia from the ancient land of Israel, and had valiantly preserved their faith for centuries. Their religion was rooted in the Old Testament, whose commandments they meticulously observed, all the while awaiting the coming of the Messiah and a return to the legendary Jerusalem.

Beta Israel's folklore has been a focus of academic study and has inspired far-reaching speculations regarding this group's unique history and identity (Wurmbrand 1971; Kessler 1982; Messing 1982; and, with different perspective, Shelemay 1989; Abbink 1992; Quirin 1992). Their folk traditions share much in common with local traditions, but also exhibit characteristics reflecting the group's Judaism and the centrality of Jewish iden-

tity, including the intensive negotiations conducted by the group with its non-Jewish Amhara and Tigrinia neighbors (Salamon 1999). These characteristics continued to evolve and change as the Beta Israel had to fight for their place within world Jewry, and even later, with the group's immigration to Israel. In Ethiopia, most Beta Israel lay community members were illiterate with a rich repertoire of oral traditions (Shelemay 1989; Quirin 1992). The Jewish religious leaders, however, like their Christian counterparts, linked religious praxis with scripture by reading publicly from the holy books written in Ge'ez, a language not understood by the majority of the community.

The Beta Israel's distinct religious rituals include the holidays mentioned in the Bible, maintained according to Ethiopian Jewish tradition and later influenced by extra-Ethiopian Jewish influences. An additional holiday not known in other Jewish communities is the Sigd. The Sigd is an annual pilgrimage holiday observed in Ethiopia on the twenty-ninth day of the eighth month of the Ethiopian calendar; it is treated as equally important as the biblically proscribed holidays. As a unique Jewish Ethiopian holiday, the Sigd is still observed by the group in Israel.

Life cycle rituals of the Beta Israel traditionally comprised two stages, a religious and a more general, social part. While the first was conducted by religious leaders and directed towards group members, the social part, particularly in weddings, funerals, and memorial services, was open to guests invited from neighboring communities and in many ways resembles celebrations held by the neighboring groups. During the social part of each religious group's celebrations, however, care was taken to separate the Beta Israel and other groups in regard to eating, particularly the consumption of meat (Salamon, 1999).

Circumcision, a ceremony that is highly symbolic in Judaism as ritualizing the special covenant between God and the Jews, was less significant in Ethiopia; Ethiopian Christians, like the Jews, conduct the same ceremony on the same day, the eighth day following the birth of a male child. An additional category of biblically based rituals is the one comprised of rituals related to female fertility and birth. During their menstrual period, Beta Israel women were confined to a separate hut ("the house of blood"), situated at the periphery of the Jewish huts in the village. A fence of stones demarcated the boundaries of this impure area as distinct from the rest of the village dwellings, and only after performing a purification ritual, was the woman allowed to rejoin the community. This practice was based on a verse from the Old Testament (Lev. 15:19). Beta Israel also considered the postbirth period as impure (forty days for a boy, eighty for a girl), in accordance with Leviticies, 12:2–6.

The Beta Israel specialized in specific crafts: blacksmithing and weaving for men, pottery for women. While they traditionally prepared vessels for agricultural work and cooking, over the past few decades, due to increased contact with international Jewry, they also began producing small clay statues, usually of biblical figures, for tourists who visited their villages.

The expressive folklore of Beta Israel is particularly rich, comprising genres similar to those of its non-Jewish Ethiopian neighbors. One example is the use of complex spoken expressions with multiple and hidden meanings known as "Wax and Gold" (Levine 1965) that require a high level of language mastery and advanced use of symbol. Most of the Beta Israel folktales overlap with pan-Ethiopian folktales such as trickster stories of Abba

Gabra-hanna or animal stories, but Beta Israel also have their own stories of historic encounters and competitions between Jews and Christians, stories of Jewish martyrs, and tales of Jewish holy sites (Alexander and Einat 1996).

The Beta Israel also have a rich repertoire of sayings and proverbs that combine Amhara and Tigrinya material with particular expressions understood only by group members, mostly regarding their Muslim and Christian neighbors (Salamon 1995).

The realm of magic is another shared, yet separate, folkloric realm. While the Jews of Ethiopia fully share popular Ethiopian conceptions of magic, their neighbors have accused them of possessing supernatural powers. Beta Israel specialization in blacksmithing and pottery making was treated with ambivalence by neighboring groups, who attributed supernatural powers to the Jewish artisans. They were perceived as Buda, the mythical Ethiopian hyena, who possesses the power to transform into human form during daytime and thus crosses the boundary between human and nonhuman. Although the image of the Buda is also associated with other groups in Ethiopia, Beta Israel's Christian neighbors related it to their Jewishness, tying it to traditional anti-Jewish accusations. As "Hyena People," the Beta Israel were feared for their "eating," that is, their sucking the blood of living victims or of recently buried cadavers, which they were said to exhume and use for alimentary and ritual purposes. The Christians took special care to protect themselves against such alleged offenses (Salamon in press).

The dramatic change undergone by the group upon their immigration to Israel takes expression in various forms of folklore, particularly those connected with language. The importance of oral tradition in Beta Israel culture is fast disappearing due to a loss of influence and close contact with the elders and replacement of traditional dialects with spoken Hebrew (Kaplan and Rosen 1993). The various spoken forms of folklore are thus undergoing dramatic changes that reflect the overall changes affecting the group. At the same time, new forms and folk traditions are emerging in Israel, the folklore of an ethnic group within a multicultural society that brings out the Ethiopian, not the Jewish, aspect of Beta Israel identity (Salamon 2003). There is a growing number of Ethiopian folk dance groups and craft objects on which the colors of the Ethiopian flag, reminders of village life in Ethiopia, and animal sculptures figure prominently at the expense of Jewish topics once expressed in Beta Israel folk art while they still lived in Ethiopia.

References

Alexander, Tamar, and Amela Einat (eds.). 1996. *Tarat Tarat. Jewish Folktales from Ethiopia*. Tel Aviv: Miskal (in Hebrew).

Abbink, Jan, G. 1992. L'enigme de l'ethnogenese des Beta Israel— Une approach anthropo-historique de leurs mytho-legende. *Cahiers d'etudes Africaines*.

Kaplan, Steven, and Chaim Rosen. 1993. Ethiopian Immigrants in Israel: Between Preservation of Culture and invention of Traditions, *The Jewish Journal of Sociology* 35 no. 1:35–48.

Kessler, David. 1982. *The Falashas—The Forgotten Jews of Ethiopia*. London: George Allen & Unwin.

Levine, Donald N. 1965. *Wax and Gold: Tradition and Innovation in Ethiopian Culture*. Chicago: The University of Chicago Press.

Messing, Simon. D. 1982. *The Story of the Falashas—Black Jews of Ethiopia*. Brooklyn: Balshon Printing and Offiet.

Quirin, James. 1992. *The Evolution of the Ethiopian Jews: A History of the Beta Israel (Falasha) to 1920*. Philadelphia: University of Pennsylvania Press.

Salamon, Hagar. 1995. Metaphors as Corrective Exegesis—Three Proverbs of the Beta-Israel. *Proverbium* 12:295–313.

———. 2003. Blackness in Transition: Decoding Racial Construct through Stories of Ethiopian Jews, *Journal of Folklore Research*, 40, no. 1:3–32.

———. In press. *The Hyena People: Ethiopian Jews in Christian Ethiopia*. Berkeley: University of California Press.

Shelemay, Kay Kaufman. 1989. *Music, Ritual, and Falasha History*. East Lansing, MI: Michigan State University Press.

Wurmbrand, Max. 1971. Falashas. *Encyclopaedia Judaica* 6, Jerusalem: Keter.

HAGAR SALAMON

See also **Music: Arab and Jewish Music of North Africa; Northeastern Africa (The Horn): Overview**

JOKES AND HUMOR

Joke may refer to any narration, action, or interaction that, judging from the response it receives from listeners or the audience, is considered to be humorous. Jokes are humorous and often evoke laughter, but performers must be very careful about when and where they are performed. A joke performed at the wrong time or place not only impoverishes discourse but it may constitute a mark of incompetence and loss of social prestige on the part of the performer. Such a joke is not likely to evoke laughter in the audience. Excellent joke performances are usually appreciated by other members of the community. It must be borne in mind, however, that excellence is not necessarily equivalent to frequency of performance. To preserve one's social prestige, one always avoids strategies that might jeopardize one's competence at telling jokes. Competent joke performers are those who have absolute control over when to joke and when to make serious points in their talk.

Humor, under which the joke genre may be subsumed, has attracted researchers from disciplines including philosophy (see Hobbes 1651, Bergson 1956); sociology (Faulkner 1987, Francis 1988); psychology (Freud 1960, Piddington 1963, Rothbart 1977, Russell 1987); literary studies (Andrews 1977, Barksdale 1984); anthropology (Apte 1985); linguistics (Raskin 1985, Attardo 1994); and folklore (Dorson 1966, Dundes 1977, Davies 1990, Oring 1992). However, the bulk of pioneering work in this field of study, as Apte (1985) points out, has been by psychologists, who began full-scale scientific inquiry into the subject in the early 1960s.

Jokes, as a folklore genre, have appeared under different names, including humorous folktale, jocular folktale, humorous anecdote, merry tale, farcical tale, and jest, in folkloristics (Baker 1986). Though it is clear that most people know and tell jokes at one time or another, jokes were still among the least collected and understood forms of folklore in the early 1970s (Baker 1986). Early works on jokes have focused on issues including subject matter (see Dorson 1966), their relationship with other genres (Dégh 1976), and their social significance (Dundes 1977, Oring 1992).

In spite of the enormous strides made so far by folklore scholars, very little work has been done on African humor in general and the joke in particular. Radcliffe-Brown (1940) discusses the joking relationship (what he describes as "permitted disrespect") as it exists in different places of the world, including Africa, distinguishing between two varieties—the symmetrical joke relationship and the asymmetrical joke relationship. He describes the symmetrical type as one in which each of the two participants teases or makes fun of the other, while asymmetrical joke relationship allows only one of the participants to joke at the expense of the other. Radcliffe-Brown's account follows earlier notes on the subject by scholars, including F. J. Pedler Henri Labouret and Denise Paulme.

Brempong (1978) makes an indirect reference to the joke genre in his folkloristic study of verbal insults among the Bono, a subgroup of the Akan people of Ghana in West Africa. He indirectly connects jokes with insults, indicating that some insults and youth game songs are known to exist in joke form. He goes on to mention that most comedy series on American television would not be humorous without insults. Broadening the scope to cover other ethnic groups in Ghana, we may mention Daniel K. Avorgbedor, who illustrates, in his essay on *haló* performance among the Anlo-Ewe, how humor, open confrontations, and insults may be conveyed through song (1994).

As argued in the latest study of jokes and joking among the Akan (see Adu-Amankwahd 2003), every mature Akan person seems to have an internal storehouse of jokes, and it takes the right audience or interaction to bring out the jokes within. Two or more people gather at a place, something happens, and a related joke heard before or a funny situation witnessed previously is remembered and told. The usual practice is for the individual to keep humorous events for use at appropriate times in future interactions with other members of the community.

The sociolinguistic factor of age is important in the performance of jokes among the Akan since jokes are normally passed from adult to adult or from adult to child, but rarely from child to adult. It is also normal for jokes to be told by one child to another. Gender is, however, irrelevant in Akan joke telling. A male teller may perform for a male or female or mixed audience and vice versa.

??? The Akan have the sister terms *aseresɛm* and *nsɛnkwaa* to refer to the joke genre. These terms are not interchangeable since the performer of *nsɛnkwaa*, unlike that of *aseresɛm*, often has laughter in mind. His or her main aim is to make a humorous statement to attract laughter from the audience, but humor or laughter is of little or no importance to the *aseresɛm* performer. In other words, *nsɛnkwaa* is a *ka-ma-yɛnsere* ("say-it-and-let's-laugh") sort of utterance, whereas *aseresɛm* may be a serious statement turned humorous. *Aseresɛm* is often based on previous events, but *nsɛnkwaa* need not have a historical base. Not only may *nsɛnkwaa* be made up on the spur of the moment, but it may also be replete with instances of exaggeration, all aimed at evoking laughter in the audience. ???

There is a close relationship between jokes and some other genres within the Akan society. For instance, joke performers may make use of proverbs for humorous effect in their narrations. The humor that such proverbs evoke is aided by the fact that the sociocultural truths contained in the proverbs are already known to the intended recipients. Unlike proverbs, however, jokes do not impose strict contextual considerations upon their understanding and appreciation. Apart from jokes in conversation, where the joke is often a response to an ongoing interaction, sociocultural background knowledge may be sufficient for a clear understanding and appreciation of most jokes.

Since jokes are often built in the form of stories, they are closely related to other narrative genres, such as folktale (*anansesɛm*). The main difference between joke narration and the narration of a folktale, however, is that *anansesɛm* often has a fixed opening formula and normally ends with the current narrator appointing someone to succeed him or her in the narration process. A joke narrative, on the contrary, has multiple opening formulae, and the next narrators are often unknown until begin their narration. Moreover, a joke may enter into intricate combinations with other genres such as folk song and graffiti.

In addition to some of the basic functions already discussed in the humor literature (such as the reflection of societal concerns, promotion of satirical statements against individuals who violate ethnic group boundaries, making light of a serious problem, releasing tension, bringing people together, and entertaining), Akan jokes may be a pragmatic tool for effecting command. Rather than give direct orders, individuals may use jokes to compel the addressee eventually to do things.

The identification of the basic characteristic features of jokes and joking among the Akan of Ghana (Africa for that matter) has set the stage for comparative studies, beginning, perhaps, with other regions in Ghana, then widening the scope to cover sub-Saharan in the Diaspora with African diasporic experiences, with the ultimate goal of examining the similarities and differences (if any) between African folklore and African American folklore.

References

Adu-Amankwah, David. (forthcoming). An Ethnopragmatic Study of Jokes and Joking in an Akan Community. Ph.D. dissertation, Indiana University, Bloomington.

Andrews, Clarence A. 1977. The Comic Element in Iowa Literature. In *American Humor*, ed. O. M. Brack, Scottsdale, Arizo: Arete.

Apte, Mahadev L. 1985. *Humor and Laughter: An Anthropological Approach*. Ithaca: Cornell University Press.

Attardo, Salvatore. 1994. *Linguistic Theories of Humor*. Berlin: Mouton de Gruyter.

Avorgbedor, Daniel K. 1994. Freedom to Sing, License to Insult: The Influence of *Haló* Performance on Social Violence among the Anlo Ewe. *Oral Tradition* 9, no.1:83–112.

Baker, Ronald L. 1986. *Jokelore: Humorous Folktales from Indiana*. Bloomington: Indiana University Press.

Barksdale, Richard K. 1984. History, Slavery, and Thematic Irony in *Huckleberry Finn. Mark Twain Journal* 22, no. 2:17–20.

Bergson, Henri. [1901] 1956. Laughter. In *Comedy*, ed. Wylie Sypher, Garden City, New York: Doubleday/Anchor, (originally, published as *Le rire. Essai sur la signification du comique*. Paris: Presses Universitaires de France.).

Brempong, Owusu. Attacking Deviation from the Norm: Insults in Bono—Ghana. Unpublished M.A. thesis, Indiana University, 1978.

Davies, Christie. 1990. *Ethnic Humor Around the World: A Comparative Analysis*. Bloomington: Indiana University Press.

Dégh, Linda. 1976. Symbiosis of Joke and Legend: A Case of Conversational Folklore. In *Folklore Today: A Festschrift for Richard M. Dorson*, ed. Linda Dégh, Henry Glassie, and Felix Oinas, Bloomington: Indiana University Press.

Dorson, Richard M. 1966. *American Folklore*. Chicago: University of Chicago Press.

Dundes, Alan. 1977. Jokes and Covert Language Attitudes; the Curious Case of the Wide-Mouth Frog. *Language in Society* 6: 141–7.

Faulkner, Joseph E. 1987. *Sociology through Humor*. New York: West.

Francis, Roy G. 1987. Some Sociology of Humor: The Joke. *International Social Science Review* 63, no. 4:158–64.

Freud, Sigmund. 1960. *Jokes and their Relation to the Unconscious*. New York: W. W. Norton.

Hobbes, Thomas. 1651. *Leviathan*. London: Crooke.

Labouret, Henri. La Parenté à Plaisanteries en Afrique Occidentale. *Africa* 2:244.

Oring, Elliott. 1992. *Jokes and their Relations*. Lexington: The University Press of Kentucky.

Paulme, Denise. Parenté à Plaisanteries et Alliance par le Sang en Afrique Occidentale. *Africa* 12:433.

Pedler, F.J. 1940. Joking Relationships in East Africa. *Africa* 13: 170.

Piddington, Ralph. 1963. *From Plato to Freud: The Psychology of Laughter*. New York: Gamut Press.

Radcliffe-Brown A. R. 1940. On Joking Relationships. *Africa: Journal of the International Institute of African Languages and Cultures* 13:195–210.

Raskin, Victor. 1985. *Semantic Mechanisms of Humor*. D. Reidel.

Rothbart, Mary K. 1977. Psychological Approaches to the Study of Humor. In *It's a Funny Thing, Humour*, ed. Antony Chapman and Hugh Foot. New York: Pergamon.

Russell, Roy E. 1987. *Life, Mind, and Laughter: A Theory of Laughter*. Chicago, Adams.

DAVID ADU-AMANKWAH

See also **Cartoons; Insults and Ribald Language**

JOKING RELATIONSHIPS

The terms *joking relationships, joking partnerships,* or *joking alliances* have been applied by anthropologists to certain institutionalized social relationships that are characterized by unusual freedom of behavior, termed *privileged license* or *privileged familiarity,* that would be inappropriate or highly insulting in any other context. Participants in such relationships may, in certain situations, joke openly, even obscenely, about each other's family, personal habits, or occupation, and "snatch" personal items from one another.

Anthropologists were interested in such relationships in many areas of the world for about fifty years, from the 1920s to the 1970s, especially when "structural" considerations were predominant in anthropological theory; such behavior was seen as integral to the social structure, as participation is obligatory in most instances and failure to reciprocate can strain a relationship. Early analyses of kin-based joking relationships, following the theory of A. R. Radcliffe-Brown (1940, 1949), presumed that the joking behavior served to alleviate some underlying tension or disjunction in the relationship, such as that between a man and his mother-in-law, or grandparents and grandchildren, or cross-cousins, or to lighten a relationship of heavy responsibility, such as between a man and his maternal uncle in a matrilineal society. Many other scholars elaborated on Radcliffe-Brown's ideas, and African studies were central in this anthropological interest in joking relationships.

Later studies focused on joking between groups or individuals in nonfamilial relationships—age-mates (see Mayer 1951), clans, residential groups, occupational groups, and whole societies— and showed that such joking may be based in a number of factors other than potential conflict, such as historical association, geographical location, shared interests which might or might not generate competition, and simple friendship. In such cases, the privileged license demonstrates the exclusive nature of the relationship, a standard function of the "in-joke" among individuals and groups worldwide. Numerous cases of interfamilial and interclan joking, like the Tanzanian custom of *utani* and others throughout sub-Saharan Africa, received much attention (see Christensen 1963). Widespread instances of "funeral friendship," irreverent joking behavior between clans at funerals— culminating in the theft for ransom of the corpse from the funeral procession—attracted early interest. Institutionalized joking between societies was found to be extensive in Africa, explained variously as arising out of situations of dominance, or stalemated hostility, or early friendly association.

From the 1940s through the 1960s, several journals, notably *Africa, African Studies, Man,* and *American Anthropologist* carried many studies on the subject.

Content of Joking Exchanges

The verbal and behavioral content of institutionalized joking conforms to specific cultural norms governing situational behavior, but it may often indicate the defining nature of the relationship. For example, members of patrilineal clans who share joking relationships with others may make derogatory comments about the others' fathers, or patrilines, since that is the basis for their clan membership and their relationship, but in their joking exchanges, they make no mention of matrilineal kin. On the other hand, age-mates joke freely about the other's mother since it is birth from their mothers and their mothers' having placed them together as children that defines their relationship; here, the father is irrelevant. The closest friendship relationships typically develop among age-mates, and, in their joking, they may make the most intimate personal references. Members of clans, residential and occupational groups, and neighboring societies joke about specific aspects of their relationship and each other's

Bachama clan joking partners rush the funeral procession and seize the bier supporting the body, which they will hold for ransom.
Photo © Phillips Stevens, Jr.

At a funeral in the kingdom of Bachama, women mock men. The woman in front has hung a calabash under her skirt to represent oversized genitals, which she swings and thrusts. Photo © Phillips Stevens, Jr.

close ties during the "times of the beginnings" (*tufo vurato*, "the traveling of the world"), the mythical times of the original settling of the people, and still maintain cooperative relations. Participants can joke publicly about one another's fathers and grandfathers, including using the generic term for the genitals, e.g., "*vo ɖo bagu* (jigu)!" (your father's [grandfather's] balls!), said in a sneering way. They may "snatch" possessions away from one another, save only articles of clothing on the body, tethered animals, or objects within the compound. A favorite theme of their joking is some unique characteristic of one or the other: "You worthless people, you never learned to (hunt, fish, make canoes, sing songs, use herbal medicines, etc.)—our grandfathers had to show you how (or do it for you)!" The word *ba*, ("worthless," or "useless,"), is a serious insult in a society in which achievement is highly rewarded.

People who share *gbouno surato* participate in funerals for one another's distinguished elders, arriving early and performing valuable tasks for the bereaved; but later, when the ceremony is under way, they group themselves near to the compound of the deceased and loudly engage in various forms of outlandish behavior (see Stevens 1991). People dress well when attending a funeral; the *gbounye* wear shabby, torn, or soiled clothes. While performing parodies of popular songs and dances, they mock the deceased, his station in life, and his clan, declaring their lowly origins, their laziness and stinginess, and making fun of the characteristics for which that clan is known: its historical accomplishments, its name, its principal occupation. Cross-dressed, men and women mock each other, and all make mockery of the noblest values of the society. They snatch away food intended by the bereaved for guests and declare how meager it is, that it is spoiled and unfit for people. And they cap off their show by roughly "stealing" the body from the funeral procession, wresting it from the pallbearers and running away with it, returning it only after extracting a sum of money from the deceased's relatives. Bachama prize cleverness of words and dramatic performance; such funeral performances are rehearsed at home, and the cleverness and originality of their routines are noted by other clans. They obviously function to alleviate grief; such behavior takes place only at the funeral of an elder. For a young person, when grief is especially deep, such behavior is inappropriate, and *gbounye* participation is completely serious. And the "ransom" paid for return of the body is recognized as compensation for the labor the joking partners have given to the bereaved.

Age-mates of the same sex share relationships of *gbouno dasoto*, according to how old their friendship may be. If it goes back to infancy (*nduwouno bo kuze*, "age-friendship from lying on a mat"), they may make verbal jokes about the persons of one another's mothers and grandmothers, even focusing on their genitals, using the second person singular pronoun to each other. In referring to other relatives, they use the third person, for example, to the other's wife: "Just listen to this worthless woman." She will laugh, but will respond only lightly: "Well then, you two just go off to your beer-house and find yourselves another woman!" The same verbal license is permitted between women as between men, but between the sexes, no genital references are made, and references to one another's bodies are generally superficial. The label "*ba*!" may be the most extreme insult tolerable in public situations.

The category of *gbouno peto* (*gboune* of meeting), operates between age-mates whose relationships began late in their lives,

alleged behavior and habits, singling out aspects of one another's history, or ecology, or capabilities, or important cultural features, but avoid direct personal references. In general, the closer the relationship, the greater the liberality of license allowed.

The permissible content of different levels, or categories, of joking relationships may be illustrated by reference to Bachama, now preferably called Bwatiye, a small kingdom along the Benue River in Adamawa Province, Nigeria (Stevens 1978, 1980, 1991). Bachama recognize several named categories of the institutionalized joking relationship, called *gboune*, each distinguished by permissible language, behavior, use of singular or plural second or third personal pronouns, and whether or not kin references are allowed in their joking exchanges. Joking in the closest relationships may be characterized by *dasoto* (insult), in which direct speech containing specific references to one's person are permissible; relationships based on looser association, between people of far different age or status, and people who meet only occasionally are restricted to *ozoto* (banter), in which no personal references are made and the third personal pronoun is used.

The most important category, *gbouno surato* (the "original joking relationship"), is shared between clans who established and between individuals and groups who have long and regular relationships based on common interests, proximity of residence, or other factors that bring them together regularly. Individual participants may abuse each other directly, using the second personal pronoun, but they indulge in a lighter form of *dasoto*; they avoid references about their fathers, and they use the third person when joking about one another's mothers. In such contexts they may refer only to visible attributes; for example, "Look at his mother's legs! His mother is bow-legged!" or "Look at his mother's breasts, how they swing and bobble!" Referring to spouses or children of their age-mates, their abusive language will refer only to the other, not to his or her family: for example, "Just look at the wife (children) of this useless man!" and the wife or children will show amusement, but will not respond.

An important relationship of *gbouno peto* exists between people who live along the banks (*zaŋe*) or tributaries of the Benue River, who have adapted to a river ecology, and people who live inland, in areas away from the river. The former are *Ji-zaŋe*, (people of the banks), the latter, *Ji-bawe* ("people of the bush"). Regardless of what other categories of *gboune* they might share, their ecology alone gives rise to earnest and popular joking competitions, most often expressed in singing contests. Group singing is a popular pastime. Local communities have their own choral groups, which meet frequently to rehearse new songs and perform publicly at a variety of social or religious occasions. Their songs extol specific accomplishments of their own members and belittle those of their rivals. Song contests provide entertainment, establish reputations, and sometimes can be the means of settling disputes between certain groups. Contests between *Ji-zaŋe* and *Ji-bawe* singers are popular and draw large crowds. Sometimes they are adjudicated by the king himself.

Relationships characterized by *ozoto* (play) and *hyesoto* (teasing) are maintained among people whose relationships are based in periodic informal meetings, between whom a casual friendship develops. This category includes those who share a more distant age-mate relationship, called *nduwouno matto* (age-friendship of maturity), which generally exists between adults whose ages are within two to four years of each other and persons of opposite sexes, who meet regularly only for public social occasions. In *ozoto* joking, no references to kin are made and references to one's personal appearance are always in the third person; the second person is used only when the object of the joke is not part of one's body or attire, and then the plural pronoun is used most often. A subcategory of *ozoto* joking is *gbouno fore* (*gboune* by day), established among people who meet together on formal occasions over long periods of time, whose relationship is based in those occasions, and who may joke only during those occasions. *Hyesoto* (teasing) is permitted downward between people of unequal status who have established familiarity after long association, that is, an employer, or a master, may make fun of his employee, or apprentice, who will show delight but will not respond.

Gboune is not recognized among kin; but a light *ozoto* is permitted during relaxed situations between children and their grandparents, including actual grandparents or elders of the grandparental generation, or elders of a clan that shares *gboune* with the clan of their fathers and who are close friends to their family. A typical exchange might be:

Children: *Jiji* (grandfather), isn't it time for you to die? Why do you want to live so long, eating up all the Guinea-corn so that your grandchildren have none? Grandfather: Just listen to these useless children! What kind of a world is this becoming, that they have no respect for their elders? It would be better that Pagla (the griffon vulture, genus *Gyps*) carries them away!

Such relationships conform to Radcliffe-Brown's (1940) observations about joking between relatives, reported among numerous other sub-Saharan societies.

Certain Bwatiye clans and villages claim joking relationships with other societies with whom they have had long historical relationships. Some of these are requited, some are not. A close relationship of *ozoto* is recognized with the Kona Jukun, Chamba Daka, and Jen, who are regarded as equals, and those societies' traditions agree. Bwatiye also practice a light *hyesoto* with the Bwaza (Bare) people to their north, who are distantly related to the Mbula, with whom the Bwatiye intermarry and who are regarded as "too close for *gboune*." Bwaza traditions acknowledge close historical relationship with Bwatiye, but they do not recognize a joking relationship with them. And both Bwatiye and Chamba look down upon the Mumuye who maintain a difficult existence in the arid hills around Chamba. Based in a legend about a culture hero who toyed with the Mumuye, Bwatiye indulge in *hyesoto* with those who come into their villages to take menial jobs, but Mumuye recognize no relationship of any sort with Bwatiye.

There are other named categories of *gboune*, obtaining among people with specific privileged relationships. All such relationships have latent sociological significance, but all serve important public functions of humor and entertainment. Bwatiye say the institution of *gboune* was given its antic attributes by ŋburum, the trickster of folktales (Stevens 1980) who claimed *gboune* with people and animals whom he was plotting to deceive, or with whom he had gotten himself into embarrassing situations. The role of ŋburum, as expressed in some well-known tale, might be evoked by any person playing the clown in a social situation.

References

Christensen, James B. 1963. Utani: Joking, Sexual License, and Social Categories among the Luguru. *American Anthropologist* 65: 1314–27.

Mayer, Philip. 1951. The Joking of "Pals" in Gusii Age-Sets. *African Studies* 10:27–41.

Radcliffe-Brown, A. R. 1940. On Joking Relationships. *Africa* 13: 195–210.

———. 1949. A Further Note on Joking Relationships. *Africa* 19: 133–40.

Stevens, Phillips, Jr. 1978. Bachama Joking Categories: Toward New Perspectives in the Study of Joking Relationships. *Journal of Anthropological Research* 34:47–71.

———. 1980. The Bachama Trickster as Model for Clowning Behavior. In *The Cultural Context: Essays in Honor of Edward Norbeck*, ed. Christine M. S. Drake. Houston: *Rice University Studies* 66:137–50.

———. 1991. Play and Liminality in Rites of Passage: From Elder to Ancestor in West Africa. *Play and Culture* 4:237–57.

PHILLIPS STEVENS, JR.

See also **Gender Representation in African Folklore; Insults and Ribald Language; Jokes and Humor**

K

KAMBA

See **Tourism and Tourist Arts**

KENYA (REPUBLIC OF KENYA)

Located on the coast of East Africa, Kenya's neighbors are Somalia, Ethiopia, Sudan, Uganda, and Tanzania. Of Kenya's more than 30 million people, 21 percent are Kikuyu, 14 percent Luhya, 13 percent Luo, 11 percent Kalenjin, 11 percent Kamba, and 30 percent belong to various other ethnic groups. The major languages spoken in the nation are English, Kiswahili, Kikuyu Luo, Kamba, Kipsigi, Maasai, and Luhya. Thirty-eight percent of the population is Protestant, 28 percent practices traditional indigenous religions, 28 percent is Catholic, and 6 percent is Muslim. With a population of 2 million, Nairobi is Kenya's capital and largest city. Kenya's climate ranges from tropical to arid.

The Kikuyu and Maasai peoples controlled much of what came to be known as Kenya, with the coastal areas under loose Arab rule from the sixteenth to nineteenth centuries. By 1895, the British gained control as the East African Protectorate and in 1920 formally established the colony of Kenya. From 1952 to 1960, the freedom struggle called the Mau Mau uprising caused the deaths of thirteen thousand Africans and one hundred English. On December 12, 1963, Kenya gained its independence from Britain after sixty-eight years under colonial rule with Jomo Kenyatta as the first president. While the ensuing years of economic growth have transformed the nation into the commercial center of East Africa, the majority of Kenya's citizens remain impoverished. In 1969, the nation reverted to a one-party state, and the government subsequently grew more repressive throughout the 1980s under Daniel T. Arap Moi, who took over after Kenyatta's death in 1978. Despite the return of a multiparty government in 1991, the nation has been marred by interethnic violence and political instability but citizens are reassured by recent elections.

Kenya's natural resources include wildlife, land, soda ash, and wattle, while agricultural production centers around tea, corn, wheat, rice, sugarcane, coffee, sisal, pyrethrum, and livestock. It is not well known that Kenya is the world's largest exporter of tea. Principle industries include petroleum products, cement, beer, automobile assembly, and food processing. Tourism is once again increasing.

Kenya's government demonstrates a strong commitment to education, as it contributes half of its annual government expenditures to educational programs. Unfortunately, culture and politics are closely tied in the country and, even today, if artistic work is not in agreement with the ideals of the government, it may be destroyed.

JENNIFER JOYCE

KONGO

See **Cardinal Directions; Central African Folklore: Overview; Divination**

KWANZAA

Kwanzaa, spelled Kwanza in the original Swahili, is a secular African American holiday based on the traditional harvest festivals celebrated by many African societies. Beginning on December 26 and ending on January 1, the seven-day holiday celebrates African American heritage, pride, community, family and culture. Its rituals and symbols combine traditional African practices with African American aspirations and ideals.

Following the 1965 Watts riots in Los Angeles, California, Dr. Maulana Karenga (later a professor at California State University at Long Beach) created Kwanzaa in 1966 as a celebration and affirmation of the virtues of an African identity and ancestry. He established the holiday based on African first-fruit harvest celebrations. The word *Kwanzaa* is derived from the Swahili phrase *matunda ya kwanza*, which means "first fruits."

According to Karenga, Kwanzaa is organized around five fundamental activities common to African first-fruit celebrations:

- the gathering of the people to reinforce the bonds between them, especially the bonds of family, community, and culture;

- special reverence for the Creator and Creation, in gratitude for the bounty and goodness of the earth and with a commitment to preserve and protect it;
- commemoration of the past, to fulfill the obligation to remember and honor ancestors, and to teach and reaffirm African history;
- renewed commitment to the highest African cultural, ethical, and spiritual values, that bring forth the best of what it means to be African and human; and
- celebration of all that is good in life, of the family, community, and culture, of relationships, of old age and youth, of knowledge and sharing, of work and wonder, and of all things of benefit and blessing (Karenga 1999,1).

Using these elements common to African first-fruit celebrations, Karenga created and placed at the center of the holiday seven principles, called Nguzo Saba, which define the meaning of the holiday and its rituals. Each day is dedicated to one of the seven principles:

December 26: Umoja (unity): a commitment to the practice of togetherness, both within the family and the community;

December 27: Kujichagulia (self-determination): the interest of developing and patterning African American lives and images after peoples of African descent instead of others;

December 28: Ujima (collective work and responsibility): working together and supporting each other on matters of common interest;

December 29: Ujamaa (cooperative economics): the habit of sharing wealth and resources within the community and among black people;

December 30: Nia (purpose-building): developing a national community;

December 31: Kuumba (creativity): inspiring black people to keep developing new ways of expressing their music and art, as well as being creative in work and industrial pursuits; and

January 1: Imani (faith): believing in the humanity of African peoples.

The Ritual

Beginning on December 26, and on each of the subsequent days, households, and even entire communities, participate in a proscribed ritual. The setting for this ritual includes a *kinara*, a candle holder with seven candles (*mishumaa saba*), which represent the seven principles, placed on a table decorated with African cloth or a straw mat (*mkeka*). The center candle is black for the color of the African American people. The three red candles symbolize their struggles and three green candles symbolize their hopes. The family places on the table a basket of fruit and vegetables (*mazao*, meaning crops), ears of corn (*vibunzi*) for each child in the household (or, if no children are in the household, one ear of corn representing the potential for children), a unity cup (*kikombe cha umola*), and other heritage symbols such as books, family pictures, and a copy of the *nguzu saba*. The black nationalist flag of red, black, and green (*bendera*) may also be hung with

the red at the top, or, if hung vertically, with the red on the flag's right. Since great emphasis is placed on rejecting the gross commercialism of Christmas gift giving, gifts are optional, usually given only to children every evening or on the last evening. Only certain types of gifts appropriate to the holiday are recommended, such as crafts, art, and handmade gifts; books about Africa and African Americans; and other cultural gifts.

On each day of Kwanzaa, an elder calls the family together. People greet each other saying, "Habari gani," meaning, "What's the news?" or "What's happening?" The response to the greeting is the name of the day. On December 29, people would respond, "Ujamaa." Water or juice is poured from the unity cup for libations (blessings and prayers) for the elders and for the family's future. A child or youth lights the candle for the day, and everyone drinks water or juice from the unity cup. In affirmation of African culture, the family discusses the meaning of the principle by reciting a story, poem, or history about Africans or African Americans.

Near the end of the holiday, usually the evening of December 31, the family or community gathers for a feast, called *karamu*. A typical *karamu* features African and African American traditional foods; wearing of African attire; and African and African American performances, music, and dancing. The feast ends with the final passing of the unity cup, shouts of "Harambee!" meaning, "Let's pull together," and prayers or blessings.

Significance

Kwanzaa is the first nonheroic African American holiday ever to come into existence. Inspired by the black power movement of the 1960s and based on ancient African celebrations, African Americans have been celebrating the holiday since 1965. By the 1990s, it had become increasingly popular and celebrated by more than 25 million people in the United States, Canada, England, the Caribbean, and Africa.

Kwanzaa is not a religious holiday. Its celebration in December, strategically placed after Christmas, does not challenge religious celebrations and beliefs; rather, it coexists with other holidays. Many African American families, if not most, celebrate Christmas and Kwanzaa. In fact, Kwanzaa's celebrants emphasize that it is a nondenominational, nonreligious, family and cultural celebration. In some communities, its secular nature has made it the only December observance that can be celebrated using public funds, as it does not challenge the separation between church and state. Since October 1997, the U.S. Postal Service has issued a Kwanzaa commemorative stamp during the holiday season.

For most African Americans, Kwanzaa, unlike the celebration of Martin Luther King, Jr. Day in January or Black History Month in February, resonates with the cultural affirmation and political confrontations of the mid to late 1960s. Yet, in spite of its origins in the 1960s black power movement and its affirmation under the philosophies of Afrocentrism in the 1980s, by the 1990s, Kwanzaa was enthusiastically embraced by American popular culture. It became more than an African American celebration; it was thoroughly integrated—some might say coopted—into the marketplace and sold to the American public in the form of Kwanzaa cards and wrapping paper; fabric for African clothing and decorations; recognition on television and radio advertisements, announcements, and programming; and incorporated into civic celebrations at public libraries, museums, performances, and schools.

Kwanzaa's commercialization has affirmed the ability of American capitalism to turn culture and philosophy into marketable goods. Yet, in spite of its commercialization, Kwanzaa's integration into every arena of America's holiday season and its acceptance and popularity among African Americans has also affirmed the reality of American society's diversity and pluralism and the impact that African American life and culture have had on American society.

References

Asante, Molefi Kete. 1999. Karenga, Maulana Ndabezitha. *Encarta Africana 2000.* Microsoft.

Copage, Eric. 1991. *Kwanzaa: An African-American Celebration of Culture and Cooking.* New York: Morrow.

Karenga, Maulana. 1980. *Kawaida Theory: An Introductory Outline.* Inglewood, Calif.: Kawaida.

———. 1998. *Kwanzaa: A Celebration of Family, Community and Culture.* Los Angeles, Calif.: University of Sankore Press.

———. 1999. Kwanzaa. *Encarta Africana 2000.* Microsoft. Kwanzaa Information Center at http://www.melanet.co/kwanzaa

Magubane, Bernard. 1987. *The Ties That Bind: African American Consciousness of Africa.* Trenton, NJ: Africa World Press.

Martin, Waldo. 1996. Maulana Karenga. In *The Encyclopedia of African-American Culture and History,* ed. Jack Salzman et al., vol. 3. New York: Macmillan, p. 1526.

Nuruddin, Mansur M., and Robyn Spencer. 1996. Kawaida. In *The Encyclopedia of African-American Culture and History,* ed. Jack Salzman et al., vol. 3, pp. 1527–28. New York: Macmillan.

Riley, Dorothy Winbush. 1995. *The Complete Kwanzaa: Celebrating Our Cultural Harvest.* New York: HarperCollins.

Yousef, Nancy, and Robyn Spencer. 1996. Kwanza. In *The Encyclopedia of African-American Culture and History,* ed. Jack Salzman et al., vol. 3, pp. 1560–61. New York: Macmillan.

LILLIE J. EDWARDS

See also **Diaspora; African Communities in the USA (African Immigrant Expressive Culture)**

L

LANGUAGES

Africa has about 1,727 languages (two-thirds of the world's languages). Africanist linguists including Joseph Greenberg (1966) have classified African languages genetically into four families: Niger-Kordofanian, Afro-Asiatic, Khoisan, and Nilo-Saharan.

Niger-Kordofanian Languages

This language family is made up of Niger-Congo and Kordofanian. Niger-Congo, spoken in the basins of the Niger and Congo Rivers, has these subfamilies: (1) Adamawa-Ubanji, spoken in parts of Central Africa and has languages such as Gbaya, Banda, and Zande. (2) (New) Benue-Congo, which includes the former Eastern Kwa—Yoruba, Edo, Nupe, Idoma, Igbo—and Bantoid (subclassified into non-Bantu and Wide Bantu.). Swahili, Kikuyu, Zulu, and Xhosa are important Benue-Congo languages. (3) Gur languages are spoken in West Africa—Ivory Coast, Ghana, Togo, Benin, and Burkina Faso. They subdivide into Oti-Volta and Grusi. Gurenne, Wali (Dagaari), Dagbani, Buli, Kusaal, Bassari, Ntrobo, Kasem, Sisaala, and Nafaanra are Gur languages. (4) Ijo is spoken by the Ijo of Nigeria and covers both Ijo and Defaka. (5) Kru languages include Grebo and Bassa. (6) Mande, spoken in parts of Mali, Coat d'Ivoire, Guinea, Sierra Leone, Guinea Bissau, Mauritania, Nigeria, and Ghana, among others, has languages like Bambara, Maninka, Kpelle, Busa, Ligbi, and Bobo. (7) (New) Kwa has languages such as Akan, Ewe (and other Gbe languages), Ga, and Togo-remnant languages, among others. (New) Kwa has undergone tremendous classification and reclassification. It includes languages spoken in southern Ghana, Cote d'Ivoire, Togo, Benin, and southeastern Nigeria. (8) West Atlantic languages are spoken in the area stretching from the Senegal River down into Liberia. They include Fula, Wolof, Diola, and Temne.

The Niger-Congo languages have vowel harmony (a system of vowel distribution in which all the vowels in a word are either rounded, unrounded, tense, or lax) tonal systems (between two and five tones), stress (Swahili), nasality, (Igbo, Yoruba), breathy voicing (Edo), dissimilation, unusual consonants, such as coarticulated consonants (e.g., [kp, gb]), implosives (e.g., bhabha / ɓaɓ /a calabash; bábā – cut, ejectives, velar fricative[kh]), consonant mutation—where certain consonant sequences such as /

mb/ change to /mm/ because of adjacent consonants—among others.

Apart from the Kru and Mande languages, most languages have serial verb constructions (where a series of two or more verbs in a given language express one action in another language), adjectives occurring after nouns, and subject-verb-object word order, but Mande has subject-object-verb. A few like Ijo and Likpe have gender systems. In Benue-Congo languages nouns are grouped into classes, and each noun class places specific affixes before or after other words occurring in the same sentence. Others, such as New Kwa, have lost most of their class forms.

Kordofanian languages are spoken in the Nuba Mountains in the Republic of Sudan. This group of languages has dental /t d/ and retroflex sounds /rr, nr/. Plosives like /t/ occurring between vowels change to fricatives /s/ and the noun class system is reminiscent of those found in other Niger-Congo languages.

Afro-Asiatic (Hamito-Semitic) Languages

This is a major language family of northern Africa and the Middle East. It has nearly 200 million speakers and is subdivided into six language groups: Semitic, Egyptian, Berber, Chadic, Cushitic, and Omotic. Egyptian, now extinct, had dialects such as Ancient Arabic and Coptic, which survived until about the fourteenth century.

Chadic is spoken in Central and West Africa south of the Sahara and includes Hausa, the official language of Nigeria and principal language of Niger, Ghana, Togo, Benin, Cameroon, and Chad. It has more native speakers than any other sub-Saharan African language including Ngizim, Warjawa, Bolewa; Kotoko (Ngala, Logone, etc.); Bata-Margi (Bachama, Gabin, etc.); and Hina, among others.

Cushitic languages are spoken in East Africa south of the Sahara in Ethiopia, Somalia, along the Red Sea, and Kenya. They have important languages like Galla, Somali, Oromo, Bedawiye, Hadya, Beja, Bogo, Kamir, Galla, Darasa, and Kambata.

Semitic languages include Arabic, Hebrew, Amharic (with over 5 million speakers, and the official language of Ethiopia) Aramaic, Akkadian, and Mehri. Other Semitic languages spoken in North Africa include Tigrinya and Tigré in Eritrea and Ancient Ethiopian, or Gecez, now extinct.

Berber, spoken in northern and northwestern Africa (west of Egypt) in countries like Morocco, Algeria, and Tunisia has languages such as Numidian, Tuareg, Iznacen, Ghadames, Riff, Shilh, and Kabyle. Berber speakers are Berber-Arabic bilingual. Omotic languages are spoken in southern Ethiopia.

Important phonological features of Afro-Asiatic languages include stress, tone, implosives (/bh, dh, gh/), and back consonants, notably velar (/k/, /g/, /kh/, /gh/) pharyngeal (/hh hg/), and glottal sounds (/ʔ, h/). Afro-Asiatic languages are subject-verb-object and have gender.

The Khoisan Languages

These languages are spoken mainly by the Khoikhoi and San peoples of southern Africa—especially in Namibia, Botswana, The Republic of South Africa, and Tanzania. There are three subgroups: South African Khoisan (SAK), Sandawe, and Hatsa. SAK has three subfamilies: Northern, Central, and Southern. Northern SAK (Bushman) has languages like !Xu and Auen. Central SAK has Hottentot (Khoi and San), Nama (with nearly 40,000 speakers) and Kxoe. Southern SAK has !Xo and other languages, some of which are extinct. Hatsa is spoken in Tanzania in an area between Lake Tanganyika and the sea. Sandawe and Hatsa are spoken by a little over 70,000 people between the Bubu and Mponde Rivers in the Kondoa District in Tanzania. Sandawe is spoken in the Dodoma region of Tanzania. Sentences in this language have subject-object-verb structure. There are three clicks (sounds during whose production air is drawn into the mouth) /t l/ dental click (the tip of the tongue touches the upper teeth), /l l/ alveolar lateral click (air escapes along the blade of the tongue) and [1811] post alveolar/palatal click (front part of the tongue touches the hard palate). Hatsa has an additional labial (kissing) click /b/. In Hatsa /b/ clicks appear less frequently and usually in the middle of words. Other consonants found in Sandawe and the other Khoisan languages but uncommon in other African languages are the voiceless and voiced lateral hissing (fricatives and affricates)—/tl, dl, hl, Hl/. Producing consonants with a breath can distinguish meaning in these languages. There are four nasals: /m, n, ny, ng/.

Nilo-Saharan Languages

Nilo-Saharan languages are spoken in pockets of areas along the Niger River in West Africa to Ethiopia, in parts of Uganda and Kenya, and throughout most of the upper Nile Valley. It has over ninety languages. Nilo-Saharan is sometimes divided into Songhai, Saharan, Fur, Chari-Nile, and Coman. Songhai is spoken along much of the upper Niger River in Niger. The Saharan languages including Kanuri—the major language with nearly 2 million people—Berti and Teda are spoken in northeastern Nigeria, throughout the Republic of Chad to the east, and parts of Libya. Chari-Nile, spoken in Chad, Sudan, Uganda, Kenya, and in the Republic of Congo, has about 1 million speakers. The Nubian languages are important Chari-Nile languages. The Nilotic languages spoken in Sudan, Uganda, and Kenya include languages such as Dinka, Nuer, Shilluk and Luo, and Massai in Kenya.

Nilo-Saharan languages have remnants of a noun-class system, and most are tonal with a two-tone system being the most common, although a few languages have three-tonal systems. The languages have vowel harmony. Nilo-Saharan languages have a five-way place consonant system (involving labials /p b/, dentals /t d/, alveolars /t d/, palatals /ky gy; hj gj/, and velars /k g/) and a strong absence of consonant clusters. Nasals generally constitute final consonants in these languages.

Other Languages

The Indo-European language of Afrikaans is an "Africanized" form of Dutch. It is spoken mainly by the descendants of Dutch settlers in southern Africa. English is native to white settlers in the Republic of South Africa and Zimbabwe and to repatriated African Americans in the nineteenth century in Liberia. Krio is an English-based Creole spoken in Sierra Leone by descendants of freed slaves. The Polynesian language of Malagasy is spoken in Madagascar. Due to colonization, English, French, Portuguese, Spanish, and Italian are also spoken in some African countries.

References

Greenberg, Joseph. 1966. *The Languages of Africa*. Bloomington: Indiana University Press.

SAMUEL GYASI OBENG

See also **Languages: Africanisms in the Americas**

Table 1   Some Consonants in African Languages

	bilabial	labio–dental	dental	alveolar	postalveolar	palatal	retroflex	velar	uvular	pharyngeal	glottal
plosive	p b			t d tp db			tr dr	k g kp gb	q G		Gg ʔ
Implosive	bh		dh					gh			
ejective	p′			t′			tr′	k′	q′		
clicks	b̬		t̬l	l̬l̬							
trill "flap				r				rr			
nasal	m	mf		n		ny	nr	ng			
fricative	pf bv	f v	t̬d̬	s z	sh zh	hj gj		kh gh	qh Gh	hh hg	h H
affricate				ts dz	ky gy						
lateral fricative				lh dlh							
lateral approximant				l				L			

LANGUAGES: AFRICANISMS IN THE AMERICAS

The question of Africanisms—that is, traits of African languages present in languages of the Americas—is actually a very complex one due, in part, to the frequent absence of the full range of information required for identifying these languages. Many West African languages varied in terms of how many speakers of each language lived in a particular area, and the extent to which the proportion of different language speakers changed over time in the same area. For example, until 1710, speakers of Ewe-Fon in Haiti comprised roughly half of the population; but only approximately one-third of the Africans arriving afterward. Additionally, many Africans, if not most, were multilingual; so, while they may have primarily spoken the language of their ethnic group, they probably also spoke at least one other language.

The major site of the study of Africanisms is Creole studies. Consequently, any discussion of Africanisms must include a discussion of Creole studies. Spears and Winford (1997) offer a recent assessment of theories, concepts, and methodologies in Creole (and pidgin) language studies. Holm (1988/1989 and 2000), the standard references, include discussions of a large number of individual Creole languages. However, it is important to note that Africanisms are found in non-Creole languages in the Americas as well.

Among the Creole languages are Jamaican, also called Jamaican English Creole and "patois;" Gullah, also called Guichee and Sea Island Creole, spoken in the United States mainly in the coastal areas of South Carolina, Georgia, and Florida and the nearby offshore islands; Haitian, also called Haitian French Creole and "Kreyòl"; and Guyanese, also referred to as Guyanese English Creole. Creole languages display a mixture of West African and European (and additionally, to a lesser extent, indigenous Native American) language input. They were created as a result of bringing together peoples with no common language, who were nevertheless compelled to interact with one another, most notably under the conditions of trade and slavery.

The West African languages that provided input into the languages of the Americas were of the Niger-Congo family, a large grouping that includes the Bantu and Kwa language families. These languages are spoken from the north of sub-Saharan Africa in the Gambia and Senegal, southward to Angola in southern central Africa. Among the languages often noted as the sources of items found in Western Hemispheric languages are KiKongo, Twi, Ibo, Mende, Yoruba, Kru, Ijo, Efik, Bambara, and Ewe-Fon (a cluster of highly similar language varieties). West African vocabulary items in the languages of the Americas are typically connected to West African cuisines, religions, and other more private, as opposed to public, areas of social life such as sexuality. The European colonial languages involved in the formation of Creole languages were English, French, Portuguese, Spanish, and Dutch.

No African language today functions as a living language in the full range of any African American community's social interaction. There are, however, instances of the use of fossilized fragments of African languages in religious rituals. As a result of the particularly heavy number of Yoruba speakers brought to Cuba, Guyana, Brazil, and Trinidad in the nineteenth century, forms of that language were spoken in these countries into the twentieth century.

There are two basic ways that one can discuss Africanisms in languages of the Americas. The first way is from the standpoint of quantity—that is, how many Africanisms these languages have relative to one another. The second way is by discussing specific Africanisms as examples of the various types of Africanisms.

With regard to quantity, we can establish roughly four levels of Africanisms based on the social history of these languages; more specifically, the extent to which they have been in contact with West African languages brought by free immigrant and enslaved Africans to Western Hemispheric shores. Since there were so few in the former category, they may well have had a negligible effect.

The first level, languages considered by linguists to have the highest amount of Africanisms, are radical Creoles. *Radical Creoles*, as the term is used by pidgin and Creole language specialists (i.e., Creolists), refers to that group of Creole languages in the Americas having less European language input, in effect, those that are more African owing to sociohistorical factors. These languages also have a number of features that must be attributed to other sources, among them putatively independently developed features that cannot be attributed to European or West African languages. All Creole languages show European language influence primarily in their vocabularies, but also show it in the rest of their grammars—phonology (the sound system), morphology (word structure), syntax (the structure of words in phrases, clauses, sentences) and semantics (meaning). West African language input shows up most in areas of grammar rather than vocabulary.

At this point, a word on the relationship between Creoleness and Africanness is needed. Creole languages toward the radical end have more features considered to be typical, for example, verb serialization, where two or more verbs share one subject. An example:

Dem da   ca   um gi dee nyong
They PROGRESSIVE carry it give the young
peepl (Gullah)
people
"They are bringing it for/to the young people."

The second verb *give* expresses the meaning of the preposition *for*. Verb serialization is frequently found in Niger-Congo languages and can thus be considered an Africanism.

Creole grammatical features are not necessarily Africanisms, but there is strong evidence that a good number of them are. Thus, grammatical features considered typical of Creole languages are often Africanisms, but they may also result from the creation of new grammatical features, neither African nor European, in the process of Creolegenesis, whereby a Creole language comes into existence, or during the subsequent evolution of the language.

The common absence of passivization in Creole languages is considered an Africanism, and is found in radical and some other Creole languages. Note the Jamaican "De rais kot" (The rice has been cut), where *de rais* appears in subject position but is the object of the act of cutting. Compare the passive sentence with the following active one: "Bob kot de rais" (Bob cut/cuts the rice), where Bob is the agent and the sentence's subject. In sum, we can take as a general rule that radical Creole, that is, those having the most Creole features of grammar, also have the most Africanisms.

As in most West African languages, adjectives are more like verbs than they are in European languages. So, for example, no copula (form of the verb *be*) is required in these languages before adjectives (cf. English "He is old"), as is the case before verbs. Kru, spoken in Liberia, and Yoruba, spoken in Nigeria, are just two examples of West African languages with this pattern, which is found in Creole languages. Observe the Haitian sentence, "Li vyè," "He/she/it is old."

The most discussed grammatical pattern found in Creole language Africanisms is the system of preverbal markers expressing tense, mood, and aspect. There are typically three of these markers, and their semantics and combinations are remarkably similar throughout Creole languages and a number of West African ones.

Among the Creole languages considered radical by most creolists are Haitian French Creole (called Haitian by Creolists), Saramaccan, and Ndjuka (the last two spoken in Suriname). Haitian's radicalness is a consequence of the Haitian Revolution, formally ended by treaty in 1804 but the result of a decades long process that won Haitian independence from France and from the normative pressure of French culture and the French language. French continued as the language of a tiny elite controlling the most important institutions, but the isolation and hindered development of Haiti contributed to keeping Haitian from becoming more Europeanized. Actually, in accord with more recent views in Creole studies, we may say that Haitian moved further away from French as a result of the revolution and the very heavy importation of slaves immediately preceding it.

Saramaccan and Ndjuka are maroon languages, in other words, languages of African descendants who escaped from slavery and formed communities in relatively inaccessible swamp, mountain, or rainforest areas. These two languages are those of Surinamese slaves who in the seventeenth and eighteenth centuries escaped from coastal areas into the interior rainforest and who were able to maintain many African traditions. These languages, with English and West African language input, were separated from the normative pressure of English for over three hundred years; and, this helps to explain their radicalness. They also have other European and no doubt indigenous language input, especially Portuguese, in the case of Saramaccan.

The second level comprises the other Creole languages, ranging from those having less African content than the radical Creoles to those having relatively few features considered typical of Creoles. Some in this group, such as Louisiana French Creole, are considered midrange Creoles in terms of Africanisms. Others are considered "lightly Creolized," and some scholars might want to argue whether they are full-fledged Creoles or not. A number of Creolists consider Trinidadian (English Creole) as very lightly Creolized due to its relatively late formation from varieties of English that were themselves very lightly or hardly Creolized. Barbadian is similar to Trinidadian in that it is also considered lightly Creolized. The Creole languages in the second level group vary in their level of Creoleness—as, indeed, Creolists believe the radical Creoles do.

Languages on the third level are not Creole languages, but they do have Creole language features, though not enough of these features for them to be classified as Creoles. Note that some varieties of the lightly Creolized languages just discussed might be put into this category. These categories do not have clear-cut boundaries since we are actually dealing with a continuum. These languages are sometimes referred to as post-Creoles or semi-Creoles. African American Vernacular English (AAVE) (the nonstandard type) and standard African American English (SAAE) are examples (Lanehart 2001). Most of the linguistic literature mentions AAVE only, but there is also a type of African American English (AAE) that can be considered standard based on the same characteristics that are used to classify other varieties of American English as standard. These characteristics include the level of education and social position of its speakers and the fact that this type of AAE has none of the grammatical features classified as nonstandard in prescriptive grammars. Among these features are *ain't*, the use of double or multiple negatives in a sentence, the use of double modals (e.g., "*He might could do that*"), and so forth. So, both types of AAE, nonstandard (or vernacular) and standard, have Creole features, but not enough of these features to actually qualify as Creole languages. Note also that the great majority of AAE varieties, standard and nonstandard, can be understood by other English speakers from around the world, but the same is not true for English-lexifier Creole languages. Those often referred to as lightly Creolized are in some instances exceptions. There are, in addition, morphological and syntactic features in AAE that can reasonably be argued to be Africanisms.

The use in AAVE of the verb *say* as a complementizer, a conjunction introducing a dependent clause, is an example of an Africanism. This use of *say* is found in a number of West African languages. Observe the AAVE sentence "He told me said they always do it." In this example the verb *say* occurs in the Simple Past form of the verb. This is one way that those varieties of AAE that have this complementizer make themselves more like non–African American varieties of English, thus camouflaging the Africanism. In Gullah, an English-lexifier Creole language spoken in the United States on the coast and offshore islands of South Carolina, Georgia, and Florida (as well as in Texas, on a much more limited basis) the uninflected verb *say* is used as the complementizer and can occur in a larger number of sentences contexts than the AAVE *said*. (*Say* occurs also in some varieties of AAVE.)

Another interesting feature, found presumably in varieties of AAE, can be strongly argued to be an Africanism. This feature is the semiauxiliary *come*, which expresses strong disapproval. It is distinct from the motion verb *come*, and both can be found, although rarely, in the same sentence; for example, "He come coming in here acting like a damn fool." In this example, the first *come* is the semiauxiliary, and the second *come* is the familiar motion verb. This disapproval form is found in many Caribbean Creoles, an indication already that it may well be an Africanism. Note also that it is found in non-English-lexifier Creoles such as Haitian, where a reflex (contemporary form) of the French motion verb *venir*, meaning "come," is used. Providing strong evidence that this form is an Africanism is the fact that it is found not only in a number of Creoles, but it has also been documented in one West African language (Bambara of the Segu area in Mali) and probably exists in more.

This discussion of the *come* of strong disapproval illustrates a fundamental point: Africanisms are such to a degree, depending on the strength of the evidence that can be brought forward to prove that a form is a survival, a transformation, or a borrowing of a West African form. Survivals are elements that have remained mostly intact in their form (sound, word structure, and syntax) and their meaning. Transformations have undergone more changes, typically in form—they are no longer recognizably West African words and phrases based on their sounds (and sometimes their grammatical patterning in sentences, too). A borrowing is incorporated into the Creole language after it has already been formed.

This last point is an important one because some Africanisms (i.e., items whose origin can be traced to African languages) were part of the material that was incorporated into Creoles in their formation process. A language can borrow only after it is in existence. Items that were incorporated into Creoles in their formation process are often referred to as retentions, in contradistinction to borrowings (or loans). Recently borrowed words in AAE such as *kwanzaa* (from Swahili, which was not spoken, or at least not spoken by any appreciable number of Africans who came to the Americas) and other terms associated with it are clear examples of borrowings. The standards of proof in linguistics are based on principles of grammatical analysis and those relating to historical/comparative linguistics and social historiography (see Mufwene 1993 and 2001 for further discussion). Some forms that have been argued to be Africanisms, for example *O.K.*, are not widely accepted as such.

Among the lexical words in AAE that are considered Africanisms are *yam, tote, banjo, gumbo, cooter* ("turtle"), *goober* ("peanut"), and many personal names such as *Cuffy* or *Coffy*, *Cudjo* or *Cudjoe*, *Zola*, and *Phoebe* (see Turner 1949 and the references in Mufwene 1993 for longer lists). *Nyam* or some variant is found in many American languages, meaning "eat" or a "yellow-orangish tuber." Linguists contrast lexical elements (words, parts of words, and sometimes phrases) to grammatical elements, those belonging to a small, closed set; *closed* meaning that those sets cannot easily take new members. Examples are prepositions, auxiliary modal verbs, articles, and verb suffixes expressing tense, aspect, and mood. Grammatical elements are more important than lexical ones in the overall grammar of languages since the grammatical ones help to provide the basic structural frame into which lexical words fit. The closed sets of which grammatical elements are a part contain elements that are tightly interrelated.

Other semi-Creoles or post-Creoles are popular Dominican Spanish, popular Brazilian Portuguese, popular Cuban Spanish, and Surinamese Dutch. (*Popular* before the language's name means the kind spoken by the great majority of the people.) It is notable that popular Dominican Spanish has a version of the *come* of strong disapproval. Popular Brazilian Portuguese has the Africanism *bunda* (buttocks).

The fourth level languages are the others in the Americas that have only a smattering of Africanisms, virtually all of which are lexical words (as opposed to grammatical ones, as discussed above). An example would be the English of the great majority of whites and some African Americans and others in the United States. (Some African Americans do not speak AAE.) This type of English, which actually includes many different varieties, has Africanisms such as *tote* (carry) and the place/person name *Cudjo* or *Cujo*. (*Cudjo* as a place name can be considered part of all American varieties of English due to the existence of Cudjo Key, Florida, apparently the only African place name in the United States.) Other languages on this level would be Argentine Span-

ish, Peruvian Spanish, and in general other languages outside what has been called Afro-America, that area stretching from the southern United States to Brazil and including the Caribbean, where African cultural and linguistic influence has historically been profound due to the density of African slaves in earlier populations.

In addition to the types of Africanisms distinguished above, there are other important ones. First, we should note that linguists make a distinction between grammar and use. *Use* refers to how speakers actually use a language, for example, to tell jokes, to insult, and to greet. *Use* also refers to characteristics such as the normal quantity of speech (do speakers typically talk a lot or not?) and speech events that are salient among particular groups of speakers (for example, sermons, cursing, praising, and storytelling). Many groups in Afro-America continue the African tradition of animal tales such as those about Br'er Rabbit. Several scholars have noted that the African element in language use may be significantly more important than that in grammar.

Second, communicative behaviors closely related to language and virtually indispensable should be considered. Among such behaviors are paralanguage and kinesics. *Paralanguage* refers to sounds that accompany speech, but that are not part of language proper: sighs, moans, imitations of nonlanguage sounds, and so forth. *Unh-hunh* (yes) and *zunh-zunh* (no) are examples. (The symbol [ʔ] stands for the sound, which is not written, at the onset of the beginning vowel of a word such as *ouch!*) Note also the sound of disgust or contempt, *hmmph*, phonetically written (hm̩), which in AAE may substitute for the semiauxiliary *come* of strong disapproval "(hm̩) coming in here acting like a damn fool." This last example shows how closely interrelated language and paralanguage are. Kinesic behaviors include face and body movements. Cut-eye and suck-teeth are examples of facial gesture Africanisms. Cut-eye involves a sharp move (cut) of the eyes far to the side with a simultaneous look of disapproval. Suck-teeth, which may accompany cut-eye, consists of pursing the lips with a small, slit opening and sucking in air; it also accompanies of look of strong disapproval. Cupped-hand-over-mouth laughter is an example of body movement combined with paralanguage, both of which may be combined with speech.

Further research into the subject of Africanisms in languages of the Americas will probably reveal more Africanisms in language use and associated communicative behaviors than in grammar itself, thus indicating that African influence is most felt today in the nongrammatical (or nonstructural) aspect of communicative behavior. Language use, paralanguage, and kinesics, being less subject to identification and labeling, have accordingly been less subject to being explicitly stigmatized. The stigmatizing of Africanisms of all types by the purveyors and upholders of Eurocentric norms has been one of the main reasons for the diminution of African influences in the cultures of the Americas. As peoples in the Americas who recognize their African descent develop more positive attitudes toward their African heritage, we may see the importation of new Africanisms, not only in language but also in other domains of culture, such as was seen during the African-American Civil Rights movement during the 1960s and 1970s in the U.S.

References

Holm, John. 1988. *Pidgins and Creoles.* Vol. 1: *Theory and Structure.* Cambridge: Cambridge University Press.

————. 1989. *Pidgins and Creoles. Vol. 2: Reference Survey.* Cambridge: Cambridge University Press.

————. 2000. *On Introduction to Pidgins and Creoles.* Cambridge and New York: Cambridge University Press.

Lanehart, Sonja L., ed. 2001. *Sociocultural and Historical Contracts of African American English.* Philadelphia and Amsterdam: John Benjamins.

Mufwene, Salikoko S., ed. 1993. *Africanisms in Afro-American Language Varieties.* Athens, Ga.: University of Georgia Press.

Mufwene, Salikoko S., 2001. *The Ecology of Language Education* Cambridge and New York: Cambridge University Press.

Spears, Arthur K. and Donald Winford, eds. 1997. *The Structure and Status of Pidgins and Creoles.* Amsterdam and Philadelphia: John Benjamins.

Turner, Lorenzo Dow. 1974 [1949]. *Africanisms in the Gullah Dialect.* Ann Arbor: University of Michigan Press. [reprinted in 1969;] University of Chicago Press.

ARTHUR K. SPEARS

See also **Diaspora; Verbal Arts: African American**

LEGA

See **Central African Folklore: Overview**

LEGENDS: EAST AFRICA

Legends are historical accounts that narrators and their audience believe to be true. They are universal in character, as they attempt to recount the true history or real life experiences of remarkable individuals in their communities. Some cannot be accurately proved, since historical details are lost due to the inadequacies of the oral modes of transmission. This results in two types of legends: first, those with a greater tendency toward fact, which are historic, and those with a greater inclination toward fiction, categorized as mythic or romantic (Okpwewho 1983).

Although the truth of legends may be difficult to ascertain, indigenous people consider them to be authentic. This is because legendary stories cover the historical deeds of human rather than mystical heroes. The storytellers and their audience accept the narrative veracity of the legend.

In traditional cultures, legends emphasize cherished cultural values, ethnic identities, and history. Legendary characters are usually human, or anthropomorphic with superhuman origins. They may be cultural heroes or chiefs who died and were later deified (Rasman and Rubel 1995). A hero is considered a historical person who is distinguished from average mortals by his or her outstanding bravery, perseverance, ingenuity, and moral or intellectual merits. The culture heroes are, therefore the personalities who have done anything to improve the conditions of human existence (Werner 1968).

This essay analyzes African legends with specific reference to the Abaluhyia (Luhyia) people of Western Province of Kenya in East Africa.

Background

The Abaluhyia is one of the subethnic groups of the Bantu peoples who inhabit the western region of Kenya. They occupy the five districts of Western Province: Bungoma, Busia, Butere-Mumias, Kakamega, and Vihiga. The Luo, Kalenjin, Teso, and the eastern province of Uganda border the community. It is composed of over fifteen subgroups: Abisukha, Abanyore, Babukusu, Abakabras, Maragoli, Abasamia, Abashisa, Abatitrichi, Abamarachi, Abatsotso, Abakhekha, Abatochoni, and Abakhayo (Fedders and Salvadori 1998, Were 1967a, b). They do not constitute a homogenous group, due to variations in some sociocultural traits. Nonetheless, their dialects are mutually intelligible and the culture manifests a higher degree of uniformity in its basic characteristics. Given the common cultural traits, the Abaluhyia form a distinct superethnic group in relation to their neighboring societies.

The Luhyia legends depict the typical traits of African historical tradition, although there are different methods of narrating the same story. These variations can be attributed to the inaccuracies of oral transmission. The patterns and points of emphasis may be altered or distorted because the narrators' memories and idiosyncratic preferences influence reporting. Unique environmental and historical experiences can also be used to account for the differences in basically similar stories from one Luhyia community to another.

Although legends purport to represent particular periods, their presentations in African oral literature have unclear outlines. Since the narratives are dependent on memorized oral traditions, their reporters may be unable to think in terms of specific dates. The Luhyia and other African legends do not claim accuracy in keeping specific time frames, dates or chronology of events. They are set in undetermined time periods and are introduced by such expressions as "Once upon a time . . ." " In the olden days . . ." and "A long time ago . . ." This may represent mythical time because the narrators' imagination is not constrained or limited by obligations to time-bound images (Okpwewho 1983).

The reenactment of accepted cultural themes, customs, and moral codes is situated in the unspecified past of outstanding personalities and their experiences. The series of tests, adventures, accomplishments, and failings of both heroes and ordinary people are cited in significant historic episodes. In some cases, narrators and their listeners supplement their legendary narratives with nonprose lore, such as proverbs and songs, which relate events and the roles of real human beings in memorable occurrences. Indigenous people recognize the chronology of important historic activities by the indelible experiences of entire communities such as droughts, famine, floods, and memorable events such as the coronation of kings, and lineage or ethnic settlement in new territories. African legends are therefore situation- or event-bound rather than time-bound in a strict sense.

The Abaluhyia have a larger population, and inhabit more territory, than other groups in western Kenya. Their culture embraces the traits of other Bantu and non-Bantu groups in the region. Since they are part of the populous Bantu ethnic groups in Africa, their legends can represent typical African folklore. The focus of Luhyia legends, as in other African societies, is on the origins and formation of genealogies and ethnic groups, ethnic migrations, wars, conquests, deeds of culture heroes and models of accomplishment, and failures according to ethnic constructions. The subject matter of legends includes themes such as the exploits of heroes, the establishment of genealogies, migrations, wars, and the formation of dynasties, all described as part of the history of living societies.

Formation of Ethnic Groups

Members of specific groups rely on historical legends to meet their identity needs in contemporary social, cultural and political contexts. Stories that trace a community's origins also identify migration legends, or personalities who led them from difficult circumstances such as drought, floods, epidemics, and oppression in their original homeland to their current location. For example, a majority of the Abaluhyia trace their original homeland to Egypt (Egebeti, Misiri). Particular individuals after whom the clans, subclans or subethnic groups were named later became part of the larger Luhyia community led each migrating group. For instance, the Maragoli were led by Mulogoli, the Ababugusu by Muvugusu, and the Abidhakho by Mwetakho. Another version of the legend is that Omuluhyia, the ancestor of the Abaluhyia moved out of Egypt with his sons and established a new home somewhere in the north, which became the point of departure for his migrating sons into the current Luhyia territory. Literary analysts hypothesize that such legends are drawn from the biblical story of the oppression of the Hebrews documented in the Old Testament.

In recounting the origins and formation of ethnic groups, genealogies or lineages, African legends take into account the personalities who gave each group their unique identities. The more authentic history of the different Abaluhyia subgroups, for instance, begins after the supposed migration from Egypt under the control of known figures in particular genealogies. Narratives describing the migration experiences form a continuum between myths and legends.

Genealogies and Migration

Oral chronicles attempt to report how ancestors of contemporary clans and ruling lineages came to have claims over their current territories as indigenous settlers. Raconteurs present the biographies of individuals who made significant contributions to the survival and continuity of their clans or subethnic groups. The narrators relate lines of succession, which are known and recognized in society (Finnegan 1970). The legends recreate the memory of how individuals brought victory or esteem to their lineage in difficult and challenging situations.

The Tiriki, for instance, believe that their ancestors conquered their present territory in the region of Kavirondo Gulf on Lake Victoria, which became their homeland. Khoba and his sons, who agreed to be initiated into the Nilo-Hamitic Terik age-groups, conquered their contemporary territory. They give credit to Diligin, a Terik elder, who first invited their clan members into the uninhabited lands (Sangree 1966). The clans, which accepted the Nilo-Hamitic initiation of the Terik, became the Tiriki (Abadiliji, Abatirichi), probably named after their first host, Diligin. Since then, the process of immigration of Abaluhyia clan segments to Tiriki land and their incorporation into the ethnic group through the acceptance of the Terik initiation and age-grade initiation systems has continued to the present. Migrants can enjoy the status of the Tiriki ethnic group.

The migration legends provide important justification for existing distributions of power within clans and lineages. Geneal-ogical stories attempt to show people's links with important past personalities who led to the establishment of influential groups in the society. In this regard, historical legends focus on distinguished culture heroes, some of whom were successful in the establishment of dynasties and ruling families. Such narratives become vehicles for expressing societal expectations, values, and morals.

Political Legends

There are narratives about individuals who founded "nations" and enhanced the social and political cohesion of ethnic groups. The narratives present distinguished personalities as having had extraordinary qualities, which enabled them to consolidate their power and unite their followers. The legends in this category present the culture heroes undertaking a series of trials and risk-taking experiences in which they triumph or lose. The historical political narratives are general recounts of the biographies of charismatic figures, with attempts to detail their exploits or failings. These narratives present what happened and attempt to explain what ought to have happened for the sake of individual and community success. The narrators focus on people who feature prominently in the annals of oral tradition. These are personages whose individual characters and achievements can be vividly remembered by the majority of the people. They are the basic actors in their clan and ethnic histories. Narrators, audience, and commentators focus attention on chief events in each person's life.

Such legends may be prominent among some subgroups of the Abaluhyia or may be acknowledged by the entire Abaluhyia fraternity. The important personalities are remembered through prose narratives, songs, and proverbs. The songs and proverbs are drawn from the episodes that narrators and their audience believe are oral records of the event. In some cases, those telling the tale may present the narrative episodes as songs (Finnegan 1970); these are occasionally sung independent of the tale-telling. Among the Ababukusu, for instance, Mango, son of Bwayo, of the Umukhurarwa clan, is one of the renowned heroes remembered in this manner. His father is said to have led the Ababukusu in earlier migration movements (Makila 1978). Mango became popular among his because of his amicable disposition and resolute character. When he was of age, he killed the most dreaded serpent in the village, Yebebe. The neighboring Barwa people rewarded him with one of their daughters as a wife after he accepted circumcision. Before Mango's circumcision, this practice was not as common and elaborate among the Ababukusu as it is today. His mother was scared of his circumcision and cried out to discourage him from accepting it. The Ababukusu are said to have turned the fateful words of Mango's mother into an initiation song, the Sioyaye chant (Makila 1978), which is still sung today during circumcision ceremonies.

The Ababukusu remember Mango for his brave deeds that astounded many people and became the basis for the revival of Bukusu identity and cultural pride. He instituted reforms in the traditional Bukusu circumcision rites to incorporate the traditions of the Tiriki and non-Luhyia groups such as the Nandi and the Kipsigis. Among the Tiriki, Sagwa is similarly remembered for having initiated changes in the traditional circumcision ceremonies to Christianize them. As a result, Tiriki Christians have composed songs, which are used today to remember his cultural and political achievement. As cultural and political heroes, both Mango and Sagwa are known as sources of inspiration, new identity, and unity for their people. They provided their subethnic groups with new approaches to political and cultural issues. Legends with political content are told to remind young and old alike of their history and the foundations of patriotism.

The Abanyore recall the story of a young man known as Tuti but nicknamed Omukhwayi. He is remembered with admiration for his determination to unite his clan and to keep it from being overwhelmed by outside influence. He defeated an enemy clan called Abasiratsi, killing hundreds of its members. Under his leadership, his Abatongoyi clan won and returned home with loot from the enemy. This marked the beginning of the new ethnocentric name Abakhwaya for Tuti's clan. Tuti Omukhwaya is remembered for his fearlessness and bravery. It is from him that the Abanyore and their Luo neighbors got the praise name *sibwori* or *sibwor mang'ang'a*, that is, "one with the fearful heart of lion."

Biographies of popular chiefs are also part of the Abaluhyia oral annals. The Tiriki, for instance, recall the successes and failures of Chief Amiani, who symbolized their unity in early colonial times. He was a giant in both physical stature and personality, renowned for instituting centralized ethnic authority and chieftaincy (Sangree 1966). Amiani ranks in Titiki history as second to Chief Mumia of the Wanga people. He had an awe-inspiring personality, which was reinforced by his fierce army of Terik warriors who acted as his ethnic police. Despite his political successes, the Tiriki recount his failures, such as the massive settlement of the Maragoli migrants in the Tiriki territory. He also attempted to divulge the circumcision rites secrets to the white missionaries. His subjects also detested his high-handedness in administration and his apparent contempt for traditional Tiriki culture. Some informants hold that Amiani's misrule toward the end of his reign was due to his domineering mother. Some of the failures of Chief Amiani are recounted in circumcision songs, which express contempt for his mother.

There are some narratives about charismatic personalities who were popular across the Abaluhyia community. These are individuals who succeeded in political, economic, and magico-religious careers. Elijah Masinde (of Bukusu descent) is one such legend. He founded the indigenous Dini ya Musambwa (religion of good spirits) sect. Through this sect, he opposed the conscription of Africans to fight in the World War II, and preached against foreign religion, particularly Christianity. Masinde's religion spread to other Abaluhyia sects, such as the Abawanga, Abatsotso, Abaidakho, and Tiriki. He became a popular nationalist during the struggle for independence and later a critic of the postcolonial government. The Abaluhyia consider Masinde a magico-religious hero due to his charisma, a distinction which bestowed him with the qualities of a messiah, liberator, and prophet. Although some people perceived him to be a troublemaker, the stories that exist about him present him as an admirable man.

The legend of Chief (Nabongo) Mumia of the Abawanga is known by the majority of the Abaluhyia people. Born into the Abashitsetse ruling clan, his charisma and leadership qualities were apparent during his childhood and youth. As a teenager,

he killed fierce animals such as leopards and lions single-handedly, using only spears and arrows. He succeeded his father Shihundu at a very critical time of attacks by the Luo, Ababukusu, and Abanyala (Were 1966b). As a leader, the Abaluhyia remember Nabongo Mumia for having successfully led the Abawanga and assisted many Luhyia subgroups through trials such as the prolonged drought that caused the historical "famine of the kikombe (cup)." Abaluhyia folk songs recall the famine.

Mumia also helped the Abaluhyia endure cattle plagues and tribal wars. He combined generosity and kindness with his skill as a warrior to extend his influence to the neighboring Abaluhyia subgroups.

Warfare Legends

Historical legends give accounts of the causes of war, and the outcome of various battles. Chief Nganyi of the Abanyore, for example, is remembered for his diplomacy in resolving conflicts with neighboring communities. His people once lost a battle to the Luo of Seme. When the Luo attacked, Chief Nganyi allowed one of them to marry his daughter as an effort toward restoring peace. He managed to mobilize his subjects to defeat the Abalogoli and the Abashisa.

Abidakho recount their war with the Abatirichi and the Maragoli over the salt lick (*isukura*) along the Lugose River, where they used to take their cattle for watering. They defeated their enemies because of their strong clan organization, which gave the elders freedom to act as war leaders (*abasesia*). Cooperation among the six Idakho clans guaranteed mutual understanding and assistance in the face of crisis. Apart from the legends with political content, there are narratives about the establishment of professional skills in particular clans or family lines.

Some of the Abaluhyia ethic segments have songs that allow them to relive past war experiences. The Babukusu, for instance, sing about Maelo Wa Khaindi, whom they believe was born of a Muwanga mother from the ruling Beshitsetse clan (Makila 1976). He led the Bukusu army to victory against many of its enemies, including the Bamia (Teso) mercenaries. A war song in praise of Maelo's exploits as a victorious commander is sung today in Bukusu circumcision ceremonies. There is also a proverb about Kitimule, a brave warrior and excellent diplomat, who led the Bukusu to victory against Kalenjin (Barwa) invaders. The proverb "reevanga Kitimule Wanyoa Ebuyumbu" ("ask Kitimule who first visited Ebuyumbu"; Were, 1967) is a moral one, encouraging reflection upon, and learning from, the experiences of brave and successful predecesssors.

Legends about Professions

African legends also include accounts of the origins and establishment of magico-religious and mundane skills. These legends justify the claim by particular lineages to specific trades. There stories of admiration for great blacksmiths, potters, house builders, medicine experts, and other specialists from whom skills are believed to have been inherited. The Abanyore, Ababukusu, and Abatsotso narrate about accomplished rain magicians (*bajimba, bakyimba,* and *bagimba*), who can induce thunder, lightning and rain. These specialists are descendants of wealthy and polygynous personalities. There are different versions, among rainmaking clans, of their lineage and the status of their ancestors. They believe that the art of rainmaking was started many generations ago and has since been transmitted from one ancestor to the next, always remaining in the same family (Wagner 1970). For the Banyore and Maragoli, the first rainmaker was a woman from the non–Bantu Nandi community; she settled among the Banyore people after being expelled from Maragoli land.

The legends about special skills generally highlight the experiences of individuals who often had some sort of contact with the supernatural. These skills are transmitted as special occasions to specific lineages. The Tiriki recount how Malongo of Munzatsi Hill acquired the blacksmith's skills from his father. He managed to maintain the skill of smelting and working iron, becoming one of the main suppliers of metal implements, such as hoes, spears, and arrows.

Conclusion

Legends among the Abaluhyia represent some of the typical features of historical narratives common in African oral literature. They are mainly expressed in prose and complemented by proverbs and songs. The legends mainly focus on genealogies, migrations, warfare, and the successes and failures of personalities whom people believe lived in particular historical contexts. These legends reflect the responses of different ethnic groups to needs that press them in contemporary circumstances. These narratives have been handed down to successive generations over the years as true accounts. Yet the passage of time and the weakness of memory may allow for fictional aspects to become included alongside factual material in the legend.

References

Fedders, A, and C. Salvadori. 1998. *Peoples and Cultures of Kenya.* Nairobi: TransAfrica.

Finnegan, R. 1970. *Oral Literature in Africa.* Nairobi: Oxford University Press.

Makila, F. E. 1978. *An Outline History of the Babukusu of Western Kenya.* Nairobi: Kenya Literature Bureau.

Okpwewho, I. 1983. *Myth in Africa.* Cambridge University Press.

Rosman, A., and G. P. Rubel. 1995. *The Tapestry of Culture: An Introduction to Cultural Anthropology.* New York. McGraw-Hill.

Sangree, W. H. 1966. *Age, Prayer and Politics in Tiriki Kenya.* London: Oxford University Press.

Wagner, G. 1970. *The Bantu of Western Kenya: With Speical Reference to Vugusu and Logoli.* London: Oxford University Press.

Were, G. S. 1967a. *A History of the Abaluhyia of Western Kenya: C1500–1930.* Nairobi: East African Publishing House.

Were, G. S. 1967b. *Western Kenya: Historical Texts.* Nairobi: East African Literature Bureau.

Werner A. 1968. *Myths and Legends of the Bantu.* London: Frank Cass.

BENSON A. MULEMI

See also **Epics; Myths**

LESOTHO (Kingdom of Lesotho)

With a temperate climate, Lesotho is a small country with a population of approximately 2.29 million people that is completely surrounded by South Africa. The capital Maseru is the country's largest city and home to 367,000 people. Lesotho is one of Africa's most homogenous nations, as the population is 98 percent Basotho and 2 percent Xhosa; most live in the rural areas. English and Sesotho are the two commonly spoken languages. Christians account for 80 percent of the population while the remaining 20 percent practice traditional indigenous religions.

Moshoeshoe I united the Basotho nation in the nineteenth century and led strong opposition to Boer invaders. On October 4, 1966, Lesotho gained independence from Britain and formed its own constitutional monarchy. Despite independence from Britain, however, Lesotho's government has been continually interfered with by South African politicians, who have strongly influenced Lesothoan politics. The country's economy has not fared well since independence, because the United Nations has listed Lesotho as one of the world's least developed countries. As a result, each year about half of the country's male population leave the country to find work in South Africa. The country has also suffered from political instability due to a series of kings and military leaders, despite the return of a multiparty democracy in 1993. Some of the commerce Lesotho is able to produce comes from the carpet, pottery, jewelry, mining, and tourism industries.

Despite its weak economic state, Lesotho is known for its high quality of schools and has produced renowned writers since the mid-nineteenth century. There is a 71 percent adult literacy rate. Many of the leading citizens of southern Africa are products of a Lesotho education.

JENNIFER JOYCE

LIBATION

Libation is a magico-religious ritual that entails pouring liquid on the ground, or sprinkling it on ritual participants or sacred objects, as a means of communication between human and spiritual beings. The liquids used and the conditions of the ritual vary by geographical, ethnic, and temporal contexts.

The word *libation* is derived from the Latin *libatio,* which denotes a sacrificial offering of drink. It is also connected with the Greek noun *loibe* (which directly translates as "libation") and the verb *leibo,* which connotes the act of pouring the libation (Betz 1987).

In traditional African cultures, libations accompany sacrifices, rites of passage, and prayers. In litany proceedings, the participants recall the meditative links between spiritual beings and people. Libations are generally intended to earn the favor of supernatural beings or spirits. In traditional African religions, (as in ancient religions, such as those of the Babylonians and the Assyrians), libations could be poured as separate offerings to spirits, gods, and God, through the ancestors. In traditional belief, ancestors dwell in the ground as masters of the land. Participants in the libation believe that the ancestral spirits can effectively receive milk, honey, oil, beer, or other beverages through the ground. The libations are poured onto the earth through natural or artificial cracks, openings, or holes. The preferred sites for religious libations are gravesides, alters, homestead shrines, and sacred groves.

The main objective of libations in indigenous African religious and social contexts is to appease ancestral and other spirits, thus encouraging their continued favor and good will. Such rituals are also meant to propitiate spirits that cause disease and other calamities. The libations are therefore intended to prevent illness or misfortune, protect human beings, and facilitate curing.

Background

Libation is a component of traditional African magico-religious belief systems. Variations in these systems reflect ecological differences, which in turn affect peoples' experience of the world, their ritualistic activities, and the material aspects related to various cultural institutions. In sub-Saharan Africa, uniformity abounds in indigenous belief systems and thought. Inasmuch as societies in sub-Saharan Africa share similar worldviews, this essay provides an analysis of libation in aspects that can be generalized to most of the African peoples living in this region.

Traditional belief systems and practices in Africa are centered on predominant modes of production and the environment. Many ethnic groups are traditionally sedentary farmers, tending food crops and rearing animals. Some societies are composed of farmers, pastoralists, and hunter-gatherers.

Different physical and socioeconomic contexts have resulted in some evaluations in religious orientation, philosophy of life, interpretation of experience and the approaches to the spiritual and supernatural worlds. Libation is, therefore, an aspect in the expression of the complex African worldview, made up of such elements as spirituality, values about the family community, ancestral beliefs, and prayer. The African understanding of contact between the visible and the invisible worlds is embedded in magico-religious rituals, in which libation plays a key role.

Libation in African Spirituality

African religious beliefs reflect a deep concern with spiritual matters. A key belief is that human beings can communicate with the spirits, and that those spirits can bring good or ill fortune to humans. Since most spirits were once human beings, people attribute human characteristics, such as anger, hunger, and craving for attention to them. People strive to appease malevolent spirits with offerings of food, milk, beer, blood, and other forms of drinks. Libation is, therefore, an integral component of spirit veneration, appeasement, and general African worship. In popular cultural practices, food and drink create mystical links between fellow human beings and between human beings and spiritual realities. In this regard, libation and food offering is a means of sustaining relationships between people and the spiritual world (Mbiti 1975).

African spirituality is drawn from the popular worldview in which the human and the spirit worlds are interconnected (Dickson 1984). The indigenous Africans perceive the world of natural phenomena as part of spiritual reality. Spirits, both good and evil, populate the universe. Interaction among these spirits may have either positive or negative consequences for human life. Due to this understanding, people live with one another in relationships of reciprocal responsibility, which they transfer to their relation with the other elements in the universe, such as the spirits. Some of the spirits—especially ancestral ones—may help the living communicate with God and guard the link between the human realm and the divine. The spirits and lesser divinities serve as messengers of God and execute His justice. As guardians of moral order, the spirits may be either benevolent or malevolent at will. They may initiate catastrophic events if the culprits do not placate them.

In most societies, the spirits that people believe to be causing trouble are appeased through offerings of beer, water, or milk.

Although blood is not a common form of libation, some believe that it is the favorite drink of the spirits. The Maragoli and other Luhyia people of western Kenya, for instance, invite spirits (Misambwa) to lick their blood during major rituals.

The ground is very significant in the African prayers that accompany libation. It is linked with spiritual power, as it is the source of livelihood and the abode of the dead. Among the Akans and the Fanti of northern Ghana in West Africa, for instance, the earth (Asase Yaa, Asase Efua) is personified as the mother of humanity. The ground, therefore, is the first to receive gestures of gratitude such as drink offerings, which the ritual participants expect to be transmitted to ancestors as secondary meditative spirits. The ground is, therefore the most important link between the living people and the invisible, spiritual world.

Libation and Worship

Worship and prayer to God are conducted through the ancestors, who inhabit a mediating role. The ancestors continue to have interest in their surviving descendants, who continue to "live" in spiritual forms. They understand the needs of their living relatives, which these ancestors are more qualified to transmit to God as they share His spiritual nature. Libations are poured on the ground in front of a shrine or an object representing the ancestors during acts of prayer (Odak 1995). In this case, offerings of drink and food are perceived by the people as ways in which the ancestors can be convinced to listen to their prayers and traffic them to the supernatural.

As an important component of spirituality and worship, libation, along with sacrifice, acts as a medium of trade between human beings and ancestors. This ritual is used to demonstrate the people's seriousness in seeking spiritual assistance. In both agricultural and pastoralist societies, beer, milk and water are poured out for this purpose to the dead and clan divinities (Leinhardt 1987). In special rituals, the libations are given as names of afflicting spirits and divinities are invoked. In such cases, libations are intended to win the favor of the spirits. Offerings of drink in most of the indigenous settings are part of the solemn activities in ancestral cults. In these contexts, the people recall their belief that there is life after death, and that the dead continue to express an active interest in everyday affairs of the living descendants. It is in appreciation of their role as watchdogs of the lineage that clan and family members offer them libations. In West African societies, fresh water or millet flour mixed with beer or palm wine is used as libations (Olupona 2000; Anti 1987). In this circumstance, libations are used to find out the ancestors' temper and influence their action in relation to the assignment to be accomplished or the help being sought. The use of alcoholic drinks is intended to produce the same effect on the ancestral spirit as it perceived among human beings. This implies that some societies use libations to manipulate the ancestors' disposition in order that they can act according to the human needs.

Sacrifice, offerings, and libations are closely related because they constitute a significant component of African worship. Sacrifices involve the slaughter of a domestic animal to God or ethnic divinities through the ancestors. Although blood is a rare form of libation, it is poured as an expression of the seriousness of calamities such as drought, floods, epidemics, and death. In both agricultural and pastoralist communities, the blood shed from the animal is the greatest and ultimate form of libation, one which reconciles people with God and other divinities. Offering as part of religious ritual involves the giving of material things, such as food, drinks, or coffee beans, as is the case in Uganda, and Kola nuts in West African countries such as Sierra Leone. Pastoralists and agriculturalists perform libations as part of supernumerary acts that accompany main rites as in the rituals that follow sacrifice (Pritchard 1974; Lienhardt 1987). Ritual specialists pour out liquids on the emblems or shrines to revere ethnic divinities, as is the case with the Nuer and Dinka of Sudan.

The mystical power of ancestors and other spiritual beings is believed to flow through the blood and other liquids to revive human vitality and welfare. Sacrifice makes it possible for the living to enter into a relationship and spiritual union with ancestors, who mediate for them. The ritual experts ensure that the intercession is possible through meals and drinks shared with the ancestors. Part of the sacrifices are eaten by the members, while some is left at the shrines or ritual spots to be "consumed" by ancestral spirits and other spiritual beings such as ethnic divinities. Among the Chewa people of central Malawi, the spirits of the dead (Mizimu) are offered portions of beer in small containers, some of which is sprinkled on the ground near the shrines. However, many African societies consider blood and other forms of valued drinks as the most important share of the spiritual beings.

In some cultures, such as the West African societies, blood of the sacrificial animal is sprinkled on the beneficiaries and the emblems of divinity. Alternatively, the participants would partake in beer or beverage drinking at the ritual spot after pouring some on the ground. The supernumerary rites, of which libation is one, create new bonds among participants, and revitalizes human relationships with deities, ancestors, and God in order to provide for human needs. Libations complement other rituals such as consecration, invocation of supernatural beings, immolation, and aspersions to malignant spirits in the acts of worship and spirit veneration.

Libation and Family Communion

The African family community is composed of the living, those yet to be born, and the dead. The dead, and especially the ancestors, are important members of the family, because their spiritual nature give them abilities to cause and prevent afflictions, depending on their perceived relationship with the living. The dead are also believed to be endowed with the power to guarantee good health and general human well-being, provided that their rapport with the living is good. Filial-parental relationships exist between the ancestors and their descendants. The living have a duty to take care of the departed, while the dead have a responsibility to protect the living and ensure that they are successful in life. Ancestors retain a practical role in the human world. In this regard, African kin groups are family communities of both the living and the dead. The ancestors may either be benevolent or punitive, even capricious, and therefore they demand acknowledgment from their descendants through various postfuneral rituals, which include libation (Kopytoff 1971).

Libation to ancestors and "feeding" of the dead in African cultures is the privilege of the elders (Kopytoff 1971; Mbiti 1990). However, libation can be poured by anybody regardless of age, gender, and social status, especially when the ritual is a personal undertaking. Traditional experts, who are mainly elders, handle libations on special occasions such as ethnic festivals, when a god requires the offering, or when it is the routine libation that requires a qualified representative of a clan, lineage, or family (Anti 1987). The rituals involve certain foods and drinks that are considered the dead persons' favorites. These tokens are offered on the basis of the understanding that good relationships are restored and sustained through the mutual care of the dead and the living. In this sense, libations symbolize commemoration, and an incitement for the departed to continue manifesting their favorable presence among the living. Elders perform memorial libations at sacred sites such as gravesides, shrines, and other religious places. In such cases, libations are accompanied by communication to the dead in the form of invocative conversational monologue. These conversations communicate gratitude, complaints, rebuke, bargains, and reminders about mutual obligations between the living dead (or ancestors) and community members. In African traditional cultures, the offering of food and libations to the dead is meant to prevent the evil deeds of the dead, as is the case the Kamba society of eastern Kenya and the Acholi of Uganda.

The theme of communion with the family community of the living and the dead through libation is also manifested in rites of passage. African rites of passage, especially initiation, are conducted with the desire for ancestral sanction, participation, and blessings in mind. Libation is an important part of the rituals that bind initiates to the lineage or ethnic community, which includes the dead. The Bantu and other groups, such as the Somali, who practice circumcision and initiation ceremonies perform public celebrations by drinking beer and making libations. Water, beer, milk, and beverages are poured on the ground or sprinkled on the initiates to invite them into the complex communion of the living and the dead. This emphasizes the solidarity of the group and the importance of their interdependence. It is through such offerings and libations that the society members renew their ties with their fellows in both the visible and the invisible worlds, of which the dead are a part (Mbiti 1990).

Libation to the ancestors for the sake of maintaining family communion in traditional societies is accompanied by prayers. Drinks and food are offered together with prayers in a few words imploring the spirits of the dead relatives to heed petitions and sentiments of gratitude. In many African societies, the presence of the dead relatives is felt on a concrete, daily basis. Therefore, people extend hospitality to the spirits of the dead through the symbolic meal of bits of food and drops of drink accompanied with incantations as recognition of the nearness and respect of the dead (Mbiti 1975). Whenever possible, elders who administer libation acts may call upon the names of particular ancestors or dead relatives. Alternatively, libation, as other magicoreligious rituals, is linked to certain words that ask the ancestors to collectively hearken to the person speaking.

When libations are linked to worship and prayer, they are either communal or individualistic practices. Individuals or groups perform worship and utter prayer rather than making them meditations. The religious orientation of traditional cultures gives a chance for both private and public libations. This is because community members are always faced with daily life problems such as illness, barrenness, and bad omens. Libations are thus part of practices that have been put in place to enable the people respond to their spiritual worlds. The practice of libation in African cultures accompanies the prayers (Mbiti 1975; Mbiti, 1990; Shorter 1975; Anti 1987), before the commencement of work, and other communal ceremonies such as naming, marriage, initiation, funerals, and during numerous religious, social, and political celebrations.

Conclusion

Libation in traditional African cultures is a magico-religious ritual and is part of worship and prayers, which expresses the indispensable spiritual unity between the living and the dead. It represents one way that the African concepts of communion among family, lineage, and clan members are reinforced. Belief in the reliance of human beings on the Supreme Being, the ancestors, and the deities is also reflected in African libation practice. However, some libations are devoid of supplication, as they are projected to influence the supernatural forces in a magical way. Adherents of African religion likewise articulate their belief in reward, chastisement, and remorse through the drink gifts intended to pacify ancestors and gods who become angry because of human wrongdoing and violation of established moral codes. Libation reminds the living about the mystery of life after death, and the mystical power which enables the living dead to guard their relatives from the negative effects of power that emanates from the invisible spiritual world. Libations, therefore, symbolize the human wish to maintain an equilibrium of interaction with supernatural forces, the physical world, and fellow human beings. The preservation of this stability augments health, success, and general well-being. In African belief systems and thought, such equilibrium can be reestablished and sustained through magico-religious rituals such as libation.

References

Anti, K. K. A.1987. *Libation in The Old Testament and Akan Life and Thought: A Critique*. M.A. dissertation, College of the Ascension, Birmingham. Available at *http://cedh.ewu.edu/faculty//ntodd/Ghana*, March 3, 2003.

Betz, H. D. 1987. "Libation." In *The Encyclopaedia of Religion*, vol. 8, ed. Eliade Mircea New York: Macmillan.

Dickson, K. A. 1984. Towards a Theologia African. In *New Testament Christianity For Africa and the World*, ed. M. Glasswell and E. Fashole-Luke London: S.P.C.K.

Kopytoff, Igor. 1971. Ancestors as Elders in Africa. *Africa*, 41: 129–41.

Leinhardt, G. 1987. *Divinity and Experience: The Religion of the Dinka*. Oxford: Claredon Press.

Mbiti, J. S. 1975. *Prayers of African Religion*. New York: Orbis Books.

Mbiti, J. S. 1990. *African Religion and Philosophy*. Oxford: Heinemann.

Odak, O. 1995. *Kemeticism: The World Religion of Black Peoples*. Nairobi: Madoa Cultural Services.

Olupona, J., ed. 2000. *African Spirituality: Form, Meaning, and Expression*. New York: Crossroad.

Pritchard, E. E. 1974. *Nuer Religion*. New York. Oxford University Press.

Shorter, A. 1975. *Prayer in the Religious Traditions of Africa*. London: Oxford University Press.

BENSON A. MULEMI

See also **Ancestors; Religion: African Tranditional Religion; Ritual Performance**

LIBERIA (Republic of Liberia)

Located on the west coast of Africa, Liberia is tropical country neighbored by Sierra Leone, Guinea, and Cote D'Ivoire. Of Liberia's population over 3.26 million peoples 95 percent are composed of indigenous groups and 5 percent are classified as Americo-Liberian. The nation's official language is English, although Kpelle, Bassa, Dan, Vai, Wee, Loma, Kru, Glebo, Mano, Gola, and Mandinka are also spoken. Seventy percent of the nation's people practice traditional indigenous religions, 20 percent are Muslim, and 10 percent are Christian. Monrovia, Liberia's capital and largest city, is home to one million people.

Liberia (along with Ethiopia) is one of only two African nations that has been spared European rule. It began in 1822 as a settlement of freed "repatriated" slaves from the United States. Later over 6,000 slaves taken from slave traders by the British and American patrols were deposited there. Between 1847 (when it formally became an independent state) and 1980, Liberia's government was composed of African American settlers. Although these "Americo-Liberians" account for only 5 percent of the population, their aggressive administration, which often, ironically, included slavery, controlled the country for decades. There was resistance by interior peoples until 1915—a resistance which anticipated the violence of the end of the twentieth century.

For much of the twentieth century, Liberia's economy was largely based on the revenue from Firestone rubber plantations (begun in 1927), iron-ore mining, and urbanization. The economic presence of the United States has always been strong—in fact, the dollar is still accepted in the country today. Almost all of the profits from these industries, however, remained in the hands of the nation's minority elite, as economic conditions for the majority of the nation deteriorated. In 1979, after years of high unemployment and inflation, riots broke out as police shot at demonstrators who protested the government's imposed 50 percent price increase of rice, the staple food of Liberians. Amid the ensuing chaos, Sergeant Samuel Doe was able to take over the government in 1980 and became the nation's first indigenous president. Despite hopes that he would bring positive changes to the country, Doe became increasingly dictatorial throughout the 1980s, and economic conditions continued to worsen.

In 1989, unrest in the country erupted in a civil war with two rebel factions, one led by Prince Johnson (whose forces brutely assassinated President Doe) and the other led by Charles Taylor, who declared himself the next president. During the fighting, thousands of civilians were killed in massacres, thousands were maimed, and thousands more fled the country. Despite the peacekeeping efforts of the Economic Community of West Africa, violence and chaos have persisted in Liberia. As a result of the war, political instability, a deteriorating economy, and a damaged infrastructure and culture have plagued the nation. In 1996, Ruth Sandra Perry became Liberia's first female president, as part of the nation's thirteenth peace accord. A year later, Charles Taylor was elected president, but peace has not yet come to the nation and its future is uncertain.

Liberia is rich in the natural resources of iron ore, rubber, timber, and diamonds. The country's main industries are iron and diamond mining, rubber processing, food processing, and lumber milling. Unfortunately, these industries have also been severely damaged by the ongoing war. Also destroyed during the civil wars were the country's universities and museums.

JENNIFER JOYCE

LIBRARIES

Throughout the world, folklore is relayed through a variety of media; for example, print, audio recordings, video recordings, or orally communication. In the African context, folklore means to a large extent oral data, which are passed on by a variety of means, for example, through storytelling, through recitations by griots, and other performances. With the effects of urbanization and the influence of Western cultures this way of passing on a culture's traditions and knowledge of the past is disappearing. Over the past two decades, attempts have been made by international organizations, as well as Western and African scholars, to record this information in either print or audio format. These attempts, however, are scattered, with much information as yet unrecorded. This, and the fact that many of the existing recordings are in private collections, has implications for African folklore researchers.

As pointed out by historian and librarian David Henige, a researcher's time in the field is usually limited by the amount of funding—doctoral students typically have funds to support one year in the field collecting their data; other researchers may have a sabbatical of one or two semesters (Henige 1989, 198–212). To make the most of their time, researchers determine before their departure which collections exist, where they exist, and the rules and restrictions of access. If a relevant collection is held by an archive or library, it could save valuable time to access the material before the actual field research, or at least get an index of its holdings. Consequently, a list of existing folklore collections would be extremely useful. Unfortunately, whereas accounts and reports of various collections exist, a comprehensive list is unavailable. Rather than attempting to create such a list, this entry discusses some strategies for, and approaches to, locating folklore collections about Africa—both in Africa and in other locations—thereby providing the tools for the location of such collections.

It is clear that the field of folklore is highly interdisciplinary with branches in literature, history, musicology, and so forth. Moreover, when trying to locate folklore collections, one has to take into account that data exist to a large extent in oral form. To conduct effective research, a combination of search strategies and approaches, as well as creativity and imagination need to be applied. Oral tradition plays an important role in the African context; in fact, one cannot talk about African folklore without considering oral tradition. Accordingly, this entry will focus largely on oral data, their collection and location, issues of access, and provide a selective list of several major folklore collections. This list is not intended to be comprehensive. In fact, considering the interdisciplinary nature of the discipline, a comprehensive list would be beyond the scope of this entry. Rather, it presents some of the largest folklore collections on Africa and is intended to point the researcher to other sources so collections relevant to research can be located.

Oral Tradition and Libraries

In cultures that are largely nonliterate, oral tradition plays an important role in transmitting information. In fact, as Ghanaian librarian A. A. Alemna points out, "with just about 40% of its people literate in the western sense, Africa is predominantly a continent where oral transmission of knowledge is still the most effective medium of communication" (Alemna 1992, 423). Scholars and researchers acknowledge that beside the "culture of the written word" there is also a "culture of the spoken word," which is called folklore, and which needs to be collected and preserved as "testimony to ways of life and areas of knowledge" (Raphael Ndiaye 1988, 45). Alemna reminds us that all African communities encourage a consciousness in their members to preserve the knowledge of their ancestry and past. Each community has its tales of how it originated, as well as other forms of social information, such as "proverbs, poetry, praise names, songs, myths, and legends" (1995, 127). There is a wealth of oral data, and the need to collect it, as well as its related issues and difficulties, has been discussed by African librarians for quite some time.

Bunmi Aleybeleye from the University of Ibadan in Nigeria, for example, points out that there is a considerable amount of literature on the collection of oral data, but surprisingly little discussion on how to make these collections available. He remarks that, although individual approaches and styles of interview techniques may vary, the methodological treatment of oral tradition is the same: (1) original data are collected in the field; (2) a primary sources base is created with the publication of the raw materials; (3) the materials are analyzed; and (4) a secondary sources is created with the publication of the analysis and interpretation (1985, 421 f). Very often, however, step 2 does not happen, for various reasons. The pressure on Ph.D. students or young faculty in U.S. institutions, for example, is to publish secondary literature which gives a critical analysis of materials. It is this kind of critical analysis that helps them advance their careers, rather than the publication of primary sources. Another reason is that in many parts of Africa, the field recordings are held by private collectors. Often, the existence of these collections is known only within a comparatively small circle of people who know the collector. Obviously, this has implications for the scholarship pertaining to these collections.

Librarians and scholars alike have commented on this issue stressing both a need to collect more data, and also to find ways of providing access. Alemna acknowledges that librarianship in Africa has for a long time focused on what he calls the " 'dead end' of the scholar's effort," that is oral information that has been recorded and exists in either audio or print format (1992, 423). Recording information through interviews in the field has so far been neglected. Similarly, other librarians/scholars, such as H. O. M. Iwuji and A. O. Amadi, both warn of condemning vast parts of cultural information to oblivion if no efforts are made to preserve it. Amadi describes the situation in strong and unmistakable terms: "The grief arising from the devastation of a library by fire or similar causes in the Western world is only comparable in intensity to the loss, through death, of an old man in Africa. The later, like the former, is the veritable embodiment of an archive or a proto-library—a library without shelves" (1981, 140; also quoted in Iwuji 1989, 205). To remedy the situation, scholars/librarians such as Aleybeleye, Alemna, and Iwuji propose a different role for both academic and public librarians. They suggest that the librarian acts as field worker who actively goes into the villages to record data and then provides access to them in the library. The library would thus become a center for a culture's oral heritage.

On the national level, several African countries have recognized the need to preserve their oral heritage and have made attempts at collecting, organizing, and disseminating oral tradition (see Appendix, *African Studies Centers and Libraries in the United States and Africa*).

Both Alemna and Aleybeleye deplore that most of these projects have not been able to fulfill all of their ambitious goals. One obvious reason for this has to do with funding. The costs for funding such projects are high and ongoing, including money for personnel, equipment, buildings, and so forth. Another issue is the training of personnel in collecting the data, recording them, and providing access. Above all, the scope of collecting a country's oral data is enormous and requires a sustained effort of governments, funding agencies, academic institutions, and libraries.

All these projects were initiated by African countries. However, not all collections of African oral data are in African libraries. There exist numerous private collections, both in and outside of Africa, collected by researchers who either store them at their homes, or deposited them at their institutions or an archive known for its focus in that area. In the case of private collections, access, or even finding out about their existence, can be problematic. However, tools for the researcher to locate archival collections exist—some of which are mentioned below.

Tools to Locate Folklore Collections

There are a number of journals devoted to improving access to African archival collections. *History in Africa*, edited by ibrarian/historian David Henige, is an example. In his article on the state of archives in Africa, Henige discusses the lack of information on archival collections in Africa and points out that as a consequence one of the goals of *History in Africa* is to publish accounts of various African or Africanist archives. Another journal worth mentioning in this respect is *African Research and Documentation*, the journal of the Standing Conference on Library Materials on Africa (SCOLMA). This journal typically publishes bibliographic articles and accounts of archival projects, such as the Oral Traditions Association of Zimbabwe (OTAZI) and the East African Centre for Research on Oral Traditions and African National Languages (EACROTANAL) which were both described in *African Research and Documentation*. Other international library journals, such as the *IFLA Journal* (International Federation of Library Associations), *International Library Review*, and *Journal of Documentation* can be expected to carry similar accounts. And too, the *African Journal of Library, Archives, and Information Science* occasionally carries reports or discussion papers on the collection of oral traditions. Other major journals in the field are the *Journal of Folklore Research and Studies and Documents (Etudes et documents)*. All these journals are indexed in several major indexes, such as *Library Literature and Information Science*, *LISA Library and Information Sci-*

ence Abstracts, and *Academic Search Premier (EBSCO)*. Using such keywords as archives, oral tradition, folklore in Africa, and so forth, articles are easy to locate.

The two major indexes for research on folklore, however, are the *MLA International Bibliography of Books and Articles on the Modern Languages and Literatures*, which is published annually. Volume 5 is devoted to folklore and, more specifically, includes folklore in Africa; and *Internationale Volkskundliche Bibliographie (International Folklore* and *Folklife Bibliography and Bibliographie internationale des arts et traditions populaires)*, which is issued twice a year. Like the *MLA Bibliography*, it is not devoted exclusively to Africa, but includes many African entries.

Apart from those very useful journals and indexes, there are various handbooks and directories that contain information about folklore collections and are worth consulting. Somewhat outdated but still one of the most useful among them is Jean Gosebrink's *African Studies Information Resources Directory*, which aims at assisting in identifying Africa-related materials and information services and their locations. Among other features, it provides extensive annotated lists of "Information Resources for African Studies" and "Resources in Church and Mission Organizations." Headings for folklore and oral data can easily be located in the index. Where available, it also lists finding aids for each collection. Equally useful is John McIlwaine's *Writings on African Archives* and its supplements in *African Research and Documentation* "of works relating to archives in African countries and to African-related material held outside the continent" (1998, 34).

Other handbooks—such as *International Guide to African Studies Research*, compiled by Philip Baker; *Africa: A Guide to Reference Material*, by John McIlwaine; *The African Studies Companion*, by Hans Zell and Cecile Lomer; and *The SCOLMA Directory of Libraries and Special Collections on Africa in the United Kingdom and in Europe*, compiled and edited by Tom French—while not focusing on folklore, provide lists of major African studies collections worldwide that include various folklore collections. More recently, Al Kagan and Yvette Scheven's *Reference Guide to Africa: A Bibliography of Sources* includes an excellent chapter on folklore, which provides an annotated list of research guides, surveys, and collections. The chapter concludes with a selective list of subject headings that are useful to locate folklore titles when searching handbooks, online catalogs, and other databases.

Last but not least, dissertations can provide useful current information on folklore/oral collections in and about Africa. Dissertations in the field are usually based on extensive field research, and, apart from representing the most current state of research, their bibliographies may provide useful hints about the existence of collections otherwise unknown. In some cases it might also be helpful to contact the author of the dissertation. The most obvious way to find out about dissertations is for the researcher to consult *Dissertation Abstracts International* and conduct a keyword search. As the title implies, however, this source covers dissertations from all areas of the world, not just Africa. Michigan State University librarian Joe Lauer's compilation of "Recent Doctoral Dissertations on Africa," which regularly appears in *ASA News*, is an invaluable resource in this respect. The compilation is drawn from *DAI* but only lists dissertations from Africa.

Please see the Appendix *African Studies Centers and Libraries in the United States and Africa* located at the back of this volume for collections on African folklore in the United States. As in Africa, there are numerous private collections with their associated problems of access, as discussed above. However, there are also numerous collections in libraries and archives, which have been donated or deposited in libraries by field researchers. (The same is true for Europe. Just like American archival collections, European collections can be located by using the handbooks and directories cited above.) The list in the Appendix is a selection of important collections and by no means constitutes a comprehensive list. The field of folklore comprises a variety of subfields, such as music, literature, history, and so forth, and in libraries throughout the United States and Europe, there are collections recorded in the field, reflecting these different disciplines.

Conclusion

Notwithstanding the projects outlined in the Appendix, the necessity to collect and record more oral data is obvious. It is equally important to provide access to existing collections by publishing reports of their existence, creating finding aids, and making them available to the public. This is particularly important for private collections, but it also applies to collections in libraries and archives. The lists of collections—for both Africa and the United States—are by no means comprehensive, and it is safe to assume that many more collections exist, unreported and therefore not widely accessible. One step in the direction of providing more information about private collections would be, as Alemna, Aleybeleye, and others have suggested, a "law enjoining researchers, masters and doctoral students to deposit copies with translations of their field tape recordings in an academic library," and all institutions collecting oral data should publish lists of their holdings (Alemna 1995, 134).

Saliou Mbaye reports that this has happened in the case of The Primary Institute of Black Africa (IFAN Cheikh Anta Diop) in Senegal, where local and foreign researchers have deposited copies of their recordings. Unfortunately, the Senegal example is the exception rather than the rule. Since academic success is based on original research, it might be hard to convince researchers to relinquish their recordings before they have had the opportunity to analyze them for publications. A more realistic proposal might be to ask researchers to deposit their materials after a certain amount of time, for example, two to five years, has elapsed. By that time, their findings have been published, and by making the field recordings accessible, a scholarly discourse can take place.

Other obstacles for the collection and dissemination of oral data, such as the sheer scope of such projects as well as costs, training issues, and maintenance of equipment, seem overwhelming. However, the fact that African governments, international organizations, as well as scholars and researchers have all recognized the need for action and are making attempts to rescue Africa's wealth of oral folklore is cause for optimism. Moreover, new information technologies, including the ability to digitize vast amounts of data and making them available in the electronic environment, may well turn out to be the solution. Particularly the increase of wireless technology may enable African librarians to digitize many of the oral collections and their finding aids, thereby bypassing a lot of the costs and issues imposed by print formats. This would serve the purposes of providing accounts of such collections and of preserving Africa's oral heritage.

References

Alemna, A. A. 1995. The Management of Oral Records by Libraries, Archives, and Other Related Institutions in Ghana. *African Journal of Library, Archives & Information Science* 5, no. 2: 127–136.

———. 1992. Towards a New Emphasis on Oral Tradition as an Information Source in African Libraries. *Journal of Documentation* 48, no. 4: 422–29.

Aleybeleye, B. 1985. Oral Archives in Africa: Their Nature, Value and Accessibility. *International Library Review* 17: 419–24.

Amadi, A. O. 1981. *African Libraries: Western Tradition and Colonial Brain-Washing.* New Jersey: Scarecrow Press.

Baker, Philip. 1987. *International Guide to African Studies Research/ Études Africaines. Guide International de Recherches.* London: Hans Zell.

French, Tom (ed.). 1993. *The SCOLMA Directory of Libraries and Special Collections on Africa in the United Kingdom and in Europe.* London, Melbourne, Munich, New York: Hans Zell.

Gosebrink, Jean E. Meeh, ed. 1986. *African Studies Information Resources Directory.* Oxford, London, Munich, New York and Paris: Hans Zell.

Hamilton, C. A. 1989. The Swaziland Oral History Project. *History of Africa* 14: 383–87.

Henige, David. 1989. The Half Life of African Archives. In *Africana Resources and Collections: Three Decades of Development and Achievement,* ed. Julian W. Witherell, Metuchen, N.J. and London: Scarecrow Press.

Iwuji, H. O. M. 1989. Librarianship and Oral Tradition in Africa. *International Library Review* 21: 201–07.

Kagan, Alfred, and Yvette Scheven. 1999. *Reference Guide to Africa: a Bibliography of Sources.* Lanham, Md.: Scarecrow Press.

Mbaye, Saliou. 1990. Oral Records in Senegal. *American Archivist,* 53, no. 4: 566–74.

McIlwaine, John. 1996. *Writings on African Archives.* London and New Jersey: Hans Zell.

———. 1993. *Africa: A Guide to Reference Material.* London, New York: Hans Zell.

Msiska, Augustine W. C. 1987. "An Attempt to Establish an Oral History Project in the University of Zambia Library, Lusaka Campus." *American Archivist,* 50, no. 1: 142–46.

Ndiaye, Raphael. 1988. Oral Culture and Libraries. *IFLA Journal* 14, no. 1: 40–6.

Pickering, David. 1999. *A Dictionary of Folklore.* New York: Facts on File.

Studies and Documents (Études et documents.) 1980–1987. Zanzibar: EACROTANAL (Eastern African Centre for Research on Oral Traditions and African National Languages).

Zell, Hans, and Cecile Lomer. 1997. *The African Studies Companion: A Resource Guide & Directory.* London and New Providence, N.J.: Hans Zell.

MARION FRANK-WILSON

See also **African Studies Centers and Libraries (Appendix); Institutional Study of African Folklore**

LIBYA

Libya is perhaps best known for its leader, Muammar Qadhafi, one of the longest-ruling heads of state in the world. The country of Libya borders the Mediterranean, and, in clockwise fashion,

Egypt, Sudan, Chad, Niger, Algeria, and Tunisia. Almost all semidesert, it is a large country covering nearly 685,000 square miles. Libya is only thinly populated with approximately 6.4 million inhabitants, 86 percent of whom live in cities, mostly in the capital of Tripoli. It is predominantly an Arab country in language and culture, although there are a few ancient Berber groups scattered throughout the country. The majority religion is Sunni Muslim (97 percent of the population).

Historically, Libya has been ruled by various foreign powers: the Turks, Italians, English, and French. Italy conquered Libya in 1911 as part of its African territorial aspirations over several decades which included today's Eritrea, Ethiopia, and part of Somalia. Eventually, the historically distinct areas of Tripolitania and Cyrenaica were united. Opposition to Italian rule began before World War II, although it was due to the war that Italy lost all its African territories. The French and English appointed a king in 1959, but by 1963, foreign oil companies were the real power. In 1969, Colonel Muammar Qadhafi led the revolt which overthrew the monarchy. Not only has Qadhafi remained in power, but he has been an active member of the League of Arab States and the Organization of African Unity. Libya's foreign policy is usually opposed by the United States and European powers, especially given Qadhafi's active support of many liberation movements around the world.

However one may view its foreign policy, internally Libya has profited greatly from its oil revenues. In addition to oil, iron ore and cement are exported. Although it has the highest standards of living in Africa, it depends heavily on imports. Farming is limited to the coast but it is highly productive. While Libya may not be democratic as it asserts, what cannot be disputed is that women are in a better position than in many Arab countries. Adult literacy is 76 percent and there are five universities.

PHILIP M. PEEK

LIMBA

See **Stories and Storytelling: The Limba**

LINGUISTICS AND AFRICAN VERBAL ARTS

Artists use ordinary language as their raw material; by crafting it, manipulating it, and shaping it with their artistry, they create language which is extraordinary, poetic, metaphorical, powerful, and esthetic.

What makes a verbal message a work of art? This is the question Roman Jakobson (1960) poses in a classic essay on linguistics and poetics, an essay which constructs a six-point model of communication with each point determining a different function of language. Jakobson defines the poetic function of language as that function that focuses on the message for its own sake. "Poetics deals with problems of verbal structure, just as the analysis of painting is concerned with pictorial structure. Since linguistics is the global science of verbal structure, poetics may be regarded as an integral part of linguistics" (1960, 350). Jacqueline M. Henkel (1996) surveys the contributions of lin-

guistics to literary theory over the past four decades. Starting with Ferdinand de Saussure's paradigm of language as a system that should be studied not only in terms of its individual parts but also in terms of the relationship between those parts (1915), she goes on to detail Jakobson's communication model, the influence of Noam Chomsky's work in generative transformational grammar, and John L. Austin and John R. Searle's work on speech-act theory. A fundamental theme running through all the models is that language is rule-governed behavior. Saussure established a distinction between langue (the language system) and parole (the act of speaking) and described the distinction by analogy to the game of chess where there is a distinction between the rules and conventions of the game and any actual game. Searle also draws on the analogy between games and speech acts. Just as a game cannot exist independently of the rules that define it, speech acts are successful only if they satisfy certain conventions or conditions. These conditions are part of what Chomsky refers to as competence, a person's knowledge of the rules of a language, as opposed to performance, the actual use of that language in real situations (Crystal 1987, 407–09). What makes a verbal message a work of art, then, is the conscious manipulation of the "rules," of the form or structure of language, for artistic purposes.

Nketia (1971) and Okpewho (1992) describe various stylistic markers in African verbal art. Repetition is a stylistic device which calls attention to form and which can also be used as a structuring mechanism. The conscious repetition of some aspect of language—a tone, a sound, a syllable, a word, a phrase—highlights that particular feature. Prosody and meter are typically defined in terms of patterned linguistic units such as number and kind of syllables, stresses or tones and thus also involve repetition. Repetition is also the organizing principle of poetry and song, both of which can be defined as "rhythmic language, divided into regularly recurring units of rhythm (or abstract time), characterizable as lines" (Bird 1972, 207). Hausa for example, makes no linguistic distinction between poetry and song, both being called *waak'aa*. Schuh (1988) has demonstrated that Hausa oral poetry is organized metrically by its musical accompaniment, which can be analyzed in terms of measures containing a fixed number of beats. The analysis of oral performance reveals that silence can have metrical value and is thus as important a structuring element as sound. An esthetic tension is created by the manipulation of the structuring elements such that expectations that are established through repetition are satisfied, withheld or even violated.

African verbal artists manipulate sound in a variety of ways for esthetic effect. The pitch of the voice may be altered so as to suggest a supernatural being or a creature that is very tiny or very huge. The Hausa ogre Dodo, for example, is performed in a very loud, low-pitched voice. Okpewho mentions that masquerades "often speak through voice modifiers . . . to further enhance the nonnatural, eerie character of the masquerades' spiritual essence" (1992, 267). Excessive nasalization or palatalization might be associated with the speech of particular characters in oral narratives. The Hausa trickster Gizo, for example, is characterized as speaking with a lisp, and the Akan Anansi as "speaking through the nose." The use of ideophones is particularly evident in performance, and ideophones generally have a distinct phonological shape. In Hausa ideophones are often marked by reduplication (*lugwi–lugwi*, "soft") or end in uncharacteristic consonants such as /f/ (*tsaf*, "completely").

Verbal art forms such as proverbs, epithets, and riddles often exhibit grammatical structure that is a deviation from that of ordinary speech. There are many Hausa proverbs with the structure: nominal phrase *sai* nominal phrase, for example, "Hakurin kaya sai jaki," Patience under a load, only a donkey [only a donkey shows patience under a load]. This construction is typically not used in everyday speech, although it is sometimes used creatively, for example in poetry. The word order of these constructions may be unusual; function words may be omitted. In the Hausa proverb: "Arziki rigar kaya," Prosperity is a coat of thorns [because of the obligations it brings with it], the word *ce* would normally be expected at the end of the sentence. The focus on irregular grammatical structure is often heightened by concurrent stylistic features such as alliteration or rhyme, as in the Hausa proverb "Zumu zuma ne," Relationship is honey [blood is thicker than water], which plays on the auditory similarity of the two words.

Verbal art is frequently ambiguous or polysemantic, especially if it involves politics, ritual, or sexual relations. Young Hausa men have praises for themselves which are called *taakee*, and which regularly allude to their sexual prowess; praise singers for royalty often criticize by means of innuendo; women obliquely abuse their co-wives (Furniss 1996). Artists capitalize on multiple lexical meanings to create ambiguity, but also exploit structural characteristics such as similarity of sound, to suggest additional meanings. The most extreme form of ambiguity occurs when messages are conveyed through speech surrogates such as drumming or gongs.

In the process of creating verbal art, a discourse about language, or metalanguage, is often created as well. The Hausa trickster Gizo, for example, provides performers with a means to discuss language through the metalinguistic terminology of his own speech: *baki biyu* ("two mouths"), deceitful speech; *romon kunne* ("ear broth"), flattering, meaningless speech; *tsammin baki* ("sour-mouth"), baby-talk, and Gizo-talk. An examination of the verses in praise of the *bori* spirit Mai Dara suggests that the voice of the spirit is powerful, as strong and fearsome as that of the ogre Dodo, of a lion. Seen as metaphorical discourse about language the verses proclaim that language is so powerful that it must by used judiciously. It can have far-reaching effects, it can convey truth, it can convey hypocrisy. Its power can and should sometimes be tempered by rechanneling it, by having a spokesperson intervene. Ournarou (1996) illustrates how Zabia Hussei and Ali na Maliki, two contemporary oral artists from Niger, create a poetic metalanguage as they create poetry itself, by using images such as the building of fences or farming to allude to the process of creating oral poetry or song.

Verbal art and the artists who create it are often believed to be endowed with exceptional power. This is in part because of the capacity of verbal art to transform, to produce an emotional response. Language which is rhythmic, metaphorical, or ambiguous is created by calling attention to linguistic form and structure. Jourdain (1997) suggests that emotion is a reaction to unexpected experience. Verbal artists craft language in unexpected ways, thereby committing what Jakobson refers to as "organized violence on ordinary speech," (1960, 353) and in so doing create language with the power to move, to impassion, and to transfix.

References

Bird, Charles. 1972. Aspects of Prosody in West African Poetry. In *Current Trends in Stylistics*, eds. Braj Kachru and Herbert Stahlke. Champaign, Illinois: Linguistic Research.

Crystal, David. 1987. *The Cambridge Encyclopedia of Language*. Cambridge: Cambridge University Press.

Elhadji Ournarou, Chaibou. 1996. *Individual Talent in Contemporary Hausa Oral Poetry*. Ph.D. dissertation, University of Wisconsin–Madison.

Furniss, Graham. 1996. *Poetry, Prose, and Popular Culture in Hausa*. Washington, D.C.: Smithsonian Institution Press.

Henkel, Jacqueline M. 1996. *Language of Criticism: Linguistic Models and Literary Theory*. Ithaca and London: Cornell University Press.

Jakobson, Roman. 1960. Concluding Statement: Linguistics and Poetics. In *Style in Language*, ed. Thomas A. Sebeok. Cambridge, Mass.: M.I.T. Press.

Jourdain, Robert. 1997. *Music, the Brain and Ecstasy*. New York: William Morrow.

Nketia, J. H. Kwabena. 1971. The Linguistic Aspect of Style in African Languages. *Current Trends in Linguistics* 7: 733–57.

Okpewho, Isidore. 1992. *African Oral Literature: Backwounds, Character, Continuity*. Bloomington, Ind: Indiana University Press.

Saussure, Ferdinand de. 1915. *Cours de linguistique Renerale*. Paris: Payot.

Schuh, Russell, G. 1988. Prealable to a Theory of Hausa Poetic Meter. In *Studies in Hausa Language and Linguistics: In Honor of F. W. Parsons*, eds. Graham Furniss and Philip J. Jaggar. London and New York: Kegan Paul International in association with the International African Institute.

LINDA HUNTER

See also **Ideophones; Proverbs; Silence in Expressive Behavior**

LUBA

See **History and Folklore: The Luba**

LUGBARA

See **Narration and Verbal Discourse: The Lugbara of Uganda**

LUHYIA

See **Legends; East Africa Medicine; Superstitions**

LUNDA

See **Festivals: Mutomboko Festival of the Lunda**

LUO

See **East African Folklore: Overview**

M

MAASAI

See **Prose Narratives**

MADAGASCAR (DEMOCRATIC REPUBLIC OF MADAGASCAR)

Madagascar, the world's fourth largest island, is a country of approximately 17 million people, located off of Africa's southeast coast. Madagascar's moderate-to-tropical climate has fostered a unique ecosystem that has produced flora and fauna found nowhere else on earth. Antananarivo, the nation's capital and largest city, has a population of 1.1 million. Madagascar's ethnic makeup consists of Malayo-Indonesian, Cotiers, French, Indian, Creole, and Comoran as well as African. The major languages spoken are Malagasy and French. Over half of the islanders practice traditional indigenous religions (52 percent); 41 percent are Christian and 7 percent are Muslim.

The Imerina monarchy ruled much of the island from 1797 to 1861, but by 1895, the French had established their control. On June 26, 1960, Madagascar gained its independence from France after fifty-six years of colonization and subsequently formed the first Malagasy Republic. This system lasted for twelve years, until, after the mounting unrest of peasants, students, and workers, a coup overthrew the government. A new constitution, implemented in 1975, allowed for controlled multiparty political competition. Since 1980, the country has suffered from a poor economy, and new political instability has emerged as a result. Elections held in 1989–1990 strengthened the multiparty democracy, and there has been an improvement in the respect for human rights and freedoms. Nevertheless, recent elections have revealed continued civil strife.

Nearly 80 percent of the Malagasy are employed in the agricultural sector, which produces rice, coffee, vanilla, cotton, and sugar. Sources of revenue come from industries such as food processing, textiles, mining, and paper. Despite its image as a tropical paradise, Madagascar is an ecological disaster, due to centuries of exploitation of the environment, and many fear for the future of its natural resources, flora, and fauna, as well as its human inhabitants.

Madagascar has produced many great twentieth-century poets. Many of these, poets such as Jean-Joseph Rabearivelo, were known for their unique writing style, which blended local Malagasy forms and rhythms (inspired by the *hainteny* form, a characteristic of popular island songs) with influences from the French literary and intellectual scene.

JENNIFER JOYCE

MAGHRIB (NORTHWESTERN NORTH AFRICA) FOLKLORE: OVERVIEW

The term Maghrib was first used by Arab geographers to designate the western part of the Arab world, as opposed to its correspondent in the east, the Mashriq. The latter, Mashriq (from *sharaqa*, "to rise"), refers to the place where the sun rises, that is, the Arab Orient; whereas the former, Maghrib (from *gharaba*, "to set"), designates the area where the sun sets on the Arab world. The Maghrib, or "Sunset," is situated in North Africa, spreading westward from Libya to the Atlantic Ocean and southward from the Mediterranean to the Sahara desert. It is composed of the countries known today as Morocco, Algeria, and Tunisia. It was originally peopled by Berbers, who still represent a high percentage of the population in Algeria (about 25 percent) and Morocco (60 percent).

From the eighth century, the Arabs began populating the Maghrib. A first wave brought their new religion, Islam, which was adopted widely. The second wave, in the eleventh century, made up of nomads (the Banû Hilâl, or "Sons of Hilal") who shared their pastoral way of life with the natives, exerted a deeper influence in the process of acculturation and Arabicization.

However, while Arabic has now become the official language, and Arabicization is total in all spheres of social life, the people of Berber origin continue to use their mother language and to claim, mostly in Algeria, the right to have their culture acknowledged. Sometimes French, the language of the former colonizers, is also spoken.

The three countries acquired independence from France (1956–1962), but the access to independence for the Algerians

A corn market in Morocco, 1960. Photo © Micheline Galley.

was at the cost of a cruel war of seven years (1955–1962). Since then, the three states of Algeria and Morocco (with approximately 30 million inhabitants each) and Tunisia (approximately 9 million) have tended towards unification. This has occurred in spite of divergences and occasional crises aroused mostly by frontier conflicts between Algeria and Morocco, and by Islamic extremism, which has been a potent force in Algeria for the last decade.

In 1989, two neighboring countries, Libya at the east (with 5 million inhabitants) and Mauritania to the southwest (2.5 million inhabitants) joined the three countries of the Maghrib in the "Union of the Arab Maghrib"; the goal was to build a vast geopolitical conglomerate (Lacoste 45–50). Now the word *Maghrib*, or phrase *Great Maghrib*, has been gradually applied

An auction in Morocco, 1960. Photo © Micheline Galley.

in political spheres to a wider area than traditionally implied. Nevertheless, this entry will focus primarily on Morocco, Algeria, and Tunisia.

Besides the Arabs and the Berbers who represent the main constituents of the Maghribian society, two other populations should be noted. First, there are the Jews, a very ancient community that was augmented by new members after their expulsion from Spain in 1492, but that has almost completely emigrated to the western countries and to Israel in recent years. Second, there is a black African population, descending from African slaves brought from the south.

These populations suggest there has been much cross-cultural fertilization within Maghrib society. For example, the narrative cycle of "The Maiden Who Seeks Her Brothers" (Arne-Thompson 1964, 451) although very popular in several pastoral areas of Algeria and Morocco, reflects a system of kinship and marriage that is common among African social groups farther south (Galley 1994, 40; Baklouti 1988, 115–21). Sometimes, on the other hand, external influences have been well integrated into the Maghribian folk culture. Their effect has produced interesting local syntheses, as illustrated in Tunisia at the time of the Ottoman Empire by the adoption of the now-vanishing shadow theater, the Turkish Karagoz. Other examples, due to contact with Mediterranean peoples, can be cited. Underglass painting, for instance, is likely to have been introduced into Tunisia by the Italians in the last part of the eighteenth century. Still a vibrant tradition, it draws its inspiration from folk beliefs (e.g., the Evil Eye) as well as religious and epic subjects. It has asserted itself as a genuine Tunisian folk art.

Main Trends of Maghribian Folk Culture: Ancient Rituals

Not surprisingly, the folklore of the Maghrib includes pre-Islamic agrarian rituals. Although they are disappearing, carnival celebrations have been widespread in the Maghrib. Those who take part in them indulge in frenzied dances and performances of a satirical nature inspired by social life. They usually give themselves the appearance of animals, hence the name *Bû Jlûd*, literally, "the one covered with hides." They may also assume some other disguise, as does the *Bû Lîfa*, "the one covered with palm fibers" and *Bû Shâyb*, "the old one." Generally speaking, the masquerade is performed on 'Ashura, the "10th day" of the first month of the Muslim year (Doutté 496–5, 10). Other fertility rites have been practiced, in order to bring rain (Galand-Pernet 1998, 88–92) or to mark the end of the harvest season, when fires are lit on the thrashing floor on the night of 'ansara, June 24th (Doutté 1984, 566 ff). The fertility and growth of plants is symbolically encouraged by placing in them "male" twigs to help bring about "impregnation." In certain areas, southern Tunisia for instance, cheerful children used to pick up some earth and throw it over a fig or palm tree, while singing:

> The earth of the 'ansara is better
> than the male tree.

Some fertility rites draw clear associations between Nature and human beings. On the feast of May in the region of Nefta (Tunisia), young girls used to take a bath in a spring, then go swinging to and fro, singing:

Pharaoh, O Pharaoh
Make my hair longer,
Make my vagina bigger.
The palm tree is
Prolific with bunches of dates.

(unpublished)

On the other hand, folk religions have developed forms of piety and rituals that exist alongside official religion, but not always in conformity with it. Among the Muslims, the sacred tombs of Marabouts—literally, those who are "linked to (God)"—are the sites of popular pilgrimages. As a matter of fact, the worship of holy men and, although less frequent, holy women has been widely practiced by Muslims and Jews alike (Zafrani 1983).

Folk Poetry

As far as the verbal arts are concerned, the various forms are, to a large extent, shared by all ethnic groups throughout the Maghrib, including proverbs and sayings (Ben Cheneb 1907; Westermarck 1930), riddles (Quemeneur 1944), lullabies and nursery rhymes (Jouin 1950). Poetic duelling has always been enjoyed by the people, along with other traditional and complex forms of poetry, among which is the highly appreciated *malhûn*, expressed in a type of poetical speech (*koine*), which exists halfway between literary and colloquial Arabic.

The themes are many. In hagiographical literature, they may deal with either meditative ecstatic thoughts or bitter (sometimes sarcastic) reflections on earthly living; striking examples are provided by the sayings and quatrains attributed to an itinerant saint called the Mejdûb (literally, "one whose mind has been ravished" from dancing; hence, a dervish). In lyrical genres, folk poets pour out their thoughts and feelings. Love poems may include Bacchic elements as in the following:

Bring the wine, waiter, and quench our thirst,
Remove our vicissitudes and, with wine, make us feel
    alive.
My gazelle has come to visit me;
She is sitting in front of me like the radiant moon . . .

(transl. from Belhalfoui 1973, 63).

But one of the most popular motives still is, as it was in the classical odes, the search for the vestiges of the encampment in the sand, associated with happy memories of the past irretrievably lost:

I wandered among the tribes of noble Arabs
Nowhere did I see El-Aalya (my beloved)
I saw no one capable of informing me
Except on the traces of the abandoned camp . . .

(transl. from Belhalfoui 1973, 149).

A popular genre, *haufi*, is improvised during ritual games by young female singers, who thus are given the opportunity of expressing social taboos attached to love and marriage.

There are also folk music and songs used as vehicles of political protest to which folk singers today resort before enthusiastic audiences, at the risk, sometimes, of their own lives. In the 1990s, a Kabyle singer, Lounes Matoub, was murdered, following the deaths of several others of both Berber and Arab origin. However, the very popular and subversive genre known as *ray* in Algeria and elsewhere has gained an international reputation through the network of show business (Virolle 1995).

Folk Narratives: A Long-Ignored Heritage

Arabian folk literature in general has long suffered from prejudice. The main reason for this negative attitude lay in the gap that existed in the minds of the grammarians and theologians between classical Arabic—the language of the *Quran* and "accepted" literature—and colloquial Arabic, the everyday spoken language of the people. It required courage to declare that the language of folk poets was rich and subtle, which is what the fourteenth century historian Ibn Khaldun did. He heard some bards in the south of Algeria sing of the adventurous migration of the Banû Hilâl to the Maghrib. In his time, in addition to attacks on its "bastard" language, the contents of folk literature were condemned as "a web of lies." The use of *khurrafa* to designate wonder tales is significant: this word is associated with lies, extravagant talk, and dotage and refers normally to a strictly feminine repertoire.

As to the "Orientalist" scholars, their views appear to be biased by standards of literary composition, in spite of the fabulous vogue enjoyed throughout Europe by Arabian narratives, such as the *One Thousand and One Nights* and the adventures of *Antar*, the famous "Prince of the Desert," both still popular in the Maghrib as well. Due to these attitudes, scientific collection and study of Maghribian narratives only began in the late nineteenth century and then essentially for linguistic purposes. We owe to linguists, such as Samuel Biarnay, Georges S. Colin, Edmond Destaing, Hans Stumme, and others, the first reliable corpuses, especially in Berber dialects.

However, for half a century, due to the efforts of specialists such as Germaine Tillion, Lionel and Paulette Galand, and David Cohen, researchers were trained in the systematic collecting of folktales, the study of performance, and all the aspects of the tales' further analyses. In the meantime, the countries concerned started to develop a new interest for their cultural identity, contributing, although not always sufficiently, to the organizing of fieldwork, scientific meetings, and publications.

Folktales

Once upon a time there was and there was not . . .
At the time when the blind used to see and the palsied
    used to jump over the walls . . .

This type of initial formulae draws the listeners into a realm of fantasy in which everything is possible, but also a world in which powerful genii and all sorts of terrifying beings prevail. This is why storytelling is regarded traditionally as potentially dangerous. A storyteller performs only at night in order to be immune from dangers. One of the risks is to have one's children affected with ringworm (El Fasi and Dermenghem 1926, 17). The world that the narrator conjures up is not answerable to the same rules and forces as the world people commonly inhabit. Time and space are measured differently: a day's walk may be like eternity, whereas it does not take long to fly over the Seven

Seas on the wings of an eagle and reach a heavenly orchard where rejuvenating apples grow (Légey 1926a, 71–3).

The narrative genre comprises other categories of tales, besides the above-mentioned *khurrâfa*. Their names suggest generally true-to-life contents (e.g., *hikâya*, "tale, account"; *qissa*, "narration"; *sîra*, "epic"). But even within narratives of a more realistic nature, no real transition separates the everyday surroundings from a supernatural environment.

Nevertheless, they grapple with problems inherent to life in society. The more recurring range from the universally tragic situation of orphans as in "Cinderella" (Aarne-Thompson 510)—whether they are secretly fed by their dead mother who takes the shape of a cow (e.g., Amrouche 1966, 55–62) or the orphan daughter flees incest from brother/father as in "Cap o' Rushes" (Aarne-Thompson 510B)—to the crucial question, for a man as well as a woman, of finding on the basis of verbal skill an appropriate mate (e.g., "The Basil Maiden," Aarne-Thompson 879, in Galley 1971: 153–80). Thus, new aspirations and ancient fears are expressed.

However, fiction also has an essential role in education: that of teaching a child, in a playful manner, how to behave within and outside the family. The basic rule is not to be cheated by others but get the upper hand in all social relations. For that purpose, he/she must be on the lookout to anticipate the others' tricks and acquire a quick flexible form of pragmatic intelligence that includes, most frequently, mastery over language.

This is illustrated in several cycles. In one of them (a combination of "The Children and the Ogre" and "The Boy Steals the Giant's Treasure," AT 327–328; e.g., Mouliéras 1892, 136–153 and Baklouti 1988, 91–4), the young hero triumphs over an ogress in spite of his physical appearance as suggested by his name ("Half Man" or "Little Smartie"). Also very small in size is the Maghribian "Rhampsinitus" (AT 950; e.g., Laoust 1912, 186–8), whose story develops into a series of challenges from the clever thief at the address of the sultan and/or his Jewish counselor.

Cunning is equally central to animal tales, in which a jackal and a hedgehog are the primary protagonists. Special mention must be made also of the funny anecdotes attributed to Joha, a many-sided complex character known throughout the Mediterranean world. Others play tricks on him, treating him like a gullible simpleton; eventually, however, he gets his revenge (e.g., Dallet 1963, 266–277).

The trickery of ruse and stratagem is generally attributed to women. Old women, in particular, excel in deceit, dealing unscrupulously at the expense of men.

Other kinds of tales represent the individual in contact with the divine. When confronted with his/her fate, the hero then accepts, fully and willingly, what he/she believes to be ordained by God. Such an attitude must not be mistaken for a fatalistic conception of life, since the individual somehow turns acceptance into an extremely dynamic force.

In a recurring cycle, the young boy who is doomed to seven years of misfortune takes, so to speak, his destiny in hand, while lending himself to God's will (e.g., Frobenius 1921,3, 208–37). In another cycle, the hero spontaneously believes in the "Good Precepts" (AT 910) delivered by a wise person and blindly follows them for his/her success. A Moroccan tale shows a youngster attracted by the discourse of a "seller of words," to whom he does not hesitate to give all the money he was supposed to spend for the food of the family (Kaddouri and Reboul 1986, 154–64).

When the tale comes to an end, the narrator sometimes uses a proverb as if to express the meaning of his story in a subtle poetical way. He also has at his disposal formulae whose function is double: protective at the time when one leaves the world of magic and aesthetic for the aural pleasure of the audience. Such phrases sound as follows:

Hiyya mshât tetkerbeb
Wa-na jît f-el-merkeb.
(My story) has gone, tumbling down its slope
And I am getting back on my boat.

(heard from Moroccan storytellers)

Epics

Folk epics play an outstanding part in Arab culture. Besides *Antar*, one of the Arabian epics whose popularity has been considerable is the *sîra* (literally, "biography") of the Sons of Hilal. The Hilalians were a nomadic people from Arabia who constituted, as was said before, the second wave of Arab conquerors in the present Maghrib. Of the complete body of the *sîra*, two narrative sequences have developed in the Maghrib, centered upon the more cherished characters of Dhyab and Jazya.

The former sequence deals with the intense, sometimes dramatic relationship between father and son, Ghanim and Dhyab, during which tests of verbal intelligence provide an unquestionable proof of paternity. The latter is focused on the antagonistic, yet close, relationship between Dhyab and Jazya themselves; in most versions, they eventually get married after she has evaluated his capabilities through various tests of cleverness.

This famous couple embodies the ethics of the group: self-sacrifice, courage, hospitality, and eloquence (Guiga 1968). A recent Algerian version reflects a nostalgia for the time when Jazya and Dhyab served as models:

In the old days people used to drink milk
as white as their hearts
And today they drink coffee
as black as their hearts.
In the old days people used to be free and true
like Dhyab and Jazya . . .
We followed their example . . .

(transl. from Nacib 1994, 269)

References

Aarne, Anti, and Stith Thompson. 1961. *The Types of the Folktale* (FF Communications 184) Helsinki: Academia Scientiarum Fennica.

Amrouche, M.T. 1966. Le grain Magique. *Contes, Poèmes et Proverbes berbères de Kabylie.* Paris: Maspéro.

Baklouti, N. 1988. *Contes populaires de Tunisie.* Sfax: I.N.A.A. (Institut National d'Archéologie et d'Art).

Belhalfaoui, M. 1973. *La poésie arabe maghrébine d'expression populaire.* Paris: Maspéro.

Ben Cheneb, M. 1907. *Proverbes arabes de l'Algé et du Maghreb.* Paris: Leroux.

Biarnay, S. 1917. *Etude sur les dialectes berbères.* du Rif Paris: Leroux

Chimenti, E. 1965. *Tales and Legends of Morocco.* New York: Aaron Benami.

Colin, G.S. 1955. *Chrestomathie marocaine. textes citadins en transcription latine* Paris: Maisonneuve.

Dallet, J.M. 1963. *Contes kaybles inédits.* Fort-National: F.D.B.

Destaing, ed. 1907/1911. *Etude sur le dialecte berbère des Béni-Snous.* Paris: (2 vol.). Leroux.

Doutté, ed. 1984. *Magie et Religion dans l'Afrique du Nord.* Paris: Maisonneuve and Geuthner.

El-Fasi, M., and E. Dermenghem. 1926. *Contes Fasis Recueillis d'apres la tradition orale.* Paris: Rieder.

El-Kasshat, M.S. 1968. *The Folk Literature of Libya.* Beyrut.

Frobenius, L. 1921. *Volksmärchen der Kabylen.* Jena: Diederichs.

Galand-Pernet, P. 1998. *Littératures berbères. Des voix, des lettres.* Paris: PUF (Presses Universitaires de France).

Galley, M. 1994. Classiques Africains. *Badr az-Zin et Six Contes Algériens.* (2nd ed.). Paris.

Galley, M., and Ayoub, A. 1983. Classiques Africains. *Histoire des Béni Hilal et de ce qui leur advint dans leur marche vers l'ouest.* Paris.

Galley, M. and Z. Iraqui Sinaceur 1994. *Dyab, Jha, La'aba. Le triomphe de la ruse.* Paris: Classiques Africains.

Gellner, E. 1969. *Saints of the Atlas.* London.

Guiga, A. 1968. *Min 'aqasis bani hilal.* Tunis: M.T.E.

———. 1968. *La geste Hilalienne.* Tahar Guiga, ed. Tunis: M.T.E.

Hejaiej, M. 1996. *Behind Closed Doors: Women's Oral Narratives in Tunis.* London: Quartet Books.

Hilton-Simpson, M.W. 1924. Algerian Folktales. *Folklore*: XXXV

I.B.L.A. (Institut des Belles-Lettres Arabes). Tunis: N. 45.

Jouin, J. 1950. Chants et jeux maternels à Rabat. *Hespéris*, XXXVII.

Kaddouri, M., and I. Reboul. 1986. *Les contes de chez moi.* Sud Maroc. Paris.

Laoust, E. 1912. *Etude sur le dialecte berbère du Chenoua.* Paris: Leroux.

———. 1949. *Contes berbères du Maroc.* Paris: (2 vol.). Leoux.

Légey, F. 1926a. *Contes et Légendes populaires du Maroc recueillis à Marrakech.* Paris: Geuthner.

———. 1926b. *Essai de folklore marocain.* Paris: Geuthner.

Mouliéras, A. 1892. *Les fourberies de Si Djeh'a.* Paris: Leroux.

———. 1965. *Légendes et Contes Merveilleux de la Grande-Kabylie,* trans. C. Lacoste-Dujardin. Paris: Maspéro.

Nacib, Y. 1994. *Une geste en fragments: la Saga hilalienne des Hauts-Plateaux algériens.* Paris: Publisud.

Noy, D. 1966. *Moroccan Jewish Folktales.* New York.

Quémeneur, J. 1944. *Enigmes tunisiennes.* Tunis: I.B.L.A.

Stumme, H. 1893. *Tunisische Märchen und Geschichtte.* Leipzig: Heinrichs.

———. 1895. *Der Arab. Dialekt des Houwara des Wad Sus in Marokko.* Leipzig: Heinrichs.

Tauzin, A. 1993. *Contes arabes de Mauritanie.* Paris: Karthala.

Virolle, M. 1995. *La chanson raï de l'Algérie profonde à la scène Internationale.* Paris.

Westermarck, E. 1926. *Ritual and Belief in Morocco.* London: Macmillan.

———. 1930. *Wit and Wisdom in Morocco. A Study of Native Proverbs.* London: Macmillan.

Zafrani, H. 1983. *Cent ans de vie juive au Maroc.* Paris.

MICHELINE GALLEY

Se also **Epics; Folktales; French Study of African Folklore**

MAGHRIB: ALGERIA

Located in the northernmost part of Africa, in the center of the Djazirat-al-Maghrib (the island of the Maghrib) of the ancient Arab geographers, between the kingdom of Morocco and the republic of Tunisia, Algeria (etymologically speaking) is the country "of the islands" (Al-Djazair). Its contemporary name dates back to the period of the Turkish occupation and refers to the establishment of the port of Algiers on a group of islets, a short distance from the coastal capital of today.

Despite Algeria's important maritime front on the Mediterranean (approximately 744 miles), the country's real center is located in its arid region, that is, in the regions of the high plains and central Sahara. At the most, the coastal areas cover only a thin strip of a few hundred kilometers in depth.

From the geomorphological point of view, as well as in terms of historical matters, it is difficult to distinguish Algeria from the rest of the Maghribian ensemble. Two imposing mountainous ridges run parallel across the country from the southwest (Saharan Atlas) to the northeast (Tellian Atlas) and then converge to form an imposing mountainous range, the Aurés. From the shores of the Mediterranean to the great stretches of desert, four major types of topography can be distinguished: (1) the discontinuous chain of coastal plains between (2) the mountainous massifs, (3) the expansive stretches of steppes, and (4) the few oases, scattered for the most part in the northern part of the Sahara.

The major cities are all located on the narrow coastal strip where most of the country's agricultural areas are located. Indeed, the extraordinary development of the oil in the second half of the twentieth century industry should not distract from the importance of Algeria's secular agricultural and pastoral traditions. From this perspective, it seems that the ancient reputation as "Rome's breadbasket" corresponded to an undeniable economic reality, that of a rich region producing high yields of cereals.

History

From an historical point of view, despite differing theories, most scholars believe that the territory that corresponds to the Algerian Republic today was probably settled, beginning in the east, through successive waves of populations. From prehistoric times on, those who defined themselves as Imazighen (sing. Amazigh, "a free man") occupied a vast region, the climate of which at that time was much more humid than it is today. Prior to the long period of the Roman domination, Algeria witnessed several occupations, the most important of which was unquestionably that of the Phoenicians (circa the twelfth century BCE), then of the Carthaginians (starting in the sixth century BCE).

Subsequently, and for more than six centuries, the Lybian populations (ancestors of the Berbers in Arabic and European historiography) would become Roman subjects, spread out between the Numids (in the east) and the Moors (in the west). The history of the Algerian peasantry has been characterized for a very long time by the experience of dispossession (Bourdieu 1958). Nevertheless, as shown by relatively recent scholarship, the resistance of the indigenous population to Romanization is a lasting and important event (Benabou 1976; Lacheraf 1988).

Later, the collapse of the Roman Empire and the arrival of the Vandals, followed by the Byzantines, would exacerbate the Algerians' spirit of independence. Yet, when the Arab-Muslim expeditionary force set out to conquer North Africa at the end of the seventh century, Algeria underwent rapid Islamization, despite the many military episodes during which the courage and pugnacity of the Berber tribes and the fierce affirmation of a secular identity were strongly displayed.

Subsequently, the representatives of the various powers—mainly the Almoravids and the Almohads—all the while seeking to preserve their autonomy, would oscillate for a long time between the influences of West and East, seeking a political balance and a coherent sociocultural structure between the great kingdoms of "Westernmost Maghrib" (Al-Maghrib-al-Aqsa), Andalusia (Al-Andalûs), the dynasties of ancient Ifriqiya (Tunisia), and those of the successive Oriental powers.

Beginning in the second half of the eleventh century, the arrival of the Hilalian tribes and their gradual settlement throughout the country initiated the definitive and massive Arabization of the indigenous Berber populations, especially the rural and nomadic ones.

In the sixteenth century, Algeria became an Ottoman province, governed by a *dey* (governor of the regency of Algiers) who was a representative of the "Sublime Port" (Constantinople, seat of Ottoman power). Whatever the real motives—a subject that has given rise to bitter debates among colonial and Algerian historians—the Turkish military intervention is best interpreted in light of the great geopolitical and economic upheavals which reestablished a power balance between West and East in the Mediterranean basin, with spectacular consequences for the whole world.

Turkish rule was applied only indirectly and was reduced, most of the time, to a mere fiscal effort aimed at regularly draining the Algerian countryside of its meager surplus of crops. There was a famous incident between the French consul and the *dey* of Algiers when, during a financial dispute, the *dey* grazed the consul's cheek with his fly-whisk. This served as a pretext for French military intervention. The fly-whisk incident aside, France's intervention of July 5, 1830, by imposing a strong and lasting presence on the southern edge of the Mediterranean, was aimed at putting a stop to the race led by the Algero-Barbaresque fleet based in Algiers and at hampering the expansionist policies of the European powers (especially England) in the Mediterranean basin.

Contrary to the thesis long perpetrated by the historians of the colonial system, the will to resist the invader was active in a violent, concerted, and permanent manner from the very first days of the French occupation. Whether it took the form of peasant jacqueries, urban insurrections, or relatively passive campaigns of disobedience at the level of the community, the region, or the entire country, the national sentiment evolved against a background of deep religiosity and political consciousness exacerbated by the increasingly expansive and violent character of the colonial mission.

From the spectacular celebration of the Centennial of French Algeria in 1930 to the onset of the armed struggle (November 1, 1954), the speeding up of events and proliferation of bloody episodes involving the Algerian nationalist movement reveal how the movement was rapidly radicalized under the pressure of the people.

From this point of view, we can argue that the contradictions with which the country struggled (and continues to struggle) probably originated in the organization of the Algerian national polity during this crucial period between the two wars and also in the blindness and intransigence (not to speak of the arro-gance) of the French administration and of a good part of the French political class.

By removing the moderate leaders along with their projects of "shared development," the "ultras" on both sides compelled the "November Revolution" to adopt radical—and often dangerous—ideological, political, and economic orientations, the consequences of which, in some cases, were to jeopardize, in a lasting way, the harmonious development of the country.

Thus, the rigidity of the state's political machinery, the unwieldiness of a centralized planning system (modeled on the Soviet system), the anarchic collectivization of the big agricultural domains, the low productivity of the so-called model of the industrializing industries, the incoherence of a "specific" socialism intended to synthesize an imported technology and a political model with the community values of a people deeply attached to their religion, language, and ancestral customs led little by little to a serious crisis that reached its climax during the events of October 1988.

At the beginning of the new century, one of the most severe aspects of the "Algerian crisis" lay in the almost neurotic relationship that Algerians had with memory and identity. Indeed, following the traumatic experience of colonialism, and confronted with the increasing influence of Western culture (especially felt through the media) and with the potency of a largely idealized Oriental referent (if only because of its religious dimension), new generations of Algerians find it difficult to define the cultural trajectory of their country. It is also difficult for them to identify the basic elements of a secular cultural project in the exhibition of devalued symbols of a local folklore.

Already in 1968, Mostefa Lacheraf made a severe assessment: "Today, 'folklore' and the abusive exploitation of the war's heroes have become the two staples in certain countries of the Maghreb. On an even greater scale, they have become successive substitutes for the exotic colonial subculture and the 'patriotic' and legionnaire epic by which the French continued to exert their protracted domination on us" (1988, 46).

It is true that, as a result of the upheavals of recent history, the postindependence youth of Algeria have lost sight of the richness of the cultural legacy of their ancestors. Yet, numerous documents written, at least since the Middle Ages, by writers and scholars of the country's various regions have left us precious information on the religious, literary, and artistic practices of the Algerians.

Anthropological Literature

Among the most prestigious of these sources remain, undoubtedly, the two great works of the scholar Ibn Khaldoun: *The History of the Berbers* and the famous *Muqaddima*, the latter, unfortunately, too often missing essential chapters (especially the linguistic and literary ones) on the specific features of Maghribian culture.

In those works we find mention of Arabo-Andalusian repertories (*Muwashshahât* and *'Azjâl*), still greatly practiced in Algeria's main cities, as well as women's songs (Hawfi) and, especially, excerpts of poems retracing the *geste* (a set of epic poems) of *Diâb the Hilalian*. Ethnographers, travelers, and other European Orientalists also published numerous (often somewhat fanciful) monographs quite early, gathering a rather impressive collection of various materials: agrarian rites, collective songs, religious customs, practices of *confreries* (pious associations established by followers of a Tariqa or "sacred path"), and so on.

We can, of course, remain, somewhat critical regarding the aims and research methodology used by those researchers who were largely influenced, if not manipulated, by the colonial system. Nevertheless, today we need to recognize that their works allow us at least to have a relatively coherent idea of the state of the Algerian cultural tradition in the first half of the nineteenth century, and this to the extent that the oral tradition was greatly disrupted by the violence of the military, political, and ideological repression.

Since we are dealing with constituent features of this tradition, we must insist from the outset on the decisive importance of the Berber "anthropological foundation," even though the syncretic phenomena are numerous and ancient (especially with the Arab world, Muslim and Judaic). Whether we are dealing with ancestral expertise (agropastoral or urban), craft industries (basketry, pottery, copperware, etc.), religious practices (connected to the orthodox worship practices as well as to the pre-Islamic rites) or with the properly artistic expression (music, literature, dance, etc.), we can readily determine the invariants of a culture specific to this region of the Mediterranean and embodied more visibly by four major human communities.

Both numerically and geographically, the Kabyles represent the most important and often the most active group in terms of identity vigilance. This was the case, for example, during the events of the "Berber spring" in April 1980, when a series of strikes and demonstrations were violently repressed, thus, marking an important chapter in the reclaiming of Amazigh identity. In sociocultural terms, they perpetuate in their mountainous regions a model of community organization characterized by family and group (*djma'a*) values founded on cohesion, on the respect of the Ancients, and on a particularly strict honor code. The systematic disinheritance of women (contradicting Quranic prescriptions) and the importance of the maraboutic cults, as well as the numerous magico-religious rituals, are a good illustration of the particular way the Berber populations have accommodated Islam and its cultural contributions.

Though the rather frequent use of Arabic as the vernacular tongue, along with Chaouia, testifies to the close contacts maintained by the Chaouia peasants and nomads with their Arabophone neighbors of the Tell and the Sahara, a certain number of features show the singularity of this steep and particularly rugged region. Thus, we encounter clearly pre-Islamic practices, and the status of the Chaouia woman (who, of course, remain formally subjected to the dominant males: father, brother, husband) presents great flexibility, a flexibility embodied quite spectacularly in the figure of the *'Azriya*. This truly "free" woman, who rejects marriage and assumes (through music, poetry, dance) a codified status of a marginal person, enjoys the group's respect and affection.

Beber Communities

The Mozabites, trace their origin in the Maghrib to the political and ideological consequences of the famous schism that occurred in the Muslim community upon the death of the Prophet. Defined as dissidents by their co-religionists, pursued throughout a great part of the Middle East, they finally chose a landscape of grandiose aridity, in the valley of the M'Zab river (northern Sahara) to develop their culture. According to Pierre Bourdieu, this culture

draws the source of its cohesion from the wealth of its historical, legendary and doctrinal traditions, from the harmonious precision of the groups' interactions within the different communities, from the ingenious functioning of the *ittifâqât*, consigned in writing and fertile in jurisprudence, finally, from a doctrine, all at once flexible and rigid, which defines a perfectly original lifestyle in North Africa. (1958, 38)

More than all the other Berberophone communities in Algeria, the *taurea* (sing. *targui*) nomads were affected (although belatedly) by the effects of French occupation and the political divisions inherited from this period. Indeed, their ancestral home, astride on several countries—Algeria, Lybia, Mali, Niger—has undergone such a fragmentation that the *targui* culture is in great danger of extinction. Yet, up to the turn of the century (date of the first incursions of the French army into central Sahara), these "lords of the desert" had been able to preserve cultural traditions inherited from their distant ancestors, the Garamante Berbers, whose symbolic representations adorn the walls of numerous underground shelters of the region. Although completely Islamized, the tuareg have adapted the Quranic message to the constraints of their lifestyle and to the rigors of their environment. Thus, the legends, the tales, and epic songs intertwine various elements of the indigenous tradition with those of Muslim popular mythology. Likewise, the status of the woman—*matriarchy* has often been used (wrongly so, it seems) to characterize the type of organization of the *targui* family—is particularly favorable. Perhaps a symbol of this very special status can be seen in the woman's right to maintain real "poetic salons" and to be the only one to play a musical instrument (*imzad*).

Mention should be made of the other Berberophone communities of lesser numerical importance scattered throughout the national terrritory and living in often mountainous (Chenoua, Beni-Snous) or desert (the Zenetes of Gourara) isolation. Despite some relatively significant variants, they all present a certain number of common cultural traits which Pierre Bourdieu summarizes as follows: "a certain independence toward Islam (with the exception of the Mzab), especially noticeable in the legal system; a peasant love for the earth and for the relentless work which fertilizes it and the predominance of direct farming, an apparently egalitarian social structure that involves the territorial concept." (1958, 7)

Care must be taken not to minimize the role of the Arabo-Muslim culture, and the significance of its models, in every milieu and in every region of the country. Whether one defines oneself as or feels oneself to be a Amazigh, an "Arabized Berber," an "Arab," an "African" or simply a "Muslim," an Algerian always positions him or herself—partly or completely, implicitly or explicitly—in relationship to a linguistic heritage (Arabic), a faith (Islam), values (pride, courage, generosity, etc.), and a political ideal (Umma), assumed to be from the Orient.

Whatever the claimed, ethnic origin, it is clear that the lived culture is a synthesis of East and West, of Africa and the Mediterranean. This syncretism is obvious in most sociocultural areas. It is manifest, for example, in the cult of the saints, which combines an Arabo-Muslim-inspired liturgy and extactic practices (often of African origin) with clearly indigenous magico-religious rituals.

Likewise, in the culinary realm, if couscous—prepared according to numerous variants—seems to belong to an indigenous tradition, pastries and certain urban dishes clearly bear the mark of the Middle East (Turkey, Iraq, Syria). Architecture is also a good example of this historic synthesis of which the Maghreb has been the stage over the centuries. Examples include the Great Mosque of Tlemcen, with its simple-shaped minaret and typically angular Andalusian silhouette, and the Ketchaoua Mosque of Algiers, with its imposing proportions, its Byzantine cupola, and its clearly oriental ornate style.

As for music, we know that Eastern, Western (Andalusian), Mediterranean, and African (sub-Saharan) have combined with indigenous Berber repertories. This stylistic plurality is expressed in the various occasions and celebrations that mark profane and sacred life: Andalusian Spain (Gharnata, Çan'a), West Africa (Fundu, Diwân), Turkey (Zorna), medieval Orient (*Muwashshah*) or contemporay Egypt (repertories of Mohamed Abdelwâhab or of Oum Kalthoum). One of the most significant popular examples of the *métissage* (a combination of cultural features within one sociohistorical field) of Maghribian musical genres and forms is Rai music, which displays both the influence of a secular tradition and a wide-ranging syncretic development.

Many of the endogenous sociocultural traits noted by Bourdieu in the 1960s have changed or simply disappeared under the weight of the socioeconomic and cultural changes that have occurred since independence. One factor contributing to this trend is the phenomenon of rural exodus and mass schooling. Thus, the relationship to the oral tradition, religion, the family (in its broadened understanding), the land, work, and marriage has changed considerably.

Urban children no longer play on swings or with marbles, but instead watch Japanese programs on TV. Young couples more frequently indulge in weddings that combine a good part of the traditional ritual with some fashionable European features at a time when newspapers often denounce the scandalous fate reserved for senior citizens, who are often placed in poorly maintained nursing homes.

Here, as elsewhere, acculturation affects increasingly broad and vital sectors of the Algerian population, exacerbating, even more, a crisis that contains a fundamentally cultural component. Yet, far from being an exclusively negative phenomenon, it is important to recognize that the *metissage* of civilizations (of which, since ancient times, Algeria has been the stage) represents a formidable wager for the future. In many sectors of intellectual and artistic life, new forms are emerging that involve a vital and creative relationship with the indigenous tradition and the often paradoxical representations of modernity.

References

Benabou, Marcel. 1976. *La résistance à la romanisation*. Paris: Maspero.
Bourdieu, Pierre. 1958. *Sociologie de l'Algérie*. Paris: Presses Universitaires de France.
Dermenghem, Emile. 1954. *Le culte des saints dans l'Islam maghrébin*. Paris: Gallimard.
Ibn Khaldoun, Abd al-Rahman. 1863–1866. *Les prolégomènes*, 3 vols. (Traduction De Slane). Paris: Imprimerie imperiale.
Lacheraf, Mostefa. 1988. *Écrits didactiques sur la culture, l'histoire, et la société*. Alger: Enterprise algérienne de presse.
Mammeri, Mouloud. 1991. *Culture savante, culture vécue (Études 1938–1989)*. Alger: Editions Tala.
Yelles, Mourad 1990. *Le hawfi. Poésie féminine et tradition orale au Maghreb*. Alger: Office des Publications Universitaizes.

MOURAD YELLES

See also **Maghrib: Berber Peoples: Their Language and Folklore; Maghrib: Northwestern Africa**

MAGHRIB: BERBER PEOPLES: THEIR LANGUAGE AND FOLKLORE

Introduction

The term *Berber* has been used in Europe by travelers and writers since the sixteenth century to designate some of the inhabitants of North Africa. It continues to be used today in scientific works and in the press. There is no "Berber race" in which one can identify common physical or physiological criteria, and there is no geopolitical entity encompassing the "Berbers." Yet, if one must eliminate labels like "the Berber race," one can nonetheless, refer to "Berber-speaking peoples," because the term *Berber* does identify linguistic commonalities.

In many African states, including Libya, Tunisia, Algeria, Morocco, Mauritania, Mali, Niger, and Burkina-Faso, there are groups of Berber speakers. The Siwa Oasis in Egypt is the easternmost location of Berber speakers, and the Canary Islands were home to speakers of Berber dialects until roughly the fifteenth century, before the Spanish Conquest. The numerical and social importance of Berber-speaking communities is rather variable. There are a few oases such as Ghadames and Ghat in Libya, only certain villages in Tunisia, and some Zenagas sparsely scattered in Mauritania. However, there are probably several hundreds of thousands of Berber-speaking nomads throughout the Sahara, specifically the Tuaregs of Algeria, Mali, Burkina-Faso, and Niger, some of whom have settled in communities due to various climatic and political conditions.

The most compact, and usually the most sedentary, Berber-speaking groups are found in Algeria (at the oases of Mzab, Aures, and Kabylies) and in Morocco (in the Rif, Central and South Atlas, Anti-Atlas, and the Sous Plain). In the western Maghrib, Berber-speaking peoples have long occupied the mountainous zones, including valleys and foothills, with the southern reaches comprised of tillable plains or barren stretches of land. As of the nineteenth century, these populations have emigrated towards urban areas, often undertaking a temporary emigration that permitted sending sustenance to village families. This emigration has accelerated in the past decades, with entire families often joining the father, not only in the large cities of the Maghrib, but also in Europe (especially in France, Belgium, Holland, and Germany). Even North America can claim a few Berber-speaking groups.

It is not easy to evaluate the number of Berber speakers because official censuses, either in African states or in the states receiving their immigrants, do not take their language into consideration. One can offer approximations by relying on estimated percentages of the total population supplied by the state, for example, 1 percent of Tunisia, 20–25 percent for Algeria, and 35 percent or more from Morocco. There are demographic fluctuations, as well as variations due to cultural and political claims of the Berber speakers, that tend to inflate the numbers. Official statistics in the states that do not recognize Berber as a national language tend to reduce the estimated number of its speakers. Although it is recognized as a "national" language in Mali and Niger, nowhere is Berber considered an official language. Around 1990, one could hypothesize the Berberophone world as numbering around fifteen to twenty million individuals.

The structural unity of the Berber language has been well established by linguistic studies, but there is no official Berber standard. Each of the different regions has its language, which can he approximately defined by dialectal traits and by zones of intercomprehension. Intercomprehension may not be complete between speakers from southern Morocco and a Kabyle or a Tuareg from the Sahara, but it may more or less easily occur because of the common linguistic foundation, despite grammatical or lexical differences. In the states where Berber is spoken, and in the areas of emigration, efforts to establish a common language, understood by all and called Amazigh or Tamazight, have begun. There is work being done currently to represent spoken Berber in the written Latin alphabet.

History of Migration and Settlement

It is commonly thought that the Berbers descend from the oldest of the Maghrib (western North Africa) populations. Excavations are more and more methodically performed by archaeologists. Their studies of bones, burial artifacts, tools, drawings, and rock paintings have permitted a tentative chronology. Around 7000 BCE, two human populations lived in the Maghrib. One of them had already been established there for a long time, while the other came from the East and presented Mediterranean characteristics of a diverse nature. Ancient cultural relations with European peoples and even more with the Eastern Mediterranean regions are also apparent. Egyptian data, in addition to that provided by Greek and Roman travelers and historians, provided the first historical accounts of encounters with Berber peoples. Several centuries before the time of Christ, the Phoenicians and then the Punics of ancient Carthage established themselves in North Africa. Their influence continued even after their defeat and the destruction of Carthage by Rome in the second century BCE. The Romans remained in North Africa from 200 BCE until 500 CE and either clashed or united with the Berber tribes, several of which were grouped into more or less stable kingdoms.

As of the seventh century, the Arabs, the carriers of Islam, also encountered Berber resistance; but by the eleventh century, Islam prevailed, due especially to repeated invasions of Hilalian Arab nomads who infiltrated throughout the western regions. Groups of converted Christians and Jews endured for a few centuries. Berber-speaking Jews remain, most notably in Morocco.

Islamization did not occur without conflict, and one of the forms of resistance—as had previously been the case for Christianity—was the constitution of heterodoxical Islamic doctrines maintained by Berber groups and sovereigns. Islamization is a determining factor in Berberophone traditions.

Language

The analysis of the linguistic structures of Berber with respect to the comparison of regional varieties and to the comparison, first with Semitic languages and then with sub-Saharan tongues, has led to formulation of a hypothetical linguistic group with different and coverging strands. Berber is a part of this network, which the French school (represented by Marcel Cohen since 1930) calls Chamito-Semitic, the American linguists name Afro-Asiatic (after Greenberg), and the Russian linguists refer to as Afrasian. This theory, supported by a number of researchers, posits that Berber is a cousin of the Semitic (which includes Arabic and Hebrew), Egyptian, and Cushitic languages, and, at least partly, of the Chadic language.

However, by emphasizing the similarities with the Semitic subfamily, the Eastern origins of Berber and the Berber-speaking peoples has perhaps been exaggerated. In effect, much work remains to be done on the substrata of Berber, in which reside elements even more archaic than Chamito-Semitic structures. This problem is similar to that of a Libyco-Berber script, of unknown origin, geometric in nature (comprised of circles, triangles, crosses, and lines) and observing only consonants, as attested to on archaic engravings (still undated) and on monument inscriptions from the Punic and Roman periods. To date, only a few words can be deciphered, thanks to comparisons to contemporary spoken Berber. The Tuaregs, who still use an alphabet of the same type, do not know how to decipher these ancient inscriptions. Several rather adventurous interpretations have only complicated the matter. Furthermore, the toponyms and anthroponyms transcribed by Greek, Latin, and Arab historians remain the most obscure. There is, therefore, much research yet to be done in this area.

Folklore

An abundant bibliography on Berber folklore exists. One of the first researchers (1829), the American consul to Algiers, W.B. Hodgson, published several studies on Berber lore and bequeathed written data to the National Library of Paris: five songs and six tales, all unedited and probably from Kabylie. But it was only about 1850 that the collection of Berber documents on language, customs, social organization, and verbal arts of Berber-speakers began in earnest. The first motivation was political. The conquest of Algeria in 1830, and of Morocco around 1910, and then the settling in of civil servants forced the French government to get to know the populations to be won, restrained, and administered. Army officers, civil servants, and then university researchers began to increase research. In 1860, an army general published the first Tuareg grammar. Descriptions of the language, the first objective in communication, often contained tales, poems, and notes on customs. In addition, until the liberation of the states of the Maghrib and of Saharan Africa (1956–1962), it was typically clerics like the White Fathers or the Brothers or Sisters of Jesus, descendants of Father de Foucauld, and civil administrators or educators (often Berbers themselves) who were close observers of the terrain, often at the heart of village activities, who left a mass of field notes, some of which has been edited. Travel narratives also constitute a source of information. Universities and other institutions have likewise provided research support and have published reviews such as *Revue Africaine* (Algeria), *Hesperis* (Morocco), and *IBLA* (Tunisia).

Around 1950, a new generation of researchers, ethnologists, and sociologists, who were preoccupied above all with analyzing the complex social structures of Berber groups (such as kinship, the mechanics of opposition and alliance among family and tribal clans, the role of Islam in the older organizations, and the role of the individual), began questioning the validity of fieldwork and that of unconscious presuppositions, all the while not only exploiting results of previous inquiry but also collecting new documents.

Documents based on observation yield information pertaining to facts and to objects: agricultural tools, agrarian practices and rituals (which follow a solar calendar, not the lunar Islamic calendar), such as the start of working the fields, the control of rain, the construction of dwellings, villages, tents, and camps, with their internal and external rules of disposition. They also include information on rites connected to harvests, family celebrations (marriages and births), religious celebrations (Quranic traditions and the cult of saints and pilgrimages). Researchers also studied architecture and the decorative arts, notably the importance accorded to geometric motifs, often archaic, placed on pottery, furnishing, weaving, tattooing, and jewelry in societies where Islam does not permit representation of the human figure.

The spoken word is an important component of these investigations. A still living oral tradition has allowed for a compilation of numerous collections of texts for more than a century (with recordings for the last few decades), whether it be of tales, hagiographic legends, riddles, proverbs, or poems. Songs have been recorded, and the music has been studied by several musicologists. This Islamization of texts is strong, but there remain important fragments of archaic myths. Poems are an integral part of agrarian and marriage rituals. Emigration has partially conserved marriage chants that survive in villages or in nomadic groups along with other ritual chants. Radio and television accelerate the rate of change, which varies according to the region. Manuscripts have also been preserved, with some containing texts of religious treaties, hagiographic legends, and fables that go back to the thirteenth century. There are, likewise, important traces of Berber folklore in the novels and poems written mainly in French by contemporary Berber-speaking authors.

References

Boogert, Nico van den. 1997. *The Berber Literary Tradition of the Sous*, with an edition and translation of *The Ocean of Tears* by Muhammad Awzai (d. 1749). Leiden: Nederlands Instituut voor het Nabije Oosten.

Bougchiche, Lamara. 1997. *Langues et littératures berbères des origines à nos jours. Bibliographie internationale et systématique*. Paris: Ibis Press.

Bynon, James. 1944/1947. Riddle Telling among the Berbers of Central Morocco. In *African Language Studies*. London: The School of Oriental and African Studies, 7: 80–104; 8: 168–97.

Galand, Lionel. 1988. Le berbère. In *Les langues dans le monde ancien et moderne*. Paris: Editions du Centre National de la Recherche Scientifique, vol. 3, pp. 207–42; 303–06.

Harries, Jeanette. 1974. *Tamazight basic course. Aït Mgild dialect*. Madison: University of Wisconsin.

Westermarck, Edward Alexander. 1926. *Ritual and Belief in Morocco*. London: Macmillian.

PAULETTE GALAND-PERNET

See also **Maghrib: Algeria; Maghrib: North Western Africa**

MAKONDE

See **Myths: Myths of Origin and Sculpture: The Makonde; Tourism and Tourist Arts**

MALAGASY

See **Cardinal Directions; Indian Ocean Islands; Malagasy Folklore and Its Study**

MALAGASY FOLKLORE AND ITS STUDY

Malagasy folklore is the product of a line of social relationships that span two and a half centuries and three continents. Fashioned by English, French, and Norwegian missionaries, agents of France's colonial projects, folklorists, ethnologists, and anthropologists, and actors from across the island of Madagascar, Malagasy folklore has in turn shaped the nature of all these groups. In exploring the productivity of Malagasy folklore discourses, it is useful to distinguish the dominant "Western" conception of folklore from what in standard Malagasy is called *vakoka-sy-fomban-drazana*. This latter notion refers to cultural forms and practices marked as traditional and performed and interpreted through such generic frameworks (again, in standard Malagasy) as *fitenin-drazana*, or "words of the ancestors"—*oha-bolana* (proverbs), *angano* (folktales and fables), *ankamantatra* (riddles), *kabary* (oratory), *tantara* (historical narratives believed to be either fact or fiction), and *hainteny* (courting poems, "art of the word"); and *fomban-drazana*, or "customs of the ancestors"—*hiragasy* (folksongs), *dihy* (dances), *fanandrona* (divination), *famadihana, famorana, tao volo*, (secondary burial, circumcision, and first haircutting rituals respectively) and so on. While *vakoka-sy-fomban-drazana* imbibe a sociality associated with a set of highly valued links between ancestors, their descendants, and land, folklore, as a discourse specific to Western modernity, has, until recently, been an uncritical, romantic reaction to capitalism's transformation of such ties between people and places. Discourses on Malagasy folklore involve a complex dialogue between both traditions, along with answers to specific demands issued by the church, the colony, and the nation-state.

The London Missionary Society

Malagasy folkloristics first emerged as an organized and sustained endeavor in the mid 1800s as part of the work of the London Missionary Society (LMS). Arriving in Madagascar in 1818, it was a relatively short time before LMS members founded the Malagasy Folklore Society in 1877, established a forum for the publication of folklore and ethnological writings in the form of the *Antananarivo Annual* (1875–1900), and published a series of important folklore texts (Cousins 1873, Cousins and Parrett 1871, Sibree and Richardson 1886). The construction of Malagasy folklore by LMS members was a remarkably complex and contradictory process. Simultaneously, folklore represented a crucial front in an intense evangelical effort and an integral part of a comprehensive, quasi-scientific discourse on Madagascar and the Malagasy that was inspired by developments in the natural sciences, historical linguistics, and the budding cultural anthropology championed by Edward Tylor. Typical of the period, James Sibree's (1880) text, *The Great African Island* (Sibree was the founder and editor of the *Antannanarivo Annual*), includes chapters on Madagascar's geology, geography, flora, fauna, and "tribes"—their languages, customs, and "folklore." Folklore, for Sibree, consisted primarily of oral literature, "superstitious beliefs," and charms. Customs, on the other hand, under which heading was included material life and "religious beliefs," were understood to be a concern of ethnology.

Perhaps the most interesting feature of Sibree's account, and symptomatic of a contradiction plaguing the work of many of the British missionaries, was the distinction drawn between religious and superstitious beliefs. For the missionaries, Malagasy religious beliefs tied their holders firmly to ancestors rather than God and led to a number of abhorrent practices such as polygamy (an offence which led the great proverb collector William Cousins to expel one of his prize native congregationists). Folklore, on the other hand, was seen as an ambivalent and intermediary realm: superstitious beliefs did not exert such a strong grasp on their subjects, and could thus lead to or away from god, and verbal art (notably proverbs, *hainteny*, and folktales) evidenced a "primitive" Malagasy monotheism. Although such folklore forms were seen by LMS members as providing a path out of fetishism and idolatry in both their content and performance (proverbs and aphorisms were often employed to enliven what many Malagasy saw as dull and artless sermons), they were interpreted by the Malagasy as "ancestral words" and, as such, steeped in traditional authority. The English missionaries were never able to resolve this contradiction.

For a majority of their tenure in Madagascar, the LMS missionaries worked exclusively with the Merina people of the island's high plateau. Insights regarding Merina culture and character were, as a rule, generalized to the rest of the Malagasy population. However, this generalization process was accompanied by two LMS activities that helped articulate the differences between the people of Madagascar. First, LMS members worked closely with the Merina royal courts of King Radama I (1810–1828), King Radama II (1861–1863), Queen Rasoherina (1863–1868), Queen Rananvalona II (1868–1883), and Queen Ranavalona III (1883–1897). From such Anglo/Merina cooperation followed the construction of a variety of schools across the Imerina countryside, the setting of the Malagasy language to Latin script in 1823, the translation and publication of the Bible, and the baptism, in 1869, of Ranavalona II and her husband, Prime Minister Rainilaiarivony. In short, a Christian Merina elite, literate and skilled in the "industrial arts," was now taking shape (Raison-Jourde 1991). Second, facing a growing competition for converts from Lutheran, Catholic, and Anglican newcomers to the island, the LMS missionaries began extending their operations to the Betsileo people in the south as early as 1862 and to the Betsimisaraka and Sinhanaka peoples to the east in the mid 1870s. The missionaries wasted no time in describing and interpreting the cultural life of these peoples and were therefore instrumental in creating and reproducing distinctions not only between a Merina elite and the Merina people more generally, but also between these and the island's other groups whom the Merina had conquered by the end of the nineteenth century.

The Colonial Period

Accompanying the emergence of Madagascar's Christian Merina elite was a rapidly expanding market for Western goods. By 1896, the year Madagascar officially became a colony of France, this market had become the point of articulation to the imperial economy. Seeking to further expand its field of opportunities, French administrators approached the island (especially its fertile coastal regions) as a "colony of exploitation" rather than one of settlement, and thus looked to indigenous recruits to help forge a Malagasy labor force (Jacquier 1904). Fresh from his colonial experiences in Indochina, Governor-General Joseph Gallieni implemented a two-fold strategy for rule in Madagascar: a *politique des races*, designed to place the burden of carrying out colonial directives on the shoulder of the indigenous leaders of the island's different groups, was wedded to a concerted effort to undercut Merina domination. Provincial oversight authority was now given to lineage chiefs and a March 2, 1902, decree legislated the village council (*fokonolona*) as the locus of tax collection and the recruitment of forced labor. These "interior protectorates" failed, however, to attain their desired objective, for a majority of their literate functionaries were Merina living away from their ancestral lands (*tanindrazana*). From the dismantling of the protectorates in January of 1926 to the end of colonization in 1960, the French experimented with a variety of means to control the movement of the Malagasy people and the object of their labor.

French folklore research throughout the colonial period was intimately tied to these changing imperial goals. In February of 1902, Gallieni established the Academi Malgache, an institution whose stated purpose was to "study the Malagasy language and the problems attached to it" (cited in Rabenoro 1982, xvii). The *Bulletin de l'Academie Malgache* quickly became an important publication venue for folklorists. In the pages of the *Bulletin*, and in independently published texts, for example, folktale collections by such authors as Birkeli (1922–1923), Dandouau (1922), Deschamps (1939), Dubois (1938), and Faublee (1947), explored the "mentality" of the Sakalava, Tsimihety, Antaisaka, Betsileo, and Bara "tribes" respectively. As the colonial period wore on, French folklore and ethnology increasingly turned to Malagasy beliefs and customs surrounding death and ancestors (Decary 1962, Berthier 1933). Gillian Feeley-Harnik (1991) has advanced the convincing thesis that an overarching concern with ancestors, widely believed to be a long-standing feature of Malagasy culture, is in fact a relatively recent development, the emergent effect of struggles over labor and loyalty that began with the expansion of the Merina kingdom and evolved through the colonial period into the present.

Nationalist Movements

Gallieni's *politique des races* had the unintended consequences of better positioning elite Merina within existing governmental structures, a consequence that led in turn to a redoubling of the colonial effort to define the divisions between the island's people. Understanding France's strategy in terms of tribalism—that is, as a "weapon used . . . to hinder the coming together of the popular masses" (Esoavelamandroso 1989, 265)—a Malagasy nationalist movement emerged that, among other things, looked to folklore to imagine a Malagasy community. Among the important nationalist groups to appear during this period were the Iron Stone Network (Vy, Vato, Sakelika)—an organization that had evolved from associations established years earlier among leaders of Madagascar's Young Men's Christian Association—and the Democratic Movement for Malagasy Renovation (MDRM), a party co-founded by the important poet from the Besimisarka region, Jacques Rabemananjara.

In his plays *Agape des dieux tritriva* (1962) and *Les boutriers de l'aurore* (1957), Rabemananjara masterfully adapted Malagasy folktales to the stage, a practice established by his older friend and colleague, the popular Malagasy poet Jean-Joseph Rabearivelo. Rabearivelo, a tragic figure who ended his own life at the young age of 36, also worked creatively with and within the *hainteny* tradition (1967, 1990). Other Malagasy artists who turned to folklore to stress the unity of the island's people included Ny Avana Ramanantoanina (1992) and Flavien Ranaivo (1949). Many of these writers worked critically with the Malagasy concepts of *embona* and *hanina*, notions that resemble the Western concepts of nostalgia and longing, and which were employed to affect a return to pre-European, Malagasy values (see Rajaobelina 1948). Finally, those Malagasy folklorists working within the nationalist, anticolonial context included Maurice Rasamuel (1950), Dama Ntsoha (1953) (both of whom carried out extensive research on proverbs), H. Randzavola (1931), and Ravelojaona (1937).

Seeking to undermine the growing nationalist sentiment, French authorities argued that such groups as the MDRM actually concealed a movement, on the part of the Merina elite, to return to precolonial forms of domination. In the summer of 1946, the French orchestrated the creation of the Party of the Disinherited of Madagascar (PADESM). The French term *desherites* was widely understood at the time to refer specifically to the island's non-Merina population, and the party was, above all else, a political arm of France's *guerre tribal* ("tribal war"). Today, a lively debate exploring the links between French involvement with PADESM (and the party's more recent political descendants) and the poverty and turmoil of contemporary Madagascar is taking place on the World Wide Web rages on.

Contemporary Scholarship

Since the end of the colonial period, discourses on Malagasy folklore have continued to be instrumental in creating and reproducing divisions and unities among the people of Madagascar. These discourses, however, have grown increasingly reflexive and complex, as scholars from Madagascar and abroad turn their attention to issues of social change and relations of domination and subordination. A few examples will suffice to illustrate this trend. Working at the formal and thematic levels with a variety of texts co-constructed by performers and collectors in the central highlands, Paul Ottino (1966) has proposed that Madagascar represents the westernmost pole of a Malayo-Polynesian culture whose characteristic "tendency" toward semantic equivocality and ambiguity emerges fully in the complex metaphorical work and generic allusions of the *hainteny*. Regarding the function of Malagasy verbal artistry, Ottino believes that by mythologizing ruling class ideologies, oral narratives have served to smooth over the contradictions between kinship and hierarchy attending the emergence of the Merina state (Ottino 1991).

The links between verbal artistry and the contradictions of state formation in Madagascar also concern the preeminent Malagasy student of *hainteny* and proverbs, Bakoly Domenichinini-Ramiaramanana, who argues that the former genre emerged, rather, to mediate such tensions. The American folklorist Lee Haring has pushed Ottino's work forward in a number of important directions. Firmly rooted in the intertextual study of Malagasy narrative (his *Malagasy Tale Index* [1982] is by far the finest in the genre), Haring is well positioned to argue that a "generative binary principle," operative in both Western Indian Ocean and Malagasy verbal art, has enabled performers and audiences in Madagascar to explore novel interpretive frameworks in resistance to hegemonic mythologies (1992).

Contemporary Current Scholarship

Distinct from Ottino and Haring's efforts to define the nature of a broad Western Indian Ocean cultural complex, scholars such as Philippe Beaujard and Lucien X. Michel-Andrianarahinjaka have instead focused on contextualizing the expressive behavior of Madagascar's Tanala and Betsileo peoples. Beaujard's (1991) analysis of some 250 *tantara* suggests that, thematically, the historical narratives provide a charter coherence to the constitutive division in Tanala society separating a late-coming "noble" class with ties to Islam from a more original group of "commoners" (*tompon-tany*, or "masters of the land"). In an earlier work, Beaujard argued that in fighting the erosion of their primary values brought about by the state's reform of the village council structure in the 1970s, many Tanala communities turned to funerals and the ceremonial construction of the lineage chief's house (the *tranobe*), both rituals "wherein the affirmation of ancient values is exacerbated" (1983, 407). In his monumental effort, *The Betsieo Literary System* (1986), Michel-Andrianarahinjaka approaches Betsileo oral literature as a complex semiological system and painstakingly defines the contours of its hierarchically related genres. Formerly the president of Madagascar's National Assembly, Michel-Adrianarahinjaka's efforts in writing the text and in deciding to publish it in the Betsileo capital of Fianarantsoa represents an attempt to thrust Betsileo artistry upon a national stage.

Finally, a number of studies building upon the ethnography of speaking and performance traditions explore the problem of social change. Elinor Ochs Keenan (1973) examines how highland Vakinankaratra participants of bride price oratories manipulate the gendered participant frameworks and other structural features of the genre to bridge intracultural differences resulting from French colonialism. More recently, in his analysis of discourses on need that link international conservation and development actors associated with the Ranomanafama National Park and area Tanala communities, Hanson (2000) demonstrates how the form/function relations specific to oral historical, oratorical, and ritual performances help mediate the contradictions attending the rapid expansion of agrarian capitalism in the region.

As Madagascar's relative insularity gives way to a variety of global horizons, Malagasy folklore is increasingly entering the realm of public culture. Many Malagasy, for example, living in the United States, France, and Japan, have established organizations that, with the help of folklore performances, allow them to define and celebrate their national and group identities (one example is the Washington D.C.-based Madagascar Cultural Alliance). Folklore is also proving to be an important part of Madagascar's rapidly developing ecological tourism industry. Ownership of and access rights to the four and a half million hectares of land now enclosed by close to forty protected areas is currently a highly contested issue. A surprising feature of this ongoing struggle over labor and land is that the folklore forms of many of the Malagasy groups living beside the enclosures have simultaneously served the interests of the groups themselves and the protected area planners (Hanson 1997). As the two preceding examples suggest, exciting directions do exist for the study of Malagasy folklore.

References

Beaujard, Philippe. 1983. *Princes et paysans: les tanala de l'kongo*. Paris: Editions L'Harmattan.

———. 1991. *Mythe et societe a Madagascar: le chasseur d'oiseaux et al princesse du ciel*. Paris: Editions L'Harmattan.

Birkeli, Emile. 1922–1923. Folklore sakalava recueilli dans la region de Morondava. *Bulletin de l'Academie Malgache* 6.

Berthier, Hugues. 1933. *Notes et impressions sure les moeurs et coutumes du peuple magache*. Antananarivo: Imprimerie Officelle.

Cousins, William. 1873. *Malagasy Kabary from the time of Andrianampoinimerina*. Antananarivo: Press of the London Missionary Society.

Cousins, William, and J. Parrett. 1871. *Malagasy Proverbs*. Antananarivo. LMS Press.

Dama-Ntsoha. 1953. *La technique de la conception de la vie chez les malgaches revelee par leurs proverbes*. Tananarive: Masoandro.

Dandouau, Andre. 1922. *Contes populaires des sakalava et des tsimihety de la region d'Analalava*. Publications de la Faculte des Lettres d'Alger; Bulletin de Correspondance Africaine, 58. Alger: Jules Carbonel.

Decary, Raymond. 1962. *La mort et les coutumes funeraires a Madagascar*. Paris: G. P. Maisonneurve et Larose.

Deschamps, Hubert. *Folklore antaisaka*. 1939. Bulletin de l'Academie Malgache 22:113–29.

Domenichini-Ramiaramanana, Bakoly. 1983. *Du ohabolana au hainteny: langue, litterature, et politique a Madagascar*. Paris: Karthala.

Dubois, Henri. *Monographie des Betsileo*. 1938. Paris: Institut d'Ethnographie.

Esoavelomandroso, Manasse. 1989. Une arme de domination: le "tribalisme" a Madagascar. In *Les ethnies ont une histoire*, pp. 259–65. Eds. Jean-Pierre Chretien and Gerard Prunier. Paris: Karthala.

Faublee, Jacques. 1947. *Recits Bara*. Paris: Institut d'Ethnographie.

Feeley-Harnik, Gillian. 1991. *A Green Estate: Restoring Independence in Madagascar*. Washington, D.C.: Smithsonian Institution Press.

Hanson, Paul. 1997. *The Politics of Need Interpretation in Madagascar's Ranomafana National Park*. Ph.D. Dissertation, The University of Pennsylvania.

——— 2000. Women in Action, Councils in Change: The Productivity of Women's Speech Styles in Madagascar's Ranomafana National Park. *Taloha* (Revue du musée d'Art et d'Archéologic, Antananarivo) 13: 263–294. *Special Issue: Rethinking 'La Femme Malgache'. New Perspectives on Gender in Madagascar*. Eds. Sophie Blanchy, Sarah Fee and Lala Raherin Jahary.

Haring, Lee. 1982. *Malagasy Tale Index*. FF Communications no. 231. Helsinki: Soumalainen Tiedeakatemia.

———. 1992. *Verbal Arts in Madagascar: Performance in Historical Perspective*. Philadelphia: University of Pennsylvania Press.

Jacquier, L. 1904. *La main-d'oeuvre locale a Madagascar*. Paris: Henri Jouve.

Keenan, Elinor Ochs. 1973. A Sliding Sense of Obligatoriness: the Polystructure of Malagasy Oratory. *Language in Society* 2:225–43.

Michel-Andrianarahinjaka, Lucien X. 1986. *Le systeme litteraire betsileo*. Fianarantsoa: Editions Ambozontany.

Ottino, Paul. 1966. Un procede litteraire malayo-polynesien. De 'ambiguite a la pluri signification. *L'Homme, revue francais d'anthropologie* 6:5–34.

———. La mythologie malgache des hautes terres. Le cycle politique des Andriambaoaka. In *Mythologies*. Ed. Yves Bonnefoy. 2 vols. Chicago: University of Chicago Press, 1991, 961–976.

Rabearivelo, Jean-Joseph. *Vieilles chansons des pays d'Imerina*. Tananarive: Editions Madprint, 1967.

———. *Poemes*. 1990. Paris: Editions Hatier.

Ravemananjara, Jacques. 1957. *Les Boutriers de l'aurore*. Paris: Editions Presence Africaine.

———. *Agapes des Dieux Tritriva*. 1962. Paris: Editions Presence Africaine.

Rabenoro, C. L'Academie Malgache octogenaire. 1982. *Bulletin de l'Academie Malgache* 60, xvii–xxi.

Ramanantaonina, Ny Avana. 1992. *Anthologie*. Antananarivo: Imprimerie Nationale.

Raison-Jourde, Francoise. 1991. *Bible et pouvoir a Madagascar au XIXe siecle*. Paris: Editions Karthala.

Rajaobelina, Prosper. Nostalgie dans la poesie malgache. *Revue de Madagascar* 3 (1948) 67–75.

Ranaivo, Flavien. Les hain-teny. 1949. *La revue de Madagascar* 7, 55–81.

Randzavola, H. 1931. *Fomba malagasy* (Work originally be W.E. Cousins with renovation and augmentation by Randzavola). Antananarivo: Imp. LMS.

Rasamuel, Maurice. 1950 *Ny fitenin-drazana*. Tananarie: Ny Antsiva.

Ravelojaona, B. 1937. *Firaketana ny fiteny sy ny zavatra malagasy*. Antananarivo: Fianinana.

Sibree, James. 1880. *The Great African Island: Chapters on Madagascar*. London: Trubner.

Sibree, James & Richardson, J. *Folk-tales and Folk-lore of Madagascar*. Antananarivo: LMS Press, 1886.

Zaikabe. 1998. Http://home.cwnet.com/zaikabe.

PAUL W. HANSON

See also **French Study of African Folklore; Government Policies toward Folklore; Myths**

MALAWI

Located in southern Africa, Malawi is a small subtropical country of some 10.98 million people. The landlocked country is surrounded by Tanzania, Mozambique, Zimbabwe, and Zambia. Lilongwe, Malawi's capital city, is home to 268,000 people. The population is predominantly Chewa, which accounts for 90 percent of the country's ethnic groups. The remaining 10 percent consist of Nyanja, Lomwe, and other Bantu-speaking groups. Chichewa, English, Nyanja, Yao, Sena, and Tumbuka are the most commonly spoken languages in Malawi. Three-fourths of the population is Christian, 20 percent is Muslim, and 5 percent practices traditional indigenous religions.

First called the British Protectorate of Nyasaland in 1841, the country has always been linked to Zimbabwe (formerly, Southern Rhodesia) and Zambia (formerly, Northern Rhodesia). On July 6, 1964, Malawi gained its independence from Britain and succeeded in forming its own one-party dictatorship. After several years of political unrest under this very repressive regime, Malawi held its first multiparty elections in May of 1994 and subsequently became a multiparty democracy. Since independence, Malawi has had a relatively stable economy, largely due to its production and exportation of agricultural products such as tobacco, tea, sugar, and cotton. Due to the poor distribution of land, however, most of Malawi's rural population has not reaped any of the benefits of the economy, as successful agricultural production has largely been the product of the country's large plantations and not the small landholders. Since 1981, the Malawian government has increased incentives to small landholders. The rural population, however, is still largely impoverished. Although adult literacy is only 56 percent, there is a good school system. As of 2003, more than 2 million people are infected with HIV/AIDS in Malawi, 60% of whom are women. This epidemic has lowered average life expectancy to 37 years.

JENNIFER JOYCE

MALI (REPUBLIC OF MALI)

Located in western Africa, Mali is an arid, landlocked country surrounded by Algeria, Niger, Burkina Faso, Cote D'Ivoire, Guinea, Senegal, and Mauritania. Mali has a population of nearly 12.5 million. Bamako, the country's capital and largest city, is home to 894,000 people. Half of all Malians are Mande, 17 percent are Peul, 12 percent are Voltaic, 6 percent are Songhai, 10 percent are Tuareg and Moor, and 5 percent are made up of various smaller ethnic groups. Mali's official language is French; however, Bamanakan, Mandinka, Voltaic, Tamacheg, Dogon, Fulde, Songhai, and Malinke are also widely spoken. The population is 90 percent Muslim, 9 percent practice traditional indigenous religions, and the remaining 1 percent is Christian.

Beginning in 1100 CE and lasting until the eighteenth century, the great Mali empire extended over much of West Africa. Sundiata Keita, the founder of the empire, is internationally recognized because the epics of his life are still performed, and several versions have been written down and published. His story is well known throughout the country and is a great source of national pride. By the late 1400s, the Songhai empire gained control over the region and reigned until the late 1500s. At the height of the empire, some of the greatest centers of learning, religion, and the arts, such as Jenne, Gao, and Timbuktu, flourished. In 1890, Mali was colonized by the French.

On September 22, 1960, Mali gained its independence from France and became a one-party republic committed to state socialism. In 1992 the country's first multiparty elections since independence were held, thereby ending the previous authoritarian political regime. Taureg insurgents have caused disruptions for the last few decades; since 1992, there has been a special administrative unit for them. These are the famous Blue Men, so-called because of their heavily dyed indigo robes, who still manage caravans crossing the Sahara.

One of the poorest countries in world, Mali has been plagued by a weak economy. Agricultural production has been hampered by drought, desertification, and locust infestation. Consequently, the country has not been successful in producing enough food for its population and has had to rely on international food donations and importation. The economy has had a recent boost, however, due to the growth of mining industries that export gold, marble, uranium, and phosphates.

Mali is internationally recognized for its great cultural diversity in which local Kora music, puppet theaters, elaborate carvings, and the songs of epic praise poems have developed and flourished. Thousands of tourists each year visit the museums, historical sites, and mosques of Bamako, Jenne, Gao, and Timbuktu. Malian musicians and singers, such as the Super Rail Band, Salif Keita, Ali Farka Toure, and Habib Koite have become some of the best known African performers in the United States and Europe.

PHILIP M. PEEK

MALINKE

See Epics

MAMI WATA IN CENTRAL AFRICA

Mami Wata, a spiritual entity, whose images and representations are widespread in Africa, continues to be the source of many popular practices and knowledge. She has been the object of much academic preoccupation for about thirty years (Fabian 1978, 315–34; Drewal 1988, 160–85), and constitutes a nexus where power relations, knowledge, and social and cultural stakes express themselves with all their contradictions in contemporary society. She also expresses the presence of a complex social imagery with a multitude of meanings. In Central Africa, more than in West Africa, her names in local languages demand the search for deeper meanings in the history and the culture of Congo River societies where Mami Wata is the fruit and the expression of ceaseless cultural transfers. This process is due to the contact between local societies themselves, and between them and Christian foreigners engaged in the sea trade from the fifteenth to the nineteenth centuries (MacGaffey 1982; Thornton 1996). In other respects, this labored cultural crossbreeding, which went on under colonization and imposed the modern state and its problems, then experienced the postcolonial society and its crises. This historical aspect ended up by allotting Mami Wata her real meaning and autonomy as social practice in a global society.

Etymology

Mami Wata, lexically derives from the English "mother of water" or "grand-mother of water" in the Agni language from Cote d'Ivoire. She is the water spirit of West Africa whose traces are also found in Surinam and in the Caribbean. In Nigeria, among some Igbo peoples, she represents Ogbwide, the female deity and spouse of the deity Urashi, the two, a divine couple living in the Oguta River. During the religious ceremonies in her honor, her followers offer her sacrifices, sing, dance, eat, and drink. The possession and the trance that Mami Wata causes reproduce, as well, the life cycle of the deity as they display her presence among living beings. The processions of disciples on the river often crown an initiation process leading to the mastery of her knowledge and its therapeutic power (Jell-Bahlsen 1991).

Mami Wata is recognized in various forms all along the Guinea Coast as well as in certain Sahel areas where there are significant lakes and rivers. Her altars such as those in Ouidah, Dahomey, or in Accra, Ghana, are splendidly decorated, and highlight the serpent, her symbol. These shrines attract many visitors, researchers, and tourists.

Links with Immigration and Urbanism

In Central Africa, her many names and her current representations are also linked to the double phenomenon of immigration of West African workers and of the birth of contemporary urbanity during the colonial period. These two phenomena favored an intensive religious acculturation between the West African religions and those of the center of Africa through Mami Wata. In this process of surrender and acquisition, Mami Wata underwent changes linked to concomitant modernization of Central Africa countries and acquired new meanings when she simultaneously adjusted to the cultures and the imaginary of the Congo River and its numerous tributaries. She was grafted to Nzondo, or Ndjonibo, the deity of the river who preceeded her. Nzondo, mentioned for the first time in the Kongo Kingdom by Cavazzi in the sixteenth century (Ceyssens 1975, 534–35), is a one-eyed fish from the Congo River that is identified with the mythical serpent producer of the rainbow. In the twentieth century Nzondo identifies itself with the protopterus, the flying fish. In the middle of the Congolese forest, called Nsembe, it easily reaches more than 6 feet. More expressively than the Kongo people from the mouth of the Congo River, the Mongo and the Luba peoples describe this spirit as being woman and fish at the same time, thus placing her within worldwide mythology, as a mermaid or siren figure. She has teats, flies through the air, and enjoys palm nuts. As soon as a person catches sight of her in a palm tree, she quickly dives again into the water. As a fish she attacks and tears to shreds other small animals and becomes a cannibal when attacked. She causes the death of any incautious person who surprises her "sleeping" when she hibernates wrapped in her cocoon within a vase. Then she punishes the offender with *fonoli*, a deadly madness. That person disappears into the forest where he or she rambles until overcome by death (Biaya 1988, 104, 118).

Even after having fallen from grace, this divine spirit has kept all the divine power and the rank of an elder among God's creatures. In Lokele society, Nsembe introduced copper as a dowry value. In Sudanese societies located between Ubangui and Congo Rivers, Mami Wata is Lufulakari, an ogre-spirit who swallows ships and urban migrant workers from this region. Her main characteristic is the ability to change shapes. She especially possesses women, whom she makes childless. The treatment expels Mami Wata from the body of the sick woman by reconciling the woman with the spirit, and it rearticulates the patient's psyche with the sacred aggressor, the Ancestor (Sow 1978, 14).

Today, these ways of thought and healing cults, which were initially located in rural areas, have became urbanized and have borrowed features from Christianity and Islam (Janzen 1992). In this process, rituals that we see occurring in Kinshasa, Brazzaville, and Bangui, without deserting their ancient premises, have accepted and integrated the West African myth of Mami Wata as a seductive water spirit as well as a means of representing modernity's conquest. However, this dimension of the seducing spirit and femininity of Mami Wata that local townspeople added shows the perverse effects of colonial ideology. As a matter of fact, these newcomers in town had to become modernized by cutting themselves off from village society and its traditional culture. They longed for the status of cultural intermediaries of the Belgian or French colonizers that West Africans called Pupu, Sawa, Sinangale, Bahuza, and so on. These individuals, often Muslims, held subordinate positions as foremen, postmen, assistants, or were independent traders and shop owners in the black cities. In this quest for modernity, the local colonized people would appeal to West Africans to give them charms to get jobs, money, fecundity charms, or love filters, thereby welcoming Mami Wata.

Portrayals

Mami Wata entered Central Africa from the realm of traditional belief and witchcraft practices made of secret knowledge and power. In West Africa, she is the object of a public cult. She borrowed the outlines and contents from local gods. Her metamorphoses led her to incarnate the metaphor and the paradigm of unusual and individual success. This social and political success, which is also mastery of modernity, is related to an exchange pact with a human life, preferably that of a close relative, which, handed over as due, guarantees an increase in established power or social benefit. It is this relationship, established between the two contractors, that constitutes the sustaining pillar of success, or the downfall of the subject that can lead to his/her own death when that relationship is broken.

Mami Wata's thirst for fresh blood did not initially have sexual or erotic connotations. In Central Africa, she is constructed like an androgynous being since her/his lovers are of both sexes, according to the discourse on witchcraft as the place of strong powers increasing mythical, pictorial and sung narrations (Fourche and Morlighern 1973; Kalanda 1993; Tonda 1988, 73–83).

In other respects, popular artists sing, dance, and picture Mami Wata in her various aspects, recounting her evolution simultaneously. In popular culture, the Mami Wata icon is read like a social fresco revealed through a pictorial narration. Her representation as a woman with a fish tail appeared around the end of colonization; she has been taking on, year after year, the appearance of a light-skinned siren with long hair and now appears in modern fashions (jewels, wrist-watch, earrings, and so on) (Jewsiewicki 1991, 130–51). Mami Wata become a combined reproduction of movie stars and advertisement bill postings that were newly offered to the urban African public after World War II. Indeed, often she is resting under the sun on an island or at the river bank. Her representation fluctuates according to the demands of the market; pictorial narrative follows the trends and impulses of social and political movements. When the economic and political situation reaches a crisis stage, Mami Wata reverts to a mythical being. She is painted in a serpent shape, copulating with a rich, naked female spinster, only to vomit money after fleshly satisfaction. The revelation of the secret by the human lover of the beautiful woman is punished by death. This vigorous return to the sacred, and its ascendancy over social belief as a means of mastering crisis, was restored after this icon underwent extensive reconsideration in better times, approximately 1974–1981 (Jewsiewicki 1995).

Mami Wata, beneath all the layers of metamorphosis, summarizes the difficulties faced daily by Central African peoples, both under colonization and in postcolonial societies, where state violence has become the only visible manifestation of power. She also denounces the presence of a wealthy elite. Paradoxically, the political bourgeoisie also has recourse to Mami Wata and her witchcraft practices, through ideologies and mystic procedures that manipulate the major symbols of ancient and modern political power to maintain and reinforce their ascendancy over the common people. The example of presidents Mobutu and Sassou Ngessou, with their political classes calling on Mami Wata as an image of the sacred, of power, and of access to wealth (Ndaywell 1993) illustrates the essential ambiguity and ambivalence of Mami Wata, whose infinite use and interpretations show that she is, above all, a polysemic metaphor and that she is open to infinite interpretations (Rush 1992, 60). Mami Wata appears as a cultural potentiality, which Central African societies with oral cultures posses manipulate as they "write" their history.

References

Bayart, J.F. 1993. *The State in Africa. The Politics Belly.* London: Longman.

Biaya, T.K. 1988. L'impasse de la crise Zairois dans la peinture urbaine. *Canadian Journal of African Studies*, 22, no. 1:95–124.

———. 1990. La peinture populaire comme mode d'action des classes dominees au Zaire, 1960–1989. *Contemporary French Civilization*, XIV:334–57.

Ceyssens, R. 1975. Mutumbala, Mythe de l'opprime. *Cultures et Developpements* 8:3–5, 485–550.

Drewal, H. J. 1988. Performing the Other: Mami Wata Worship in West Africa. *The Drama Review* 118: 160–85.

Fabian J. 1978. Popular culture in Africa: Findings and Conjectures. *Africa.* 48:315–34.

———. 1996. *Remembering the Present. Painting and Popular History in Zaire.* Berkeley: University of California Press.

Fourche J., and H. Morlighem. 1973. *Une Bible Noire.* Bruxelles: M. Arnold.

Janzen, J. M. 1992. *Ngoma. Discourses of Healing in Central and Southern Africa.* Berkeley: University of California Press.

Jell-Bahlsen, S. 1991. *Mami Wata: In Search of the Water Spirit in Nigeria.* Film. Berkeley: University of California. Extension Media Center.

Jewisiewicki, B. 1991. Painting in Zaire. From The Invention of West to Representation of Social Self. In *Africa Explores: Twentieth-Century African Art,* ed. S. and I. Ebong. Vogel New York: Center for African Art.

———. 1995. *Cheri Samba. The Hybridity of an Art.* Montreal: The AGAA Publication.

Kalanda M. 1993. *La revelation Tyakani.* Kinshasa: L.A. S.K.

MacGaffey. W. 1982. *Modern Kongo Prophets.* Bloomington: Indiana University Press.

Ndaywell, I. 1993. *La societe Zairoise dans le miroir son de discours religieux (1990–1993).* Bruxelles: CEDAF Institut africain.

Rush, D. 1992. The Convulsive Beauty of Mami Wata. MA Thesis in Art History, University of Iowa.

Sow, I. 1978. *Psychiatrie dynamique africaine.* Paris: Payot.

Tonda, J. 1988. Marx et l'ombre des fetiches d'un pouvoir local contre *njobi* dans le Nord-Congo. *Politique africaine* 31:73–83

Thornton, J.K. 1996. *The Kongolese Saint-Antony: D. Beatriz Kimpa Vita, 1684–1706.* Cambridge, U.K.: Cambridge University Press.

T.K. BIAYA

See Also **Cosmology; Gender Representation in African Folklore; Government Policies toward Folklore**

MANCALA

Mancala (also Mankala or Manqala) refers to a group of board games in which counters are distributed in order to make a move. Mancala is frequently encountered in the shape of a board with rows of holes and a proportionate number of counters. During the game, the players, usually two or two teams (with rare variations allowing for three or more parties), take turns in distributing counters around the board. The counters, commonly seeds, shells, or stones are of equal value and may change ownership during the game. In most cases, players start with the contents of a hole at their side of the board. In all Mancala variations, these contents may be distributed one by one in consecutive holes. The holes may be carved in a board or dug in the sand but are also found as drawn circles. The configuration of these holes divides Mancala into two main variations. In the first variation the holes form one circle in which the counters are distributed or spread around. In most of those examples, the holes will be lined up in two rows, although three-row, circular, and rectangular configurations are also known. In the second variation, the holes form two separate circles in which the counters are distributed, shaping the board in four, or even six, rows of holes. Counters often remain in one of the two circles except when captures are being made.

The object of Mancala is to capture the majority of the counters. In some variations, one can also win by immobilizing the opponent. Two types of capture can be distinguished. In one, the capture is made when a specific number of counters, commonly three or four, is accumulated in one hole. The other type of capture is made when a certain position is reached, and, for instance, the contents of neighboring holes are captured. Captured counters are taken from the game or, as in some four-row games, are spread back in the rows of the player who captured them.

Both the materials, the boards and counters, and the rules of Mancala have provided insight into the history of this group of games. Material evidence has so far provided the earliest evidence of Mancala. Museum collections of predominantly wooden boards date back to the beginning of the nineteenth century. The data on boards in museum files only indicate the date they entered the collections and sometimes stipulate the purpose of the object or the name of the game. They rarely identify the owners, former players, or dates of making or using the board, which would predate the acquisition of the board by the museum. If these factors are taken into account, it would date these wooden boards back to perhaps the late eighteenth century.

Archaeological evidence suggests that the occasional terracotta and stone Mancala boards date back to the first centuries CE. In these cases, it is not always clear that the objects were used for playing Mancala. Although the precise age of stone boards appears difficult to determine, it is generally believed that some examples go back to the sixth century CE or earlier. Boards found in ancient Egypt would predate existing evidence by a few thousand years. The absence of game rules and the possible

The game known as *Owela*, which is popular in Namibia, is one of the largest mancala games and often is played with two teams. Photo © Alex de Voogt.

recently has Asian Mancala received serious attention, and large parts of the Middle East and Central Asia are poorly investigated. The thesis that Mancala originated in Africa is largely based on speculation and limited evidence from Asia.

Among the many descriptions of Mancala rules, specific sets of rules are found to be similar across large parts of the Asian or African continent. These distribution patterns follow known migration or trade routes. Rules found in the Caribbean have also been described for West African games and date back to the African slave trade; the Swahili-speaking people along the East African coast appear to play the same Mancala variation that is linked to the Swahili trade routes; and rules found in the Philippines are almost identical to those in parts of Indonesia, Malaysia, and the Maldives, which date back to contact prior to the thirteenth century.

The Caribbean game of Wari, a two-row Mancala game, and the East African game of Bao, a four-row Mancala game, are best known for tournaments and players' clubs. Other games are played at home by women and children or during particular ceremonies. Such ceremonies or rituals include weddings, funerals, divination, or ceremonies involving royalty. In some areas, this means that the game is never played at night, as has been recorded for the Caribbean. In other areas, the game is played during any festive occasion, as long as there is time to play. Certain sculptured boards became prestige gifts for royalty and were never played or intended for play.

The distribution of counters around the board and the distribution of Mancala rules around the world have been central in Mancala studies. Mancala boards are also part of art historical studies, which concentrate on the aesthetic qualities of Mancala boards rather than the distribution or history of Mancala. Sculptured Mancala boards have played a role as prestige gifts, particularly in West Africa. Plain boards appear to gain aesthetic value when intensive play smoothens the surface, providing wooden boards with an attractive shine.

A recent use of Mancala in computer science and psychological studies has augmented the use of Mancala outside Asia and Africa. The computational aspects of some Mancala variations puts them in the same league as draughts and certain strategic Asian board games. The distribution of counters around the board has made Mancala the most volatile group of board games, compared to games recently programmed by computer scientists. In psychology, Mancala is used in studies on human memory and problem solving and also in developmental and educational studies. It appears that the moves particular to Mancala require cognitive skills that differ from skills studied in players of other board games.

Mancala is defined primarily by the distribution of counters in consecutive holes. Simple and complex rules exist for different Mancala variations, but the purpose of the game, or even the boards, cannot be generalized. Hundreds of variations of rules and boards have been recorded, while, at the same time, similar rules may be found across the continents. At present, Mancala is thought to be older than most board games, and evidence suggests that Mancala has been, and still is, the most widespread group of board games in the world.

References

Deledicq, A., and A. Popova. 1977. *Wari et solo. Le jeu de calcul Africain*. Paris: Cedic.

confusion with other Egyptian board games prevent conclusions in this direction. Since Mancala is also played in the sand, it is not inconceivable that Mancala predates all other existing board games; evidence to this effect is not available.

Mancala rules have been recorded since the 1650s. Earlier mention of the game in Arabic sources has given it the name Mancala, derived from the Arabic *naqala* meaning "to transfer" or "to move things about." The written sources do not predate the archaeological finds, but recent studies of Mancala rules have given insight into the distribution of Mancala. This distribution has been linked to migration routes, which may go back several hundred years. Mancala is played in most parts of Africa, the Middle East, parts of Central, and most of South and South East Asia. The game was introduced to South America and the Caribbean during the African slave trade. Immigrants have played the game in Europe and North America, and commercial and souvenir versions have also reached the Europeans and Americans themselves.

The two-row variation is found in all the above regions of the world. Three-row versions are known mostly in Ethiopia and four-row in East and Southern Africa with few exceptions. Hundreds of variations have been described in Africa, a few dozen for Asia, and only a handful for the Caribbean. Only

Murray, H. J. R. 1952. *A History of Board Games other than Chess.* London: Oxford, at the Clarendon Press.

Townshend, P. 1979. Mankala in Eastern and Southern Africa: A Distributional Analysis. *Azania* 14:109–38.

Voogt, A.J. de 1997. *Mancala Board Games.* London: British Museum Press.

Walker, R. A. 1990. Sculptured Mankala Gameboards of Sub-Saharan Africa. Ph.D. dissertation. Indiana University.

ALEX DE VOOGT

See also **Bao; Wari**

MANGBETU

See **Body Arts, Hair Sculpture**

MAQALAT: CONCEPTS OF FOLKLORE IN THE SUDAN

The Muslim-Arab Rubatab of northern Sudan identify an array of their discourse genres as *maqalat* (singular, *maqala*). The word *maqalat* is the passive participle of the verb *yaqul* ("to say"). *Maqalat* are described by the Rubatab as anonymous, traditional, and orally transmitted artistic or fictitious discourses. Unarguably, these Rubatab criteria are congruent with these contemporary folklore scholars use in defining the materials of their discipline. One can therefore argue that maqalat is a folk gloss on the academic idea of folklore itself (Herzfeld 1983).

Rubatab emphasize the anonymity of *maqalat*. An informant said a *maqala* is handed down and "Ma maqtu'a min al-ras" (lit., "cut from the head," not created by a known individual), and its anonymity is defined as the futility of trying to *tasinda* (attribute them) to known creators.

To underline the traditional aspect of maqalat, the Rubatab insist that *maqalat* do not qualify without having a chain of transmission. They are described as "kalam ba'id aw tarikh aw qadim" (past, historical, or ancient discourses). An informant even broke down *maqalat* to its root, *qal* (said), and repeated "qal, qal, qal" to emphasize the chain of its transmission. Telling about one's firsthand experience, according to an informant, is not a *maqala* but a *wanasa* (casual talk). To clarify the importance of oral transmission, a literate informant referred to the *'an'ana* (chain of transmission) in Prophet Muhammad's *hadith* (his sayings and practices). To verify the authenticity of a *hadith*, Islamic scholars would scrutinize its chain of transmission and accept it or dismiss it on the basis of the character and authority of the men who recorded it for posterity.

With respect to the oral transmission of *maqalat*, Rubatab emphasize their circulation as a consequence of people applying them to current situations. Three processes are mentioned by which these old creations are reproduced in the present: *ta'qib* (repetition), *jar* (dragging one to illuminate a current situation), and *darb mathal* (to analogize). One would say "y 'mlat al-maqala" (as the maqala said) as a key to applying a maqala to an emerging situation.

Rubatab are so intrigued by their maqalat that they often engage in discussing their artistic nature. There is a gender difference in understanding maqalat. Men are inclined to view maqalat as fictitious and thus doubt their veracity. An informant said the maqala can be "hasla wa mahasla, mafi zul yaqdar" ("It could have happened and it could have not. No one can be certain"). Another informant said a maqalat can be truthful, but he did not feel contradicted when someone else said it could also be false.

The ambiguity of maqalat is revealed in conversations and in Rubatab folktales. One folktale tells about a young man who could not find a match in any of the village girls paraded in front of him by a matchmaker, an old woman. In desperation, the old woman rebuked him saying:

"You will only be married to al-Lu'ayb, I think."
"And who is this Lu'ayb?"
"Don't be ridiculous. This is a mere maqala"
"You wouldn't have mentioned her to me had it been only so."

The young man cajoled the old woman to reveal the place of al-Lu'ayb. He ultimately found her after being subjected to severe trials and tribulations.

However, maqalat become pure fiction in two distinct cases. *Huja* (folktales), a genre performed largely by women narrators, is seen by men as a collection of fantasies. Men describe huja variously as "lies," "fiction," "myths," and "maqalat of old wives, based solely on lies." Women are said to "cut huja from their heads." Women, on the other hand, are less interested in the ethical implications men have in distinguishing between truth and lies. Instead, women foreground the mechanics of the genre as stories not attributable to anyone in particular and handed down from one generation to the next. A woman narrator said that, as a mother, she found huja handy in *ghashghish* (lit., "deceiving," "taking one's mind off something"), as when distracting her children until supper was ready.

Fiction creeps into maqalat through the embellishment of wordy entertainers. These entertainers, who pepper casual talk with artistic tendencies, are described as maqalat tellers, humorists, mimics, and *buda'i*, that is, "tellers of buda" ("things not known to people before"). *Bud'a* are thus defined by a Rubatabi as discourses an entertainer creates. It is also defined as saying things, largely understood to be humorous, that have never been said before. However, the buda'i builds a creation on kernels of realities or occurrences of maqala. The process by which the creation is spun off is called *ta'liq* ("comment") or *talhin* ("embellishment"). A *buda'i* is thus defined by Rubatab as one who makes a short, old story long by embellishment and ornamentation.

Here, for example, is a story told by one al-Sheikh al-Sayim, a *buda'i*, about a situation in which he embellished a story he had been told so as to produce a totally different maqala: He lived once for a month or so in a Rubatab hostel in Atbara town in Sudan. For dessert, after lunch, the cook served bananas every day. Not being particularly fond of bananas, Al-Sayim refused to take them one day. Asked why, al-Sayim told the story of the homosexual, the bananas, and the monkey. In the story, the homosexual would invite boys to his place, give them bananas, and have sexual relations with them in front of his monkey. One day his date did not show up and, in desperation, he ate some of the bananas and threw some to the monkey. Revolted, the monkey swung his head, body, and hands violently and refused to take the bananas.

When asked how he came to learn the story, al-Sayim said he heard it from Salman, the Rubatab chief. However, in reproducing it in the hostel context, he took only the frame of Salman's story and improvised the rest of it. The story he heard was about a blacksmith, a kid goat, and a monkey. The blacksmith wanted his monkey to learn how to fan the fire with bellows. To teach it by example, the blacksmith would bring a kid, order it to fan the fire, and beat it when it failed to do so. The blacksmith did this with the kid repeatedly and ultimately killed it with a knife when it failed to learn. The "moral" of the story did not escape the monkey. Asked to work the bellows, the monkey, having learned the lesson, complied and did well.

It is fair to conclude from this representation of maqalat that Rubatab not only have an emic name for the material scholars categorize as "folklore," but also engage with these materials based on a set of criteria with which a folklorist can comfortably relate.

References

Ibrahim, Abdullahi Ali. 1994. *Assaulting with Words: Popular Discourses and the Bridle of Shari'ah*. Evanston: Northwestern University Press.
Herzfeld, Michael. 1983. An Indigenous Theory of Meaning and Its Elicitation in Performative Context. *Semiotica* 34:113–41.

ABDULLAHI ALI IBRAHIM

See also **Folktales**

MASKS AND MASQUERADES

In the Western popular imagination, masks and masked dances are probably the single most representative symbol of art making and performance in Africa. The very nature of African masquerade—encompassing a disguise of the human face, elaborate costuming, choreography, and musical accompaniment—imbues masquerade performance with aesthetic power and mystery.

The term *mask* usually defines the object that hides the human face or head. However, scholars routinely study the entire ensemble including the mask, the costume, the dance, and the musical and song accompaniment within its ritual or ceremonial context in order to fully understand the meanings and intent of the performance.

It is not known when masking was first enacted on the African continent, but rock engravings and painted decoration at sites in southern Algeria, in Lesotho, and elsewhere suggest that masquerade is very ancient. For example, at Tassili-N-Ajjer in Southern Algeria, rock painting suggests that masked performances were enacted by the fourth or fifth millennia BCE.

Today, masks and masquerades are found in many parts of the sub-Saharan African continent. In part, this relates to the ancient movement of Bantu peoples, who occupy a vast region of the continent south of the Sahara Desert. Throughout this region, masks, their costumes, and other paraphernalia, are made exclusively by men. Even in cultures where women may actually perform masked dances, such as the Mende of Sierra Leone, men make the masks (Phillips 1995). This relates in part to the division of labor in Africa, as men exclusively carve wooden objects. It also relates to the dominant position of men's secret societies in the governance structure of many African communities. It is these societies that often produce masks and sponsor their appearance. Masked appearances are often an overt assertion of male dominance and authority. Women, however, may still be important participants in some aspects of the masquerade, even if they only appear to have a passive role as observers.

Masquerade as Transformation

Many masquerade performances may be thought of as secular, valued solely as sources of entertainment. More often, however masquerade transforms the masked dancer into a powerful animated spirit force. As masquerade suppresses human identity, it also transforms the dancer into a new and often powerful entity that suggests the supernatural realm. Two entities and realms are often evoked in masked performance. The first are ancestral spirits, who are thought to return to the temporal world to aid living members of the community. The other are localized nature spirits who, like ancestral spirits, demand respect, but also reward the community with good health, a bountiful harvest, and many children.

The characters created in these transformations are not arbitrary. They follow the hierarchy of mask types that have developed within a particular community or culture. The form and style of the mask and its costume directly relates to the character or personages that the animated figure is suppose to represent. Masked characterizations are drawn from a cross-section of human society. They are human and animal, male and female, benign and dangerous, flamboyant and youthful, or solemn and elderly. They may represent the respected pillars of the community such as important rulers, warriors, or other historical figures, or conversely, those that represent human frailties and are therefore despised or ridiculed, such as prostitutes or drunkards. Mask characterizations may also represent specific wild or domestic animals, or a combination of both human and animal characteristics that represent revered ancestral or feared and dangerous nature spirits. The names given to masks suggest deceased forebears, famous personages, or animals such as birds, crocodiles, antelopes, or collective spirit forces.

Masquerade Forms, Styles, and Materials

African artisans have employed tremendous ingenuity in their attempts to disguise and alter the shape, size, and color of the human body. The body's characteristic movements and voice are disguised in the desire to create a new animated spirit being.

The basic face covering, so highly prized by museums and collectors, is often made of wood. It may also be made in part or entirely of more perishable organic material such as fiber or cloth. Other mask types cover the entire head or even the entire body of the dancer. The addition of a crest, horns, feathers, or a more elaborate projection to the top of the mask increases its aesthetic power and clearly helps to identify the particular character or personages being represented. Often masks are a synthesis of various human and animal characteristics that are enlarged or reduced to create entirely new and imaginative kinetic sculpture. Elaborate masquerade costumes and the accessories they carry further obscure or alter the profile of the human form and help to define the personage being represented. Stilts, long poles, or other devices may be employed so that the dancer can increase the height of the figure at will. When performing, the dancer may abruptly spin, causing the body of the masked figure to expand in size and then suddenly fall to the ground, suggesting to an observer that the body animating the mask has suddenly disappeared. For example, masked dancers performing Egungun masquerades among the Yoruba of western Nigeria are called "miracles" because they can literally turn their costumes inside out to dramatically change the entire color of the costumes at will. This is done with such finesse that even after repeated viewing, it continues to amaze and delight the viewer.

Masks, their costumes, and accessories are fabricated from materials or carry objects that are associated with, or symbolic of, the temporal or supernatural realms from which they emanate. For example, masks may carry paraphernalia associated with the forest world such as bows and arrows, spears, hunting nets, or bells. On the other hand, masks may wear or display certain leaves, fibers, pigments, quills, bird beaks, feathers, animal horns, or teeth that are symbolically associated with ancestral or nature spirits that are believed to reside in the forest, or in rivers or lakes. Alternately, other masked figures may carry objects that are chosen for their symbolic power relating to one's elevated status in life such as a sword, staff of office, or flywhisk (all objects that are associated with leadership). The masked figure *ngady mwaash*, produced by the Kuba of the Democratic Republic of the Congo, displays high status by carrying a flywhisk and wearing a decorated vest and several elaborately embroidered textiles (see illustration). In addition, *ngady mwaash* displays a beaded triangular hat on top of the head that is only worn by Kuba female diviners. This further illuminates the status and authority of the masked figure, as a female diviner derives her source of clairvoyant and healing power directly from powerful nature spirits called *ngesh*.

A *ngady mwaash* masked dancer performing at a funeral in the Southern Bushoong community, 1982. Photo © David A. Binkley.

An elder instructing a novice in the painting of the initiation mask Kamakengu, Northern Kete initiation camp, 1981. Photo © David A. Binkley.

The forms and styles of masked figures describe in visual terms the supernatural worlds they intend to evoke. They run the stylistic gamut from those that represent idealized physical beauty and moral authority to characters that represent grotesque, disfiguring disease, deformity, decay, and even death (Cole 1985). In many African cultures, there is thought to be a direct link between an individual's outward physical beauty and his or her inner moral and spiritual purity. Masquerade figures depicting good character and moral fortitude usually display the marks of social status, wealth, achievement, and good health. Conversely, figures that represent human degradation or disease are dark and often grotesque in appearance and suggest malevolent forces at work to serve as a warning against antisocial or immoral behavior.

Whatever the personage being represented, the masked dancer performs the appropriate dance movements, gestures, and sounds that befit the intended characterization. If the masked figure represents a wild animal or nature spirit, its performance may be threatening and unpredictable. In so doing, the figure may threaten onlookers or be beaten back by attendants in an attempt to control its behavior. If the mask is regarded as uncivilized or a fool, it may talk nonsensically and meander aimlessly through the community—behavior completely inappropriate for a properly socialized individual. Masked figures that represent women will often wear false breasts and clothing appropriate to women. The dance movements may appear nurturing. They may imitate women's roles, or mime behavior associated with women, such as preparing food or nursing a child. Conversely, the dance may be overtly erotic, miming women as sexually unrestrained and immoral beings.

Preparation and Performance

Elaborate preparations accompany the appearance of masked dancers. Masquerades require the skills of many individuals. Since masked dancers often do not appear alone, a number of masks and costumes must be fabricated or refurbished. Skilled craftsmen prepare the masks and costumes in a secluded location away from the prying eyes of nonmembers. Other individuals, including retainers who accompany the dancers throughout their performances, must also be selected. Retainers are important because they make certain that the mask and costume of each dancer is secure and remains in place and that the dancer does not stumble or fall during the performance.

Musical accompaniment is also an important aspect of masquerade. Indeed, drums or other percussive, stringed, or wind instruments may actually direct the tempo and duration of the masquerade performance. Several singers, or even an entire choral group, may also be present during masked performances. But even if singers are not required, individuals observing the performance may be familiar with praise songs associated with the masked figure and begin an impromptu song honoring the power of the masked figure, or during a funeral, extolling the qualities of the deceased and his family.

Depending on the purpose or context, masked dancers circulate throughout the community, perform on a central dancing area set aside for such purposes, or perform at a particular home or compound if, for example, a masked performance is required before a deceased individual can be buried.

The relationship between the masquerade figure and its audience is not spatially defined by a stage as it is in Western theatrical presentations. During African masquerade, the audience and the participants may on occasion mingle. For example, a drummer may leave the performance and be replaced by a member of the audience. Or, an unmasked member of the masking society may enter the dancing area and mime the movements of the masked dancer. In this regard, masquerade performance is both fluid and dynamic. The masked dancers, musicians, and others participating in the performance follow a loosely choreographed program, obeying the culturally proscribed rules of presentational style and decorum. Variations often occur that allow for creativity and innovation. Having seen masks perform on a number of occasions, the audience attending a masked performance is aware of the range of characters that appear and vocalizes its praises or criticism regarding the quality of the masked performance. Competitions between individual dancers, masking societies, or families who own masks are a vital and dynamic part of African masquerade.

Masquerade may take place during the day or only at night, depending on the nature of the performance. Often more then one masked dancer may appear on an occasion, each fulfilling a particular role or function within the masquerade sequence.

Masquerade figures are often arranged into a hierarchy that corresponds to a similar hierarchy of leadership in the masking society or in the larger community. When several masks perform on the same occasion, there may be a specific sequence of activities lasting several days in which masks of a lesser rank or status perform before the final performance by the senior masquerade figure.

Masquerade performance often accompanies serious occasions that rally the entire community into action. These occasions include initiation and funeral rituals or cyclical occasions such as the onset of the planting season or harvest time. One of the most frequent occasions for masquerade in west and central Africa is during funeral rituals, especially to honor deceased members of the masking society. During funeral performance, masks are regarded as intermediaries between the living members of the community and those recently departed. Masked dancers honor the memory of the deceased and conduct the spirit safely to the land of the dead. Among the most elaborate masked performance are those held in the western Sudan for the Dogon peoples of Mali, and the Bwa, Bobo, and Nuna peoples of Burkina Faso (Van Beek 1991; Roy 1987).

Masked dancers also appear during initiation rituals in which young men (and sometimes young women) learn the secret knowledge that allows them to become participating members of the community. (Binkley 1990; Phillips 1995) In many communities, membership in a esoteric cult or society is mandatory for all individuals who have reached the appropriate age. Masked dancers appear to escort the uninitiated youth to a bush or forest enclosure. On these occasions, masked figures serve as guardians and, together with the elders, discipline and instruct the youth. They are also part of the secret lore taught to the youth and help to safeguard their physical and spiritual well-being. When masked figures perform for women and children in the community, they express the pride of membership in the society and the prestige of those who have undergone the rite (Binkley 1987, 1990).

Masks also form part of the prestigious regalia of aristocratic rulers and their families and appear at festivals or rituals surrounding the splendor of the royal court. Elaborate masked performances have been documented at the Bamum royal court in the Cameroon Grassfields and at the capitol of the Kuba kingdom in the Democratic Republic of the Congo. Among the Kuba, several masks are reported to form part of the ruler's patrimony (Geary 1983; Cornet 1982).

Masked figures also perform on a variety of other occasions in sub-Saharan Africa. Elaborate masking traditions developed among the Bamana of southern Mali. The *ciwara* society is primarily concerned with fertility of the fields. Society members hold masked performances during agricultural rituals to honor a mythic creator who was instrumental in bringing agriculture to the Bamana (Wooten 2000). Among the Yoruba of western Nigeria, several masking traditions appear in dramatic presentations of mythic or historical tales relating to village or clan histories. During Epa performances, masked dancers remember and honor important chiefs, warriors, or culture heroes, and during Gelede performances, powerful elder women are called out for special veneration (Drewal and Pemberton 1989).

Masked dancers also perform on the occasion of festivals associated with political or religious observances, such as Christmas or New Years Day, or for the tourist trade. Indeed, because of both external influences and internal change, some African masking traditions have lost their initial ritual importance and appear now in more secular events or as entertainment. However, one should not overlook humor as a vital and creative aspect of African masquerade. During the most somber of ritual occasions, such as during the funeral of a respected community leader, a satirical masked figure may appear to help lighten the solemnity of the occasion.

Regardless of when masked figures appear—whether to help initiate youth, honor the recently dead, promote agricultural and human fertility, or simply to amuse onlookers—they express the dominant values of the community. As noted earlier, masquerades are often sponsored or associated with centers of political and/or spiritual authority in the community. These include secret or semi-secret societies that require members to have passed through a period of initiation and instruction. Other masks are owned by certain important families, lineages, or clans who control their appearance and safeguard the masks and their paraphernalia when they are not in use. Masquerade ultimately acknowledges leadership within the community and expresses the value of membership in the secret society that sanctioned the performance, as well as the aesthetic values of the entire community who witness this most dramatic of African artistic expressions.

References

Arnoldi, Mary Jo. 1995. *Playing with Jime: Art and Performance in Central Mail.* Bloomington Indiana University Press.

Binkley, David. 1987. Avatar of Power: Southern Kuba Masquerade Figures in a Funerary Context. *Africa,* 57 (1):75–97.

———. 1990. Masks, Space and Gender in Southern Kuba Initiation Ritual. *Iowa Studies in African Art,* vol. III:157–76.

Cole, Herbert M., and Chike C. Aniakor. 1984. *Igbo Art: Community and Cosmos.* Los Angeles, Museum of Cultural History, UCLA.

Cornet, Joseph. 1982. *Art royal kuba.* Milano: Edizioni Sipiel.

Drewal, Henry John, and John Pemberton, III, with Rowland Abiodun. 1989. *Yoruba: Nine Centuries of African Art and Thought.* New York: Center for African Art & H. N. Abrams.

Geary, Christraud. 1983. *Things of the Palace: A Catalogue of the Bamum Palace Museum in Foumban (Cameroon).* Wiesbaden: Franz Steiner Verlag.

Lawal, Babatunde. 1996. *The Gelede Spectacle: Art, Gender and Social Harmony in an African Culture.* Seattle: University of Washington Press.

Nunley, John. 1987. *Moving with the Face of the Devil: Art and Politics in Urban West Africa.* Urbana: University of Illinois Press.

Phillips, Ruth B. 1995. *Representing Woman: Sande Masquerades of the Mende of Sierra Leone,* Los Angeles: UCLA Fowler Museum of Cultural History.

Roy, Christopher D. 1987. *Art of the Upper Volta Rivers.* Meudon, France: A. et F. Chaffin.

Tonkin, Elizabeth. 1979. "Masks and Power," *Man* 14 (2):237–48.

Wooten, Stephen R. 2000. Negotiating Meaning and Identity Through the Bamana *Ciwara* Complex. *African Arts,* 33, no. 2: 18–33, 89–90.

Van Beek, Walter E.A. 1991. Enter the Bush: A Dogon Mask Festival. In *Africa Explores: Twentieth-Century African Art,* ed. Susan Mullin Vogel, New York: Center for African Art: Munich: Prestel-Verlag.

DAVID A. BINKLEY

See also **Performance in Africa; Puppetry; Ritual Performance**

MASQUERADING BY WOMEN: EJAGHAM

Ejagham peoples live on both sides of the contemporary Nigeria-Cameroon border in West Africa in the area surrounding the Cross River. The Ejagham are made up of several subgroups who share a similar language, similar cultural traditions, and a belief in a common origin. The Ejagham also have a dual-gendered ritual system in which both men and women perform masquerades. Ejagham women perform several masked dances that provide them with numerous possibilities for ritual expression.

Aside from the seemingly unique masquerades of the women's Sande Society in Sierra Leone, scholars had at one time believed that women did not perform masquerades and that masquerades were the sole territory of men. This assumption was based on the fact that there were few documented cases of women's masquerades, resulting in part from the tendency of researchers to focus on male ritual activity. Therefore, until the late twentieth century, a general understanding of masquerades was shaped by the characteristics of men's masking traditions, which tend to use full-body costumes and masks to conceal the identity of the dancer. As a result of our expanding knowledge about women's masquerades, scholars must rethink previous assumptions that were fueled in part by complex cultural narratives that place restrictions on the ritual activity of women.

Mythology

In Africa there are many variations of a myth that attempts to explain why women do not perform masquerades. In these myths, women were the original possessors of masquerades, but were not capable of controlling them. Thus, men took them for themselves. While we can not be certain of what actually happened in the distant past, these myths reflect the fact that gender symbolism and gender restrictions play a significant role in masquerades. While masks and costumes that conceal the identity of the wearer have been strictly forbidden to women in many parts of Africa, some women have developed alternative forms of masquerade.

Classification

In an attempt to classify the characteristics of women's masquerades, scholars have emphasized the fact that women do not conceal their identity and rarely use carved wooden masks. Therefore, scholars have expanded the definition of masquerade to include face painting, acoustic masks, and other transformative techniques that are used by women in danced performances. Judith Bettleheim (1998) has suggested that the fact that female performers do not completely conceal their identity is a unifying issue for women's masquerade and performance, distinguishing them from male masquerades. However, examples of women's masquerades among the Ejagham suggest that the strategies of concealment and revealment cannot be assigned solely to men or women.

The Ejagham have two different types of women's masquerades; Ekpa masquerades *reveal* the dancer's identity, and Agot masquerades *conceal* it. However, it is most likely that the use of masks by women has been a site of controversy between the genders. And, how women have negotiated this performance strategy is not entirely clear. It may be a result of the powerful role that women, such as those in the Ekpa association, play in the ritual life of the Ejagham.

Ejagham Ekpa, or Njom-Ekpa (cult of Ekpa), is a women's association that can perform masquerades and is known for its ability to provide social purification for the community, spiritual healing, and insight into the future. For example, if a war is pending, Ekpa women might communicate with the spirit world in order to predict the outcome. The community could then plan accordingly. In Ekpa rituals, women's spiritual abilities have the potential to both heal and harm, but should be used for the good of the society or to check the power of male community leaders.

During festive daytime performances, an Ekpa woman will dance with an elaborately carved headdress mask that sits on top of her head, fastened with strings, allowing her face to be seen. The masks may look slightly different from place to place, depending upon the carver and the stylistic preferences in the region. The main components appear to be the representation of multiple faces or figures, the use of mirrors, the use of scarves

Ekpa-Nkim masquerade, Efraya village, Etung-Ejagham Ikom, Cross River State, Nigeria. Photo © Amanda Carlson.

or cloth, and the use of colorful pigments or paints. In a documented case in Cameroon, the main figure represents a woman with a snake, who is understood in many parts of Africa and the world as Mami Wata. However, in this case, the figure represents a female ancestor and the powers associated with her that give Ekpa women their power (Roschenthaler 1998).

Aside from the masked dances, Ekpa women also perform nighttime displays in which women sing, dance, and communicate with the spirit realm. Men are forbidden to witness these events, which may occur on a regular basis or may be called upon because of special circumstances (such as in the event of a war). On the most serious of occasions, the women perform completely naked. In this context, the naked female body has a symbolic power that is associated with female sexuality and reproduction, whose meanings are deeply rooted in an Ejagham philosophy and worldview.

Among the Bakor-Ejagham, an Ejagham subgroup, based between the towns of Ikom and Ogoja in Nigeria's Cross River State, the Ekpa association does not perform a masked dance. However, the Bakor-Ejagham women do have other masking associations, such as Agot. These masking associations are social groups that provide women with a form of entertainment, with camaraderie, and with opportunities for public ritual expression. Membership may be linked to an age-grade or it may be open to anyone who would like to join and is deemed socially respectable.

Agot maskers use carved wooden headdresses and full body costumes (see photographs). The identity of the dancers is concealed under long cloth robes that cover the entire body, except

Agot masquerade, Ogomogom village, Bakor-Ejagham Cross River State, Nigeria. Photo © Amanda Carlson.

for the hands and feet. Cut-out eyeholes allow the dancer to see. Tied to the top of their heads, each masker wears a carved wooden headdress painted with glossy enamel paints. The two characters look more or less the same, with variations in the details of the headdresses and in the type of cloth used to make the costume. One headdress represents a woman and one represents a man. The female character can be easily recognized by the fact that she usually carries a white European-looking doll.

Agot refers to the type of masquerade and to the name of the dance group. In some cases, the names of individual dance groups may be modeled after aspects of daily experience that are important to Ejagham women, such as beauty, agriculture, and the market. One group named their dance after fermented cassava, *Akpu*. Their performance celebrates the introduction of cassava, which revolutionized women's ability to feed their families. These women begin with a pantomimed demonstration that precedes the entrance of the masked dancers and reenacts women toiling in the fields, discovering a cassava root, and bringing the food product back to the village, which results in the prosperity of the community.

As Satirization of Male Behavior

Both the Ekpa and the Agot women's masquerades comment upon, or satirize, male behavior. Describing an Ekpa performance in Cameroon, Ute Roschenthaler writes,

[T]he dance group, composed of at least nine women, appears. Some of them imitate and satirize typical male roles to the delight of the spectators: two or four "guards" run around carrying swords and machetes to control the dance floor; the "protocol leader" shakes his rattle; the "hunter's dog" searches for prey; the "soldier" points his gun at the audience; the "policemen" (called "blue bottoms") frighten with their large rods. . . . (1999, 45).

In this humorous display, women are making fun of men and the ways in which they behave. Likewise, Agot masquerades sometimes include songs that critique male behavior. For example, in 1994 a chorus of Agot women sang:

Life
Emanuel
Emanuel feeds his children
Emanuel feeds his children fat.
Fathers feed your children like Emanuel
Emanuel feeds his children however from other people's
    sweat
Emanuel reaps where he has not sewn
Fathers do not allow your kids to starve
Fathers do not feed your kids like Emanuel

(Translation by Ngoro Agibe)

In this verse, women sing about men's roles as fathers and their obligation to provide food for their children. They can even use these songs to voice their opinion about a particular person in the community. While these performances are for entertainment, they also offer women an opportunity to articulate their concerns and to form bonds of solidarity around women's issues.

History

Masquerades such as Agot probably originated in the twentieth century, but oral history suggests that women's masquerades in general have a much longer past. Bakor elders at the end of the twentieth century remember women's masquerades that their mothers and grandmothers had performed, which are no longer danced. The fact that Ejagham women have been able to acquire masquerades may in part be due to the tradition of women's associations and their danced rituals, which have played a significant role among the Ejagham and in the surrounding region. These associations typically involve women, who possess the power to heal and to foresee the future. Many of their ritual performances are characterized by dancing naked in the night and the required exclusion of men. There are several instances, such as in the Anlu Uprising (1958–1959) in Cameroon and The Women's War of 1929 in Nigeria, in which women in this region have used these ritual strategies to confront patriarchal forces, including colonial and Christian institutions. The considerable power that Ejagham women have gained through ritual associations such as Ekpa may partially explain how women have acquired the social, artistic, and spiritual skills necessary to use these masking strategies that are so often attributed to men.

References

Adams, Monni. 1993. Women's Art as Gender Strategy Among the We/Guere, Canton Boo, Cote d'Ivoire. *African Arts* 26:4, 32–43, 84.

Bettleheim, Judith. 1998. Women in Masquerade and Performance. *African Arts* 31:2, 68–70, 93–4.

Kasfir, Sidney L. 1998. Elephant Women, Furious and Majestic. Women's Masquerades in Africa and the Diaspora. *African Arts* 31:2, 18–27, 92.

Philips, Ruth B. 1995. *Representing Woman: Sande Masquerades of the Mende of Sierra Leone.* Los Angeles: UCLA Fowler Museum of Cultural History.

Roschenthaler, Ute M. 1998. Honoring Ejagham Women. *African Arts* 31:2, 38–49, 92–3.

Tonkin, Elizabeth. 1983. Women Excluded? Masking and Masquerading in West Africa. In *Women's Religious Experience.* ed. Pat Holden, London: Croom Helm.

AMANDA CARLSON

See also **Gender Representation in African Folklore; Performance in Africa**

MAURITANIA (ISLAMIC REPUBLIC OF MAURITANIA)

Mauritania is a country of some 2.58 million located on Africa's west coast whose neighbors are Western Sahara, Algeria, Mali, and Senegal. Nouakchott, a city of 480,400, is the country's capital. Mauritania's climate ranges from arid to semiarid, and approximately three-fourths of the country is covered by sand. Forty percent of Mauritania's population is mixed Maure and darker-skinned Africans from farther south, while it is estimated that Maures account for 30 percent of the population. "Maure" gives us the name of the country as well as "Moor." The remaining 30 percent is black. Arabic and French are the country's official languages, although Hasanya, Bamanankan, Fulani, Sarakole, Wolof, and Berber languages are spoken as well. More than 99 percent of the country is Sunni Muslim.

Mauritania gained its independence from France on November 28, 1960, and subsequently formed an Islamic republic. The government has stressed Islam as a source of national cohesion and unity, as it is the religion that many of the country's diverse ethnic groups share. Most individual freedoms are restricted in Mauritania. It was only in 1980 that slavery was officially abolished, and some traces can still be found.

In recent years, Mauritania has suffered from social tensions and economic problems. In a move to alleviate such problems, the country held its first multiparty elections in decades in 1992, but they were boycotted by opposition groups. Mauritania suffers from the problems caused by the International Monetary Fund's/World Bank's policies of structural adjustment that have burdened so many African nations.

For decades Mauritania's climate has become increasingly drier, and as a result of desertization, less than 1 percent of the land can be cultivated, and only 10 percent is usable for livestock grazing. Such environmental conditions have resulted in great migrations to urban centers, where employment problems abound and poverty is prevalent. Despite such economic woes, Mauritania receives high revenue from its fishing industry (as its coastal waters are among the richest in the world) and iron ore.

Some of Mauritania's ancient cities, once trade and Islamic learning centers, are currently in the processes of restoration. Located on traditional routes from North Africa to Sudan, the cities were points of origin for pilgrimages to Mecca and were known throughout the Middle East. The town of Chinguetti, for example, is ranked as the seventh city of Islam, and scholars, poets, and priests have gathered there for centuries.

JENNIFER JOYCE

MAURITIUS (REPUBLIC OF MAURITIUS)

Mauritius is an island of 1.18 million, located off Africa's southeast coast. Its capital is Port Louis, a city of 142,000 people. The ethnic population of the country is mostly made up of Indo-Mauritians and Creoles. English, French, Creole, Hindi, and Urdu are the most widely spoken languages. Over half of the country is Hindu (52 percent), 28 percent are Christian, 17 percent are Muslim, and the remaining 3 percent is made up of various smaller religious groups.

Although the Portuguese "discovered" the island around 1510, it was the Dutch who named and first settled on Mauritius. After a long colonial history of French and British rule, Mauritius gained its independence from the British on March 12, 1968, and subsequently set up its own parliamentary democracy. Political pluralism and human rights are widely respected in the country. More than thirty political parties exist, and the country's labor movement is one of Africa's strongest.

Until the 1970s, the Mauritian economy was largely dependent on its sugar industry. While this is still a source of revenue for the country, Mauritius has since transformed itself into a successful industrial and manufacturing state, exporting clothing

and chemicals. The exporting of flowers is also very profitable. There is a strong service sector as well. Along with other Indian Ocean islands, Mauritius's main source of foreign revenue now comes from tourism. Mauritius has become one of the developing world's greatest economic successes.

PHILIP M. PEEK

MEDICINE: OVERVIEW

Folk medicine refers to the traditional resources used in the maintenance and restoration of health, drawing from traditional, rather than modern, biomedical knowledge. African folk medicine encompasses the indigenous cultural knowledge and practices used in diagnosis, treatment, and prevention of illness. The knowledge on which African folk medicine is based is acquired from concrete experiences in local environments and transmitted orally from one generation to the other.

Folk medicine varies with social, cultural, and physical environments. This means that African folk medicine is a variety of culture-specific responses to health concerns in human experience. Ethnomedicine is a component of a people's culture and refers to the beliefs and practices relating to diseases that result from indigenous cultural evolution. In this sense, folk medicine is not derived from the conceptual framework of modern medicine. In this essay, the terms *ethnomedicine*, *traditional medicine* and *folk medicine* are used synonymously. These terms do not necessarily denote archaic or obsolete medicine, but refer to medical resources that are indigenous to the Africans, holistic environments. This is the medicine that existed before the introduction of Western medicine and was suited to the needs of African cultures (Makinde 1988,91).

African Worldview and Folk Medicine

Different environmental contexts provide Africans with various resources, which they have incorporated in their folk-medicine practice. Within specific environments, local communities have evolved integrated systems of beliefs, strategies, and behaviors to prevent illness and restore health. The material and nonmaterial resources used to maintain health constitute African folk medicine, which is associated with a uniform worldview found in the sub-Saharan region.

Most traditional African societies perceive the universe as an entity that encompasses pervasive vital powers. These powers, or forces, are hierarchically ordered and exist in a state of equilibrium. The conceptually perceived harmony among the elements of the universe ensures the well-being of humankind. When the harmony is enhanced, the balance and order that determine health result. For human beings to stay healthy, the perceived equilibrium among the elements of the universe should be sustained and restored at all costs (Magesa 1997; Mbiti 1969).

The traditional African worldview has at least six categories of elements with have vital power. The power that issues from these elements can either diminish or augment the life force in human beings. God is the ultimate source of the vital force that affects human life and health. The lesser deities, such as minor gods and autonomous spirits, have a share of the supernatural power that emanates from God. There are also spirits of the underworld, the waters, and the air whose power is ambivalently revered. Below God and the semiautonomous spirits are the people who died a long time ago, but are still actively remembered by their descendants. These ancestral spirits have their own demands on the living, and when these demands are fulfilled, the ancestors reciprocate with good health, general well-being, and prosperity.

Living human beings are also part and parcel of the African traditional perception of the universe. This category of beings is sustained by the power of life drawn from the other elements, as well as from their own activities. Human beings sustain their life and health by tapping power from greater elements that include God, the lesser deities, and the autonomous, as well as the human, ancestral spirits. Plants, animals, and other biotic elements are also perceived as resources that enhance human life and health. These elements constitute the core sources of material for medicine. Other natural phenomena and objects are also believed to be potential sources of medicine because they possess life-enhancing or life-threatening forces, which ultimately are controlled by the high God. Nonbiotic elements also have medicinal value, especially when they are associated with sacred places and inherent mystical power. Other natural objects attain the property of having a healing power through ritualistic animation with spiritual strength.

From the African conception of the universe, therefore, there exist phenomena that have the potential to provide the force essential to human vitality and perpetuation of life. Lay medical practitioners can tap this power, although experts who have supernatural endowments maximize the efficacy of the curative and healing force in natural health-promoting resources. God, spirits, and ancestors constitute part of the African cosmology that comprises the powers of the invisible world. Conversely, human beings, animals, plants, and other tangible phenomena are part of the visible world. Traditional Africans believe that both the visible and invisible elements have power that can be manipulated or harnessed to affect human beings negatively and positively.

The principles of African folk medicine are, therefore, founded on the traditional perception of a pervasive power in the universe. Traditional medical practice is concerned with the cosmic power that is advantageous to human beings, especially when there is a balance in the universe. Diagnostic and therapeutic practices among traditional African medical experts reflect the anthropocentric nature of the African cosmological perspective (Mbiti 1969; Magesa 1997). In the African traditional conceptualization of the universe, everything is perceived to exist so as to benefit human beings. In this regard, the world comprises a convergence of powers, whereby health, prosperity, controlled suffering, and minimum misfortunes in human experience reflect the desired equilibrium for achieving abundant life. From the African folk explanatory models for illness, there is the popular belief that powers in the universe affect each other reciprocally. Folk medicine, is therefore, an attempt by practitioners to restore balance in the universe, keep a good relationship with the powers from the visible and invisible worlds, and eradicate illnesses that result from an existing lack of equilibrium.

Folk medicine in indigenous African societies is also concerned with the disharmony that results from human interactions and activities in their visible social world. Human beings have the potential to manipulate the invisible spiritual power in the universe to harm others out of jealousy and vengeance. In this regard there are medicines to counter the undeserved misfortune and suffering meted by witches, sorcerers, and the "evil eyed." Some of the medicines associated with the social agents of disease and misfortune are either protective or curative. Traditional Africans with diseases and illnesses originating from the invisible spiritual world also associate the social world with misfortune. Health problems, which emanate from the African social world, are culturally constructed by the local people as the consequence of a breach of taboos and the disruption of social equilibrium that enhances human well-being in one way or another. Diseases that indigenous Africans directly or indirectly associate with breaches in the moral social order include those that are linked to lineage inheritance, malevolent spirits, and curses. In traditional belief systems, illnesses contracted through these agents and mechanisms mainly represent a disruption in spiritual equilibrium.

Traditional medicines, addressed to the spiritual causes of illness, underpin the folk notions about a person's dual nature. The belief that a human being is both corporeal and nonmaterial is ubiquitous in sub-Saharan Africa. The invisible human life force in the African worldview is the intangible air or breath-like force given by God. This aspect of a person forms the human spiritual dimension, which stretches to eternity. This spiritual force, integrated with the human body, is usually affected by the consequences of evil deeds, naturally occurring cosmic imbalances, and human misbehavior. This conception of the double nature of human beings in traditional beliefs accounts for the application of organic matter to cure the organic person and the use of "nonempirical" medicines as spiritual remedies. This implies that African folk medicine draws from a traditional view in which good health goes beyond a simplistic perception of a healthy body only (Ngubane 1977).

The perceived integrated nature of the African universe influences traditional medical practice, which is based on an understanding of health as a holistic phenomenon. In this perspective, health involves a state of comprehensive mental, psychological, spiritual, physical, and cosmic equilibrium. As such, good health is a condition of harmonious coexistence between people and fellow human beings, people and invisible spiritual forces, and people with rest of the natural world. Health is not an isolated phenomenon but part of the entire magico-religious and social fabrics. It is an intricate physical condition as well as a religious matter (Appiah-Kubi 1981; Mbiti 1969). Illnesses are indicators of an ontological imbalance, which requires restoration through the use of both tangible and intangible medicines.

The traditional African worldview provides a framework for perceiving the origin of illness. Understanding the causality of ill health has enabled the people to discover resources derived from their environments to combat undesirable health conditions. The most common resources that constitute African folk medicine are leaves, herbs, barks, and the animal substances that were revealed to the forebears of medical practice before the contact with Western and other foreign medical systems.

For Africans, the human world is conceived as a field of forces. The two opposing features of the cosmos are life and death. In this sense, medical practices comprise the use of all known empirical and nonempirical resources aimed at combating death and other enemies of life. There is also the world of spiritual beings and powers that intervene in human affairs. Among spiritual forces, some are good, others ambiguous or evil. People consider these powers as living realities, which can be solicited and can influence human destiny. According to this perception, there is hidden power in plants, human beings, animals, inanimate objects, and some specific parts of fauna and flora. Material and nonmaterial phenomena can be used as intermediaries of invisible spiritual and cosmic powers to affect health. Various types of traditional medicines and related practices are applied on the basis of folk theories about the relationship between the powers of the visible and the invisible worlds as well as God, ancestors, the spirits, and human beings. Folk medicine practiced by Africans, therefore, is classified as curative, preventive, tonics, or remedies for spiritual illnesses. Each of these categories of medicine is based on folk knowledge about strategies for restoring balance in human organic and social experiences.

Curative Medicine

Curative medicine is applied to alleviate or remove bad health conditions, which are practically conceived in the human body. The traditional cures in this case involve herbal leaves, stems, bulbs, barks, roots, decoctions, and animal substances, which traditional Africans believe have the power to treat illnesses linked to natural causality (Kokwaro 1976; Appiah-Kubi 1981). Practitioners use these medicines as purgatives, enemas, and emetics with regard to cultural knowledge of illness as a consequence of body intrusion. Traditionally, where illnesses are associated with culture-bound theories about the attack of undesirable foreign objects or conditions that should be removed, medical resources would involve the use of bitter medicines, egg yolk, and other ingredients of ethnopharmacopeia local people believe are opposed to the illness-causing elements. Indigenous treatment is also effected through rubbing herbs into the skin, inhaling medicated air or vapor, and administering cures through body incisions.

Traditional cures also include the material used to deal with the nonorganic spheres of illness. Folk medicines used in this case are believed to have the power to combat illnesses resulting from mystical causes that are not easily predicted or managed. To traditional Africans, therefore, the most efficacious medicines are those they believe possess vital forces that restore health at both metaphysical and physical levels. In this sense, there are medicines, used to cure conditions caused by human agents such as witches and sorcerers, and by supernatural punishments for breaches of moral order and taboos (Maclean 1971). Traditional healers ameliorate conditions with perceived natural and supernatural causality using oral incantations, spells, and physical medicines. Special herbs and material medicine may also be used in the process of spiritual exorcism. The behaviors of the members of the community and good relationships with spirits are important in keeping cosmic harmony. Those who strictly observe the norms of social life and fulfill the religious and customary duties, can succeed in confronting the threats to life emanating from spiritual powers.

Folk cures among Africans also include the use of medicines they believe have either similar or the exact opposite qualities of the effects of an illness. As an example, herbs with milklike saps would be used to cure conditions involving milk production among humans and livestock. Similarly, herbs that produce red decoctions are applied in various societies to enact the power of blood. Ethnomedical practice in Africa gives importance to blood, which is regarded as one of the agents of good health. Folk medical theories and practices imply that blood is the main beneficiary of all medicine addressed to naturally caused diseases and illnesses (Makinde 1988). The principle that blood carries life is the basis for practices such as rubbing medicines in incisions and letting out bad blood from the body through suction.

Protective Medicine

Traditional Africans also apply medicines with the power to ward off misfortunes, suffering, and bad luck, which they perceive as disease or illness. Illness in this sense is understood to result from forces in the environment, the spiritual world, human malice and envy, and the power of the spoken word. Chewing herbs from the areas where the diseases are perceived to originate prevents diseases and illnesses, which result from potent environmental emissions. Protection of human health is based on notions about magical or countermedicine. In this context, various types of charms and amulets are used to ward off the effects of curses, witchcraft, and sorcery. Medical preparations from herbs and animal substances are also applied to protect people from unknown causes of illnesses that are generally attributed to superhuman forces. Ritualistic practices in sacrifices, divinations, incantations, and spells invoking the names of ancestors also have preventive effect in the traditional health-seeking behaviors among rural Africans. On the same plane, ethnomedicine is applied to prevent accidents, defeat in legal cases, possession by evil spirits, anger of ancestors, and other health dangers.

Apart from tapping the protective power of traditional medicines, these substances are also used as tonic herbs for revitalizing social, physical, mental, and spiritual vitality. The decrease of the life power in this regard is perceived in all spheres of health through direct or indirect manifestations of malfunction. At the social level, quarrels, hatreds, and other forms of conflict that eventually affect human well-being are indicators of diminution of health. Reduction in physical health is recognized through perceived dysfunction of the body as an organism. The negative effects of mystical forces on mental and spiritual health are realized through culturally constructed reduction of normalcy. Syndromes associated with the mind and spirit are sometimes manifested in conditions defined as madness, nightmares, and ominous visions. Preventive medicine in such cases includes substances that are believed to have repulsive power to ward off agents of illness. This medicine is constituted of herbs and animal substances with strong scents, which would either attract benevolent protective spirits or repel bad ones. Health protection also requires medicines that are applied to ensure fertility among men and women. Various types of aphrodisiacs, foods, fruits, and traditional beers are perceived differently by various people as health-revitalizing substances. Spiritual strength may also be rejuvenated through a mixture of herbs and incantations.

Human and Livestock Medicine

African ethnomedical practice, as applied to human beings and domesticated livestock, is based on similar knowledge about sources and operation of cures and healing. It is believed that the cosmic and spiritual forces that are against one's own health and prosperity would also affect one's possessions, of which livestock and especially cattle are the most valued. Therefore, to treat livestock diseases, some people resort to herbal preparations with both curative and preventive power. The same herbal medicines may be used to treat other illnesses among human beings and their livestock. The Digo of the Kenya coast, for example, use the *mkawalafisi* or *mpalafisi* herb as a treatment for pneumonia, as well as a charm to protect their livestock from predators. The Meru, the Swahili, and the Kamba use *muatha*, *muhasa*, and *muvatha* (*Veronia lasiopus*), respectively, to treat stomachache among people and sores on cattle (Kokwaro 1976). The principles behind the use of some types of medicines, such as purgatives, also apply to livestock. Ritualistic medicine also alleviates the ill health of livestock and is part of holistic health, of which some indicators are the success and well-being people seek from supernatural powers.

Conclusion

African folk medicine is based on indigenous cultural knowledge and practices used in diagnosis, prevention, and treatment of diseases and illnesses. This medicine existed in Africa before the introduction of modern medicine and relied on concrete experiences and observations transmitted orally through the generations. The focus of African ethnomedicine is the power in the universe, which can affect life positively or negatively. Traditional medical practice depends on the expert's or lay practitioners' spiritual endowment of the power to discover causes of illnesses and prescribe efficacious remedies. Traditional medicine is ultimately concerned with restoring and maintaining equilibrium among all elements in the universe. When equilibrium is lacking in the human organism, and in the cosmic, social, and spiritual spheres, health is disturbed and illness results. Alleviation of ill health depends on how the power of the universe can be tapped and balanced successfully, using tangible and nonempirical medicine. The efficacy of this medicine is realized simultaneously at both the psychological and physical or organic levels of human experience.

References

Appiah-Kubi, Kofi. 1981. *Man Cures, God Heals: Religion and Medical Practice among the Akans of Ghana.* New York: Friendship Press.

Devisch, Rene. 1993. *Weaving the Threads of Life: The Khita Gyn-Eco-Logical Healing Cult Among the Yaka.* Chicago: University of Chicago Press.

Feierman, Steven, and John M. Janzen, eds. 1992. *The Social Basis of Health and Healing in Africa.* Berkeley: University of California Press.

Janzen, John M. *Ngoma: Discourses of Healing in Central and Southern Africa.* Berkeley: University of California Press.

Katz, Richard. *Boiling Energy: Community Healing Among the Kalahari Kung.* Cambridge, Mass.: Harvard University Press.

Kokwaro, J. O. 1976. *Medicinal Plants of East Africa.* Nairobi: Kenya Literature Bureau.

Maclean, Una. 1971. *Magical Medicine: A Nigerian Case Study.* London: Penguin Press.

Magesa, Laurenti. 1997. *African Religion: The Moral Tradition of Abundant Life.* New York: Orbis Books.

Makinde, M. Akin. 1988. *African Philosophy, Culture and Traditional Medicine.* Athens, Ohio: Center for International Studies, Ohio University.

Ngubane, Harriet. 1977. *Body and Mind in Zulu Medicine: An Ethnography of Health and Disease in Nyuswa-Zulu Thought and Practice.* London: Academic Press.

Twumasi, Patrice A. 1975. *Medical Systems in Ghana: A Study in Medical Sociology.* Accra, Ghana

Yoder, P. Stanley, ed., 1982. *African Health and Healing Systems.* Los Angeles

BENSON A. MULEMI

See also **Cosmology; Divination; Religion: African Traditional Religions; Spirit Possession**

MEDICINE: FOLK MEDICINE OF THE HAUSA

To someone unfamiliar with medical practices in rural West Africa, the sight of a young girl with strings of leather-bound amulets around her waist and neck being led by her mother to a Western dispensary for therapy might be incongruous. But to the Hausa of southern Niger, combining seemingly incompatible therapeutic approaches is far from paradoxical. It is, in fact, standard procedure for those who face the threat of illness on a daily basis. No one will be surprised to hear from a woman who describes herself as a pious Muslim that she has enlisted the services of a spirit medium to ensure her brother's success in finding a job.

In this impoverished, drought-ridden country, where many struggle to eke out a living from the sandy Sahelian soil, there are many paths available to those who seek relief from their ailments, whether they are suffering from hepatitis, diarrhea, or sleeplessness. Exposure to Western beliefs has meant that some villagers regularly visit the local dispensary to receive quinine for malaria or to get a shot that will cure what they call *ciwon likita* ("illness of the doctor," that is, treatable by biomedical means). Although certain conditions require visits to specialized practitioners such as bonesetters, midwives, or herbalists, other afflictions are not so easily classified. In such cases, diviners and spirit mediums often play a critical role because, whether they identify an ailment as an "illness of evil" (caused by sorcery) or as an illness caused by spirits, their diagnosis ultimately helps patients make sense of their problems by concretizing the roots of the affliction.

The domain of *lahiya* (health), as the Hausa see it, extends well beyond the limited boundaries of the Western concept of health to include a sense of harmony with one's social and physical environment. From this perspective, health refers as much to personal well-being as to the fertility of the land and the prosperity of the community. Absence of *lahiya* thus entails not only wasted bodies and individual sickness, but also social strife, climatic disasters, or business failure. Quranic scholars who provide Islamic medicine to ward off evil often derive a substantial income from the manufacture of amulets or potions destined to insure success while taking an exam or protection from competition on the job market. Similarly, spirit mediums who advertise their skills as healers may receive requests to call on the spirits on behalf of patients who are complaining of stomach aches, suffer from insomnia, or require protection before traveling. While most of those who claim to be Muslim generally seek advice and treatment from Quranic healers, they occasionally—and discreetly —resort to the services of spirit mediums when they suspect a spirit attack, or when all other options have been exhausted. Muslims shun spirit possession and the practice of dealing with spirits to cure afflictions. They insist that prayers to Allah are more effective than sacrificial offerings to the spirits. While both Quranic science and the medicine of spirits have proven their effectiveness, they are of no avail against certain afflictions, such as *darme*, that are attributed to human agency.

Now that cash has become the indispensable means of exchange, individuals who find that money "burns holes in their pockets" or who feel unable to keep a job often suspect that they have been "tied" (*darme*) through sorcery by a resentful colleague or competitor. Successful civil servants who draw a regular income are particularly fearful of *darme* attack in a country where scarce administrative positions are coveted by many. In such contexts, one's inability to hold on to a salaried position or, more generally, to maneuver within one's social and professional world may be diagnosed as a symptom of *darme*. *Darme* sometimes proves fatal because the victims are so reluctant or unable to absorb food that they slowly wither and die, besides losing all interest in money or professional matters. Restoring the patient to health involves removing surgically, or through the absorption of a special concoction, the knots that have formed in the ailing body as a result of the "tying." Some healers who specialize in such procedures pull out a foreign substance—such as knotted cotton threads—from a small incision in their patients' necks or backs. Others provide potent medicines that, once absorbed orally, will dissolve the knots or flush them out of the victim's body. Once the crippling knots—whose numbers indicate precisely how many years the victim has been afflicted—are destroyed, patients are soon able to eat normally again and resume their former activities. Nevertheless, there may be lasting effects depending on the duration of the illness. Recognizing *darme* as a debilitating condition whose emergence is rooted in a context of thwarted ambitions, intense competition, and economic wants is a way of symbolically dealing with the corrosive impact of money. By translating monetary failure and uncertainty into the accessible experience of physical wasting, Hausaphone Nigerians can devise cures to reverse the visible effects of economic forces that insidiously threaten their current well-being and prosperity.

References

Abdalla, Ismail H. Neither Friend, Nor Foe: The Malam Practitioner-Yan Bori Relationship in Hausaland. In *Women's Medicine: The Zar-Bori Cult in Africa and Beyond*, ed. I. M. Lewis, Ahmed Al-Safi, and Sayyid Hurreiz. Edinburgh: Edinburgh University Press.

Last, Murray. 1979. Strategies Against Time. *Sociology of Health and Illness* 1, no. 3: 306–15.

Masquelier, Adeline. 1999. Money and Serpents, Their Remedy Is Killing: The Pathology of Consumption in Southern Niger. *Research in Economic Anthropology*, 20: 97–115.

Wall, Lewis. 1988. *Hausa Medicine: Illness and Well-Being in a West African Culture*. Durham: Duke University Press.

ADELINE MASQUELIER

See also **Divination; Spirit Possession**

MEDICINE: INDIGENOUS THERAPEUTIC SYSTEMS IN WESTERN KENYA

The term *therapy* is drawn form the Greek word *therapeia*, which connotes the ideas related to health care practices and cure of diseases. Traditional therapeutic systems are the organized, indigenous strategies of caring for those in ill-health conditions, constructed from culture-bound medical knowledge. This knowledge is integrated with beliefs and practices that have evolved as part of specific cultures for the maintenance and restoration of health. This implies that traditional therapeutic systems existed before the development of, and contact with, modern medicine. In this sense, traditional therapies in indigenous African societies convey, in a symbolic way, their beliefs and attitudes towards the strong mystical powers that underpin their culturally constructed universe.

The traditional therapeutic systems in western Kenya are embedded in the indigenous cultural knowledge related to notions about good health, causes of disease and illnesses, the courses and duration of illness episodes, the sources of cures, and the importance of social groups in health care and restoration. The Luhyia (or Abaluhyia) and the Luo (or Jaluo) of western Kenya in East Africa provide typical indigenous African models of health care and treatment of diseases and illnesses. These models reflect a system of therapy, supported by shared beliefs and myths about etiologies of different diseases and ailments.

The Luhyia and Luo ethnic groups are linguistically different, but they share many cultural aspects such as economic, social, and religious institutions. The Luhyia form part of the linguistic group in Kenya known as the Western Bantu. The other Bantu-speaking ethnic groups in this region are the Abakuria and Abagusii. The Luhyia is the second largest ethnic grouping in Kenya and includes at least fifteen known subcultures with mutually intelligible subdialects. The Luo are the only representatives in Kenya of the linguistic and cultural group in Eastern Africa known as the River-Lake Nilotes. They are the third largest ethnic group in Kenya and are also found in other countries of eastern Africa such as Uganda and Tanzania.

One of the most significant differences between the Luo and Luhyia is found in their myths of origin. Oral tradition among the Luhyia elders and other sage informants claim that their original homeland is a place to the north called Misri, which is a local equivalent of Egypt. Conversely, the Luo mythology indicates that the original homeland of this group was some fertile area where one of the Nile river tributaries originates. These differences in myths of origin account for the cultural variations between the two communities; however, these ethnic groups share some significant cultural traits due to their long coexistence. The Luhyia have integrated cultural traits of the Nilotic Luo speakers and other Bantu-speaking groups (Fedders and Salvadori 1976). Similarly, some elements of the indigenous medical knowledge among the Luhyia and Luo can be found among other neighboring ethnic groups.

The Cultural Construction of Health

The traditional methods of treatment and prevention of disease and illness among the Luhyia and Luo reflect the typical perception of health among the indigenous societies in this region. These societies view health as the holistic well-being of human beings, which entails psychological, physical, spiritual, and cosmic equilibrium. Good health is a condition positively associated with stability and increment in all the visible and invisible forces that enhance human life and prosperity. The Luo and Luhyia description of health is couched in phrases and terms that imply wholeness, harmony, and an integrated force of life. Members of these communities who consider themselves healthy use terms centered around the roots *-lamu* (*mulamu*) and *ngima* (*a-angima*) respectively to refer to a comprehensive state of being without disease and illness. This means that the indigenous strategies to cure illness are integrated with the myths and beliefs regarding the enemies of the wholeness of human life. Among the Luo, for instance, ethnomedical remedies and therapies are varied and all encompassing because there is no aspect of life that exists independent of health (Kawango 1995, 81).

Both Luhyia and Luo have evolved health care and restoration strategies based on their cultural knowledge and cultural ecologies. In this context, health is perceived as a state of equilibrium with all the visible and invisible elements in the universe. These elements are animated with mystical powers, which affect human life either directly or indirectly. These communities locate antagonists to human life and well-being in the natural, social, and spiritual worlds. Health action, therefore, involves comprehensive efforts to restore both perceived and unknown areas of imbalance in the ethnocosmology. This approach to disease or illness treatment is founded on culturally constructed synergetic activity of combined herbal medicines, incantations, spells, and magico-religous rituals. In this sense, the local people would use multiple treatment strategies to increase the probability of addressing all the possible causes of disease or illness (Wandibba 1995; Kawango 1995). To achieve the goal of comprehensive health care and treatment of disease, the Luyo and the Luhyia resort to simultaneous or sequential use of herbal remedies and appeals to the mystical sources of help, depending on the perceived causes of ill health.

Notions of Disease Causality and Therapeutic Patterns

Indigenous illness etiologies in western Kenya typify African ideas and myths about the sources and origins of illness as manifestations of misfortunes in human experience. Disease and illness etiologies are usually attributed to a multiplicity of human, superhuman, and naturalistic factors. This holistic perception of disease causality gives rise to determinations of human causes, natural and inherited diseases, misfortunes associated with God and spirits, and syndromes that are explained with reference to breach of taboos and customs.

Human-Caused Illnesses and Diseases

In many traditional African societies, all human beings are potential sources of evil. Both the Luo and Luhyia believe that some human beings can tap the pervasive power in the universe either to harm or augment the person's life force. Among the Luhyia, sorcerers (*balyuli*, *babila* or *basijeteri*) apply medicines to harm others, and their victims may get ill and even die. For the Luo and Luhyia, sorcerers are people who oscillate between harmful and protective activities by using potent medicine. Their positive role in human well-being is realized when they are consulted to provide preventive medicine and material for revenge.

Disease and illness in this society are also attributed to human agents who practice witchcraft (*vulogi*, *vulosi*). Witches are essentially the agents of evil, and their activities never have aspects which local people describe as positive in relation to human well-being. The local people believe that the art of witches and sorcerers is transmitted through specific clans and lineages. The human agents in such descent groups have access to mystical power and can manipulate potent medicines and spells against other people because of jealousy (*imbodokha*) or vengeance (*burima*).

The Luhyia perceive the negative health effects of the witches (*jojuok*) among the Luo in a similar way. Among the Luo, chronic chest pains, coughing, or conditions that cannot be treated by herbal and other tangible medicines are attributed to the evil practices of witches. Such illnesses and other culture-bound syndromes that cannot be easily treated by empirical remedies include the effects of the "evil eye." The evil eye is usually blamed for persistent health problems such as stomachache and stitch (*hima*, *rihima*). Victims of diseases caused by personal agents seek treatment from people they believe to have some supernatural powers. These specialists include diviners, oracles, and seers. The basic role of such thearapists and curers, especially the herbal specialists, is diagnostic. The specialists include the general traditional practitioners (*ajuoga*), diviners (*jodilo*), and those who remove bewitchment medicine and other objects of the evil eye from the patient's stomach. Others include experts who propitiate evil spirits (*jodilo*) and traditional specialists who can determine by scent where bad medicines are hidden or buried (*jamorieri*) (Ocholla-Ayayo 1976).

The traditional herbal pharmacopoeia incorporates the treatment of conditions that the local people associate with personal agents of illness causality. Among the Luo, there are herbal remedies for *sihoho*, a syndrome believed to result from the bewitchment of cooked food eaten in the presence of a special evil-eyed witch called *jasihoho*. This witch is believed to have powers that cause indigestion, stomachache, and swellings of the stomach and legs. To remedy this condition, pounded leaves of herbs, such as *nyalwet kwach*, *ohingla-thiang'*, and *olandra*, are taken orally. The Luo and Luhyia also treat this illness through incisions made to remove the objects of intrusion by using a suction pad or the specialist's mouth.

The Luhya, especially the Bukusu subgroup, also believe that body intrusion is effected through bewitchment of food. Body intrusion techniques include the throwing of harmful objects called *ebilasila*. *Ebilasila* consist of tiny objects such as hairs, bits of grass, beans, bone splinters, and pieces of broken bottles. In the traditional Luhya belief systems, such objects are mysteriously transmitted into the body of the witch's victim. When these objects have entered the victim's body, they cause acute illnesses such as a swollen stomach and cramps, accompanied by vomiting, intense headache, hot forehead, and unbearable fever. Apart from herbal remedies and consulting *valumiki* (those who specialize in suctioning foreign objects or illnesses from the stomach), the Luhyia treat this condition through rituals and spells conducted by doctors and oracles or seers, whom they believe have access to mystical powers to counter the effects of witches.

Naturally Caused Diseases and Illnesses

Traditional therapeutic practices in western Kenya are also based on beliefs and myths about natural or environmental causes of illness. Some ailments are believed to result from environmental pollution or emissions with harmful elements that alter the cosmic equilibrium. Most of the people believe that when *muya* (bad air) is inhaled, illnesses such as fever, thrush, flu, scabies, and nose bleeding may result. The local people perceive changes in wind and weather patterns as ominous and disruptive to health also. Among the Luo, *yamo* (boils) and skin diseases are believed to come with winds from other places. Seasonal changes, environmental pollution, and contamination of the air are traditionally associated with cosmic cycles among the Luo and Luhyia. These changes, when accompanied by other natural occurrences such as rains, maturation of food crops, and eclipses, have been associated by local peoples with invisible mystical powers that are potentially dangerous.

Symbolic cosmic liminality is explained in myths as having hidden power that disrupts the existing equilibrium in the human corporeal and spiritual spheres of life. The Luo, the Luhyia and their neighbors perceive the resulting cosmic imbalance as having negative consequences for health. In this sense, illness is usually associated with natural events such as the flowering of food crops and other vegetation. The changes in seasons manifested in perceptible natural phenomena such as rain, earth tremors, migration of birds, and floods are linked with different illnesses. The indigenous Luo and Luhyia, for instance, associate sudden increase in cases of mental illness, diarrhea, fever, and stomachache with potent emissions in the environment resulting from natural cosmic rhythms.

The belief that some health problems are caused naturally among societies in western Kenya entail the traditional notions about pollution. In the Babukusu and Abatachoni Luhyia subcultures, the people also believe that there are times when the air is contaminated, and if such air is inhaled, the victim becomes ill (Wandibba 1995). There is also belief that some illnesses may be caused by crossing foreign rivers and environments. These people believe that rivers, swamps, ashes from the hearths of mothers who are weaning twins, and valleys have potent powers that cause illnesses. For the indigenous Luhyia, flu and illnesses whose signs are rashes around the mouth result from emissions in such environments. Some Luo and Luhyia groups also believe that disease may result from symbolic pollution caused by activities that are against human life, such as bloodshed, and immoral sexual behavior, such as incest and adultery.

Diseases or illnesses that these communities attribute to natural or environmental causes are treated empirically through natural and herbal remedies. In the Luhyia medical ecology, the myths about the forces behind natural illnesses imply that some personified mystical forces collaborate with cosmic events and rhythms to affect human health. In such cases, treatment strategies would include multiple therapeutic practices (Nyamwaya 1986). Local perceptions about naturally caused diseases and ailments are linked to the culture-bound conceptualization of intrusion of pathogens and conditions that oppose existing equilibrium in the human internal and external environments.

In order to cure the conditions of naturally induced body intrusion, the people of western Kenya seek therapeutic resources they believe have mystical potency to expel the resulting disease.

The Luo believe that the most potent therapeutic resources to counter the effects of natural illnesses are bitter herbal medicines. Following this local perception of efficacy, communities in western Kenya use emetics, purgatives, and herbal medicines, which they squeeze into incisions that are intended to let out "bad blood." Therapists also use different medicines to induce vomiting or diarrhea, in which case, purgation and emesis are believed to signify the expulsion of the disease from the body. Some of the Luo and Luhyia communities also interpret the appearance of rashes on the mouth of patients after taking medicines as indicators that the pathogens or opposing conditions that caused illness are leaving the body. In the traditional therapy management groups, participants believe that therapeutic efficacy for any kind of disease is determined by the power possessed by the practitioners of that medicine. The most effective practitioners are those whom the people believe are the legitimate heirs of the curing and healing vocation acquired through special lineages. Ethnomedical practice is sanctioned by myths, which attribute the healers' treatment abilities to the mystical powers conferred by ancestral spirits and God to specific clans and individuals.

The other strategy used by these communities to treat illnesses associated with natural causality includes the process of steam inhalation (*fundo/humo*). The leaves, bark, and roots of certain herbal medicines are boiled, and part of the solutions is taken orally while the rest is used to steam bathe the patient. In the folk explanatory models, steam bathing and inhalation help the patient recover from illnesses such as fevers and flu through sweating. They also resort to induced sneezing by the use of herbal powder from herbs such as *obuo madongo* and *indama* to expel body intrusions they believe cause fevers, headaches, colds, flu, dizziness, and nose bleeding. Among the Luhyia, diseases of the chest are also treated by steam inhalation involving herbal solutions from a herb called *litoto*.

Illnesses Linked to Spiritual Causes and Breach of Taboos

As in the beliefs of other African communities, personified supernatural agents may cause disease among the Luhyia and Luo. Some misfortunes, described as disease in the folk explanatory models, are caused by malevolent spirits. The Luo and Luhyia people believe that spirits may send sickness and death to express their demands. When the indigenous people attribute illnesses to spiritual causes, they always explain the origin in terms of displeasure of ancestral spirits or God. People who are afflicted by the supernatural agents of illness resort to spiritualistic healing. This type of healing is, to a large extent, based on the belief that there are some people who are endowed to cure certain diseases revealed to them through the help of spiritual powers. The traditional therapeutic procedures in this case involve special rituals and gestures to propitiate the spiritual forces so that they can restore human health. When such rituals are ignored, the spirits send more punishment in the form of illness. In this regard, the traditional people perceive disease and illness as reminders to the living that they should accord the spiritual powers the respect they deserve. Diseases in this sense sanction the living to maintain proper relations with the dead and the invisible world.

The people of western Kenya believe that supernatural punishment also results from breach of taboos and contravention of moral order. When people go against established social norms, it is tantamount to disrespect to the ancestors who are guardians of tradition and morality. In this sense, disease and therapy are important in harmonizing personal and social experiences that are affected by visible and invisible interactions. For the Luo, *chira* is the consequence of a breach of both known and unknown taboos. The symptoms of *chira* include persistent headache, *wichbar*, coughing, and diarrhea. More specifically, illnesses that gradually cause body wasting are linked to *chira*. Other diseases that the traditional Luo and Luhyia associate with the breach of taboos are infertility, early death of children, and the contraction of incurable diseases among children and adults.

The breach of taboos is against social and moral codes that are necessary for the perpetuation of life. Among the Luhyla, immorality exposes individuals and their lineages to conditions of ritual impurity and danger, referred to as *luswa*. They have mythical explanations of *luswa*, which, in some cases, result in inherited diseases such as chronic skin ailments. Health conditions, which the people associate with breach of taboos and supernatural causality, are treated through traditional sacrificial rituals. Victims of ritual impurity spread illnesses, and traditional practitioners of health care would advise that these people should be avoided until cleansing rites are performed. Therapeutic techniques in such cases also include the use of assorted medicines derived from vegetation, animals and other potent natural resources.

Conclusion

Indigenous therapeutic practices in western Kenya are part of an integrated system of belief and thought. These systems provide the local people with the myths and folk theories about the origins of disease and illnesses. The people in this region believe that the etiologies of disease and illness are numerous. A multiplicity of origins of illness create infinite forces that are antagonistic to human welfare and life. Therefore, in these traditional societies, there exist different therapeutic approaches and options as an adaptation to the perceived threats to life. The myths about the origins of diseases and illnesses provide the people with lay conceptual frameworks of analyzing diseases and health. Folk explanatory models allow the local people to contextualize the health-endangering forces within the natural, social, and spiritual worlds that underpin holistic human existence and survival.

References

Fedders, Andrew, and Cynthia Salvadon. 1979. *Peoples and Cultures of Kenya*. Nairobi: Transafrica Book Distributors.

Kawango, Evelynes Agot. 1995. Ethnomedical Remedies and Therapies in Maternal and Child Health among the Rural Luo. In *Traditional Medicine in Africa*, ed. Sindiga Isaac, Chacha Nyaigoti Chacha, and Mary Peter Kanunah. Nairobi: East African Educational Publishers.

Nyamwaya, David. 1986. Medicine and Health. In *Kenya Socio-Cultural Profiles: Busia District*. ed. Gideon S. Were, Nairobi: Ministry of Planning and National Development and the Institute of African Studies.

Ocholla-Ayayo, A.B.C. 1976. *Traditional Ideology and Ethics among the Southern Luo*. Uppsala: Scandinavian Institute.

Wandibba, Simiyu. 1995. Traditional Medicine among the Abaluyia. In *Traditional Medicine in Africa*, ed. Sindiga Isaac, Chacha Nyaigoti-Chacha, and Mary P. Kanunah. Nairobi: East African Educational Publishers.

BENSON A. MULEMI

See also **Cosmology; Divination; Spirit Possession**

MENDE

See **Prose Narratives: The Mende; Silence in Expressive Behavior**

METALLURGY AND FOLKLORE

Precolonial and early colonial African societies that depended on metals and complicated metal technology also relied on folklore to teach about and reinforce the social significance of metals. Folklore explained, justified, and, in some cases, manipulated ideas about metal production and use. Iron and copper have a long history and wide significance across Africa and, therefore, will be the focus of this discussion. Gold, silver, and alloys of copper, such as bronze and brass, were also important to some societies.

Folktales, songs, oral traditions, and more formal oral histories involving metalworking, metal workers, and metal objects communicate and explain. Significant topics included the origins of society, the origins of kingship and royal dynasties, the origins of metals and metallurgy, the social status and activities of metal workers, and why metal production succeeded or failed. Many different people created and used traditions about metallurgy, including the political and social elite, official historians, storytellers, villagers, and metal workers themselves, depending on the purpose of a desired message and the context in which it was told or sung.

Importance of Metallurgy

Reference to metals, particularly iron and copper, in such diverse folklore genres and sources is a result of several factors. First, these metals were highly valued in everyday life. For centuries, iron has been critical to the fundamental subsistence activities of many African societies, including hoe agriculture, hunting, building, and food preparation. Copper was used for personal adornment and to symbolize significant life changes, social status, and political power. Furthermore, these metals were valued for the complex technical process involved in their manufacture: at a minimum, mining the requisite ore, smelting the ore into a mass of raw metal in a furnace, and hammer-forging it on an anvil to make an object.

Second, particular properties of iron and copper, such as color, luminosity, malleability, corrosion resistance, storability, and sound, carried symbolic meaning in many African societies. These physical properties were often used as descriptive metaphors in stories and orations about various matters. The red color of copper was widely associated with blood (related to war and/or fertility), heat, and power, but also had many other meanings depending on its context of use. Iron was most often associated with strength and hardness, such as among the Luba

(Congo) and Oromo (Ethiopia, Somalia). Some folklore even explained the differences between metals based on physical properties. The Yoruba (Nigeria) origin myths present iron, brass, and lead as the children of the same mother. When they were all told to make a sacrifice to prevent death, brass and lead obeyed. Iron did not, saying that the Sky God had proclaimed that everything would last forever. To punish iron for its disobedience, it rusts away with time while brass and lead do not.

A final factor is tied to the widespread belief system that explained iron and copper production in terms of human procreation. Despite enormous variety in the ways it was expressed across Africa, the complete transformation of iron or copper ores into shiny metal during smelting was related to human gestation and birth. Although iron smelting was a carefully controlled technical operation, it also often involved rituals and song that simulated significant times in the life of a productive woman, such as marriage, pregnancy, and birth. The Fipa (Tanzania) adorned and treated a newly built furnace as a bride who would have many children. The Phoka (Malawi) furnace was perceived as a "wife" to the iron smelters.

Symbolism and mythology

Furthermore, various parts of furnaces were often given the same names as female body parts, particularly those related to sexuality and birth. The Shona (Zimbabwe), Chokwe (Angola), and other cultures were more explicit and built their furnaces as women. They decorated the walls with breasts and scarification, denoting fertility, and the bloom was sometimes extracted between leg-like projections. Rituals were also used to consecrate new iron forges or tools during which relationships were drawn between the hammer (the most important tool of a smith) and a second wife, such as among the Nyoro (Uganda), or a child by the Ondulu (Angola). This powerful imagery of fertility and procreation was evoked in folklore for a wide variety of uses by people in many different social roles.

All peoples have a need to explain the origins of humans and their society. Metals and metal workers sometimes played significant roles in the stories about such events. Among the Dogon (Mali), the smith was semidivine and the twin of Nommo, the son of the creator god and earth, having been created from Nommo's placenta. When the smith descended from the sky, he brought three essential ingredients of society: iron, seeds, and fire. The Mvet (Cameroon) speak of the emergence of humanity from a cosmic mother-stone, called Nana Ngawgaw. They relate the creation of life to a stone anvil, Ngawg-Si, which was related by genealogy to the mother-stone. The Baguirimi (Chad) associate the origin of human society to a time when an anvil fell from the sky during a primordial sacrifice. In a song sung by the Yatenga (Burkina Faso), the smith was key to the origin of life since he freed humans from their natural condition and, although he could not stop death, he made an ax to build a village and forged a razor to cut umbilical cords.

Smiths were sometimes portrayed as bringing civilization to African societies, particularly in relation to the advent of royal dynasties. Ndagara, a smith, became the first king of Karagwe (Tanzania) and made all the royal regalia passed down to his successors. Similar oral traditions about "smith-kings" are known for the Kongo (Democratic Republic of the Congo),

Twanda (Rwanda), and Rundi (Burundi). For the Babungo (Cameroon), the founders of the chiefdom were iron smelters who came from a cave behind a waterfall while carrying special medicines. These medicines allowed the founders to induce productivity from the earth and make iron blooms and children, that is, the society's wealth. Among the Luba (Democratic Republic of the Congo), Kalala Ilunga, a technologically superior hunter and visitor from the east, competed with Nkongolo, an uncultured king, for leadership. When Kalala Ilunga won, he introduced civilization to the Luba; this included bringing a master iron smelter from the east to teach the Luba how to smelt and forge. In a similar way, the Nupe (Nigeria) culture hero Tsoede is said to have brought workers of iron and brass with him to teach the locals. Women were occasionally linked to introducing metalworking to a society, such as among the Hausa (Nigeria).

Oral tradition was also used to explain the origins of metallurgy. The Babungo (Cameroon) explain that iron smithing, in contrast to smelting, started when the ancestor of smiths fell from the sky or descended on a spider's web, carrying a hammer, the "mother-thing" for all. Pieces of this hammer were forged into other hammers of smiths and represent connections between the earth and the powerful spirits in the sky. The Fipa (Tanzania) tell how a piece of star, *nbanda*, fell from the sky into a medicine basket, and then people knew how to smelt iron. Among the Taberma (Togo), God made humans out of clay and antelopes out of iron ore. Iron was the exclusive privilege of antelopes. They owned the first forges, which they lit with their hooves. The antelope is now the sponsor of any new smith and his forge. For the Bariba (Benin), God gave the knowledge of smithing to the crab who then gave it to man. The crab lives in the stone anvil at the forge.

Metal workers

Iron and copper workers were specialists in African societies. Mining, smelting, and forging were complex tasks, requiring considerable expertise in and control over both technical knowledge and ritual. Metal workers imparted measured doses of information about their craft through folklore and songs to explain what they did, why they did it in particular ways, and how to ensure success through various rules and taboos. Age and gender played prominent roles in the choices made during metalworking and in the explanations provided about the activities, including the significant influence of ancestral spirits, the technical and ritual expertise of elders, the work load of the youth, and the exclusion of women. Although women often mined iron ore during times of labor shortage, such as occurred among the Shona (Zimbabwe) and Babungo (Cameroon), they were almost always excluded from smelting operations, particularly women who were pregnant or menstruating. If a menstruating woman came by an operating furnace in Lopanzo (DR of Congo), it would "menstruate" forever and never produce iron. One exception seems to be among the Barongo (Tanzania), who allowed menstruating women at a smelt. Prepubescent girls and postmenopausal women were sometimes allowed to participate in presmelting rituals, or they cooked and transported food to the smelters. Strong taboos existed to prevent men from having sexual relations prior to a smelt in order to ensure its success. Such behavior represented infidelity to the furnace; adultery was often thought to cause miscarriages in pregnant women, as well as furnaces. Furnaces were usually placed far away from villages to minimize this potential threat.

African iron and copper workers were revered, respected, feared, and/or despised depending on factors often related to their contributions to the economic foundations of their society. The metal workers used traditions, including some of what is presented above, to perpetuate those attitudes, often to ensure a craft monopoly and to control access to their specialized knowledge. The Banjeli (Togo) spoke of a chief from an iron-smelting lineage who also had rain-making abilities. He was banished at one point, but a drought developed and worsened. When he was recalled, rain fell. Babungo (Cameroon) smiths were said to have powerful medicines useful against foreign witches who entered their fields during planting, as well as against any pollution they left.

In other societies, stories were told to reinforce the more negative images of metal workers for social, political, and economic purposes. The Kapsiki (Cameroon) said that smiths were not fully adult. Gurage (Ethiopia) smiths were forbidden to plant or herd cattle because they would negatively affect the fertility of the earth and the cows. Similar attitudes prevailed among the Dimi (Ethiopia), where iron workers were not allowed to be involved in agricultural rituals. Among the Tuareg (Niger), iron workers were associated with chiefly lineages and groups of warriors, based on the critical objects they made, although their patrons portrayed them as lazy and liars. Tuareg folklore, however, related how the society could not function without them.

A considerable amount of African folklore exists involving metallurgy. Some of this is still alive, but much is fast disappearing as the crafts of iron and copper smelting, in particular, are lost to modern technology and international trade. Furthermore, few elder metal workers are still alive who possess the technical and ritual knowledge of metal production and will share it. Blacksmiths, as well as workers in tin, aluminum, and scrap metal, still contribute to the local economy of many societies, however, where important traditions survive and have meaning. New lore often replaces the old, such as the importance of copper for preventing sickness among the Luba (Democratic Republic of the Congo).

References

Childs, S. Terry, and David J. Killick. 1993. Indigenous African Metallurgy: Nature and Culture. *Annual Review of Anthropology* 22: 317–37.

de Maret, Pierre. 1985. The Smith's Myth and the Origin of Leadership in Central Africa. In *African Iron Working*, ed. R. Haaland and R. Shinnie, pp. 73–87. Oslo: Norwegian University Press.

Herbert, Eugenia. 1984. *Red Gold of Africa*. Madison: University of Wisconsin Press.

———. 1993. *Iron, Gender and Power: Rituals of Transformation in African Societies*. Bloomington: Indiana University Press.

Miller, Duncan, and Nikolaas van der Merwe. 1994. Early Metal Working in Sub-Saharan Africa: A Review of Recent Research. *Journal of African History* 34: 1–36.

Schmidt, Peter. 1996. *The Culture and Technology of African Iron Production*. Gainesville, Fla.: University of Florida Press.

S. TERRY CHILDS

See also **Blacksmiths**

MOROCCO

Morocco lies in the far northwestern corner of North Africa, a region that comprises the Maghrib, a designation used by Arab geographers for "the place where the sun sets." To the south is the still disputed territory of the western Sahara, once a Spanish colony, which still seeks its independence, but has been appropriated by Morocco. Morocco's western and northern borders are the Atlantic Ocean and Mediterranean, respectively; Algeria is to the east.

More of North Africa's original inhabitants, the Berbers, live here than anywhere else on the continent, as they were pushed westward by the Arab invasions starting in the seventh century. It was the Almoravid movement, coming out of Mauritania and Morocco, that conquered North Africa and southern Spain by 1056 CE. The only country in North Africa not controlled by the Ottoman Turks, Morocco was one of the earliest independent nations, having fought off the Portuguese, as well, in 1578. Pushing their control further south, the Moroccan army destroyed the great Songhay Empire in 1591. The eighteenth and early nineteenth centuries saw the prominence of the infamous Barbary Pirates. Although the French had general control over the area in the nineteenth century, France and Spain formally divided the country in 1912, with Tangier becoming an international zone. Nevertheless, Morocco's military powers remained, and it defeated the Spanish army in 1921. This arrangement stayed in place until the mid 1950s, when the country became an independent kingdom under Mohammed V. Throughout the late twentieth century, Morocco grew increasingly democratic, setting up a constitutional monarchy.

There remain two areas of contention. Spain still controls the cities of Ceuta and Melilla on the Mediterranean, and Morocco continues to fight the Polisaro, the freedom fighters of western Sahara. While Morocco occupies most of this territory (despite a United Nations referendum in 1990), there has not been a final resolution.

Reflecting their early dominance, Berber is still the first language for 30 percent of the country, while 75 percent speak Arabic, and, as elsewhere, French is the language of commerce and government. Spanish is still spoken in parts of the country, and increasingly, English is used. Berbers continue to press for more recognition, especially in the schools; since 1994, Berber has been a permitted language in the schools.

While Fez and Marrakesh are still recognized as traditional capitals, Rabat is the international capital, with Casablanca as the financial center. Although Morocco has no oil deposits, it exports a wide range of minerals (phosphate, lead, zinc, and silver, among others). The nation has some of the richest farm land in Africa, as well as good fishing. Moroccan wines are sold worldwide. It has also become highly industrialized with busy air and sea ports. A thriving tourist industry welcomes many visitors who come for the beautiful old cities, ceramics, woodwork, and rugs.

Although a constitutional monarchy and firmly Muslim (98 percent of the population), Morocco has developed as a relatively "liberal" society, with sizeable, and very old, Jewish and Christian communities. Morocco continues to play an important mediating role between Europe and the United States, and the Arab world of North Africa and southwestern Asia.

PHILIP M. PEEK

MOZAMBIQUE (PEOPLE'S REPUBLIC OF MOZAMBIQUE)

Located on the coast of southeastern Africa and bordered by Tanzania, Malawi, Zambia, Zimbabwe, South Africa, and Swaziland, Mozambique is a country with a climate that ranges from tropical to subtropical. The nation's population of approximately 19.5 million is composed predominantly of Bantu-speaking groups. Major languages spoken in the country are Portuguese, Yao, Tubbuka, Batonga, Makua, and Shona. Sixty percent of the nation practices traditional indigenous religions, and 30 percent is Christian. The remaining 10 percent are either Muslim or belong to various other religious traditions. Maputo, Mozambique's capital and largest city, has a population of 931,000. Although 66 percent of the people live in rural areas, urbanization is increasing.

Mozambique was first ruled by Portugal as part of Portuguese India, but in 1752, a separate administration was established. After a long liberation struggle, on June 25, 1975, Mozambique, one of the world's poorest countries, gained its independence after nearly four hundred years of occupation. FRELIMO, the major freedom movement, formed the new government, but another group refused to join the government and continued to wage a tragic and devastating civil war. Unfortunately, the years since independence have been difficult, both politically and economically, and it was only in 1992 that the nation's thirty-year period of war was ended with a cease-fire agreement. The subsequent multiparty elections of 1994 have given the country a renewed sense of hope that peace and prosperity may finally come to the nation, whose rebuilding has also been hampered by environmental disasters such as floods.

Mozambique's natural resources include coal, iron ore, tantalite, fluorite, and timber, while the agricultural sector produces cotton, tobacco, cashews, sugar, tea, copra, sisal, and subsistence crops. Principal industries include processed foods, textiles, beverages, refined oil, chemicals, tobacco, cement, and glass. A major new export is shrimp.

Mozambican women, who played an active role in the struggles against the Portuguese, have become increasingly involved in the nation's social causes in the years since independence. The Organization of Mozambican Women has successfully fought against gender discrimination and has opened up educational and job opportunities for the nation's women. Mozambican women now have laws guarding them against sexual harassment, as well as protection in divorce, desertion, and child custody. The nation is also seeking to improve its higher education system.

JENNIFER JOYCE

MUSIC IN AFRICA: OVERVIEW

Research on musical traditions in Africa requires examination of a complex web of activity that involves not only music, but all of life. Because music is intertwined with so many other parts of life in Africa, many studies of social, economic, political, or other [orientations issues] involve discussion of music. Anthropologists, historians, folklorists, dance ethnologists, and linguists, as well as ethnomusicologists and musicologists, have written on aspects of music in Africa. African musicology also

has developed into its own field, concerned with music in itself and also with the role of music and musicians in African society, the relation of music to other arts in Africa, and issues such as education, gender, and musical developments in the African diaspora (for an overview of developments in African musicology, see DjeDje and Carter 1989). Publications that focus specifically on music in Africa range from overviews of musical features and traditions of the continent (for instance, Nketia 1974; Bebey 1975; Merriam 1982, Stone 1998) to detailed studies of particular musical traditions.

Overviews of Africa

Researchers have struggled, and continue to struggle, in presenting overviews of music in Africa. Musical traditions vary even within geographic regions and contemporary political nations. Differences depend on factors such as physical environments (influencing, for instance, which materials are available for instrument construction), social and political structures, religious beliefs, dominant occupations (such as whether ethnic groups are nomadic or sedentary), musical aesthetics, and foreign influences from within and outside Africa. Investigators have attempted to classify culture areas according to these factors as well as according to race and language groups (see, for instance, Murdock 1959, Greenberg 1959; Merriam 1982; Kubik 1994), yet most recognize that generalizations break down as soon as particular traditions are examined.

Africa often is divided into *at least* two areas: North Africa and sub-Saharan Africa (Merriam 1982, 61; Nketia 1974, 3). Predominantly reflecting Arab influence, though also bearing some influences from East and West Africa, musical traditions of North Africa frequently are considered in studies of the Middle East or Mediterranean rather than in studies of Africa. Several recent studies on Africa, however, have included discussions of North Africa (Kebede 1982; Stone 1998; DjeDje 1999). Music of white settlers in South Africa sometimes is also excluded from general writings on music of Africa, again due to its development through predominantly European rather than indigenous African influences.

Alan Merriam, in his work on Africa, divides the continent into several areas: Bushman-Hottentot, East Africa, East Horn, Central Africa, West Coast, Sudan Desert (divided into two areas, Sudan and Desert), and North Coast (Merriam 1982, 99). Other scholars recognize similar culture areas, with the following changes: Khoisan is preferred to the term Bushman-Hottentot and is included within the larger area of Southern Africa; the East Horn is included as part of East Africa; and Sudanic regions are referred to as Sudanic Africa. Some studies do not separate Sudanic Africa from West Africa, but divide the area into a savanna belt and a forest belt.

Music of North Africa, as previously noted, is distinguished by its dominant Arab characteristics. Some musical traditions of Sudanic Africa and coastal areas of East Africa also demonstrate significant Arab influence, though generally mixed with indigenous African traditions. West Africa is known for its dominance of large drum ensembles and "hot" rhythms, Central Africa for a combination of smaller drum groups and use of a variety of other types of instruments, and Southern Africa for thick-textured vocal traditions in addition to instrumental ensembles (for a discussion of these areas, see Merriam 1982, 97–100).

Certain areas and ethnic groups are sometimes are discussed separately due to their distinctive histories or musical styles. These include Ethiopia, Madagascar, the so-called Pygmy peoples of Central Africa, and the Khoisan peoples of Southern Africa (Kebede 1982 offers information on these and other areas of Africa).

While nation states cannot be used as cultural units for considering traditional African music, as ethnic groups often are spread over two or more nations, they have been used as units for considering popular music (for discussions of African popular music, see Manuel 1988 and entries on Africa in Broughton et al., 1999). Some countries, such as the Democratic Republic of Congo, have become particularly known for their popular musical traditions.

Characteristics of Music in Africa

Traditional and contemporary musical genres co-exist in Africa today. Traditional music often is defined as music performed by groups linked by factors such as kinship, ethnicity, and cultural beliefs. Contemporary music is music performed by groups linked through more contemporary factors such as urban spaces and nation states. Both traditional and contemporary music are dynamic traditions, for music in Africa has always been characterized by variation and transformation. While contemporary genres have emerged in response to modern social and political developments, traditional genres also continue to thrive and are being transformed to fit into modern settings.

Many writings on Africa focus predominantly on traditional musics. Although traditions vary across the continent, researchers note that many do share certain characteristics. These characteristics relate both to the relationship of music to other aspects of culture and to music itself. In discussing the music and in classifying musical instruments, scholars have tended to use Western musical concepts and terminology, though recognizing that African peoples have different concepts and terminologies relating to their music.

Traditional music in Africa frequently serves as part of daily life and rituals. Much music originally was associated with kingdoms or religious ceremonies, accompanied work, or announced

A member of the band Kambazithe plays on a traditional xylophone in Malawi. Photo © Hal Noss, www.halnoss.com.

Kenyan musicians perform contemporary and traditional songs in Nairobi, Kenya. Photo © Hal Noss, www.halnoss.com.

events such as births, deaths, and wars. Today, music often remains a central aspect of funerals, festivals, and religious celebrations. However, in contemporary contexts, performances may combine elements from various traditional contexts and may be played outside any of these contexts.

African music usually is practiced in conjunction with other arts, such as dance or drama. African arts rarely can be considered as distinct elements, for they often function together as a unified whole. An instrumental performance, thus, may also involve singing and dancing (the videos on Africa in the *JVC Video Anthologies* of music and dance are useful resources for those interested in viewing different music and dance traditions). As various researchers have pointed out, some African languages do not even distinguish between types of music or differentiate music from other arts. Ruth Stone notes, for instance, that the Kpelle people of Liberia use the same word, *sang*, to describe well-executed dance movements, sung phrases, and drumming (Stone 1998, 7).

Many African musical events are communal. Although particular musicians may be singled out as master performers, all individuals present at an event might participate by playing accompanying instruments, singing, clapping, or dancing. Ewe musical performances at funerals in Ghana, for example, often involve one or more master drummers, various accompanying drummers, and a bellplayer. In addition, individuals from the community join by playing rattles, singing, and dancing.

Ensemble organization is structured in various ways in Africa, depending on the combination of instruments involved and on personal and group aesthetics. Chopi xylophone orchestra music of southeast Africa involves xylophones and xylophone players. In other regions of Africa, however, one or a few xylophones may be combined with drums or other instruments. Because much music is communal, often more than one musician is involved. Nevertheless, solo performances by individuals also may be heard.

While scholars note the dominant use of drums and complex rhythmic structures in some regions of Africa, and particularly in West Africa, African musical traditions demonstrate use of a wide range of instruments and interest in melodies as well as rhythms. Instruments range from membranophones (drums with stretched membranes) and idiophones (such as bells, rattles, xylophones, lamellophones, and slit-drums) to chordophones (including musical bows, fiddles, harps, lutes, lyres, and zithers) and aerophones (flutes and horns). Much contemporary music also includes electrophones (such as electric guitars and keyboards). The number of melodic instruments, also including voice, and the frequency with which they are performed together and with nonmelodic instruments, demonstrate the importance of melody in Africa. When patterns of drum tones are used to imitate spoken language in some regions of Africa, such as in some music of the Ewe of Ghana and the Baganda of Uganda, these patterns also often sound melodic.

Much vocal music uses what J.H. Kwabena Nketia has called "homophonic parallelism," involving parallel movement in intervals of thirds, fourths, or fifths (Nketia 1974, 161–2). Some vocal music in Africa, including the *iscathamiya* style made famous by groups like Ladysmith Black Mambazo, is based on thick homophonic texture include in parentheses: (the term *iscathamiya* denotes the dance movements that accompany the vocal harmonies; see Allingham 1994, 383). Researchers differ in their opinions as to whether or not homophony is indigenous to certain parts of Africa, for some homophony reflects the influence of Christian church music introduced by missionaries. Researchers often note the prevalence of pentatonic scales in African musical traditions, but other scales also may be used (for a discussion of vocal melody and polyphony, see Nketia 1974, 147–67). Vocal music also may involve other vocal effects, such as the mimicking of animals and birds, and, as amongst the so-called Pygmy peoples of Central Africa, vocal hocketing (the combining of short musical patterns, generally performed by different musicians, to create a lengthier and unified composition) and yodeling techniques.

Call-and-response forms are prevalent in many parts of Africa. Call-and-response occurs both in instrumental and vocal music, and between unequal and equal numbers of performers. When call and response is performed between a soloist and a chorus, the soloist frequently is provided freedom to improvise while the chorus repeats the same response after each solo. This type of interaction demonstrates two other important characteristics associated with much music in Africa: repetition and improvisation. While much music involves repeated phrases or patterns, improvisation (of all musicians or at least of solo or leading musicians) is also highly valued.

Traditionally, much African music was not notated, but was passed on orally from generation to generation through musical apprenticeships or observation of professionals by young musicians. Some musicians and scholars now have transcribed traditional songs, and composers are notating new compositions.

Continued Transformation

Although elements that characterize much music of Africa have been identified, it is impossible to provide an accurate general definition of so-called African music. One definition cannot describe all the musical traditions of such a large continent, traditions that are so complex structurally and that serve so many functions in African cultures. Furthermore, as already noted, different musical traditions in Africa continue to evolve and blend with musical influences from other parts of Africa and from outside Africa. Traditional musics reflect the influence of African ethnic groups upon each other and, in many regions, influence from the Arab world, Europe, and Asia. Increased radio and television broadcasting, production of cassettes, compact discs, and video recordings, and travel to other regions and countries for performances has led to continued musical experimentation, adaptation, and creation on the continent. Contemporary productions range from Western-style art forms to pop fusions that incorporate elements from around the world, often with heavy influence from the Americas.

Attention must also be drawn to the role of African musicians. Scholars increasingly are focusing on the musicians composing and performing music in Africa, rather than on just the music they produce (DjeDje 1982; Stone 1998). Traditionally, African musicians have served in many roles, including as oral historians, educators, political mediators, and entertainers. Contemporary musicians continue to serve in these capacities. Musicians such as the Nigerian Fela Anikulapo Kuti are known not only for producing music for entertainment but also for using music as a tool for social and political commentary.

References

Allingham, Rob. 1994. Township Jive: From Pennywhistle to Bubblegum: The Music of South Africa. In *World Music: The Rough Guide*, ed. Simon Broughton, Mark Ellingham, David Muddyman, and Richard Trillo. London: Rough Guides.

Bebey, Francis. 1975. *African Music: A People's Art*. New York: Lawrence Hill Books.

Broughton, Simon, et al. 1999. *World Music: The Rough Guide*. Vol. I. London: Rough Guides.

DjeDje, Jacqueline Cogdell. 1982. The Concept of Patronage: An Examination of Hausa and Dagomba One-String Fiddle Traditions. *Journal of Africa Studies* 9, no. 3:155–63.

DjeDje, Jacqueline Cogdell, ed. 1999. *Turn Up the Volume! A Celebration of African Music*. Los Angeles: UCLA Fowler Museum of Cultural History.

DjeDje, Jacqueline Cogdell, and William G. Carter. 1989. African Musicology: An Assessment of the Field. In *African Musicology: Current Trends*, Vol. I, ed. Jacqueline Cogdell DjeDje and William G. Carter. Atlanta Ga. Crossroads Press, African Studies Association, UCLA.

Greenberg, Joseph H. 1959. Africa as a Linguistic Area. In *Continuity and Change in African Cultures*, ed. William R. Bascom and Melville J. Herskovits. Chicago: The University of Chicago Press.

The JVC Video Anthology of World Music and Dance. 1990. Rounder Records.

The JVC/Smithsonian Folkways Video Anthology of Music and Dance. 1995. Multicultural Media.

Kebede, Ashenafi. 1982. *Roots of Black Music: The Vocal, Instrumental, and Dance Heritage of Africa and Black America.* Englewood Cliffs, NJ: Prentice-Hall.

Kubik, Gerhard. 1994. *Theory of African Music*, Vol I. Wilhelmshaven, Germany: Florian Noetzel Verlag.

Manuel, Peter. 1988. *Popular Music of the Non-Western World: An Introductory Survey.* New York: Oxford University Press.

Merriam, Alan P. 1982. *African Music in Perspective.* New York: Garland.

Murdock, George Peter. 1959. *Africa: Its Peoples and Their Culture History.* New York: McGraw-Hill.

Nketia, J. H. Kwabena. 1974. *The Music of Africa.* New York: Norton.

Stone, Ruth. 1998. African Music in a Constellation of Arts. In *Africa: The Garland Encyclopedia of World Music*, ed. Ruth M. Stone. New York: Garland.

Wachsmann, Klaus P., ed. 1971. *Essays on Music and History in Africa.* Evanston, Ill. Northwestern University Press.

KATHLEEN JENABU NOSS

The author would like to thank Dr. Jacqueline Cogdell DjeDje for her suggestions during the writing of this entry.

See also **Dialogic Performances; Musical Instruments: Focus on Namibia; Performance in Africa**

MUSIC: AFRICAN MUSICAL TRADITIONS IN THE UNITED STATES

To the perceptive observer, reminders of African cultures echo throughout American life. Body language, verbal patterns, styles of social interaction, dress, color preferences, foodways and, particularly, music and dance, all bear witness to the persistence and vitality of traditions with roots in African cultures. American music draws most heavily from the Savannah region of West Africa (including Mali, Senegal, Gambia, and Burkina Faso). But, whether viewed as retentions, modifications, or extensions, African music traditions are part of a dynamic African American culture and, like all traditional expression, must adapt to the changing needs of the communities which sustain them. African American music embraces change, but it also consistently refers back to deeply held and traditional values, aesthetic choices, and rules of performance that have provided structure, style, and meaning for African American creativity for generations.

A Group Activity

Both African and African American music have been characterized as a group activity, collective or communal in nature, and as an aspect of daily life, connected with a wide range of social activities. Secondly, African and African American–derived music commonly employ antiphonal structures, particularly patterns of overlapping call-and-response, which can be found in religious songs, worksongs, gamesongs, and by extension, blues, jazz, and even dance performance. Call and response comes in many forms: a solo voice and responding chorus, a solo voice and the answering voice of an instrument, an instrumental solo and the supporting instrumental voices of a jump band, or a solo dancer or couple supported by the energy of a band and dance hall community. Antiphony allows self-expression within a communal or participatory context, setting boundaries for individual creativity within traditional norms. Antiphonal patterns provide group support, which allows for improvisation. Whether in a jazz combo or at a corn shucking party, improvisation connects with antiphony as the call-and-response form suits the criteria of collective participation.

Multiple Rhythms

The interactive participatory nature of African-derived performance also dovetails with the use of multiple rhythms. While polyrhythms may be found in the performance of a solo blues guitarist, they are more common in group performance. Such rhythmic complexity underlies common practices such as keeping a vocal line independent of, yet connected to, instrumental backing, or dancing different rhythms with different parts of the body. This ability to work with multiple rhythms separates West African music tradition from Western European tradition and is found to some degree throughout the African-Atlantic diaspora. African instrumental music also tends to employ a percussive attack and a variety of techniques for rhythmic variations such as hitting the body of an instrument, or, in the case of stringed instruments, stopping notes by dampening the sound with one's hands, creating rhythmic tension by abruptly cutting off the sound. Musicians should be sophisticated enough to play off the beat, on the beat, around the beat, or against the beat. The use of polyrhythms, as well as the interactive nature of African American music, allows for such rhythmic dialogue and helps create the tension of suspending the beat or pushing it forward, contributing to the overall propulsive feel of African American dance music.

In contrast to European preferences for clear tones, African musicians draw on a wide tonal range, both instrumentally and vocally, using sounds derived from the community soundscape to reflect and express life through sound. This auditory range includes buzzing, burred tonalities, sizzles, rasps, moans, groans, shouts—all of which add up to a nearly tactile aesthetic, often described in terms of feeling. Feeling encompasses the range of human emotions expressed in sound—particularly, those performed on talking instruments—guitars, harmonica, saxophone, trumpet—but it also refers to physically feeling sound with one's body as well as one's ears. African American music also employs a wide tonal spectrum and, tellingly, African American musicians have greatly expanded the tonal properties of various instruments from the harmonica to the saxophone.

Just as musicians may literally play with the rhythm or the beat, they also play with the pitch, sliding up to or down to a note or employing various pitchbending techniques to work within a system of microtones different from European scales. It is not just one or two notes that can be "worried," but almost any note or pitch. Musicians playing in African American style "worry" or play around with time and pitch as well as timbre to successfully communicate feeling. Moreover, African vocal and instrumental music often use the same language. The well-known talking drums, in conjunction with West Africa's tonal languages, allow drums to simulate speech. In the Americas, instruments "talk" as well, both in sacred instrumental music and the blues. For example, the United House of Prayer Bands employ brass instruments, particularly a trombone, along with percussion to accompany ceremony and induce religious fervor. The Holiness Churches in Florida have developed a tradition of using electric steel guitars and drums for similar purposes. In both cases, the key characteristic of performance is the emulation of the human voice. The range of talking instruments—guitar, banjo, harmonica, trombone, trumpet, pedal steel guitar, or tuba made to stimulate speech patterns with mutes, plungers and a variety of playing techniques—testifies to the ongoing preference for this particular African value in American music.

Instruments

Although drum traditions were suppressed in North America, African preferences for percussion and rhythm persisted. Pseudo drums included barrels, buckets, plow points, or other household goods. In place of drums Africans in America used their bodies to provide rhythms for ceremony and recreation. More recently this had been called "Hambone," a combination of songs and improvised verses with complex hand, patting rhythms, but during slavery, it was often referred to as "patting Juba" or even "dancing Juba." Drum traditions were also transposed to string instruments. Prior to the twentieth century, the most common folk instrument in the United States, and that most commonly associated with slave and free African American musicians, was the violin or fiddle. While the standard violin comes from Europe, a remarkable array of similarly bowed lutes are common to West Africa. These include the Fulani *nyanyer*, the Hausa *kukuma*, the *soko* from Burkina Faso and the *gonge* or *godgi* common to Northern Ghana. These instruments have one, two, or more strings, are bowed and fretted with the left hand. Their timbre is generally harsher than the sweeter tone of the European fiddle, and they can sound quite like the human voice. Ensembles of bowed instruments and other percussion instruments provide instrumental backing for vocal song and dance, foreshadowing the development of the African American string band tradition in which violin, banjo, and other percussion instruments served as the soundtrack for dances. In the plantation-era American South, fiddle players sometimes employed what is called a "straw beater" to hover over the fiddle and beat on the fiddle strings with two lengths of straw adding a pronounced percussive effect and complicating the rhythm.

Apart from bowed instruments, a remarkable array of string instruments, such as lutes, lyres, and harps, are also widely used throughout Africa. However, once the guitar became readily available, it tended to obscure older traditional instruments, and the availability of mass-produced commercial instruments eroded traditional methods of construction. Nevertheless, the traditional playing techniques were often transported to the guitar, and continue to echo through African music today.

African American musicians utilize comparatively short, rhythmic, melodic building blocks, typical of the savannah region of Africa. These short, rhythmic, melodic phrases, or riffs, were enhanced by various African techniques such as bending notes, hammering on, pulling off, damping the strings for rhythmic effect, or hitting on the body of the instruments. Violin, banjo and later the guitar were all subjected to these African-

derived techniques, altering European musical ideas and creating distinctly different styles. Various finger-picking and strumming techniques also drew on African traditions.

Another widely distributed African and African American string instrument is the so-called diddley bow or one-string guitar. Countless blues artists recall making them as children, a crucial step in the learning process prior to acquiring a standard model. Often constructed of broom wire, they were characteristically nailed "upside the wall" and raised by a makeshift bridge at the top and bottom often using a tin can as a resonator. The playing technique involved using a glass or metal slide, or perhaps a knife. This method of sliding on the string allowed the player to slide up or down to a note rather than hitting a pitch dead on. The technique, when translated to the six-string guitar, allowed the artist to work within the traditional African American scale rather than depend on fret placement, which corresponded to a European scale. It also allowed the instrument a greater capacity for emulating the human voice. Moreover, early guitar open tunings connected the guitar with earlier banjo tunings, and from the banjo back to Africa.

Yet another popular blues instrument, the harmonica, also exhibits a range of African-derived playing techniques. African reed instruments such as the Fulani *tiorumba* or the *bounkam* from Burkina Faso produce sounds much like the harmonica. But, unlike the harmonica, the *bounkam* is a single reed instrument, which means one needs to use tongue pressure and mouth shape to bend the notes, to produce a melody. The harmonica was initially designed to be played in the key or the blow notes and that is how European or white musicians initially used the instrument. But "cross harp," which depends on draw notes rather than the blow notes, was an African American innovation in which the instrument was literally played backwards. By utilizing note bending and hand cupping, African Americans reshaped the harmonica to a traditional aesthetic rooted in African practices. Furthermore, African American style is predicated on the instrument's ability to approximate the sound and emotional nuances of the human voice.

Harmonica riffs also echo vocal traditions such as field hollers. Hollers can be found throughout Africa and the African diaspora and were once common to the soundscape of southern agricultural work. Through blues musicians, from Tommy Johnson to Howling Wolf, they became part of the vocal repertoire of American popular music. Other vocal techniques suce as falsetto snaps, moaning, the heavy use of melisma, and various yodeling techniques likewise inform blues, gospel, soul, and rock. Indeed, today's popular music draws heavily on African American tradition and, by extension, African roots. In turn, African music is influenced by both North and South American traditions, and contemporary technology has increased the rate of change and the range of possible influences. Nevertheless, African musical traditions remain readily discernible and will continue to shape world music into the twenty-first century.

References

Charters, Samuel. 1981. *The Roots of the Blues: An African Search.* New York: Perigee Books.

Chernoff, John Miller. 1979. *African Rhythm and African Sensibility: Aesthetics and Social Action in African Musical Idioms.* Chicago: University of Chicago Press.

Kebebe, Ashenafi. 1995. *Roots of Black Music: The Vocal, Instrumental, and Dance Heritage of Africa and Black America.* Trenton, N.J.: Africa World Press.

Maultsby, Portia. 1990. Africanisms in African-American Music. In *Africanisms in American Culture,* edited by, Joseph E. Holloway, Bloomington: Indiana University Press.

Oliver, Paul. 1970. *Savannah Syncopators: African Retentions in the Blues.* New York: Stein and Day, 1970.

BARRY LEE PEARSON

See also **Carnival; Diaspora; Polyrhythms; Verbal Arts: African American**

MUSIC: ARAB AND JEWISH MUSIC OF NORTH AFRICA

The musical and dancing traditions of Arabs and Jews in North Africa plays a prominent role in all walks of life. These traditions represent a conglomerate of tribal, rural, and urban musical and dancing styles, which display old and new characteristics. They involve multiple uses, encompassing religious and ritual functions that enhance events related to annual and life cycles, as well as entertaining purposes. They are partly of a traditional and folk nature, partly conceived in an artistic sophisticated manner strongly affiliated with the so-called Andalusian musical and instrumental style, and partly represent a mixture of traditional and art repertories. A common trait is the predominance of vocal music—with or without instrumental accompaniment. The latter would include, in the case of folk music, various drums, rhythmic instruments, and a few melodic instruments like the flute, the oboe-like (*ghaita*) and simple stringed instruments, whether plucked (*gunbri*) or fretted (*rabab* and *amzad*), and, in the case of art music, an ensemble of a *rabab*, or violin, *kuitra* or *'ud* (short-necked lute), and drums.

In the realm of performance practice, the poet-musician has a uniquely important position. Those belonging to this class, both male and female, are poetically and musically gifted and articulate the moods and aspirations of their compatriots. The sung texts in the whole repertory are either in classical Arabic and Hebrew, in one of the various local vernacular Arabic and other recognized idioms, or in combinations of classical and vernacular languages. Texts in classical Arabic, Hebrew, and a large part of those in two or more idioms or languages exist in written form, but the others, including women's songs, are orally transmitted.

In the category that includes written texts, is another salient musical trait—the blurring of the borderline supposedly separating art and folk modes of expression. Such an intermingling and interpenetrating of those expressions is to be found mainly in religious music of both Jews and Muslims.

Religious and "Serious" Music

There is a basic distinction in North African music between two major classes: serious and light. In Morocco these are called, respectively, *klem el-djed* and *klem el-hazel*, which mean discourse of a religious and ethical nature as opposed to jesting or lighthearted banter. The musical aspect of these categories should roughly correspond to "long songs" which are rhythmically free and ornamented, and single out the meaning of the words and "syllabic melodies," which are distinguished by strictly measured and scanned rhythm, short verses, and a limited use of embellishments.

The major genre belonging to the first class is the Maghribian *qasida*, also called *nashid* in Tunisia. The *qasida* derives from the classical, prestigious poetical genre of the same name, which was based on a union of meter and rhyme, with the same rhythmical structure repeated in each line of the poem. Connected essentially with religious ceremonies, the Maghribian *qasida* is performed by specialized singers, the *qassadin*, at various feasts, celebrations, and specific ceremonies, including those held by the mystic orders. Its musical rendering can embody a simple form or a very sophisticated one. In a religious context, it is, as a rule, essentially vocal and simple, but there are cases of recourse to art secular forms and tunes drawn from the *nuba* (compound composition) repertory, with or without instrumental accompaniment. This way of combining formal and secular tunes was, despite the devotional and serene approach of the performers, criticised by certain theologians. On the other hand, the sophisticated rendering of the *qasida* and *nashid* under the same respectful character can be found in events that are not part of a formal religious context.

A simple form of the genre is widely known through the performance of the class of itinerant singers called *meddah* (panegyrist). Their songs, which encompass a great variety of themes, begin and terminate with a long formula of piety and creed.

Jewish Music

While the musical component of the major Maghribian categories and genres is shared by male and female Jewish musicians and performers, the distinguishing traits of Jewish music should be sought in its linguistic, thematic, and functional particularities. First and foremost are the liturgical Hebrew poems written by the most famous poets of the Jewish people, as well as by locally distinguished ones. These include hymns of praise, imploration, invocations, supplications, lamentations, Jewish holidays, principles of creed, and moral values. Under the influence of kabbalistic ideas and doctrine, a ceremony called *baqqashot* (supplications) was established. The singing of *baqqashot* is sophisticated, borrowing its main components from the art of the compound secular form the *nuba*, but completely avoiding instrumental accompaniment. In the framework of this ceremony were introduced dozens of *qasida*, composed by local poets borrowing their tunes from Arab *qasidas*. These themes deal with historical or happy and tragic events concerning local communities or the Jewish people as a whole. Most of the *qasidas* exist in written form and in Arabic or Judeo-Arabic dialects. The Jewish repertory of sung poetry includes interesting genre called *matruz* ("embroidered") in which verses in Hebrew, Aramaic, Arabic, and Judeo-Arabic are combined in different ways. This genre, as well as the fact of their sharing an indigenous musical language, may be considered symbolic of the cultural encounter between Jews and Muslims.

Mystic Orders and Healing Rituals

The mystics of the Muslim world developed complex congregational rituals and spiritual exercises designed to send participants into religious ecstasy. Music and dance are essential in this ecstatic procedure. The ritual of some North African groups is called *hadra*, the name usually given to the North African Sufi ritual that assists adepts to attain mystical union with God. It may involve extravagant behavior such as tearing one's clothing, sitting on hot coals, self-mutilation and exorcism, or magico-religious heating rituals.

Such healing rituals are usually performed at special therapeutic *hadra*, mainly by the 'Isawiyya, or 'Isawa, one of the most popular religious confraternities founded by Ahmed ben 'Isa (d. 1523); the Hamadisha, a society more aptly described as a community of exorcists founded by 'Ali ben Hamdush (16th century); and the Gnawa in Morocco, or the *soudanis*, as they are known in Algeria and Tunisia, a brotherhood comprised of descendants of slaves who placed themselves under the patronage of Bilal, the Prophet's black *muezzin*. Frequently, the 'Isawa and Ghnawi collaborate in performing therapeutic *hadras*, held in the houses of patients in need of a cure for some disease, or seeking release from an evil spirit that has possessed them.

The chief aim of their *hadra* is to induce trances in themselves and in the sick in order to clear a path for certain spirits to pass through the soul and depart from it, that is, to release psychic blockages. The healing process depends very much on the use of exciting music and frenzied ecstatic dancing by both healers and patients. The predominance of a rhythmic component is an essential agent of the stimulation sought. In the Hamadshi *hadra*, the melodies played by the oboe-like *ghaita* usually allude to the particular spirits that should be pacified or exorcised. In the performance of the Ghnawi *hadra*, the player on *gunbri* (a long-necked lute), is considered as a knowledgeable person who assumes, in this capacity, the role of the ritual's master; he also beats the *ganga* (a big side-drum). The other musicians of the group are four or six *qeraqeb* (a pair of iron clappers) players. Those musicians also take part in the dancing and can beat a small drum. To the metallic beat of this ensemble the dancers display their skills in a sequence of acrobatic figures performed with impressive rapidity. Finally, it should be noted that the effect of the music is tremendously increased when a subtle gamut of perfumes (incenses) is being used at a precise moment of the ritual.

Dance

Communal dances, which are more participatory activities than performances, characterize the sequence of dances of various Berber groups. Women are frequently included among the large number of participants in the *ahidou* and *ahwash* dances. A sequence of dances, linked to each other and progressing from slow to a more rapid movement, are frequently performed by mixed groups, either in two lines, one of women and the other of men, or in a circle with men and women alternating. Standing shoulder to shoulder or holding hands and bending backward and forward, the performers move while singing and clapping hands. They are accompanied by an ensemble of frame-drum (*bendir*). The *bendir* players hold the drum horizontally and beat the skin stretched underneath with an upward movement.

In Algeria, there is an interesting couple dance called *saadaoui*. The two dancers perform basically the same patterns, moving to the sounds of the *ghaita* and the *bendir*, without jumping or sliding. In the Algerian Sahara, a ritual dance is performed in front of men by young girls who have reached puberty. The girls dance in couples facing each other, their arms engaging in a kind of dialogue.

In another interesting dance, young unmarried Tunisian and Lybian girls perform in front of young men a "hair" dance, called *nakh*. Kneeling with their hair loose, the girls sway, moving the head and upper torso in time to the accompanying music.

Individual dancing is fairly typical of folk dances in urban and semiurban centers. The dancers usually treat the torso as two separate units, the hips gyrating or shaking. In Morocco, professional itinerant musician-dancers travel as troupes throughout the country. They often perform at Marrakesh where, clad in white robes, they dance, sing, and play on the *gunbri* and a single-stringed, skin-bellied fiddle.

Women's Songs

As in other parts of the Islamic world, North African women singing for other women on various occasions encouraged the emergence and crystallization of songs in which Muslim and Jewish women could express their world of experiences and the female values they upheld.

Their songs in the vernacular languages pertain exclusively to the realm of oral tradition. They reflect themes of everyday life, individual personal experiences, and various communal happenings. Among the latter, wedding ceremonies and rituals are the most important. The woman fortifies her spirit by singing to herself, and perhaps to her infant who absorbs the mother's confessions, longing, complaints, and dreams. This kind of singing presents a different, lyrical aspect, virtually not found in men's singing. The songs are sung in public on occasions of a folk nature by either a group or one individual with a good voice. Particularly notable is the performance of funeral laments and dirges, which are considered the province of women who excel as keeners.

The female poet-singer draws her poetical material from tradition and from a repository of themes, idioms, and images, which she adapts to a given situation. The same holds true for the music, which is always taken from the reserve of traditional melodies.

Among the widespread female folk lyric genres are the *'arubi*, the *mawwal*, and the swing songs; all of them are more or less associated with urban and semiurban life. The Tunisian *'arubi* is a strophic quatrain song; the Moroccan and Algerian are more flexible and have five to six lines in a strophe. The themes of both the *'arubi* and *mawwal*, whose shorter strophe includes three to six lines, describe sorrow, loneliness, unsatisfied love, betrayal, separation, and life and death in exile. The performers are usually gifted nonprofessional women; sometimes two women compete, exchanging improvised verses bound by strict rhythmic and melodic conventions.

Swing songs represent an important female repertory, which has existed in North Africa for many centuries. These songs are performed in various local vernacular languages on the occasion of magic, hagiographic, and games-playing rituals. In their poetical structure close to the *'arubi*, the swing songs are performed collectively in an alternating manner in a natural environment (meadow, waterfall, garden); their slow rhythm is more or less molded to the range of the swaying human form. The form of the swing songs is a good way of alleviating tension and bringing hearts together.

References

Crapanzano, Vincenzo. 1975. *The Hamadsha*: *A Study in Moroccan Psychiatry*. Berkeley: University of California Press.

Guettat, Mahmud. 1980. *La musique classique du Maghreb*. Paris: Sindbad Lièvre, Viviane: Karthala. 1984. *Danses du Maghreb d'une rive a l'autre*. Paris.

Lachmann, Robert. 1940. *Jewish Cantillation and Song in the Isle of Djerba*. Jerusalem: Azriel Press.

Lortat-Jacob, Bernard. 1980. *Musique et fêtes au Haut-Atlas*. Paris: Mouton/EBESS. Cahiers de l'Homme.

Schuyler, Philip. 1974. *Al-Milhun: The Fusion of Folk and Art Traditions in a Moroccan Song Poem*. Washington, D.C..

Schuyler, Philip. 1984. Berber Professional Musicians in Performance. In *Performance Practice. Ethnomusicological Perspectives*. ed. G. Behague, London: Greenwood Press.

Shiloah, Amnon. 1992. *Jewish Musical Traditions*. Detroit: Wayne State University Press. [Reprint in paperback 1995].

Shiloah, Amnon. 1995. *Music in the World of Islam: A Socio-Cultural Study*. London: Scolar Press

Yelles-Chaouche, Mourad. 1996. Les chants de Pescarpolette au Maghreb. *Journal of Mediterranean Studies*, 6, no. 1: 120–34.

AMNON SHILOAH

See also **Maghrib; North Africa**

MUSIC: ATALAKU OF CONGO (ZAIRE)

The term *atalaku* is said to have come from a Kikongo expression meaning "Look here, look at me", and first appears in common parlance in Kinshasa (capital of former Zaire, today known as the Democratic Republic of the Congo) in the early 1980s. The term is not only part of an expression associated with a popular music dance step from that period, but it has also come to be the primary term used to refer to the performing disc jockeys who sing and shout during the dance sequences which have come to stand for contemporary Congolese music.

Since the 1970s, most popular dance music in Congo-Zaire has been made up of songs which have a unique two-part song structure: a slow, lyrical introduction followed by a fast-paced dance sequence (usually referred to as *seben*). During the first part of each song, couples will dance close together with their arms around each other, listening to the fluid melodies and parallel harmonies of the vocalists. Several minutes into the song, when the lead guitar and the change in rhythm announce the arrival of the *seben*, couples separate, and individuals begin to express themselves as part of a larger, loosely organized, whole (Tchebwa 1996, 339). The *seben*'s particular mood of controlled frenzy is maintained in great part by the *atalaku*, who, having taken the microphone of one of the now dancing singers, improvises a careful combination of shouts, melodies, and various other vocal gymnastics which are intended to drive people in the audience (and on stage) to dance.

The emergence of the role of *atalaku* is intimately tied to the presence of urban traditional styles of music in Kinshasa. Musicians that play ethnic-based traditional music are often hired to play at funeral parties (*matanga*) and other important life-cycle ceremonies, but not many groups can earn a regular income from this kind of work. In the late 1970s, when some of these groups began to perform in the bars and concert venues associated with "modern" dance music, they immediately at-

tracted the attention of a wider urban audience. In 1982, two members of the Zaiko Langa Langa (the flagship group of the Zairean new wave and the most successful band at the time) approached several musicians from an urban traditional group named Bana Odeon and asked them if they wanted to join Zaiko. They would play their signature rhythm on homemade maracas (an emptied insecticide spray can with soundholes for resonance and hardened seeds inside), and during the *seben* they would flood the microphone with the shouts and proverbs which were a large part of urban traditional music's appeal.

The first shout they sang began with the phrase "atalaku mama" ("look here, woman") and it is from here that these performing disc jockeys were given the name *atalaku* (in French *animateur*). Although shouts have always been a part of popular music in the Congo region, it was not until this period that they became used in any systematic way. Most shouts are sung in coded language, either using obscure expressions from one of the many Kikongo languages in the region or drawing from creative forms of urban slang (on the Kinshasa youth slang known as *hindubill*, see Tchebwa 1996). Thus it is not uncommon, even with very popular shouts, for people to create their own meanings based on the little they are able to understand. At any given moment there is a pool of favorite shouts which circulate and from which almost all bands will draw to complete their own repertoire of shouts. This habit of borrowing shouts (usually from younger, less well-known bands) is one of the reasons why Congolese music has been criticized for being repetitive. Since the early 1980s, shouts have gone from being shouted to being shouted and sung, to being completely sung, finally culminating in the recent practice of some lead singers (Koffi Olomide, General Defao, J.P. Buse) who croon shouts with "care" (*atalaku va soin*) or "charm" (*atalaku va charme*).

Today, very few bands in Kinshasa perform without one or more *atalaku*. Given the music's emphasis on a lively stage show, the *atalaku* has become an indispensable part of the modern dance band phenomenon. He is an instrumentalist, a vocalist, and a dancer; but he is most valued for his ability to punctuate the music with the often hysterical shouts and melodies that guide the audience through the various dance steps that occur in live performance. The *atalaku* is interesting not only for his shouts and stage antics which make him a sort of live-time trickster, but also because the material he uses very often comes from traditional or at least urban-traditional music forms, and thus his creative borrowing gives important clues about how traditional forms of cultural knowledge become tied up in the process of commercialization. Unfortunately, the *atalaku*'s association with traditional music is somewhat of a stigma, and this limits not only his position within the band hierarchy, but also within society (White 2000). Following the first atalakus, Nono and Bebe Atalaku (Zaiko Langa Langa), only a handful of musicians have been able to make a name for themselves in this musical role. They include Diuna Mumbafu (Empire Bakuba), Ditutala (Choc Stars), Robert Ekokota, and more recently Tutu Kaludii (Wenge Musica BCBG) and Bill Clinton (Quartier Latin).

The phenomenon of *atalaku* was certainly influenced by Mobutu's elaborate propaganda machine which used "traditional" music and dance from the various regions of Zaire to sing his praises and those of his one-party state. In this context, the "animateur" took on a political as well as a musical role (Kapalanga 1989) and various accounts have discussed the way that the *atalaku* is implicated in the violence of youth culture (Biava 1997) and patron-client relations (White 1997). Popular accounts of the *atalaku* also relate this phenomenon to the shouts and dances of James Brown, whose visit to Kinshasa had a huge impact on youth music and dance in the 1970s (Nkashama 1979). If the *atalaku* is often compared to hip-hop's "M.C.," it is probably because he shouts in a highly percussive manner and combines words and song in an impressive, often improvised, display of verbal skill. Although the *atalaku*'s art differs significantly from that of the M.C., it shows important commonalities with rap and other musics of the African diaspora, and suggests that the resilience of African contemporary music is, in part due to its ability to creatively draw from the past.

References

Bemba, Sylvain. 1984. *Cinquante ans de musique du Congo-Zaire: (1920–1907): De Paul Kamba à Tabu Lev.* Paris: Présence Africaine.

Biaya, T.K. 1997. Kinshasa: Anomie, "ambiance" et violence. In *Youth, Street Culture, and Urban Violence in Africa.* ed. Georges Hirault and Pius Adesanmi. pp. 329–82. Proceedings of the International Symposium, Abidjan, May 1997. Ibadan: Institut Français de Recherche en Afrique.

Kapalanga, Gazungil Sang'Amin. 1989. *Les spectacles d'animation politique en Republique du Zaire.* Louvain-la-Neuve: Cahiers theatre Louvain.

Lonoh, M. B. 1969. Essai de Cammentaire sur la Musique Congolaise Moderne. Kinshasa: S.E.I.M.N.C. in collaboration with the Zairean Ministry of Arts and Culture.

Nkashama, P. Ngandu. 1979. Ivresse et Vertige: les nouvelles danses des jeunes au Zaire. *L'Afrique litteraire et artistique* 51: 94–102.

Tchebwa, Manda. 1996. La Terre de la Chanson: La musique zäiroise hier et aujourd'hoi. Brussels: Duculot.

White, Bob W. 2000. "Modernity's Trickster: 'Dipping' and 'Throwing' in Congolese Popular Dance Music." In *Research in African Literatures.* Vol. 30, no. 4. (Winter): 156–175.

———. 1997. Singing the Sponsor: Popular Music and Micropolitics in Mobutland and After. CAAS Working Paper Series: Q44 (October): 1–30. Ann Arbor, Michigan: Center for Afroamerican and African Studies.

ROBERT W. WHITE

See also **Dialogic Performances Call-and-Response in African Narrating**

MUSIC AND DANCE STYLES OF THE EWE

The Ewe people live in southeastern Ghana, southern Togo, and southwestern Benin. The Ewe are said to have migrated to Ghana from more eastern regions. Locke (1992, 11) suggests the Ewe migrated to Ghana from Nigeria in the sixteenth century, while Ladzekpo and Ladzekpo (1980, 216) argue that Notsie in Togo served as the final home of the ancestors of Ghanaian Ewe prior to their move to Ghana in the seventeenth century. Between the sixteenth and nineteenth centuries, conflicts arose between these Ewe and other ethnic groups, including the Akan and the Ashanti (Manoukin 1952, 13). The British became involved in 1874, determined to help the Ewe and other ethnic groups quiet the Ashanti, who had by then invaded and ran-

sacked Ewe territories. Although the British signed peace treaties with several ethnic groups, they defeated Ewe subgroups and established their own rule. In 1899, Ewe territories were divided under the rule of the British and Germans. After World War I, these territories were split between the British, in what became Ghana, and the French, in Togo (Manoukin 1952, 13).

Traditionally, the Ewe worked primarily as agriculturalists and fishermen, and many Ewe in rural areas of Ghana still serve in these capacities. Other professions among the Ewe include making handicrafts and trading. Land ownership and some political and religious offices traditionally were passed down patrilineally. Both traditional religious beliefs and Christianity are practiced in Ewe areas today. Madeline Manoukin describes three types of supernatural beings: the supreme god Mawo, spirits or *trowo*, and ancestral spirits (Manoukin 1952, 46–9). Alfred Ladzekpo and Kobla Ladzekpo discuss worship of the Afa and Yewe gods among the Anlo Ewe in the Volta Region of Ghana (1980, 218).

Music functions as an integral part of Ewe culture. Today, traditional music ensembles are heard most often at religious ceremonies and funerals. Instrumental music, singing, clapping, and dancing usually are performed together, as elements that draw from, and communicate with, each other, forming a complete whole. While particular musicians may be chosen as instrumental and vocal soloists, the entire community participates in performances by singing choral responses, clapping along to the music, or dancing. Ewe music and dance styles include Kinka, Atsiagbeko, Brekete, Kete, Gahu, and Bobobo.

Gahu

Gahu is one of the styles most researched by scholars and, already popular among the Ewe, it is becoming increasingly popular outside Ghana. Bobobo is perhaps unique in the extent to which it is associated with Christianity, although other styles are also said to contain Christian elements.

Gahu is a recreational drumming, dance, and song style. According to Ewe drummers in Kopeyia, in the Volta Region of Ghana, the style, originally called Kokosawa, was created by the Yoruba in Nigeria. These drummers explain that the Ewe borrowed the style from the Yoruba, eventually increasing the tempo of the music and changing the name of the style to Gahu, meaning "money drum." The Ewe supposedly chose this name because the costumes for the dancers were so expensive that the dancers could not afford them. Kobla Ladzekpo and Alan Eder, however, argue that this theory is incorrect. Gahu, or Agahu, they explain, came from the Egun people of Ketonu in Benin. Known first as Gunbe, the style spread to the Badagry region of Nigeria and, through Ewe fisherman, then to Ghana (Ladzekpo and Eder 1992, 181–2). The name Agahu, according to Ladzekpo and Eder, was given to the style when an airplane flew over a performance of Gunbe and an individual exclaimed "*aga-hun*," meaning "air vessel" or "airplane" (1992; 183–4). In a more recent work, Christian Horton suggests that Gahu developed from the style *gumbe*, which was brought from Jamaica to Sierra Leone by freed slaves and later spread to other countries (Horton 1999).

The Gahu instrumental ensemble incorporates the following instruments: the *gankogui* double bell; the *axatse* rattle, made by hanging cowry shells or beads on the outside of a gourd; *kagan*, *kidi*, and *sogo* supporting drums; and the *gboba* or *agboba* master drum. The drums are barrel-shaped instruments of different sizes and pitches. Each instrumentalist has basic rhythmic patterns upon which he or she may improvise to a greater or lesser extent. The master drummer is responsible for signaling changes between rhythmic patterns to the remainder of the ensemble. Communication between drummers functions as call and response, for the supporting drummers must respond with the appropriate rhythmic patterns to calls given by the master drummer. The drums thus communicate in much the same way people converse orally or in written literature. Furthermore, drum tones are directly related to speech tones. Differing drum tones, which the drummers produce and alter, using a combination of one or two drumsticks and their hands, mimic the sound of speech tones, so the drums truly "speak" phrases.

The words that the Ewe in Ghana now associate with the drum variations of Gahu consist of a mixture of Yoruba, Ewe, and other languages from Benin and Togo. The drummers in Kopeyia who argue that Gahu originated with the Yoruba note that many of the Ewe who played Kokosawa did not speak Yoruba. They learned to play the Kokosawa drum patterns and memorized the Yoruba words associated with these patterns, but they did not understand the meanings of the words and thus mispronounced or eventually forgot many words. Tradition did not allow young musicians to ask questions of the few elders who did understand Yoruba; thus, knowledge of the correct pronunciations and meanings of the Yoruba words died with those elders.

The Gahu instrumental ensemble is usually accompanied by call-and-response singing. The Gahu dance, a circular dance for a group of men and women, also may be performed.

Bobobo

Bobobo is an Ewe music form that originated in Pando, in the Volta region of Ghana. Bobobo supposedly was founded by a Christian named Mr. Nuatro and was created as a style of traditional music that would be accepted in churches. It still is associated with Christianity, particularly with Christmas. Musical ensembles form before Christmas and play until after the New Year, each day competing with one another in different villages. Judges are brought from Pando to judge the groups.

Two bells, called *toke*, are used for Bobobo; one is considered female and the other male. Downbeats are added by an *adjijiwa*. A rattle made by filling a gourd with seeds, or an *axatse* rattle with a string that can be tied around the neck, follows the *adjijiwa*. There are supposed to be two supporting drums called *adzima*, playing different rhythms, but sometimes only one may be used. A tall drum that is hung around the neck, sometimes substituted by a *kagan*, also may be played. Traditionally, only one master drum, called an *agodome*, was used, but today, three master drums may be played in order to produce a louder sound. If three drums are used, all drummers play the same variations, each one signaling changes to the others. Some Bobobo drum patterns correspond to particular songs, but other patterns may accompany any song. Bobobo songs usually center on love, death, and the Christian faith.

Traditional Ewe drumming and dance styles continue to be performed frequently in Ewe regions of Ghana today. The migration of some Ewe to other countries and increased collaboration among musicians and scholars, with non-Ghanaian musicians traveling to Ghana to study and Ewe traveling to other regions of the world to live and perform, has led to Ewe music also being performed quite frequently outside Ghana. Ewe ensembles, for instance, can be heard practicing and performing on many university campuses in the United States.[1]

Notes

[1] Portions of this article were published in "Traditions and Transformations: Ewe, Ashanti and Baganda Drumming, Dance and Song in Contemporary Africa" (Noss 2000). This information was provided by drummers at the Dagbe Cultural Centre, founded by the late master drummer Godwin Agbeli, during fieldwork in Ghana in 1997. Unless otherwise noted, information presented in the remainder of the article is also according to these drummers.

References

Horton, Christian Dowu Jayeola. 1999. The Role of the Gumbe in Popular Music and Dance Styles in Sierra Leone. In *Turn Up the Volume! A Celebration of African Music*, ed. Jacqueline Cogdell DjeDje. Los Angeles: UCLA Fowler Museum of Cultural History.

Ladzekpo, Alfred, and Kobla Ladzekpo. 1980. Anlo Ewe Music in Anyako, Volta Region, Ghana. In *Musics of Many Cultures: An Introduction*, ed. Elizabeth May, Berkeley: University of California Press.

Ladzekpo, Kobla, and Alan Eder. 1992. Agahu: Music Across Many Nations. In *African Musicology: Current Trends*, ed. Jacqueline Cogdell DjeDje, Vol. 2, Los Angeles: Regents of the University of California.

Locke, David. 1992. *Kpegisu: A War Drum of the Ewe*. Tempe, Au: White Cliffs Media Company.

Manoukin, Madeline. 1952. *The Ewe-Speaking People of Togoland and the Gold Coast*. London: International African Institute.

Noss, Kathleen. 2000. Traditions and Transformations: Ewe, Ashanti and Baganda Drumming, Dance and Song in Contemporary Africa. *Percussive Notes* 38, no. 4: 34–8.

KATHLEEN JENAKO NOSS

See also **Music; Music in Africa**

MUSIC AND DANCE: UGANDA

Uganda displays a diversity of folk performing arts traditions that combine aspects of music, dance, and drama. The southern kingdom of Buganda is the most thoroughly studied region, but significant research has also been undertaken in Busoga, Ankole, and Acholi. This article classifies the instruments of Uganda and outlines some of the major dance features of the country.

Musical Instruments

Uganda retains an unusually large number of musical instruments and performance styles, which vary according to region. Musical form is closely tied to linguistic structure, and speakers of the same language family often share common performance features.

Membranophones:

Drums figure prominently in almost every region of Uganda. In addition to providing the primary accompaniment for a variety of dance forms, drums were an important part of the royal regalia in many kingdoms and chiefdoms of East Africa. There are two general varieties of drums in Uganda—double membrane (often called "Uganda" drums) and single membrane. Dimensions and construction techniques vary according to region, but cowhide is widely used for double-membrane drums, while monitor lizard skin is often used for single-membrane drums (as well as for a variety of string instruments).

Idiophones:

This class of instruments includes xylophones, lamellaphones (thumb pianos), bells and clappers (usually worn and activated by dancing), rattles, half gourds, clay pots, and percussive troughs. The southern Ugandan xylophone complex (found in Buganda and Busoga), in which multiple artists combine interlocking parts on a single instrument to create larger, more complex melodies, is one of the best studied of Uganda's musical traditions.

Chordophones:

A wide variety of string instruments exist in Uganda, including bow harps, lyres, tube fiddles, zithers, and musical bows. Poetic recitation by solo performers is most often accompanied by such instruments, but ensembles are also common. Notable research has been conducted on the string traditions of Buganda, including the *ennanga* (bow harp), *endongo* (lyre), and *ndingidi* (tube fiddle).

Aerophones:

Notched flutes, panpipes, transverse flutes, transverse trumpets, end-blown trumpets, and a variety of small horns are found throughout Uganda. Aerophones are often played together in sets, with several people combining intricately interlocking parts. The related traditions of royal transverse trumpet ensembles (*amakondere*) of the Interlacustrine kingdoms has been particularly well studied, as have the royal flute ensembles of the Kabaka of Buganda (called *ekibiina ky'abalere*).

Dance Traditions

As with Uganda's music, dance traditions vary widely throughout the country. It is possible, however, to identify choreographic

Members of the Nebbi Community Adungu Group performing social dance music on *adungu* bow harps, Uganda, 1995. Photo © Wade Patterson.

motifs that prevail in certain areas. In general, dance formations may constitute lines, circles, or compact groups.

Waist-Centered Dances:

Dance traditions of the southern regions of Buganda and Busoga emphasize gyrating waist movement. Upper body motion is minimized while specific foot patterns create the desired waist movements, which are further accentuated by cloth and skin adornments worn around the hips.

Leaping and Stamping Dances:

Western Ugandan dances often accentuate movements that bring the feet into forceful contact with ground. In Bunyoro, for example, activated rattles worn around the ankles during the *ekitaguriro* dance emphasize such action. In the northeast, among the Karamojong, dances in which performers wearing ankle bells leap in place are common.

Dances Emphasizing Arm, Leg, and Head Movement:

Dances of northern and northwestern Uganda use combinations of arm and leg movements, which often reflect work-related motion. The use of ankle bells is common, but foot movements are not generally as pronounced as with the western stamping dances. Waist movement is usually linear (either front to back or side to side) and not gyrating, as in southern Uganda. Many of the northern regions (such as Acholi and Karamoja) also use a variety of head adornments that emphasize subtle neck and head movements.

References

Kubik, G. 1964. Xylophone Playing in Southern Uganda. *Journal of the Royal Anthropological Institute* 94: 138.

Kyagambiddwa, Joseph. 1955. *African Music from the Source of the Nile.* New York: Frederick A. Praeger.

Mbabi-Katana, S. 1982. *The History of Amakondere (Royal Trumpet Set) of the Interlacustrine States of East Africa.* Kampala: n.p.

Mukasa, Edward G. 1977. *A Brief Anthology on Uganda Musical Instruments.* Kampala: Ministry of Culture and Community Development.

p'Bitek, Okot. 1974. *Horn of My Love.* Nairobi: Heinemann Kenya.

Herbert Bakesigaki performing on *enanga* trough zither in the region of Kigezi, southwestern Uganda, 1995. Photo © Wade Patterson.

Van Thiel, Paul. 1977. *Multi-Tribal Music of Ankole: An Ethnomusicological Study Including a Glossary of Musical Terms.* Belgium: Musee Royal De L'Afrique Centrale.

Wachsmann, K.P. 1971. Musical Instruments in Kiganda Tradition and Their Place in the East African Scene. In *Essays on Music and History in Africa*, ed. K.P. Wachsmann, Evanston: Northwestern University Press.

———. 1950. An Equal-Stepped Tuning in a Ganda Harp. *Nature.*

WADE PATTERSON

See also **Music; Music in Africa**

MUSIC: MUSICAL INNOVATION IN AFRICAN INDEPENDENT CHURCHES

Music and religion are two interrelated sites of cultural production in Africa, as shown in examples from precolonial to contemporary times. It is, however, within the various appropriations and manifestations of Christianity in Africa that we find intense creativity and innovation in sub-Saharan Africa. Important areas of this production of culture include: music and dance, legends, social ethics, plastic arts, language use and script, oratory, ethnic and gender relations. Several factors and processes account for the significant emphasis on music (or the performative) in independent churches in Africa. For example, in addition to the general affective and symbolic imports of music in ritual settings, music making in African societies generally aims at a composite or unified experience; it embraces sound, movement, and verbal and visual arts in spectacular ways. This comprehensive approach to music is now best illustrated in the musical traditions of various churches in contemporary Africa. The great variety of musical traditions encountered in the churches can be attributed also to the appeal of plural musical traditions, that is, secular or popular musical cultures, which are easily co-opted into the church repertory. The religious/sacred and secular are, however, not totally separate domains, as articulated in African systems of thought and daily practice. The close relationship between the performative and religious traditions in Africa is, therefore, due in part to the widespread practice of music as an integrated art form and in part to the fluid boundaries between the sacred and secular.

Contemporary Christian musical traditions in the independent church, as examined below, continue and extend these fundamental principles and practices concerning the nature of music and its relations to other aspects of life and living in Africa.

The Independent Church in Perspective

A multitude of terms and designations are employed interchangeably to refer to independent churches in Africa, particularly those that integrate beliefs and practices from the Old and New Testaments and their accompanying indigenous traditions. Some of these designations are: "spiritual churches," African Independent Churches, African Indigenous Churches, and African Initiated Churches (AIC is the acronym for the last church). These churches are, however, now described simply as "independent," mainly because they have gained autonomy or broken away from a mainline or denominational church, or they have been founded by an independent visionary who had no previous denominational affiliation. Their emphasis on innovative liturgy and music distinguishes them also from the older denominations, which increasingly have been adopting the practices and beliefs associated with the independent churches.

David Barrett, in his seminal texts, outlined the basic features of over six thousand African independent churches (Barrett 1968, 1971, 1989). In 1986, Bennetta Jules-Rosette predicted—with the independent church in mind—that, "[b]y the year 2000, it is expected that Africa will house 351 million Christians, 31.2 percent of the world's total Christian population, representing a shift in the center of Christianity from north to south" (1986, 159–85). The following observations from a chapter, "Indigenous Expressions of Christianity in Africa," by Charles Forman sums up the situation of the African independent church:

> The mid-twentieth century has witnessed the most rapid indigenization of Christianity in Africa . . . The most radical reinterpretation of the faith and Africanization of forms of Christianity has taken place, however, not in Roman Catholic or Protestant circles but in the independent movements initiated by African "prophets." In some cases the reinterpretation has been so sweeping as to raise doubts whether the result can still be called Christian (1967, 122ff.).

Music in the Independent Church

Music and the related arts have constituted the core of ritual performance among the independent churches, from the early stages of their development in the late nineteenth century to the present. Music remains a vibrant site of cultural production, especially as the churches strive to keep up with both the old and new and as they (re)define themselves and justify their existence in relation to the avant-garde, popular culture, and local politics of culture. These tendencies, articulated succinctly in the areas of music and visual arts, not only reflect and challenge the vestiges of the past, but they also validate the realities and complexities of postcolonial identities in Africa.

Musicians are preparing local and imported musical instruments to accompany music and dance in this Bethel congregation of the Evangelical Presbyterian Church in New Town, Accra. Photo © Daniel Avorgbedor.

Mr. T.V.O. Lamptey, former music director of the non-denominational Ministry, Joyful Way Incorp. (Ghana) creates synthesized accompaniment tracks for independent choral and church groups in his home music studio. Photo © Daniel Avorgbedor.

Early accounts of indigenous initiatives in church music are usually traced to the 1815 conversion and resulting songs of Ntsikana Gaba (c.1780–1828; Dargie 1982 7–28; Hodgson, 1980). The roots of the current dynamic and intense musical creativity associated with independent churches can, however, be associated with two fundamental sources of influence: local initiative and input from foreign mission work in Africa. A close interaction between these two sources is partly responsible for the phenomenal growth and diversity of music in the independent church. (This mutual exchange is often overlooked in the related literature.) The current situation shows a clear emphasis on selective integration of indigenous, popular, and innovative musical forms. This expanded and varied musical diet constitutes a creative response to the colonial and missionary heritage; it also represents an important process in constructing musical—and hence cultural—autonomy. This idea of autonomy is, however, best understood in light of some early missionary efforts that sought to suppress or discourage a wide range of cultural and musical practices, most of which were labeled "paganistic." The music and dance forms concerned were usually those originating, directly or indirectly, from indigenous recreational or rituals contexts, or from song traditions that encoded insult or obscene themes.

Even in contemporary postcolonial times, creative musical expressions in some local congregations are still first reviewed by overseeing foreign and local missionaries, as reported among the Dinka (Nikkel 2001,285). It can, however, be misleading to overemphasize the negative consequences of the suppression of music and customary practices without acknowledging the important contributions that church missions have made to the revival, innovation, and adaptation of specific musical and ritual traditions (for example, Haazen's *Missa Luba* became a model for local composers, as reflected in Cajetan Lunsonga's *Missa Bemba*, David Fanshawe's *African Sanctus*, and Reverend Anthony Okelo's *Missa Maleng*.)

It is primarily through the agencies or interventions of specific missionary enterprises that certain innovative musical practices were initiated in mainline and independent churches in Africa. Today, there are continuing musical interventions in which foreign mission and musical experts collaborate with local congregations to compose, adapt, and recontextualize music and dance forms for congregational use. A summary of significant sources that inform musical creativity and diversity in the independent church is presented below.

Sources of Influence on Musical Creativity in the Independent Church in Africa

1. Extant and extinct indigenous or ethnic musical traditions as background resource. Common features in African musical practices that are emphasized in the independent church include predominance of percussive texture, call and response, repetition, emphasis on timbral variety and "pitch-bending" (in contradistinction to pure or exact pitches, by Western tempered scale standards), polyrhythm (several layers of rhythm sounded at one time), "offbeat" phrasing, music as integrated art form (i.e., combines sound, movement, costume, and verbal and visual arts), active participation and audience input, music as an integral part of rites of passage and daily life, employment of three basic timbral levels in drum ensembles, influence of speech tone (especially in tone-language societies), inventiveness and improvisational skills, and music as a medium for social criticism and competition. In addition, spontaneous musical expression (or invention) is highly characteristic of church independency and autonomy. This spontaneity and related traditions of orality are rooted in indigenous practices and are partly responsible for the ephemeral and anonymous nature often identified with the printed music of independent churches. Where hymnbooks are compiled, these are usually quickly superseded by subsequent "editions," or they simply go out of print. The unsystematic methods of collecting and assembling, and the low-quality mediums of preservation, are also responsible for their transient nature. In their efforts to engage and emphasize indigenous heritage, some congregations study and reproduce existing music and dance forms in new church contexts. A consistent practice is, however, to rework existing materials and forms in light of global and local popular practices, and in relation to the colonial and missionary experiences.

The independent churches emphasize their indigenous musical roots and cultural traditions differently, both within one congregation and across churches. The various, shifting ways in which music articulates independency, musical and social-religious progress, and postcolonial identity are indicated also in the adoption of hybrid repertories that transcend indigenous roots (with varying degrees of revision and instrumentation), music of local composers (i.e., along Western art music models), popular music, spontaneous compositions by members, and selective continuation of Protestant hymnody, all of which can be experienced in one congregational service. The heritage of the African church is thus articulated through the practice of hybrid or plural musical styles, which ultimately constitute effective and affective mediums for establishing and communicating autonomy and progress.

2. Initiatives of the Catholic Church, Vatican II, beginning with Pope Paul VI in 1963. These initiatives were later formulated under the theme Musical Indigena: Native Music and its Possible Use in Liturgy and Proclamation (Overath 1976). Foreign mission workers actively pursued the adaptation and recreation of locally derived musical practices, as seen in *Missa Luba* (1965) by Reverend Father Guido Haazen. Although the Catholic Church in Africa and elsewhere has often been perceived as a conservative religious establishment, it has witnessed the development of myriad splinter congregations (for example, the proliferation of Catholic charismatic groups whose modes of worship and music share many elements in common with existing independent churches, as seen the classic case of Kimbaguism, led by Prophet Simon Kimbangu, 1889–1951). The Catholic Church and its semiautonomous laities sponsor workshops on church music; these workshops are not limited to members.

3. Church music workshops sponsored by All Africa Church Conference, the World Council of Churches, and by independent congregations.

4. Church and secular music workshops, festivals, and competitions sponsored by local government agencies, and by local institutions of higher learning.   These are a common feature of postindependence African countries.

5. Workshops by the African regional unit of the traditional media unit of the International Christian Media Commission to encourage the integration of dance, drama, and poetry in the liturgy.

6. Christian ethnomusicologists.   Ethnomusicologists and local evangelists, who collaborate to encourage the creation of new music by and for local congregations, draw on indigenous models.

7. Art music composers.   There are imposes, self-taught, or trained in Western academies, whose repertoires and texts orient toward Christian messages. Many of these compositions become integral part of popular music genres and transcend denominational boundaries and hierarchies.

8. Church and Popular Culture Interaction.   The situation of church autonomy and popular music (culture) is a dialectical one, a creative space for the common interchange and negotiation of musical ideas, with important musical repercussions, as summed up in the following examples. (The term *gospel* is employed rather loosely in the African Christian context to refer to a wide range of music that incorporates evangelistic and Biblical themes.):

> I [have] noted the importance of Christianity not only as a source of musical inspiration but as a training school for musicians. There can be no doubt that the Christian religion played a significant role in the development of highlife music. . . . Many bands were created in indigenous churches and were provided with instruments and ready markets in the process. In a sense, during the late 1970s and the early mid-1980s, highlife adopted a distinctly religious flavour. (Graham 1988, 104)

[G]ospel music might come from small ensembles like guitar bands, but playing songs with religious or inspirational content.

Several of Nairobi's most famous stars have gone from pop to gospel. Joseph Kamaru, a pillar of Kikuyu pop music since the 1960s, recently disbanded his band and reformed a gospel group. The style is so popular at the moment that the newspapers have added a top ten weekly gospel chart to their African and International top ten lists.

[A] growing trend in the Nairobi music industry in the last six years, [is] the solo gospel singer. While the phenomenon of the solo singer is not new in Nairobi, this development was made more obvious due to a sudden influx of kiosks selling this music on cassette. The style became so popular that people began to buy new cassettes instead of relying on the traditional practice of pirating. Out of this popularity came the development of professional church musicians in Nairobi (Kidula 1995, 1–16). At the start of the twenty-first century local gospel music constitutes around 75 percent of the popular music output in Ghana (Collins 1996, 1503 [reporting on the state of popular music in Ghana]).

Another important source of influence regards conscious efforts in privileging African American performance culture, both sacred and secular, within the context of the worldwide popular culture. (See, for example, Veit Erlmann's accounts of African American presence in South African Christian and popular music, beginning in the early 1890s, *The Early Social History of Zulu Migrant Workers' Choral Music in South Africa* 1990; *Migration and Performance: Zulu Migrant Workers' Isicathamiya Performance in South Africa, 1890–1950*, 1990; and *Nightsong: Performance, Power, and Practice in South Africa*, 1996). The active exchange and symbiotic processes between church and popular music are illustrated further by an increasingly pervasive culture of cassette trading and fame surrounding individual musicians. Both the name and several musical elements identified with *juju*—a popular Yoruba music genre—explain this symbiosis very well; *soukous, highlife, mbube* (e.g., Ladysmith Black Mambazo) and rap are some of the popular music sounds that are reproduced in the church contexts, often with techniques of *contra facta* and parody (i.e., replacing "secular" texts and sound configurations with contextually appropriate ones). New converts who were former popular musicians often bring to the church their talents and skills, thus enriching church music and bringing it closer to the public domain.

9. Workshop and conference proceedings and independent scholarly works—including theses in theological institutes—that address the situation of African culture and Christianity, with emphasis on music, and often with prescriptions.   For example, see Nketia 1958, Weman, 1960; the occasional *All-Africa Church Music Journal*, Olson 1971, 61–67, Dargie 1979, 18–32; and the African contributors in Overath, 1976.

10. Syncretism, Directions, and Conclusions.   Almost all published texts dealing with African Christianity—employ the paradigm of syncretism in characterizing the constitution and identity of expressive culture in the church. Although syncretism has served important analytical goals, it falls short of explaining the dynamic and active negotiations associated with music, ritual, and general performance culture in the independent churches. Syncretism thus seems to privilege products over important processes.

New musical products arise when song and dance styles, musical instruments, and the universe of symbols unique to each ethnic group are reworked together with musical elements and practices associated with the Western institutions and practices, according to the tenets of syncretism. The processes and products identified with the independent African church cannot, however, be easily classified into African and Western, as often suggested in the related literature. In addition, the music and ritual traditions of these churches have been so imaginative that they not only transcend the African–Western dichotomy, but they also challenge the established canons of global Christianity. (Consider, for example, controversies and debates among charismatics and mainline churches on the issue of the "Christian" contents of the music, ritual, doctrines, and beliefs of Bwitism, Kimbaguism, Zulu Zionism, and Cherubim and Serafim [or Aladura].)

The intensity, frequency, and variety of music encountered in the independent church depend also on the demographic characteristics of the congregation, the leader's background, levels of competition among the churches as they strive to increase membership, and the general politics of culture of the times. In some mainline churches such as Methodist, Evangelical Presbyterian (E. P.), Anglican, Baptist, and Pentecostal, musical independence is cultivated (or achieved) in many ways, but without secession or formation of a completely separate or independent church. For example, when the E. P. church of Ghana broke away from the mother E. P. church constellation in the 1980s, the move was motivated mainly by the need to emphasize the "gifts of the Spirit" and avant-garde music and liturgy. The mother church, however, now co-opts these "new" forms of music and liturgy, partly to win back dissenting members who left for the new church, and partly in response to the general wave of renewal in churches all over Africa. Except for the messages of the song texts and interethnic populations, there are moments when music, musical instruments, symbolism and ritual, costume, and dance in the independent church approximate indigenous performance practices. Some of these churches have thus achieved unique identities, mainly due to their express emphasis on these performance practices. For example, the Apostolic Revelation Society (founded in 1939 in Ghana by the late Prophet Charles Koblavi Mawufeame Wovenu Nutornutsi, 1921–1999) adopted Ewe music and dance genres, which are recontextualized and renamed globally as *tutudo*). In the Church of the Nazarite of Isaiah Shembe (d. 1935), Zulu-Nguni philosophy, rites of passage, and music have been revised and institutionalized in the church (Muller 1999). Although many Western sources—as well as innovative forms of music and dance—have been identified in Nazarite performance practices (Mthethwa 1982/83, 34–7), it is important to pay attention to the processes of incorporation and translation of indigenous concepts and ideals that inform these practices. For example, a close study of the music accompanying the reinterpreted Nguni *umgonqo* puberty rite of the church shows high preferences for rich timbres, polyrhythmic structures, heterophonic and percussive textures in the drums and trumpets employed (Muller, 1999, 179ff.); these elements are among those often associated with indigenous musical traditions in Africa. Even in mainline churches elsewhere in Africa, a certain level of autonomy is realized through a selective integration of indigenous musical instruments and songs composed in local popular idioms, as exemplified in the adoption and revised tuning of *adungu* (harps) in Catholic churches in the Nebbi district of Uganda.

Women's leadership roles and musical creativity have been elevated significantly in the independent churches, as summed up in the examples of Mrs. Grace Tshabalala (Sundkler 1976, 1978), Prophetess Alice Mulenga Lenshina Lubusha (Jules-Rosette 1974, 1975), the evolution of *ebibindwom* (song type deriving from indigenous styles) in the Methodist Church among the Fante of Ghana (Mensah 1960; Williamson 1958, 126–34), and others. These comments on Dinka Christianity summarize the situation well: "Women figure more prominently than ever before and are consistently among the most gifted composers. . . . Over one-third of the new compositions are by women who, with many of their menfolk in combat or dead, have played prominent roles in every aspect of church life" (Nikkel 2001, 303, 313). Finally, it is within the independent churches that we see an increasing number of women who play lead drums, even if these drums are modeled after those employed in school and military bands.

Independent churches in Africa provide a fruitful context for researching and understanding mutual relations between religion, performing arts, and social conditions; these relations influence, in many significant ways, the continuity, reconstitution, and reinvention of music and dance, both within and outside of the church. Distinctions between church and popular musical practices are becoming more difficult to draw, as both are actively engaged in the production and reproduction of expressive culture in Africa.

References

All-Africa Church Journal. Nairobi: All-Africa Church Conference.

Barrett, David. 1968. *Schism and Renewal in Africa: An Analysis of Six Thousand Contemporary Religious Movements*. Nairobi: Oxford University Press.

———. 1971. *African Initiative in Religion: 21 Studies from Eastern and Central Africa*. Nairobi: East African Publishing House.

———. 1989. *Rise Up and Walk! Conciliarism and the African Indigenous Churches, 1815–1987: A Sequel to Schism and Renewal in Africa (1968)*. Nairobi: Oxford University.

Bond, George, Walton Johnson, and Sheiler Walker, eds. 1979. *African Christianity: Patterns of Religious Continuity*. New York: Academic Press.

Collins, John. 1996. [Untitled news report] *West Africa*.

Dargie, David. 1979. African Church Music, New and Old. *WACC Journal* 26: 18–32.

———. 1982. The Music of Ntsikana. *South African Journal of Musicology* 2: 7–28.

Erlmann, Veit. 1990. *The Early Social History of Zulu Migrant Workes' Choral Music in South Africa*. Berlin: Arabische Buch.

———. 1990. Migration and Performance: Zulu Migrant Workers' *Isicathamiya* Performance in South Africa, 1890–1950. *Ethnomusicology* 34: 199–220.

———. 1996. *Nightsong: Performance, Power, and Practice in South Africa*. Chicago: University of Chicago Press.

Fernandez, James. 1982. *Bwiti: An Ethnography of the Religious Imagination in Africa*. Princeton, N.J.: Princeton University Press.

Forman Charles W. 1967. *Christianity in the Non-Western World*. Englewood Cliffs, N.J.: Prentice-Hall.

Graham, Ronnie. 1988. *The Da Capo guide to Contemporary African Music*. New York: Da Capo Press.

Hodgson, Janet. 1980. *Ntsikana's Great Hymn: A Xhosa Expression of Christianity in the Early 19th Century Eastern Cape.* Cape Town: Centre for African Studies, University of Cape Town.

Jules-Rosette, Bennetta. 1974. Ceremony and Leadership: The Influence of Women in African Independent Churches. Paper presented at the UCLA African Studies Center colloquium, "Women and Change in Africa, 1870–1980."

———. 1975. *African Apostles: Ritual and Conversion in the Church of John Maranke.* Ithaca N.Y.: Cornell University Press.

———. 1986. The Influence of Missions on the Rise of Africa's New Religions: Case Studies from Central and Southern Africa. In *Christian Missionarism and the Alienation of the African Mind,* ed. Ramadan S. Belhag and Yassin A. El-Kabir, 159–185. Tripoli: African Society of Social Sciences.

Kidula, Jean Ngoya. 1995. The Appropriation of Western Derived Music Styles into Kenyan Traditions: Case Study of Some Nairobi Christian Musics. *Pacific Review of Ethnomusicology* 7:1–16.

Mensah, Attah Anan. 1960. The Akan Church Lyric. *International Review of Missions* (April).

Mthethwa, Bongani. 1984. Western Elements in Shembe's Religious Dances. In *Papers Presented at the Third and Fourth Symposia on Ethnomusiciology, 1982/1983,* ed. Andrew Tracey, 34–37. Grahamstown: International Library of African Music.

Muller, Carol Ann. 1999. *Rituals of Fertility and the Sacrifice of Desire: Nazarite Women's Performance in South Africa.* Chicago: University of Chicago Press.

Nikkel, Mark. 2001. *Dinka Christianity: The Origins and Development of Christianity among the Dinka of Sudan with Special Reference to the Songs of Dinka Christians.* Nairobi: Paulines Publications Africa.

Nketia, J.H. Kwabena. 1958. The Contribution of African Culture to Worship. *International Review of Missions* 47: 267–278.

Olson, Howard S. 1971. African Music in Christian Worship. In *African Initiative in Religion: 21 Studies from Eastern and Central Africa.* Workshop in Religious Research, University College, Nairobi, 1967–1968, ed. David Barrett, 61–67. Nairobi: East African Publishing House.

Overath, Johannes, ed. 1976. *Musica Indigena: Einheimische Musik und ihre Verwendenung in Liturgie und Verkundigung. Symposium Musico-Ethnologicum Romae 1975.* Rome: CIMS.

Sundkler, Bengt. 1976. *Zulu Zion and Some Swazi Zionists.* Glasgow: Oxford University Press.

Weman, Henry. 1960. *African Music and the Church in Africa.* Uppsala: Svenska Institutet för Missionsforskning.

Williamson, Sydney George. 1958. The Lyric in Fante Methodist Church. *Africa* 28(2, April): 126–134.

DANIEL AVORGBEDOR

See also **Music in Africa: Overview; Performance in Africa; Popular Culture**

MUSIC: POPULAR DANCE MUSIC IN CONGO (ZAIRE)

Since the early 1950s, the success of the guitar-based popular dance music of Brazzaville and Kinshasa has made it a sort of "musica franca" of sub-Saharan Africa. Known by various names outside of the Congo Region (such as, Congo Jazz, Lingala Music, Congo Music, La Musique Zairoise, Zairian Rumba, Soukouss), in former Zaire (now the Democratic Republic of Congo) the music is usually referred to as *la musique moderne.* Apart from its particular combination of Afro-Cuban and Afri-can dance rhythms, Congolese popular music is most easily identified by its fluid parallel harmonies and distinctive layered guitar sound.

Origins

The exact origins of the musical style are difficult to trace, but most historical accounts explain that the music has drawn inspiration from many sources since its emergence beginning in the 1930s (Bemba 1984; Lonoh 1969). The earliest forms of popular music in the region are thought to have emerged in the colonial labor settlements, which were organized around the newly forming industrial centers at the turn of the century. The transport industries of Kinshasa (at that time, Leopoldville) and mining interests in Lubumbashi (then Elizabethville) brought together male laborers and musical traditions from various parts of Africa (Congo, Rhodesia, Angola, Cameroun, Liberia, Cabinda). Musicians from this period tell stories about how they used to marvel at the highlife guitar style of the West African "Coastmen" who came to work in Leopoldville. But this external presence did not arrive in a musical vacuum. Local musical traditions had already been transformed through the creation of new urban dance styles such as the *agbaya* ring dance or the *maringa,* which was the first form of partnered dancing in the region (Martin 1995). The primary influence in modern Congolese music, however, is the family of Afro-Cuban music, which, after World War I, was becoming increasingly popular in North America and Western Europe, and which was being marketed in Central Africa as early as the 1920s on 78" records bearing the label "G.V." (Graviation Victor). This early imported music, most of which was Cuban *son* or *son-montuno,* had a profound influence not only on the music of Kinshasa, but also on the various highlife musics of West Africa and on the "dry" guitar style of urban centers in East Africa and in the Copperbelt region (White 2002).

According to Kazadi (1979), despite the fact that many Congolese consider Kinshasa to be the cradle of modern Congolese music, there is reason to believe that the musical style actually emerged in different places at more or less the same time. If Kinshasa is today the undisputed center of Congolese (or even Central African) music, it is due not only to the city's size (more than five million people) and cosmopolitan nature, but also to post colonial policies, which promoted Kinshasa as a part of a larger strategy to suppress regionalism in other parts of the country. Nonetheless, the history of the musical style is intimately linked to the history of Kinshasa. People in Kinshasa often say that the music and the city "grew up" together and that their special relationship is an expression of what it means to be "modern." In Kinshasa, it is difficult to separate popular music and everyday life in the city, especially as it seems that everyone is a musician there, and everything happens with a song (Tchebwa 1996).

The first people in Kinshasa who were recognized as professional musicians began playing in the 1930s, animating public spaces and events in the lower income neighborhoods of Congo's rapidly growing urban centers. When the first recording houses (Olympia, Opika, Loningisa) were opened by foreign merchants in the early 1940s, these musicians were recruited and offered individual full-time contracts: Wendo Kolosov, Adou Elenga, Leon Bukasa, Tino Baroza, Emmanuel d'Oliveira, and Lucie

Eyenga, to mention only a few. When a second generation of musicians came onto the scene in the 1950s, their newfound success enabled them to break away from the foreign-owned recording houses to form independent musical groups of their own. This was the classical rumba period of the 1950s and 1960s which saw the rise of big band style orchestras such as Kabasele's African Jazz, Franco's O.K. Jazz, and the African Fiesta groups of Tabu Ley and Dr. Nico. The rivalry that developed between African Jazz and O.K. Jazz was accentuated by the emergence of two distinct musical styles or "schools," one considered modern, sophisticated and romantic (African Jazz) and the other traditional, raw and erotic (O.K. Jazz). This period was also characterized by increasing professionalization and a more systematic use of Western instruments such as the clarinet, the saxophone, and the electric guitar.

The strength of these two musical empires would not be challenged until the late 1960s, when a new generation of musicians emerged. Taking cues primarily from *les Belgicains* (Congolese students living in Belgium whose music drew from classic rumba but also from African American soul music), young musicians in Kinshasa created a new musical idiom that clearly marked the arrival of a third generation. With the formation of the youth super group Zaiko Langa Langa in 1969, the Zairian new wave ushered in a series of stylistic innovations such as the use of drum kits, the distinct two-part song structure, and the choreographed dancing which appealed widely to a growing urban youth (Nkashama 1979). Although this period produced a large number of commercially successful "stars" such as Papa Wemba (Viva la Musica), Pepe Kalle (Empire Bakuba), and Koffi Olomide (Quartier Latin), it was not until well into the third generation that Congolese music took on its most commercialized form, that of Congolese dance music intended for non-Congolese audiences, *soukouss*. This subcategory of Congolese popular music was pioneered by Congolese musicians living and working in Europe in the 1980s who adapted the two-part words/dance song structure by shortening the words part and extending the dance part, since this was what most pleased non-Congolese audiences in Europe and North America (White 1998).

DjoDjo and Lidjo Kwempa of Viva La Musica. Photo © Seth Cashman.

As Cultural Expression

Popular forms of cultural expression such as music, not only provide valuable information about larger historical and political processes, but also are windows onto Kinshasa's collective soul. Discourse about the two schools (one traditional, one modern) reveals how local categories of modernity reflect a "double consciousness" (to borrow a term from Paul Gilroy), and the importance of generational categories shows how personal identity in Congolese society is often expressed in relation to elders or "spiritual ancestors" (Tchebwa 1996). The romantic veneer of Congolese music, a music filled with lyrics about matters of the heart (love, marriage, infidelity, etc.) covers a political subtext, not only since many songs contain masked political messages, but also because of the music's particular form of commercialized praise singing, in which musicians cite the names of powerful state and commercial elites. Thus the tendency to avoid lyrics that are perceived as politically engaged is, in part, a function of the need to maintain good patron client relations, but musicians also sing about love in order to appeal to a wider audience. Male and female audiences alike express a preference for lyrics that are considered romantic, and despite an important number of female vocalists since the early years of the musical style (Abeti Masikini, Mpongo Love, Mbilia Bel), male musicians often compose songs in which they assume the female voice and sing from what they believe to be a woman's point of view.

Recent discussions of popular arts in Africa have called attention to the fact that "popular" tends to be used as a residual category, applying to all forms of artistic expression that do not fall neatly into the categories of "elite" or "traditional" (Barber 1987). This observation is important given the undeniable presence of popular arts in Africa as well as for what these art forms tell us about cultural practice and meaning (Fabian 1978; Jewsiewicki 1991). After modern music, by far the most important category of popular music is religious music. In fact, in recent year, as the country has gone deeper into political and economic crisis, religious music has taken on an increasingly important role for many Congolese. Religious music ranges from informal prayer group songs to commercially produced evangelical dance music, which, in some cases bears a striking resemblance to the words/dance song structure of modern music, or what they call the "music of this world." Variations on the fanfare ensemble (or mini-marching band) are used in some local churches (Kimbanguiste, Salvation Army, etc.) and for various types of lifecycle ceremonies. This style is preferred by those families that, because of religious convictions or an elevated class status wish to distance themselves from the stereotypes of witchcraft and backwardness that are often associated with "traditional" music.

Ethnic-based forms of "traditional" music are often heard at the end-of-mourning funeral parties (*matanga*) in Kinshasa. Where families cannot find a group of musicians who specialize in the music from their home region or ethnic group, sometimes a prerecorded cassette of this music is used. Groups in this category use traditional instruments, which are sometimes adapted for use in an urban setting (strings made from steel belting in tires, metal containers instead of gourds, electric amplifications of some sort). In some cases, folklore musicians use electric instruments and perform not in ceremonial circumstances, but in the bars and bistros scattered throughout the city. It was from these urban traditional groups (such as ana Odeon, Kintweni

National, and later Swede Swede) that the category of *tradi-moderne* was born, a style whose form draws from "modern" music but whose lyrical-melodic content comes directly from folklore. Thus, there is a great deal of overlap between what at first seem like stylistically and analytically distinct categories of popular urban music. What is most interesting about these locally produced musical styles is the extent to which they are locally consumed. In fact, it is very uncommon to see or hear foreign music of any kind in 1990s Kinshasa. Even with regards to rap music, one of the only imported styles that received regular airplay on local private television, a dynamic local rap scene had emerged in which young artists infused an increasingly global aesthetic form with local motifs, meanings, and language (*Revue Noire* 1996).

References

Barber, Karin. 1987. Popular Arts in Africa. *African Studies Review* 30, 3: 1–78.

Bemba, Sylvain. 1984. *Cinquante ans de musique du Congo-Zaire: (1920–1907): De Paul Kamba à Tabu Ley.* Paris: Présence Africaine.

Fabian, Johannes. 1978. Popular Culture in Africa: Findings and Conjectures. *Africa* 48, 4: 313–334.

Jewsiewicki, Bogumil. 1991. Painting in Zaire: From the Invention of the West to the Representation of Social Self. In *African Explores.* New York: Center for African Art.

Kazadi wa Mukuna. 1979. The Origin of Zairean Modern Music: A Socio-Economic Aspect. *African Urban Studies.* Winter, 6: 31–39.

Lonoh, M.B. 1969. *Essai de Commentaire sur la Musique Congolaise Moderne.* Kinshasa: S.E.I./A.N.C. in collaboration with the Zairian Ministry of Arts & Culture.

Martin, Phyllis. 1995. *Leisure and Society in Colonial Brazzaville.* New York: Cambridge University Press.

Nkashama, P. Ngandu. 1979. Ivresse et Vertige: les nouvelles danses des jeunes au Zaire. *L'Afrique litteraire et artistique* 51: 94–102.

Revue Noire. 1996. Kinshasa, Zaire. Vol. 21. June/July/August. Paris: Cooperation Francaise.

Tchebwa, Manda. 1996. *La terre de la chanson: La musique zaïroise hier et aujourd'hui.* Brussels: Duculot.

White, Bob W. 2000. *Soukouss* or Sell-Out? Congolese Popular Dance Music as Cultural Commodity, in Angelique Haugerud, M. Priscilla Stone and Peter D. Little (eds.), *Commodities and Globalization: Anthropological Perspectives.* New York: Rowman and Littlefield. P. 33–58.

White, Bob W. 2003. Congolese Rumba and Other Cosmopolitanisms, in Bob W. White (ed.), special issue of *Cahiers d'études africaines*, XLII (4) 168: 663–686.

ROBERT W. WHITE

See also **Music: Atalaku of Central Africa**

MUSIC: SOUKOUSS

Since the mid 1950s, the popular music of Congo-Zaire has been widely distributed and sold throughout sub-Saharan Africa and farther abroad (Ewens 1990; Tchebwa 1996). Over the years this unique musical style has been known by various names outside its native region: Congo music, Congo jazz, Lingala music, Zairean music, Zairean rumba, and most recently, *soukouss*. *Soukouss* refers to a particular type of Congolese popular music which was developed by Congolese musicians living in Europe in the 1980s and is virtually unknown within the Congo itself.

Increasing disillusion with Mobutuist politics, and local perceptions of improved financial opportunity abroad, led to a rise in the number of Zairians attempting to emigrate to Europe in the 1980s (especially France, but also Belgium and Great Britain). Among this new wave of immigrants were a number of professional musicians, a social-occupational category that had been particularly hard hit not only by the government's neglect of the music industry infrastructure, but also by the arrival of cassette technology and the subsequent flood of music piracy in the region (White 1998). By relocating to Europe, musicians believed they would have access to state-of-the-art recording equipment, well-developed distribution networks, and an entirely new consumer audience that, compared to consumers in Kinshasa, had considerable disposable income.

By this time, Congolese music had already undergone several important stylistic transformations, most notably the development of a distinct two-part song structure in which a slow, lyrical introduction is followed by a fast-paced dance sequence. Responding to their new audience's preference for dance music, Congolese musicians in Europe further altered the music by shortening the words, extending the length of the dance sequence, and speeding up the tempo. This new style, which appealed mainly to Europeans and non-Congolese Africans, became known as *soukouss*, a term that was originally the name of a dance from the late 1960s and said to have come from the French verb *secouer*, "to shake." Groups such as the Soukouss Stars, Kanda Bongo Man, and Loketo were among the first to win over mostly French audiences from their bases in Paris, but their touring circuits also included Brussels, London, Montreal, New York, and many cities in sub-Saharan Africa. The late 1980s saw a flurry of interest and journalistic writing on Congolese popular music (see for example, *The Beat* 1989), much of which tended to blur the distinction between *soukouss* and classic Zairian rumba.

Despite its initial success, however, interest in *soukouss* music in Europe and North America seemed to wane in the 1990s,

Congolese guitarist Dizzy Manjeku. Photo © Seth Cashman.

especially with the arrival of new Congolese artists who have strayed from the conventional Congolese format in more innovative ways (Papa Wemba, Lokua Kanza, J. P. Buse). With a few exceptions (Lokassa va Mbongo, Daly Kimoko, Gouma Lokito), *soukouss* musicians are generally unknown in Kinshasa, where audiences place a great deal of emphasis on remaining close to the local sources of modern Congolese music.

References

Ewens, Graeme. 1990. *Africa O-ye!* London: Guiness Books.
Tchebwa, Manda. 1996. *La terre de la chanson: la musique zaïrose hier et auiourd'hui.* Brussels: Duculot.
The Beat. 1989. Vol. 8, no. 6, Special issue on Zairian popular music.
White, Bob W. 2000. *Soukouss* or Sell-Out? Congolese Popular Dance Music as Cultural Commodity, in Angelique Haugerud, M. Priscilla Stone and Peter D. Little (eds.), *Commodities and Globalization: Anthropological Perspectives.* New York: Rowman and Littlefield. pp. 33–58.

ROBERT W. WHITE

See also **Music: Popular Dance Music in Congo (Zaire)**

MUSIC: WEST AFRICAN "HIGHLIFE"

The term *highlife* is an umbrella term for various styles of local transcultural dance that evolved in Ghana beginning in the late nineteenth century. All involved a fusion of traditional African musical and performance elements with imported ones from Europe, America, and the African diaspora.

The earliest was *adaha*, which emerged in the 1880s in the Cape Coast area. This highly syncopated form of local brass band music had its imported origins in the nineteenth century European and West Indian regimental bands of the colonial forts. A more indigenous variety of adaha known as Konkoma Highlife appeared in the 1930s, spreading inland and as far east as the Volta Region (influencing Ewe *borborbor* music) and Nigeria.

A second source of highlife evolved just after the turn of the twentieth century, out of small, low-class, coastal groups that used local percussion instruments and sailors' instruments (banjo, concertina, and, particularly, guitar). These groups played *osibisaaba*, *annkadan-mu* and *yaa amponsah* of the Fanti, Sierre Leone–derived asiko, and the mainline, dagomba, and fireman songs of visiting Liberian Kru seamen. As the coastal guitar styles moved inland, they became influenced by the music of the Akan *seprewa* harp-lute, which resulted in Odonson or Ashanti Blues. Both the coastal and inland styles, what later came to be called "Palmwine music" (i.e., played in palmwine bars), became immensely popular from the late 1920s. At this time, artists such as Kwame Asare, Mireku, Kwesi Menu, and Appiah Adjekum made many recordings.

The umbrella term *highlife* itself (i.e., "high-class life") was coined during the 1920s, when the ballroom dance orchestras of the Ghanaian elite (such as the Excelsior Orchestra, Cape Coast Sugar Babies, and Jazz Kings) began to orchestrate local Adahas, street-songs, and palmwine tunes.

After World War II, the large dance orchestras were reduced in size and, pioneered in the 1950s by E. T. Mensah and the Tempos, played a calypso/swing/Afro-Cuban–influenced form of dance-band highlife. This became the vogue for other dance bands in Ghana (Black Beats, Rhythm Aces, Ramblers, Uhuru, Red Spots, Broadway) and in Nigeria (such as those bands led by Bobby Benson, Victor Olaiya, Rex Lawson, A. C. Arinze, and Eddie Okunta). The small palmwine groups had meanwhile evolved into what are called guitar bands. Initiated in 1952 by E. K. Nyame, guitar-band highlife became the music of the concert party.

The concert party is a Ghanaian form of popular drama or comic opera that goes back to the early twentieth century. In the early days, it was based on imported vaudeville and was performed in English for the black coastal elite. In 1930 the comedian Bob Johnson hijacked the genre from the elite and took it into the rural hinterland where he created the genre's central "Bob" character, a fusion of the imported black minstrel and the mischievous trickster hero of Akan folklore, Ananse the Spider. It was with the formation of E. K. Akan Trio in 1952 that the genre was fully Ghanaianised, with performances entirely in Akan and, with their guitar band, highlife music replacing the ragtime and foxtrots of earlier groups. Subsequently, many other guitar bands-cum-concert parties were formed: Kakaiku's, Onyina's, Kwaa Mensah's, Yamoah's, the Jaguar Jokers, Dr. Gyasi's, the African Brothers, and later, the City Boys, Kumapim Royals, and Obra.

During the 1950s and 1960s, highlife music was supplied mainly through urban dance bands and more lower-class and rustic-oriented guitar bands, until around 1970, when offshoots began to appear. Afro-rock and Afro-beat were created by the Ghanaian members of Osibisa and the Nigerian Fela Anikulapo-Kuti, all of whom were ex-dance-band highlife musicians. At the same time "roots" versions of highlife were being explored by the acoustic guitarist Koo Nimo in Kumasi and Wulomei and other Ga cultural groups in Accra. During the early 1980s, Burgher highlife, which combines disco and electronic music with highlife, and was created by Ghanaian musicians who had settled in Hamburg, Germany during Ghana's economic decline of the 1970s, became popular with the youth

E.T. Mensah and his Tempos, Highlife dance band, 1952–3. Photo © John Collins/Bokoor African Popular Music Archives (BAPMAF).

Some members of Kwaa Mensah's Concert Party in 1959 (Kwaa is in drag with a guitar). Photo © John Collins/Bokoor African Popular Music Archives (BAPMAF).

of Ghana. This decline also resulted in many commercial dance musicians moving into the Ghanaian separatist Christian churches that allow dance for worship, thus producing a new genre of highlife, gospel highlife.

References

Agovi, K. E. 1989. The Political Relevance of Ghanaian Highlife Songs Since 1957. *Research in African Literature* 20, no. 2.

Bame, K. N. 1985. *Come to Laugh: African Traditional Theatre in Ghana.* New York: Lillian Barber Press.

Barber, K., E. J. Collins, and A. Ricard. 1997. *West African Popular Theatre.* Indiana University Press/James Currey.

Collins, E. J. 1976. Comic Opera in Ghana. *African Arts* 9, no. 2: 50–7. Republished 1988. in *Ghanain Literature*, ed. R. K. Priebe, pp. 61–72. Greenwood Press; Conn.

———. 1976. Ghanaian Highlife. *African Arts* 19, No. 1: 62–8, 100.

———. 1985. *Music Makers of West Africa.* Washington, D.C.: Three Continents Press.

———. 1986. *E. T. Mensah: The King of Highlife.* 1996. London: Off the Record Press. Republished Accra: Anansesem Press.

———. 1987. Jazz Feedback to Africa. *American Music* (Sonneck Society Journal) 5, no. 2: 176–93.

———. 1992. *West African Pop Roots.* Philadelphia: Temple University Press.

———. 1996. *Highlife Time.* Accra: Anansesem Press.

Collins, E. J., and P. Richards. 1989. Popular Music in West Africa. In *World Music, Politics and Social Change*, ed. S. Frith, pp. 12–46. Manchester University Press.

Coplan, D. 1978. Go to My Town Cape Coast: The Social History of Ghanaian Highlife. In *Eight Urban Musical Cultures: Tradition and Change*, ed. B. Nettl. Urbana: University of Illinois Press.

Mensah, A. A. 1971–92. *Jazz the Round Trip.* Jazz Forschung/Research, Universal Ed. No. 3/4, pp. 124–137. Graz, Germany: International Gesellschaft Fur Jazzforschung.

Sutherland, E. 1970. *The Original Bob.* Accra: Anowuo Educational Publications.

Yankah, K. 1984. The Akan Highlife Song: A Medium for Cultural Reflection or Deflection? *Research in African Literature* 15, no. 4: 568–82.

JOHN COLLINS

See also **Concert Parties; Music: Soukouss**

MUSICAL INSTRUMENTS: FOCUS ON NAMIBIA

Much of the information that exists on musical instruments in Africa describes instruments as works of art or as objects of scientific study (organological studies). Fewer studies really look at instruments as extensions of peoples' lives, as concrete expressions of philosophy, and personal and societal values. In any society it is important to understand the elements that give music continued meaning. As Nketia (1998, 14) has stated, it is important that our goals are not only the "quest for knowledge and understanding of human beings in Africa as makers and users of music, but also in regard to practical issues related to music as a language or mode of communication, music as an object of aesthetic interest, and music as culture." This entry briefly explores the congruence and consonance between the values of people and the implicit values of the music systems, with a special focus on Namibia. The information is based mainly on research undertaken between 1993 and 2001 and describes current practices in Namibia.

Musical instruments in Africa are imbued with meaning. They are constructed not only to create musical sounds, but as instruments of communication with people, spirits, and gods. For this reason, only special trees are selected for the making of drums, and all over Africa drums for use in important events are always dedicated to the ancestral spirits or the gods. In similar ways, some instruments are believed to contain the actual spirit of god or of an important animal. As a general introduction, musical instruments will be described in terms of the manner in which sound is produced, commonly referred to as the Hornböstel-Sachs system (Sachs 1978).

Classification

Chordophones are instruments utilizing strings at tension. Manipulation of the strings by means of plucking, striking, scraping, or bowing brings forth the sound. The diversity of different kinds of chordophones in Africa is simply astounding. They range from simple hunting bows to multiple bows, from lyres, harps, lutes, and guitars to zithers. The different forms of *kora*, a harp-lute found in west and northwest Africa, are superb examples of chordophone development. The music of the kora has found its way into popular world music. These magnificent instruments may be played solo or as part of a larger mixed ensemble or orchestra, such as the L'Orchestre Symphonique de la Guinea Con Akry.

Idiophones are instruments of inherently resonant material where the material itself produces the sound when shaken, struck, or subjecting the object to friction. African examples include a huge variety of rattles, sticks, bells, gongs, bottles, iron plaques, slit (log) drums, lamellaphones, and xylophones. These instruments take on different shapes and forms depending on the materials available in a certain area. While xylophones (e.g., balafon in Senegal and marimba in Mozambique) and lamellaphones (e.g., *mbira* in Zimbabwe) are capable of producing melodic and harmonic music, most idiophones serve to add texture and color to song, dance, and other instruments. Some African idiophones are invested with secrecy and special power, only brought out for special occasions such as healings or exorcisms.

Membranophones are instruments where the sound generator is a stretched membrane that may be struck, beaten, or rubbed. This includes the many different forms of drums and mirlitons, which are membranes attached to other instruments' resonators to create a buzzing effect. Drums take different shapes and sizes throughout Africa, and may be used in drum ensembles (most common) or singly. While most drums consist of a wooden body, some might be made of clay. Some drums have chords attached to the membrane and the other end of the drum. As these are tightened and loosened by arm pressure, the pitch of the drum changes when struck. In this way, speech, or voice inflection and rhythm, can be imitated, hence the term "talking drum" of countries such as Ghana, Nigeria, Senegal, and others. The compelling sound of drums is vital to most African dances and is also a means through which one may enter the spirit world through trance or the dance. Drums also have fertility connotations and, especially in the past, were often performed during harvest and fertility rites.

Papaya stem flutes. Photo © Minette Mans.

Aerophones are instruments that utilize the vibration of air to produce sound, for examples, flutes, trumpets, horns, reeds, whistles, and also, whirling instruments. Very often, African aerophones were constructed from natural materials such as animal horns (which could be side-blown or end-blown like a trumpet), or bones, or reeds, or even the bark of trees. In Namibia, Uganda, and South Africa, for example, there are flute ensembles where each individual plays only one note in a set sequential turn. The whole thus creates an extended melody while flautists perform a circular dance. These performances have much social significance in the metaphoric recreation of egalitarian spaces for each individual within the total system.

It is important to note that musical instruments in the large and diverse continent of Africa are used in specific circumstances. Whether used singly or in combination with other instruments, voice, or dance, musical instruments have their own repertoires and form part of a greater cognitive schema or constructed musical world. These schemas are culture-specific, and the relationships between people, their instruments, their dance, and their values and beliefs are constructed in unique ways. Yet, there are commonalities amongst different cultures, for example, certain kinds of instruments, such as drums or rattles, are typically related to certain kinds of events, rituals, or entertainment. Typically, instrumental music forms part of a complex understanding of music as part of life, as a living force that can be utilized for its power and positive influence.

Namibia is a fairly large, arid, and lightly populated country on the southwestern side of Africa, north of South Africa, and south of Angola. It has, at different times, been a German and British colony and was later occupied by South Africa. The population is made up of Khoekhoe-speaking people (e.g., Nama, Damara, and Hai//om), different San (Bushman) language groups (e.g., Ju/'hoansi, !Kung, Kxoe, Nharo, and ≠Khomani), different Bantu-speaking groups (e.g., Ovaherero, Owambo, Vakwangali, Valozi, Batswana, Hambukushu, Vasambyu, Vagciriku, and Ovazimba), and European-based language groups (e.g., German, Afrikaans, English, and Portuguese). The country is, therefore, linguistically, culturally, and musically diverse. It has only been politically independent since 1990. Because of its occupation and dominance by South Africa, very little research was undertaken on Namibian folklore, and especially limited information is available on its diverse musical heritage. What follows is a brief generic listing of some Namibian musical instruments, followed by a discussion on the importance of bows.

Namibian idiophones include ankle rattles, hand-held rattles, and rattles worn around the upper body; bottle, brush, lamellaphones; a xylophone; percussion plaques of iron and wood (one of which is attached to the foot and stamped on the ground); concussion bars of wood; bells; and a scraped calabash idiophone.

Membranophones include tubular conical drums (usually used in sets of two or three), a clay pot drum, wooden pot drum with wet handheld membrane, friction drums, mirlitons. *Aerophones* include end-blown and side-blown animal horns, one with a wax bulb extension, stopped and unstopped flutes from reed, animal horn, and papaya stems, with and without finger holes, bullroarers and whistles from bark or metal. One horn with a wax bulb extension is used to inform people that cattle are being moved.

Chordophones include various forms of bows, single or multiple (pluriarcs), lutes, and zithers. The importance of the drum in Africa is often expressed as the birth and heartbeat of Africa, the source of the dance, the sound that draws people together from afar, and it serves as a metaphor for male-female relations. Yet, in certain parts of the continent, the bow is far more common. Simply put, if the drum is the symbol for community, the bow(s) is the symbol of the philosopher and lonely traveler—the sages of the past. In Namibia and Botswana, where the populations are small but the areas large, arid, and open, people travel for long distances either alone or in small groups. They are, by and large, pastoralists who have to move their goat, sheep, and cattle herds from one watering and grazing spot to another. The herding lifestyle of the past continues in contemporary times and has contributed to an abundance of bows and other string instruments. It is still customary for young men to look after the cattle in the long treks. Their only protection from predators and their solace has always been the bow, providing a weapon as well as a musical instrument. It is interesting that amongst Khoesan-speaking people of the south, the generic term for bow, *!goma* (different orthographies), is a term similar to the generic Bantu language root term *ngoma* for drum. But, *ngoma* refers to far more than just the drum, as it also includes reference to Life Force, food, dance, first fruits, and more (see Bjørkvold, 1992; Mans 1997; etc).

Bows

Musical bows may be performed without or without vocal music as song, praise, and other percussive or ornamental sounds. Within these songs, one can trace histories of different groups of people and cultures, as well as the often poignant stories of individuals. Humorous incidents are retold and stretch the imagination. Within the narrative songs, one hears about the migrations of people and about ancestors and their heroic deeds; the texts contain insights about the meanings assigned to many aspects of life and the hereafter. In nearly all the bow songs in this region, cattle (for the Bantu-speaking peoples) and game, especially eland (for Khoesan-speaking peoples) feature prominently. Whereas the playing of drums in Africa has traditionally been reserved for men (with exceptions in southern and south-

western Africa), bows are quite often played by women as well as men.

Various mouth- and gourd-resonated bows are found all over Namibia, Botswana, southern Angola, and South Africa and are commonly played as boys walk along herding cattle or sit and rest under a tree. Older men often play for "loneliness" reasons. Some bows are simply played by inserting one end into the mouth (cheek) and beating the string with a small stick while creating different overtones by changing the shape of the buccal cavity (inside mouth). Others are tied with a small piece of sinew or wire to create two (or more) different lengths of string, giving different tones. When an external resonator is attached, a more resonant sound can be created. The social significance of hunting bows (which have dual purpose—hunting and music) and gourd-resonated bows (only for music) differs.

Hunting bows used as musical instruments may be braced or unbraced and are mouth resonated. In Namibia these bows are common amongst Bantu-speaking as well as Khoesan-speaking cultures. Some of these bows are large and may be played by two persons, in which case they are called *n!aoh* in Kxoe language. These hunting bows are often played in a manner that emphasizes rhythm above melody. It is important to note that these bows are not constructed or played in an identical fashion by all Namibian cultures. For example, the player's mouth may surround the wood in the center of the bow, or the end of the bow may be inserted into the mouth. Strings may be made of sinew or of steel, and are usually single, although there is an unusual form of *!gomakhās* in northwestern Namibia that is constructed with two metal strings. The second (higher pitched) string is metaphorically referred to as the female voice, and it provides sympathetic vibration for the longer (male voice) string.

When playing the long hunting bow, one end is clamped between the toes on the ground, while the other end is inserted into the mouth. But bows can be played while seated, lying on one's back, or while walking, and may be held either vertically in front of the body or transversely (horizontally). It is more common in San (Bushmen) cultures to hold the bow vertically and among Khoekhoe and Bantu cultures to hold it horizontally. In some cases, the bow is used for hunting as well as musical entertainment.

The value that the instrument holds is evident in the care taken to name each part of the instrument. Special words in each language describe the string, its material, the way it is tied, the stick with which it is beaten, the wood of the bow, and the parts of the bow.

Music performed on the hunting bow may include narratives, prayers or praise incantations. The musical use of hunting bows is said to be ancient and filled with potential power. It may be played before a hunt, when the hunter prays to the spirits of deceased relatives to obtain help in the hunt (Kxoe). But the bow is also played after a successful hunt (Kxoe, !Kung, Hai// om) and to give thanks after killing one's first eland (Kxoe). It is played for one's own pleasure and to calm the animals when herding cattle (Ovazimba, Ovahimba, Ndonga) and for social entertainment (Hai//om, Ovazimba, Ovahimba, Ndonga). Among some of the people, the bow is far more than mere musical or hunting instrument, and good playing is powerful enough to ensure a successful hunt. According to Olivier's field observations, two or more Ju/'hoansi are not allowed to play their hunting bows at the same time as it could be dangerous. The men could inadvert-

Tjisuta playing omburumbumba. *Photo © Minette Mans.*

ently kill each other because they would be musicians, hunters, and animals at the same time. The scarification ritual that takes place after the first hunt ensures that the hunter's body contains *n/om* that strengthens him and enables him to see the animals. Each of the players possesses this *n/om* which may only be used for hunting or to become a shaman. If they play their bows at the same time the *n/om* might cause one to kill the other.

The braced, gourd-resonated bow exists among several cultures in Namibia, each language having its own vernacular name for the instrument. In northwestern regions the calabash (*otjikola*), or plastic resonator, is placed on the chest and opened and closed rhythmically to create different sound effects. In the northeast the resonator is made of a dried melon, a tortoise shell, a metal tin, or, occasionally, a plastic or wooden bowl. The placement of the brace that ties off the string at different lengths might differ from player to player, and culture to culture. It may appear anywhere from about one-fifth of the string to the middle. Like the larger hunting bows, these bows are also held either vertically to the front of the player or horizontally at chest level. The string is struck with a small stick, usually held in the right hand while the left hand holds the bow and creates partials by touching the string with the nail of the thumb or index finger. In Ovazimba music there are many vocal sounds such as aspirations, clicks, shouts, and a drone that enhance the quiet songs and bow playing.

Although not used for hunting, the social circumstances for playing resonated bows include preparation for the hunt, announcing a successful hunt, praying for the dead, herding, and entertainment. Interestingly, this bow is also played for seduction because (Ju/'hoan) women like good hunters (and, by implication, players of the musical bow) because they like meat! Hence, the different lifestyles and social circumstances of various cultural groups are reflected in the songs. Some songs tell tales of hardship and travel. One song by a master *ombulumbumba* player, Petrus Tjisuta, tells of walking on the long road between Johannesburg, South Africa, and Opuwo in Namibia. On the road he finds a lion sleeping. He pokes at it with his finger. The lion gets such a fright, it jumps up and runs away. He sings that the music of the bow gave him the courage to chase the lion away.

In certain circumstances, a bow can be is played by more than one person. The end of the bow is placed on or in a resonator on the ground. The man holding the bow usually creates different tones by touching the string, and also plucking the string with his forefinger, while another man strikes the lower part of the string in a rhythmic pattern with handheld sticks. Another adds vocals. Up to five people can play one bow, although three is more common. The end result, with its deep rhythmic bass, can be quite amazing!

A bow with a completely different sound is scraped, not struck or plucked. Its "string" is made of a strip of palm leaf, and it is played by scraping a small stick across the notches on the bow in a rhythmic pattern, while, at the same time, placing one's open mouth over the strip of leaf to create different timbres. As one of the few instruments traditionally played by women, it is not surprising that one form of this bow has associations with the feminine ritual transformation, or "traditional marriage" (*ohango*), of Ngandjera (Owambo) people. In times past, when the large gathering of young "brides" travelled north to Ombalantu for this initiation, some of them played the *okaya-*

gayaga bow while walking the 20 or 25 miles to their destination. Occasionally, a girl might take a few dance-like steps to the music as they walked, although it is now more common to be seated when playing. It is generally played when "feeling lonely and thinking about far-away things," according to informants. Because it is used for no other purpose than music, this instrument is not considered to contain the same spiritual power as a hunting bow, which is one of the reasons it is customary for a woman to play it.

For musical situations where musicians seek more melodic development, pluriarcs are used. The term *pluriarc* infers an instrument with several bows with strings attached; these in turn are tied down over a soundboard on a resonator. In Namibia the most common form has five bows with attached strings, ranging in size from quite small to large wooden pluriarcs nearly a meter in total length. The tuning of the strings differs from area to area, to fit with the tonal organization of the music of that area. For this reason, it would be a mistake to see all of these instruments as identical. In purpose as well as music they are as different from another as a guitar from a banjo.

Pluriarc

The four-string Ju/'hoan pluriarc, which is played by women, has metal strings and a metal resonator. It is accompanied by singing and sometimes by dance and is played for entertainment, although when dancing and playing healing songs with this pluriarc, shamans can go into trance. Tradition says that this instrument came to the Nyae Nyae area in the northeast of Namibia from further south about four generations ago, when a Ju/hoan couple brought the instrument and its playing technique from the Nharo people.

The five-string pluriarc goes by different names in different cultures, and this instrument is played only by men. Among Ovahimba and Ovazimba, the pluriarc (*otjihumba*) is a very important instrument for accompanying praise songs (*omutandu*)—a form of orature that is fundamental to lifestyle and ancestor remembrance of the people of this northwestern part of the country. Here, the pluriarc forms a rhythmic ostinato accompaniment during the praise incantations. This is interspersed with instrumental solos that expand and vary the basic musical material. This is where the musician demonstrates his instrumental skill, while in the singing part, it is his poetic skill in praising ancestors, places, cattle, heroes, and modern day events, that is important. In Ju/hoan and Hai//om playing, the voice part performs the same melody in imitation of the pluriarc. Ju/'hoansi relate that their five-string pluriarc originated in the Nyae Nyae area. Its history is sacralized in a myth about Kxao N//ae, who used the instrument to create his own inner peace after having tragically killed his wife. The music he played also served to calm others who might have punished him in revenge.

Lute

Traditionally, young men of that northwestern area played a lute or ramkie. The lute played amongst Ovazimba, Ovacuvale, and Ovangambwe is called an *otjindjalindja*. It has three metal or animal sinew strings, a resonator box, a neck and fingerboard, and the head is fitted with three tuning pins. The fingerboard has two raised nuts, allowing only a single change of pitch for each string. The strings are generally plucked or strummed with the right hand while the left stops and releases the strings. Young men play to accompany their singing or praise incantations when they are traveling, although the instrument can be played without song as well. They say that the sound of the *otjindjalindja* keeps them company. Some people say it is played by "gamblers" or young men who take chances. When groups of young men gather to talk, drink, or play games of chance, this instrument is sometimes passed from one to another and the songs are for entertainment. Others might join in the music by rhythmically tapping a walking stick on the ground and creating quiet vocal sounds to accompany the song.

Zither

In Namibia and Botswana there are board and trough zithers of various shapes and sizes (cf. Norborg 1987). Zithers have been reported among Ju/'hoan, Hambukushu, Batswana, Sambyu, and Khoekhoe people. The single string of this instrument is scraped (bowed) with a small bow held in the right hand, while the left touches the string to create partials. The trough or board to which the string is attached is topped by a loose tin resonator (in the past, a tortoise shell).

The Ju/'hoan zither is imbued with special meaning, even though it may be played purely for entertainment as well. Like the other bows, it is played the evening before a hunt, to announce a successful hunt, or even after an unsuccessful hunt in order to ensure that the next one will be successful. The musician is said to pray, and the music of the bow goes up to the god who can help the hunter.

Musical bows and other stringed instruments in Namibia are some of the ways in which people use music to pray, to praise, and to create joy and happiness. For these purposes, stringed instruments are considered very important, even in present times when urban living is reducing the use of bows. They are instruments that give meaning to life, and they are a means of communicating with ancestor spirits and gods, animal spirits, and people. As such, they have always made an important contribution to the spiritual welfare of the people and deserve an important place in the framework of African folklore. It is likely that in the future, the use of bows, lutes, and zithers will go into decline and be replaced with more "modern" instruments such as guitars and violins.

References

Bjørkvold. J-R. 1992. *The Muse Within: Creativity and Communication, Song and Play from Childhood through Maturity.* Tran H. Halverson. Aaron Asher Books. New York: HarperCollins.

Kirby, P. R. 1968/1938. *The Musical Instruments of the Native Races of South Africa.* 2nd ed. Johannesburg: Witwatersrand University Press.

Mans, M. 1997. *Ongoma! Notes on Namibian Musical Instruments.* Windhoek: Gamsberg Macmillan.

Mans, M., and E. Olivier. (forthcoming). Scientific Report for the Project: The Living Musics and Dance of Namibia: Exploration, Publication, Education. Prepared for the French Department of Cooperation and Cultural Affairs in Namibia.

Nketia, J. H. Kwabena. 1998. *Africa. The Garland Encyclopedia of Music,* pp. 13–73. New York: Garland.

Norborg, Å. 1987. *A Handbook of Musical and Other Sound-Producing Instruments from Namibia and Botswana.* Stockholm: Musikmuseets skrifter 13.

Sachs, S. (Ed.) 1980/1940. *The History of Musical Instruments.* London: J. M. Dent.

MINETTE MANS

See also **Music; Music in Africa**

MYTHS: OVERVIEW

The variety of cultures across the African continent offers an equal variety of mythical narratives of all types and genres. A myth is defined here primarily as a sacred narrative involving divine, superhuman, or ancestral figures and the processes that have shaped the world of human observation and experience. The definition addresses content more than context or form, and the range of examples would include the sometimes comic etiological narratives told in casual settings, as well as more formalized and even ritual utterances associated with a restricted or qualified listenership. There are, in practice, few hard and fast rules for identifying a narrative as a myth rather than a folktale or a legend. Local terminology may or may not distinguish types of stories that correspond to recognized global mythical narratives from other sorts (distinctions may involve the perceived age of the stories as well as their truth value). Context may be the most reliable guide: the need for a specialized narrator, a ritual occasion, or other such preconditions marks the narrative with a significance above and beyond that of the ordinary story. The requirement of religious belief, rather than literary enjoyment, may also be another useful criterion, although one not entirely necessary in those parts of the world where myths are seen principally as the narrative relics of extinct belief systems. In Africa, the term applies not only to simple etiologies, but to the narrative infrastructure of living belief systems.

The documentation and description of African myths still leaves much to be desired. Although some studies have identified themes found across sub-Saharan Africa (for instance, the story of the origin of death as due to the tardiness of a messenger [Abrahamsson 1977], or variants on the *enfant terrible* narrative), they are relatively few in number, nor are they accompanied by reliable anthologies. The study of regional groupings is hindered by the language divisions that are a legacy of the colonial era, but which continue to divide students of neighboring regions. Moreover, the continuing functionality of African myths raises the question whether specific narratives should be approached through their Africanness or through their operative context (e.g., hunter-gatherer narratives, etiologies of divination systems or healing cults, royal rituals). However, sub-Saharan African offers ample scope for studies in comparative mythology, be it on a regional level (e.g., among the various peoples of the Niger river) or on the basis of linguistic affinity (the many Bantu-family languages in southern Africa) or on a combination of both (e.g., among the several kingdoms of the Great Lakes region).

It may be helpful to distinguish different sorts of myths, occurring in different contexts and fulfilling different functions: creation myths, charter myths, cult myths, and etiological narratives. Creation myths, perhaps the most widely recognized type of myth, tell how the world came into being; charter myths have more social importance and explain the establishment of human institutions; cult myths explain the origin of specific beliefs and practices, often invoking the available symbolism of creation myths; etiological narratives occur in a variety of less formal contexts and reflect attitudes and interpretations of the teller's world.

Creation myths of all sorts are found across the continent, in a variety of contexts. Some are told casually, others are surrounded in ritual secrecy and performed only on special occasions (e.g., the reroofing of the *Kama Bloñ* of the Mande [Dieterlen 1955]). Creator figures tend to exist at a remove from their creation and function most identifiably in the modern world as guarantors of a world order discernible through divination (e.g., Mawu-Lisa of the Fon pantheon). The world may have come into being as an egg, or through the separation of waters, or it simply exists. Many narratives, from early Egypt to the present, describe the departure of the creator-figure to a home in the sky: people were ungrateful, people imposed on him, he became old or sick. Within the general category of creation myths, the actual creation of the land is often less important than the division of space and the allocation of responsibilities such as the rules of the world and the regulation of rainfall. The creator-figures themselves appear in all configurations: as single males or females, as couples, as androgynous beings, and, occasionally, as partial or half-bodied entities.

More active in the world than the original creators may be the demiurges, the second-generation gods, culture heroes, and tricksters. They are the ones whose stories really establish the parameters of human existence on this planet in every way, from the appointment of foodstuffs and modes of production to the rules of kinship, marriage, and gender relations; they are the ones whose wanderings define the spatial world of their descendents. Some of these figures emerge on earth without antecedents, such as the Khoi-San figure of the Mantis, whose family is the prototypical hunter band; others are descendents of divine figures, such as Nyikang of the Shilluk, who leads his people to their current home along the Nile. Frequently, some part of the process involves a descent from heaven on a rope, a chain, or a vine. The culture hero may later return to the earthly realm, and other adventures may involve a descent into the underworld or the world of the dead. The numerous individual stories featuring the culture hero may occasionally form a loose cycle or sequence, as is the case with Lianja of the Mongo.

Culture heroes are rarely ordinary figures; they often share the characteristics of the trickster, and tricksters in turn show an ability to shape the world as they guide our perception of it. Tricksters may be human or theriomorphic, or indeterminate. One widespread type is the spider (Ananse of the Asante, Ture of the Zande, Nden-Bobo in Cameroon); another is the hare (Leuck in Senegal, Kalulu in Zambia). Tricksters play a significant role in challenging the established world order or in subverting it; they are also particularly important in the context of divination systems because they provide a factor of unpredictability. Ananse the spider brings the sun, the moon, and darkness into the world while proving his boast to Nyame, the sky-god. In Fon narratives from old Dahomey (now Benin), the trickster Legba sets brother against brother to bring about the current regime of uncertain rainfall; in a Yoruba myth of Ifa divination, the trickster Eshu finds a way for Obatala, the god of divination, to escape the coffin that is fated for him. The trickster may also

serve in the same way as a violation of an interdict or an accidental transgression to express and explain the difference betwee the world as it is and the perfect world that might have been.

Charter myths are more human-centered, although they may derive some of their power from association with creation mythology. Typically, the myths that explain and justify the establishment of human social institutions deal with migrations and the progenitors of dynasties. Since the time of Malinowski, it has been accepted that such myths are a reflection of, and upon, the contemporary society, and that they do not necessarily preserve ancient traditions; where old lore and modern practice differ, modern practice will shape the modern narrative. Stories about figures such as Sunjata of the Manding, or the Bachwezi of the Buganda kingdoms, would be obvious examples of such charter myths, but the narratives need not be sober and historical. Stories about the origin of marriage almost always have a humorous tone to them, and stories expressing the tensions in kin-relations may also play with comic effect.

Cult myths are very specific in their scope and application: they serve to explain and justify a specific and localized set of beliefs and practices. The extensive literature of the Ifa divination system among the Yoruba (and beyond) involves a large number of such narratives, explaining and justifying the methods and practices of divination; the various Thunder cults of Nigeria, Benin, and the upper Niger offer different narratives, shaped to the perspective of the believers, to explain the power of their deities. The Bagre ritual of the LoDagaa of northern Ghana offered an extensive creation narrative to accompany the ritual practice (the narrative had changed, however, when Jack Goody went back to record a new version some twenty years after the first). The Sorko explain and justify at least one possession cult with reference to a nineteenth century Muslim figure who is said to have accepted the practice, and Mande hunters' associations have a number of myths of origin involving their deities Sanen and Kontron. One might include in this category the newer narratives that ground world religions such as Islam and Christianity in a localized form and the various syncretic beliefs that have spread beyond Africa in the world of the diaspora.

Etiological narratives in general partake of the ordinary folktale and are distinguished by their subject matter. Such narratives rarely claim profound authority (as would a cult myth), but reflect popular beliefs about the process of creation while focusing narrative attention upon a specific feature or institution: the behavior or appearance of certain animals, the location of geographic features, elements of human behavior. Among etiological narratives, the topic of sex and the human acquisition of sexual characteristics and behavior may deserve special mention. Many such narratives are set in the animal world, where the human parallels can be focused upon specific behaviors or moral principles.

A significant feature of African mythology is the way in which multiple belief systems may coexist within a given community. An effective illustration of this flexibility is found in the corpus of Dahomean narratives (Herskovits and Herskovits 1958) in which the myths of the different cults (sky-*Fa* divination, earth, thunder, hunters) may share characters and protagonists united through projected family relationship, but still follow their specialized interests. Such polymorphic, nonexclusive belief systems are widespread and would defy any attempt to reduce a culture's beliefs to a coherent whole. Another noteworthy feature is the adaptibility of mythical systems and the extent to which beliefs and practices may change radically in a relatively short span of time.

One particular problem is that of identifying possible influences from imported religions such as Christianity and Islam. For example, many peoples of southeastern Africa recount a narrative in which humans attempt to build a tower with which to ascend the heavens. The motivations vary; the effort is unsuccessful. Is this an echo of the biblical narrative of the Tower of Babel or simply a similar but unrelated narrative? The problem has, as yet, no solution, but the question should be asked. The vehicle need not have been Christianity or Judaism; Islam, present along the coasts of eastern Africa, uses the same narratives, and, in fact, many of the biblical parallels that missionaries and others have observed in African mythology may more easily be explained through the contact with Islam than through diffusion from Egypt or Ethiopia.

The study of African mythology has suffered a number of handicaps. Early collections were often made by missionaries, colonial administrators, or converts, and show scorn, distaste, and discomfort for the traditions they document (e.g., Bishop Samuel Johnson's *History of the Yorubas*). In many collections, the seemingly innocuous animal tales are overrepresented at the expense of more revealing, more problematic, and often more graphic narratives (the collections of Frobenius and Pettazzoni are exceptions). Sensitivity on the value of traditional religious belief in distinction to imported monotheisms has led to an overvaluation of creation figures at the expense of more significant human actors, and perhaps to an exaggeration of the coherence of traditional belief. Despite the efforts of collectors such as Leo Frobenius (and perhaps because of his attempts to link African cultures with classical sources), African mythology has not been integrated into the study of world mythology, which has shown a greater fascination for the Indo-European complex and its relations with Middle Eastern religions. Racism and a disregard for apparently primitive African cultures explain much of this bias, and the effects can still be seen in the work of such scholars as Joseph Campbell. Students will find some useful studies (Werner 1933; Tegnaeus 1950; Abrahamsson 1977; Pelton), but in some cases, the methodology displaces the material from center stage (de Heusch 1982) and in others (e.g., Griaule 1965), there are serious questions about the underlying ethnographic basis of the work. Much work remains to be done on all aspects of African myths.

References

Abrahammson, Hans. 1977. *The Origin of Death*. (1951). New York: Arno Press.

Bascom, William. 1969. *Ifa Divination: Communication Between Gods and Men in West Africa*. Bloomington: Indiana University Press.

de Heusch, Luc. 1982. *The Drunken King*. Trans. Roy Willis. Bloomington: Indiana University Press.

Frobenius, Leo. 1921. *Atlantis: Volksmärchen und Dichtung Afrikas*. 12 vol. Iena: Eugen Diederichs.

Griaule, Marcel. 1965. *Conversations with Ogotemmeli: An Introduction to Dogon Religious Ideas*. International African Institute/ Oxford University Press.

Herskovits, Melville, and Frances Herskovits. 1958. *Dahomean Narrative*. Evanston Ill.: Northwestern University Press.

Parrinder, Geoffrey. 1986. *African Mythology*. New York: Peter Bedricks Books.

Pettazzoni, Raffaele. 1948. *Miti e leggendi*. Vol. 1, *Africa*. Torino.

Scheub, Harold. 2000. *A Dictionary of African Mythology*. Oxford University Press.

Tegnaeus, Harry. 1950. *Le Héros Civilisateur*. Studiathographica Upsaliensia II.

Werner, Alice. 1933. *Myths and Legends of the Bantu*. London: George Harrup. Repr. *Africa: Myths and Legends*. London: Studio, 1995.

STEPHEN BELCHER

See also **Cosmology; Epics; History and Cultural Identity: The Chokwe; History and Folklore: The Luba; History and Religious Rituals: Bemba Traditions**

MYTHS: MYTHOLOGY AND SOCIETY IN MADAGASCAR: A TAÑALA EXAMPLE

Like Ariadne's threads stretched between man and the hereafter, Malagasy myths create necessary connections among the various realms of the universe. The alliance between the lands of the living and the dead occurs either through a union or a sacrifice. The Melusinian universal theme of a woman from another world whom the hero weds by promising to respect a prohibition takes on a special importance in Madagascar. The Tañala from the Southeast region of this island have developed three myths from this plot line, all expressing a certain view of the world and society.

Koto the Bird Hunter

Youngest son of a king, hated by his family, Koto lives on hunting birds in the forest. At the edge of a lake, he captures a "princess of the sky," the daughter of the celestial god Zañahary, whom he marries after having sworn never to drink rum. That night, the daughter of the god appears suddenly with her servants; Koto's shelter becomes a royal palace in the middle of a huge village. Jealous, the brothers—also rivals—of the hero visit him, bringing rum. They intoxicate Koto, who reveals the origin of his wife. Princess and riches disappear.

Wandering in the forest, Koto meets an old woman at the intersection of eight roads. With a fragment of bamboo, he removes the sticky matter that blinds her. She then reveals to him the road to Zañahary's village, a path strewn with trials over which Koto will triumph. He ignores a fat eel's request to be grilled with salt [a *tona* eel, the reincarnation of ancestors of ancient inhabitants of the Eastern coast, but abhored by today's nobility], crosses a deep lake filled with crocodiles, lets himself be attacked by a skeleton, a silver cock, and so on. In the house of the deity, he avoids gold objects and, thanks to a mosquito, he recognizes his wife among three women who look alike. Zañahary grants him his daughter's hand. She brings a chicken with her which she lets nibble some paddy rice. The rice that Zañahary had refused to give to the young people thus arrives on earth.

On their way to visit Zañahary in their turn, the elder brothers transgress the prohibitions of the road. The deity changes them into dogs. Hence, the origins of royalty, rice, and pariahs are explained.

Koto the Sharpshooter

While hunting birds in the forest, a king comes upon two women seated on a stone in a clearing. He captures the younger one, Rasôrôva ("Beautiful Lady Blackbird"), and marries her, after having sworn never to reveal her origin. Rasôrôva gives birth to a son. When the people of the village have gone to the fields, she sings a lullaby that recalls her "animal" origin. The king's mother hears the song and alerts her son. Rasôrôva flees away, pursued by her husband. They arrive at a cave where Rasôrôva's sisters and mother live. Her mother orders her daughter to return to the world of the humans. They say to Rasôrôva, "If the child falls ill, call us, and we will treat him with plants."

Koto the Fisherman

A poor fisherman, Koto, catches a "princess of the waters" (water sprite or undine) in a deep hole of a river. She agrees to marry him if he respects the prohibition of rum and does not call her "daughter of the salt." That night, Koto's shelter becomes a beautiful house. Along with the water sprite (undine), oxen and boxes filled with riches emerge from the water. The undine gives birth to three children, a boy and two girls. During a circumcision, the jealous king of the village intoxicates Koto, who reveals his wife's origin. She returns to the realms of the waters. At the conclusion of a test imposed on the children (eating bananas underwater), the daughters follow their mother, and the son remains on earth with his father, who falls back into poverty.

Sacrifice of a bull at the inauguration of a "large house" (*tranobe*) of a chief. With two pairs of horns (made of wood) on the roof, the house expresses the connection between house, chief, and bull. The sacrifice takes place on the east of the "large house", where two trees grow: a ficus and a kind of *Albizzia* (a post connected with the cult to the ancestors and the spirits of the earth, that took root). Photo © Philippe Beaujard.

A procession toward the mouth of the river Mananjary preceding a circumcision. A man chosen by the lineage bears a gourd containing "holy water" (*rano masina*, or *rano manoro*). His forehead and cheeks are marked with white clay. Fathers bear their sons, dressed in red, with a cap decorated with a white cross. White and red are the colors of the aristocracy on most of the island. Here the king, dressed in a red robe, with a "three colored material" (*lamba telo soratra*) over it signifying his kingship, sprinkles the gourd bearer and the whole congregation with *rhum* (blessing) before the procession starts. Photo © Philippe Beaujard.

The Universal Order

These three myths express the structure of the universe: sky, earthly world of the living, and the lower world divided between earth and water. Liminal sites of passage, the sites of capture of the three women, reveal their connections with the elements, the beings, and the realms with which these elements are associated. The stone (associated with death) of the "Beauty of the Forest" corresponds both to the lake in which the princess of the sky descends to bathe and to the abyss of water from where the princess of the waters emerges. Both the princesses appear connected to the waters, but in an inverted relationship. From the lower realm, two women arise, whose status differs: the water spirit is a princess, while the "Beauty of the Forest" is a commoner, connected with the earth. The split of the lower realm between earth (or stone) and water is related on the social level with a schism between aristocrats and indigenous peoples expressed by the funerary customs of the two groups composing the Tañala society (slaves were on the margins of the society, and outside were the pariahs, deemed to have sinned with a dog). The bodily fluids of a king (who carries the title of Lord of the River) are thrown into a deep hole of a river (where they are changed into a crocodile), while the bodily fluids of the indigenous people—who carry the same title, Masters of the Earth, as the spirits of the earth—are allowed to run at the foot of a stone table erected near the collective tomb of the lineage.

In the character of the princess of the sky, sky merges with water. This merging appears clearly in other Malagasy versions of the myth. In a tale from the highlands, Faralahy, the "Last-Born," sets up snares at the edge of a lake and catches a box containing a princess of the sky, her maid, and a wild duck. From this box, an image of a "fertile" coffin, like the stomach of the "Swallowing Monsters" (an ogre—Trimobe, name of Bantu origin—or a seven-headed snake), which contains a kingdom, people and oxen emerge when the daughter of God breaks the box. In a legend from Imerina, the goddess Andriambavirano ("Princess of the Waters") falls from the sky into a lake in the form of a perfumed leaf that a prince captures uttering, "If I am noble through my father and noble through my mother, I shall capture her easily."

Rum, forbidden to the princesses, offered in rituals to the ancestors, and consumed at funerals, is not mentioned by the "Beauty of the Forest." In Madagascar, as in other countries, mythical thought establishes a connection between the process of alcoholic fermentation and the decomposing body. We should note that in the ancient Javanese classification, alcoholic beverages are symbolically connected with the West and therefore opposed to the ladies of the sky, who are connected, as in Madagascar, with the East; here emerges an opposition between Death (West) and Life (East) (Ottino 1986, 261).

Beyond the oppositions (Culture/Nature and Nobility/Autochthony) among the three ladies, their respective connections with the three substances (rice, zebu, and rum, respectively associated with the three realms of the universe), which are offered in the sacrifice to Zañahary, to the ancestors, and to the spirits of the earth, a central ritual of the Malagasy religion, highlights their fundamental complementarity.

The prohibition of salt, common to the Tañala water spirits and to the Merina water spirit Ranoro seems to evoke a maritime origin for these "daughters of the waters." To mention salt would be to refer to their origins, which is prohibited in all Melusinian tales. We find the term *noro* again in the name of the water used in circumcision, *rano manoro*, also named *rano masina* ("holy water," or "salted water"; *masina* has these two meanings). Circumcision is evoked explicitly or figuratively in the myth of the water spirit (the test of the bananas to be eaten; with the Zafiraminia Antambahoaka, the maternal uncle of the child eats the cut prepuce in a banana). In the Highlands, the Antehiroka, of Vazimba ascendance, had the privilege of fetching water for the royal circumcision near the lake in which Ranoro threw herself. A "Princess Defeated" (an epithet given to Ranoro) on the political level, the water spirit recovers importance on the religious level. The triple alliance of water, light, and salt in circumcision and the character of the water spirit may be related to the Fatima of Shiite Islam, whose name we encounter in a "Bara-Tañala" version of the myth of the water spirit (Ottino 1986, 532). A collective ritual of integration into the group, controlled by the king, the circumcision on the southeast coast has been influenced by the Islamicized aristocrats who came from Indonesia around the thirteenth century and may have played a role in the development of the kingdom of the Southeast and the South, and of the Highlands. Circumcision appears in most of the texts where a male hero grows from childhood into adulthood. In the story of the bird hunter, it is transferred onto the character of the old woman (the cutting of the sticky matter with a fragment of bamboo), and onto the bull of Zañahary, from which Koto wrests the single horn without shedding any blood.

Cosmic Dualism, Social Dualism

The acquiring of rice, oxen, and healing plants symbolically emphasize that union with a woman from the other world always proves to be beneficial. The three Melusinian myths, whose endings are inseparable, express different lessons, however, on the social and political level, although within the same aristocratic logic. Along with the alliances with the three hierarchized realms, the tales explore the possible unions for the nobility. The merging of sky and water in the daughter of Zañahary makes her marriage with the hunter-prince of the earth the only alliance capable of uniting the three worlds, as well as the only one that is at the source of a noble lineage on both paternal and maternal sides. The "three colors" (red—sky, white—waters, black—earth) of the toga in which the Malagasy kings drape themselves symbolize the universal sovereignty that issued from this alliance. The marriage of the king with the "Beauty of the Forest" is at the origin of a disparaged aristocratic lineage, for it is noble only through the male line, whereas the *hasina* (sacred power of divine origin) is ideally transmitted through the female line. As a warrant of this *hasina*, the king's mother obviously opposes her son's marriage. The undine leaves on earth only an indigenous lineage since it is noble only on the female side (since the eighteenth century in Tañala country, aristocratic status has been passed through the male line and no longer through both lines).

The tragic conclusion of the myth of the water spirit, furthermore, illustrates the prohibition of the hypogamy of the princesses, known throughout Madagascar. This prohibition also explains Zañahary's anger with the bird hunter. First, he must endure his initiation voyage in a country where there is a confusion of the realm of the dead (where the hero comes to draw wisdom and legitimacy from the ancestors) and that of the sky, dispenser of sovereignty (which, on a political level, constitutes the stakes of the voyage into the other world). Then Koto (in some versions of the myth) must confront additional trials (he struggles against a unicorn bull, wrests a lightening-tree, carves a pirogue from stone and makes it float) and prove his mastery over the three elements connected to the three realms of the universe (fire, water, stone), with which the three metals (gold—solar metal reserved for the king—silver, and copper) are associated.

This tripartite conception of the universe is combined with a cosmic and social dualism, which is expressed in color distinctions: red (political power) and white (religious power) are associated with nobility, black with the indigenous people (and with the slaves). There is a parallel between the correlative oppositions of the sky (united with waters) and of the earth (earth-world of the living and earth-world of the spirits), of Life and Death, of the Upper and the Lower, and aristocrats—connected to the sky—masters of the waters, and indigenous "masters of the earth."

Tañala society renews with schemas well known in western Indonesia (for example, the Ngaju of Kalimantan, studied by Schärer 1946). Evoking Tañala and Merina, Condominas (1989) has spoken of "Malagasy variations on the Malaysian theme of the sovereign as husband of his people." The product, perhaps, of more recent Indonesian influences in Madagascar, the structure of the center and the cardinal points (i.e., the intersection of eight roads in the myth of the bird hunter), bringing into play a hierarchization of the space underlying a political project, shows the combination of the ternary system with a quaternary system. In a Sakalava myth, the son of a king "in the middle of the earth," who raises yellow, white, red, and black dogs, goes to confront trials in the four directions of space (Dahle and Sims 1971,116). Seated in the "middle of the earth," the god-king combines in his person the four colors, along with the four elements connected with the cardinal points: red and fire in the North (direction of the nobility's political power), white and water in the East (direction of the divinities, of socialized Death), black and earth in the South (direction of the political power of the indigenous people), and yellow and stone in the West (direction of wild Death). Thus, two axes structure space: North–South, axis of the political, and East–West, axis of the religious. This quaternary system is reduced again to a binary system with a North-East-Upper/South-West-Lower opposition, connected to the aristocrat/indigenous split, an opposition that we find also in the Korawasrama, a Javanese cycle of the Mahabharata, and the *wayang* theater of shadows (Ottino 1986,245). For the cycle of the Andriambahoaka ("Lord of the People," a royal title found in the myths and the tales and in the historic kingdoms of the Southeast coast and of the Highlands), Ottino notes that the West and South, unfavorable directions for the nobility, house monsters "belonging to Bantu mythology," an observation that takes on a special meaning in the "Indonesian" context of the aristocratic symbolic system.

The myth of the bird hunter illuminates the inner workings of Tañala society. The wife (or the sister) of the king, who bears the title of "Princess of the Sky," attends palavers and participates in decisions. During the sacrifice, and even before the divinities are invoked, she and her "sisters" of the noble group eat part of the prepared offerings. Since the eighteenth century, princesses and relatives through the female line have elected new kings (among the relatives through the male line). In the nineteenth century, a king still chose, preferably, a first wife of noble origin. The image of the population of "servants," who accompany the princess of the sky to earth, is contrasted with the primordial myth of the bird hunter, which is the political opposite of the Tañala kingdoms of the nineteenth century, characterized by a sharing of power between the nobility and the indigenous people. Even if, before the eighteenth century, matrilineal filiation dictated the royal line, the myth of the bird hunter, like the other Melusinian tales, represents a model with which the nobility has dealt with the establishing of an original dualist power. The alliance of a commoner with a princess, though condemned in the myth of the water spirit, has been a social practice since the eighteenth century. Yet, up to the present time, the model continues to permeate the nobility's worldview.

Other myths, focused on the relationship between the nobility and the common people, also split from social reality. An aristocratic version of the myth of the "Seven-Headed Snake" (*fañany*, a creature of the underworld who devours a kingdom as a result of a sin committed by an indigenous man) warns against excessive power granted the "masters of the earth," whom the snake symbolizes (the myth follows the plot line of the Bantu tales dealing with the "Swallowing Monsters," Werner 1968, 206).

An indigenous version, in which the initial sin is ascribed to a member of the nobility, illustrates the legitimacy of the rise of the indigenous people, who triumph over the monster after the sacrifice of wild boars, which are taboo for the nobles (the myth reflects ancient beliefs or practices that were eliminated under the influence of the Islamicized aristocrats). The two social strata, at once allies and rivals, use the plot line of the same myth but endow it with opposing political interpretations. The

indigenous people seem, in fact, to be caught between two contradictory desires: the taking on of, and denial of, power. The myth of the two Zañahary, "from Above" and "from Below," struggling for universal power, expresses an irreducible opposition between two social strata. Although, in some versions, the celestial god triumphs, in others, he is ridiculed by the god from the underworld, who personifies both the spirits of the earth and the indigenous people, and who sometimes carries the name of Mbodisy (Iblis, the devil of Islam, who here has lost some of his evil character), or that of "the Child looking for misfortune." Like a hero of the Bara tales, Tinaimboaty, the "god from below" here borrows features of the African "clever child" who defies the authority of the chief. The two versions of the myth of the Zañaharys expressed the absolute domination one social stratum wants to have over another, and a rejection (desired or feared) of the royal power by the indigenous people. Conflicts and violence proscribed by social practice are sublimated in the realm of the myth.

Other tales, however, show the two divinities as allied in the creation of man—the Zañahary from Below shapes the bodies with clay; the celestial Zañahary sets them in motion—thus presenting an image of cooperation and unity between the sky and the earth.

In a version where the two Zañahary share the world between them, the rice ("white" plant) and the humans belong to the celestial god (who symbolizes the "whites," the nobility), while the tubers ("black" plants) and the wild beasts belong to Mbodisy (who represents the "blacks," the indigenous people). Here we see an opposition between white and black, undoubtedly of Islamic origin, but inserted into an Afro-Indonesian symbolic system. In the myth of the bird hunter, we remember that the daughter of the celestial god steals rice from her father. This motif throws light on the social place of this divine food, a female plant, associated with royalty. In Imerina in the nineteenth century, the king Andrianampoinimerina said, "The rice and I, we are but one."

Other well-known myths connect the arrival of rice on earth with that of death. Granted by god, rice is exchanged for the life of the "Ninth" of the primordial men, or grows miraculously on the tomb of an immolated child. This name of "Ninth" (reference to the ninth case in geomancy—of Arab origin—which represents the spirits in a general way) is also given to the "spirits of the earth." These two mythical systems—rice of the sky, rice of the earth—are related to two logics of power, aristocratic and indigenous, to different agricultural techniques (wet-rice growing for the nobility, dry-rice growing for the indigenous populations), and to two types of rituals.

Like the water spirit and the "Beauty of the Forest," the "Ninth" and the sacrificed child express the fertility that emanates from the world of the dead—here through sacrifice—and the continuity of death with life, of the ancestors with the spirits of nature (merging with the souls of the first inhabitants). To these spirits, Faublée (1954) gave the lovely name "spirits of life," not seeing, however, their essential connection with the lower world. In Madagascar, in fact, the symbolic conceptions oppose ancestors and spirits of nature less than spirits of the earth, connected with the indigenous people, and spirits of the waters, associated with the princes.

The problematic and shifting relationship between the nobility and the common people appears at the center of most of

Madagascar's mythic tales. Although the myths shed light on social reality, they are not mere reflections of this reality. A production of the "pensée sauvage" (Levi-Strauss 1962), myth is both a conscious construct and a dream, an expression of desires and anxieties. The Malagasy myths, in which the Indonesian legacy seems to dominate, characterized by an "Indo-Islamic encounter" no doubt already achieved in Indonesia (Ottino 1986, 15–80), testify furthermore to the richness and the complexity of the syncretic folklores of this region.

References

Beaujard, Philippe. 1991. *Mythe et société à Madagascar (Tañala de l'Ikongo). Le chasseur d'oiseaux et la princesse du ciel*. Paris: L'Harmattan.

Beaujard, Philippe. 1993. Religion et société à Madagascar. L'exemple tañala. In *L'Etranger intime. Mélanges offerts à Paul Ottino*. pp. 181–217. Université de la Réunion: Océan Editions.

Condominas, Georges. 1989. Le souverain époux de son peuple: variations madécasses sur un thème malais, In, H. J. M. Classen (ed), *Variant Views: Five Lectures from the Perspective of the "Leiden Tradition" in Cultural Anthropology*, Leiden: ICA Publicatie.

Dahle, Lars, et John Sims. *Anganon'ny Ntaolo* [contes des anciens]. 1971. Antananarivo: Trano Printy Loterana. (Ière éd. L. Dahle, *Specimens of Malagasy Folk-Lore*, Antananarivo, 1877).

Faublée, Jacques. *Les esprits de la vie à Madagascar*. Paris: PUF.

Haring, Lee. 1982. *Malagasy Tale Index*. FF Communications no. 231. Helsinki: Suomalainen. Tiedeakatemia, Academia Scientiarum Fennica.

———— 1992. *Verbal Arts in Madagascar: Performance in Historical Perspective*. Philadelphia: University of Pennsylvania Press.

Lévi-Strauss, Claude, 1962. *La pensée sauvage*. Paris: Plon.

Mack, John. 1986. *Madagascar: Island of the Ancestors*. London: British Museum.

Ottino, Paul. 1986. *L'etrangère intime. Essai d'anthropologie de la civilisation de l'ancien Madagascar*. 2 Vol. Paris: Editions des Archives Contemporaines.

Schärer, Hans. 1946. *Ngaju Religion. The Conception of God among a South Borneo People*. The Hague: M. Nijhoff.

Stöhr, Waldemar. 1968. Les religions archaïques d'Indonésie et des Philippines. In *Les religions d'Indonésie*, ed. Waldemar, Stöhr, et Piet Zoetmulder. 7–255. Paris: Payot.

Werner, Alice. 1933. Myths and Legends of the Bantu. London: Frank Cass.

PHILIPPE BEAUJARD

See also **Cosmology; Color Symbolism: The Akan of Ghana; French Study of African Folklore**

MYTHS: MYTHS OF ORIGIN AND SCULPTURE: THE MAKONDE

The Makonde live in southeastern Tanzania and northern Mozambique. Their original home seems to have been to the south-west of this region. There is a debate about whether the Makonde of Tanzania and those of Mozambique are the same people linguistically and culturally. Some people prefer to use different names for the two groups of Makonde.

The literature on Makonde folklore mentions a myth of origin, about a man who lived alone in the bush. He carved a statue, which, in the night, became a woman. He married her, and together they went to the river to bathe. She gave birth to three children, the first two of whom died. The third and susbsequent children survived. These are the ancestors of the Makonde.

This myth is supposed to account for various aspects of Makonde culture. The mythical first ancestor directed his descendants to bury their dead upright, since their mother came to life from a statue that was standing. The myth also helps to account for the fact that the woman occupies such an elevated position in Makonde society. There is a distinct cult of feminine ancestors, who are sometimes deified. The mother plays a very important role; in time of death or distress, the Makonde pray to their mothers.

The founding myth seems to be the original inspiration of the tradition of wood carving, for which the Makonde are famous. This art is very important in Makonde life. It projects the diversity of life's themes so comprehensively that it can be considered a discursive tradition in its own right.

Makonde folktales present a wide array of characters. These may be human, human-like, or nonhuman. Hare, the main trickster in the folklore of eastern and southern Africa, appears in this role in Makonde folklore. Other characters from this region, such as Lion, Hyena, Elephant and Antelope are also prevalent in Makonde folktales.

There are close linkages between Makonde folklore and sculpture. Makonde sculpture often represents themes, characters, and episodes from Makonde folklore. One of the most prevalent and memorable characters represented in the sculpture is a devil figure popularly known as *shetani*. Makonde sculptures have been adept at representing this grotesque, indefinable, but persistent figure of Makonde folklore and consciousness. The mask, a special and most noticeable form of Makonde sculpture, is regularly used in dances. The dancers wearing such masks represent human or animal spirits.

References

Dias, Antonio Jorge. 1961. *Portuguese Contribution to Cultural Anthropology*. Johannesburg: Witwatersrand University Press.

Kingdon, Zachary. 1996. Chanuo Maundu: Master of Makonde Blackwood Art. *African Arts*, XXIX, 4: 56–61, 95–6.

Nang'umbi. A. A. 1998. Mystical forces and social relations in Makonde oral literature. *In The Making of a Periphery: Economic Development and Cultural Encounters in Southern Tanzania*, ed. Pekka Seppälä and Bertha Koda, pp. 265–84. Uppsala: Nordiska Afrikainstitutet.

JOSEPH L. MBELE

N

NAMIBIA

Located on the southeast coast of Africa, Namibia is an arid country bordered by Angola, Zambia, Zimbabwe, Botswana, and South Africa. Of the nation's 1.73 million people, 50 percent are Ovambo, 9 percent, Kavango, 7 percent, Herero, 7 percent, Damara, and 27 percent are composed of various other groups. English, Ovambo, Kavango, Nama/Damara, Herero, Khiosan, German, and Afrikaans are the country's most widely spoken languages. Seventy percent of the nation is Christian, and 30 percent of Namibians practice traditional indigenous religions. Windhoek, the nation's capital, is also its largest city, with 161,000 inhabitants.

Germany declared southwestern Africa its protectorate in 1884, soon establishing a rigidly segregated society and initiating diamond mining. The Union of South Africa occupied the territory in 1915 and was granted a mandate by the League of Nations five years later. South Africa continued to rule Namibia (as it was officially renamed by the United Nations in 1968) in defiance of the UN for decades. Namibia, Africa's last colony, gained its independence on March 21, 1990, after 106 years of colonial rule. But South Africa did not leave Walvis Bay, prized as a deep water port and once center of the American whaling industry, until 1994.

After a twenty-six-year war for liberation, during which thousands of civilians died by South African death squads, it was expected that it would take a long time to establish a stable society and economy. Despite the nation's rich natural resources and strong economic potential, Namibia's government continued to suffer from an unstable economy in its postcolonial years. Although the apartheid rule of colonialism had been abolished, much of the nation's wealth remained in the hands of the white minority. At the turn of the century, the government was attempting to encourage economic development, as well as the redistribution of wealth. Adult literacy stood at only 60 percent.

Namibia's many natural resources include diamonds, copper, lead, zinc, uranium, silver, cadmium, lithium, coal, fish, and possible oil reserves. Agricultural production revolves around corn, millet, sorghum, and livestock. The nation's principle industries and sources of revenue include meat canning, dairy products, leather tanning, textiles, clothing, and mineral concentrates. Two of the country's harshest and most interesting areas,

the "Skeleton Coast," a strip of desert along the Atlantic coastline, and the Kalahari Desert, may prove destinations for Namibia's growing tourist industry.

JENNIFER JOYCE

NAMING CUSTOMS IN AFRICA

In Africa, a range of social, religious, and cultural circumstances determines the naming of a child (Skhosana 2001). The naming of a child is a very important event among Africans, and the names bestowed on children have definite meanings. Hence, parents, relatives, and neighbors are very careful when choosing the name of an individual. Madubuike remarks, "Names are not merely labels or simple tags which the individual carries along with him. They have a deep social significance, and many names studied collectively express a worldview, the *Weltanschauung* of the people" (1976, 13–14).

Experts on names and naming practices, such as Koopman (2001) and Ledzekpo (2001), illustrate the functions of African personal names in social and cultural bonding. [Most examples in this entry are taken from the works of the above onomasticians, as they represent West, Central, East, and Southern Africa.]

Ladzekpo (2001) notes that an African personal name offers insight into one's cultural origin. It may personify the individual by alluding to a story about the family or the immediate parents of the bearer. It signifies the values, beliefs, convictions, traditions, hopes, fears, and conceptions of the whole group. In Africa a child is given a name with a deep-rooted meaning. In the fashion handed down through generations, a name is selected after careful reflection and consultation and with the hope that the child will grow up in fulfillment of the name provided. Many Africans will seek guidance from ancestors or spiritual entities by consulting with a diviner about the proper name for a child. Some families may consult the naming traditions of Christianity or Islam or baby name books, while others may find such European or Arabic names offensive. Surnames or clan names were originally personal names that have since been adopted by the people descended from that particular clan.

A name is the identity of and window into one's culture and self. A name exerts an influence for better or for worse on the life of the child. Quartey-Papafio (1910) reports that a Ga man would even die for his family name. If someone misused his name, it was considered an insult, not only to the person to whom the affront was offered, but also to the family to which he belonged. It is considered an unpardonable defamation to call a man or a woman by a name other than the one given to him or her by parents or relatives. African names are very close and dear to one's heart, because they connect one with one's ancestors and are a part of one's spirituality. Moreover, African names offer the first insight into a person's cultural origin.

Some famous African leaders have jettisoned their Euro-Hebraic names in favor of pertinent African ones: Kwame Nkrumah discarded Johnson, Mobuto Sese Seko discarded Joseph, and Jomo Kenyatta discarded Johnson, to select just a few examples from a long list. Even in South Africa, some politicians have reverted to their original African names. The adoption of African names demonstrates a sense of cultural independence. On the other hand, in an interesting anticolonial reaction, some parents in Nigeria, during World War II, named their sons Hitler.

Names given by an ethnolinguistic group in Africa depict a significant character as well as an exposition of the circumstances of the birth of the name bearer (Ladzekpo 2001). The name of the Zulu king Shaka bears testimony to this. Koopman (2001) explains that reasons for giving names on the African continent can be divided roughly into four categories: These are in no particular order of priority, and many names overlap two or more categories. Two are discussed here:

One type of name derives from a handed-down family name or a name given to commemorate a deceased relative or friend. Koopman (2001, 3) says the choice of a relative's or friend's name to be thus commemorated ranges from purely arbitrary—the whim of the father or mother of the child—to a highly rigid structure common to all members of the society. For the Gikuyu of Kenya there is a rigid system of naming, in which the first son is named after his father's father (Madubuike 1976, 95). The Nuer people seem to have the same practice, in that, according to Evans-Pritchard (1948, 167), personal names sometimes occur in lineal descent, as is the case with monarchies. Interestingly enough, even in southern Africa, monarchies follow this practice; for example, the reigning Swazi king in 2002 was Mswati III, and in Lesotho, it was Letsi II. Ladzekpo (2001) notes that African names have the capacity to reveal a person's original clan. People knowledgeable of these traditions can decipher a person's clan status and birth rank by analyzing the etymology of the names.

Another system of naming focuses on the circumstances surrounding the birth. Ladzekpo states that "historically, African people of all ethnic persuasions can identify and recount past events by naming children in accordance with the event or circumstance at the time of birth" (2001, 4). Children may be called names that suggest famine, earthquake, harvest, thunderstorm, and any natural phenomenon. In South Africa, for example, when the identity document was introduced for blacks, many parents were not too sure about the exact date on which they were born, but the main events of the time helped them to approximate the year for the document. Even the bearer of the name will boast that he or she was born on the day of such and such an event. As Molema notes, "Names of children were taken from events that were taking place about the time of their birth. Thus, children born, say, during the South African War might be called Leburu

(Boer), Ntoa (War), Maksone (Maxim), Kganelo (Siege) and so forth" (1928, 128).

References

Evans-Pritchard, E. E. 1948. Nuer Modes of Address. *Uganda Journal* 12.

Koopman, A. 2001. *Zulu Names*. Durban: University of Natal Printers.

Ladzekpo, E. 2001. *African Personal Names: Their Historical and Cultural Significance*. From http://www.soi.city. (web project/introduction).

Madubuike, I. 1976. *A Handbook of African Names*. Washington D.C.: Three Continents Press.

Molema, S. S. 1920. *The Bantu, Past and Present*. Edinburg: Edinburgh Press.

Skhosana, P. B. Names and Practices Amongst Southern Ndebele Male Persons. *Nomina Africana* 15, nos. 1 and 2.

Quartey-Papafio, A. B. 1910. The Use of Names among the Ga or Acra People of the Gold Coast. *Journal of the African Society* 10.

PETROS MAFIKA LUBISI

See also **Birth and Death Rituals among the Gikuyu; Gender Representation in African Folklore**

NAMING CUSTOMS, EAST AFRICA

East African communities have different ways of naming children. While some systems are fixed, others are rather flexible. This flexibility allows some communities to capture certain natural and social phenomenon and encode it in their culture through names. Thus, names constitute East African communities' folklore inasmuch as they exhibit the artistic characteristics of accurate observation, vivid imagination, and ingenious expression. The differences in naming systems of East African communities calls for separate discussions for some selected communities.

The Maragoli of Western Kenya

In this community, children are named either according to circumstances surrounding their birth or according to the names of their clans. Generally speaking, "good" people will be named after their death, but people will try to forget the name of a person who was considered "bad" during his lifetime. Examples of Maragoli names and their meaning are given below.

A child who is born at night may be called Avukidu, meaning "of the night."
A child born during the time of famine is called Anzala.
A child born outside the house is called Chavulimu, meaning "wild."
A child born during corn harvest time is called Kaduma, meaning "maize."
A child who is the only one in the home is called Muderwa.
A child born when locusts are threatening the country is called Asige, meaning "of the locust."
The first twin is usually called Malonge.
A child born during planting time is called Vutagwa.

The Bagisu of Western Kenya

The natural seasons in agriculturalist communities provide an important reservoir of names in several East African communities. Among the Bagisu, male and female children born during a famine are named Wantsala and Nanzala, respectively, after *insala*, meaning "hunger." Similarly, the male and female children born during a drought are named Nasimiyu or Simiyu—after Simiyu, meaning "drought." A boy born in the rainy season is named Wafula, and a girl is named Nafula. A girl born during the time of sowing may be called Nakhumitsa, during the weeding time, Nekesa, and during the ploughing time, Nelima.

Some names among the Bagisu have significant meanings. The firstborn is called Bakoki, meaning "the first to give pain to the woman." The name is not used publicly. The last-born boy or girl has a pet name, Mutuwa, meaning "the one who closed the path." Kuloba is the name given to a baby boy who follows the death of another child. Liloba is the earth, and since the earth has swallowed the other child, the next newborn is, therefore, given the name Kuloba. Wepukhulu is the name given to a baby boy if he is the only one in the family. Nabisinyo is the name given to bastards of either sex. Other names describe beauty. Matiinyi, meaning "well proportioned," is the name given to a beautiful girl. Naluhende, meaning "slender," is another name given to an attractive girl.

The Gĩkũyũ of Central Kenya

The Gĩkũyũ have a formulaic way of naming their children, one based on their extended family relations. The name given to a child depends on sex and birth position. The formula (shown below) is fixed, and therefore a child's name is known before he or she is even born. If the ninth child is a boy, he will be named after the father's second brother. If the father had only one brother, then the boy will be given the name that the father's mother would have given her third son if she had had one. In this case, the boy would be named after the father's father (grandfather's) first brother.

Twins are named either on the mother's side or the father's side depending on their position and sex. For example, if male twins are firstborns, the first will be named after the father's father and the second after the father's first brother. If a child— for example, a third son—dies and another son is born soon after, three naming options exist. The newborn could be given the same name that had been given to the dead child; in this case, he would be named after the father's first brother. Alternatively, he could be given the name Kariuki or Muriuki, meaning

Table 1

Position and Sex	Named after
1st male	Father's father
1st female	Father's mother
2nd male	Mother's father
2nd female	Mother's mother
3rd male	Father's first brother
3rd female	Father's first sister
4th male	Mother's first brother
4th female	Mother's first sister

"the one who has risen from the dead," implying that the parents feel that the dead child has "risen" in the newborn. A third option is that he could be given the name of the next relative in the order given in the chart above (e.g., what would have happened if his predecessor were still alive), and, in this case, be named after the mother's first brother. The same case would apply to a girl born immediately after the death of a sister, the difference being that, in the second option, the name given to a girl is Njoki, meaning "the one who has returned."

If a child is born outside marriage and the man responsible refuses to marry the girl, the child is named after its relations from the mother's side according to the above formula. If the woman later marries, it means that her parents or relations will be named before those of the husband, and any one conversant with the Gĩkũyũ naming customs will know that the children were born out of wedlock.

The Luo of South Western Kenya

Among the Luo, there is a traditional naming of children, based on the time of birth and sex. Generally, names starting with the letter "O" refer to males and those starting with "A" refer to females. A child born in the early morning is named Omondi or Akinyi. One born in midmorning is called Onyango or Anyango. One born in broad daylight is called Ochieng' or Achieng'. A child born in the evening is named Odhiambo or Adhiambo. One born at night is Otieno or Atieno, while one born at midnight is named Owuor or Awuor. Other Luo names correspond to the place where one is born. One born by the roadside is Oyoo or Ayoo. One born in the bush is named Olum or Alum. Twins are Apiyo and Adongo and Opiyo and Odongo, depending on whether they are boys or girls. Their follower is named Akelo or Okelo, depending on sex.

Naming systems in East Africa portray the diversity of African culture and the richness of its folklore. Names remain a fairly stable category of African oral traditions. Although East Africans were forced to take European names as a mark of Christianity during colonialism, European names have never achieved meaning in the naming systems. African names continue to carry lineage, tribal, and cultural meanings. They remain an integral system of the African oral traditions.

References

Lo Liyong, T., eds. 1972. *Popular Culture of East Africa: Oral Literature*. Nairobi: Longman Kenya.
Nandwa, J., and A. Bukenya. 1983. *African Oral Literature for Schools*. Nairobi: Longman Kenya.

MICHAEL WAINAINA

See also **Linguistics and African Verbal Arts**

NARRATION AND VERBAL DISCOURSE: THE LUGBARA OF UGANDA

The Lugbara are a Central Sudanic–speaking people of northwest Uganda and the adjacent areas of the Democratic Republic of the Congo and the Sudan Republic. They numbered about a quarter of a million in the 1950s, the era with which this entry is concerned. They were densely settled farmers, growing mainly sorghums as staples and keeping some livestock. There were some sixty dispersed patrilineal clans, segmented into territorially compact subclans, each of some four thousand people, and in turn divided into several levels of lineages. The minimal lineage was the core of a joint family, the basic residential group (Middleton 1960). They traditionally lackedcentralized political authority; those with the greatest authority were the rainmakers, one in each subclan. Beneath them were the elders of joint families. The British and Belgian colonial administrations appointed chiefs. This "traditional" social organization was greatly changed by the turn of century, but the situation remained uncertain. In the 1950s most Lugbara were illiterate. Although many younger people could read and write; theirs was not a literate culture. Formal behavior was dependent upon verbal communication, in which narrative skill, nuances of speech, use of proverbs, subtle allusion to local events, and preciseness in choice of words were necessary for the speaker to be counted as a mature person.

The Lugbara community of shared communication included the living, the dead, and spirits. Lugbara saw themselves as creatures of the Creator divinity, Adroa, with whom they lost contact long ago. They once lived together in the sky, but, due to a woman's action, fell to earth. Adroa was given the attributes of omnipotence, ubiquity, and atemporality, and of being beyond human understanding. Divinity communicated with the living by sending good and bad fortune and death.

The living came into regular contact with lesser powers. These included a'bi (the ancestors) of several kinds: the male lineage ancestors and firstborn female ancestors were known as ori, "ghosts," and were given greater authority, depending largely on how long ago they had lived (Middleton 1960). Very old living men and women might be called a'bi also, a sign of how thin was the boundary between them, but the distinction was invariably made. The other powers were the many kinds of spirits, not tied to localities and beyond counting. They contacted the living by possession of their bodies and minds; offerings were then made to them, and their random power was transformed into authority over particular individuals, many of whom thereby acquired the mystical ability of divination.

Men in general had more formal authority than did women, but postmenopausal women held greater informal authority than did younger men; youths and children had little or no authority, except among themselves. The superficially rigid lineage structure, paradoxically, allowed for much fluidity in local patterns of settlement and behavior (Evans-Pritchard 1961). A person's authority was constantly changing with age, genealogical position, and wisdom and reputation. People competed for high lineage and neighborhood position, and in this nonliterate society, genealogies, which validated the exercise of authority, could rapidly be changed over time. This was reflected in speech, which although seemingly subject to rigid rules, in fact, followed the looseness of everyday relationships.

The occasions when the living communicated with other people and with nonliving powers were each accompanied by differences in the identities of speech participants and in kinds and degrees of formality of speech. Communication was never entirely verbal, but was accompanied by forms of gesture and bodily stance, all being expressions of closeness or distance.

Five main categories of occasion might be distinguished by the degrees of formality, of distance between the living and between them and nonliving participants, and so the distance from the sacred. The most sacred occasion for traditionalists was that of a rainmaker beseeching Divinity for help for the community in the secrecy of his rain grove, alone; rainmakers have said that they addressed Divinity but without actual words, as Divinity understood their thoughts. This was known as a'izu, "to beseech," the word adopted by Christians for prayer. A rainmaker also used great formality when making peace of feuds or when telling his people to begin sowing or harvesting, thereby defining the flow of the seasons, a godlike activity. The rainmakers were given many attributes of sacredness and were symbolically counted as having died socially when succeeding to the office (Middleton 1971, 1978). With this occasion may be classed that of prophetic utterance. When a prophet spoke as emissary of Divinity, his words, being Divine and so highly powerful and dangerous, were expressed in glossolalia translated by his nonprophetic assistant. These words were thus, in a sense, also secret, although uttered aloud. The great prophetic leader among the Lugbara was Rembe, a Kakwa prophet who lived among them in 1915 and 1916 and was still vividly, although mythopoeically, remembered in the 1950s (Middleton 1963, 1971).

The second category included the words and gestures used in rites of sacrifice to ancestors and ghosts by elders and other senior men. These words were supposed to be a'da, the "truth," as far as the speaker knew it; only a rainmaker knew more of the truth, and even then, he never knew everything, as only Divinity knew that. Sacrificial speech included many conventional phrases used to "please" the ancestral listeners; it also included silences the listeners understood represented respect and subservience to their power. There was no reference to detailed occurrences that had to do with the offence that was the original reason for the sacrifice; the dead and the spirits knew the facts in any case, and to include them would merely destroy the intended amity between the living to be brought about by the sacrificial rite.

The third category was communication with spirits by diviners. Each diviner had her repertoire of actions and phrases that were taken to be the expression of the thoughts of the possessing spirit that guided her and that often needed to be "translated" to her clients. These words were also spoken within a hut and so were semisecret. Diviners were almost always women who had been possessed by certain spirits at puberty; they were also typically women who had been mistreated by their husbands and had shown themselves possessed as a means of asserting their independence as women (Middleton 1969a).

The fourth occasion was that of funerals. Death dances were the most important rites of passage of any, and those for an important man might last for many months (Middleton 1982). The words used by mourners were highly competitive and usually antagonistic between those fighting to succeed to the deceased's social position. They were accompanied by brawling and heavy drinking, and although uttered aloud and often in song, were "secret" in the sense that the allusions were rarely understood by nonmourners.

The last category of occasions in which formal speech was necessary included those of legal cases, the naming of an infant by its mother, the public weeping of a mother for a dead child (a very different expression than the crying of a bereaved woman), and even drunken "speech," which, in fact, followed certain conventions of allusion and intelligibility.

There was a corpus of myth dealing with the beginning of the world and society, the coming of the Heroes, and their establishment of proper patterns of settlement, production, marriage, and feuding. An elder, relating a myth, included carefully chosen and "traditional" words and much gesture when telling his story.

The only other occasions of formal "speech" were those of singing and dancing. There was an immense repertoire of everyday songs that were an integral part of dances. Both death dances and courtship dances contained proverbs, elliptical phrases, and topical and obscene references to well-known persons and happenings of the day. Death and courtship dances were the main dances that attracted large numbers of participants from a wide area (Middleton 1985).

The terms *formal* and *informal* in speech and behavior need explication. Formality was characterized by what the Lugbara call "slowness." Slowness was proper in age and in relations of respect, whereas young men and women were expected to behave with some impetuosity. Besides actual speech, the choice of words, gestures, and respectful demeanor was always considered important. The kinds of narration, speech, and gestures used between living and between living and nonliving were never rigidly fixed by changes in age and genealogical position, respect, personal ability, and, of course, degree of acceptance of Christianity. In fact, the same pattern was carried over into Christian religious behavior.

In summary, the degree of formality in speech was determined by the degree of sacredness of the "persons" being addressed by the living, and/or by the dignity or the "slowness" of the speakers. These factors were linked in that only those reputed to be "slow" could address the more sacred personages, which helped validate their achieved social positions in this loosely organized society.

References

Evans-Pritchard, E.E. 1961. *Kinship and Marriage among the Nuer.* Oxford: Oxford University Press.

Middleton, John. 1960. *Lugbara Religion: Ritual and Authority among an East African People.* London: Oxford University Press.

———. 1963. The Yakan or Allah Water Cult among the Lugbara. *Journal of the Royal Anthropological Institute* 93: 80–108.

———. 1969. Oracles and Divination among the Lugbara. In *Man in Africa*, ed. M. Douglas, and P.M. Kaberry, London: Tavistock Press.

———. 1969. Spirit possession among the Lugbara In *Spirit Mediumship and Society in Africa*, ed. J. Beattie, and J. Middleton, pp. 220–31. London: Routledge and Kegan Paul.

———. 1971. Prophets and Rainmakers: The Agents of Social Change among the Lugbara. In *The Translation of Culture*, ed. T.O. Beidelman. London: Tavistock Press.

———. 1978. The rainmaker among the Lugbara of Uganda. *Systemes de Signes: Textes Reunis en Hommage a Germaine Dieterlen*, In ed. M. Cartry, pp. 377–88. Paris: Hermann.

———. 1982. Lugbara Death. In *Death and the Regeneration of Life*, ed, M. Bloch, and J. Parry. Cambridge: Cambridge University Press.

———. 1985. The Dance among the Lugbara of Uganda. In ed. P. Spencer, *Language in Africa*. Cambridge University Press.

JOHN MIDDLETON

See also **Cosmology; East African Folklore: Overview; Gender Representation in African Folklore**

NDEBELE

See **Children's Folklore: Ndebele; Southern African Oral Traditions**

NGBAKA MA'BO

See **Central Africa; Proverbs; Riddles; Songs**

NIGER (REPUBLIC OF NIGER)

Landlocked in western Africa, Niger is an arid country surrounded by Mali, Burkina Faso, Benin, Nigeria, Chad, Libya, and Algeria. Of Niger's 10.8 million people, 56 percent are Hausa, 22 percent, Djerma/Songhai, 10 percent, Fulani, 8 percent, Tuareg, and 4 percent are composed of various other groups. French is the official language, with Hausa, Djerma, and Fulani the "national" languages; Songhai, Kanuri, and Tamacheg (Tuareg) are also spoken. The majority of Niger's people are Muslim (80 percent), and 20 percent practice traditional indigenous religions. Niamey, a city of 398,000, is the nation's capital.

The area was first colonized by the French in 1883. This rule was never accepted by the Taureg, who continued to oppose the government. On August 3, 1960, Niger gained its independence from France after decades under colonial rule. In 1974, after drought and economic decline, the country's government of civilian rule was overthrown by Lieutenant Colonel Seyni Kountche, who instituted a Supreme Military Council. The nation returned to a multiparty system in 1993, but it continued to be plagued by periodic coups and counter coups.

In the latter part of the twentieth century, Niger's government spent a large percentage of its national budget on agriculture programs, which aided the harvests of Niger's farmers, despite the recurrent problem of drought. Nearly 82 percent of the population is rural. Niger's natural resources include uranium, coal, iron, tin, and phosphates, while agricultural production centers around millet, sorghum, peanuts, beans, cotton, and cowpeas. Principle industries include mining, textiles, cement, agricultural production, and construction.

Niger's government has a strong commitment to the preservation of the nation's cultural heritages, and the country's primary schools often instruct students in their traditional languages. The National Museum and the annual youth festival in Agades also serve to reinforce the traditions of Niger's many cultures. These are bright spots in an otherwise difficult situation, because in 2002 Niger had Africa's highest fertility rate (7.4 children per woman), and the lowest adult literacy rate in the world, at 14 percent.

JENNIFER JOYCE

NIGERIA (FEDERAL REPUBLIC OF NIGERIA)

Nigeria, located on the coast of West Africa and bordered by Benin, Niger, Chad, and Cameroon, is the continent's most populated country, with nearly 129 million citizens. Twenty-one percent of the population is Hausa; 21 percent, Yoruba; 18 percent, Ibo; 11 percent, Fulani; and 29 percent is composed of various other groups. The most commonly spoken languages in the country are English, Hausa, Yoruba, Ibo, and Fulani nearly 250 other languages have been recognized by the government. Half of all Nigerians are Muslim, 40 percent are Christian, and 10 percent practice traditional indigenous religions. Abuja, a city of 339,100, is the nation's official capital, that Lagos remains the commercial center. Nigeria's climate ranges from tropical to arid.

Nigeria was one the major sources of the slave trade in the eighteenth century. By the mid 1800s there was much trading activity in the Niger Delta and, as throughout the British Empire, the flag followed the traders. By 1914, the northern and southern provinces of Nigeria had been linked in a federated colony. On October 1, 1960, Nigeria gained its independence from Britain after more than a century of colonial rule. Unfortunately, the years since independence have been plagued with interethnic violence (most dramatically during the Biafran War in the late 1960s), economic deterioration, and mostly military rule.

In the 1970s, Nigeria's economy grew tremendously with the increase of oil revenues. During this oil boom, however, agriculture and nonpetroleum exports were virtually abandoned and suffered a severe decline. Along with the financial success of the 1970s came much corruption and wasteful spending within the government. When oil prices declined in the 1980s, Nigeria suffered severe economic losses. One of the saddest episodes in this tragic history was the execution of writer Ken Saro-Wiwa and eight others, the leaders of the Ogoni protest movement in the Niger Delta. Opposition to national corruption and foreign exploitation continues in the Niger Delta, with the women's movement taking a leadership role. Ironically, the source of Nigeria's vast oil wealth, the Niger Delta, has suffered so much pollution that the people can no longer farm, fish, or drink the water in the area. Despite its economic and political woes, Nigeria maintains one of Africa's largest economies, second only to South Africa. At the start of the new century, under elected leadership, President Olusegun Obasanjo was moving the country ahead, and many people were becoming somewhat optimistic about Nigeria's future. Another area of concern has developed, however, as the northern states instituted Islamic Sharia law, and periodic outbreaks of violence between Christian and Moslem fundamentalists took hundreds of lives.

The Niger River has been the foundation for communication and trade with much of West Africa for centuries. The mobility that the river offers has, throughout the millennium, fostered the emergence of a vast array of cultures in the region. Before the onset of colonialism, Nigerian artists produced and traded many types of crafts, such as sculpture, metalwork, glass, textiles, and leather. Colonial rule and the slave trade, however, disrupted these trades and industries.

Over 90 percent of Nigeria's income in 2002 was derived from oil and gas. Other natural resources included timber and various minerals, while the agricultural sector produced cotton, cocoa, rubber, yams, cassava, sorghum, palm kernels, millet, corn, rice, and livestock. Principle industries and sources of revenue were mining, crude oil, natural gas, coal, tin, columbite, the processing of palm oil, cotton, rubber, and petroleum, and the manufacturing of textiles, cement, building materials, chemicals, and beer brewing.

Nigeria is internationally renowned for its writers, artists, musicians, and athletes. Famous writers include novelist Chinua Achebe and Wole Solyinka (Nobel Prize for Literature winner for his poems, plays, and novels). Fela Anikulado Kuti, a Nigerian musician, achieved world fame with his "Afro-Beat" style of music. "King" Sunny Ade is another renowned musician who is known for his popularization of Nigeria's Juju music. Nigeria was also successful in the 1996 Olympics when the nation's female track and field team won five medals and the soccer team competed in the finals. Many traditional and contemporary painters, sculptors, metal workers, and textile artists are active in the outcomes.

JENNIFER JOYCE

NILOTIC PEOPLES

See **Animals in African Folklore; Origin and Culture Heroes**

NORTH AFRICAN (WESTERN SECTION) FOLKLORE

See **Maghrib**

NORTH AFRICAN (EASTERN SECTION) FOLKLORE: OVERVIEW

The northeast corner of Africa comprises Egypt and Libya. Egypt's Sinai Peninsula offers one of three major bridges linking Africa to Asia and Europe (the others are the Bab al-Mandab Straits on the Red Sea between Yemen and Ethiopia and Gibraltar on the Mediterranean between Morocco and the Iberian Peninsula). Prior to the opening of the Suez Canal in the nineteenth century, the Sinai Peninsula provided the only land route to Africa. From time immemorial, traders, travelers, conquerors, and migrants moved in or out of Africa via Egypt. Eventually, with the advancement of shipping and sailing technologies, other routes into Africa, especially around the Indian Ocean, became available.

Today, after sixty centuries of recorded history of population mobility, Egypt represents a microcosm of the Afro-Arab World. Its population is about 70 million, almost 99 percent of whom live in the Nile Valley, which constitutes about 4 percent of Egypt's total land mass. The composition of the cultures of its population and the distribution of the various social groups on the land form four distinct culture areas, described below.

The Nile Valley

The Nile Valley is represents an essentially *fellah* (peasant) culture. The population is predominantly Sunni Muslim, with a Coptic (Christian) minority; small numbers belong to other Christian sects, such as the Greek Orthodox, Roman Catholic, Armenian, and various Protestant churches. Egypt also has a very small Jewish community. The primary language spoken is

Arabic, although the Fâdidchî, Kunûzî Nubian, and Berber (Siwi) languages are spoken in the extreme south, and in the Siwa Oasis in the west of the country, respectively. Several metropolises are found in this area, many of which (such as Cairo, Alexandria, Tanta, Asyout, and Aswan) are industrial centers, with more than 1 million inhabitants.

The Northeastern Oasis

This region includes Siwa and extends into Libya, where the influence of Berber groups is noticeable. Practically all the nomads, as well as the great majority of the farmers, are Arabs, with a small Berber element also present. The nomads' domain extends both to the west (the coast of Libya) and to the east (the Libyan plateau of western Egypt), as well as to the Mediterranean coast. The dominant religion is Islam, with the Senussi sect predominating in the central part of the area.

The Beja

The Beja lies between the Upper Nile and the Red Sea. Most Beja tribes have retained their own Hamitic language, although Arabic has been adopted by many. The grazing conditions are poor; consequently, they must move continually, in very small groups.

The North Arabian Desert

This region is the cradle of Islam and the Arabic language. Its center is Western Asia (Saudi Arabia). The Egyptian Eastern Desert and Sinai belong to this culture area; the nomadic way of life dominates.

Although the number of nomads in Egypt is fairly small, there have been major demographic changes in terms of detribalization and the adoption of sedentary life styles.

Folklore and Scholarship

Considering Egypt's long history and its position as "cradle of civilization," presenting a detailed description of its cultural phases and transformations is a demanding task. Traditionally, the Egyptian countryside, with its villages and perennially irrigated small fields, remained outside the spheres of cultural influences of those non-Egyptian rulers residing in urban centers, such as the Persians, Romans, Mamelukes, Ottomans, French, and British. Arab-Islamic influence began to penetrate rural areas only as late as the fourteenth and fifteenth centuries. Moreover, folklore and similar aspects of expressive culture were viewed by ruling authorities as too insignificant to affect the cardinal religious, linguistic, and political orientations of the dominant demographic category of the population. Thus, the culture and lifestyle of the Egyptian peasants were almost totally ignored.

For millennia, allusions to Egyptian folkloric forms have appeared in various literary works. Yet, it was not until the emergence of nationalistic independence movements in the twentieth century that interest in the "folk" and their lore was emphasized by scholars and governments. The uncovering of ancient Egyptian civilizations and the possible connections between that marvelous stage in Egypt's history and the contemporary era gained momentum. In the late nineteenth century, *Aida*, an opera by Italian composer Guiseppe Verdi to celebrate the new Egyptian Opera House and the inauguration of the Suez Canal, and the sounding by an Egyptian of *fellah* background of the horn (bugle) found in King Tutankhamun's tomb, had profound nationalistic implications for Egypt's independence and her deep-rooted history and culture.

The first center in the Arab world for the study of folklore was established in Egypt in 1958: the Center for Folklore at the Ministry of Culture (CFMC) in Cairo. It was composed of the following specialized departments: folk literature, customs and traditions, music, dance, museum, archives, and library.

In the early 1970s, the Arts Academy, Ministry of Culture, was inaugurated. Beside such institutes for the elite (academic) arts such as music, ballet, opera, and theater, the Academy also included the High Institute for Folk Arts. Today several Egyptian colleges and universities have academic folklore programs that award the M.A. and Ph.D. degrees in a variety of specializations within the discipline. Among these are Cairo University, Ain-Shams University, The Girl's College (Cairo), and Alexandria University.

Although once limited to mainly "folk literature," the scope of interest in folklore has expanded in accordance with recent developments in international academic institutions. Thus, the discipline currently incorporates a variety of fields: oral literature, material culture, social folk customs (e.g., rites of passage, folk medicine, etc.), folk arts (e.g., dance, festivals, etc.), and music and ethnomusicology.

Vernacular Arabic and Folk Groups

As part of the Arab-Islamic world, Egypt's culture is anchored to the Arabic language, spoken by all its religious groups, Muslim and Christian alike. Serious and sustained interest in orally communicated lore may be attributed to the impact of Western scholarship. During the nineteenth century, European students of Arabic dialects (including J. Seldon Willmore and Wilhelm Spitta) collected and published oral texts as examples of representative dialectical utterances. This foreign emphasis on the study of vernacular Arabic had virtually no appreciable impact on indigenous Arab and Moslem scholars; their concern with Arabic dialects and dialectical narrative lore remained dormant (or hostile) until the middle of the twentieth century when radical political changes in attitudes toward folk groups took place.

Since the 1950s, significant attention has been paid to indigenous, orally transmitted lore. This new interest was generated by a number of factors: First, there was the emergence of the modern nationalistic ideologies stressing political entities referred to as the state. Under the previous forms of ideal Islamic government, namely the Caliphate, the independence of such entities was not tolerated, and they were referred to only as ʾaqâr ("regions") or ʾamâr ("territories"), or even shuQiqûb (national or ethnic populations; singular, shaQiqb (i.e., a people of a specific nationality). Second, a companion force of nationalism and the emergence of the modern populist state is the reliance on the jamâhîr (masses) and local communities and their cultures (i.e., regional cultures, or culture areas). Such social groups were previously referred to as Qiqâmmah (i.e., commoners, or al-ghawghâʾ, or al-sûqah, the vulgar classes). A third force has been the introduction into the academic realm of modern scholarly theories, which justified the study in Arab universities of folk literature in vernacular Arabic.

Consequently, folklore centers have been established in virtually every Arab country over the course of the past thirty years. Academic institutions and other government-sponsored establishments (e.g., folklore centers, and "mass culture" divisions in ministries of culture) were created in order to address the need to collect, study, preserve, and process folklore materials.

Adverse Attitudes Toward Dialects

The current strong interest in folk and regional cultures in the Arab world (including Egypt and Libya) is countervailed by the viewpoint held by many Arab nationalists and formal religious authorities that paying attention to folk dialectical literatures erodes the primacy of classical Arabic and encourages the institutionalization of regional differences and developing identities separate from that of a unified Arab Nation. Thus, it is feared that bestowing academic legitimacy on Arabic dialects will ultimately lead to the eroding of the primacy of al-fushâ (classical Arabic, the language of the Quran), and contribute to the emergence of new languages out of these dialects (as in the case of Italian and French, for example, evolving from, and eventually replacing in common usage, Latin). Eventually, the fear is that these developments would further fragment Arab unity. In this respect, and with reference to pan-Arab nationalism, the study of verbal folklore is seen as promoting regionalism, and is therefore perceived as antinationalistic and, in some circles, antireligious. Additionally, the label turâth shaQiqbî (folk tradition), which folklorists have been using to designate the subject matter of their field of inquiry, generates apprehension, especially among fundamentalist Muslims. Folklore conferences and symposia held under the title turâth shaQiqbî generate feelings of ill will. The main source for concern is the use of the word turâth ("traditions", or "legacy"), as, for the past fourteen centuries, this word has designated theological and related writings other than the Quran and hadîth ("traditions", i.e., sayings and descriptions of deeds attributed to the prophet Muhammad).

Arab folklorists have attempted to assuage these fears. In some symposia, resolutions were adopted calling for translating folk literature invariably expressed in lahajât ("dialects") or in al-Qiqarabiyyah al-dârijah ("vernacular Arabic") into al-fushâ ("classical Arabic"); the neutral term ma'thûrât ("traditions" or "legacy") has been adopted as a substitute for the religion-bound term turâth.

Typology, Indexes, and the Study of African Folkore

A presentation of Egypt's folklore as part of the lore of Africa requires a comparative approach. Considering the present academic separation between northern and southern Africa, researchers in the field of folklore rely on reference works that serve as guides to the vast amount of data involved.

There are two relevant indexing and classificatory systems that treat folk traditions in general, and narrative data in particular: Antti Aarne and Stith Thompson's The Types of the Folktale, and Stith Thompson's Motif-Index of Folk Literature; this latter index, which is more inclusive of social and cultural materials, addresses smaller units of analysis that may be found in religious belief, family life, government, and so on.

In spite of the intended universality of coverage, both works paid negligible attention to sources addressing Egyptian materials, ancient as well as modern. Consequently, an inaccurate state of affairs dominates the academic scene in this area of scholarship. For example, the pivotal anthology, Popular Tales of Ancient Egypt, by Egyptologist Sir Gaston Maspero, does not appear at all in The Types of the Folktale. Actually, no "Egyptian" texts are cited in relation to other tale types that were known to exist in ancient Egyptian literature.

Similarly, Stith Thompson's Motif-Index of Folk Literature contains only two peripheral motifs from Maspero's Contes. Thus, the absence of Maspero's work from the Aarne-Thompson tale-type index and Thompson's motif index is total. Consequently, ancient Egyptian narratives and related traditions remained outside folklore indexes. The rich data and constructive thoughts that Maspero's work offered played no significant role in the development or the testing of folklore theories especially with reference to Africa. As will be shown below, research on sub-Saharan lore, including Egyptian materials, typically makes no significant references to possible connections with the north.

Ancient Egyptian Legacy

The earliest recorded literature in history, depicted in hieroglyphic and temple wall paintings, reveals strong exchanges between the African north and south. Ancient Egypt's maritime routes extended from the Nile eastward to the Red Sea via marshlands (hence, the Nile was labeled "The Ocean River"). Their purpose was to conduct trade and secure incense and other African goods; their destination was what is now Somalia and adjacent countries. Also, the internal migrations within sub-Saharan Africa provided for early close interactions between the North and the South (with the Sahara chosen as the dividing point in prevalent academic literature). Some Bantu-speaking groups are reported to have lived as far north as Singa in the Sudan.

Sub-Saharan Influence on the North

Numerous aspects of ancient Egyptian lore seem to be found throughout Africa. Although many Africanists typically argue in favor of one-way cultural borrowing by sub-Saharan groups from "higher" cultures north of the Sahara, such a viewpoint might not be quite accurate. Recorded examples of lore spreading in the opposite direction, though not numerous, indicate significant impact of sub-Saharan cultures on the inhabitants of the North.

One of the most important figures in this respect is the ancient Egyptian deity Bes, who has been authoritatively characterized as "certainly African" (see Budge 1904). In addition to being a deity of song, dance, and merrymaking, he was also a warlord. Presumably through syncretism, the character of the ancient Afro-Egyptian Bes, along with his cult, came to be identified with a powerful Muslim saint named El-Sayyid El-Badawi (1200?–1276), especially among folk groups. Currently, the cult of this saint is centered in Tanta, in peasant communities in the middle Delta. The crusaders, it has been argued, borrowed the character of El-Badawi and carried it to Europe where it became Saint Nicholas, or Santa Claus (see El-Shamy, "The Story of El-Sayyid Ahmad El-Badawî with Fatma Bint Berry").

Another case that may be cited in this regard, though from Morocco in the western part of North Africa, is a modern oral text of a trickster tale titled "My Uncle the Spider":

My uncle, the spider, went hunting and entered the body of a fat cow, eating her fat and carrying home some for his family. He didn't touch the cow's heart for that would have killed her. Tiger's wife visited Spider's wife and saw all their food. She returned home and told her husband to become Spider's friend so they can hunt together.

Tiger went to Spider, but Spider didn't want to let him hunt with him for Tiger would kill the cow. Tiger swore that he will not. Both hunt and Spider gets enough food for Tiger and himself. Next day they hunt, but Tiger kills the cow. Spider tells Tiger to get inside cow's stomach; Spider gets inside her bladder.

Shepherd found dead cow and searches for cause of death. He cut open cow's belly; he threw away the bladder. Spider got out. He told the shepherd to remove cow's stomach and beat it. Shepherd did this. He opened it and found dead Tiger.

Grateful shepherd gave Spider half the cow. Spider was happy (Légey 1926, no. 69, pp. 247–48).

Since spiders do not appear in the folk narratives of the region, the text must be judged as a recent development on the North African scene. Clearly, the tale's persona, stage, and plot are typically sub-Saharan, probably about Ananse, the Akan spider-trickster. This conclusion is reinforced by the fact that the narrator was a black slavewoman in the harem of the sultan; she had presumably heard it from another black slavewoman.

Other instances of cultural transfer from the South to the North may be found in such spheres as music (*zâr*), exorcism, and mythology. The *zâr* cult is argued to have entered Egypt and other Arab countries during the eighteenth century, when it was carried into Egypt by Ethiopian slaves and into the harems of rich rulers and their army generals (Klunzinger).

The Ancient Egyptian Narrative

The genres and topics of verbal lore in contemporary Africa as a whole may be said to parallel the recorded literary legacy of ancient Egypt. The literature of ancient Egypt consisted of sacred accounts of the deeds of gods and demigods (myths), other sorts of historical narratives, proverbs and counsels by viziers and other wise men, poetry, songs, hymns, lamentations, funerary spells (typically labeled "magical" by modern writers), and practical solutions to enigmas such as dreams.

Notably absent are the fairy tale, humorous anecdotes, and similar nonserious narratives. Also absent are the equivalents of the modern short story, the novel, and the play. However, the absence of these genres may be normal at the developmental stage of literature of a certain time period, or as result of disdain by scribes and copiers for the nonserious in general. The celebrated "Tale of the Two Brothers," treated in folkloric circles as the first *märchen* (ordinary tale), is thought to have been an account dealing with two deities rather than two persons. If true, for the ancient Egyptians, the narrative would have been a myth rather than an ordinary tale (see El-Shamy in Maspero, 2002).

The *Märchen* among Non-Aryans

In the absence of data from Egypt and other non-Aryan cultures, folkloristic circles in Europe had accorded the *märchen* (fairy tale) and its presumed creators a privileged status. This assumption formed the basis of such theories as Wilhelm Grimm's, which attributed the origins of folk narratives to Indo-European (Aryan) peoples. This claim acquired powerful influence at the beginning of the twentieth century through the assertion that true *märchen* existed only within Indo-Germanic linguistic boundaries and that non-Aryans distorted the *märchen*, which they had essentially copied from the Indo-Germanic groups. Similarly, the "Indianist" theory, suggested by A. Loiseleur-Deslongchamp in 1838, and developed by Theodor Benfey and E. Cosquin, was based on the principle of citing India as the original source of all folktales except Aesop's fables; other nations, it was presumed, had derived their tales from Indian sources. Objective research based on representative field collections reveals that such views are impressionistic and inaccurate.

Egyptian narrative genres (and genres from other parts of the Arab world), include: fantasy narratives (*haddûtah, khurraifah, hujwah, hikâyah*), the novella/romantic tale, the animal tale (fable), humorous narratives (*nuktah, nâdirah, haddûtah*), the legend (*'usûrah, qissah*), religious tales, myth (*khurâfah qasasiyyah*) (mislabeled *'ustûrah* by most Arab writers), the epic (*malamah*, poetic *qaîdah* ["ode"], typically a versified religious belief or quasi-religious belief account, a historical-legendary account), and the ballad (*mawwâl qasasî*).

Ancient Egyptian Tale Types

Numerous narratives reported from ancient Egypt manifest typological qualities. The similarities between the ancient texts and modern ones indicates possible direct descent. Irrespective of how each of these narratives originated, Maspero concluded that "everything in them is Egyptian from beginning to end, and even the details that have been pointed out as being of foreign provenance appear to us to be entirely indigenous when closely examined" (2000, lxxiv–lxxv). Stith Thompson, perhaps influenced by Maspero's views, arrived at a similar conclusion: "The tales are given a definitely Egyptian setting and are closely related not only to the known history and geography of Egypt but to its religious conceptions and practices as well" (273).

The Aarne-Thompson Type Index and Egyptian Folktales

The overwhelming majority of Egyptian folk narratives manifest the defining components of international tale types. The Aarne-Thompson type index is, however, seriously limited with regard to the treatment of Arabic and Berber folktales, and especially, Egyptian tales.

Three major deficiencies limit the applicability of the type index to Middle Eastern materials (including Egypt and Libya). First, only a fragment of the published collections from the Middle East was included. Arabic and Berber collections available before 1961, 1928, and 1910 were abundant. Second, only a fraction of the tales that comply with the designated contents of the tale types in the works treated in the type index were recognized in the list of references to a tale type. For example, Wilhelm Spitta's *Contes* includes twelve tales, of which ten are of indisputable typological character: these are nos. 1 (AaTh 325, *The Magician and his Pupil*),

4 (AaTh 465, *The Man Persecuted Because of His Beautiful Wife*), 5 (AaTh 621, *The Louse-Skin*), 6 (AaThs 881, *Oft-proved Fidelity*; and 883A, *The Innocent Slandered Maiden*), 7 (AaThs 706, *The Maiden without Hands*; and 872, *Brother and Sister*), 8 (AaTh 410, *Sleeping Beauty*), 9 (AaTh 567, *The Magic Bird-heart*), 10 (AaTh 590, *The Prince and the Arm Bands*), 11 (AaTh 707, *The Three Golden Sons*), and 12 (AaTh 314, *The Youth Transformed to a Horse*. None of these tale types was acknowledged in the index.

The sub-Saharan African tale is closely related to its counterpart in the North. Indeed, it is difficult to distinguish between North and South with regard to certain areas that have served as melting pots for various social and cultural groups: Sudan, Somalia, the Swahili coast of east Africa, south Arabia, Mauritania, Mali, and the entire southern strip of the Sahara.

Factors that affect the placement of a group or individual include race and color of skin, language, religion, and political and kinship-group affiliation, as well as geographic location. There is one geographical area in which Arab and African traditions intermingle: shaped like an arch, it extends from the tip of the African Horn and Dar es-Salaam in the east across the continent to the northern borders of Mauritania and some diffuse point south of Dakar in the West. With regard to narratives and other traditions, many groups in this area manifest varying degrees of similarity to groups in the extreme north of the African continent.

Nevertheless, we find that some of the renditions most similar to tales told in Egypt come from the Hottentots, the Basotho, and other southern Bantu-speaking groups.

The nature of these parallels to contemporary as well as ancient traditions in Egypt awaits further research. Yet, attempting to establish the relationship between contemporary narratives and their ancient Egyptian counterparts constitutes not a quest for origins but, rather, an effort to ascertain the stability of a tradition and its social, cultural, and emotional relevance. Had these ideas and values not been of continuous significance to their bearers, they would have survived only in the form of scrolls or rock paintings.

Conclusion: Lore and Theory

The folklore of northeast Africa in general, and Egypt in particular, manifests qualities that allows it to the play the role of a bridge between Africa and the rest of the world. Only within this inclusive context can the various dimensions of folkloric phenomena in Egypt and Africa be meaningfully understood. Studies that are based on partial or exclusionary approaches, which view Africa as composed of a North divorced from the South, are likely to lead to biased or inaccurate conclusions.

A dilemma faced in folklore scholarship is the presence of powerful theories that seem to make sense from an abstract perspective, but fail when applied to real life uses of folklore. An example of this situation is pointed out by Hasan El-Shamy in his review of Peter Gilet's *Vladimir Propp and the Universal Folktale: Recommissioning an Old Paradigm—Story as Initiation* (1998). When applying the "theory" to North African/Berber and sub-Saharan Hausa tales, with distinct ties to ancient Egyptian counterparts, the outcome repeatedly fails to substantiate the "theory." Gilet concludes the actual life in Africa is wrong,

and has been for thousands of years, but the European theory is right, no matter what.

In the study of folklore, African or otherwise, the first and final objective must be the folklore itself, in its relevant and applied context.

References

Aarne, Antii, and Stith Thompson. 1961. *The Types of the Folktale.* FF Communications no. 184, Helsinki: Academia Scientartum Fennica.; first published by Aarne in 1910.

Budge, Ernest A. W. 1904. *The Gods of the Egyptians*, 2 vols. London: Methuen.

Coult, Lyman H. 1958. *An Annotated Bibliography of the Egyptian Fellah.* Coral Gables, Fla: University of Miami Press.

El-Shamy, Hasan M. January, 1988. Belief and Non-Belief in Arab, Middle Eastern and sub-Saharan Tales: The Religious-Non-Religious Continuum. A Case Study. *al-Ma'thûrât al-Sha'biyyah* 3, no. 9: 7–21.

———. 1980. *Folktales of Egypt, Collected, Translated and Edited with Middle Eastern and [sub-Saharan] African Parallels.* Chicago: University of Chicago Press.

———. 2001. Review of Peter Gilet's *Vladimir Propp and the Universal Folktale: Recommissioning an Old Paradigm—Story as Initiation. Asian Folklore Studies* 61, no. 1: 153–57.

———. 1976. The Story of El-Sayyid Amad El-Badawî with Fama Bint Berry, part I, An Introduction. *Folklore Forum* 10, no. 1:

———. 1976. The Story of El-Sayyid Amad El-Badawî with Fama Bint Berry, An Egyptian Folk Epic, part II, text and explanatory notes. *Folklore Forum* 11, nos. 3–4: 140–63.

Ions, Veronica. 1968. *Egyptian Mythology.* Middlesex, U.K.: Hamlyn.

Klipple, May Augusta 1992. *African Folktales with Foreign Analogues*, with an Introduction by Alan Dundes. New York: Garland.

Klunzinger, C.B. 1878, [1984]. *Upper Egypt: Its People and Its Products.* New York : AMS Press.

Légey, Françoise. 1926. *Contes et légendes populaires du Maroc, recueillis à Marrakech*, no. 69. Paris.

Maspero, Gaston C. 2002. *Popular Stories of Ancient Egypt*, edited and with an introduction and classification by tale type and motif by Hasan El-Shamy. Santa Barbara, Calif: ABC-CLIO.

Murdock, G.P. 1959. *Africa: Its Peoples and Their Culture History.* New York.

Patai, Raphael. 1969. *Golden River to Golden Road: Society Culture and Change in the Middle East.* Philadelphia.

HASAN EL-SHAMY

NORTHEASTERN AFRICAN FOLKLORE (THE HORN): OVERVIEW

The Horn of Africa (or Northeast Africa, as it is sometimes called) is composed of Djibouti, Eritrea, Ethiopia, Somalia, and Sudan. The region is one of the most unstable on the African continent. Much of its instability is a direct consequence of its geographic location, which has historically been both a boon and a curse to the inhabitants of the area. Its proximity to the Middle East has engendered narratives that have shaped and informed the internal and external topographies of the region's identity. This identity—complex, tortuous, and beautiful—is expressed in its folklore.

The Horn of Africa is home to all three monotheistic religions of the world, and the folktales of the Horn are a mosaic of its history. They are suffused with the elements of pre-Islamic African religion, Egyptian and Arab civilizations, Christianity, Judaism, Islam, and especially Sufism.

In the beginning was the myth, even before it could be told or written as story. The myth just was, in the way that the sky *was* the god whose thunder and lightning were immediate, fierce, and unavoidable. The myth belongs to what Vico calls, labelling our human understanding, the age of gods—an age in which there is no distance from the gods. There is no understanding of an "I" who is a distinct, autonomous being who can create a story that then becomes a thing unto itself and can be told for generations.

It is only once we pass from the age of gods, and gain perspective and distance, that we are able to recognize ourselves as separate and to narrate that mythic experience. The myth, then, is born in this period of new perspective and is already separate from the time in which it was everything.

At these various stages of our human development, our relation to our gods and our heroes and indeed to ourselves changes, so that the "we" who tells and the "we" who listens are not the same as they were when the telling was fresh. Our minds have changed, and with them the sense of awe in which we hold the mythic elements. The myths themselves could not have begun to be told until the teller could see himself as a story-creator, a different entity from the sky/god about which he speaks. The sky/god is diminished in power and in his mind.

A story from Somalia illustrates the point: "In the beginning of time the sky hung so low over the earth that a person standing on the ground could touch it with his fingers." But women pounding millet with a mortar disturbed the sky until it "could no longer stand the pain caused to it by the women and receded further and further away from the earth to where it is now" (Hanghe 1988, 110). The actions of human beings caused the sky to retreat and to become, in the process and in the telling, less fearsome and less awesome.

The belief in a sky god, or *Waaq*, is common to the Cushitic groups in the Horn of Africa. These include the Oromos and the Somalis. The notion of God's retreat from the world, however, is also found among the Dinka of the Sudan, who also blame women for the retreat. To finalize the withdrawal, the finch is sent by God to sever "the rope that still linked Heaven and Earth, thus ending the complete happiness that had prevailed and turning man into a suffering and mortal being" (Deng 1972, 62). A Somali proverb, mostly used by women, anticipates the blame: "All that is bad, belongs to Hawa (Eve)."

After the myth and the age of gods comes the age of heroes, of people who are larger than life; their exploits become the plots of legends. This is the age of poetry, the age of epics and of metaphorical tropes and modes of expression. This age has given us the *Iliad* and the *Odyssey*. Similarly, it brings us a story from the Borana of Ethiopia. Thus begins one of many stories of Dido Gawole, the strong man (Kidane 2002, 140):

Dido Gawole was strong. One cannot find a brave and strong man like him. Wise too he was. At that time the Borana were fighting the Arsi. They used to fight with shield and spear. In battle even fifty men couldn't be a match for him. He was full-hearted. When he fought, if he missed with his lance, he struck and killed with his shield. Such was the man Dido Gawole.

Finally, the age of men arrives. This is the age in which we understand ourselves to have a history and to want to tell the story of that history. This is the age in which we understand ourselves to have a society we want our children to join and a past that we want them to appreciate. Our stories begin to have different meanings and different purposes. Now come stories for their own sakes, stories for amusement, stories for edification, stories to make children laugh and to frighten them into not disobeying their parents or straying from home. And stories for adults, too: stories of wisdom that act as guideposts by which to live a life.

Folklore in the Horn of Africa, as elsewhere, helps humans to come to terms with ontological and etiological issues. Cattle are important to the psychological, social, and economic fabric of the Dinka. A Dinka myth accounts for the troubles caused to people by their need to own and defend cattle. The cow is said to have the last laugh, forever. Since the Dinka killed the mother of the cow, the cow has perfected the best revenge on man. It opted "to fight man within man's own system: to be domesticated to make man slave for her; to play man off against man; and to cause him to fight and kill for ownership, possession, or protection of her" (Deng 1972, 2).

Not all encounters between humans and animals are violent. The folklore of the region is replete with tales that emphasize the connections between the two. There is always some kind of debt that is due to the animal kingdom. Some animal or another is implicated in the proliferation of a group. The animal becomes the group's guardian and, by extension, its totem. The dispersal of the Nuer in the Sudan is, for example, attributed to a blue heron. Latjor, a Nuer chief, led his people to new places: "In their search for a new land, the band, without boats, came across the Nile. A blue heron in the midst of the river gave Latjor the idea to wade through the water" (Huffman 1970, 2).

Animals endowed with human consciousness feature prominently in the folklore of the Horn. Animal stories cover the whole range of human emotions, sentiments, and ideas. Even though blatant forms of chicanery are not accepted, the stories test and set limits to accepted behavior. The sly but witty are given a space to flout rules and regulations and to flaunt their intellectual prowess. In the stories, there is subtle or direct contest of wills between adversaries. In most cases, the weak and the small dupe the strong. The fox always outwits the strong and the weak. In the lore of the Amhara in Ethiopia, the dwarf, Sinzero, outwits his stalwart brothers.

Some tales come to life when the human foibles they were meant ward off are repeated by the living. Thus, new tales are fashioned out of old tales to suit local needs and motives. A Tigray tale tells how two friends lose their friendship, sown over the years and sustained by deep commitment to one another. The two paupers stumble upon what seems to be a shining treasure on the ground. Each lunges at it. A nasty fight ensues. A local priest comes to their rescue and shows them the object of their quarrel: an old and cheap metal comb. The two bald men cringe as the priest asks them which one would go first to have his hair combed. (Incidentally, this story has come to symbolize the recent bloody war between Eritrea and Ethiopia. The two heads of state were, before the war, good friends, and when their disagreements over a barren piece of land came to blows, people sought solace in the old Tigray tale. Both presidents belong to Tigrinya-speaking groups and should have been aware of the travesty of the bald heads.)

Another cautionary tale from the Borana of Ethiopia concerns three cows, one black, one red, and one white. One day the black cow whispers to the red one that it would be wise to dissociate themselves from their white companion because he stands out and is so obviously an attraction to predators. The red cow agrees, and the two abandon the white cow. Very soon, he is eaten by a lion. The black cow then thinks to himself that it would be best to leave the red cow, for he, too, stands out and can attract predators. The red cow, too, disappears. The black cow stands alone, and his solitude guarantees that it does not take long for him to be eaten in his turn. It is a story clearly meant to knock sense into the heads of ornery humans.

This order of things—myth, followed by legend, followed by history—is the precise opposite of euhemerism, which is the idea that history fades in memory, and transforms in the fading, to become legendary, and then mythic.

Folktales, whether they are stories of the sky and the earth (myths), stories of great deeds of warriors or queens (legends), or stories of battles or proverbs or morality tales, are all stories that are about our very humanness. They are variants on our attempts to place ourselves in the galaxy and to explain our very existence. It is important to grasp this so as not to turn these stories into curios brought back from forays into other people's cultures.

Like the minds that hold and receive the stories, the stories themselves change and evolve over time, reflecting the particular histories of the people who hold them. The folktales of the Ja'aliyyin of the Sudan illustrate how the influences of various civilizations affect the telling of folktales. There are folktales that show the influence of the great Sudanese Meroitic kingdom, whose heart was also the center of the land of the Ja'aliyyin. The kingdom, which thrived for some six hundred years until the year 320, was ruled at one point by a queen, and there are hints that lineage among the Ja'aliyyin was once matriarchal. Folktales that entered the lexicon during a later period, after the introduction of Islam to the region, clearly show a different orientation, and yet these stories co-exist peacefully. One of the most popular concerns a young woman whose brother vows to wed her. In her escape from an intolerable situation, the queen reverses the gender roles common to European tales. She leads a band of female companions fearlessly, outwits an evil ogre, disguises herself as an old man, and eventually wins the heart of a wealthy and desirable young man. (Hurreiz 1977, 83; Moore 1978, 110).

Famous, as well, is the story of Arraweelo, a powerful Somali queen. There are many versions of the Arraweelo story, in both Somali and Oromo lore, and the version told often depends upon the gender of the teller. Arraweelo is sometimes depicted as a cruel queen who castrated men in order to ensure she would have no opposition. Other versions—told increasingly in the light of recent events in Somalia—emphasize that the reign of this woman brought peace and prosperity to a land that sorely needed it.

In the folktales, as well, can be read the story of the minds that created them because it is important to recognize that our human minds—as we are conceptual thinkers, indeed, as we are readers and writers—could not have developed the way they have without the oral traditions and the folktales that underlie them. There is a direct line from understanding the sky as a god, to seeing that a hero is *like* a god, to telling the cautionary tales of foxes, lions, and snakes, to holding an intangible concept in one's head and to having a symbol on a piece of paper represent that concept.

The folktales—myths, legends, stories, and wisdom—are the bedrock upon which our ability to think in the way we do rests. And in that sense, the folktales of the Horn of Africa have everything in common with the folktales of Russia or the British Isles or the Australian outback, however their specifics might differ.

References

Aboker, Axmed Cali. 1987. *The Camel in Somali Oral Traditions*. Uppsala, Sweden: Somali Academy of Sciences and Arts and Scandinavian Institute of African Studies.

Adera, Taddesse, and Ali Jimale Ahmed, eds. 1995. *Silence Is Not Golden: A Critical Anthology of Ethiopian Literature*. Lawrenceville, N.J.: The Red Sea Press.

Al-Shahi, Ahmed, and F. C. T. Moore. 1978. *Wisdom from the Nile: A Collection of Folk-Stories from Northern and Central Sudan*. Oxford: Clarendon Press.

Andrezewski, B. W. 1962. Ideas about Warfare in Borana Galla Stories and Fables. *African Language Studies* 3:16–36.

Bader, Christian. 2000. *Mythes et legends de la Corne de l'Afrique*. Paris: Editions Karthala.

Courlander, Harold and Wolf Leslau, Comp. 1950. *The Fire on the Mountain and Other Ethiopian Stories*. New York: Henry Holt.

Davis, Russel and Brent, Ashbranner. 1959. *The Lion's Whiskers: Tales of High Africa*. Boston: Little, Brown.

Deng, Francis Mading. 1972. *The Dinka of the Sudan*. New York: Holt, Rinehart, and Winston.

Hanghe. Ahmed Artan. *Folktales from Somalia*. 1988. Uppsala, Sweden: Somali Academy of Sciences and Arts and Scandinavian Institute of African Studies.

Huffman, Ray. 1970. *Nuer Customs and Folk-Lore*. London: Frank Cass.

Hurreiz, Sayyid. 1977. *Ja'aliyyin Folktales: An Interplay of African, Arabian and Islamic Elements*. Bloomington: Indiana University.

Johnson, John William. 1974. *Heellooy, Heelleellooy: The Development of the Genre Heello in Modern Somali Poetry*. Bloomington: Indiana University Press.

Kennedy, John G., ed. 1978. *Nubian Ceremonial Life: Studies in Islamic Syncretism and Cultural Change*. Cairo and Berkeley: University of California Press and The American University in Cairo Press.

Kidane, Sahlu. 2002. *Borana Folktales: A Contextual Study*. London: Haan.

Levine, Donald N. 1970. *Wax and Gold: Tradition and Innovation in Ethiopian Culture*. Chicago: University of Chicago Press.

Okpewho, Isidore. 1994. *African Oral Literatures*. Bloomington: Indiana University Press.

Vico, Giambattista. 1984. *The New Science of Giambattista Vico: Unabridged Translation of the Third Edition (1744)*. Thomas Goddard Bergin and Max Harold Fisch, trans. Ithaca, N.Y.: Cornell University Press.

Verene, Donald Philip. 1981. *Vico's Science of Imagination*. Ithaca, N.Y.: Cornell University Press.

ALI JIMALE AHMED
RIMA BERNS-MCGOWN

See also **Folktales; Maqalat; Myths; Origins and Culture Heroes; Women's Folklore: Eritrea**

NSIBIDI: AN INDIGENOUS WRITING SYSTEM

The Ejagham of southeastern Nigeria and southwestern Cameroon have developed a nonverbal form of communication, *nsibidi* [pronounced *in-sib-eh-dee*], which is displayed as two-dimensional signs, three-dimensional forms, and pantomimed gestures. In its material form, this graphic writing system consists of pictographs and ideographs based on line drawings, many of which are formed with geometric shapes. Nsibidi differs from many Western forms of writing in that it is intricately linked to art and ritual. Individuals may present nsibidi signs in a variety of ways: drawn in the air (gestures) or on the ground, on the skin (tattoos), and on art forms (dance costumes and masks, stone monoliths, cloth, funerary sculpture, and jewelry).

Scholars believe that nsibidi originated among the Ejagham, who use it more extensively than any other group in the region. The spread of *nsibidi* may have been a result of Ejagham migrations or their practice of selling the secrets of the Ejagham men's Leopard Society (Ngbe) to their neighbors (the Igbo, Efik, Ibibio, Efut, Banyang, and others). In 1904, T. D. Maxwell, a British colonial officer, recognized the writing system, which soon became an interest of other Westerners as well. Other reports of *nsibidi* appeared at the beginning of the twentieth century by European missionaries, colonial officers, and ethnographers. Scholars believe that *nsibidi* is very old, but it is difficult to determine exactly when it began. Similar signs that appear on carved stone monoliths (possibly created as early as 200 CE) may provide a clue.

Nsibidi is an esoteric form of knowledge that can only be fully understood by a select group of people. Various secret societies utilize this system to guard information that can only be known by its members through lengthy processes of initiation that may take a lifetime. While the meanings of these signs are often secret, the signs may be seen by the general public. Some of the most well-known examples of *nsibidi* have been produced by the male Leopard Society.

Leopard Society members, who pursue excellence and expertise in the artistic and intellectual facets of *nsibidi*, create brilliant displays with their secret knowledge, which once gave them the power to enforce the laws of the society at large. On ritual occasions, members create a dramatic presence by wearing an *ukara* cloth, which they tie around the waist to form a long skirt. The cloth may be hand-woven or produced mechanically in a factory, the latter being more common today. Nsibidi signs are created by stitching and tying the cloth, which is then dyed in indigo. After drying, the stitching and ties are removed to reveal the white designs that appear against the deep blue background. Ukara cloth has an array of signs that uniformly cover the surface of the cloth and refer to titled positions within the society, secret rituals, and philosophical concepts. Read as a whole, the cloth is a synopsis of the Leopard Society and a symbol of membership. Today, the *ukara* cloth continues to be an important symbol of the Leopard Society, which remains an important aspect of ritual life and major component of cultural identity for many Ejagham communities.

Nsibidi can also be understood as a spiritual action that is used to govern, punish, and control individuals and resources. For example, among the Bakor-Ejagham, an Ejagham subgroup

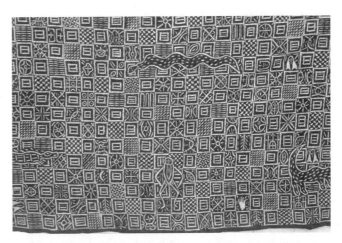

Ukara cloth purchased in Watt Market, Calabar, Cross River State, Nigeria. Photo © Amanda Carlson.

who are based between the towns of Ikom and Ogoja in Nigeria's Cross River State, the Ntim society (a traditional policing unit) was using *nsibidi* to punish people. It could cause a person to get lost in the bush by using actions like nodding the head or drawing on the ground. In this way, it could be used to make an injunction for a spiritual manhunt. This means that no physical action would be directed at the man, but he would be hunted down and killed in the spiritual realm. To the uninitiated, these actions would go unseen or undetected. However, this would lead to his eventual death in the physical world.

While much of the literature suggests that *nsibidi* is the sole prerogative of male secret societies, it is becoming more apparent to scholars that women may use it as well. While there are many restrictions limiting women's knowledge of *nsibidi*, there are many examples of women using decorative, coded signs. Talbot (1912), with the crucial assistance of his wife Dorothy, published some of the earliest of accounts of women's use of signs. Thompson (1984) has also noted many female art forms that are encoded with this writing system, such as serving trays, calabashes,

Calabashes, Enyi village (Ekajuk clan), Bakor-Ejagham, Cross River State, Nigeria. Photo © Amanda Carlson.

women's bodies, and ritual dress. Recent research suggests that *nsibidi* may be used by the women's secret society Ekpa.

An important aspect of the *nsibidi* system involves encoding signs with an element of indirection. The aesthetic of indirection refers to the process of twisting language and meaning so as to conceal knowledge. Therefore, *nsibidi* can at times resemble a trick or a riddle. Talbot writes that "the Ekoi [or the Ejagham] explanation of the name nsibidi, or more properly Nchibbidy, is that it is derived from the verb *nchibbi*, 'to turn,' and this has taken to itself the meaning of agility of mind, and therefore of cunning or double meaning" (1912, 305). For example, when Ekpa women give the sign for "talk," it actually means "don't talk." Noninitiates would therefore be tricked into doing the wrong thing.

Individual signs often have multiple layers of meaning that may change over time and are affected by the context in which it is displayed. For example, one of the most popular signs is composed of two linking semicircles, one semicircle symbolizing a man and the other symbolizing a woman. As it appears on ancient carved stone monoliths, this sign probably referred to the combining of male and female reproductive forces—an important concept within ritual systems that ensured the fertility of the community in terms of agriculture and children. In contemporary times, this sign continues to signify the male and female union. A woman may tattoo this sign on her upper arm, which she would use to cradle her lover. Here, the design signifies the contemporary concept of "romantic love." Several creative individuals have inscribed the symbol onto wedding bands, incorporing the sign into a Western-based concept of marriage.

Nsibidi has proven to be an adaptable and fluid system, cap-able of meeting the needs of changing times and circumstances. Expanding beyond the Cross River region of Africa, *nsibidi* use was brought to Cuba via the trans-Atlantic slave trade and into America along the paths of former slaves. In these new contexts, *nsibidi* flourished among the Abakua, a Cuban version of the Ejagham Leopard Society. More recently, *nsibidi* has been used by contemporary artists in the international arena. Artists in Nigeria, Cuba, and the United States have incorporated these signs and infused them with new meaning through the media of painting, print making, and photography. For many people, *nsibidi* symbolizes one of Africa's many cultural accomplishments, challenging the stereotype of Africa as a continent without writing.

References

Kalu, O. U. 1978. Writing in Pre-colonial Africa: A Case Study of Nsibidi. In *African Cultural Development*, ed. Ogbu U. Kalu, pp. 76–83. Enugu: Forth Dimension.

Macgregor, J. K. 1909. Some Notes on Nsibidi. *Journal of Royal Anthropological Institute* 39: 209–19.

Talbot, Percy Amaury. 1912. *In the Shadow of the Bush*. London: Heinemann.

Thompson, Robert Farris. 1983. *Flash of the Spirit*. New York: Vintage Books.

AMANDA CARLSON

See also **Languages; Orality and Literacy in Africa; Textile Arts and Communication**

NUER

See **Animals in African Folklore; Evans-Pritchard E. E.; Northeastern African Folklore (The Horn): Overview**

NYANGA

See **Central African Folklore: Overview**

O

OKYEAME

Okyeame, an Akan (the major language family in Ghana) title, refers to the position of the chief's speech intermediary, or royal orator. He is the liaison between the chief and his addressees and occupies the most crucial diplomatic and communicative position within the traditional political hierarchy. Besides being the royal spokesman, the *okyeame* is also the chief's confidante, personal assistant, ambassador, and judicial advocate. He has also been referred to as the chief's prime minister and prayer officiant.

The position has sometimes been mistranslated as "linguist" by scholars, in apparent reference to the *okyeame*'s skills in public speaking. In formal situations, a chief does not speak directly to an audience in his presence; he speaks only through an *okyeame*, who relays or repeats his words to the audience the latter's message to the chief must also pass through the *okyeame*.

The position of okyeame was first established by the Adansi, the first Akan state in the latter part of the sixteenth century. This institution with the same title has since spread to many of the ethnic groups of Ghana. It exists among the Ga, Adangme, and Ewe of southern Ghana, and evidence suggests that it has parallels among ethnic groups in the northern and upper regions of Ghana. In certain parts of northern and upper Ghana, particularly among the Mamprusi, Dagomba, and Gonja, there are clues to the existence of royal spokesmen—possibly borrowed from the Ashanti, even though designations given to the position in the north are not cognates of the Akan or Ashanti term. Outside Ghana, parallels of the *okyeame* may be found among certain groups throughout West Africa, for example, in Burkina Faso, Benin, and parts of Nigeria.

Speech Mediation

While the institution of speech intermediary in Africa may have originated within the royal domain, it has spread to all communicative settings where social status and verbal wit can be asserted for social and political advantage. Any formal, traditional proceedings in Ghana involving communication between two or more parties require the use of an *okyeame*. Parties at formal meetings may instantly call on one of their numbers to fulfill the intermediary role of an *okyeame*, announcing the purpose of the meeting, pronouncing a party's donation, or putting across consensus reached. Likewise, he first receives all messages intended for his party. The position has been adopted within lineage groups, who all have *abusua akyeame* (lineage spokespersons). Similarly, deities and their priests have *abosom akyeame*, who interpret the words of the priests to their clients. The institution was adapted from traditional to modern politics in 1962 by Kwame Nkrumah, who appointed an *okyeame* for the state and modified his original functions.

The practice of using speech intermediaries in royal discourse is partly aimed at creating opportunities for the flowering of language in the relay process. *Akyeame* (plural of *okyeame*) often say "We embellish the chief's words," and they compare the treatment of the chief's words with the act of making *fufu* (a basic food made by pounding plaintain and cassava in a mortar) to facilitate consumption. Besides this, the deployment of *akyeame* in formal discourse is an avoidance strategy to preserve the sanctity of royal space. The very sacredness of kingship among the Akan, and in Africa in general, often refered to as "divine kingship," encourages royal seclusion from the world's dangers. Chiefs in Africa are considered in close relation to spirits of the ancestors. At the farthest extreme are the Yoruba kings, whose bodies upon installation are imbued with powers of dynastic ancestors or gods. Because the king is sacred, care is taken to preserve his person and maintain his sanctity, through the avoidance of direct contact. It is reported among the Ijebu of Southern Nigeria, for example, that in the nineteenth century the king was never seen and, until recently, any communication was made to him through a screen.

The adoption of various distancing strategies is partly meant to preserve the sanctity of royal space. It insures the monarch against the perils of face-to-face interaction, where his person could be defiled, and where speech directed at him may be spiritually potent. The royal orator, then, becomes not only a mouthpiece, but also the buffer on which all dangerous words are deflected. Through him, the potency of the incoming spoken word is palliated and rendered safe for royal consumption.

From another perspective, the issue of speech mediation may be seen to benefit both parties of royal discourse. The concept of kingship in Africa carries with it associated beliefs in a king's spiritual potency, which could be used for destructive ends and which has to be contained in the interest of order. Among certain groups, including the Akan, a chief's slap or curse is believed capable of causing madness. In moments of royal wrath, an agent is needed to contain the destabilizing forces capable of being activated. Thus boisterous or undignified remarks indiscreetly made by the chief are instantly softened and passed on without retroactive damage; for since the royal speech act is not complete until relayed by the chief's *okyeame*, it does not take effect until then.

Speaking through an *okyeame* leaves room for possible modification, addition of omitted detail, and the elevation of discourse to a poetic level. Indeed, formal discourse within the royal domain scarcely qualifies as communication without an intermediary, who diplomatically rephrases any potentially controversial statements or enlivens bland language. In the *okyeame*'s care, royal words may be paraphrased, elaborated, punctuated with history, ornamented with metaphor, enlivened with proverbs and allegories, or even dramatized outright. Through the okyeame, royal words are refined, poeticized, and made more palatable for public consumption.

The *okyeame*'s role as speech intermediary is made possible because he witnesses all official transactions involving the chief. He represents him at funerals, reminds him when he forgets, receives his guests, prosecutes offenders, pronounces judgment, and is familiar with all official transactions. He is, indeed, the only functionary who has access to the royal chambers. The official intimacy between the chief and his *okyeame* is such that the latter is referred to as *nana yere* "the chief's wife." Indeed, prior to the installation of the *okyeame*, he is "wedded" by the chief and given a ring. On the death of his master, the *okyeame* may go through the same rites of widowhood as the chief's spouse.

Importance in Society

Prior to the emergence of modern nation states in West Africa, royal spokesmen were so important that their image at home and abroad was of special concern. Among the Ashanti, *akyeame* on royal missions had access to a public wardrobe from which they dressed in a manner befitting royal emissaries. As ambassadors, they needed to carry symbols of authority and comport themselves as men of dignity. The practice of *akyeame* holding staffs of authority still prevails today. Among the Akan, the staff is covered in gold or silver leaf.

Akyeame perform their duties holding the staff, on which is embossed an appropriate symbol conveying a cryptic proverbial statement that depicts royal policy. Every chief has two or more staffs for his *okyeame*. The higher a chief's status, the wider his range of staffs since an important chief deals with a greater variety of situations and has to match various occasions with appropriate messages. Inherent ambiguities in such icons of diplomacy are sometimes exploited to make subtle political comments, which, when deciphered by the intended target, may lead to a diplomatic crisis. To avert such crises, royal spokesmen strive to steer clear of ambiguity where no malice is intended. They strive to comply with norms of propriety to ensure that harmony prevails between occasion and staff symbolism.

Two examples follow. The symbol of two birds with their beaks touching reminds all that "When two mouths meet, conflict does not arise." This is used in settling disputes. It advocates the use of diplomacy, rather than physical confrontation, in solving problems. Mutual talk dissipates conflict, it says. Another example has two men seated on a long bench. This means that "The royal stool is not long enough to seat two." Such a staff is taken to judicial sittings dealing with disputes over inheritance. It implies that rules of succession do not permit joint occupancy; heirs succeed one at a time, and there cannot possibly be two occupants of a stool.

References

Okpewho, Isidore. 1992. *African Oral Literature: Backgrounds, Character, and Continuity*. Bloomington: Indiana University Press.

Peek, Philip M. 1981. The Power of Words in African Verbal Arts. *Journal of American Folklore* 94: 371, 19–43.

Yankah, Kwesi. 1983. To Praise or Not to Praise the King: The Akan Apae in the Context of Referential Poetry. *Research in African Literatures* 14: 3, 382–400.

———. 1989. *The Proverb in the Context of Akan Rhetoric: A Theory of Proverb Praxis*. New York: Peter Lang.

———. 1995. *Speaking for the Chief: Okyeame and the Politics of Akan Royal Oratory*. Bloomington: Indiana University Press.

KWESI YANKAH

See also **Chiefs; Oratory; Proverbs**

OLD MAN AND OLD WOMAN

According to Westermarck, old age in Morocco traditionally "inspires a feeling of mysterious awe which tends to make the man a saint and the woman a witch" (1930, 46). Indeed, Moroccan proverbs make it clear that respect is due to the males' "white hairs" (*ibid.*). To designate elderly men, apart from precisely the term "white-haired" (*shâ'ib, shîbâni*), the following are used in the folktales of the Maghreb: *shikh*, to indicate and address, with reverence, a learned gentleman (mostly in religious matters); *hakîm*, for a "doctor" in the occult sciences (e.g., Desparmet 1910, 90–122); *Qdîm ar-Rây* (lit., "old opinion") from the narrative cycle of the Banu Hilal, who, because of his perception of the hidden implicit meaning of things, plays a specific role of mediation among his people (e.g., Galley and Ayoub 1983, n. 57, 154). Of equally common use in the Arabian tales of Algeria is *mudabbir*, a form whose meaning suggests the ability to clear entangled situations and find pragmatic solutions (e.g., Desparmet 1909, 91, 226; Bencheneb 1946). An interesting aspect of his function in society lies in his choice of the metaphorical language to be used appropriately in questions of great issue; such choice being founded on tacit rules of decency (due to age, sex, kinship) as well as on aesthetic criteria (Breteau and Galley 1970, 57–66). In brief, whatever status the old man is given in the tales, he seems to have not only stored knowledge and wisdom from a lifetime of experience, but also acquired a deep insight into sociability. He intervenes within the family, or at a wider social level, thus contributing to safe practical settlements among the members of the group.

In North African folktales, the old man, generally, in his relations with young individuals, plays the role of the helper (El-Shamy 1995, N 825.2, N 835). As such, he exercises an important determinant influence, perceptible, for example, from the treatment of these recurring themes: In one, a young hero, at a crucial stage of his/her solitary journey (by the spring, at a crossroads, on a faraway mountain, and so on), comes across an old man. As a reward for a favor asked and fulfilled, the latter gives him precious, sometimes enigmatic, advice which, if blindly obeyed, ensures success and, ultimately, social recognition (e.g., Baklouti 1988, 106, 118–121). Another common sequence has an old peasant or fisherman rescuing abandoned infants from a trunk that he finds floating on the river or sea. He adopts, feeds, and educates them (e.g., Desparmet 1910, 241–64). Also, there are tales about an old huntsman/sultan who saves a young maiden lost in the Wasteland. He takes her under his protection and sometimes marries her and builds a family with her (e.g., Galley and Iraqui Sinaceur 1994, 86–91). In these three samples, the old man seems to find himself exactly where he is needed, whether he shows the way to the inexperienced hero and helps him/her to overcome forthcoming perils, gives a home and education to forlorn babies, or provides a shelter and security in married life to a desperate girl. In all these circumstances, the old man appears to be the bearer of a whole system of values, which he has the privilege and duty to transmit, exemplify, and perpetuate (Baklouti 1988, 13–15).

The old woman is portrayed as the complete opposite of her male counterpart. In several proverbs from Morocco, she is said to beat the Devil himself, to do in an hour what he does in a year, to possess a cunning (*kîd* or *kayd*, typical of women) superior to the Devil's (e.g., Westermarck 1930, nos. 12, 20, 21). She is apparently such an evildoer that, as the phrase goes, "May God not forgive her on the day of her death" (e.g., Marçais and Guiga 1925, 2553).

To designate her in the tales, the *'ajûza* (aging, weakening) is used with no real pejorative meaning. But more common is *settût*, literally the "sixty-year-old" one; a term that is notably restricted to females and synonymous with "witch." Apart from few rare occasions when she assists the hero (El-Shamy 1995, N 825.3.2) or some other character (e.g., Destaing 1911, 39; Baklouti 1988, 103), she is invariably a troublemaker (e.g., AT 1353, "The Old Woman as Trouble Maker" and AT 1406, "The Merry Wives Wager"). Strikingly, while, in this society, a woman is traditionally considered asexual when past child-bearing age, in the folktales, she is either personally or indirectly involved in love affairs. A widow in the former case, she marries an ogre and, very likely in order to satisfy her sexual appetite without opposition, persuades him to murder her own son (e.g., El-Shamy 12.1; AT 590, 11, "The Treacherous Mother;" Lacoste and Mouliéras 1965: 72–87; Lacoste-Dujardin 1970, 503). In the latter, the so-called *settût* plays the role of a clever unscrupulous procuress (El-Shamy, 452) who treacherously introduces a man into the privacy of young maidens while their father has gone on a pilgrimage (e.g., Basset 1897, 156–61; Légey 1926, 7–13; Galley 1971, 185–95). In order to be admitted into a private house, she may pretend to be a midwife and, as such, achieve her criminal deeds (El-Shamy, 1947; K 2292.5.1; e.g., Desparmet 1910, 231–64). Thus, the most sacred values, which are the cement of family life, are defiled by such old women.

Mention should also be made of the way the old woman manipulates her listener(s) in the dialogues of the tales: she uses all the potentialities of language, from the short enigmatic, sometimes nonsensical, phrases (as in AT 408, "The Three Oranges;" e.g., Destaing 1911, 145–48; Baklouti 1988, 41) to the ceaseless outpouring of words (Galley and Iraqui Sinaceur 1994, 138–93). She then arouses an immediate irrational desire for something or somebody, at the risk of the victim's life (e.g., Biarnay 1917, 154–70; Légey 1926, 40). The protagonist of a Maghribian narrative cycle, a variant of Dalilah in *The Arabian Nights*, resorts to such verbal stratagems; she is known in several versions (Galley and Iraqui Sinaceur 1994, 232–3) under the name of La'âba—an intensive form which means, literally, "great player" (at the other's expense); in other words, "expert in deceit." She is described "girdling herself" to go out in town, ready for cheating. Although she claims to be justified in provoking disorder throughout the city, she seems to destroy, systematically, the belongings of her preys—all males—as well as their dignity. In this respect, she is not only the antithesis of the old man, but his ruin.

References

Baklouti, N. 1988. *Contes populaires de Tunisie*. Tunis: I.N.A.A.

Basset, R. 1897. *Nouveaux contes berbères*. Paris: Leroux.

Bencheneb, S. 1946. *Les contes d'Alger*. Oran: Ed. Henrys.

Biarnay, S. 1917. *Etude sur les dialectes berbères du Rif*. Paris Leroux.

Breteau, C., and M. Galley. 1970. La pastèque et le couteau, In *Littérature orale arabo-berbère*, no. 4:57–66. Paris: C.N.R.S.

Desparmet, J. 1909–10. *Contes sur les ogres recueillis à Blida*. 2 vol. Paris: Leroux.

Destaing, E. 1911. *Etude sur le dialecte berbère des Beni-Snous*. 2 vol. Paris: Leroux.

El-Shamy, H. M. 1995. *Folk Tradition of the Arab World: A Guide to Motif Classification*. 2 vol. Bloomington: Indiana University Press.

Galley, M. 1971. *Badr az-Zin et six contes algériens*. Paris: Classiques Africains.

———, and A. Ayoub. 1983. *Histoire des Beni Hilal et de ce qui leur advint dans leur Marche vers l'ouest*. Paris: Classiques Africains.

———, and Z. Iraqui-Sinaceur. 1994. *Dyab, Jha, La'aba . . . Le triomphe de la ruse*. Paris: Classique Africains.

Hilton-Simpson, M. W. 1924. Algerian Folktales, *Folklore* XXXV.

Lacoste-Dujardin, C. 1965. *Légendes et contes merveilleux de la Grande-Kabylie recueillis par Auguste Mouliéras*. 2 vol. Paris: Impr. Nat.; Geuthner.

———. 1970. *Le conte kabyle*. Paris: Maspéro.

Largeau, V. 1879. *Flore saharienne. Histoires et légendes traduites de l'arabe*. Paris.

Laroui, A. 1978–79. *Vieux contes de Tunisie*. Alger: SNED and Tunis: MTE.

Légey, D. 1926. *Contes et légendes populaires du Maroc recueillis à Marrakech*. Paris: Leroux.

Marcais, W., and A. Guiga. 1925. *Textes arabes de Takrouna*. Paris: Leroux.

Taos-Amrouche, M. 1966. *Le grain magique*. Paris: Maspéro.

Thompson, Stith. 1964. *The Types of the Folktale*. Folklore Fellows Communications, no. 75 and 184. Helsinki: Academia Scient.

Westermarck, Edward. 1930. *Wit and Wisdom in Morocco. A Study of Native Proverbs*. London: Routledge.

MICHELINE GALLEY

See Also **Folk Tales; Gender Representation in African Folklore; Maghrib; Typology and Performance**

ORAL LITERARY RESEARCH IN AFRICA

Some of the formative work on oral literature in Africa was done by scholars who analyzed the texts they collected from basically nonliterary perspectives. Evidence of this extraliterary interest may be seen from a brief sampling of the works of, especially, European collectors and scholars. The most striking quality of these early publications is the sheer curiosity felt by the visitors at encountering something strange, a curiosity that may be gleaned even from the titles they gave to their works. We see this trait in Equilbecq's *Essai sur la litterature merveilleuse des noirs* (1913–1916). Even Bleek's *Reynard the Fox in South Africa* (1864) strikes us as much with the author's amazement at discovering an ostensibly European tale type in Africa, as by his arguably genuine desire to explore cultural commonalities between widely separated peoples. No doubt also, the works of the German Leo Frobenius, such as *Atlantis* (1921–1928, in twelve volumes), stand as an epitome of that ecstatic pursuit of vanished worlds and other exotica that may help European students of culture trace the stages of growth of human civilization.

History

The curiosity is also recognizable in that collecting zeal, whereby the scholar sought to put together everything he could find of the oral traditions of a whole people within the covers of one volume or a few. Henry Callaway's *Nursery Tales, Traditions, and Histories of the Zulus* (1868) comes to mind, as do those catch-all collections of Hausa lore by scholars like Schon (1885), Rattray (1913, in two volumes) and Tremearne (1913). Subtitled *An Introduction to the Folklore and the Folk*, Tremearne's work, in particular, gives some evidence of the way this curiosity converged with a certain condescension, which enshrined the concept of the folk as a (mostly) rural people, judged unsophisticated or uncouth simply because they did not have the wisdom that Western education supposedly confers. Although Alan Dundes addressed this prejudice in a classic essay over two decades ago (1977), it is one that had a very good run in humanistic scholarship and may still be very much alive in certain circles.

In time, however, this career of peregrine collectivism gave way to a more realistic concentration of interest—identified with the growth of social anthropology as a discipline—in the ways of life of manageable or fairly well-integrated ethnic or linguistic communities. The study of traditional texts as literature may not have recorded significant gains thus far, but the narrowing of the scholar's focus somehow guaranteed that the foundations were slowly being laid for the due recognition of the aesthetic sophistication of those texts. The perception of the literary character of these texts is revealed as early, indeed, as the mid-nineteenth century, when Bleek observed that the "literary activity" of the traditions "has been employed almostm in the same direction as that which had been taken by our own earliest literature" (1864, xiii). Bleek may, as we have noted, be considered no more than a bemused amateur. But in the work of scholars like Marcel Griaule, we soon move from an interest in the cherished traditions of a people like the Dogon, to a recognition of the idiosyncratic articulation of it by their most distinguished savant, Ogotemmeli (1948). This singular figure of the traditional wit or artist was clearly the last to gain its freedom, thanks largely to the old view of "tradition" as a body of knowledge handed down from generation to generation in virtually word-perfect form and its bearers as largely uncreative conduits. Still, in the work of a scholar like William Bascom, there is clear evidence, in the coinage *verbal art* (1955), of a gradual shift

from an obsession with the functional value of the oral tradition, to an acknowledgment of its artistic sophistication.

This recognition of the artistry of African traditional texts was facilitated by other factors. As scholars trained their gaze on ways of life within manageable societies, it soon made sense to explore the relationships between various traditional forms as components of a coherent system. Griaule's appreciation of the complexity of Dogon thought certainly gained much from his study of their games (1938a) and masks (1938b). This integrative insight was to reach considerable maturation in the search for traditional aesthetic principles guiding the artistic life of a people, amply demonstrated by the work of Robert Farris Thompson. To that extent, the meeting in 1965 of scholars of various traditional African arts—music, the plastic arts, narrative and song—in a symposium, later edited by Warren d'Azevedo as *The Traditional Artist in African Societies* (1973), may be judged a turning point in the recognition of the artistic quality of African oral traditions.

It is in this light that we can fully appreciate the services of Kwabena Nketia to the discipline of African oral literature. A musicologist by training, he recognized early enough not only the sophisticated texture of the music played by his people but also the varied contests—the royal court, funeral rites, and other social settings—of the songs and chants interweaving the sounds. Together with European scholars like Tracey and Carrington, he trained our ears to listen to the music *in* words and within the enabling context of the instrumentation and the total moment of the event. The benefit of this interest in enabling context or moment was to be seen in the work of scholars who trained under Nketia's guiding genius. Thus in a rather groundbreaking essay, Avorgbedor (1990) guides us to appreciate that the import of a song text for an audience changes accordingly as the performer shifts his attention from one auditor to another.

The idea of text brings one to another factor that has helped our appreciation of the literary or artistic quality of African oral traditions and the contribution of native African scholars to this development. In the nineteenth century and earlier decades of the twentieth, there was a great deal of careful classification and analytical study of various African languages by European scholars. Much of this was done in the service of Christian missions, striving to win the souls of the "heathen natives" by co-opting the resources of their unfamiliar speech; still more was work commissioned by colonial and settler administrations in the interest of adequate understanding and thus effective control of peoples whose land and resources they had usurped and were exploiting; while others were an extension of the eighteenth-century interest in tracing the history of civilization through the comparative study of languages. The efforts of these scholars may be seen in studies of various southern African languages by Casalis (1841), Madan (1911), Doke (1933, 1948), and Lestrade (1937); of central African texts by Stappers (1953) and Boelaert (1955); of Hausa and Kanuri by Prietze (1904) and Lukas (1937–38); of Igbo by Green (1936) and Ward (1941); of Dogon by Calame-Griaule (1965); as well as the classification of African languages by Greenberg (1955, 1963) and others.

There is little doubt that most of this foreign effort has advanced our understanding of the linguistic basis of the literary or imaginative quality of African oral literature; Doke's work, in particular, would seem to be a classic effort in this regard. But the severe shortcomings and unfortunate consequences of these studies have equally begun to be recognized, as may be seen in the examination of the situation of Igbo by Afigbo (1981). Thus, while we celebrate the pioneering effort of foreign scholars in drawing attention to the sophisticated texture of African languages, the insights brought to bear on the subject by native African scholars, analyzing the internal dynamics of their native speech forms as well as external influences upon them—for example, Mofokeng (1945) and Kunene (1965) in south Africa, Lasebikan (1955) and Babalola (1964–65) among the Yoruba of Nigeria, and Sow (1965) among the Fulani of Senegal—achieves special significance in the acknowledgment of the imaginative quality of African oral literature.

The participation of indigenous African scholars in the field study of their peoples' oral traditions may be traced mostly from the 1950s and 1960s, which was both the heyday of colonial activity in Africa and the period when several African youth were beginning to graduate in moderate numbers from colonial academies inside and outside the continent. As various intellectuals—anthropologists, art historians, linguists, musicologists, literary critics, writers, and others—directed their focus on fairly integral communities, their insights became increasingly more representative of the subjects of their attention. If the quality of texts of African oral literature appearing from this period is anything to go by, we may safely say that the literary character of this tradition was no longer much in doubt.

This is what makes Ruth Finnegan's work *Oral Literature in Africa* (1970) such a landmark in oral literary research in Africa. We should bear in mind, of course, that she was not the first to use the word *literature* in characterizing the subject of her study. The foundations for such a concept were laid by the praises lavished by much earlier scholars like Junod (1913) on the creative genius of African narrative performers and Smith and Dale (1920) on the virtuosity of their representations. And the word itself has been applied to indigenous texts by observers and analysts all the way from Koelle (1854), Bleek (1864), and Burton (1865) to Doke (1934) and Lifchitz (1940). The geologist Eno-Belinga's book, *Litterature et musique populaire en Afrique noire* (1965) is a modest survey, mostly of the Cameroonian field, but it should be recognized as among works that preceded Finnegan in drawing attention to the literary quality of the traditions. Even if we dismissed these usages as limited perceptions of the claims of the traditions to be judged on equal terms with literate classics, we should at least credit them with settling the debate promoted by the likes of Walter Ong (1982, 10–15) even before it had begun.

Finnegan's work takes full account of a vast array of the work of scholars across the field, from the earliest generations of the study to its heyday in the 1960s, using the term *literature* not only with the merit of historical insight but also with the benefit of training in the relevant disciplines. Armed with a B.A. in classics and a doctorate in social anthropology, she earned her stripes with fieldwork in various West African communities but especially among the Limba of Sierra Leone, from which she published a number of ethnographic studies and, particularly, the delightful *Limba Stories and Storytelling* (1967). This work, in fact, established Finnegan as a key player in the field, for it helped promote those factors we have come to recognize as ingredients of the peculiar artistry of the oral narrative performance: the imaginative use of words and the images they conjure, the idiosyncratic genius of the narrator, and the fervent dialogue between that genius and the context (human and otherwise) within which it plays.

Only a scholar with such a background could have produced a work of the scope and depth of *Oral Literature in Africa*, a solid ethnography of the subject that brings a sense of history to bear on a moment when African intellectuals, not least the literati, were basking in the hard-won liberation of their proud cultural traditions from the prejudices of the past. Partly in deference to this cultural pride but partly also in honest representation of the full dimensions of her subject, Finnegan strikes a just balance between content, form, and context even as she casts an enormous historic and geographic net across the entire sub-Saharan Africa.

Finnegan's book is pivotal because it put a final stamp of authority on our recognition of the oral traditions as literature, and even more because it brought a certain sense of self-assurance to further endeavors in this field. It might not be far-fetched to state that the establishment of courses in oral literature—and even their designation as compulsory—in various universities in Africa, including the last bastions of colonial indoctrination like Ibadan, owe much to the publication of Finnegan's book. Her work coincided, incidentally, with the growth of the so-called science of folklore, especially in the American academy, and one could sense a certain disciplinary stress in the attempt by Richard Dorson, the doyen of the discipline there, to undervalue Finnegan's book in his superfluous differentiation of the concerns of "folklore" from those of "oral literature" (1972, 10–18).

Whatever one's disciplinary outlooks or prejudices, Finnegan's book has been responsible, in no small way, for the immense strides taken in the study since the 1970s. The countless citations of the book by contemporary scholars amply bear this out, as does the fact that most of their works give the sort of acknowledgment of the literary texture of the traditions that Finnegan has encouraged.

Collections and Anthologies

The list of these works is long, but a random sampling gives a sense of the generic and geographic coverage of the oral-literary interest promoted by Finnegan, even when she is not specifically identified as a source of inspiration. We may conveniently start with collections and anthologies, which have gained fresh impetus from the entry of native African scholars in the field. The Ghanaian poet Awoonor was one of the first to celebrate the literary merit of the oral traditions with his translations first of a collection of Ewe poetry (1974), then of the oral narratives (1981). East Africa gave us Okot p'Bitek's delicate renditions of Acoli poetry (1974) and later of the narratives (1978), as well as Rose Mwangi's collection of Kikuyu folktales (1982). There have been several collections of tales and songs from Francophone countries, among which may be cited Thoyer-Rozat's editions of hunters' chants from Mali (1978 and 1984). Loretto Todd's collection of trickster tales from Cameroon (1979) is introduced by a brief treatment of the literary and imaginative quality of the oral tradition, and Roger Abrahams's collection of *African Folktales* (1983) also has a very stimulating discussion of matters of form and performance as well as the key concerns of the tales. Harold Scheub's *The African Storyteller* (1990) organizes its Africa-wide collection of tales thematically; there is no general introduction but, as in most of Scheub's work, several photographs of narrators in performance give vivid notice of the fact that these tales are products of imaginative histrionic as well as verbal representation on the part of the living artists.

Scheub may, in fact, be counted among the first to consolidate the interest in oral-literary research in more recent times with his masterly study (1975) of the Xhosa oral narrative tradition (*ntsomi*), a work that appeared in the same series—Oxford Library of African Literature—as Finnegan's 1967 and 1970 studies. His work is pivotal in foregrounding performance as the lifeblood of the oral text. It also epitomizes the flourish of structural analyses of the oral tradition that we see in studies by Arewa and Shreve (1975), Anozie (1981), as well as such Scheub alumni as Ropo Sekoni (1990, 1994) and Rassner (1990). This intensive analysis, especially of the oral narrative, may also be seen in the works of scholars like Seitel (1980), Cosentino (1982), and Jackson (1982), the latter two following Finnegan in exploring the Sierra Leonean field. Among other area studies, we may especially recognize Wande Abimbola's insider's view of *ifa* divination poetry (1976) which takes William Bascom's work in this area (1959) one step further; Olatunji's careful treatment of the major features of Yoruba oral poetry (1984); Kwesi Yankah's masterly discussions of Akan proverbs (1989) and court rhetoric (1995); and the analyses of South African oral poetic traditions by Jeff Opland (1971, 1983) and Elizabeth Gunner (1990). Studies of the oral narrative traditions of Zambian communities by David Bynum (1978) and Clement Okafor (1983) have also benefited from literary insights gained from the Harvard school of Milman Parry and Albert Lord. And Zinta Konrad's study of Ewe trickster tales (1994) is especially laudable for the way it explores issues of content and style along with the philosophical and educational significance of this oral narrative tradition.

Surveys

These studies of national traditions have been supplemented by survey discussions, both at the local and the continental levels. Eno-Belinga was one of the first in this regard, following his 1965 work with one that replaced the concept of "popular literature" with the more professional identification *oral literature* (1978). His fellow countryman Kashim Tala gave us a modest view of the field of Cameroon oral literature (1988), while from eastern Africa, Kipury provided a bird's-eye view of the *Oral Literature of the Maasai* (1983). Lee Haring has offered a quite readable account from an African subregion with his study of what, following the likes of Bascom and Crowley, he called the "verbal arts" of Madagascar (1992).

There have also been Africa-wide studies of specific genres. Here, we need only mention Francoise Tsoungui's general work on the folktale (1986), which discusses form and structure as evidence of the artistic merit of the tales and also explores their relevance to the enabling culture. Of continental surveys of African oral literature, there is the modest but lucid volume targeted by Jane Nandwa and Austin Bukenya at East African secondary schools (1983), but very useful beyond that market. Jacques Chevrier's *L'arbre a palabre* (1986) as well as *African Oral Literature* (1992) by Isidore Okpewho are a general introductions to African oral literature, devoted special attention to oral narratives and poetry, recognizing the imaginative qualities of the forms and setting them within the universe of social and cultural life.

My own *African Oral Literature* (1992) also belongs in this group of works.

Essays

The above survey concentrates on published books, and mostly monographs at that. But one should bear in mind that a lot of very useful work has been published in numerous journals, both in Africa and abroad, concerned generally with African society and culture, but sufficiently hospitable to issues in African oral literature. There have also been edited collections of essays that were either presented at special gatherings, such as Görög-Karady's Oxford symposium (1983), or else published as special issues of established journals, such as the issue on Oral Literature edited by Lilyan Kesteloot for *Research in African Literatures* (1993).

Whether or not these works acknowledge Finnegan as their source of inspiration, they are, in fundamental ways, extensions of the program to which her work has been dedicated: a recognition of the imaginative texture of African oral literature, as well as its significance in mirroring people's outlooks and aspirations. Finnegan's work has been equally pivotal in a rather different direction. Given its enormous coverage, and the crudeness of some of the evidence on which it relied, *Oral Literature in Africa* was given to some errors of judgment, which some scholars, armed with more dependable material and the benefit of analytical tools that Finnegan had not fully consulted, were led to challenge.

Influence of Finnegan

By far the most critical issue on which dissident scholars have revised Finnegan's judgment on African oral literature is the epic. "All in all," she concludes from the evidence of texts she has reviewed, "epic poetry does not seem to be a typical African form" (1970, 110). It seems unreasonable to suggest, as did Lee Haring, that "Finnegan's argument was misread" (1994, 34) by those who took her to task for it. To be sure, the texts on which she based her conclusions were poor records of the traditions they had set out to represent. But then Finnegan, with a background in European literary classics like Homer, was obviously swayed by such influences as she engaged traditions in which the line between poetry and prose was even less marked than contemporary scholars like Dennis Tedlock (1971) have endeavored to suggest.

Right or wrong, Finnegan had, in her brief addendum, dropped a bombshell which caused an explosion of scholarly effort, from scholars including the author (1977, 1979) and John William Johnson (1980, 1986), who fundamentally disagreed with her, and from others moved less by the spirit of controversy than by the urge to contribute to a growing body of information in a new field. There is now a large corpus of edited texts of the African oral epic, of which Gordon Innes's editions of various epics from the Gambian Mandinka (1974, 1976, 1978) are as representative of the Anglophone initiative as Lilyan Kesteloot and A. H. Ba's edition of the Da Monzon epic (1972) and Christiane Seydou's editions on Silamaka (1972) and Hambodedio (1976)—within the series of Classiques Africains published by Armand Colin in Paris—are of the Francophone. Daniel Biebuyck's translation of three more versions of the Mwindo epic (1978) than he had earlier produced (1969) may not have impressed Finnegan, since it sported many of those errors of representation that she had recoiled from (justifiably, in some cases). But J. P. Clark's edition of the Ijo epic of Ozidi (1977) offered a resounding counterpoint both to the prose/poetry dichotomy and to the question of episodic structure that seem to have guided Finnegan's reservations about the epic in Africa.

There have been other revisions of Finnegan's views on African oral literature. She doubted that myths were, "on the evidence we have, . . . a characteristic African form at all" (1970, 362); the author of this essay, in a book on the subject (1983), sought not simply to demonstrate the contrary but even to review the parameters on which the genre was conventionally understood. She also grudgingly conceded—and some African critics like Echeruo (1973) have echoed her misgivings about—the existence of drama in Africa's traditions (1970, 500–17). Studies by Enekwe (1981) and Ugonna (1984) on Igbo dramatic masques and by Conteh-Morgan (1992, 1994) on Francophone African traditions have been very useful in throwing light on evidence that Finnegan may not have fully exploited in her difficult job of surveying the entire field of Africa's oral literary tradition.

Whether a piece of oral literary study is designed purposely as an elaboration of Finnegan's insights or as a revision of her view, she was seminal to much of the work that has been done in this discipline in the last three decades of the twentieth century. Indeed, the latter kind of effort is perhaps the greater credit that anyone might hope to give her; for knowledge grows better when an idea or a proposition draws visceral responses than when it elicits merely a cheerful smile or an appreciative nod.

But what does the future hold for oral literary research in Africa? What resources are available for further study, and what should scholars working in this field be concerned with today and tomorrow?

Future Directions

The above survey reveals that, from the dawn of political independence, African scholars have risen to the task of investigating the oral traditions as their contribution to the intellectual and cultural liberation of their peoples. But, in the twenty-first century, there are still far fewer Africans engaged in this study than non-Africans. This is a truly unfortunate state of affairs, but it is clear why the situation is as it is the available resources can hardly satisfy the needs of those trained or inclined to do what needs to be done. Although there are centers and institutes in various African countries charged with encouraging the recording and preservation of African oral traditions, African governments have not given them adequate support, partly because the resources have been mismanaged by successive leaders, and partly because the programs of structural adjustment imposed upon Africa leave too little for the pursuit of interests that, sadly, appear to be luxuries.

Some lines of inquiry need to be pursued in this field of study. One in particular deserves emphasis, and this is the program of recording and documenting oral literature in ways that respect the oral character of it, by using modern technologies of recording and preservation. These audiovisual tools are expensive, but doing fieldwork with pen and paper will take us not much further than the days when the peculiar imaginative qualities of the oral literature were missed or ignored by scholars with a somewhat different agenda.

There are two other lines of investigation. In an issue of *Research in African Literatures* devoted to women as oral artists (1994), the editors, Omolara Ogundipe-Leslie and Carole Boyce Davies, charged scholars with ignoring women in studies of African oral literature. There is no denying that much work needs to be done to correct the imbalance that earlier works may have encouraged. Happily, some groundbreaking work has been done in this direction. Harold Scheub led the way early with his almost total attention to female narrators of the Xhosa *ntsomi* tradition. Edris Makward's charming portrait of a female Wolof griotte (1990), in a tradition many had long considered a male preserve, is also a notable addition to this necessary service. Thomas Hale's study (1998) of male and female artists in the same tradition is a noteworthy work of true scholarly dimensions. Karin Barber also published a most stimulating account of female *oriki* (praise) poets in a Yoruba community (1991). Finally, in his study of the *tebra* poetic tradition of Mauretanian women, Georges Voisset (1994) extended the work of Norris (1968) and others in rescuing from obscurity the contribution of women to the maintenance of the artistic traditions of a society lodged curiously between *africanite* and *arabite*.

A final line of investigation focuses on the external relations of African oral literature. Ethnologists and folklorists have long drawn attention to African folktales as prototypes of African American traditions, and in the 1960s and 1970s, there was a great controversy between two groups, led by William Bascom on the one hand and Richard Dorson on the other, as to how much of that tradition was actually traceable to African origins (see Crowley 1977 and Bascom 1992).

Without joining the controversy, any African scholar who has had occasion to examine the oral traditions of the Black Atlantic will have been amazed at how much common stock there is between the two regions. Two lines of approach are suggested by some publications in this area. In their book *Two Evenings in Saramaka* (1991), Richard and Sally Price present narrative performances from Suriname (South America) in which audience members interject nuggets of song and tale as often as they please until the main narrator has quite finished his/her performance. Although the Prices provide no cultural glosses for this phenomenon, one immediately thinks of similar traditions, especially in West Africa (for example, the *mmoguo* among the Akan), and is drawn to a viable intellectual curiosity: Where do the Saramaka come from?

An equally interesting line of approach is suggested by the posthumous publication (1992) of narratives whereby William Bascom had tried to prove the African origins of oral traditions in the African diaspora. One is especially struck by images of the mother figure in the section titled "Dogs Rescue Master in Tree Refuge," containing tales (recorded both in African and diasporic societies) dealing mostly with characters who find themselves in dire circumstances from which they desperately seek to be rescued. The mother in the African stories fails to organize this rescue in two instances, while in the diasporic stories, she fails in eleven, so painfully that she is roundly scolded in three of the eleven and actually strangled to death in one! Bascom's collection does not, of course, pretend to be exhaustive, but here the intellectual curiosity takes on the character of a political concern: why has the image of mother suffered such a deterioration with the movement of these stories from Africa to the New World? And who, by the way, is responsible for such representations of it? In the continuing studies of Afro-diasporic oral traditions by scholars like Daryl Cumber Dance (1978), John Roberts (1989), Carolyn Cooper (1995) and others, there is promise of a valuable intellectual fellowship between scholars committed to exploring the creative traditions of black peoples across time and space.

We owe it to ourselves and to future generations to keep alive the flames of Africa's cultural history. The urgency of this duty is, indeed, forced upon scholars by the steady indigenization of artistic expression in various media. In art, Nigeria's Uche Okeke and Twins Seven Seven, as well as Congo's Trigo Piula and Cote d'Ivoire's Ouattara, have championed the exploitation of mythical themes. In fiction, Ousmane Sembene, Ngugi wa Thiong'o, and Ben Okri have taken ample strides in exploiting formal patterns of the oral narrative, while Chinua Achebe and Amadou Kourouma have not hesitated to deconstruct the dominant European languages of their novels with elements of indigenous spoken art. In poetry, the early adoption of oral modes by Leopold Sedar Senghor, Mazisi Kunene, and Kofi Awoonor has been sustained by the late Tchicaya U'Tamsi and by Atukwei Okai as well as by Kofi Anyidoho and Niyi Osundare. In drama, Wole Soyinka's use of ritual and mythic elements has been a key influence on the work of his countrymen Femi Osofisan and of the Cameroonian Werewere Liking and the Ivoirian Senouvo Zinsou. Special credit must be given to those writers who have chosen to express their creative thoughts in the medium of the indigenous speech: writers from the earlier generations like the Sotho B. M. Khaketla, the Zulu B. W. Vilakazi, the Igbo Pita Nwana, and the Yoruba D. O. Fagunwa to the many who followed them. Nor should descendants of the disapora like Kamau Brathwaite and Paule Marshall, who in their works have highlighted African traditions enshrined in the racial memory, be omitted.

Works Cited

Abimbola, Wande. 1976. *Ifa: An Exposition of Ifa Literary Corpus.* Ibadan: Oxford University Press.

Abrahams, Roger D. 1983. *African Folktales.* New York: Pantheon.

Afigbo, Adiele. 1981. *Ropes of Sand: Stufies in Igbo History and Culture.* Ibadan: University Press.

Anozie, Sunday. 1981. *Structural Models and an African Poetics.* London: Routledge.

Arewa, E. Ojo and G.M. Shreve. 1975. *The Genesis of Structure in African Narrative: Vol 1. Zande Trickster Tales.* Owerri: Conch Nigeria.

Avorgbedor, Daniel. 1990. The Preservation, Transmission, and Realization of Song Texts: A Psychomusical Approach. In Okpewho 1990.

Awoonor, Kofi. 1974. *Guardians of the Sacred Word.* Enugu: Nok Press.

———. 1981. *Fire in the Valley: Ewe Folktales.* Enugu: Nok Press.

d'Azevedo, Warren L., ed. 1973. *The Traditional Artist in African Societies.* Bloomington: Indiana University Press.

Babalola, S.A. 1964–65. The Characteristic Features of Outer Form of Yoruba Ijala Chants. *Odu,* 1 and 2.

Barber, Karin. 1991. *I Could Speak Until Tomorrow: Oriki, Women, and the Past in a Yoruba Town.* Washington, D.C.: Smithsonian Institution Press.

Bascom, William. 1955. Verbal Art. *Journal of American Folklore,* 68: 245–252.

———. 1969. *Ifa Divination: Communication Between Gods and Men.* Bloomington: Indiana University Press.

———. 1992. *African Folktales in the New World.* Bloomington: Indiana University Press.

Biebuyck, Daniel P. 1978. *Hero and Chief: Epic Literature from the Banyanga.* Berkeley: University of California Press.

——— and Kahombo C. Mateene. 1969. *The Mwindo Epic from the Banyanga.* Berkeley: University of California Press.

P'Bitek, Okot. 1974. *Horn of My Love.* London: Heinemann.

———. 1978. *Hare and Hornbill.* London: Heinemann.

Bleek, W.H.I. 1864. *Reynard the Fox in South Africa.* London: Trubner.

Boelaert, E. 1955. De Structuur van de Nkundo-poezie. *Kongo-Overzee,* 21:142–160.

Burton, R.R. 1865. *Wit and Wisdom from West Africa.* London: Tinsley Brothers.

Bynum, David. 1978. *The Daemon in the Wood: A Study of Oral Narrative Patterns.* Cambridge, MA: Harvard Center for the Study of Oral Literature.

Calame-Griaule, G. 1965. *Ethnologie et Langage: La Parole chez les Dogon.* Paris: Gallimard.

Callaway, Henry. 1868. *Nursery Tales, Traditions, and Histories of the Zulus.* London: Blair.

Casalis, Eugene. 1841. *Etudes sur la Langue Sechuana.* Paris: Imprimerie Royale.

Chevrier, Jacques. 1986. *L'Arbre a Palabre: Essai sur le Contes et Recits Traditionnels d'Afrique Noire.* Paris: Hatier.

Clark, John Pepper, ed. 1977. *The Ozidi Saga: From the Ijo of Okabou Ojobolo.* Ibadan: Ibadan and Oxford University Presses.

Conteh-Morgan, John. 1992. French-language African Drama and the Oral Tradition: Trends and Issues. *African Literature Today,* 18: 115–132.

———. 1994. *Theatre and Drama in Francophone Africa.* Cambridge: Cambridge University Press.

Cooper, Carolyn. 1995. *Noises in the Blood.* Durham: Duke University Press.

Cosentino, Donald. 1982. *Defiant Maids and Stubborn Farmers.* Cambridge: Cambridge University Press.

Crowley, Daniel J., ed. 1977. *African Folklore in the New World.* Austin: University of Texas Press.

Dance, Daryl Cumber. 1978. *Shuckin' and Jivin': Folklore from Contemporary Black Americans.* Bloomington: Indiana University Press.

Doke, C.M. 1933. A Preliminary Investigation into the State of the Native Languages of South Africa With Suggestions as to Research and the Development of Literature. *Bantu Studies,* 7:1–98.

———. 1934. Lamba Literature. *Africa,* 7:351–370.

———. 1948. The Basis of Bantu Literature. *Africa,* 18:284–301.

Dorson, Richard, ed. 1972. *African Folklore.* Bloomington: Indiana University Press.

Dundes, Alan. 1977. Who Are the Folk? in *Frontiers of Folklore,* ed. W.R. Bascom. Boulder: Westview Press.

Echeruo, M.J.C. 1973. The Dramatic Limits of Igbo Ritual. *Research in African Literatures,* 4: 21–31.

Enekwe, Ossie. 1981. Myth, Ritual, and Drama in Igboland. In *Drama and Theatre in Nigeria,* ed. Yemi Ogunbiyi. Lagos: Nigeria Magazine.

Eno-Belinga, S.M. 1965. *Litterature et Musique Populaire en Afrique Noire.* Paris: Cujas.

———. 1978. *La Litterature Orale Africaine.* Issy-les-Moulineaux: Edition St-Paul.

Equilbecq, Francois-Victor. 1913–16. *Essai sur la Litterature Merveilleuse des Noirs, suivi des Contes Indigenes de l'Ouest Africains.* 3 volumes. Paris: Maisonneuve et Larose.

Finnegan, Ruth. 1967. *Limba Stories and Storytelling*. Oxford: Clarendon Press.

———. 1970. *Oral Literature in Africa*. Oxford: Clarendon Press.

Frobenius, Leo. 1912–28. *Atlantis: Volksmarchen und Volksdichtungen Afrikas*. 12 volumes. Jena: Eugen Diedrichs.

Gorog-Karady, Veronika. 1983. *Genres, Forms, Meanings: Essays in African Oral Literature*. Paris: Maison des Sciences de l'Homme.

Green, M.M. 1936. The Present Linguistic Situation in Ibo Country. *Africa*, 9: 68–77.

Greenberg, J.H. 1955. *Studies in African Linguistic Classification*. New Haven: Compass.

———. 1963. *The Languages of Africa*. Bloomington: Indiana University Press.

Griaule, Marcel. 1938a. *Jeux Dogons*. Paris: Institut d'Ethnologie.

———. 1938b. *Masques Dogons*. Paris: Institut d'Ethnologie.

———. 1948. *Dieu d'Eau*. Trans. by T.M. Wright as *Conversations with Ogotemmeli* 1965. London: Oxford University Press.

Haring, Lee. 1992. *Verbal Arts in Madagascar*. Philadelphia: University of Pennsylvania Press.

———, ed. 1994. *Ibonia: Epic of Madagascar*. Lewisburg: Bucknell University Press.

Innes, Gordon. 1974. *Sunjata: Three Mandinka Versions*. London: SOAS, London University.

———. 1976. *Kaabu and Fuladu: Historical Narratives of the Gambian Mandinka*. London: SOAS, London University.

———. 1978. *Kelefa Saane: His Life Recounted by Two Mandinka Bards*. London: SOAS, London University.

Jackson, Michael. 1982. *Allegories of the Wilderness: Ethics and Ambiguity in Kuranko Narratives*. Bloomington: Indiana University Press.

Johnson, John William. 1980. Yes, Virginia, There Is An Epic in Africa. *Research in African Literatures*, 11: 308–326.

———. 1986. *The Epic of Son-Jara: A West African Tradition*. Bloomington: Indiana University Press.

Junod, Henri. 1913. *The Life of a South African Tribe: Vol. 2*. Neuchatel: Attinger Freres.

Kesteloot, Lilyan and A.H. Ba, eds. 1972. *Da Monzon de Segou*. Paris: Nathan.

———, ed. 1993. Special issue on Oral Literature. *Research in African Literatures*, 24, no. 2.

Kipury, N. 1983. *Oral Literature of the Maasai*. Nairobi: Heinemann.

Koelle, S.W. 1854. *African Native Literature; or, Proverbs, Tales, Fables, and Historical Fragments in the Kanuri or Bornu Language*. London: Church Missionary House.

Konrad, Zinta. 1994. *Ewe Comic Heroes: Trickster Tales in Togo*. New York: Garland.

Kunene, D.P. 1965. The Ideophone in Southern Sotho. *Journal of African Languages*, 4: 19–39.

Lasebikan, E.L. 1955. Tone in Yoruba Poetry. *Odu*, 2:35–36.

Lestrade, G.P. 1937. Traditional Literature. In *The Bantu-Speaking Tribes of South Africa*, ed. I. Schapera. London: Routledge.

Lukas, J. 1937–38. Sprichworter, Aussprache und Ratsel der Kanuri. *Zeitschrift fur Eingeborenen-Sprachen*, 28.

Madan, A.C. 1911. *Living Speech in Central and South Africa: An Essay Introductory to the Bantu Family of Languages*. Oxford: Oxford University Press.

Makward, Edris. 1990. Two Griots of Contemporary Senegambia. In *Okpewho* 1990.

Mofokeng, S.M. 1945. Notes and Annotations of the Praise-Poems of Certain Chiefs and the Structure of Praise-Poems in Southern Sotho. Honors Thesis, University of the Witwatersrand, S. Africa.

Mwangi, Rose. 1982. *Kikuyu Folktales*. Nairobi: Kenya Literature Bureau.

Nandwa, Jane and Austin Bukenya. 1983. *African Oral Literature for Schools*. Nairobi: Longman Kenya.

Norris, H.T. 1968. *Shingit Folk Literature and Song*. Oxford: Clarendon Press.

Ogundipe-Leslie, Omolara and C.B. Davies, eds. 1994. Special issue on Women as Oral Artists. *Research in African Literatures*, vol. 25.

Okafor, Clement A. 1983. *The Banished: A Study in Tonga Oral Literature*. London: Folklore Society.

Okpewho, Isidore. 1977. Does the Epic Exist in Africa? Some Formal Considerations. *Research in African Literatures*, 8:171–200.

———. 1979. *The Epic in Africa: Toward a Poetics of the Oral Performance*. New York: Columbia University Press.

———. 1983. *Myth in Africa: A Study of Its Aesthetic and Cultural Relevance*. Cambridge: Cambridge University Press.

———. 1992. *African Oral Literature: Backgrounds, Character, and Continuity*. Bloomington: Indiana University Press.

———, ed. 1990. *The Oral Performance in Africa*. Ibadan: Spectrum Books.

Olatunji, Olatunde. 1984. *Features of Yoruba Oral Poetry*. Ibadan: University Press.

Ong, Walter J. 1982. *Orality and Literacy: The Mythologizing of the Word*. London: Methuen.

Paulme, Denise. 1916. Litterature Orale et Comportements Sociaux en Afrique Noire. *L'Homme*, 1: 21–44.

Prietze, Rudolf. 1904. *Haussa-Sprichworter und Haussa-Lieder*. Kirchhain N. -L.: M. Schmersow Vorm. Zahn und Bandol.

Rassner, Ronald. 1990. *Narrative Rhythms in Agyriama Ngano: Oral Patterns and Musical Structures*. In Okpewho 1990.

Rattray, R.S. 1913. *Hausa Folk-Lore, Customs, Proverbs, etc., Collected and Transliterated with English Translation and Notes*. 2 volumes. Oxford: Oxford University Press.

Roberts, John. 1989. *From Trickster to Badman: The Black Folk Hero in Slavery and Emancipation*. Philadelphia: University of Pennsylvania Press.

Scheub, Harold. 1975. *The Xhosa Ntsomi*. Oxford: Clarendon Press.

———, ed. 1990. *The African Storyteller*. Dubuque: Kendall/Hunt.

Schon, J.F. 1885. *Magana Hausa: Native Literature, Proverbs, Tales, Fables and Historical Fragments in the Hausa Language*. London: Society for Promoting Christian Knowledge.

Seitel, Peter. 1980. *See So That We May See: Performances and Interpretation of Traditional Tales from Tanzania*. Bloomington: Indiana University Press.

Sekoni, Ropo. 1990. *The Narrator, Narrative-Pattern, and Audience Experience of Oral Narrative Performance*. In Okpewho 1990.

———. 1994. *Folk Poetics: A Sociosemiotic Study of Yoruba Trickster Tales*. Westport: Greenwood Press.

Seydou, Christiane. 1972. *Silamaka et Poullouri*. Paris: Armand Colin.

———. 1976. *La Geste de Hambodedio*. Paris: Armand Colin.

Smith, E.W. and A.M. Dale. 1920. *The Ila-Speaking Peoples of Northern Rhodesia*. 2 volumes. London: Macmillan.

Sow, Abdoul Aziz. 1993. Fulani Poetic Genres. In Kesteloot 1993.

Stappers, I. 1953. Toonparallelisme als Mnemotechnisch Middel in Spreekwoorden. *Aequatoria*, 16:

Tedlock, Dennis. 1971. On the Translation of Style in Oral Literature. *Journal of American Folklore*, 84:114–133.

Thoyer-Rhozat, A. 1978. *Kanbili: Chant de Chasseurs du Mali, par Mamadou Jara*. Paris: n.p.

———. 1984. *Nyakaken la Forgeronne: Chant Recit de Chasseurs du Mali, par Mamadou Jara*. Paris: n.p.

Todd, Loretto. 1979. *Tortoise the Trickster and Other Folktales from Cameroon*. London: Routledge.

Tremearne, Arthur John Newman. 1913. *Hausa Superstitions and Customs: An Introduction to the Folk-Lore and the Folk.* London: J. Bale, Sons, and Danielsson.

Tsoungui, Francoise. 1986. *Cles Pour le Conte Africain et Creole.* Paris: Conseil International de la Langue Française.

Ugonna, Nnabuenyi. 1984. *Mmonwu: A Dramatic Tradition of the Igbo.* Lagos: Lagos University Press.

Voisset, Georges M. 1993. *The Tebra' of Moorish Women from Mauritania: The Limits (or Essence) of the Poetic Act.* In Kesteloot 1993.

Ward, I.C. 1941. *Ibo Dialects and the Development of a Common Language.* Cambridge: Cambridge University Press.

Yankah, Kwesi. 1989. *Proverbs in the Context of Akan Rhetoric.* New York: Bern.

———. 1995. *Speaking for the Chief; Okyame and the Politics of Akan Royal Oratory.* Bloomington: Indiana University Press.

ISIDORE OKPEWHO

See also **Institutional Study of African Folklore; Oral Literature: Issues of Definition and Terminology; Oral Narrative; Prose Narratives**

ORAL LITERATURE: ISSUES OF DEFINITION AND TERMINOLOGY

The term *oral literature* has been central to the analysis of the many unwritten forms in Africa that can be regarded as in some way possessing literary qualities. It normally refers to such genres as narratives, myths, epics, lyrics, praise poetry, laments, and the verbal texts of songs; also sometimes to oratory, drama, riddles, proverbs, or word play. Anthropologists, historians, linguists, and literary scholars have interacted with folklorists in the study of these forms (well exemplified in this volume), thus laying the basis for an informed and appreciative analysis of African arts and creativity.

However, *oral literature* is neither a neutral nor an undisputed term, and, in common with other potential cross-cultural concepts, it carries its own implicit assumptions. This entry gives a brief account of the kinds of theoretical issues and controversies it raises and some of the contending arguments involved.

The Controversial Concept of Oral Literature and Its Background

Contrary to what is sometimes assumed, there is no single "natural" terminology to describe or classify the arts or technologies of human expression, whether in literate or nonliterate settings, European or African cultures. The subjects treated in this volume are no exception. Indeed, due both to their evaluative status and to the historical circumstances in which African topics were initially studied, issues about appropriate terminology have attracted particularly heated debate.

Readers of this volume will already have moved beyond an uncritical acceptance of concepts such as primitive culture, savage communalism, tribal customs, artless nature, "passive tradition," "stone-age culture," and "primitive mentality," all once used as terms for describing African cultures. While there is no need to unpick these derogatory and ill-founded terms in detail here, it is worth noting that they are still occasionally encountered. They also form the backdrop to the development of more recent and carefully considered terminologies.

By the mid-nineteenth century, a few scholars and collectors were already using the term *oral literature* to describe African forms (for examples, see Finnegan 1970, chapter 2). The term was brought into wider academic circulation in the Chadwicks' comparative work (1932–1940), which treated not just European and Eastern literatures but also the oral literatures of Polynesia and Africa. From the 1960s, it attained further visibility through the influential oral-formulaic school, leading to numerous studies of oral literature world wide (mainly Eurasian, but also some from Africa). Equally important in an African context was the growing self-confidence from the mid 1960s, as now-independent African countries organised university-based studies of their own cultural arts. Here the heading oral literature was often felt to provide a more accurate and dignified approach than other currently available terms (and certainly more than the earlier dismissive terminologies) and to set this form within the highly regarded international currency of *literature*. The term is now widely accepted and has been used extensively by literary scholars, sociolinguists, folklorists, anthropologists, and others over the years (see references below, and also the influential journal *Cahiers de littérature orale* and the International Society for Oral Literature in Africa [ISOLA], founded 1998).

The concept, however remains contentious. Some scholars reject oral literature as a self-contradiction: how could something defined as written (Latin *litterae*, letters) be simultaneously defined as spoken? Others point out the term's negative connotations, implying a failure to reach some supposed norm of [written] literature, and prefer the more positive *orature*. Some query the need to be constrained by culture-bound etymologies or criticize the West-centered elitist stance of excluding African forms from international literary scholarship. There is also the argument that comparative analysis regularly relies on extending terms from their "original" referents, and that if oral literature proves an illuminating phrase, this is more important than philological pedantry.

Other controversies focus on whether it is either productive or accurate to refer to "literature" when studying *oral* expression and communication. One powerful argument—worth treating seriously—is that this imposes narrowing ethnocentric *written* models on forms that may include other elements than the purely verbal and/or aesthetic. It risks overemphasizing textual features, downplaying the magic moment of performance, or introducing potentially misleading parallels to genres from the Western written canon. As against this, the concept of "literature" has been helpful in relating African forms to a widely recognized scholarly tradition, rather than marginalizing it as something "different" and "other." It also encourages an interest in literary and artistic dimensions, individual creativity, new as well as old forms, and a range of genres (rather than the undifferentiated "oral tradition"), aspects overlooked in many earlier functionalist, and even folkloristic, approaches.

The concept of *oral* itself can be problematic, however. The word is actually ambiguous, meaning either "unwritten" (thus opposed to written) or "spoken/verbal" (thus opposed to sign language, visual communication, material culture, etc). African forms studied under the head of "oral literature" may or may not be oral in both these senses. In any case, there remain issues about the relative balance in, say, storytelling between the linguistic and the nonverbal elements (e.g. musical, choreographic, visual, artifactual). The "oral" qualifier can also be taken to imply a (debatable) distinction between what is written and what is not, suggesting that it is justifiable to separate the two or study the one without the other. Even if this was ever acceptable, it certainly seems inappropriate now as researchers increasingly reveal the complex and multifaceted ways through which oral and written modes overlap and flow into each other both now and in the past. (This doubtless applies throughout the African continent, but perhaps most notably in the areas where Islamic literature has had such a long presence.) On the positive side, the term *oral*, where used with due caution, has led into a heightened awareness of the qualities of unwritten forms and alerted scholars to the rich and varied artistry of performed literary events.

The term *oral* sometimes additionally evokes deeply evaluative assumptions, surfacing in the so-called literacy–orality debate. It was once conventional wisdom to assume a generalized contrast between orality and literacy, in which the former was associated with an early stage of human development and characterised by particular social and cognitive properties, supposedly typical of "primitive culture", oral literature was thus envisaged as intimately bound in with that cultural stage. This viewpoint is still occasionally found in comments on African forms. However, most scholars of African oral literature now see this position as yet another example of outdated evolutionist or colonialist ideologies. They point to the varying ways that oral communication and expression are used in many differing contexts and periods (including in highly "literate" modern cultures), and argue instead for nonjudgemental empirical analyses of oral genres and their multiplicities rather than generalising prior judgement.

Those using the term *oral literature*, therefore, need to bear in mind its complex and value-laden background and the debates and counterdebates it has provoked. In one sense, this is one of its strengths. For assessing the benefits and limitations of the term leads analysts of African oral forms into a set of substantive and fruitful issues, offering a challenging focus for scholarly investigation and discussion.

Alternative Terminologies?

The strengths and weaknesses of the concept oral literature are further illuminated by comparing it with other influential terminologies in the study of African arts and folklore. For although *oral literature* is indeed an accepted and convenient general phrase, it is only one among several competing terminologies. Looking briefly at these can be useful, not for prescribing some illusory right choice, but for highlighting further issues.

Oral tradition is one familiar term, either for the totality of unwritten material within a culture or for particular genres such as stories, songs, or historical accounts. It helpfully reminds us of the cultural expectations and settings of such genres (they are not arbitrary one-off productions created by individuals in a cultural vacuum) and has been used in a number of valuable studies of African forms (for example, Haring 1994). The term is not without its problems, however. It still sometimes carries the implication that the topic so described is "old," is shared equally by everyone, and/or has arisen from "the community" in some "natural" nonpolemical way; its use can therefore lead the unwary researcher into a number of probably unsupported assumptions. *Tradition* is also often envisaged as something precious and deeply rooted. Thus, when participants and/or analysts

class something as part of *tradition*, this can sometimes be less a cool analytic assessment than an (implicit) personal evaluation—one that might be misleading, furthermore, as demonstrated in the research into the processes through which *traditions* are created or maintained in specific historical conditions to fit particular interests or values. Statements about *tradition* are often intertwined with emotive questions of national or group identity, so here too a detached assessment can be difficult. If not used cautiously, the term thus sometimes distracts from other equally interesting issues for investigation, like a genre's changes over time, its differential relation to specific interest groups, or its degree of openness to individual creativity.

Folklore and its various derivatives (*folk art, folktales, folksongs, folk narrative*, etc.) form another influential cluster of terms, plentifully illustrated in this volume. Nowadays, these substantially coincide with the field studied under the label of oral literature. For while *folklore* is sometimes understood in the broad sense of all forms of orally transmitted tradition, including material culture, its central emphasis has commonly been on verbal genres. As such, it has long inspired the study of forms that might otherwise have remained hidden to scholarship, resulting in colossal efforts in collecting and analyzing narratives, poetry, song, riddles, and proverbs in much the same way as under the head of oral literature. However, in the past, the two sets of terminology have carried somewhat different overtones. Earlier work under the rubric of *folklore* was often in the antiquarian style, amassing extensive texts with little analysis. The term occasionally still carries echoes of its original evolutionist focus on survivals, communal creation, and/or the rural and unlettered "folk." Apparently, new or topical forms or those created by individuals that had not yet "sunk into tradition" were, for a time, eschewed by those using the folklore terminology (for example, Dorson 1972), thus making *oral literature* the preferred term for those interested in such aspects of African cultures. However, these older associations of folklore, while occasionally still surfacing, are now rejected by leading folklorists, who normally follow a broader definition of the folk and actively pursue questions about individual creativity, modern forms, and urban as well as rural contexts.

Verbal art is another often-used term, summarized in Bascom's classic article as "a convenient and appropriate term for folktales, myths, legends, proverbs, riddles, and other "literary forms" (1955, 245). Substantial work has been conducted under this stimulating concept, which usually also covers songs and poems, together with verbal processes like naming, rhetoric, or tongue twisters. It tends to highlight aesthetic aspects and challenges the (sometimes) limited focus of oral literature on lengthy textually articulated forms by its attention to small-scale spoken arts. It thus facilitates the treatment of all forms of verbal art together while avoiding the loaded associations of the term *oral*. The cost is the loss of parallels with literary approaches, so some researchers still prefer *oral literature*, particularly for analysing "literary" genres like heroic poetry or lengthy narratives. If taken literally, *verbal art* implies a limitation to *words*, but most scholars using the term are now also sensitive to nonverbal aspects of performance.

"Performance" is another key concept, leading to the popularity of terms like *performed art, performed genres, performance literature*, and so on. Such terms usefully alert us to the multiplex processes by which oral literary forms are circulated and realized, rather than focussing just on the "products" or the texts (see Okpewho 1990). This terminology thus challenges the model of the essentially verbal, one-line, and single-voice basis sometimes read into the term *literature*, by raising questions about the other elements—and participants—in the performance event as a whole and bringing African practices within the now-flourishing transdisciplinary field of performance studies.

A more recently developed concept is that of "popular culture." This raises interesting issues. It has some advantages over arguably backward-looking terms like *oral tradition, folklore,* or even *oral literature*, looking to new forms and technologies that are of immediate interest to people today, not least to young people (see, for example, Barber 1996, Furniss 1996). It emphasises the new, not the old, draws attention to everyday, not just "traditional" settings, avoids the temptations of romantic nostalgia, and widens the focus into variegated media, including the mass media, and into (among others) the musical, artifactual, theatrical, and choreographic dimensions of communication and expression. The term perhaps has limitations too. Forms regarded as older or more elitist may get ignored, and a focus on mass media and mass audience sometimes edges out studies of less visible forms. Another influential trend among some (not all) scholars using the term is to set an ideological delimitation for its application in relation to social class and power, or to look almost exclusively to issues of class, gender, or ethnicity, thus turning attention away from the aesthetic attributes analyzed under other terminologies.

Given these problems, some avoid aiming for an overarching term at all and instead turn either to (arguably) less-loaded terms like *prose, poetry, song, oral texts*; to more precise words for particular genres or practices; or to the native terms themselves. There is much to be said for specific and localized terms. They avoid imposing outsiders' terminology, open the door to new combinations and practices that take us beyond the limiting oral/written dichotomy, and bypass what some still regard as colonialist terminological dominance; *some* local terminology will, in any case, be needed for any detailed work on African literatures and arts. On the other hand, folklorists, anthropologists, and linguists alike tend to share a commitment to the values of translation and of a comparative perspective on humankind so as to complement and transcend the divisions between cultures for the mutual enrichment of both sides. To avoid parochialism, some cross-cultural terms will probably continue to be sought and used.

Building on the Concept of Oral Literature

With all its controversies and competing terminologies, an approach to African oral texts and performances in terms of "literature" still has the valuable advantage of linking into the spectrum of perspectives within literary studies more generally. Which of those many perspectives turn out to be most fruitful depends on both the analyst and the nature of the specific subject under study. But the important—if obvious—point is the availability of numerous *alternative* perspectives. Given the earlier picture of African forms as essentially simple or artless, this is worth stressing. By now, it is acknowledged that, no more than for conventional written literatures, can African oral literatures (plural rather than singular) be fully comprehended by simplex expla-

nations. Their rich multiplicities can respond to analysis from a whole series of competing or overlapping literary perspectives.

Thus, the insights and controversies developed in, for example, structuralist, poststructuralist, feminist, psychological, historicist, narratological, or postcolonial approaches to literature can equally be applied to oral literature. So too can the various theories inspired by Marxist or by postmodernist and "cultural studies" perspectives on literature and culture. The study of African forms also both benefits from, and contributes to, comparative work, drawing on such concepts as intertextuality, reader-reception interactions, genre, "discourse," power, ideology, meaning, imagination, textuality; the significance of social attributes like gender, age, or locality; or the "poetics" and politics of texts. It can interact with long-debated issues such as how to define the boundaries of literature or of art, the relation between individual originality and tradition, or the essential nature and role of literature. There are perhaps special problems about how to delimit literature when it is oral and thus not differentiated through the demarcating symbol of writing, perhaps with no unambiguous divide between lengthy performed genres at one end and, at the other, minor forms of verbal art, short textual nodes, or everyday but arguably poetic salutations, witticisms, or anecdotes. But this issue itself is now being linked into the increasing recognition of the ideological, situational, and relative nature of the borders that are or have been drawn around the term *literature* more generally.

The oral, or performed, qualities of much African literature can also invoke challenging issues and a range of possible perspectives. There are questions, for example, about the processes of composition, "communicative events," or the mechanisms for dissemination and representation. By now many theorists are sensitive to the multiplicity rather than uniformity of the "oral": a complex and differentiated cluster of features, realized differently in different contexts and genres and interacting differentially with other media. The arts and settings of performance also raise questions for debate. How far, for example, is a prime focus on the lead performer or on the words (as in many traditional literary approaches) realistic in the face of performance features like music, dance, auditory, and vocal qualities, kinesic features, visual aspects, multivocality, communicative setting, multiple performers/participants, or the active role of audiences? Are written transcriptions and translations still acceptable for representing these performance features, given the increasing availability of other media besides the written word? Does the concept of "performance literature" have implications for literary theory more generally (see Gerstle and Hermans 2000-)? Many scholars are currently turning towards more intensive investigation and debate about the active, multidimensional and nonneutral *processes* by which literary forms—written as well as oral—are both produced and studied.

New developments in information technology raise further issues, extending scholars' vision beyond written or transcribed words-on-a-page to other media of expression and leading to an increasing appreciation of the "materiality" of texts. There are new questions too about the nature of "text." Once seen as something fixed, bounded, and stable, the experience of "soft" computer text has uncovered issues about malleability, relativity, and nonboundedness (issues that will actually cause little surprise to those acquainted with oral literature).

These varied questions provide a meeting point between the kinds of issues long of interest to students of oral literatures and those now treated in, for example, media studies, literary theory, performance studies, or popular culture. The informed study of African oral literatures has much not just to learn from but also to contribute to the comparative international study of literature in the widest sense of that term, not least in its insight into the significance of processual, multimodal, and performance dimensions, the problematics of textuality, and the role of active—and heterogeneous—participants. Indeed, it could be claimed that some recent transdisciplinary developments are merely ways in which other academics are now beginning to catch up with established insights in the study of African oral literature and performed arts.

Conclusion

None of the terminologies or approaches can be applied in any mechanical way to the African forms analyzed and celebrated in this volume. The final choice must be for individual scholars, weighing up the costs and benefits in the light of particular genres, settings, questions, or theoretical aims, while, at the same time, recognizing the complexity of a subject matter that is too dynamic, subtle, and multifaceted for single-line dogmatic reductionism. Contemporary analyses thus need to—and increasingly do—take account of the insights and challenges summed up in the many contending terminologies and perspectives. *Tradition* and *folklore* remind us that literary genres, whether oral or written, are not just the asocial creation of isolated individuals, and that artistry may not lie in words alone. *Verbal art* and *performance* usefully direct us to the performed qualities of art and warn against confining our view just to verbalisation or high art forms. *Popular culture* brings in a wider range of media and new developments in the present, challenging elitist and backward-looking preconceptions. *Oral literature* focuses attention on aesthetic, literary, and personal facets, which have sometimes been obscured in other terminologies as well as in the more blinkered prejudices of an earlier era. Above all, it brings the analysis of oral forms, whether from Africa or elsewhere, into the framework of other studies of those accepted riches of human expression described as literature, both drawing from and enlarging those studies.

References

Andrzejewski, B. W. 1985. Oral Literature. In *Literatures in African Languages. Theoretical Issues and Sample Surveys*, ed. B. W. Andrzejewski, S. Pilaszewicz, and W. Tyloch, Cambridge: Cambridge University Press, and Warszawa: Wiedza Powszechna.

Barber, Karin, ed. 1996. *Readings in African Popular Culture*. London: James Currey.

Barber, Karin. and Farias, P. F. de M., eds. 1989. *Discourse and Its Disguises: The Interpretation of African Oral Texts*. Birmingham, U.K.: Centre of West African Studies, Birmingham University African Studies Series 1.

Bascom, W. R. 1955. Verbal Art. *Journal of American Folklore* 68: 243–52.

Ben-Amos, D., ed. 1987. *African Art and Literature*. Special Issue, *Word and Image* 3 no. 3.

Bukenya, Austin. 1994. *Understanding Oral Literature*. Nairobi: Nairobi University Press.

Chadwick, H. M. and N. K. Chadwick. 1932–1940. *The Growth of Literature*. 3 vols. Cambridge: Cambridge University Press.

Dorson, R. M. ed. 1972. *African Folklore*. Bloomington: Indiana University Press.

Finnegan, Ruth. 1970, 1977. *Oral Literature in Africa*. Oxford: Clarendon Press; Nairobi: Oxford University Press.

Finnegan, Ruth. 1992. Reflecting Back on *Oral Literature in Africa*: Some Reconsiderations after 21 Years. *Southern African Journal of African Languages* 12 no. 2: 39–47.

Furniss, Graham. 1996. *Poetry, Prose and Popular Culture in Hausa*. Edinburgh: University of Edinburgh Press.

Furniss, Graham, and Liz Gunner, eds. 1995. *Power, Marginality and African Oral Literature*. Cambridge: Cambridge University Press.

Gerstle, Drew and Hermans, Theo. 2000-. Reports on Research Projects at AHRB Centre for Asian and African Literatures, University of London. http://www.soas.ac.uk/literatures

Görög-Karady, V, ed. 1982. *Genres, Forms, Meanings: Essays in African Oral Literature*. Oxford: JASO.

Gunner, Liz., ed 1994. *Politics and Performance. Theatre, Poetry and Sang in Southern Africa*. Bloomington: Indiana University Press.

Haring, Lee, ed. 1994. *African Oral Traditions*. Special issue, *Oral Tradition* 9, 1.

Kaschula, Russell H., ed. 2001. *African Oral Literature: Functions in Contemporary Contexts*. Claremont: New Africa Books.

Okpewho, Isidore, ed. 1990. *The Oral Performance in Africa*. Ibadan: Spectrum Books.

Okpewho, Isidore. 1992. *African Oral Literature: Backgrounds, Character, and Continuity*. Bloomington: Indiana University Press.

RUTH FINNEGAN

See also **Electronic Media and Oral Traditions; Folk Tales; Oral Literary Research in Africa; Oral Narrative; Oral Performance and Literature; Oral Traditions; Orality and Literacy in Africa; Performance in Africa; Popular Culture; Prose Narratives; Radio and Television Dramas; Theater: African Popular Theater; Typology and Performance in the Study of Prose Narratives in Africa; Verbal Arts**

ORAL NARRATIVE

The utility of the term oral narrative is based in its apparent neutrality in designating a story or narrative that is spoken rather than written or read. There are numerous types of narrative that need to be examined in order to understand the range of this term and how it applies to African verbal art forms.

A story can be conceived as a string of words that conveys events having a beginning, a middle, and an end. A common type of story is found in the orally performed narrative, describing events that move a character or characters through one state of existence into another. Narratologists would generally depict these stages as a movement from ignorance to knowledge, from poverty to wealth, from single to married status, from youth to adulthood, from life to death, or variations of these changes of state or status. These developments are at the heart of almost all known stories, from the briefest tales to the longest epics. In written literature, the short story, novel, and other post industrial prose genres adhere to these basic elements of narrative.

Narratives can be comprised of everyday speech interactions, as basic as a lone person telling another what happened that day or at some time in his or her life. Some societies preserve their significant historical information in primarily oral formats, with historians or even non specialists being able to recount important events and characters from memory. These narratives are often in the form of heroic actions and/or significant migrations from one place to another. Individuals are able to tell their own life stories in the form of narratives of achievements and/or failures, and these, in turn, become a part of local or family histories.

Generically, oral narratives come in many forms. These have historically been labeled folktales, legends, fables, parables, *cante fables*, myths, epics, histories, origin tales, and so on. In the study of oral societies, it is clear that each society has named its narratives and that these terms are often not exactly equivalent to the generic terms provided by outside scholars. For example, the Bemba people of Zambia distinguish two types of imaginative narrative: *ulushimi* (*inshimi*, pl.) and *umulumbe* (*imilumbe*, pl.). Though both types of tale are similar in many ways, the former often contains a song or songs and is mostly told to children, while the latter usually does not contain songs and is most often told to adults. The categories are familiar to the Bemba, although there is also no great care taken to keep the classifications "pure," in any sense of enforcement of rules of performance or strictures against certain people telling the respective stories.

Narratives are also classified by the context in which they are performed. For example, certain narratives focus on past kings or spirits who are important to a society. If they are recounted at special occasions, sometimes as a part of a ritual, they may be seen to have religious or even curative significance. Certain forms of divination, such as the Yoruba Ifa system, include narratives or proverbs in their body of knowledge that are then linked into the process of establishing the appropriate responses to specific cases. Some tales of heroes or hunters may be linked to ceremonies of purification for initiation rites or specific preventative measures, such as before a hunt or a particularly hazardous journey. In post colonial times, these journeys may include travel to a distant town to work in mines, industry, or agriculture, or even wayfarers going abroad for study or commercial reasons.

Sacred or secular, the narratives often have similar plots and activities. In some cases, the same story may take its particular value from the characters involved. In one set of tales, the characters may be animals, and all their actions, attitudes, and accomplishments may be simply seen as humorous and somehow removed from real human concerns. If the same plots and actions are carried out by human characters, the tales might be seen as more important or significant in their relationship to the world of people. Even some of the most intricate or important tales are subject to repetition by anyone who has heard them. In fact, the continuity of some narratives over time depends on this kind of transmittal and repetition.

Africa is particularly replete with narratives that treat the adventures of trickster characters. Though societies from other parts of the world sometimes produce stories centered on trickster activities, many have inherited the stories from the African diaspora. Trickster narratives found in the Caribbean, South America, and in the southern United States can be identified as having African origins. There is a Native American tradition of trickster stories, but these are often quite different from the African narratives in terms of characteristics of the trickster and the tone and tenor of the tales. Nonetheless, African tricksters tend to be small, clever creatures, such as Kwaku Ananse, the spider of Akan tales; Sungura and Kalulu, the hares of East African and Zambian narratives, respectively; Mantis, the San

trickster; or the tortoise of several Nigerian traditions. The character of the trickster, the small, clever, and, at times, amoral figure, is often diluted a bit and found in the person of the young child who is beset by ogres or brutal villains in other kinds of narrative.

Narrative in Africa reaches a particularly complex, highly textured form in the performance of epic, which involves a combination of narrative, poetry, and song; the epic is often sung or chanted to musical accompaniment. The content of these narratives is usually historical, at least in part, and focuses on a crucial period in the society in question's past.

References

Bascom, William. Oba's Ear: A Yoruba Myth in Cuba and Brazil. In *African Folklore in the New World*, ed. D. J. Crowley. Austin: University of Texas Press.

Cancel, Robert. 1989. *Allegorical Speculation in an Oral Society: The Tabwa Narrative Tradition*. Berkeley: University of California Press.

Okpewho, Isidore. 1983. *Myth in Africa: A Study of Its Aesthetics and Cultural Relevance*. Cambridge: Cambridge University Press, 1983.

ROBERT CANCEL

See also **Folktales; Legends: East Africa; Myths**

ORAL PERFORMANCE AND LITERATURE

Oral performance and literature are often regarded in contrast to one another. The relationship between the two types of discourse is a complex one and depends in many cases on the researcher's interest and what he or she is seeking. On the one hand, studies from the 1960s onward have been exploring the concept of "orality" as opposed to "literacy." On the other hand, there are many qualities of narrative, form, and imagery that clearly overlap between the spoken and written word.

It is important to emphasize the differences between oral performance and literature because, for many years, the former was seen as the progenitor (and less "advanced" relation) of the latter. This relationship is clear in the earliest evidence of literary activity, from the Dead Sea Scrolls, to the Epic of Gilgamesh, the Old Testament, and Homeric epic. At the same time, these seminal works posed problems in form and style that were only answered when scholars began to see them as products of oral societies. Qualities often seen as flaws in contemporary literature—repetition, parallel constructions, episodic structure, rambling speeches, or apparent digressions—were common in these early texts.

Work begun by Milman Parry in the 1920s, and later carried on by Albert Lord and others, compared a living epic tradition from Yugoslavia with the remnants of the oral epic tradition of the Homeric corpus. The similarities were impressive enough to allow scholars to solve some of the oldest questions about Homer's compositions. The repetition, digressions, even the obvious errors due to losing one's train of thought, were explained by the dictates of narrating and composing poetic narrative as the performer went along. Methods of composition were discovered that were based upon the rhythmic activities of bardic instruments such as the lute. Oration, furthermore, came to be seen as a living, interactive art form. (Lord 1960)

Later scholarship by Walter Ong (1967) pointed to similar qualities of composition and performance in other literary works, in particular, the Bible, and went further to hypothesize an entirely different sensory mode of perceiving the world. Oral societies were based in an orally and aurally dictated environment that was three-dimensional and founded on sound and its various emotional/intellectual properties. The literate world had evolved into a visual culture, depending on the private and isolating environment of reading and writing to keep history, store knowledge, and even argue ideas. The oral world was a communal one, where ideas had to be voiced in order to be understood, argued, and perpetuated. The great orators were also among the most respected intellectuals, the most powerful people in society. In the literate world, ideas flowed in books and on paper, and they could be read repeatedly for understanding and critical examination. The spoken word was powerful, though vaporous. Once spoken, it disappeared. It is difficult for someone to say the exact same thing more than one time. Therefore, ideas were subject to perpetuation only if they were spoken over and over again.

Some scholars argued that orally composed and performed narratives were, in fact, not prose at all. Tedlock (1977) and his contemporaries in the field of ethnopoetics contended, that prose is a product of literacy. What oral performers of narrative did was much closer to what literary scholars call poetry. The rhythms of speech, the types of imagery, the power of the spoken word, and the close proximity of song to speech in oral performance all moved towards poetic composition rather than prose. This is a particularly valuable way to discuss the dynamics of performance, which often include many techniques and interactions that allow speech to approach song and body movements to approach dance.

Yet it is also important to acknowledge the elements of spoken narratives and poems that approach literary production. In imaginative narrative, there are crucial elements of plot, character, action, and theme that are linked to the appreciation of these performances. Some scholars acknowledge this vital connection by referring to the art forms as *oral literature*. Other scholars, treating mostly African verbal arts, who are wary of a certain degree of ethoncentricity intrinsic in even the term literature, choose to call the activity and its products *orature*. Both schools of thought explicitly acknowledge the equivalent processes of creativity in language, character development, intricacies of plot or structure, and related factors that go into orally performed narrative or poetry. Oral performance and literature employ symbolic forms that create metaphor and allegory. Both oral and written arts are potentially transformative in the ways they can move audiences/readers.

Early African writers, mission-educated and often working in their own languages, reproduced tales, proverbs, and riddles as subjects of their literary efforts. Although they lacked evidence of the dynamic oral spontaneity and verbal interactions between audience and performer, these works did, in an inadequate way, suggest the themes, characters, and concerns of African oral traditions.

Contemporary African writers, working in English and French, often include elements of oral traditions in their literature. In his novels, Nigerian Chinua Achebe has made the prov-

erb a key formal and thematic device of his art. Nigeria's Nobel laureate Wole Soyinka combines ideas from Yoruba myth, religion, song, and ritual within modernist frameworks in his plays, novels, and poems. In a controversial groundbreaking novel, Yambo Ouologuem, from Mali, uses a particularly sarcastic evocation of the traditional epic bard to set the sardonic tone of his novel *Le devoir de violence*. In their efforts to create an "African" literature, writers take a syncretic approach, selecting from several artistic traditions, oral and written.

References

Cancel, Robert. 1993. Literature in African Languages: Perspectives on Culture and Identity. In *A History of Twentieth-Century African Literature*, ed. Oyekan Owomoyela. Lincoln: University of Nebraska Press.

Finnegan, Ruth. 1992. *Oral Traditions and the Verbal Arts: A Guide to Research Practices*. New York: Routledge.

Lord, Albert B. 1960. *The Singer of Tales*. Cambridge, Mass.: Harvard University Press.

Ong, Walter J. 1967. *The Presence of the Word: Some Prolegomena for Cultural and Religious Studies*. Cambridge, Mass.: Harvard University Press.

Tedlock, Dennis. 1977. Toward an Oral Poetics. *New Literary History* 8: 507–19.

ROBERT CANCEL

See also **Gesture in African Oral Narrative; Oral Literature; Orality and Literacy in Africa**

ORAL PERFORMANCE DYNAMICS

Oral performance is the means by which numerous genres of verbal arts are externalized through the interaction between performer(s) and audience(s). There is no verbal art outside of performance. Storytelling, singing, formal orations of any type exist only in people's minds until they are spoken, shared. The techniques employed by performers and the context within which the performances occur comprise the dynamics of oral performance.

On one level, performance dynamics are linked to the methods or techniques the performer employs in externalizing the particular genre at any one time. A simple example of these techniques is the choice of demeanor by a storyteller or bardic performer of epic poems. This choice is often dictated by the individual's personality: serious or comical, authoritative or open to audience concerns. This demeanor is also influenced by the context of the performance: tied to an important ritual/festival, an informal gathering around a fire, a competitive situation between performers, and so forth. Both the qualities of the individual and the elements of context of performance are also mediated by the expectations of the audience. Do they know the performer and expect him or her to satisfy their expectations of style or technique? Does the context suggest a well-known performer should, for reasons of decorum, alter his or her approach in deference to the situation?

Looking more specifically at techniques that make up any one performer's style, certain elements can be catalogued. Does the performer prefer the lengthy exposition of certain commonly known kernels of imagery, plot, or character development, or is he or she prone to concise evocation that allows the audience to fill in details on their own, based on past performances? A simple example can be seen in the performance of the epic

Sunjata among the Mande people of the Gambia. One bard performed the epic in the framework of 1305 lines, while another extended the same basic plot and events into an exposition of 2065 lines (Innes 1974). Some people opt to chant rather than sing their performances, while others avoid the poetic genre entirely in favor of songless narratives or the more concise, more compact genres of proverb and riddle.

Another dimension of performance is the methods by which performers learn their skills and shape them into individual styles. Basically, performers learn in two ways: formal and informal. The latter is by far the most common for most types of oral performance. The most common genre of performance is probably song, and songs are sung at many occasions, from solemn rites to boisterous beer-drinking gatherings. Singers simply learn from hearing certain songs repeatedly sung over time. Since some individuals are creatively gifted or inspired, they become singers and composers of songs. A similar process holds true for storytellers, who learn tales by listening and participating in the various contexts that spur performances. Most storytellers have heard narratives performed since birth and begin by repeating tales, some going no further than telling the same few stories they know over and over. Other performers move to more intricate manipulation of tales by adding new scenes or episodes and altering them to fit certain occasions or conditions of performance.

The formal education of oral performers is not common in all African societies, but the instances of such education are not rare. Often this kind of education is dictated by the nature of the art form or genre. For example, the singer of Yoruba Ijala poetry often is apprenticed to an experienced bard. The apprenticeship begins with the student listening to and learning to repeat what the master sings. After a while, the student is allowed to perform in concert with the bard, singing along during performances. The final stage is reached when the student is allowed, or decides, to go out on his or her own (Okpewho 1992). This kind of training is most often tied to the more esoteric forms of oral traditions: genres such as divination, epic singing, forms that require instrumental accompaniment, or specialized ritual performances.

The question of audience response and interaction is vitally tied to the notion of performance dynamics. The oral performer must share the art, or there is no performance; and part of the sharing is in the response of the audience and the counter response of the performer. Some generic forms by definition require immediate and continual response. This includes songs that employ the well-known call-and-response pattern, in which the singer depends on a chorus to either repeat or augment the lyrics he or she sings. There are narrative genres that often employ antiphonal cooperation between storyteller and audience. The riddle and proverb genres depend almost entirely on responses to initial statements or problems set out by the performer. In fact, in these particular art forms, the distinction of who is a performer and who is the audience is almost completely blurred. Further, audiences respond to performers in widely varied ways. This again depends on the context of the situation and the relationship between the individuals involved. Sometimes audience support for the performer is strong and encouraging, egging him or her on with positive comments. On other occasions, the performer is discouraged from continuing in no uncertain terms.

Although the term *oral performance* suggests a verbal activity, there are important nonverbal techniques employed by performers. These are termed by some "histrionics," composed in part of gestures, mime, or the general acting out of portions of a narrative. Indeed, it is these very elements that create the greatest difference between a text of an oral performance and the actual event. Much can be communicated by the tone of voice given a particular piece of dialogue, or the acting out of activities in a tale. A written text is therefore a mere scenario, the equivalent of a script in a play or film, of the living performance.

References

Bauman, Richard. 1977. *Verbal Art as Performance*. Prospect Heights, Ill.: Waveland Press.

Ben-Amos, Dan. 1975. *Sweet Words: Storytelling Events in Benin*. Philadelphia: Institute for the Study of Human Issues.

Innes, Gordon. 1974. *Sunjata: Three Mandinka Versions*. London: School of Oriental and African Studies, University of London.

Okpewho, Isidore. *African Oral Literature: Backgrounds, Character, and Continuity*. Bloomington: Indiana University Press, 1992.

Scheub, Harold. 1971. Translation of Oral Narrative-performance to the Written Word, *Yearbook of Comparative and General Literature* 20: 28–36.

ROBERT CANCEL

See also **Dialogic Performances: Call-and-Response in African Narrating; Gesture in African Oral Narratives; Griots and Griottes; Typology and Performance; Silence**

ORAL TRADITIONS

This term is made up of two words. *Oral* is associated with the spoken or sung word, as well as the verbalization of sound in general. It is also associated with the reception of those sounds, that is, the aural activity of listeners. Modes of speaking and interacting verbally are often given the generic term *orality*. This term is often opposed to, or seen as the opposite of, *literacy*, the latter concept having to do with the written word.

Tradition has historically been employed by several scholarly disciplines. The word is most commonly used to refer to longterm practices and beliefs of groups of people. It was often contrasted to the notion of "modern" or contemporary practices. Therefore, when one spoke of a people's traditions, the implication was that these were practices located in the past that had persisted over time, somehow fixed in the social memory, and at times outlasting their practical relevance into the present. In early anthropological discourse and later folkloric designations, traditions were associated with the idea of "survivals" from antiquity.

Long seen as a product, the term *tradition* has come to be applied to processes since the later twentieth century. In ethnography and related disciplines, there is a current of thought that focuses on the ways tradition is continually created and adapted by contemporary, living cultures. Rather than static, fixed anomalies, traditions are considered to be linked to the activities that allow cultures to grow and change in order to perpetuate themselves. If the products of societies are the result of ongoing creation and transformation, both the products and their processes can be considered traditions.

When the words *oral* and *traditions* are therefore combined, the resulting term connotes the verbal arts of a society *and* the creative activities that surround their production. The range of oral traditions is therefore broad. It includes imaginative oral narrative, song, proverbs, riddles, and epics. It also designates the more "realistic" verbal genres such as history, personal narrative, formalized speech, and informal daily speech that employs tropes or standardized explanations. In all cases, the notion of transmission by performance and preservation in living memory are important elements of oral traditions.

These traditions conform to the tenets of verbal arts, whereby they must be performed in order to be experienced. They otherwise exist only in people's memories, until they are verbalized. This is not to say that the traditions are exclusively learned through memorization or internalization of the words and images that comprise the specific traditions. In fact, some sources of stories or histories may originate in books, radio broadcasts, films, or formal schools. The material is, however, transformed into oral knowledge when it is presented as part of a larger store of ideas, imagery, or forms.

Most genres of African oral traditions generally conform to the categories found in other parts of the world. One form of oral tradition, which today is not often found outside of Africa, is the epic narrative. These long, intricate poems, intended for performance, have been recorded in West, central, and East Africa. Generally, they are tales of individual heroes who founded states or created new social orders. Most recorded African epics are sung or chanted to the accompaniment of music. They are, therefore, impressive combinations of narrative, poem, and song.

A genre that exists on the border between epic and poetry is the praise poem, which, in some cases, can reach epic length, but sometimes does not have the linear continuity of a narrative. This genre is found in many areas of Africa, most notably in southern Africa.

Oral traditions perform several societal functions. On the one hand, they constitute living representations of significant cultural information: history, values, instructions, and ritual activities. On the other hand, they are a dynamic form of entertainment based in the development and appreciation of artistic skills of speech, song, mime, gesture, dance, and instrumental music. Indeed, the elements of social function and aesthetic pleasure combine in oral traditions to make a highly effective network of cultural expression, educating and entertaining at the same time. The blurred line between artifice and reality is the space in which individuals create their statements on cultural issues, confirming or challenging old and new assumptions, depending on their respective points of view. These ongoing statements and debates are the means by which the culture renews, reaffirms, and regenerates itself in words and music.

References

Finnegan, Ruth. 1992. *Oral Traditions and the Verbal Arts: A Guide to Research Practices.* London: Routledge.

Okpewho, Isidore. 1979. *The Epic in Africa: Toward a Poetics of the Oral Performance.* New York: Columbia University Press.

———. 1992. *African Oral Literature: Backgrounds, Character and Continuity.* Bloomington: Indiana University Press.

Ong, Walter. 1982. *Orality and Literacy: The Technologies of the Word.* London: Methuen.

ROBERT CANCEL

See also **Prose Narratives; Southern African Oral Traditions**

ORAL TRADITIONS AND ORAL HISTORIOGRAPHY

As recently as fifty years ago, some western historians considered African historiography nothing better than ethnohistory or folk history, worthy of the attention of anthropologists, but not of professional historians, due to an assumption that the African continent still lay in a prehistoric period lacking writing systems, civilization, or a proper sense of history. Such historians mistook the predominance of oral cultures and traditions and the close relationship of African historical sources to folklore to mean a lack of historical consciousness.

Indeed, African historical sources are predominantly oral traditions, reported through time as part of the knowledge, literature, language, and cultural resources of communities. Yet other sources are contemporary traditions remembered as part of the personal experiences of people living within a generation. Professional historians classify this second category of oral sources as oral history. These oral sources represent the baseline, internally derived data that carry the ideology, philosophy, history, and worldview of communities. Through the multidisciplinary method, historians are able to apply the insights of history, historical linguistics, archeology, and the resources of other disciplines to enrich the evidence of oral traditions, oral history, and folklore.

Africa has not always been a continent more reliant on orality than the written word. Ancient Egypt was a primary center of origin of the art of writing, and parts of northern Africa and northeastern Africa have known varieties of writing over many centuries. The arrival of the Arabs in the seventh century brought Islamic scholarship and a culture of writing extending from North Africa across the Sahara to the western, central, and eastern Sudan, and from across the Indian Ocean to the Swahili coast of East Africa. Western Christian traditions of writing spread inland from the coasts of West, Central, southern, and East Africa starting in the late fifteenth century. But local and indigenous forms of writing have also been reported for some of these regions.

Oral historiography has not been an exclusively African mode of historical expression, nor does oral tradition operate to the exclusion of writing. On the contrary, oral tradition has been a universal form of historical consciousness, which usually operated alongside writing. This was, indeed, the case in ancient Egypt, and in ancient Greece, a secondary center of innovation in the development of writing. When Herodotus visited Egypt (c. 454 BCE), he collected oral traditions from the priests, who were also the custodians of the archives. The Greek father of the western historiographical tradition was himself a practitioner of oral tradition and oral history. Historians of Africa use historical footprints wherever they can find them, and in whatever form: oral traditions, oral history, folklore, ethnography, the linguistic record, archaeological artifacts, and other sources of evidence.

Practice

The antiquity of the use of oral traditions in Africa reported by Herodotus is confirmed by the record of its use in practice. Manetho the priest (c. 285–246 BCE) wrote the first extant history of ancient Egypt from hieroglyphic records and from oral traditions. His chronology of Egypt, based on pharaonic dynasties, has remained the basis of the discipline of Egyptology. Manetho was followed in the Christian era by a number of fathers of the early African church, including St. Augustine of Hippo (CE 430). The Islamic tradition, with its developed systems of *hadith* and *tarikh* (traditions and formal history), quickly produced contributions to the recording of African oral traditions, and the construction of histories such as Ibn Batutu (1303–1368), Leo Africanus (c. 1494–1552), Ahmad Baba of Timbuktu (1556–1527), Al-Sa'di (1596–1656), Ibn Fartuwa of Borno, and others. The Islamic tradition did, in fact, produce a great many local historians in the western, central, and eastern Sudan, and in East Africa, and northern Africa. In some of these regions, the chronicle or *tarikh* became a preferred form of recording local traditions and interpreting them in an Islamic context. The Kano Chronicle of northern Nigeria is among the most celebrated, coming down in written form from the nineteenth century.

The Christian tradition gave birth to a great many written interpretations of African oral traditions from the late nineteenth century, after the missionary effort took root. Many of these efforts by African converts were first done in local languages, and later translated into European languages. The principal examples of these are, from East Africa: Sir Apolo Kagwa (*The Kings of Buganda*, 1901, and others), John William Nyakatura (*The Kings of Bunyoro-Kitara*, 1939), and from West Africa, Carl Christian Reindorf (*The History of the Gold Coast and the Asante*, 1898/1966), Samuel Johnson (*History of the Yorubas*, 1897/1921), Jacob Egharevba (*A Short History of Benin*, 1934/1960), and Akiga Sai (*The Tive Tribe*, 1939/1965). In the same tradition were the prolific works of Alexis Kagame of Rwanda in Central Africa, and the writings of Solomon Plaatjie and others of South Africa, Boubou Hama of Niger, and Hampate-Ba of Mali.

In the 1950s, a number of remarkable professional historians, trained in western universities, took up the cause of oral traditions in mainstream academic historiography. Kenneth Onwuka Dike of Nigeria founded the Historical Society of Nigeria, and preached the validity of oral traditions as historical evidence. His classic work, *Trade and Politics in the Niger Delta, 1800–1885* (1956), although grounded in archival sources, provided support for the complementary use of oral traditions. Another Nigerian, Saburi O. Biobaku, used oral traditions more rigorously to support written documents in his *The Egba and their Neighbors* (1957). The most thorough use of oral traditions for the reconstruction of history was carried out by Bethwell A. Ogot of Kenya in *A History of the Southern Luo: Migrations and Settlement* (1967). These African founding fathers were followed by a crop of other scholars, including K. Y. Daaku of Ghana, Isaria Kimambo of Tanzania, and D. T. Niane of Guinea, who recorded the epic *Sundiata* from the griots of the western Sudan region of West Africa.

Crucial support came from western scholars, the most influential being the theoretical and substantive work of Jan Vansina, beginning with his publications in the 1960s, including *Oral Tradition: A Study in Historical Methodology* (1961, 1965). He became even more effective as the trainer of a whole generation of graduate students at the University of Wisconsin. The other significant theoretical publication was Daniel F. McCall's *African in Time Perspective: A Discussion of Historical Reconstruction from Unwritten Sources* (1964). We note that a great deal of the early studies of oral traditions were based on recordings or collections made by European colonial anthropologists administrators, missionaries, or visitors. In Nigeria, the most viable source were the so-called Intelligence Reports of the 1930s, created by the colonial authorities to provide information on the history and government of various communities.

Theory

Vansina integrated the general advocacy and practice of oral tradition in Africa into a systematic theory of its use in the construction of professional academic history according to the rules of mainstream western historiography. He worked from his own research in the field in the Kuba kingdom of Congo and among other communities in Central Africa, and from earlier collections of oral traditions going back into the past. He defined oral traditions as "testimonies of the past which are deliberately transmitted from mouth to mouth," and distinguished them from other accounts, that had not been transmitted over a period of time, being eyewitness accounts, rumors, and so forth, had not been accepted into the corpus of community traditions. These have now received the technical title of *oral history*. Vansina, thus, laid down the essential elements of oral traditional methodology, especially for centralized states similar to those in Central Africa, from which he directly derived his theories.

Some of Vansina's students, his critics, and others working in other parts of Africa provided complementary insights that led to elaborations and revisions of his theories in detail. In particular, the consideration of oral traditions as "testimonies" or simple evidence or source material and the raconteurs or narrators of oral traditions as mere "informants" had to be revised. Oral traditions had to be seen as interpreted and not innocently transmitted so that they were histories in their own right and their narrators were historians rather than informants. Vansina eventually embodied these and other insights in his *Oral Tradition as History* (1985).

Case Study

The Niger Delta region of Nigeria is occupied by a variety of ethnic communities, but predominantly by the Ijo. Their culture reserves a place of honor for elders, the oldest male being selected as village head in the western delta. Among the eastern delta city-states, special ancestral houses cover the graves of lineage founders and kings. These ancestral houses become virtual museums for historical relics, regalia, and other memorabilia of the ancestors, including, among the Kalabari, sculptural figures representing specific ancestors, named *duein fubara* or "foreheads of the dead."

Among the generally noncentralized Ijo communities of the Niger Delta, knowledge of the past was not considered the preserve of any specialist, expert, or court historian, except for elders, priests, and drummers, who had to learn the drum praise poetry (*kule*), the equivalent of the Yoruba *oriki*. The general knowledge view of oral traditions among the Ijo reflects the multiple forms in which historical information came down from the past, so that the oral traditions were not strictly demarcated from folklore or oral literature. Indeed, oral historical narratives were rendered with the same opening and closing gambits or formulae as were used in the telling of folk tales. As well, folk tales and historical narratives were both termed *egberi*, "stories," only differentiated by the modifiers *lugu*, and *elemu kura*, that is, "stories of the imagination," and "stories of former times." Yet the genres cannot be completely separated since there were also historical folk tales. Songs (*numo*), riddles (*duu*), and proverbs (*kabu*) were accepted as repositories of history. Thus, a corpus of riddles among the Nembe are known to recount the history of the ancient community of Onyoma and of its mythical priest king, Onyoma-pere.

Prospects

The growing sophistication of studies in African oral traditions and historiography can gain from further deepening and expansion of its multidisciplinary bases. Historians have yet to take up Richard M. Dorson's invitation (1972) to integrate into their work some of the standard methods of folkloristics. Progress in Africa is stunted by poor funding of the universities, and in the West, by the low priority accorded African studies in recent times.

The Western cult of theory appears to be currently exercised, among others, by postmodernism, keen to challenge and attack what proponents term the totalizing metanarratives of the mainstream, without presenting alternative constructions of African historiography. The attention seems still to be fixed on methodology and questions of the truth value of oral traditions. African historians, on the other hand, continue to be exercised by the practical problems of constructing community histories, and, therefore, with the problems of dialogue between the academy and the people, and with the ideology and philosophy of the practice of oral traditions and historiography on the ground.

References

Alagoa, E. J. 1966. Oral Tradition among the Ijo of the Niger Delta. *Journal of African History* VII, no. 3:405–19.

———. 1968. The Use of Oral Literary Data for History: Examples from Niger Delta Proverbs. *Journal of American Folklore* 81: 235–42.

———. 1968. Songs as Historical Data: Examples from the Niger Delta. *Research Review* (Legon) 5, no. 1: 1–16.

———. 1971. Ijo Drumlore. *African Notes* (Ibadan) 6, no. 2: 63–71.

———. 1975. Riddles in Nembe. Oduma (Port Harcourt) 2, no. 2: 17–21.

———., ed. 1990. *Oral Tradition and Oral History in Africa and the Diaspora: Theory and Practice*. Lagos: Centre for Black and African Arts and Civilization.

———. 1994. An African Philosophy of History in the Oral tradition. Paths towards the Past: African Historical Essays in Honor of Jan Vansina, ed. Robert Harms, Joseph C. Miller, David S. Newbury, Michelle D. Wagner. Atlanta: African Studies Association Press.

Vansina, Jan. 1960. Recording the oral history of the Bakuba, I. Methods. *Journal of African History* I, no. 1: 45–53.

———. 1961 [1965]. Oral Tradition: A Study in Historical Methodology. Chicago.

———. 1985. Oral Tradition as History. Madison.

E.J. ALAGOA

See also **Myths; Oral Traditions**

ORAL TRADITION: ORAL HISTORY AND ZAMBIA

Mbili salala, or *mbili sagona*, is a Zambian proverb that translates as "history does not sleep," meaning that explanations of the past are often revised based on the contingencies of contemporary events. This proverb speaks about the dynamics of knowledge in cultures of orality. It also speaks about the consequences of ecological conditions of radical scarcity, characteristic of much of the central African plateau. In this part of Africa, low population density and intense competition for survival drives a traditional political system based on the competing interests of myriad alliances. It is a politics of contingency, which authorizes revisions of political alliances to keep pace with strategic decisions about resources. Old alliances are undermined to make way for new ones, and stories of the past, which must justify new political relationships also are revised to cover up the old and reveal the new.

The proverb "history does not sleep" identifies history telling as a form of political argumentation. This is a characteristic of explanations of the past observed by scholars on the central African plateau since at least 1951 when Ian Cunnison wrote about the contingent qualities of *ilyashi* as a northern Zambian (Bemba) idiom for "history telling." Cunnison described *ilyashi* as carrying connotations of "gossip," "affairs," and "stories, as well as "history." The same is true of the term *mbili* in the Nyanja-based languages. This does not mean that past historical circumstances have no value to people who recall them, but that public determination of their value is a political process.

In rural Zambia, investigation into the past is often referred to as "digging deep" (*kukumba pansi*), a description of an activity that looks to resurrect old circumstances in argumentation about new circumstances. In rural Zambia, it is also said that people only remember what is useful. In the sedimented layering of passing time, things not useful are forgotten, tossed aside like rubbish from the village that is tossed into bordering fields. Recovery of what was not useful yesterday, if it is decided it might be of use today, must be dug up from the debris accumulated in village fields. The verb "to remember" (*kukumbukila*, literally, "to dig for us") comes from a practiced analogy between memory and the verb "to dig" (*kukumba*).

There are approximately seventy-three ethnic political groups in Zambia, each with its own distinct identity and history of origins. What one hears of those seventy-three distinct histories in the palaces of Zambia's chiefs, however, is less determined by events in the remote past than by contemporary political circumstances.

These idiomatic practices relating to memory and history telling in Zambia resonate with Walter Ong's discussion on the psychodynamics of oral language practices and knowledges of radical contingency in *Orality and Literacy* (1989).

References

Cunnison, Ian. 1951. *History on the Luapula*. Rhodes-Livingstone Papers no. 21. Manchester University Press.

———. 1963. Kazembe and the Arabs to 1870. In *History of Central African Peoples*. Lusaka: Rhodes-Livingston Institute.

Marks, Stuart. 1976. *Large Mammals and a Brave People*. Seattle: University of Washington Press.

Ong, Walter. 1989. *Orality and Literacy*. London: Routledge.

Strickland, Bradford. 1995. *Knowledge, Power, and Agency Among the Kunda of Eastern Zambia*, Ph.D. dissertation, University of North Carolina.

BRADFORD STRICKLAND

See also **Identity and Folklore: The Kunda; Oral Traditions**

ORALITY AND LITERACY IN AFRICA

The pair of terms *orality* and *literacy* is used less to denote a definition of two phenomena than an area of debate based on a concern with the implications of technology for societies. At the heart of the extensive literature in the field lies a set of questions about whether technologies of communication have intellectual consequences. Do particular systems of handling information affect thought and social organization? In debates on orality and literacy, this broad agenda of questions is explored in relation to how literate technologies interact with, and are shaped by, oral systems of handling information.

The lineage of these debates is generally traced to the work of Milman Parry and Albert Lord on the nature of Homeric epics. Drawing on fieldwork among South Slavic practitioners of oral heroic poetry, this work established a theory of oral composition that happens in and around formulas and formulaic devices. These are the mnemonic kernels that performers activate and from which they unfurl their oral texts. This idea of formulaic composition came to be extremely influential and prompted many studies into the performance context and formulaic "being" or oral literary genres from a range of different societies.

In some instances, generalized claims about the universality of an oral style were made. Such claims suggested an invariable relationship between modality (medium of delivery) and stylistic characteristics. If there was an oral style, then there could also be entire thought worlds shaped around oral poetic formulas. With the introduction of writing and printing, such modes of thought would shift to produce new ways of thinking and forms of social organization. In its cruder manifestations, these ideas suggest a "great divide" between oral and literate societies. These dualities of orality and literacy, in turn, superseded others like developed/underdeveloped, magical/scientific, *Western*/non-*Western*, and so on. In such scenarios, it often appeared that literacy *by itself* was capable of bringing about changes in government, political ideas, economic development, and abstract thought. It often became something of an article of faith that widespread literacy would precipitate economic "lift off" in non-literate societies.

This idea of a great divide between oral and literate cultures has been challenged from many directions. Ruth Finnegan has questioned the confident, generalizing claims that are made about the changes attributed to literacy. Instead, case studies from different historical periods and geographical areas indicate that literacy is taken up and used in diverse ways with manifold consequences. Literacy should not be viewed in isolation since technologies are socially embedded and are shaped by the social relations into which they migrate. It is, consequently, difficult to establish any general or universal patterns for the impact of new technologies on societies.

This set of ideas was also explored in the field of linguistic anthropology and applied linguistics and came to be known as the New Literacy Studies. Research in this field has uncovered the rich multitude of literacy practices, multiliteracies, and literacy events in and across societies.

In terms of African oral literary studies, the initial phase of the debate on oral formulaic composition-in-performance influenced a great number of scholars. Many notable works appeared as a result of the application of these ideas and included Isidore Okpewho (*The Epic in Africa*) and Harold Scheub (*The Xhosa Ntsomi*).

Another field in which formulaic analysis of oral texts had an influence was in the arena of oral history in Africa. As historians came to rely on oral history as a source for reconstructing the precolonial past, the question of how to historicize information in such data became important. Vansina, in his pioneering work, adapted ideas of the formula to suggest that the most conventionalized forms of speech might be the oldest. The question of how, or indeed if, one can locate such kernels in sheets of testimony has produced much active debate.

These literary and historical investigations into the oral realm have been important, but they highlight the extent to which questions of literacy have been sidelined in discussions of African orality. Indeed, analyses of oral literature in Africa often screen out wider social forces (including literacy) so that, at times, oral forms appear to exist in a ringfenced world, cut off from history and social change. Karin Barber, a noted scholar of Yoruba literature, has suggested that the current field of African cultural studies is somewhat artifically divided between studies of oral literature on the one hand and, on the other, analyses of mainstream canonical writers working in Europhone languages.

Barber has instead suggested that the bulk of popular cultural production in Africa occupies the zone between these two points. Such cultural production also invariably entails a complex interweaving or "genetic engineering" of oral and written forms. To engage properly with popular culture in Africa is to come to terms with forms that straddle not only the modalities of the verbal and written but also forms like cinema, radio, video, and the like.

Finally, another outgrowth of the debates on orality and literacy has been felt in the field of the study of written African literature. Central to this field of study has been the question of how oral narrative forms interact with written genres. Very often, the presence of oral forms in written literature was understood simply as the importation of oral forms into printed guise. Such forms were furthermore often seen as providing the "essence" that could confer Africanness on texts. Critics like Eileen Julien, drawing indirectly on debates on orality and literacy, has changed this perception. Oral forms cannot simply be imported into writing but must be invented anew through the artful management of linguistic style and register. The way, then, in which oral and written forms intertwine is multilayered and needs to be the subject of detailed study if we are to capture the complexities of African cultural production.

References

Berber, Karin, ed. 1996. *Readings in African Popular Culture*. Bloomington: Indiana University Press.
Finnegan, Ruth. 1988. *Literacy and Orality: Studies in the Technology of Communication*. Oxford: Basil Blackwell.
Ong, W. J. 1982. *Orality and Literacy: The Technologizing of the Word*. London: Methuen.

ISABEL HOFMEYR

See also **Oral Literature: Issues of Definition and Terminology**

ORATORY: AN INTRODUCTION

Persuasive communication is used in many spheres of life in both traditional and contemporary Africa. Where persuasive speaking extends to the public domain, the challenges are enormous, for the speaker has to deal with audiences of varied social and political standings.

Oratory, or public speaking, is of tremendous importance in oral societies such as Africa. This is not surprising since, in the relative absence of writing and modes of electromagnetic communication, speaking constitutes the single most important mode of interaction.

In the African world, speech is considered to be free, distinct from the trickster's monopoly. Despite his greed and selfishness, Ananse (the Akan trickster who takes the form of a spider), the source of cultural phenomena, did not make speech the monopoly of one man. The Dogon people in Mali trace the origin of speech to the fox, while for the Fang of Gabon, it is the parrot who first brought to man the capacity to speak. Within the mythology of Akan lineages, the parrot stands supreme. The eloquence associated with one of the eight lineages follows from their being saved long ago by the cackling talk of the parrot. The timely speech intervention by the parrot saved the lineage from extinction. The parrot, that lineage's emblem, depicts the essence of eloquence. The Akan say, "The mouth is used to protect the head." Speech, judiciously used, can save lives.

The Akim, an Akan-speaking group, believe their eloquence is partly derived from the natural environment. They believe that the Birim River, of which they drink gave them the gift of oratory; thus the appellation, "The Akim born, that drinks of the Birim River."

The power of the spoken word is well recognized in African societies. Being the embodiment of acoustic energy, the spoken word has an immediate impact, the capacity to make or break. According to a Yoruba proverb, "Speech is an egg: when dropped, it shatters." The Akan of Ghana say, "When the mouth slips, it is more suicidal than the foot."

In everyday life, those endowed with the power of effective speech are held in high social esteem, due to the facility with which they bring stressful situations under control through persuasion. Despite the importance of good speaking in Africa, most cultures do not organize formal training in the art, since it comes naturally with exposure to traditional speech. Children often attend forums for debate and acquire speaking skills, customary lore, and genealogies by listening to elders. Skills in oratory also come with certain social and political positions. Several traditional offices require forensic skills in the exercise of duties. Positions like chieftaincy, headship of lineages, and membership of juries require considerable rhetorical skills in conflict management. Chiefs, prior to their installation, go into several weeks of seclusion where their attention is drawn to certain formal norms of communication. Even so, most chiefs and elders acquire rhetorical abilities on the job. In Ghana, there are occasional instances of chiefs who have been dethroned on account of oratorical incompetence.

Rare instances of formal training in oratory may be found among the Tutsi in Burundi, and also in the West Indies. In Burundi, where the ideals of oratory are stressed among the upper classes, aristocratic boys are given formal education in speech making from the age of ten. The content of the training includes impromptu speeches, formulas for petitioning a superior for gift, funeral orations, self-defensive rhetoric etc. (Finnegan 1970, 449). As a result, Tutsi aristocrats are well known for their elegance in speech. Among the people of St. Vincent, in West Indies, where "talking sweet" is highly valued in certain forums, parents not only encourage their children to learn techniques of oratory, they enter into agreement with men of proven oratorical abilities to formally train their children in delivery, fluency, and self-comportment in public speaking (Abrahams 1977, 123).

To help contain the hazards of public speaking, the exercise of rhetoric in Africa may be delegated by dignitaries to surrogates and other speaking agents. Professional orators, in several cultures of Africa, speak on behalf of patrons, who may be chiefs or other important personages. This is common particularly in West Africa among the Akan, Kru, Ga, Ewe, and several other ethnic groups in northern Ghana, Burkina Faso, Benin, and Cote d'Ivoire.

In Ghana, frequent references have been made by past scholars to the "linguist," or intermediary, locally known as *okyeame*, through whom the chief receives messages from his audience and speaks to them. On receiving the chief's message, the orator has the discretion to edit the royal word—elaborate it with metaphor, proverb, and other rhetorical devices, paraphrase it, or merely repeat it if well spoken. Without the orator's supplement, the patron's speech act is incomplete as a formal utterance.

Gender

Rhetoric in many African communities is male-dominated. In certain cultures, women are forbidden to express themselves in public. Among the Akan, the virtues of ideal womanhood include abstinence from speaking within the public domain. Women are believed to be repositories of wisdom and knowledge. Yet, society has considerably restrained woman's speech. The chief's palace, where most public debates are done, is not always open to women. They are prohibited from entering the premises when they are in their menses. Communication roles in mixed gender situations are often deferred to men. According to the Akan, "The hen knows that day has broken, yet it looks to the cock to announce it."

Even so, current trends point to a gradual recognition of women in speaking roles. Not only are women chiefs occasionally found but there are a few instances where male chiefs have appointed women as their orators (*akyeame*), on the basis of rhetorical excellence.

Occasions for Oratory

Occasions that attract rhetoric range from litigation in court, where persuasive speeches are given by litigants to influence juries, to macaronic diction given by men of words in the West Indies at feasts and tea meetings. In St. Vincent, home ceremonies and send-offs provide fitting occasions for speech making, and at tea meetings, speakers may present the gospel and emancipation stories in ornate speech. Among several ethnic groups in Africa, sermons, funerals, marriage ceremonies, and even public donations provide fitting opportunities for speakers to assert oratorical skills. Among the Akan, a public donation or drink gift is not merely presented. It is accompanied by a brief speech, often replete with proverbs, archaisms, idioms, and other rhetorical devices. The speaker's widow's mite may be compared with that of the housefly: "A poor fellow I am, not rich enough to lavish presents; yet even where the housefly had nothing to give, it scraped its offer from its bare limbs." A flowery acceptance speech is also expected from the recipient or his orator.

In Malagasy, marriage requests attract the most elaborate use of *kabary*, ceremonial speech, which is highly allusive. Here, two speech makers, representing both parties, start a contest in which they try to outdo each other in speaking skills (Keenan 1974). Generally, though, rhetoric pervades most verbal interaction. A beggar in Burundi may petition a patron for a new pair of shoes in poetic style, referring to his ragged shoe held together by a safety pin: "One does not hide one's misfortunes; if one tries to hide them they will nevertheless soon be revealed. Now I know a poor old man, broken in health and ill; there is a spear stuck in his body, and he cannot be saved" (Finnegan 1970, 450).

References

Abrahams Roger. 1977. The Training of the Man of Words in Talking Sweet. In *Verbal Art as Performance*, ed. Richard Bauman. Rowley, Mass.: Newbury House.

Albert, Ethel. 1972. Rhetoric, Logic, and Poetics in Burundi: Cultural Patterning of Speech Behaviour. In *Directions of Sociolinguistics*, ed. John Gumperz and Dell Hymes, pp. 35–71. New York: Holt, Rinehart and Winston.

Finnegan, Ruth. 1970. *Oral Literature in Africa*. Oxford: Oxford University Press.

Keenan, Elinor. 1974. Norm Makers and Norm Breakers: Uses of Speech by Men and Women in Malagasy Community. In *Explorations in the Ethnography of Speaking*, ed. Richard Bauman and Joel Sherzer, pp. 125–43. Cambridge: Cambridge University Press.

Yankah, Kwesi. 1995. *Speaking for the Chief: Okyeame and the Politics of Akan Royal Oratory*. Bloomington: Indiana University Press.

KWESI YANKAH

See also **Gender Representation in African Folklore; Okyeame; Oral Traditions; Performance in Africa**

ORATORY: POLITICAL ORATORY AND ITS USE OF TRADITIONAL VERBAL ART

Political oratory is the practice of public speaking. In Western societies it is defined as a formal, polished discourse that is usually written down and published. Most great orations in the traditional African context normally are neither written nor published. The fundamental purpose of political oratory is to influence the audience's beliefs and attitudes politically. As in many other societies worldwide, political oratory in African societies is immediate in its relationship to audience response. As a genre, political oratory subsumes such categories as speeches of political leaders, praise poetry, propaganda, and laws.

Okyeame

Africa is a heterogeneous continent that includes thousands of ethnic groups with diverse linguistic, social, political, and economic systems. Consequently, the distribution of the types of political oratory is varied. The role of the *okyeame* among the Akan of Ghana (Yankah 1995) is different from the compositions and performances of the Shona *marombe* of Zimbabwe (Hodza and Fortune 1979). While the *okyeame* is a leader in his own right, the *marombe*, who is a special praise singer to the chief, appears to revel more in sycophancy than in building alternative bases of authority. These variations among actors in political oratory do not, however, negate the fact that all of them intend to use traditional verbal arts either to transform their audience's dispositions or to reinforce their already held beliefs and attitudes. Through the use of verbal arts, political orators attempt to construct frameworks that encourage favorable responses to their speeches within the broad contexts of their hearers' perceptions and preconceptions.

Political oratory in Africa, past and present, varies from place to place. A category of political oratory is performed according to the situation. Skills that are demanded of elders who preside over worship are not exactly the same as those that are required of a dispenser of justice. Similarly, a panegyric suggests different oratorical expectations than a eulogy. In some cases, however, a political speaker may combine characteristics of distinctive subcategories of political oratory.

The *okyeame* (Yankah 1995) exemplifies a multifaceted political actor who, as the chief's diplomat, counselor, and orator, accentuates the rhetorical powers of the words of the chief. Moreover, the *okyeame* is a symbol who helps to create and sustain the power and mystery surrounding the chief. The *okyeame* (Yankah 1995; Obeng 1997) effects a rhetorical strategy that enables the individuality of the chief to seen indirectly into the diverse strata of society. The Yoruba of Nigeria have a similar institution. They have a king, *oba*, who is regarded as the representative of gods (Karade 1994). The king rules all living creatures. Due to the preeminence of the king, oratory is used to depict his distinction from other creatures. Like the Ashanti chiefs, the Yoruba king sends messages to his subjects through other people and rarely speaks publicly.

Among the Shona of Zimbabwe, the *marombe*'s role is to elaborate, in hyperbolic terms, the authority of the chief, calling him, for example, "Lord of the Sun and the Moon" and "King of the Land and the River" (Hodza and Fortune 1979, 3–4). Masizi Kunene (1979, xxv–xxvi) reports that literature in the era of King Shaka of the Zulu and after was used to reaffirm approval and disapproval of the whole nation. The poet and the singer not only praised leaders but also criticized and evaluated them based on their deeds.

Public Debates

Political oratory in traditional African societies was also employed in public debates. In complex land disputes, purpetual marital disagreements, or clan quarrels, each party of the contending groups invested its victory or the possibility of being heard honorably in the oratorical prowess of its representative or representatives. Chinua Achebe's *Arrow of God* (1964) dramatizes a protracted land dispute in which the rhetorical supremacy of Ezeulu (the principal character) determines its conclusion in favor of one the villages. The village of Okperi wins the case because Ezeulu fearlessly and eloquently testifies in its favor, notwithstanding the fact that he hails from the enemy village of Umuaro. In the same vein, Jomo Kenyatta (1938) uses his oratory to defend Kenyans' land rights in the face of its alienation by the British.

Ceremony

Finally, political oratory is employed to fulfill ceremonial functions. An orator may speak in recognition of a leader's achievements or on an important occasion. Conversely, an orator may speak deprecatingly about a leader or a situation. The Xhosa of South Africa have imbond yesizwe, literally, "the voice of the people," whose duty it is to praise and criticize as the circumstances demand (Diko 2001).

To Communicate Political Agendas

Contemporary African leaders have used traditional verbal art during the struggle for independence and after to communicate their political agendas effectively. Kwesi Yankah (1989) demonstrates how Nkrumah's post adopted and adapted traditional formulas and expressive devices to talk about current sociopolitical events. Nkrumah's speaker graced presidential functions with appellations meant to boost the image of Nkrumah and elicit fear in his opponents. In pursuit of this goal, the poet scrutinized the appellations of all other chiefs in Ghana and applled them to Nkrumah. Yankah reports that it is against this background that Nkrumah got his title Osagyefo, which means "savior at war." Although the title was originally identified with the King of Akim Abuakwa state, it was relevant to Nkrumah because of his opposition to British colonialism.

Poetry

In Tanzania, traditional poetry was also molded anew and employed to agitate for political freedom. Saadani Kandoro (1972) wrote an anthology of poetry in Kiswahili entitled *Mashairi ya Kandoro*, ("Poems of Kandoro"). Traditionally, Kiswahili poets could compose poetical epistles to their friends for any number of reasons, including expression of love, hatred, and apology. In one such poetic letter, Kandoro (1972, 138) informs a fellow poet about the political happenings in Tanzania. The image of the colonialist that Kandoro creates is embodied in a snake, which is being attacked by numerous insects (fighters for independence) united by their common objective of immobilizing the snake. In the late 1960s, during the politicization and mobilization of the Tanzanian citizenry to embrace socialist politics, the same poetic traditions were employed. An example of such a poem is titled "Which Type of Punishment":

Adhabu gani tuwape, wenye kosa la kunyonya
Wanyonyaji kama kupe, wagande wafe kunyonya
Hawauchi hata kope, vipi tutavyowaonya
Adhalni gani tuwape, wanyonyaji Tanzania?

(Honero 1980, 29)

How do we punish them, those whose crime is to
    exploit
Those who exploit like ticks, how do we freeze and kill
    them
They don't spare even an eyelash, how do we chastise
    them

Which punishment do we give these, exploiters of
    Tanzania?

(author's translation)

The metrical pattern of this poem is a popular traditional renddition, which was developed and popularized by the nineteenth century Kiswahili poet, Muyaka wa Muhaji (Abdulaziz 1979). Here, however, it is used to preach the policies of socialism as enshrined in the ideals of Arusha Declaration of 1967 and, at the same time, attack opponents of the new political and economic dispensation.

Songs

Songs are also used rhetorically to communicate political messages. Crane (1971) points out that, during the struggle for independence in the Democratic Republic of Congo, a religious group, Kimbangu, was suspected of composing the following subversive song:

Greetings, Lulua people
The white people came and put us in a fence
We who stand a strong column of the Congo
We have our own meetings
Our president walks around with white people
But our chief Kalarnba is only a puppet
He is like a leopard who is fed on dog meat instead of
    goat

(1971, 42)

Traditionally, it was a humiliation for a leopard, a traditional symbol of royal power, to eat dog meat, the food for beggars. This song was among other messages that were sent across the country and culminated in the 1959 riots in the Congo.

Other Rhetorical Devices

Many rhetorical devices are used in political oratory. Tropes such as proverbs, euphemisms, evasion, circumlocution innuendo, hyperhole, irony, metaphor, periphrasis, paradox, and personification are applied selectively and opportunistically to bring the points home. These tropes are highly intertextual in that they rely on other texts, which are either being affirmed or subverted. Furthermore, the intertextual nature of political oratory is manifested in its semantic and pragmatic vagueness, ambiguity, and indirectness (Yankah 1995; Obeng 1997). The proliferation of these devices in political oratory enables actors within it to construct cognitive structures with alternative ramifications, possibilities, and combinations as the observer encounters new situations. Yankah (1995) discusses third-party talk as a pervasive system of rhetorical indirection in West Africa, expressing itself in circumlocution and metaphorical and proverbial speech.

Samuel Obeng (1997) subscribes to the same view when he observes that politicians, when talking about risky topics, avoid the direct and obvious and communicate obliquely in order to protect their interests and gain leverage over their foes. They do so by engaging in indirect references. Besides using oblique speech, politicians use circumlocution and evasion to avoid responding to questions or situations without apologizing.

Metaphorical language in political oratory has two functions, which in some cases are mutually exclusive. It may used to vivify a point affectively, it may also be deployed to nonceal meaning. Kenyatta fabricates a fairy tale in *Facing Mount Kenya* (1938, 47–52) and allegorically uses it to describe how Kenyan lands came to be alienated through the insidious trickery of hypocritical treaties initiated by the British. The fairy tale is Kenyatta's explanation of the causes of the two world wars and of Kenya's fight: for independence. So many stylistic devices in political oratory are associated with traditional verbal art that each political event marshals its own as the context demands.

History of Scholarship

Political oratory, and its use of traditional verbal arts, is finally receiving serious scholarly attention. Nonetheless, the power of traditional cratory was recognized as early as 1888 (Freeman 1958, 13). Freeman reports on how highly developed an art form cratory was in West African societies. E. W. Grant (1929) and G. P. Lestrade (1935) have done studies of praise poetry directed to chiefs and sung by official bards in Southern Africa. Ruth Finnegan (1970, 1992) has amplified scholarship in the field by identifying and analyzing various types of oratory in different parts of Africa. Specifically, Finnegan analyzes the formalized praises, directed publicly to kings, chiefs, and leaders, which are composed and recited by members of the king's court (1970, 111–46). D. P. Kunene followed closely with his *Heroic Poetry of the Basotho* (1971), in which he describes the heroic deeds of warriors and kings. Early scholarly efforts in political cratory mainly focused on the thematic and formal characteristics of the genre.

By far, the most significant work after these early efforts is that of Maurice Bloch and others (1975). Eloch's study is intended to demonstrate how traditional cratory indexes the unquestionable and unchallengeable nature of traditional authority. In cradional societies, argues Bloch, authority is suggested and evoked by the very language that is evoked by speakers. Bloch begins his discussion from the assumption that the notion of a conscious exercise of power is not applicable in a society where socialization permeates in an unconscious and acceptable way. Consequently, formalization of cratorical discourse, the repeated emphasis of topic, adumbrates the absolute authority of elders over other members of the society. For example, in Bloch's view, there is a direct correspondence between fixed formal styles among the Merina of Madagascar and the stringent social control that obtains in that society.

Other studies disagree with Bloch. According to Paine (1981), even in communities that are said to be authoritarian, language is used in a flexible way. Paine insists that formalization is a rhetorical device through which speakers stimulate audiences to go on listening to them. Formal cratory creates and sustains the power of royalty, and any political center has symbols that help it to extend power beyond its immediate confines. These symbols may be verbal or physical objects, which are either handed down traditionally or constructed in the course of time or both.

Kwesi Yankah's study of the *okyeame* (1995) is perhaps the most authoritative statement to date on political oratory and its use of traditional verbal art. Applying insights drawn from pragmatics, anthropology, and folkloristics, Yankah demonstrates that the study of communication is governed by culture-bound rules. The description and analysis of the role of the *okyeame* in the context of message production and reception foregrounds the significance of senders and receivers of messages as primary actors in communication. Beneath this sender/receiver relationship, there is a dynamic that traditional verbal arts are perpetually subjected to as contexts of communication change. Based on insights gained from linguistic anthropology, such as Durant (1997), and Yankah's studies, researchers in political rhetoric, such as Samuel G. Obeng (1997), seek to illustrate how metaphors and other devices of speech are opportunistically used by political functionaries, speak without taking responsibility for the many conflecting interpretations of their speeches that may be result.

References

Abdulaziz, M. K. 1979. *Muyaka: 19th Century Swahili Popular Poetry*. Nairobi: Kenya Literature Bureau.

Achebe, Chinua. 1964. *Arrow of God*. London: Heinemann.

Bloch, Maurice, ed. 1975. *Political Language and Oratory in Traditional Societies*. London: Academic Press.

Crane, Louise. 1971. *The Land and People of Congo*. Philadelphia: J. B. Lippincott.

Diko, Nolutho. Personal communication, April, 2001.

Durant, Alessandro. 1997. *Linguistic Anthropology*. Cambridge: Cambridge University Press.

Finnegan, Ruth. 1970. *Oral Literature in Africa*. London: Oxford University Press.

———. 1992. *Oral Poetry. Its Nature, Significance and Social Context*. Bloomington: Indiana University Press.

Freeman, R. A. Journey to Ashantee, 1988. In *Pageant of Ghana*, ed. Freda Wolfaon. London: Oxford University Press, 1958.

Grant, E. W. 1927. The Izibongo of the Zulu Chiefs. *Bantu Studies* 111, no. 3: 201–44.

Hodza, A. C., and G. Fortune. 1979, *Shona Praise Poetry*. Oxford: Clarendon Press.

Honero, L. N., et al. 1980. *Matunda ya Azimio*. Dar es Salaam: Taasisi ya Lugha.

Kandoro, Saadani. 1972. *Mashairi ya Kandoro*. Dar es Salaam: Mwanachi.

Karode, Ifa. 1994. *The Handbook of Yoruba Religious Concepts*, York Beach, ME: S. Weiser.

Kenyatta, Jomo. 1938. *Facing Mount Kanya*. London: Martin Secker and Warburg.

Kunene, Daniel P. 1971. *Heroic Poetry of the Basotho*. Oxford: Oxford Library of African Literature.

Kunene, Mazisi. 1979. *Emperor Shaka the Great: A Zulu Epic*. London: Heinemann.

Lestrade, G. P. 1935. Bantu Praise Poems. *The Critic* IV, No. 1: 1–10

Obeng, Samuel G. 1997. Language and Politics: Indirectness, in Political Discourse. *Discourse and Society* 8, no. 41: 49–82.

Paine, Robert, ed. 1981. *Politically Speaking: Cross Cultural Studies of Rhetoric*. Philadelphia: Institute for the Study of Human Issues.

Yankah, Kwesi. 1995. *Speaking for the Chief*. Bloomington: Indiana University Press.

———. 1989. Creativity and Traditional Rhetoric: Nkrumah's Personal Poet and His Son. In *Literature and National Consciousness*, ed., Ernest Emenyou. Ibadan: Heinemann Educational Books.

RICHARD M. WAFULA

ORIGINS AND CULTURE HEROES: NILOTIC PEOPLES

Broadly considered, folklore refers to cultural traditions that are passed from generation to generation. This brief essay attempts to illustrate some common themes in the folklore of the Nilotic-speaking peoples of the southern Sudan. Although we do not possess a detailed account of Nilotic history, it is agreed that peoples of this region of Africa—the Shilluk, Anuak, Dinka, Nuer, and Atuot—share a common historical affinity. It is thus more reasonable to call attention to common themes in Nilotic folklore than to focus solely on any single ethnic group.

Though the Nuer possess elaborate means of bodily adornment and finely crafted utilitarian artifacts, their material culture is fairly sparse. In this light, Evans-Pritchard (1956, 43) suggested that "lacking plastic and visual arts, the imagination of this sensitive people finds its sole expression in ideas, image and words." The same can be said of all Nilotic people, and it can be added that, given the significance of oral tradition to guide and interpret life's offerings, folkloristic genres often have pragmatic as well as mnemonic consequences. Lienhardt (1975, 213–14) suggests that many oral traditions are, in their substance, held to be historical by those who tell them and may thus be regarded as legends, a term that reflects their historical validity.

Nilotic creation myths have common cross-cultural themes. The most common is that in a world prior to this one, known by common experience, the normal order of existence was inverted. For example, at some point in the past, life was timeless and carefree, but with the advent of human agency, death emerged. And with this came the essential perplexities of human existence: time, consciousness, mortality, and sin.

This general theme appears in Nilotic folklore on the origins of human beings and death—the two seem ever contingent. Among the Shilluk, the legend exists that many generations ago a culture hero (or in metaphorical language, a "spiritual image") emerged from a river in the form of Nyikang, the spiritual manifestation of Shilluk ethnogenesis. Nyikang is thought of as a spiritual agent that created the Shilluk people as well as the legitimizing agent that gave rise to the tradition of divine kingship in Shilluk society. In each human generation, the spirit of Nyikang is reborn in each succeeding Shilluk king or *reth*, the embodiment of the Shilluk polity. Likewise among the Anuak, tradition holds that village headmen share a common agnatic affinity with a founding riverine spirit, shared across generations by closely related patrilineal kin. For the Dinka, Nuer, and Atuot, this notion takes on a slightly different permutation. Dinka assert that their traditional religious and political leaders, *beng bith* or "masters of the fishing spear," can trace their origin and descent to an original master of the fishing spear called Aweil Longar, a spirit in human form that emerged from a river to promote or extinguish life. Atuot traditions closely parallel this notion in asserting that their own traditional healers and political leaders are descended from an ancestor that emerged "from the river." Likewise, among the Nuer, traditional political/spriritual leaders, known as "priests of the leopard skin," are said to have had a common origin with river spirits. These themes are discussed in greater detail by Lienhardt (1975) and Burton (1980).

There exists a considerable literature on the oral traditions of Nilotic peoples of the southern Sudan. In 1912, D. Westermark published a lengthy account titled *The Shilluk People: Their Language and Folklore* and in 1931, the missionary R. Huffman completed his *Nuer Customs and Folklore*. F. M. Deng published *Dinka Folktales: African Stories from Sudan* in 1974 as well as *The Dinka and their Songs* (1973). T. Svoboda in 1985 wrote a small book titled *Nuer Song*. These works represent only a small fraction of work in print on the general topic of Nilotic folklore; common themes in this literature address pan-human dilemmas: how parents treat their children, fears that children have of the unknown, how life's sorrows may be confronted, and why death haunts all human action.

For the Nilotic peoples of the Sudan, whose cultural traditions have been passed on by word of mouth rather than by the written word, the interested reader will find a wealth of material written by a number of generations of foreign authors. In this literature the reader will find local answers to dilemmas all human beings face, with a focus on kinship, the patrilineal family, spiritual agents, and cattle herding as a central economic activity.

References

Burton, John W. 1980. The Wave is My Mother's Husband: A Piscatorial Theme in Pastoral Nilotic Ethnology. *Cahiers d'Etudes Africaine* 21: 1–21.

Evans-Pritchard, E. E. 1956. *Nuer Religion*. Oxford: Claredon Press.

Lienhardt, R. G. 1975. Getting Your Own Back: Themes in Nilotic Myth. In *Studies in Social Anthropology*, ed. J. H. M. Beattie and R. G. Lienhardt. Oxford: Clarendon Press.

JOHN W. BURTON

See also **Hero; Myths; Northeastern African Folklore (The Horn): Overview**

ORISHA

For the Yoruba of western Nigeria, *orisha* is a generic name used to refer to the divinities. There are various accounts concerning the origin of the word *orisha*. One myth asserts that it was first used in designating the archdivinity of Yorubaland. The archdivinity and Orunmila, another orisha, descended into the world to accomplish the divine tasks allotted them by Olodumare, the Supreme Being. The affairs of the world were going on smoothly until the archdivinity decided that he needed a slave. He went to the market, where he bought a slave named Atowoda (meaning "that which was created by one's hand"). Atowoda was submissive and hardworking, and he was well loved by his master, the archdivinity.

Atowoda put a request before his master. Specifically, he asked for some land for farming. The archdivinity readily gave Atowoda a portion of land on the hillside near his home. However, all along, Atowoda had a sinister motive; he intended to kill his master. The archdivinity regularly visited Atowoda on his farm. Atowoda hatched a plan of loosening the soil under one of the embedded stones at the hilltop of his farm with a view to rolling it downhill to crush his unwary master when he climbed the hill during one of his visits. The plan was successful, and the archdivinity was crushed, his remains scattering everywhere.

When the news reached Orunmila, he performed certain rituals, gathered together the archdivinity's remains, put them in a calabash, and took it to Iranje, the city of the archdivinity. At Iranje, he deposited a portion of the body; he then distributed the rest all over the world, calling it, *ohun ti a ri sa*, ("what was found and gathered"). It is from *ohun ti a ri sa* that the term *orisha* is derived.

There is another account, which traces *orisha* from the word Orí-sè, which literally means "Head-Source." The Yoruba use *ori* to refer symbolically to the spiritual being; that is, the soul or individual ego. Thus, when the Yoruba says "Ori mi" ("my head"), he is not referring to the physical head; he is referring to his soul. The word *se* means to "originate," "to begin," or "to derive or spring from." The word *orise* would therefore mean "*Ibi ti ori ti se,*" ("the origin or source of *ori*") This source is Olodumare himself, the great ori from whom all ori originate.

In Yoruba, the name Orise (the original form) refers originally to Olodumare. In many parts of Yorubaland, even though Olodumare is not part of the divinities, the name Orisha is applied to Him. In the Owo district, Itsekiri and western Ijaw, the original form, Orise, is Olodumare's common name. The archdivinity, the Orisha-nla, and some of the primordial divinities are referred to as the offspring of Olodumare, in the sense that they are all entitled to the generic name of divinities. Therefore, the divinities would be the small orise, taking their name from their origin from Orise Olodumare himself. *Orisha*, therefore is a corruption of *orise*.

It is pertinent to distinguish *orisha* from *imole*. *Imole* is used to designate the spirits. *Imole* are dreaded, while the *orisha* are hallowed and respected. *Imole* are appeased due to fear of retribution, rather than worshipped in reverence. *Orisha* are localized and familiar; they have their shrines inside the city. On the other hand, *imole* shrine are restricted to the dark groves in the bush.

The *orisha* form the Yoruba pantheon, from which Olodumare is distinct, for he is a higher being than they are. Sometimes, however, their fuctions overlap. For example, Orisha-nla (Obatala) is in charge of creation (molding human beings); Ogun is the god of iron responsible for war, hunting, and blacksmithery; Oshun is the goddess of the river, responsible for fertility in women; and Yemoja is the goddess of deep sea. Jakuta and Sango are the gods of thunder and lightning. Orisha-Oko is the god of fertility, responsible for success in agriculture. Orunmila is the Yoruba god of wisdom.

In all, there are estimated to be four hundred orisha who form the Yoruba pantheon. Of all these, only very few are worshipped throughout the entire Yoruba region. Most are worshipped locally. Therefore, the orisha can be classified as either the greater *orisha* or the lesser orisha. The greater orisha are those with principal functions; the lesser *orisha* are those who are worshipped locally or might have overlapping functions. *Orisha* can also be classified as primordial and nonprimordial. The primordial *orisha* are those that Olodumare sent down from heaven, while the nonprimordial are those that were heroes or heroines who were later deified.

The *orisha* can also be classified into "hard" and "soft" groups. For example, while Ogun is regarded as a strong or "hard" *orisha*, Osun is regarded as a "soft" and gentle *orisha*. All the orisha have favorite foods, which their adherents must offer as sacrifice to them. One can incur the wrath of an *orisha* if the wrong food is offered as sacrifice. For example, Esu does not like shea butter or the oil extracted from palm kernels. His favorite is red palm oil (from the outer covering of palm nuts). People who use Esu for wicked purposes offer shea butter to him in the name of the person they want Esu to attack. Each *orisha* also has its own emblem and, at times, its own color and number.

KAYODE FANILOLA

See also **Diaspora: Cosmology; Religion: African Traditional Religion; Santeria in Cuba; Vodou**

ORPHAN MOTIF IN AFRICAN FOLKLORE

The traditional reverence for family and community so prominent in cultures throughout Africa gives the folk image of the solitary orphan a tragically symbolic significance. The orphan appears in oral tradition's across the continent as the hero of folktales and the subject of proverbs and insults.

The orphan as featured in most West and Central African folktales generally displays stock characteristics. The male or female orphan lives with an adoptive guardian (often the biological mother's co-wife). This guardian is cruel, depriving the orphan of food, sending her on impossible, dangerous missions, or forcins her to undertake difficult or demeaning work. Often the orphan embarks on a journey, usually to complete an impossible task at the guardian's bidding (e.g., fetching water from a dangerous well inhabited by genies). On the way to accomplish the task, the orphan meets and accepts challenges (e.g., rubbing the razor sharp back of a dead grandmother) without question, reluctance, or complaint. A dead mother, father, or grandmother often shows the orphan the key to the task. Because the orphan is obedient and modest, she successfully completes the mission and gains riches and status.

In the northern East African cattle area (e.g., Somalia and Uganda), folktale types involving orphans display common characteristics that depart from the West and Central African pattern (Arewa 1980). The orphan is in the care of her father's second wife. The adoptive mother despises the orphan and tries to kill her by burying her alive while the father is away. Either a half-sibling or the father hears the orphan singing from her trap and rescues her. The father punishes the stepmother by killing her or driving her away.

Across the continent, the orphan prevails, but she is tragic, representing solitude in cultures that place family and community in high esteem. Indeed, membership in a family unit is absolutely essential for any individual's proper growth and success in life.

Although it is limited to three southern Cameroonian ethnic groups, Charles Binam Bikoi's 1975 dissertation, "L'orphelin dans la litterature orale des Basaa, Beti et Bulu du Cameroun," is the most complete study of the orphan motif. Bikoi places the orphan tale within the realm of serious tales, as opposed to light tales, which means that tales about orphans carry a profound moral message about vital cultural knowledge (Bikoi 1975, 4). For example, throughout traditional African cultures, parents and guardians teach children to be obedient and to defer to age; these are highly valued childhood traits. Because she succeeds by doing what she is told, the orphan is the ultimate model for childhood obedience. On the other hand, the cruel stepmother serves as an example of how not to treat another member of the human family since her cruelty toward the orphan is rewarded with punishment at the end of the tale. The moral at the end of a Fon orphan tale from West Africa reflects this lesson in communal responsibility: "And this is why one never mistreats orphans. For once you mistreat them, you die" (Herskovits 1958, 293).

Bikoi examines this compelling image of family in African cosmology and orphan solitude as cosmic metaphor for all human tragedy:

> A number of African people, indeed, consider that the universe has a unique, supreme father, and that each group in nature constitutes a family, with ancestors, parents, brothers. . . . Everything that involves one single member of this family involves, beyond the specific group to which the member belongs, the whole universe. Also, in the case of human beings, the tragedy of orphans becomes a tragedy of life and their solitude, the solitude of the society.

> (1975, 121) (author's translation)

Proverbs and insults from Basaa, Beti, and Bulu oral folklore reveal this universal regard for community as it contrasts with the solitude, and ultimately the misery, that the orphan represents. The Beti proverb, "Unfortunate orphan: never eats good food," reflects the literal and symbolic hunger that routinely befalls the orphan (Bikoi 1975, 110). And the Basaa insult, "Mangy like an orphan," vividly demonstrates the miserable condition understood by the symbol of the orphan (Bikoi 1975, 104). The Guerze people of Guinea refer to nice, durable shoes as "orphan's shoes," a metaphor that shows multifaceted cultural understanding of the orphan motif; everyone knows that the orphan is too poor to afford more than one pair of shoes and that she has to walk everywhere, so it is normal to assume that an orphan would covet a single pair of shoes that would last a long time.

The orphan motif, with its themes of alienation, abuse, and journey, appears frequently in postcolonial African literature. In her 1981 article "The Orphan in Cameroon Folklore and Fiction," Susan Domowitz looks at the theme of orphanhood in Mongo Beti's *Le pauvre Christ de Bomba* and Ferdinand Oyono's *Une vie de Boy*. Both novels have orphan protagonists who journey away from their traditional values and landscapes toward a new world transformed by colonialism. However, unlike the orphan heroes of oral tradition whose journeys have joyous endings, the fate of the literary orphans is not so sanguine. Because they are "[b]ereft of the protection and familiar rules of traditional society, the orphans of the novels stumble determinedly toward ruin" (Domowitz 1981, 355).

This variation of the traditional orphan motif echoes throughout Chinua Achebe's *No Longer at Ease*, in which the protagonist journeys away from his village (a kind of self-imposed orphanhood) and a multilayered set of traditional and colonial Christian values, to make his way in the city under a new set of rules. This literary orphan journey also ends in ruin rather than self-actualization. The urban landscape in postcolonial African literature (e.g., Thomas Akare's *The Slums*, Alex LaGuma's *A Walk in the Night*, Mongo Beti's *Remember Ruben*, Buchi Emecheta's *The Joys of Motherhood*) is often the setting where tragic themes of orphanhood, that "vivid metaphor for colonialism" (Domowitz 1981, 355), are played out. Under traditional social systems, it is the orphan who experiences hunger, solitude, alienation, and abuse. But for people living under colonial and postcolonial systems, those challenges and abuses once reserved for orphans permeate everyday existence.

There are multifarious orphan themes throughout contemporary African cultures. The image of orphanhood in oral tradi-

tion—folktale, proverb, and insult—reinforces traditional values of family and community. As systems of education, technology, and government work to transform traditional social structures, the orphan presents a compelling topic for folklore scholarship in Africa.

References

Arewa, Erastus Ojo. 1980. *A Classification of the Folktales of the Northern East African Cattle Area by Types*. New York: Arno Press.

Abrahams, Roger D., comp. 1983. The Orphan and the Cloak of Skin. In *African Folktales: Traditional Stories of the Black World*. New York: Pantheon Books.

Babale, Chaibou, and Robert S. Glew, trans., eds. 1993. The Cruel Stepmother. In *Hausa Folktales from Niger*. Athens, Ohio: Ohio University Center for International Studies, Monographs in International Studies.

Beling-Nkoumba. 1985. Les Trois Orphelins. In *Contes du Cameroun II*. Yaounde: Editions CLE.

Berry, Jack, and Richard Spears, ed. 1991. The Orphan's Revenge, and How the Crab Got His Shell. In *West African Folktales*. Evanston, Ill: Northwestern University Press.

Binam, Bikoi Charles. 1975. L'orphelin dans la litterature orale des Basaá, Betí et Búlu du Cameroun. *Memoire de Diplome d'Etudes Superieures*, Université de Yaounde.

Domowitz, Susan. 1981. The Orphan in Cameroon Folklore and Fiction. *Research in African Literatures* 12: 350–8.

Ferry, M. P., trans. 1983. L'orpheline de mère. In *Les dits de la nuit: Contes tenda (Sénégal Oriental)*. Paris: Karthala.

Herskovits, Melville J., and Frances Herskovits. 1958. Orphan Twins Visit Dead Mother: Market of the Dead: Mistreatment Avenged, The Good Child and the Bad, and Orphan Outwits Trickster: Why Orphans are Not Mistreated. In *Dahomean Narrative: A Cross-Cultural Analysis*. Evanston, Ill.: Northwestern University Press.

Magel, Emil A., trans. 1984. Kumba the Orphan Girl. In *Folktales from the Gambia: Wolof Fictional Narratives*. Washington, D.C.: Three Continents Press.

Meyer, Gerard. 1988. L'Orpheline Devenue Reine, and L'Orpheline et le Grand Génie de la Brousse. In *Paroles du soir: Contes Toucouleurs. Sénégal, Mauritanie, Mali, Guinée*. Paris: Editions L'Harmattan.

Storzer, Gerald H. 1977. Abstraction and Orphanhood in the Novels of Mongo Beti. *Présence Francophone* 15: 93–112.

KATHERINE ROBERTS

See also **Folktales**

THE OXFORD LIBRARY OF AFRICAN LITERATURE

This substantial scholarly series was published between 1964 and 1979 by the Clarendon Press (of Oxford University Press), with the following aims:

> The task of recording oral compositions before they are lost to memory, and of providing a basis for future literary studies of Africa, is a specially urgent one for scholars of the present generation, for African literature which has appeared in print is only a tiny fragment of the whole. This library offers a selection of African poetry and prose chosen irrespective of time and place of composition. Each

volume from a particular people introduces the society in which the works have been created, and describes their literary and linguistic characteristics. Annotated translations, often with the complete text facing in the original language, enable readers to compare varied expressions of African thought and imagination.

Compositions in local languages will thus find their place in the literary heritage of the whole continent, and the styles of African authors, many of them unfamiliar, may make their impact on the world of literature as those of India and China have done for many years.

(General editors' statement in first volume)

The series' initial impetus largely came from social anthropology. Of the three general editors, two were at the Institute of Social Anthropology, University of Oxford (Professor E. E. Evans-Pritchard, one of the preeminent anthropologists of his generation, and Godfrey Lienhardt); Wilfred Whiteley, Professor of Bantu Languages at the University of London, had a background in both anthropology and linguistics. All had carried out fieldwork in Africa and also shared an interest in literature (Lienhardt's original discipline) and in the humane aspects of anthropology. However, the series was not wedded to any one theoretical stance; authors came from multiple disciplines, backgrounds, nationalities, and viewpoints, and several were native speakers.

The volumes typically consisted of translations, commentary, and original texts (in full or selective). The series was innovative for its time, moving away from the narrow functionalism and lack of interest in verbal art or individual creativity then dominant in British anthropology, to celebrate and analyze African thought and imagination. It went beyond the established philological tradition of presenting texts appropriate for linguists by including substantial treatment of specific cultural settings and/or of literary themes, style, and performance. The preview emphasized "oral compositions," but this was not interpreted in a restrictive sense; some written texts and oral/written interactions and overlaps were featured too. The series also carried some of the preconceptions of its time and place. The series title echoed the then-standard model of literature as verbalized products whose reality lay essentially in texts (though some volumes implicitly challenged this and/or included striking accounts of performance or composition processes). There was, initially, an understandable focus on dictated and/or transcribed texts (nineteenth as well as twentieth century, occasionally earlier), and it was only gradually—and selectively—that reliance on audio-recordings became established; nor was there often much comment on collection or transcription issues. While the series was ahead of its time in avoiding a fixation on the traditional, its laudable aim of documenting older forms before they were lost undoubtedly affected the selection and treatment; there was less coverage of contemporary forms, popular culture, or mixed media that might nowadays seem an obvious goal. The series had some success in achieving its ambitious and imaginative aims. And if it did not wholly manage to gain for African literatures the visibility of those of India or China, this was in the face of (still continuing) obstacles, which, perhaps, no series could totally overcome. Comparable to the French *Classiques*

africains, the volumes remain an invaluable resource for scholars and admirers of African literary arts.

As the list of volumes below indicates, the series covered a wide (if clearly not comprehensive) geographical, historical, and generic range:

Whiteley, W. H., comp. 1964. *A Selection of African Prose. Vol. 1 Traditional Oral Texts. Vol. 2 Written Prose.*
Andrzejewski, B. W. and Lewis, I. M. 1964. *Somali Poetry. An Introduction.*
Morris, H. F. 1964. *The Heroic Recitations of the Bahima of Ankole.*
Schapera, I. 1965. *Praise Poems of Tswana Chiefs.*
Huntingford, G. W. B. 1965. *The Glorious Victories of 'Amda Seyon, King of Ethiopia.*
Mbiti, John S., ed., trans. 1966. *Akamba Stories.*
Johnston. H. A. S., comp., trans. 1966. *A Selection of Hausa Stories.*
Babalola, S. A. 1966. *The Content and Form of Yoruba Ijala.*
Finnegan, Ruth, ed., trans. 1967. *Limba Stories and Story-Telling.*
Evans-Pritchard, E. E., ed. 1967. *The Zande Trickster.*
Lienhardt, Peter, ed., trans. 1968 *The Medicine Man. Swifa ya Nguvumali, by Hasani Bin Ismail.*
Cope, Trevor, ed. 1968. *Izibongo. Zulu Praise Poems.*
Norris, H. T. 1968. *Shinqiti Folk Literature and Song.*
Coupez, A., and Th. Kamanzi, 1970. *Littérature de cour au Rwanda.*
Finnegan, Ruth, 1970. *Oral Literature in Africa.*
Kunene, D. P. 1971. *Heroic Poetry of the Basotho.*
Goody, Jack. 1972. *The Myth of the Bagre.*
Norris, H. T. 1972. *Saharan Myth and Saga.*
Deng, Francis Mading. 1973. *The Dinka and their Songs.*
Damane, M., and Sanders, P. B., ed., trans. 1974. *Lithoko. Sotho Praise Poems.*
Shack, William A., and Habte-Mariam Marcos. 1974. *Gods and Heroes. Oral Traditions of the Gurage of Ethiopia.*
Scheub, Harold. 1975. *The Xhosa Ntsomi.*
Willis, Roy, ed., trans. 1978. *There was a Certain Man. Spoken Art of the Fipa.*
Al-Shahi, Ahmed, and F. C. T. Moore. ed., trans.. 1978. *Wisdom from the Nile. A Collection of Folk-Stories from Northern and Central Sudan.*
Hodza, A. C., comp., and G. Fortune, ed., trans. 1979. *Shona Praise Poetry.*

RUTH FINNEGAN

See also **Classiques Africaines, Oral Literature: Issues of Definition and Terminology**

OYO TUNJI: A YORUBA COMMUNITY IN THE USA

Religious beliefs and ceremonies, visual culture, and social organization closely based on traditional Yoruba prototypes from Nigeria and Benin Republic are embraced by African American members of Oyo Tunji in Beaufort County, South Carolina, as viable alternatives to mainstream American culture. Oyo Tunji ("Oyo Returns" or "Oyo Rises Again") is a metaphor for the reconstruction, in the United States, of the ancient kingdom of old Oyo, which flourished in Nigeria (c.1600 to 1830 CE).

Oyo Tunji is popularly referred to as "the African village." The current leader, known as Oba (king) Efuntola Oseijeman Adefunmi I, along with a handful of priests and priestesses, established Oyo Tunji in 1970, near the town of Sheldon, where routes 17 and 21 intersect.

Oyo Tunji encompasses ten square miles of semi-forest, agricultural land in a rural, agricultural terrain. It follows a traditional town plan that can still be seen in the outlying areas of small Yoruba villages in West Africa. Oyo Tunji's land is partitioned into precincts radiating from the central focus where the palace (called the Afin) is located. Oba Adefunmi I apportions the land to male and female householders who pay annual taxes to the Oba for this land. All the dwellings adhere to the traditional Yoruba architectural plans, which consist of small, usually windowless, enclosed dwelling units (used for storage and sleeping), built around large, open, square courtyards where most daily tasks are performed (Ojo 1966). The size and elaboration of architecture signifies status, ranging from the sprawling, immense palace through the middle-size homes of the chiefs to the small houses of the general populace.

Oyo Tunji is, first and foremost, a religious community. The primary criterion of membership is initiation into "Yoruba" religion, which, in fact, while foregrounded there, accommodates an intertextual blend of borrowing from other African religions including Fon, Asante, Edo (ancient Benin kingdom), and ancient Egyptian. The king's name is an excellent example of the influence of multiple African elements: *Efuntola* signifies his initiation into Yoruba religion as a priest of Obatala (in Nigeria, the Yoruba deity credited with human creation through his modeling of human bodies from primordial clay). *Efun* in Yoruba is white chalk and *ola* denotes abundance. *Oseijeman* (or "savior of the people" in Akan) is a customary name for chiefs in Ghana. *Adefunmi* ("crown for me") builds upon the Yoruba traditional of designating all royal lineage families by prefixing their names with *ade* ("crown"). Funmi is a conscious signifier of Oyo Tunji's king's (formerly Walter Serge Roy King of Detroit, Michigan) proactive appropriation of Yoruba royal names and a conceptual pun on his "slave" name. Adefunmi can thus be seen as a "New World" *oriki* (Yoruba praise name) that puns on the fact that Walter Serge Roy King originated the "kingdom" of Oyo Tunji and created a royal lineage for himself and his family, with the right to rule and wear the crown (*ade*, the sign *par excellence* of royalty among the Yoruba in West Africa).

A very large number of African American men and women have been initiated in Oyo Tunji by Kabiyesi (Yoruba, "royal highness") Queen Iy Orite and others since 1970. These priests and priestesses maintain close and continuous ties with the community, although many have chosen not to remain permanently in Oyo Tunji. They have dispersed throughout the United States to found small religious satellites of Oyo Tunji in Chicago, Indiana, Wisconsin, New York, Virginia, Florida, and Los Angeles. The major deities (*orisha*) are conceived as embodiments of organic, supernatural, and mortal power that often calibrate with numerology and astrology. Thus, Orunmila (while equated with the domain of Ifa divination among the Yoruba in Africa) is associated with the Sun. Olokun (a deity associated with rulership and wealth in the ancient Nigerian Benin kingdom) is identified with the planet Neptune and the sign Pisces. In Oyo Tunji, Olokun is also conceptualized as the ecumenical deity representing the souls of all descendants of Africans transferred from their homeland by ships sailing the Atlantic Ocean and, as such, serves as the patron deity of all African Americans. Obatala (the creation deity who first molded humans from earth) is the patron deity of Oyo Tunji and the one with the most initiates. Obatala

is linked with the planet Jupiter and the sign Sagittarius. Sango (whose domain is thunder and who was a former king of old Oyo, an ancient Yoruba city) is governed by Uranus and linked to Aquarius. Yemoj (the mother of deities not born by Nanan), seen in Oyo Tunji as a powerful *iyami* (enchantress), governs the Gelede society organized by men to honor elderly women of tremendous spiritual authority. As a moon goddess, Yemoj is connected with the sign of Cancer and the numbers 4 and 7. Esu-Elegba, the prankster, is seen as, simultaneously, the youngest and the oldest of all the deities. He is linked to the planet Mercury, the signs Gemini and Virgo, and the numbers 1, 3, 11, and 21. His domains are the marketplace and the crossroads. He possesses the spiritual force to open and close roads and place or remove obstacles, all metaphors for positive or negative opportunities and success or failure.

In Oyo Tunji, a separate temple complex exists for each deity, which includes the main shrine, a smaller shrine for the Esu-Elegba of the deity, and a building where initiates are housed during their seclusion. Priests and priestesses function as diviners and herbalists who provide guidance for the inhabitants of Oyo Tunji, as well as visitors or local South Carolinians. They combine healing with herbs, fasting, divination, palmistry, tarot cards, numerology, and astrology.

Known ancestors are honored by paintings, photos, and Egungun cloth ensembles, as in Africa, while unknown ancestors are determined by roots-reading divinations and honored by fresh water, flowers, candles, and prayers. An innovation introduced in Oyo Tunji is the initiation of women into the Egungun society.

Finally, the visual culture of Oyo Tunji exemplifies a deliberate creative project that departs from the mainstream, exhibition-directed arts created by many African American artists, who position themselves within the American mainstream. In contrast, Oyo Tunjians look toward conventional Yoruba art forms still commonplace in the African homeland and available through African art books, journals, or early ethnographies.

In sum, Oyo Tunji occupies a unique place among African diaspora communities; it is a uniquely intellectual entity, consciously created by African Americans as a counterpoint to, and revitalization effort within, mainstream American society and culture. Rooted in West African Yoruba religious, sociopolitical, and artistic epistemologies, Oyo Tunji testifies to the agency and activity of African Americans in the diaspora.

References

Gregory, Steven. 1999. *Santeria in New York City: A Study in Cultural Resistance*. New York: Garland.

Murphy, Joseph M. 1988. *Santeria: An African Religion in America*. Boston: Beacon Press.

———. 1994. *Working the Spirit: Ceremonies of the African Diaspora*. Boston: Beacon Press.

Hunt, Carl. 1979. *Oyo Tunji*, Ph.D. dissertation, University of Virginia.

Ojo, G. J. A. 1966. *Yoruba Culture: A Geographical Analysis*. London: University of London Press.

Omari, Mikelle Smith. 1984. *From the Inside to the Outside: The Art and Ritual of Bahian Candomble.* Monograph Series no. 24. Museum of Cultural History, University of California, Los Angeles.

————. 1989. The Role of the Gods in Afro-Brazilian Ancestral Ritual: *African Arts Journal* XXIII, no. 1.

————. 1990. Creativity in Adversity: Afro-Bahian Women, Power, and Art. The International Review of African American Arts 9, no.1: 35–41.

————. 1991. Completing the Circle: Notes on African Art, Society, and Religion in Oyo Tunji, South Carolina. *African Arts*, July, 66–75, 96.

————. 1994. Aesthetics and Ritual of Candomble Ago. In *African Religions: Experience and Expression*, ed., Thomas Blakely, pp. 135–9. London: James Curry; Portsmouth, N.H.: Heineman.

————. 2002. *Manipulating the Sacred: Yoruba Art, Ritual and Resistance in Brazil.* Detroit: Wayne State University Press.

Pinn, Anthony. 1998. *Varieties of African American Religious Experience.* Minneapolis: Fortress Press.

MIKELLE SMITH OMARI-TUNKARA

See also **Diaspora**

P

PALAVER (KINZONZI) IN KONGO LIFE

Among the Kongo peoples of the Democratic Republic of Congo, life is in constant flux, and palaver (*kinzonzi*)—the art of settling matters through talk—is an essential ingredient in human affairs. *Kinzonzi* marks the moment when conflicts and social realities are subjected to scrutiny. In the Kongo context, it suggests the power of the word. The term derives from the verb *zonza* (to quarrel), but it also indicates a distinguished oratory and dialogical expertise. The performer is described as *nzonzi* or *zonzi*, a judge, an orator, or a defender (Laman, 1936 831). The quest for an orator is familiar, as the well-known Kongo expression indicates: *A mono nkondolo nkazi nani kumvovila* (As I do not have an uncle [or brother], who will speak for me?). The art of mastering words has very functional demands. Although there are women with such skills, being a *zonzi* is first and foremost a man's profession.

The family home and the traditional community courts are the social arenas where palavers take place. In the family context, there are two instances, or levels, of palavers: the household and the extended family. They are the only means to address a conflict (e.g., someone's behavior or an illness) or to discuss a project (such as a wedding proposal or taking a journey). The parents and the eldest son are the primary decision makers in Kongo families, and the eldest son is responsible for decisions about issues related to his parents' behavior or health. Regarding siblings, parents and the eldest child are cojudges.

Decisions drawn from palavers require the household's unanimous consent. The household is not made up of parents and children alone, but also includes nephews, uncles, and other relatives of the extended family as well. This would explain the impossibility of confidentiality. Relatives of the extended family would be aware of the household issues before an extended familial court is convened. Whenever issues to be dealt with are beyond the scope of the household, the extended family is approached. In the case of a child's wedding or sickness, the social and philosophical organization of Kongo society obliges the father to consult first his own maternal and paternal family. An appointed member of the father's family is given the power to lead the palaver, and the principal interlocutor is the eldest of the child's maternal uncles. Friends, or anyone concerned with the issue to be discussed, can attend this gathering. They are *mbangi* (witnesses) to the decision that is made, and they constitute the "therapy managing group" that Janzen discusses (Janzen 1978, 4).

The traditional community judicial system deals with issues involving people without familial bonds. In some circumstances such courts serve as the last recourse for the familial judicial system. The issues most discussed by the community judicial system involve land disputes, witchcraft accusations, interclan conflicts, robbery, and other social conflicts.

A palaver can last from one day to many months, depending on the nature of the case to be scrutinized. There are three primary aspects of every palaver. The first section is the introduction, when participants are given an exhaustive account of the situation. In the context of the community judicial courts, the event starts with a prelude by the judge and his team, during which the reason for the gathering is explained. The representatives of the people involved in the issue to be discussed are then given time to narrate their versions in detail. The second section is the discursive period, which includes interrogations and interventions of *mbangi*. Judges can ask people involved in the conflict to consult with each other separately in order to resolve the issue. This is expressed in words such as *Luenda ku nima nzo or, loenda ku fongo* (Go to the backyard). These discussions are led by the wisest people of each group.

The third and the last component of a palaver is the deductive, or concluding, period. This moment is enriched by what is known as *Fongo dia zi nzonzi*. These are the secret consultations of judges, where, in the light of the evidence and their interrogations, they find ways to address the conflict. When there is a disagreement among the judges, a majority decides, or else the case is referred to other *nzonzi*. Such a referral also occurs when the judges' conclusions are disputed by those involved in the conflicts.

There is a similar structure of *kinzonzi* on issues of marriage in the familial context. The difference lies in the fact that this is a happy event, which should mean less time and fewer complications. Nevertheless, when some members of a family express disagreement about a marriage a long process of negotiation is necessary.

Palavers require the relevant use of appropriate metaphors, parables, songs, and legends. Such speech and verbal art forms are regarded as signs of knowledge and wisdom. Yet, apart from their oratory performance, judges are to be impartial and confidential. This is the basis of their authority.

Palavers have therapeutic, pedagogic, and ethical functions (Mampolo 1976, 70–4). The therapeutic dimension of palavers is related to the fact that the Kongo have a social concept of health and disease (i.e., physical sickness is caused by social disharmony) (MacGaffey 1983, 148). Palavers lead to confession and repentance, which are essential in the Kongo's quest for health. In their pedagogic function, palavers provide an occasion when legends, proverbs, questions about life, and the art of using words effectively are learned through participant observation. Their ethical function is seen in the insistence to seek what is socially and morally accepted.

In a country decimated by the consequences of three decades of a vicious political system, it is more than an obligation to rejuvenate palavers and redeem them from the inhumane politics to which they have been subjugated since 1965. This will return *kinzonzi* to their central place in the judicial systems of the Kongo and other Congolese peoples. For the Kongo, as for all Africans, parables are not only a means of communication, but a medium through which vital forces are expressed.

References

Laman, K. E. 1936. *Dictionnaire Kikong-Français, avec une étude phonetique decrivant les dialtectes les plus importants de la langue dite Kikongo.* Brussels: Georges Van Campenhout.

MacGaffey, W. 1983. *Modern Kongo Prophets: Religion in a Plural Society.* Bloomington: Indiana University Press.

Mampolo, M. 1976. *La liberation des envoutes* (traduit de l'anglais par Jean Geli). Yaoundé, Camaroon: Editions Cle.

ADRIEN N. NGUDIANKAMA

See also **Gossip and Rumor; Oral Traditions; Personal Narratives**

PERFORMANCE IN AFRICA

Among the best known of the many performance genres in Africa are storytelling, masquerades, and playwriting. For the most part, these are carried out by men, although there are exceptions.

Masquerades present nonhuman beings in visible form. These beings may be deities, spirits, or ancestors not normally visible to ordinary people. Most masquerades have spiritual associations and are sacred. While much performance in Africa is designed to be efficacious—that is, to have "power" and be able to affect humans, not simply to entertain—certain masquerades are much more powerful or efficacious than others. It can be said that there are "sacred" masks and "secular" or "entertainment" masks. Some masks are held to be so powerful that those members of society considered to be more vulnerable—usually women and children—cannot even see them in any but the most circumscribed situations. The penalty for a woman who transgressed was often said to be that she would not bear children or even, formerly, must suffer death. Masked figures often have the right to chase women and children with whips or batons—reputedly to keep them in order. Other, more lighthearted masks mock strangers, condemn drunkenness, or exhort people to be socially responsible (and thus uphold the status quo).

The word *mask* is generally used to refer to the face and head covering, while *masquerade* refers both to the individual masked figure and to the entire performance event in which masked figures appear. Masks can be carved from wood or made from cloth or raffia, and they are often regarded as being imbued with real power, even when they are being worn or stored. Frequently their storage place is kept secret from everyone but a few, and often women may not see the most sacred masks even when they are in storage. When the mask is worn, the identity of the wearer is officially kept secret, and the masked figure assumes a sacred status. This is because when a masked figure appears in public it is no longer a human being disguised as a spirit, but has taken on the attributes and power of what it represents, and thus it has *become* the spirit, deity, or ancestor. This transition from human to something "other" is one reason that masquerades are regarded with awe and respect and are often a central form of articulation in systems of belief.

Masquerade events are divided by gender. Although the characters represented by the masks can be male or female, mask wearers are almost always male. An exception is the Mende women of Sierra Leone, who have an elaborate masking practice as part of the Sande society, an organization designed to inculcate appropriate social and sexual behavior in women. Among the Sande masks is Sowei, the most powerful mask, which epitomizes the ideal of beauty. Sowei has a comical mimic, Gonde, whose antics highlight the elegance and beauty of Sowei. Although Sowei is powerful and can only be worn by initiates of the Sande society, Gonde is not, and can be worn by noninitiates. The masks of the female Sande Society are paralleled by those of the male Poro Society, a powerful organization whose focus is on economic and political behavior.

Masquerade performances do not take place randomly, but are tied to specific events such as the annual Egungun masquerade of the Yoruba of Nigeria. The Egungun spirits are said to be the ancestors. The Dogon people of Mali have a variety of occasions for masking, including the great Sigui, which only takes place every sixty years, and the Dama, which takes place every two or three years and has also been adapted as a secular entertainment. Among the Chewa of Zambia and Malawi, the masquerade figures appear at collective funerary remembrance ceremonies honoring recently deceased persons. The Chewa masquerades, part of the Nyau Society duties, include the Kasiyamaliro, which covers the entire body of the wearer. Many masquerade performances are part of rites that mark the transition of the newly dead to the world of the ancestors.

Storytelling also forms a part of the performance repertoire of most societies in Africa. Storytelling usually takes place in the evenings, when the day's work is complete and people can relax together. If it is an occasion when more than just the children and close family are present, then it is the men who tell stories and perhaps mimic the antics of the characters. If it is mostly just children around, then women will often tell the stories. Many tales are designed to educate younger members of society, and they often end with a moral. Storytelling has a very earthy aspect to it, and many ribald tales of sexual exploits are told—mostly about the animals of the forest or savannah, or else about magical creatures who take semihuman forms and who can affect the lives of humans.

In most societies there is a set format for opening the story, which usually gives the listeners a sense of venturing in search of a story until an appropriate one is found (one that is interesting and likely to be well told). Among the Idoma people of Nigeria, storytelling is called *ocha*. A storyteller opens with the phrase, *Ocham ta kpa, kpa kpa . . .* (My *ocha* went out looking, looking, looking . . .), and then, having decided on a story, he begins.

Among the Mende of Sierra Leone, storytelling is divided into historical narratives called *Ngawovei* and fictional narratives called *Domei*. Adherence to historical fact is sought in the *Ngawovei* and, therefore, they are recounted in a straightforward manner. The *Domei*, however, rely on the style, skill, and imagination of the storyteller to capture and hold the attention of the audience. Whereas participation is slight in the Ngawovei, vociferous singing and clapping are an essential feature of the art of Domei.

Performance activities such as storytelling, singing, and dancing focus primarily on presenting the self as skilled, whereas performing in masked events emphasizes the presentation of the "other" and deliberately diminishes the degree to which the self is present. In some cases this extends to total effacement, where the performer is not seen, may not be seen, and is not officially acknowledged even to be present.

Orally transmitted dramatic dialogue has long been a feature of African performance, particularly at funerary ceremonies celebrating the lives of the newly dead and their exemplary deeds. There are also dialogues within the performances of people in a trance, such as the *bori* cults of northern Nigeria or the *hauka* (madness) practices in Niger, where, in certain circumstances, the *hauka* pave the way for the public to encounter the spirits. These dialogues are fleeting and take place with individuals in the crowd—often placing unsuspecting spectators in an unwanted spotlight. In the early part of the twentieth century, the *beni* dance forms, a mock-militaristic genre popular in East African countries, also made use of dialogue to heighten the interaction between the performers.

Playwrights make use of several long-established forms of performing in dialogue drama. The literary form gives playwrights the opportunity to address issues in a more prolonged way. Early playwrights include the Nigerian James Ene Henshaw, a medical doctor whose best-known play is the ever-popular *This is Our Chance* (1956). By the late 1950s and early 1960s, literary giants from Nigeria had appeared on the world scene. Wole Soyinka's early works include *The Lion and the Jewel* (1963), in which a young woman whose beauty is revealed through the visit of an urban photographer—and which in turn brings her to the lascivious attention of the local chief—is a tale of the victory of established practice over social change. This tension remains pervasive in Soyinka's work and is evident even in his later masterpieces, including *The Road, Death and the King's Horsemen*, and *Madmen and Specialists*. The plays of J. P. Clark (John Bekederemo Clark) include *Song of a Goat* and *The Raft* (Three Plays, 1964) and the recent *All for Oil* (2000). His greatest works lay in documenting a storytelling performance of the Ijo of the Niger Delta (his own people), in which the deeds of the legendary Ozidi are recounted and published as *The Ozidi Saga* (1977), and in his play called simply *Ozidi* (1966), which is based on the story of Ozidi.

Other Nigerian playwrights include Femi Osofisan, whose works include *Another Raft* (1988) and *Morountundun* (1984), and Bode Sowande, whose work includes *Farewell to Babylon, The Night Before*, and *Sanctus for Women* (all published in 1979). Ghana has provided the most prolific women playwrights of world standing, particularly Ama Ata Aidoo, who wrote the play *Anowa* (1965) and Efua Sutherland, who wrote *The Marriage of Anansewa* (1975), in which the relationship between storytelling and playwriting is addressed in the form as well as the content.

Later, the Kenyan playwrights Ngugi wa Thiongo'o and Ngugi wa Mirii addressed the same issue in the play *I Will Marry When I Want* (1982). This play famously arose from a collaborative project with ordinary people in Kamiriithu, Kenya, starting in 1976. The playwrights responded to the request of the local people to help them articulate their concerns at the ways in which, they were being unjustly exploited as laborers and peasants. The resulting play was created orally by the people themselves and formed into a written text using the skills of wa Mirii and wa Thiongo'o.

South Africa has a distinct history of playwriting, and the early play texts of H. I. E. Dhlomo highlighted Zulu and Xhosa heroes and heroines. Credo V. Mutwa, Gibson Kente, and, later, Zakes Mda also emerged as key dramatists. The South African actors John Kani, Winston Ntshona, and Mbogeni Ngema are internationally famous.

Performances are determined by access to, and use of, such resources as materials, performers, audience, and venue. The movement from orally transmitted work to literary texts is just one part of an ongoing process of change that has always taken place in African societies. No performance is ever exactly the same as a previous one. Key elements in performance are retained, but these may be embellished as individual preferences alter and different opportunities occur. Key elements may be a text, a storyline, or a sacred ritual. New features are incorporated to accommodate individual talent, but, in the absence of someone capable of fulfilling a specific role, some features may have to be dropped, perhaps temporarily, perhaps forever. Performance in Africa, like performance anywhere, relies on the presence of skilled, knowledgeable, and willing performers.

Long-established performance genres are now made use of in contemporary media, especially in video, films, and television drama, which provide new and fertile fields of expansion as performance moves between a position of efficacy and one of entertainment. This does not, however, concomitantly reduce its efficacy in the original setting. Similarly, the use of familiar forms of performance, including dialogue drama, in contexts directly related to social mobility, environment, agriculture, health, and other aspects of contemporary life is increasing. Known as community theatre or theater for development, it is being widely used to challenge undesirable aspects of social change, as well as to support those which are advantageous. People continue to use familiar forms—sometimes in new contexts, sometimes in established contexts. Changing opportunities, features, and meanings because African performance, like performance worldwide, is creative in form and context.

References

Arnoldi, Mary Jo. 1995. *Playing with Time: Art and Performance in Central Mali*. Bloomington: Indiana University Press.

Barber, Karin, J. Collins, and A. Ricard, eds. 1997. *West African Popular Theatre*. Bloomington: Indiana University Press.

Drewal, Margaret Thompson. 1992. *Yoruba Ritual*. Bloomington: Indiana University Press.

Harding, Frances, ed. 2002. *The Performance Arts of Africa*. New York: Routledge.

Kerr, David. 1995. *African Popular Theatre*. London: James Currey.

Kruger, Loren. 1999. *the drama of south africa*. New York: Routledge.

Mda, Zakes. 1993. *When People Play People*. Development Communication Theatre. Johannesburg, S. Africa: Witswatersrand University Press; London, ed.

Plastow, Jane. 1996. *African Theatre and Politics: The Evolution of Theatre in Ethiopia, Tanzania, and Zimbabwe: A Comparative Study*. Amsterdam: Rodopi.

wa Thiong'o, Ngugi. 1981. *Decolonizing the Mind. The Politics of Language in African Literature*. London: James Currey.

Spencer, Julius. 2002. Storytelling Theatre in Sierra Leone: The Example of Lele Ghomba. In Harding, ed.

FRANCES HARDING

See also **Dialogic Performances, Call-and-Response in African Narrating; Drama; Masks and Masquerades; Puppetry; Theater**

PERFORMANCE STUDIES AND AFRICAN FOLKLORE RESEARCH

The first folklorist to understand the inextricable link between performance and folklore was the African-American folklorist and writer Zora Neale Hurston (1903–1960), who, in the 1920s, claimed that, "every phase of Negro life is highly dramatized. No matter how joyful or how sad the case there is sufficient poise for drama. Everything is acted out" (1981, 49). She understood the deep connection between African diaspora mimicry and parody and its manifestation in virtually all forms of folk expressions, and she concluded that the best way to transmit these characteristics was on the stage, rather than in print (Hill 1993, 295). She followed this idea through quite literally in her productions of *Color Struck* (1925) and *The First One* (1927), as well as in musical revues and concerts that, according to performance studies scholar Lynda Hill, "showcased the forms of folk expression she sought to introduce to the larger white public" (1993, 298). Hurston's understanding of the "characteristics of negro expression" as constituting the drama of everyday life directed her interests to performer and audience interactions, to the audience's assessment of the performance, and to her own role as a self-reflexive participant-observer (Davis 1998, 14–15). According to performance studies scholar and folklorist Mella Davis, Hurston used storytelling in such texts as *Mules and Men* to evoke the temporality and contingencies of performance. It would be nearly five decades before folklorists returned to performance as a critical concept applicable to folklore. Hurston's work, Davis has pointed out, anticipated contemporary ethnography (Davis 1998, 15–16).

As the application of embodied skill and knowledge, performance is behavior twice behaved, repetition, or "restored behavior" (Schechner 1985), in which performers often, but not always, have some responsibility either to an audience or to each other, as in participatory performances such as public festivals and rituals. Since the mid-1940s, scholars from a range of disciplines have theorized human action using dramaturgical paradigms and metaphors. Some of the influential perspectives include: Kenneth Burke's rhetorical, performance-oriented theories that take stock of the effects of performance on audiences, which was influential in anthropology, sociology, and folklore from the 1950s on, Victor Turner's models of social drama and the ritual process, which employ his notions of liminality and communitas, Gregory Bateson's work on metacommunication in performance and play, and Erving Goffman's dramaturgical model of the presentation of self in everyday life, as well as his frame analysis that seeks to explain how audiences recognize that a performance is in progress (influenced by the work of Bateson and Richard Schechner). Other significant work includes Milton Singer's concept of "cultural performance" as an encapsulation of a larger, unmanageable whole, and Clifford Geertz's concepts of thick description, deep play, and blurred genres. Turner, Goffman, and Geertz, who were strongly influenced by Burke, never actually researched drama per se, yet, ironically their perspectives have been instrumental in shaping research on performance in Africa. In addition, English translations of Mikhail Bakhtin's work have begun to influence the study of performance, especially his treatment of the carnivalesque and heteroglossia, that is, the layering of different languages and voices in speech and writing. Late-twentieth-century works that engage some of these performance theorists include Abdullah Ali Ibrahim's *Assaulting with Words* (1994) and Kwesi Yankah's *Speaking for the Chief* (1995).

As a result of these works, certain key concepts have become part of a standard vocabulary in research on performance—in particular, Goffman's analysis of performance frames, cueing or keying, and frontstage/backstage; Turner's concepts of communitas, liminality, and social drama; and Bakhtin's dialogics and multiple voicedness.

In *Power, Marginality and African Oral Literature* (1995), Graham Furniss and Liz Gunner observe that folklorists and others have been working with the concept of performance and its implications for the field of folklore studies since the early 1970s. They, and the advocates of performance-centered research to whom they refer, neglect Hurston's pioneering work. At the same time, Furniss and Gunner's wording is intriguing; for example, the phrase "the exploration of the term performance and the broadening of its implications" (2) seems rather tentative and hints at an ongoing struggle to understand performance's relation to folklore, a struggle that Hurston appears never to have experienced, probably because she grew up with the very people she went back to study, and thus already had an embodied knowledge of their practices as performance—indeed, she was herself a performer. The problem of applying performance to folklore research is methodological, posing a challenge for the researcher to find a way to treat the temporality and contingency of performance.

In the 1970s, folklorists such as Dan Ben-Amos, Americo Paredes, Richard Bauman, and Kenneth S. Goldstein initiated the call for a performance-centered approach to verbal art, and Roger Abrahams began to develop a theory of enactment. Like some of their predecessors, these folklorists combined sociolinguistics and folklore, privileged language over other forms of performance, and neglected history. At the same time, however, they developed a more multidimensional analysis of the interrelationships of form, function, and meaning for studying the discursive constitution of social life. This strand of performance theory drew on the concerns of J. J. Gumperz, Dell Hymes, Richard Bauman, and Joel Sherzer about formality, patterning, and communicative competence in speech acts, and about treatments of performance in terms of an event or enactment. This work has in turn been influential on those studying African oral performance, approached variously as performative utterances, verbal art, oral literature and poetry, oral texts, oratory, oral discourse, and orature (oral literature).

Folklore scholarship has had an uneasy relationship with what has been termed *performance*, though Hurston fully embraced performance not only as expressive drama in everyday life, but also as an essential mode of knowing the world and engaging the communities she studied. For many post-Hurstonian folklorists, socially situated performance meant nothing more than a normative, ahistorical description of "context." As Charles L. Briggs has pointed out, "most definitions of context are positivistic, equating it with an 'objective' description of what exists in the situation of a performance" (1988, 14). The question context raises, then, is: Where does text leave off and context begin, and how does a researcher methodologically delimit "a context"?

Folklorists could not have established the boundaries between text and context without genre theory, which serves to frame a text and block it off from everything outside it. The text/context field establishes a perspectival view reflecting the objectivist gaze of the folklorist. This perspectival view is akin to foreground and background in realist painting; it sets the text off as a singular object of study against a background necessarily delimited by the folklorist. It ignores intertextual relations between performances, between different social groups, between genres, and between the genre and what is outside its frame. This approach highlights "product" in the same way the procedures of earlier preservationist folklorists did, and it devalues the ongoing processes of production, reproduction, and transmission. Equally significant is that the text/context frame does not lend itself to the study of African folklore in diaspora, or of the broader intertextual relations between folk performances of various African derivations throughout the Americas and beyond. For example, in Yoruba divination practices, which have found their way to Brazil, Cuba, and the United States, among other places, the same basic material can be recast by performers in radically different genres and styles of performance, from poetic chanting to melodious singing with musical accompaniment to storytelling. The study of a particular genre of divination orature would miss the multiplicity of purposes, uses, diverse media, and situations for which the same material is often reconfigured.

Performance-centered approaches in folkore that, prior to 1986, strove to integrate history, society, and culture in their particularistic studies of events remained, in the words of I. E. Limon and M. I. Young, "still a promise to be fulfilled" (1986, 440). One of the problems was that, as L. Honko has noted, performance folklorists relied heavily on observation rather than "face-to-face knowledge of the speaker or vivid perception of the scene and participants of communication" (1985, 43). In response, Bauman and Briggs advocated a move from "context" to "contextualization," which "involves an active process of negotiation in which participants reflexively examine the discourse as it is emerging, embedding assessments of its structure and significance in the speech itself" (1990, 67–68). Understanding performance as discourse, however, demands approaches that can accommodate more than speech acts, oral tradition, oratory, and conversation, which tend to regard all other related action (facial expression, gesture) as secondary or paralinguistic.

Hurston never struggled with the text/context dichotomy, since she narrated in a way that conveyed the chains of communication in which she herself was fully present as a participant, and in which one person's rendition of a story could be understood to precipitate or remind a participant of another. In this way, Hurston gives the reader a sense of the temporal flow of exchanges and transactions, capturing a sense of a multivocal community of divergent voices in tension around issues of racism, colorism, gender, and other power relations.

Subsequent to Hurston's groundbreaking work, folklorists continued to treat oral performance in Africa as literature or literary text. As literature, oral performance in Africa was transcribed and translated, frozen on the printed page, and treated as a fixed text until 1980 (Seitel 1980). Turned into artifacts and objects for study, the verbal texts were thus decontextualized, stripped from the performative situation in which they were uttered, and rendered statically. The politics of this practice seems to have been an attempt to put the verbal arts in Africa on equal footing with Western literature. Represented by Judith Gleason, Veronika Gorog-Karady, John W. Johnson, Thomas A. Hale, among others, this practice continues alongside situated studies of oral performance (see Isidore Okpewho's critique, "How Not to Treat African Folklore"). Although useful, the transcription and translation of texts do not address performance per se in any direct way.

Another problem in applying a performance paradigm in African folklore studies is the legacy of disciplinary boundaries. This legacy has forced performance in the West, and by extension folklore research in Africa, into arbitrary dissected and compartmentalized categories of disparate media such as oral literature, theater, folk art, dance, music, and so on. Such compartmentalization does not reflect African performance practices. Media rarely exist in isolation in Africa, yet they are often treated as if they do because scholars trained in Western disciplines are incapable of dealing with more than one medium, whether it be oral literature, sculpture, music, dance, song, or ritual symbols. As a reflection of this general state of affairs, Africanists and others became interested in various ways different media function together both in performance and in their interrelationships. The irony is that had the disciplinary tradition not dissected performance into disparate media in the first place, there would be no need for scholars to reintegrate them. On the other hand, studies concerned with how various media function tend to stress their autonomy by drawing distinctions between them, thus maintaining an illusion of exclusivity (see Bloch 1974). But a gesture or a look can alter the intent and reading of an utterance, and vice versa. Indeed, either a gesture or a look can comment on or contradict the other, creating ambiguity. Dancers and musicians, for example, communicate with and comment on each other during performance. Performance is in this way not only multivocal, but multifocal.

The overall effect of disciplinary boundaries is that scholars fail to comprehend performance as a web of multiple and simultaneous discursive practices, and they reduce performance to a unidimensional, normative sequence of events.

Performance studies as a formally institutionalized area of study in academia emerged from two distinct historical contexts: (1) nineteenth-century elocutionism and (2) the avant-garde and political protest movements of the 1960s (see Drewal 1991, 7–8). Until the 1960s, the field of drama focused largely on written texts. Performance theorists such as Richard Schechner thus turned to the social sciences, where scholars were engaged with the study of human behavior. Schechner and Willa Appel's volume *By Means of Performance: Intercultural Studies of Theatre and Ritual* (1990) marks a collaboration that began in the spring of 1977 and included conferences in 1981 and 1982. The conferences and the volume that grew out of them brought together practitioners, theater scholars, anthropologists, and others, including Heather and Anselmo Valencia, Monica Bethe, Phillip Zarrilli, Herbert Blau, Du-Hyun Lee, Victor and Edie Turner, Colin Turnbull, Barbara Myerhoff, Barbara Kirshenblatt-Gunblett, Yi-Fu Tuan, James Peacock, and Ranjini Obeyesekere. From the conjunction of these interests in theater and anthropology, the Graduate Drama Program at New York University changed its identity in 1980, reconstituting itself as the Department of Performance Studies so that students might rigorously pursue the interdisciplinary, intergeneric, and intercultural study of performance (Zarrilli 1986a, 372; 1986b).

The institutionalization of performance studies as an academic discipline in its own right is particularly significant because it opened up the definition of performance to incorporate the practice of everyday life, defying disciplinary constraints and boundaries in order to forge a more truly interdisciplinary research practice. Implied here is that performers have been either formally or informally trained in body techniques in order to restore or revive a particular style or mode of performance. Meanwhile, from the 1970s on, other institutions of higher learning became centers for performance-oriented research, understood initially as the study of context in folklore. The most notable of these were the folklore programs at the University of Texas at Austin, the University of Wisconsin, Madison, and, especially, Indiana University (see Stone 1988). In this approach, performance often involves what Bauman and Briggs call "the enactment of the poetic function" (1990), as well as the authoritative display of communicative competence—features of performance that have been of particular concern in sociolinguistics and folklore. Paralleling the performance-centered approach in folklore was a similar movement in African art studies to examine the contexts of the use of objects, particularly evident in the journal *African Arts* from the late 1960s onward. These studies likewise involved objective descriptions of performance as the context of African art forms.

In Africa, performance is a primary arena for the production of knowledge. It is where philosophy is enacted and where multiple and often simultaneous discourses are employed (Drewal 1990). In addition, performance is a means by which people reflect on their current condition, define or reinvent themselves and their social world, and either re-enforce, resist, or subvert the prevailing social order. Indeed, both subversion and legitimation can emerge in the same utterance or act.

Since performance is temporal and, in Africa, often improvisational, participatory, and contingent, three simultaneous paradigmatic shifts are required for a performance-studies approach to African folklore: (1) from structure to process (i.e., from an essentially spatialized, distanced, objectivist view to a temporal, participatory, and interactive research practice); (2) from the normative to the particular and historically situated (i.e., from the timeless to the time-centered); and (3) from the collective to the agency of named individuals in the continuous flow of social interactions. Only through these shifts can performance

as practice be historicized and long-term transformations be revealed.

The reason such a shift has not occurred in African studies is twofold: (1) the tendency in the social sciences (until fairly recently) to search for regularity, pattern, and convention in societies, and (2) the inadequacy of researchers' performance and other skills, including the lack of fluency in African languages, which has precluded any research method other than distanced observation. The problem is, as Karin Barber has noted, "the kind of collaboration that social science, in its shift from positivistic observation of social facts to participatory interpretation of human experience, now enjoins, is usually easier to propose than to perform, not least because the researcher has so little to offer her proposed partners, the subjects of her study" (Barber 1987, 65). This would be true of highly formalized practices that require apprenticeships and years of training to master, such as drumming, dancing, or woodcarving. Harold Scheub makes a very similar argument with regard to the compartmentalization of oral tradition and the written word, which he sees as grievous because it has "led to misconceptions about the verbal arts" (1985, 45). He suggests more attention should be given to the relationship between the oral and the written.

Given that performance in Africa is temporal, tactical, and improvisational, it demands an approach that can accommodate human agents in the process of constructing ongoing social realities. The embodied practices and actions of performers as human agents situated in time and place in Africa—both constituting, and constituents of, ongoing social processes—remain largely unresearched. As long as researchers continue to privilege one medium, genre, or context, that is, to view a performance as an isolated event, rather than as part of an ongoing process in continual dialogue and flux, the concept of performance will remain static and reductive. And it is in this area that a performance paradigm as a research method can advance folklore research.

Performance challenges the notion of an objective social reality, as well as the notion that society and human beings are products. Not only is performance production, but both society and human beings are performative, always under construction. As restored behavior, both performance and research entail repetition—not as reproduction, but as a transformational process involving acts of re-presentation with critical differences. As such, both performance and research necessarily involve relations between the past and individual agents' interpretations, inscriptions, and revisions of that past in present theory and practice.

Instead, however—strongly reflecting a materialist-objectivist bias—most research in Africa renders performance "thinglike"—by turning it into structures and sets of symbols, in the case of ritual; graphic notation, in the case of music; and the printed word, in the case of oral literature. Olabiyi Yai takes issue with folklorists who rely substantially on transcriptions:

> Thus, the "text" of an oral poem is fixed and mummified, paralinguistic elements being the only elements of variation. This, in our view, imposes drastic limitations on the generative latitude of the translator-performer, thereby ignoring the essence of oral translation which is re-creation. In our model, improvisation is basic and the translator-performer may even add "lines" of his/her own making to the "text" which is never closed, once he/she

is inspired by the mood or the muse of the genre. (1989, 68–69)

To involve oneself in the production of performance means learning techniques and styles and, above all, learning to improvise. Yai's model, in fact, would be a good model for fieldwork on performance generally.

In focusing on transcriptions of texts, research reifies performance as a spatialized representation for mental cognition alone, as if detached from the human bodies that practice it. Ruth Finnegan has shown how this works in the study of music:

> Musical art too tends to be equated with its written form, so that if something is not written it is assessed as not "really" music, or at any rate not worth serious scholarly study. In traditional western musicology "music" is usually defined as the musical work, itself in turn defined as its written formulation—the score—rather than, for instance, the process of playing or singing or the act of performance. This emphasis on text is reinforced by the western educational system . . . where formal music training even in unassuming local schools as well as in conservatoire settings is usually taken to consist in learning to read music: to cope with notation, learn musical theory, and pass written (not just practical) music examinations. . . . As with oral literature, this definition of music as text leaves out essential elements of the art form as actually practiced by performing musicians and experienced by audiences. (Finnegan 1988, 125)

As music notation becomes the object studied, the graphic description becomes the context. With few exceptions, most research renders performance static rather than dynamic by adhering to normative structural models (perhaps from a desire for fixity) in spite of occasional invocations of creativity, invention, and play. Performance process and the embodied practices and actions of performers as human agents situated in time and place remain largely unresearched.

Yai blames "the new concept of performance" for this problem:

> The common flow of all theories of performance is that by portraying oral poetry performance not as one moment in its mode of existence but as the absolute event they unconsciously reify it and endow it with attributes of finiteness typical of written literature. Oral poetry is thus equated with an "oeuvre" and a monument, an attitude which blocks the way for perceiving critical activities outside the "event." The truth is that a literary work in oral form is never "bounded" and that we can grasp oral criticism of oral poetry before, during and after "performance." To be able to understand the oral poetics of oral poetry, we must dismiss any theory which presents this poetry as a "product" or a "work" that has the features of finitude and closure as implied by these concepts. Instead, we should talk of uninterrupted "production." (Yai 1989, 63)

Although Yai refers specifically to oral performance, his observations could easily apply to the study of all modes of performance in Africa. It was perhaps folklore's methods of studying performance as a fixed and bounded event, rather than as unin-terrupted processes, that drew Yai's critique. And if Hurston's folklore studies seemed unconventional, it is because she brought a sense of this process into her writing, conveying a sense of the temporal flow of storytelling and of her own role in that process.

A more participatory practice in folklore fieldwork means placing the emphasis on the participant side of the participant observer paradigm; breaking down the boundaries between self and other, subject and object, subjectivity and objectivity; and engaging in a more truly dialogical relationship with the subjects of study so that both researcher and researched are equal participants in performance discourse (Fabian 1983). This has been accomplished most successfully in the past by ethnomusicologists who have mastered African instruments and music styles, and who therefore can join in the music production. Paul Berliner, John Chernoff, David Locke, and Michelle Kisliuk are only a few exemplars of this.

Because most performance in Africa is participatory, there are many diverse kinds of roles researchers can take. What performers understand cross-culturally is that anthropologist Michael Jackson's notion of "practical mimesis" is only an initial stage in learning to perform. The more a performer performs, the more embodied the practice becomes, so that at some point performing becomes second nature and performers can begin to "play" with the practice—they can begin to improvise. This is analogous to acquiring fluency in a foreign language.

The paradigm shift advocated here means changing from the normative to the particular by focusing on how performance practitioners and other participants operate, observing *what* they actually do in specific performances, and then listening to what they say about what they do (their intentionality). Since much performance in Africa is participatory, the distinctions between performers and spectators are blurred. All participants are in dialogue with each other, and they frequently shift their standpoints within the performance. Very little research in Africa deals specifically with reception. Part of the difficulty is that the idea of reception implies some sort of distanced separation and a unidirectional relationship between performer and audience (see Nkanga 1995 for a corrective to this perception). Shifting to the particular also means distinguishing particular performances situated in time and place from performances as events encapsulating a culture or an ideology.

Adopting a temporal perspective means following repeated performances of the same kind by the same people, but between different groups of people (different audiences). It means focusing on individuals in specific performances as they use structure and process, and then locating that performance within a larger body of performances and in history, society, and politics. This is a fundamental reorientation in the study of performance. But rather than losing sight of social structure, as skeptics might imagine, the performances illuminate structuring properties all the more brilliantly, indicating at the same time how performers handle them.

Studies of the particular should also include specific instances of the transmission of modes, techniques, and styles for generating performance and constructing authority. Given the contingent nature of unscripted performance, it is not sufficient to observe that performance is emergent; rather, it is crucial to understand how particular performances situated in time and place emerge through the discursive practices of agents (and through the rhetoric of their actions). With these shifts to the particular and the individual, it is possible to study performance as transformational process, in contrast to the more standard approach to certain kinds of performance, such as ritual, as a process of regularization in which the performance is viewed more or less as reproducing the past or the cosmos in a stable fashion with relatively little, or only gradual, change. But in shifting methodologically to the particular and the individual in the study of performance, what becomes readily apparent is that there are no predictable or verifiable constants in performances endlessly or mindlessly repeated by performers. This is precisely why change is possible. Performance is a multilayered discourse employing multiple voices and perspectives continuously under negotiation. It is crucial to understand transformative practices and processes in order to understand change in the long term.

Folklore research in Africa can benefit from performance studies by understanding the interactive, intertextual, intergeneric, and intercultural processes characteristic of African and diaspora practices. Hurston acknowledged these practices and could be said to be the unrecognized precursor of contemporary performance theory. Ahead of her time, Hurston's methodology reflected these suggested paradigm shifts—against the grain of conventional Boasian anthropology. Her practices disoriented the academic and literary community of the time, and to this day scholars still struggle to classify her work generically (see, for example, Gates and Appiah 1993, Williams 1994, Domina 1997, and Jacobs 1997). Hurston's faithfulness to African-American culture indeed provoked some bourgeois literati of the Harlem Renaissance, for she embraced her African legacy unconditionally (Williams 1994). Richard Wright accused her of "the minstrel technique that makes 'white folks' laugh" (1993, 17). Hurston's work appeared in the wake of the popularity of Joel Chandler Harris's *Uncle Remus*, and, misrecognizing her style, critics drew an unfortunate connection between the two (see Moon 1993, 10, and Gannett 1993, 11).

However, the emerging field of performance studies is moving closer to Hurston's model of performance as both an interactive method for research and a subject of study. Hurston's interactive approach to folklore did not freeze tales on the printed page as bounded objects of study. She understood the intersubjective, intertextual, and intergeneric practices at the heart of African American mimicry and parody, and she also used and played on these relations in her own theatrical and written work. She already knew what Olabiyi Yai understood and advocated in 1989, that "from the point of view of oral poetics, oral poetry strictly speaking should not even be described. We know it by practicing it and by contributing to its making" (Yai 1989, 68). As a bearer of African-American tradition herself, Hurston was true to the practice. She did not describe or explicitly analyze so much as she practiced her embodied knowledge of oral poetics, albeit in written form through her translations, but she also contributed to its making (in Yai's sense) by restaging it in both literary and theatrical forms for broader audiences. Hurston's participatory practice in the study of folklore, no doubt based on her first-hand experience of it from childhood, gave her access to the processes of its production, which enabled her to subvert the objectivist bias in folklore. As D. A. Boxwell put it:

According to [objectivist] standards, *Mules and Men*, with its highly visible, intensely subjective, and active narrator and distinctly felt "author image," appears to be a willful

violation of long-held and persistent attitudes to social-scientific writing. Yet it is now possible, I think, to view Hurston's work as a striking prefiguration of theories articulated in Clifford Geertz's recent writings about the limitations of Boasian attitudes toward ethnography. (1992, 607)

It is also this very unconventional practice, and the impact of the legacy of objectivism on contemporary folklore, that all too easily allows Hurston to be consistently ignored as the quintessential folklorist employing performance theory. For, while she set out to translate storytelling into literature, her mode of presentation documented the ongoing processes of communal interactions as performance.

References

Bakhtin, Mikail. 1968. *Rabelais and His World*. Tr. Helen Iswolski. Cambridge, Mass: MIT Press.

———. 1981. *The Dialogic Imagination*. Ed. M. Holquist. Tr. Caryl Emerson. Austin: University of Texas Press.

Barber, Karin. 1987. Popular Arts in Africa. *African Studies Review* 3, no. 3:1–78.

Bateson, Gregory. 1958. *Naven*. 2d ed. Stanford, Calif.: Stanford University Press.

———. 1972. *Steps to an Ecology of Mind*. San Francisco: Chandler.

Bauman, Richard. 1977. *Verbal Art as Performance*. Prospect Heights, Ill.: Waveland.

Bauman, Richard, and Charles L. Briggs. 1990. Poetics and Performance as Critical Perspectives on Language and Social Life. *Annual Review of Anthropology* 19:59–88.

Ben-Amos, Dan. 1971. Toward a Definition of Folklore in Context. *Journal of American Folklore* 84:3–15.

———. 1987. Introduction. *Word & Image: A Journal of Verbal/Visual Enquiry* (Special Issue on African Art and Literature) 3, no. 3:223–4.

Ben-Amos, Dan, and Kenneth S. Goldstein, eds. 1975. *Folklore: Performance and Communication*. The Hague: Mouton.

Bloch, Maurice. 1974. Symbols, Song, Dance, and Features of Articulation. *European Journal of Sociology* 1511:55–81.

Boxwell, D. A. 1992. "Sis Cat" As Ethnographer: Self-Presentation and Self-Inscription in Zora Neale Hurston's *Mules and Men*. *African American Review*, 26, no. 4:605–18.

Briggs, Charles L. 1988. *Competence in Performance: The Creativity of Tradition in Mexicano Verbal Art*. Philadelphia: University of Pennsylvania Press.

Burke, Kenneth. 1945. *A Grammar of Motives*. Berkeley: University of California Press.

Davis, Mella. 1998. African Trickster Tales in Diaspora: Resistance in the Creole-Speaking South Carolina Sea Islands and Guadeloupe, French West Indies. Ph.D. diss., Northwestern University.

Domina, Lynn. 1997. "Protection in My Mouf": Self, Voice, and Community in Zora Neale Hurston's *Dust Tracks on a Road* and *Mules and Men*. (Autobiography and Ethnography by Zora Neale Hurston.) *African American Review* 31, no. 2:197–210.

Drewal, Henry John. 1980. *African Artistry: Technique and Aesthetics in Yoruba Sculpture*. Atlanta: High Museum of Art.

Drewal, Henry John, and Margaret Thompson Drewal. 1990. *Gelede: Art and Female Power Among the Yoruba*. 2d ed. Bloomington: Indiana University Press.

Drewal, Margaret Thompson. 1990. (Inter)text, Performance, and the African Humanities. *Text and Performance Quarterly* 10, no. 1:72–86.

———. 1991. The State of Research on Performance in Africa. *African Studies Review*. 34, no. 3:1–64.

———. 1992. *Yoruba Ritual: Performers, Play, Agency.* Bloomington: Indiana University Press.

Drewal, Margaret Thompson, and Henry John Drewal. 1987. Composing Time and Space in Yoruba Art. *Word and Image: A Journal of Verbal Visual Enquiry* 3, no. 3:225–51.

Fabian, Johannes. 1983. *Time and the Other. How Anthropology Makes Its Object.* New York: Columbia University Press.

Finnegan, Ruth. 1988. *Literacy and Orality. Studies in the Technology of Communication.* Oxford: Oxford University Press.

Furniss, Graham, and Liz Gunner, eds. 1995. *Power, Marginality, and African Oral Literature.* Cambridge, England: Cambridge University Press.

Gannett, Lewis. [1935] 1993. "*The New York Herald Tribune Weekly Book Review*, October 11, 1935." In *Zora Neale Hurston: Critical Perspectives Past and Present.* Ed. Henry Louis Gates Jr. and K. A. Appiah. New York: Amisted.

Gates, Henry Louis, Jr., and K. A. Appiah, eds. 1993. *Zora Neale Hurston: Critical Perspectives Past and Present.* New York: Amisted.

Geertz, Clifford. 1973. *The Interpretation of Culture.* New York: Basic Books.

———. 1980. Blurred Genres. *American Scholar* 49, no. 2:165–82.

Gleason, Judith. 1981. *Leaf and Bone, African Praise Poems: An Anthology with Commentary.* New York: Viking Press.

Goffman, Erving. 1959. *The Presentation of Self in Everyday Life.* Garden City, NY: Doubleday/Anchor.

———. 1974. *Frame Analysis: An Essay on the Organization of Experience.* NY: Harper & Row.

Gorog-Karady, Veronika, ed. 1982. *Genres, Forms, Meanings: Essays in African Oral Literature.* Paris: MSH.

Hale, Thomas A. 1990. *Scribe, Griot, and Novelist: Narrative Interpreters of the Songhay Empire Followed by The Epic of Askia Mohammed Recounted by Nouhou Malio.* Gainesville, University of Florida Press.

Hill, Lynda M. 1993. Staging Hurston's Life and Work. In *Acting Out. Feminist Performances.* Ed. Lynda Hart and Peggy Phelan. Ann Arbor: The University of Michigan Press.

Honko, L. 1985. Empty Texts, Full Meanings: On Transformal Meaning in Folklore. *Journal of Folklore Research* 22:37–44.

Hurston, Zora Neale. 1981. *The Sanctified Church.* Foreward by Toni Cade Bambara. New York: Marlowe.

Ibrahim, Abdullah Ali. 1994. *Assaulting with Words: Popular Discourse and the Bridle of SharTah.* Evanston, Ill.: Northwestern University Press.

Jackson, Michael. 1989. *Paths toward a Clearing: Radical Empiricism and Ethnographic Inquiry.* Bloomington: Indiana University Press.

Jacobs, Karen. 1997. From "Spy-Glass" to "Horizon": Tracking the Anthropological Gaze in Zora Neale Hurston. *Forum on Fiction* 30, no. 3:329–60.

Johnson, John William. 1986. *The Epic of Son-Jara: A West African Tradition.* Text by Fa-Digi Sisoko. Bloomington: Indiana University Press.

Limon, J. E., and M. J. Young. 1986. "Frontiers, Settlements, and Development in Folklore Studies, 1972–1986." *Annual Review of Anthropology* 15:437–60.

McNaughton, Patrick R. 1987. Nyamakalaw: The Mande Bards and Blacksmiths. *Word & Image: A Journal of Verbal/Visual Enquiry* 3, no. 3:271–88.

Moon, Henry Lee. [1935] 1993. "*The New Republic*, December 11, 1935." In *Zora Neale Hurston: Critical Perspectives Past and Present.* Ed. Henry Louis Gates, Jr. and K. A. Appiah. New York: Amisted.

Nkanga, Dieudonné-Christophe Mbala. 1995. Multivocality and the Hidden Text in Central African Theatre and Popular Performances: A Study of the Rhetoric of Social and Political Criticism. Ph.D. diss., Northwestern University.

Okpewho, Isidore. 1996. How Not to Treat African Folklore. *Research in African Literatures* 27, no. 3:119–29.

Opland, Jeff. 1983. *Xhosa Oral Poetry: Aspects of a Black South African Tradition.* Cambridge Studies in Oral and Literate Culture. Cambridge, England. Cambridge University Press.

Ortner, Sherry B. 1984. Theory in Anthropology Since the Sixties. *Comparative Studies in Society and History. An International Quarterly* 26, no. 1:126–66.

Paredes, Américo, and Richard Bauman, eds. 1972. *Toward New Perspectives in Folklore.* Austin: The University of Texas Press.

Schechner, Richard. [1966] 1988. Approaches. In *Performance Theory.* Rev. ed. Ed. Richard Schechner. New York: Routledge.

———. 1985. *Between Theatre and Anthropology.* Philadelphia: University of Pennsylvania Press.

Schechner, Richard, and Willa Appel, eds. 1990. *By Means of Performance: Intercultural Studies of Theatre and Ritual.* Cambridge: Cambridge University Press.

Scheub, Harold. 1985. A Review of African Oral Traditions and Literature. *African Studies Review* 2, no. 8:1–72.

Seitel, Peter. 1980. *See So That We May See: Performances and Interpretations of Traditional Tales from Tanzania.* Bloomington: Indiana University Press.

Singer, Milton. 1972. *When a Great Tradition Modernizes: An Anthropological Approach to Indian Civilization.* New York: Praeger.

Stone, Ruth M., ed. 1988. *Journal of Folklore Research* (Special Issue, Performance in Contemporary African Arts) 25, nos. 1 and 2.

Turner, Victor. 1957. *Schism and Continuity in an African Society.* Manchester: Manchester University Press.

———. 1969. *The Ritual Process: Structure and Anti-Structure.* Chicago: Aldine.

Williams, Donna M. 1994. Our love-hate relationship with Zora Neale Hurston." *Black Collegian* 24, no. 3:86, 91.

Wright, Richard. [1937] 1993. "*New Masses*, October 5, 1937." In *Zora Neale Hurston: Critical Perspectives Past and Present.* Ed. Henry Louis Gates, Jr. and K. A. Appiah. New York: Amisted.

Yai, Olabiyi. 1989. Issues in Oral Poetry: Criticism, Teaching, and Translation. In *Discourse and Its Disguises: The Interpretation of African Oral Texts.* Ed. K. Barber and F. de Moraes Farias. Birmingham University African Studies Series 1. Birmingham: Centre of West African Studies, University of Birmingham.

Yankah, Kwesi. 1995. *Speaking for the Chief. Okyeame and the Politics of Akan Royal Oratory.* Bloomington: Indiana University Press.

Zarrilli, Phillip B. 1986a. Toward a Definition of Performance Studies: Part I. *Theatre Journal* 38, no. 3:372–76.

———. 1986b. Toward a Definition of Performance Studies: Part II. *Theatre Journal* 38, 4:493–96.

MARGARET THOMPSON DREWAL

See also **Drama; Festivals; Gesture in African Oral Narrative; Oral Performance Dynamics; Oral Traditions; Performance At Theater**

PERFORMING ARTS OF SÃO TOMÉ AND PRÍNCIPE

São Tomé and Príncipe, located in the Gulf of Guinea, is a twin-island republic with a total area of 372 square miles, making it the second smallest independent state in Africa. The islands have a total population of 170,000 (2002), of which about 5,000 live on the smaller island of Príncipe. Portuguese navigators discovered the two uninhabited islands around 1471. In the late fifteenth century, Portuguese settlers and convicts, deported Jewish children, and African slaves from the mainland settled the islands. The Portuguese introduced sugar cane, making the islands the first plantation economy in the tropics. Since the late nineteenth century, cocoa has dominated the local plantation economy. The African slaves were taken to the islands as individuals and not as social groups so they did not retain their various cultures and languages intact.

The Culture and Language

The five-hundred-year-long blending of elements of the dominant Catholic Portuguese culture and the African cultures resulted in the development of a distinctive Creole society with its own culture and languages. The majority of Creoles are descendants of the early settlers and slaves and are called Forros, a term derived from the Portuguese word for "letter of manumission." In the sixteenth and seventeenth centuries, runaway slaves formed a small maroon community in the south of São Tomé, and their descendants are known as Angolares. They are now primarily fishermen. Both Forros and Angolares have always refused to do manual field labor on the Portuguese *roças* (plantations), as they historically considered it demeaning and beneath their status as free blacks. Because their number was insufficient to supply the necessary labor, between 1875 and the 1950s the Portuguese recruited thousands of contract workers from Angola, Mozambique, and Cape Verde. These indentured laborers, called *serviçais*, constituted a new sociocultural category on the islands and outnumbered the native Forros up until the 1940s. The contract workers were considered second-class citizens under colonial law, which discriminated between natives (indigenous) and citizens until it was abolished in 1961. Their descendants born on the archipelago, known as Tongas, still live predominantly on the plantations, whereas the Forros live in the capital and in the few small towns and dispersed communities, locally called *lucháns*. Since the country's independence in 1975, the Tongas have been assimilated by the Forro community through migration, acculturation, and marriage, and the sociocultural differences between the groups have been blurred. Consequently, some realignments have occurred among the sociocultural categories entailing the development of new cultural forms and changing modes of participation in social life.

Besides the official language of Portuguese, three distinct Afro-Portuguese creole languages are spoken: Ling'lé on Príncipe, Lunga Santomé, or Forro, on São Tomé, and the Lunga Ngola of the Angolares. The first two are mutually intelligible; however, due to the isolation of the former maroons, Lunga Ngola is unintelligible for Ling'lé and Forro speakers, although the three languages are closely related in terms of phonology, lexicon, and syntax. The local creole languages have no generally accepted and written orthographies, and instead rely on oral literature. During the colonial period, the Portuguese considered the local Creoles as inferior and primitive. After independence, however, the government promoted the Lunga Santomé to *língua nacional* (national language). In daily life at home the Creole is used and spoken by the majority of the people. Only the upper class speak Portuguese in their private lives. Portuguese remains the official language, however, as well as the language of education. Except for a few lyrics, literature on the islands is in Portuguese. Due to its physical, historic, economic, and sociocultural characteristics, São Tomé and Príncipe is more akin to the Afro-Creole societies in the Caribbean than to the nearby African societies.

Oral Literature

There are four distinct forms of local oral literature in the archipelago. A riddle (*aguede* in creole), such as "I have gone and come, but have not left the place" (door) or "House without door or window" (egg) often serves for entertainment at night. A *vessu* is a proverb or proverbial saying derived from historic or fabulous facts, traditional stories, and theater plays. These are used in conversation and songs. A *contagi* (tale that is well known) is a sad or happy narrative and can be told on any occasion. Such popular folktales feature figures familiar from both African and European folktales, such as royalty, giants, and witches, and frequently deal with encounters of men and animals. The turtle often plays a prominent role as a sympathetic, intelligent, and bright animal, comparable to the fox in European stories. The tales reflect important aspects of social life in the archipelago, such as the natural environment, the plantation, hunting, traditional medicine, and beliefs. *Soia* are fictional stories exclusively narrated by storytellers at night during the Nozado, the memorial ceremony for the dead. According to local belief, angry spirits are likely to cause the death of a family member if a *soia* is told outside the Nozado.

Theater

The best-known manifestations of local folklore are popular theater performances that include colorful costumes and anachronistic properties. Forros on the island of São Tomé perform the most famous play: *The Tragic Story of the Marquis of Mântua and Emperor Charlemagne*, locally known as *tchiloli* and based on text written around 1540 by Baltasar Dias of Madeira, a blind playwright. He based his drama on six Castilian novels, which were in turn derived from the eleventh-century Charlemagne cycle. Most probably, the Dias drama was introduced from Portugal and first performed in the mid-nineteenth century. Around that time such texts reappeared and circulated in Portugal as *literatura de cordel*, a form of cheap literary produc-

Anto de Floripes theater (the troops of the Moors), Santo António, Príncipe.
Photo © Lourenço Silva.

tion. It has also been suggested that the play was introduced by sugar planters from Madeira as early as in the sixteenth century; however, its existence on São Tomé is not mentioned in the literature prior to the twentieth century. The drama has also been taken to the Sertão, Brazil's northeast interior. The medieval play tells the story of Dom Carloto, the son and heir of Charlemagne, who kills his best friend Valdevinos, the Marquis' nephew, during a hunting party because he has fallen in love with Valdevinos's wife, Sibila. The two families and their representatives debate questions of law, justice, and good government. The key subjects are treason and equality before the law. The emperor is confronted with the classical dilemma to choose between the *raison d'état* (reason of state) and his paternal love. Finally, his son Dom Carloto is sentenced to death and executed in the imperial fortress.

Presently there are more than ten *tchiloli* groups, known as *tragédias*, with about thirty amateur actors, each coming from a particular Forro locality. Within certain dramaturgic limits, each troupe performs its particular version of the play. According to the medieval tradition, men exclusively play and dance both male and female roles. The same actor always performs the same parts. The roles, costumes, and texts are passed down within families. It is not uncommon for actors to be addressed by their *tchiloli* names in daily life. Usually the performances last about six hours and take place in the open air during the dry season, called *gravana*, predominantly on the occasion of religious feast days and other festivals. The African influence, in terms of the notion of time, has extended the few pages of the original to what is often a very long performance. However, during official inaugurations, expositions, or guest performances abroad, the drama can be condensed to a few scenes (about ninety minutes). The open stage, some 15 to 20 yards long and 5 to 10 yards wide, can be watched from all sides. The spectators participate actively in the performance by making comments during the various scenes of the play, which many islanders know well. On one side of the open space rises the *corte alta* (high court) on wooden stakes and roofed with palm-tree branches, representing the imperial palace. On the opposite side is a cabin on the ground made of green branches representing the *corte baixa* (low court) of the mourning Mântua family. During the entire play a small coffin placed on a stool in the midst of the stage symbolizes the dead Valdevinos.

Most of Dias's sixteenth-century seven-syllable verses are used in their original version, but additional modern Portuguese prose texts have been integrated into the performance. The latter dominate the parts concerning the criminal investigation and the legal procedures. Contrary to the original text, these modern additions are constantly adapted and extemporized by the actors. Three drummers, three bamboo flute players, and four men shaking *sucalos* (wicker-rattles filled with seeds) provide the music that accompanies the actors when they dance across the stage. The music is rather monotonous, for the same melody is repeated constantly. The dance, dumb-show, and music dominate the performance, rather than the verse and prose texts. Charlemagne's family members are dressed up in splendid, colorfully decorated costumes, and his ministers are in Napoleon-style hats and uniforms. The Mântua family members wear black mourning dresses, while the two lawyers, Anderson and Bertrand, appear in three-piece suits and carry briefcases. The actors use wire-screen masks until after sunset. The masks, commonly painted in a white-face style, can be understood as manifestations of the spiritual world, for in Africa white is the color of the dead. Certain characters wear long colorful ribbons, a symbol of wealth. Particularly during the 1950s, additional figures, such as the two lawyers, derived from the twentieth-century colonial administration, have been integrated alongside the medieval royal personages. In addition, some actors wear sunglasses and fashionable rucksacks, and the imperial court is equipped with a telephone and a typewriter.

The *tchiloli* is an exciting example of cultural creolization and syncretic theatre. It comprises elements stemming from different cultures and times that seem to be incompatible at first sight. The play has always given the local people the opportunity to have debates on justice, the confrontation between the strong and the weak, a fair trial, and the stamina of those who are right and finally win. As this popular play developed in a plantation colony marked by slavery and forced labor, the search for justice and truth has been an important aspect of its production. It has even been argued that the *tchiloli* originally represented a form of political resistance against colonial oppression, serving both playful and therapeutic functions.

The *Auto da Floripes*

Another medieval drama, the *Auto da Floripes*, is played every year on August 10, the feast day of Saint Lawrence on Príncipe. The play probably stems from the sixteenth or seventeenth century, and its author is unknown. As this play has been performed annually for five centuries on August 5 in the village of Neves in the Portuguese Minho province, it is not unlikely that an emigrant from that region took it to Príncipe. Against the background of the battle between Christians and Muslim Turks, or Moors, the play tells the story of the revolt of a daughter against her father. Princess Floripes, the daughter of the Moor commander admiral Balão, has fallen in love with the Christian knight Gui de Borgonha. The action takes place in the small town of Santo António, and the thirty actors wear colorful, decorated costumes, with many wearing artificial moustaches and beards. The Christians are dressed in white and blue, and the Moors in red. A wooden platform in front of the parish church represents the castle of Charlemagne. On the opposite side of the street rises the castle of the Moor admiral Balão. The performance lasts a whole day, and the dramatic climax is a two-and-a-half-hour fight between the Christian nobleman Oliveiros and the Turk Ferrabrás, Floripes's brother and the son of admiral Balão. During a hand-to-hand duel with swords, both men try to convert each other to his own beliefs. Finally, Ferrabrás surrenders, becomes converted to Christianity, and joins the army of Charlemagne. In one of the many battles, Balão himself succeeds in capturing Gui de Borgonha and detains him in his castle. Floripes is torn between her love for Gui and her father. She asks her father to convert to Christianity like her brother, but Balão rejects her proposal. After the Christians defeat Balão in a final battle, a large pageant, accompanied by singing people, drums, horns, and hooters, moves through the streets of Santo António. The part of Floripes has to be played every year by a different girl, whereas the other roles are articulated by the same male actors and passed down from year to year. Formerly, the girl had to be a virgin, but this rule has become difficult to maintain. As there is no fixed version of the text, the actors performances, called *congos* or *congadas*, constitute an integral part of the festivals of religious brotherhoods in Brazil. Blacks performed a Congo festival in Lisbon as early as the sixteenth century. The theme probably stems from the coronation of the Mani-Congo in Angola. The dance may have come to São Tomé directly from Africa or indirectly from Bahia, where the local Creole clergy was educated from 1677–1845, when São Tomé belonged to the archdiocese of Bahia.

The Danço Congo is enacted in the open air by permanent associations domiciled both within Forro and Angolar communities. It symbolizes the story of four incompetent sons (the Bobos), who have to give the *roça* they inherited from their father to the captain of Congo. During a festivity on the plantation both the Bobos and the Captain invite the Sorcerer and his assistant, who then are captured and compelled to participate in the dance. The Captain, however, constantly fears that the two might kill the Anso Molê. Finally, the Sorcerer and his assistant succeed in escaping. In the meantime the Pés-de-Pau begin to dance, surrounded by all the characters. Thereupon, the Devil starts jumping and moving convulsively. The Sorcerer reappears and succeeds in killing the Anso Molê. The Captain is shocked and asks the Logoso why he allowed the flight of the sorcerer and the Devil. Meanwhile, the Bobos and the others, unmoved by the murder of the angel, continue to dance, for they see no reason to interrupt the party. The Danço Congo can last about six hours, and it is perhaps the most lively, colorful, and noisy manifestation of local folklore. Like other theater and dance, it is performed on religious feast days and official festivals.

Other Dances

While many of the older dance forms of the Forros have definitively disappeared, the *ússua* and the *sócópé* are still performed by community-based cultural groups. Their members pay fees, and the groups also function as associations of mutual assistance in the case of funerals, illness, and other misfortunes. The steps and the music of the *ússua* are similar to a slow waltz or a minuet. The musical instruments accompanying the dance are one accordion, two *canzás*, two *caixas* (drums), and a *bombo* (large drum). The *mestre-sala* (dancing master) conducts the dancers with his horn. The women dancers wear colorful robes, long skirts with laces, albs (full-length linen vestments), laced clerical collars, long and wide sleeves, and headscarves. The men are dressed in black trousers, black shoes, white blazers, a tie, and straw hats.

The *sócópé*, literally meaning "only with the foot," developed from the *ússua* and first appeared on the island of São Tomé around 1900. Within the *sócópé*, dance troupes of both men and women have a complex hierarchy consisting of numerous functions ranging from president to singers. The groups carry their own standard and the country's national flag during the performance. The men are dressed in showy uniforms with stripes and badges, or else in black trousers and white shirts; while the women wear uniform colorful skirts, white blouses, and scarves. The instruments are three *caixas*, *canzás*, one *pito* (bamboo flute), and two *bombos*. Currently the *sócópé* is still performed by only a few groups.

The *puíta* (or semba) is a dance introduced by Angolan contract workers. It was once performed all night long by the African contract workers and the Tongas on the plantations during a

Danço Congo masquerade, Sáo Tomé.
Photo © Lourenço Silva.

extemporize and continuously develop new themes, motives, intrigues, and fragments. Music, dance, pantomime, and properties play important roles in the performance of the *Auto de Floripes*.

The Danço Congo

Other distinct cultural societies on São Tomé, comprising twenty to thirty members each, perform the Danço Congo, acted out in a dumb show with dances, acrobatics, whistles, and drumming. Typically, the characters are the Capitão (captain) of Congo and his soldiers playing Canzás (bamboo bows), the Logoso (plantation guard), the Anso Molê (the dying angel), two Anso Cantá (singing angels), two Pés-De-Pau (men walking on stilts and wearing red trousers), four Bobos (buffoons), the Feiticeiro (sorcerer), the Zugozugo (assistant of the sorcerer), and the D'jabo (devil). The sorcerer, his assistant, and the devil are dressed in red, while the other actors wear colorful costumes, dominated by green. The costumes stem directly from African styles with high, large circular headdresses made of iron wire and decorated with colored paper strips.

The Danço Congo remind one of performances dedicated to the king of Congo in Brazil, Columbia, and Panama. Such party in honor of a deceased person. The guests eat and drink the deceased's health before they dance to the sound of the percussion music. *Puíta* is also the name of the large drum used for the dance. The other instruments used are two small drums, one *micoló* (can beaten with wooden sticks), three *sucalos*, an iron rod, and an ox horn. The songs are both in local Creole and African languages. Since independence, many plantation workers have migrated to the capital, and the *puíta* can now be found in the neighborhoods of São Tomé city. The *bulauê*, which developed after independence among Tongas living in urban neighborhoods, has been adopted by the larger Forro community and can now be found in all corners of the island. However, the *bulauê* is more popular among low-status Forros, while the elite often disdain this dance. Its songs are in the Forro creole. Unlike the older Forro dance societies, the *bulauê* society does not offer mutual assistance to its members.

References

Ambrósio, António. 1985. Para a história do folclore São-Tomense. *História*. 81: 60–88.

Espirito Santo, Carlos. 1988. *A Coroa do Mar*. Lisbon: Editorial Caminho.

Fablier de São Tomé. 1984. Collection Fleuve et Flamme. Paris: edicef.

Perkins, Juliet. 1990. A Contribuição Portuguesa ao tchiloli de São Tomé. *Revista do património histórico e artístico nacional*, Especial Issue. 131–141.

Reis, Fernando. 1965. *Soia, literatura oral de São Tomé*. Braga: Editora Pax.

———. 1969. *Povô flogá, o povo brinca: folclore de São Tomé e Príncipe*. São Tomé: Câmara Municipal de São Tomé.

Rosa, Luciano Catano da Rosa. 1994. *Die Lusographe literatur der inseln São Tomé und Príncipe: Versuch einer literaturgeschichtlichen darstellung*. Frankfurt am Main: Verlag Teo Ferrer de Mesquita/Domus Editoria Europaea.

Shaw, Caroline. 1996. Oral Literature and Popular Culture in Cape Verde and in São Tomé and Príncipe. In *The Postcolonial Literature of Lusophone Africa*. Ed. Patrick Chabal. Evanston, Ill.: Northwestern University Press.

Seibert, Gerhard. 1991. O Tchiloli de São Tomé. *História* 142, 66–73.

Tchiloli de São-Tomé et Príncipe. 1990. *Internationale de l'Imaginaire*. 14 (special edition).

Valverde, Paulo. 2000. *Mascara, mato e morte em São Tomé*. Oeiras, Portugal: Celta Editora.

Pereira, Paulo Alves. 2002. Das Tchiloli von São Tomé. Die Wege des karolinischen Universums. Frankfurt: IKO.

GERHARD SEIBERT

See also **Performance in Africa; Theater**

PERFORMING ARTS OF THE TIV

The Tiv people live in Benue State in the area known as the Middle Belt, situated between the north and southeastern parts of Nigeria. In spite of the fact that they also occupy substantial parts of other states and that other peoples, particularly the Idoma, occupy a large part of it, they are largely synonymous with Benue State. The Tiv population, regardless of state boundaries, is variously said to be between 3 and 4 million, making them the largest settled minority population after the "big three"

(Igbo, Yoruba, Hausa) in Nigeria. This has made the Tiv important in the political stakes of Nigeria, and their power is never ignored.

The Tiv people are renowned as farmers. Yam is the main crop and Tiv cuisine depends largely on well-prepared pounded yam served with meat in a variety of sauces. Tiv men and women both engage in farming and take great pride in their farms. Almost all Tiv people have a farm, and even those living far away in one of the towns do their best to maintain one in their home village through joint ownership.

Dance, song, storytelling, riddles and proverbs, and puppet and masquerade theater are among the many forms of creative performance in Tiv society. All these forms have some aspect which is available for men and women to perform, though not necessarily at the same time. Neither gender has full access to the range of possibilities. Within dance (*amar* or *ishol*) and song (*acam* or *imo*), women are expected to display grace and elegance (*legh*, or *lugh*). These and other Tiv words emphasize the desirability of smooth movement in women's dancing and singing. For men, strength and energy are the most desirable attributes.

As well as being gender-specific, some dances are also particular to specific occasions, such as the *ibiamegh* ceremony (the most prestigious of all ceremonies), or the *girnya*, a dance performed at the death of significant leaders and said formerly to require the taking of heads as part of the ceremonial preparations.

Not all dances are equally popular throughout Tivland. Some, like the *ivom*, which is a competitive display of status and wealth staged by young men, are preferred in certain, but not all, parts of Tivland. The *girnya* is not widely performed, although most people know of it. *Ingough* is a dance which parodies the movements of people distressed by disease, their limbs dangling helplessly, their stomachs distended, until at a musical signal they return to normal. It is more widely performed as a means of deflecting a sense of hopelessness during illness. The *agatu* graphically displays the putative movements of witches as they avoid touching each other, which would bring about their death. This illustrates an important point about all Tiv performance arts: they are not uniform throughout the area, nor across time. The *shamanja* (sergeant major) and *dasenda* dances, for example, reflect more recent military influences. Tiv people relish, encourage, and reward innovation in the arts.

Instrumental music is also a significant part of Tiv expression in the arts, and can accompany dance, song, or the puppet and masquerade theater, known as *kwagh-hir*. *Kwagh-hir* is based partly for its content and its competitive organizational form on a long-established storytelling practice, also called *kwagh-hir*, or sometimes *kwagh-alom*. *Kwagh-hir* means "something wonderful" or a "fabulous thing." It refers both to storytelling and to the content of the story. *Kwagh-alom* means "thing" of the "hare." Alom is the trickster character in Tiv storytelling who always survives even the direst fate, prompting the saying "Alue kwagh alom une wua yo, myanga une hom ga" (A story where Alom is killed is not humorous).

As with all Tiv performances, new dances, saying, styles of music, masquerade and puppet characters, and stories are continuously being created. The performer is a prestigious figure in Tiv society, so that when a singer, dancer, or puppeteer introduces a new creation, it may be immediately imitated, and perhaps elaborated on, to often become popular beyond the performer's own immediate area and may retain the name of the artist who created it no matter how often it is repeated and interpreted. While the masked performers and the puppeteers in the *kwagh-hir* are men, women are essential to the performance as accompanying singers, and they can also be the *shuwa* (narrator), whose task is to call out to the audience a synopsis of the ensuing masked or puppet item.

References

Bohannan, Laura & Paul. 1953. *The Tiv of Central Nigeria.* London: International African Institute.

Hagher, Iyorwuese, Harry. 1990. *The Tiv Kwagh-Hir.* Lagos, Nigeria: The Centre for Black Arts and Civilisation.

Harding, Frances. 1978. To Present the Self in a Special Way: Disguise and Display in Tiv Kwagh-Hir Performances in *African Arts.* Vol. XXXI, no 1, University of California, Los Angeles.

Keil, Charles. 1979. *Tiv Song: The Sociology of Art in a Classless Society.* Chicago: University of Chicago Press.

FRANCES HARDING

See also **Dance; Performance in Africa; Puppetry**

PERFORMING ARTS OF UGANDA

Introduction

Uganda is a landlocked republic of East Africa bordered on the east by Kenya, on the west by the Democratic Republic of Congo, on the north by Sudan, on the south by Tanzania and on the southwest by Rwanda. Located along the northern shores of Lake Victoria, Uganda straddles the equator atop the plateau created by the two arms of the Great Rift Valley. The climate is mainly tropical, with the exception of the arid northeast. Rainy and dry seasons are each experienced twice a year. Precolonial social organization was remarkably diverse, including centralized kingdoms (such as Buganda in the south and Ankole in the west), confederates of chiefdom states (such as Acholi in the north) and noncentralized, segmentary societies (such as Kigezi in the southwest and Karamoja in the northeast). Economic pursuits were primarily agricultural, with the exception of populations in the western and northeastern regions, who raised cattle; a small number of gathering communities along the mountainous western border, and vibrant fishing enterprises around the many lakes and rivers.

Uganda gained its independence from Great Britain in 1962, and in 1996 there was a population of about 20 million (50% of which was 0 to 14 years old). The majority of the population is involved in agricultural pursuits, with the primary exports being coffee, tea, cotton, and copper. While the nation is administered as a system of districts, linguistic and cultural features (including complex clan systems) continue to emphasize precolonial social groupings as important markers of ethnicity.

Language

As a site of migration and settlement since the first millennium BCE, the region of what is today Uganda has been the converging point of populations speaking a variety of Bantu (Benue-Congo) and Nilo-Saharan (specifically eastern Sudanic) languages. Estimates have placed the number of distinct linguistic communities in Uganda at over forty, with the Bantu speakers located primarily to the south of Lake Kyoga and Lake Albert and making up about 70 percent of the total population. Language structure has a significant impact on the nature of Uganda's oral folklore, and similar modes of expression may be found among speakers of related languages. The Nilo-Saharan speakers of the North, for example, maintain many linguistic ties to southern Sudan and western Kenya, with whom they share many similarities in expressive culture. Multilingualism is widespread, especially since independence and with the growth of urban centers, such as the capital city of Kampala. English and Kiswahili are recognized as the two official languages of Uganda, but a myriad of local linguistic communities continue to thrive.

Folklore

Research in Ugandan folklore has primarily emphasized material culture, oral literature, and the performing arts. Material culture studies have focused on the archaeological record, as well as the application and distribution of contemporary production techniques. The examination of pottery techniques in the former kingdoms of Ankole and Bunyoro, for example, has yielded detailed information concerning the migration patterns of nomadic pastoralist communities in the early fifteenth century. Additional research (carried out primarily in the 1950s) has focused on the countrywide distribution of a variety of local technologies such as building construction, weaving techniques, iron working, body adornment, and instrument construction.

Uganda retains a remarkable diversity of oral literary forms, including tales, proverbs, riddles, games, and poetry. Additionally, each of these forms maintains a large set of subcategories, which vary in different regions of the country and are especially significant with respect to poetry. A small but important body of work exists on the country's oral literature, with the central kingdom of Buganda being the most thoroughly studied (folklore materials were published in Luganda as early as 1908). Significant folklore research has also been conducted in Acholi, Ankole, Busoga, Kigezi, and Lugbara. The style and content of oral forms in Uganda varies primarily in relation to distinct linguistic communities, but similarities between speakers of related languages, as well as local variation within single-language groups, is notable. For example, many western Bantu speakers (such as the Banyankole, Bakiga, Banyoro, and Batoro) share a form of heroic poetic recitation that exploits their languages' elaborate grammatical potentials, often drawing upon deliberately archaic imagery, including cattle-keeping imagery. Generally speaking, oral literary forms tend to be gender-specific and associated with particular stages in the life cycle (that is, specific forms are considered the domain of particular age groups). As with many African societies, the right to perform particular genres, as well as the appropriate social conditions for the application of oral forms, is determined largely by an individual's position in the hierarchy of society.

Uganda displays a diversity of performing arts traditions that combine aspects of music, dance, and drama. The southern kingdom of Buganda is the most thoroughly studied region, with significant research also having been undertaken in Busoga, Ankole, and Acholi.

Members of the Tebifanana Abifuna Cultural Group performing dances from the Kiganda tradition in south-central Uganda, 1995. *Photo © Wade Patterson.*

Musical Instruments

Uganda retains an unusually large number of musical instruments and performance styles, which vary according to region. As with the other arts mentioned, musical form is also closely tied to linguistic structure, and speakers of the same language family often share common instrumentation and performance features.

Membranophones

Drums figure prominently in almost every region of Uganda. In addition to providing the primary accompaniment for a variety of dance forms, drums were an important part of the royal regalia in many kingdoms and chiefdoms of East Africa. Royal drums were often given human names, housed in special locations, and were only beaten on special ceremonial occasions. With the recent reinstatement of some precolonial polities (as cultural icons with limited political powers), these royal drums are once again an important feature of group identity.

There are two general varieties of drums in Uganda: double membrane (often called Uganda drums) and single membrane. Dimensions and construction techniques vary according to region, but laced cowhide is widely used for double-membrane drums, which are generally conical in shape and played with sticks, hands, or a combination of the two. Pinned and glued monitor-lizard skins are often used for single membrane drums, which resemble an elongated goblet and are played with the hands.

Idiophones

This class of instruments includes xylophones, lamellaphones (thumb pianos), bells and clappers (usually worn and activated by dancing), rattles, half gourds, clay pots, and percussive troughs. The southern Ugandan xylophone complex (found in Buganda and Busoga), in which multiple artists combine interlocking parts on a single instrument to create larger, more complex melodies, is one of the best studied of Uganda's musical traditions, although other xylophone traditions exist elsewhere in the country. Large ensembles of thumb pianos, which incorporate instruments of differing size, are found in Teso, Lango, and Acholi and have received some scholarly attention.

Chordophones

A wide variety of string instruments exist in Uganda, including bow harps, lyres, tube fiddles, zithers, and musical bows. Performances by solo performers in poetic, narrative, or topical formats is most often accompanied by such instruments, but ensembles are also known, particularly as they relate to the harp and fiddle. Zithers are common in the west and among the Acholi in the north, harps are mostly found in the north and northwest (and as a royal instrument of the Baganda in the south), lyres are common in the south and east, and fiddles are found throughout the country. Notable research has been conducted on the string traditions of Buganda, including the *ennanga* (bow harp), *endongo* (lyre) and *ndingidi* (tube fiddle).

Aerophones

Notched flutes, panpipes, transverse flutes, transverse trumpets, end-blown trumpets, and a variety of small horns are found throughout Uganda. Aerophones are often played together in sets, with several people combining interlocking parts in a hocket style. The related traditions of royal transverse trumpet ensembles (*amakondere*) of the Interlacustrine kingdoms has been particularly well studied, as has the royal notched flute ensemble of the Kabaka of Buganda (called *ekibiina ky'abalere*).

Dance Traditions

As with Ugandan music, dance traditions vary widely throughout the country. Each cultural group retains its own distinct set of dances—many of which accompany specific community events, such as life transition (birth, initiation, marriage, death, etc.) or seasonal celebrations. Within each cultural setting, there is also a notable degree of local variation, and performances by specific communities can differ from one another while still being recognizable as belonging to the same overall form. Beyond this regional variation, there are some general motifs that are exhibited in the traditional dances of various regions of the

Wat Mon Cultural Group performing the "larakaraka" courtship dance from Acholi in northern Uganda, 1995. *Photo © Wade Patterson.*

country. In general, dance formations may constitute lines, circles, or compact groups.

Waist-Centered Dances

Dance traditions of the southern regions of Buganda and Busoga emphasize complex waist movements, while upper-body motion is minimized. Specific foot patterns create the desired waist movements, which are further accentuated by cloth and skin adornments worn around the hips. Dances such as the *baakisimba* of Buganda and the *tamenhaibuga* of Busoga have been well documented.

Leaping and Stamping Dances

Western Ugandan dances often accentuate movements that bring the feet into forceful contact with ground. In Bunyoro, for example, activated rattles worn around the ankles during the *ekitaguriro* dance emphasize such action. Similarly, dancers of the *ekizino* from Kigezi speak of "raising dust" and "punishing the ground" when describing spirited performances. In the Northeast, among the Karamojong, dances in which performers execute dramatic leaps with their arms held firmly at their sides are common and closely related to similar dances performed by the Massai of Kenya.

Dances Emphasizing Arm, Leg, and Head Movement

Dances of northern and northwestern Uganda use combinations of arm and leg movements that often reflect battle-inspired or work-related motion. The use of ankle bells is common, but foot movements are generally more subdued and complex than the stamping dances of the west and northeast. Many of the northern regions (such as Acholi and Karamoja) also use a variety of head adornments that incorporate feathers and emphasize subtle neck and head movements. The best documented of these is the chiefly *bwola* dance from Acholi, which may incorporate more than one hundred performers in a carefully choreographed dance-drama.

References

Anderson, Lois. 1984. Multipart Relationships in Xylophone and Tuned Drum Traditions in Buganda. In *Studies in African Music*, eds. Nketia, K. and Djedje, J. C., Los Angeles: UCLA.

Cohen, David W. 1972. *The Historical Tradition of Busoga: Mukama and Kintu.* Oxford: Clarendon Press.

Cooke, Andrew, and James Micklem. 1999. Ennanga Harp Songs of Buganda: Temutewo Mukasa's "Gganga Alula." In *African Music* 7, no. 4: 47–65.

Cooke, Andrew, James Micklem, and Mark Stone. 1999. Xylophone Music of Uganda: The Embaire of Nakibembe, Busoga. In *African Music* 7, no. 4: 29–46.

Cooke, Peter. 1990. Fieldwork in Lango, Northern Uganda, Feb–Mar 1997. In *African Music* 7, no. 4: 66–72.

Kagwa, Apolo Sir. 1928. *Uganda Folklore and Proverbs.* In Engero za Baganda. London: Religious Tract Society.

Kubik, G. 1964. Xylophone Playing in Southern Uganda. In *The Journal of the Royal Anthropological Institute of Great Britain and Ireland* 94: 138–159.

Kubik, G. 1984. Uganda. In *The New Grove Dictionary of Musical Instruments.* Ed. Stanley Sadie. London: Macmillan.

Kyagambiddwa, Joseph. 1955. *African Music from the Source of the Nile.* New York: Praeger.

Mbabi-Katana, S. 1970. Similarities of Musical Phenomena over a Large Part of the African Continent as Evidenced by the Irambi and Empango Side-Blown Trumpet Styles and Drum Rhythms. In *African Urban Notes* 4: 25.

Morris, H. F. 1964. *The Heroic Recitations of the Bahima of Ankole.* London: Oxford University Press.

Mukasa, Edward G. 1977. *A Brief Anthology on Uganda Musical Instruments.* Kampala: Ministry of Culture and Community Development.

Ngologoza, P. 1969. *Kigezi and its People.* Kampala: East African Literature Bureau.

P'Bitek, Okot. 1974. *Horn of My Love.* Nairobi: Heinemann Kenya.

Roscoe, J. 1911. *The Baganda: An Account of their Native Customs and Beliefs.* London: Macmillan.

Trowell, Margaret, and K. P. Wachsmann. 1953. *Tribal Crafts of Uganda.* London: Oxford University Press.

Van Thiel, Paul. 1977. *Multi-Tribal Music of Ankole: An Ethnomusicological Study Including a Glossary of Musical Terms.* Belgium: Musee Royal De L'Afrique Centrale.

Wachsmann, K. P. 1971. Musical Instruments in Kiganda Tradition and their Place in the East African Scene. In *Essays on Music and History in Africa.* Ed. K. P. Wachsmann. Evanston, Ill.: Northwestern University Press.

Wachsmann, K. P. 1950. An Equal-Stepped Tuning in a Ganda Harp. *Nature* 4184: 40.

WADE PATTERSON

See also **Dance; East African Folklore; Music and Dance—Uganda; Music in Africa**

PERSONAL EXPERIENCE NARRATIVES

Personal narratives are first-person prose narratives based on the performer's own experiences. In everyday conversation, people tell stories about the ordinary, and sometimes extraordinary, events that shape our lives (see Stahl 1978 and Langellier 1989). Telling personal-experience narratives is therefore part of normal life and a component of daily discourse. However, this simple definition and the fact that these stories often go unnoticed as "story" belie the importance personal narratives play in people's lives. It is often in the mundane and the ubiquitous that the profound and meaningful is to be found (Adler 1994). As they are told and retold, these personal, individual stories begin to reflect public and social norms, values, and concerns on an intimate, private level.

In folkloristics, personal-experience narratives are performed, single-episodic stories that are part of a performer's storytelling repertoire (Stahl 1977). They are told as true stories since they are based on the teller's own, unique, lived experience—although elaboration and exaggeration sometimes occur in order to make the narrative more humorous or increase its emotional impact. As single-episodic narratives, personal-experience narratives are different from personal oral histories and illness narratives, which often narrate different and multiple events and experiences occurring over time. Personal-experience narratives tend to focus on one particular event or experience and have a more defined narrative structure.

Furthermore, illness narratives are often consciously elicited by professionals, such as doctors, researchers, and social workers. Personal-experience narratives are part of an individual's store of stories and arise within normal conversation. These personal accounts of the mundane, humorous, or traumatic emerge out of a "felt need" to share the experience at the heart of the narrative (Stahl 1977).

Psychologists and social workers have found personal-experience narratives to be a useful tool in restoring people's self-esteem and positive self-identity (Adler 1994). Moreover, for people who have suffered a traumatic experience or something out of the ordinary, personal-experience narratives can be therapeutic, for they operate as an informal post-traumatic stress debriefing. The work of Eleanor Wachs (1988) and Tim Tangherlini (1998), on the narratives of crime victims and paramedics, respectively, show how these personal stories facilitate coping, making sense of traumatic experiences, and can help the individual to regain a sense of control over events and emotions. The teller benefits from the experience of narrating a personal event—as does the audience. The listener participates in a direct experience that leads to what Donald Baird calls "experiential meaning," defined as a process of engagement with the narrative that results in the narrated experience becoming part of the listener's own "resource for living their own lives" (1996, 26).

In Africa, personal-experience narratives are an overlooked genre of everyday expression. In research presented in 2001, Mbugua wa-Mungai and David Samper found that personal-experience narratives about extra-ordinary events on Kenya's privately owned minibuses (called *matatu*) help Nairobi residents cope with traumatic experiences and successfully manage their anger and frustration. Stories about theft, verbal and physical abuse, hijacking, sexual harassment, and even rape are first and foremost part of an informal information system that serves to warn fellow commuters about which vehicles, routes, and times to avoid. Also, sharing these stories not only psychologically prepares Nairobi residents to deal with these experiences, but also provides them with possible strategies and courses of action when faced with similar situations. Anger and frustration are two common emotions of Nairobi commuters, and narration helps to vent and create emotional distance. In Nairobi, personal-experience narratives about *matatu* are an informal mode of psychological debriefing. Narrating these events to a sympathetic audience allows people to release some of the emotional impact of the trauma they experienced. Storytelling gives structure and imposes order on chaotic experiences, emotions, and events, which restores to the narrator a sense of personal control (see Bendix 1990). At the very least, storytelling is a mark of survival.

In her 1995 study of Hutu refugees in Tanzania, Liisa Malkki encountered harrowing personal narratives of murder, genocide, and escape. Over time, these narratives began to reveal the emergence of similar patterns, suggesting that these personal stories of survival are part of a process in which the social and communal meaning of the Burundi holocaust is being defined.

References

Adler, Herbert. 1994. The Psychotherapeutic Use of Personal Experience Narratives. Ph.D. dissertation, University of Pennsylvania.

Bendix, Regina. 1990. Reflections of Earthquake Narratives. *Western Folklore* 49:331–347.

Baird, Donald. 1996. Personal Narrative and Experiential Meaning. *Journal of American Folklore* 109:5–30.

Langellier, Kristin M. 1989. Personal narratives: Perspectives on Theory and Research. *Text and Performance Quarterly* 9:243–276.

Malkki, Liisa. 1995. Purity and Exile: Violence, Memory, and National Cosmology among Hutu Refugees in Tanzania. Chicago: University of Chicago Press.

Stahl, Sandra. 1977. The Personal Narrative as Folklore. *Journal of Folklore Research* 14:9–30.

wa-Mungai, Mbugua, and David Samper. 2001. *"No Mercy. No Remorse": Personal Experience Narratives about Public Transportation in Nairobi, Kenya.* Paper presented at the American Folklore Society Annual Meeting in Anchorage, Alaska.

DAVID A. SAMPER

See also **Gossip and Rumor; Leyonds: East Africa; Oral Traditions; Palaver (Kinzoni) in Kongo Life**

PIDGIN AND CREOLE LANGUAGES

A pidgin is a reduced language that results from extended contact between groups of people with no language in common. Pidgins evolve from the need for some means of verbal communication, often for the purpose of trade.

Creole languages, by the most general popular account, arise when a pidgin becomes the native language of a new generation of children. In other words, a pidgin becomes a creole when it acquires native speakers.

English-Based Pidgins and Creoles

English-based pidgins and creoles are spoken in West Africa from the Gambia to the Cameroon. They are spoken in countries where English is an official language. These countries are, from west to east, Gambia, Sierra Leone, Liberia, Ghana, Nigeria, and Cameroon. According to Gilbert Schneider, "Pidgin-English is the most common name given to a lingua franca spoken throughout West Africa from Sierra Leone to the Gabon." It is a medium of communication for African peoples who have no first language in common, for white men of various ethnic backgrounds, and for the working man, trader, and transient peoples of West Africa. Pidgin English is not a mere simplification of English, but a separate and describable language. Its vocabulary is predominantly English based, but the lexical forms have changed their meaning to fit into the value system and world view of the African people.

Gambia

Gambian Krio (locally called Aku or Patois) is spoken as a home language by some 3,500 Creoles in Banjul, and by others as a second language (Hancock 1969a, 8).

Sierra Leone

Krio is an English-based lingua franca used throughout Sierra Leone as an intertribal language of trade and social communication. It is the mother tongue of the descendants of freed slaves who settled in the Sierra Leone peninsula between 1787 and the early years of the nineteenth century. It is a second language for other residents of the area whose mother tongue is one of the Sierra Leone languages. It has also spread throughout the country, principally to the more urban areas, as an additional language (Jones 1971, 66).

Liberia

Liberian English encompasses several restructured varieties. There is a creole spoken as a home language by the descendants of settlers from the United States (3 percent of the total population of 2,180,000 in 1984), who live largely in and around the capital, Monrovia (306,000 inhabitants). There are also second-language varieties of this speech used as a lingua franca throughout the rest of the country. One of these, Kru Pidgin English, is more similar than the other varieties to West African English because of its distinct historical origins. All of the varieties in Liberia have influenced one another and appear to form a continuum rather than discrete entities (Holm 1989, 421).

Ghana

The major speakers of Ghanaian Pidgin English (GPE) are males, students, military and police personnel, youngsters, co-workers, and friends. Educational institutions, urban areas, workplaces, lorry stations, military and police barracks, and entertainment venues are the most obvious places where one will hear GPE. The usage of GPE is mostly in the spoken mode; there is little usage of GPE in the written mode. Speakers of GPE use it for communication, entertainment, politics, socialization, and fun (Amoako 1992, 143).

Nigeria

Nigerian Pidgin English is a lingua franca for many, and thus a true pidgin in Hall's sense; it is also a mother tongue for a number of families in certain areas and communities, and as such might be defined as a creole language (Mafeni 1971, 95). Many Nigerian novelists, playwrights, advertising agents, trade unionists, and even politicians have realized, and are exploiting, the great potentialities of the language as a medium of mass communication. The various broadcasting corporations in Nigeria have done much to popularize pidgin by allowing its use in advertisement. In addition, the NBC radio serial *Save Journey* has been running with great success for a number of years, and Albert Achebe and other writers have used pidgin in their novels and poems (ibid.100).

Cameroon

Cameroon Pidgin English is widely used along the East Cameroon coast, especially in the Douala area. Though it has little official recognition, it is still an important medium of communication for Cameroon's political, social, religious, and economic life (Barbag-Stoll 1983, 38).

Pidgin and Creole Varieties Based on African Languages

Fanakalo

Fanakalo, which is also called Fanagalo, Isikula (Coolie language), Kithen Kaffir (also a pejorative term), or Basic Zulu, is a pidginized variety of Zulu spoken in southern Africa, especially in the gold, diamond, coal, and copper mines, where the workers come from many different language backgrounds (Holm 1989, 555). D. T Cole estimates that about 70 percent of its lexicon is derived from Zulu, 24 percent from English, and 6 percent from Afrikaans (1964, 549).

Kituba

Kituba, which is also called Kikongo-Kituba, Kikongo *simplifié*, or Kileta, is a simplified form of Kikongo. It is estimated that Kituba is spoken as a first or second language by some 5 million people in the Democratic Republic of the Congo (DRC) and in the city of Brazzaville in the Republic of the Congo (Holm 1989, 557). Kituba enjoys the prestige of a big-city language associated with modern life, while ethnic Kikongo is associated with the Bakongo people and their traditional culture.

Lingala

Lingala, also called Ngala, Mangala, Bangala, and Lingala, is spoken along the Congo River in western and northern DRC, in Brazzaville, and in the Central African Republic by an estimated 10 to 12 million speakers. As Belgian traders, soldiers, and colonial officials arrived in increasing numbers toward the end of the nineteenth century, they used Mangala for contact with the native population, leading to a pidginized variety of reduced structure and vocabulary called Bangala. By the first decade of the twentieth century a creolized form, which came to be called Lingala, emerged in urban centers of interethnic contact (Holm 1989, 559).

Sango

Restructured Sango is a lingua franca spoken by over one million people in the Central African Republic as well as the bordering areas of the Democratic Republic of the Congo, Brazzaville, Cameroon, and Chad. It is a pidginized variety of one or more closely related dialects used as a second language by most of its speakers; however, it is gaining a growing number of native speakers in the capital of the Central African Republic, Bangui. It is based on Sango and possibly other dialects of the cluster known as Ngbandi of the Adamawa Eastern branch of the Niger-Congo family; the restructured variety is also known as Sango (Holm 1989, 562). Pidginized Sango emerged from the contact between the native people and Africans from other areas brought into this area as laborers (by Europeans).

Swahili

Swahili is the first language of some 5 million people who live mainly in a narrow strip along the coast of Kenya and Tanzania and on offshore islands such as Zanzibar. Varieties of Swahili that have been restructured to varying degrees are spoken as a lingua franca by over 30 million people in East Africa and the Democratic Republic of the Congo. The importance of Swahili as a lingua franca grew under the Belgian administration of the Congo, which recruited soldiers in Zanzibar and used Swahili for training them. In Katanga, Swahili became the lingua franca of a multilingual population drawn in to work in the copper mines from the Luba-speaking areas of northern Katanga province, from Rwanda and Burundi, and from Zambia and Zimbabwe. Swahili became a creole in Katanga (Holm 1989, 565).

A pidginized variety of Swahili called Kivita ("war language") was used in the former British East African army, while British and other European settlers in the Kenyan highlands used a variety called Kisetla with their servants or farm laborers (Vitale 1980). I. F. Hancock notes two mixed, and possibly creolized, varieties of Swahili on the Somali coast: Banjuni on the islands of the same name near the Kenyan border, and Ci-miini (or Kilambizi or Chilambuzi) in the coastal town of Brava (or Barawa or Miini), believed by its speakers to be a mixture of Swahili and Portuguese (Hancock 1979b, 390).

Pidginization and creolization will no doubt continue as speakers of different languages come in increasing contact.

References

Amoako, Joe K. Y. B. 1992. *Ghanaian Pidgin English: In Search of Diachronic, Synchronic, and Sociolinguistic Evidence*. Ph.D. dissertation, University of Florida at Gainesville.

Barbag-Stoll, Anna. 1983. *Social and Linguistic History of Nigerian Pidgin English as Spoken by the Yoruba with Special Reference to the English Derived Lexicon.* Tubingen, Germany: Stauffenberg Verlag.

Cole, D. T. 1964. Fangalo and the Bantu Languages in South Africa. In *Language in Culture and Society: A Reader in Linguistics and Anthropology,* ed. Dell Hymes. New York: Harper and Row.

DeCamp, David. 1971. Introduction: The Study of Pidgin and Creole Languages. In *Pidginization and Creolization of Languages,* ed. Dell Hymes. New York: Cambridge University Press.

Fasold, Ralph. 1990. *Sociolinguistics of Language: Vol. 2, Introduction to Linguistics.* Cambridge, England: Basil Blackwell.

Hall, Robert A. 1954. *Hands off Pidgin English.* Sydney: Pacific Publications Limited.

Hancock, I. F. 1969a. A Provisional Comparison of the English-Based Atlantic Creoles. *African Languages Review* 8:7–72.

Hancock, I. F. 1979b. *The Relationship of Black Vernacular English to the Atlantic Creoles.* Working Paper of the African and Afro-American Studies and Research Center, University of Texas at Austin.

Holm, John. 1988. *Pidgins and Creole Vol. 1.* New York: Cambridge University Press.

Holm, John. 1989. *Pidgins and Creole Vol. 2.* New York: Cambridge University Press.

Hymes, Dell. 1971. *Pidginization and Creolization of Languages.* New York: Cambridge University Press.

Jones, Eldred. 1971. "Krio: an English-Based Languages" of Sierra Leone. In *The English Language in West Africa,* ed. John W. Spencer. London: Longman.

Lyons, John. 1981. *Language and Linguistics.* New York: Cambridge University Press.

Mafeni, B. 1971. *Nigeria Pidgin English.* In *The English Language in West Africa,* ed. John W. Spencer. London: Longman.

Mühlhäusler, Peter. 1986. *Pidgin and Creole Linguistics.* Oxford: Basil Blackwell.

Schneider, Gilbert D. 1966. *West African Pidgin-English: A Descriptive Linguistic Analysis with Texts and Glossary from the Cameroon Area.* Ph.D. dissertation, The Hartford Seminary Foundation, Hartford.

Todd, Loreto. 1974. *Pidgins and Creoles.* London: Routledge.

Vitale, A. J. 1980. KiSetla: Linguistic and Sociolinguistic Aspects of a Pidgin Swahili of Kenya. *Anthropological Linguistics* 22, no. 2: 47–65.

Wardhaugh, Ronald. 2001. *An Introduction to Sociolinguistics.* Malden, Mass.: Blackwell.

JOE AMOAKO

See also **Languages**

POLYRHYTHM

Polyrhythm is the simultaneous use of two or more contrasting rhythms in a musical texture. Constituent rhythms are typically assigned to individual instruments or instrumental groups within an ensemble, or to individual voices or voice parts in a chorus. Each rhythmic pattern has a clear profile that is reinforced by extensive repetition. The simultaneous sounding of individual rhythms produces a resultant rhythm that is different from, but fully compatible with, its constituents. Although they are frequently discussed in tandem, polyrhythm and polymeter are different techniques. A musical texture is polymetric if it uses two or more meters simultaneously. Meter denotes a fixed, recurring temporal unit with a prescribed accentual scheme. Thus, 2/4 means two quarter-notes in a bar with the normative pattern stressed-unstressed, while 3/4 means three quarter-notes in a bar in the sequence stressed-unstressed-unstressed. Although polymetric music often features polyrhythm, polyrhythm normally operates within a single governing meter, not two or more.

Although it has appeared sporadically in European and American music (fourteenth-century French music and American jazz, respectively), polyrhythm is most strongly prominent in the traditional music of Africa. From the earliest writings to recent ethnomusicological studies, rhythm looms large as a salient and defining feature of African music. Since music making is typically communal rather than individual, it is natural for African repertories to feature ensemble music with distinct layers of rhythmic organization. In addition, the close association between music and dance means that movement patterns and other choreographic constraints exert an influence on the organization of ensemble music.

Two well-documented instances of polyrhythmic usage are the ensemble drumming of the Ewe of southern Ghana (studied in the 1950s by the British scholar A. M. Jones, and more recently by the American ethnomusicologist and performer David Locke) and the music of horn ensembles in the Central African Republic (written about by the French scholar Simha Arom). In Eweland, the music of community dances like *agbadza, atsiagbekor,* and kpegisu is performed by an ensemble of instruments comprising, typically, a bell, rattle, small drum, larger drum, and largest, or lead, drum. Handclaps provided by dancers, singers, and some onlookers reinforce the basic meter. The bell plays a distinctive and memorable pattern that provides a rhythmic foundation for the ensemble as a whole. Small and larger drums beat patterns of greater complexity, some of them accentually distinct from the prevailing meter. The lead, or "master," drum performs the freest and most complex patterns. Relying on the foundation supplied by the other instruments, the lead drummer instructs or converses with the dancers, ensures the rhythmic security of the ensemble, and, most important, exposes rhythmic patterns of considerable musical interest with appropriate virtuosity.

The horn ensembles of the Banda-Linda of the Central African Republic feature over a dozen instruments, each playing a distinctive rhythm. Although individual patterns sometimes resemble one another, none of them is wholly identical with another. Patterns are typically brief and subject to extensive repetition. Holding the ensemble together is a grand tactus, akin to the beat of an invisible conductor. This ensures that the timing of individual horn entrances is precise and metrically constrained, and the polyrhythmic effect is thus guaranteed. A similar pattern of organization is evident in the singing of various so-called pygmy groups. Among the Baaka, for example, distinct layers of sung motives unfold simultaneously, sometimes in hocket fashion (different voices sing different notes of the same melody in turn) and often responding to externalized movement or dance. Although the ensemble's controlling beat is not necessarily prominent (if sounded at all) it is nevertheless felt by performers.

These are but brief instances of a technique of musical organization that occurs with surprising consistency in a variety of repertoires across the African continent. Although polyrhythm is used most authentically in traditional music, it is occasionally found in popular music, as well as in so-called art music, despite the challenges posed by transcribing African rhythms in staff notation. Non-African composers such as Steve Reich and Gyorgy Ligeti have drawn, respectively, on the polyrhythmic techniques of Ghanaian ensemble musics and Central African horn orchestras. The vitality of polyrhythm as an organizing principle is unquestioned. Its regular use in daily musical life in Africa will doubtless continue, even as the forces of modernization impel a transfer of the technique from ensembles of drums, bells, and elephant horns to guitars, trumpets, drum sets, and pianos. Gathering more ethnographic data about its repertorial provenance will not only serve as a record of musical thinking in traditional Africa, but provide a valuable resource for composers and scholars.

References

Arom, Simha. 1985. *Polyphonies et polyrythmies instrumentales d'Afrique Centrale: structure et methodologie.* Paris: Selaf. English translation, Cambridge, England: Cambridge University Press, 1991.

Jones, A. M. 1959. *Studies in African Music.* 2 vols. Oxford: Oxford University Press.

Locke, David. 1987. *Drum Gahu: A Systematic Method for an African Percussion Piece.* Crown Point, Ind.: White Cliffs.

KOFI AGAWU

See also **Dialogic Performances; Call-and-Response in African Narrating; Music in Africa; Silence in Expressive Behavior**

POPULAR CULTURE

There is not a clear and generally accepted concept of popular culture in Africa. Many scholars have given different definitions or interpretations, which are sometimes contradictory, and some specialists are convinced the term *popular culture* should not be used at all. Nevertheless, a useful agreement is growing, mainly based on the work of Karin Barber. Her approach is followed here. The most powerful argument for using the term is that it makes things visible that would otherwise be ignored. Barber defines *popular culture* as the area between traditional culture and elite culture—a vast area that is flexible and ever changing, representing a loose collection of different cultural expressions. It often escapes the attention of the outside world, but it forms the ingredients of the lifestyle of the major part of the African (mainly urban) population. In spite of the great variety in expression and the apparent tendency of all kinds of popular arts to change constantly, there are common denominators.

Essentially, what all forms of popular culture have in common is that they are a product of a dialogue with Western culture and modernity. It results from a selective and creative rearrangement of specific elements (forms, themes, materials, techniques) of Western culture and indigenous culture, which form a new product that is adapted to new times, surroundings, and audiences.

Popular culture grew naturally in Africa's cities, especially in coastal towns, industrial centers, and seats of colonial government. Colonial culture had its greatest impact in these areas because imported products came to them first, and because sailors and tradesmen were available to introduce new products and ideas. New techniques and novelties, such as radio and the

Middle Art, sign painting. Onitsha, Nigeria, 1981. *Photo © Paul Faber.*

cinema, were launched in the cities. For the urban population, the city offered new impressions, new possibilities, and new lifestyles. Also, the population itself was changing. Young and enterprising people left the villages for the cities, leaving at least a part of their strong social and ethnic network behind. The new arrivals came into a new social fabric with people of different regions and different religions, all speaking different languages. They moved from a predominantly agricultural life to one with all kinds of new jobs and businesses, all based on a monetary economy.

In the cities, people found themselves in a new exciting environment, with new challenges and new possibilities, but never in very luxurious circumstances. The producers of popular arts, music, literature, and theater all found themselves in a narrow space, constantly forced to come up with new ideas, new products, and new markets due to heavy competition. Few succeeded in making a living that freed them from worries.

The producers belonged to the urban masses. They generally had some basic general education, and were either self-taught or trained by practicing colleagues in their field. They shared the same social and cultural background with their clients, audience, and fans.

The urban environment, spreading more and more to the countryside, forms the location where popular theater thrives, but it also forms the subject of many different forms of popular art. In songs, plays, and paintings, people deal with aspects of living in the city and all the complications that come with it.

In this close relation to social and economic development, popular history has a specific history. Many early outbursts of popular art forms started in the early decades of the twentieth century, sometimes even in the nineteenth century. But it was especially in the years after World War II that African popular culture matured. The economic growth in the cities was relatively high then, the war itself had shown the colonial powers to be more vulnerable than previously thought, and independence seemed a viable possibility. Popular culture thrived in the 1960s and 1970s. In the following decades, the influence of mass media became more noticeable, changing the character of popular culture in a possibly decisive way.

This was also the era of a growing feeling of national and continental pride. Black intellectuals and political leaders stressed, in articles and speeches, the concepts of negritude (particularly Leopold Senghor), black consciousness (Kwame Nkrumah), and later Authenticite (Sese-Seko Mobutu). This growth of awareness led to an emphasis on traditional African heritage.

Visual Arts

The visual popular arts in Africa are dominated by painting. The choice for this medium was in itself an expression of modernity, as it was relatively new in the African context. It involved the use of new materials such as boards and canvas, brushes, and imported paints in many bright colors. Several painters were active before World War II, but painting became a serious affair only in the 1950s when materials were more readily available and a class of people emerged that could afford to buy or commission paintings for purposes of commercial advertising, public decoration, or private contemplation.

Painted signs for commercial advertising were directly linked with urbanization and the growth of economic activities. Countless people set up small enterprises in the informal economy that dominated many areas, especially West Africa. They needed to underline their presence, due both to competition and the need to establish their individuality. Painters fulfilled their needs. These were, of course, small businessmen themselves, usually self-taught, who drew their models from photographs, magazine pictures, calendars, and posters. Barber signs were seen everywhere. These were painted advertisements made for small-scale barbers who set up under a tree and needed something to draw attention to their business. This grew into a large field of indigenous portraiture, with a mixed message. The main idea was to draw attention to the barber, but it drew attention to the capacities of the painter as well. At the same time it reflected contemporary fashion and hairstyles, and showed how people saw themselves. Other customers followed, such as tailors and mechanics. Painters worked to make large posters for concert parties, and eventually for the cinema.

The demand for painters continued to grow, and owners of shops, bars, and restaurants have used their services to embellish their buildings. This has enabled painters to work on a large scale, as the painter is often asked to fill one or more walls and to create an ambiance where the clients feel at ease and see their identity confirmed. Portraits of popular heroes have also appeared, such as musical stars. Elements of landscape and village life are used to evoke a harmonious world, where one can find peace from the hectic town life.

Another form of public art was painted on the trucks and cars that transport people or goods. Specific vehicle body parts were decorated with painted scenes and texts, following rules that were invented locally for each genre. Nigerian "mamy wagons"—trucks converted into buses—are famous for their brightly painted adages such as "God Dey" and "No Condition Permanent."

Apart from these paintings in the public space, artworks have also been made for private use. Portraits are popular, though largely confined to private interiors and made only on commission. People order portraits for reasons of commemoration: parents that passed away, for example, are sometimes memorialized on canvas. The painter starts from a small photograph and translates it into a full-size painting. The unique techniques of the painter are the selling point, especially as color photography has become widely available. The painter can also beautify the subject—the target is not realism, but realistic idealism.

Three-dimensional forms of modern, individual portraiture have been devoted primarily to commemorative sculpture. Figurative grave sculptures have been a feature of mourning since the 1950s. In Nigeria this trend became fashionable mainly through the activities of Jack Sunday Akpan, who produced life-size cement statues of deceased persons. This trend in grave art has a parallel in Ghana, where a similar fashion developed in making figurative carved and brightly painted coffins. The shapes of these coffins—made by Kane Kwei beginning in the 1950s, and later by his former pupil Paa Joe—refer to the profession of the deceased. When an onion farmer had passed away, he might find his last resting place in an onion-shaped coffin, while an important or wealthy man might repose in a wooden Mercedes.

Another important category of art for private use are story paintings, which are painted scenes that usually have a narrative context. The genre-paintings made in Shaba, in former Zaire, beginning in the 1950s are a well-researched example. Here an urban middle class, economically connected to the copper mine industry, developed the habit of decorating their private space with paintings of meaningful scenes. Certain themes or "genres" were very popular, regardless of how they were made, making it clear that it was not esthetics that counted, but content. Themes such as "Mami Wata," "Colonie Belge," or images of the civil war, have been made and sold in vast numbers. The detailed analyses of J. Fabian and I. Szombati show that these works represent and reflect collective memories that are interpreted for the present social situation. Social shifts in society have led to changes in meaning of old themes and the generation of new ones.

These paintings are linked to literary forms of popular culture. The popular historiography finds a remarkable example in the paintings of Tshibumba Kanda, which present an overview of national history from the precolonial past into a distant future. This project, however, was only realized due to the financial resources of a Western researcher.

Barbershop, Lapos, 1981.
Photo © Paul Faber.

Popular Music

In the vast field of African music, there is a similar history of new inventions originating in the hybridization that went on in the early centers of urbanization. From the nineteenth century on, there has been an interaction of local music styles with different forms of Western music, such as church hymns, sea shanties, and military brass-band music. The early dance orchestras played Western music on instruments that were new to the continent.

The guitar has made a deep and lasting contribution to many different kinds of African popular music. Sailors, mainly Kru from Liberia, introduced the instrument in coastal ports all the way to Zaire. Often, the guitar replaced sounds and effects of comparable traditional instruments. The new music was popular in the industrial cities, with their mixed populations of Africans from different regions, descendants of freed slaves from Brazil and Cuba, and migrant workers from different countries. The cities also changed where and how the music was played. Music had traditionally been a community affair, performed in village centers. Now it moved into the streets, the bars, and dance halls.

The development of a recording industry helped to spread the music across large distances, made musicians famous, and lead to followers and reactions elsewhere. Radio, which started in Africa in 1924, supported this diffusion very effectively. Again, the first big impact came only after World War II. This was mainly due to the importation of many recordings of rumbas, chachas boleros, and mambos from Cuba. This started a Latin craze, particularly in the French colonies and the Belgian colony of Congo. Part of the reason for the success was, of course, that listeners recognized the African roots of this music. It was therefore greeted with great enthusiasm, and music with strong European characteristics lost ground quickly.

The 1950s saw the rise of highlife in Ghana, with E. T. Mensah as one of the heroes of the genre. This was the emergence of a truly popular music, and it had a large impact on the whole West African region. In Nigeria, the well-known juju music was changed with the added power of electrical amplification. Immensely influential was the musical boom that took place in the Congo. The first modern band here was African Jazz, founded in 1953. This band absorbed and reinterpreted Afro-Cuban rhythms in a purely African way, adding sweet harmonies along the way. This Congolose guitar music swept across the continent, dominating the musical scene in several countries for a long time.

But popular music was not the simple result of the introduction of novelties. It was rather the successful blending of traditional rhythms, patterns, instruments, and songs with new possibilities and selective aspects of the new international styles. The 1960s and 1970s saw the rise of the electrical kora, the reuse of instruments such as the *balafon* and *sanza* in an electronic context, new adaptations of old song traditions by Salif Keita and others, and the emergence of songs sung in local languages rather than English and French. South Africa is an exception, however, for here apartheid and white Bantu politics made traditionalization suspicious. The music scene here was dominated by an urban culture based on American models of jazz and swing.

More than any other medium, the music scene is internationally oriented and influenced. Such African American music trends of the 1980s and 1990s as reggae and hip-hop quickly found their way to Africa, and they were recognized and adapted in much the same way that Latin American music was in the 1940s.

Popular Theater

The story of the theater reflects, and in fact incorporates, the development of popular music. A first impulse for a new popular variety of dramatic performances came from the Western musical genre that was launched in the early decades of the 20th century in the coastal cities of West Africa. The combination of music, dance, and vaudeville acts formed a new type of entertainment only to be found in the new cities. Successful groups toured the area, and school concerts produced a new generation of musicians and entertainers. After World War II, new forms of music joined in, especially the Ghanaian highlife. Imported musical genres were adapted to African needs and according to African fashion. In the booming 1950s, audiences grew, and a thriving form of popular theater was formed. Groups called concert parties toured the nations of Ghana and Togo. The Yoruba in Nigeria developed a comparable brand of popular theatre based on traditional stories.

These theatrical performances combined humor and drama using songs, acting, music, and sometimes even film. The theater troupes traveled around, spreading new themes and ideas from the city to the countryside. The interaction of the audience with the stage performance was strong and intense. The public was amazed and thrilled by the spectacle, but they also recognized in the plays their own experiences and uncertainties, mainly resulting from conflicts with modernity. Apart from working on the social and psychological level, the theater presented a new form of entertainment. The monetary economy made this form of African show business possible, but technological developments created the major competition and threat: television. Competition pushed the companies toward new inventions and improvisations, but in the end the popular theater slowly lost ground.

One of the reasons for the success of the popular theater was its use of language. Language in Africa was changed extensively through urbanization, colonization, and modern education. New languages developed in different mixtures, creating new ways of communicating between different language groups. Popular theatre used the language of the people, as did other textual expressions, such as the Onitsha Market literature, which comprise small cheap pamphlets with lurid stories that convey an enlarged vision of modern city life, as well as Kenyan chapbooks and Tanzanian detective stories.

Photography

While urbanization brought many social changes, it also introduced technological advances that influenced popular culture deeply. The influence of radio and the record industry on music has already been noted. Even earlier, photography was a new invention that made its mark on the African visual world. Africa has a long tradition of local photography that goes back to the early twentieth century, when, in the wake of traveling Western photographers, Africans learned the technical aspects of photography, as well as the Western standards of formal portraiture. Later, when the group of potential customers grew, African photographers set up studios. The heyday of the trade was between the 1950s and 1980s.

The idea of portraiture is a powerful one. Owning a lifelike portrait of oneself, and of loved ones who had departed or passed away, created new ideas about death. These photographs gave a physical and visual symbol of family ties and relations with friends that could be shown in an album.

In the 1980s, black and white photography was slowly replaced by color photography. Hand printing lots its appeal, and photographers were reduced to being snapshot makers, bringing their film to labs. Most studios closed down, but in some cases the competition led to new inventions. Philip Kwame Apagya in Ghana ordered painted backdrops by local painters and created situations that visualized the dreams, ambitions, and hopes of his clients. Through the medium of the photograph, a dream would seem to come true for eternity. In a similar fashion, the Likoni Ferry photographers in Kenya embellished their studios with many different images and decorations that could transform the photographed person into a fantasy world, expressing the hopes and dreams of a poor class of workers who often migrated from the interior of the country to Mombasa.

Film and Television

Photography was, in its early phase, a sophisticated and expensive technological miracle, but in the hands of Westerners it created products that fast became popular. It took some decades for local photographers to meet this demand. They were aided in this by the invention of a cheap and easy-to-make wooden camera that was produced in large numbers from the 1940s onward. The cinema followed a similar development. The African movie industry was at first a high-tech medium that required enormous sums of money, limiting the number of African productions to a handful that could hardly compete with cheap imports from the United States, India, and Hong Kong. Television was more adaptable to national and regional tastes and programs, but there was also limited room for local production. Developments in video, however, made the medium more economical and helped improve quality. Production costs were reduced, and new players came into the market.

Television became a popular medium, in the sense that it reached wherever a television set could be found. Theater companies have tried to compete, but have found it difficult. Many African "soap operas" have been based on the activities of popular theater groups.

Volatile and fluctuating, popular culture has many forms, appropriating a wide variety of media genres. Due to social, political, and economic changes, popular culture shifts constantly.

References

Barber, Karin. 1987. Popular Arts in Africa. *African Studies Review* 30:3.
Barber, Karin, ed. 1997. *Readings in African Popular Culture.* Bloomington: Indiana University Press.
Barber, Karin, John Collins, and Alain, Ricard. 1997. *West African Popular Theatre.* Bloomington: Indiana University Press.
Bender, Wolfgang. 1991. *Sweet Mother, Modern African Music.* Chicago: University of Chicago Press.
Fabian, Johannes. 1998. *Moments of Freedom. Anthropology and Popular Culture.* Charlottesville: University Press of Virginia.
Vogel, Susan, ed. 1991. *Africa Explores, 20th Century African Art.* New York: Centre for African Art.

PAUL FABER

See also **Cartoons; Decorated Vehicles; Electronic Media and Oral Traditions; Music: Soukous; Radio and Television Drama; Theater**

PORTUGUESE STUDY OF AFRICAN FOLKLORE

Very little folklore research has taken place in the former Portuguese colonies of Africa. This is directly related to the development of the discipline in Portugal. Two issues stand out in this connection: (1) the needs that folklore in Portugal was supposed to meet, and (2) the role it was to play in the colonial enterprise. Together, these issues illuminate the field as it currently stands. It is especially worth examining the relationship between folklore and anthropology, for in Portugal, unlike in many other European colonial powers, both scientific pursuits went hand in hand and sought to lend legitimacy to one another within the context of Portugal's self-perception as a nation with a civilizing mission.

Donato Gallo, an Italian social scientist who has produced perhaps the best analysis of Portuguese anthropology, argues there is no such thing as Portuguese anthropology, but rather a Portuguese form of knowledge (the word for *knowledge* in Portuguese is *saber*, which has a similar meaning to the French word *savoir*). This form of knowledge articulated many of the concerns that, elsewhere, made anthropology an ally of the colonial enterprise.

The immediate context for the emergence of anthropology and folklore in Portugal was the historical period running from the middle of the nineteenth century to the early part of the twentieth. This was a turbulent political period for Portugal, during which there was a succession of constitutional-monarchical, republican, and dictatorial governments. This political instability came into conflict with the country's colonial ambitions. Most of Portugal's colonial claims in Africa, particularly in Mozambique and Angola, came under attack from England, Belgium, and Germany. Consequently, as the nineteenth century drew to a close, much of the intellectual and political activity in Portugal centered around the need to define the country's role in the world. This was the time when important national institutions saw the light of day, most of which were to play a crucial role in the development of the scientific study of mores and customs.

It is worth mentioning, in this connection, the Geographic Society of Lisbon and the Ethnological Museum. The circumstances under which each emerged say much about the rationale behind anthropology and folklore. It is, therefore, worth taking a closer look at each of them.

The Ethnological Museum and the Emergence of Portuguese Folklore

The Ethnological Museum was founded in 1893 by a well-known *homme des lettres*, José Leite de Vasconcelhos. The creation of this museum was part of a growing national awareness within Portuguese society. Although Spain's geographic proximity had long provided important impulses for the coalescence of a national identity, this identity was translated into a sense of missionary duty and colonial fate that took little notice of the burgeoning and impoverished rural population. Jorge Freitas

Branco, a folklorist, has equated the creation of the Ethnological Museum with the "nationalisation of the people" (1999, 27).

This statement requires elaboration. The Ethnological Museum was going to be the place where Portuguese popular culture would be publicly represented. This popular culture was derived mainly from the ways of life of rural people. These included not only economic activities such as farming and handcrafts, but also rituals, festivities, tales, and dress. By bringing all these aspects of rural Portuguese life under the banner of a single Portuguese culture, the hitherto ignored peasant was firmly integrated into an imagined Portuguese community. This move was further emphasized by a growing interest in the description of rural ways of life as part of a national culture. Folklorists such as Teófilo Braga (1985), who in 1885 published a book in which he sought to describe the "Portuguese people" through its common customs, beliefs, and traditions, played as much of a role in the nationalization of the people as Vasconcelhos.

Little occurred, however, between the creation of the museum and the rise to power of António de Oliveira Salazar's fascist regime in the late 1920s. Portuguese scientific interest in cultural matters, in the meantime, was dominated by physical anthropology. At the University of Oporto, in particular, there was a burgeoning interest that translated into an effort to understand human evolution through the analysis of the physiological constitution of humans. It took an alliance between the dictatorship's national chauvinism and the rise of cultural anthropology to rekindle an interest in folklore.

Salazar's dictatorship drew some of its legitimacy from the argument that it was acting on behalf of the national interest to recover Portugal's past glories. It sought to give the impression that its power was directly inspired by Portuguese cultural traditions. Both domestically and abroad in the colonies the dictatorship pursued policies based on the need to reassert the national interest. The economies of the colonies, for example, which until then had been under the control of capital interests from other European colonial powers, were increasingly brought under Portuguese control. Portugal became the main recipient of exports from these countries, as well as the main source of their imports. Politically, African possessions, especially under growing international pressure for decolonization, changed their colonial status to being part and parcel of Portugal as "oversea provinces." In Portugal itself, there was an effort to wrest control of important economic sectors from mainly British interests.

It was within this context that there was renewed interest in folklore. The National Propaganda Secretariat, an official body of the fascist state, was charged with representing Portuguese national culture not only at home, but also abroad, at the various world exhibitions in Geneva (1935), Paris (1937), and New York and San Francisco (1939). According to Vera Marques Alves, these exhibitions were to be the backbone of the 1940 "Portuguese World Exhibition," which not only represented Portugal's metropolitan culture, but also the culture of subject peoples around the world. The 1940 exhibition was the culmination of a process started in 1935 with the creation of a national ethnographic commission with the "priority task" of carrying out a national folklore and ethnographic exhibition in which "the most representative and typical aspects of each province would be present" (Alves 1997, 239). There were regular contests in Portugal for "Portugal's most Portuguese village" in which

popular culture was further harnessed to the notion of a single Portuguese national culture.

The Lisbon Geographical Society and the Emergence of Portuguese Anthropology

The Lisbon Geographical Society was founded in 1875 under the initiative of Luciano Cordeiro, a very active geographer and public commentator. Cordeiro, as indeed all those who joined him, identified the role of the society with raising awareness in the nation of the need to preserve its past glory as an imperial power. This was to be achieved through a greater concern with Portugal's colonial enterprise. The general mood toward the end of the nineteenth century in Portugal was one of discomfort with the place of the country in the concert of nations. Some argued that the country had overstretched itself and should pull back from its overseas commitments. Others, like Cordeiro, felt that the problem was that the country lacked a clear identity. They argued that Portugal could define itself by producing and promoting better knowledge of its world. The Lisbon Geographical Society, as a scientific institution profoundly influenced by positivist ideas of science, held to the belief that knowledge was the solution to Portugal's identity crisis.

The society was interested in mapping the world according to Portugal's centrality. Apart from strictly cartographic knowledge, the society aimed at producing scientifically based accounts of the cultures of the societies under Portugal's colonial rule. There was, however, a political motive behind this. The Lisbon Geographical Society linked Portugal's potential to return to its former glories with its ability to make better use of its colonies. In this sense, knowledge about other cultures could help formulate a clearer colonial policy, which in the long run would have positive consequences for the country. From its inception the society encouraged anthropological research and developed very close links with anthropologists, some of whom, such as Mendes Côrrea, served at some stage as its executive secretary.

The general framework within which anthropological knowledge was deployed was the regulation of native labor. Indeed, as a French commentator once remarked, making natives work was the golden rule of Portuguese colonial policy (Aurillac 1964, 243). This was premised on the twin ideas that Africans should be brought under the tutelage of the colonial state, and that their relationship to the state should be based on the enforcement of their obligation to work. The tutelage idea found expression in the policy of denying Africans citizenship status by confining them to "traditional" political and social institutions, within which they were expected to develop the ability to assimilate Portuguese culture.

The obligation to work was derived from the belief that Africans were lazy by nature. If Portugal was to fulfill its civilizing mission, it had no choice but to compel them to work. Knowledge about the culture of subject populations was, therefore, geared towards bringing the above-mentioned twin ideas to fruition. Portuguese descriptions of African culture had an instrumental character—they served the purposes of colonization. At the same time, however, such descriptions placed these cultures firmly within the fold of the Portuguese nation, albeit far down in the evolutionary scale. Soon after being founded, the Lisbon Geographical Society presented a petition to the government for a scientific expedition to the colonies that was to gather knowledge that would allow the country to do justice to its imperial claims. In 1945 the Board for Geographical Missions and Colonial Investigations published a report entitled *The Scientific Occupation of Portuguese Overseas Territories*, in which it argued for more resources to be invested on research of this type (Junta das Missões Geográficas 1945). More than fifty years had passed between the first and second plea, and yet the content was the same.

The reason for this was that, in spite of the perceived need to do something, Portugal's political course for much of the relevant historical period was highly unstable. One practical suggestion made by the Lisbon Geographical Society was for the creation of a school for training colonial officials. As with most other policy recommendations in Portugal, this lay dormant for nearly a quarter of a century. Having recognized the role of anthropological knowledge for the colonial enterprise, the authorities developed a sort of relationship with anthropologists. Indeed, through the agency of Mendes Corrêa (who, along with António de Almeida and Rodrigues Santos Júnior, was part of the famous Oporto School), the ministry of the colonies funded anthropological research (see Pereira 1989, 68). This was mainly in the area of physical anthropology and dealt with issues such as the size of the African cranium, the reaction times of Africans, and the physical build of Africans. While meeting some of the concerns of the colonial authorities, the interest in physical anthropology was more dominant within the ranks of anthropologists themselves. The change of emphasis from physical to cultural anthropology came much later with Jorge Dias, a Portuguese language teacher in several European universities, who had completed a doctorate in folklore studies at the University of Munich. Dias was invited by Mendes Corrêa to lead a research group that was expected to carry out an ethnographic and ethnosociological survey of the country. His marked interest in cultural, as opposed to physical, anthropology led Dias to finally introduce an ethnographic section within the Portuguese Anthropological and Ethnological Society (see Pereira 1989).

As far as the society was concerned, there were three major ways in which it mediated between anthropology and colonialism. The first was through scientific expeditions to the colonies. These were major undertakings involving not only anthropologists, but also (and mainly) geographers, cartographers, oceanographers, and natural scientists from a whole range of disciplines. In 1936 and 1937–8, two anthropological missions led by Rodrigues Santos Júnior, an anthropologist, were sent to Mozambique, where they mostly collected archaeological material that was complemented by a few kinship studies and observations of burial rituals. Later, in the 1950s, further missions were sent to Guinea-Bissau, Angola, and Mozambique under the supervision of Jorge Dias. Chief among the objectives of this later mission was an attempt to find out the reasons behind the budding nationalism in nearly all the Portuguese colonies, which in Angola, Mozambique, and Guinea-Bissau soon translated into armed rebellion against the Portuguese.

These anthropological missions were significant in two important ways. First of all, they bore testimony to a closer cooperation between academic anthropology and the colonial authorities. This had been made possible by institutional developments within the colonial bureaucracy with the creation, in 1954, of a research unit on colonial ethnology at the Center for Political and Social Studies in Lisbon. Jorge Dias, who had been teaching cultural anthropology at the Center, seems to have aroused colonial officials' interest in the role that cultural anthropology could play in furthering the goals of colonial administration. Indeed, most dissertations written by final year students were social-anthropological monographs with a heavy functionalist bias that reflected Dias's own analytical inclinations and were consistent with the colonial concern of reinventing traditional African society.

Secondly, this cooperation signalled a paradigm shift within Portuguese anthropology itself, which up until then had seen its contribution toward the colonial enterprise more in terms of physical anthropological. The emphasis on cultural factors reflected the growing importance that cultural anthropologists had acquired since Jorge Dias had introduced an ethnological section into the Portuguese Ethnological and Anthropological Society in 1949.

Whereas physical anthropological research had emphasized an interest in the physical features of subject peoples, which often translated in the presentation of actual people as exhibits in the colonial exhibitions, interest in cultural anthropology focused attention on native artifacts. Dias's influence was behind the rise of Makonde art (wood carvings), Tchokwe ritual artifacts, and, to some extent, Tchopi music (xylophone). These were increasingly seen as manifestations of a vibrant cultural life, which Portugal had the obligation to mold to its cultural understanding. Eduardo Mondlane, a nationalist leader in Mozambique, wrote that Makonde artists resisted Portuguese orders to carve the Madonna by placing a monkey instead of a baby in her lap (Mondlane 1970).

The second way in which anthropology sought influence before the colonial authorities was through the so-called colonial congresses. These were major events organized both by the society and the overseas ministry in Portugal itself, and in which the problems of the colonies were discussed and their natural, human, and cultural resources were exhibited. There were four such colonial congresses, solemn occasions during which physical, social, and cultural anthropologists were given the opportunity to produce scientific facts in support of their relevance to the colonial enterprise.

Finally, anthropologists were also given the chance to participate in the training of colonial officials. At the founding of the Geographical Society of Lisbon, one of the suggestions made by its founders was to set up a school for the preparation of colonial officials. This suggestion met with the suspicion of the government department in charge of overseas affairs at the time, which set up its own geographical commission to look into such matters. With the normalization of relations toward the end of the century, the Geographical Society, with financial assistance from the government, set up a school for the preparation of traders and settlers for their encounter with African reality in 1906. In 1927 this school became the Colonial High School, where from 1946 onwards courses in "advanced colonial studies" were administered to colonial officials. While academic anthropologists did not play a very important role in the design of the syllabus of these courses, their expertise was very much in demand, for the main drive in the content of the courses was toward understanding African society within the framework established by the regulation of labor, which saw African society in primordialist terms and sought to reconstruct it along those lines. Most of the final projects produced by those attending these courses dealt with matters dear to social anthropology at the time, and they reveal a concern with the reconstruction of the exotic side of African life from the Portuguese perspective of the time.

Folklore in Portuguese-Speaking Africa

The development of folklore in Portuguese-speaking Africa is intimately connected to developments in Portugal. As suggested above, interest in the symbolic and material culture of subject African societies was a direct result not only of the assertion of a Portuguese identity, but also of the country's need to make the best use of its colonies. This instrumental interest led to an emphasis on those aspects of African culture that could deliver insights to help render these societies amenable to Portuguese control. One reason behind the second ethnographic mission to Africa, for example, was the collection of empirical material that could help the authorities come to terms with budding nationalist feelings in those countries.

Throughout the colonial period, the colonial authorities remained the major producers of accounts of the symbolic and material culture of African society. Colonial administrators, amateur anthropologists, and professionally trained anthropologists produced a considerable number of monographs on various aspects of African folklore. These ranged from mores and customs, food, farming techniques, and language to warfare techniques, dress, religion, and oral literature. Missionaries of both Catholic and Protestant persuasion were also very instrumental in registering African folklore. In Mozambique the best known missionary-anthropologist was Henri-Alexandre Junod, whose account of the life of the Tsonga of southern Africa provided considerable material to Sir James George Frazer's *Golden Bough* and remains the richest ethnographic account ever written on any African community in Portuguese-speaking Africa.

It has been claimed that Portuguese colonialism was "softer" than that of the British or French, in as much as it ignored racial boundaries and sought to adapt to the tropical environment. This was the central theme in the notion of "Lusotropicalism" put forth by the Brazillian Gilberto Freire. Several authors have disputed this by showing, for example, that the proportion of mixed-race offspring was much higher in South Africa than in the Portuguese African colonies. Portugal may have believed it was practising a softer form of colonial rule because it was genuinely convinced that it had a mission in Africa. This meant that there was a much more overt attempt to integrate Africans into an all-encompassing notion of Portuguese culture. This culture did not make room for African culture in its own right. Makonde art and Tchokwe ritual artifacts were not symbols of this all-encompassing culture, but rather symbols of subject cultures. The real colonial culture, the one that was also presented at colonial exhibitions in Portugal, was the culture of Portuguese settlers abroad.

The context within which interest in African symbolic and material culture arose has had an impact on the general perception of folklore in these countries. At the time of independence in the mid-1970s, for example, there was a general mistrust toward anthropology. In Angola and Mozambique, where the ideological orientation towards Marxism was much more pronounced, this mistrust translated into more importance being attached to history, for example. In both countries, history came to fulfill the function of anthropology. This served two purposes. On the one hand, history was expected to provide historical legitimacy to the new nations by constructing an ideologically correct past. On the other hand, this ideologically correct past was to be the basis upon which a sense of nationhood would be instilled in the postcolonial period.

Generally speaking, the arts have reflected this ambivalence. Twentieth-century writers and artists such as Pepetela, Bonga, Castro Soromenho, and Rui Mingas from Angola, and José Craveirinha, Mia Couto, Luís Bernardo Honwana, and Malangatana from Mozambique drew their inspiration from their respective cultures, but they also sought to express a national culture. In their novels Pepetela and Mia Couto (both Africans with European ancestors) articulate this ambivalence in a very forceful, yet beautiful, manner. Both seek to write in a style that is closer to the way the average person on the street perceives the world around him. To this end, they rely on a language style that is neither Portuguese nor broken Portuguese, achieving thereby a highly effective aesthetic effect. In the process, however, what they produce is not a revelation of native culture, but rather something purporting to be a national culture. Mia Couto has been unjustly accused of misrepresenting Mozambican culture (Muianga 1991), but this only shows how difficult it is to represent culture in the aftermath of colonial rule.

As a general rule, folklore research in the period after independence was politically motivated. In Mozambique, Angola, and Guinea-Bissau, the description of the material and symbolic culture was constrained by the need to provide arguments for national unity. Only those aspects which could be used in the nation-building effort were emphasised, much like the way in which Portugal, a century earlier, had "nationalized" its own people. From 1975 to the early 1990s, there were hardly any monographs on individual ethnic groups. With the exception of work carried out by foreign researchers (Lerma et al. 1989; Geffray 2000), no attempt was made to continue the tradition set by the colonial authorities (see, for example, Oliveira 1978; Parsons et al. 1968; Reis 1969). One honorable exception is the work of Rui Duarte de Carvalho, an Angolan anthropologist, who has been studying the way of life of the pastoral community of Kuvale (Carvalho 2000). São Tomé and Príncipe and Cape Verde are exceptions to this. Their main concern in the period after independence has been less to stave off the spectre of tribalism, but rather to bring diverse former slave and forced-labor communities under the same national umbrella.

The political changes that took place in Africa at the end of the eighties have led to a reassessment of the role of folklore in these societies. In Mozambique and Angola, anthropology has been introduced as an academic discipline in the universities. In all of these countries there is an increasing reliance on anthropology within the area of official policy formulation. In the area of government reform, in particular, anthropologists have been playing a major role in advising governments on culturally appropriate forms of political participation. Development agencies rely on anthropological knowledge for an appreciation of the sociocultural dimensions of their interventions. While these developments are controversial, they at least illustrate a reassessment of the role of folklore studies, a reassessment essential to the development of the discipline.

References

Alves, Vera Marques. 1997. Os etnógrafos locais e o Secretariado da Propaganda Nacional—um estudo de caso. 1, no. 2:237–257.

Ataíde, Alfredo. 1934a. Tempos de reacção de indígenas das colónias portuguesas. In *Trabalhos do 1 Congresso Nacional de Antropologia Colonial.* Porto: Exposição Colonial Portuguesa.

———. 1934b. Ergografia nos indígenas das colónias. In *Trabalhos do 1 Congresso Nacional dé Antropologia Colonial.* Porto: Exposição Colonial Portuguesa.

Aurillac, M. 1964. Les provinces portugaises d'outre-mer ou la "force des choses." In *Revue Juridique et Politique* 18, no. 1:239–262.

Braga, Teófilo. 1985. *O povo português nos seus costumes, crenças e tradições.* Lisbon: Publicações Dom Quixote.

Branco, Jorge Freitas. 1999. A fluidez dos limites: discurso etnográfico e movimento folclórico em Portugal. *Etnográfica* 3, no. 1:23–48.

Brito, Joaquim Pais de. 1982. O estado novo e a aldeia mais portuguesa de Portugal. In *Autores vários.* Lisbon: A Regra do Jogo.

Carvalho, Rui Duarte de. 2000. *Vou lá visitar pastores: explicação epistolar de um percurso angolano em território Kuvale (1992–1997),* 2d ed. Lisbon: Cotovia.

Cordeiro, Luciano. 1980. *Questões Coloniais.* Lisbon: Editorial Vega.

Dias, Jorge. 1956. *Relatório da Campanha de 1956.* Lisbon: Missão de Estudos das Minorias Étnicas do Ultramar Português.

———. 1964a. *Portuguese Contribution to Cultural Anthropology.* Johannesburg: University of Witwatersrand.

———. 1964b. *Os Macondes de Moçambique. Vol. 1, aspectos históricos e económicos.* Lisbon: Agência Geral das Colónias.

———. 1964c. *Os Macondes de Moçambique. Vol. 2, Cultura Material.* Lisbon: Agência Geral das Colónias.

Dias, Jorge, and Margot Dias. 1964. *Os Macondes de Moçambique. Vol. 3, Vida Social e Ritual.* Lisbon: Agência Geral das Colónias.

Dias, Jorge, and M. V. Guerreiro. 1959. *Relatório da Campanha de 1958 (Moçambique e Angola).* Lisbon: Missão de Estudos das Minorias Étnicas do Ultramar Português.

Dias, Jorge, M. V. Guerreiro, and M. Dias. 1960. *Relatório da Campanha de 1959 (Moçambique, Angola, Tanganhica e União Sul-Africana).* Lisbon: Missão de Estudos das Minorias Étnicas do Ultramar Português.

Dias, Jorge, M. V. Guerreiro, and M. Dias. 1961. *Relatório da Campanha de 1960 (Moçambique e Angola).* Lisbon: Missão de Estudos das Minorias Étnicas do Ultramar Português.

Duffy, J. 1959. *Portuguese Africa.* Cambridge, Mass.: Harvard University Press.

Gallo, Donato. 1988. *O saber Português—antropologia e colonialismo.* Lisbon: Heptágono.

Geffray, Christian. 2000. *Nem pai nem mãe—crítica do parentesco: o caso macua.* Lisbon: Caminho.

Gómez, Luis Ángel Sánchez. 1999. Cien anos de antroplogías en Espana y Portugal. *Etnográfica* 3, no. 1.

Harries, Patrick. 1981. The Anthropologist As Historian and Liberal: H. A. Junod and the Thonga. *Journal of Southern African Studies* 8, no. 1:37–50.

Junod, Henri-Alexandre. 1913. *The Life of a South African Tribe.* 2 Vols. Neuchatel, Switzerland: Attinger Fréres.

Junta das Missões Geográficas e de Investigações Coloniais. 1945. *Ocupação Científica do Ultramar Português.* Lisbon: Agência Geral das Colónias.

Leclerc, Gerard. 1972. *Anthropologie et colonialisme—essai sur l'histoire de l'africanisme.* Paris: Fayard.

Liesegang, G. 1967. *Beiträge zur geschichte des reiches der gaza nguni im südlichen Moçambique 1820–1895.* Ph.D. dissertation, University of Cologne.

Mendes Corrêa, A. 1954. *Antropologia e História.* Porto: Instituto de Antropologia do Porto.

Mondlane, Eduardo. 1970. *The Struggle for Mozambique.* Harmmondsworth, England: Penguin.

Muianga, A. 1991. *Literatura e Moçambicanidade.* Lisbon: CIDAC.

Munido, F. F. O. 1949. La Orientacion etnologica en ele proyecto definitivo de codigo penal para indigenas de Mozambique. *Cuadernos de Estudios Africanos* 6:9–34.

Oliveira, Fernando de. 1978. *Contos populares de Angola—folclore quibumdo.* Porto: Nova Crítica.

Parsons, Elsie Clews, et al. 1968. *Folclore do arquipélago de Cabo Verde.* Lisbon: Agência Geral do Ultramar.

Pereira, Rui. 1989. A questão colonial na etnologia ultramarina. *Antropologia Portuguesa.* 7:61–78.

Pina, Luís. 1931. Materiais para a antropologia de Moçambique. *Arquivo Anatómico e Antropológico de Moçambique* 14:114–125.

Pires de Lima, J. A., and Constáncio Mascarenhas. 1926. Contribuição para o Estudo Antropológico de Moçambique. *Arquivo de Anatomia e Antropologia.* 10:699–716.

Reis, Fernando. 1969. *Pôvô Flogá o povo brinca: Folclore de São Tomé.* São Tomé: Câmara Municipal.

Santos Júnior, J. R. 1947. Alguns Aspectos da 4. Campanha da Missão Antropológica de Moçambique. *Boletim da Sociedade Portuguesa de Ciências Naturais* 15:128–151.

Silva Cunha, J. M. 1952. *O sistema português de política indígena—princípios gerais.* Lisbon: Agência Geral do Ultramar.

ELÍSIO MACAMO

See also **French Study of African Folklore; Government Policies toward Folklore**

PRAISE POETRY: SOUTHERN AFRICAN PRAISE POETRY

Since praise poetry is historically an oral genre, it remained unwritten until the arrival of missionaries and colonial settlers. It is for this reason that, as attested to by records left by these people in former British colonies, the praises of those native peoples who came into contact with the West first have the longest and most varied historiography.

Despite this relatively new written form, designed for study by both scholars and amateurs, praise poetry is primarily an oral art that remains inextricably tied to performance. It is an art that is actualized in performative creation. The written version lacks, and cannot capture, the extralinguistic aspects of performance, such as gestures, the intricate interplay between performer and audience, and the general, elusive ambience of the occasion (the spirit of place). The link between the emergence of the written form and the arrival of settlers has been remarked on by many who have studied the praises of the Nguni group, especially those of the Zulu and Xhosa. The history of the collection and analysis of various types of this genre stretches from the first half of the nineteenth century to the late twentieth century when new research perspectives and analytical paradigms galvanized scholars into forging pride of place for the discipline among other pursuits in academia, both in South Africa and elsewhere on the continent.

Many studies of Zulu and Xhosa praises have been published over the years, the most recent being by Liz Gunner and Ma Fika Gwala (1991) for Zulu, and by Jeff Opland (1983) for Xhosa. The Ngoni of Malawi and the Ndebele of Zimbabwe are offshoots of the Zulu. The praises of the latter have been studied by Alfred Mtenje and Boston Soko (1998), by Moyo (1978) for Ngoni, and by Caleb Dube (1988) and Temba Nkabinde (1990) for Ndebele. Isaac Schapera's (1965), Sam Guma's (1967), and Daniel Kunene's (1971) works on the praises of the Sotho-Tswana group remain classics even today. The best-known works on the praises of the Shona group are those by Aaron Hodza and George Fortune (1979), and Alec Pongweni (1996).

The Nature and Functions of Praise Poetry

Praise poetry has several subgenres. While all the groups have clan praise poems as well as those for the chiefs, the Nguni and Sotho-Tswana have personal ones composed either by an individual for himself or herself, or for a peer. This includes praises for both civilians and war heroes. They also have praises for their domestic and wild animals, to which the Sotho-Tswana add those of divining bones. Particularly among the Nguni and Sotho Tswana, praise poetry is not to be viewed as consisting only of "ossified texts" composed long ago, but also as a contemporary and vibrant oral art form that is readily responsive to current sociopolitical developments.

This contemporaneity of the genre is the reason for its adaptability and symbiotic relationship with other oral art forms, so that there is constant multidirectional "borrowing" between it and these others, but especially between it and contemporary African music. For example, the songs of Zimbabwean liberation war choirs of the 1970s incorporate praises of Nehanda, Kaguvi, and Chaminuka, heroes of the nineteenth-century liberation struggle, and those of contemporary leaders Mugabe, Chitepo, Takawira, and Nkomo. These praises are in contrast with those directed derisively to leaders who were cooperating with the colonial system, namely Chirau, Muzorewa, and Sithole. Among the Nguni, Gunner and Gwala report that modern acculturated township music incorporates the famous war leader Shaka's praises.

In view of the double-edged character of the genre, the term *praise* is misleading, especially when applied to compositions for the powerful: the praise singer does praise, but he or she also pillories the subject if the latter is guilty of misconduct. Thus, a notoriously licentious Chief of the Bomvana clan was "praised" with the lines: "Below the rocks it is very dreadful to behold/ For there are the handsome and their concubines," (Jordan, 26). Further, the colonial power was not spared by the poet Mqhayi when the Prince of Wales visited the Zulu in 1925: "Ah! Britain! Great Britain! She sent us the Bible, and the barrels of brandy; She sent us the breechloader, she sent us the cannon; 0, Roaring Britain! Which must we embrace?" (Jordan, 27). Vail and White observe that among the Ndebele of Zimbabwe, the praises of their ancestors Mzilikazi and Lobengula discriminated between the two on the basis of the sociopolitical legacies which each left his descendants. The first was a warrior who "had raised himself from nothing" when he led his people away from the hostile Shaka and across the Limpopo River into present day Zimbabwe, managing to establish an empire. Lobengula, on the other hand, compromised that empire in his dealings with the settlers. So Mzilikazi is "the bush buck that strikes carefully on the rocks," while Lobengula is "the bush buck that strikes with hooves and damages the stones" (White and Vail, 1984, 55–

56). Mzilikazi managed to maintain his empire's independence through skillful diplomacy, and without provoking confrontations with the white settlers, while Lobengula exposed it to their superior firepower and they vanquished him. The Ngoni of Malawi, nineteenth-century migrants from Zululand, have acculturated praises for their founding father: "He ate the people along the Zambezi/King Zwaryendaba, who beat the waters of the Zambezi with a short staff/And the waters parted" (Mtenje and Soko, 1998).

Praise and criticism in this poetry points to the traditional Bantu people's preference for conformity over deviance in the conduct of both ordinary folk and their leaders. This emphasis on the golden mean is echoed in the proverbial lore, where aphorisms that urge apparently opposite courses of action are to be found. For example, in a parallel to the English proverb "Many hands make light work," the Shona have the saying, "One finger cannot crush a louse," which urges cooperation. But they also have one that says, "To benefit from other people's wisdom, you must have some of your own," which encourages individualism.

Clan Praises

Just as the poems of rulers accord individuals both the praises and the criticisms due them, so do those of the clans and ordinary people. The praises of the clans serve to remind members of who they are, where they came from, the vicissitudes of their lives, how they overcame challenges to their existence, and so on. The poems are thus biographical sketches as well as being a means of portraying the subject's self-image. In all instances, the heroism of both individuals and the clan as a whole are praised, just as their antisocial conduct is pilloried. The language used is laconic and full of archaisms, ambiguities, and hyperbole. The Lion clans of Zimbabwe have a line in their poem that praises them as "Those who do not subsist on plunder." Yet their history shows that they once behaved like their totemic animal, regularly going on cattle-raiding forays for self-aggrandizement. The "praise" line is thus to be read as "Those who should NOT subsist on plunder," because their old ways led to their being banished from their original home after their founding father had been executed. This latter catastrophe is referred to only in the line, "Those who scattered when the father died." Further, Chief Mpangazitha of the Hlubi clan was praised as "the wielder of the brain-weighted club" (Jordan, 24–25). Was his club covered by the brains of the enemy whose skulls he crushed in battle, or was he a brilliant military strategist?

The Ovambunderu of Botswana are cousins of those in Namibia, having been dispersed from there by the colonial German war machine in the nineteenth century. Even today the two groups hold an annual festival to commemorate their survival and to celebrate the value of peace. Their black, green, and white flag is the symbol around which they rally as they sing its praises: "It came on feet; It has gone through the taste/test of time; It is a tree on fertile soil; Cultural richness is its fruit; Every generation flocks to one."

While the clan praise poem found in some of the other southern African groups is derived from certain commendable characteristics of the totemic animal, it also incorporates those that would be unacceptable if literally transposed from the animal kingdom to human society. There is no biological connection between the animal and the clan. Claude Levi-Strauss says "totemic origins are applications, projections or dissociations; they consist of metaphorical relations the analysis of which belongs to an ethno-logic rather than an ethno-biology" (1963, 31). Thus, while the poem serves to "place" the subject of praise by references to his clan's history, it binds him to follow in the footsteps of the ancestors in the philosophy that guides his dealings with other people. Praise is meant as criticism when it is sung for one who clearly is not behaving in ways that earned his ancestors that accolade in the first place. The subject of praise must therefore dissociate himself from the deviant ways of the totemic animal.

The Nguni generally do not have animal totems. The exceptions are some Swazis, such as the Fakudze, who are of the Baboon totem. The baboon is believed to have originated from them. Instead of weeding their crop fields, the Fakudze sat on their hoes until the handles grew onto their hind-parts, and long hair began to cover their bodies. The indolence which this myth implies is reflected in the poem of the Baboon clans of Zimbabwe, who are sarcastically praised thus: "They who subsist on stolen food; They who eat what others have cultivated; They who boast, 'we sit on cattle melons: While we eat pumpkins; As for watermelons, we carry under the armpit like everyone else: Corn we just munch. With cucumbers on our mouths, We remove the sugarcane bark'" (Hodza 1985, 7 my translation). This poem also says that the members of this clan must distance themselves from the behavior of their totemic animal.

San Praises

San oral forms focus on the activities of their ancestors, who are closely linked to animals since, as Duncan Brown notes, in San cosmology all animals were once people. One such text is the story "The Jackal and the Hyena." Brown says this story is partly etiological since it is used to "explain" why the hyena's rear end is small. The Jackal cheats the Hyena out of the meat of an animal which the latter had killed, using a trick that results in the Hyena falling from the roof of a hut (where the Jackal had placed the meat) because the rope the Jackal gave the Hyena to use for climbing is so weak that it snaps. The story is about the ownership of a kill. In order for the San to survive, there was a need to ensure that a carcass was fairly distributed. The San thus have a custom designed to maintain human life. The story portrays the Jackal's legendary trickery and selfishness so that he emerges as the villain of the piece. In another story, however, the Jackal comes out as a hero. In "The Jackal and the Lion" he loses his meat to the marauding lion, but manages to kill it "with the help of a sorceress and his own cunning" (Brown 1998, 61). This exploit restores peace and the "people" live life to the full.

By portraying the same character in one instance as a villain and in another as a hero, these two stories are thematically parallel to the praise poem in its combination of praise and criticism of its subject. Whatever the jackal may have represented in precolonial times, the antisocial conduct has come to be associated with the way that the colonizer dislocated Bushman society economically, politically, and culturally. Indeed, because the story of the Jackal and the Lion expresses a yearning for peace and restitution, it "may stand as an early exemplar of what has come to be our national narrative: colonial intrusion; dispossession;

and the brutal destruction of whole societies," (Brown 1998, 62). These stories begin with formulaic expressions such as "Mama/Father used to tell me . . ." which are parallel to those used by the Shona when they quote a proverb to warn someone against acting unwisely. Such formulas lend authority to what follows them for they represent wisdom handed down through the generations, and are thus not to be taken lightly.

Being an egalitarian, hunter-gatherer society, the San traditionally had much time to devote to artistic creation: including engraving, making necklaces and beads, dancing, singing songs, and storytelling. Their egalitarianism, which contrasts with the stratification found in the other communities in the region, prevented "the emergence of a literary elite comprised of individuals specifically recognized and rewarded for their talents" (Brown 1998, 48). This is reflected in the performance of their songs, which address religious themes and personal experiences. Those on religion and medicine are believed to come from god. The performance of songs takes place at trance dances, with women clapping and singing while the men dance in order to enter a state of trance. Although San stories do contain metaphors, trance songs make extensive use of them for both aesthetic purposes and for expressing social and personal concerns. An example is the /Xam San //Kabbo's song, in which the loss of his tobacco pouch causes him "famine."

Another important feature of San oral forms is their repetitiveness. The "Mama/Father used to tell me" formula is strategically placed in performance. This way, as Brown states, the performer "could have lent rhythm to his delivery, thus creating an anticipatory structure into which his listeners could then have fitted each new section to ensure coherence, even if a line or two had escaped them" (Brown 1998, 65–66). Repetition also gives these forms the circularity that is commonly found in the oral forms of the other groups in the region. It has a wider philosophical significance in that it can be viewed as one way in which the San are saying "even the seasons turn-turn"—things will come full circle. That is to say, their conquerors will one day have to account for their dislocation of San society.

Some of those who have studied the foregoing types and functions of praise poetry have not paid much attention to the others, which some would say, are even more important, particularly those for the ordinary individual. Even private people achieve, suffer setbacks, and have hopes and ambitions. Further, they yearn to be recognized as people who occupy space in the scheme of things. This poetry thus has an autobiographical function. The very adaptability of praise poetry allows such persons to compose or to have others compose poems in their praise. There are thus both official public praises and private individual ones. Once a praise has been given to the individual, it sticks such that the subject has no control over its use. It survives the subject's physical death and may be inherited by his or her offspring, thereby serving as an instrument of social control for the latter.

Praises for the Young and for Women

Among the Sotho-Tswana there are praises composed for and by graduates of the initiation school, the ritual after which the young are admitted into adulthood. These youngsters adopt new praise names, both coined and borrowed from traditional heroes and chiefs. The source of inspiration may be the individual's difficult childhood, or it could be the initiates' view of themselves as the custodians of cultural values, which their peers who have become Christians have abandoned. So their praises will incorporate lines that pillory the modernists. There are also praises for women, such as one recently recorded in Lesotho, that praises the woman for the munificence of her heart: "Her back is wide enough to take those who are lonely; She collects all those who have lost hope, Elders and orphans." She is also praised for her beauty: "Her beauty cannot be measured; As if God had created her on the first day of the week; When people come back from the weekend with their minds alert. It was not a hurried work" (recorded at my request in Maseru, Lesotho, by Julia Tsoenyo in 1996). Among the Nguni, women's praises are generally confined to the mundane concerns of daily survival, avoiding the robust and violent epithets that men earn in war. They are about economic progress and hardships, the imprisonment of loved ones in distant jails, and so on.

Among the Shona there are praises for young men and women. Because they have not crossed the rite of passage into marriage, they have not lived long enough to deserve clan praise for whatever commendable deeds they may perform. So they are praised by the recitation of their totem, which is theirs by virtue of having been born into a particular family, and not by the praise poem.

These contrast with those praises for the traditional Shona woman, which are recited for her only when she demonstrates her knowledge of how to reciprocate her husband's advances in the consummation of their marriage. He in turn must know his wife's praise poem appropriate for the occasion. Outside this context, the woman is praised for her commendable deeds by her husband's praise name.

References

Brown, Duncan. 1998. *Voicing the Text: South African Oral Poetry and Performance.* Oxford: Oxford University Press.

Dube, Caleb. 1988. "Ndebele Oral Art: Its Development within the Historico-socio-economic Context." M.Phil thesis. University of Zimbabwe.

Guma, S. M. 1967. *The Form, Content, and Technique of Traditional Literature in Southern Sotho.* Pretoria: J. L. vam Schaik.

Gunner, L, and M. Gwala. 1991. *Musho! Zulu Popular Praises.* East Lansing: Michigan State University Press.

Hodza, Aaron. 1985. *Mitupo Zvidawo Zvamadzinza.* Harare: Longman Zimbabwe.

Hodza, A. C., and G. Fortune. 1979. *Shona Praise Poetry.* Oxford: Clarendon Press.

Jordan, A. C. 1973. *Towards an African Literature: The Emergence of Literary Form in Xhosa.* Berkeley: University of California Press.

Kunene, D. P. 1971. *Heroic Poetry of the Basotho.* Oxford: Clarendon Press.

Levi-Strauss, Claude. 1968. *Totemism.* Tr. R. Needham. Boston: Beacon Press.

Moyo, S. 1978. *A Linguo-Aesthetic Study of Ngoni Poetry.* Madison, University of Wisconsin.

Mtenje, A, and B. Soko. 1998. Oral Traditions among the Northern Malawi Ngoni. *Journal of Humanities* 12:1–18.

Nkabinde, Temba. 1990. Modern Ndebele Poetry: Characteristics and Development. M.Phil. thesis. University of Zimbabwe.

Opland, Jeff. 1983. *Xhosa Oral Poetry: Aspects of a Black South African Tradition.* Cambridge, England: Cambridge University Press.

Pongweni, A. 1996. *Shona Praise Poetry as Role Negotiation: The Battles of the Clans and the Sexes.* Gweru, Zimbabwe: Mambo Press.

Rycroft, D. 1976. Southern Bantu Clan-Praises: A Neglected Genre. *Bulletin of the School of Oriental and African Studies* (University of London) 39, no. 1: 155–159.

Schapera, Isaac, ed. 1965. *Praise Poems of Tswana Chiefs.* Oxford: Clarendon Press.

Vail, L, and L. White. 1984. The Art of Being Ruled: Ndebele Praise-Poetry, 1835–1971. Literature and Society in Southern Africa. Ed. L. White and T. Couzens. Cape Town, South Africa: Maskew Miller Longman.

ALEC J.C. PONGWENI

See also **Ancestors; Linguistics and African Verbal Arts; Oral Performance and Literature; Yoruba Oriki (Praise Poetry)**

PRAISE POETRY: PRAISE POETRY OF THE BASOTHO

Located within the borders of the Republic of South Africa, the country of Lesotho is home to most of the Basotho people. Derived from a Swati nickname ("Abashuntu"), Basotho was taken as the name of the new kingdom in the nineteenth century. Sesotho refers to the language and customs of the Basotho people.

Praise poetry (*lithoko*) is a type of spoken communication that is dedicated to chiefs and warriors because of their heroic deeds, especially during a war. It was popular for relating historical events to an audience in a stylistic manner using a condensed and captivating poetic language. Praise poetry, often called heroic poetry, is still popular for celebrating the achievements and other good qualities, of chiefs and outstanding personalities in the society.

Lithoko is performed by distinguished artists who have proven themselves as talented poets in the society. Although praise poems of different chiefs are passed from elders to young men, there are cases of spontaneous production. The artists can recite praise poems for the chiefs on various occasions, while at the same time adding their own verses. In some cases, such as when returning from the battlefield, an artist could produce praise poetry based on the outcome of the war. During the performance the artist makes himself audible, while the audience listens attentively to the message communicated. The artist moves to and fro in a dramatic manner displaying his devotion and talent. Today, with the availability of technology, movements are restricted because the artists use microphones, which generally confine them to one place.

Unlike written poetry, it is difficult to pin down the form or structure of praise poetry. In general, the praise poem has an introduction, a body, and a conclusion. The introduction, in some cases, is a conventional opening that introduces the person to be praised, either by name or associating him with his relatives. The introduction may also employ metaphors that call for the audience's attention. The body of the poem relates to various events that the artist wishes to emphasize when praising the hero. The conclusion is marked by a traditional closure formula, which signifies that the artist has come to an end of the praises. Different aspects of form in praise poetry, particularly stylistic forms such as parallelism and stanzas, are easily understood when it is written.

As indicated earlier, the content will refer to events or subject matter that the artist wants to put forward to the audience. After the great wars, the artists adopted a stylized formula in order to summarize the events. Initially, the preparation undertaken by the army is described, then the setting out for the battlefield, followed by episodes of the war. In addition, poems may refer to the following: the birth of the chief, his upbringing, his administration, the places under his ward, his physical appearance, the problems he encountered in life, his relatives, his achievements, and his good qualities. The contents are worded in a dramatic and patriotic manner that calls for unity, as well as submission to and love for the chief. The praise poet is an important public figure whose major role is to enhance stability and a peaceful atmosphere in society. The contents of his praises are, sometimes, about the social, economic, and political issues of the society.

The following praises are examples of praise poems based on war events.

1. Tlali e nts'o ea habo Seeiso
   Ea chesa Maseru tsatsi le rapame.

Translation:

The Black Lightning of the house of Seeiso
Burnt Maseru in the late afternoon.

2. Semamarela sa Mohato, Lekena.
   Semamarela—batho,
   Semamarela batho ba ha sepiriti!
   O tlang batho ka nare ea lithebe
   Mekoetla e ba fahle.
   Koena ea sheba ka har'a boliba,
   Ea sheba ka mahlo a mafubelu,
   Bashanyana ba makhooa ba oela!

Translation:

The Gripper of Mohato, Lekena.
The Gripper on the people,
Gripper on the people of Sprigg!
Strike people by means of buffalo shields
That the white class dust should blind them.
The Crocodile looked into the deep pool,
It looked with eyes that were red.
And the European boys fell in!

The following example illustrates praises concerning the physical appreciation of the hero.

3. Naleli e ts'oeu-ts'oeu ea Ramatheola.
   E ts'oeu—ts'oeu ea Ramakhoba
   O mosehla moshemane oa Ts'akajoe,
   O bosehla, o ts'oana le lehlabathe,
   Ka bosoeu o ts'oana le linaleli,
   Bongata ba na ba hana boa latola,
   Bo re o ts'oana le mafube hantle.

Translation:

The White-Shining Star of Ramatheol.
The white-shining of Ramakhobalo,
He is yellow-coloured, the son of Ts'akajoe,
His yellow colour resembles the sand,
His whiteness resembles that of the stars.
The majority refuse and dispute

They say he is identical with the dawn.

The language of praise poems is different from everyday language. It is condensed, economic, and has a special flavor that arouses the interest of the audience. It inspires and stimulates audience attention because it is full of poetic devices. Basotho praise poems are known for employing eulogies, repetition, and archaic language. The most common devices are metaphorical, where chiefs are identified with a variety of animals, plants, objects, or any other natural phenomenon. This likening of human beings to nonhuman objects such as natural phenomenon is considered to be a justification of the character of the person praised. Praise poetry is said to be public speeches in stylized form, and because of the powerful nature of its language, it is highly appreciated by the Basotho.

The following praises demonstrate the use of metaphorical references to physical characteristics and natural phenomena.

1. Makatolle oa khoro li katiloe
   A katolla khoro li katiloe,
   li bile li bateloa, li etsoa bothata,
   Ho thoe ho koaloa ka Baroanvana,
   Ho koaloa ka Baroana ba Chere.

Translation:

Unblocker of gates that are blocked.
That were secure and hard to penetrate.
In vain they were blocked with the Little-Sans,
They have been blocked with the Little-Sans of Chere.

2. Tsukulu ea Lekena, Lehlaba ts'oana,
   Sebata sa rora meroro se ts'abeha,
   Tau ea rora e ba bona haufi.

Translation:

The Rinocerous of Lekena, Lehlabats'ooana,
The Wild beast roared roarings because it is fearful,
The Lion roared, seeing them near.

References

Damane, M., and Sanders, P. B. 1974. *Lithoko Sotho Praise Poems.* London: Oxford University Press.
Finnegan, Ruth. 1976. *Oral Literature in Africa.* Nairobi: Oxford University Press.
Guma, S. M. 1967. *The Form, Content, and Technique of Traditional Literature in Southern Sotho.* Pretoria: J. L. Van Schalk.
Kunene, D. P. 1971. *Heroic Poetry of the Basotho.* London: Clarendon.
Mangoaela, Z. A. 1981. *Lithoko tsa Marena a Basotho.* Morija Sesuto Book Depot.
Okpewho, Isidore. 1992. *African Oral Literature,* 3d ed. Bloomington: Indiana University Press.

MAKALI I. MOKITIMI

See also **Animals in African Folklore; Linguistics and African Verbal Arts; Performance in Africa**

PRAISE POETRY: PRAISE POETRY OF THE XHOSA

Traditions of oral poetry were well-established among the Xhosa-speaking peoples who inhabited the coastal seaboard of southeastern South Africa at the time of their first interaction with European settlers late in the eighteenth century. The first references to Xhosa praise poetry (called *izibongo*), by Christian missionaries, date from the 1820s. During the previous two decades the earliest recorded Xhosa poem was composed. The prophet Ntsikana taught his followers a hymn in praise of Jesus in the traditional form of poems in praise of rulers. It was transmitted orally by them after his death in 1821, and first transcribed in 1822 by John Bennie. Bennie set about systematically transcribing the Xhosa language after his arrival at Tyhume in 1821, and printed this poem for the first time in December 1823.

Poems may treat animals and familiar objects, but essentially they concern people and their social and political affairs. They are composed by individuals about themselves or their associates, commemorating physical qualities, character traits, and deeds. Men, women, and children are all potentially composers of these izibongo, which contain praise references coined by themselves or by others. The poems may be added to in the course of a lifetime, but they tend to verbalize stability. A son may therefore learn the izibongo of his father and grandfather, which he will use as ritual invocations (*izinqulo*) of his ancestors after their deaths. Lineage poems of royal ancestors become the clan poems (*iziduko*) known widely throughout the community. All these varieties may be employed by the reciter to express pride or to exhort or honor the hearer.

Izibongo may include both flattering and unflattering references, usually formulated in the mode of hyperbole or caricature. The dominant image is the metaphor, frequently drawn from the animal kingdom. The irreducible core of the line is nominal, either a personal name or a metaphor (distinguished only by a variation of a prefix). In their simplest form, clan praises may consist of a list of names in a lineage. Each of these nominals may be extended into a qualifying phrase, and the qualification may in turn be extended, producing a recognizable expansible structure of praise names, verses, and stanzas. Izibongo consist of a concatenation of these "praises" of their subjects. For example, the izibongo of the nineteenth-century warrier-chief Matanzima includes the lines:

> Conqueror, he hurls a grey rock.
> Cannon that thundered in the Mathole,
> So cowards fled and entered this land,
> So cowards fled in headlong.

Here the core nominals are the personal name "Conqueror" extended to a verse, and the metaphor "Cannon" extended to a three-line stanza. This mode of poetic expression exploits the Xhosa naming system, which provides for a variety of alternative names and nicknames for individuals.

Historically, the common structure of clan and popular izibongo also underlay the elevated *izibongo* produced in honor of the chief or dignitaries by the court poet, or *imbongi* (pl. *iimbongi*), who was always a male. The imbongi was attached to the chief's court, but seems to have enjoyed a degree of independence from authority that accorded him the license to criticize the chief with impunity. The imbongi was thus both herald, cheerleader, and social critic, and he sustained in his poetry the social norm. He praised achievement but condemned excess, and was loyal not so much to the person of the chief as to the chieftainship. In confirming the rule of the chief, he was promoting the well-being of the polity. In this respect his poetry was essentially political, a function modern izibongo retains to this day.

The izibongo of the imbongi refers not only to the chief and his ancestors, but also to the social and political context of the performance. The Xhosa imbongi composes his poetry spontaneously in performance: as the poet Melikaya Mbutuma put it, "an imbongi is eyes." As with all izibongo, the performance is solo, unaccompanied by musical instruments, and produced in a distinctively gruff voice. Among the poets in the community, only the imbongi wears an animal skin cloak and hat and carries two spears or fighting sticks.

Despite the gradual spread of literacy—and the frequently articulated fear that oral traditions were under threat—the primary collection of izibongo, published in 1906, is entitled *Zemk'inkomo, magwalandini!* (Preserve your heritage!). Xhosa *iimgongi* continued to operate throughout the nineteenth and twentieth centuries, and they have flourished in the independent South Africa that has emerged from the apartheid years. Worker poets active in the period just prior to independence drew on traditional modes of expression and performance, and following independence Xhosa iimbongi have performed publicly at the opening of parliament in praise of President Nelson Mandela, the British Queen, and the Pope.

References

Brown, Duncan. 1996. South African Oral Performance Poetry of the 1980's: Mzwakhe Mbuli and Alfred Qabula. In *New Writing from Southern Africa: Authors Who Have Become Prominent since 1980*, ed. Emmanuel Ngara. Cape Town: David Philip.

Mafeje, Archie. 1967. The Role of the Bard in Contemporary African Community. *Journal of African Languages* 6:193–223.

Ndawo, H. M. 1939. *Ixiduko zama-Hlubi*. Lovedale, Colo: Lovedale Press.

Opland, Jeff. 1983. *Xhosa Oral Poetry: Aspects of a Black South African Tradition*. Cambridge, England: Cambridge University Press.

———. 1998. *Xhosa Poets and Poetry*. Cape Town: David Philip.

Rubusana, W. B. 1911. *Zemk'inkomo magwalandini*. 2d ed. London: Author.

JEFF OPLAND

See also **Griots and Griottes, Southern African Oral Traditions**

PRAISE POETRY: XHOSA PRAISE POETRY FOR PRESIDENT MANDELA

South Africa's presidential inauguration on May 10, 1994, was an impressive occasion. It took place after years of the infamous apartheid system, which was finally dismantled in 1994. Deliberations between the National Party, under the leadership of former President F. W. de Klerk, and the African National Congress (ANC) led by President Nelson Mandela, began in 1990, when Mandela was released from prison. A peaceful settlement was finally reached in 1994.

It is against this historical backdrop that contemporary Xhosa oral poetry is performed. The Xhosa are the second largest ethnic group in South Africa, and they live mainly on the eastern shores of South Africa. They have an extensive body of spoken arts, including folktales, proverbs, and praise poetry. Over the years, there have been many performances of poetry praising Nelson Mandela. The poetry performed in honor of him at his inauguration as president of South Africa is of particular importance.

Dignitaries from all over the world were present in order to witness this momentous event. Thousands upon thousands of people gathered at the Union Buildings in Pretoria to take part in the festivities and to see President Mandela taking his presidential oath. Special places were reserved on the podium for the president's two *iimbongi* (oral poets).

Archie Mafeje defines the *imbongi* (as "[a] praise poet who frequented the chief's great place and traveled with him in traditional Nguni society. His distinctive feature is that he can recite poems without having prepared them beforehand" (1967, 193).

Although this definition may have sufficed in the past, it is no longer accurate. The presence of an *imbongi* at occasions such as the presidential inauguration or the opening of parliament show that the *imbongi* are no longer simply limited to praising chiefs. They have managed to adapt to contemporary political contexts, and thus have remained relevant and powerful political and social commentators.

Urbanization, the impact of Western education, the formation of the independent homelands, the changing nature of chieftainship, the emergence of black nationalism, the struggle for freedom, the release of political prisoners, and more recently, the election and installation of a new democratic government have all had an effect on the tradition of praise singing. Despite so many influences, the custom remains an important part of contemporary culture in South Africa.

This tradition formed an important part of what was called protest literature during the years of struggle for equality and independence in South Africa. Hence, there are poets such as Mzwakhe Mbuli, who performs in English and Zulu and uses the tradition of oral poetry as inspiration for commenting on contemporary events.

One of the poets who performed at Mandela's inauguration was Zolani Mkiva, a young man who was then a student at the University of the Western Cape. Both his uncle and his grandfather are recognized as *iimbongi*. Mkiva sees himself as "a traditional praise singer who is dynamic" and his presence at the inauguration is a clear indication of his growing acceptability among the people of South Africa. At the beginning of 1995 he returned from a tour of Germany, during which he performed his poems. For many, he represents a new era that requires a "liberated" oral literature not necessarily subsumed within the realms of political protest poetry, but which can provide commentary on national as well as international events as they relate to South Africa. The following is an extract taken from Mkiva's lengthy inauguration poem:

Yaghawuk' imbeleko . . .
Zghawuk' i-ankile zentiyo nengcinezelo . . .
Hlambani intliziyo bantu baseMhlabuhlangene,
Kuba ide yafika imini enkulu.
Ubekiwe ngokusesikweni uMongameli wenene nenvaiso
    weli lomdibaniso. Ndithetha goMandela wodumo,
    odume ngobulungisa eluntwini . . .
Kaloku ingcombolo yamathambo, iqala ngoNkosi
    Bambatha,

Wazithath' intambo uBambatha wazinikela
    kuLangalibale Dube,
Wazithat' uDube wazinikela kuNkos' Luthuli,
UAlbert Luthuli wazinikela kuOliver Reginald Tambo.
Namhlanje singena ebhantini sihamba noMandela,
Inamb' enkulu ecandi iziziba . . .
Iqadi likaJongintaba . . . unyana kaNosekeni . . .
    Ndimvile uFidel Castro—the Commandant General
    of the International Cuban Forces esithi:
    "Victoire c'est."
Watheth' uYasser Arafat . . . wathi:
    "Solidarity in action and solidarity forever."
Ndimvile uBoutros Boutros Ghali . . . esithi:
    "L'union c'est la force."
Waphendula noKanel' Gadaffi ngelithi:
    "Karambanin akuya ta kayi ta kwa."
Nguye lowo ke uMandela—the living legend and the
    international figure.

Translation:

The umbilical cord has snapped . . .
The anchors of hate and oppression have snapped . . .
Wash your hearts people of Mhlabuhlangene (united
    South Africa),
Because the great day has arrived.
The leader of truth has been placed by custom to lead
    this united society.
I am speaking about Mandela, the great one, who is
    known for healing society . . .
Because the process began with Chief Bambatha and
    his ancestors,
Chief Bambatha took the reigns and gave them to
    Langalibalele Dube,
Dube took these and gave them to Chief Luthuli,
Albert Luthuli gave them to Oliver Reginald Tambo.
Today we are entering the destined area (new South
    Africa) together with Mandela,
The powerful one who has crossed many oceans . . .
From the house of Jongintaba . . . the son of
    Nosekeni . . .
I have heard Fidel Castro—the Commandant General
    of the International Cuban Forces saying:
    "Victory is ours."
Yassar Arafat spoke:
    "Solidarity in action and solidarity forever."
I have heard Boutros Boutros Ghali saying:
    "Unity is strength."
Colonel Gadaffi answered:
    "Honour the people of the world."
This is Mandela—the living legend and the
    international figure.

This poem has an international flavor appropriate to the occasion, but it is also influenced by Mandela's credibility in the eyes of the rest of the world. It is a poem encapsulating the past history of the ANC and its leaders, but it also possesses a contemporaneity which is interwoven with history to form a complex literary tapestry. It is evident that the poem is mainly about praise, and that the critical element is reserved for apartheid and those who upheld it. There is also a strong "unity" theme in the poem. This can be seen as the beginnings of what could be termed "reconciliation" literature and a movement away from "protest" literature in South Africa.

It remains to be seen, however, to what extent these oral art forms will be manipulated or appropriated by those in control of power in South Africa, especially politicians. There have been attempts by rulers in other African countries to exploit this art form for their own good, and there is evidence of "the manipulation of oral art for the benefit of the ruling classes, leading to the domestication and disempowerment of oral art" (Mlama 1991).

Cultural bodies and those guarding freedom of speech in South Africa will have to be vigilant against this danger if the poet is to remain a critic and mediator. Furthermore, one can assume that there will be further shifts in power in South African politics in the future, and it will be interesting to observe how oral poets will fit into the new dispensation.

It is clear, however, that those who hold power, and the *imbongi*'s ability to be innovative as a contemporary sociopolitical commentator (as well as the people in general, who legitimize power) will continue to influence the tradition of oral poetry, which remains a context within the wider strategy of power and ideology in South Africa.

References

Kaschula, Russell H. 1991a. The Role of the Xhosa Oral Poet in Contemporary South African Society. *South African Journal of African Languages* 11, no. 2:47–54.

———. 1991b. Power and the Poet in Contemporary Transkei. *Journal of Contemporary African Studies* 10, no. 2:24–43.

———. 1995. Mandela Comes Home: the Poets' Perspective. *Oral Tradition*.

———. 1997. The Interface Between Orality-Literacy With Particular Reference to the Xhosa Imbongi. *Research in African Literatures*. 28, no. 1:173–191.

Kaschula, Russell H., and Mandlakayise Matyumza. 1996. *Qhiwu-u-ula—Return to the Fold*. Pretoria: Via Afrika.

Mafeje, Archie. 1967. The Role of the Bard in a Contemporary South African Community. *Journal of African Languages*. 6:88–89.

Mlama, Penina. 1991. Oral Art and Contemporary Cultural Nationalism. Paper read at an International Oral Literature conference hosted by the School for Oriental and African Studies, University of London.

Opland, Jeff. 1983. *Xhosa Oral Poetry. Aspects of a Black South African Tradition*. Cambridge, England: Cambridge University Press.

RUSSELL H. KASCHULA

See also **Oral Performance and Literature; Popular Culture; Praise Poetry**

PRAISE POETRY: YORÙBÁ ORÍKÌ

Oríkì are attributive epithets or praise poetry that are central in the social, religious, and political life of the Yorùbá of southwestern Nigeria. They are vocative in address and namelike in form, disjunctive both in relation to each other and internally, and condensed and allusive in reference.

A text or performance of *oríkì* is an assemblage of potentially separate and diverse units, which can be performed in varying orders and combinations and which are held together by their common application to a specific subject. Nominalized sentences feature prominently, and there are ways in which the grammar of ordinary speech can be extended to yield namelike forms of great length and internal complexity. Long passages of text can also be attributed to the subject through the use of expressions such as "Ọmọ . . . " (Child of . . .) or ". . . ni wọ̩n ń pe Lágbájá" (. . . is what they call so-and-so). The *oríkì* are understood to "belong" to the subject—and to have an intimate connection with the subject's social and moral being.

All entities, whether human, spiritual, or inanimate, have *oríkì*. The most elaborated and culturally valued bodies of *oríkì* belong to: (1) prominent individuals of the past (ancestors); (2) towns of origin (*orílè*) and the large, dispersed kin groups identified by common membership in them; and (3) the *òrìsà* (gods).

Every baby is given an *oríkì* name at birth and will be saluted with the *oríkì orílè* of its father's lineage. These are the most ancient and best known *oríkì*. They form the bedrock of social identity and can arouse profound emotions of pride and gratification when performed. As a person grows up, he or she will gradually acquire more *oríkì*, reflecting his or her qualities, characteristics, and actions as they take shape. These personal *oríkì* are composed by drummers, professional praise singers, and fellow townspeople. Some of them may be drawn from a common stock shared by all to whom they are applicable, such as *oríkì* praising tall people, generous people, excellent farmers, or medicine men. Others are idiosyncratic and may commemorate obscure and even shameful or embarrassing incidents in the person's life. *Oríkì* remark on what is distinctive in a person, rather than simply flattering him or her. Men tend to acquire more *oríkì* than women, and prominent people in the community acquire more than obscure people.

Profusion and variety are of great importance in a performance, for the more prolonged and intense the salutation, the more the aura of the subject is enhanced. Material may be borrowed from a range of textual sources—including other bodies of *oríkì*, proverbs, Ifa divination verses, and even riddles—and converted into attributions to heap upon the subject. The performance of *oríkì* is galvanizing and empowering, heightening a human subject's social well-being, spurring a masquerade into action, and inspiring the *òrìsà* to make their presence felt among the human community.

Oríkì may be recited in a normal speaking voice to greet or congratuate a subject, in which case they are simply called *oríkì*. But they also form the basis for a wide variety of named chants or chanting modes, some very localized and others widely found among Yoruba-speaking people. Among the most widespread and best known are *ìjálá* (hunters' chants), *iwì egúngún* (ancestral masquerade chants), and *ẹ̀kún ìyàwó* (bridal chants). Chanting modes are distinguished by intonation and voice quality, by the focus of the address (thus, in *ìjálá*, the subjects are often animals, while in *iwì egúngún* there are usually long passages addressing the legendary founder of the ancestral masquerade cult, and in *ẹ̀kún ìyàwó* the focus is on the performer herself, who is the bride), by the nature of the additional textual materials that supplement the *oríkì*, and by the people who perform the chant (and the contexts in which they do so). But there are also many styles of *oríkì* chanting that are not distinguished by name, as genres. These are often performed by the daughters and wives of a household, who may achieve unparalleled mastery of the art.

Both men and women may be professional or specialist performers who earn an income by attending major life-cycle celebrations, festivals, and other events in their area, praising the celebrants using whatever portions of their *oríkì* they are familiar with. Some become famous through performance on television and radio, or through records and cassettes.

The meaning of *oríkì* is often obscure, requiring an explanation from knowledgeable elders. This often involves the parallel and interdependent tradition of *itàn* (true narrative). In many cases, women are more expert than men in *oríkì*, while male elders are better versed in the *itàn* that can explain them.

References

Babalọlá, S. A. 1966. *The Content and Form of Yorùbá Ìjálá*. Oxford: Oxford University Press.

Babalọlá, Adébóyè. 1966. *Àwọn Oríkì Orílè*. Glasgow: Collins.

Barber, Karin. 1991. *I Could Speak Until Tomorrow: Oríkì. Women, and the Past in a Yoruba Town*. Edinburgh: Edinburgh University Press.

Ọlatunji, Ọlatunde. 1984. *Features of Yoruba Oral Poetry*. Ibadan, Nigeria: University Press.

KARIN BARBER

See also **Okyeame; Praise Poetry**

PROSE AND POETRY OF THE FULANI

The Fulani (also called Fulbe or Peul) are found in the Sahelian zone, from Senegal in the west to the south of Sudan in the east, and into the Central African Republic to the south. Over time, they have formed varied communities, ranging from groups of shepherd nomads to vast states in the eighteenth and nineteenth centuries, which the colonial conquests eradicated. They share a common language, with diversified dialects and a common culture. Their literary production, whether oral or written, is uncommonly abundant. There is a tradition of scholarly literature inherited from Islam and written in *adjami* characters adapted from Arabic. They are a people of nomadic origins, who lack statuary or permanent architecture, and they have left the art of instrumental music to castes. So it is primarily in the field of language that they have invested their artistic and creative faculties. Their literature is, in fact, one of the richest in western Africa, with the genres varying within each group according either to historical or ecological conditions.

Prose Genres

As elsewhere, tales (*taalol*) are the most commonly found genre. However, under the impact of neighboring populations, themes and interpretations may differ according to regions. Told and heard by everyone, prose forms such as legends, fables, song tales, proverbs, and riddles serve as purveyors of social norms and systems of thought. It is through these genres, and the countless linguistic acrobatic and pedadogic puns and plays on words, that children learn language.

Intended for adults rather than for youths, the *janti*, among other narratives, are long philosophical stories or great parables marked with esoteric symbolism. They seem to bear witness

to systems of thought or to ancient initiation rituals. Amadou Hampâté Bâ published several magnificent examples of these narratives, including *Koumen*, *Kaïdara*, and *l'Éclat de la grande étoile*. For the two latter he gave poetical versions.

Another narrative genre of considerable importance is the epic, which flourishes in the western part of the Fulani area (even though the nomadic Fulani ignore it) and those who are sedentary in Cameroon and Nigeria do not know of its use). Restricted to griots (specialists in verbal arts) the oration of epic narratives is accompanied on a lute by musical passages which are associated with specific heroes. The epic genre offers three orientations. The most common exalts the feats and doings of historical characters, such as Samba Guéladio Diégui, Silâmaka and Poullôri, Ham-Bodédio, and Boûbou Ardo Galo, in addition to all those heroes of the *Dìna*, the Massina Empire, that was established by Seku Amadu. All of these characters are transmuted by legend into prototypes of the representative heroes of *pulaaku* (the Fulani ideal way of being, centered on the assertion of absolute independence). A second type of epic is related to professional occupations: *sulalbe* (fishermen), *sebbe* (warriors from Senegal), and Fulani shepherds. The epic narratives about the latter group deal exclusively with raids on cattle, while the narratives of the fishermen form part of an annual ritual for a crocodile hunt in which they are sung, not by griots, but by the possessors of knowledge of magic (healers and diviners). A final type of epic, of religious inspiration, praises the heroes of the jihad, particularly El Hadj Umar, the founder of the Tukulor Empire in the nineteenth century. This character was also praised in an epic in verse in the same pattern as Arabic poetry.

The common goal of these epics is to foster a sense of community in the audience. This is accomplished by exalting the form of both text and music. By representing extravagant characters, this form is reminiscent of the specific traits on which Fulani identity is based. Therefore, it is the genre which best ensures the perpetuation of the behavioral ideals for the Fulani.

Among the prose narratives, there are also historical chronicles called *tarikhs*. When delivered orally, their style is close to that of epics, but when written they are often reduced to genealogies, with schematic and conventional biographies and stark descriptions of events presented without elaborations.

Finally, in addition to the translations of the Quran into Fulani, the cultural heritage from Islam is represented by an abundant literary output, including scholarly, academic, and didactic written works, either in Arabic or in Fulani. These works are by learned intellectuals anxious to transmit, at a high level of competence, teachings in the fields of theology or exegesis, and to spread them among the Fulani.

Poetic Genres

There are many poetic genres, which serve to illustrate the foremost traits of Fulani culture, mainly pastoralism and Islam. This a rich, pastorally-inspired poetry takes different forms depending on the region. There are *askooji na' i* (cattle genealogies) in Sénégal, recited in contests between shepherds while they water their cattle. There are *cooraaji* and *diisi*, which are spells and propitiatory incantations sprinkled with Muslim invocations to God and the Prophet. These are ritually repeated by the master owners of the pastoral secrets in the Futa-Jalon. There are also *jammooje na' i* (praises of cattle), which are endless poems using sound sequences composed by the young shepherds from Mali during their solitary migrations to water sources and pasture land. They declaim them, at the top of their voices, while they publicly march their herds at the annual feast in celebration of their return. The sophisticated composition of these poems reveal, as oral creations, a stylistic refinement, an outstanding linguistic awareness, and an extraordinary artistic knowledge.

Other poetical genres, more eclectic in their themes, are just as refined in their style. The *mergi* in Mali are recited in monotone rhythm by their authors, while in Cameroon the *mbooku* requires the participation of a troupe of performers who repeat each verse after the narrator, adding a balancing movement to the rhythm of the recital. Here, each poet puts his talent into practice in a fictitious rivalry ranging across diverse subjects and in the most varied tones, so that these poems act as conservatories of language and culture.

Islam has lead to some rich poetical productions in Arabic, but most are in Fulani. Using metrics and a prosody inspired from Arabic patterns, a great variety of religious poetry has developed, intended, at times, to be performed in a militant matter or at other times, as a more personal mystical aspiration. This poetry is sung without instrumental accompaniment in the *zaouias* by *talibes*, by groups of pious women in private, or in public by blind men who are professional singers.

A modern secular poetry has also appeared. This verse deals with ordinary subjects. In conjunction with this poetry a certain professional enacting of literature has also appeared. These can be testimonies of the colonial period, circumstantial pamphlets or panegyrics, or lyrical, satirical, or dramatic evocations.

Genres of Song

Song is so important to the Fulani that it cannot be dissociated from literary creation. Alongside religious poetry, there is an extensive range of sung secular genres, which are performed with instrumental accompaniment or a cappella with only the clapping of hands and tinkling of bracelets as accompaniment. There are many public or private opportunities to express oneself in song. Lullabies, young girls, songs, and marriage songs are widely performed. There are war odes (*buruuji*), praise songs, and satirical or parodic songs taken up by profession griots with lute accompaniment. One also hears languorous and evocative shepherd elegies accompanied by a monocord lute. And there are songs of defiance preceeding rituals of flagellation.

Besides these genres, each professional group develops a type of traditional song of its own, such as the *fantang* of cattle breeders in Sénégal, the *gumbala* of warriors, and the *dillere* of the weavers. Certain songs like the *direere* of the farmers (in Mali) or the *gerewol* of the nomads in Cameroon and Niger, are accompanied by specific dance steps. Among the epic texts, the *pekaan* of the fishermen is also sung a cappella. The more ancient genres continue to be perpetuated while new ones are being born (like the *uumarayel* in Sénégal).

Literary activity is strongly implicated in the functioning of society, and the repertoires are distributed according to sex, age, professional function, and social status. For example, a certain pastoral poem will only be used among young shepherds, who, however great their talent, will forsake this style as soon as they are integrated into adult life. The same occurs with other song genres. As for epic narrations, they are performed by the griots.

However, among the learned classes, some Fulani-speaking authors have emerged, such as the great Malian writer Âmadou Hampâté Bâ, who, besides his production in the French language, has written texts in a superb poetical form. There is also the Senegalese writer and poet Yêro Dôro Diallo whose work, exclusively written in Fulani, is less known. Within the younger generation a movement of artists and modern poets has developed. They still imitate the traditional songs, but have also inaugurated new styles and written poems of a more personal nature.

The vitality that the Fulani people show in their literary creation has not waned with time. It remains a symbol of their unfailing capability to adapt themselves to new situations, and it has enabled them, through all their migrations, to preserve their cultural identity.

REFERENCES

Abdoulaye, O. D. 1988. *Mbooku, poesie peule du Diamaré*. Vol. 1. Paris: L Harmattan.

Arnott, D. W. 1985. Literature in Fula. *In Literatures in African Languages. Theoretical Issues and Sample Surveys*, ed. B. W. Andrzejewski, S. Pilaszewicz, and W. Tyloch. Cambridge, England: Cambridge University Press.

Bâ, A. H. 1974. *L'eclat de la Grande Etoile, suivi du Bain rituel, récits initiatiques peuls*. Paris: A. Colin, Les Belles Lettres, Classiques Africains, 15.

———. 1985. *Njeddo Dewal, Mère de calamité*. Abidjan-Dakar-Lomé. Les Nouvelles Editions Africaines.

Bâ, A. H., and Dieterlen, G. 1961. *Koumen. texte initiatique des pasteurs peuls*. (Paris: La Haye, Mouton, Cahiers de l'Homme.

Bâ, A. H. and Kesteloot, L. 1968. *Kaídara. récit initiatique peul rapporté par A. H. Bâ*. Paris: A. Colin, Les Belles Lettres, Classiques Africains 3.

Correra, I. 1992. *Samba Guéladio, épopée peule du Fuuta Tooro*. texte pulaar par Amadou. Kamara Dakar, initiations et études africaines no. 36. Université de Dakar-Ifan Cheikh Anta Diop.

Eguchi, P. K. 1978–84. *Fulfulde Tales of North Cameroon*. 4 vols. Tokyo: Institute for the Study of Languages and Cultures of Asia and Africa.

Gaden, H. 1931. *Proverbes et maximes peuls et toucouleurs. traduits, expliqués, annotés*. Paris: Travaux et mémoires de l'Institut d'ethnologie.

———. 1935. *La vie d'El Hadj Omar, qacida en poular de Mohammadou Aliou Tyam*; Paris: Travaux et mémoires de l'Institut d'ethnologie.

Haafkens, J. 1983. *Chants musulmans en peul: textes de l héritage religieux de la communauté musulmane de Maroua, Cameroun*. Leiden: Brill.

Labatut, R. 1974. *Chants de vie et de beauté peuls. Becueillis chez les Peuls nomades du Nord-Cameroun*. Paris: Publications orientalistes de France.

Lacroix, P. F. 1965. *Poésie peule de l Adamawa*. éditée par. Paris: Julliard, Les Belles Lettres, Classiques Africains 3.

Meyer, G. 1988. *Paroles du soir. Contes toucouleurs*. Paris. L'Harmattan.

———. 1991. *Récits épiques toucouleurs. La vache, le livre, la lance*. (Paris: Karthala-ACCT.

Mohammadou, E. 1980. *Traditions historiques des Foulbés de l'Adamaoua*. Paris: CNRS.

Ndongo, S. M. 1986. *Le Fantang. Poémes mythiques des bergers peuls*. (Karthala: IFAN-UNESCO.

Ngaide, M. L. 1983. *Le vent de la razzia. Deux récits épiques des Peuls du Jolof*. Dakar: IFAN.

Noye, D. 1976. *Blasons peuls. Eloges et satires du Nord-Cameroun*. Paris: Librairie orientaliste P. Geuthner.

———. 1983. *Baba Zandou raconte.* Paris: Edicef, Fleuve et
Flamme.

Seydou, C. 1992. *Silâmaka et Poullôri. récit épique peul raconté par
Tinguidji, édité par.* Paris: A. Colin, Les Belles Lettres, Classiques
Africains 13.

———. 1973. Panorama de la littérature peule. *Bulletin de 1
I.F.A.N.*, 35, no. 1:176–218.

———. 1976. *Contes et fables des veillées.* Paris: Nubia.

———. 1976. *La geste de Ham-Bodêdio ou Hama le Royge.* traduite
et éditée par. Paris: A. Colin, Les Belles Lettres, Classiques
Africains 18.

———. 1991. *Bergers des mots. poésie peule du Mâssina présentée et
traduite par* Paris: Les Belles Lettres, Classiques Africains 24.

Sow, A. I. 1966. *La femme, la vache, la foi. écrivains et poètes du
Foûta Djalon.* Paris: Julliard, Les Belles Lettres, Classiques
Africains 5.

———. 1968. *Chroniques et récits du Foûta-Djalon.* Paris: G.
Klincksieck.

———. 1971. *Le filon du bonheur éternel. par Tierno
Mouhammadou Samba Mombéyâ,* Édité par. Paris: A. Colin, Les
Belles Lettres, Classiques Africains 10.

Sy, A. A. 1978. *Seul contre tous.* Dakar-Abidjan, NEA.

CHRISTIANE SEYDOU
TRANSLATED BY SUZANNE RUELLAND

See also **Epics; Songs**

PROSE NARRATIVES: THE MAASAI

As if intrinsic delight is not enough, oral traditions also provide
commentary on a people's history and society. Given the mischief of cultural imagination, however, the relation of oral literature to a people's past and present is elusive, as it may serve to
reflect or distort, to explain or rationalize, to assert or deny, or
to describe or satirize history or the social order.

Fortunately, the formal properties of oral production often
convey something of the truth claims implicit in given genres.
Maasai oral culture includes both the sung and the spoken word.
Apart from ordinary songs, several forms of lyric poetry and
recitation, the most noted being the sweet *Eoko* and the rapid,
tongue-twisting *Enkijuka*; the concise *en'dung'eta erashe* (skin
cutter) or proverbs; riddles called *il-ang'eni* (for the clever), and
numerous genres of oral narrative, described below.

In *The Masai: Their Language and Folklore* (1905), A. C.
Hollis distinguished between "stories" (*inkatinin* [pl.], *enkatini*
[sing.]), "news of long-ago" (L-Omon Li-Opa), and mythic narratives, also termed "beginnings" (*inkiterunot* [pl.], *enkiterunoto*,
[sing.]). Narrative speech in general is called "news" (*il-omon*
[pl.]), and just as one is said in the Maasai idiom to "eat the
news" (*ainosa ilomon*), in its recounting one also "eats" or "consumes" a story (*ainos enkatini*) (Mol 1996, 39). Within Maasai
narrative, Naomi Kipury distinguishes myth and legend, as well
as Ogre, Trickster, and Man stories.

Maasai tales of the "beginning" describe the origins of social
multiplicity. Best known are "The Origin of Cattle" and "Ascending the Escarpment," each of which involves movement
along a vertical axis that signifies a transit between the human
and the supernatural worlds and the origins of Maasai culture.

The Origin of Cattle

One day God called Maasinta, who had no cattle, and told him
to make a large enclosure, and to wait early in the morning. At
the appointed hour, God dropped down a long leather strap,
down which cattle descended into the enclosure. The Dorobo
woke up, saw the cattle coming down, and expressed surprise,
saying "Ayieyieyie." At this, God said to Maasinta that if these
were enough, then he would receive no more, and that he should
love the cattle. Maasainto cursed the Dorobo, that he should
remain poor, live off animals in the wild, and find milk to be
poison (Kipury 1983, 30–31).

Here, the genesis of cattle explains the social distinction between the Maasai pastoralist and the Dorobo hunter, their economic status, and the dominance of one and subordination of
the other, which are all seen to originate through supernatural
intervention, and to be explained by, and justified by, the myth.

Ascending the Escarpment

Long ago, the Maasai found themselves in a dry, craterlike country during drought, but it was noticed that birds flew down the
steep escarpment with green grass. Climbing the escarpment,
scouts found a lush, green pasture, empty of people. At that
time there were no social divisions, and everyone spoke Olmaa.
They constructed a "bridge" out of a strap, up which people
and livestock began to climb, but when only half the people had
reached the top, it collapsed, throwing the other half down to
the dry plains. Those people became Ilmeek, the non-Maasai,
while those who reached the top became the Maasai, and at
that time clans, age-sets, diviners, blacksmiths, and other social
differences originated (Sankan 1971, 67–69).

"Coming up" the escarpment (*enkilepunoto endigir*) defines
the moment of historical "becoming" for Maasai, who trace their
origin as a people to "when they came up." On the one hand,
their becoming "people of cattle" (Galaty 1983) occurred with
the movement of cattle from sky/heaven (*enkai*) to earth (*enkop*),
while, on the other hand, they became cultured Maasai by the
movement of people and cattle from below (*abori*) to above
(*shumata*). In the first case, divinity descends to the Maasai,
while in the second the Maasai ascend to divinity; nonetheless,
in the beginning of social difference, it is being favored by divine
blessing that above all distinguishes the Maasai.

In Maasai myths of origin, dramatic personae exemplify social
categories—the protagonist, for instance, being the Maasai as
pastoralist—and plots hinge on vital ruptures in cosmic time
that give rise to distinctions crucial to the world as it is known:
between men and women, between herders, hunters, and farmers, between ordinary folk, blacksmiths, and prophets, between
moieties and clans, between age groups and language groups,
between a world where God mingles with people and sky and
earth are one, and one where the natural and supernatural are
properly distinguished—in short between original cosmic homogeneity and subsequent mundane differentiation (Galaty 1982,
1986).

In legend, however, prototypical characters are personifications of actual groups (e.g., Maasai or Olarinkon as representatives of the Maasai or Ilarinkon groups). Through the use of
symbolic images, legendary episodes seem to represent social
processes more than historical events, and they exemplify social
relations rather than actualities (Willis 1981, 101; Kipury 1983,
18). Historical groups with whom Maasai came into early conflict (e.g., Ilarinkon, Iltatwa, Iloogolala) are recalled as the stuff
of legend, their warrior giants defeated by the small but swift

Maasai only due to the latter's intelligence and audacity. Similarly, the Inkidong'i narrative, which recounts the origin of the Maasai *Iloibonok* (Laibon) diviners and prophets, dramatizes the lineage's history as a series of magical actions that lend its members credibility as ritual leaders of the Maasai (Galaty 1977, 280–284). Oral history, finally, makes reference to actual age-sets and named heroes, details actual times and places, and describes events with vivid imagery. Thus, in the continuum from myth to legend to history, narrative dimensions evolve from a vertical cosmic axis (along which the mortal engages with the divine) to a horizontal north-south historical axis, signifying a migratory trajectory of the long term.

Maasai stories, in contrast to narratives of "long ago," occur along a cultural axis, which contrasts the domestic and the wild in proximal, social space. Prototypes of the "wild" may be animals, monsters, enemies, or simply the greedy or cruel, but all are associated with the wilderness (*entim*) that lies outside domestic space and beyond civilized norms of everyday Maasai cultural life. Human stories often portray human foibles and predicaments against the backdrop of Maasai social patterns and conflict with generic opponents.

The Shepherd Boy

A shepherd boy used to soothe a goat that did not like its kid, encouraging it to nurse. One day he was taken by warriors, who had come to steal the livestock he tended. Later, he saw warriors from his own home and arranged to meet them when he was soothing the goat. He prepared a big gourd of milk for them to drink. Because he was watched by a suspicious woman, he gave instructions to his comrades indirectly, by singing a song to the goat he was soothing, explaining to the woman that this was how it was done where he came from. Then the warriors jumped over the gate and killed everyone except those who had been kind to the boy, and retrieved their cattle and sheep (Kipury 1983, 115–118).

In some human-based stories, specific animals interact with humans as dramatic agents, these often being birds of character, whose stereotypic attributes define their roles in folklore (Galaty 1998).

The Girl Who Married a Crow

A disgusting bird disguised himself as a person and married a girl, despite her misgivings and apprehensions. Out of sight of her home, the Crow threatened to eat her and went to fetch wood. She sung a lament which was heard by her brother, her former lover, and several others, who gave her a club and hid nearby. Crow was struck and crushed to death, and the girl returned to marry her lover (Hollis 1905, 198–201; Kipury 1983, 59–60)

Here, Crow plays the role often attributed to monsters or ogres.

Old Sayialel and Eagle

Ole Sayialel was killed in a raid, but after being left by his comrades he was revived by Eagle's beating wings. His lover mourned his supposed death and refused to marry anyone else. When, upon returning, Ole Sayialel killed one of his own fat

he-goats for Eagle, the herders ran to report the loss and described the warrior. Ole Sayialel sung a praise song to Eagle. His lover, hearing it, suspected it was Ole Sayialel, and dressed in her finery to receive him (Kipury 1983, 93–95).

In contrast, Eagle here is a quasi-divine agent, a helper, even a savior. The final example represents one of the few cases in which the fable and story are mixed, with human destiny intersecting the cohort of the usual fabulous animals.

The Warrior and Dove

All except one in a hungry group of warriors killed and ate a dog. Fearing the one who did not eat the dog would tell and shame them, the warriors made him fall in a well and left him to die. When Zebra, Jackal, Hyena, and Rhino asked to drink at the well, the warrior said that they could do so only if they could relate the incident properly so he would be rescued, but they were unable to do so. Only Dove appropriately told how she would sing a song telling of the accident, asking for "eight straps and eight hooks." She was allowed to drink and departed to call for help. Dove was finally understood at the warrior's village, and after the warrior was rescued he slaughtered a ram for Dove, who became his close friend (Kipury 1983, 97–100).

Here, Dove resembles Eagle in serving as a human partner.

In Maasai fables, ordinary birds and game animals rarely figure as characters; rather, social scenarios are played out by unique animals like Hare (*enkitejo*, the "speaker"), Hyena, Snake, and Elephant, with stand-ins provided by Lion, Jackal, Giraffe, Rhino, Ostrich, and Turtle. Here, an alternative society is created, homologous to the human world, in which talking animals are endowed with human personalities, motives, and foibles. One type of Maasai fable pits a subtle, humorous, and cunning protagonist (Hare, Jackal, or Mongoose) against an manipulative and greedy bully (Hyena or Lion). The protagonist invariably overcomes the villain through trickery or with the assistance of other animals, and the latter is often killed. In a second, lighter fable, the protagonist—incorporating some of the greedy attributes of an absent villain—plays a trick on one of the larger, stupider, but well-intentioned characters, and, after failing, escapes. In a third variation, the villain tries to exploit one of the larger but harmless animals, but is thwarted by the cunning protagonist, who takes the latter's part.

Interestingly, the lead characters are all medium-sized, well-proportioned (on a human scale), and—like Maasai—generally share some human predatory consumption traits, including an appreciation of meat. Naive foils, on the other hand, tend to be large and grotesque, like Elephant or Ostrich, or, if not unusually shaped, equally harmless and gullible, like Cow or Antelope. Across fables, a pattern of systematic replacement can be seen of animal characters by their thematic counterparts. The most common dramatic partnership (of protagonist and antagonist) is of Hare and Lion, though Jackal and Hyena or Mongoose and Lion are also common. The naive Elephant is often paired with a wily foil, such as Snake or Bird. The great is thus paired with the small, the high with the low, and the gullible with the shrewd.

Hare and Other Animals

Hare, Elephant, Snake, Tortoise, and Hyena owned a herd of cattle and donkeys, and when Elephant was herding, Hare told the others that to avoid having their animals stolen by Elephant one day, they should kill him. Snake bit Elephant's trunk when he drank water and he died. When Snake took his turn herding, Hare told the others that since Snake had been so brave, he would take all the cattle for himself, so should be killed. Tortoise rolled down the hill and killed Snake. When they moved their home to look for better pastures, Hare said that since Tortoise was so slow they should leave him behind, which they did. Then Hare suggested to Hyena that they divide their cattle, and asked to take the cattle without horns so she wouldn't get butted. Hyena insisted on himself taking the cattle without horns, which were of course donkeys. Later, Hyena ate Hare's mother, and to avenge her Hare told Hyena that the diviner said they should jump over a big fire, Hare when it was smoking, Hyena when it was burning. Hyena plunged into the fire, and when he asked Hare to rescue him, Hare turned him over with a rake, saying "Did you ask me to turn you over?" And that is the end (Kipury 1983, 68–71).

Maasai fables balance between the fantastical and the allegorical: animals that speak form communities of human proportion. Neither small nor gregarious herd animals play crucial roles, for neither are truly distinctive. The characterization intrinsic to animal roles tends both to be ethologically sound and humanly persuasive, making fables convincing junctures between the human and the bestial. Animal characters speak, connive, hold meetings, go herding, and adorn themselves, manifesting human traits and acting out human scenarios. Major players seem male, while vulnerable foils are female (often mothers with young). Themes of the smaller, weaker, and younger overcoming the larger, stronger, and older are common to Maasai stories, as well, and the contrast between the restrained and cunning protagonist and its impulsive, greedy, and cruel counterpart is not unlike the contrast implicit in the Maasai idealized self-image (exemplified in myths of origin) of being superior to lesser non-Maasai. Fables are at once fantastic renderings of an autonomous animal world humanized, and allegorical representations of a human world bestialized. The animal and the human serve, in Erich Auberbach's terms, as *figura* of one another, each signifying and fulfilling not only itself but the other (2003, 64).

The very fact that folklore is entertainment does not tell us why it is entertaining. Maasai folklore performs a sort of cultural work; it worries and plays at the question of identity by crafting a plethora of personae that dramatize attributes (embodied in *figura* as memorably grotesque), which define, through contrast, opposition, and satire, the self-endowed traits of the self. In this way, there is a peculiar unity running through radically diverse genres, connecting hunters and blacksmiths in social life, preternatural ogres and monsters (giants dramatizing enemies), cowards and the selfish in "man" stories; and, in fables, portraying species as individuals. Folklore and oral traditions do more than stage a society already defined and known, for through the diverse genres of the oral imagination, scenes, characters, and scenarios are scripted and brought into play, constructing in thought and images a social world that is then lived out.

References

Auberbach, Erich. 2003. *Mimesis: The Representation of Reality in Western Literature* (1953), tr. Willard R. Trask. Princeton, N.J.: Princeton University Press.

Galaty, J. G. 1977. *In the Pastoral Image: The Dialectic of Maasai Identity*. Ph.D thesis, University of Chicago.
———. 1982. Being "Maasai"; Being "People-of-Cattle": Ethnic Shifters in East Africa. *American Ethnologist* 9, no. 1:1–20.
———. 1986. East African Hunters and Pastoralists in a Regional Perspective: An "Ethnoanthropological" Approach. *Sprache und Geschichte in Afrika* 7, no. 1:105–131.
———. 1998. The Maasai Ornithorium: Tropic Flights of Avian Imagination in Africa. *Ethnology* Summer.
Hollis, A. C. 1970. *The Maasai: Their Language and Folklore* (1905). Westport, Conn.: Negro Universities Press.
Jacobs, Alan. 1968. A Chronology of the Pastoral Maasai. In *Hadith I*. Ed. B. Ogot. Nairobi: East African Publishing.
Kipury, Naomi. 1983. *Oral Literature of the Maasa*. Nairobi: Heinemann.
Mol, Frans. 1978. *Maa: A Dictionary of the Maasai Language and Folklore, English-Maasai*. Nairobi: Marketing and Publishing.
———. 1996. *Maasai Language and Culture*. Lemek: Maasai Centre.
Sankan, S. S. 1971. *The Maasai*. Nairobi: East African Literature Bureau.
———. 1979. *Intepen e Maasai*. Nairobi: Kenya Literature Bureau.
Willis, Roy. 1981. *A State in the Making: Myth, History, and Social Transformation in Precolonial Ufipa*. Bloomington: Indiana University Press.

JOHN G. GALATY

See also **East African Folklore; Folktales; Myths**

PROSE NARRATIVES: THE MENDE

The Mende people, numbering more than one million, live in villages and towns clustered into chiefdoms throughout the low forests of southern Sierra Leone, in diaspora communities of Freetown (the national capital), and in adjacent areas of western Liberia. The Mende have occupied these areas for at least the last 500 years, although traditional settlements and social structures have been profoundly affected by a civil war that ravaged Mendeland and the rest of Sierra Leone in the 1990s.

The Mende refer to their oral tradition collectively as *njepe wovei* (old talk), which includes such diverse genres as history, the dilemma tale, myths of the trickster (Kaso), the hero (Musa Wo), and the folktale (*domei*). Despite this genre diversity, all Mende narrative forms are related through common plots, which are the building blocks of *njepe wovei*.

History is divided by the Mende into two epochs: ancient times, when present patterns of life were established, and the past, which is in the memory of the oldest people in the town. This division corresponds to the distinction between the nameless dead (*ndebla*), and the remembered fathers (*kekenl*), who together constitute the *ndoobla* (ancestors). Mende history is simply called *njepe wovei*, and so is related to all the other forms of storytelling, although it is held to be an accurate account of historical fact. The oldest and most respected men, the *kpakoisla*, who do not perform other narratives, take pride in telling histories, especially stories about the founding of their towns.

According to the *kpakoisla*, dilemma tales hold a position of prestige midway between narrative histories and the folktale proper (*domei*). In the dilemma tale, plots borrowed from *njepe wovei* are subordinated to the framing of a conundrum. Possible resolutions to the conundrum are then presented to an audience, which must either choose among them or recognize the dilemma as irresolvable. Open-endedness is thus the distinguishing mark of this type of narrative; the narrator purposefully creates a conflict of choice. The point of the narrative is the cleverness of the argument.

Dilemma and history are kinetic: they release their energies outward. Their appeal is directly to the intellect, and their recitation is altogether a respectable affair. Both genres lack the leader/chorus singing which characterizes the performance of the *domei*. This absence is crucial, since the Mende maintain that music is incompatible with truth (*tonya*), and so they categorize the *domei* as separate from other narrative genres on this basis alone.

If *tonya* is further glossed as "objectivity," then the sense of the Mende classification becomes more apparent. The *domei* is a subjective art form for women. The *domeigbuamoi* (performer) uses leader/chorus singing as an emotional net with which to trap her audience. By joining in the song, everyone participates in her performance. In order to generate the energy necessary to so ensnare her audience, the *domeigbuamoi* must commit her body to the performance. Such uninhibited behavior is not in keeping with the emotional austerity expected of male elders. *Domei* performance is thus left to women, and to those males willing to take chances with their reputations.

Domeisia (pl.) fit into the universal category of folktale. Although all Mende would agree that they are fiction (and in fact are commonly called *nde* [lies]), domeisia are the only narratives that deal exclusively with basic human problems. In their coupling of everyday issues with fabulous, contrived plots, *domeisia* might also be compared to the conventions of the television soap opera. In performance, they seem tangentially related to such contemporary theatrical forms as the American burlesque or the English music-hall review. Like other genres of *njepe wovei*, *domeisia* are created out of an inherited body of narrative images that are brought to ephemeral life through the words, song, dance, and dramatic mime of a performer in dramatic harmony with her audience. Together, and out of a common tradition, performer and audience realize the most intensely personal form of all Mende narrative artistry.

There is a final genre of *njepe wovei* that must be considered in relationship to the *domei*. This is the continuum of tales that stretches from Kaso, the spider-trickster, to Musa Wo, the trickster-hero. In structure, these narratives are simpler than the *domei*, following an invariable violated injunction-punishment pattern. It may be this simplicity of form that makes these tales so popular, for Kaso is undoubtedly the most re-created character in Mende folklore, especially favored by children. The tales are also easier to perform, since they generally lack the songs that would otherwise ensnare an audience in the unfolding plots. Through the boundless repetition of tricks, which on the animal level seeks to despoil rice pots and on the human to obliterate chiefdoms, this narrative complex defines what is below and above accepted standards of social order.

Kaso and Musa Wo thus generate the narrative body of Mende mythology. They express the ineffable in the form of a spider and a willful child. As mythological characters, trickster and hero sharpen the concepts of order that underlie the rest of *njepe wovei*. These myths represent a counterpoint to that order. The world of trickster and hero is a chaos without boundary, evoking the laughter of Mende audiences because it belies the categorical borders they have devised to maintain the rest of their folklore.

References

Cosentino, Donald. 1980. Lele Gbomba and the Style of Mende Baroque. *African Arts* 13, no. 3:54–57, 75–78.

———. 1982. *Defiant Maids and Stubborn Farmers*. Cambridge, England: Cambridge University Press.

———. 1988. Image, Parody and Debate: Levels in Mende Narrative Performance. *Journal of Folklore Research* 25:1–2; 17–34.

———. 1989. Midnight Charters: Musa Wo and Mende Myths of Chaos. In *Creativity of Power*. Ed. W. Arens and I. Karp. Washington, D.C.: Smithsonian Institution Press.

Hinzen, James, and Tamu Sorie. 1987. *Fishing in Rivers of Sierra Leone Oral Literature*. Freetown: People's Educational Association of Sierra Leone.

Innes, Gordon. 1965. The Function of Song in Mende Folklore. *Sierra Leone Language Review* 4:54–63.

Kilson, Marion. 1976. *Royal Antelope and Spider, West African Mende Tales*. Cambridge, Mass: Langdon Associates.

Philips, Ruth. 1995. *Representing Woman*. Los Angeles: Fowler Museum.

Winch, Julian. 1971. Religious Ideas of the Mende towards Land. *Africana Research Bulletin* 2:17–36.

DONALD COSENTINO

See also **Folktales; Gesture; Oral Performance Dynamics**

PROSE NARRATIVES: THE TABWA

Tabwa folklore was studied during the colonial period by several able amateur ethnographers. At the turn of the century, Father Joseph Weghsteen collected cosmological myths, including an important account of an anthropomorphic aardvark. As a culture hero, Aardvark instigates the introduction of human life and culture to the world before retiring to the underworld obscurity he has occupied forever after. Aardvarks are preposterous beasts by Tabwa reckoning, combining physical and behavioral features of many different animals. Aardvark proves an especially appropriate hero, for order is established through his efforts, but never to the exclusion of aardvark-like ambiguities in cosmic and social domains. The protagonists of this story have changed to meet the needs of the new circumstances in which Tabwa find themselves in postcolonial times, but the tale's structure remains an important vehicle for discussing radical social change and necessary human innovation (Roberts 1986).

Proverbs were collected by Stefano Kaoze, a Tabwa seminarian who, in 1917, became the first citizen of the Belgian Congo to be ordained a Catholic priest. Many of the proverbs have yet to be published, but one selection edited by Genevieve Nagant in 1973 contains both humorous nuggets of wisdom and politically pointed proverbs used in the course of heated debate. "Kalimba ngawana ta kapwa musango" (One can never play a melody on a borrowed thumb piano [plucked ideophone]) bespeaks a Tabwa sense of personal identity, ability, and achievement that cannot be borrowed or otherwise gained from someone else. "Unge walaviziwe na mwezi kutota" (Someone has been fooled by the moonlight) brings to mind midsummer nights' dreams and

Shakespearean insight into the uncertainties of perception and knowledge. "Mweni ubika buta, tabika matwi" (A stranger will lay down his bow, but never his ears) is a double-edged warning, for one must be careful when venturing abroad and vulnerable by listening to what is being whispered by one's hosts, and those receiving a visitor must beware not to speak too openly in front of strangers whose motivations and affiliations are not yet known.

Tabwa enjoy telling riddles and "dilemma tales" (Bascom 1975) when paddling their canoes or walking long distances. These are familiar to everyone, and the same narrator may present a different argument or defend a different protagonist from one telling to the next. Take, for instance, this riddle: "A man is traveling in a canoe with his sister, wife, and mother-in-law. None but the man can swim. When the canoe is overturned and sinks in a storm, the man can only save one passenger. Which should he rescue?" This simple device can provide hours of raucous debate, for it reveals conflicts inherent to Tabwa social structure, the consequences of which are known all too well to everyone concerned. Tabwa observe matrilineal descent, so a man must look to his sister to give birth to his heirs. Tabwa marriage is arranged, but is often long-lived, stable, and enlivened by love. One's wife is a helpmate, lover, and mother of one's children—for whom one cares with all parental intensity, even though they are not one's heirs. A man courteously avoids his mother-in-law, for his relationship to her is critical to conjugal happiness. How can the unfortunate man allow any of these women to perish? And yet hard choices are the stuff of life, and so time is passed wondering what the man should do.

Fables (nsimo) are told by parents, grandparents, and neighbors to entertain children and teach them the precepts and responsibilities of Tabwa society. Many tales concern animal tricksters and those they dupe. Kalulu, the wily hare, regularly deflates the pomposities of Lion and avoids the silly schemes of Hyena. Like many African tricksters, Kalulu's hilarious duplicity is both shocking and admirable. As a proverb has it, "Kwatumwa Kalulu lwendo kene kalinu lwa kako" (There where Kalulu has been sent, he wanted to go in the first place) (Nagant 1973, 749). The lesson is this: if someone whom you know to be untrustworthy readily agrees to do you a favor, it is because he has already recognized some personal gain most likely to prove to your own disadvantage.

Zambian Tabwa narratives are the ongoing subject of Robert Cancel's writing and videography. The "living enactment that is storytelling" is brilliantly presented, and as Cancel explains the circumstances and purposes, stylistic flourishes, and audience interactions that animate and motivate a given performance, the reader is transported to join the audience's circle in rapt attention.

References

Bascom, William. 1975. *African Dilemma Tales*. The Hague: Mouton.

Cancel, Robert. 1989. Allegorical Speculation in an Oral Society: The Tabwa Narrative Tradition. *Modern Philology* 122.

Nagant, Genevieve, ed. 1973. Proverbes tabwa. *Cahiers dEtudes Africaines* 52, no. 4:744–768.

Roberts, Allen. 1986. Social and Historical Contexts of Tabwa Art. In *The Rising of a New Moon: A Century of Tabwa Art*. Ed. Allen Roberts and Evan Maurer. Ann Arbor: University of Michigan Press.

Weghsteen, Joseph. 1962. Origine et dispersion des hommes d'apres les legendes tabwa. *Annali del Pontifico Museo Ethnologico Lateranensi Vaticano* 26:213–219.

ALLEN F. ROBERTS

See also **Dilemma Tales; Folktales; Proverbs**

PROSE NARRATIVES AND PERFORMANCE: THE TUAREG

The Tuareg are a socially stratified, seminomadic people who speak a Berber language (Tamadheq), adhere to Islam, and predominate in the contemporary nation states of Niger and Mali, as well as parts of Libya, Algeria, and Burkina Faso. Tuareg verbal art specialists, although characterized by some flexibility and overlap, generally follow inherited social stratum, age and gender categories.

Tuareg Folklore: The Roles of Specialists

Blacksmiths often provide social commentary in folktales and songs, and act as "gate-keepers," helping to arrange noble marriages, given their status outside nobles' descent system. Blacksmiths also serve as artisans and general handy persons. Their music specialty is praise singing and percussion instrumentals, namely small drums called *acanza*. They are played at rites of passage, while the *tende* drum is played at festivals and female spirit possession rituals. Smiths tell animal tales illustrating human social situations and moral points.

Young noble men, and in some regions, also women, specialize in sung poetry, sometimes accompanied by a one-stringed, bowed lute call *anzad*, which is played by a woman. Men sing poems outside villages and camps in the company of age-mates and those with whom they share familiar joking relationships.

Young girls of diverse social origins tell origin tales of female matrilineal clan ancestors and animal stories. Women often tell tales as they weave mats at night, inside the maternal tent that a married woman owns, with close kinspersons present. Women also tell tales while they are in the pastures herding their livestock. Some tales have sung verses embedded within the plots, at intervals; these usually represent lamentations. *Messelane*, or riddles, are more formalized, always told by a pair of persons, each alternating in the rhyming couplet question and answer. Tuareg call riddles the "brother of tales" (*amadray n imayen*) because they are "next to (i.e., similar to) each other." Children learn riddles from their mother. Old women sing songs in each other's company on gathering expeditions and perform Islamic liturgical music near the mosque on Islamic holidays. There are certain tales only women should learn, tell, and hear, in particular, the matrilineal origin myths (Pottier 1946).

Themes and Motifs in Tuareg Folklore: Local Typologies of Oral Traditions

Many Tuareg tales feature motifs of brothers searching for lost sisters, female founding ancestors/culture heroines, animal tricksters, and geographic features of the local desert and mountain environment. For example, a series of tales about a hero called Aligouran in the Air Mountain region of the Sahara in northern Niger depicts the adventures of an uncle and his sister's son: the uncle sends his maternal nephew on difficult and dangerous journeys and the nephew overcomes these dangers. There is the belief that the nephew inherits his intelligence from his mother's brother. Some Tuareg explain this folklore theme as referring to the uncle's role as a teacher, testing his nephew's skill at survival. Some scholars interpret this motif as representing the undercurrent of tension between matrilineal and patrilineal inheritance forms in Tuareg society (Casajus 1987). The Tuareg believe that Aligouran created the rock art in the Sahara; much of this rock art has been dated back to the Neolithic age and is contemporaneous with an ancient Tuareg group of the region called the Itesen. Natural geographic features are also popular subjects of Tuareg folklore: elders tell stories about mountains—which are personified as being like humans—standing in kinship relationships to each other, marrying and divorcing one another, and moving from place to place.

Among the Kel Ewey political confederation of Tuareg, where Islamic scholars called *marabouts* are influential and respected, myths about female ancestors coexist alongside alternate myths about Islamic-related male founder/heroes. An elderly woman in a noble, *maraboutique* family related a story about Tagurmat, the local mythical female ancestress, but she did not mention her name directly due to respect (Tuareg refrain from mentioning the names of deceased ancestors for this reason, and also from fear that to pronounce their name would invoke their souls). Perhaps this woman also omitted Tagurmat's name because her husband, a marabout, was present. Her version of this tale, also related by many female herbalists around Mount Bagzan in Air, is as follows:

> There was a man named Mohammed of Ibil. He and his wife were at their house, and the woman saw some cameliers who were passing and she went inside to watch them. She looked at them to see them clearly. The husband slapped his wife, who died. He then cut open her stomach, and took out two little girls, whom they called "Those girls who were cut." The little twin girls (of Tagurmat), it was they who founded all the Igurmaden (a descent group within the Kel Ewey political confederation of Tuareg, predominant around Mount Bagzan in Air). One made the Igunnaden of the Kel Bagzan. All the Kel Igurmaden are from these two girl twins who created them.

Many Kel Ewey Tuareg men tend to downplay matrilineal ancestor mythology told by women (Rasmussen 1996). When a schoolchild mentioned Kahena, a Berber woman heroine depicted in myth as having fought against Arabs and resisted Islam, older men present quickly dismissed her as "not important." Only female herbalist healers explicitly mentioned Tagurmat by name, when they related the story of Tagurmat as founder of the local Igurmaden clan and also the founder of the herbalist medical profession. One elderly female herbalist, for example, related another variant of the Tagurmat myth:

> There was a woman who had a very jealous husband. He transferred her very far away. They lived so that other men would not see her. One day, he saw people coming toward them on their camels, elaborately decorated. They said,

"Look at the men who are going to war." The woman looked and she said, "I see a very handsome man among these men, one with an indigo robe." As soon as he heard this, the husband killed the woman with a knife and she died. He straightened her body out for burial. The woman's stomach moved. He tore it open and took out two small twin girls. The two little girls each held something in their hands. He cut the umbilical cords. He arranged these girls, and after that he united the people for taking the dead woman to the cemetery. And he told the people afterward, "Look at what is in the hands of the little girls." The people said, "These small objects held, you must hide until the girls grow up to learn about them. If they die, the information will also die." The small objects were in wood. These were hidden until the girls grew up. They replied, "That is the beginning of medicine." They even had medicine of *icherifan* (clans claiming descent from the Prophet) and they taught how the medicine is made: one touches, they explained, everything. They were named Fatane and Fatoni. All the women on their side of the family learned to make medicine from them, and taught this to those women who were interested. That was the beginning of healing. Since being taken out of their mother's womb, these girls held medicines.

In discussions of local mythical/historical heroes, many men expressed admiration for Boulkhou and also Kaousan: the former was a founding marabout/warrior hero, the latter was the leader of the 1917 Tuareg Senoussi Revolt against the French in the Sahara. They also emphasized the sinking of the first well and the building of the first mosque in the area by a patrilineally traced male ancestor. A marabout, insisted that myths about the mythical female founding ancestress were "not true history, but like a children's tale." Instead, he emphasized a legend relating the exploits of Boulkhou, a male marabout/warrior hero who resisted enemies in the Air region by wearing Quranic amulets, suspended by a thread, inside a well for forty days. Many local men cited folklore sources they identified with the Quran in order to validate legal practices. Marabouts, for example, explained the custom of bridewealth as deriving from a local variant of the Adam and Eve myth: "Adam gave the first bridewealth for Eve by reciting the Islamic *ezeker* (songs praising God)" (Rasmussen 1997, 138). Among many Air Tuareg groups, the traditional purpose of bridewealth is to protect women socioeconomically, for it is considered ungallant for a husband to request a reimbursement on divorce. Kel Ewey fathers hold the bridewealth in trust for brides, and marabouts decide who keeps the bridewealth on divorce (whoever is not at fault, according to the marabout's ruling). This interplay of counter-myths is not surprising in a society characterized by bilateral descent and inheritance institutions, with more recent patrilineal influence from Islam and neighboring sedentary agricultural peoples, superimposed on former matrilineal institutions (for example, some non-Quranic inheritance forms of some property transmitted among women), and current high status and economic independence of Tuareg women (Murphy 1967; Nicolaisen 1963; Bernus 1981; Claudot-Hawad 1993).

The Performance Style of Folklore

Women sometimes tell tales in pairs, debating plots, correcting each other, and completing sections for each other. The audience laughs and comments freely throughout these folklore perform-ances. In narrative gestures during storytelling, there is the idea of *sikbar* (lit. "imitation"), central to performative competence (Calame-Griaule 1977, 311). The perceived complementarity of the gesture to the spoken word in performance is expressed in a musical metaphor that compares the gesture to the *asakalabo* instrument, a calabash floating in water, beaten with a stick, which accompanies the *tende* mortardrum struck with the hands during festivals and spirit-possession rituals. A Tamacheq prov-erb states, "Gestures are the *asakalabo* of the spoken word." Perhaps because gestures are so important, they are sharply re-stricted in usage, according to the social status and roles of the speaker. A noble, for example, should not make as many gestures as a smith, a woman should not make as many gestures as a man, and women are obliged to avoid equivocal, suggestive gestures altogether. Smiths use gestures to make people laugh, contrary to nobles' dignity and reserve. Their gestures are labeled, in effect, as a kind of nonverbal obscenity or at least given poetic license. Men and women of all social origins are constrained in storytelling before certain relatives. Children and all young women stop all performance of tales and riddles when elderly men and women approach because, they explain, they are "ashamed" to continue, from respect (in their reserved relation-ship with these persons, particularly elders on the paternal side). Women may not tell stories in front of their mother-in-law. A man may tell stories before his father-in-law, provided the latter has asked him to do so. One does not initiate talk in front of a parent, a parent-in-law of either sex, an elder sibling, or elders on the paternal side, without having been invited. Another con-straint is that some elderly persons do not wish to have their voices recorded because they do not wish them heard by their descendants after death. A few Islamic scholars declined to be recorded on tape because, in the words of one, "Marabouts are not supposed to seek glory. They should not say things pro-found. Rather, they should be a reflection of God." (Rasmussen 2001, 52).

Folklore and the Transfer of Historical and Cultural Knowledge

Among the Tuareg, verbal arts are used to transfer but also dispute, historical knowledge. Both written and oral forms of expression remain vital today. There exist two types of written channels: Arabic literacy of the Quran and the Tifinagh script of Tamacheq used in love messages, poetry, and on musical instruments and jewelry. There are several types of oral tradi-tions. First, there are those stories called *imayen*, translated into French as *contes folkloriques* or folk tales; examples include the stories about Aligouran and Tagurmat. These are primarily iden-tified with young women, smiths of either sex, and children. *Imayen* in general are viewed by some Tuareg—namely Islamic scholars, or marabouts and noble men—as "not true history." This type of tale portrays what men and Islamic scholars or marabouts consider fictional. Whereas by contrast, accounts called *idamen iru*, denoting legends of the past, are viewed by these persons as "true history," and are associated with elders, noble men, and Islamic scholars, who relate these latter stories, for example, the legends about Kaousan and Boulkhou. Many people, particularly youths, deny that they know origin tales. Some types of these *idamen iru* are esoteric knowledge, and

their telling is restricted by values of respect toward elders and deceased ancestors. The elderly know them, and sometimes, after long acquaintance and proper approach through intermediaries, agree to relate them. Youths say only old people should tell some kinds of tales. But asking them to do so is a delicate matter for youths cannot pronounce names of deceased ancestors, and youths are not supposed to ask questions of old people. These legends are also linked conceptually to official Islam. One elderly gardener and marabout indicated that, since growing old, he had ceased telling the other oral traditions, called folktales or *imayen*, and now only told historical legends or *idamen iru*. He expressed the view prevalent among men that the *imayen* were "not Islamic and therefore not true." However, the tellers of *imayen*, women and blacksmiths, have much informal influence; for women educate small children by telling tales that have a clearly didactic purpose, and smiths control nobles' reputations through their social commentary contained in their publicly per-formed tales and songs.

Among the Tuareg, therefore, social roles based on gender, social stratum, occupational specialty, and age are associated with different types of folklore and the transfer of different types of knowledge. Different specialists and interest groups seek to "own" certain forms of oral traditions which promote their own interpretation of history and culture. Noble divisions, for exam-ple, formerly had copyrights over forms of poetry and their asso-ciated drum patterns and *anzad* melodies. Folklore conveys dif-ferent forms of knowledge and interpretations of history which are linked to age, descent, and gender. Among the Tuareg, these reveal social tensions, conflicts, and change, but also the long-standing adaptability and flexibility of a culture and its capacity to accommodate and incorporate diverse ideologies and institu-tions into its framework.

References

Bernus, Edmond. 1981. *Touaregs Nigeriens: Unite d'un Peuple Pasteur*. Paris: Editions de l'Office de la Recherche Scientifique et Technique d'Outre-Mer.

Calame-Griaule, Genevieve. 1977. *Langage et culture africaines: Essais d'ethnolinguistique*. Paris: Maspero.

Casajus, Dominique. 1987. *La Tente dans l'Essuf*. Paris and London: Cambridge University Press.

Claudot-Hawad, Helene. 1993. *Touareg: Portrait en fragments*. Aix-en-Provence; Edisud.

Murphy, Robert. 1967. Tuareg Kinship. *American Anthropologist* 66: 163–70.

Nicolaisen, Johannes. 1963. *Ecology and Culture of the Pastoral Tuareg*. Copenhagen: Royal Museum.

Pottier, Jeanne. 1946. *Legendes Touaregs*. Paris: Nouvelles Editions Latines.

Rasmussen, Susan. 1996. The Tent as Cultural Symbol and Field Site: Social and Symbolic Space, Topos, and Authority in a Tuareg Community. *Anthropological Quarterly* 69:1: 14–27.

———. 1997. *The Poetics and Politics of Tuareg Aging Life Course and Personal Destiny in Niger*. De Kalb, Ill.: Northern Illinois University Press.

———. 2001. *Healing in Community: Medicine, Contested Terrains, and Cultural Encounter Among the Tuareg*. Westport Ct., Bergin and Garvey.

SUSAN J. RASMUSSEN

See also **Maghrib**

PROVERBS

Pithy and terse sayings are very much appreciated in Africa. These gnomic utterances are recognized as a distinct genre with a specific name in the local taxonomies of the written and spoken word. The closest English equivalent is the proverb. While similar to the genre in Europe, African proverbs emanate from a repertory preserved by the community of speakers. Their form is elliptical and figurative, which easily allows for their recognition in discourse.

The characteristic traits of the genre may vary from one society to the next, yet the proverbs share a certain degree of similarity because of shared properties that confer a relative homogeneity among them throughout the continent. There are similar properties of content, which is understandable given the task of the proverb to express general truths that are the fruits of experience of the society as a whole. In Africa, as elsewhere, these universal "truths" can be of a practical, ethical, social, or philosophical nature.

What is nevertheless striking is the remarkable resemblance of themes and points of view in collections of African proverbs, not only throughout the continent, but also with respect to other civilizations. The same subjects are discussed, often in the same terms, and despite certain specific tendencies, the homogeneity of the discourse is quite remarkable. Africa hardly deviates from the rest of the world on this point, even if the proverb sometimes refers to customs unfamiliar to other continents, such as polygyny.

The other properties that characterize the African proverb are likewise inherent in what is universal in the genre. However, they sometimes display specific traits that allow one to identify them as African.

Their stylistic properties conform more or less to their homologues from other continents. In Africa, as elsewhere, the proverb can be recognized by its formulaic turn of phrase, which is characterized by notable expressions. In many communities, the giveaway of a terse and pithy utterance as belonging to the genre of proverb is established straightaway by a formulaic introduction: "Our ancestors said that . . ." or "In the past, it was said that . . ."

From a rhetorical perspective, the genre is identified by the frequency of binary constructions, which creates a logical relationship between two statements, such as: "Struck forehead, prudent neck." Here the Dyula intend that the neck will learn to be careful from the wound suffered by the head. This example also demonstrates that, like its European homologue, the African proverb favors the ellipsis.

Even when there is only one proposition, it generally brings to light a relationship of symmetry, in one way or another, between a pivotal element and, for example, a verb: "The brilliance of the sun eclipses the light of the moon" (Minianka, West Africa). These phenomena of symmetry (e.g., parallelisms, chiasmus) are frequently reinforced by an exploitation of the proverb's sonority through rhymes, puns (paronomasia), alliteration, and assonance, which are obviously apparent only if the proverb is expressed in its language of origin.

The metaphorical dimension distinguishes the genre among many African societies in an undoubtedly more systematic fashion than in Europe. The proverb is indeed considered a saying that is necessarily circuitous, as it must certainly not express directly what it has to say. Consequently, among the Manianka a gnomic saying that does not contain an image or metaphor will not be included in the category of *sanda*, a term by which the group designates the repertory of sayings that constitute the cultural heritage of this group. The same is true of the *nsana* of the Bambara, the *lantara* of the Dyula, the *bitaru* of the Kassena, the *wo* of the Ngbaka, and the *cingala* of the Vili. The genre thus emerges as a verbal art form valorized by the staying power of its metaphors to express a more general and abstract situation.

A few examples of Ngbaka *wo*, with possible explanations, illustrate the complexity of some proverbs' imagery, as well as the fundamental nature of their message. "The termite has fooled everyone, but the day ends without his knowing it," is an expression one might use when someone has been fooled by a friend, but the day ends without the friend realizing it, and yet retaliation is taken against the friend. The fragile nature of one's reputation is demonstrated by the proverb "You're like the back hoof of a goat that erases the imprint of the front hoof"—even if one is a good person, one bad action erases the good. A third example, "To guard the child is not to change the mother," is used to comment on the persons who attribute to themselves actions that they have never performed.

In Africa, the proverb is undoubtedly used more than in present-day Europe, where it is rarely heard in conversation, and it is characterized by well-defined properties of expression. The proverb is characterized by the interlocutors of this type of discourse: it will always be uttered by the elders to the younger group members, who may themselves reply with a proverb.

Proverbs are often encountered in everyday conversations among Africans, but they can also have several ritualistic uses. In many African cultures, the proverb is indispensable to customary judgment. Likewise, it is the centerpiece of verbal jousts in which the two adversaries "exchange" proverbs that must progressively neutralize each other. There is yet another rather widespread practice, reserved for the specialists, consisting of reciting, in order, an entire repertory of proverbs with the help of a "reminder" prop in the form of bits of gourds strung on a cord. This is referred to as a "proverb cord." Finally, the genre is characterized by its inclusion in most of the other genres: folktales, chronicles, and epics are usually full of proverbs. As for sung genres, some are nothing more than a string of proverbs set to music.

The last defining trait of the African proverb concerns its cultural function. As witnesses and caretakers of the body of accumulated wisdom of the group, proverbs express the norm, the point of view, and the philosophy of the group, taking into account its tensions as well, since different proverbs can express contradictory theses. This function of the proverb with respect to the group is evident in the repertory of normative and connotative formulaic expressions such as "it is necessary that . . ."; "better to . . . than to . . ."; "do this,"; and "do not do this."

The proverb in Africa is a highly valued mode of discourse that functions as an indication of cultural status. In Europe, someone who uses or speaks in proverbs is likely to be regarded as backward and intellectually limited for using hackneyed expressions instead of having a more personal and original discourse. In African societies, on the other hand, where an oral tradition of discourse exists and where memory is the sole guarantee of conservation of this verbal culture, proverbs are held in esteem. The individual who demonstrates a knowledge of proverbs distinguishes himself as the inheritor of his ancestors' cumulative wisdom, as well as a master of the poetic dimension of the language. As the Nigerian novelist Chinua Achebe has pointed out, according to the Igbo, "Proverbs are the palm oil which 'seasons' words."

References

Thomas, J. M. C. *Contes, proverbes, devinettes ou enigmes, chants et prieres Ngbaka Ma'bo.*

JEAN DERIVE

See also **Children's Folklore; Riddles; Textile Arts and Communication**

PROVERBS: SESOTHO PROVERBS

The Basotho people, of the kingdom of Lesotho in southern Africa, live not only in Lesotho but also in the Free State Province and some parts of the Gauteng Province in the Republic of South Africa. The word Sotho is derived from the Swazi word Abashuntu, which refers to people who wore their loincloth with the knot tied at the back. It was a nickname that later became Basotho. The term was later adopted by King Moshoeshoe I as the unifying political term for his emerging kingdom in the nineteenth century. Mosotho is the singular form of Basotho. Sesotho is the language, as well as any custom, of the Basotho.

As among so many African peoples, the Basotho of southern Africa use proverbs extensively. Sesotho proverbs are examples of stylized language expression. *Maele* is the Sesotho term which refers to both proverbs and idioms, which are normally classified under the same genre because they are similar communicative expressions. However, scholars have shown that proverbs and idioms are distinct in that they differ from one another in form and significance. Proverbs are fixed-form expressions, whereas idioms or proverbial phrases are open or free-form proverbial phrases that can be extended or changed in both number and tense during their application. Proverbs are normally used by older and skillful members of the society in their daily interaction to impart authority and truth to their utterances and communication.

Sesotho proverbs originate from observations of the community's daily activities. Proverbs deal with the wide spectrum of the people's experience with the physical environment, including animal and plant life, as well as the people's way of life, attitudes, values, feelings, and emotions. While most proverbs are coined by an individual, they eventually come to represent the wisdom of the group.

The meaning of Sesotho proverbs is best understood when they are studied in the context of their actual use. The social factors surrounding the application of a particular proverb may also clarify its meaning which, more often than not, is metaphorical or figurative. An outsider's initial understanding of a proverb might not be the meaning intended by the Mosotho. Take, for example, the following proverb: *Tsa ha se mele poea* (The site does not grow amarunthus). According to the situation, this proverb could be used to communicate a positive or negative message by the speaker. And, demonstrating a familiar phenomena, proverbs often convey opposite meanings. For example, "Tieho e tsoala tahleho" (Hesitation begets loss) conveys exactly the opposite message of "Mamello e tsoala katleho" (Patience begets success). The meaning of Sesotho proverbs, therefore, is determined by the contextual usage when the speaker is communicating with the audience in a particular situation.

Proverbs are regarded as vehicles of communication in dialogue, and their performance entails the different levels at which they are applied in practical situations. The first level occurs when circumstances trigger the use of a proverb. The second level occurs when the participants or the audience respond to the use of a proverb in a way that shows the proverb to be appropriate or inappropriate. The audience may sometimes respond with another proverb that connotes either approval or disapproval of the speaker's proverb. For example, a speaker may assert "Marabe a jeoa ke bana" (Parents make sacrifices for their children), which may elicit an opposing proverb, such as "E a shoa, mahe a bole" (If a parent dies, the children suffer).

Sesotho proverbs are concise, pithy, reflective statements that are both simple and complex, and that follow certain poetic patterns. They are composed in poetic language, which makes them memorable to their users. This poetic language is governed by metaphor, repetition, direct or indirect parallelism, elision, and omissions. The proverb foregrounds itself through its structure and its connotative significance, and is governed by its syntactic patterns and linguistic modifications coupled with tone and rhythm. They compactly express large, abstract ideas or concepts.

The following illustrate the nature of the poetic devices of Sesotho proverbs.

> *Repetition:* Motsoalle oa lesholu ke lesholu (A friend of a thief is a thief) Tieho e tsoala tahleho (Hesitation begets loss)
> *Direct parallelism:* Bo ts'oloa bo chesa, bo tsoha bo folile. (Tempers cool with time)
> *Elision of prefix:* (Se) Ts'a ha se mele poea (The site does not grow amarunthus) (Le) Ts'oele le beta poho (A crowd can easily overpower a bull)
> *Coalescence:* Mesa-mohloane ha a panye (The locust-roaster does not blink)

A number of objectives encourage the use of proverbs. A speaker may choose to apply a particular proverb from his repertoire to advise, console, or comment on socially accepted norms. He or she may use a particular proverb to condemn those who deviate from the accepted societal norms. Being microtexts, proverbs may occur in macrotexts, where their purpose would be to illuminate or enhance the theme, content, and style of those texts.

The use of proverbs as social commentary use is demonstrated by the following examples. In accepting a helping hand, one might say, "Ts'oele le beta poho" (A crowd can easily overpower a bull). If a speaker disapproves of the relationship of a good person with a bad person, he might observe "Motoalle oa lesholu ke lesholu" (A friend of a thief is a thief).

Basotho use of proverbs continues, with new ones being created to express and come to terms with contemporary issues and new technology. They are still employed today, even though in some languages they may be regarded as archaic, with no place in modern society.

References

Guma, S. M. 1992. *The Form, Content, and Technique of Traditional Literature of Southern Sotho.* Pretoria: J. L. Van Schaik.

Mokitimi, M. I. P. 1997. *The Voice of the People: Proverbs of Basotho.* Pretoria: University of South Africa.

———. 1998. *A Literary Analysis of Ssotho Proverbs (maele).* Pretoria: J. L. Van Schaik.

Okpewho, Isidore. 1993. *African Oral Literature.* Bloomington: Indiana University Press, 1993.

Sekese, A. 1978. *Mekhoa le Maele a Basotho.* Morija: Morija Sesotho Book Depot.

Yankah, K. 1989. *The Proverb in the Context of Akan Rhetoric.* New York: Peter Lang.

MAKALI I. MOKITIMI

See also **Linguistics and African Verbal Arts; Riddles; Southern Africa**

PUPPETRY

From Egypt to South Africa, and from Senegal to Tanzania, puppetry is a continental phenomenon, with historical and contemporary puppet traditions performed in more than forty African countries. African puppets take a variety of forms, including hand and toe puppets, rod puppets, string puppets, shadow puppets, and full body puppets. They are used in ritual contexts, as well as in games and in dramatic plays that are produced primarily for entertainment. Puppets are also increasingly being used as part of an educational outreach strategy to inform and instruct communities about a variety of political, public health, and development issues.

History and Ritual

Historically, among a number of West and Central African peoples, puppets of various degrees of complexity and elaboration played a significant role in divination rites. Among the Lobi and Birifor, in Cote d'Ivoire and Ghana, respectively, diviners used two wooden figures, which they articulated by means of a string. The string passed through the puppets and was secured to the toes of the diviner seated on the ground facing his clients. As the diviner manipulated the puppets, he posed questions to the figures and interpreted the answers by reading the puppet's movements according to a designated code. Songye diviners in the Congo (region) manipulated a carved wooden figure by means of two strings that passed through the statue's knees. The figure responded to the diviner's questions with yes or no answers. If the figure fell forward, the answer was affirmative; if backwards, it was negative.

In searching out a guilty party by divination, Pende diviners from the Congo region used a carved wooden head attached to a flexible lattice-stick frame. When divination revealed the identity of the transgressor, the puppet shot forward in the direction of the accused. In Ijebu Yoruba communities in Nigeria, a carved wooden puppet with one leg, one arm, and one eye plays a central role in divination rituals surrounding Osanyin, the god of herbalism. During the ritual, the puppet speaks with a high-pitched squeak and responds favorably (or not) to questions that the diviner poses about herbs, medicines, and healing.

Puppets appear on other ritual occasions as well, including men's and women's initiations and during funerals. Historically, among the Fang of Gabon, carved wooden heads functioned as guardian figures placed on reliquary bundles in ancestor shrines. During men's initiation they were removed and used as puppets. The reliquary heads appeared at the top of a cloth screen and danced to a musical accompaniment. During Senufo male initiation in Cote d'Ivoire, the Kagba puppet masquerade performs. This rod puppet represents the head of an antelope. The puppet head appears out of the front of a costumed square armature meant to represent the animal's body. The puppeteer hidden underneath the costume raises and lowers the puppet head, twirls it around, and moves it from side to side as the masquerade dances.

In Yoruba communities in western Nigeria and Benin, the Gelede ritual masquerades honoring women often open with a short puppet performance. String puppets appear on a platform and are operated from below. Later in the performance, masks with articulated figures attached to the mask dance. In Mali, among the Bamana, some Komo men's associations use a rod puppet representing Komo during its annual masquerade ritual. This wooden Komo head is an amalgamation of several animals, with antelope horns, porcupine quills, and bird feathers attached to its surface. The Komo dancer-puppeteer hidden within the animal's costume manipulates the rod puppet head, sometimes extending it six or more feet into the air, then pulling it down into the costume and close to the ground in a dramatic display.

Elders among the Zaramo of Tanzania recall that small wooden puppet figures that praised the deceased were once a central part of gravesite rites. In the Congo, during funerals for chiefs, the Bwende danced a larger than life-sized cloth figure through the community. This figure contained the mummified remains of the deceased. Dressed like a chief with flexed arms and legs in a dance pose, the figure was manipulated from below by six men as it moves through the village. When it stopped, everyone in the procession would freeze, only to begin the dance again as the figure moved forward. Guns were fired in praise of the deceased, women approached the figure to sing laments as he made his way one last time through the community.

In northern Togo, the Bassar continue to fashion a figure of plaited fiber to substitute for the body of a deceased elder woman as part of her second funeral rites. During these rites the puppet figure is carried to the deceased natal home by women. The figure directs its bearers as to the direction and the pace of their journey, sometimes directing the bearers to walk sedately, at other times directing them to break into a fast walk, or even to run.

Puppets as Entertainment

Some puppets once performed on ritual occasions have now been incorporated into entertainment events. For example, in the opening decades of the twentieth century the Kuyu and Mbochi living in Brazzaville used a finely carved and painted dummy-head puppet in divination and for ritual dances. By the 1960s the performance had become a popular competition, primarily defined as an entertainment. During the dance competition, the puppeteers raise and lower the dummy heads while whirling in a tight circle.

A Bamana youth association puppet masquerade from the Segou region in Mali. The large rod puppet animal head represents Sigi, the bush buffalo. Out of its back several small rod puppets appear, representing people engaged in daily activities. Photo © Mary Jo Arnoldi.

Similarly, Ekon society puppets, once used by the Ibibio for divination and in men's initiation rites, are performed today in satiric skits. These carved wooden-rod puppets have articulated jaws and limbs and represent both sexes and all ages and social groups. Manipulated from below, the puppets emerge from the top of, and from behind, a cloth stage. The skits have no narrative plot, but consist of a series of monologues or dialogues. The majority of the characters represent social types, although only rarely are individuals represented. The skits deal with family discord, adultery, political corruption, religious frauds, and excesses.

Other puppet traditions, like those performed in Egypt, Tunisia, and Algeria, and among the Bamana in Mali, the Tiv in Nigeria, and the Kanuri and Hause in Nigeria, Niger, and Chad, originated as popular entertainment forms. The shadow puppet plays performed in North Africa are believed to have developed in Egypt and Turkey in the eleventh and twelfth centuries. These plays still include the exploits of the popular character, Kharagoz. Dating from at least the nineteeth century, Kanuri and Hausa itinerant puppeteers use hand puppets in satiric performances.

Plays include the exploits of the coquette, the trickster, the foreign woman, the greedy man, and the charlatan, among others.

Puppets of the pantin type, popular in Europe in the nineteenth century, were also incorporated into festivals and masquerades along the coast of West Africa. In Senegal, pantin puppets (xouss-maniap in Wolof) were carved of wood and painted with their limbs articulated by strings. They were performed during the Lantern festivals that took place at Christmas. Placards that carried a variety of messages were added to these carnivalesque figures. In the 1950s, in the years leading up to independence, the festival and the puppets were banned for a number of years because the messages the puppets and floats carried became more strident and carried political party slogans. Among the Bamana living in the Segou region in Mali, young men's associations stage annual festivals that include both puppets and masks. The puppet repertoire consists of rod puppets, dummy heads, miniaturized rod and string puppets, and an occasional hand puppet. Like the Ekon puppet skits, there is no narrative plot; each character performs individually. In the ninetieth century, animal and spirit characters predominated, but by the 1920s characters representing different social types began to gain prominence in the theater. The song sung for each puppet masquerade includes the character's name, a praise line, and a reference to some quality or behavior associated with this animal, spirit, or personage. The audience brings to the event their knowledge of folktales, legends, and historical epics. Phrases in the songs make reference to this rich body of oral literature. Bamana puppet troupes have regularly participated in regional and national arts festivals, and several local troupes have traveled abroad. The puppet masquerades have also been incorporated into the repertoire of the National Theatre and performances can now occasionally be seen on Malian television.

The Kwagh-hir puppet masquerade is a more recent performance form created by the Tiv in Nigeria. The genre seems to have emerged in the mid-twentieth century and is a combination of two distinct Tiv traditions: storytelling and men's masquerades. The puppets appear in vignettes and include characters such as Mami Wata, a female water spirit, the woman grinding grain, the man smoking a cigarette, musicians, and disco dancers. Hunting scenes, executions of criminals, and Catholic priests conducting religious services may be included as well as various animals, such as birds and tortoises. Characters and scenes from folktales are interspersed with vignettes that make a commentary on the contemporary scene. A narrator introduces the vignette and the scene to be played, and the puppets perform to a chorus of songs and drumming. These puppet skits are interspersed with other masquerade performances, the two elements constituting the Kwagh-hir event. Like the Bamana troupes, Tiv troupes compete in regional and national arts festivals. Their performances have been aired on the national television network, and some troupes have performed internationally.

There are also a growing number of newer urban-based puppeteers and puppet troupes in Mali, Togo, Benin, the Cote d'Ivoire, Burundi, the Democratic Republic of the Congo, South Africa, and elsewhere. While many of these troupes draw upon local puppet traditions for inspiration, they tend to be highly innovative in their performances. Their plays have a well-developed narrative plot line and are often produced from written scripts, rather than proceeding as conventionalized short skits and vignettes. Some troupes, such as the Troupe Sogolon in

Bamako, Mali; THEMAZ in the Democratic Republic of the Congo; Troupe de la Savane in Bujumbura, Burundi; and the Togolese puppeteers DANAYA Kanlanfei and Massimo-Wanssi have introduced string marionettes borrowed from European puppet traditions into their repertoires. These troupes perform their plays in a variety of urban venues, including cultural centers, schools and libraries, and on national television.

Increasingly, puppets are also being used in countries like Mali, Botswana, Zimbabwe, South Africa, and elsewhere in popular plays that are part of community outreach efforts. These plays are performed in cities and in rural areas in order to raise awareness of AIDS prevention, encourage participation in immunization campaigns, inform people about strategies to fight deforestation, and to encourage voter registration.

References

Arnoldi, Mary Jo. 1995. *Playing with Time Art and Performance in Central Mali*. Bloomington: Indiana University Press.

Dagan, E. A. 1990. *Emotions in Motion Theatrical Puppets and Masks from Black Africa*. Montreal: Galerie Amrad African Arts.

Darkowska-Nidzgorska, Olenka. 1980. *Theatre populaire de marionnettes en Afrique sud-Saharienne*. Bandundu, Zaire: Centre d'Etudes Ethnologiques.

Hagher, Iyorwuese Harry. 1990. *The Tiv Kwagh-hir*. Lagos, Nigeria: Center for Black and African Arts and Civilization.

Malkin, Michael. 1977. *Traditional and Folk Puppets of the World*. South Brunswick, N. J.: A. S. Barnes.

Scheinberg, Alfred. 1978. *Ekon Society Puppets: Sculptures for Social Criticism*. New York: Tribal Arts Gallery II.

Thompson, Robert Farris. 1975. Icons of the Mind: Yoruba Herbalism Arts in Trans-Atlantic Perspective. *African Arts* 8, no. 3:(Spring): 52–9, 89.

———. 1988. *Unima informations special: l'Afrique noire en marionnettes*. Charleville-Mezieres: Presses de L'Imprimerie de Nevers.

MARY JO ARNOLDI

See also **Drama; Performance in Africa; Theater**

Q

QUEEN MOTHERS

Queen mothers of Africa, warrior queens, and many other titled women have held positions of authority and exercised leadership throughout the history of African societies. The fearless Queen Njinga of Ndongo and Matamba (Angola), who dominated international politics and led her people against the Portuguese in the seventeenth century, and the courageous queen mother Yaa Asantewaa, who inspired and led the Asante of Ghana against the British in 1900, are representative of women who led the opposition to Western occupation. Although it was their leadership in warfare that endowed these women with a place in history, the authority they wielded was based on the position they occupied.

Dual-Gender Systems

Most African societies define a specific position of authority for a woman, and through it women may play a significant role in political leadership. Like male leaders, these women are chosen from a select group of individuals who occupy a privileged position in a hierarchical society. While matrilineal societies afford women leaders greater authority than patrilineal ones, royal women generally hold positions of authority in the latter as well. The term *dual-gender system* refers to those societies in which the political system includes one or two female leaders who occupy positions of authority in parallel with the male leader, usually considered a chief or a king. These female roles are complementary to, rather than the same as, the male roles in their functions. In many societies a woman who qualifies for the position of female authority can also assume the male position, that of chief, should circumstances favor that solution. She often occupies the position as a regent, but in some instances she assumes the position permanently.

A significant number of precolonial societies were structured on this dual-gender principle, but the changes resulting from colonization and modernization have weakened the role of female authority considerably, and in many instances it has disappeared or survives only as a vestige of the earlier one. In her impressive 1971 survey article, "The Role of Women in the Political Organization of African Societies," Annie M. D. Lebeuf acknowledges the wide variety of indigenous political systems found throughout Africa and discusses the many examples of powerful women who exercise leadership through their positions of authority. Notable among precolonial systems, and the one that seems to have the greatest continuity into the present, is the system based on joint sovereignty.

In some examples a female and a male represented sovereign authority (a king and a woman of high rank), and in others this authority consisted of a king and two women. Generally defined in terms of kinship, the woman in the dual-gender system represented the figure of mother, whether or not she was the biological mother of the king. When two women represented female authority, one usually represented the mother and the second one would likely be classified as sister of the king. The majority of the societies with joint sovereignty are matrilineal, though some patrilineal societies have specific roles of authority defined for royal women.

The term *queen mother* often raises objections in Africa today, because it does not represent a direct translation from the native language of any society; nevertheless it is the term widely used in English to describe the female counterpart to the chief throughout Africa. In contemporary African societies, the term will likely translate as aunt-nephew, uncle-niece, sister-brother, or cousin. Though rare, the literal relationship of biological mother and son does still occur among African rulers, as it has most recently in the case of the Asante, in which the Asantehemaa is the actual mother of the Asantehene, enthroned in 1999. In most instances, however, the female ruler is regarded as a metaphorical mother, and she advises and guides the chief in all affairs. For this reason, perhaps, the term for these female leaders has most often been translated as *queen mother*.

Each society defines the role of female authority, or queen mother, with particular practices that may differ from those in other societies. Yet, there are a cluster of characteristics that are widely associated with the role wherever it occurs in Africa. These concern the relationship between the queen mother and her chief, their complementary duties and responsibilities, the space they occupy, and the conceptualization of the roles. The two leaders are expected to work together for the welfare of their communities, but they each have their own stool, the symbol of authority. Though they must belong to the same kin group, they are each selected at separate moments in time, on the basis of their own qualifications for leadership from among those who qualify for the position. (A queen mother is not a wife to the male leader.) Their dual leadership operates, then, in parallel.

Motherhood

The concept of motherhood, a powerful force in African societies, shapes the role of queen mother and many of its functions. Especially important in this capacity, the queen mother has responsibility for the welfare of women in her domain. While the functions vary from one society to the next, this responsibility may extend to the supervision of women's labor, and it almost certainly determines that queen mothers are important figures in dispute settlement. Women, and sometimes men, bring disputes and conflicts arising from everyday life to the queen mother for litigation and resolution.

Political Roles

To some observers, the queen mother's most significant political role concerns the selection of a new chief. Most societies organized on a dual-gender system endow the queen mother with a major role in selecting a new chief. Depending on the particular society, and also on the traditions of specific locations, the new chief may be determined because he is the son of a queen mother, but in some societies she must nominate an individual from her kin group to the elders for the position of chief, even though she has the option to nominate her own son in many instances. Once the new chief has been agreed upon by the queen mother and her elders, he will undergo the important rituals that will confirm him as king or chief. From that time forward the queen mother will advise him on political matters, as well as those concerning religion, custom, and law.

Among the most essential of the queen mother's duties will be the performance of powerful rituals honoring her ancestors and the deities of her culture. Consistent with traditional religious practices in each location, such rituals are generally believed to provide protection for her people, and will probably be performed in her palace, if she has one, or in the compound of her kin group. Queen mothers have their own palaces, or compounds, where they live and hold court, resolve disputes, and may provide protection for individuals who are at risk of losing their lives. In addition to her own space, a queen mother will have her own entourage and household servants. As the female leader in her society, the queen mother enjoys many privileges and assumes many responsibilities. This position extends to the domain of marriage and sexuality. Generally, queen mothers are allowed to exercise sexual freedom, much the same as royal males—and unlike other women of her society. Economically, both the chief and queen mother should receive support from the financial resources of the royal position. These may include the resources of specific villages or lands that have been designated for the queen mother or chief.

While female leaders have received scant attention from scholars and writers, a careful search nevertheless reveals that this institution is quite widespread throughout sub-Saharan Africa. In some cases, female leaders may have ceased to exist, but were strong institutions in the past, having been destroyed by colonization and modernization. Other societies may have continued the institution, but they may be only barely visible to outsiders. A few societies discontinued the practice and have now reconstituted it. In a few instances, among the Akan of Ghana, in particular, the institution has been continuous through time with no breaks in history, though it must be emphasized that all institutions of female leadership were affected negatively by colonialism.

Among those societies that are believed to have functioned with dual-gender systems in the past was Ruanda (now Ruanda), where the mother of the king shared responsibilities of power with him. In another example, the Bemba of Zambia define a female ruler who is either the mother or the oldest uterine relative of the king. She participates in tribal councils, governs several villages, and enjoys sexual freedom. Also regarded as the mother of the kingdom is the female leader of the Lunda of the Democratic Republic of the Congo. A kinswoman of the chief, she takes part in the administration, has her own court and her own officials, and collects her own taxes.

In Cameroon, the queen mother (*mafo*) of the Bamileke, who is the mother of the *fong*, or *mfong* (the chief), has been considered by some scholars to be an equal to him. She has her own residence and her own estates (which can serve as refuge, since they are outside the jurisdiction of the king), and she directs female activities, which, because the women are the farmers, means that she controls the agriculture of the whole community. She takes part in the administrative council and presides over the women's secret societies. Like many other queen mothers, she can exercise sexual freedom. Her children belong to her and not to the father, as do other children of the society.

Among the neighboring Kom, one of the independent kingdoms of the Tikar people, the queen mother's position is very similar to that described above for the Bamileke, who share the Cameroonian grasslands with the Tikar. The Kom are a matrilineal society, however, unlike most of the other Tikar and Bamileke, who are patrilineal in descent. The *nafoyn* (queen mother) was usually not married, but enjoyed the privileges of sexual freedom, according to Paul Nkwi. Moreover, some scholars argue that she had the choice of whether or not to have a husband. Her children belonged to her and not to their father. This situation has been explained in terms of a mid-nineteenth-century decree prohibiting queen mothers from marrying. Intended to counter the implications of brideprice (a fee paid at the time of marriage by the husband) that endowed the husband with rights over the children, the decree ensured that no man/husband/father could marry a woman who might become the mother of a Fon (king), and thus create the situation where a man would have the right to command obedience from the king because of the conditions of marriage. Eugenia Shanklin reports that the queen mother of the present day continues to direct women as a workforce on her farms, adding to her economic power. Among the queen mother's responsibilities, her ritual duties are particularly important. The significance of her ritual powers serves as strong evidence for the argument that complementarity was, and continues to be, the organizing principle for the ritual sphere in Kom society. Complementarity in one domain suggests the same in other domains, including the political, especially since sources have reported that in the past the queen mother sat with village leaders and challenged them at times. Considering the full range of a queen mother's powers, the argument that the Kom were organized by a dual-gender system seems persuasive. In the past, according to Caroline Ifeka Grassfield, royal women were more visibly powerful than they are today. The royal women of Bamum, like the royal men, killed fearlessly and were killed. Among the Nso', queen mothers perform a variety of constitutional functions including the role of *interrex*. More importantly, Caroline Ifeka emphasizes that a dual-gender system, based on a complementarity of both mystical and political power, defines the entire Nso' social system, encompassing all ranks from commoners, who use titles to demonstrate respect to the "mother" (*yeela'*) and "father" (*taala'*) of the compound, to the Fon and his queen mother (*yeefon*), who is his real mother.

Swaziland

Especially well known among the queen mothers of Africa is the mother of the king in Swaziland, the *Ndlovukazi* (also called the *Indlovukati*). Like other queen mothers, she has her own residence, her own court and officials, and functions in complementary relations to the king. Metaphors for her include the Great She Elephant, the Earth, the Beautiful, and the Mother of the Country, while the king is the Lion, the Sun, and the Great Wild Animal. The king owes his position to the queen mother, usually his biological mother. She is expected to train him and hand over power to him when he reaches maturity. In spite of their close relationship, they serve as a check on each other's powers. Hilda Kuper in her book *The Swazi* (1963), described the political structure of the Swazi as a dual monarchy, a system in which the power and privilege of each monarch is held in check by the other. For example, the male monarch is revitalized in the annual ritual of kingship, which is held at the home of the queen mother. Moreover, he is entitled to use the royal cattle, but if he wastes the national wealth she can rebuke him publicly. Mahmood Mamdani also notes the restriction placed on administrative authority when he describes the queen mother's position as strategic enough to act as a check on any absolutist royal pretensions the king might develop. For example, in the past the king controlled the army, but the commander-in-chief resided at the queen mother's village.

The Ndlovukazi can act as regent, in place of a dead king, until a new one is prepared to assume the position. During a particularly crucial era in Swazi history (1889–1921), the queen mother, Labotsibeni Mdluli, held this position for a lengthy period and was in full charge of the political affairs of the polity. Described as "a woman of outstanding intellect" and "the shrewdest and most astute of the Regents who ever controlled the destinies of the Swazis," she is credited with having protected the Swazi from the colonial powers during this period, and with bringing new order and strength to the monarchy. She also laid the groundwork for independence, so that when her grandson, Sobhuza II, became king he could bring the country to independence in 1968.

The Kpojito of the Fon

History points to the Kpojito as one of the most interesting queen mothers of the past. The female leader in the Fon kingdom of Dahomey (dated from the seventeenth century until the dissolution of its monarchy by the French in 1900), she was the wealthy and powerful double of the King of Dahomey. According to Edna Bay, the term *Kpojito* translates as the one who whelped the leopard (the leopard represents the king), but she was not necessarily the biological mother of the king. She could hear appeals from the court of the minister of religion, with final appeal to the king himself, and she acted as intercessor with the king, pleading on behalf of his subjects. She had her own entourage, but she was forbidden all contact with men. Supported by tributary villages and plantations of slaves, she was reported to be very wealthy. After death, a female descendant in her family of birth replaced her, and she was honored in annual rituals.

Benin

In another of the historical West African kingdoms, Benin, queen mothers exercised impressive power. According to Paula Ben-Amos the Iyoba (queen mother) of the Edo-speaking peoples of southwestern Nigeria was considered one of the senior chiefs, or Town Chiefs, and had her own palace and court. The first Iyoba of Benin was Idia, the mother of the Oba, or king of Benin, who reigned from 1504–1550 (Kaplan 1997). Often described as the only woman who went to war, oral tradition credits her with having raised an army and employing magical powers to aid her son in defeating his enemies. However, a special problem developed in Benin. According to Bay, the king was considered to be divine, and therefore he could not prostrate himself before any person; yet a child was required to subordinate himself before his or her mother. The resolution of this problem was that the queen mother and her son, the king, could never see each other after he became king, though she is believed to have exercised considered political power from her palace.

Many other West African societies also operated with dual-gender systems, characterized by queen mothers or female leaders, prior to colonialism. Of particular note were the female leaders among the Igbo, known as the *omu* (the male leader was the *obi*). Kamene Okonjo (1976) tells us that the *omu*, like the male *obi*, had her own cabinet of counselors (generally women), and they could challenge male authority if necessary. Among the duties of the female leader and her counselors was oversight of the community market, a predominantly female space. Their oversight included judging cases of dispute that occurred in the market. The precolonial Yoruba also recognized female leaders, although they were a patrilineal society. Many women were endowed with the title Iyalode (a woman designated as a political leader) for their contribution to war efforts. The Iyalode, like the Igbo *omu*, was considered the head of market women, but the title indicates responsibilities much broader than just the market. It translates to "mother in charge of external affairs" (Awe 1977, 144). And indeed, the Iyalode of each town was a chief in her own right, with her own servants, drummers, and bell ringers, and she held jurisdiction over all women. (Each Yoruba town created a more specific title as well for their female leader.) She seems to have acquired her office through achievement as a leader, rather than through heredity. Women brought their quarrels to her court for resolution, and she met with groups of women to determine their stand on various political and economic issues.

Among the matrilineal Akan of Ghana, the queen mother (*ohemaa*) is a thriving institution in contemporary society. As with the examples cited above, the queen mothers of the Akan have suffered a loss of power since colonialism because the colonial forces failed to recognize female authority. Yet, Akan queen mothers have unbroken continuity with the past, and they continue to exercise their authority in Ghana today, especially in the Asante region (Stoeltje 1997; 1998). In fact, the dual-gender system has proven to be so attractive that neighboring patrilineal societies, ones that have never had queen mothers (the Ga and the Ewe), began to create the position during the 1990s.

The Asante

The Asante (the largest of the Akan societies) replicate this dual-gender system throughout the Asante region, so that every paramountcy is led by a queen mother and chief (*ohemaa* and *ohene*), and every village and town has both a chief and a queen mother (*odikro* and *oba panin*). The Asantehene and the Asantehemaa are the king and queen mother of the Asante, and they occupy the position of greatest authority. Next in the hierarchical system are the paramountcies, each of which has a powerful chief and queen mother. Small towns and villages are located within a division and serve a particular paramountcy, but each of them has its own chief and queen mother. Consequently, Ghana has many queen mothers of differing status. To explain that a chief and queen mother each have their own authority, it is said that the chief and the queen mother each have their own stool. The stool is the symbol of authority in all Akan societies, functioning much like a throne for European monarchies.

A queen mother of the Asante (and the other Akan groups) is considered to be the mother of the chief and of the particular clan and community, whether or not she is the biological mother of the chief. Therefore, like the queen mothers of other societies, she has specific responsibilities associated with the roles of mothers and female leaders. When the position of chief becomes vacant, she nominates an individual from the royal family to become the new chief. Her nomination goes to the elders of the royal family, and ultimately to the subchiefs (who represent the clans other than the clan of the royal family). Once the new chief has been enstooled, the queen mother is expected to advise him, drawing upon her wisdom and knowledge, and he is expected to consult her. Her responsibilities also encompass the welfare of the women in her domain. One of her major responsibilities includes the settlement of disputes. The Asantehemaa maintains her own court, with elders (predominantly male) that meets once a week to hear cases brought primarily by women concerning the conflicts of everyday life. Other queen mothers hear cases as well, but with a smaller court. A queen mother has her own living space separate from the chief, and she will meet with people to resolve disputes and conduct other business at her own "palace."

A queen mother and a chief must both be members of the same royal family, so they will be sister and brother, uncle and niece, aunt and nephew, cousins, or distant relatives, and in some instances, mother and son. Queen mothers are not only expected to have children, but it is unlikely that a woman would be chosen, from among those qualified, for the position if she did not have children, because of the importance of the concept as well as the reality, of motherhood. However, a queen mother need not be married. She may also divorce, and she may remarry if she wishes. Unlike every other woman, a queen mother can exercise freedom in matters of sexuality, whether or not she is married. In this domain, as in other domains of her life, she has autonomy. Her position as symbolic mother of the clan and of the chief, and her position as procreator, is enhanced by her autonomy with regard to matters of sexuality, procreation, and marriage. These combine with her political, ritual, and juridical authority to create a position (like that of chief), that integrates elements of kinship, politics, and religion, creating strong positions of traditional leadership that have endured, with modification, through colonization and modernization.

Most African societies display flexibility, adaptability, and even creativity in their political and religious systems. This can certainly be observed in regard to the Asante. It is illustrated by the fact that some of the most well-educated and wealthy individuals in the society also hold positions as chiefs. The king of the Asante, Osei Tutu II, enstooled as Asantehene in 1999, was an active and well-educated businessman in London when he was nominated by the Asantehemaa, his biological mother, for the position. Enthusiastically received by the Asante people, he has established an educational fund for the enhancement of the schools in Asante and has given it a high priority.

Although queen mothers have not enjoyed the same privileges of education that their male counterparts have, the culture is now encouraging education and is placing educated women on the stool as queen mothers whenever possible. Due to contemporary influences, then, it is not unusual today to observe queen mothers participating in efforts to bring education to illiterate queen mothers, to support young women's football teams, or to organize events that illustrate the need for planned parenthood. In contemporary African societies, the role of traditional authority seems to be expanding as indigenous systems exercise flexibility in regard to modernization, and as the state slowly recognizes the need to cooperate with traditional systems. It appears that the twenty-first century version of this encounter may be more hospitable to female authority than the colonial encounter, with the value of queen mothers as female leaders being recognized in the indigenous sociopolitical system.

References

Aidoo, Agnes Akosua. 1982. Asante Queen Mothers in Government and Politics in the Nineteenth Century. In *The Black Woman Cross-Culturally*, ed. F. C. Steady. Cambridge, Mass: Schenkman.

Awe, Bolanle. 1977. The Iyalode in the Traditional Yoruba Political System. In *Sexual Stratification*, ed. Alice Schlegel. New York: Columbia University Press.

Bascom, William. 1973. *African Art in Cultural Perspective*. New York: Norton.

Bay, Edna. 1997. The *Kpojito* or "Queen Mother" of Precolonial Dahomey. In *Queens, Queen Mothers, Priestesses, and Power*, ed. Flora Kaplan. New York: New York Academy of Sciences.

———. 1998. *Wives of the Leopard*. Charlottesville: University of Virginia Press.

Ben-Amos, Paula Girshick. 1983. In Honor of Queen Mothers. In *The Art of Power/The Power of Art*, ed. P. Ben-Amos and A. Rubin. Los Angeles: Museum of Culture History, UCLA.

Feeley-Harnik, Gillian. 1997. Dying Gods and Queen Mothers: The International Politics of Social Reproduction in Africa and Europe. In *Gendered Encounters*, ed. Maria Grosz-Ngate and Omari H. Kokole. New York: Routledge.

Farrar, Tarikhu. 1997. The Queenmother, Matriarchy, and the Question of Female Political Authority in Precolonial West African Monarchy. *Journal of Black Studies* 27, no. 5:579–597.

Ginindza, Thoko. 1997. Labotsibeni/Gwamile Mduli: The Power behind the Swazi Throne 1875–1925. In *Queens, Queen Mothers, Priestesses, and Power*, ed. Flora Kaplan. New York: New York Academy of Sciences.

Ifeka, Caroline. The Mystical and Political Powers of Queen Mothers, Kings, and Commoners in Nso', Cameroon. In *Persons and Powers of Women in Diverse Cultures*, ed. Shirley Ardener. New York: Berg.

Kaplan, Flora. 1997. *Iyoba*, The Queen Mother of Benin. In *Queens, Queen Mothers, Priestesses, and Power*, ed. Flora Kaplan. New York: New York Academy of Sciences.

Kuper, Hilda. 1947. *An African Aristocracy: Rank Among the Swazi*. New York: Holmes and Meier.

———. 1963. *The Swazi*. New York: Holt, Rinehart and Winston.

———. 1978. *Sobhuza II: Ngwenyama and King of Swaziland*. New York: Holmes and Meier.

Lebeuf, Annie. 1971. The Role of Women in the Political Organization of African Societies. In *Women of Tropical Africa*, ed. Denise Paulme. Berkeley: University of California Press.

Mamdani, Mahmood. 1996. *Citizen and Subject*. Princeton, N.J.: Princeton University Press.

Nkwi, Paul Nchoji. 1974. The Origin of Kom Matrilineal Institutions. In *Symposium Leo Frobenius. Deutesche UNESCO Kommission*. Koln: Verlag Dokumentation.

O'Barr, Jean. 1984. African Women in Politics. In *African Women South of the Sahara*, ed. Margaret Jean Hay and Sharon Stichter. New York: Longman.

Okonjo, Kamene. 1976. The Dual Sex Political System in Operation. In *Women in Africa*, ed. Nancy J. Hafkin and Edna G. Bay. Stanford, Calif.: Stanford University Press.

Stoeltje, Beverly J. 1997. Asante Queen Mothers. In *Queens, Queen Mothers, Priestesses, and Power*, ed. Flora Kaplan. New York: New York Academy of Sciences.

———. 1995. Asante Queenmothers: A Study in Identity and Continuity. In *Gender and Identity in Africa*, ed. Mechtild Reh and Gudrun Ludwar-Ene. Bayreuth: Lit Verlag.

Shanklin, Eugenia. 1991. Women of Power, The Power of Women. Paper delivered to African Studies Association meetings, St. Louis, Mo.

Wipper, Audrey. 1984. Women's Voluntary Associations. In *African Women South of the Sahara*. New York: Longman.

BEVERLY J. STOELTJE

See also **Ancestors; Chief; Gender Representation in African Folklore; History and Culture: The Ashanti**

R

RADIO AND TELEVISION DRAMA

Many African radio stations were first set up in the 1920s, but they did not carry extensive programming specifically designed for African listeners until the early 1940s. African television stations were first established in the late 1950s. Drama programs in both African and European languages have been an important part of broadcasting content since colonial times.

Dramas are among the most popular of all broadcast genres. Successful dramas draw some of the most devoted audiences, and are typically equaled only by the broadcast of soccer matches and presidential press conferences in their ability to attract very large audiences. For example, in South Africa, Zulu musical dramas based on folk songs were first aired in the mid-1940s and have aired regularly since the late 1950s. One of the longest running radio dramas can be heard on Radio Zambia. Entitled *Malikopo*, this Tonga language program about the adventures and mishaps of an urban man began in the late 1940s, and continues to air to this day.

The form and content of African radio and television dramas are quite diverse, as are the inspirational sources for these creative works. Some programs are dramatizations of traditional folktales and myths. Others are broadcast versions of original works, which were first scripted and produced for the theater, or which first appeared as novels. In addition, countless dramas are written explicitly for television and radio. Many are long-running serials, with a melodramatic (or soap operalike) plot construction. One of the first serial dramas on South African radio, *Deliwe*, ran for twenty-five episodes in March 1964, and was followed by a fifty-nine-episode sequel two months later.

Melodrama plots typically revolve around unfolding personal relationships, marriage and romance, power struggles, schemes for financial success, rivalries between families, moral transgressions, and stories about ambition and betrayal. One example from Egypt is the long running serial *Hilmiyya Nights*, which aired every year between 1988 and 1992 during the Muslim holy month of Ramadan. This immensely popular television show told the story of the intertwined lives and fortunes of a group of characters over a forty-year period. A hybrid product reflecting the influence of imported melodramas from Latin America and the United States, *Hilmiyya Nights* was distinguished for its glamorous and fashionable women characters and its lavish sets.

In addition to melodramas, numerous other dramatic genres are represented in African broadcasting, including comedy, romance, suspense, social realism, myths, and historical drama. Recent examples include a feminist Egyptian television serial in Arabic about a women's retirement home, a comic Zambian radio drama in Bemba about the exploits of an urban playboy, a multilingual South African television drama with health education messages, and a Nigerian situation comedy in Nigerian English about household servants and their corrupt employers.

For many media professionals, drama is not just a form of entertainment, but a vehicle for social and political communication. Many dramas convey, for example, the importance of good citizenship, formal education, literacy, and the appreciation of the arts. Others present challenges to those in power, through commentary on oppressive political conditions or social inequalities. Such messages tend to be conveyed indirectly, through multiple layers of meaning and allegorical characterizations. Despite the high degree of media surveillance by contemporary African states, these dramas with critical messages often escape censorship due to indirection, as well as other complex linguistic nuances which may not be understood by the censors.

In recent years, radio and television dramas have been used to educate people about family planning and about HIV/AIDS. One example is the Tanzanian radio soap opera entitled *Twende na Wakati* (Let's Be Modern). Episodes depict the outcomes of different lifestyle choices and health attitudes, and focus in particular on the positive values of monogamy, spousal communication, joint decision making, and safe sex. The story is structured around three basic character types: positive and negative role models, who embrace or reject, respectively, the educational messages of the program, and transitional characters, who undergo a positive attitudinal and behavioral change over the course of several episodes.

Soul City, an immensely popular South African-produced TV serial, is another example of a program that addresses health issues through the format of social realist drama. Themes such as smoking, HIV/AIDS, childcare, and domestic violence are depicted within the context of the unfolding lives of the main characters. The program is also distinguished for its use of language, which mirrors urban realities. Characters are multilingual and South African English is heard alongside languages such as isiZulu and SeSotho. Set mainly in a community clinic, *Soul City* represents a very interesting hybrid genre as it incorporates visual and narrative elements from American hospital melodrama, Hollywood thrillers, glamorous American soap operas, and didactic theater-for-development.

A great deal of entertainment content on African radio and television is imported from the United States, and from Western European nations, and to a lesser extent from Latin America, India, and the Middle East. Particularly when it comes to television in Africa, one finds that a very high percentage of drama programming is not locally produced; rather, it comes from outside sources. One very popular American import across Africa is the soap opera, *The Bold and the Beautiful*, set in the Los Angeles fashion world. Both male and female fans in Egypt are reported to have become enamored with the characters, making discussion of their lives, looks, and fates part of everyday conversation. Women viewers in South Africa seem to embrace the program for many of the same reasons as viewers worldwide: it depicts a glamorous fantasy world that one can escape into. But South African women also see *The Bold and the Beautiful* as a vehicle for thinking about their own lives. They are particularly drawn to the strong female characters in the program and they relate the actions and choices of different characters to those of people that they know.

Some critics of radio and television dramas in Africa worry that they have replaced older forms of entertainment, such as listening to elders tell traditional stories or to musicians sing about folk heroes. They fear the erosion of traditional culture and the influx of foreign influences. Others have argued that, in many cases, older forms of entertainment were available only to men and thus the availability of dramatic entertainment for wider audiences on television and radio is a welcome development. Drama on African radio and television brings to the forefront important social issues that can be engaged and reflected upon. It allows for a new type of creativity to flourish, one that incorporates both modern and timeless themes, as well as newer and more traditional storytelling devices. And finally, radio and television dramas in African languages are vital for promoting the continued use and value of these languages. This is a particularly pressing issue, as European languages (typically English, French, or Portuguese) are used pervasively by most African radio and television stations, and are also accorded very high prestige through other dominant institutions of society such as education and government.

References

Abu-Lughod, Lila. 1995. The Objects of Soap Operas. In *Worlds Apart: Modernity Through the Prism of the Local*, ed. Daniel Miller. London: Routledge.

Abu-Lughod, Lila. 1997. The Interpretation of Culture(s) after Television. *Representations* 59:109–34.

Barber, Karin. 2000. *The Generation of Plays: Yorùbá Popular Life in Theater*. Bloomington and Indianapolis: Indiana University Press.

Coplan, David. 1985. *In Township Tonight!: South Africa's Black City Music and Theatre*. London, New York: Longman.

Gunner, Liz. 2000. Wrestling with the Present, Beckoning to the Past: Contemporary Zulu Radio Drama. *Journal of Southern African Studies* 26, no. 2:223–37.

Kruger, Loren. 1999. Theater for Development and TV Nation: Notes on an Educational Soap Opera in South Africa. *Research in African Literatures* 30, no. 4:106–26.

Lyons, Andrew P. and Harriet D. Lyons. 1985. "Return of the Ikoi-koi": Manifestations of Liminality on Nigerian Television. *Anthropologica* 27, no. 1–2:55–78.

Lyons, Andrew P. 1990. The Television and the Shrine: Towards a Theoretical Model for the Study of Mass Communications in Nigeria. *Visual Anthropology* 3, no. 4:429–56.

Lyons, Harriet D. 1990. Nigerian Television and the Problems of Urban African Women. In *Culture and Development in Africa*, eds. Stephen H. Arnold and Andre Nitecki. Trenton, N.J.: Africa World Press.

Powdermaker, Hortense. 1962. *Copper Town: Changing Africa*. New York: Harper and Row.

Rogers, Everett M., Peter W. Vaughan, Ramadhan M. A. Swalehe, et al. 1999. Effects of Entertainment–Education Radio Soap Opera on Family Planning Behavior in Tanzania. *Studies in Family Planning* 30, no. 3:193–211.

Tager, Michele. 1997. Identification and Interpretation: "The Bold and the Beautiful" and the Urban Black Viewer in KwaZulu-Natal. *Critical Arts* 11, no. 1–2:95–119.

Valente, Thomas W., Young Mi Kim, Cheryl Lettenmaier, et al. 1994. Radio Promotion of Family Planning in the Gambia. *International Family Planning Perspectives* 20, no. 3:96–100.

DEBRA SPITULNIK

See also **Electronic Media and Oral Traditions; Popular Culture; Theater**

RASTAFARI: A MARGINALIZED PEOPLE

Rastafari emerged in Jamaica in the turbulent 1930s in the context of social, political, and cultural conflict in a dying colonial order. In Jamaica, European social, political, and cultural hegemony held sway over the masses of people of African descent. This meant that their lives were governed by British social and political institutions and cultural values, which were projected as the marks of civilization. In contrast, African culture (religion, language, music and dance) and folkways were denigrated as the marks of incivility and backwardness. Of course, British hegemony faced unrelenting opposition from the masses as they struggled for political freedom and cultural identity. In the early twentieth century, the conflict intensified and came to a critical juncture in the 1930s. One manifestation of the conflict was widespread labor unrest, leading to the crystallization of a powerful trade union movement. Another manifestation was a growing demand for enfranchisement, leading to universal adult suffrage in 1944 and culminating in political independence in 1962. Yet another manifestation was the emergence of the Rastafari movement that rejected the whole colonial establishment with its institutions and values, calling instead for a revitalization of Jamaica's African heritage and a return to Africa, the ancestral home of black people.

Both the early teachings of Rastafari and the early relationship between the movement and the wider society indicated the reality of cultural conflicts. Rejecting institutional religion (Christianity), Rastas instead proclaimed Haile Selassie, the newly crowned emperor of Ethiopia, as the reincarnated Christ returning to earth as the black messiah and liberator. Ironically, they used the Bible, the source of authority for European Christianity, to prove that Selassie was the messiah, "King of kings, Lord of lords, the Conquering Lion of the Tribe of Judah," as his titles read. In the same vein, Rastas drew on the biblical imagery of Babylon to reject the vaunted British institutions and values that were considered the hallmarks of civilization. Instead, they indicted Jamaica as a contemporary manifestation of the spirit of ancient Babylon and the Roman (dubbed "Babylon the Great" in Book of Revelation) for its structures of oppression and its alienating values. Whites, who instituted and managed the colonial system for their own benefit, were condemned as oppressors and, therefore, considered enemies of God and black humanity.

Unlike the working class, who simply desired more of the fruits of the economic system, and the middle class, who were heirs apparent to the sociopolitical system, Rastas wanted to opt out of a system they viewed as beyond redemption. For them redemption meant repatriation to Africa. In this respect, while Jamaica was regarded as the land of exile, Babylon, Africa became the land of redemption, Zion in biblical terms. Repatriation was to come about either by Selassie's sending ships to Jamaica to transport the displaced Africans back to their ancestral homeland, or by Rastas pressuring the British (in the UN if necessary) to finance their return to the land from which they were forcibly taken. While they awaited repatriation, Rastas withdrew their support from the established order. Refusing to work in the exploitative economy of Babylon, some turned to subsistence farming, craft making, or street peddling. Others moved into self-governed and self-sufficient communes (Howell's "Pinnacle in St. Catherine" was the first and the most famous).

The rejection of the legitimacy of the social institutions and cultural values bequeathed to Jamaica by the British colonialists continues today, in the symbols and lifestyle Rastas have embraced as expressions of their determination to fashion their own esthetics and cultural identity. For example, the use of the colors red, green, and gold symbolizes an identification with Africa (these colors are the colors of the Ethiopian flag). Along with dreadlocks, these colors have become the most visible expressions of Rastafarian identity and unity.

The dreadlocks hairstyle is a bold affirmation of the beauty of African hair against a tradition that values straight hair and labels kinky hair as unattractive. Moreover, the matted locks have became a symbolic assertion of a lion-hearted and "lionized" African identity, proclaiming connection of Rastas to the Ethiopian emperor whose emblem was the lion. On one hand, "dreadtalk," the Rastafarian argot or in-group speech, is a symbolic rejection of one of the most significant features of Jamaican middle class respectability, the ability to master the English language. On the other hand, it is appropriation of the right to determine one's vehicle of self-expression, rather than the expression of one's self in the terms of others. Another element of Rastafarian lifestyle is *ital* (natural) living. This represents an abandonment of Babylon's culture of artificiality, which deals in the chemical, synthetic, counterfeit, and ersatz. *Ital* living is a commitment to using things, especially foods, in their natural states. It also applies to the use of herbs for their healing properties. Foremost amongst herbs is, of course, marijuana or *ganja*, which is believed to have not only physical but spiritual and social healing properties. It is smoked ritually to aid the individual in shaking off the shackles of alienation and inducing unity between the individual and Jah (God), as well as generating a feeling of peace and love toward other human beings.

The Rastafarian rejection of Jamaica's institutions and values brought the movement into conflict with the existing power structures. The authorities labeled them as seditious subversives, a criminal underclass, or a lunatic fringe. These labels were accompanied by campaigns of repression against members of the Rastafarian movement from the early 1930s to the 1960s. For example, Leonard Howell, one of the founders of the movement, and his lieutenants were indicted, convicted, and jailed for seditious activities in the 1930s because in their preaching they disavowed any loyalty to the colonial establishment, claiming instead that they were subjects of only Emperor Haile Selassie. During the forties and fifties, Howell's commune at Pinnacle was repeatedly raided and eventually destroyed (1954) on the pretext that the Rastas were behaving in an intimidating manner toward people in the adjoining neighborhoods. However, the real motive for the destruction of Pinnacle was the government's persistent fear that the commune would become a breeding ground for guerrilla activities. The authorities unleashed waves of repression against the movement, especially in the urban areas, after Rastafarian leader, Claudius Henry, and his son were charged for plotting an insurrection in late fifties, and after a few Rastas burned a gas station in Montego Bay in 1963, killing an attendant in the process. Repressive measures included arrests, beatings, shaving Rastas' locks, and various other means of harassment and intimidation. In fact, the famous slum, "Back O' Wall," where Rastas were concentrated in the greatest numbers, was eventually bulldozed in 1966 as part of a campaign against the criminal threat it harbored. Over the years, a number of Rastas, including Howell, were committed to mental institutions. As late as the 1970s, a young person declaring an acceptance of the Rastafarian worldview or starting "to grow locks" was regarded as exhibiting the first sign of mental deterioration.

The conflict between Rastas and the wider society started to lessen after a 1960 study (Smith, Augier, and Nettleford) found that Rastas were essentially peaceful persons who suffered disproportionately from the inequities and the lack of opportunities in the Jamaican society. After this study, the government sought to address Rastafarian concerns through various gestures: a mission to Africa to explore the possibility of repatriation issue, the invitation of various African leaders, including Haile Selassie, to Jamaica to demonstrate Jamaica's link with Africa, and an invitation of the Ethiopian Orthodox Church to establish missions in Jamaica in the hope of channeling Rastafarian religiosity into more structured and acceptable forms.

By the late 1960s, growing disenchantment with the economic and political progress of the newly independent nation (1962) led to a greater acceptance of Rastafarian views concerning the corruption and exploitative nature of Jamaica's social and political institutions. In fact, disenchanted middle-class youths started to embrace Rastafari, and radical intellectuals started to embrace their critique of the social system. Some of these intellectuals (most notably, university professor and Black Power advocate, Walter Rodney) also established collaborative relationships with various Rastafarian groups. Sensing the diffusion of Rastafarian sensibilities among the poor, the young, and radical intellectuals, politicians started to use Rastafarian symbols, imagery, and language in an effort to attract the support of the masses. Therefore, the national election campaigns of the 1970s drew heavily on the popular music, speech, and symbols which showed the distinct influence of Rastafari on Jamaican street culture. Then and now, some scholars have argued that such manipulation of the Rastafarian elements in the culture smacked of opportunistic cooption for the selfish ends of shrewd politicians and did not reflect a genuine embrace of Rastafarian causes. That may be the case. However, by using Rastafarian elements so openly, the politicians succeeded (probably inadvertently) in conferring legitimacy on the movement, to such an extent, that continued middle- and upper-class dislike notwithstanding, Rastas now enjoy a peaceful coexistence with the rest of the society.

Perhaps of more significance than the legitimacy conferred on Rastafari by the political use of symbols is the role of the movement in the development of Jamaica's expressive culture over the past forty years. By now it is common knowledge that Rastafari has been an essential force in the development and dissemination of reggae music, which most Jamaicans embrace as a national treasure. The rhythmic content and character of popular Jamaican music is traceable to Rastafarian ritual drumming called Nyabinghi. A good example of this is one of the earliest local recordings, "O Carolina," whose accompaniment features the Nyabinghi drumming of Count Ossie's drummers. The lyrics of reggae also show an indebtedness to Rastafari. The "conscious lyrics" of reggae abound with Rastafarian philosophy and rhetoric. These "conscious lyrics" were the trademarks of vintage reggae from the late 1960s to the early 1980s (Bob Marley, Peter Tosh, Bunny Wailer, Third World, Jimmy Cliff, and Jacob Miller). The latter half of the nineties is experiencing a return to serious, Rasta-inspired lyrics with scathing social criticisms, unrelenting calls for social change, and frightening warnings of apocalyptic destruction of the structures of oppression and exploitation (Sizzla, Anthony B., Luciano, Tony Rebel, Buju Banton). Furthermore, those who embrace the beliefs and lifestyle of Rastafari are heavily represented among the artists who have created, shaped, and taken reggae music around the world. In fact, the majority of the most celebrated artists have been Rastas or have embraced significant elements of Rastafari, and they have brought their conviction to their musical creativity.

Rastafarian contribution to Jamaica expressive culture extends far beyond popular music and touches every creative artistic endeavor. The performing arts (popular theater and dance) have dealt with Rastafarian themes and employed Rastafarian speech for decades. Literature, both novel and poetry, bears the marks of Rastafarian influence on contemporary Jamaican society. Rastafarian iconography appears frequently in the visual arts and the broader visual culture. A visit to Jamaica's National Gallery will reveal the growing influence of Rastafari on and its representation in local paintings and sculptures. Artists, both trained and intuitive, have used Rastafari to represent Jamaica's social reality or to express their African consciousness. Broader visual representations reveal an identification of the indigenous culture with Rastafari. This is particularly evident in graphic arts that make liberal use of Rastafarian colors (red, green, and gold), speech, and other symbols to advertise just about everything from rum to reggae concerts. The association of Rastafri with local culture is even more pronounced in the tourist wares sold in the various craft markets in the island. These run the gamut from carvings depicting Rastas and painted in Rastafarian colors, to T-shirts with Rastafarian images or symbols and well-known expressions such as "Irie," "One Love," and "Peace and Love."

Amazingly, the once maligned Rastafari has not only become the most significant force in Jamaica's expressive culture, but also has evolved into a movement with a worldwide following. It first spread to other Caribbean islands and to metropolitan centers in Europe and North America where many Jamaicans have migrated since the fifties. But with the popularity of Reggae and the charisma of Bob Marley and others, Rastafarian ideas have found favorable reception much further afield. At the beginning of the twenty-first century, Rastafari has significant representation in most major population centers of North America, Europe, Brazil, Cuba, and West and Southern Africa, and followers among the Maoris in New Zealand, the indigenous Australians, and the Pacific Islanders. In various other places and among other social groupings around the world, there are individuals committed to the Rastafarian way of life. There are even web pages on Rastafari in Russia. Beyond the full-scale adoption of Rastafarian philosophy and lifestyle, many have been influenced by Rastafari in various ways. The attraction of Rastafari to various peoples seems to be its trenchant criticism of the forces of oppression and its clear articulation of a vision of human liberation. Thus a movement, started by a marginalized people struggling against British social, political, and cultural hegemony, has been embraced by other marginalized peoples around the world to express their opposition to oppression and repression and their desire for freedom and human dignity.

References

Barrett, Leonard E. 1988. *The Rastafarians: Sounds of Cultural Dissonance*. Rev. and Updated. Boston: Beacon Press.

Chevannes, Barry. 1994. *Rastafari: Roots and Ideology*. Syracuse, N.Y.: Syracuse University Press.

Lewis, William F. 1993. *Soul Rebels: The Rastafari*. Prospect Heights, Il.: Waveland Press.

Murrell, N. Samuel, William D. Spencer, and Adrian A. McFarlane, eds. 1998. *Chanting Down Babylon: The Rastafarian Reader*. Philadelphia: Temple University Press.

Smith, Michael G., Roy Augier, and Rex Nettleford. 1960. *The Rastafarian Movement in Kingston, Jamaica*. Kingston: Institute of Social and Economic Studies.

ENNIS B. EDMONDS

See also **Diaspora; Caribbean Verbal Arts; Vodou**

RATTRAY, R. S. (1881–1938)

Captain Robert Sutherland Rattray M.B.E was a barrister at law, and held a diploma in anthropology from Oxford. Rattray did considerable anthropological research on African people, especially the Ashanti; he also worked on the Hausa. Rattray's main area of investigation included tradition, culture, religion, customs, folklore, proverbs, and art. His valuable works on Africa include the following: *Ashanti* (1923); *Religion and Art in Ashanti* (1927); *Ashanti Law and Constitution* (1929); *Ashanti Proverbs— The Primitive Ethics of a Savage People* (1916); *The Tribes of Ashanti Hinterland* (1932); *An Elementary Mole Grammar* (1918); *A Short Manual of the Gold Coast* (1924); *Some Folk-lore Stories and Songs in the Chinyanja with English Translation and Notes* (1907); *Hausa Folk-lore, Customs, Proverbs* (1913).

When a new Anthropological Department was set up in Ashanti in the 1920s, Rattray was charged with the task of researching the law and constitution of Ashanti, to assist the colonial administrators in ruling the Ashantis. With his office in the Anthropological Department in Ashanti, Rattray set out to do detailed and voluminous research on Ashanti religion, customs law, art, beliefs, folktales, and proverbs. His personal contact with the people of Ashanti afforded him an intimate knowledge of their culture, which is reflected in his thoughtful and nuanced writing on them.

Rattray undertook research into Ashanti law, and then proceeded to look into religion and other social matters in Ashanti; finally, he examined Ashanti arts and crafts. When he began researching Ashanti legal customs, he was constantly confronted with words in the Ashanti language which, although primarily associated with religion, were nonetheless continuously found in connection with legal and constitutional procedures. Meanwhile, the exact significance of these words needed to be determined to ensure an accurate and useful study. Rattray discovered that Ashanti law and Ashanti religion are intimately associated. He realized that a thorough understanding of the religion would assist him in his study of law. Rattray then wrote first *Ashanti*, followed by *Religion and Art in Ashanti*, and finally, the last of the trilogy, *Ashanti Law and Constitution*.

Ashanti deals with social anthropology. It gives detailed accounts of the social mores, religious beliefs, and rites and customs of the Ashantis. It also includes an article on the Golden Stool of the Ashantis.

In *Religion and Art in Ashanti* Rattray described religion and other customary practices of the Ashantis. Here, he tried to shed light on the motives and reasoning behind some Ashanti practices that seemed appalling or horrific from a Western perspective. Rattray described himself as a student of anthropology from its practical and applied, rather than its academic, standpoint.

Ashanti Proverbs is a translation of and a commentary of a work by Reverand J. G. Christaller. Here, Rattray selected approximately eight hundred proverbs from an existing collection of proverbs by Christaller. His aim here was to illuminate some customs and beliefs through proverbs, which were of interest to anthropologists, focusing on the contextual meanings of proverbs cited.

Ashanti Law and Constitution treats the constitution and the history of the Ashanti legal tradition. Special attention is drawn to the land tenure system. Rattray also traced the growth of the "individual household" and its head from its original humble origins, to the present-day territorial groupings under a head-chief. According to Rattray, this system directly reflected concepts of the ruler and ruling office in West Africa.

The Tribes of Ashanti Hinterland focuses on the people of the northern territories of Ghana (then known as the Gold Coast). It is essentially a linguistic survey of these tribes, and deals with the ethnological and historical relationship among the tribes of Mo, Nchumuru, Kratchi, Nanumba, Gonja, Dagomba, Konkomba, Chokosi, Bimoba, Mamprusi, Kusasi, Nabdom, Talansi, Nankanni, Kassena, Builsa, Isala, Dagati, Wala, and Lobi.

Hausa Folklore is a two-volume book that deals with Hausa folkloric customs. Part One is a short history purporting to give the origin of the Hausa nation and the story of their conversion to Islam. Part Two contains various stories of heroes and heroines. When Rattray wrote this work, he had never been in the Hausa country before. He studied Hausa in the Gold Coast colony, where he was in constant touch with Hausa. Significantly, the book's publication was financed by the Gold Coast government.

An Elementary Mole Grammar (1918) is a revised and enlarged edition of *A Mole-English Vocabulary with Notes on the Grammar and Syntax* (1912). *Some Folklore Stories and Songs in Chinyanja* (1907) contains works in the Chinyanja language, with English translation and notes. It contains examples of native life, habits, and customs of the native peoples inhabiting central Angoniland. Finally, *A Short Manual of the Gold Coast* contains statistical information on the Ashanti, covering such topics as ethnology, administration, resources, education, communication and transport, and trade.

KWESI YANKAH

RELIGION: AFRICAN TRADITIONAL RELIGION

Africa's traditional religious heritage traces its origins to the human quest for meaning and self-understanding. The same questions which every people have asked about themselves and the world in which they live since the dawn of human consciousness—how was the world created? How did human and non-human forms of life come to be? What is the meaning of life, and death?—were also posed by our African forebears, and the answers given to these questions came out of their own unique experiences and reflections. The answers, pregnant with philosophical and theological meaning, took the form of myths and stories, and it is clear that these myths and stories would not have come about if people had not asked questions about their existence.

The quest for meaning led to the apprehension of an underlying reality that our African forebears experienced, and in acknowledging and accommodating themselves to this reality, the religious institutions in African societies originated. But while African societies are characterized by a considerable degree of diversity, there is at the same time a remarkable degree of unity in terms of spirituality. To describe the religious heritage as *African* is not to imply that there is complete uniformity of belief and practice; it is only to suggest that such beliefs and practices have an African provenance. But even where beliefs and practices may be extremely divergent, they have nevertheless come out of the African experience and can therefore be legitimately called African.

Although there is no word in many African languages which may be exactly translated as the English word *religion*, the concept of religion does exist everywhere in African and Africans in their own way, under the influence of their various cultures, have given expression to this universal phenomenon. The closest equivalent to the word *religion* that is found in African languages are words such as *custom*, *tradition*, *rule*, or expressions such as the "way of the ancestors," "our way of life," and so on. But this is a pointer to a continent-wide reality in Africa, which is that religion does not stand by itself apart from other aspects of life, rather it is related to every aspect of life and links all aspects of life into a coherent system of thought and action. It gives meaning and significance to life and provides abiding and satisfying spiritual values. And, in the crucial moments of life, such as birth, puberty, marriage, and death, as well as in matters relating to human welfare and destiny, religion provides answers that are helpful and satisfying to the human spirit.

A main problem for Western scholars studying traditional religions in Africa has been a lack of familiar scholarly resources, such as a holy book. Except for a few instances, such as Coptic Christianity in Egypt, Ethiopia, and Eritrea, there are no sacred written scriptures in traditional African religions. Few African peoples have rigidly fixed creeds. Still, for most African societies, there are abundant sources for the study of religious traditions, for the ancestors devised many ways of recording their experiences and passing them on from one generation to the other.

One can begin by studying the life of African people, since religions pervades every facet of African life. The myths that abound in African societies tell of the origin of things, the creation of the world and humans and the relationship between the creator or divinity and humans and other spirit beings. Rituals and festivals convey religious ideas and from them one can learn of the relationship between humans and the spiritual and physical worlds. In the rites prescribed for public worship, one learns the attributes given to divinity and other spirit beings, the devotion which people express when they worship either in public or in private and the confidence expressed in the constancy of spirit beings.

Religious experiences are also expressed in songs and dances; from these the history, joys, sorrows, aspirations, and hopes, as well as the philosophical and religious outlook of African peoples, can be ascertained. Proverbs, adages, and wise sayings represent a rich source for the study of African beliefs and practices as well as moral values. Furthermore, aspects of religious heritage have been preserved in art. Art may express social values, deep religious ideas, feelings, and experiences of the people. Carvings, emblems, moldings, shrines, and sacred places all convey religious truth. Even names of people reflect religious beliefs. The whole spectrum of African life provides a rich source for the study, understanding, and appreciation of the religious traditions of Africa.

To say that the religious traditions have been passed on from generation to generation is not to suggest that they have remained static or unchanged. As social constructs, these traditions have changed with the succeeding generations. Since these traditions are deeply connected to African people and their histories, they have undergone many changes in tandem with human experiences, development, and adaptation.

Again, to refer to the religion as "traditional" is not to suggest that it is a thing of the past, rather it is to express the view that it is based on a fundamentally African or indigenous value system and that it has its own pattern, with its own historical legacy from the past. But at the same time, the religion is a contemporary reality, since it continues to influence the lives and thoughts of millions of people, not only on the African continent, but also throughout the African diaspora. The religions of African provenance in the Americas, such as Candomble, Umbanda, Macumba, Vodou, Santeria, and others illustrate that African religious traditions are as relevant as ever.

The singular form of the word *religion* is not employed to downplay the many variations and differences in belief and practice found in African societies. On the contrary, it is a reference to the core of beliefs and ideas which provides a unifying element and that warrants the use of the singular with reference to the religion. But having said this, it must also be pointed out that

the adjective *African* essentially refers to origin and provenance, rather than to uniformity.

That the scholars who first wrote about the religious heritage of Africa came mostly from Europe as missionaries, explorers, colonial officials, and anthropologists, led to the development of a primary view of that heritage derived from the perspective of nonpracticing, non-native individuals. Many African scholars who have written on the subject are products of European education and, in many instances, are nonpractitioners, and converts to Christianity or Islam. The perspective of the practitioners was deemed not important and the observers' views essentially became the religion itself. Thus the traditional religious heritage became synonymous with the idea of "otherness," and similarities were, in the past, and to a considerable extent, even up to the present, attributed to influences from Christian or Islamic contact. Such conclusions, no doubt, originate from the assumption of Africa as a tabula rasa, but serious scholars ought to do better than perpetuate age-old misconceptions, even though they were originated by venerable writers. The African practitioners' own views of their beliefs and actions should be the guiding factor in any consideration of the subject of African traditional religion.

In such a crucial area of human life and culture, knowledge of the indigenous languages of the people whose religion is being studied is absolutely critical to an informed interpretation of the material. And yet, in the case of Africa, many scholars have written authoritatively about the religions of societies in Africa, without a thorough or working knowledge of the languages of those societies. Scholars studying Eastern religions go to the extent of studying languages that are no longer spoken in order to read ancient scriptures; and yet those studying Africa do not often bother to thoroughly understand spoken languages of the people whose religion they are studying, and rely on translators whose knowledge of the researcher's language may be limited, to say the least.

African traditional religion generally holds that the universe did not come into being on its own accord, and that there was a time when it did not exist. Many myths tell of the activities of a Creator, Moulder, Sculptor, Fashioner, Great Weaver, or Originator, who brought everything that exists into being. In some cases, the Creator used agents to carry out the task of creation, but the myths make it clear that those agents merely carried out orders and were not independent agents who acted on their own volition. The universe is one, but it has two aspects, visible and invisible, and these aspects constitute the reality of the universe.

The universe is populated by beings and beings presuppose relationships; there is an interconnectedness between all that exists. These beings are hierarchically arranged, and they all originate from one source. There are mystical powers whose existence is borne out by the practice of witchcraft, sorcery, medicine, rainmaking, and curing. These forces can be used to bring about pain and suffering and they can also be used to fight evil.

Death is not the end of life, and the dead ancestors continue to be members of their families and societies and to wield influence over the living. The involvement of the dead in the affairs of society continues without interruption and there is a sense in which death increases a person's powers, for the dead can punish or reward the living. Communication with the dead is possible, through libations and offerings, dreams and possession.

The dead are believed to return into the world and to be reborn and this belief is given concrete expression in the names given to children indicating the return of a deceased person into life. Life therefore is a cycle of birth, maturation into adulthood and finally death, and the life cycle is renewable.

The spirit world is real and is inhabited by Divinity, the ancestral spirits, and agents, children, or messengers of Divinity called *orishas* by the Yoruba, Vodun by the Fon, and Abosom by the Akan. These latter spirits may take up residence in rivers, rocks, mountains, or shrines. As agents and messengers of Divinity, these spirits interact regularly with human beings and are interested in what happens in the human world.

In spite of the powers attributed to them and the worship and service offered them, these spirits are limited beings with circumscribed powers. Each has an area of competence which is limited to the specific attribute for which it is known. Shrines are maintained by priests or priestesses as places where sacrifices or prayers may be offered to these spirits, who are believed to protect, bless, and punish.

God does not have a generic name, but unique names and attributes. Shrines, temples, and statues dedicated to God are rare, nor are there priests or priestesses dedicated to the service of God. This implies that no human can stand in as the messenger or mouthpiece of God, no human can have such a direct link to the ultimate divinity. And because God is not conceived of in physical terms, there are no shrines, physical or visual representations such as sculptures or paintings. Rather, God is portrayed as a great spirit without any physical representations. The Akan proverb: "If you want to speak to Onyame (Divinity), speak to the winds," suggests that God is invisible but everywhere. The various names for God in African languages bring out the wide variety of ideas and attributes for the ultimate divinity.

The belief that humans will enjoy peace and tranquility in this world if they act in accordance with the moral sanctions of their societies, which and are supervised by the divinities and ancestors, constitutes a core idea of African traditional religion. Religion is for this world and its purpose is to make life more comfortable and prosperous. It enables people to find meaning in life, and resonates with the power to improve life.

These core ideas have been given concrete expression in a variety of ways in African societies, and each society's religious practices constitute elaborations on these common beliefs. The forced emigration of millions of Africans into the Americas during the era of the slave trade led to the introduction of African religious beliefs and practices in the New World; these beliefs continue to be a vital part of the religious and cultural life not only of African descendants, but also of other American people.

African traditional religion is part of the religious heritage of humankind and shares essential similarities with other world religions. Like all religions it deals with the supernatural and springs from humanity's eternal quest to comprehend the universe, and humankind's place in that universe. It is, like all religions, a profound expression of the apprehension of a truth that defies adequate verbalization. Studies of traditional African religion will undoubtedly continue to provide knowledge of not only this specific tradition, but of basic religious impulses and beliefs adhered to throughout the world.

References

Abimbola, Wande. 1997. *Ifa Will Mend Our Broken World: Thoughts on Yoruba Religion and Culture in Africa and the Diaspora.* Roxbury, Mass.: Aim Books.

Blakeley, Thomas D., Walter E. A. van Beek, and Dennis L. Thomson, eds. 1994. *Religion in Africa: Experience and Expression.* London.

King, Noel Q. 1986. *African Cosmos: An Introduction to Religion in Africa.* Belmont, Ca.: Wadsworth.

Magesa, Laurenti. 1997. *African Religion: The Moral Traditions of Abundant Life.* Maryknoll, New York: Orbis Books.

Mbiti, John S. 1969. *African Religions and Philosophy.* London: Heinemann.

Mbiti, John S. 1991. *Introduction to African Religion.* Second Edition. London: Heinemann.

Opoku, Kofi Asare. 1978. *West African Traditional Religion.* Accra et al: FEP.

Ray, Benjamin C. 1976. *African Religions: Symbol, Ritual, and Community.* Englewood Cliffs, N.J.

Some, Malidoma Patrice. 1998. *The Healing Wisdom of Africa: Finding Life Purpose Through Nature, Ritual and Community.* New York: Tarcher/Putnam.

Zahan, Dominique. 1979. *The Religion, Spirituality, and Thought of Traditional Africa.* Chicago and London: The University of Chicago Press.

KOFI A. OPOKU

See also **Cosmology; Divination: Overview; Healing; Spirit Possession**

RELIGIONS: AFRO-BRAZILIAN RELIGIONS

The African religious heritage is rich in Brazil. From the north to the south, manifestations of African deities can be detected. These religions are generally known as Candomblé. Candomblé reached Rio de Janeiro by the end of the nineteenth century and, more recently, the city of São Paulo.

It is important to stress that in the southeastern part of Brazil (especially in the states of Rio de Janeiro, São Paulo, and Minas Gerais), there is also Macumba, a generic term that also includes the Umbanda. Both Macumba and Umbanda are popular religions resulting from a similar syncretic process. In the state of Maranhao, in the "Casa das Minas" church, one can find the worship of *vodun*, divinities of Fon origin from Dahomey's ancient kingdom (now Benin). In the city of Cachoeira in Bahia state, there is also the service of *vodun* at the Ceja Undê church; however, this rite is originally from Mahi, in Benin. In Pernambuco, we can find Xango being served, originally a Yoruba *orisha*, mainly in the city of Recife.

The word Condomblé is etymologically derived from the Kimbundu language: *Ka + ndumbe + mbele*, which translates as "indoctrination house." Its cult is based on worshipping forces of nature (*Orisis*) and ancestors. The sacerdotal structure obeys a hierarchy, in which the main priests are called *babalorixa* ("*pai-de-santo*," a male religious leader) or *ialorixa* ("*mãe-de-santo*," a female religious leader). It dates back to the time of the slave trade, when Africans were brought by force to Brazil to serve as laborers in the plantations and cities. The three main groups that formed Candomblé were the Nago, the Jeje, and the Bantu-speakers. The Nago or Yoruba came from several regions in what today is called Nigeria. The Jeje, or Fons, came originally from Daome's (Dahomey) ancient kingdom (current Benin Republic), Ghana, and Togo while the Bantu speakers arrived from the wide territory of Portuguese colonization in southern Africa, such as Angola, Mozambique, and Congo.

These ethnic groups brought the Yoruba, Ewe-Fon, and Kimbundu languages to Brazil. The emergence of African sects in the New World was an unforeseen consequence of the slave trade. Candomblé is fundamentally an initiatory religion, in which the neophyte (iaô) must undergo seclusion for about three weeks. During this time, the initiate undergoes rituals to consecrate the body in preparation for possession by his or her orixá (protector and the "owner of their head"). In general, the most popular aspects of Candomblé are the public celebrations (xire), in which, through singing and dancing, the orixas are summoned to be praised, and to bless their devotees.

Orixás

Orixá, the name by which the African deities worshiped in Brazil are known, stands for the many cosmologic principles or divinities which command the forces of nature. There are many orixás worshipped in Brazil today. Not only does the general name, orixá, come from the Yoruba, but many of the individual names are Yoruba as well.

Exu, the "African mercurial divinity" and first-born, is the great communication agent according to the Yoruba religious system, where he is known as Eshu. Exu is the speech itself. Holder of epithets of Ojixé, "the messenger," and of Enubanrijô, "the collective mouth," he is the one who provides humans with the knowledge of the orixis' will and with the offerings that should be made for obtaining their benevolence. Therefore, he is the agent of trading relations and of exchange. The idea of exchange in Candomblé expresses one of the most important liturgical and conceptual concepts of this religion, since the devotional act implies a restitutional process involving energy (axé) and reaching balance. This deity also commands sexual impulses; he is represented by an erect penis. Monday is Exu's day of reverence. His colors are black and red, his place of service is the crossroads, and his favorite foods are the rooster and farofa de dendê (a mix of manioc meal and azeite de dendê African palm oil). He also likes to drink cachaga (alcoholic beverage derived from skimmings of boiling sugar cane).

Ogun is the divinity of war and the lord of the paths. He created technology and metallurgy. In Africa, he was originally an agrarian divinity. Therefore, his symbols are the sword and agricultural tools. Tuesday is his day, his color is blue, and he is worshiped on the railroads and highways (because trains and motor vehicles are made of iron). Yams are his favorite food.

Oxossi is the deity of hunting and forests. He is represented by a bow and arrow. He also holds an ox tail which he uses to command the forest spirits. His votive day is Thursday, his colors are blue and green, and he likes axoxo, a food made of boiled corn decorated with coconut strips.

Ossaim is the mysterious deity of herbal medicine and is deeply connected to African healing traditions. He knows all the plants' power for liturgical and healing purposes, and lives in the virgin forests: He eats honey, corn, and peanuts. This deity likes to smoke and to drink cachaga. His colors are green and yellow; the bird is one of his symbols.

Omolu cures victims of plagues, epidemics, and contagious diseases. He is called "the poors' doctor." He is a mysterious and gloomy divinity, covered with straws that hide his face. Monday is his day for worship. His colors are black, red, and white, and his favorite food is popcorn.

Xangô might be said to resemble Zeus, the ancient Greeks' supreme god. He is the orixá of thunder and lightning god. His cult is originally from the Yoruba city of Oyo. He would have been one of this African city's historic kings and, therefore, is also called Obi and Alafin, which in Yoruba means "king" and "palace lord," respectively. His element is fire and his symbol is a double ax. He appreciates a rich diversity of food, such as lamb and turtle, but his favorite dish is made with okras. Thursday is his votive day, and his colors are red and white.

Oxumara is represented by the serpent and the rainbow. Among the Yoruba, he is the deity who transports water from rivers and seas to Xango's palace, which is located in heaven. He is also a mighty fortune-teller. The Fon call him Bessem, and he is represented by an iron snake. His colors are yellow and black. Oxum is a beautiful seductress, and is associated with water in all forms, sweat, rivers, waterfalls, and so on. She is vain and proud, always wearing copper bracelets, combing her hair, and admiring herself in the mirror. Her color is golden yellow, and her favorite dish is omolucum, a food made of beans, shrimp, and eggs.

Iansa's the orixá of wind, lightning, and storms. She rules the spiritual realm. A fearless warrior, she is a brave woman who follows her husband into battles. She is one of Xango's wives, as is Oxum. Her color is red or coral. She holds an ox tail with which she commands the world of the dead. Her favorite food is acaraja (bean rolls with shrimp fried in azeite de dendi).

Iemanjá is the "Lady of Sea Water," who lives at the mouth of rivers where the rivers' water and the seas' water blend. She is the great mother of all orixás. Her connection with childbirth is signified by her large breasts. All sea fishes are also her children. Her objects are silver plated and her color is transparent. Her day of worship is Saturday. One of her main foods is made of honey and rice. She holds a silver fan in one of her hands. She is usually represented as a mermaid.

Naná Buruku is the oldest female divinity. This deity is connected with still waters, swamps, and mud, and is also associated with the dead. An old, slow, and introspective orixá, her colors are dark blue and white.

Oxalá is the great god of creation, and father of all orixás. An ancient divinity, he is represented as an old hunchbacked man, walking very slowly, and supported by his staff (opaxorô). His ritual objects are white, a color associated with the beginning of time and death. (White is the mourning color for the Yorubas.) Oxala's day of worship is Friday. It is a tradition of Candomblé followers to use white on Fridays in homage to the ancient orixá devotion. This deity's main dishes are canjica (white corn), white pigeon, and igbin (edible land snail).

Service to the Ancestors

The homage to the community's dead members is a separate rite in Candomblé. The spirits of eminent deceased people are called Baba Egun (ancestors' fathers). The central site of these services is on Itaparica Island, next to Salvador (Bahia). When the spirits manifest themselves by possessing their devotees, they give advice and highlight the groups' solidarity. They also answer questions and heal the sick. The dead cannot be touched. Only the clerics of the cult of the dead have the power to communicate with these spirits.

Divination

In Candomblé, communications are established between the physical world (*aie*) and the spiritual world (*orun*). Thereby, the multiple instances of interaction are revealed: between human and orixas, between human and ancestors (*egun*), among human themselves during services (*egbe*), in the destiny revealed by *odu* (the signs of Ifá), by the nature of their own *Ori* (divinity head), and by the other forces of supernatural world. Ifá is the Yoruba's oracle or divinatory system, which is headed by the deity Orumila, who is aware of humans' destiny, and by Exú, the orixá linked to communication. The oracle is one of the main foundations of the Afro-Brazilian religions belief system. This divination system is composed of a set of sixteen cowrie shells. Divination is made by throwing the shells on a white cloth; the configurations are interpreted for their oracular messages.

Macumba

The term Macumba is probably the result of the acculturation of Bantu-speaking African slaves. The term's etymology is controversial, even though it is known that it is originally from the Kimbundu language: *ma* (everything that scares) + *kumba* (to sound). This derivation seems to refer to the sounds of musical instruments used in this religion, which are mainly percussion, such as *atabaques* (drums played with the hands which were probably assimilated from the Yoruba cultural group). There is also a record of the melding of the plural prefix *maku* + the word *mba* meaning "sortilege." The term Macumba also refers to an ancient African musical instrument, consisting of a bamboo pipe with transverse cuts, over which two slender sticks were grated. Another reference identifies the word Macumba as the name given to the initiates in the nation of Cabinda, a Bantu-speaking group brought to Brazil as slaves.

Macumba was the dominant form of Afro-Brazilian worship in Rio de Janeiro up to the beginning of the twentieth century. Its influence was also present in the states of Minas Gerais and Saõ Paulo. Religious practices usually took place in sanctified areas where the spirit entities were evoked. These entities were called Pretos Velhos (old slaves' spirits), Caboclos (native Brazilian spirits) and Beijadas (children's spirits), among many other names. Such rituals were celebrated by *chefe de terreiro* (lounge leader), which could be either a *pai-de-santo* or *mae-de-santo* (a male or a female religious leader, respectively), always helped by an assistant called *cambone*. Macumba was a strongly syncretistic worship, a deep blend of Catholic religious practices and Allan Kardec's spiritualism. This religious denomination practically disappeared around 1910, due to the emergence of Umbanda. A word derived from Kimbundu and Kikongo idioms, Umbanda means "witchcraft" and "sorcery" in the city of Rio de Janeiro. Like Candomblé and Macamba, Umbanda is also composed of various cultural elements, such as native Brazilian and African beliefs, Catholicism, spiritualism, and Eastern rituals. It is practiced in urban centers in southeastern Brazil. Throughout Brazil, African-derived faiths remain vital for their devotees.

References

Bascom, William. 1991. *Ifa Divination: Communication Between Gods and Men in West Africa*. Bloomington: Indiana University Press.

Bastide, Roger. 1959. *Sociologia do Folclore Brasileiro*. São Paulo: Editora Anhambi.

Bastide, Roger. 1989. *As Religioes Africanas no Brasil: Contribuição para uma Sociologia das Interpenetraçoes de Civilizaçoes*. São Paulo: Livraria Pioneira Editora.

Santos, Cristiano H. R. dos. 2001. Candomblé. In *The Concise Encyclopedia of Language and Religion*, ed. John F. A. Sawyer and J. M. Y. Simpson. Oxford, England: Pergamon / Elsevier Science.

Santos, Cristiano H. R. dos. 2001. Macumba. In *The Concise Encyclopedia of Language and Religion*, ed. John F. A. Sawyer and J. M. Y. Simpson. Oxford (UK): Pergamon / Elsevier Science, 2001. pp. 73–74.

Santos, Juana Elbein. 1993. *Os Nàgô e a Morte: Pàde. Àsèsè e o Culto Égun na Bahia*. Petropolis: Editora Vozes.

Verger, Pierre Fatumbi. 1957. *Notes sur le Culte des Orishe et Vodoun à Bahia, la Baie de Tous les Saints au Brasil et à l'Ancienne Côte des Esclaves*. Mémoire 51 de l'Institut Frangais pour l'Afrique Noir. Dakar: IFAN.

Verger, Pierre Fatumbi. 1993. Orixás: *Deuses lorubés na África e no Novo Mundo*. São Paulo: Corrupio.

CRISTIANO HENRIQUE RIBEIRO DOS SANTOS

See also **Diaspora; Santeria; Vodou**

RELIGIOUS CEREMONIES AND FESTIVALS: SÃO TOMÉ AND PRÍNCIPE

The island republic of São Tomé and Príncipe is the second smallest state in Africa. After five hundred years of Portuguese colonial domination the country became independent in 1975. The native Creole population, descendents of African slaves and European settlers, have become known as Forros. Roman Catholicism has always been the dominant religion in the archipelago. However, African religious forms have always persisted side by side with Christian beliefs or have been merged into local syncretic religious rites.

The Catholic Church has been rooted on the archipelago since the formation of the Creole society in the late 15th century. Particularly the Forro community adheres to the Catholic religious manifestations and associations. Every parish has a *confraria*, a religious brotherhood with membership of both men and women. The members are not obliged to have had a church wedding. Every *confraria* has a president, a secretary, and a treasurer. The senior members often play important roles in the local Forro community. The brotherhood gathers every Sunday, collecting money among the members who jointly attend the mess. The brotherhood gives money to the poor and supports members in case of illness or other misfortunes. The *confraria* organizes the parish festival annually to commemorate the local patron saint. Against a small contribution other persons can become *juiz* (assistant) in order to participate in the organization of the festivity. On Thursday in the week preceding the festival the president hoists the flag. During the novena the brothers and the *juizes* attend the special prayers in the church. After the principal mass there is a banquet of fraternization with typical dishes behind the church where everybody can participate free of charge. Eight brothers who are dressed in red carry the figure of the patron saint through the streets of the town. The same day the theater and dance societies perform simultaneously on different places in the town. Modern popular bands playing the local version of Congo-style dancing music like Africa negra, sangazuza, and os úntués perform at night on the *terraço*, the local enclosed open dancing floor. The major festival Deus Pai on June 13 in the town of Trindade attracts thousands of people from all over the island. Another important festival takes place on December 21 to commemorate Saint Thomas, the patron saint and name-giver of the major island.

Many Forro families have their own wooden chapel with a picture of a Catholic saint on their quinté (compound). Once a year on a particular day the family brings the picture in a little procession to the parish church to be blessed by the priest. After a few days, they take it back to their chapel where it remains until the following year. On the day when the picture is back in the chapel, the family gives a banquet with traditional dishes. The fixed date is the anniversary of the very first blessing of the family saint in the church.

The local population considers baptism and funeral as the most important sacraments, whereas only the small elite practices the Christian-style wedding and marriage. However, even formally married men are very unlikely to stick to the monogamous rule. A mother's first-born is called *bilibega*, the last-born is referred to as *codabega*. After childbirth a woman is not allowed to maintain sexual relations until she has effected the *flêcê* (offering), preferably in the church Madre de Deus. Forty-five days after childbirth at daybreak, the mother wears a black shawl and carries her baby to the church, taking a candle, charcoal, and half a bottle of palm oil, which she puts at the foot of the altar where she prays and presents her child to God. On the way to the church and back home, the woman, sometimes accompanied by her own mother, may not turn her head backward. After having prayed, the mother walks seven times around the church collecting leaves of plants, which she needs for a ritual bath at home. Thereafter she may resume her sexual activity. Baptism is a family feast engendering considerable expenses. Therefore, the ceremony is often postponed and frequently children are a few years old when they are baptized in the church. Apart from the Christian godparents whose duty it is to pay for the layette of the godchild and for the sacristan, sometimes there are an additional godmother and godfather, referred to as the *mandjam lu-lu-lu* and *pandjam lu-lu-lu*, who bury the placenta of the newborn. The godparents often come from the same family and can be children, while the Christian godparents often come from outside the immediate family and used to be of higher social status. A Catholic saint can also serve as godparent.

When a person has died, the family members light candles in the room of the deceased. The mournful news is spread by the local radio station. The following day a truck takes the coffin of the dead and the singing and crying relatives and friends dressed in black to the graveyard. Usually they bury the dead without the presence of a priest. A deceased adult who has not bore or fathered a child is buried with a flower on the coffin. Following the funeral, the mourning family stays together during a *velório* (wake) of seven days in the yard of the deceased, where the *kispa*, a covering made of palm tree branches, has been erected. Friends and neighbors constantly express their sympathy and contribute to the expenses of the funeral. The contributions

Catholic brotherhood during procession of feast of Deus Pai (June 13), Trindade, São Tomé.
Photo © Gerhard Seibert.

are registered in a copybook. In the night of the seventh day the *nozado*, a gathering in memory of the dead, takes place. However, there is no *nozado* if the dead is a child or a person without offspring. At the invitation of the mourning family the litany group (*ladaínha*) sings, the women serve coffee and food, while the men drink palm wine and *aguardente* (gin), playing the popular cardgame *bisca* 61. The following morning, the eldest son knocks three times against the wall saying: "Come with me." Thereupon, all attendants go to the church celebrating the seventh day mass. On their way to the church they may not turn backward. When they return from mass, the most intimate relatives of the dead walk three times around the house. The *nozado* recurs after the thirtieth day mass and at the end of the time of mourning. This period, during which women are dressed in black and men sometimes only wear a crape, lasts one and a half year in the case of a mother, one year and three months following a father's death, and six months for the grandparents, an aunt, uncle, parents-in-law, and elder siblings. If a young child has died, neither the parents nor the elder siblings are in mourning. The surviving dependants may hold a *nozado* annually on the day of death of the late family member. These gatherings are announced through the local radio station.

A ritual called *bócadu* held on Ash Wednesday unites all family members in the house of the oldest relative, mostly a woman. After the attendants have sung the litanies, the old woman puts dishes with the local festive food upon a mat on the ground: *angú, djogó, calulú, cozido de banana, izaquente,* and maize pudding, giving everybody a mouthful (*bócadu*) and her blessing. Due to the beginning of Lent the dishes may not contain meat. A favorite drink is palm wine, termed *vipema* in creole. One dish containing all delicacies is set apart for the relative who has died most recently. During the meal the family members entertain each other with anecdotes and small stories. The *bócadu* symbolizes the passage of the elder's wisdom to the younger generation and strengthens the unity of the family members with each other.

References

Ambrósio, António. 1985. Para a história do Folclore São-Tomense. *História* 81:60–88.

Espírito Santo, Carlos. 1998. *A Coroa do Mar*. Lisbon: Caminho.

Egzaguirre, Pablo. 1986. *Small Farmers and Estates in São Tomé, West Africa*. Unpublished Ph.D. thesis. Yale University.

Nordlund, Solveig. 1990. *An Immortal Story*. 16mm film, Torromfilm.

Perkins, Juliet. 1990. A Contribuição Portuguesa ao Tchiloli de São Tomé. *Revista do Património Histórico e Artístico Nacional*. Rio de Janeiro: Especial Issue 1990, pp. 131–141.

Reis, Fernando. 1969. *Povô Flogá. O Povo Brinca. Folclore de São Tomé e Príncipe*. São Tomé: Câmara Municipal de São Tomé.

Rosa, Luciano Catano da Rosa. 1994. *Die Lusographe Literatur der Inseln São Tomé und Príncipe: Versuch einer Literaturgeschichtlichen Darstellung*. Frankfurt on Main: Verlag Teo Ferrer de Mesquita/Domus Editoria Europaea.

Shaw, Caroline. 1996. Oral Literature and Popular Culture in Cape Verde and in São Tomé and Príncipe. *The Postcolonial Literature of Lusophone Africa*, ed. Patrick Chabal. Evanston, Ill.: Northwestern University Press.

Seibert, Gerhard. 1991. O Tchiloli de São Tomé. *História* 142:66–73.

———. 1990. Tehiloli de São Tomé et Príncipe. *Internationale de l'Imaginaire*. 14.

Tenreiro, Francisco. 1961. *A Ilha de São Tomé*. Lisbon: Junta de Investigações do Ultramar.

———. (1990) [special edition]

GERHARD SEIBERT

See also **Birth and Death Rites among the Gikuyu; Diaspora; Carnival**

REUNION

See **Indian Ocean Islands: The Process of Creolization**

RIDDLES

All African societies reveal a distinct taste for enigmatic games. These come in many forms, of which two are especially common. The first consists of a brief, enigmatic definition calling for one right answer, which in English is called a riddle. The second is a short narrative, called a dilemma tale, which proposes an unsolvable enigma for the audience to debate. Often such a tale revolves around three heroes, who accomplish extraordinary feats. The puzzle's solution may be determined by deciding which of the three is the bravest and/or the strongest. In many societies these two forms are considered as evolving from the same genre and are, in fact, designated by the same term.

Riddles are often associated with folktales; they are often told to an audience waiting for a performance to begin. The riddles sometimes carry the same name as that of the tales, although this is not the most common practice. On the other hand, they are frequently the object of the same taboos of recitation, particularly during the daytime. This genre is primarily presented as a diversion for children, with adult participation occurring only for the benefit of the children. It has all the characteristics of a game. The riddles are presented in a series of organized sessions. The search for a solution to each riddle implies competition, as everyone wants to see who will emerge victorious: the one who proposed the riddle, or the audience who guesses the correct answer.

This game often adheres to ritualistic formulas. One must formally confess to losing when one has not found the answer to the riddle. For example, with the Dyula, to express the powerlessness of the audience, one of the members of the audience says to the riddler, "Here is your house." The questioner might provide the key to the enigma when it has not been solved. The author of the riddle replies in a ritualistic manner, "I am shaking it; it bursts open," before giving the answer.

Yet behind these playful appearances, the riddles also play a pedagogical role. The enigmatic nature of these riddles rests upon a process of "veiling" through metaphor. The audience's job in coming up with the correct answer is to search for the causal relationship between the image and the object or the image and the situation it represents. The relationship between the two can be demonstrated by two forms of comparison.

A formal analogy might be used as in the following riddle which is well known in West Africa (e.g., among the Manding and Fulani [Peule] peoples). "On the road, a black thread?" with the answer: "Soldier ants." These large ants are indeed black, and they move in narrow columns which give the impression of a long thread stretching across the road. This is the most elementary degree of metaphorical analogy and therefore is the type of riddle told early on to the young.

The other type uses a functional analogy. Here it is a common function attributed to the metaphorical element and to the object to be guessed at which establishes the relation between them. For example, another Dyula riddle goes, "I went to throw out the wood. He told me to give him some water?" and the answer is "Shit." The metaphorical process at work here is found in metonymy, in the evocation of the hygenic gesture which follows defecating. To the extent that it is not simply the object which is metaphorically suggested by one of its properties but rather a function which is contingent to it, the relationship is a little more difficult to discover and a riddle of this type represents a greater degree of sophistication in the mechanism of figurative imagery.

Another form utilizes an analogical structure depending on a series of objects as well as on their relations. A Mandinka riddle proposes "The skinny bird perched on the puny tree" and its proper response is "Repayment of a debt between two bums." In this example, the skeletal nature of the tree and of the bird is the very image of poverty, whereas their respective positions (the bird perched on the tree) metaphorically recalls the relationship of creditor (the bird) to his debtor (the tree). Here is an even more elaborate degree of the metaphor process.

This game will thus be an example of a veritable exercise of reflection on the principles of the functioning of visual expression that is a fundamental trait of other more respected genres such as poems and proverbs, to which riddles are stylistically rather close. Like them, riddles are short and formulaic, frequently marked by opening formulas that function as a marker for the genre. Thus, among the Dyula, riddles almost always begin by conventional statements such as, "I went to my parents-in-law and I saw. . ." or "I went to the village" (or "to the fields" or "in the meadows") "and I saw . . ."

Riddles in African societies function, therefore, like a sort of initiation into poetic expression, fundamental and introductory to most other genres. There is a sensitivity to the formulaic properties of the signifier (symmetry, paronomasia [word play, especially puns], and alliterations) and, above all, the learning of the complex mechanisms on which the use of metaphor rests. To this effect, examining a riddle session as it takes place naturally in the center of a community is doubtlessly more revealing than analyzing a corpus of riddles classified by a theorist according to formal or thematic criteria. In effect, apart from the fact that one can often discern an agenda of progression, from simple metaphors to more complex ones, for example, the efforts of the audience to find the correct answers is likewise very instructive. In this respect, incorrect answers are often as interesting as correct answers because they reveal the inductive mechanisms by which the listeners attempt to decode the images. It is thus a truly active learning process by which the intelligence of the individual is solicited.

Riddles respond particularly well to this pedagogical function to the extent that their game-like character renders them more appealing and that the brevity of their subject matter allows them to be memorized without great difficulty by children. Children must, therefore, be exposed to this type of learning in order to be adept at subsequently comprehending what certain societies refer to as *la parole pilee* ("the compressed word," from the Gbaya of CAR) or *la parole a coque* ("the encased word" from the Mossi of Burkina Faso), that is, the word which must be broken open because it is bursting with meaning. This learning process supported by creative speech and verbal arts assists individuals in the process of socialization.

References

Bentolila, F. 1986. *Devinettes berberes*. Paris: CILF.

Dalfovo, Albert Titus. 1988. Lugbara Riddles. *Anthropos* 83:811–30.

Derive, Jean. 1980. La maison eclatee: quelques devinettes dioula de Cote d'Ivoire, In *Recueil de litterature manding*, ed. Gerard Dumestre. Paris: ACCT.

Giray-Saul, E. 1983. A West African Riddling Tradition: The Solem Kueese of the Mossi of Upper Volta. In *Cross Rhythms: Papers in African Folklore*, eds. K. Anyidoho, et al. Bloomington, Ind.: Trickster Press.

Kabira, Wanjiku, and K. Muthah. 1988. *Gikuyu Oral Literature*. Nairobi: Heinemann Kenya.

Knappert, J. "Rhyming Riddles in Swahili Songs of Secrets," *Afrika und Ubersee* 71:2.

Thomas, J. M. C. *Contes, proverbes, devinettes ou enigmes, chants er prieres Ngbaka Ma'bo*.

Yankah, Kwesi. 1983. The Poetics of the Akan Riddle, In *Cross-Rhythms: Papers in African Folklore*, eds. K. Anyidoho, et al. Bloomington, Ind.: Trickster Press.

JEAN DERIVE

See also **Folktales; Proverbs**

RIDDLES: SESOTHO RIDDLES

The Basotho are the people of the Lesotho Kingdom, which is centered in the country of Lesotho. Their name derives originally from a Swazi word, which was later adopted by King Moshoeshoe I as the unifying political term for his emerging kingdom. Sesotho refers to the language and any customs of the Basotho.

This essay is a discussion of Sesotho riddles, focusing on their source, meaning, performance, structure, and function. Sesotho riddles are games based on offering puzzles and guessing their solutions. The game is normally played by two teams of children;

one team proposes the riddles, while the other attempts to answer them. Sesotho riddles exist as a distinct and self-sustaining genre.

In some societies, the riddle consists of a question and answer; this, however, is not the case with Sesotho riddles. The first part of the riddle is always a statement. However, some riddles are interrogative in form. In such cases, the proponent requires not an answer but a solution to the proposition made.

Like proverbs, Sesotho riddles draw upon daily activities common within society. The observation of the life of familiar animals and plants is very important for the creation of riddles. Their different characteristics, features, and behaviors contribute significantly to the creation of most of the riddles. It is not only plant and animal life that is the source of riddles, but also the natural environment, material culture, and some parts of the body. New riddles are also being created from the observation of modern material culture and the new technology.

Sesotho riddles are normally played in the evening, and around the fire, especially in the winter when it is cold. The young members of the family are normally all present. An older member present does not take part, but may arbitrate if there is a misunderstanding among players. Since riddling is a competitive game, at the end of each game there is always a winning and a losing team.

The first part of the riddle is poetic; the rhythm is sustained by several poetic devices. These devices, which contribute to the poetic nature of riddles, include contrast, reduplication, ideophones, personification, repetition, and parallelism, among others. There are short and long Sesotho riddles. The first part of the riddle, which is the puzzle or the proposition, may be two words, phrases, and simple or complex sentences. The solution, which is the second part of the riddle, may also be one word, a phrase or a sentence. The following examples illustrate the various stylistic devices employed.

Contrast: Ke eloa, ke enoa.
He is there, he is here.
Solution: A road

Alliteration: Kahqa, khiqi, khopo tsa Satane.
Tightly, closed ribs of Satan.
Solution: Lehlafi la Sesotho
A traditional door made of twigs

Ideophones: Qaa, pote!
Quickly biting, it disappeared!
Solution: the flea

Repetition: Khomo ea ka ea raha le'na ka raha.
My cow kicked and I too kicked.
Solution: a pair of trousers when one dresses up

Personification:
Linese tse ngata tse kolokileng ka sepetlele li sa sisinyehe.
Many nurses standing in a row in a hospital but not moving.
Solution: teeth

First Person: Ka khanna koloi ke sa e palame.
I drove a vehicle without sitting in it.
Solution: a wheel barrow

Animalisation: Poho ea khonya mohlakeng.
The bull bellowed at the meadow.
Solution: an adze

Augmentative: Thota e shoeshoe e'ngoe.
A valley with one flower.
Solution: the moon or the navel

Parallelism: Se re se ea koana e ke se tla koano.
Going that way as if coming this way.
Solution: vehicle

Metaphor: Bukana-se-bula-likeiti.
The booklet, the opener of gates.
Solution: passport

Sesotho riddles are games of entertainment and excitement, which teach players to be observant of their surroundings and the society's daily activities. Riddling creates a spirit of competitiveness among players and a spirit of togetherness for those who find themselves in the same team. Like proverbs, riddles are stylistic in form. Their performance has much social importance as well as entertainment value for the children who participate in their enactment.

References

Guma, S. M. n.d. *The Form, Content and Technique of Traditional Literature of Southern Sotho.* Pretoria: Van Schaik.
Mokitimi, MI. 1993. The Sesotho Proverb as a Poetic Text. *South African Journal of African Languages* 3:96–100.
Okpewho, Isidore. 1993. *African Oral Literature.* Bloomington Indiana University Press.
Segoete, Everitt. 1995. *Raphepheng.* Morija. Morija Sesuto Book Depot.

MAKALI I. MOKITIMI

See also **Linguistics and African Verbal Arts; Proverbs; Southern Africa: Overview**

RITUAL PERFORMANCE

A ritual performance marks a meaningful social event or transition through various kinds of coordinated and individual actions. As occasions or events, ritual performances are often considered emotionally or esthetically heightened occasions as well. Performance and performance analysis also have more specialized, technical senses in fields such as folklore, anthropology, religious studies, and art history, where they refer to a mode of analyzing rituals and ceremonies.

Types of Ritual Performance in Africa

Ritual performances in Africa exhibit even greater diversity than African cultures and histories in general. In different African societies, different changes and occasions may be recognized through ritual performance as culturally important. Cultural definitions and understandings of these changes and occasions vary widely in different places and times, although some types of rites manifest structural similarities and have some symbolic themes in common. At any point in history, people in particular African societies also recognize and practice a number of different ritual performances. These might be concerned with religion, healing, political and family relations, individual and social transformations, and other matters as well. In most cases, ritual performances involve several of these domains at once. They could include initiation into new statuses, associations, or offices, funerals, marriages, other rites of passage, calendrical rites, healing rituals, masquerades, and other kinds of ritual occasions.

Ritual performances often include diverse ritual events, activities, and objects, special ways of speaking, songs, dances, and distinctive costumes, built structures, and locales. In different regions and different African societies, these diverse media are organized in particular dramatic configurations, incorporating distinctive meanings and references to specific social environments, histories, and cultural philosophies. Feasting and celebration are normally part of the occasion as well, which increases the number of people involved.

The Otjiserandu Commemorations of the Herero people of Namibia and Botswana provide one example. During this ceremony, Herero communities come together to remember those who died in the war with the German colonial presence in the territory (a war which saw the first genocide of the twentieth century, in which 80 percent of the Herero nation perished). Practiced annually since the 1923 death of paramount chief Samuel Maherero, the commemorations are also known as "flag ceremonies" because the several communities that comprise the Herero people are commonly referred to as different "flags." These ritual performances take place over several days and include dancing, marching, horseback riding, striking dress, praise songs, prayers, speeches, and observances at ancestral graves. The Otjiserandu Commemorations focus on remembrance and identity, at once honoring nineteenth and twentieth century heroes, and constituting contemporary social groups and relations; they are also deeply enmeshed with contemporary political life in Namibia.

Initiation into adulthood is one of the most widespread rites of passage in Africa. Many societies have a history of both male and female initiation, including Maasai and Kikuyu in Kenya, Ndebele in southern Africa, and Kuranko in Sierra Leone. While others practice male initiation only (e.g., Afikpo Igbo in Nigeria, Wagenia of the Democratic Republic of the Congo), initiation for women alone is rare. In all cases, notions of personhood and ethnic identity are fundamental to initiation into adulthood. Initiation marks social maturity and the end of childhood, but people in different societies see adulthood as beginning at different ages and stages of biological maturation. In Kenya, for example, Kisii people initiate their children at around eight years old (younger than in precolonial times), while Maasai initiate children into adulthood between fifteen and eighteen years of age. Ritual performances associated with initiation into adulthood are a focus of elaborate attention in some societies, while for others they are a relatively minor occasion.

Political transitions are also occasions marked by ritual performances, illustrating another type of initiation and rite of passage. These performances help to legitimate the office involved, whether it is chief, king, association head, or another position. They also validate the person who assumes office as an appropriate office bearer and confer on them both rights and duties of office. The person involved thus takes on a new social identity and enters into social relations that make him or her accountable to various constituencies (and vice versa). At the same time, these ritual performances might provide occasions through which participants contest issues of succession and influence and reinterpret historical relations and precedents. They might also be seen as ritually cleansing and restoring society after an uncertain interim between office bearers.

Herero women in distinctive dress watch men preparing to march during the Otjiserandu Commemorations at Okahandja, Namibia, 2001.
Photo © Casper W. Erichsen.

Many such roles and ritual performances in Africa have combined political, economic, and religious concerns, from precolonial times to the present, though the specific nature of these concerns may change over time. This can be seen, for instance, in installation ceremonies for the Oba of the Yoruba people in Nigeria, the king of Bamum in Cameroon, or the Kabaka of the Baganda people of Uganda (recently allowed to hold office again by the national government). The pageantry of the ritual performance represents and invokes the range of social groups and relations involved, as well as the moral values that support the office and relations. In Swazi society, the king participates in an elaborate annual ritual performance called Nc'wala that strengthens him and his position and renews and cleanses the entire kingdom. In contemporary African nation states, presidential inaugurations and national celebrations are also related ritual performances. Initially created at and after independence, they often draw on the symbolism of these other, long-standing political rituals as well as aspects of European state pageantry and more recently developed ceremonial forms.

Healing rituals constitute another important and extremely varied kind of ritual performance common throughout Africa. In many cases these are relatively small-scale ceremonies that chiefly involve close family members and perhaps a consulting medical specialist. One such example from the Ga people in Ghana is the cleansing rite called *naabu daimo*, which might be prescribed by a spirit medium for various ailments. Participants in the ritual performance might include only two or three family members in addition to the spirit medium. Like other ritual performances, however, it has a complex structure combining many elements and media, including incantations, libations, proverbs, and ritual acts, objects, and places. In other cases, however, healing rituals can be elaborate events that incorporate entire village sections, extended families, or draw people from a number of different villages and towns. Anthropologist Victor Turner has described such occasions of ritual performance in Ndembu villages in northwestern Zambia in the early 1950s. These "rituals of affliction" included many different kinds of performance, including specific rites for various maladies and

misfortunes, such as hunting problems or reproductive troubles. In each case diagnosis drew attention to certain ancestor spirits. The patient was treated by people who once suffered the same problems themselves, and who had thus become adepts in the ritual, forming an association or cult defined by their common affliction. The entire process could take several days, and rituals could be repeated or new ones tried if the patient did not improve. After going through the performance, the patient also became a member of the group, and could participate in ritual performances for healing others.

In many parts of Africa, spirit possession cults are also related to healing, with members recruited in a similar way. The presence of a spirit is initially manifested through health problems. These are treated through ritual performance in which the spirit involved possesses the patient for the first time, is identified and appeased, and the patient is incorporated into the group. In most cases, the patient develops a continuing relation with the possessing spirit, as in Bori cults in Niger. In different societies, the spirits may represent gods, ancestors, or be associated with other historical beings. Among the Iteso of western Kenya, for instance, there are two sorts of possession spirits, local spirits of the dead (*ipara*), and spirits of other ethnicities, said to be the spirits of strangers once killed by Iteso and named after rivers and spirits found among neighboring peoples. During ritual performance, a number of different spirits may possess those attending. This is common in many other parts of Africa where possession exists as well, such as *zar* cults in the northern Sudan. In most cases, these ritual performances include singing, dancing, special forms of speech, offerings, types of dress particular to individual spirits, and objects with symbolic meanings specific to their cultural settings.

Though far from exhaustive, this brief set of examples provides an initial sense of the range, variety, and importance of ritual performance in Africa. Ritual performance usually represents and recreates key moral values and social relations. The precise nature of those values and relations and the ways that they are represented and invoked vary in different African societies and depend on the type of ritual performance. Through performance people give these values and relations an embodied sense that differs from (but draws on) other contexts and experiences of daily life. At the same time, ritual performance heightens their emotional and aesthetic impact. In this way, ritual performances can often help produce a sense that the existing organization of social life is a natural order, the way it should be. At the same time, however, ritual performances can also provide a forum where contradictions of social organization and problems in social relations can be raised and addressed, if not resolved. Similarly, while the social transformations accomplished through ritual performances can simultaneously help create and legitimate differences of status, power, and authority based on gender, age, caste, wealth, ethnicity, or other criteria, the performances might also incorporate settings where such differences and values are challenged by people who usually have no opportunity to do so. People participate in diverse social interactions during ritual performances, which can also become occasions through which participants continue and sometimes mediate social conflicts over many issues. Ritual performances also contribute to a number of other social and psychological processes, which vary according to specific context, society, and occasion.

It is important to note that at times ritual performances can also be enormously entertaining social events for those participating.

Some events, activities, songs, speech genres, and so forth, might be unique to a particular kind of ritual performance in a community. However, other aspects of the many media and events combined in ritual performance may not be limited to those contexts, forging links to other occasions and types of expressive culture. For instance, the Okiek people of Kenya sing dozens of songs of several different genres when they initiate children into adulthood through ritual performance. Many of these are particular to initiation, with some specific to ceremonies for either boys or girls. Yet other songs are sung during other ritual performances as well, creating continuities and relations between initiation and other Okiek life cycle rituals. Similarly, the ritual *mabwaita* shrine is constructed not only during initiation, but on a wide range of other occasions.

Masquerade performances common in many parts of western Africa provide further examples of the ways that expressive forms and media can both distinguish particular types of ritual performance and link them to other domains of life and performance. One of the best known art works of the Baga people in Guinea, for example, is D'mba, a female figure that idealizes the role of mother (and known in most art historical literature as Nimba). Worn and danced with a raffia and cloth costume, D'mba appears at a number of life cycle events (births, marriages, and wakes) and harvest festivals, as well as secular receptions held to welcome visiting dignitaries. The way that D'mba is incorporated into each type of ritual performance, however, and the other aspects with which it is combined in each case identify and differentiate the occasions. In Nigeria, the masquerades of the Igbo peoples show enormous regional variety in form, history, and particular characters represented, though most masks are understood to be manifestations of supernatural and ancestral spirits. Different age-grades of men dance different masks, each with specified occasions for performing, such as agricultural festivals and life cycle rituals.

People throughout Africa often consider some of their ritual performances to be central to their cultural tradition, history,

Herero men wear uniforms that indicate their "flag" to march to the grave of late Paramount Chief Samuel Maherero, during the Otjiserandu Commemorations at Okahandja, Namibia, 2001. *Photo © Casper W. Erichsen.*

and ethnic identity, but ceremonies are not unchanging. As historical and social circumstances alter over time, people may change aspects and interpretations of their ritual performance. Igbo masquerades, for instance, incorporated many new characters and costume types during the twentieth century, and the size of masks themselves also increased. Some Igbo masquerade performances have also increasingly become a kind of secular entertainment.

The Nc'wala ceremony of the Ngoni people of eastern Zambia also illustrates historical transformations in a ritual performance regarded as an icon of tradition and identity within the community. Related to the Swazi Nc'wala ceremony described above, the Ngoni developed their own version of Nc'wala after they settled in this area in the late nineteenth century. Originally a first fruits celebration, the Nc'wala ceremony was one way through which they established and maintained political control there. Colonial and postcolonial governments banned Ngoni ritual performance from about 1900 until 1980, when the annual ceremony was revived. In its current form, the Nc'wala is a ritual performance that displays and helps to create Ng'oni identity within the Zambian state, but the performance also includes political officials in ways that simultaneously evoke images of national unity. Some Ngoni have made efforts to promote the event as a tourist attraction as well.

Writing the histories of the diverse traditions of ritual performance in Africa is an important task for further research in folklore, anthropology, and art history. An essential element of that, and equally important in its own right, is scholarly work that seeks to understand the structures, meanings, and experience of ritual performance as expressive culture and social action. Both of these tasks are included by the approaches in the fields of folklore and anthropology known as performance analysis.

Performance Analysis

Performance analysis seeks to understand the ways that people produce structure, process, and meaning in ritual performance by examining particular occasions and specific examples. This concern with actual performances foregrounds processual and temporal processes and emphasizes empirical, ethnographic research. The approach situates the occasions in their cultural and sociological contexts, analyzes the multiple expressive forms, media, and actors involved, and usually considers poetic and aesthetic aspects of ritual performance. Performance analysis also recognizes the emergent and creative aspects of ritual, exploring the imaginative variation, adaptation, and improvisation incorporated into ritual performance in different cultures and settings. Performance analysis diverges from approaches that define ritual as tradition-bound repetition, unchanging in form and sequence. Performance analysis has also been applied to storytelling, music, dance, festivals, and other expressive forms.

Performance analysis emerged as a recognized approach in the 1970s, initially rooted in attempts in folklore and anthropology to incorporate greater concern with context and move away from approaches that relied chiefly on text analysis, in dramaturgical models in social theory, and in the contrast between competence and performance drawn by linguist Noam Chomsky. Later, scholars in theater studies such as Richard Scheckner also contributed to the emerging synthesis. In folklore and anthropology, Dell Hymes, Richard Bauman, and Roger Abrahams were particularly central at the time in developing this mode of performance analysis. Earlier anthropological work on myth, ritual, and symbolism provided a strong foundation for them, including work by two prominent Africanists: Victor Turner's analyses of Ndembu ceremonies in Zambia in the early 1950s, and Audrey Richard's study of Bemba girls' initiation in Zambia (then Rhodesia) in the 1930s. Both Richards and Turner described and analyzed actual ceremonies in detail, including indigenous commentaries on ritual symbols and procedures. Turner's work in symbolic analysis converged with a growing concern with communicative and semiotic frameworks, bringing greater attention and prominence to performance analysis in ritual studies.

Considering specific ritual performances as actualized can show the ways that ritual structure emerges and changes. At the same time, it can also highlight less-structured, unexpected, and contradictory aspects of ritual. The multiple perspectives and experiences inherent in ritual performance should be prominent in performance analysis. At times these different perspectives diverge and can reveal tensions among the actors and interests involved, differences of power, contradictions within the cultural values and social relations that inform the ritual, and historical shifts in ritual procedures and interpretations. Further development of performance analysis in the 1990s has included greater attention to wider scale political, economic, and historical processes that help to shape ritual performance, as well as continued attention to the relations among esthetics, cultural values and meaning, and social life.

References

Abrahams, Roger. 1972. Folklore and Literature as Performance. *Journal of the Folklore Institute* 8:75–94.

Bauman, Richard. 1977. *Verbal Art as Performance*. Rowley, Mass: Newbury House.

———. 1992. Performance. In *Folklore, Cultural Performances, and Popular Entertainments*, ed. Richard Bauman. New York: Oxford University Press.

Bauman, Richard, and Charles Briggs. 1990. Poetics and Performance as Critical Perspectives on Language and Social Life. *Annual Review of Anthropology* 19:59–88.

Beidelman, T.O. 1966. Swazi Royal Ritual. *Africa*. 36, no. 4:373–405.

Boddy, Janice. 1989. *Wombs and Alien Spirits: Women, Men, and the Zar Cult in Northern Sudan*. Madison: University of Wisconsin Press.

Cole, Herbert, and Chike Aniakor. 1984. *Igbo Arts: Community and Cosmos*. Los Angeles: Museum of Cultural History.

Drewal, Margaret. 1991. The State of Research on Performance in Africa. *African Studies Review*, 34, no.3: 1–65.

Fitzgerald, Dale. 1975. The Language of Ritual Events among the Ga of Southern Ghana. In *Sociocultural Dimensions of Language Use*, ed. M. Sanches and B. Blount. New York: Academic Press.

Fortes, Meyer. 1962. Ritual and Office in Tribal Society. In *Essays on the Ritual of Social Relations*, ed. M. Gluckman. Manchester: Manchester University Press.

Hendrickson, Hildi. 1996. Bodies and Flags: The Representation of Herero Identity in Colonial Namibia. In *Clothing and Differences*, ed. Hildi Hendrickson. Durham: Duke University Press.

Karp, Ivan. 1990. Power and Capacity in Iteso Ritual Possession. In *Personhood and Agency: The Experience of Self and Other in African Cultures*, ed. Michael Jackson and Ivan Karp. Stockholm: Almqvist and Wiksell International.

Kratz, Corinne A. 1993. *Affecting Performance: Meaning, Movement, and Experience in Okiek Women's Initiation*. Washington, D.C.: Smithsonian Institution Press.

Lamp, Frederick. 1996. *The Art of Baga*. New York: The Museum for African Art.

Richards, Audrey. 1956. *Chisungu*. London: Faber and Faber.

Turner, Victor. 1967. *Forest of Symbols*. Ithaca: Cornell University Press.

———. 1968. *Drums of Affliction*. Oxford: Clarendon Press.

———. 1969. *The Ritual Process*. Chicago: Aldine.

———. 1982. *From Ritual to Theater*. New York: PAJ Publications.

CORINNE A. KRATZ

See also **Divination; Initiation; Islamic Brotherhoods; Performance in Africa; Spirit Possession; Theater**

RWANDA (REPUBLIC OF RWANDA)

Located in southeastern Africa and landlocked by Uganda, Tanzania, Burundi, and the Democratic Republic of Congo, Rwanda is a temperate country of over 7 million people. Kigali, the capital and largest city, has a population of 257,000. The majority of Rwandans are of the Hutu group (89%), while 10 percent are Tutsi, and 1 percent are Twa. The nation's major languages are Kinyarwanda, French, Kiswahili, and English. Sixty-five percent of the population is Roman Catholic, 25 percent practice traditional indigenous religions, 9 percent are Protestant, and 1 percent is Muslim.

Once a harmonious multiethnic hierarchical society, Rwanda began to unravel in 1959 when the Hutu overthrew the Tutsi monarchy. On July 1, 1962, Rwanda gained its independence from Belgium after forty-six years of colonization. Within ten years, ethnic violence began. The years since independence became increasingly violent and, in the 1994, the Hutu-dominated government, assisted by French military "advisers," initiated a hundred-day genocide, during which an estimated one million Tutsis and politically moderate Hutus were murdered. Animosity between the Hutu and Tutsi groups is a result of the nation's colonial history. In precolonial times, the Tutsi traditionally acted as the aristocratic "protectors" of the Hutu "clients" who herded cattle and provided other services for the Tutsi elite, while the Twa, a pygmy group, were the hunters. This feudal system was manipulated by Rwanda's German colonizers and later by the Belgians, who used as the popular "divide and conquer" tactic of administering colonial rule.

In 1961, pre-independence elections implemented Gregoire Kayibanda's Hutu Emancipation Movement; the Tutsi lost their dominant position to the Hutu. Upon this reversal of powers came violent backlashes against the former Tutsi elite. Violence escalated for over thirty years and culminated in the 1994 genocide. It is estimated that over one million were killed in 1994 and approximately 2 million of the nation's citizens live in exile in neighboring countries. Despite recent trials of the War Crimes Commission, peace has not yet returned to the war-torn country. Rwanda's health system, infrastructure, government, economy, culture, and society have all suffered traumatic losses as a result of 1994's violent events.

Rwanda's natural resources include tungsten, tin, and cassiterite, while the agricultural sector produces coffee, tea, pyrethrum, beans, and potatoes. Principle industries of the nation are mining, food processing, and light consumer goods.

Rwandan poet Abbe Alexis Kagame is internationally renowned for his poetry and studies of traditional Rwandan poetry. Some of his works have been translated into French from Kinyarwanda, Rwanda's official language.

JENNIFER JOYCE

RWANDA: TALES OF GENOCIDE

Folklore has it that Watutsi (or Tutsi) cattle breeders began arriving in this area of central Africa from the Horn of Africa in the fifteenth century, whereupon they gradually subjugated the majority Hutu inhabitants. The Tutsis established a monarchy headed by an *umwami* (king) and a feudal hierarchy of Tutsi nobles and gentry. Through a contract known as *ubuhake*, the Hutu farmers pledged their services and those of their descendants to a Tutsi lord, in return for the loan of cattle and use of pastures and arable land. Thus, the Tutsi reduced the Hutu to virtual serfdom. The earliest known inhabitants of what is now Rwanda were the Batwa Pygmies, an ethnic group that still lives in the country today but makes up only 1 percent of the population. The Batwa held sway over much of the mountainous terrain until around the eleventh century, when Hutu farmers migrated into the region and displaced them. A few hundred years later, the Hutus were subjugated by the warriorlike and pastoralist Tutsis, who established their harsh system of feudalism on the area.

The Tutsi reign was characterized by the absolute rule of the *umwami* who, with a great amount of religious ceremony and formal conqueror's pomp, oversaw the extraction of labor from the Hutus and determined which of them received land, and how much was allotted to them. The status quo remained until a couple of European powers, namely Britain and Germany, decided to apportion large swathes of eastern Africa in the late nineteenth century. The British gained Uganda and Kenya, while the Germans took Burundi and Rwanda.

German colonialism was accompanied by the coming of Christian missionaries in this area. The influence of Germany on the territory came to an abrupt halt in the second decade of the twentieth century, when the end of World War I forced it to hand over all of its African territories to the League of Nations.

The League of Nations promptly allotted Rwanda to Belgium; apparently this was an earnest token of reparation to Belgium for its suffering during the war. No such political compassion was applied to the Africans, however, who subsequently remained the victims of European colonialism.

The Belgians found it administratively convenient to not only uphold, but also increase, the power of the Tutsis in Rwanda, allowing the tribal minority to enjoy even fuller control of the country's bureaucratic, military and educational systems and, by extension, the large Hutu population. The Belgian-backed Tutsi leadership began to unravel in the late 1950s, when Hutus started demanding improvements in their living conditions and an easing of their ethnic suppression. The response from a newly empowered and particularly ruthless Tutsi clan in 1959 was to resist. However, this course of action failed to subdue the Hutus. In the ensuing conflict, an estimated 100,000 Tutsis were massacred, and many fled into exile. The restive Hutu population initiated a revolt in November 1959, resulting in the overthrow of the Tutsi monarchy. Since then, there have continued to be periods of violent turmoil.

With some 8 million inhabitants, Rwanda was until recently one of the world's most densely populated countries. The Batwa make up only 1 percent, whereas the Hutu and Tutsi comprise 85 percent and 14 percent, respectively, of the total population in Rwanda.

Rwandans speak Kinyarwanda, and most of them are Christians, although some still practice their traditional religion. Nevertheless, the Batwa people stand out in terms of cultural distinctiveness. Batwa tradition is rich in song, dance, and music, and cultural gatherings are firmly integrated in the social life of the Batwa. The Batwa form an isolated and marginalized group in Rwandan society. Traditionally, other groups look down upon them as uncultured and unclean. It is within this political and cultural atmosphere that folklore of the Rwandans is created and celebrated.

The Rwandans, like other African peoples, have a rich tradition of folkloristic materials. These materials serve as the reservoir of the people's values and history. Being an oral culture, with very few individuals literate, these materials serve to also express the ethical code and hopes of the people. Folklore is deeply embedded in Rwandan daily life.

It is notable, however, that scholarly studies of folkloristic material remain sparse. Despite having oral folktales, riddles, proverbs, and songs, which are integrated in the peoples' way of life, very little meaningful study has been carried out on these materials. New genres of folklore, such as the confession or the individual life experience story, have evolved in the tumultuous era of genocide, but these developments have not been extensively studied by folklorists.

In terms of material culture, the Rwandans produce many beautiful crafts. Women weave baskets and mats from banana leaves, grasses, and papyrus fibers. Geometrical designs, usually in black, white and red, are often woven into these objects. It is considered a sign of wealth and status to own many decorated baskets and mats. Men do wood carving and make drums pipes for smoking, as well as stools, knives, handles, bowls, and jugs.

Many traditional musical instruments are played in Rwanda. Stringed instruments such as the *lulunga* (an eight-stringed instrument similar to a harp) accompany singing and dancing. The *mbira* or *kalimba* is a thumb piano. Flutes are made from reeds. Drums are very important in Rwandan music and drummers often play in groups of seven or nine. The drums are of different sizes and each produces a distinct tone. Together the drummers produce a complex rhythm.

Rwanda also has a rich tradition of stories and folklore. Storytelling and public speaking are much admired and good storytellers are honored. Many stories have a message and are used to teach values such as cooperation or generosity. Other stories tell of the exploits of heroes or the suffering caused by evil spirits. Some stories are deliberately suppressed, however, since they glorify the Tutsi feudal system that was overthrown by the Hutu in 1959.

Rwandan ethnic groups, namely the Batwa, the Hutu, and the Tutsi, have a well-developed and sophisticated folklore, which embodies their history, traditions, mores, worldview, and wisdom. Their legends recount the movement of people to and from the rift valley, into the hills, the grasslands, and the lake regions. Famous historical individuals are represented in myths and legends. Myths include accounts of how cattle were given to a certain people by God, so when they went on cattle raids they were merely taking back what was rightfully theirs. Folktales try to answer etymological questions, such as why the hyena has a limp, and the origin of death. In Rwandan culture the message that men would not die was given to a chameleon, but he was so slow that a bird got to man before him and gave them the message that men would die. Folktales also recount the adventures of tricksters. In Rwanda, tricksters are usually the hare or the tortoise.

The Rwandans have a large store of riddles, proverbs, and sayings, which are still an important aspect of daily speech. Riddles are usually exchanged in the evening before a storytelling session. Riddling sessions are usually competitions between two young people who fictionally bet villages, or cattle, or other items of economic life on the outcome. In Rwandan culture, as in other African cultures, riddling during daylight hours is prohibited.

Proverbs are social phenomena; they can be defined as messages coded by tradition and transmitted in order to evaluate human behavior. Proverbs reveal key elements of a culture, such as the position and influence of women, morality, what is considered appropriate behavior, and the importance of children. The proverbs are woven in day-to-day speech.

The Rwandan Muslims have a rich oral tradition that has been influenced by Islam. Stories of genies are told along with stories of the Hare and the Hyena. There is also a very rich tradition of popular poetry that has been part of Swahili cultural life for over four centuries.

Rwandan radio and television shows use folklore as part of their daily programming. Oral literature is part of the university syllabus. Part of the requirement in these classes is for students to collect folklore from their community and subject them to analysis—the beginning of a scholarly tradition. Literate Rwandans believe that folklore is an important part of their heritage and culture and are taking steps to preserve and encourage folklore and education. While global culture in the shape of movies, music, and written literature is replacing folklore, Rwandans are actively involved in its maintenance. These materials call for critical study.

References

Finnegan, Ruth. 1970. *Oral Literature in Africa*. London: Oxford University Press.

Knappert, Jan. 1979. *Four Centuries of Swahili Verse: A Literary History and Anthology*. London: Heinemann.

Okpewho Isidore. 1983. *Myth in Africa*. Cambridge: Cambridge University Press.

EGARA KABAJI

See also **Central African Folklore: Overview; East African Folklore: Overview; Folktales**

S

SAHIR (EVIL MOUTH)

Gaze and Utterance in Evil Eye Scholarship

Sahir (Evil Mouth) is a concept related to the Evil Eye, a belief of the Muslim Arabs of northern Sudan. The casting of the Evil Eye is attributed to utterances in the form of metaphors, rather than the literal gaze of one's eye. A common situation in which these dramatic metaphors are used is a speech event involving the speaker (*sahhar*) of the metaphor, a victim (the subject of the metaphor), and an audience. In a sahir situation, a sahhar attempts to cast the metaphor at persons or objects by comparing them to something else. One example involves the story of a sahhar who saw two healthy children dressed in red shorts and shirts. He said to their father, "Your children look like Union Carbide batteries (commonly red in color)." The children are said to have then caught a strange stomach disease, and they died two days later. Accounts of these situations circulate in the form of a genre called *sahra*.

The evil mouth has been regarded as "subordinate to [the Evil Eye] and a marginal relative to it" (Flores-Meiser 1976). The emphasis in Evil Eye scholarship has been on the gaze rather than on the evil mouth. This emphasis may be because the European perspective is more vision-centered—looking and staring are said to have a more constant and generally defined value than the utterance (Spooner 1976). The existence of the phenomenon of the evil mouth in Arab and Muslim contexts has been noted by Edward Westermarck (1926, Vol. 2). He points to the belief in the evil mouth among the Moroccans, and how they greatly feared the utterance when combined with a look.

A Performance-Centered Approach to Sahir

Ideally, sahir is a performance in which a competence, albeit deadly, is displayed. It involves an actor, an audience, a subject, and a judgment. As a performance, it is keyed and can be disclaimed (Bauman 1977). Besides the social risks that sahhars take, sahir involves the common risks of performance, in that it is an assumption of responsibility for a display of competence before an audience.

A sahhar initiates a sahir event by offering a simile that likens the physical attributes and actions of a subject (person or object) to something else. When the subject is a person or the property of a person, that person will normally utter or perform traditional invocations to protect himself or his property from the adverse consequences of sahir. The audience, on the other hand, laughs at good similes, though they are not unaware of the evil consequences that may result, or that the subject claims may result, from sahir.

Situations of Sahir

The sahhar may utter the sahir voluntarily, or he may be pressured into uttering it. Understandably, sahhars concur that they are at their best in the former situation. People agree that a sahhar wears on his face an expression that shifts between a smile and suppressed laugh when he has finished mentally conjuring up his simile. Recognizing this expression as a key to performance, the audience then urges him to utter his sahir.

Sahir emerges out of a variety of situations. A sahhar may be invited to speak sahir. Occasionally people ask him to *yashar* (bewitch) persons or objects that look a little odd or different. Furthermore, a sahhar may be provoked into saying sahir. One man with curled, grey hair got on the nerves of a sahhar, who then said, "Get off my back with your hair that looks like the vapor arising from hot porridge." Those who are exceptionally scared of sahir are the most exposed to this kind of sahir. Sahir may also arise from a competition between sahhars called for by a leading practitioner of their art. People of a village may also ask a visiting sahhar to compete in sahir with their local sahhar. Interestingly, a victim may hire a sahhar to cast the Evil Eye on a sahhar who hurt him or her before.

There are two typical situations in which a sahhar may disclaim his or her performance. The first is when he has been asked by the audience to bewitch somebody or something. The sahhar may begin by saying "Ashar layk or layh shinu" (What am I to bewitch you/him/it for, a sahir would be wasted on you/him/it), and then utter the sahir metaphor anyway. The second situation in which disclaimers are used to preface sahras is when someone, either in anticipation of sahir or because he is exceptionally afraid of sahir, asks the sahhar in advance "Ma tasharni" (Don't bewitch me).

Response to Sahir

The responses of the targets of sahir range from laughing to actually fighting with the sahhar. A laughing response, however,

Wad al-Tom of Atmur village and the "dean" of *sahhars* (those who assault with words).
Photo © Corinne A. Kratz.

A plate plastered above a door to divert the evil eye.
Photo © Abdullahi A. Ibrahim.

does not mean that the subject may not later have second thoughts about the effect of sahir. Occasionally, the subject can react with violence. A sahhar may actually find it necessary to flee the scene to avoid retaliation. A subject may choose to reprove a sahhar for making him a target of his metaphor. He may tell the sahhar that he is genuinely scared of sahir and indicate to him the kind of miseries it causes him, such as headaches and the like. Another possible tactic for victims is to complain to the sahhar's elders. Villagers may, however, impose unannounced sanctions, such as "taking another road if they happen to meet with sahhars," as it is usually expressed. The magnitude of such sanctions may account for the decision of many aging *sahhars* to quit this particular vocation.

In order to stop the *sahra*, or to forestall its adverse consequences after its utterance, the target or victim may perform various prophylactic rituals. The *sahhars*, who are especially insulted by these prophylactic measures, make these countermeasures in turn the object of their ridiculing "meta-sahra."

Evaluation of Sahir
Audiences penalize incompetent sahhars for flaws in their display of competence, either by token laughter or by not laughing at all. Poor sahir metaphors are ignored, and therefore do not become popular. When someone attempts sahir, but fails with the audience, he may be asked to take it to Wad al-Tom, the master of the genre, to "grade" it for him. There is a hierarchy within the sahir profession. *Sahhars* apparently always have a "dean," recognized by his peers and by the people at large. To test and "license" sahhars, a dean may identify bewitching targets for them to see how well they do. A meta-sahra acknowledges one of these deans as "the gas tank from which other sahhars pump gas (that is, sahir)" (Ibrahim 1994).

Besides laughter, a successful sahra is rewarded with praise for its precision. The criterion of exact similitude in guessing out analogues is paramount for the audience. For example, one sahhar was asked by some of his audience to show them exactly how the terms of one of his sahir metaphors matched.

The audience expresses its appreciation of sahir through gun metaphors. Their delight in the exactitude of the metaphor is expressed in terms of "shooting the target dead," and audiences normally punctuate their laughter with expressions such as "he killed him," "have mercy on him," or "you are really bad!" An audience may also praise the power of sahir metaphor by uttering the *tawidhah* (a religious prophylactic). *Sahhars* themselves sometimes take such utterances as indicators of the audience's appreciation of their satanic power.

Sahir emerges as a continuum ranging from the evil gaze to the articulated metaphor. However, the most evil sahir is held to be the staring kind, that is, the one that has not been articulated. It is likened to a shot from a pistol with a silencer.

Debating Sahir's Efficacy
Northern Sudanese debate the efficacy of sahir. Sahhars, of course, object to being accused of possessing the *'ayn hara*. Instead, they argue that sahir stems from an irresistible imaginative urge, and is not from *fakr* (envy). For them, sahir is the creation of an artful mind. It is *wanasa* (whiling away time), or a joke that is meant to make people laugh. Sahhars may concede a degree of evilness to their sahir (they usually confess this rather jokingly). A sadhar may argue that his own sahir metaphors are mild, attributing more dangerous powers to rival *sahhars*. A sahhar jokingly described the sahir of one of his colleagues as *kaab* (really evil), like the sting of a scorpion, while his own was only like a prick of a water crab. A sahhar may similarly describe his sahir as buckshot compared to the bullet shot of other sahhars.

An attractive hypothesis, espoused mainly by the sahhars themselves, speculates that affliction falls only on those who are really scared of sahir. It is either a coincidence or a sabab (cause or agency), referring to the belief that every occurrence is predestined by Allah, and that natural causation and people's actions are mere agents for the predestined to take place. *Sahhars* may also point to a rational cause for an inadequacy or a misfortune held to result from sahir.

References
Bauman, Richard. 1977. *Verbal Art as Performance*. Rowley, Mass.: Newbury House.

Flores-Meiser, Enya. 1976. The Hot Mouth and Evil Eye. In *The Evil Eye*. Ed. by Clarence Maloney. New York: Columbia University Press.

Ibrahim, Abdullahi. 1994. *Assaulting with Words: Popular Discourses and the Bridle of Shari'ah*. Evanston, Ill: Northwestern University Press.

Spooner, Brian. 1976. Anthropology and the Evil Eye. In *The Evil Eye*. Ed. by Clarence Maloney. New York: Columbia University Press.

Westermarck, Edward. 1926. *Rituals and Belief in Morocco*. Vol. 2. London: Macmillan.

ABDULLAHI ALI IBRAHIM

See also **Evil Eye; Insults and Ribald Language; Performance in Africa**

SAN

See **Dance; Music in Africa; Southern African Oral Traditions**

SANTERIA IN CUBA

Afro-Cuban Santeria, also known as La Regla de Ocha, La Religion Lucumi, and El Santo, is a highly systematized and dynamic modern African diaspora religion that is widely practiced well beyond the island of Cuba, by tens of thousands of ethnically diverse people in the United States, Puerto Rico, Panama, Venezuela, Columbia, Mexico, and Spain. The religion is grounded in reworked Yoruba patterns of cosmology, philosophy, initiation, priesthood, divination, sacrifice, pharmacology, ritual language, praise song repertoire, drumming, dance movement, spirit possession, iconography, and altar assemblage. During the period of Spanish colonial rule, which ended in 1898, Santeria incorporated elements of Cuban popular religion and material culture, including the devotions of local Catholic saints, their festival calendar, and their Baroque religious esthetic. It drew on other religious systems, such as the Kardecian Spiritist system of mediumship for communicating with the dead. However, many initiates since the 1960s, particularly the descendants of the nationalist Black American Yoruba Movement and other ideologically antisyncretic Cuban, American, and Puerto Rican constituencies, have sought to realign the practice with its West African origins.

History

Members of the Yoruba-speaking subgroups, as well as many of their close neighbors to the west and north who also embarked from the Bight of Benin, became known as Lucumi, an ethnonym derived from the name of an ancient West African kingdom between Ardra and Benin (Ulcumi, Oulcoumi), an early nickname for Yoruba-speaking peoples, and the Yoruba greeting, *olukumi* (my friend). The Lucumi organized themselves into societies and clubs called *cabildos*, some of which were attached to the Catholic church and tended devotions of patron saints, such as the Sociedad de Socorros Mutuos Nacion Lucumi bajo la advocacion de Santa Barbara (Society of Mutual Aid of the Lucumi Nation under the Advocation of Santa Barbara) founded in Havana in 1820 (Ortiz 1951). The *cabildos* were "incubating cells" of the modern *casa-templos* (house-temples) of Yoruba-derived religious practice in Cuba (Palmie 1993). The emergent modern Afro-Cuban religious systems became known as *reglas* (orders), after the *relamentos* (charters) that governed *cabildo* life (Murphy 1988, 33). The Lucumi religion was called La Regla Lucumi or La Regla de Ocha (a contraction of the Lucumi term for deity, *orisha* [Yoruba, *orisha*]) or Santeria (the way of the *santos*). The modern *reglas'* criterion of membership was not African ethnic affiliation but ritual initiation; their constituencies became heterogeneous as the religions spread among the black, mulatto, and white working classes in the late nineteenth and early twentieth centuries.

Institutions and Personnel

The "Lucumi religion" is comprised of two distinct but related *reglas*, each with its own priesthood, initiations, and ranking specialists. Priests who tend the pantheon of orishas, or *santos*, are called *santeros*, although many consider this term—along with Santeria—pejorative, and prefer the formal Lucumi titles. Male and female orisha priests make up the *casas* (houses) of Ocha's genealogical branches (*ramas*), while the *babalawos*—the male diviners of the Ifa oracle, whose tutelary deity is Orunmila—make up the houses of La Regla de Ifa. Both *reglas* count on master herbalists and drummers of the sacred two-headed *bata* drums. The professional diviner and master of ceremonies of Ocha is the *oba-oriate* or *italero*, who, along with his fellow Ocha priests, may divine with the orisha's 16-cowrie-shell system (*'dilogun*). All initiates of Ifa and Ocha may divine with the *obi-coco* oracle, the four shards of coconuts that replaced the Yoruba kola nut system. The Ocha and Ifa systems are highly systematized, theologized, and textualized, given this century's educated priesthood, which has produced a corpus of published "manuals" (e.g., Angarica 1955; Pichardo 1984; Castillo).

Cosmology

Modern Ocha cosmology and ritual represent a condensation and reworking of West African religious principles. The African and Creole founders in Cuba organized the prominent kingdom-based deity clusters of the Yoruba into a unified hierarchical Lucumi pantheon of orishas under a High-God trinity. More than twenty orishas are called in the protocols of invocation, the *oro del santo*, during single ritual events, such as drummings, initiations, and divination sessions. Each orisha of the pantheon played a determinate role in God's Creation; each was delegated by God a dimension of the human and natural worlds and their associated processes; and each orisha "owns" a determinate functional domain in a highly codified system of symbolic classification. Of the High-God Trinity, Olodumare is the All-Powerful and most otiose (without specific functions); Olorun (Owner of the Sky) is the firmament and embodies the powers of Olodumare as reflected in the Sun; and Olofin (Owner of the Law) is the beginning, the end, and the evolution of existence. Of the three, only Olofin is materially enshrined—within the secret altars of *babalawos*, the priests of Ifa's interpreter, the orisha Orunmila. Of these deities, Oduduwa created the world and established the relation between the celestial realm and human beings, including the mystery of human life and death; the immaculate Obatala, an earthly extension of Oduduwa, is the arch-divinity, "highest" authority, and "father" of the orisha pantheon; that is, he created, and is the "owner of" the orishas and human beings; Olokun, the mysterious owner of the depths of the sea, is the great counterpart of Orisha Oko, the Earth (la Tierra). The one-legged Osain is the owner of the earth's forest (*el monte*) of sacred plants (the religion's pharmacology). Very close to the human world are the omnipresent Elegba, the universal mediator, interpreter, and mischievous trickster who opens the road, as well as puts a stone in the path; Ogun, who is war, blood, eternal labor, and the creative and destructive force of iron technology; Oshosi, the brainy pathfinder-hunter-magician who provides daily nourishment and keeps one out of traps. The macho Shango, a great king, warrior, healer, dancer, and prophetic speaker carries (and carries away) fire and problems on his head; the mendicant Babalu Aye (or Asojuano) controls skin and internal diseases and is the beloved patron of the poor. Yemaya, the all-embracing Seven Seas, is the great Mother of the World, including all the orishas, and human beings. Oya-Yansan, the erstwhile warrior-spouse of Ogun and Shango, controls meteorological changes and the swift transition between life and death—figured in her patronage are the dead *egun* and ownership of the cemetery's perimeter. Ochun is the sensual *mulata*, the owner of the "river" and of "the blood that runs through the veins"—three metaphors that define her as the nurturer and mediator of relationships among and between people, families, human cultures, and supernaturals.

Modern Ritual System

Ocha initiates "make" a single tutelary orisha and "receive" a standard group of four to six other orisha protectors, all in a ceremony called the *kariocha*, which is phased over a seven-day ritual period and is followed by a year of apprenticeship. Each initiation reproduces, and thereby ensures the posterity of, the core orisha pantheon and its associated bodies of specialized knowledge (e.g., prayer, herbalism, oracular narratives, sacrificial formulae, and shrine arts). Initiation, along with day-to-day Ocha ritual, restores health and well-being through the rigorous implementation of oracular prescriptions, such as cleansings and sacrifices (*ebo*), graded acquisitions of the orishas' spiritual power (*ache*), and attention to the family and priestly ancestors (*eguns*). Such periodic ritual events also include drummings, which act as problem-solving *ebo*. Annual events include the anniversary of priests' initiations (*cumpleanos*) and the orishas' calendrical festivals, celebrated on the feast days of their Catholic saint counterparts (December 4, for example, is the feast day of both Shango and St. Barbara). The great annual *cabildo* processions for Yemaya and the Virgin of the Havana seaport town of Regla brought tens of thousands of followers out in the streets each September 7.

Altars and Arts

The orishas' enshrined objects consist of sets of consecrated stones (*ota*), cowrie shells, and small cast, cut-out, or carved iconographic *herramientas* (tools), which are contained in metal, wood, earthenware, and porcelain vessels, the last of which are imitations of the soup tureens that used to grace the dining room sets of the Cuban nobility and bourgeoisie. Priests hierarchically

Canastillero cabinet for *orishas*, Marianao, Havana, cuba, 1989. The Yoruba-Cuban *orishas* are hierarchically organized in vertical cabinets, which serve as domestic altars.
Photo © David H. Brown.

arrange their *soperas* in multishelved, often glassed-in, cabinets called *canastilleros*, which can mask as decorative domestic displays. For periodic and annual celebrations, the orishas' vessels are brought out, elevated on pedestals under dazzling canopied "thrones" of satin, velvet, lace, chiffon, and lamé, and are draped with decorative squares of brocaded and sequined fabric, called *panos*, which recall the *mantos* (capes) of the Catholic saints. On the Middle Day of the Ocha initiation, the throne is occupied by the *iyawo*, who wears the orisha's royal regalia. This formal consecration garment, called *ropa de santo*, includes a jewelry-encrusted pasteboard crown and a satin gown or jacket-and-pants ensemble. These Spanish colonial-era outfits are combined with Yoruba-derived garlands of thick beadstrands and cowries (*collares de mazo*) and iconographic hand-held dance wands (e.g., Shango's thunderaxe, Yemaya's and Ochun's fans, Ogun's cutlass).

References

Angarica, Nicolas Valentin. 1955. *Manual de Orihate: Religion Lucumi*. Havana.

Bascom, William. 1952. Two Forms of Afro-Cuban Divination. *Acculturation in the Americas*. Vol. 2, Proceedings and Selected Papers of the XXIX International Congress of Americanists. Chicago: University of Chicago Press.

———. 1950. The Focus of Cuban Santeria. *Southwestern Journal of Anthropology* 6, no. 1:64–68.

Brown, David. 1993. Thrones of the Orishas: Afro-Cuban Altars. *African Arts* 26, no. 4: 44–59, 85–87.

Cabrera, Lydia. 1983. *El monte: igbo-finda, ewe Orisha-Vititi nfinda; notas sobre las religiones, la magia, las superstitiones, y el folklore de los negros Criollos y el Pueblo de Cuba*. Miami: Coleccion del Chichereku en el Exilo.

Castellanos, Jorge, and Isabel Castellanos. 1992. *Cultura Afrocubana*. Vol. 3, *Las religiones y las lenguas*. Miami: Ediciones Universal.

Castillo, Jose M. 1976. *Ifa en la tierra de Ifa*. Miami.

Gleason, Judith. 1992. *The King Does Not Lie: Initiation of a Shango Priest*. Video 50 min. Arlington, Va.: American Anthropological Association

Hunt, Carl. 1979. *Oyotunji Village: The Yoruba Movement in America*. Washington, D.C.: University Press of America.

Mason, John and Gary Edwards. 1985. *Black Gods: Orisa Studies in the New World*. Brooklyn, N.Y.: Yoruba Theological Archministry.

Murphy, Joseph. 1988. *Santeria: An African Religion in America*. Boston: Beacon Press.

Omari, Mikelle Smith. 1991. Completing the Circle: Notes on African Art, Society, and Religion in Oyotunji, South Carolina. *African Arts* July:66–75, 96.

Ortiz, Fernando. 1951. *Los Bailes y el Teatro de los Negros en el Folklore de Cuba*. Havana: Ediciones Cardenas y Cia.

———. 1921. Los Cabildos Afrocubanos. *Revista bimestre Cubana* 16:5–39.

Palmie, Stephan. 1993. Ethnogenetic Processes and Cultural Transfer in Afro-American Slave Populations. In *Slavery in the Americas*. Ed. Wolfgang Binder. Wurtzburg: Konigshausen Un Neumann, 337–63.

Pichardo, Ernesto. 1984. *Oduduwa/Obatala*, Miami, Fla.: Rex Press.

Thompson, Robert Farris. 1993. *Face of the Gods: Art and Altars of Africa and the African-Americas*. Exhibition Catalog. New York: Museum of African Art.

DAVID H. BROWN

See also **Diaspora; Religion; Vodou**

SÃO TOMÉ AND PRÍNCIPE (DEMOCRATIC REPUBLIC OF SÃO TOMÉ AND PRÍNCIPE)

São Tomé and Príncipe are small tropical islands located off central Africa's west coast. The two islands have a combined population of 170,000 (2002). São Tomé is the nation's capital and largest city, with approximately 60,000 inhabitants. The population is predominantly composed of a Portuguese-African mixture, with an African minority. The most commonly spoken languages are Portuguese, Fang, and Kriolu. The majority of people are Christian (80%), while 20 percent practice traditional indigenous religions.

Originally a slave depot, the islands were among the first to grow cocoa. Beginning with riots in 1953, a liberation movement was active through the 1960s, with aid from the mainland. But it was not until a revolution in Portugal in 1974 that independence came to the Portuguese African colonies. After approx-imately four-hundred years of Portuguese rule, São Tomé and Príncipe gained independence on July 12, 1975, and subsequently formed a one-party republic committed to Marxist-Leninism. In January 1991, the nation's first multiparty elections were held as part of a process of democratization. Part of this political reform has been the development of a market economy in which former state farms have been privatized. Such changes have made the country a more desirable place to visit, and the tourist industry has subsequently benefited from increased revenue. Fishing, coffee, cocoa, palm oil, bananas, and copra (dried coconut) are the major exports.

A good deal of Portuguese culture was absorbed by the people, and festivals continue to mark the Roman Catholic calendar. São Tomé and Príncipe are renowned as the place of origin for the Luso-African artistic tradition. The poets Jose de Almeida and Francisco Tenriero have brought recognition to the country, as they were the first poets to write about African pride in the Portuguese language.

JENNIFER JOYCE

SECRECY IN AFRICAN ORATURE

Secrecy is a powerful esthetic strategy underlying many forms of African orature. A dialectic of concealment and revelation is implicit to narratives, legends, proverbs, riddles, puzzles, songs, and praise poems—and to the visual arts related to these oral media. Exploration of the uses of secrecy in African orature lends insight into the ways secrecy embodies, protects, and selectively transmits knowledge in diverse contexts, including initiations and gender dramas, royal rites and performances, processes of divination and healing, and encounters with foreigners. By activating the tension between clarity and obscurity implicit to knowledge itself, secrecy can structure experience so that it mirrors and invokes the partiality of human understanding.

In Western societies, the word *secrecy* tends to summon sinister stereotypes. In Africa, however, secrecy is considered to be a useful and positive strategy for the control of knowledge (Nooter 1993). Knowledge is currency; like money, too much can be dangerously abused and manipulated. Knowledge should therefore be acquired progressively over the course of a lifetime. Expressive arts are often the mechanism for the incremental transmission of such knowledge, whether in the form of proverbs, masquerades, or songs. Yet, these are not literal or direct sources of information. Rather, such art forms articulate and convey knowledge through metaphorical, allusive, and polysemic signifiers. In such contexts, indirectness is a virtue, and ambiguity and multivalent meanings are sought and valued.

In his book on the Poro secret association in Liberia, Beryl Bellman discusses the "language of secrecy" that defines membership in exclusive institutions associated with government, education, and healing. This "language" is composed of the procedures for disclosing the presence of concealed information without revealing the information itself (1984, 50). Ever since Georg Simmel's 1908 landmark study of secrecy, it has been recognized that the power of secrets lies not in their disclosure, but rather in the paradoxical advertisement of secret knowledge that occurs while the secrets themselves are protected.

Secrecy in Initiation Rites

Initiation is often surrounded by a veil of secrecy. Yet most of what is learned during initiations is not a "profound revelation of new knowledge," but rather a "poetic and imaginative reconsideration of the familiar" (Beidelman 1993, 43). Among the Lega peoples of eastern Democratic Republic of the Congo, for example, Bwami is an association of ethical conduct, and its teachings are generated through initiation objects and accompanying proverbs, maxims, and songs, which grow more complex and multi-referential with each ascending level. New configurations of objects produce new and more complex meanings and associations (Biebuyck 1973, 93).

Frequently, initiations are ways of setting up boundary markers between genders, age-grades, or classes. The solidarities and the divisions that secrecy creates between members and non-members often hold more importance than the actual content of the secrets themselves. Jan Vansina recounts, for example, that the secret of Kuba initiation was that there was no secret (1973, 304). Yet dramatic tales of the ordeals to which novices are submitted are a means of aggrandizing and mystifying male power through the possession of "secrets" forbidden to women.

Secrecy and Gender

A language of secrecy often underlies gender dynamics. During Yoruba Gelede masquerades, men personify women through mask performances and sing verses about "our mothers, the witches, the nightbirds," in reference not only to the secretive powers of women themselves, but to a more general conception of individuality that is based on both exterior and interior aspects (Lawal 1996). All people are believed to have both an outer head and an inner head, and as one Yoruba proverb states, "May my inner head not spoil my outer one." The true being, character, and intentions of a person are in constant conflict with that person's outward social persona. Women are perceived to be especially capable of concealing their inner being with a composure and coolness that emanates from their enhanced life force, and Yoruba men stress this distinction in the following way: "Women are more secretive than we. . . . But we men usually open our secret to anybody. . . . Women have many secrets they will never tell . . . except [to] their mothers" (Drewal and Drewal 1983, 73).

In addition to the boundaries set by spoken language, secrecy may delimit space and social difference through the sounds and silence of other-world beings (Peek 1994). Initiation rites are often conducted outside of the view of women and noninitiates, but not outside the range of their hearing. Auditory masks, spirit voices conveyed through musical instruments such as bullroarers, and other aural signals may convey the presence of the spirits to those who are excluded from the rites, or to initiates of lower ranks (Lifschitz 1988). Likewise, silence is a powerful signifier of sacred or occult powers (Peek 1994, 477–478). The space around a king, for example, may be rendered sacred by the absence of verbal communication. Not only is a Benin king confined to the palace, secluded from the public eye, but he is never heard to utter ordinary speech. The absence of sound indicates the presence of the secret, erecting a boundary: "What is unknown must be made present by an awareness of its absence" (Poppi 1993, 196–203).

Secrecy and Society

Through these dialectics of absence and presence, concealment and revelation, secrecy structures the hierarchies that separate royals from nonroyals. In the Akan kingdom of Akuapem, the king is accompanied by spokesmen, or counselors, who "mediate in all verbal discourse with the king and protect him from danger and pollution. They are visible metaphors of the invisible royal person" (Gilbert 1993, 134), and provide an "extra authority of remoteness" for the king (Peek 1994, 477). Their emblems—gold-leaf-covered staffs with representational imagery on their finials—are made to "speak," for they evoke proverbs about leadership, moral conduct, and the dangers of power. One staff depicts an egg to convey the idea that the state is like an egg: if handled carefully, it will not break. Meaning emerges from the interplay of the visual, proverbial, and the "nonverbally implicit." Just as the power of proverbs comes from their ambiguity, there may be more than one meaning for a single form.

Secrecy and Divination

Such indirect and implicit language also characterizes divination and spirit mediumship in many parts of Africa. Diviners who become possessed by a spirit often speak with nonhuman voices in an esoteric language (Peek 1994, 479). The language is perceptible only to certain titled officials who intercede between the patient and the spirit. Among Luba peoples of southeastern Democratic Republic of the Congo, for example, a diviner becomes possessed by singing the songs for twins, esoteric songs that invoke the spirits' attention. Once a spirit has come to mount the diviner's head, the diviner's own voice becomes subsumed by that of the spirit, and only the diviner's assistant, called a *kitobo*, can translate for the participants in the consultation (Roberts 1999). The ability to speak in such tongues is referred to as glossolalia, and serves to reinforce the diviner's linguistic access to realms inaccessible by most other people. Diviners, in other words, like royals and initiates, acquire a literacy that defines social status and spiritual prerogative (Peek 1991).

Other forms of divination serve as repositories of esoteric verse and secret prayers. Muslim diviners recite the ninety-nine names of God and saintly poetry to invoke divine blessing, while Yoruba Ifa diviners, called "fathers of the secrets," defer to the 153,600 Ifa verses for secret directives of healing and guidance. *Awo* is a collective term for the four classes of secret information in Yoruba culture. All *awo* categories of knowledge revolve around Ifa divination practice, which provides the oral literature through which they are defined and interpreted (Hallen and Abimbola 1993, 217).

Finally, the interactions that foreigners have sustained with Africans over the course of several centuries have produced a body of secret knowledge and oral history. Secrecy is implicit to every field researcher's experience, whether in posing questions about highly guarded arenas of knowledge or simply in the mythology of ethnography, which presupposes the revelation of some "within." Western epistemology posits that all knowledge must be obtainable, and that scrutiny is the key to scientific discovery. African aesthetic systems, by contrast, stress the inaccessibility, partiality, and dangers of knowledge. As one Mende proverb states, "Beauty is best perceived from a distance," and as a wise Dangme official states, "Keep what you know not in your head, but in your kneecap" (Murphy and Quarcoopome, quoted in Nooter 1993).

References

‹Abimbola, Wande, and Barry Hallen. 1993. Secrecy and Objectivity in the Methodology and Literature of Ifa Divination. In *Secrecy: African Art that Conceals and Reveals*, ed. Mary H. Nooter. New York: Museum for African Art.

Beidelman, T. O. 1993. Secrecy and Society: The Paradox of Knowing and the Knowing of Paradox. In *Secrecy: African Art that Conceals and Reveals*, ed. Mary H. Nooter. New York: Museum for African Art.

Bellman, Beryl L. 1984. *The Language of Secrecy: Symbols and Metaphors in Poro Ritual*. New Brunswick, N.J.: Rutgers University Press.

Biebuyck, Daniel P. 1973. *Lega Culture: Art, Initiation, and Moral Philosophy among a Central African People*. Berkeley: University of California Press.

Drewal, Henry John, and Margaret Thompson Drewal. 1983. *Gelede: Art and Female Power Among the Yoruba*. Bloomington: Indiana University Press.

Finnegan, Ruth. 1970. *Oral Literature in Africa*. Oxford: Clarendon Press.

Gilbert, Michelle. 1993. The Leopard Who Sleeps in a Basket: Akuapem Secrecy in Everyday Life and in Royal Metaphor. In *Secrecy: African Art that Conceals and Reveals*, ed. Mary H. Nooter. New York: Museum for African Art.

Lawal, Babatunde. 1996. *The Gelede Spectacle: Art, Gender, and Social Harmony in an African Culture*. Seattle: University of Washington Press.

Lifschitz, Edward. 1988. Hearing is Believing: Acoustic Aspects of Masking in Africa. In *West African Masks and Cultural Systems*, ed. S. L. Kasfir. Tervuren, Belgium: Musée Royal de l'Afrique Centrale.

Nooter, Mary H., ed. 1993. *Secrecy: African Art that Conceals and Reveals*. New York: Museum for African Art.

Peek, Philip M. 1991. *African Divination Systems: Ways of Knowing*. Bloomington: Indiana University Press.

———. 1994. The Sounds of Silence: Cross-World Communication and the Auditory Arts in African Societies. *American Ethnologist* 21, no. 3:474–494.

Poppi, Cesare. 1993. Sigma! The Pilgrim's Progress and the Logic of Secrecy. In *Secrecy: African Art that Conceals and Reveals*, ed. Mary H. Nooter. New York: Museum for African Art.

Roberts, Mary Nooter. 1999. Proofs and Promises: Setting Meaning before the Eyes. *Artistry and Insight: A Cross-Cultural Study of Divination in Central and West Africa*, ed. John Pemberton III. Washington, D.C.: Smithsonian Institution Press.

Simmel, Georg. [1908] 1950. "Secrecy" and "Secret Societies." In *The Sociology of Georg Simmel*. Tr. Kurt H. Wolff. Glencoe, Ill.: Free Press.

Vansina, Jan. 1973. Initiation Rituals of the Bushong. In *Peoples and Cultures of Africa*, Ed. Elliot P. Skinner. Garden City, N.Y.: Natural History Press.

MARY NOOTER ROBERTS

SENEGAL (REPUBLIC OF SENEGAL)

Located on the coast of West Africa, the Republic of Senegal is a tropical country neighbored by Mauritania, Mali, Guinea, Guinea-Bissau, and The Gambia. Of Senegal's 9,490,000 people, 36 percent are Wolof, 17 percent Fulani, 17 percent Serer, 9 percent Toucouleur, 9 percent Diola, and 9 percent are Mandingo. The remaining 3 percent are composed of Europeans, Lebanese, and other ethnic groups. The major languages spoken in the country are French, Wolof, Fulde, Oyola, Mandinka, Sarakole, and Serer. The majority of Senegal's people are Muslim (92 percent), while 6 percent practice traditional indigenous religions and 2 percent are Christian. Dakar, the nation's capital, is also its largest city, with a population of 1,730,000.

On April 4, 1960, Senegal gained its independence from France. French influence, however, has continued to prevail throughout the country. The Senegalese educational system, for example, has retained a French character, while France maintains a military force in the country and continues to invest in Senegal's economy. Since the 1988 election of President Abdou Diouf, Senegal has fortified its system of a multiparty government. Diouf's task has not been easy, however, as the nation has suffered from a weak economy, regional separatism, disputes with neighboring countries, and sectarian pressures.

Senegal's natural resources include fish, phosphates, and iron ore, while agricultural production revolves around millet, sorghum, manioc (cassava), rice, cotton, and groundnuts. Principle industries and sources of revenue are fishing, food processing, and light manufacturing. Dakar, Senegal's capital and once the capital of French West Africa, has long been a center for West Africa's cultural affairs. Negritude, a Francophonic African tradition, was founded by Senegalese writers; most notably Senegal's first president, poet, and statesman, Leopold Senghor, was one of the leading exponents of negritude, a political and artistic assertion of African identity primarily associated with Francophone African Caribbean writers and leaders. The ancient traditions of the griots, historian bards found throughout Senegal, as well as Mali and Guinea, continue to inspire contemporary musicians and singers. Youssou N'Dour and Baaba Maal are among the many musicians who have gained international reputations.

In recent years, increasing numbers of African Americans have traveled back to West Africa in search of their heritage. Goree Island, one of the major shipment points during the centuries of slavery, is a major historical site, along with the slave forts of Ghana.

JENNIFER JOYCE

SENUFO

See **Speaking and Nonspeaking Power Objects of the Senufo; Tourism and Tourist Arts**

SEYCHELLES

Located off the east coast of Africa, the Republic of the Seychelles is Africa's smallest country in terms of both size and population. The 115 subtropical islands of Seychelles consist of a number of scattered archipelagos that collectively are home to approximately 80,000 people. The country's capital is the city of Victoria, which has a population of 25,000. The country is predominantly composed of the Seychellois, who are a mix of Asians, Africans, and French. English, French, and Creole are the most widely spoken languages. Ninety-eight percent of the population is Christian, while the remaining 2 percent is made up of various other religious groups.

In 1771 the French formed a settlement in Seychelles and created spice plantations. It was the British, however, who officially colonized the country, in 1814. On June 29, 1976, Seychelles finally gained its independence and formed its own republic. In 1993 the one party government ended its fifteen year rein, and a multiparty system was established.

Since gaining its independence, Seychelles has benefited from a solid economy and positive social progress. The economy received a substantial lift in 1971 with the opening of an international airport, which led to a great rise in tourism, the country's major source of foreign revenue. In addition to its tourism industry, Seychelles has gained revenue from its shrimp, cinnamon, and copra (coconut meat) exports, as well as its vanilla processing and coconut oil industries. Seychelles has also become a world leader in wildlife preservation and environmental conservation. The islands also take pride in their adult literacy rate of 84 percent.

JENNIFER JOYCE

SHENG: EAST AFRICAN URBAN FOLK SPEECH

Sheng is the dynamic, protean combination of Swahili and English, but it also borrows from Kenyan ethnic languages such as Kikuyu, Luo, and Luhya, from the Indian languages of Hindi and Gujarati, from foreign films, from the news, and from the languages of Kenya's many tourists. It is primarily localized in Nairobi, Kenya's capital, but it has also moved to other large urban areas, such as Nakuru. Sheng has become a symbol of urbanity and is used as a marker for nonethnic identity—the use of Sheng distinguishes parking boys (street urchins), soccer players, market sellers, and many other societal groups. Toward the end of the twentieth century, a new form of Sheng, called Engsh, developed. It contains more English words, and is more heavily influenced by English grammar and sentence construction. As English is a marker of education, Sheng and Engsh have become signifiers of class distinctions as well.

Sheng contains structural elements of slang, and it reflects the processes of pidginization and creolization, as well as intense code-switching, word borrowing, and meaning shifts. Sheng speakers most commonly embed English words that have undergone a meaning shift through the adjustment to Swahili grammar and sentence structure. For example, a word such as *imedeadisha* contains the English word *dead*, here meaning "to break," within the standard Swahili grammar of constructing a causative verb. The following exchange provides numerous other examples:

Mike: Aa maze John ninje maze hukinishow ati ulikuwa unaishio movie?
Nilikuchekicheki hulu na huku lekini sikujua ulikrosigi weikya.
John: Wee la Mike usiworry sikuwe ne chope lekani nili-one man mwingini we kwengu nikomkolic man hate ako-cough kasomething.

Translation:

Mike: Aw man John how is it man you didn't tell me that you were to be at the movie? I looked for you here and there but I didn't know where you were.
John: Oh, no Mike don't worry, I didn't have any money but saw another friend from my place I hit him up until he coughed up something.

Close examination of the construction of some of the above words shows that the sophistication and density of language processing work is quite high. Even a common and often-used word such as *Mzee* (an honorific term used when referring to elders) can change to *Maze* without mixing with English, but its traditional connotations are inverted, as it is used in referring to a youth. *Hukinishow* is an English verb embedded in a Swahili verb construction. In Swahili, personal pronouns, verb tense, and direct-object identification are represented in verbs as prefixes and infixes. *Hu* is the negative personal pronoun ("you did not"), *-li-* is the past tense marker, and *-ni-* is the first person prefix. *Show* is the English verb *show*, but in this usage the meaning of *show* has been shifted to *tell*. *Nilikuchekicheki* also contains an English verb within standard Swahili verb usage. The verb in this case is *check*, which has been shifted in meaning to "looking for you," or "checking out for you." The English word *check* is Swahilized by adding an "i" at the end. *Akacough* means to "cough up" some money. The *-a-* is the third-person prefix, and the *-ka-* is the connective tense. In *kasomething*, however, *-ka-* appears to be present for alliteration, not as the connective tense.

References

Achuhi, Roy. 1985. Using 'am red, its Sheng! *The Standard* August 30: 17.
Akungu, John. 1988. Sheng: the Language That Keeps Changing for Survival. *Kenya Times* September 9: 23.
Icheru, Catherine, and Roy Gachuhi. 1984. Sheng: New Urban Language Baffles Parents. *Daily Nation* March 14: 11.
Aitin, Davide, and Carol Eastman. 1989. Language Conflict: Transactions and Games in Kenya. *Cultural Anthropology* 4, no. 1:51–72.
Ioga, Jacko, and Dan Fee, eds. 1993. *Sheng Dictionary*. 2d ed. Nairobi: Ginseng.
Ikangi, Katama. 1985. Sheg-flag of a "Peoples' Culture." *The Standard* August 30: 17.
Utahi, Wahome. 1990. Its the Age of Sheng and I Just Dig the Talk. *Sunday Nation* September 30: 13–14.
Spyropoulos, Mary. 1987. Sheng: Some Preliminary Investigations Into a Recently Emerged Nairobi Street Language. *Journal of the Anthropological Society of Oxford* 18:125–136.
Sure, Kembo. 1990. The Coming of Sheng. *English Today* 32, no. 8: 26–28.

DAVID A. SAMPER

See also **Linguistics and African Verbal Arts; Popular Culture; Urban Folklore**

SHONA

See **Southern Africa; Tourism and Tourist Arts**

SIERRA LEONE (REPUBLIC OF SIERRA LEONE)

Located on the coast of West Africa and neighbored by Guinea and Liberia, the Republic of Sierra Leone is a tropical country with a population of 4,870,000. Freetown, the country's capital, is also its largest city, with 469,000 inhabitants. Thirty-one percent of Sierra Leone's population is Temne, 34 percent is Mende, 5 percent is Krio, and 35 percent is made up of various other groups. English, Krio (Creole), Temne, Mende, Vai, Kru, Fulde, and Mandinka are the most widely spoken languages. Over half of the population still practices traditional religions (60%), while 30 percent are Muslim and 10 percent are Christian.

In 1787 the settlement of Freetown was initiated by freed black slaves from England, Jamaica, and Nova Scotia. A British Protectorate was established in 1896. It was not until April 27, 1961, however, that British rule ended, giving Sierra Leone its independence. In 1978 a new constitution made Sierra Leone a one-party state. Since the overthrow of the long-governing All People's Congress in April 1992, Sierra Leone has suffered from severe political instability and civil war. The 1996 elections were followed by a coup the next year. In response, West African nations sent a peace-keeping force, led by Nigeria; nevertheless, the brutal civil war started again. The ongoing war has worsened the state of human rights in the country and created hundreds of thousands of refugees, both within the country and in surrounding nations. As was the case in Angola, "blood diamonds" (illegally mined and sold diamonds) have financed the competing rebel groups.

Although the country was rich in natural resources at independence, the smuggling and depletion of resources, particularly gold and diamonds, has cost the country much in potential revenue. The country produces coffee and cocoa, but international prices for these have not been stable. Such economic conditions have resulted in Sierra Leone's present status as one of the world's poorest countries. In the mid-1990s, Sierra Leone had the highest infant mortality rate and lowest life expectancy in Africa.

In 1814, Fourah Bay College was founded in Sierra Leone as a Christian school. It became a renowned educational institution for all of West Africa, and before 1918 it provided the only higher education in the region. During colonial times, the college produced many important West African leaders. The indigenous peoples of Sierra Leone such as the Mende, Limba, and Temne, have extensive visual and verbal-art traditions.

JENNIFER JOYCE

SILENCE IN EXPRESSIVE BEHAVIOR

The numerous instances of cultural silences in African societies cluster in two basic, although not unrelated, areas. Ritual uses of silence seem to refer fundamentally to the realm of deities, spirits, and ancestors. Although in full experience the spirit realm is not really silent, it cannot be heard easily, and often necessitates intermediaries such as diviners (Peek 2000). The other basic realm of signification is the representation of wisdom and respect. For cultures throughout Africa, silence and the reticence of a speaker is commonly understood to convey respect, sagacity, esoteric knowledge, and serenity.

Silence can be the manifestation of social power, where control over others is demonstrated by silencing them. Those in power can prevent others from speaking—they can, in fact, cause silence. But these instances, except in clear cases of despots and dictatorships, often overlap with situations of ritual, sacred uses of silence, or situations where respect or wisdom is evidenced by the silence.

African religious beliefs and practice provide numerous instances for such manifestations of silence. The Yoruba of Nigeria have proverbs about a deity who is so powerful that it does not have to acknowledge humankind's puny existence: *Akii je nii gb'orisa niyi* (It is the silence of the deity that confers dignity on it). Periods of silence often protect critical rites of birth and death, as well as initiations.

African masquerade traditions often include fearsome silent masks that do not speak or make any sound, and in their silence reveal even more potency than they would if they were loud. Sometimes masks may have no mouths depicted at all. In other instances, masks which do "speak" seldom do so in normal voices, but rather use instrumental means or voice disguisers to communicate. Others may use exclusively visual languages of gesture and sign language to communicate. While the treatment of masqueraders' voices may comment on the fearsomeness of spirit speech, a closed or absent mouth may demonstrate the wisdom of silence. One who could speak instead chooses, wisely, to remain silent.

Among the Mende of Sierra Leone, a person's silence is understood to demonstrate composure and quality of judgment, a prominent quality of elders. Thus, just as the wise person seldom opens his mouth, the chief is quietly aloof, and the proper woman is discreetly silent, masks representing these figures are therefore depicted with small, pursed mouths, as appropriate to their exalted status. Images of ideal, perfect silence permeate the society, occurring in all possible contexts to continually remind people how to behave as proper Mende women or men (Boone 1986).

Perhaps the epitome of the overlap of sacred and secular realms with regard to silence occurs with divine kings. In many African societies, a defining feature of the king is that he does not speak in public—one could not even see the king's mouth move in the ancient courts of Benin City, Nigeria. One interpretation of such instances of prohibited speech stems from the acknowledged power of words, especially those related to taboo topics and highly potent individuals. If to speak is to act—if words actualize ideas, then to not speak is to prevent something unwanted from happening (Peek 1981). For example, among the Yoruba, one never speaks the "real" name of smallpox out loud.

Another important reflection of the associations of silence and wisdom is the striking presence of silent animals in a variety of contexts. In West Africa, spiders and tortoises are portrayed both as trickster figures and as emblematic of wisdom. The "silent" spider, known as *Anansi* among Akan speakers of Ghana, is considered the origin of tales. Many divination systems employ silent animals as agents of oracular messages from the other world, such as mice among the Baule, crabs in northern Cameroon, and the desert fox for the Dogon of Mali.

The presence of silence is also a part of folktales and their performance. Indicative of the importance of silence, the Kuranko of Sierra Leone actually employ an ideophone to signify silence. The Shona in Zimbabwe also recognize that silence is not simply absence or "nothing," for they use a specific gesture to indicate silence's presence in a narrative (Klassen 1999). An extraordinarily poignant tale from the Yoruba of western Nigeria brings forth the subtlety of thought on these matters, both in regards to divine kings and to the concepts of silence:

> The king invited the animals to a great feast, and offered a prize to the best dancer. The animals danced energetically before him, each showing off its own most striking qualities—the elephant its grave dignity, the leopard its beautiful coat and sinuous agility, the gazelle its spectacular leaps and so forth. When, at the end of the dance, they gathered around the king to hear his judgment, to their surprise and displeasure he awarded the prize to the tortoise. Answering their complaints, the king asked them who had provided the feast, and who was giving the prize, to which they could only reply "It is you, O King!" "And so it is that I awarded the prize to the tortoise," said the King, "for it is only I who can see the dance of the tortoise: his dance is entirely inside him!" (Lienhardt, 1985, p. 143).

This is an exceptional testimony to the importance of the unstated, to the superior quality of the inner state. This is not a singular testimony, however. In eastern Nigeria, for example, the Igbo have an adage: "It's not the sound you hear that I will dance to."

The natural world that cultural beings inhabit is one of sound. Noise is natural; it is silence that must be created. Humans are genetically programmed to speak and to hear. Normally, people cannot not speak; therefore, to choose silence is a significant act of humanness. The cessation of sound, the stopping of speech, the choice of silence, this is always noteworthy. This condition is generally understood to be one of respect and wisdom among African, as well as traditional American and Asian cultures. As the Bamana say: "If speech burned your mouth, silence will heal you."

References

Alberts, Ethel M. 1972. Culture Patterning of Speech Behavior in Burundi. In *Directions in Sociolinguistics*, ed. D. Hymes and J. Gumperz. New York: Holt, Rinehart and Winston.

Boone, Sylvia A. 1986. *Radiance from the Waters: Ideals and Feminine Beauty in Mende Art*. New Haven, Conn.: Yale University Press.

Hunter, Linda. 1982. Silence Is Also Language: Hausa Attitudes about Speech and Language. *Anthropological Linguistics* 24, no. 4: 389–409.

Klassen, Doreen. 1999. You Can't Have Silence with Your Palms Up: Ideophones, Gesture, and Iconicity in Zimbabwean Shona Women's Ngano (Storysong) Performance. Ph.D. dissertation, Indiana University.

Lienhardt, Godfrey. 1985. Self, public, private. Some African representations. In *The Category of the Person*, edited by M. Carrithers, S. Lukes, and S. Collins. Cambridge, UK: Cambridge University Press.

Peek, Philip M. 1981. The Power of Words in African Verbal Arts. *Journal of American Folklore* 94, no. 371:19–43.

———. 1994. The Sounds of Silence: Cross-World Communication and the Auditory Arts in African Societies. *American Ethnologist* 21, no. 3:474–494.

———. 2000. Re-Sounding Silences. In *Sound*, ed. P. Kruth and H. Stobart. Cambridge, England: Cambridge University Press.

Samarin, William J. 1965. Language of Silence. *Practical Anthropology* 12, no. 2:155–119.

Tannen, Deborah, and M. Saville-Troike, eds. 1985. *Perspectives on Silence*. Norwood, N.J.: Ablex.

PHILIP M. PEEK

See also **Animals in African Folklore; Divination; Gesture in African Oral Narrative; Ideophones; Performance**

SIYAR: NORTH AFRICAN EPICS

While the epic is absent from classical Arabic literature, the genre, although long ignored by academia, plays an important role in popular culture throughout a vast area of Northern Africa.

A Narrative Genre: the *Siyar*

The genre is called *siyar* (biography). The term is used as a title of epic narratives: *Sîrat 'Antara, Sîrat Banî Hilâl, Sîrat al-Zîr Sâlim, Sîrat Sayf ibn Dhî Yazan*, and so on. Interestingly enough, *siyar*, as derived from *sarâ* (to walk, or to behave) applies, in its physical and moral senses, both to movement and behavior. Thus, the genre lends itself to a biographical (or allegedly biographical) narrative about a distinguished figure of the past. The narration follows the course of an entire life, or even of successive lives through several generations within a family, extended sometimes to a whole people. Perceived as biographical, a *siyar* represents, in the eyes of its most fervent devotees, their true history. These are legendary biographies, in which history is reinterpreted for the purposes of the genre.

Diffusion of the *Siyar*

These epic narratives have been spread through various modes of transmission, including oral performances (with or without musical accompaniment), manuscript, and (at least from the eighteenth century onwards) printed versions. Unlike the others, one *siyar*, the story of the Banû Hilâl (the Sons of Hilal) is still a living oral tradition. In Upper Egypt, the musician-poets (*shu'arâ*) sing versions entirely in verse, using the local dialect and skillfully combining memory and improvisation (Canova 1996). In a village of the Nile Delta, a hundred hours, on average, are needed for one of the fourteen "poets" to sing this epic to an audience (Reynolds 1995). In Tunisia, the Hilalian oral tradition, which is no longer musical, survives in the form of poetry or, more frequently, prose interspersed with rhymed prose (*saj'*) and poetry. In Algeria and Morocco, the *siyar* is broken into small tales centered on two main sequences that deal with antagonistic relationships, one between the favorite hero, Dhyâb, and heroine, Jâzya (usually before they get married), and one between father and son, Ghânim and Dhyâb (Nacib 1994; Galley and Iraqi-Sinaceur 1994). In the societies south of the Sahara (e.g., Darfour, Kordofan, Bornou, Chad, Mali) several episodes of the *siyar* have been popular (MacMichael 1912; Carbou 1913; Patterson 1930; Connelly 1973).

Sîrat Banî Hilâl: Its Historical Substratum

The most popular cycle of the Hilalian tale is the third and last part of the whole *siyar*, known as the March Westwards (*tagh-*

rîba). Historically, the Banû Hilâl constitute the second wave of Arab conquerors who spread westwards and settled in northern Africa in the fifth century of the Hegira. They were originally a nomadic people who, in the previous century, had arrived in Egypt in great numbers, fleeing the deserts of Arabia because of drought. There, they were exhorted by the Fatimid ruler of Cairo to head for Ifrîqiyya (present-day Tunisia). Strikingly enough, the various sociopolitical reasons for the event are completely absent from the narrative. Stress is laid, instead, on their living conditions as the cause of their migration. They have suffered drought for years at a stretch:

> During seven entire years
> Not a single lightning announcing the rain,
> No cauldron placed on the tripod
> Nor grain stirred on the fire.
> A bushel had grown dearer,
> It cost a three-year she-camel.
> (transl. from Galley and Ayoub: 50–51)

Although the decision to migrate is vital, it is perceived first as an exile (*taghrîba*):

> Where is the tribe of the famous name?
> Their drinking troughs are dry,
> They have exiled themselves, bringing their camps far
> and wide.
> (transl. from Galley and Ayoub 1994: 48–49)

An Epic of the Desert

The key factor in the story of this march is the search for a land hospitable to men, women, children, and herds. The goal to be reached at the end of all ordeals is Tunis, a synonym for Paradise on Earth. The very name of Tunis conveys a dream of abundant food, water, and greenery; everywhere the *taghrîba* is recounted,

Glass painting from Tunis, Jazya, or al Zazya.
Photo © Micheline Galley.

An underglass painting inspired by a folk epic in which the hero Bu Zid triumphs over his enemy, Tunisia (black & white photo of a color print of a warrior).
Photo © Micheline Galley.

including in Darfour and Kordofan; and among the Yesiye of Bornou and the Toundjour of Chad, the place dreamed of by these nomadic herders is none other than "Tunis the Green" (*Tûnis al-khadrâ*), "the Prosperous," "the Blessed," "the Well-Named."

The journey is long and full of hardships, with inevitable confrontations with the sedentary peoples they encounter. Sometimes the impressive tide of Hilalian riders is described by a local (Zenâti) hunter:

> And behold!
> Waves of horsemen, squadron after squadron,
> Their burnooses flapping in the wind
> Like birds with ruffled feathers.
> And behold!
> Waves of horsemen, squadron after squadron,
> Deep in sockets,
> Their black eyes sparkling like fragments of pottery.
> And behold!
> Waves of horsemen, squadron after squadron . . .
> The first one leading a bridge of horsemen across the
> ford,
> The last one still distant amidst the dunes . . .
> (Galley and Ayoub 1994: 119–121)

Bloody battles ensue, which "turn the hair of little children white." Yet, most versions of the oral tradition end relatively happily, the Promised Land having finally been reached. However, in some cases, especially in manuscript and published versions, the narrative develops into real tragedy (Saada 1985): power struggles break out within the Hilalian community, leading to the dispersion of a people and the death of its most prestigious members.

The heroes die, but their memory lives in the hearts of men who recognize themselves in these models of heroism, virility, and dignity. Those who sing or recite the *siyar* have exalted these models for their audience, particularly at times when there is a need to reinforce feelings of identity. During the Algerian War of Independence, the exploits of the familiar heroes, brought back to life by means of oral performances, contributed to the strengthening of Algerian national pride.

The Laws of the Desert

Beyond their individual prestige, the heroes of the Hilalian *siyar* embody a communitarian ideal linked to the way of life of the desert people. This ideal conveys a particular sense of honor that seems to determine all the individual behaviors and regulate social life, serving, in essence, as a moral code.

What are the essential components of this code reflected by the *siyar*? First, family solidarity or *esprit de corps* (*as̱abiyya*), which demands self-denial. The heroine Jâzya must sacrifice herself by accepting to be given in marriage to a foreign prince: the very survival of the group takes precedence over individual consideration. In this case, exogamy (marriage outside the group) is practised: normally, endogamy is preferred (as the proverb says, "Knead your own clay"). The necessity of bearing male descendants also involves the honor of men. The sons of Hilâl owe it to themselves to perpetuate their lineage. Therefore, female barrenness is a calamity. Emir Rizq, still without a son after seven years of marriage, says to his wife, Khadrâ':

> I married you an honourable woman to increase my
>   honor
> It turns out you are barren, in you there are no
>   offspring . . .
> Woe to him whose strength Fate has destroyed.
> (Reynolds 1997: 236)

Another basic virtue in which the Hilalians take pride is eloquence. They refer to themselves as *ahl al-mʿâna* (people of allusion). The Banû Hilâl of pre-Islamic Arabia are known to have attached great importance to the art of poetry, organizing verbal contests in periods of truce, when feats of war gave way to rhetorical exploits. In the *siyar*, the characters themselves seem to evince a taste for language using linguistic subtleties, playing on word sounds and polysemy (multiple meanings).

Death entails a codified ceremony. The body is surrounded by ritual cares, ceremonial laments are sung, and respect is paid to the deceased in keeping with his prestige, even if he is a foreigner. Such is the case of Khwâja ʿAmer, the valorous ally. At his death, the expression of mourning takes the form of sacrificed animals and the destruction of wealth. However, it may happen that the Hilalian Jâzya remains clearly indifferent to the death of one of her people. She then justifies her behavior before the Council of Elders:

> O Hilâl Bû Ali, three kinds of men deserve to be wept
>   and mourned for.
> The first faces danger so that war be extinguished.
> The second offers hospitality in years of drought and
>   famine when giving a sip of water to the thirsty one
>   requires great efforts.
> The third is witty and eloquent, imposing his own
>   rights as well as the others'.
> The rest, o Hilâl Bû Ali, are nothing more than the
>   dim glitter which a blind man can hardly perceive.
> They deserve neither tears nor laments.
> (transl. from Guiga 1968: 28).

Such is the law of the desert, an absolute imperative that makes men great.

References

Canova, Giovanni. 1996. The Epic Poet in Egyptian Tradition. *Journal of Mediterranean Studies* 6, no. 1:7–14.
Carbou, Henri. 1913. *Méthode pratique pour l'étude de l'arabe parlé au Ouadaï et à l'est du Tchad*. Paris.
Connelly, Bridget. 1973. The Structure of Four Banî Hilâl Tales. *Journal of Arabic Literature* 4:18–47.
Galley, Micheline and Ayoub, Abderrahman. 1983. *Histoire des Bani Hilal et de ce qui leur advint dans leur marche vers l'ouest. Classiques Africains* 22. Paris: Belles Letters.
Guiga, Abderrahman. 1968. *Min ʿaqâsîs banî hilâl*. Tunis.
MacMichael, H. A. 1912. *The Tribes of Northern and Central Kordofan*. Cambridge, England: Cambridge University Press.
Nacib, Youssef. 1994. *Une geste en fragments*. Paris: Publisud.
Patterson, J. R. 1930. *Stories of Abu Zeid the Hilali in Shuwa Arabic*. London.
Reynolds, Dwight. 1995. *Heroic Poets, Poetic Heroes*. Ithaca N.Y.: Cornell University Press.
Reynolds, Dwight. 1997. The Epic of the Banî Hilâl. In *Oral Epics from Africa*, eds. J. W. Johnson, T. A. Hale and S. Belcher. Bloomington: Indiana University Press: 228–239.
Saada, Lucienne. 1985. *La geste hilalienne*. Paris: Gallinard.

MICHELINE GALLEY

See also **Epics; Maghrib; Oral Performance and Literature**

SOMALIA (SOMALI DEMOCRATIC REPUBLIC)

Located on the coast of northeast Africa, Somalia is an arid country neighbored by Djibouti, Ethiopia, and Kenya. The country's nearly 11,530,000 people are predominantly Somali. With a population of 900,000, Mogadishu is the nation's capital and largest city. The major languages spoken in Somalia are Somali, Arabic, Oromo, Italian, and English. The majority of the nation's people are Sunni Muslim (99%), while the remaining 1 percent is composed of various other religious groups.

In 1884, Britain took over northern Somaliland; Italy gained control of southern Somaliland a few years later. In 1936, Italy merged this territory with Eritrea and Ethiopia to create Italian East Africa, which it lost in World War II. After seventy-five years of colonial rule by Britain and Italy, Somalia gained its independence on July 1, 1960. Unfortunately, in the years since its independence Somalia has been plagued by war, famine, and economic and social turmoil. Between 1991 and 1992, hundreds of thousands Somalis starved to death before the United Nations intervened and administered relief supplies. Somalia has had no functioning government or formal economy since Mohammed Siad Barre, the nation's dictator for over twenty years, was overthrown in 1991. As of 2003, the country was still divided by armed contingents, which are organized by clan membership, and several attempts at reunification had failed.

Somalia is an arid country, and famine has therefore been a problem for its people for centuries. Because agricultural conditions are poor, 25 percent of the nation's people now live in cities. Unfortunately, there are more people than jobs and unemployment in the country has become increasingly problematic. Despite such poor economic conditions, Somali industries include sugar refining, tuna and beef canning, textiles, iron-rod plants, and petroleum refining. The country's natural resources are uranium, timber, and fish, while agriculture revolves around livestock, bananas, sugarcane, cotton, and cereals.

Despite Somalia's tumultuous economic and political history, the nation is renowned for its poets. Scholars believe that the strength of the nation's poetry is a reflection of the strong oral traditions of Somali nomads, and poetry has played a vital role in the nation's social and political arenas.

JENNIFER JOYCE

SONGHAY

See **Spirit Possession**

SONGS FOR CEREMONIES

The song is a widespread mode of expression in African societies. Although songs are usually accompanied by music and dance when they are performed, numerous distinct types of songs can be distinguished. Some songs are performed purely for pleasure, and singers are in no way restricted by time or place. Examples of these types are cradle melodies, children's nursery rhymes set to music, and love songs, which are often interpreted in many societies by young girls during the drought season. There are songs associated with specific activities, such as hunting, farming, blacksmithing, warfare, and so on. In addition, there are ceremonial songs produced solely, at least in principle, for a particular celebration, of which the song is but one element of the whole ritual. It is this last type of song that is the subject of this discussion.

Under the rubric of "ceremony," it is helpful to distinguish the various types with which certain songs are associated. First, there are ceremonies dependent on seasonal events marked by the local calendar, such as ceremonies to mark the new year, the new moon, the arrival of the rainy season, and the anniversary of a special celestial event. There are also ceremonies linked to the different religious calendars, such as the end of Ramadan or the feast of the lamb in Muslim societies. Songs are also associated with masquerades and the rites associated with honoring ancestors.

Songs are also heard during ceremonies designed to celebrate the momentous stages or moments of human life, or the rites of passage marked by each society. These include rituals of birth,

of naming, of circumcision or excision, of marriage, and of funerals. Among the Sanan of Burkina Faso, this song might be heard at funerals:

If I don't accompany you, mother,
  you won't arrive under the tree of death.
If I, Kuma, speaker of words, don't accompany you,
  mother,
  you'll never arrive under the tree of death.
(Nieba and Platiel, 1980)

On the whole, a majority of a society's repertory of ceremonial songs are those composed for these various ceremonies. In addition, there are songs accompanying the various stages of the initiation ceremonies of different initiatory societies, such as the songs of the Komo and of the Kore of Bamana initiatory societies. One also finds a repertory of religious songs, such as those in Islam that celebrate the completion of Quranic school or the return from the obligatory pilgrimage to Mecca.

Ceremonies tied to certain aspects of social life are marked by song as well. An important event in any community is the crowning of a chief or the arrival of a visiting government official. The following song is heard at the enthronement of a Bambana chief:

Here's the trunk,
Here's the great trunk,
Here's the white trunk,
A chief is enthroned . . .
Guardian spirits of the town respect him!
Dwarfs of the town fear him!
Bad sicknesses are appeased by his reign!
(Bungener and Dieterlon)

Frequently, at such occasions, praise songs are performed. These are especially valued in the cultures of southern Africa (e.g., Xhosa and Zulu). Certain types of songs peculiar to specific activities may also fall into this category of ceremonial songs. Hunting songs, for example, can be produced for a specific hunting-related activity—a song may accompany the admission of one of the members of a society of hunters to a superior grade of that society. Similarly, some agricultural songs may be performed during the sowing or harvest seasons. As noted earlier, even these songs are accompanied by music and dance.

The themes of ceremonial songs are obviously closely connected to cultural functions. Songs that are sung at feasts related to celestial events or at religious ceremonies are usually characterized by a more philosophical tone. Either they are addressed to deities or they evoke, through maxims or aphorisms, the laws of nature. Fulani weavers offer this prayer:

I beg authorization from God where the sun rises.
I beg authorization from God where the sun sets.
At the beginning is God, at the end is God.
Who doesn't begin in your name, will finish in your
  name.
All things except God are a lie.
(Dieterlen 1965)

Ceremonial songs celebrating life's rites of passage, from birth to death, usually focus on conspiring against bad luck, administering benediction, giving advice about what behavior to adopt in a new stage of life. For example, songs of marriage will remind the bride of her new duties, both as a housewife and as a mate. By the same token, songs associated with circumcision call on the candidates to muster up courage before the knife. From the Bamana of Mali we have the following:

Go speak to my father and to my mother,
   they aren't ashamed,
Oh! He! to be ashamed.
At the assembly place, the child is courageous!
He, he, he! What joy!
(Luneau, 1980)

Even though the themes of songs may differ from one type to the next, the stylistic properties of ceremonial songs are relatively homogeneous, both for the genre as a whole and for the different societies of the African continent. Most often, the song's infrastructure rests upon short aphorisms, many of which come from the repertory of proverbs. These are usually repeated several times, according to a more or less elaborate ritual, and most often punctuated by the alternation of a solo (or duo) and a chorus in a call-and-response fashion. The artistic element in these songs emanates from the subtle counterpoint of repeated lines, both textual and musical.

What distinguishes the specific genre of the ceremonial song depends on the mode of expression (i.e., the melody and instrumental accompaniment). It does often happen, for example, that the same wording in a song may be used for a marriage or mask song or for a funeral chant. Yet, upon hearing the interpretation, those listening will be able to tell exactly which occasion is targeted. Each type of ritual song will be defined by a strict set of parameters reflecting what is authorized to be composed (and sung), as well as to be consumed (heard) by the public. For this same reason, there are frequently forbidden aspects, in particular with respect to initiatory songs. Some can be sung only by the head of the family, some by women, and some by the initiators of the neophytes.

Of all the genres, except those that are the prerogative of specialists, these are certainly the ones which are the most closely regulated. As they are often linked to sacred rites, they are less susceptible to variation than the others. In effect, religious songs are frequently sung exactly the same, word for word, from one performance to the next. On the other hand, certain types of ceremonial songs allow for the creativity of the interpreter, whose artistic contribution consists of introducing variants of the canonical models. This is often the case for songs of praise, which are sung at many different ceremonies.

Thus, the repertory of ceremonial songs represents an extremely important part of the storehouse of verbal folklore of many African societies, one that must not be neglected. Furthermore, these songs are often a source of real inspiration for the ritual theater and for modern popular songs in Africa.

References

Bungener, Youssouf Cisse, and Germaine Dieterlen. *Priere pour l'intronisation d'un chef bambara.*
Dieterlen, Germaine, ed. 1965. *Textes sacres d'Afrique Noire.* Paris: Gallimard.
Luneau, R. 1980. Chants d'excision bambara. In *Recueil de litterature manding.* Paris: ACCT.
Nieba, A. and S. Platiel. 1980. Chants de funerailles Sanan. In *Recueil de litterature manding.* Paris: ACCT.
Rodegem, F. 1973. *Anthologie Rundi.* Classiques Africains Paris: Belles Lettres.

JEAN DERIVE

See also **Birth and Death Rituals among the Gikuyu; Children's Folklore; Music**

SONGS OF THE DYULA

The Dyula occupy a savanna area covering northern Cote d'Ivoire and southern Burkina Faso. This society is part of the Manding ethnic grouping, a significant cultural complex in West Africa. Their gradual Islamization, occurring between the seventeenth and nineteenth centuries, has had important repercussions on their traditions.

Dyula folklore is essentially comprised of words, music, and dance. Whereas certain genres of their oral repertory can be performed without dance or music, it is quite rare for the dances to be produced without sung accompaniment. Furthermore, singing is conceptually linked to dance, as the Dyula term *donkili* illustrates with its etymological connotation of "a call to dance." As far as music is concerned, it is inconceivable to perform it without recourse to words or dance.

Twenty instruments are used by the Dyula. Percussion instruments include drums (*baa, butu, dagadundun, domisi, dundunba, jembe, karanamentu, korokoto, kotodundun, longan,* and *perende*), metal gongs (*daworo, kagayan,* and *lato*), and *balafons*. Their wind instruments are horns (*gbeni* and *gbofe*) and whistles (*filen* and *sinbon*). They also use cattle-bells, bracelet bells (*gbanyan*), and rattles (*yanbara*).

The specific combinations of these various instruments constitute the proper musical accompaniment for each type of song and dance. In effect, it is the great variety of songs that creates the originality characteristic of Dyula folk music. The occasions for their performance include calendar holidays, celebrations of each Dyula community's historical events, occasions in the Islamic calendar (e.g., Ramadan, Tabaski), or events in the pre-Islamic calendar.

The dances that are common among the Dyula of Kong use masks (*Do donkili*). A song which accompanies the Safo mask goes:

He, sorcerers, don't stop here!
Safo comes, Safo comes to take you,
   today is the day!
The Sorcerer was snared today, it's Safo who knew it!
The Sorcerer wasn't snared today, it's Safo who knew
   it!
Korodugu's Safo is coming out today,
sorcerers, know it quickly!
Korodugu's child is coming out today,
children, know it quickly!

Another mask song is for Domuso, a female mask that aids women's fertility, especially those previously childless. In this song, women's uteruses are likened to a cooking pot that has been dried up by the fire, but *beno*, the power of the Domuso mask (which is rich with gold and silver), will bring children, the ultimate wealth:

> Beno, owner of gold, come, he doesn't inspire disgust.
> Beno, owner of silver, come, he doesn't inspire disgust.
> The cooking pot of some women is dried by the fire
> They all stay to look at Beno for a bargain.

There are also ceremonies to mark the important ritual moments of human life, such as baptism, circumcision, marriage, and return from pilgrimage. A favorite wedding song reflects the negative feelings by women about marriage (the "little bone" it refers to is the husband's penis). Traditionally, Thursday night is the night of first sexual intercourse for the couple, and because women (in this case Majuman) usually are married against their will, the event is characterized as a "battle":

> There's the little bone, there's the little bone!
> I don't give it to anyone.
> If you don't see Majuman,
> it's she who's in the Thursday night battle!

Songs and music are associated with particular activities linked to farming and hunting. One song demonstrates the competition farmers wage in preparing their fields. This song challenges Vali to work harder:

> He, Vali, you who advances quickly, come back, settle,
> I proclaim your name!
> Make your mounds quickly and stop!
> He, Vali, I proclaim your name!

This next song honors great hunters of the past, such as Nyapon:

> Ohe, bush dog
> Nyapon who kills the animal at your place,
> hunter who kills meat at your place!
> I ask you to let me proclaim men's names,
> of men who are in the bush,
> of hunters who are in the heart of the bush.

Still other songs can sometimes be performed on an individual basis to celebrate a personal event, or simply to provide amusement and entertainment, as in the case of *bondolon donkili*, the little love songs sung by young girls in moonlight:

> Certainly render an account that is my beloved's,
> he who's learning in college,
> the author of the letter which pleases me so is at
>   college.
> Certainly render an account that is my beloved's,
> and myself I see that it's my beloved's.
> My beloved is a good speaker,
> he who makes a beautiful speech is my beloved.

The last example is of children's nursery rhyme songs (*Tolon donkili*):

> The little partridge, dyendyen oh!
> Dyendyen!
> There's a little partridge,
> dyendyen!
> It isn't snared by the thread,
> dyendyen!

> It will however be snared by the thread,
> dyendyen!
> The partridge isn't being watched over.
> the partridge flies away—frou, frou!

A specific Dyula name is assigned to each of these different songs. Most often the name is a combination of the word *donkili* (song) and the term for the ceremony, mask, activity, or dance with which it is associated: examples include *densagali donkili* (baptismal song), *safo do donkili* (song of the Safo mask), *donso donkili* (song of hunters), and *kurubi donkili* (song of the Kurubi dance). This system used for naming allows the distinction of forty individual types of songs, which can be grouped into several generic categories. For example, marriage songs (*konyon donkili*) can be further divided into ten types; the same goes for songs for dance (*don donkili*).

Even though the majority of songs are closely linked to dances, some songs can be performed without musical accompaniment, such as the hunting songs and the *bondolon* (love songs). Strict rules of etiquette govern both the performers and audience of these songs, especially with respect to the criteria of gender, age, or social class—such as a nobleman (*horon*) or a captive (*woloso*). Certain songs can also be restricted to certain community members, such as the Kong mask songs, which women as well as the uninitiated are forbidden to hear.

Although the majority of the Dyula oral repertory is to be sung, there are more classical oral genres whose performance is spoken rather than sung. Nonetheless, there are certain tales (*ntalen*) that do contain parts to be sung. They may be recited by either gender, but some distinctions are made for more strictly masculine or feminine repertories. The Dyula oral repertory often contains appended riddles and enigmas (*ntalenkorobo*), which in principle can only be recited at night and are differentiated from the etiological narratives and myths (*ngalen kuma*), which may be told during the day as well as at night.

The Dyula also possess a large repertory of proverbs (*lamara*), which the eldest members are at liberty to recite on various occasions, and which also show up frequently in the songs and in the folktales. When they are lacking professional artists to perform the epic narratives, to which they sometimes listen in the company of their Maninka and Bambana cousins, they love to hear the telling of their own glorious family histories (*ko koro*), which can only be narrated by the head of the family.

The Dyula have been meticulous in circulating their oral repertory within their society through the proper channels of circumstance and spokesperson (by whom the institutional message can be spoken and transmitted) and this has rendered their verbal folklore a most effective tool of social regulation.

References

Derive, Jean. 1987a. Parole et pouvoir chez les Dioula de Kong. In *Journal des Africanistes* 57:19–30.

———. 1987b. *Le fonctionnement sociologique de la litterature orale: l'exemple des* Dioula de Kong. Paris: Institut d'Ethnologie.

———. 1989. Le jeune menteur et le vieux sage. In *Graines de paroles*. Paris: CNRS.

———. 1990. La chanson dans une societe de tradition orale. In *Contemporary French Civilization* 15:191–202.

———. 1992. The Function of Oral Art in the Regulation of Social Power in Dyula Society. In *Power, Marginality, and Oral*

Literature, ed. G. Furniss and E. Gunner. Cambridge, England: Cambridge University Press.

Derive, Marie-Jose, Jean Derive, and Balemory Barro. 1980. *Jula ntalen. Contes dioula*. Abidjan: CEDA.

Nebie, Marc. 1984. Et si on disait un conte? (Jula, Haute Volta). *Cahiers de Litterature Orale* 16:35–38.

JEAN DERIVE

See also **Birth and Death Rituals among the Gikuyu; Gender Representation in African Folklore; Initiation; Masks and Masquerades**

SONGYE

See **Visual Arts**

SOUTH AFRICA (REPUBLIC OF SOUTH AFRICA)

South Africa, located at the southernmost tip of Africa and neighbored by Namibia, Botswana, Zimbabwe, Mozambique, Swaziland, and the Atlantic and Indian Oceans, is a country of over 46 million people. Its climate ranges from temperate to arid. Pretoria, a city of one million people, is the nation's capital. Three-quarters of South Africa's population is black, 14 percent is white, 9 percent is colored, and 2 percent is Indian. The major languages spoken are Afrikaans, English, Ndebele, Pedi, Sotho, Swati, Tsonga, Tswana, Venda, Xhosa, and Zulu. Eighty-one percent of the nation is Christian, while the remaining 19 percent are either Hindu or Muslim.

South Africa has suffered a long and tumultuous history of institutionalized racism and white supremacy, which began with the first Dutch settlement at Cape Town in 1652. The Dutch Cape Colony depended on the slavery of nonwhites for its domestic economy. While indigenous populations resisted their enslavement during the eighteenth and nineteenth centuries, the white settlers eventually conquered their land and robbed them of their freedom. To the dismay of the Dutch, the British gained possession of the Cape Colony in 1815. Between 1899 and 1902, the Boer War erupted between the British and the Afrikaners (white Dutch, or Boers), each of whom were vying for control of the colony. On May 31, 1910, the Afrikaners and the British Empire came to an agreement that granted rule to the Union of South Africa's white minority.

South Africa's ensuing years of white supremacy culminated in the implementation of apartheid, or "separatehood," in 1948 by the nation's National Party. Under apartheid, preexisting patterns of racism and inequality between the whites and nonwhites were enforced and legalized in a vast body of laws and legislation. In the face of the growing international protest during the 1980s, the dismantling of apartheid began in 1989, and Nelson Mandela was released from prison in 1990. In April of 1994, the nation held its first nonracial elections. This election resulted in the overwhelming victory of the African National Congress (ANC), which cooperated with its past rivals, the National Party and the Inkatha Freedom Party, in forming the Government of National Unity (GNU). Nelson Mandela, the nation's first black president, served as head of the GNU.

South Africa is rich in natural resources such as gold, diamonds, mineral ores, uranium, and fish. Based in the fertile farmlands, the nation's agricultural sector produces corn, wool, sugarcane, wheat, tobacco, citrus fruits, and dairy products. South Africa's principle industries and sources of revenue are mining, automobile assembly, metalworking, textiles, iron and steel, and fishing. South African wines have become world famous. Tourism is another major industry, with South Africa the twenty-fifth most popular tourist destination in the world in 1998.

Despite apartheid's end, the legacy of three and a half centuries of inequality have not been erased, and South Africa remains a deeply divided nation. Whites still control much of the nation's industry and have comfortable lives, while nonwhites often suffer from economic hardship. The end of apartheid has, however, ended international cultural and sporting boycotts against the nation, and South Africa's artists and athletes have become increasingly prominent.

Contemporary South African artists from all ethnic groups have rejoined the world art scene. Traditional verbal artists, especially the famous praise poets of the Xhosa and Shona, continue to create and adapt their work. Women's literacy, at 82 percent, is the highest in Africa.

HIV/AIDS is South Africa's greatest challenge as it enters the twenty-first century. Not only does South Africa have the highest rates of infection and death in all of Africa, but response to the epidemic is hampered by debate over which strategies to follow. In 1999, 250,000 died of AIDS in South Africa and in 2000, 40% of those 15–49 years old died from AIDS. With an estimated 4.7 million suffering from HIV and AIDS in 2003, South Africa has the highest number of infected individuals in the world.

JENNIFER JOYCE

SOUTH AFRICA, ORAL TRADITIONS

The African oral tradition distills the essences of human experiences, shaping them into memorable, readily retrievable images of broad applicability, with an extraordinary potential for eliciting emotional responses. These images are removed from their historical contexts so that performers may recontextualize them in artistic forms. The oral arts, containing this sensory residue of past cultural life and the wisdom so engendered, constitute a medium for organizing, examining, and interpreting an audience's experiences of the images of the present.

The major oral genres—riddle and lyric poem, proverb, tale, heroic poetry, and epic—are characterized by a metaphorical process, the product of pattern and image; and, being prescriptive rather than descriptive, they resolve themselves into models for human and cultural behavior, falling into a cyclical, not linear, mode. History, a part of heroic poetry and epic, appears in fragmentary form.

The oral categories are interwoven; a common internal structure characterizes them, each with a rhythmical ordering of image and motif, which controls the ties between the art tradition and the real world. It is by means of this common structure, and it is because of the metaphor or its potential (the organizing factor in each of the genres), that vital links are established with the visual arts, as well as with dance, mime, and music. Each of the forms in some way nourishes the other.

Riddles

The riddle is a figurative comparative form. A problem is fathomed, but perhaps more important, the attributes of each side of the comparison are transferred to the other. Because the riddle involves paradox as well as imagery, it exercises both the intellect and the imagination of the audience; in its attempts to find the answer, it becomes a part of the metaphorical transformation. The delight in discovery characterizes the riddle, prepares members of an audience for the more complex coupling that occurs in the tale and epic, and reflects the relations among images in lyric poetry. The riddle operates in two modes, much as lyric and tale do; one is literal, the other figurative, with a tension and an interaction between them. The literal level of interpretation interacts vigorously and creatively with the figurative; that is the full experience of the riddle. It is not simply a solution that is wanted; it is the prismatic experience of figurative imagery placed against the literal; the play is between fantasy and reality, between the figurative and the literal. In the riddle, the audience's imagination, made active during performance, is also made visible.

The riddle establishes a model for all oral art. The relationship between images has at least the potential for metaphor and complexity. In the African lyric, it is possible to see a set of riddles operating as the separate images in the poem relate to one another metaphorically. The combination of figurative images creates the final experience of the lyric poem. It is often more complex than the riddle because it embraces a number of riddling connections, and a single riddle relationship may become more complex when it is introduced into the context of yet another, and so on, as the riddling images of the poem interact. The poet supplies a series of images that repeat aspects of a basic theme or examine an emotion with intensity. Each metaphorical set, in itself a riddle, acts as a kind of clue, bringing the audience closer to an understanding of the poet's intent. The lyric poet repeats the image, establishes the boundaries of the varieties of imagery that may be introduced into the poem, and creates the rhythm; these ensure that the different sets of images will be experienced by the audience in a similar way.

Myth

Myth is not a theology or body of dogma or a worldview; it is not so much a story as that which moves the story, and we find it in incipient form in the riddle, lyric, and proverb. In the latter, metaphor is achieved when a somewhat hackneyed expression is brought into contact with reality. The proverb is a metaphorical relationship, tying an old saying to a situation with which it may or may not have a clearly perceived relationship, but that, with thought, reveals a reference for that real life experience. The proverb in this respect behaves similarly to the way image operates in lyric poetry, in which diverse images are brought into contact with one another. The audience knows what it must do, and it works toward an understanding of the relationship; the proverb form, and the audience's experiences with it, force a movement toward reason. Proverbs are tired clichés only when viewed in isolation, but when they are placed into realistic con-

texts, they become vital, even dynamic. What gives them freshness is the experience to which they are giving form. In the lyric, linkages must be understood within the poem before they can be comprehended in a realistic context. In the proverb, the only way for the metaphor to be realized is by means of the instant connection between the art form and reality. The proverb is similar to the riddle in the sense that metaphor is intended, as the ancient truth of the culture touches contemporary experience. More, perhaps, than the riddle, the proverb establishes ties with the culture's sages; ancient wisdom is carried by the proverbial expression that, through constant use, becomes easily remembered, and hackneyed, until given new life. The proverb gives cultural and artistic form to present action. The riddle does much the same thing when problem and solution are harmonized.

Patterning of Images

The single most important characteristic of African oral performances is the patterning of images. In the simple tale, patterns are built on the actions of a single character, as fantasy and reality are linked in a linear movement from conflict to resolution; at the same time, the metaphorical structure, not unlike that which governs the movement in lyric poetry, controls the patterning, providing the possibilities for complexity, for meaning, and for the revelation of the mimetic relationship. That lyrical core ensures that the potential for expansion and development are not lost. Out of a triangular relationship that includes a central character, a helper, and a villain, the basic movement is developed. The tale at this stage will not necessarily be metaphorical; it may simply bring like image sets into contact with one another for no purpose other than to move the tale effectively to its resolution. But the possibilities for metaphor are a part of the form because of the existence of patterning.

Links among Tales

Many tales have a built-in capacity for linkage to other tales; a number of them, when placed in a narrative frame, produces a complex story. When two tales or more are thus joined and the parts harmonized by the metaphorical process, an epic matrix, if not an epic, is created. It is at this stage that organizing activities similar to those found in the proverb assume importance. In the shorter tales, a process like that of the riddle and poem is sufficient, but, as organization and theme become more involved, the metaphorical movement found in the proverb becomes crucial because it supplies the structure necessary to carry a complex theme. The proverb-type activity establishes the ties between past and present; the type found in the riddle and lyric can then continue to supply the internal ordering of the larger forms. When the number of tales develops to a complexity no longer supportable by the simple structure of the story, and when that set of tales is brought into a context that includes history and the hero, epic is the result.

In heroic poetry, or panegyric, the relationship among images seems also obscure at times. The images are indeed connected; a discourse is initiated by the poet, and the panegyric assumes lyrical form. As in the lyric poems, the rhythm of the poetic performance, its single subject, the thematically designed boundaries, bind the diverse images. Of all African art forms, heroic poetry is the closest to history in its choice of images. It frequently concentrates on historical figures. Panegyric poetry examines heroic aspects of humans—positively, in the rush of pleasure in recounting the affairs in the lives of authentic culture heroes; negatively, in the comparison of the flawed contemporary leader with the great heroes of the past. While the raw material of this poetry is, by and large, realistic, it is history made discontinuous, then placed in novel frames. Within this new context, the hero is described, then judged. It is in the measurement of the poem's subject against the ideals of the society that the work has its metaphorical power. While such poetry is not a historical rendering, it nevertheless has no existence outside history. Images, selected at least partially for their power to elicit strong feelings from an audience, are first removed from their mainly historical contexts, as in the tales. Certain emotions associated with such subjects as heroism and the kingship are intensified and reordered. Because contemporary events are thus routinely measured against cultural values, history is constantly being revived and revised. The poems depend on this enhanced narrative, reproduced, atomized, and redefined. It is a subjective accounting, but the poet, using all his magic to convince his listeners otherwise, contains these, as yet unchannelled, bursts of energy and gives history a new gloss.

Fragmented history, which addresses the adventures of both historical and fictional characters, is also frequently a part of African epic. It is not historical veracity in the linear sense that determines epic, but rather the insight into history and culture provided by this confluence of oral genres. Now, within a pretext or setting that makes possible the merging of various frequently unrelated tales, the metaphorical apparatus—the controlling mechanism found in the riddle and lyric, the proverb, and heroic poetry—coordinates this set of tales to form a larger narrative. All of this centers on the character of the hero and a gradual revelation of his frailty, uncertainties, torments: he often dies, falls, or is deeply troubled, in the process bringing the culture into a new dispensation often prefigured in his resurrection or coming into knowledge. The mythical transformation caused by the creator gods and culture heroes is reproduced precisely in the acts and cyclical, tortured movements of the hero.

Epics

When the tale is at the heart of epic, significant changes occur. The epic is a complex reshaping of the tale. Heroic poetry provides a grid, helping to organize the narratives and narrative-fragments that are transported into the epic framework; it also supplies the specific historical and geographical data for certain epics. What African epics owe to the tale tradition is not difficult to discern. Less obvious is the role that heroic poetry plays in their construction. The simple tale weaves through the historical fragments trapped in images and given new context in the fictional activities. A strong sense of realism thus invests the imaginary character and his actions, even though they are taken directly from the imaginary tale tradition.

In some works, data about geography and history are injected into the narrative, tying the imaginative tales that compose the epic to the real world, to historical place, event, and time. The emphasis on praise-names singles out the hero, his character, his ideals, his struggles. This is not the case in the tale, where characters are not as important as the actions they perform; indeed,

they are often not even given names. The stress in epic is on character, and the praise-names are evidence of this. Epic thus has a grander sweep than either the tale or heroic poetry. It enshrines the themes and emotional experiences of the tale on a broad scale; it embodies the details and historical and cultural specificity of panegyric poetry.

HAROLD SCHEUB

See also **Electronic Media and Oral Traditions; Oral Tradition and Historiography; Ideophones; Oral Literature: Issues of Definition and Terminology; Oral Performance and Literature; Oratory; Performance Studies and African Folklore Research**

SOUTHERN AFRICAN FOLKLORE: OVERVIEW

A Historical Background

The part of the African continent called southern Africa lies between 10 and 35 degrees south of the equator, encompassing the nations of Zambia, Malawi, Zimbabwe, Botswana, Lesotho, South Africa, Swaziland (all former British colonies), Namibia (formerly a German colony, and later a South African colony), Mauritius, Seychelles (former French colonies), Angola, and Mozambique (former Portuguese colonies). These are now all sovereign states, having gained their independence at various stages beginning in the late 1950s. Their systems of government are democratic, although each has its own local variety approximating, to some degree, those of various Western countries.

In all of them, the language of the former colonial power is used as an official medium of communication, with one or more vernaculars serving as national languages. They, together with the Democratic Republic of the Congo in central Africa and Tanzania in East Africa, belong to the Southern African Development Community, a forum designed to encourage trade and political cooperation.

Ethnic Composition

The area is extremely complex in terms of ethnic composition. The peoples of the area are united by the common historical origin of the various vernacular languages spoken by the native citizens. By far the greater majority of the peoples of this region speak languages that belong to the Bantu group. With minor morphonological variations, these languages have a common core vocabulary. For example, the name of the language group comes from the root, *ntu*, the words *mu-ntu* (person) *ba-ntu* (people). There is a usage of this word that restricts its meaning to "black person," which can thus be extended to "a person is one who is black in color." So a *mu-ntu* is distinct from a *mu-rungu*, *mu-zungu*, *um-lungu*, *mu-kiwa*, *le-koa*, *i-khiwa*, which are all terms used in these languages for "white man." It is common to hear an utterance such as "I met two people and three white men," said without any intention to convey racial prejudice. Bantu languages are subdivided into smaller clusters that have more in common with themselves than with languages in other clusters. The degree of mutual intelligibility is the factor that binds the following clusters: the southern Bantu Nguni cluster, which includes Zulu, Xhosa, Swati, Ndebele, (and Ngoni of Malawi); the Tswana-Sotho cluster of South Africa and Botswana, which includes Tswana, southern Sotho, Northern Sotho, and also Lozi of Zambia. Further north there is a cluster that includes Shona of Zimbabwe, Nyanja and Bemba of Zambia, Chewa and Tumbuka of Malawi, and Sena of Mozambique. In Namibia and Angola the two major clusters are Herero and Mbundu, respectively. There is also Venda of northern South Africa and southern Zimbabwe, and the Tswa-Ronga cluster of South Africa. The national language of Tanzania is Kiswahili, which is also spoken in many other countries in East and central Africa, including the Democratic Republic of the Congo, where Chiluba, Kikongo, and Lingala are the major languages.

Speakers of the above language are relative newcomers to the region when compared to the San (Bushmen), who live in parts of South Africa, Namibia, and Botswana. The San are the original denizens of southern Africa and are now concentrated in these three countries after a long history of war, conquest, and displacement in their struggles to retain their land against African immigrants into the region and European settlers. Their folklore, including praise poetry, songs, folktales, and other lore about their hunter-gatherer life, are the first articulations of the nature of colonial experience from the point of view of the colonized. Duncan Brown (1998) recognizes these oral forms as the most original and earliest contributions to world literature to come from southern Africa. Their stories are about the life of the Early Race who, according to their myths, are the San's ancestors. Failure on the part of newcomers to the region to listen to and understand San folklore denied them the opportunity to be guided in their interaction with the San by the latter's rich cultural heritage as conveyed in that folklore. Instead, a perception of the San as prehistoric, static, and, therefore, anachronistic led not only to the neglect of their oral literature by researchers and colonial administrators but to their near decimation.

Folklore Scholarship

Of all the genres of folklore to be found in the communities of southern Africa, the ones that have been most extensively researched, and on which many publications have been produced, are the verbal, which many in the field call "orature." These include legends, songs, proverbs, riddles, and tales. But folklore encompasses many other genres, including nursery rhymes; traditional rituals performed to "celebrate" rites of passage, such as birth, initiation into adulthood, marriage, death, and settling the spirit of the dead, and the dances and various forms of drama that accompany and complement all of these other forms. Since the communities among which these forms flourished continue to be rural, there is folklore about the weather, domestic and wild animals, and traditionally prescribed rewards and sanctions governing the individual's conduct in the family and in the wider society. For example, drought or pestilence can visit a community if the chief or one of his subjects desecrates a shrine that is dedicated to the ancestral spirits, or if he persistently flouts the proscription that no one should till the land on a certain holy day. In such a case, a diviner will be consulted so that the offender is identified. Depending on the enormity of the offense, and on the social standing of the culprit, appropriate sanctions, ranging from imposing a fine on the of-

fender, exiling him, to requiring the community as a whole to hold a propitiation ceremony at which a beast is sacrificed, may be the only way out.

These and other practices and beliefs are what the first students of folklore in southern Africa, including missionaries, travelers, colonial administrators, and anthropologists, sought to come to terms with—at a time when folklore was still passed on from generation to generation by word of mouth in nonliterate societies. They constitute what traditional scholarship originally demarcated as folklore. But more recent research on the subject has led scholars to realize that folklore does not serve to define only a worldview that was prevalent in preliterate societies, and which today is confined to those that are still illiterate or who have become semiliterate. It is the quintessential component of the ways in which the "folk" view themselves and their place in the universe; and it informs and prescribes the ways in which they can both nurture and exploit their material environment in order to meet their secular and spiritual needs. Society—whether literate or not, whether rural or urban, whether industrialized or pastoral—both consciously and unconsciously creates and thrives on folklore. This is the inspiration behind Alan Dundes's expansion of the definition of the term *folk*, and, by extension, of what constitutes *folklore*. To Dundes, "The term *folk* can refer to *any group of people whatsoever* who share at least one common factor. It does not matter what the linking factor is—it could be a common occupation, language, or religion—but what is important is that a group formed for whatever reason will have some traditions which it calls its own." Pointing out that a group will consist of at least two people, he claimed that the domain of folklore can range in size from a family to a whole nation adding that given the inclusive nature of folk and folklore, "it would be absurd to argue that there is no folklore in the United States and that industrialization stamps out folk groups and folklore" (1980, 6–8).

Research and interest in folklore in southern Africa began with the arrival of Westerners in the region, whether they were missionaries, colonial administrators, hunters, or anthropologists. Given the culture-bound nature of folklore as outlined above, the various genres individually and collectively presented the newcomers to the region with intractable epistemological problems. Many dismissed them as indices of the backwardness of the natives in the march from the dark past toward civilization, on a road along which they themselves and their societies back home had made giant strides. This was partly because they had been schooled in an intellectual milieu that had done little to enable them to accommodate difference.

Leray Vail and Landey White (1991) provide one of the most detailed surveys of the theories that informed the work of Western-trained scholars and missionaries on southern African folklore. The year 1840 marked the four-hundredth anniversary of the invention of movable type. This was celebrated by Mendelssohn in his Second Symphony *Hymn of Praise*, as indicating that "The night has passed away/and the day has come." Vail and White comment that for the composer, and also for the intellectuals of the time, those societies "possessing print literacy are truly blessed by God, while those without it are indeed benighted." Thus the division between races was clear-cut. There developed a belief, with a pseudoscience to buttress it, that since the races had different origins, they had nothing in common. The possession and use of the technology to write things down became a litmus test for being viewed as civilized (this served as an elaborate justification for slavery for some time). But, in the 1850s, Christian thinking took centerstage in writings about race, and the belief in polygenesis was discarded. It also came to be realized that races with a common origin could develop along fundamentally different lines, and at different rates, due to evolution, an influential paradigm by which such phenomena were explained in this period.

This paradigm influenced the work of Edward Tylor who, in studying nonliterate cultures, also used the comparative approach. Vail and White say his book was concerned essentially with "the mental life of non-literate peoples." This was the focus of Sir James George Frazer's *Golden Bough* (1890). He theorized that all societies, and the individuals within them, came to understand themselves and their place in the universe by using their mental capacities. Whereas primitive societies, "encased in a world of mystery and magic, and with mental processes much inferior to those of [their] educated contemporaries" (Vail and White 1991, 6), were still far behind.

One of the earliest studies of southern African societies informed by the works of Tylor and Frazer is Dudley Kidd's *The Essential Kafir* (1904). This was specifically focused on the African peoples of the southeastern region of the continent, namely those in the Cape Province, Mozambique, Rhodesia, and Nyasaland (Malawi). Vail and White point out that Kidd's work was influenced by that of Tylor and Frazer in having an evolutionist and comparative thrust. He is quoted as writing that "when we come to understand the silliest of their customs we are surprised to find how it fits *with human customs* the world over, and forms some of the primordial stuff out of which modern European usages have evolved" (Vail and White 1991, 7). It is as if he half-suspected that his subjects might not be human.

Vail and White also comment that Kidd's portrayal of the African would have found ready acceptance among the white settlers, since it echoed their own racial stereotyping of the natives. Some of his assertions about his subjects could not have been entertained if he had conducted a thorough study of local folklore. Kidd is reported as having said that the African could not be trusted to be truthful, not out of malice, but because, "childlike, he could not grasp the importance of truth." Further, Kidd claimed that because the native African had undeveloped mental capacities, he had no sense of logic and was thus "capable of entertaining contradictory ideas at the same time" (Vail and White 1991, 7–8). It was also believed that the native African lacked the ability to classify phenomena, was unable to think in abstract terms, and was weak in grasping causal relationships.

Modern Scholarship

Modern scholarship has come a long way since *The Essential Kafir*. All the epithets with which Kidd labels the southern African native have since been shown to be contradicted by various aspects of the folklore of the region. No society, in Africa or anywhere else, could survive unless it placed a premium on the value of truth. Communities in the region have proverbs that emphasize this fact, that the truth cannot be hidden. The Shona of Zimbabwe say: "That which has horns cannot be concealed (by covering it) in a bundle of grass." To emphasize the importance and stubbornness of the truth, the Shona pronoun for "that which" is in the augmentative form, *ri-*, instead of the

diminutive *chi-*. Further, parallel to the English saying, "Cash talk breaks no friendship" a Shona proverb proclaims "The truth does not destroy a relationship."

As for being comfortable with entertaining two contradictory ideas at the same time, the African's answer is that this ensures that extremes are avoided. Things must be done in moderation, with the individual always striving to achieve the golden mean in his or her conduct. Thus, both cooperation and individualism are recommended in the proverbial lore, with circumstances determining which one to choose: "What is mine alone is food/ when it comes to a court case, I call others," which is in apparent contradiction to "Too many mice make no lining for their nest" (which is very similar to the English saying: "Too many cooks spoil the broth").

Above all, the very fact that a community has its own proverbial lore, riddles, tales, and religious beliefs means that its members have the mental capacity to think in abstract terms and to philosophize about the human condition. The observation of human conduct, of the flora and fauna in the ecological environment, and of the seasons, together with the dialectical interrelations of these and other phenomena, has inspired the African (as it has done others beyond Africa) to develop a complex, multigenre folklore. This folklore serves to regulate social behavior even as it educates citizens about opportunities for self-fulfillment, their responsibilities and rights, about sanctions for aberrant conduct, and the rewards for conduct that bolsters the integrity of the social fabric.

Praise Poetry

Many studies of the praise poetry of southern African societies have been conducted. For the Xhosa there are the works of A. C. Jordan (1973) and Jeff Opland (1983): Liz Gunner and Mafika Gwala's Musho (1991) is a generously illustrated discussion of Zulu popular praises, as opposed to those of the rulers, which have been studied more recently by, among others, Duncan Brown (1998). The latter covers several genres besides praise poetry. Beginning with the oral literature of the Xam Bushmen, Brown analyzes the praises of King Shaka, and he then dwells at length on the hymns composed and performed by Isaiah Shembe's Church of the Nazarites. He comments on the vitality of this oral genre, which arises from its merging of texts from both Zulu traditional praises and the Bible. This hybridity of South African poetry was carried over into the writings and oral performances of the poets of the black consciousness movement in the 1970s. These poets, because they were addressing issues arising from the ravages of the apartheid system, conveyed their messages partly orally and partly in writing. Written versions of their work were always in danger of being censored or banned altogether (and they often were), because they were seen by the authorities as subversive.

The Ngoni of Malawi and the Ndebele of Zimbabwe are offshoots of the Zulu. The praises of the latter group have been studied by Caleb Dube (1988) and Themba Nkabinde (1990), while Vail and White devote a whole chapter to Andrew Smith's study of the praises of Mzilikazi, the Ndebele king who led his people from Zululand to present-day Zimbabwe in 1834–1835. Alfred Mtenje and Boston Soko (1998) and Moyo (1978) have written studies of the praises of the Ngoni. Saac Schapera's (1965) and Daniel Kunene's (1971) works on the praises of the

Sotho-Tswana group remain classics even today. The best known works on Shona praises are those by Aaron Hodza and George Fortune (1979), and by Alec Pongweni (1996).

Other Folklore

In addition to work on the praises, many publications have appeared on other types of folklore, such as riddles (Pongweni and Chiwome, 1995), music (Coplan 1985; Pongweni 1982), folktales (Scheub 1999), and on aspects of the folklore of women's household work (Seloma 1998). David Coplan's book is on the music and theater of black people in the townships of apartheid South Africa, while Pongweni's is on the songs sung by Zimbabwe's liberation war cadres. Each of those books deals with the creative responsiveness of the genre to contemporary political and economic issues under oppressive and undemocratic regimes. This same responsiveness of music is evident today, when the region is threatened with extinction by the scourges of famine and AIDS.

While the more established breakaway church denominations have been inundated with new converts in unprecedented numbers, new ones have sprung up, as people turn to religion to find explanations and solutions to their problems. They do this in songs whose lyrics merge messages from the scriptures and from traditional religion. On the other hand, Michael Bourdillon (1998) has written an authoritative and wide-ranging study of the Shona peoples of Zimbabwe, covering their folklore regarding the individual's and society's obligations and rights in many aspects of life, such as marriage, land "ownership," the traditional roles of men as opposed to those of women, chieftainship, witchcraft, the roles of the medicine man and the diviner in times of sickness and other misfortune, and religion. Each of these studies, and others mentioned here, carry long lists of references and bibliographies that show just how much work has been done by scholars from various backgrounds on the folklore of southern Africa.

It is clear to modern scholars that, far from providing evidence that southern African societies lived in a state of homeostasis, as Dudley Kidd and others claimed, folklore is decidedly responsive and adaptive to changing sociopolitical developments. This is evident in many of its genres, particularly in the ones on which most research has been done. In 2001, Russell Kaschula published a collection of essays from a 1998 conference under the title *African Oral Literature: Functions in Contemporary Contexts.* Omit the colon in the title and you have Kaschula making a statement about the perennial relevance to African life of one genre of folklore. Or, perhaps not one genre, when one considers the chapter headings in the book, about which he writes:

> The chapters in this book comment on various aspects of contemporary African existence and how orality permeates our daily lives. These chapters are grouped under the following appropriate headings: orality and music; orality and gender; orality and medicine; orality, theatre and cinema; orality and religion; orality, text, texture and context, as well as orality, history, and politics (2001, xvi).

Folklore permeates the lives of the people of southern Africa, in the sense that its knowledge is like that of a nonverbal language, particularly as it serves what Michael Halliday (1971) called the "ideational" and the "interpersonal" functions in one's life. Of the ideational function he wrote, "the speaker or writer embodies in language his experience of the phenomena of the real world," for himself and others. The interpersonal function serves to position the individual in relation to others who have knowledge of the folklore shared by the community to which they all belong. Folklore serves to guide, to evaluate, and to criticize conduct, providing a running commentary on human behavior. The leader of Zimbabwe's war veterans, who in the first years of the twenty-first century violently dispossessed white farmers of their land, was asked by journalists what he planned to do with the two or more farms that he allegedly acquired. The story goes that he replied, "I plan to become a successful white farmer."

References

Brown, Duncan. 1998. *Voicing the Text: South African Oral Poetry and Performance.* Cape Town. Oxford University Press.

Coplan, David B. 1985. *In Township Tonight: South Africa's Black City Music and Theatre.* New York: Longman.

Damane, M. and P. B. Sanders, eds. 1974. *Lithoko: Sotho Praise Poems.* Oxford. Clarendon Press.

Dube, C. 1988. *Ndebele Oral Art: Its Development within the Historico-Socio-Economic Context.* M. Phil. thesis. University of Zimbabwe.

Dundes, Alan. 1980. *Interpreting Folklore.* Bloomington, Indiana University Press.

Guenther, Mathias G. 1989. *Bushmen Folktales: Oral Traditions of the Nharo of Botswana and the Xam of the Cape.* Stuttgart. Franz Steiner Verlag Wiesbaden GMBH.

Guma, Sam M. 1967. *The Form, Content, and Technique of Traditional Literature in Southern Sotho.* Pretoria: J. L. van Schaik.

Gunner, Liz and Mafika Gwala. 1991. *Musho! Zulu Popular Praises.* East Lansing: Michigan State University Press.

Halliday, Michael, A. K. 1971. Linguistic Function and Literary Style. In *Literary Style: A Symposium,* ed. Seymour Chatman. New York, Oxford University Press.

Hamutyinei, Michael, and Albert Plangger. 1987. *Tsumo-Shumo: Shona Proverbial Lore and Wisdom.* 2d ed. Gweru: Mambo Press.

Hodza, Aaron C. and George Fortune. 1979. *Shona Praise Poetry.* Oxford: Clarendon Press.

Jordan, Archibald C. 1973. *Towards an African Literature: The Emergence of Literary Form In Xhosa.* Berkerley, University of California Press.

Kaschula, Russell H. 2001. *African Oral Literature: Functions in Contemporary Contexts.* Claremont, South Africa: New Africa Books.

Kidd, Dudley. [1904] 1971. *The Essential Kafir.* Freeport, N.Y.: Books for Library Presses.

Kunene, Daniel P. 1971. *Heroic Poetry of the Basotho.* Oxford: Oxford University Press.

Levy-Bruhl, Lucien. [1926] 1985. *How Natives Think.* Princeton, N.J.: Princeton University Press.

Lewis-Williams, David. 1981. *Believing and Seeing: Symbolic Meaning in Southern San Rock Paintings.* New York: Academic Press.

Mapanje, Jack, and Landey White, eds. 1983. *Oral Poetry from Africa: An Anthology.* New York: Longman.

Moyo, S. 1978. *A Linguo-Aesthetic Study of Ngoni Poetry.* Madison: University of Wisconsin Micro-film.

Mtenje, Alfred and Boston Soko. 1998. Oral Traditions among the Northern Malawi Ngoni. *Journal of Humanities.* 12:1–18.

Nkabinde, Themba. 1990. *Modern Ndebele Poetry: Characteristics and Development.* M. Phil. thesis. University of Zimbabwe.

Opland, Jeff. 1983. *Xhosa Oral Poetry: Aspects of a Black South African Tradition*. Cambridge, England: Cambridge University Press.

Pongweni, Alec. 1996. *Shona Praise Poetry as Role Negotiation: The Battles of the Clans and the Sexes*. Gweru: Mambo Press.

Pongweni, A. 1982. *Songs that Won the Liberation War*. Harare: The College Press.

Pongweni, A., and Emanuel M. Chiwome. 1995. *Zvirahwe Zvakare Nezvitsva: Traditional and Modern Shona Riddles*. Eiffel Flats. Zimbabwe: Juta Zimbabwe.

Rycroft, David. 1976. Southern Bantu Clan-Praises: A Neglected Genre. In *Bulletin of the School of Oriental and African Studies* (University of London) 39, no. 1:155–159.

Schapera, Isaac, ed. 1965. *Praise Poems of Tswana Chiefs*. Oxford: Clarendon Press.

Scheub, Harold. 1999. *The African Storyteller: Stories from African Oral Traditions*. Dubuque, Iowa: Kendall/Hunt.

Seloma, Pearl S. 1998. *When Women's Worlds Collide: A Folkloristic Study of Household Work in Botswana*. Ph.D. Diss., University of California, Los Angeles.

Stuart, James. 1968. *Izibongo: Zulu Praise-Poems*. Ed. Trevor Cope. Oxford: Clarendon.

Vail, Leray, and Landey White. 1991. *Power and the Praise Poem: Southern African Voices in History*. Charlottesville: University Press of Virginia.

———. 1984. The Art of Being Ruled: Ndebele Praise-Poetry, 1835–1971. In *Literature and Society in Southern Africa*. Ed. L. White and Tim Couzens. Cape Town: Maskew Miller Longman.

ALEC J. C. PONGWENI

See also **Callaway; Oral Literature; Praise Poetry**

SOUTHERN AFRICAN ORAL TRADITIONS

Most branches of the Khoisan people (the Korana, Ng'huki, Seroa, Xam, Xegwi, and Xiri) are either extinct or nearly extinct. The Nama survive, mainly in Namibia—there are some 146,000 (1995) in Namibia and South Africa. The ancient rock paintings of the San people, thousands of years old, are the evocative, if sometimes enigmatic, repositories of the mythic system of the San. The graphic images tell a story of intrepid San hunters, magnificent herds of animals, and the gods. These ancient "museums" are a part of southern Africa's storytelling treasure.

Early Studies

Contemporary oral storytellers have continued the tradition. In the mid-nineteenth century, the German philologist W. H. I. Bleek, with the help of Lucy Lloyd, collected, annotated, and translated San myths and tales. Among the great storytellers and mythmakers they encountered was Kábbo, a prisoner being held on Robben Island. Other San storytellers have been documented, including those encountered by Lorna and John Marshall in 1955 (Stephens 1971), Marguerite Biesele (1975), and J. M. Orpen (1874). Bleek worked with other estimable San storytellers, including Día!kwain, a!kúnta, and Kásin. But Kábbo (the name means "dream") was, without question, the most imaginative and poetic of these storytellers, and he remains, in the midst of a people moving towards extinction, a golden thread weaving from the middle of the nineteenth century back to those ancient rock paintings that burst in splendor in caves and on walls throughout southern Africa. In one of the rock paintings, one sees the San hunters in pursuit of magnificent elands, moving through the space of time. In the background, masked and mysterious, are the figures of the gods, observing, and perhaps orchestrating, the ancient relationship between human and animal. It is that metaphorical relationship between images that adorns the walls and caves, inspiring poetic interpretations by contemporary observers (see Lewis-Williams 1981, 1982; and Vinnecombe 1976). And it is this metaphorical relationship that is used in words by Kábbo in such stories as that of the creator god, Kággen, or Mantis, and a swallowing monster, Khwái-hemm (Bleek and Lloyd 1911, 30–40). Kággen, a divine trickster, has played an unworthy trick on ticks, and when he is beaten by the ticks for his deed, he dreams that he robs the heavenly ticks of all of their possessions and ways of life, transporting these to earth, thereby establishing San civilization. When God awakens, his dream has come to fruition. But Kággen has also invited into this new world the fiery Khwái-hemm: that is, he has created the force of fire. That force proceeds to devour everything that God has created, even God himself in the end, leaving behind only two children and their teacher. In the second part of the story, the teacher instructs the children on how to withstand the destructive force of Khwái-hemm, and they destroy the monster, releasing all from within its belly. The humans have thus re-created the world that God had given them. The storyteller is making the point that God creates, but humans must themselves learn to deal with the great forces that God has given them, or else they will perish.

In a Tswana myth, the Creator of all things sends the chameleon to earth to tell the people that when they die they will be reborn. But because Chameleon was slow, a lizard overtook him and gave his own message to the humans: "Whenever people die, they die for good" (Jones and Plaatje 1916, 1–2). And so it was that death came into the world. Xhosa myth celebrates Qamatha, "master of everything, father of all things, . . . the creator of old" (Sinhanha Mbalo 1967, Scheub collection). Death means a movement to the heavens: "Guide me, O Hawk! / That I may go heavenward. / To seek the one-hearted man, / Away from the double-hearted men, / Who deal in blessing and cursing." With irony, the commentator adds, "We trust that there were some of our people in heaven before the missionaries came" (Callaway, 1880, 59). The storytelling tradition unfolds within this mythic frame. In a Zulu origin myth, Umpondo Kambule (Callaway, 1868, 89–95) effectively blends a contemporary kidnapping tale and a mythic parting of waters and emergence from reeds: the past is destroyed and a new world born. Callaway's Zulu informants provide some detail regarding this mythic system. In the Zulu religious system, Nkulunkulu is God: "The old men say that Unkulunkulu is Umvelinqangi [the first being, the creator], for they say he came out first; they say he is the Uthlanga [potential source of being] from which all men broke off" (Ufulatela Sitole, quoted in Callaway, 1913, 7).

Heroic Poetry

Heroic poetry is popular throughout southern Africa. A Ndebele poem reads: "News of the nation of Matshoban', *dzi dzi*! / Come and see, come and see! / Here is news of Matshoban'! / No other nation will come, *dzi dzi*!" (Trask 1966, 85). The continued influence of such oral poetry can be seen in contemporary literature by Ndebele poets. Of the various categories of oral tradition among the Sotho people, heroic poetry is highly valued. Everitt Lechesa Segoete found emotional power in the Sotho national poem, "Mokorotlo (Song of the Enemies) and notes in his *Raphepheng* that the words are so sad that "There is no Mosotho who listens to them without feeling his heart rise" as the song causes him to remember other times: "It is an ageless war song, unchanging. It treats of death and war, of vultures eating the bodies of men: 'Boy child, offering to the vultures, and to Jackal and Crow.' Although the song is about men, its words have a poignant effect on women as well. When they hear it, they utter shrill cries. As long as the Basotho remain a nation, the song will be sung" (1913, 37).

Azariele M. Sekese described how Sotho warriors, during times of war, composed praise songs for themselves. Some leaders, among them Lejaha Makhabane, also composed poetry for themselves. A warrior would recount the details of his valorous behavior on the day of battle. Having done so, he would stab the ground a number of times equal to the number of enemy soldiers he had killed: "If it was one, he would stab the ground once; if two, then he would stab twice . . ." As he did so, the group that surrounded him would join in, crying, "Hii! Hii! Hii! Hii!" each time he stabbed the ground. Then, as he ended his activity, he would point with his spear the number of times equivalent to the number of those he had killed, pointing towards the enemy. And he would continue to sing his praises: "Whirlwind of the enemies of Lejaha, / The whirlwind finished the people, / People were swept away in a shower of spears, / Summer floods, whirlwind, / Hail with hard drops" (Sekese 1931, 69–70).

S. K. Lekgothoane wrote that the Sotho "are taught hundreds and even thousands of lines of prase-poems, for everything that we see with our eyes we can praise, and besides, such things as we know from thinking about them or hearing about them, without seeing them, all these we call praise." Oral poems, he argued, "refer to past history, to present events and to the future. There is great prophecy in them, they are a prayer. . . . Furthermore, it is deep learning. We are enabled to establish harmony between ourselves and God and the departed spirits by means of praises. It is rejoicing and it is weeping with which we cry unto God. The praises reveal what a man thinks in his heart" (1938, 191–193). Eugene Casalis wrote, "The hero of the piece is almost always the author of it. On his return from war he cleanses himself in the neighboring river, and then places his lance and his shield in safety. . . . He recounts [his exploits] in a high-flown manner. He is carried away by the ardor of his feelings, and his expressions become poetical" (1859, 328–329). Moshoeshoe I, the founder of the Sotho nation, has been praised in poetry by such bards as Lishobane Mpaki Molapo, a great-grandson of Moshoeshoe: "You who are fond of praising the ancestors, / Your praises are poor when you leave out the warrior, / When you leave out Thesele, the son of Mokhachane; / For it's he who's the warrior of the wars, / Thesele is brave and strong, / That is Moshoeshoe-Moshaila" (Damane and Sanders 1974, 73).

Swati heroic poetry sometimes treats a leader who "was always known by his men, who would praise him for any act of generosity, in battle and in the chase. The praises were not recited in an ordinary voice, but were called out at the top of the voice in as rapid a manner as possible" (Cook 1931, 183). In a poem dedicated to King Ludonga I, the bard sings, "They are hungry in the kraals and they want a king to be born, / The news of him is sweet to the people" (Cook 1931, 196–197). On October 9, 1972, at the royal residence of Sobhuza II, in Entonjeni, Swaziland, Mtshophane Mamba, a Swati bard, then about sixty years old, sang of "The-long-eared-Bhuza-who-hears-no-news: / When he does hear news, he hurries to the shield, / Thundering shield!" He cries, "You move like the thundering birds of the sea. / The cold of your arrow / Is like an open grave. / You are like a lion that eats men." Hilda Kuper writes, "Traditional African history is recorded in such *tibongo* (praises) recited on public occasion. Different bards, or oral historians, present their own selections of events and the same events may receive different emphasis and conflicting interpretations" (Kuper 1978, 16). "The rumbling is deep and reverberates like the tramping of many feet," sings the Tswana bard, "Splendid young man that you are, Modingwane" (Ellenberger 1937, 7), This is a heroic poem dedicated to the leader, Modingwane a Mokgoywe a Pooe. If there are poems heralding the acts of kings, there are also poems celebrating the deeds of commoners: "I entered within, I smote the ox [to be slaughtered at his marriage] / with a crooked shin" (Norton 1922, 256).

To Edison Bokako, the Tswana oral heroic poem is "a story of endeavor, of resistance overcome, of something accomplished. In it an individual was glorified, a momentous occasion recalled, or the achievement of victory celebrated." Such poetry, he argued, aroused the national consciousness, "and the atmosphere it created of ancestral might and liberty kindled the desire for the greatest effort" on behalf of the nation. It was no trivial matter, "rather was the highest distinction conferred for valor and for safeguarding tribal permanence and security. To the soldier it was a highly coveted prize, the highest reward for courage and manliness." The heroic poem, Bokako continues

> is laudatory. The poet freely indulges ornament, entertaining contrasts between major and minor personalities. No man is presented under ordinary light, no man is allowed to appear only with what strictly belongs to him, no circumstance in which he appears is presented except as a swelling spectacle. There is no lack of embroidery. The might of heroes is exaggerated. This is because heroic poetry is not bare realism. For two reasons. Firstly, because the poet must secure that largeness of atmosphere which will produce the illusion of heroic ampleness. Secondly, because the "grim resolution of heroic despair" does not allow him to use a less self-conscious style. Hence there can be no question of whether this insistence on the wonderful vitiates the sobriety of heroic poetry. An actual antidote to counteract the demoralizing effects of the relentless and blighting militarism of that day was found in the spirit of poetry which in Matthew Arnold's words "attaches its emotion to the idea" (Bokako, Appendix A, 1–2).

Ernest Sedumeli Moloto insisted that more is involved in such poetry than praising a leader. He tells of how Montshiwa, the leader of the Tshidi branch of the Barolong people, with his fellow warriors, assassinated Ndebele King Mzilikazi's emissaries in about 1832. The bards commemorated the event, in part, as follows: "Those men were the emissaries of Mzilikazi. / He had sent Boya and Bhangele to visit us / But you crafty son of Tawana ate them up: / Yours will be similarly eaten up craftily— / Remember you are not a made dog, but a man." Moloto notes, "The point at issue . . . is that there was intertribal suspicion simmering between the Rolong and the Nguni." He asks, "Who says Mzilikazi's intentions were honest? And who says the denigration of Montshiwa by his bard is not intended to forewarn and therefore fore-arm him? That is the role of the bard. The bard is a constructive institution. He is a loving critic" (1970, 81–82).

Isaac Schapera observes that boys undergoing rites of passage "were gathered every evening round the camp fire, and took turns in reciting their compositions." The men responsible for the education of the boys offered suggestions when their poems were weak. At the end of the ceremony marking the close of the rites, the boys returned to their homes with their fathers, "where, to the applause of the people assembled to welcome them back, . . . 'they praised their names,' i.e., each in turn recited his composition" (1965, 2–3). A. C. Jordan speaks of the creator of heroic poetry as composer and public reciter with a background in the history and culture of his people, a person honored by his community. Such a poet was S. E. K. Mqhayi, who created in both oral and literary genres. H. M. Ndawo and D. P. Yali-Manisi collected such poems.

Elements of Oral Poetry

Xhosa oral poetry has also been the subject of study. Archie Mafeje states that the poet "celebrates victories of the nation, sings songs of praise, chants the laws and customs of the nation, he recites the genealogies of the royal families." He notes that praise is not the only attitude taken in the poetry; the bard also "criticizes the chiefs for perverting the laws and the customs of the nation and laments their abuse of power and neglect of their responsibilities and obligations to the people" (Mafeje 1967, 195). Samuel Mqhayi writes of the great silence when the poet begins his work, his voice purposely kept low, not strident, his tone in sympathy with people's hearts made tender by the day's event. So elegant is his poem, so forceful its imagery, that men weep, while women do not attend to their cooking and the food burns. Some who have been smoking burn their pipe stems. No one among them moves, some unknowingly stand naked, others pull their garments too tightly around their bodies and tear them.

Dumisani, the bard, reminds the people

In olden days when mountains appeared,
One person was placed as ruler of us all.
It was said this was a person of royal blood,
It was said this was the child of the nation,
It was said this person must be submitted to by all,
And he in turn must submit to God
Whence law and custom emanate, / And when the king
    is wrong it will not be good:
Trouble and confusion will result

(Mghayi 1931, 32–35).

W. B. Rubusana contended that the poetry is composed of "speech which concentrates all of the eloquence of the Xhosa language, comprising all the figurative aspects of Xhosa" (1911, vi). Jordan adds that the language of the poetry is elegant, "highly figurative," and "abounding in epithets" (Jordan, 1973b, 21). B. W. Vilakazi describes a Zulu poet in this way:

A Zulu man who is considered to have a natural gift of seeing and feeling most in the wake and experience of life, will look at his king, survey him in the light of his ancestors, and again turn over in his mind the heroic deeds of his king and even his weaknesses. Suddenly he will spring up in a crowd with his shield pointed to the sky and the whole of his body tingling with emotional excitement. The crowd is bound to listen to him. Such a man is never requested to do his duty, but stirred by the performance of his tribal ceremony and imbued with national pride, feels it most opportune for him to express his feelings, and thus fulfills his self-imposed duty. He cries out, "Bayede!" (Hail, O King!) And the crowd is all silent (Vilakazi 1937, 12).

Referring to the oral stories of the Zulu, Callaway argued in 1868

If carefully studied and compared with corresponding legends among other people, they will bring out unexpected relationships, which will more and more force upon us the great truth, that man has everywhere thought alike, because everywhere, in every country and clime, under every tint of skin, under every varying social and intellectual condition, he is still man,—one in all the essentials of man,—one in which is a stronger proof of essential unity, than mere external differences are of differences of nature,—one in his mental qualities, tendencies, emotions, passions" (Callaway 1868, preface).

Mvingana, the bard of Zulu King Dinuzulu (1870–1913), working within the Zulu poetic tradition, weaves some ten patterns into a unified whole. Within this richly textured design of the poem are brief unpatterned passages. In this work, the king is criticized even as he is being praised. The poet speaks of a war of total destruction: everything is being pulverized, even the grinding stone, the propping stone, the tobacco fields, the wrapping mats— all homely images, destroyed utterly. "Dinuzulu does not kill," exclaims the poet, "He destroys even the grinding stone" (Grant 1927–1929). In contemporary times, the poetry tradition continues to flourish. Umhle Biyela of Yanguya in kwaZulu remembers the mythic founders of the Biyela people: "Ndaba stepped hard, and a lake appeared," he sings. He calls the subjects of his poems "Stabber-into-the-mist" and "Awesome cliffs-of-the-wilderness." And he describes "Beauty as revealed in houses: / They are beautiful, including the one at Mbuyeni, / Because they are beautiful and black" (Scheub 1972).

The San poet Día!kwāin sings of a man shot by a Boer commando. As he dies, he teaches his songs to the father of the poet. One of the songs is a lament, sorrowful because "the string is broken" and the "ringing sound in the sky" is no longer heard by the singer. Typically, the poem opens with a strong image that is repeated, as the poet carefully works new images from it, repeating it with variation. He develops a companion image, peeling a new image from the juxtaposition. The first two lines, "People were those who / Broke for me the string," establish the problem of the poem; the poet then explores lyrically what this has meant for him, formulating his basic set three times, incrementally revealing his feelings with each repetition. The sense of loss, of alienation, is the emotion being expressed here, not the actual history of the event. The finest example of Venda oral tradition is the epic *Ngoma-lungundu*, about the drum of the dead. An especially dramatic version of the story was created by E. Mudau (Van Warmelo 1940).

Oral History

Among the Tsonga, Sikwaazwa, remembering an event that occurred to him in the final years of the nineteenth century, creates an oral history about the death of his father: "I know you. Your name is Sikwaazwa. Your father is no longer alive, he is dead, it was the Ndebele who killed him. Your mother is the one who is alive. Now she is married, Choka is the one who married her. Thereupon I wept," and, recalling the Anglo-Boer War: "we heard that the war of the whites had arrived. As soon as it reached Johannesburg . . . , we heard the guns firing very loudly, they fired, there was fighting" (Jones and Carter 1967, 96–102).

Oral history is also a significant part of the Xhosa oral tradition. Mdukiswa Tyabashe, a Mpondomise, re-creates Mpondomise history, effectively and daringly bringing history and fantasy into a viable relationship (Scheub 1996, 227–274). This Xhosa historian and poet details the entirety of the history, weaving the fantasy storytelling tradition into the historical account in order to give dimension, resonance, and meaning to history. Ndumiso Bhotomane, another Xhosa historian, builds his account around a generational timeline of kings, working into the timeline anecdotal historical accounts (Scheub 1996, 31–47).

Proverbs and Riddles

Proverbs and riddles are important parts of southern African oral traditions. The Ndebele oral tradition, like its Zulu and Xhosa counterparts further south, also includes poetry, history, riddles, and proverbs. "Unyathela inyoka emsileni" (You tread on the snake's tail) and "Izolo liyembelwa" (Yesterday is buried) are Ndebele proverbs (Pelling 1977, 23, 85). *Vutomi i norho*, "Bya hundza tani hi norho" (Life is a dream. It passes like a dream) is a Tsonga proverb (Junod 1936, 294–295). Venda oral tradition includes poetry, narrative, song, riddle, proverb, and history. "If a great one is lame, his subjects limp," is one Venda proverb, while another states, "The heart is the elder brother of man" (Wessmann 1908, 76–77). Riddles include: "A chief presided and the people surrounded him" (The moon and the stars) and "An old man whose grey hair is inside his belly" (The grey fibers inside a pumpkin) (Stayt 1931, 359). "The proverbs," the Zulu writer C. L. Sibusiso Nyembezi has written, "are a collection of the experiences of a people, experiences some of which have been learned the hard way. Those experiences are stored in this special manner, and from generation to generation they are passed on, ever fresh and ever true. The new experiences of the younger generations are themselves embalmed in this special manner, and in that way the language is enriched more and more" (1954, xii).

The Narrative Tale

As in most societies, the tale is by far the most popular of the genres of the real tradition. Ndebele performers emphasize the necessity of retaining linkages with the past. In a story having to do with girls moving to womanhood, Eva Ndlovu warns, "People who do not heed custom are consumed, they have not followed the patterns of behavior prescribed in ancient times. Nothing goes well for those who do not listen to the values of the people of old." In a tale by Mercy Sidile, an old woman, an old man, and a frog test two sisters, determining if they are prepared to move to womanhood; and in a story performed by Clevis Gumpo, a phantom of the forests ravages the countryside, destroying the children of his wife: "Never again did she return to her husband's place. But she never lived happily, because her heart was always remembering her children" (Scheub 1972). The hare is a popular Ndebele trickster: "Well is he named 'The Clever One of the Veld.' Only once that I know has the laugh been against him" (Savory 1962, 52). In 1908, Edouard Jacottet of the Sotho wrote that "Africa has treasures, for the most part still hidden, in store for the student of folk-lore" (1908, xiv). Among the Sotho storytellers who provided the rich materials for Jacottet's collections were Moshe Mosetse and 'Mamangana: "I have taken great care to reproduce them exactly in the form they were dictated to me," he wrote, "and have not tried to reduce them to any given standard" (1908, xxii). Among the stories in his collections is "Kumonngoe," the story of Thakane, a girl who grows to womanhood, struggling first against her restrictive father (he decides to have her destroyed because she cut into his *kumonngoe* [milk tree]), and then against a nation of swallowing monsters; in the process, she moves to completeness as the storyteller simultaneously develops dramatic arguments having to do with proper human relations. Jacottet's collection is one of southern Africa's finest, the stories detailed and full, the images resonant and profound.

Swati tales have much in common with those of the Zulu and Xhosa. Chakijana (a mongoose), for example, is a trickster to both the Swati and the Zulu (Engelbrecht 1930, 7–10). A boy in a story by Sarah Dlamini (Scheub 1972) eats a medicinal herb and becomes pregnant in a whimsical dramatization of the growth of the boy to adulthood. She also tells a poignant story of a young man who, seeking to kill another, ends up destroying his own child (Scheub 1972). Ntombinde is abandoned by her fellows in an ocher pit in a tale told by Albertine Nxumalo (Scheub 1972). "The Unnatural Mother" is a tale about a woman who "sinned against nature" and is exiled to "strange countries, and [was told] you must never come back till you have found the water in which there are no frogs, no fishes, and no animals of any kind." In a far-off land, she finds the water but she cannot rise, and the limbs of a tree grow around her "and hold her fast." A rabbit releases her, and she takes the water to him soon. When she gives it to him, the world is transformed: "All the little paths became winding streets, and the trees became beautiful round houses, woven with great skill. The animals became men and women. . . ." The hare is the typical Tsonga trickster (Fell 1–35): "And the lion died. The hare deceived him" (Bourhill and Drake 1908, 58–65). "Basiangandu" is the story of a young woman who seeks a husband but whose mother, opposed to any marriage, sets out to destroy the men the young woman marries. The old woman kills the first husband, but the young woman and her second husband outwit the old woman, destroying her: "Now then he molded wax. He threw it down to the ground. Whilst the old woman was still cutting [the tree], the wax became a leopard. It bit the old woman" (Fell 140–145). So it is that the girl moves into womanhood, severing her ties with her childhood past. There is also the brief story of Muloba:

> A certain boy used to live on an island. And he was always playing his fiddle. All the people wished to see him. But there was no canoe. Now he was longing for one girl only, because that girl was poor. But nevertheless all the girls used to sing about him, they said, "O Muloba, / Siasai. / O Muloba, / It is the bow which glitters, / For which we cry. / Try, can you not bottom it, / O Muloba, the beautiful, / It is the bow which glitters, / For which we cry." Continually, they were singing about him thus, and were trying to reach where he was. But they kept going to him until, yes, that very girl, the very one crossed over herself alone (Fell 145).

There are also stories of a boy named Drum who has a sister in a community in which girl-children are to be destroyed. The story centers on the survival of the girl due to her harmonious ties with nature (Torrend 1910). Among Tswana tales are the story of a man who had a tree growing on his head (Curtis 40–41) and stories of the trickster tortoise and his various dupes (Jones and Plaatje 1916, 8–9). Sankhambi, the tortoise, is a typical Venda trickster, and tales include the story of a beautiful girl who had no teeth (Stayt 1931, 339–341) and a strange story of Malambatata, the child who died grinning (Lestrade 1949, 29–31).

The Xhosa

The Xhosa oral tradition ranges from ancient myths to tales of heroic deeds to poetry of eminent kings. Storytellers argue that these ancient traditions are a crucial means of connecting members of contemporary society to the traditional past. Stories range from heroic activities of such men and women as Sikhuluma and Mityi (Theal 1882; Zenani 1992) to the antic behavior of tricksters, including the diminutive Hlakanyana and the wily jackal. In the oral poetry of the Xhosa (Rubusana, 1911; Opland 1983), the subject matter is broad, from descriptions of rulers to evocations of everyday life. Also included in the Xhosa oral tradition are riddles and proverbs (Soga 1931; Matsebula 1948). There were some early compilations of Xhosa stories (e.g., Theal 1882); one of the most impressive collections is that of A. C. Jordan, including a poignant love story, "The Turban," a tale of a boundless passion that leads to tragedy. More recently, a set of stories performed by Nongenile Masithathu Zenani impressively reveals the poetic possibilities of the Xhosa tradition. In her story "Nomanaso," Zenani takes an ancient story of Qwebethe, a persistent pursuer, and builds a complex story around it, detailing the tensions between a mother and her daughter (1992a, 438–458). By using the fantasy imagery of the pursuer, and by metaphorically juxtaposing mother, daughter, and fantasy pursuer, the performer takes her audience into the tormented psyche of the central character, showing her moving with uncertainty, but also with determination, to her new status as a woman. Other inventive Xhosa storytellers include Noplani Gxavu (Scheub 1975, 334–367; Scheub 1996, 163–186) and Emily Ntsobane (Scheub 1996, 187–201).

The Zulu

Among the Zulu, common forms of oral tradition include tales, poetry, histories, proverbs, and riddles. Parts of the Zulu oral tradition have been preserved in print by researchers, ranging from Henry Callaway in the mid-nineteenth century to such contemporary Zulu scholars as C. L. S. Nyembezi and B. W. Vilakazi. Significant storytellers whose work is available in print include Lydia Umkasethemba (Callaway 1868) and Sondoda Ngcobo (Scheub 1996). The work of a number of talented poets has survived, including that of Mvingana, a poet of Dinuzulu, and Gwebisa, a poet of Zibebu, a Madlakazi ruler (both in Grant 1927–1929). James Stuart published the work of a number of poets, including Magolwana, the poet of Mphande. Umhle Biyela, a forty-year-old Zulu poet, in Yanguya, kwaZulu, was recorded in September, 1972.

The Zulu writer C. L. Sibusiso Nyembezi compiled an impressive collection of proverbs. The finest Zulu storyteller recorded by Callaway, and arguably the most accomplished Zulu performer yet recorded, was Lydia Umkasetemba. Callaway transcribed and translated eight stories by Umkasetemba, the most impressive being "Umxakaza-wakogingqwayo" and "Untombi-yaphansi." In the former, a princess is exposed as not being ready for her purification ritual; nature, in the form of a monster, removes her from her home and takes her to a far-off place where, in the realm of fantasy and the psyche, she undergoes a proper initiation into adulthood. In the process, the moral grotesqueness of her childhood, dramatically revealed by fantasy characters and imagery, is cleansed, and she emerges a woman, an emergence marked by an act of selfless generosity (Callaway 1868, 181–216). In "Untombi-yaphansi," a living girl is brought into metaphorical relationship with a fantasy character, as the girl's agonizing, but ultimately triumphant, movement into womanhood is signaled and revealed by the antics of the imaginary character in the realm of fantasy (Callaway 1868, 296–316).

References

Biesele, Marguerite Anne. 1975. Folklore and Ritual of !Kung Hunter Gatherers. Ph.D. dissertation, Harvard University.

Bleek, Wilhelm Heinrich Immanuel, and Lucy C. Lloyd. 1911. Specimens of Bushman Folklore. London: George Allen.

Bokako, Edison M. Bo-Santagane, An Anthology of Tswana Heroic Verse. Unpublished manuscript, University of Cape Town Library.

Bourhill, E. J., and J. B. Drake. 1908. Fairy Tales from South Africa. London: Macmillan.

Callaway, Henry. 1868. Nursery Tales, Traditions, and Histories of the Zulus. Springvale, Natal: John A. Blair.

———. 1880. A Fragment Illustrative of Religious Ideas among the Kafirs. Folk-Lore Journal (South Africa) 2, no. 4:56–60.

———. 1913. The Religious System of the Amazulu. Mariannhill: Mariannhill Mission Press.

Casalis, Eugene. 1859. Les Bassoutos ou vingt-trois années d'études et d'observation au sud de l'Afrique. Paris: C. Meyrueis.

Cook, P. A. W. 1931. History and Izibongo of the Swazi Chiefs. Bantu Studies, 5:181–201.

Curtis, Susheela. 1975. Maimaine, Tswana Tales. Gaborone: Botswana Book Centre.

Damane, M., and P. B. Sanders, eds. 1974. Lithoko, Sotho Praise-Poems. Oxford: Clarendon Press.

Ellenberger, Vivian. 1937–38. Di Rebaroba Matlhakola—Tsa Ga Masodi—a-mphela. Transactions of the Royal Society of South Africa, 25:1–41.

Engelbrecht, J. A. 1930. Swazi Texts with Notes. Annals of the University of Stellenbosch, 8, sec. B, no. 2.

Fell, J. R. *Ingano Zya Batonga e Zimpangaliko Zimwi, Folk Tales of the Batonga and Other Sayings.* London: Holborn.

Grant, E. W. 1927–1929. The Izibongo of the Zulu Chiefs. *Bantu Studies,* 3:201–244.

Groenewald, H. C., and Staupitz Makopo. 1992. Urban Folklore—The Political Song. *South African Journal of African Languages* 12, no. 4: 131–138.

Gunner, Liz, and Mafika Gwala. 1991. *Musho! Zulu Popular Praises.* East Lansing: Michigan State University Press.

Jacottet, Edouard. 1908. *The Treasury of Basuto Lore.* London: Kegan Paul.

Jones, Daniel, and Solomon Tshekisho Plaatje. 1916. *A Sechuana Reader.* London: University of London Press.

Jones, A. M., and Hazel Carter. 1967. The Style of a Tonga Historical Narrative. *African Language Studies,* 8:103–126.

Jordan, A. C. 1973a. *Tales from Southern Africa.* Berkeley: University of California Press.

———. 1973b. *Towards an African Literature: The Emergence of Literary Form in Xhosa.* Berkeley: University of California Press.

Junod, Henri Philippe. 1936. *Vutlhari bya Vatsonga (Machangana), The Wisdom of Tsonga-Shangana People.* Braamfontein: Sasavona.

Kuper, Hilda. 1978. *Sobhuza II, Ngwenyama and King of Swaziland.* London: Gerald Duckworth.

Lamplough, R. W. 1968. *Matabele Folk Tales.* Oxford: Oxford University Press.

Lekgothoane, S. K. 1938. "Praises of Animals in Northern Sotho." *Bantu Studies* 7:189–213.

Lestrade, Gerard Paul. 1949. *Some Venda Folk-tales.* Lovedale: Lovedale Press.

Lewis-Williams, and James David. 1981. *Believing and Seeing: Symbolic Meanings in Southern San Rock Paintings.* London: Academic Press.

———. 1982. The Economic and Social Context of Southern San Rock Art. *Current Anthropology,* 23, no. 4:429–449.

Mafeje, Archie. 1967. The Role of a Bard in a Contemporary African Community. *Journal of a African Languages.* 4, no. 3: 193–223.

Matsebula, J. S. M. 1948. *Izakhiwo zamaSwazi.* Johannesburg: Afrikaanse Pers-Poekhandel.

Moloto, Ernest Sedumeli. 1970. The Growth and Tendencies of Tswana Poetry. D.Litt. and D.Phil. dissertation, University of South Africa, Pretoria.

———. 1942. *Inzuzo.* Johannesburg: Witwatersrand University Press.

Mqhayi, Samuel Edward Krune. 1931. *Ityala lamawele.* Lovedale: Lovedale Press.

Ndawo, H. M. 1928. *Izibongo zenkosi zamaHlubi nezamaBhaca.* Mariannhill: Mariannhill Mission Press.

Norton, W. A. 1922a. Sesuto Praises of the Chiefs. *South African Journal of Science,* 18:441–453.

———. 1922b. Sesuto and Sechwana Praises. *Transactions of the Royal Society of South Africa,* 10:253–266.

Nyembezi, C. L. Sibusiso. 1954. *Zulu Proverbs.* Johannesburg: Witwatersrand University Press.

Opland, Jeff. 1983. *Xhosa Oral Poetry.* Cambridge, England: Cambridge University Press.

Orpen, J. M. 1919. A Glimpse into the Mythology of the Maluti Bushmen. *Folk-lore,* 30:139–156.

Pelling, J. N. 1977. *Ndebele Proverbs and Other Sayings.* Gwelo: Mambo Press.

Rhodesia Literature Bureau. 1969. *Kusile Mbongi wohlanga.* Salisbury: Rhodesia Literature Bureau.

Rubusana, W. B. 1911. *Zemk' Inkomo Magwalandini.* London: Butler and Tanner.

Savory, Phyllis. 1962. *Matabele Fireside Tales.* Cape Town: H. Timmins.

Schapera, Isaac. 1965. *Praise-poems of Tswana Chiefs.* Oxford: Clarendon Press.

Scheub, Harold. 1975. *The Xhosa Ntsomi.* Oxford: Clarendon Press.

———. 1986–1987. "Oral Poetry and History." *New Literary History,* 18:477–496.

———. 1996. *The Tongue Is Fire: South African Storytellers and Apartheid.* Madison: University of Wisconsin Press.

Segoete, Everitt Lechesa. 1913. *Raphepheng* (Father of the Scorpion). Morija: Sesuto Book Depot.

Sekese, Azariele M. 1931. *Mekhoa Le Maele a Ba-Sotho* (Customs and Proverbs of the Sotho). Morija: Sesuto Book Depot.

Soga, John Henderson. 1931. *The Ama-Xosa: Life and Customs.* Lovedale, South Africa: Lovedale Press.

Stayt, Hugh Arthur. 1931. *The Bavenda.* London: H. Milford.

Stephens, Jean B. 1971. "Tales of the Gwikwe Bushmen." M.A. Thesis, Goddard College.

Stuart, James. 1924a. *uBaxoxele.* London: Longmans, Green.

———. 1924b. *uHlangakula.* London: Longmans, Green.

———. 1925. *uKulumetule.* London: Longmans, Green.

———. 1926. *uVusezakiti.* London: Longmans, Green.

———. 1929. *uTulasizwe.* London: Longmans, Green.

Theal, George McCall. 1882. *Kaffir Folklore.* London: W. Swan Sonnenschein.

Torrend, J. 1910. Likenesses of Moses' Story in the Central African Folk-Lore. *Anthropos,* 5:54–70.

Trask, Willard R. 1966. *The Unwritten Song.* New York: Macmillan.

Van Warmelo, N. J., ed. 1940. *The Copper Miners of Musina and the Early History of the Zoutpansberg.* Pretoria: Government Printer.

Vilakazi, Benedict Vilakazi. 1937. "Conception and Development of Poetry in Zulu." M.A. thesis. University of the Witwatersrand.

Vinnicombe, Patricia. 1976. *People of the Eland.* Pietermaritzburg: University of Natal Press.

Wessmann, R. 1908. *The Bawenda of the Spelonken (Transvaal).* London: African World.

Yali-Manisi, D. P. 1982. *Izibongo zeenkosi zamaXhosa.* Lovedale, South Africa: Lovedale Press.

Zenani, Nongenile Masithathu. 1992. *The World and the Word.* Madison: University of Wisconsin Press.

HAROLD SCHEUB

See also **Callaway, Bishop Henny; Oral Traditions; Praise Poetry; South Africa**

SOUTHERN AFRICA: CONTEMPORARY FORMS OF FOLKLORE

The debate surrounding oral literature in South Africa is a vibrant one. The new political order has introduced a renewed pride in what it is to be African, and there has been a revival in the status and role of oral literature. This form of literature is taking its rightful place alongside written literature and is now being taught at schools and universities. Furthermore, it is also being used in innovative ways to teach people about national issues such as AIDS, agriculture, and family planning. The didactic nature of this material is ensuring its recognition in the new educational structures in South Africa. But if the traditional verbal arts are to serve any long-term useful purpose, then they must be taught and recognized as dynamic, living traditions that have much to offer.

Oral literature in South Africa finds itself at the center of the debate addressing the questions, "What is literature?" and "How is it to be taught?" The orality-literacy debate and the relevance of the oral word alongside the written word are the focus of much discussion worldwide. David Coplan talks of extending terms such as *orature* and *oral literature* to "auriture," which encapsulates not only the oral and the written, but the aural as well (1994, 8). In a similar way, Elizabeth Gunner (1989) discusses the mixing of genres in terms of the orality-literacy debate. The crux of the matter is that these debates impact on the definition of oral literature in South Africa, and whether it is in fact necessary to classify and define it in the first place.

Earlier scholars, such as G. P. Lestrade (1959), who are recognized as pioneers in the classification of oral literature generally outline three separate areas of oral literature in southern Africa: folktales, wisdom-lore, such as riddles and idioms, and oral poetry. These traditional genres are explored further in Russell Kaschula's *Foundations in Southern African Oral Literature* (1993), but this volume also cautions against a prescriptive approach: "It may be necessary not only to reclassify aspects of oral traditions (and not to be prescriptive in this regard) but also to redefine certain of these aspects" (Kaschula 1993, viii). But it should be remembered that definitions (even contemporary ones) may in themselves become prescriptive. In any event, a more liberal and liberated approach to the study of African oral literature is required.

It is important to note that poetry, folktales, and wisdom-lore should not be seen as hard and fast "categories" of oral literature. For example, a novel may contain a folktale, and contemporary trade-union poetry may involve song, dance, and music (Gunner 1989, 49). A more flexible approach is therefore required when viewing contemporary oral literature in South Africa.

All of this should be seen against the backdrop of the commercialization of spoken art forms in South Africa. This is one of the most important factors influencing the development of oral literature in South Africa today, whether it be the making of wood carvings for the tourist market or the release of an Mzwakhe Mbuli oral poetry and song compact disc.

In terms of contemporary oral forms, it would seem that there are three areas of prominence in South Africa. These are contemporary stories (including the Internet and television), entrepreneurial oral art, and oral poetry (forms such as riddles, idioms, and proverbs are now generally regarded as less prominent). The underlying link between the three is that they all have commercial value.

Contemporary Stories

The urban legends dealing with the South African elections compiled by Arthur Goldstuck in 1994 is perhaps the most important recent example of contemporary oral literature. It is a collection of stories told (and sometimes believed) around the time of the 1994 South African elections. Perhaps the most famous tale is the "Ink in the Porridge." In this legend, Major-General Bantu Holomisa (then leader of the old Transkei homeland) told his mainly Xhosa-speaking audience that the National Party offered porridge (pap) laced with ink to black voters. The intent was that the ink would show up under the ultraviolet lamps on election day, and black people who consumed it would then be disqualified from voting for the African National Congress (the main opposition to the National Party).

Another example of an urban legend that nearly destroyed the South African citrus industry concerned the AIDS virus. Rumors flew in the cities that oranges had been infected with HIV-positive blood by the Afrikaanse Weerstands Beweeging (AWB), a conservative right-wing organization. This story quickly spiraled out of control and instantly became a national legend with many variations.

The art of storytelling is therefore alive and well in South Africa. Legends are told in English, Xhosa, Afrikaans, Zulu, and Sotho—indeed, in all of the languages of South Africa. What seems significant is that these legends are fueled by modern-day technology, namely television and the Internet. Afrikaans comedy television programs, such as *Spies and Plesie* (which aired in the 1980s), are examples of contemporary Afrikaans narratives, drawing largely on Afrikaans oral stories and traditions. Likewise, Gcina Mhlophe's televised Xhosa stories keep the tradition of folktales alive. Again the message is clear: oral art represents a thread by which humanity is bound, and its development can be influenced by a number of factors. In Arthur Goldstuck's words, "A large proportion of the material I collected would not have reached me were it not for the Internet" (Goldstuck 1993, x1). The real question is: To what extent does this secondary orality (written book) experience become an oral one? (Ong, 1982:68). The existence of a postsecondary orality via, for example, the Internet now becomes an issue. The Goldstuck collection proves the three-way dialectic between orality (the telling of stories), technology (the Internet) and the written word (his book).

Another important development in the folktale tradition in South Africa is the reinterpretation of both modern and traditional tales in order to comment on the role of women in society. The tales are told in such a way that they show the oppression of women. In this regard, Neethling comments as follows on a well-known Xhosa folktale: "A dog, which is a low-status animal in Xhosa society, becomes a symbol of male dominance when he satiates his sexual appetite by raping the luckless victim, a young girl. The narration represents a distinctly feminist outcry and protest against forced sexual relationships." Therefore, folktales have a lot to offer when interpreting the sociological point of view.

Entrepreneurial Folklore

One of the generally accepted definitions of folklore is that it is something that is handed down from one generation to another by word of mouth. Arguably then, the modern artwork that is sold at craft markets also falls into the category of folklore. An example of this is wirework. Wire baskets, wire flowerpot holders, wire candlestick holders, and other wire products are sold at these informal markets, which have become extremely popular in South Africa. Most of the people involved in this craft gained their knowledge of wirework as children, as they grew up making wire toys, such as car replicas. This art form has been passed down from generation to generation, just as traditional oral forms of folklore are transmitted. In this process, the art form has been commercialized, and it now forms an integral part of South Africa's emerging entrepreneurial market.

There are many other examples of contemporary entrepreneurial folk arts that have blossomed since the 1994 elections, including beadwork (in which the new colors of the South African flag are featured very prominently) and wood carving. This is an area in need of research, however.

Contemporary Oral Poetry

Oral poetry represents the richest and most fertile area of contemporary oral literature in southern Africa. David Coplan (1994) shows how Basotho migrant workers who work on South Africa's gold mines have adapted this art form to reflect the hardships and challenges they face as migrants. Likewise, Elizabeth Gunner (1989) has shown how Zulu *izibongo* (oral poetry) has been used within the Congress of South African Trade Unions in order to educate workers about their rights and other matters. She provides the example of Alfred Qabula, a poet based in Durban, who began performing oral poetry in the 1980s. In one instance Qabula refers to the trade union as: "a hen with wide wings which protects its chickens" (Gunner 1989).

This tradition is also particularly vibrant among the Xhosa-speaking people. *Izibongo* is performed at most important occasions and gatherings, whether they are cultural, religious, political, or educational—the four contemporary pillars of power in Xhosa society. It is also clear that the *imbongi* (oral poet) has kept pace with shifts in power. For example, from a political point of view, as power gravitated away from traditional chiefs to new leaders within the Congress of South African Trade Unions and the African National Congress, the *iimbongi* (plural form of *imbongi*) shifted their focus to the new leaders. This direct link between the *imbongi* and power, as well as the ability of *iimbongi* to adapt to these new power bases, has ensured their survival within South African society.

The adaptability of oral tradition is not a new phenomenon, but it has been reinforced by recent shifts in political power in South Africa. For example, by 1827, Ntsikana, a Xhosa oral poet, was converted to Christianity and used the tradition to praise God in the same way as he would have formerly praised the chief (Kaschula 1995). Among the Zulu people the same type of figure emerged about forty years later when Isaiah Shembe began producing hymns in the traditional poetic style. The dynamic nature of this form of literature is therefore not new, and it allows for this form of "auriture" to feed on and mould itself within present-day happenings. *Iimbongi* can be heard at the openings of new schools, circumcision ceremonies, graduations, political gatherings, funerals, and weddings—indeed, they permeate the lives of South Africans at just about every level. Bongani Sitole, an *imbongi* living in the Eastern Cape, recently referred to Nelson Mandela as: *Yinkunz' ethi ya-kugquba kulal' amatye* (A bull that kicks up dust and stones).

This is a recurring image in his poetry about Mandela, as well as about the late Joe Slovo (the former leader of the South African Communist Party and Minister of Housing in Mandela's cabinet).

Conclusion

In this short synopsis of contemporary forms of South African folklore an attempt has been made to contextualize the work within two areas: the orality-literacy debate and the commercialization of folk art, spoken and otherwise. If one views South African oral literature against this backdrop, one finds that the tradition is alive and well. While some aspects of the oral tradi-

tion are no longer emphasized (such as riddles), the capability of oral literature, or "auriture," to adapt to new power bases and societal change is ensured by its relevance within what one could call South Africa's complex postprimary, presecondary, and secondary oral society (Ong, 1982).

References

Coplan, David. 1994. *In the Time of Cannibals: The Word Music of South Africa's Basotho Migrants.* Chicago: University of Chicago Press.

Goldstuck, Arthur. 1994. *Ink in the Porridge: Urban Legends of the South African Elections.* Johannesburg: Penguin.

Gunner, Elizabeth. 1989. Orality and Literacy: Dialogue and Silence. In *Discourse and Its Disguises.* Eds. Karin Barber and P. F. de Moraes Farias. Birmingham, England: Centre for West African Studies, University of Birmingham.

Kaschula, Russell H. 1993. *Foundations in Southern African Oral Literature.* Johannesburg: Witwatersrand University Press.

———. 1993. Preachers and Poets: Oral Poetry Within the Religious Cosmology of the Xhosa. *South African Journal of African Languages*, 15, no. 2:65–73.

Lestrade, G. P. 1935. Bantu Praise Poems. *The Critic, A South African Quarterly Journal*, 4:1–10.

Neethling, S. J. 1991. Eating Forbidden Fruit in a Xhosa Oral Narrative. *South African Journal of African Languages*, 11, no.1: 83–87.

Ong, Walter. 1982. *Orality and Literacy: The Technologizing of the Word.* London: Methuen.

RUSSELL H. KASCHULA

See also **Electronic Media and Oral Traditions; Popular Culture; Praise Poetry; Radio and Television Dramas**

SOUTHERN AFRICA: SHONA FOLKLORE

The Shona, defined as a distinct southeast African ethnicity, are a modern invention of postcolonial nationalism based on their common language, ChiShona. This is a Bantu language subdivision first utilized by the South African linguist Clement Doke in 1931 to consolidate and unify the diverse collection of dialects spoken within what was then known as Rhodesia. ChiShona, however, is not a singular or uniform language, but is instead an amalgamation of mutually intelligible dialects, which include six dominant groups: Kalanga, Karanga, Zezuru, Ndau, Korekore, and the Manyika.

Geographically, the majority of ChiShona speakers reside within the national republic of Zimbabwe and the northwestern region of Mozambique. However, there are also a number of isolated scattered segments in South Africa, Malawi, Botswana, and Zambia. Although the label of Shona ethnicity was politically imposed, the Shona do, in fact, constitute a unique cultural cluster of common social traditions, norms, practices, values, and beliefs. The Shona are primarily subsistence farmers whose kinship structure is characterized by localized patrilineages and exogamous clans (*matobos*). Descent, inheritance, and succession are patrilineal, while the administration of villages, wards, and chiefdoms are often hereditary positions. Shona traditional culture, which is in fast decline, was first noted for its superior ironwork, pottery, and musicianship. Shona religion and cosmology are rooted in the belief in a creator/God (Mwari) and the practice of propitiation of ancestral, tribal, and other spirits to ensure good health, rain, and success in business. Finally, a belief in magic, witchcraft, and sorcery continues to play an important role in everyday life, despite rigorous efforts to eradicate it by Christian missions and elementary education.

Those seminal studies that are germane to the study of Shona folklore include Hamutyinei and Plangger's (1987) comprehensive collection of Shona proverbs; Paul Berliner's (1978) study on Shona musical traditions; David Beach's (1980, 1990, 1994) thorough analysis of Shona oral literature, through which he reconstructs the prehistoric past of Zimbabwe's Shona and their neighbors; H. Ellert's (1984) extensive study on Zimbabwe's material culture; M. F. C. Bourdillion's classic ethnographic survey of the contemporary Shona (1976), their changing society (1993), and religion (1990); and Michael Gelfand's extensive studies on Shona customs and traditions (1979, 1973), affinity (1981), system of health and healing (1944), ritual (1959), medicine and magic (1962), ethics, religion, and spiritual beliefs (1968, 1964, 1977), traditional healers (1964), witchcraft (1967), and ethnopharmacopeia (1985).

In general, Shona folklore materials and traditions are primarily verbal, musical, visual, three-dimensional, and perceptual in form and content. However, for the purpose of this summary, Shona folklore can be reduced into the three broad genres: oral literature, material culture, and customs and traditions.

Shona Oral Literature

The majority of Shona folklore scholarship has focused on the study of Shona oral literature, which is divided into the three large groupings of narratives, speech, and song. Shona folk narratives include the generic subcategories of *nhango* (prose narratives), *madetembedzo* (praise poetry), *tsumo-shumo* (proverbs), and *chirahwe* (riddles). *Mango* can be further subdivided into *ngano* (folktales), *nyaya* (myths and urban legends), *magamba* (legends), and *makuhwa* (tall tales). *Rungano* (the plural form of *ngano*) were traditionally told by the older members of society as a form of evening entertainment and instruction for children about Shona beliefs and customs. They focus on the everyday practices of common social personalities, such as *mhizha* (craftsman), the *n'anga* (traditional healer), and the *mambo* (chief). There are three basic types of *ngano*: the story with a song, the story punctuated by interjections, and the straight narrative, with the first and second types requiring the active participation of the audience to collaborate with the *sarungano* (storyteller). *Rungano* that call for interjections from the audience often have a *mushauri* (leader) to motivate and guide the *vadaviri* (chorus).

Madetembedzo (praise poems) are particular to a clan or subclan, which are typically identified by specific totem. *Madetembedzo* are performed at specific social gatherings, such as a *bira* (ritual feast to propitiate ancestral spirits), wedding, or funeral, or less formal gatherings such as the celebration of a successful hunt or family accomplishment. *Detembo* (praise) are described as being mostly praise with subtle criticism. Those individuals responsible for performing the *madetembedzo* are called *musvitsi* or *mudetembe*, and are traditionally the most senior wives of a clan. Likewise, the sons of a daughter of that particular clan are also responsible for learning and performing the *madetembedzo*. In addition to totemic praise poetry there is

also *ndyaringo*, the poetry of admiration or for lovers, performed at courtship rituals such as the formal exchange of the *labolla* (bride price). Finally, Zimbabwe has a national praise poem, called the Mupiro, which is performed at national celebrations by either a *mhondoro* (the region's guardian spirit) or *svikiro* (tribal spirit medium).

Tsumo-shumo ("sense" or "wisdom" accepted by all, as in proverbs), similes, and idioms are sometimes referred to as *zvirungwnutauro* (utterances that add salt to speech), and are highly regarded speech acts in Shona society. Their authoritative power emanates from the supposition that they are the views and opinions of the ancestors, which is also emphasized through the formulaic introduction "*Vakuru vakati . . .*" (as the elders say . . .). Proverbs were traditionally used to inculcate Shona customary law and rules of conduct, and even though they can be utilized in everyday speech, they continue to be employed within jural or educational contexts. Structurally, *tsumo-shumo* have two distinct, or parallel components, with a pragmatic emphasis on the independent use of the first part as a truncated proverb.

Riddles are called *chirahwe* in Zezuro, while in Karanga they are *chirabwe*, and in Manyika and Korekore they are called *chipari* and *chirapi*, respectively. *Chirahwe* are not interrogative in form, but appear more commonly as declaratives. In the past, *Chirahwe* were also used as a form of evening entertainment for children in between *ngano* sessions. They are no longer considered children's entertainment and can now be commonly found in songs, poetry, narrative, and coded messages of adults.

In addition, under the rubric of Shona oral literature, there is a distinct genre of Shona folk speech called "Deep Shona," which is the ritualistic coded language used during the Shona spirit-medium divination. Deep Shona is different from divination poetry, which is an amalgam of archaic Shona lexicons and related Bantu contact or loan words that are "not readily intelligible" (Bourdillion 1991, 236).

Songs, like riddles, are used as an important method of teaching children about culture, society, and group identity. The most common form of song within oral literature is the *nzio dzoku-punza*, the category of songs that conclude a storytelling session (Hannan 1954). Another important subcategory of song is *kude-ketera*, which Paul Berliner describes as the sung poetry that occurs with *mbira* (thumb piano) music. Berliner identified three distinct and mutually inclusive types of *kudeketera*: the fixed-line, the narrative, and the mosaic. The fixed line type has a core set of lyrics that are repeated throughout the composition, while the narrative type is a "long and involved, rapidly sung, storytelling style" that adheres to more conventional composition strategies (1978, 162). Finally, the mosaic style is an improvisational style of sung poetry, which can include proverbs, praise poems, and oral history.

Material Culture

Shona material culture encompasses all physical objects produced in traditional ways, which embody the broad categories of folk architecture, folk arts and crafts, and foodways. Shona folk architecture is a symbolic spatial representation of Shona culture and society. The traditional circular or womb-like building design corresponds with the importance the Shona attribute to procreation in maintaining the growth and development of the lineage. Within the *musha* (rural home compound) are other symbolic spaces segmented by gender, such as the *dare*, which is an exclusively male social space, or the *chikhova*, a display shelf for a woman's pots (which are a sacred representation of woman/motherhood).

Studies of Shona folk art today focus primarily on modern stone sculpture and paintings, overlooking the important production of folk crafts. Shona artistic genius was traditionally expressed through other mediums, such as metal, wood, textiles, and clayware. Precolonial textiles included *gudza* (bark fiber) cloth, reed mats, basketwork, pipe production, pottery, and ceramics. Shona wooden crafts included secular wooden products such as combs, jewelry, and other forms of body ornamentation. In addition, there are certain sacred objects such as the *mutsago* (headrest), *hakata* (divining implements), doors, walking sticks, and ritual weapons (bows and arrows). Traditional metal crafts included basic farming tools and implements. Musical instruments in both the past and present include the *mbira*, *marimba* (xylophone), *mahlwayi* (leg rattles), and *goma* (drums). These instruments constitute an important part of Shona material culture. Finally, Shona foodways, which are traditions shared by other southeastern Bantu-speaking people, include the traditional processes of brewing of *hwahwa* or *doro* (traditional millet beer) and the inhalation of snuff. This finely grained tobacco is used to enhance spirit possession, as a commodity exchanged as a gift in the *labola* (bride wealth payment), or as a ritual offering to appease angry spirits.

Shona Customs And Traditions

Between oral and material folklore is a middle ground filled by custom, ritual, festival, children's games, folk drama, rites of passage, folk dances, and all other genres involving action, performance, and paraphernalia. Shona musical traditions are an extension of the Shona culture, folklore, wisdom, and spirituality. The *mbira* (thumb piano) is an essential element in Shona folk music and spirituality.

Paul Berliner's survey, *The Soul of the Mbira: Music Traditions of the Shona People of Zimbabwe* (1981), is the most complete ethnomusicological study of the Shona. Berliner illuminates the dynamics of the socioreligious context, function, and aesthetic qualities of the *mbira* instrument and its use in religious and secular performance.

Included under the rubric of folk customs are traditional systems of health and healing. *Un'anga* is a loosely linked set of beliefs, practices, and institutions that pertain to the Shona cultural domain of health and healing. Shona therapeutics are an integral part of politics, kinship relations, religion, trade, farming, and sexual life, and they reflect not only Shona beliefs and values but also serve to illuminate power relations related to illness and the management of misfortune. The Shona traditional healer (*n'anga*) is not only a medical practitioner but also "a religious consultant, a legal and political adviser, a police detective, a marriage counselor, and a social worker" (Chavunduka 1978, 19). In recent history, the *n'anga* has also played the role of nationalist hero, activist, and revolutionary.

Un'anga is a binary system of disease etiology that attributes the cause of disease or misfortune to either nature or human or superhuman agency. Metaphorically, Shona health is maintained through a balance of coolness and purity. The Shona have three basic dichotomies of illness etiology: (1) natural versus supernatural; (2) normal versus abnormal; and (3) African versus foreign. Natural/normal/African illnesses (such as colds, coughs, slight fevers, stomachaches or headaches) are generally regarded as normal because they occur from time to time in everyone's life and appear and disappear according to expected lengths of time. In contrast, abnormal illness is primarily determined by its lack of responses to treatment or to its unusual lengthy duration. Abnormal, supernatural, or foreign illnesses are believed to be caused by the following supernatural forces: *vadzimu* (familiar ancestor spirits), *mhondoro* (clan or tribal spirits), *ngozi* (angered spirits), *mashave* (alien spirits), or *muroyi* (witches). These illness are only treatable through traditional therapeutics.

There are five different types of *n'anga*: a diviner, a diviner-medium, a herbalist, an injectionist, and a midwife. The primary methods of diagnosis for the *n'anga* is spirit possession and divination, and traditional therapeutic treatments include the proscription of herbal medicines, incisions (*nyora*), inhalation of steam or smoke, sucking (*murimiko*), and transference. Healing knowledge and spiritual authority emanates from the *n'anga*'s custodianship of an inherent healing spirit derived from either a *mudzimu* (a deceased healer in the family) or a *shave* (an alien spirit).

Shona Popular Culture

Contemporary Shona folklore has been modified through tourism and global commodification. *Chimerenga* music and Shona stone sculpture are two forms of contemporary Shona folklore that blur the contested boundaries of popular culture and folklorisms. Thomas Mapfumo, one of Zimbabwe's most prominent musicians, first coined the phrase *Chimurenga* music to describe his revolutionary music, which evolved during Zimbabwe's struggle to gain independence in the early seventies.

The roots of Mapfumo's musical style are in the traditional Shona *mbira* music, which is juxtaposed with modern electric instrumentation. *Chimurenga* music gained national and international acclaim as the primary vehicle for the artistic expression of the political sentiments of a nation fighting for its self-determination. Mapfumo's *Chimerenga* music, which is characterized by sharp social and political commentary, has become synonymous with the struggle for human rights, political dignity, and social justice.

For thirty years, Shona stone sculpture has been perceived as a modern artistic tradition with an imagined mythicalized historical past (Zilberg 1995), as a revival of the superior stone work found at the Great Zimbabwe ruins (McEwen 1972, 1991). As a result of a debate over authenticity, art critiques have unfairly dismissed it as an invented tradition, and therefore unworthy of serious aesthetic analysis (Umbani 1992; Chikove 1990). Although Shona stone sculpture is argued to be firmly located within a modernist discourse, its content and form are informed by traditional spiritual beliefs, myths, legends, oral history, customs, and rituals, which impart a new function and modernist aesthetic for creative expression in stone (Winter-Irving 1993, 15–16).

References

Beach, D. N. 1994a. *The Shona and Their Neighbors*. Oxford: Blackwell.

———. 1994b. *A Zimbabwean Past: Shona Dynastic Histories and Oral Traditions.* Gweru, Zimbabwe: Mambo Press.

Berliner, Paul F. 1978. *The Soul of Mbira: Music Traditions of the Shona People of Zimbabwe.* Chicago: University of Chicago Press.

Bourdillon, M. F. C. 1976. *The Shona Peoples: An Ethnography of the Contemporary Shona, with Special Reference to their Religion.* Gwelo: Mambo Press.

Chavuduka, G. L. 1978. *Traditional Healers and the Shona Patient.* Gwelo: Mambo Press.

Chikove, Syne. 1990. Distortions of Shona Sculpture. *The Artist,* 1, no. 6:3–5.

Fortune, G. 1980. *Ngano.* Salisburg, Zimbabwe: Mercury Press.

Gelfand, Michael. 1944. *Sick African, A Clinical Study.* Cape Town: Post-Graduate Press.

———. 1956. *Medicine and Magic of the Mashona.* Cape Town: Juta.

———. 1959. *Shona Ritual.* Cape Town: Juta.

———. 1961. *Northern Rhodesia in the Days of the Charter: Medical and Social Study.* Oxford: Blackwell.

———. 1962. *Shona Religion.* Cape Town: Juta.

———. 1964. *Witch Doctor: Traditional Medicine Man of Rhodesia.* London: Harvill.

———. 1965. *African Background: Traditional Culture of the Shona-speaking People.* Cape Town: Juta.

———. 1967. *The African Witch; with Particular Reference to Witchcraft Beliefs and Practice among the Shona of Rhodesia.* Edinburgh: Livingstone.

Gelfand, Michael, et al. 1985. *The Traditional Medical Practitioner in Zimbabwe: His Principles of Practice and Pharmacopoeia.* Gweru: Mambo Press.

Hodza, A. C. 1987. *Ngano, dzamatambidzanwa.* Gweru, Zimbabwe: Mambo Press.

Hamutyinei, M. A., and A. B. Plangger. 1987. *Tsumo-Shumo: Shona Proverbial Lore and Wisdom,* Gweru, Zimbabwe: Mambo Press.

Limbani, Ester. 1992. Shona Sculpture vs. Airport Art: Which way Zimbabwe? *Africa Calls* October: 7–8.

McEwen, Frank. 1972. Shona Art Today. *African Arts* 1, no. 2:8–11.

———. 1991. Rebirth of an Art. In *Zimbabwe Shona Sculpture: Spirit in Stone.* Exhibition catalog 34.

Winter-Irving, Celia. 1993. *Contemporary Stone Sculpture in Zimbabwe: Context, Content, and Form.* Harare: Craftsman House.

Zilberg, Jonathan. 1995. Shona Sculpture's Struggle for Authenticity and Value. *Museum Anthropology* 19, no. 1:3–24.

TONYA TAYLOR

See also **Popular Culture; Praise Poetry; Proverbs; South Africa**

SPEAKING AND NONSPEAKING POWER OBJECTS OF THE SENUFO

The Senufo of West Africa are comprised of thirty subgroups, distinguished by dialects, customs, and geographical location, with each subgroup identifying itself by a different name. Therefore, one cannot speak of the Senufo as a monolithic people with the same art, traditions, and lifestyles. In Burkina Faso, there are nine Senufo subgroups, which reside in the southwest part of the country. They do not have centralized political structures, but they have a social organization based on family heads, a council of elders, and leaders of secret societies.

The Tagwa-Senufo, who number nearly 30,000, occupy the Tagwara plateau in the Koloko prefecture, about 68 miles northwest of Bobo Dioulasso in Burkina Faso. They are divided into clans and specialized occupational groups. The farmers, by far the largest group, are the village founders and leaders of religious institutions. Blacksmiths, called Toutoun or Noumou, are both ironworkers and woodcarvers, while their spouses are basket makers. The Tagwa-Senufo do not have the male initiation system, known as Poro, that is generally associated with Senufo people. Instead, the Tagwa have Komo, a male secret association, usually seen as distinctly Bambara (a neighboring ethnic group).

Cosmology

The Tagwa use two types of power objects: the "nonspeaking" power objects and the "speaking" power objects. All power objects that do not "speak" directly to people and need the interpretation of a diviner or a priest are nonspeaking power objects. Nonspeaking power objects are made of different types of materials and can have different forms, including carved wood, kitchen stone, pottery, or animal tail and skull. Individuals, families, and the entire village possess nonspeaking power objects. They protect the people from malevolent neighbors, evil forces, disease, and various calamities. Individuals keep their personal power object on their person, in the front of their house or in their bedroom. A Tagwa man's house always has two rooms: a living room for the visitor and the bedroom, and some men do not allow anyone, even their wives, to go inside their bedroom without their authorization. A family power object is kept inside the ancestors' house and is only seen by circumcised males of the family. The power object is the responsibility of the family head. The secrets of the objects are taught to the young boys of the family as a part of the traditional educational system.

A village's power object is generally located inside the limits of the village and is the responsibility of the village's Tarfolo (Chief of the Earth). Any person in the village can consult the object. Its function is to protect the entire village from social calamities and natural disasters. If it has a very good reputation, people from other villages will consult it. Both the family and village power objects are always out of the sight of women and children and located in places with visible signs to warn visitors in the village.

The speaking power objects "speak" directly to people through a masquerade, trances, and divination. They are in the form of objects or masks worn by male performers who speak to the audience in the name of the power object. The performers symbolize the power object and are possessed by the spirits. In the Tagwara, the most well-known speaking power objects are Wara, Kono, and Komo. All speaking spirits belong to the families or clans and are available to circumcised men of the village after a special initiation ceremony.

Komo Soddy

The Komo is considered to be the most fearful and dangerous of all the speaking power objects. According to the Tagwa, the Komo was a speaking wild animal with two feet, feathers, and a head like a buffalo. It lived in the bush. One day a hunter met this strange animal and killed it. When he cut it open, he found in its mouth a tube of bamboo closed at the two extremities with a very fine membrane, which gave the animal a sweet voice. The hunter took the head of the animal and the skin full of feathers back to the village. He built a small house and placed the head inside. One morning, a song coming from the small house awakened the hunter. When he listened carefully, it was the same voice and the same song that he had heard the day he killed the strange animal. When be opened the door, he found the singing was coming from the head. The song asked him to name it Komo and to take it to entertain the men and the women in the village. He took the head, along with musicians, to the villagers and entertained them.

One day, women took control of the Komo and excluded all the men from the performance. However, the men fought back, and the hunter, the owner of the Komo, killed a chicken, put the blood on the head, and locked it up again in the small house. Since that day, men excluded women from being part of the Komo performance.

Komo performances take place only at night in a specified area. Generally, this specified area is either the place in front of the house of the Komo owner or at the public place of the village, if there is a large audience. When the masker is preparing himself inside the Komo house, the musicians and the Komo accompanists prevent those who are not allowed to see him by playing the Komo music. The Komo does not enter the village before midnight. Once in the village, the Komo sings "A yi sira bila mousolou, na ma sira bila wara na do dun" (Women, leave the path; otherwise the wild animal will eat you). The song is a warning for women to go inside their houses while the Komo is in the village. The Komo first greets the Komotigui, who generally is inside his house or in front of his door. The Komo, accompanied by the Yelema, his translator, continues to greet the oldest men and women. The Yelema responds to the songs of the Komo and interprets them because he is the only one who understands the Komo language. Besides the Yelema, the language is only understood by the senior initiates. The Komo masker does not cover his face. All audience members are initiated and immediately told during the initiation not to talk about the Komo in front of a noninitiated person.

The masker, guarding his anonymity from noninitiated persons who may recognize his voice from their houses, holds in his month the iron tube closed to the extremities by a spider web. The tube gives the Komo a strange voice similar to the one of the original animal killed by the hunter. It cannot be recognized by the noninitiated, especially by the women. The Komo has a terrifying voice that keeps women and noninitiates inside their homes. The Komo mask is the visible symbol of the secret nature of the Komo institution. Once the masker wears the mask, he loses his own identity and becomes the Komo, who has authority over anyone in the village. He becomes the voice of the ancestors and the spirits.

References

Barbier, Jean-Paul, ed. 1993. *Art of Côte d'Ivoire*. Geneva: Barbier-Mueller Museum.

Binger, Louis-Gustave. 1892. *Du Niger au Golfe de Guinée par le pays de Kong et le Mossi*. 2 vols. Paris: Hachette.

Bochet, Gilbert. 1965. Les masques Sénoufo, de la forme à la signification. *Bulletin de l'Institut Fondamental d'Afrique Noire* B, 27, no. 3–4:636–677.

Brett-Smith, Sarah. 1994. *The Making of Bamana Sculpture: Creativity and Gender*. Cambridge, England: Cambridge University Press.

Coulibaly, Sinali. 1978. *Le paysan Sénoufo*. Abidjan, Cote d'Ivoire: Nouvelles Editions Africaines.

Delafosse, Maurice. 1909. Le peuple Siéna ou Sénoufo. *Revue des Etudes Ethnographiques et Sociologiques*.

Dieterlen, Germaine. 1972. *Les fondements de la société d'initiation du Komo*. Paris: Mouton.

Förster, Till. 1988. *Die Kunst der Senufo*. Zurich: Rietberg Museum.

Glaze, Anita. 1981. *Art and Death in a Senufo Village*. Bloomington: Indiana University Press.

Goldwater, Robert J. 1964. *Senufo Sculpture from West Africa*. New York: Museum of Primitive Art.

Holas, Bohumil. 1957. *Les Sénoufo (y compris les Minianka)*. Monographies Ethnologiques Africaines. Paris: Presses Universitaires de France.

Knops, Pierre. 1980. *Les anciens Sénufo (1923–1935)*. Berg-en-Dal: Afrika Museum.

McNaughton, Patrick. 1979. *Secret Sculptures of Komo: Art and Power in Bamana (Bambara) Initiation Associations*. Working Papers in the Traditional Arts, 4. Philadelphia: Institute for the Study of Human Issues.

Rondeau, Chantal. 1980. La société Sénoufo du sud Mali (1870–1950) de la "tradition" à la dépendance. Paris: Université de Paris.

Zahan, Dominique. 1960. *Sociétés d'initiation Bambara, le N'domo, le Koré*. Paris: Mouton.

BOUREIMA TIEKORONI DIAMITANI

See also **Masks and Masquerades; Silence in Expressive Behavior; Voice Disguisers**

SPIRIT POSSESSION DANCE IN GUYANA: COMFA

Comfa is the principal ritual of a folk religious complex (also called *cumfa or cumfo*) whose defining elements include ecstatic, trancelike dancing, and spirit possession, induced by drumming. It is practiced in Guyana, South America, mainly by the descendants of enslaved Africans. Comfa appears to have evolved from West African sacred performances remembered and reinterpreted by enslaved Africans, as they encountered European and Asian culture bearers in the New World. According to sociolinguist Kean Gibson, the foremost expert on Guyanese Comfa, the religion is currently practiced by about 10 percent of the country's African-Guyanese population.

Guyana, formerly British Guiana, lies in the northeast corner of South America and enjoys sociocultural, linguistic, and political as well as geographic proximity with other Caribbean basin territories. More than any other Caribbean territory, however, Guyanese vernacular culture and identity have been influenced by Asian and Native American and African and European components. Contemporary Comfa cosmology and ritual reflect the many diasporic communities to which Guyanese people claim membership, even though Comfa is indigenously regarded as essentially African in derivation.

A Comfa dance is staged when human beings desire direct spiritual intervention in their everyday lives. In the modern Comfa worldview, God is the Creator and the Beginning and End of all things. He can be accessed through prayer. Living human beings, however, dwell outside God's domain. They exist at the center of the universe, below a realm called Heights in which reside angels, biblical prophets, and apostles. Below living humans is the terrestrial realm where disembodied souls (demigods) who are designated according to nationality make their homes in water or in graveyards. Because these spirits have already "mastered the challenges of the natural plane of existence . . . they are . . . in a position to advise on how to deal with everyday problems" (Gibson 1995:164). The seven terrestrial spirit groups are African, Amerindian (Buck), Chinese, Dutch, East Indian, English, and Spanish.

A ceremony given in honor of an English terrestrial spirit is called an English Dinner; one given to honor a Chinese or Indian spirit is called a Chinese or an Indian Work. An African Work shows appreciation for the earth and is therefore also referred to as Earth Work. Celestial services that are also called "Thanks," short for "Thanksgiving," are given to God's glory and to advise Him of the participants' wishes and desires. A celestial service usually precedes a terrestrial Work. Neither of these categories of Comfa dance are simply a display of gratitude to God or to the terrestrial spirits whom He directs. The primary purpose of the dance is for a particular sponsor to make an offering and petition to one spirit or all seven in what is called an All Nation Work for continued assistance in the form of advice, healing, information, or the mending of a breached relationship.

Music and dance form the core of Comfa performance. The specific type of music, dance, as well as food, candles, water, alcoholic beverages, and clothing, all which are also important elements of the ritual, is dictated by a stereotyped understanding of the national identity of the terrestrial worker being invoked and by the extant purpose of the ceremony. Drumming, especially the use of the 2-foot high cylindrical African drum called a Comfa drum, facilitates manifestation of the spirit through the medium of the living human, often the sponsor. Other participants may also exhibit signs of possession. Musicians are overtly responsible for summoning and disbursing the spirit to whom the ceremony is directed, though uninvited spirits may attend. Comfa songs, which may include Anglican hymns, *sankies* or hymns of the Reform churches, traditional Guyanese songs and popular songs, frame and pace the ceremony. Apart from the music, it is the dancing which enables the performer/sponsor to "move from one state of consciousness to another" and which "communicates the dancer's experience to the audience" (Gibson 1993, 103).

Although a critique by participants is a meaningful aspect of Comfa performance, the success of a Comfa dance is measured by the manifestation of the spirit during the ritual and by the tangible fulfillment of the desires expressed by the sponsor throughout and subsequent to the ritual. These wants and needs are often material in nature and arc a principal reason for the continued vitality of the religion in poverty-ridden postcolonial Guyana. About 90 percent of Comfa practitioners are women to whom the religion offers a viable alternative for attaining personal power, positive economic prospects, fellowship, and observable solutions unmatched by governmental promises or Christian doctrine. On the other hand, the fees of the religion's mothers and elders as well as the demands of the three main spirits, called entrees, to whom practitioners are beholden, can add financial burden to individuals who are already desperately poor. Nevertheless, as recently as 1993, when Kean Gibson completed her fieldwork, the Comfa dance retained a central role in the spiritual lives of a small but significant portion of the African-Guyanese population.

Cultural historian Brian Moore derives the term Cumfo from the Dahomean *kumfo*. He characterizes Cumfo as an affirming and subversive practice for newly emancipated Africans and black Creoles in late-nineteenth-century British Guiana. According to Moore, Cumfo always consisted of a dance and often included spirit possession achieved through invocation by a designated actor or medium. He indicates that in postcolonial Guyana, the religious practices designated by the term Cumfo were also referred to as Watermama in honor of the river gods or Wind (pronounced wine), in reference to the kind of dancing that reportedly took place during these ceremonies. Moore notes the West African tendency to view certain deities as being of or residing in water and suggests that this religiocultural continuity "achieved further relevance and significance to the African slaves and their descendants by virtue of the fact that rivers are so numerous in Guyana" (1995, 138). Then as now, Cumfo sessions were generally held "when misfortune had befallen a family or district, or when information was required . . . [and] the watermama was thus normally invoked either to remove evil or to divulge information" (1995, 139).

Historical and contemporary accounts of Comfa dance suggest that it is but one iteration of religiocultural complex found throughout the Caribbean. For example, while there are significant differences, the Comfa dance shares with the Jombee dance of Montserrat central elements that include the invocation of the ancestors actuated through drumming, dancing, and feasting for the benefit of a financially obligated sponsor who often offers his or her body as a vessel for spiritual mediumship. Moreover, though the principal objective of the Grenadian Shango ceremony is to induce physical and psychic possession of worshippers by Orisha, like the Guyanese Comfa dance, it is also referred to African Work or Thanksgiving Feast. In addition to shared terminology, anthropologist Patrick Polk also links the origins of Shango ritual in Grenada to the worship of the Watermama, who is mostly likely a localized version of the female Yoruba water Orisha, Yemanja. Only further research will determine whether the similarities between these and other folk rituals found throughout the Caribbean basin are surface manifestations of deeply structured cultural continuities with African origins.

References

Abrams, Ovid. *Guyana Metagee*. Buxton: Guyana.

Dobbin, Jay. 1987. *The Jombee Dance of Montserrat: A Study of Trance Ritual in the West Indies*. Columbus: Ohio State University Press.

Gibson, Kean. 1993. An African Work: The Guyanese Comfa Dance. *Journal of Cribbean Studies* 9:99–111.

———. 1995. An English Dinner: An African-Guyanese Religious Dance. *Lore and Languages* 13:163–89.

———. 1993. *A Celebration of Life: Dances of the African-Guyanese*. (videotape) Cinema Guild.

———. 1996. An Analogy Between the Continuums of Guyanese Creole and Guyanese Comfa. *Journal of Caribbean Studies* 11:3–13.

Dobbin, Jay. 1987. *The Jombee Dance of Montserrat: A Study of Trance Ritual in the West Indies*. Columbus: Ohio State University Press.

Moore, Brian. 1995. *Cultural Power, Resistance and Pluralism: Colonial Guyana 1838–1900*. Montreal and Kingston: McGill-Queen's University Press; Barbados: The Press University of the West Indies.

Polk, Patrick. 1993. African Religion and Christianity in Grenada. *Caribbean Quarterly* 39:73–81.

Smith, Raymond T. 1962. *British Guiana*. London and New York: Oxford University Press.

HAYLEY S. THOMAS

See also **Diaspora: Santeria in Cuba; Vodou**

SPIRIT POSSESSION: KUNDA

Since at least 1831, Europeans have reported an association in central African between lions and the spirits of deceased chiefs. The Portuguese explorer Gamitto, while passing through the Luangwa River Valley on his way to Kazembe's palace in Katanga in 1832, commented on Africans in the valley being able to chase lions away from animals they had killed and take the meat for themselves. Local Africans explained that this was possible because the lions were really benevolent chiefs' spirits. Gamitto also described seeing similar practices among inhabitants of Monomotapa's country (Zimbabwe), including offerings being made to lions.

More difficult to document is a spirit possession cycle called *Nfumpas*, which enacts the practical association between chiefs and lions. The *Nfumpas* spirit-possession cycle of the Kunda (the term is a Kunda adaptation of *mfumu mpashi* [chief's spirit] in Bemba/Bisa language) in the central Luangwa River Valley may be an example of the lion-chiefs spirit cult that was practiced over much of central Africa into the mid-nineteenth century. The cult presumably has dwindled with the disappearance of lions from most areas, while it continues in the Luangwa Valley, which still has a large population of wild animals, including lions.

Some Kunda elders explain that when dangerous lions disturb an area, it is the local chief who is responsible for stopping them. The chief dispatches local hunters, who kill the lion or lions and bring the carcass to the chief in a celebration generically called *malaila* (calling together), which all the chief's now-liberated inhabitants might attend. After the presentation of the lion carcass, the elder relatives of the chief save the most vital parts of the lion and, when possible, preserve the skin for the chief. The chief may assume some of the power of the lion through traditional medicines made from the lion. This process is repeated each time a lion is defeated by a chief.

Upon a chief's death, the elder relatives of the chief may secretly place certain items from the lion in the coffin with the chief's body. The entrails of the chief may be replaced by preserved lion entrails. The claws may be tied on each finger, the teeth strung round the chief's neck, and the tail of a lion is tied to the waist of the chief. When the chief's coffin is buried, the chief's relatives make libations at the gravesite with beer, raw eggs, and maize flour. A straw is inserted into the ground, and after some time a small grub may be seen to exit from the grave. This grub goes off into the bush and grows into a lion (a spirit lion). Spirit lions, who are incarnations of chiefs, are recognizable by their light-colored faces and benevolent actions toward people. Wild lions and lions sent by witchcraft also roam the bush, but they behave with animosity toward people.

Kunda description of the *Nfumpas* spirit-possession cult explains that these spirit lions sometimes need people to continue doing "jobs" for them. They are chiefs, after all, who may want things which they cannot get on their own in the bush. When they need something they come to certain people in dreams and apparitions and command things of them, such as an all-night dance at which offerings are made, applications of certain herbal medicines in the village, or hoeing a certain plot of land. The person that the lion spirit comes to is made to feel sick until the job is completed; symptoms usually involve heaviness in the chest and difficulty breathing. If the person does the bidding of the lion spirit he or she usually feels well again and acquires a special skill, such as expertise in drumming, knowledge of medicines for healing, or extraordinary skill and strength for hoeing in the garden. Their special skills and medicines are gifts from the lion-chief's spirit and are guarded in secrecy, as are many of their specialized practices. *Nfumpas* spirit possession runs in families, and one cannot suffer from it unless someone in the family did before.

It is worth noting that there are very old chiefs' praise songs that reflect these dangerous and beneficial relationships between lions, chiefs, spirits, and people. One nineteenth-century Kunda praise song for the Kakumbi chiefs states:

> We are so happy we are yours,
> we are so happy we are yours!
> We are so happy we are yours
> that you can kill us and eat us,
> kill us and eat us!

This is a sentiment sung to living chiefs but directed to their deceased forbears who have assumed the shape and status of lions. It is a joyous song. The opening lines are sung in a somber mood but give way to excitement and happiness in the closing refrain. Because the songs are sung at occasions for dancing, their words are few, repeated in driving rhythms to the accompaniment of drums, clapping, and rattles.

Another song associated with the *Nfumpas* complex deals with the preparation of herbal medicines for healing those affected by the spirits. This song, like the Chief's praise song above, is a joyous one and is sung as an occasion for dancing. Its words are also few and sung to drumming, clapping, and rattles. To fast rhythms the words are sung:

> Lay them, lay them!!
> Lay down the roots, my mother!!
> Lay them, lay them!!
> Lay down the roots, my mother!!

References

Gamitto, A. C. P. 1960. *King Kazembe and the Marave, Cheva, Bisa, Bemba, Lunda, and other Peoples of Southern Africa, 1832*, tr. Ian Cunnison. Lisbon: Junta de Investigacoes do Ultramar.

Marks, Stuart. 1984. *The Imperial Lion: Human Dimensions of Wildlife Management in Central Africa*. Boulder, Colo.: Westview.

Strickland, Bradford. 1995. *Knowledge, Agency and Power among the Kunda of Eastern Zambia*, Ph.D. dissertation, University of North Carolina, Chapel Hill.

BRADFORD STRICKLAND

See also **Ancestors; Animals in African Folklore**

SPIRIT POSSESSION: TUAREG AND SONGHAY

The term *possession* has been applied to contexts in which humans are said to be temporarily displaced, inhabited, or "ridden" by particular spirits in Africa, the African diaspora (especially Brazil and the Caribbean), the Middle East, the Pacific, and sometimes South and Southeast Asia. During these episodes, voice and agency are attributed to the spirit rather than the host, who is not held accountable for what occurs—and indeed may claim subsequently to have no knowledge of it, or at least no ability to have influenced its direction. The spirits are generally conceptualized and experienced as discrete persons, whether ancestors, foreigners, historical figures, gods, or members of an alternate species. These persons may be viewed as more or less distinct from their hosts, according to the particular performance tradition at issue, as well as to the stage the relationship between an individual host and spirit has reached. In Africa, some commonly recognized cultural forms (which may cover a broad range of local variations) of possession include *zar* in northeast Africa (Lewis 1971, 1986; Boddy 1989), *bori* among the Hausa of northern Nigeria and southern Niger, *hauka* among the Songhay of Niger (Stoller 1989, 1992), and *goumaten* among the Tuareg of northern Niger (Rasmussen 1995). As in other regions of the world, terms, if not pantheons, often overlap. As Ivan Karp has noted, a single researcher would have difficulty in reviewing the literature on spirit possession in Africa alone (1989, 91). Presented here is a brief review of approaches to possession, followed by two examples from the western Sahelian region: studies of spirit possession among the Tuareg and the Songhay peoples of Niger.

Early Studies

Many earlier studies of spirit possession suffered from efforts to place possession in one or another Western category, particularly medical, religious, or ethnopsychological. What is important is to understand its multiple significance within the particular contexts in which it occurs. Possession is about meaning. During the late 1900s there was a move away from positivist, decontextualizing approaches and toward cultural interpretation (Lambek 1981, 1993; Boddy 1989; Stoller 1989; Kramer 1993; Rasmussen 1995). Possession intersects with numerous cultural domains, including medicine and religion, but is itself reducible to none. Several authors remark on how spirit possession thickens social ties. Spirit assertions of difference or identity are metastatements: coded moral and political acts of the humans they possess, derived from thinking about one's relationships to others by thinking through the "Other" writ large (Boddy 1994, 423). This point accommodates a widening of perspective from specific spirits to their imagined worlds, which are in various and subtle ways alien to their hosts.

To some investigators, spirit mythologies constitute reservoirs of cultural knowledge—about illnesses and medicines, but also about ethnicity, history, domination, social propriety, and caprice. In her 1995 study of Tuareg spirit possession, Susan Rasmussen accents its comedic and aesthetic dimensions by comparing possession to satirical allegory, where historical and cultural consciousness is vividly dramatized in challenging, but also reinvigorating, the embodied, engendered, moral order. Among the Kel Ewey Tuareg of northeastern Niger, a seminomadic, socially stratified, Islamic people, persons undergoing spirit-possession rituals called *tende n goumaten* come from diverse social strata, but are predominantly women. Local residents believe that certain illnesses, if they persist, are caused by spirits (variously called *goumaten, eljenan,* or *kel essuf*) passed from mother to daughter, causing a trance. A cure requires songs, jokes, and music provided by the *tende,* a drum made from a mortar used to crush grain. These rites are usually staged in the evening. They feature a drummer (generally a smith or descendant of a slave); a female player of the *asakalabo* (a calabash floating in water, struck with a cloth-covered baton); a chorus of young women from diverse social origins who sing songs identified with possession ritual; and usually, one patient, called a *gouma.* Present at all possession rituals is a large, mixed-sex audience, ranging in age from about ten to twenty-five years. Audience, chorus, and patient evaluate the ceremony's effectiveness through jokes that criticize various singers for transgressions of codes of personal conduct, as well as for shortcomings in performative competence—that is, whether they are lazy, whether the chorus and drum drown out the solo singer, whether too much crying and shouting overwhelm the performance, and whether singers forget words or fail to use the "proper" Tamacheq, the language of the Tuareg. Only women learn these songs. In their verses, there are themes of social commentary and criticism, as well as references to past and current events and conditions in local history and culture.

Tuareg Rituals

Tuareg spirit-possession rituals are noisy public events where a degree of license is allowed in personal conduct. At the beginning of the ceremony, the patient lies prone beneath a blanket. As the songs and drumming quicken in pace and become rhythmically more elaborate, the patient rises to a sitting position and begins shaking her head from side to side, slowly at first, and then faster and more vigorously. Tuareg refer to this as the "head dance." Soon the motion includes the shoulders and upper torso, although the patient never dances on her feet. Throughout the rite, she remains seated, facing the drummer, surrounded on one side by the women's chorus and on the other by the general audience. In her hand, the patient grips a man's sword, usually borrowed from a close male relative (in everyday life, Tuareg women do not carry swords; they do, however, inherit property in livestock and own the residential tent). She rocks upon this sword, holding it perpendicular to the ground throughout her dance. Over her head she wears a black face veil (also contrary to everyday practice, in which Tuareg men, not women, wear the face veil), and a white cloth band, attached to her veil by a female friend or close kinswoman.

Men and women generally associate these possession rituals with women, ridicule the few men who have undergone them as effeminate, and say women's love and worries cause spirit-possession attacks. Women say spirits attack them when they are "touched in the heart" by beautiful music. Overt symptoms include refusal to eat, sleep, and speak, and sometimes running wildly through the desert. Some women become possessed on Islamic holidays, though the Muslim clergy oppose this rite as "anti-Islamic." The clergy do not, however, forbid these ceremonies and often refer women to them, though limiting their enactment to neighborhoods far from the mosque and to times that do not coincide with religious events. A large number of frequent patients are older women and adolescent girls who are wives and daughters of prominent Islamic scholars.

Although Tuareg men and women alike may become possessed, men's spirits and women's spirits differ: those of men respond to verses from the Quran, while those of women require music of the *tende*. Thus, men's manner of curing spirits, not their affliction, is gender-specific. However, Rasmussen argues that female spirit possession cannot be reduced to simple rebellion, "sex-warfare," or compensatory behavior (Rasmussen 1995, 86).

The dance motions of trance (associated with women) and the music of the *tende* (traditionally played by persons of low social status, such as smiths and formerly servile or client peoples—in the precolonial social order of nobles, tributaries, smith/artisans, and slaves) evoke key, contradictory themes in Tuareg culture. Specifically, these conflicts are the freedom to conduct illicit affairs outside marriage (which are still officially arranged by parents and ideally take place within one's own social stratum), restrictions imposed on men and women as they age, and jural ambiguities and constraints associated with older persons' authority roles in property ownership. As a parent-in-law, an aging person's conduct must ideally be reserved and dignified, with increasing devotion to Islamic ritual and withdrawal from festivals defined as secular, and arrangement of children's marriages, which are ideally endogamous (within the same some social stratum).

In their aesthetic elements, Tuareg spirit-possession rituals reveal two interrelated themes: one concerns the possession ritual negotiation of social power and of redefinitions of self; the other juxtaposes an individual patient's trance solitude and the music of the ritual. The sounds of spirit exorcism enable, not solely the possessed patient, but also diverse participants, to find a voice by alternately reflecting and subverting social values. Enactment of the musical cure, as well as commentary on it during and following these rituals, in effect allows a recasting of the possession experience and, concomitantly, becomes a lens through which social experience is analyzed and, to an extent, controlled. Sound mediates the remoteness of the patient and the free sociability of audience, transforming an experience normally incongruent into a state in which needs coincide with circumstance. The possession idiom for the Tuareg encapsulates the ironies and contradictions for persons at the margins and thresholds of life in Tuareg society, such as adolescent girls, older women, and members of different social strata, as they freely interact with each other and communicate directly with one another at the possession ritual. They cannot do this so freely or openly in everyday social life. But the interplay of aesthetic form and intention in possession cannot be reduced to conscious manipulation or be seen as directly causal. Rather, the enactment of possession enables commentary on the human condition in an expressive style articulating with, rather than completely overturning, socially structured beliefs about personal identity.

These processes are clearly shown in the ludic, or carnival, elements of the possession ritual. The songs and other behavior during the possession rituals display the inversion typical of "rituals of reversal." For example, men and women of diverse social strata, who in principle normally do not marry, may flirt with one another and initiate romantic liaisons. Contrary to the usual value in Tuareg culture placed on concealing one's true desires, the patient indicates nonverbally her song preference. The head dance of a patient who is an elderly woman presents a further inversion of normal behavioral roles, for older women usually

do not dance in public, particularly not in mixed company or at events featuring ribald entertainment (the verses of some songs contain sexual innuendoes and sometimes even mock official Islam). Young boys play on the sidelines, sometimes dancing like grown men, sometimes causing considerable mischief. They speak to adults without the usual reserved respect, often teasing them, but this behavior provokes little reprimand during a possession ceremony. Outside the possession ritual, there is not such openly direct expression or free social interaction between youths and older persons, or between members of different social strata.

In the Tuareg possession ritual, there are also symbolic parallels with rites of passage, particularly marriage. For example, at the beginning of a possession rite, the possessed patient always appears in a prone position on the ground, with her entire body covered by a blanket. This is also the dominant symbol at weddings, seen in the central image of the wedding tent: for the first days of the eight-day wedding ritual the bride lies prone beneath a blanket in her mother's tent. During this phase of the wedding, for several successive nights, the older female relatives of the bride take down and reconstruct the nuptial tent, making it larger each night. This tent image is associated with both the spirit-possession ritual and rites of passage. The tension between the inversion and the correspondence of symbols in spirit possession and the wedding rite of passage reflect certain contradictions in Tuareg social relationships. The alternating frames of nonserious joking and serious healing seem to parallel the frames associated with relationships over the life course that are transformed, such as the transition from courtship (involving a degree of sexual license and frequently illicit liaisons) to marriage (featuring behavioral restrictions and economic obligations), as well as in-law roles (which involve increased reserve in relationships and participation in devotion to Islam). The transition to marriage affects kinship behavior: the joking and horseplay of cousins become the reserve and formality of husband and wife.

Thus, the *tende n goumaten* possession ritual, through its setting (which encourages relaxing of the usual daily social restrictions) and its jokes and songs (which express alternatively criticism and praise on social stratum, age, gender, and official religion) provides a forum for reflection and discourse on Tuareg culture, society, and history. Its ritual imagery not only encapsulates contradictions but also reveals compromises between ideals and actual conditions of existence. For example, the imagery expresses a contradiction between the local ideology of the elevated and independent status of nobles—particularly women—and their actual position amid economic transformation and uncertainty in contemporary social change (sedentarization and tensions with the central state government) and ecological crisis (recurrent droughts), both of which threaten long-standing Tuareg beliefs, practices, and social institutions.

Therefore, during possession rites, when human and spirit realities most obviously interpenetrate, or fuse, as Stoller (1989) suggests, cultural knowledge is momentarily embodied, expressed indirectly via the images and antics of the alien performance, and undoubtedly changed.

Songhay Rituals

Without denying their seriousness to participants, possession ceremonies have been described in aesthetic terms as theater, allegory, satire, and burlesque, and as witty and historically perceptive metacommentaries on the human world. Among the Songhay of western Niger, myths constitute the charter of the spirit-possession cult: there are myths about the origin of the various families of spirits. Each has a genealogy, with names and ethnic origins for all the families of the Songhay pantheon. Human beings are never far from the domain of the spirits, and the spirits often intervene in the social affairs of human beings.

Spirit incantations take the form of praise poems in which the *sorko*, a bard of the spirits, first indirectly declares his power-lessness—a kind of prostration before the spirit world—and then sings about the great exploits of the spirits. The most important set of praise songs is called *Tooru che* and is recited for the nobles of the Songhay spirit world. Entrance into a spirit-possession cult occurs, not by personal choice, but when a person is struck by an illness that does not respond to any kind of treatment, thus signifying that the sickness is extraordinary, precipitated by a spirit.

Ritual elements of Songhay possession include music (especially songs), dance, costumes, altars, stones, hatchets, antelope horns, and dolls. The Songhay state that the *godji* violin or the drum carries the words. Songhay say that the sound of the *godji* "cries" for all Songhay, penetrating them and making them feel the presence of the ancestors. It is the most sacred of instruments. The sound of the *godji* is a tangible link between Songhay present and past, for this wailing sound revivifies deep-seated cultural themes about the nature of life and death, the origin of the Songhay, and the juxtaposition of the social and spirit worlds. These themes, in turn, reinforce Songhay cultural identity.

Ritual music is a veritable support for the phrases of the praise poem. Stoller explores the power of sound in Songhay spirit possession. The *sorko*, the praise-singer to the spirits of the Songhay pantheon, is a healer in his own right: he knows the words that can repel witches and sorcerers. The *zima*, or ritual priest, is the impressario and healer associated exclusively with the Songhay possession cult. These men and women know the words that have the force to beckon the spirits from the spirit world to the world of social life. All these practitioners must undergo a long apprenticeship, during which they memorize scores of ritual incantations and learn to apply these special words to the substances they prepare for clients. A magical substance (a vine, a tree bark, a stone, or a cowry shell) is without power unless a possession-ritual specialist has imbued it with force.

It is clear that esthetic and performance dimensions of possession are inseparable from its spirituality, from its capacity to reformulate identity or to heal. Since possession is embodied in usually public rituals, it constitutes a specific performance. Performances may be comic or dramatic, suspenseful or joyful, and establish hierarchies or invert them. They make use of music, dance, distinct clothing, and unusual speech patterns and body movements. Possession, therefore, may be understood as a system of communication, providing alternative, authoritative voices and critical distance, but also antilanguage and ambiguity (Boddy 1989) and the possibility for the simultaneous transmission of opposed messages (Rasmussen 1995). Possession is truly heteroglossic. Recent studies have tried to break through prior restrictions to examine possession on its own terms, in the societies where it is found. These studies locate it in wider social and historical contexts, describing how it acts as a prism through which naturalized constructs (e.g., of person, gender, or body) are refracted or undone.

References

Boddy, Janis. 1989. *Wombs and Alien Spirits.* Madison: University of Wisconsin Press.

——— 1994. Spirit Possession Revisited: Beyond Instrumentality. *Annual Review of Anthropology* 23:407–434.

Karp, Ivan. 1989. Power and Capacity in Rituals of Possession. In *The Creativity of Power: Cosmology and Action in African Societies,* eds. William Arens and Ivan Karp. Washington, D.C.: Smithsonian Institution Press.

Kramer, F. 1993. *The Red Fez: Art and Spirit Possession in Africa,* tr. M. R. Green. London: Verso.

Lambek, Michael. 1981. *Human Spirits.* Cambridge, England: Cambridge University Press.

———. 1993. *Knowledge and Practice in Mayotte: Local Discourses of Islam, Sorcery, and Spirit Possession.* Toronto: University of Toronto Press.

Lewis, I. M. 1971. *Ecstatic Religion: An Anthropological Study of Spirit Possession and Shamanism.* Harmondsworth, England: Penguin.

———. 1986. *Religion in Context: Cults and Charisma.* Cambridge, England: Cambridge University Press.

Rasmussen, Susan. 1995. *Spirit Possession and Personhood among the Kel Ewey Tuareg.* Cambridge, England: Cambridge University Press.

Stoller, Paul. 1989. *Fusion of the Worlds: An Ethnography of Possession among the Songhay of Niger.* Chicago: University of Chicago Press.

———. 1992. *The Cinematic Griot.* Chicago: University of Chicago Press.

SUSAN J. RASMUSSEN

See also **Gender: Representation in African Folklore; Medicine; Performance in Africa; Zar; Spirit Possession in the Sudan**

SPIRIT POSSESSION: WEST AFRICA

Spirit possession in West Africa is important for a number of reasons. It is a significant aspect of local healing and social systems in much of the region, and it is the source of many of the possession practices that traveled to the Americas via the Atlantic slave trade. It has also been the site of some of the most distinctive academic studies of possession.

The distribution of spirit possession is uneven, but covers most of West Africa from Senegal to Nigeria with the exception of the coastal strip from Guinea Bissau to Cote d'Ivoire. Though there are some scattered reports of possession seances in Guinea, Liberia, and western Cote d'Ivoire, they are rare and seem likely to have been introduced recently from neighboring areas.

In the Sahelian region on the southern border of the Sahara, possession is common and ranges from Senegal, across Mali, and into Niger and northern Nigeria. Here, possession usually coexists with Islam, as in much of North and East Africa, though it is officially discouraged. Indeed, it seems likely that North African spirit-possession cultures may have had a strong influence on their analogues in West Africa, especially given the presence of possession among the Tuareg, who cross the Sahara regularly, sharing in the culture of both regions (Rasmussen 1995). Other types of spirit possession in the Sahelian region include the *ndop* possession groups among the Wolof of Senegal, *djine don* possession rites of the Bamana people of Mali, *Holey* possession among the Songhay of Niger, and the *Bori* possession cult among the Hausa of Niger and Nigeria. Two characteristics link these various forms of possession: Possessing spirits are usually either spirits or animals of the surrounding land and water, said to have lived there "always," in implicit distinction from the Muslim or Christian high God, who has been introduced relatively recently. Secondly, adepts—those who actually "take the spirit"—are most often women, a characteristic trait of possession throughout the continent.

Spirit possession in West Africa has been studied by both French and English speakers. Anglophone anthropologists have tended to link spirit possession to its causes in the wider society. Explanations have included compensation for women's lack of power in male-dominated societies to nutritional deficiencies and "automatic" responses to certain types of music. Many of these approaches have been criticized for reducing complex situations and practices to single-cause explanations.

Francophone writers have tended to focus primarily on the experience and the expressive aspects of possession. This has encouraged a much broader range of analyses than those that fall within the domain of British social anthropology. While some authors have approached possession from a psychoanalytic perspective (Ortigues and Ortigues 1966), others have focused on the multifaceted role of music in possession ceremonies (Rouget 1990). Still others have focused on the theatrical aspects of the possession seance, which typically attracts a large (interactive) audience of nonadepts, who become involved in the proceedings much in the same way as they might during a masquerade or a performance involving music and dance. Most famous among these researchers is Jean Rouch, whose 1954 film *Les maîtres fous* (The Mad Masters) portrays a group of young migrant workers from Niger living in Accra, Ghana (then the Gold Coast), and acting out the roles of colonial officials in a violent Hauka possession seance. The film is probably the most dramatic ever made on spirit possession, but it does have its critics.

Recent analyses by American writers have focused on issues of gender, and especially the links between possession and women's health and fertility (Masquelier 1995, 2001; Rasmussen 1995). This research follows the insight from other parts of the continent that many possession communities have gender, sexuality, and conception as primary foci.

Finally, possession is one of the strongest links between the cultures of the West African coast and those of the African diaspora. As nonmaterial valuables, possessing spirits were among the "belongings" African slaves were able to bring with them across the Middle Passage. Important coastal possession cultures exist in Southwest Nigeria, where Yoruba speakers share possession by deities such as Shango and Ogun with practitioners of religions such as Candomble in Brazil and Santería in Cuba (Verger 1957). The Vodun religion and possession practices of present-day Benin and Togo continue there and in a recognizably similar form across the Atlantic in Haiti. In Africa and the diaspora, cultures and religions of possession coexist with and borrow from monotheistic religions such as Catholicism, Protestant Christianity, and Islam.

References

Bessmer, Fremont. 1983. *Horses, Musicians, and Gods*. South Hadley, Mass.: Bergen and Garvey.

Gibbal, Jean-Marie. 1994. *Genii of the River Niger*. Chicago: University of Chicago Press.

Kramer, Fritz 1993. *The Red Fez*. London: Verso.

Masquelier, Adeline. 1995. Consumption, Prostitution, and Reproduction: The Poetics of Sweetness in Bori. *American Ethnologist* 22, no. 4:883–906.

———. 2001. *Prayer Has Spoiled Everything: Possession, Power, and Identity in an Islamic Town of Niger*. Durham, N.C.: Duke University Press.

Ortigues, Marie-Cecile, and E. Ortigues. 1966. *Oedipe africain*. Paris: Plon.

Rasmussen, Susan. 1995. *Spirit Possession and Personhood among the Kel Ewey Tuareg*. Cambridge, England: Cambridge University Press.

Rouch, Jean. 1978. On the Vicissitudes of the Self: The Possessed Dancer, the Magician, the Sorcerer, the Filmmaker, and the Ethnographer. *Studies in the Anthropology of Visual Communication*, 5, no. 1:2–8.

———. 1989. *La religion et la magie Songhay*. Brussels: Editions de l'Universite de Bruxelles.

Rouget, Gilbert. 1990. *Music and Trance*. Chicago: University of Chicago Press.

Verger, Pierre. 1957. *Notes sur le culte des Orisa et Vodun a Bahia: la Baie de tous les saints au Brasil et l'ancienne Cote des esclaves en Afrique*. Dakar: IFAN.

MICHAEL MCGOVERN

See also **Diaspora; Comfa Healing; Santería in Cuba; Vodou**

STORIES AND STORYTELLING: THE LIMBA

According to the Limba of northern Sierra Leone, their storytelling is not as significant as their music, songs, and dances. Nevertheless, it still plays important roles. Scholarly knowledge is largely based on Ruth Finnegan's 1960s extensive storytelling research among eastern Limba, Gugelchuk's generative-transformational analysis of twelve tales collected by Finnegan (1985), and Ottenberg's unpublished notes from 1978 to 1980 on the northeastern Limba in Wara Wara Bafodea chiefdom. Stories are called *mboro*, a term also used for riddles, proverbs, parables, analogies, metaphors, and, occasionally, historical narratives.

According to Finnegan, Limba stories are usually short, untitled, uncomplicated, and not rigidly fixed. The narrators, mostly males, alter and embellish them, and occasionally create new stories or take them from elsewhere. According to Finnegan, "there is no *one* form of any Limba story that could be called the fixed or 'correct' one" (1967, 91). The Limba possess little specialized vocabulary to describe stories and storytelling, and there is no special term for the narrator. Story vocabulary is like everyday speech, and action in the tales usually take place in a Limba village, though the texts are sometimes obscure. Some stories are told in the daytime, but most are presented at night in Limba villages, occasionally at the farms, and palm wine is often drunk during the storytelling. Narrator and audience sing in a call-and-response pattern in the midst of the tale, with audience clapping. The narrator often appoints a responder from the listeners, who supports or comments as the story unfolds. Narrators are of all ages, and stories are not owned by individuals, families, or clans, as is the case among Native Americans of the Northwest Coast of the United States. The audience is normally composed of males and females of various ages with plenty of children also in attendance.

Storytelling is but one aspect of the emphasis on speaking well among Limba. Muslim influences on tales through Mandingo and Fulani living in Limba country occur, as well as Western influences. Stories refer to past times, but flashbacks within them are rare. The inner feelings of characters in the stories are rarely developed; the emphasis is on action. Limba are proud of their stories, which serve as ethnic markers for them, even though similar tales occur in neighboring cultures. Historical narratives are not usually found at Limba story sessions but rather in the context of court cases and political conflicts, where songs and clapping do not occur. While many stories have moral elements, aesthetic features such as humor and fantasy are very significant. Finnegan believes that Limba stories not only reflect life but influence it.

Types of Stories

Finnegan classifies stories into those about people, those about religion and the high God, Kanu (also called Kanu Masala, Masala, or, occasionally Allah) and those based on animals. She indicates there is much classificatory overlap, however, and the Limba themselves do not classify their tales. People stories, the most popular and elaborate form, often involve marital or parent-child conflicts, where women play strong, aggressive, and sometimes treacherous roles, more so than in everyday Limba life. Love and spouse-wooing themes and competitions are common. Killings, beatings and revenge, adultery, and the plight of orphans are also frequent themes, suggesting underlying family tensions in Limba life. Some people stories involve chiefs and succession to chieftaincy, where chiefs may act poorly and are punished, suggesting some anxiety among the Limba over leadership. Little reference occurs to colonial or modern political situations. Hunter tales are common, as are stories involving twins and triplets.

Religious stories are often explanatory tales about how death came about, why Kanu is in the sky, or the origin of chieftaincy, but few stories concern the origin of natural phenomena. Kanu generally plays a friendly and supportive role in the tales. Stories of Kanu meld with Christian and Muslim beliefs—both religions exist among the Limba, in addition to their own. Some religious tales involve spirits other than Kanu, often living in the bush. But though ancestors play important roles in every day life, few references to them occur in stories. Witch beliefs and supposed practices, endemic among the Limba, find expression in some tales.

Animal stories are metaphoric of human behavior. Animals often have specific characteristics: the antelope is retiring, the leopard dangerous, the finch a diviner. The key story figure, Wosi the spider, who, unlike the case in many other West African animal trickster tales, is an unsuccessful trickster. Arrogant and selfish, his tricks are defeated by honorable animals, often by his larger and stronger, but honest and forthright, wife Kuyi. Slander is not uncommon in Limba life and occurs in both animal and people tales.

Storytelling Sessions

Storytelling sessions are spontaneous occasions, growing out of sociability in public, and they are not a private activity. Finnegan stresses the importance of understanding storytelling as a performance, in its particular settings, where the narrators' gestures, dancing, and other body movements; changes in voicing and facial expressions; singing ability; skills in mimicry of people, animals, Kanu, and other spirits; use of dramatic repetition; and the interaction of teller and audience, are as important as the text. Storytellers are often skillful drummers, singers, and diviners, sometimes even blacksmiths. But they do not travel, as do musicians and diviners; theirs is not a truly professional role.

Ottenberg's unpublished researches at Wara Wara Bafodea suggest variations. There, songs often open and close the story, as well as occurring within it. There is frequently a wood gong (*nkali*) player in addition to the narrator, or the narrator plays the instrument himself. Females are active as storytellers, and tales are told less in the dry season, in the villages, where other performative activities occur, than at the more isolated, farm residences in the rainy season.

References

Bockarie, Samura, and Heribert Hinzen. 1986. *Limba Stories and Songs*. Stories and Songs from Sierra Leone, no. 13. Freetown: People's Educational Association of Sierra Leone.

Chopping Boy (Momodu Mansaray). 1986. *"Aw fish kam na dis wol" en da stori den we Chopin Boy pul (How Fish Came into the World and Other Stories by Chopping Boy)*. Stories and Songs from Sierra Leone, no. 8. Freetown: People's Educational Association of Sierra Leone.

Finnegan, Ruth. 1965. *Survey of the Limba People of Northern Sierra Leone*. London: H.M.S.O.

———. 1967. *Limba Stories and Story-Telling*. Oxford: Clarendon Press.

———. 1969. Attitudes to Speech and Language among the Limba of Sierra Leone. *Odu, A Journal of West Africa, Studies* 2:61–77.

———. 1970. *Oral Literature in Africa*. Oxford: Clarendon Press.

———. 1982. "Short Time to Stay." Comments on Time, Literature and Oral Performance. Bloomington: African Studies Program, Twelfth Annual Hans Wolff Memorial Lecture.

———. 1992. Reflecting Back on Oral Literature in Africa: Some Reconsiderations after 21 years. *South Africa Journal of African Languages* 12, no. 2:39–47.

Gugelchuk, Gary M. 1985. A Generative Transformational Analysis of the Plots of Limba (West Africa) Dilemma Tales. Ph.D. dissertation Ohio State University.

Ottenberg, Simon. Unpublished field notes, Wara Wara Bafodea, 1978–1980.

SIMON OTTENBERG

See also **Performance in Africa Storytellers; West Africa**

STORYTELLERS

"Kwathi ke kaloku ngantsomi . . ." ("And now for a story . . ."): The storyteller pronounces the familiar formulaic words, and moves her audience into the riches of the cultural past into a world charged with fantasy. But in the process, the members of the audience never leave the tangible, perceptible world. The storyteller moves them into antiquity, scrupulously making the connections between past and present, and in that nexus shapes their experience of the present. When the opening words are pronounced, the audience realizes that an enchanting fusion of the two worlds is about to transpire, that time is about to be arrested, and that history is about to be experienced.

The Tools of the Storyteller

The stuff of the storytelling profession has been around from the beginning of recorded time. These materials include the remnants, relics, and shards of the human experience. These are snatches of the lived life, images that reflect it, and the mythic images that define and shape it. It was only the presence of the storyteller that was required to knit these materials into stories that gave meaning and context to it all, forming the emotions of those in the audience into worlds of illusion, creating stories out of the air itself—tales that would never relinquish their mesmerizing hold on audiences.

Storytellers sing of humanity's triumphs and record humanity's debasements. They embody and engage both sides of the human condition—its beauty and its monstrousness—keeping both alive. That is the troubling pact, at once glorious and odious, that is made with the storyteller, who unlocks a people's collective memory, allowing listeners to both celebrate and revel in their past. The storyteller knows sadness and has experienced hate, and, although the storyteller never turns her eyes from melancholy, her words give us hope. The images of the youth whose love was plain and whose quest was right gives people hope. And these most ancient of artists focus their efforts and the attention of their audiences on the changes they regularly experience.

The Great Storytellers

"Africa," wrote Edouard Jacottet "has treasures, for the most part still hidden, in store for the student of folk-lore" (1908, xiv). Among the Sotho storytellers who provided the rich materials for Jacottet's collections were Moshe Mosetse and 'Mamangana, who told stories about the movement of young people to completeness, the rites of passage moving them to adulthood. The finest storyteller encountered among the Zulu in the mid-nineteenth century by Henry Callaway, and arguably the most accomplished Zulu performer yet recorded, was Lydia Umkasetemba. Callaway transcribed and translated eight stories told by Umkasetemba. Among the most impressive is "Untombi-yapansi," a story in which a real-life girl is brought into metaphorical relationship with a fantasy character, as the girl's agonizing but ultimately triumphant movement into womanhood is signaled and revealed by the antics of the imaginary character in the realm of fantasy. Storytellers in Africa have traditionally been a major means of making connections with the past, of enabling members of audiences to view themselves and their worlds within an ancestral context, a context that makes sense of their world, that charts their lives for them, that records and manipulates their movements through the great changes that mark their arc from birth to death.

We "are in the . . . market place which lies within the casbah of a Moroccan town. Blind Mahjoub, the storyteller, is in the center of a circle of spellbound listeners who are eagerly drinking in his tales of caliphs, jinns and saints, of enchanted gardens and alabaster palaces" (Chimenti 1965, 1). The storyteller is the crucial figure. Margaret Read argues that "her imagination and her personality illuminate the ancient stories with her own turns and phrases. The story is the same, but its telling is ever changing" (Elliott 1968, vii). Observers document the performances of great storytellers: "One listens to a clever storyteller, as was

our old friend Mungalo," noted Edwin E. Smith and Andrew Murray Dale. "Speak of eloquence! . . . [E]very muscle of face and body spoke, a swift gesture often supplying the place of a whole sentence" (1920, 2, 336).

Ahmad Abd-al-Rahim M. Nasr tells of Musa al-Tahir from northern Nigeria who used a *fahami* charm given to him by his father, a charm that enabled him to remember things in detail, and he became a renowned professional singer of stories. He used a tin drum as accompaniment, becoming known as Maitanaka, the possessor of a tin, and he told stories to his 104th year. "Anyone may tell a story," asserts Alta Jablow, "but there is usually one, noted for his skill as a raconteur and for his wide repertory of tales, who carries much of the performance. There are also special times when stories are told during the day in the market-places, as when a noted teller of tales comes to a Hausa village. The usual market activities slow down or cease altogether while the storyteller performs" (1961, 29–30).

Among the Lamba people of Zambia, Mulekelela from Kawunda Chiwele was a great raconteur. The stories that he performed, he said, were passed down through the generations. He started his story with the words, "Mwe wame! After each sen-

A Xhosa woman, Nongenile Masithathu Zenani, performing a story, 1975.
Photo © Harold Scheub.

tence he pauses automatically for the last few words to be re-peated or filled in by his audience, and as the story mounts to its climax, so does the excitement of the speaker rise with gesture and pitch of voice. A good storyteller will tell over again a story, well-known to all, in such a way that they will leave their pipes and crowd nearer to him around his fire, so as not to miss a single detail" (Doke 1927, xii–xiii). Said S. Samatar tells of ʿAb-dille ʿAli Siigo, who would chant poetry "late into the night before a captivated audience of men, women, and children. He was a dramatic chanter who seemed to command even the atten-tion of the camels which sat nearby, lazily chewing their cuds" (1982, x). Abbakar Hasan of Maiurno, Sudan, was both musi-cian and actor. He played a two-stringed musical instrument as he performed, using ideophones and proverbs, and he was careful "to link fictitious events with his people's day to day life" (Abu-Manga 1985, 9–11). Ross and Walker tell of the Nkundo story-teller, Tata Manga, who, "regardless of the size of his audience, entered fully into the spirit of each tale he told, dramatizing the dialogues, varying his tone and his speed, utilizing the full range of Lonkundo locutions, and employing every opportunity for the increasing of suspense" (1979, 50).

One of the greatest of Africa's storytellers was //Kabbo, a San performer, who said, "A story is like the wind. It comes from a far-off place, and we feel it." He continued:

> I am waiting for the moon to turn back for me, so that I may return to my home and listen to all the people's stories when I visit them. When the weather gets a little warmer, I sit in the sun, sitting and listening to the stories that come from out there, stories that come from a dis-tance. Then I catch hold of a story that floats out from the distant place—when the sun feels warm and when I feel that I must visit and talk with my fellows (Bleek and Lloyd 1911, 298–301).

When he said those words, //Kabbo was a prisoner being held on Robben Island. His name means "dream," and he was without question the most imaginative and poetic of these storytellers.

Observers tell of how storytellers create character, the tools that they use as they construct their tales: "His variation of speed and tone, vocabulary, persuasion of his listeners, vehemence and drama, are all knit into an aesthetic whole" (Kabira 1983, 16). Writing of the Nigerian Edo people, H. L. M. Butcher com-mented, "The narrative holds the audience enthralled, though most of the tales will be familiar, and the eloquence of the teller receives instant appreciation. The various actions described are imitated, and onomatopoeic sounds are freely used" (1937, 342). And Edward Evans-Pritchard emphasizes nonverbal aspects of performance among the Azande people of the Sudan, noting "the tone of voice, the singsong of the chants, and the gestures and mimicry which give emphasis to what is being said and are sometimes a good part of its meaning" (1967, 18–19). Masks and costumes may be used as well, as in Ijo epic performances in Nigeria (Clark 1977, xxiv). Writing of the creation of Nyanga epics in Congo, Daniel Biebuyck and Kahombo Mateene note that, "while singing and narrating, the bard dances, mimes, and dramatically represents the main peripeties of the story" (1969, 13).

Performance is the thing: "The artist changes the voice de-pending on whether he/she was imitating the ogre or a bird. In this way, he/she can shape the audience's emotions" (Kabira and Adagala 1985, xvi). Words are not the only aspect of storytelling. "It is in performance that a storyteller makes a tale his or her own," writes Robert Cancel. "When the performer is not only in command of his or her stage presence but also an inventive embellisher of narratives, the results can be both entertaining and transforming" (1989, 19–20). Writing of storytellers in Sierra Leone, Modupe Broderick describes "the dynamic relationship existing between performer and audience engaged in the manip-ulation of emotions and in the creation of suspense, the vital non-verbal features such as the rhythmic swaying of the body during the rendition of a song, a subtle facial expression to con-vey sorrow, joy, or surprise, or the imitation of the movement of stock characters" (1980, 7–8).

Such a storyteller "can conjure up an atmosphere, and carry his audience with him, and thus provide a thrilling entertain-ment. Some are good mimics and add to the enjoyment by emulating the sounds of the animals and birds they impersonate" (Basden 1938, 424). The role of the storyteller is to keep the society alive, to create a conduit to the past. But, as John Mbiti has pointed out, "each person will tell the same story differently, since he has to make it personal and not simply a mechanical repetition of what he had heard or narrated before. He becomes not only a 'repeater' but also a 'creative' originator of each story" (1966, 26).

Nokavala, a Xhosa storyteller.
Photo © Harold Scheub.

The Role of the Audience

The audience has a crucial role to play. "The narrator commences the story with the formal beginning of the story. This said in a slightly high-pitched voice. It appears to be done in order to prepare the audience: it proves to be an effective way of drawing their attention and arousing their interest" (Nkonki, 91–93). The audience "acts as a stimulus, a catalyst, to the creativeness and imagination of the artist since . . . each performance before each particular audience constitutes a new creation. The mood of the audience, whether sad or gay, will most likely infect the artist; likewise the mood of the artist will affect the audience" (Akivaga and Odaga 1982, 10). Those audiences are varied, not just "of tender years, but grown men and women, who listen to the well-worn recitals" (Maugham 1910, 380–381). In Cameroon, the Gbaya performer always places the ancient story within the context of the contemporary world, and "The audience also participates in the performance by breaking in with questions and comments and by singing the chorus that accompanies the song" (Noss 1967, 35). What is being revealed here is that stories are a major means of remembering the past: "The most respected women of each community had assumed the responsibility of passing on the culture of the Bura by telling stories to the younger children in the evening time. The older children carried on by reciting the stories to one another" (Helser 1930, 9).

The Power of Stories

"When those of us in my generation awakened to earliest consciousness," said a contemporary Xhosa storyteller, "we were born into a tradition that was already flourishing" (Zenani 1992, 7). Walter Benjamin, having read an African tale, commented, "This story from ancient Egypt is still capable after thousands of years of arousing astonishment and thoughtfulness. It resembles the seeds of grain which have lain for centuries in the pyramids shut up air-tight and have retained their germinative power to this day" (1973, 90). Storytelling is entertainment, always, and it is seldom openly or obviously didactic. But it routinely embraces the breadth of human experience, providing emotional excursions into experiences that shape audiences and reveals to them the contexts of the worlds in which they live, as well as their place in those worlds. Stories are ancient, relying on emotion-evoking images that come from the past, yet stories are always contemporary, constructing around those ancient images the world of the present. These images from the past become a storyteller's means of exploring and shaping the audience's experiences of the world that it inhabits. If a member of the audience cannot move beyond the literal level of the story, then the power of the tale is denied him. It is the rhythm of the tale that seduces him, lures him into the story, to the characters and their relationships, and, in the end, it is that emotional participation in the activities of the tale that make the audience a part of the transforming metaphor that is at the core of all storytelling. That is where messages can be found; it is the reason one cannot ignore the wiles of the tale-teller.

The Role of Fantasy

Fantasy, to which audiences respond, is complex, comprised as it is of mythic images, patterns, and relationships within the context of artistic performance. Contemporary images are not fantasy until they are introduced into the parallel mythic world; they then retain their real-world significance, but are brought into relationships with fantasy images. All are encompassed in performance, which is, of course, fantasy, comprised of dance, music, and relations with audience. So fantasy is defined as an image, an action, a pattern, a relationship that occurs within a tightly manipulated and controlled narrative environment that partakes of the real world but is itself a parallel world. That parallel world can only occur within the context and embrace of the real world, so that there is always an ironic encounter between them. But the relationship is only ironic: it is not a one-to-one relationship.

The fantasy parallel world is fed by the real world; indeed, everything in the parallel world can be seen to have its origins in the real world. But it is not the real world in its organization, in the relationship between images, or in the images themselves when those images transcend in some way their real-life counterparts. This parallel world exists in its own right, with its own rules and laws. These rules and laws can be stated in broad terms, but they can only be worked out by an analysis of the individual narrative that exists within that parallel world.

The patterns are needed because they give emotions form, shaping them. Patterns work the evoked emotions into designs that, while having little to do with the surface movement, are composed wholly of those images. The body and voice of the storyteller and nonverbal elements of performance play large roles in this shaping process. Patterns are the chief organizing devices of storytelling. Images, which are sensed actions, are organized into patterns, and theme (or meaning) grows out of these patterns.

Metaphor

The power of a tale is not that one emerges with a glimmering, memorable metaphor. The tale is itself a metaphor, and that is its power. To attempt to summarize the tale in the form of a single metaphor would be to paraphrase that which cannot be paraphrased. Fantasy tales are a form of reasoning, a way of looking at things. The move from reality to fantasy is useful—things do not obey normal routines because they are not normal routines; they are the stuff of normal routines brought together in poetic form to reveal new relationships. Because tales use the materials of the known world, audiences have a tendency to be sensitive to their interrelationships, and when those relationships do not correspond to the way we behave in their routine world, they are confused. This is the world of art, a closed world, and normal experiences of images are given new forms and new relationships and linkages. The result is a new measure of the real world. The blending of the real and fantasy is the key, not simply fantasy. Without the moorings of the real world, fantasy would be dull. Fantasy breaks the world into artificial pieces, for one thing. It forces thinking about those matters into new modes.

It is the figure in the mask that links African stories and, in turn, provides connections to stories throughout the world. That mask, whatever shape it takes, becomes the chamber for transformation, which is at the heart of the tale-telling tradition. It may be a literal mask, or it may be figurative, but it is present in all stories that have to do with change.

What is universal in the African stories is this metamorphosing of humans, a change revealed by a mirroring process, by journeying, by dualism—in short, by metaphor, which is at the heart of the tale. This inner metaphorical core universalizes the stories, whether it be stark trickster stories (which contain the amoral energy necessary to the transformation), the seemingly obvious journeying stories, or the more complex tales in which characters are poetically layered. It is this process that envelopes members of audiences, so that they have a shimmering sense of the path that lies before them.

References

Abu-Manga, Al-Amin. 1985. Baakankaro, A Fulani Epic from Sudan. *Africana Marburgensia* 9:9–11.

Akivaga, S. Kichamiu, and A. Bole Odaga. 1982. *Oral Literature*. Nairoibi: Heinemann.

Basden, George Thomas. 1938. *Niger Ibos*. London: Cass.

Benjamin, Walter. 1973. *Illuminations*. Tr. Harry Zohn. Glasgow: William Collins.

Biebuyck, Daniel, and Kahombo C. Mateene. 1969. *The Mwindo Epic*. Berkeley: University of California Press.

Bleek, W. H. I., and Lucy C. Lloyd. 1911. *Specimens of Bushman Folklore*. London: George Allen.

Broderick, Modupe. 1980. *Go Ta Nan* 1:7–8.

Butcher, H. L. M. 1937. Four Edo Fables. *Africa* 10:342.

Callaway, Henry. 1968. *Nursery Tales, Traditions, and Histories of the Zulus*. Springvale, Natal: John A. Blair.

Cancel, Robert. 1989. *Allegorical Speculation in an Oral Society*. Berkeley: University of California Press.

Chimenti, Elisa. 1965. *Tales and Legends from Morocco*. New York: Ivan Obolensky.

Clark, John Pepper. 1977. *The Ozidi Saga*. Ibadan, Nigeria: Ibadan University Press.

Doke, Clement M. 1927. *Lamba Folk-Lore*. New York: G. W. Stechert.

Elliot, Geraldine. 1968. *The Long Grass Whispers*. New York: Schocken Books.

Evans-Pritchard, E. E. 1967. *The Zande Trickster*. Oxford: Clarendon Press.

Helser, Albert D. 1930. *African Stories*. New York: Fleming H. Revell.

Jacottet, Edouard. 1908. *The Treasury of Ba-Suto Lore*. Morija, Lesotho: Sesuto Book Depot.

Jablow, Alta. 1961. *Yes and No, The Intimate Folklore of Africa*. New York: Horizon Press.

Kabira, Wanjiku Mukabi. 1983. *The Oral Artist*. Nairobi: Heinemann.

Kabira, Wanjiku Mukabi, and Kavetsa Adagala. 1985. *Kenyan Oral Narratives*. Nairobi: Heinemann.

Maugham, Reginald Charles F. 1910. *Zambezia*. London: J. Murray.

Mbiti, John S. 1966. *Akamba Stories*. Oxford: Clarendon Press.

Nasr, Ahmad Abd-al-Rahim M. 1977. Maiwurno of the Blue Nile: A Study of an Oral Biography. Ph.D. dissertation, University of Wisconsin-Madison.

Nkonki, Garvey. "The Traditional Prose Literature of the Ngqika," M.A. dissertation. University of South Africa.

Noss, Philip A. Noss. 1967. Gbaya Traditional Literature. *Abbia*, 17–18:35.

Ross, Mabel H., and Barbara K. Walker. 1979. *"On Another Day. . ." Tales Told among the Nkundo of Zaire*. Hamden, Conn.: Archon Books.

Samatar, Said S. 1982. *Oral Poetry and Somali Nationalism*. Cambridge, England: Cambridge University Press.

Smith, Edwin E., and Andrew Murray Dale. 1920. *The Ila-speaking Peoples of Northern Rhodesia*. London: Macmillan.

Zenani, Nongenile Masithathu. 1992. *The World and the Word: Tales and Observations from the Xhosa Oral Tradition*, ed. Harold Scheub. Madison: University of Wisconsin Press.

HAROLD SCHEUB

See also **Initiation; Oral Performance Dynamics; Oral Traditions; Performance in Africa; Stories and Storytelling: The Limba**

SUDAN

Located in northeastern Africa, Sudan, with 967,500 square miles, is the continent's largest country. Sudan's climate ranges from desert in the north to tropical in the south. Of the nation's 31,100,000 citizens, 52 percent are black, 39 percent Arab, 6 percent Beja, and 3 percent are from other ethnic groups. The major languages spoken in the country are Arabic, Nuer, Dinka, Shilluki, Masalatis, Fur, Nubian, and English. While Arabic is the official language, only 60 percent of the nation speak it. Christianity and traditional indigenous religions are practiced throughout the country, though the population is mostly Sunni Muslim in the north. Khartoum, a city of 924,500, is the nation's capital.

Sudan's modern history is traced from 1821, when it was conquered by Egypt. In 1881, Muhammad Ahmad, the Mahdi, a powerful religious leader, overthrew the Egyptian government. An Anglo-Egyptian army defeated him in 1899, and the country was then ruled by the two nations jointly. Sudan gained its independence on January 1, 1956. Due to the country's vast size, great ethnic diversity, and ongoing north-south warfare, however, the nation's subsequent governments have had tremendous difficulty in building a cohesive nation. This situation was worsened in 1989, when the fundamentalist National Islamic Front took control of the government and implemented a repressive military regime. Despite its potential for growth, Sudan has become an increasingly divided society.

The Nile River runs through Sudan, supplying water to almost all of the nation's farmers (some 80 percent of the population). Sudan is rich in the natural resources of oil, iron ore, copper, chrome, and other industrial metals, while the agricultural sector produces cotton, peanuts, sesame, gum arabic, sorghum, and wheat. Principle industries include textiles, cement, cotton ginning, edible oils, distilling, and pharmaceuticals. Despite such exceptional potential for economic growth, Sudan remains one of the world's poorest nations.

Mohammed Wardi, Sudan's most popular musician, is internationally renowned for his songs about injustice. His music, however, has been banned in Sudan and he has been forced to live in exile.

JENNIFER JOYCE

SUPERSTITIONS

Superstition is an aspect of belief, and it is often connected with daily human experiences. It is found in all human cultures and can be linked with people's attempts to apprehend mysterious experiences and happenings in their world, reflecting people's curiosity about the future or unknown realities. In common usage, the term *superstition* connotes beliefs about phenomena that people find difficult to explain in rational terms. Superstitions are, therefore, beliefs and practices that are apparently lacking a rational basis. People in different cultures assign seemingly superficial explanations to occurrences whose causes are not easily visible. Most often, the explanations are accompanied by various practices and observances, which the concerned people believe may cause desirable effects or prevent detrimental consequences from natural and social events. Many analysts of traditional belief systems consider superstition to be a false, groundless belief that stretches beyond the actual limits of faith (Schmidt 1963, 13). The causes and effects, which are beyond ordinary human explanation, are sought in speculative accounts. A reductionist definition of superstition refers to nonempirical and nonscientific beliefs about good and bad luck.

Credulity, fear, a sense of vulnerability, and perhaps ignorance are the main hallmarks of beliefs, practices, and rituals that are popularly linked with superstition. In most cases, people find themselves obliged to observe certain prescriptions, observances, and proscriptions. In this regard, people are guided by their acceptance of mysterious and supernatural forces that invisibly affect their lives. Superstition has also been connected with nontheistic beliefs, through which human beings are convinced that they can influence and manipulate the invisible forces in the universe to their benefit. This approach contradicts religious beliefs about supplication to God, who is the ultimate source of power, which human beings cannot control or tap as they please. This aspect usually depicts superstition as the opposite of religious belief; however, there are religious, cultural, personal, and magical aspects of superstitions.

Superstition is a dynamic component of culture. Superstitious tradition manifests persistence and change in any culture. This results in the coexistence of popular and artificial superstitions. Popular superstitions preserve ancient customs and traditions of a people, especially as they have developed among those sections of the community who live closest to nature, such as farmers, shepherds, and boatmen, as well as fishermen and craftsmen (Schmidt 1963, 15). Popular superstitions contrast with artificial ones, which do not have links with old ethnic customs. Artificial superstitions are false notions about ritualized behaviors involving modern aspects of life such as brushing teeth with a brush with a particular color or wearing a certain kind of attire on specific days. In this distinction, one can talk about indigenous and modern superstition, both of which are products of human experience in concrete environments.

Modern education and religions, such as Christianity and Islam, have had the greatest impacts on the traditional Africans, leading them to abandon most of their popular superstitions. Superstitions may be limited to countries, regions, villages, families, social or vocational groups, and individuals. Individuals, both in the past and the present, develop personal superstitions related to their own perspectives and experiences about success and failure. This implies that "irrational beliefs" or superstitious ideas may endure regardless of the facts that reject their accuracy.

The Bantu

The Bantu of western Kenya have various superstitions that present a pattern that is arguably representative of the entire Bantu and other African ethnic groups. The Bantu is one of the largest ethnic groups in Africa, with many expansive dialects that are mutually intelligible. They occupy over one-third of the continent and are well represented in territories of other indigenous ethnic groups as either immigrants or sojourners.

The Bantu of Kenya are part of a larger group that is believed to have come from the Cameroon highlands in West Africa (Murdock 1959; Osongo 1976; Werner 1968). Historians have used linguistic evidence to locate the original home of the Bantus at the Cameroon-Nigeria border in the Cameroon mountains. The term Bantu is derived from the linguistic uniformity that characterizes the Bantu people of Africa. The people who speak the Bantu languages have the common suffix "-ntu" in their words, representing a person, place, modality, or being. In most of the Bantu languages, the word for "people" is Abantu (or variants of it maintaining the common root "-ntu"). Bantu languages may differ in vocabulary and pronunciation, but they have uniform grammatical structure and main linguistic outlines. As such, the Bantu have close genetic relationships, indicating their differentiation from a single speech community (Murdock 1959; Wagner 1970).

Apart from the linguistic homogeny, the Bantu have many common beliefs and customs. Commonality in Bantu cultural traits is attributed to the historical process of union and absorption of fellow Bantu-speaking peoples. They also have common patterns in their indigenous forms of social, economic, and political organization. The sociocultural characteristics of the Bantu and their adjacent communities reflect the consequences of intermingling and the process of acculturation. The Bantu occupy territories that were once inhabited by hunters and gatherers (Murdock 1959; Fedders and Salvadori 1979), whom they have gradually absorbed.

The Bantu of western Kenya have patrilineal, patrilocal communities, and people are related to each other through a system of minimal patrilineages, which are the main descent groups. The descent groups are land-owning units and the basis of kinship in Bantu societies. Polygyny is a prescribed form of marriage union. However, an increasing number of monogamous marital ties are evident among the young generation.

Typically, the Bantu believe in God, ancestors, and the existence of good and bad spirits. Magico-religious beliefs are also evident in the Bantu conceptualization of the mystical powers that may increase or decrease human vitality. Superstitious beliefs among the Bantu manifest the desire by traditional Africans to maintain an equilibrium among all the mystical forces that have consequences for their prosperity, success, happiness, and health. In this regard, the people are always conscious of, and on the look out for, auspicious and inauspicious behavior and phenomena.

Good and Bad Omens

The Bantu of western Kenya, like other Bantu peoples, believe that they can predict imminent events and occurrences through omens and warnings. The omens may be auspicious, making one confident in his or her undertakings. If the omens are perceived as inauspicious according to popular beliefs, those concerned either abandon their plans or engage in rituals to ward off looming evil spirits (Wagner 1970). In the popular superstitions, community members infer omens from short- and long-term bodily processes; natural occurrences in the cosmos; certain days and timing of events; dreams; encounters with, and cries of, particular animals; and encounters with people whom the community associate with good or bad luck.

Superstitions and Body Processes and Functions

From the time one is born until one's death, he or she experiences bodily changes to which the culture attaches certain meanings. The people interpret some of the alterations in body functions and unique aspects of growth with impending success, prosperity, or good health, and vice-versa. Among the Abagusii, Abasuba, Abatiriki, and Abalogoli, when a child is born, family members are keen to detect the signs that may hint at the future success of the child and the lineage. The community members construe specific birthmarks as indicators of either bad or good qualities inherited from the ancestors. Some birthmarks are manifestations of either negative or positive endowments. The Abaluhyia believe that a child born with mysterious scars (*tsimbala* or *etsimbala*) is gifted with special skills or qualities that will help in such careers as medicine, leadership, rainmaking, divining, or craftsmanship. For the Abanyore, for example, rainmakers belong to the *Abajimba* lineage, although unique birthmarks or other features can identify the specific practitioners at birth.

In some communities, inauspicious signs at birth and during childhood include early teething, persistent crying, and habitual use of the left hand. When families become aware of these omens, they suppress them through the performance of rituals, negative reinforcement, and the application of herbal and animal medicines. In both childhood and adulthood, the Bantus of western Kenya interpret a shaking of the eye (*khudejera imoni* in Luhyia), a sudden sharp noise in the ear (*khutiya shirhoi*, *kudiya gutu*), repeated sneezing, and watering of the eyes (*zimoni khulila*) as inauspicious signs. In these cases, community members believe that they are warned of people talking ill of the victim, or merely of "something evil about to happen." The victims and their families resort to ritualistic practices to ward off the imminent evil. Similarly, when an individual suddenly becomes too anxious or restless, members of his or her social network remind him or her that the condition is an indicator that, in one way or the other, all is or is not well.

Perceptions of Natural Rhythms and Occurrences

There is a degree of uniformity among the Bantu people of western Kenya in relation to superstitions about natural occurrences in the universe. The weather provides the most regular omens that guide economic activities, particularly agricultural production. The people's knowledge about tropical rain patterns is also linked to a number of beliefs that are irrational from the outside observers' perspective. The Abaluhyia, for instance, suppose that complaining about the rain after a long dry spell sends the rain away. Similarly, people do not walk in the first rains after a drought, because the rains cause fever (*ludejera*), or, in modern times, the disease known as malaria.

Like the Bantu of southern Africa, the Bantu of western Kenya believe lightning comes from a mystical living being in the form of a red cock (Werner 1968). They believe that thunder that is preceded by lightning results from the flight of the cock. They also believe that thunder is the voice of a powerful spirit whose medium is the red cock. From time to time some community members claim to have seen the cock eating insects during heavy rains. The people who manage to see the flash of the cock go unhurt by lightning. Only those who are unable to see this flash in good time are struck dead or injured by lightning. Similarly, since the medium of thunder and lightning is red in color, the people believe that those in red attire attract it.

There are also superstitious beliefs related to celestial bodies and other phenomena in the sky. The moon, for example, is the subject of magical rites among the Abagusii and the Abaluhyia. The Maragoli and the Abatiriki throw *kitatula* or *shitatula* sticks in the direction of the full moon to heal long-term illnesses, especially among children. If a mother has an invalid child, she throws the sticks to the moon and runs back into the house without looking back. The Abaluhyia believe that these rites lead to a gradual disappearance of illness as the moon gets smaller each night (Wagner 1976). Similarly, most of the Luhyia communities believe that they can treat mumps (*tsindendei*), a common childhood illness, by throwing miniature bundles of firewood onto the *mutembe* or *elitembe* tree after dancing around it. As is the case with throwing sticks at the moon, the mumps patients do not heal if they look back in the course of running back home.

The western Kenya Bantu consider the sight of a comet to be an evil omen. In most cases, it is viewed as a sign of imminent war with a community that lives in the direction of the comet. Defeat in the foreseen war is prevented by offering sacrifices.

Among the rainmaking communities, certain people can prevent hailstorms and make rain when there is need. The rainmaker is a person with the foreknowledge and power to avert the harmful effects of rain, and to make it when there is a shortage of water. The art of rainmaking among communities such as the Abanyore is an inheritable property (Akong'a 1987). People send petitions to them and pay tribute to guarantee that they use their knowledge to bring rain. The participants in rainmaking perceive the process as real and true, although this may be based on false notions. The expert can also stop the rain when it is undesirable, using medicines and spells, especially when the people think there has been too much or when it interferes with essential activities or ceremonies. The rainmaker will petition for rain, or for rain to stop, if he is pleased with the tribute paid to him. In popular Bantu superstition, nonexperts can also participate in controlling rain or hailstones. For instance, it is common among the Abaluhyia and Abagusii for people to scatter ash and fix an axe in the ground to prevent or stop hailstorms. The Abaluhyia also believe that the rainbow is an instrument that God sends to discontinue the rain. The rainbow is therefore generally perceived as malignant and dangerous.

Other superstitions associated with cosmic rhythms are those related with dawn, dusk, night, and other times of the day. The break of the day is a sign of prosperity. In most of the traditional communities in western Kenya, the elders would offer prayers for their families by spitting in the direction of the rising sun (*ivwagwi*, or *ivugwi* in Luhyia). When a death occurred in the family, the elder would throw an egg to the east at night to inhibit its return. In most of these communities, dusk symbolizes the end, especially of unfavorable events or experiences. Community members in traditional Bantu cultures say prayers for the end of misfortune by beseeching the setting sun to "sleep" with the bad luck. The night represents evil, and activities that the people relate to bad omens are reserved for the night. Such activities include burial of people who commit suicide or are struck by lightning. Among some western Kenya Bantu, responding to a call by an unknown person at night is taboo, because it is believed that it could be from an evil spirit. The people suppose that if one responded to such a call, it would result in death or illness in the family. Similarly, rituals that are meant to cleanse the society of impending evil are done at night or just before dawn. In most of these cases, the west—the direction of the sunset—is believed to be capable of arresting all evil forever. Therefore in magical spells to ward off evil, the west, which is coincidentally the direction of Lake Victoria, is believed to be the recipient of exorcised evil.

Superstitions and Dreams

The link between dreams and superstitions in most of the Bantu communities of western Kenya are the themes of death, life hereafter, and success. The people believe that distressing dreams come from evil spirits. Dreams are considered auspicious if they are related to common values about prosperity. Ill-omened dreams revolve around death, which is the greatest form of evil to befall families, lineages, and clans. In death-related dreams, people talk of having seen and eaten roast meat or seen or heard mourners and other funeral-related experiences. People chronically predict their imminent death if they dream about roast or raw meat on sticks (*minyama khuvisala* in Luhyia), or about havng participated in meat-eating feasts. Community members abhor similar dreams even among healthy members. However, when those who are very sick have such dreams regularly, they are comforted by the thought of imminent death.

Among the Tiriki, Maragoli and Banyore, impending death, which is communicated through dreams, can be averted through various rituals. If a person dreams that one of his or her relatives is dead, he or she must look for a branch of a *lisazi* or *elisatsi* tree and beat the relative with it. After doing this, the person expresses regret for having dreamt that the other was dead. The people believe that this ritual prevents such a bad omen from coming true. The Bukusu and the Maragoli seek advice from a specialist called *omunyosi* or *mulyuli* when such dreams persist. All the Bantu groups predict looming death by dreams in which a sick person talks of having been turned away from the land of the ancestors by one of his or her living-dead relatives, especially by a grandparent. In this case, it is believed that the dreamer will have a longer life than had been imagined. Paradoxically, the Abaluhyia believe that dreams about the death of members of a social group are not necessarily ill omens. At times, such dreams may indicate that the person dreamt about is experiencing momentary prosperity. In such cases, the person depicted as dead in the dream is described metaphorically as having been "too satisfied after a meal" (*yegurhe, yiguti, yakwiguta,* or *yigurhi*).

There are also superstitions about nightmares, especially among children. People perceive nightmares as communications from ghosts or evil spirits about unknown misfortune. They are signs of disasters expected to befall individuals, lineages, families, or the community as a whole, due to the neglect or offence of the living dead. Bad dreams are therefore warnings about impending calamity meted out on human beings by supernatural forces. People often become troubled about such dreams and seek recourse after consultation with dream prophets, referred to as *bayoti* by the Bukusu. When the prophets and other members of the therapy management group believe that evil spirits cause nightmares, they apply medicines with strong scents. These medicines are put under the pillows of the victims. Apart from dreams, the Bantu of western Kenya also correlate people and other organisms with omens in various ways.

People, Animals, and Insects as Omens

Popular superstitions link the first person one meets in the morning with either good or bad luck. If a person leaves his or her home, he or she becomes mindful of meeting a person who represents the gender of his or her first-born child. In the traditional societies, if they do not meet such a person, the journey would be postponed. For the Abagusii, a person setting off on a journey or going on a special undertaking has to ask the first person he or she meets the gender of his or her first born. If it happens to be the same as that of the inquirers' first-born child, it is a good omen. If the two children happen to be of different sexes, it is a bad omen, and the person who was traveling is made aware of the imminent bad luck. To avoid postponement of an urgent trip in such a case, one would try to keep a safe distance from the person who symbolizes bad luck.

The same superstitions apply to encounters with people who are culturally constructed as abnormal or ritually impure. This may include coming across nude, quarrelling, or fighting people while pursuing important matters. The people also link bad luck and impending failure with human behaviors such as giving or receiving gifts with the left hand, children eating with one hand on the floor, and making faces at others. Many of the Bantu communities in western Kenya construe meeting certain animals early in the morning or while on important assignments as ill-fated. The Maragoli, for example, believe that running into a certain type of rat (*ilivegi* or *ulunihi*), an antelope (*ikisusu*), a red hawk (*ikimindwa*), or a squirrel (*ikijemanye*) are bad omens. Among the Bukusu, if one comes across a species of big ants called *nafusi* it is a good omen (Wagner 1970). Other Bantu societies in western Kenya associate the presence of bees, cockroaches, and migrating birds with wealth and prosperity in homesteads and villages.

In popular superstitions, it is portentous for an owl to hoot near a homestead. For the Abaluhyia, this implies that a member of the homestead or family will die soon. Driving away the owl with a firebrand prevents this impending misfortune. The Abaluhyia also associate bad luck with the cries of the *enyiru* bird and the hyena. In other Bantu communities, people view some chance occurrences, such as repeated stumbling, as bad omens. If one stumbles on consecutive occasions, he or she becomes anxious about an unknown number of looming predicaments. The Wanga strongly believe that stumbling with the left foot forecasts bad luck, while the right foot foretells good luck.

Conclusion

Bantu superstitions reflect the influence of cross-cultural interaction with neighboring societies. Popular African superstitions are, therefore, replicated and reflected in Bantu beliefs. The people observe outstanding auspicious and inauspicious signs in ordinary cosmic rhythms, human physiological processes, dreams, and beliefs about times of the day. Encounters with people, animals, and various animal sounds are also attributed to good or bad luck due to a history of life experiences with such phenomena.

References

Akong'a, Joshua J. 1987. Rainmaking Rituals: A Comparative Study of Two Kenyan Societies. In *African Study Monographs* 8, no. 2: 71–85.

Fedders, Andrew, and Cynthia Salvadori. 1998. *Peoples and Cultures of Kenya*. Nairobi: TransAfrica.

Osogo, John N. B. *East Africa's People in the Past*. Nairobi: Longman.

Schmidt, Phillip. 1963. *Superstition and Magic*. Westminster, Md.: Newman Press.

Wagner, Günter. 1970. *The Bantu of Western Kenya: With Special Reference to the Vugusu and Logoli*. Oxford: Oxford University Press.

———. 1976. The Abaluhyia of Kavirondo. In *African Worlds*, ed. Daryll Forde. Oxford: Oxford University Press.

Werner, Alice. 1968. *Myths and Legends of the Bantu*. London: Frank Cass.

BENSON A. MULEMI

See also **Dreams**

SUPREME BEING

See **Cosmology; Religion**

SURROGATE LANGUAGES: ALTERNATIVE COMMUNICATION

A surrogate language is defined as a method for communicating through a spoken language but by means other than speaking. In contrast with speaking, which is the uttering of words or the articulation of sounds with the human voice, a surrogate language involves the uttering of words or the articulation of sounds through an alternative or surrogate voice. Through the use of instruments, a surrogate language employs sounds that substitute for spoken words. In exceptional cases, a surrogate language may even substitute written text (Nketia 1971, 699). Instruments that produce surrogate languages include the "talking drum" (which may or not be an actual skin-headed membranophone), gongs, horns, the lips (for whistling), hand-made whistles, and even guitars (Carey 1949, 74–80). These surrogate language instruments have been found in the Republic of the Congo, the Democratic Republic of the Congo, Ghana, Nigeria (Carrington 1949, 26–29), and Cameroon (Finnegan 1970, 484).

Surrogate languages communicate actual speech by sounding out the stress and tones of syllables. As technologies, they may be described as a cross between the telegraph and the radio. They transmit information by being beaten, blown, strummed, or tapped upon.

Surrogate languages differ from musical instruments. Although musical instruments may be acoustic media, they normally communicate generalized emotions via nonverbal signifiers, not exact linguistic terms. Surrogate languages communicate exact words. Secondly, musical instruments usually communicate through melody. In comparison, any melody produced by a surrogate language is merely a by-product of its instrumentation, not the method through which communication occurs.

Surrogate languages "talk" by producing words, as in the case, for example, with "talking drums" by being struck. A talking drum is capable of emitting words when it is struck because the language being expressed is tonal. In general, spoken languages are distinguished by three auditory characteristics: (1) vowels and consonants, (2) stress placed on the vowels and consonants, and (3) tone or musical intonation of the vowels and consonants. All spoken languages possess the first two characteristics, but only tonal languages possess the third. Surrogate languages emit words because they replicate the stress and tone of tonal languages. By "tone," it is not meant "a tone of voice," but rather a phonemic tone, which is a key feature of many African languages. There is a change of meaning with a shift from a high to a low tone on a syllable of a word. For example, in the Twi language, spoken by the Akan people in Ghana, the use of a high note on both letters "a" in the word papa (pápá) creates the meaning "good." In contrast, if the first "a" is pronounced with a low note and the second with a high note (papá), its meaning is changed to "father." Without such tonality, which does not exist in many world languages, such as English or French, surrogate languages would be rendered incapable of transmitting a discernible language (Carrington 1949, 15–20).

The best-known and most widely used surrogate language instrument is popularly called the "talking drum." A talking drum usually designates an instrument whose sounding occurs when its membrane is caused to vibrate; but many "talking" instruments, such as the wooden slit gong, depend on the vibration of their whole body. Words are ascribed meaning on such instruments by the pitch, force, rhythm, and context in which they are sounded.

One type of talking drum is the Akan *atumpan* pair found in Ghana. This type of talking drum produces surrogate speech through its use of two separate drums, each tuned to a different pitch. A second type of drum, the double gong, works along the same lines, emitting different pitches, in this case through the use of high and low sections. The most frequently used instrument for such communication in Africa is a wooden slit-gong. It has one of the sides of its slit, or opening, tuned high, and the other low. The amount of force used to beat the drum creates the distinction between the male and the female form of a word, that is, the application of great force is associated with the male form and less force is analogous to the female form (Carrington 1949, 23–24). Another type of membrane-headed drum is the pressure drum. An example of a pressure drum is the *dundun* used by the Yoruba in Nigeria. The pressure drum "speaks," through the exertion of pressure on strings that hold the two drum heads together. By alternating pressure between the two strings, both low and high tones can be emitted. Different words are sounded out by altering the rhythm, the duration, or the configurations of beats. Long syllables are simulated by allowing the drum to continue vibrating, whereas short syllables are simulated if it is stopped (Nketia 1971, 717–720). "Stereotyped," or short, phrases are employed in order to contextualize the meaning of words that share the same stress and tone patterns (Nketia 1971, 707).

A drum language, like all surrogate languages, is not, however, a perfect substitute for spoken language. Speech is slightly modified by its use. The use of stereotyped phrases greatly lengthens the message and the time necessary for its relay. An Akan drum can only produce approximately 500 words, excluding proper names and titles (Nketia 1971, 711). As a result, some topics are difficult to communicate. The drum has a limited capacity to conquer time because it can only be heard up to about twenty miles away. If the destination of a message is greater than twenty miles (or, in some cases of dense forest, only seven miles), the message must be relayed from one drummer to another (Carrington 1949, 28–31). As a result, instantaneous communication across a greater distance is not possible.

Surrogate languages are extremely important because they transmit special messages. They allow for "secret" communication to occur publicly. The talking drum transmits information "secretly" through segmented public space. Like a radio, it sends messages that can be listened to by anyone within its range. At the same time, it can only be understood by those who understand the language in which the message is transmitted. Unlike radio, however, only those who can recognize the use of tones on the drum are actually aware that messages are even being transmitted. As a result, African groups have used the drum and other surrogate-language instruments to convey warning messages and mobilize their people.

Africans used the talking drum as a strategic method to warn against the arrival of slave catchers during the slave trade. Once their use became known to non-users and as a mark of their effectiveness, slave masters in the Americas (Yankah 1997, 7) and colonial governors in Africa (Carrington 1949, 76) outlawed their use. Despite this, black Africans ingeniously found their way around the problem by using other instruments, such as whistles, to communicate. For example, during the 1940s, Yakusu schoolboys in the former Belgium Congo (present-day Democratic Republic of the Congo) secretly warned each other that their white African schoolmasters were approaching by whistling words (Carrington 1949, 76).

During the period of slavery in the Americas, surrogate languages were used by African slaves to organize riots and rebellions, despite the great ethnic and linguistic differences that existed among them (Yankah 1997, 7). Africans in the Americas had come from a diverse array of locations and backgrounds throughout the whole of the continent of Africa. The drum, therefore, served as an extremely powerful substitute for language. It made communication across the plantations in the new world, otherwise forbidden, possible. As a result, it provided African slaves with a tool to try to integrate themselves into a new identity—that of African American.

In spite of their great legacy, use of surrogate languages has decreased (Carrington 1949, 81–85; Finnegan 1970, 408). Modern technological advances in communication have overshadowed their traditional importance. Subsequently, new generations are less interested in their appeal, although some contemporary musicians, such as King Sunny Ade of Nigeria, make use of the Yoruba pressure drum.

References

Carrington, J. F. 1949. *Talking Drums of Africa*. London: Carey Kingsgate Press.
Finnegan, R. 1970. *Oral Literature in Africa*. Oxford: Clarendon Press.
Nketia, J. H. Kwabena. 1971. Surrogate Languages of Africa. *Current Trends in Linguistics* 7:699–732.
Yankah, Kwesi. 1997. *Free Speech in a Traditional Society. The Cultural Foundations of Communication in Contemporary Ghana*. Accra: Ghana Universities Press.

YAEL WARSHEL

See also **Linguistics and African Verbal Arts; Musical Instruments**

SWAHILI

See **Epics: Liongo Epics of the Swahili; Urban Folklore**

SWAZI

See **Queen Mother**

SWAZILAND (KINGDOM OF SWAZILAND)

Landlocked between Mozambique and South Africa, Swaziland is a small country of 984,000 people. The climate ranges from temperate to subtropical to semiarid. Swaziland's capital is the city of Mbabane, which is home to 46,000 people. The population of Swaziland is predominantly African, with English and Swazi being the most commonly spoken languages. Christians account for 60 percent of the population, while the remaining 40 percent practice traditional religions.

The Swazi Kingdom was created in the late eighteenth century. Several conventions in the 1880s guaranteed the kingdom's independence, but South African continued to control it. Not until September 6, 1968, was full independence granted. Throughout the country's history, Swaziland has suffered a precarious relationship with neighboring South Africa. In the past, Swaziland was able to maintain political autonomy while relying on economic support from South Africa. Since the end of apartheid, however, the Swazi government has sought political support from South Africa's new African National Congress government.

Since independence, Swaziland has had a relatively secure economy due to the expansion and diversification of its agricultural products. Other industries such as tourism, mining, and paper milling, have contributed to Swaziland's economic growth. Until the early 1990s, Swaziland's economy was also aided by international investors seeking a market comparable to that of South Africa. However, since the political reforms in South Africa, investors are now more willing to take their business there. Swaziland's attraction as a center for corporate relocation has therefore been greatly reduced.

Swaziland is renowned for its elaborate festivals. Many of these festivals take place during the lunar month of *Ncwala*, which lasts from December to January. It is during this time that the nation reaffirms its bonds with the country's royal leaders. In addition to ritual dancing and other festivities, the king traditionally tastes the season's first fruits, blesses the ancestors, and prays for rain.

JENNIFER JOYCE

T

TABWA

See **Animals in African Folklore; Central African Folklore; Prose Narratives**

TAÑALA

See **Madagascar; Myths: Mythology and Society in Madagascar: a Tañala Example**

TANZANIA (UNITED REPUBLIC OF TANZANIA)

Located on the coast of East Africa, Tanzania is neighbored by Kenya, Uganda, Rwanda, Burundi, Democratic Republic of Congo, Zambia, Malawi, Mozambique, and the Indian Ocean. Its territory includes the islands of Zanzibar and Pemba. The nation's 33,690,000 citizens are classified as African. English and Swahili are the official languages. Although the Swahili constitute only 8 percent of the population, over 90 percent of the inhabitants of the country speak the language. Other commonly spoken languages Chagga, Gogo, Ha, Haya, Luo, and Maasai. Most of the nation's people are Christian, Muslim, or practice traditional indigenous religions, while the Tanzanian island of Zanzibar is predominantly Muslim. Dar es Salaam, a city of over 1.4 million people, is the nation's former capital and largest city; Dodoma is the new capital. Tanzania's climate ranges from tropical to arid to temperate. Its most famous physical feature is Mount Kilimanjaro; at 19,340 feet it is Africa's tallest mountain.

In the seventeenth century, local peoples and Arabs drove out the Portuguese. In 1887, the British established a protectorate but gave it over to the Germans the next year. Tanganyika, as it was known after the Germans lost control following World War I, was a League of Nations mandate, managed by Britain, until 1946, when it became a UN trusteeship. On December 9, 1961, Tanzania gained its independence from Britain with Dr. Julius Nyere, one of Africa's greatest leaders, as the new president. Pemba and Zanzibar were unified with Tanzania in 1964. In the years since independence the nation has suffered from a deteriorating infrastructure and weak agrarian economy. A 1990 World Bank loan of $200 million, however, has improved the nation's agricultural marketing system. In 1995, the nation's first multiparty elections were held, although the nation's Revolutionary Party (Chama Cha Mapinduzi) still maintains much control over the government and media.

Tanzania's natural resources include hydroelectric potential, unexploited iron and coal, gemstones, gold, and natural gas, while the agricultural sector yields cotton, coffee, sisal, tea, tobacco, wheat, cashews, livestock, and cloves. Principle industries include agricultural processing, diamond mining, oil refining, shoes, cement, textiles, and wood products. Ninety percent of the population are farmers. With twelve national game parks, Tanzania's economy depends heavily on tourism. One of the world's most famous archeology sites for human evolution, Olduvai Gorge, is located in Tanzania.

Tanzania's government has encouraged the use of Swahili as the nation's national language. Through educational programs subsidized by the government, mass literacy in Swahili has promoted the rise of a cohesive national culture. Consequently, Tanzania is now one of Africa's most culturally unified nations.

JENNIFER JOYCE

TELEVISION

See **Electronic Media and Oral Traditions; Radio and Television Dramas; Women Pop Singers of Mali**

TEXTILE ARTS AND COMMUNICATION

In African societies, where oral traditions take precedence over written ones, visual arts play a vital role in their function as language. Included among these arts is that of textiles, which is an exceptionally rich and varied medium on the sub-Saharan continent.

The cloth medium lends itself particularly well to this function. Cloth is an inherently flat surface; thus it operates as the page onto which language and related symbols are written, and within which varying textures and motifs are incorporated. It also has a rich and varied "syntax." It comes in any variety of fibers woven in any number of ways, depending on the type of loom used. Its specific technology determines its relative size, its overall density (whether it is loosely or tightly woven), the texture (its quality of smoothness or nubbiness), and its surface patterns (geometric or representational designs achieved through a supplemental patterning system). Pattern can also be achieved by resist-dying or painting the cloth surface (much like the page onto which a scribe applies his script). Finally, cloth is a pliable, portable medium that can be wrapped around the body, or cut and tailored to fit. Worn either way, the cloth functions as a kind of billboard for the transmission of information.

Text and Textile

Cloth bears a structural parallel to language in many ways. Threads are interwoven to produce cloth, much in the same way that words are interconnected to create syntax. Not coincidentally, this connection is also suggested by the apparent relationship between the words "text" and "textile," both of which share a common root in a concept involving building, either literally or figuratively. Language involves the building of written symbols or sounds to communicate an idea. Similarly, weaving requires the gradual addition of weft-threads to the warp as the process progresses. And, just as warp threads interconnect with those of the weft, words interrelate to make up the syntax of a sentence.

The connection suggested here between language and cloth structure is particularly pertinent to nonliterate cultures, such as those from Africa, that traditionally rely on visual forms over written ones to communicate their ideas. The Dogon of Mali are among a number of African cultures that readily acknowledge the existence of speech in cloth (Calame-Griaule 1986). They would say that "to be nude (that is, without cloth) is to be without speech." The Dogon word for cloth, *soy*, even has its roots in the word *so*, their word for the speech of their creator god, Nommo.

The Dogon also equate the weaving process to the nature of language, believing that the threads on their loom interconnect to produce fabric just as words are combined to make speech. They, like many groups throughout West Africa, weave on a horizontal, foot-treadle loom that produces a long, narrow strip of cloth. The Dogon claim that speech came about through weaving on such a loom. They refer to the entire loom apparatus as *so ke ru*, meaning "secret speech," and equate its individual components to the physiology of an individual's speech mechanism. For example, the reed is equated to teeth, the shuttle to the tongue (because of its constant back-and-forth motion inside the mouth) and the heddles to the uvula that rise and fall like the words themselves. Even the creaking sound of the loom during the weaving process itself is likened to the sound of the first manifestation of the word from the creator.

Dogon cloth design generally consists of white and indigo checks, either uniform or varied in size. The color and design elements in the cloth carry or connote a specific meaning. For example, the white characterizes truth and the speech of the creator god, whereas the black refers to falsehood, obscurity, and the secret speech of male initiates. The check designs refer to the cultivated field (which resembles such a configuration), the

white checks being fields on the plains (i.e., easy to cultivate), and the black ones being those of the plateau, where cultivation is difficult. In sum, cloth and its production for the Dogon is a metaphorical expression of their worldview, a view that encompasses the dichotomies of village/bush, plant/animal, daily/ritual, male/female.

The Dogon are not alone in equating weaving with speech. The Tukolor of Senegal believe weaving to be an incantation directed to their mythical ancestor, Juntel Jabali. Jabali was responsible for expelling bush spirits—once the owners of weaving—from the loom, thus making weaving a human prerogative (Dilley 1987). Moreover, the Tukolor, a traditionally Muslim people, say that "weaving is like praying" in the sense that both processes must be oriented toward the east, in the direction of Mecca. The Tukolor loom and the weaver seated at it must conceptually face in an eastern direction so as to pay their respects to the spirit realm as they weave. The weaver even impregnates the spun cotton with the power of words by first uttering incantations into knotted threads and then spraying saliva on them to bind the words to the threads.

Just as the process of making cloth is equated with speech, so too are its woven products, many of which serve as ideal forms of praise to the spirits, not unlike verbal prayer. For example, when the Dogon priest speaks to the spirits during the formal planting ceremony, an imitation of the checkered cloth he is wearing is painted on the facade of the cult house as a metaphorical offering to the spirits. At the appropriate moment he utters the following phrase, "nama of millet, enter into the drawing of Nimu's blanket" as if the blanket pattern could speak of fertility and continuity similar to the incantations of the priest who wears it.

The Yoruba of Nigeria are also known to view cloth as a visual prayer. Henry Drewal (1977) outlines the various ways that Yoruba initiates praise and honor Orinyla, the Great Mother. As with devotees of other gods (*orisha*), those honoring Orinyla must make an incision in their heads to allow the deity to enter (mount) them. In addition, the devotees must collectively purchase a white cloth which they present as a "visual prayer to the mother of us all." Drewal's reference alludes to what appears to be a common practice in Yoruba culture of using cloth to sing the praises of individuals, whether spiritual or human.

Such is the case among the Ijebu Yoruba (Aronson 1992). Ijebuland, located in southeastern Yorubaland, is the center of the Oshugbo (Ogboni), a secret society whose power derives from *onile*, the Earth Mother. Through privileged contact with the *onile*, Oshugbo members are able to exercise spiritual, political, and judicial authority in Yoruba society. Membership requires the wearing of certain attire ritually presented to the initiates during the initiation process. Most notable are the figurative bronze staffs (*edan*) either worn around the neck or placed in the ground when judicial decisions are being made. Oshugbo attire also included armlets, staffs, and, for the purposes of discussion here, textiles.

The Oshugbo cloth repertoire involves basically two pieces, a large wrapper (Iborun-nla) worn toga-style and the much smaller cloth (Itagbe) worn over the shoulder. Although different in size, each type is embellished with a complex array of weft-float patterns that include a number of animal forms important to Oshugbo cosmology such as the frog (*ofolo*), crocodile (*ooni*), or the mudfish (*agbarieja*). In addition, some of the designs refer to speech-imitating objects such as the big drum (*gbedu*) and the smaller pressure-type variety (*gangan*), the latter marvelously portrayed by a series of repeated triangular marks resembling the rhythmic tapping of the stick on the drum head.

Like the patterns on it, much about the ritual use of the Itagbe cloth suggests it functions as a visual form of prayer. One ritual involves the decorated fringe. Initiates ordained into Oshugbo ceremonially receive an Itagbe from the king (Awujale). At this crucial moment in the presentation of the cloth, the tassels are lowered to the ground as though to be invoking the earth goddess Onile. From that point, the cloth becomes the official and privileged possession of the initiate receiving it.

Itagbe are also presented as offerings at shrines, to gain the good wishes of the spirits. The most convincing evidence of the cloth's prayerlike function derives from the recent tradition of weaving itagbe with English words in place of visual imagery. The words *jebemi oluwa* woven on one Itagbe documented in 1978 mean "answer my prayer," thus acknowledging, in this newly symbolic system, its function as a prayerlike invocation to the spirits.

Cloth as Written Text

Just as cloth is used as a kind of surrogate for speech, it functions as a surface onto which words and word-derived imagery are applied. Although nonliteracy is traditionally the norm in sub-Saharan African, some systems of writing have prevailed, a few dating back quite early in time. Among them are a host of indigenous writing systems, the most well-known examples being found among the Vai, Loma, Efik, Bamum, and Kongolese. Such systems are ritually charged forms of writing intended more for efficacy and action than for explication of pictures or the mere recording of information. Several textile patterns, including those on the mud-painted cloths (*bokolanfini*) of the Bamana of Mali, may be inspired by such script, as Sarah C. Brett-Smith (1984) has suggested.

An even more influential form of writing, as far as textiles are concerned, is Islamic script, which may be among the earliest forms introduced to sub-Saharan region. Exactly how early Islamic script appeared in sub-Saharan Africa is uncertain. But, recognizing the vital role that Islamic script serves in promoting Islam (for one must learn to read and recite the scriptures to become one with Allah) it may have appeared as early as the eighth century C.E., when Islam first reached sub-Saharan African soil.

Scholars of Islam have noted that the Quran differs from the Bible in that it does not narrate stories about God but is the actual speech of Allah himself. Therefore, to be reciting passages of the Quran is to be appropriating and uttering Allah's very words, with all the potency and eloquence that they carry. Likewise, the written version of Allah's sacred speech serves as an ideal if not honorable form of artistic embellishment, again as an embodiment of Allah's speech more than a mere reference to it.

Islamic traditions throughout North Africa produce cloths with words encoded in them. One North African type, called *tiraz*, has prayers or praises to rulers woven into the cloth itself. Indeed, in some cultures, such as those of Algeria, the very name for weaver (*reggam*) has its roots in a word meaning to write.

The suggestion from all of this is that cloth serves as an important carrier of Allah's speech. Along with the advent of Islam into West Africa came an influx of Quranic-inscribed protective garments and other forms of body adornment bearing Quranic script. Evidence of this is seen in the vast array of garments and other forms of body adornment which bear Quranic writing as a form of protection.

The amulet charm serves as a useful introduction to the topic of the wearing of ritual script. Traditional African charms (of non-Islamic origin) can be made up of natural substances (bones, horns, or other medicinal materials) that are tightly if not elegantly bound together. However, the charms of Islamic inspiration will often contain Islamic-derived script written on paper by a marabout or other bearer of Islamic ritual knowledge. To be worn, the substances are inserted into leather-tooled or metal encasements and then worn around the neck or at other areas of the body.

When opened, these amulets reveal what Labelle Prussin calls "magical square constructions" (1986, 75) in either a uniform checkerboard design or in squares with a pronounced centralized element. Whatever the specific configuration, the images can be read as conceptualized models of the universe, with Allah at the center. They are believed to enhance the mystical powers of the written prayers they enclose.

The aesthetic of a number of textiles from West Africa draws its influence from these charm motifs. To cite one example, it is seen on much West African strip weaving, particularly in the areas where Islam is pervasive. Common designs for strip-woven coverlets from Islamized regions of West Africa often bear either a checkerboard or an overall grid design with a centralized element not unlike the magical square configurations on charms.

Cloth as Proverb

Proverbs can be defined as short, poetic axioms of truth, or wisdom often characterized by their sharp wit, sarcasm, humor, or rhetoric. In sub-Saharan Africa, where proverbial speech is a highly developed art form, it can be used to embellish all types of speech, from oratory to everyday conversation. Furthermore, the number of proverbs in any one culture can number four thousand or more. Given the importance of proverbial speech throughout sub-Saharan Africa, it is not surprising that it should make its appearance on cloth, particularly through the recent introduction of roman script.

However, it is not only through the writing of proverbs on the cloth surface that proverbial speech is transmitted. Before the introduction of Western-influenced writing, and even in the present, certain African cultures have relied on the cloth designs themselves to communicate proverbial thought. This is particularly true of Akan speakers of Ghana and Cote d'Ivoire.

It has long been known that the woven patterns on Kente, the famous royal cloth of the Ashanti, can often have proverbial meaning. One particular Kente design bears the proverb, "There is fire between the two factions of Oyoko clan," a reference to the civil war that ensued over the subsequent heir to the throne after the death of the first Ashanti ruler, Osei Tutu, in 1731. A sense of conflict is created by the clash of colors and patterns, the two background colors of the cloth representing those of the two battling clans.

The Akan-speaking Agni of Cote d'Ivoire, like many African cultures, now favor factory-printed cloths over locally woven ones for daily and even ceremonial use. Susan Domowitz, in particular, has done significant research emphasizing the rich proverbial meaning that even these cloths can carry (Domowitz 1992). For the Agni, the patterns on factory cloth bear social messages intended for someone else to read. For example, a cloth with brown and white abstract patterns addresses the conflicts among cowives under such a marital arrangement. Its proverb is as follows: "Cowife rivalry is like cow dung" (meaning that it looks fine on the outside but sticky on the inside).

Domowitz notes that cloth designs are selected very often for the proverbial speech that they communicate, rather than for their colors and patterns. One woman who had recently ended a disastrous marriage selected a cloth with cornstalk patterns because of the appropriate proverb that pattern would elicit. The proverb read, "Men are not like corn" (meaning if they were corn, one could pull off the husks and examine the interior kernels before buying them).

One could say that factory cloths for the Agni function like certain aspects of language. The linguist Ferdinand de Saussure (1966) identifies what he calls the quality of "mutability," by which he means that the linguistic sign, being dependent on a rational principle, is arbitrary and can be organized at will. This suggests that linguistic signs change their meaning over space and time. Similarly, we see that the proverbial cloth messages shift in meaning relative to the context in which they operate. For example, when a divorced Agni man saw his new lover wearing a cloth with a spider motif, he immediately thought of the proverb, "What one does to *cendaa* (a small harmless spider), one does not do to *bokohulu*" (a large spider considered dangerous), for him a grim reminder that he should not be unfaithful to her, as he had been to his former wife. In other words, it was his experiences from the past, combined with circumstances of the present, that gave meaning to the cloth design. Were she to have worn her spider cloth in the presence of neighboring Akan groups, they might have gleaned very different proverbs from the designs.

This essay has highlighted a number of ways in which African textiles encode thought and speech. It is only the beginning of a potentially rich exploration into the ways in which textiles in Africa can be, and are, used as language.

References

Aronson, Lisa. 1992. Ijebu Yoruba Aso Olona: A Contextual and Historical Overview. *African Arts* 25:52–63, 101.
———. 1995. Threads of Thought: African Cloth as Language. In *African and African-American Sensibility*, ed. Michael W. Coy, Jr. and Leonard Plotnikov. Pittsburgh: Dept. of Anthropology, University of Pittsburgh.
Brett-Smith, Sarah, C. 1984. Speech Made Visible: The Irregular as a System of Meaning. *Empirical Studies of the Arts* 2:127–47.
Calame-Griaule, G. 1986. *Words and the Dogon World*, Philadelphia.
Dilley, R. 1987. Myth and Meaning in the Tukulor Loom. *Man* 22: 256–66.
Domowitz, Susan 1992. Wearing Proverbs: Anyi Names for Printed Factory Cloths. *African Arts* 25:82–7.
Drewal, H. 1977. Art and the Perception of Women in Yoruba Culture. *Cahiers d'Études Africaines* 17:545–67.
Prussin, L. 1986. *Hatumere: Islamic Design in West Africa*. Berkeley.
Saussure, Fredinand de. 1966. *Course in General Linguistics*. New York.

LISA ARONSON

See also **Body Arts; Gender Representation in African Folklore; Nsibidi; Proverbs**

TEXTILES: AFRICAN AMERICAN QUILTS, TEXTILES, AND CLOTH CHARMS

Some African American quilts are the visual equivalent of jazz or blues, rich with color and symbolism. Characterized by strips, bright colors, large designs, asymmetry, multiple patters, improvisations, and symbolic forms, these African American quilts have their roots in African textile technique and cultural traditions.

The antecedents of contemporary African textiles and African American quilts developed in Africa as long as two thousand years ago when cotton was domesticated along the Niger River in Mali, where it was used for fish nets and woven cloth.

The actual links between African and African American textile traditions were forged between 1650 and 1850, when Africans were brought to Latin America and the United States. It is possible to trace African textile techniques, aesthetic traditions, and religious symbols that were adapted by African American textile innovators to the needs and resources of the new world.

Four African civilizations had profound influences on African American folk arts: the Mande-speaking peoples of West Africa (the modern countries of Guinea, Mali, Senegal, and Burkino Faso), theYoruba and Fon peoples from the Republic of Benin and Nigeria, the Ejagham peoples of Nigeria and Cameroon, and the Kongo and Kongo-influenced peoples of Zaire and Angola.

African American quilts are unique, resulting from the creolization of various African, Native American, and European traditions that took place in Brazil, Surinam, Haiti, Cuba, other Caribbean island, Mexico, and the southern United States. Although men had traditionally been the primary textile artists in Africa, American plantation owners adhered to the European system of labor division. Thus African women became the principle weavers, seamstresses, and quilters in southern society in the United States.

African American women produced utilitarian and decorative quilts for both African and white households. Many of their quilts were done in what we think of as traditional Anglo-American styles, even though some of these styles were adapted from traditional African designs. However, some quilts made for personal, often utilitarian, uses by African Americans were designed and stitched with definite African traditions in mind. Thus African American women preserved many African textile traditions and passed them on from generation to generation over several hundred years. Because improvisation is basic to many African aesthetic traditions, this African American heritage is not static. Each generation—indeed each quilter—is free to borrow from other traditions and add elements from his or her own cultural history.

Many contemporary African American quilters are unaware of the continuities between African textiles and their quilt designs, but the designs and symbolic similarities are so striking as to prompt some historical explanation. In examining the African history underlying certain African American quilt traditions, we can look at three aspects: technological similarities, the religious symbols in writing systems, and charm traditions.

Technological Traditions

Strips

The use of strips is a chief construction technique, a dominant design element, and symbolic form in West African, Caribbean, and African American textiles. Beginning in the eleventh century, most cloth in West Africa had been constructed from strips woven on small portable men's looms. These long, narrow strips, once used as a form of currency, are woven plain or with patterns. Some strips are lightly tacked together, so as to allow air through while hung up as screens. The Tuareg use such cloths as tent hangings. Woven strips are sometimes sewn together into larger fabrics to be worn as clothing or displayed as wall hangings and banners.

Blue and white designs, as in the earliest cloths, are still made with domestic cotton and dyed blue from a native indigo plant. Later, more colorful fabrics were made by unraveling European cloth and reweaving the bright colors, African-style. Nadsuaso cloth, made by the Asante weavers in Ghana, is the best known of the colorful West African textiles. It was once made from silk, but had been made with rayon since about 1946.

A new preference for strip textiles continued in the New World. In Surinam, African women continued African textile traditions when they ran away from plantations to Maroon societies in the Surinam rainforest. Both Djuka and Saramaka women continued to cut strips from imported commercial cloth, and save the strips until they wanted to make an African style of cape for their men, called *aseésènte*. They then sewed the strips together in an aesthetic fashion, the aesthetic being determined by conversation among various women.

While men did most of the weaving in Africa, in all probability it was women who most often created textiles in the New World, and it was women who maintained strip aesthetic. West African women who came to the United States would have remembered West African cloth made from narrow strips sewn together. Some strips quilts made from blue denim scraps are called "Blue Jean quilts" by African Americans and "Britchy quilts" by white people. Many strip quilts are made from the smallest usable rectangles of cloth, called "strings." Many African American quilters speak of "strips quilts," "to strip a quilt," and of how strips bring out the design.

Large Shapes, Strong Colors

Large shapes and strong contrasting colors, such as the indigo blue and white found in historic and contemporary West African cloth, insure the pattern in a cloth is recognizable from a distance and in strong sunlight. It can be important to recognize patterns from a distance if one needs to give a proper greeting to someone.

Important people wear cloth with complex patterns and more color. Because colors are prestigious in cloth, Africans eventually imported European cloth so as to unravel it and reweave the colored threads into their own bold cloth. African American women in Surinam value strong colors in their pieced textiles. They say that the colors should "shine" or "burn" and that the color of one piece should "lift up" the one next to it—that is, provide strong contrast.

Many African American quilters, when discussing their use of bright colors, explain that they look for maximum contrast when piecing scraps together. Often scraps are pieced together as they come out of a bag or box, with last-minute decisions as to whether the pieces show up well next to each other. A Mississippi quilter, Pecolia Warner, speaks of colors which must "hit" each other right, and of "whooping" together contrasting colors.

Asymmetry

In West Africa, when woven strips with patterns are sewn together to make a larger fabric, the resulting cloth may have asymmetrical and unpredictable designs. "Off beat" patters are one option in West and Central African fabrics. When strips are sewn together, the colored or patterned weft blocks are staggered in relation to those in other strips. Roy Sieber has noted that "the careful matching of the ends of the cloth dispels the impression of an uncalculated overall design."

Women's Weave

African women also weave, but on wide stationary looms in their homes where they cook and care for children. "Women's weave" features wide panels with vertical designs that may look, from a distance, like the strips of the older "men's weave." While "men's weave" is abundant and sold commercially, "women's weave" is more for personal use.

African wide-loom weaving frequently features asymmetrical alignments. Wide-loom weaving was also once done by black women in the United States, the same women who made quilts and probably transmitted and preserved African textile traditions.

Improvisation

Asymmetrical arrangements of cloth are a form of improvisation, found in West and Central African textiles. Kongo people praise talented expressions of sound and vision with the phrase, *veti dikita*, meaning the mind plays the pattern strongly. Improvisation, break-patterning, or flexible patterning in Kuba raffia cloth and painted Mbuti textiles has also been linked to spirit possession. The Kongo scholar Fu-Kiau Bunseki says, "every time there is a break in pattern (it) is the rebirth of (ancestral) power in you."

African American quilters often adapt what we think of as traditional European-American quilt patterns, and "African-Americanize" them by establishing a pattern in one square and varying it in size, arrangement, and color in successive squares. Their use of lines, designs, and colors varies with a persistence that goes beyond a possible lack of cloth in any particular size, color, or pattern.

Multiple Patterning

Improvisation, as seen in asymmetrical textiles, shades into multiple patterning, also described as flexible patterning. Improvisation and multiple patterning form another aesthetic tradition shared by the people who made African American quilts. Multiple patterns are important in African royal and priestly fabrics, for the number and complexity of patterns in a fabric increase in accordance with owner's status. Cloth woven for priests and kings may feature various woven patterns within each strip, as well as a variety of strips each featuring a different pattern. Multiple patterned cloth communicates the prestige, power, and wealth of the wearer, for only the well educated and the wealthy can name the different patterns and afford to pay master weavers.

African cloth thus has social and political significance, for it is worn and displayed as an indicator of wealth, occupation, social status, and history. Robert Farris Thompson (1983) has suggested that certain West African asymmetrical and multiple-patterned strip cloths have more than an aesthetic function: the complex designs serve to keep the evil spirits away, because "evil travels in straight lines." If the patterns do not line up easily, the belief is that evil spirits will be confused and slowed down. Thus some textiles become protective.

Contemporary African American quilts often are made with four different patterns in four large corners. Plummer T. Pettway of rural Alabama believes that many different patterns and shapes make the best quilts. "You can't match them. No. It takes all kind of pieces to piece a quilt."

Many contemporary African American quilts may not communicate an owner's status or religious identification, but they do retain an African aesthetic preferences for improvisation, for variations on a theme, and for multiple patterns. Improvisation and multiple patterning are also protective, for copying is impossible. Although ostensibly reproducing European-American patterns, many African American quilters maintain African principles of asymmetry, improvisation, multiple patterning, and unpredictable rhythms and tensions similar to those found in other African American arts, such as jazz.

Appliqué Traditions

Besides piecing, in which strip patterns may dominate, another basic quilt top construction technique known in Europe, Africa, and the United States is appliqué, the art of sewing cut-out shapes onto a surface. While European-American appliqué quilts are primarily decorative, African American appliqué quilts often express stories and ideas in the same manner as appliqué textiles do in Africa.

With bold appliqué shapes, African cultures recorded court histories, religious values, and personal histories of famous individuals, using designs symbolizing power, skill, leadership, wisdom, courage, balance, composure, and other personal and religious qualities. The best-known African appliqué cloth was made by the Fon people of the Republic of Benin (formerly Dahomey).

In the nineteenth century, Fon appliqué banners were made by a guild of male artisans to decorate the walls of the royal palace and to depict historical events. The technique was similarly used to decorate royal umbrellas, flags, costumes, and banners.

African American appliqué quilts often mirror the diverse influences that shape the lives of black women in the United States. Contemporary African American quilters appliqué quilts with shapes drawn from their imaginations, from black culture and from popular American culture shaped by magazines, television, and advertising. Some women cut out magazines illustrations and reproduce them in cloth. Others are inspired by animal pictures and search for appropriate animal like fuzzy materials; a few make paper templates from dreamed designs; and some (like Pearl Posey and Sarah Mary Taylor) use people or doll forms, as well as hands.

Protective African Scripts

In Africa, among the Mande, Fon, Ejagham, Yoruba, Kongo, and other cultures indigenous and imported writing is associated with knowledge, power, and intelligence, and thus is considered sacred and protective.

Various African graphic systems were designed in precolonial times to express and transmit ideas or to convey messages. Some use pictures or pictograms; others use ideograms or ideographs to represent ideas and other phonological (syllabic, hieroglyphic, or phonemic): based on language and sounds. African graphic signs were painted or drawn on the ground or on buildings; sewn, dyed, painted, or woven into cloth; and Central African artifacts were often read as aspects of a Kongo religious cosmogram.

In West Africa, Bamana women paint cloth, called Bogolanfini (which has been woven by men on a narrow loom and then sewn into fabrics) with designs similar to a syllabary invented by the Vai people in the nineteenth century but a syllabary which is thought to have much older precedents. Bogolanfini fabrics are used for women's wrapper-skirts and protective clothing for hunters. Bamana women coded, in discretionary irregularities of design, ideas too serious to speak of directly.

Many West African peoples encase little scraps of religious writing (from the Bible, the Quran, or indigenous writing) in protective charms covered with cloth, leather, or metal, which are worn around the neck or sewn to cloth gowns, quilted war shirts, and quilted horse armor.

In Nigeria, the Ejagham people are known for their four hundred-year old writing system, called Nsibidi. It was most likely invented by women since you see it in their body painting and tattoos, and on their Nimm secret society buildings and ritual fans, calabashes, stools, skin-covered masks, textiles, and woven, dyed, and pieced costumes made for the men's Ngbe (Leopard) secret society. For the Ejagham, the leopard is the symbol of power, intelligence, and cool leadership. Ejagham women make woven costumes and resist-dyed appliqué cloths featuring checks, triangles, and other Nsibidi signs. These textiles are worn by dancers or hang in shrines.

Ejagham men make stools and skin-covered masks decorated with Nsibidi signs learned from the women. Six hundred and ninety Nsibidi symbols are known. Light and dark triangles or squares represent leopard spots; intersecting arcs represent love or marriage. Arcs separated by a line stand for divorce. A circle bisected with a cross, with a small circle in each quadrant, represents the Ejagham belief in spiritual as well as physical vision.

Central African peoples, influenced by the religion of the Kongo people, practiced a healing, curing religion, promoted by priests who used symbolic art forms related to the Kongo cosmogram, a circle, or a diamond with four points representing birth, life, death, and rebirth in the world of the ancestors under the sea. The top of the circle can be considered the noontime of life, the peak of power and potential. Its opposite, the midnight sun at the bottom, represents the power and position of the ancestors below the sea. To the left is the position of dusk, death, and transition from the land of the living to the watery world of the ancestors. To the right is the position of the rising sun, or birth. The horizontal axis represents the transition between air and water. The Kongo priest draws the cosmogram on the earth, and Kongo and related peoples bury their dead chiefs in red cloth mummies, often decorated with the sign of the cosmogram. Images like these red mummies appear in African-Latin America arts, in Vodun dolls in the United States, and in African American quilts.

New World Scripts

In the New World, various mixtures of West African (Vai, Fon) and Nigerian (Nsibidi) scripts, the Yoruba concept of a crossroads, and the Kongo cosmogram, fuse to create numerous new scripts, which are seen on folk arts, including textiles. African-Brazilian signs, called marked "Points" (*pontos riscados*, or points drawn) can be found in ground paintings, and on textiles for the Yoruba gods.

In Surinam the Maroon ideographic system, called Afaka, is embroidered by women onto loincloths and capes for their men, and painted by men onto houses and paddles, as well as carved on stools and houseparts.

Cuban Anaforuana signs are seen on contemporary banners that often feature four eyes for real and for spiritual vision, and in the reappearance of the men's secret society costume featuring Nsibidi checks to represent leopard's spots and power. Similar costumes are now seen in Miami, and some of these signs continue in African American quilt top designs.

Haitian ideographic signs, called Veve, derive from a mixture of Fon, Yoruba, Ejagham, and Kongo traditions. People from all these cultures were taken to Haiti in the seventeenth and eighteenth centuries, and gradually their religions and their graphic forms merged with Catholicism into the Vodun religion. In Haitian art we see the reappearance of the Kongo cosmogram, in textiles, groundpainting, cut steel sculptures, and in paintings depicting marriages, ceremonies, life, death, the watery ancestral world, and the rebirth of souls.

African American Signs

After Haitian independence in 1804, many free Africans came to New Orleans, and the Vodun religion spread throughout the United States' south. Vestiges of African American protective writing traditions, often incorporating Masonic symbols also, occur in African American folk arts. As in Brazil, Cuba, Haiti, and Surinam, African American use symbols on many levels. On one level symbols can be explained as Christian or Masonic, while on another level, the same symbols have deeper African meanings revealed only under special circumstances, to special people.

It was the manipulation of secret symbols, Prince Hall Masonic symbols, by African American secret society members, which contributed to the success of the American Underground Railway. Gladys-Marie Fry (1990) writes that quilts were used to send messages through the underground railroad. Log Cabin Quilts made with black cloth were hung on a line to indicate a safe house of refuge. Joyce Scott reports that "My mother was told that slaves would work out a quilt, piece by piece, field by field, until they had an actual map, an escape route. And they used the map to find out how to get off the plantation."

Protective Writing

Writing continued to have protective symbolism in African American culture, even when the writing was in English. Newsprint has been placed on the walls of southern homes, and in shoes as well, partly for protection against the weather, but in African American homes, to protect against evil enslaving spirits, in the belief that "evil spirits would have to stop and read the words of each chopped up column" before they could do any

harm. This concept derives from the African American practice of leaving a Bible open at night so that the power of religious words would protect a family.

Checks

Checks are another popular old African American quilt top pattern remembered from early childhood. Checked designs can be made from the smallest scraps, and also allow for maximum contrast between squares without elaborate preplanning. Checked designs are transformed into the popular "Nine-Patch" block design also often seen in Anglo-American quilt-making traditions. Perhaps the ancestors of some African American quilters adopted "Nine-Patch" and other checked and triangular patterns, like "Wild Goose Chase," because they resembled the nine-square patterns of West African weaving, the Nigerian leopard society resist cloths, or the checked designs so often seen in Kuba raffia cloth.

Crosses

Crosslike patterns also occur frequently in African-American quilts. Although now interpreted as Christian crosses, they could once have been adopted because of a resemblance to the Yoruba belief in sacred crossroads, or the Kongo symbol for the four points of the sun. Circular designs, like crosses, may have once been a means for remembering the Kongo cosmogram. A Pinwheel pattern evokes the circular nature of the cosmogram, the rebirth of souls into the bodies of grandchildren. A Wheel quilt and a Double Wedding Ring quilt could have the same function.

Contemporary quilters do not speak openly of quilts as protective coverings or as confusing to evil spirits, but their aesthetic choices do imply traditions that once had protective significance, and that may well show a continuation of protective African ideographs.

Protective Charms

Various African traditions of healing or protective charms also experience a renaissance in African American visual arts in the New World, including African American quilt patterns. As these protective concepts were retained in the New World, the took different forms and different meanings, partly because ideas from West and Central African fused and then further creolized with Native American and European ideas, and because of new cultural environments.

Charms are made in Africa or the New World by men, women, priests, priestesses, spirit-diviners, and folk artists on commission from clients with political, personal, physical, emotional, or religious problems. Priests and priestesses make charms to suit needs so each charm is different; each is an improvised solution to an individual need. Some are more protective; others are to heal. Charms are accumulated arts; arts made with magical ingredients, on the inside or the outside. Beads, buttons, coins, claws, feathers, and shells are attached to cloth and costumes to imbue them with protective powers.

West African Charms

In West Africa, there is a tradition of enclosing writing in charms because writing is considered protective due to its inherent knowledge. These small square packets, often red leather, cloth or metal, enclosing script, are worn around the neck and sewn on hunting, religious, and war costumes as protection against evil spirits. The Tuareg peoples enclose charms in intricate leather and metal designs. Textiles are key a ingredient in making charms, whether made in Africa or the New World.

Kongo Minkisi

In Central Africa, the Kongo Minkisi, the medicines of God, appear in numerous forms usually activated by reciting verbs of action, to conjure the powers that ancestors had to make charms work. Minkisi medicines fall into two classes: spirit-embodying materials such as shells, graveyard earth, and clay and spirit-directing medicines such as animal claws. Northern Kongo people often asked Mbute experts to make famed good luck charms for hunters and athletes.

Ceramic vessels with liquid medicines were an early type of Kongo charm, as were Kongo graves with symbolic objects-references to the watery world of the ancestors. Cloth forms, usually red, could be tied at the neck, with feathers at the top. The ultimate charms were large cloth figures, wrapped in red blankets, "used to transport the smoke-mummified bodies of the most important persons from this world to the next," and often protected with the cosmogram sign to insure the prosperity of the Kongo nation. A wooden charm often took a human or animal shape, with a hollow in the center for the magical curing substances. This cavity was sealed with glass, a shell, mica, or a mirror, all references to the watery land of the Kongo ancestors. Nails were sometimes used to activate these wooden charms.

New World Charms

When African charm traditions were transplanted to the New World, they took on different forms and different meanings, partly because ideas from West and Central Africa fused and then further creolized with American Indian and European ideas, and partly because of new cultural environments.

African-Brazilian charms for love and war called *ponto de seguar* (securing points) are small cloth containers designed to stop a spirit or attract a person. They are sealed with tight criss-crossing cords. Protective charms also take the form of wooden hands, called *figas*. Some are large while small ones are often attached to a necklace.

In Surinam, numerous charms, called Obia, are used to protect, warn, and heal members of secret societies. Other specially prepared necklaces, armbands, and belts were worn for protection against sickness and evil spirits.

In African-Cuban cultures one finds beaded charms, tied charms, and pots with cosmogram-like signs and magical ingredients. Many African-Cuban examples are now appearing in Miami.

Pacquet Kongo

In Haiti, the Kongo cloth charms are still very much alive in the form of *pacquets kongo*, small tightly wound charms, enclosed in cloth, with arms, beads around the neck, ribbons, and sequins. Some have earrings or lace ruffles and are meant to represent female spirits. Maya Deren noted that "Pacquets Congo . . . are bound as magical safeguards . . . whose efficiency depends on the technique of careful wrapping (the idea being to enclose the soul well, so as to keep it from evil)."

Vodun dolls

In the United States, these African and African-Caribbean cloth charm traditions evolve into several new forms. One is the Vodun doll, which can be traced back from New Orleans, to the Haitian Pacquet Congo, Kongo red mummies, Kongo wooden Minkisi with nails, and other Kongo cloth charms. One also sees these spirit figures in contemporary African American folk paintings.

For some quilters, the protective symbolism of Vodun dolls may have been forgotten but they continue to use the form in new ways. Sarah Mary Taylor and her mother Pearl Posey's appliqué designs feature red figures reminiscent of Vodun dolls, on quilts and pillows. They name their patterns "Men," "Dolly Dingle Dolls," "Cowboys," "Man with Two Dogs," and "Fashionable Ladies."

Mojo

The African American term Mojo refers to a hex or spell, healing medicine, and the charm or amulet used to lift a spell or protect one from evil forces, as in the folksong "Got My Mojo Working," popularized by the blues singer Muddy Waters. A small square red African American cloth charm called a Mojo, or a Hand (in the sense that a charm is a helping hand), fuses West African and Central African charm concepts. Zora Neal Hurston (1931) collected this information about a "hand":

> Take a piece of the fig leaf, sycamore bark, John de Conquer root, John de Conquer vine, three paradise seeds. Take a piece of paper and draw a square and let the party write his wishes. Begin, "I want to be successful in all my undertakings." Then cut the paper from around the square and let him tear it up fine and throw it in from of the business place or house or wherever he wants. Put the square in the "hand" and sew it all up in red flannel. Sew with a strong thread and when seams are closed, pass the thread back and forth through the bag 'til all the thread is used up. To pour on "hand:" oil of anise, oil of rose geranium, violet perfume, oil of lavender, verbena, bay rum. "Hand must be renewed every six months."

During the Civil War, triangles in a quilt design signified prayer messages or a prayer badge, a way of offering a prayer, or asking for protection. Many African American quilters prefer patterns, such as the "Nine Patch," or the "Log Cabin," which incorporate small red squares to look like a Mojo. Some are decorative; others may be allusions to protective charms.

African American quilts have been described as protective baffles to guard loved ones in the night. We are just beginning to examine the many ways in which African American artist use textiles to protect, heal, and encode ideas.

Conclusions

African American quilt patterns involve aesthetic decisions, but many of those aesthetic choices derive from rich cultural traditions. In their choice of techniques, textiles, forms, design names, and colors, African American quilters perpetuate African techniques and cloth forms. Strip quilts reflect the strong West African textile traditions that are also evident in African-Caribbean fabrics. Many quilt patterns may have been chosen because they awakened a memory of ceremonial textiles.

If only one or two African forms occurred in African American quilts, it could be coincidental. But the numerous instances of similar forms, and sometimes similar meanings, is evidence of a cultural heritage that is stronger than any one lineage. Like many other African American folk artists, quilters are inspired by dreams. Not the dreams of idiosyncratic artists, quilters' dreams, like those of other folk artists, revive visual imagery from the culture of their childhood. Their dreams are culturally conditioned.

African American folk artists have often been labeled idiosyncratic because they do not always know, or care to explain, the African traditions that shape their visions, dreams, and arts. African men and women remembered African artists techniques and traditions when they came to the New World. They mixed and sorted their own traditions, then combined them with European-American and Native American ideas to create their unique creolized arts. Their combined ideas were passed down from generation to generation, thus preserving many African art traditions, even when unspoken.

Some well-known quilt patterns may have been adapted by African Americans because they resemble important ideas in African religions. Some Anglo American pattern names such as Flying Geese, Rocky Road to California, and Drunkards Path are indicative of action; while forms such as in Bears Paw, imply action, as in Kongo charms. In Kongo religion, it is important to activate a charm to make it work, and words are often part of the process. Certain "Anglo" patterns may appeal to African-American quilters for numerous historic cultural reasons, visual and verbal.

Improvisation

Most ideas highly valued by cultures are encoded in many forms. Such seems to be the case with African protective religious ideas which have been encoded into visual arts, songs, dance, and black speech in Africa and the New World. All these forms recognize improvisation as a style; and many refer to West African and Central African religious concepts that survive in contemporary African American cultures because they have been encoded so many ways. The redundancy indicates high value and insures survivability. This article attempts to explain the survival and transformation of African writing and charm traditions in one form, African American quiltmaking. The evidence is equally rich, powerful, and eloquent for continuities between African writing and charm traditions in African American architecture, ceramics, painting, sculpture and environments.

The African American Art Quilt

In recent years, African American quilt making has evolved in a new direction. Jesse Lane, Faith Ringold, Wini McQueen, Joyce Scott, and others have drawn on traditional folk designs for inspiration in creating their fine arts. These are trained artists who are proud of their mothers' arts, proud of family heirlooms, and they chose to build on family cultural traditions in creating contemporary arts.

African American folk arts provide evidence that American folk arts are not naive, primitive, or simplistic. African American arts are unique in America, fusing various international traditions to produce new ones.

African American artists maintaining this creolized aesthetic demonstrate the power and vision of African cultural traditions in contemporary American society, affirming the extraordinary tenacity of African religious ideas over hundreds of years.

References

Benberry, Cuesta. 1992. *Always There: The African-American Presence in American Quilts*. Louisville: The Kentucky Quilt Project.

Dorsey, Frances. 1991. *For John Cox's Daughter*. Ann Arbor: The Jean Paul Slusser Gallery, University of Michigan School of Art.

Ferris, William, ed. 1983. *Afro-American Folk Arts and Crafts*. Boston: Hall.

Fry, Gladys-Marie. 1990. *Stitched From the Soul: Slave Quilts from the Anti-Bellum South*. New York: The Museum of American Folk Art and Dutton Studio Books.

Grudin, Eva Ungar. 1990. *Stitching Memories: African American Story Quilts*. Williamstown, Mass.: William College Museum of Art.

Hurston, Zora Neal. 1931. Hoodoo in America. *Journal of American Folklore* 44:414.

Leon, Eli. 1987. *Who'd a Thought it, Improvisation in African American Quiltmaking*. San Francisco: San Francisco Craft & Folk Art Museum.

———. 1992. *Models in the Mind. African Prototypes in American Patchwork*. Winston-Salem, N.C.: Winston-Salem State University.

Thompson, Robert Ferris. 1983. *Flash of the Spirit: African and Afro-American Art and Philosophy*. New York: Random House.

Vlach, John Michael. 1978. *The Afro-American Tradition in the Decorative Arts*. Cleveland: The Cleveland Museum of Art.

Wahlman, Maude Southwell. 1974. *Contemporary African Arts*. Chicago: The Field Museum.

———. (with John Scully) 1980. *Black Quilters*. New Haven: Yale Art and Architecture Gallery.

———. 1980. The Art of Afro-American Quiltmaking: Origins, Development, and Significance. Ph.D. dissertation, Yale University.

———. 1981. Afro-American Quilt Aesthetics. In *Something to Keep You Warm*, ed. Patti Carr Black. Jackson: The Mississippi Department of Archives and History.

———. 1983. *Ten Afro-American Quilters*. University, Miss.: The Center for the Study of Southern Culture.

———. (with John Scully) 1983. Aesthetic Principles in Afro-American Quilts. In *Afro-American Folk Arts and Crafts*, ed. William Ferris. Boston: Hall.

———. 1986. African Symbolism in Afro-American Quilts. *African Arts* 20, no. 1.

———. 1989a. African-American Quilts: Tracing the Aesthetic Principles. *The Clarion* 14, no. 2:44–54.

———. 1989b. Religious Symbolism in African-American Quilts. *The Clarion* 14, no. 3 36–43.

———. 1993. *Signs and Symbols: African Images in African-American Quilts*. N.Y.: Penguin.

MAUDE SOUTHWELL WAHLMAN

See also **Diaspora; Textile Arts and Communication; Vodou**

THEATER

See **Drama: Anang Ibibio Traditional Drama; Festivals: Mutomboko Festival of the Lunda**

THEATER: AFRICAN POPULAR THEATER

African popular theater is a contested but useful term that critics have applied in many contexts. This survey takes a broad definition, which incorporates mimetic performances involving some portrayal of character and an explicit or implicit narrative, presented to an audience that is representative of the majority, rather than elite groups in a community.

Despite authorative suggestions that drama in the European sense of the term is virtually unknown in precolonial Africa (Finnegan 1970, 516), there is broad consensus that scriptless theater or paradramatic oral performances were very widespread in the precolonial era. Indeed, European drama may have had an African origin in the Osiris mysteries of first millenium Phaeronic Egypt, which transferred to Greece through Orientalist cults.

A useful categorization of African popular theater can be based on a simple diachronic periodization into pre- and postcolonial eras. This, however, is rather misleading. Arabic domination of indigenous peoples in North and East Africa conceivably constitutes both cultural and political colonialism. Similarly, Jane Plastow (1996) has argued convincingly that Ethiopian theater in Amharic during the Haile Selassie regime was tantamount to a colonial form of theater, dominating subordinate languages and cultures. For the purposes of simplicity, however, it is useful to keep a periodization based on precolonial, colonial and postcolonial traditions, with colonial referring to the seventeenth, eighteenth, and nineteenth century incursions by English, Portuguese, French Spanish, and German missionaries, armies, administrators, and educators.

Precolonial Popular Theater

Scholars frequently make distinctions within precolonial theater between ritual and secular performance, with ancestral masquerades, hunting dances, and spirit-possession rituals given as example of religious theater, and entertainment dances and oral narratives as examples of secular performances. The distinction is useful with the proviso that very few secular performances were without some ritual elements, and that ritual performances had enormous variations in their levels of sacredness. Moreover, a diachronic analysis of forms shows that they were capable of changing their functions, with, for example, some ritual forms becoming gradually more secular over the years.

In most precolonial masquerades, such as Egungun, Ekoe, Okukmpa (West Africa), and Makishi and Nyau (Central Africa) worshippers considered masked dancers to be the spirits of ancestors who returned to earth during sacred rituals in order to sustain the living souls' links with the dead, and to cleanse the community of spiritual and physical impurities.

The masked dancers had a hierarchical grading, with some considered very sacred, and others, less sacred. In Yoruba Egun-gun, the "elder" masks, which covered the whole body (including the face) with richly embroidered cloths were the most sacred, while more approachable, comic masks (such as *onidan*) were more representational and considered much more secular. Similarly the zoomorphic, Chewa, Nyau masks represented ancient, powerful spirits, while the anthropomorphic masks were more minatory and parodic.

African masquerades usually associated themselves with single sex secret cults, such as the Poro society in West Africa or the Nyau in East Central Africa. These cults were usually all male, but female cults with associated masquerade theater forms were not uncommon. Occult ceremonies of a predominantly ritual nature took place in secluded parts of the forest, while the theatrical performances involving ceremonies and dance mimes geared to public entertainment took place in the open squares of the village or town. The latter often contained satirical sketches, which lampooned physical departures from community norms, such as ethnic outsiders or those afflicted with deformities like smallpox. More frequently, however, they encouraged social control by satirizing moral weaknesses, such as promiscuity, drunkenness, laziness, or the breaking of taboos.

Many ritual forms of masquerade developed secular variants. Adedeji (1978, 35–9) gives a detailed accounts of fairly secular masquerade forms of theater which arose in the eighteenth and nineteenth centuries among some Yoruba peoples. These forms, variously called Alarinjo or Apidan, were originally aristocratic entertainments, but acquired a progressively more popular form as troupes of traveling players took the dramas out of the courts and into the public squares of Yoruba towns.

There were many other secular precolonial forms of dramatic entertainment that did not necessarily evolve from rituals. Perhaps the most influential is that of narrative drama. Oral narratives in Africa almost always had a theatrical element, not only because of the presence of an audience, but owing to the incorporation of participatory songs as structural devices, and because of the verbal and kinesic skills of the narrators in making the characters come alive.

In some parts of Africa, oral narratives developed into more obviously dramatic forms. In Mali, the Koteba were dramatized oral narratives performed at night by young men, organized in agricultural work teams, based on age-sets. The plays were usually satiric, making fun of such individuals as lazy farmers, submissive husbands, or negligent polygamists. In Ghana, Anasesem were semidramatized performances that portrayed the exploits of the Akan trickster hero, Anase (spider), using a combination of narrative, song, drumming, and mime (by a specialized troupe of mime artists).

The principle function of narrative drama was entertainment, but there were still strong didactic elements, which made the stories suitable for accompanying such rituals as initiation ceremonies.

There were many other types of precolonial performance, including spirit-possession dances, dramatized songs and hunting dances. All incorporated marked theatrical elements into aesthetic forms which mixed such different types of art as music, song, dance, sculpture, costuming, and mime. The tendency for most precolonial African theater was not to valorize drama as a specialized genre but to use it as one approach in a wider, synesthesia.

Popular African Theater in the Colonial Period

One traditional view of colonialism is that it totally suppressed indigenous African theater. This is far from the truth. Although the efforts of missionaries and colonial administrators to eradicate "heathen" or "immoral" manifestations of African performance undoubtedly had a major impact, African theater was capable of adapting itself to mediate, and often resist, the changes brought about by colonialism. There are many accounts of masquerades that used the tradition of satirical stereotyping in song and mask creation to lampoon white colonial officers. The same is true of spirit possession and dramatized songs (Kerr 1995, 50–8).

In addition, however, various new genres of performance emerged which, owing to their synthesis of European and indigenous African traditions, are henceforth termed syncretic. These created cultural tools for communities to mediate the social problems associated with urbanization, labor migration, and the rise of the cash nexus.

One of the strongest and most widespread forms of syncretic theater is the militaristic mime, a parody of colonial military armies. Variants of these emerged from the late nineteenth century onward in several colonial cities, especially on the coast. They include Soja and Goge (Nigeria), Goumbe (Cote d'Ivoire), Beni (Tanganyika [now Tanzania]), Kenya and Nyasaland [now Malawi], Kalela (northern Rhodesia [now Zambia] and Congo), and Muganda (Northern Rhodesia and Nyasaland) (Kerr 1995, 59–71). Very closely related to these were the carnival parades in South Africa, such as the Coon Carnival in Cape Town (derived from minstrel shows from the United States and religious militaristic mimes, such as those of the South African Zionist church.

Although the militaristic mimes imitated colonial armies in their earliest manifestations (often using real uniforms and military paraphernalia), the music and songs derived from indigenous traditions. Moreover, as the mimes developed, and especially as they moved back to the home villages of the migrant workers, they appropriated other indigenous traditions of song, dance, costuming, and mime, as well as local functions. In the towns they provided group solidarity for migrant workers, but in the "up-country" villages their function was much more that of allowing new elites an outlet for asserting their modernity in the face of traditional authority, or mediating between the conflicting demands of modern and traditional value systems (Kerr 1998).

The militaristic mimes tended to emphasize group solidarity rather than individual expression, and thus relied on an aesthetic of ensemble mime. The kind of individual creativity that could lead to characterization and dramatic dialogue emerged in a rather later form of syncretic popular theater, the concert party.

The concert party is most closely associated with Ghana and some neighboring countries (especially Nigeria and Togo), although similar forms can be found in other parts of Africa. Concert parties originated in Ghanaian schools during the 1930s when teachers like Master Yalley and former students like Bob Johnson mixed Western forms such as vaudeville songs, silent movies, and slapstick routines with indigenous forms of stylized satire, such as Halo. In its early stages the concert party was fairly upmarket with performances at schools and exclusive clubs, but by the 1950s it had become a much more popular art form, with professional troupes touring their plays around community halls and bars.

The concert party used melodramatic or farcical plots with all-male casts and stylized costumes and makeup to project stereotyped characters, such as the good-time girl, the country bumpkin, or the faithful wife, in plays that relied heavily on domestic conflicts or rags-to-riches/riches-to-rags formulae. Highlife singers and instrumentalists integrated their musical performances with the dialog, as well as providing post-performance dance music (Barber et al. 1997, 12–14).

Similar syncretic drama forms emerged during the colonial period in other parts of Africa. In Western Nigeria, Yoruba opera had its origins in the independent Christian churches. Christian choirmasters or teachers like Hubert Ogunde, Ola Ogunmola, and Duro Ladipo combined a Western Christian cantata style with indigenous theatrical and musical traditions, such as Alarinjo, to create a syncretic form of popular theater. Dialogue (usually in Yoruba), music, singing, and mime were mingled in plays that ranged through themes concerning history, Christian morality, the supernatural, crime, and domestic conflicts (Barber, et al. 1987, 38–54).

In East Africa, Vichekesho theater had more secular origins. Itinerant professional, almost invariably male Zanzibari mime artists during the 1930s used Indian film-acting techniques, Taarab music, and indigenous African *ngoma* music and dance mime to create stylized farces which satirized aspects of modern urban life.

A similar mix of music, singing, dialogue, and stereotyped characterization emerged in South Africa during the 1960s in the township musical, with Gibson Kente as the most prominent artist/entrepreneur. The township musical combined the traditions of Western dialog drama with African choral music and township jazz (itself a syncretic form of music) (Kavanagh 1985, 135–44).

Yoruba opera and township musicals differed from concert parties and Vichekesho in that they used female as well as male actors, although male actors and entrepreneurs still maintained aesthetic and financial domination. All these forms tended to concentrate on domestic situations (usually from a male perspective), relying on an appeal to precapitalist community moral values to mediate and judge the rapid transformations brought about by modernization.

Post-Colonial Popular African Theater

In the postcolonial period, existing forms of indigenous and syncretic theater not only survived, but often flourished. The heyday of concert parties and Yoruba opera was probably in the 1960s and 1970s, with a massive expansion of traveling theater troupes well after independence.

Other forms of popular theater, however, also emerged in the postcolonial period. One of the most potent, if apparently unlikely sources was the elitist tradition of literary theater in schools and universities. Although in its early stages this tended to be rather unadventurously close to European models of theater (with aesthetic dependence reinforced by financial support from the British Council and Alliance Française), eventually many of these art theater institutions initiated programmes that attempted to widen their appeal, particularly through the performance of plays in African languages, using dramatic techniques and plot motifs drawn from indigenous folklore. University traveling theaters, such as those found at the universities of Ibadan, Legon, Makerere, Zambia, and Malawi, began taking plays out of the university cities into the rural towns and villages (Kerr 1995, 133–48).

As a result of this interaction between literary drama and mass audiences, a form of popular urban improvised drama emerged among amateur troupes, mobilizing the vast labor reserve of unemployed college graduates. In Uganda, for example, during the 1970s, playwrights like Wycliffe Kiyingi and Byron Kawadwa built up a strong Luganda popular theater, based on a mixture of school drama techniques and popular paradramatic performance, until the movement was crushed by Idi Amin's reign of terror (Kerr 1995, 127–29). Similar phenomena occurred, though in less repressive circumstances, in many other African countries.

A slightly different form of popular theater is associated with the efforts of postcolonial governments and non-governmental organizations (NGOs), to use local language drama as a tool of communication for development purposes. Although there were many colonial precedents, the orgins of "Theater for Development" are often traced to the Laedza Batananai movement for adult education in Botswana in the early 1970s. By the 1980s, partly due to the donor funds it attracted, several varieties of "Theater for Development," "Animation Theater," or "Community Theater" became pervasive throughout sub-Saharan Africa. These ranged in style and ideology from the nakedly instrumental tools of NGOs to communicate sectoral messages about health, agriculture, literacy and so on, to a more community-oriented focus on indigenous cultural renewal and social mobilization (Mda 1993). The most famous, radical variant of the latter is the Kamiriithu experience in Kenya during the late 1970s and early 1980s, which was vigorously crushed by the Kenyan Government (Ngugi 1986, 59–62).

Another form of theater which became increasingly popular during the postcolonial period is that associated with the mass media. Even drama forms which appear to be totally Western in their origins, such as television and radio drama, acquired very different structures, styles, and techniques when adapted to African radio and television stations. Syncretic forms of popular theater such as the concert party and Yoruba opera found a fruitful expansion on Ghanaian and Nigeria television in the 1980s (Jeyifo 1984). Less obviously, African traditions of narrative structure and presentation became essential to the success of the radio plays, especially through the technique of collective improvisation as a play-creation device (Kerr 1998).

The entire history of postcolonial popular African theater, both mediated and nonmediated, is testimony to the resilience and adaptive capacity of indigenous African performing arts, despite the transformations caused by capitalism, urbanization, and modernization.

References

Adedeji, Joel. 1978. Alarinjo: The Traditional Yoruba Tavelling Theatre. In *Theatre in Africa*, ed. Oyin Ogunba and Abiola Irele. Ibadan: Ibadan University Press.

Barber, Karin, John Collins, and Alain Ricard. 1987. *West African Popular Theatre*. Bloomington and Indianapolis: Indiana University Press; Oxford: James Currey.

Finnegan, Ruth. 1970. *Oral Literature in Africa*. London: Oxford University Press.

Jeyifo, Biodun. 1984. *The Yoruba Popular Travelling Theatre of Nigeria*. Lagos: Nigeria Magazine.

Kavanagh, Robert. 1985. *Theatre and Cultural Struggle in South Africa*. London: Zed Books.

Kerr, David. 1995. *African Popular Theatre: From Precolonial Times to the Present Day*. London: James Currey; Portsmouth, NH: Heinemann; Nairobi: EAEP; Cape Town: David Philip, Harare: Baobab.

———. 1998. *Dance, Media Entertainment and Popular Theatre in South East Africa*. Bayreuth: Bayreuth University Press.

Mda, Zakes. 1993. *When People Play People: Development Communication Through Theatre*. London: Zed Boooks; Johannesburg: Witswatersrand University Press.

Ngugi wa Thiong'o. 1986. *Decolonising the Mind: The Politics of Language in African Literature*. London: James Currey.

Plastow, Jane. 1996. *African Theatre and Politics: The Evolution of Theatre in Ethiopia, Tanzania and Zimbabwe*. Amsterdam and Atlanta: Editions Rodopi BV.

DAVID KERR

THEATER: DURO LADIPO AND YORUBA FOLK THEATER

Duro Ladipo was born in Oshogbo, Oshun (Nigeria) on December 18, 1931. His father was an Anglican clergyman who tried to raise his son according to Christian ideals. Ladipo was an active member of the church choir and exhibited a rare talent for song composition, especially during the annual cantata (Service of Songs). In his compositions, he deviated from the normal tradition of songs composed according to the pattern of English hymns. He adapted traditional Yoruba religious tunes to Christian religious songs. This was not well received by the mainstream church leaders. He was sharply criticized and was forced to incorporate songs from English hymns into his composition during a particular service of songs.

Ladipo, however was not to be discouraged by the criticism of the church leaders. He introduced the traditional *dundun* (talking drum, which was then regarded as appropriate only for the sacred Yoruba music of services for Shango, and for Egungun masquerades) to his composition of Christian songs. He was not only criticized for attempting to covertly introduce "paganism" into Christianity; he was barred from presenting his composition during the cantata. He realized that the church was not the right place for his music and decided to find a more secular site for his work.

In December, 1961, Ladipo was invited to perform a Christian cantata, at the newly founded Mbari Club in Ibadan. The notable founders of this organization for artists included Wole Soyinka, J. P. Clark, Christopher Okigbo, D. O. Fagunwa, and Ulli Beier. Ladipo's performance was well received. This encouraged him not only to compose more songs but also to establish a similar club in Oshogbo. He converted his Oshogbo home into a center for cultural activities. The center was later named Mbari-Mbayo (If I should see it, I would be happy). The center was formally opened on March 17, 1962, with the performance of his first musical drama, titled *Oba Moro*.

Apart from more than one hundred episodes of *Bode Waasimi*, a popular television drama series composed for the Western

Nigerian Television Services (WNTV/WNBS), he composed more than twenty full-length plays. The establishment of his cultural center was an epoch in the history of Yoruba folk theater. Before this time, no Nigerian dramatist or performer had ever established their own cultural center and theater.

Most theater practitioners at this time made the urban centers of Lagos and Ibadan their base where there were many wealthy patrons. Duro Ladipo was dedicated to his theater profession without making material or financial gains his focus, the major factor that motivated most of his contemporaries to remain in the big cities. He realized that culture is dynamic; thus, his decision to remain with his people. In fact, it could be said that Duro Ladipo and his cultural center were essential ingredients of transformation of Oshogbo from a traditional Yoruba town to an internationally acclaimed cultural tourist center.

Almost all Duro Ladipo's plays were premiered at his Mbari-Mbayo cultural center, where the local audience passed their judgment about the plays. Ladipo then revised most of the plays taking into consideration the criticisms and comments of the people before taking his performances to the big cities and colleges. Before long, the Mbari-Mbayo cultural center had outgrown its initial purpose of a theater center. Its transformation occurred with the professional encouragement from Ulli Beier and Suzanne Wenger.

Wenger, a German batik artist who became a priestess of Osun, a river goddess, is known by her adopted Yoruba name of Adunni Olorisa. She became the major artistic influence of the Mbari-Mbayo center as it became a training school for young Yoruba artists from Oshogbo. Wenger still lives and works in Oshogbo where she has created many extraordinary shrines.

A series of experimental workshops were conducted at Mbari-Mbayo by Dennis Williams and Georgiana Beier for young artists. Local talents who were brought into the limelight as a result of these workshops were Twins Seven-Seven, Jimoh Buraimoh, Muri Oyelana, Adebisi Fabunmi, and Asiru Olaatunde.

All Duro Ladipo's plays (*Oba Koso, Moremi, Eda, Oba Moro, Oba Waja, Ajagunnla*) are very popular, but his masterpiece is *Oba Koso*. This play put Duro Ladipo in a class of internationally acclaimed playwrights. It has been performed more than two thousand times in Nigeria and in more than fifteen foreign countries; it won first place at the Berlin festival in 1964. The play later went on to win seven other awards at international theater and cultural festivals. A television version of the play was produced successfully by CBS in the United States.

For his role in propagating Nigerian culture at home and at abroad, Duro Ladipo was honored by the Nigerian government with the award of the Member of the Order of Niger (M.O.N.). He was a research fellow at the University of Ibadan's Institute of African Studies; the focus of his research was the Yoruba mythologies and history.

Duro Ladipo was initiated into several Yoruba *orisha* cults and in fact became a Shango priest (Shango is the Yoruba *orisha*, or deity, of thunder). Many observed that Duro Ladipo was possessed by the spirit of Shango each time he performed *Oba Koso*, which is a play about Shango. In some quarters, he was regarded as Shango's reincarnation. This view was reinforced when there was an all-day downpour of torrential rain and devastating thunderstorm when he died on March 11, 1978, marking the thunderous exit of a theater giant, a profound cultural ambassador, composer, and historian.

KAYODE FANILOLA

References

Owomoyela, Oyekan. 1977. Folklore and Yoruba Theater. In *Forms of African Folklore*, ed. B. Lindfors. Austin: University of Texas Press.

See also **Performance in Africa; Theater**

THEATER: POPULAR THEATER IN SOUTHERN AFRICA

In the precolonial period, many of the drama forms typically found in other parts of sub-Saharan Africa also flourished in southern Africa. These included ritual dance mimes connected with hunting rituals (particularly among the Khoisan peoples), masquerade theater, such as *makishi*, among the Lunda, Luvale, and Lozi peoples, and narrative drama, such as *nthano* among the Chewa and Manganja peoples. Owing to the strength of semimilitarized kingdoms among the Nguni-speaking peoples, the Sotho/Tswana, and the Shona, performances associated with heroic poetry constituted a particularly widespread form of civic entertainment in southern Africa.

However, the social effects of widescale colonial wars, land appropriation by white settlers, commercial agriculture, mining, and urbanization had a particularly deracinating effect on southern African culture. For example, the preference for foot stomping and clapping as a form of syncopation in dance forms south of the Limpopo, may be partly due to the ecological devastation caused by settler agriculture, causing a shortage of suitable timber for the construction of drums.

Racism became the catalyst for forcing many indigenous forms of popular theater to acquire characteristics of protest. Work songs, once removed from the context of community agriculture or fishing and put into use on the colonial estates, frequently deplored work conditions (Vail and White 1997). Similarly, spirit mediums during Zimbabwe's Chimurenga war associated veneration for ancestors with the cleansing potential of ZANU freedom fighters' military struggle, either in traditional spirit possession dances, Mapira (Ranger 1985), or in the propaganda performances, Pungwe, created by ZANU militants in the rural areas (Pongweni 1982).

The cultural impact of colonialism also had an impact on southern African performance. Imported European forms of popular theater (such as vaudeville, Christian morality plays, and at a later stage, cinema and radio drama), as well as European rituals (such as military parades and Christian worship) all had a strong impact on African performance. Examples of syncretic forms, mixing indigenous and imported artistic styles (discussed by Coplan 1985 and Kerr 1996), include the morality plays associated with Catholic festas in Angola and Mozambique, the dance mimes of such independent Christian sects as the Zionist Christian Church, the Coon Carnivals of Cape Town, militaristic mimes like Muganda and Kalela of Malawi and Zambia, South African township musicals, such as those of Gibson Kente, and improvised African language radio plays.

More elitist forms of European performance, such as the literary play, opera, and ballet, also had an influence on popular African theater, particularly in the late twentieth century. Literary drama, promoted through the formal school system, tended to be elitist when performed in European languages. When schools' drama festivals began to open up to plays in African languages (like Setswana in Botswana and Seswati in Swaziland), or when university theater programs (such as the travelling theaters of Zambia and Malawi) began to use indigenous languages, on their own, or mixed with English, this became the catalyst for popular drama, not only in educational institutions, but also among amateur (and occasionally professional) troupes.

Theater for Development schemes, promoted by government departments, educational institutions or donor-assisted, nongovernmental organizations (NGOs) contributed much to this type of popular theater. The Laedza Batanani Popular Theater movement in Botswana, through a series of local and regional workshops, provided an influential model for a theater that strategized solutions to socioeconomic problems through community-based, participatory, didactic theater.

Examples of independent popular drama groups, performing plays that ranged from commercial domestic farces through sociopolitical melodrama, through Theater for Development to agit-prop, include Kanyama (Zambia), Kwathu (Malawi), Amakhosi and Zambuko/Izimbuko (Zimbabwe), and Magosi (Botswana). In Lusophone Africa, professional theater troupes tended to restrict themselves to plays in Portuguese in the urban areas. The spread of the popular theater ideology, however, through the cultural activities of the Southern African Development Community, has seen groups like Producoes Ola of Mozambique, attempting to make their theaters more accessible to popular audiences.

Language in South African theaters has been complicated by the apartheid government's attempt to link African languages to the Bantustan concept, where each so-called nation (such as English, Dutch, Zulu, Xhosa, and Sotho), had its own cultural forms. The black consciousness theater movement in the 1970s tried to break down these stereotypes by valorizing English as a pan-South African medium of communication.

By the 1980s, however, more varied forms of protest theater emerged, linked, for example, with the Trade Union movement in Durban (the collectively created, Ilanga Le So Phonela), the liberal urban professional theater (such as Woza Albert! by Ngema, Mtswa, and Albert), or township protest theater (such as Matsamela Manaka's Pula). These varied forms of theater, though using different ideological and dramatic strategies, tended to have in common, an antiapartheid perspective and a multilingual code-switching flexibility.

The victory of the democratic struggle in South Africa has had a catalytic role not only in that country, but throughout the region. Within South Africa it has widened the scope of popular theater to include themes other than anti-apartheid protest. Within the region, it has given impetus to a growing cross-fertilization of popular theater ideas, techniques, and movements.

References

Coplan, David. 1985. *In Township Tonight: South African Black City Music and Theatre*. Harlow: Longman.

Kerr, David. 1996. *African Popular Theatre from Precolonial to Modern Times*. London: James Currey, Portsmouth, N.H.: Heinemann; Nairobi: EAPH; Harare: Baobab; Cape Town: David Philip.

Ranger, Terence. 1985. *Peasant Consciousness and Guerrilla War in Zimbabwe*. London: James Currey.

Pongweni, Alex. 1982. *Songs that Won the Liberation War*, Harare: College Press.

Vail, Leroy, and Landeg White. 1997. Plantation Protest: the History of a Mozambican Song. In *Readings in African Popular Culture*, ed. Karen Barber. Bloomington and Indianapolis: Indiana University Press, Oxford: James Currey.

DAVID KERR

THEATER: THEATER FOR DEVELOPMENT

Theater for Development is a technique of drama building which rests on an interaction between people who are affected by development projects, and those who initiate such projects. It has been used in many countries of Africa since the 1970s. There are two basic forms.

Firstly, it can be initiated by a government or non-government agency (NGO) as a means of promoting a particular message suited to its purpose. This is sometimes called Campaign Theater because it has been widely used in campaigns with specific goals such as the promotion of good health (vaccination, clean water, safe sexual behavior) and in HIV/AIDS information campaigns, as well as in education-oriented strategies. This approach is didactic in orientation and seeks to communicate a message from the agency to the recipient people.

The second form is as an open-ended strategy for giving people an opportunity to identify, address, and analyze issues that they consider to be of primary importance to their daily lives. This is a participatory strategy, seeking only to provide an opportunity and a platform for people to focus their concerns and to articulate them in familiar forms of performance. In this latter approach, the people are in control of both the technique and the content. It is oriented toward interrogating issues arising in response to the presence or absence of "development," that is, the social and physical changes brought about by national and international agency, whether governmental or nongovernmental.

Within government social departments and donor aid agencies, this form of Theater for Development has found itself frequently (and perhaps increasingly) constrained by a direct cause-analysis-action paradigm identifying it as a theater of social information and social education. This form of Theater for Development reverses the direction of the flow of information between "developers" and the "developed." It does this by using familiar forms of performance that help to instill in people a sense of their own worth, respect for their own forms of articulation, and gives them the confidence to explore beyond present knowledge. By its very nature, dramatization approaches the unknown. It is creative, theatrical and spectacular. This form of Theater for Development not only goes beyond a simplistic didactic mode, but also eschews didacticism altogether in favor of a theater that is neither mechanical nor prescriptive, but exploratory and forever incomplete, open to new interpretations and new developments.

Theater for Development is not a technique in the service of the development industry. On the contrary, it is a technique of interrogating approaches to development so that those most affected can intervene in top-down approaches and determine the extent and nature of their engagement.

The lineage of Theater for Development is usually traced from Paulo Freire's *Pedagogy of the Oppressed* (1972) through Augusto Boal's experimental theater work in Brazil as recounted in his book, *Theater of the Oppressed* (1979). These very general beginnings were themselves part of the shift in arts practice and in the thinking about the arts that took place during the 1960s from arts for the people to arts by the people. The content and personnel of Theater for Development derive from "on-the-ground" situations and embrace the logic of a Freireian-Boalian paradigm of direct fictionalizing and dramatizing that lead ideally to action in real life.

Theater for Development provides a fictional framework within which people explore their own real lives and is designed to create a deeply affecting encounter between its participant-audience and its participant-performers, so that each individual acquires a changed mode of interacting with reality. In Freireian parlance, this is called "conscientization." Boal describe the technique as a "rehearsal for life," but in many instances, people have used it not only as a "rehearsal" but as an actual defining moment for coming to terms with and taking control of change in their society.

The early experiments in "community" theater that took place in Botswana, Zambia, Malawi, and Sierra Leone were developed more fully in Nigeria over many years in Amadu Bello University by Oga S. Abah and his team. They emphasized and developed a fully interactive process of drama building between local people and "resource persons," the experienced personnel of the Theater for Development.

Gradually, this interactive form has become the most successful and is now the most sought after by development agencies keen to explore "participatory processes." Besides these first few countries, nowadays, Theater for Development takes place in most countries of Africa: Ghana, Cameroon, Burkina Faso, Senegal, Eritrea, Zimbabwe, Tanzania, Kenya, Uganda, Ethiopia, and many others. Along with Oga Steve Abah and Jenkeri Okworri in Nigeria, among the best-known directors are Rose Mbowa in Uganda, Penina Muhando Mlama in Tanzania, Stephen Chifunyise in Zambia, and Gonche Materego in Tanzania.

Theater for Development relies at every stage of the process on the contribution of participant-spectators to create the drama. Their interactions and reactions are not optional extras without which the drama will go ahead anyway, but rather the sine qua non, without which there is no drama. In Theater for Development, everyone who is physically present at rehearsal or performance is a participant-performer and a participant-spectator. The opportunity to shift more than once between the two positions is one of the mechanisms which gives Theater for Development its special appeal and power, because spectators can intervene in the unfolding "plot" and change it as it is being performed. In its shifting, nonliterate, analytical approach, Theater for Development is a committed, open-ended theater.

At its best, it operates through a series of very simple principles:

1. It recognizes people's existing skills in performance, analysis and articulation;

2. It uses as its story-line, the experiences of the people within the community where it is being created;
3. It fictionalizes that account so that no one is compromised by being personally named or identified;
4. It contributes through discussion to an understanding of the issues raised;
5. Its performers are from within the community;
6. Its audience is the community;
7. It offers no fictional resolution to the crisis within the drama, but interacts in a direct manner with the community throughout the performance and in post-performance discussion and action.

References

Abah, Oga Steve. 1997. *Performing Life: Case Studies in the Practice of Theater for Development*. Zaria, Nigeria: Shekut.
———. 2002. Creativity, Participation and Change in Theatre for Development Practice. In *The Performance Arts in Africa: A Reader*, ed. F. Harding. NY: Routledge.
Boal, Augusto. 1979. *Theater of the Oppressed*. London: Pluto Press.
Freire, Paulo. 1972. *Pedagogy of the Oppressed*. London: Penguin Books.
Harding, Frances. 1998. Neither "Fixed Masterpiece" nor "Popular Distraction": Voice, Transformation and Encounter in Theatre for Development. In *African Theatre for Development: Art for Self determination*, ed. K. Salhi, Exeter, UK: Intellect Press.
———. 1998. Fifteen Years Between: Benue & Katsina Workshops. In *African Theatre in Development*, ed. M. Bnaham, J. Gibbs, and F. Osofisan. Oxford, UK: James Currey.
Kilo, Asheri. 2002. The Language of Anglophone Cameroon Drama. In *The Performance Arts in Africa: A Reader*, ed. F. Harding, NY: Routledge.
Mda, Zakes. 1993. *When People Play People: Development Communication through Theatre*. Johannesburg, South Africa: University of Witswatersrand; London: Zed.

FRANCES HARDING

See also **Government Policies toward Folklore**

THEATER: YORUBA FOLK THEATER

Centered in western Nigeria, the Yoruba folk theater has its origins in Alaringo (traveling dance troupe). Alaringo first emerged from the dramatic roots of the Egungun masquerades, which honored the ancestors, and initially all participants came from the same patrilineage. But when Ologin Ologbojo, the head of the court entertainment during the reign of Alaafin Ogbolu, died, the kingship was given to Esa-Ogbin, a maternal relation. Esa-Ogbin is generally credited with the professionalization of masquerades. Although Ologbojo only performed for Alaafin and his royal guests by flattering and amusing them, Esa-Ogbin took the theater to the masses. Through him, the theater became popular and attracted people from other lineages who wished to work in theater. These performances continue to entertain Yoruba communities.

The acting troupes move from one town to another; they have historically often been exposed to dangerous situations. As a result of this, they relied heavily on the Egungun association for protection. In some villages, members of the troupe are regarded as lazy rogues and vagabonds. Nevertheless, they are usually well received when they arrive for their performances.

The nature of the troupe's performance depends on whether the troupe is invited to the village, and if invited, who sponsors the troupe. On certain occasions, the troupe may be invited by the Oba (traditional ruler). The audience is usually limited to the Oba's royal guests and the nobles in the village. The troupe may also be invited by Alagbaa, the head of the Egungun association in the town. However, it may also go to a village to perform without actually being invited. Either way, the troupe must first go to the house of the Alagbaa to pay homage and gain permission to perform. Without this important step, the troupe will not be allowed to perform in the community. Usually, the performance venue is the market square or the front yard of the Alagbaa's house. The role of the Alagbaa is crucial before, during, and after the troupes's performance. All necessary groundwork and preparations prior to the arrival of the troupe should be done by the Alagbaa. When the troupe arrives, the Alagbaa also accompanies the troupe while they dance around the village to publicize their arrival and to announce the venue of the performance.

The venue is an open ground and not an elevated or raised platform, and it is encircled by the audience. The space within the circle depends on the type of dance or dramatic sketch the troupe is performing and also on how orderly the audience is. Therefore, the circle formed by the audience can sometimes contract or expand. No entrance fee is charged because it is a sort of open show. However, a good performance is rewarded by the appreciative audience with money and gifts, such as new cloth and even new wives.

The presentation of the drama can be divided into three parts. The opening comprises the signature tune of the troupe, which pays homage to Olodumare (Almighty God), homage to Esa Ogbin (the founding father of the Egungun association as a professional entertainment guild), and homage to the other pioneers of the profession. The opening must also include the introduction of the leader of the troupe, who is usually the lead chanter/vocalist. This introduction usually includes a list of activities and attributes which portray him as a hero and a great performer. Lastly, the opening must include greetings and the welcoming of important members of the audience to the show.

After the opening is the actual performance, which usually comprises different types of acrobatic dances, dramatic sketches, and at times magical displays of various sorts. The closing is the grand finale, which comprises the farewell songs and expressions of gratitude to the patrons, not only for the money and the gifts but also for patiently staying until the end of the performance.

In certain situations, the drama sketches may be a social or political satire, which may be too critical or controversial, and thus displease the ruler. The traditional ruler in such a situation may order the performance to be brought to an abrupt end and order the troupe out of his domain.

The first Yoruba professional theater group was that of Hubert Ogunde, formed in 1946. The name of the group at its formation was the Africa Music and Research Party. Among his earlier plays are *Tiger's Empire, Darkness and Light,* and *Mr. Devil's Money.*

Ogunde, a former police constable, was born in 1916 at Ososa, Ogun State of Nigeria. He gradually shifted the focus of his plays from biblical themes to politics. This shift is explained by the fact that this period following World War II was marked by the political activity of various nationalist movements fighting for political independence throughout Africa. Ogunde's plays were his contribution to the struggle against colonialism. Among Ogunde's plays with political themes are *Strike and Hunger* (1946), *Towards Liberty* (1947), *Worse than Crime,* and *Bread and Bullet* (1950).

For a long time, Ogunde dominated not only the Yoruba theatrical scene, but that of all of Nigeria. His audience grew to include various ethnic groups of Nigeria. The reason for this is in part due to the fact that he performed most of his plays at this time both in Yoruba and English. Because of the popularity of his plays and their impact on the public, the colonial administration attempted to suppress Ogunde's work. *Strike and Hunger* and *Bread and Bullet* were both banned at various times, and Ogunde was fined.

Even after Nigeria gained independence, Ogunde's plays continued to focus on political themes. His monumental play *Yoruba Ronu* (Yoruba Think) satirized the intraparty crises that engulfed the Action Group, the political party that was controlling the Western Nigerian government. *Yoruba Ronu* is a clarion call for unity among the Yorubas in the face of divisive external forces. The play was not well received by the government; it was banned and Ogunde was barred from performing anywhere in the region.

Ogunde's popularity continued to rise. The ban on Ogunde was lifted by the military government in 1966. In 1967, Ogunde's theater represented Nigeria in EXPO '67 in Montreal, Canada after which the group undertook a much acclaimed tour of the United States. In the 1970s, Ogunde decided to try filmmaking. His first movie was a monumental success; it was not only shown throughout West Africa, but in many European cities. This film, *Aiye,* was followed by *Jaiyesimi, Aropin ni tenia,* and *Ayanmo.* Ogunde is generally regarded as the "Father of Nigerian Theater."

Another towering figure in Yoruba theater is Akin Ogungbe. Most of the second generation of Yoruba theater practitioners were trained by Akin Ogungbe, including Isola Ogunsola, Jimoh Aliu, and Baba Ijesa.

Kola Ogunmola is another important artist of the Yoruba theater. Very popular among the people, his most famous play is *Omuti,* which is based on Amos Tutuola's *Palmwine Drunkard* which was loosely based, in turn, on Yoruba folktales. Notable Yoruba theater practitioners trained by Ogunmola include Ray Ejiwumi and Fabusola.

As Ogunmola's popularity continued to grow, a great tragedy struck. He became paralyzed on stage during one of his performances. For years, his theater group was dormant because he was being carried from one healing home to another in search of cure. In 1972, the news of his recovery was received enthusiastically by all theater lovers. In a short time, Ogunmola staged a come back. He was again on the road, taking his theater from one city to another. In all the cities where he performed, the halls were always packed full; but at the height of his popularity, his death was suddenly announced. It was believed in many quarters that he worked too hard too soon after his recovery.

Another aspect of Yoruba folk theater is comedy. In this regard, Moses Olaiya, a.k.a Baba Sala, is a pioneering Yoruba theater comedian. His Alawada group became so popular that many of the theater groups which formed in the early and mid-1970s followed the pattern of Moses Olaiya's Alawada group.

The high degree of literacy among the Yoruba, particularly in the Yoruba language, has contributed to the popularity of *atoka*, a Yoruba "photo play" magazine which was introduced in the 1970s by West African Publishing Company, also publishers of *Spear* and *Drum* magazines. Yoruba theater practitioners were selected every month for performance of their play, during which all the scenes in the play were recorded in photographs and every character's utterances were transcribed. The "photo play" magazine became a great commercial success.

Another important factor that has contributed to the growth of Yoruba folk theater is the role of Western Nigerian Television, Ibadan, which happened to be the first television station in Africa. Theatrical productions were often shown in prime time slots. The television station also embarked on a program of talent hunts, whereby many new talents were discovered. Also, the television station commissions theater groups to produce special plays for the station's yearly anniversary, which lasts an entire month every October. Drama presentations usually constitute about 60 percent of the anniversary's programs.

However, radical changes are taking place in the production of Yoruba folk theater. These changes are being brought about by the effects of a profound media transformation. With the advent of cinematography and video production of most plays, most theater groups are disintegrating. Most artists now see themselves as individual stars and no longer a members of a particular theater group. They are free to star in or feature in any movie or video production of any play. Live stage performances of drama are growing more rare. Instead, Yoruba movies are shown, and videotapes of drama productions can either be bought at video stores or rented at video clubs which can be found in every corner of most Nigerian cities. Most of the producers of these movies and video plays find active financial support from businesses, which consider movie and video plays another valuable medium for advertising.

KAYODE FANILOLA

References

Owomoyela, Oyekan. 1977. Folklore and Yoruba Theater. In *Forms of African Folklore*, ed. B. Lindfors. Austin: University of Texas Press.

See also **Performance in Africa**

TIGRINYA

See **Northeastern Africa ("The Horn") Overview; Women's Folklore: Eritrea**

TIV

See **Performing Arts of the Tiv; West African Folklore: Overview**

TOGO (REPUBLIC OF TOGO)

Located on the coast of West Africa and neighbored by Benin, Burkina Faso, and Ghana, Togo is a tropical country of 4.7 million people. Lome, the nation's capital, has a population of 513,000. The ethnic makeup of the country consists of more than forty groups, including the Ewe (44 percent), Mina, and Kabye. The major languages spoken are French, Ewe, Mina, Dagomba, and Kaybe. The majority of the country practices traditional indigenous religions (70 percent), while 20 percent are Christian and 10 percent are Muslim.

The Portuguese first settled here in 1471. The British and French jockeyed for control years, but it was the Germans who formally colonized the territory in 1884. After World War I, Britain and France coadministered it for the League of Nations and later for the UN. In 1956, British Togoland voted to join the then Gold Coast (Ghana), while French Togoland voted for full independence in April 27, 1960. In the years since independence, the nation has suffered from political violence and an unstable economy and government. Although a civilian government was implemented in 1963 after a military coup, in 1967 General Gnassingbe Eyadema assumed the presidency and still rules the country. In recent years, however, prodemocracy demonstrations have renewed hope that Togo will return to a multiparty system.

Togo's natural resources include phosphates, limestone, and marble, while agricultural production yields yams, manioc, millet, sorghum, cocoa, coffee, and rice. Principle sources of revenue come from the industries of phosphates, textiles, agricultural products, and tourism.

Lome, Togo's capital, is known internationally for its association with the Lome Convention, an association through which products of African, Caribbean, and Pacific nations are given advantageous access to European trade markets.

JENNIFER JOYCE

TONGUE TWISTERS: EAST AFRICA

Tongue twisters fall under the short forms of oral literature in East Africa. Other categories in this group include proverbs and riddles. These short forms share a number of characteristics, which include invariability, compactness, word play, and informality. These characteristics are related in tongue twisters. Since tongue twisters rely on word play, they generally appear in fixed patterns nearly all the time and there is very limited scope for improvisation or invariability. Since they do not change over time, they are able to retain their compactness. This compactness makes it possible for these forms to be so easily incorporated into ordinary conversation or performed in intimate and informal situations.

Despite these characteristics—or perhaps because of them—tongue twisters are among the most memorable of all the forms of performance in the East African oral tradition. This is especially so among young audiences. This can be attributed to their versatility and utility in play.

Tongue twisters also have the function of testing a speaker's fluency in a language. They require the speaker to utter without hesitation or faltering, a sequence of words with particular difficulties in articulation. The words themselves have a basic meaning, usually of a jocular nature, and part of the fun of performing tongue twisters consists in the likelihood that distortion of the utterance, due to the articulation problems, will result in distortion or confusion of meaning.

Structurally, tongue twisters hinge mainly on both alliteration, the repetition of a series of consonants, and assonance, the repetition of a series of vowels. Below are examples from selected communities in East Africa. Since tongue twisters depend on grammatical structures of the language, they loose their structural arrangement and artistic appeal upon translation. An effort is however made to provider a phonological transcription to enable nonnative speakers experience the effect of the tongue twisters.

Akawala akaawa Kaawa kaawa akaawa ka wa?
Transcription: /akawala aka:wa ka:wa ka:wa aka:wa ka wa/
Translation: The girl who gave Kaawa bitter coffee, where is she from?
Community of origin: Buganda, central Uganda.

Wale wale watu wa liwali wala wali wa liwali?
Transcription: /walɛ walɛ watu wa liwali wala wali wa liwali/
Translation: Those very people of the headman eat the rice of the headman.
Community of origin: Swahili, Kenyan coast.

Khaba, orakhaba khaba obabakha esibakhwa ta, khulabakha abene.
Transcription: /xaba, oraxaβa xaβa oβaβaxa ɛsβaxwa ta, xulaβaxa aβene/
Translation: No. Do not bother about maids, we shall do it (wedding) ourselves.

Omulukha khwomulukha kuno kwolele khubalukhi bemilukha ta.
Transcription: /omuluxa xwomuluxa kuno kwolele xubaluxi βemiluxa ta/
Translation: The arrangement of this occasion was not reviewed by the experts.

Tora butora okhutora khwabatori khwakhuhenga.
Transcription: /tora βutora oxutora xwaβatori xwaxuhenga/
Translation: Go on getting thin we have left the world of the slim to you.

Olakhalaka akhalaka khanje khesilaka.
Transcription: /olaxalaxa axalaka xandʒɛ xesikala/
Translation: How he is tearing to pieces my piece of cloth meant for mending.
Community of origin: Bunyore, western Kenya.

Kaana ka Nikora kona kora kora, nako kora kona kana ka nikora kora.
Transcription: /ka:na ka nikora kona kora kora nako kora kona ka:na ka nikora kora/
Translation: Nikora's child saw a tadpole and ran away and the tadpole saw the child and ran away too.

Kĩrĩgu kĩhungu kĩna kĩronda kĩa ndĩira kĩrahaica kĩhingo ta kĩhĩĩ.
Transcription: /kerego kehongo kena kero(n)da kea (n)dera kerahaisa kehingo ta kehee/

Translation: A huge, uncircumcised*, mannerless girl with a putrescent wound scales over the gate like an uncircumcised boy. (Circumcision was a compulsory rite of passage to adulthood for both boys and girls in traditional Gĩkũyũ society)
Community of origin: Gĩkũyũ, central Kenya.

Atud tond atonga, tond atonga chodi.
Transcription: /atud tond atonga tond atonga tʃodi/
Translation: I tie the rope of the basket, the rope of the basket breaks.

Apon ng'op ong'owo, ng'op ong'owo luar.
Transcription: /apon ŋop oŋowo ŋop oŋowo luar/
Translation: I pick up the fig fruit that falls down.

Acham tap chotna malando chotna cham tapa malando
Transcription: /atʃam tap tʃotna malando tʃotna tʃotna tapa malando/
Translation: I eat from the red dish of my lover and my lover eats from my red dish.
Community of origin: Luo, southwestern Kenya and southeastern Uganda.

References

Lo Liyong, T., ed. 1972. *Popular Culture of East Africa: Oral Literature.* Nairobi: Longman Kenya Limited.
Nandwa, J., and A Bukenya. 1983. *African Oral Literature for Schools.* Nairobi: Longman Kenya Limited.

MICHAEL WAINAINA

See also **Linguistics and African Verbal Arts**

TONGUE TWISTERS: YORUBA

Yoruba tongue-twisters are enjoyed by people of all ages. Although primarily intended as forms of entertainment, they can nevertheless have a serious purpose as well. During the Nigerian civil war in the late 1960s, military checkpoints used tongue twisters in order to verify a person's identity. Yoruba is a tonal language, which means that words that are identical in terms of vowels and consonants will have totally different meanings if pronounced with different tones. Thus, tongue twisters rely on not only acomplex series of consonants, but changing tones as well. The following tongue twister plays with the words *míràn* (another), *òmìràn* (another one), and *òmìrán* (giant).

E wa wo òmìrán
To ti ibomirah wa wo
òmíràn òmìrán wa
(Come and behold a giant
who comes from somewhere to see
another giant from elsewhere!)

Another example:

Gbógbó igbó fi gbó gbin gbòngbò.
(All the forest used all forest land to grow its roots)

AKINSOLA AKIWOWO

TOURING PERFORMANCE GROUPS

State support of folkloric troupes has led to the development of music, dance, and theater performances at a number of levels. Although some groups perform locally and relatively informally, others perform throughout a nation, and still others tour the world. These groups are different in function, and to some extent in form, from either the "traditional" cyclical performances linked to rites of passage and other ceremonies, or the professional popular theatrical troupes that perform dramatic, acrobatic, or puppet theater from town to town. However, the government troupes often borrow liberally from the themes and performance styles of other forms of theater. These troupes seem most often to operate in one or more of three modes: political, commodified, or educational.

Probably the most common function intended for folkloric groups is an educational one. According to the setting, governments sometimes call upon these troupes to illuminate a group's cultural heritage for them, especially to younger generations. At other times, the groups may have to represent the culture of one region or ethnicity within a nation to others, promoting tolerance and national cohesion. In international performance, they educate foreigners about their homeland's rich cultural heritage.

As in all nations, the line between educational functions and political ones is blurred, such as when national performance troupes are meant to create a sense of national identity and belonging across groups that are otherwise considered to have ethnic or religious differences. More explicitly political uses include theatrical and musical performances that are parts of political mobilization spectacles. These are dramatic performances meant to transmit party doctrine, and cultural performances representative of specific (but politically dominant) ethnicities, which are portrayed as representing the whole of a nation's traditional or folkloric culture.

Finally, commodified folklore is frequently part of the cultural landscape in countries with large tourist industries. African artists have been extremely flexible and successful in meeting outsiders' demands for aesthetic goods and performances, some of the earliest examples being the Afro-Portuguese ivory salt cellars carved by West African artists in the sixteenth century for European traders. During the colonial period, entire genres of carving emerged in response to European taste and demands, leading into ever more complex negotiations between buyers and sellers where "authenticity" became a major criterion of value. Similarly, displays of masked dances and other performances have been perfected for nonritual purposes since the colonial period, when masquerades were often used to welcome important personages, including colonial officials. Today, in countries including Kenya, Zimbabwe, and Ivory Coast, capital cities and other tourist sites offer numerous folkloric "shows," each attempting to provide the most authentic experience possible for its audience.

The international touring troupes combine elements from each of these three modes, often trying to educate, entertain for profit, and promote a political program at the same time. Les Ballets Africains of the Republic of Guinea is one of the most popular and successful folkloric groups in the world, and since the early 1960s, its annual tours of Africa, Europe, and North America have played to large audiences. Education has probably been the number one consideration in these performances, showing peoples from other nations, both in Africa and elsewhere, the tremendous richness of Guinean musical and dance styles and genres. In this way, the troupe achieves one of the major objectives of many African states' cultural policies: to recuperate the rich traditional culture that is said to have been lost during the colonial period. The claim is somewhat problematic, since it assumes that Africans did not continue to practice their religions, music, and performance genres (even secretly, when necessary) during the colonial period. Moreover, it accepts the opposition introduced during the colonial period between the realm of folklore and "tradition," and that of art and modernity. This dichotomy is well represented by the assumptions of some countries that local festivals and ceremonies are in no need of state support, while the state's artificial folkloric festivals and events require funding beyond what the public is willing to contribute.

This educational-recuperative program becomes increasingly political as the organizers try to negotiate the balance between ethnically specific and nationally inclusive performances. The Guinean troupe, for instance, made it a point to recruit performers from all over the nation, and to have them participate in the performance of songs in the languages and rhythms of every region of the country. The Bomas of Kenya, a cultural/folkloric group based in Nairobi, organized its performances in the same way, arguing by example that the various ethnic groups of the nation were not separated by any essential qualities, and could, in fact, understand and perform one another's music, theater, and dances within the context of their shared national identity.

There is some question as to the extent to which this approach to folklore has been convincing to differing groups. Although the history of aesthetic innovation throughout Africa shows a consistent willingness to borrow, quote, and appropriate both neighboring and faraway styles, the decontextualized juxtaposition common to the performances of national folkloric troupes may be less convincing to rural African audiences. As hybrid performance genres, they often present African "tradition" within the context of European conventions (proscenium stage, lack of larger social significance surrounding the performances, costume changes). In this respect, the troupes often receive warmer receptions from urban elites, international African audiences in other countries or at festivals such as FESTAC, or Euro-American audiences overseas.

It is this decontextualizing dynamic that raises the question of commodification as it relates to cultural politics. Les Ballets Africains, for instance, has been criticized for the exotic manner in which it portrays Africa, with scenarios of "primitive" rites, and the female dancers dancing topless through the 1960s. These qualities no doubt added to the troupe's economic success, while simultaneously undercutting the intended educational aspect of the performances. Although there are no easy answers to questions regarding the proper functions and forms of state folkloric performances, they are central to each African nation's choices about how to portray history, and how regionally specific cultures articulate their relationship to the nation as a whole.

References

Andrade, Mario de. 1982. Communication for Cultural Decolonization in Africa. *Culture* 8, no.(3):15–25.

Arnoldi, Mary S. 1995. Playing with Time: Art and Performance in Central Mali. Bloomington: Indiana University Press.

Kapalanga, Gazungil Sang'Amin. 1989. *Les spectacles d'animation politique en République du Zaire*. Special number of *Cahiers theatre Louvain*.

Kirshenblatt-Gimblett, Barbara. 1990. Objects of Ethnography. In *Exhibiting Cultures: The Politics and Poetics of Museum Display*, eds. Ivan Karp and Steven Lavine. Washington, D.C.: Smithsonian Press.

Ministry of Culture, People's Revolutionary Republic of Guinea Cultural Policies. 1979. Paris: UNESCO.

UNESCO Cultural Policies: Guidelines. 1969. Paris: UNESCO.

MICHAEL MCGOVERN

See also **Education: Folklore in Schools; Popular Culture; Tourism and Tourist Arts**

TOURISM AND TOURIST ARTS

Tourism in Africa has impacted indigenous expressive culture in many different ways, both positive and negative. The two primary categories of expressive culture that have been affected by tourism are the visual arts and performance. This essay will focus on the visual arts, which have variously been referred to in the literature as tourist art, airport art, popular art, export art, souvenirs, ethnokitsch, or curios.

Evaluations of African tourist arts have always been divided between those that view such work as having a negative impact on the artistic traditions of Africa, and those that consider it vital to the survival of both traditional styles and the spirit of creativity. The former, which regards tourist art as a threat to the cultural survival of "traditional" arts, posits that commercialization encourages shoddy workmanship through the limitations imposed by mass production and the decreasing expectations of tourist patrons with putatively "undeveloped" taste. Critics of commercialism argue that tourist art leads inevitably to the cultural demise of true artistic genius. Frank McEwen, the first director of the National Gallery of Zimbabwe, coined the term *airport art* in 1960 to reflect his disapproval of all aspects of commercialism in African art, which he described as one of "the saddest forms of art prostitution that ignorant tourists support" (1960, 39).

Admirers of African tourist art, on the other hand, value commercial developments for at least four reasons. First, they argue that the rise of a tourist art trade often leads to the continuation, or even revival, of earlier art forms that might otherwise have vanished. In certain areas, for example, where missionary conversion may have suppressed the religious practices which once employed masks and statues, banished art forms persist only as a result of their secular, commercial production for outsiders. Second, defenders of tourist art suggest that commercial production for export encourages young artists to develop their skills and aptitude as workshop apprentices and "line" carvers. Such abilities may then be transferred back into more traditional artistic practices for indigenous consumption. Third, from an economic perspective, tourist arts are championed as a financial survival strategy in areas where other forms of income may be hard to find. Tourist art networks employ not only artists but a vast array of related personnel, including itinerant street-hawkers, marketplace traders, wholesale and international middlemen, gallery employees and owners, and government bureaucrats. Finally, some argue that tourist art should not be viewed

as a degraded or inferior version of "traditional" African art, but rather analyzed as a category of artistic production with its own aesthetic sensibilities, merits, and values. Turning to a linguistic parallel to underscore this point, Paula Ben-Amos suggested (1977) that tourist art might even be compared to a pidgin language, since both are created as means of communication in transcultural exchange. Just as linguists confirm that pidgin languages are not "simplified foreigner talk" but complex language systems, so too one could argue that tourist art represents a sophisticated form of cultural expression which can be accorded equal intellectual (and aesthetic) value, and studied at the same level of analysis, as traditional arts.

History of Tourist Art in Africa

Although most African tourist art emerged after World War II, in response to greater numbers of foreigners working and traveling on the continent, examples of commercial production go back to the earliest encounters between Europeans and Africans. Among these are the so-called Afro-Portuguese ivories, dating to the late fifteenth and early sixteenth centuries. Mainly ivory horns and saltcellars, these works were commissioned by Portuguese sailors to bring home as tribute to their royal sponsors in Europe. Since the first monograph on the subject (Fagg 1959), these ivories have been treated as early hybrid commercial art forms; yet because of their age, rarity, and stunning technical virtuosity, they have not generally been grouped into the broader category of tourist art.

Until recently, art historians and collectors alike have often assumed that any art object acquired in Africa prior to the twentieth century must be "authentic." This term is understood in the literature to mean something "produced by a traditional artist for a traditional purpose and conforming to traditional forms" (Cornet 1975, 55). There is, however, a growing body of evidence to suggest that art objects have been manufactured commercially for sale to outsiders prior to the twentieth century. In the late nineteenth century, for example, the ethnographic museum in Rome acquired a collection of masks and statues assembled in 1887 along the mouth of the Congo River by explorer Giuseppe Corona. Given their early date, it was assumed that these objects were intended for indigenous use. Yet they were in fact made for sale to outsiders, and they cater to European stereotypes of Africans, especially the two unclothed male figures with exaggerated sexual organs. In a 1979 article ironically entitled "Nineteenth-Century Airport Art," Ezio Bassani concludes that "this unknown artisan must have worked on order, creating sculptures for sale to foreign sailors and travelers who wished to bring back from Africa curios and 'typical' objects" (1979, 35).

As the production of tourist art grew in scale and quantity as a result of increased foreign demand following World War II, different categories and styles of tourist art slowly began to emerge across the continent. Today, tourist arts might usefully be divided into two broad categories: (1) those derived largely from traditional object types (mainly copies of canonical styles of masks and sculptures from West and Central Africa), and (2) those developed purely for external trade due to newly formed associations with European and American buyers (the most notable examples of these developed first in East and Southern Africa).

West and Central Africa

Most commercial production in West and Central Africa consists of reproducing "classic" examples of traditional art forms, mainly wooden masks and statues, but also elaborately carved wooden spoons, game boards, stools, door locks, and headrests, terra-cotta vessels and figurines, as well as cast bronze figures, goldweights and other forms. Since the early decades of this century, artists have produced increasing quantities of objects for sale to outsiders. Much of this production has been spurred by the need for cash income, as the spread of colonial taxation rapidly disrupted the internal structure of subsistence economies. Although many artists produce for both local and foreign markets, novice and less skilled artists are often limited to producing for outsiders, because their work is not of sufficient quality to be desired by local patrons.

Among the oldest and best-organized commercial networks in West Africa is that of the Kulebele, a Senufo subgroup living in northern Cote d'Ivoire. Kulebele artists have long produced masks and statues for use in traditional religious activities. By the early 1900s, however, they also began selling copies to French colonial administrators. Since the 1940s Kulebele production has expanded to accommodate a much wider tourist market (see Richter 1980). Today shipments are dispatched throughout Africa and the world. To keep up with growing demand, Kulebele men carve in large, collective workshops where they often use such nontraditional tools as chisels, saws, mallets, vises, sandpaper, and shoe polish. As the market continued to expand and become more competitive in recent years, it became evident to the Kulebele that certain ethnic styles sold better than others. Thus, in addition to carving Senufo art, enterprising Kulebele carvers have added to their repertoire Dan masks, Asante combs, Baule figures, and other forms highly sought after by tourists. In her research on ebony carvers in Benin, Paula Ben-Amos remarked on this capacity of commercial artists to go beyond the limits of their own inherited style: "Carvers produce whatever sells, regardless of their personal preference or sense of pride in knowing traditional patterns" (1976, 327).

One feature that distinguishes commercial art markets in West and Central Africa from those of other parts of the continent is a large traffic in fake objects. Many foreign buyers are aware (through what they read in guidebooks, for example) that collectors value age and signs of indigenous use in their definition of "authentic" African art. Thus tourists often demand objects that look old and appear to have served (or been "danced") in a ritual context. In response, artists and traders have become adept at sophisticated techniques of artificial aging and creating fake patinas. Mashed kola nuts, for example, are applied to masks and figures to imitate the encrustation of sacrificial materials. Objects are held over flames to replicate quickly the smoke and soot residue that would accumulate over time on objects stored in rafters above cooking fires. Carvings are buried in termite mounds to stimulate decay. Sculptures covered with grain are set out in open compounds enabling chickens to peck at the wood, creating random "evidence" of age and distress.

While many commercially produced objects in these areas are replicas of classic styles (sometimes copied from dog-eared books on African art that for years have made the rounds of carving workshops) some objects have been invented or modified in direct response to consumer demand. Because tourists are limited in the amount of luggage they can carry, a high demand exists for small, portable objects. This has led, for example, to a lively trade in so-called passport masks, carvings that reproduce on a small scale the identifiable styles of larger masks. Some objects, such as Baule "spirit" figures and Asante *akuaba* images have been embellished by additions of beads applied with resin to wood surfaces. Many such designs are applied by traders or less skilled artisans after the carvings are acquired from workshop artists. This indicates that commercial manufacturing is often an incremental process not limited to the work of a single artist or to conventional time frames for artistic production.

Finally, tourist art in these regions is not limited to non-African buyers; it appeals also to a culturally diverse and growing body of African elite and middle-class consumers in urban centers, who acquire art forms as household decorations and gifts for relatives and friends. Many such buyers are not interested in replicas of traditional forms, objects they do not believe can be disassociated for them from village contexts and often potent religious associations. Rather, they favor nontraditional styles, including carved ivory fruit, malachite boxes and chessboards, ebony busts or animal figures, and wildlife, scenic, or narrative paintings, among other forms.

East Africa

Although there is some evidence that the Kamba of Kenya carved spoons, stools, and small ritual objects in the nineteenth century, prior to the 1920s, the Kamba certainly did not have a well-developed woodcarving tradition. A number of different stories recount the roots of Kamba commercial woodcarving in the twentieth century. Some locate the origins of this art after World War II, influenced by Icelandic Lutheran missionaries. Others attribute the birth of Kamba art to a single artist, Mutsiya wa Munge, a veteran of World War I who fought for the British in German East Africa (now Tanzania) and returned to Kenya, where he began carving copies of Maconde masks and statues he had seen abroad. A district officer is said to have seen his fine carvings and commissioned him to sculpt a walking stick with a human figure on the handle. Other administrators placed orders with Mutsiya, and slowly, by word of mouth, a small industry was born. In order to supply the growing market, Mutsiya trained his sons, relatives, and fellow villagers.

During World War II, soldiers looking for souvenirs in East Africa began purchasing increasing quantities of Kamba carvings. Artists responded by developing new styles and object types, including carved ebony letter openers and salad servers crowned with Maasai heads, sculpted warriors bearing spear and shield, bookends with elephant motifs, antelope napkin rings, and models of giraffes, rhinoceroses, and leopards. Although no two objects are exactly alike, the rapid production in Kamba woodcarving encourages stylistic homogeneity through imitation. This overwhelming quantity of uniform, assembly line–produced carvings has often aroused skepticism in the aesthetic judgments of connoisseurs. For example, John Povey, former editor of *African Arts* magazine, remarked during a visit to Kenya on the contradiction between "the pretensions of 'artistic' hand carving and the repetitious copies so unashamedly exposed in bulk." Yet, he went on to observe, "the little Volkswagen safari buses with their cheerful zebra painted stripes seem to deliver the visitors in unceasing hoards" (1970, 1).

As the Kenya government began to realize the financial significance of Kamba art within the overall framework of international tourism, the carving industry was reorganized by the Kenya External Trade Authority (KETA) beginning in 1977. This new arrangement helped to centralize production into four carving cooperatives now capable of systematically filling even the largest export orders. KETA provided links to international marketing organizations so that orders could be placed more efficiently, and encouraged "product development" so that greater varieties of types and styles were produced. By the mid-1980s, it was estimated that six thousand Kamba artists produced more than one million carvings a year, both sold locally and exported. In relation to this flourishing market, Tony Troughear suggested, "the day is approaching when it will no longer be possible to dismiss even much of the mass-produced carving as 'airport art' " (1987, 21).

While the Kamba had little woodcarving experience prior to their involvement with a foreign market, the Maconde, from the border region between Tanzania and Mozambique, have a long carving history. In precolonial times the primary patrons of Maconde carvers were local. Objects produced for consumers included masks danced at initiation rites, ancestral female figures, and elaborately carved snuff boxes. The Maconde continue to produce objects for local use, but starting in the early decades of the twentieth century—perhaps inspired in part by the Kamba example—artists began adding to their repertoire many objects intended for Europeans, whose presence was steadily increasing. Colonial officials commissioned animal-motif souvenirs, while missionaries encouraged sculptures of the Virgin and relief panels depicting the Stations of the Cross.

Over time the Maconde developed three distinct carving styles: a naturalistic one, known in Swahili as *binadamu* ("son of Adam," or human beings), in which individuals are portrayed in typical village scenes engaged in daily activities (an elder smoking a pipe, a woman carrying a cooking pot, etc). A second, agglomerate style, *ujaama* or "people pile," depicts figures stacked one on top of each other, suggesting perhaps a lineage founder and his descendants. Finally a more abstract style, *shetani* (in reference to evil or mischievous spirits found in Maconde religious beliefs), depicts deliberately misshapen bodies and distorted faces, sometimes with several figures entwined in a single sculpture. Some have argued that these images of wild demons and frightening spirits are "a response to the tourist's view of Africans as superstitious and spirit-ridden," and that Maconde art generally is "made to satisfy the expectations of customers who do not share the values or assumptions of its makers" (Vogel 1991, 238). Others suggest that *shetani* images are indeed an authentic, integral part of the Maconde worldview, and that those who intimate otherwise are motivated by their desire to degrade Maconde art simply because it falls outside the conventional canons of African art. Maconde art is "often seen as 'grotesque' by connoisseurs of traditional art—a normative judgment, based on the preference for the more 'classic', self-contained precolonial styles" (Kasfir 1992, 48).

Southern Africa

The modern Shona stone sculpture from Zimbabwe dates back to the early 1960s, when British-born gallery director and entrepreneur Frank McEwen provided the initial catalyst in establishing the National Gallery Workshop School in Salisbury (now Harare). He encouraged local artists to develop their skills in his studios, where he deliberately did not teach or offer models to copy, but simply provided an environment in which they could "draw out an inner personal vision" (Zilberg 1996, 83). The artists quickly began to specialize in the production of stone carvings, mostly of abstracted faces emerging out of a single block of cut steatite, which some have interpreted as the artist's personal reading of the traditional Shona spirit worlds. Although this art was developed purely for commercial purposes, McEwen took great pains to distinguish Shona stone sculpture from other African commercial art production, all of which he deplored.

What made Shona sculpture unique or "authentic," according to McEwen, was its presumed deep, spiritual connections to primeval Shona traditions found in the carved stone birds at the ancient ruins of Great Zimbabwe, its pure, mythological subject matter inspired by dreams and visions that reportedly appeared to the artist in spirit possession, and its independence from any external influences or market demands. Those who disagree with McEwen's position suggest instead that Shona stone sculpture is no different from any other type of commercially produced art. These critics take the view that McEwen was largely responsible for "inventing" the idea of Shona sculpture, and for concocting a corpus of Shona symbols and totemic myths with which to interpret the works, with little input from the artists themselves. Critics also point out that the term *Shona sculpture* itself is a misnomer, as most of the artists are not Shona, but rather migrant farm laborers of diverse ethnicities from Mozambique, Malawi, Zambia, and Angola. This ongoing debate over the art-historical status and quality of Zimbabwe sculpture is highly instructive, as it points to both the complexity and contentiousness of commercial production in African art history.

Conclusion

African artists involved in commercial production continue to be caught in a web of conflicting agendas imposed on them by those who consume, and those who critique, their works. Although some would like to stimulate artistic creativity among artists by encouraging experimentation with new styles and mediums, others, driven perhaps by a nostalgia for Africa's precolonial past, discourage any type of aesthetic change or innovation. Although some would like to elevate certain forms of commercial art to the Western category of "high" art, others insist that commercial works are unworthy of such honor and must be relegated to the status of mere craft. Finally, while some champion the economic success of struggling commercial artists, others view the financial aspects of the art trade as defiling the supposed purity of authentic African art. Against this polemical backdrop, artists across the continent nonetheless maintain their successful production of a vast array of art objects destined to satisfy the demands of the tourist trade.

References

Bassani, Ezio. 1979. Nineteenth-Century Airport Art. *African Arts* 12, no. 2:34–5, 90.

Ben-Amos, Paula. 1976. "A la Recherche du temps Perdu": On Being an Ebony-Carver in Benin. In *Ethnic and Tourist Arts: Cultural Expressions from the Fourth World*, ed. by Nelson H. H. Graburn. Berkeley: University of California Press.

Ben-Amos, Paula. 1977. Pidgin Languages and Tourist Arts. *Studies in the Anthropology of Visual Communication* 4, no. 2:128–39.

Cornet, Joseph. 1975. African Art and Authenticity. *African Arts* 9, no. 1:52–5.

Fagg, William. 1959. *Afro-Portuguese Ivories*. London: Batchworth Press.

Kasfir, Sidney Littlefield. 1992. African Art and Authenticity: A Text with a Shadow. *African Arts* 25, no. 2:41–53.

McEwen, Frank. 1960. Art Promotes Racial Understanding. *Museum News*. 36–9.

Povey, John. 1970. First Word. *African Arts* 3, no. 2:1–2, 92.

Richter, Dolores. 1980. *Art, Economics, and Change: The Kulebele of Northern Ivory Coast*. La Jolla: Psych/Graph Publishers.

Troughear, Tony. 1987. Kamba Carving: Art or Industry? *Kenya: Past and Present* (Nairobi) 19:15–25.

Vogel, Susan. 1991. Extinct Art: Inspiration and Burden. In *Africa Explores: 20th Century African Art*. New York: Center for African Art

Zilberg, Jonathan. 1996. *Zimbabwean Stone Sculpture: The Invention of a Shona Tradition*. Ph.D. dissertation, University of Illinois at Urbana-Champaign.

CHRISTOPHER B. STEINER

TRANSLATION

Translation, from the Latin *trans-latus*, "carried across," is described in some African languages as "changing" (Gbaya *kpai*, Lingala *-bongóla*; Swahili *-geuza*). Translation refers to the process in which a message that was expressed in one language for a first audience is "changed" or transferred into a second language for communication to a second audience.

Translation has been important throughout Africa's history, from the time of early migrations and empires up to the modern era of nationhood. The significance of oral translation from one African language to another is implicit in the central African phenomenon of secret languages that were spoken by young initiates, for whom the only communication with noninitiates was through interpretation. The role of written translation is evident in the history of travelers, merchants, missionaries, and colonial powers who communicated their message from their own language through translation to African communities and kingdoms over many centuries.

Among the world's earliest records of the history of translation is Herodotus's reference to young Egyptian boys who were taught Greek in order to serve as interpreters in the fifth century B.C.E. kingdom of Psammetichus III. The Rosetta Stone inscribed with Egyptian hieroglyphics and demotic writing together with the translation in Greek dates to the reign of Ptolemy V in the second century B.C.E. In the third and second centuries B.C.E., in Alexandria, the Hebrew Scriptures were translated into Greek, and during the early centuries C. E. the Bible was translated into Latin in Carthage, into the Coptic languages of upper Egypt, and into Ge'ez in Ethiopia and Eritrea.

The earliest written records of translations of Bantu words date to the Arab writers Hamadani and Masudi of the tenth century. The first known translation of African folklore into a European language is an Inhambene song in a letter by the Portuguese priest Andre Fernandez dated December 5, 1562 (Doke 1969, 2–5):

Gombe zuco virato (Cattle have shoe-leather)
ambuze capane virato. (goats no shoe-leather)

During the nineteenth century, at a time of great interest in Europe in missionary activity and in folklore scholarship, numerous collections of African oral traditions were translated into European languages (Scheub 1977). For example, in 1852 the Nigerian Bishop Samuel Ajayi Crowther published *A Vocabulary of the Yoruba Language*, which included over five hundred Yoruba proverbs in English translation. In 1854 the German missionary Sigismund Koelle published *African Native Literature, or Proverbs, Tales, Fables, and Historical Fragments in the Kanuri or Bornu Language, to which are added a translation of the above and a Kanuri-English Dictionary.*

The translation of African oral traditions continues up to the present day. Scholars transcribe and translate texts in an extremely literal fashion for scientific analysis. Writers retell folktales remembered from childhood and publish them for foreign audiences, as A. C. Jordan has done in *Tales from Southern Africa* (1977). Modern authors draw inspiration from traditional motifs and form as in the novels, poems and plays of the Nigerian writers Amos Tutuola and Nobel Prize winner Wole Soyinka. Or, an artist may adapt and illustrate a popular African folktale for a children's book.

As a result of translation under a variety of guises, it is true, as Roger Abrahams asserts, that "the oral repertoire of Africa is better known than that of any other area of the world" (1983, xiv). But translation raises serious issues (Okpewho 1992, 347–54). In addition to the practical problems to be solved, such as how to translate ideophones and whether to retain extensive repetition in written text, classic distinctions of genre may become blurred. Prior to translation, the oral text is transcribed, thereby transposing it from spoken rhythms to formatted lines. Is the artist's tale then to be presented as narrative text or as prose poetry? Is the song to appear as free verse or is it dance?

Ethical questions also arise. Folklore by definition belongs to the people, but an oral performance is created by an artist for an audience. In recording a tale by writing, by audio recording or by video, a record is made of an event, but what is that event and to whom does it belong? When a translation is made, does it reflect the social event of the performance, or is it merely a skeletal storyline? What recognition is owed to the performer who is all too often lost in the anonymity of translation? What degree of freedom may an editor exercise in modifying a translation to meet the expectations of a new audience?

Modern African writers and critics have brought translation into literary discussion as well. Some argue that their works should be written first in the mother tongue and only secondly be translated into international languages (Ngugi 1986, 27). Many authors, however, prefer to create their works in a language like English or French that will reach a wider audience both in and outside the continent of Africa.

In the polyglot nations of modern Africa, translation is a prominent feature of everyday life. The mother tongue is spoken in the home, a trade language is spoken in the market place, a regional language is spoken for business and politics, and an international language is taught in the schools and is used on a national level. Translation in a myriad of forms ensures communication in all spheres of life, from the artistic and religious to the commercial and political.

References

Abrahams, Roger D., ed., 1983. *African Folktales*. New York: Pantheon.

Doke, C. M. 1969. The Earliest Records of Bantu. In *Contributions to the History of Bantu Linguistics*, eds. C. M. Doke and D. T. Cole. Johannesburg: Witwatersrand University Press.

Jordan, A. C. 1973. *Tales from Southern Africa*. Berkeley: University of California Press.

Okpewho, Isidore. 1992. *African Oral Literature*. Bloomington: Indiana University Press.

Scheub, Harold. 1977. *African Oral Narratives, Proverbs, Riddles, Poetry, and Song*. Boston: Hall.

Thiongo, Ngugi wa. 1986. *Decolonising the Mind: The Politics of Language in African Literature*. London: James Currey.

PHILIP A. NOSS

See also **Callaway, Bishop Henry; Linguistics and African Verbal Arts; Ideophones**

TRICKSTERS IN AFRICAN FOLKLORE

A significant number of African folktales feature the trickster figure, whose exploits appeal to the people's imagination. No precise data exist on the percentage of the corpus of any culture's folktales the trickster subgenre represents, but by one estimate three out of five Yoruba folktales are about Àjàpá the trickster (Sekoni 1994, 1). The Asante, for their part, hold Anansi, their trickster, in such high regard that they assign the generic name *anansesem* (spider stories) to all their folktales.

Although strikingly human in his habits and tendencies, the trickster is usually an animal. In some cultures the spider is the primary trickster figure, as is Anansi, Ture of the Zande, and Gizo among the Hausa. In other cultures it is the Hare, for example among the Kikuyu Wakaboko, and elsewhere in East and Central Africa, Sungura and Zomo. The Tortoise enjoys wide popularity especially in western and central Africa; the Yoruba Àjàpá is a tortoise, as is the Kalabari Ikaki, the Mpongwe Ekaga, and the Ila Sulwe. Other tricksters are the Gazelle and the Jackal, who hold sway in certain southern African cultures.

Characteristically, tricksters possess some exceptional physical properties that awe their human observers, who, as a result, invest them with extraordinary capabilities in other regards. The Spider impresses humans presumably because it emits yards upon yards of fine, silky thread from its body, and with it spins webs that seem much larger in total mass than the body that manufactures them. The Tortoise performs no such magical feat, but its apparent agelessness, which its wrinkled, scrawny neck and its deliberate (dignified) gait suggest, and the hard protective shell that always carries with him, are impressive enough to qualify him as a trickster. As for other tricksters, like the Hare and the Gazelle, their qualifying asset is their physical agility. In all cases, however, regardless of the trait that initially qualifies the animal for trickstership, once it has attained that status it takes on other characteristics of the trickster.

The tricksters' endowments are such as confer on them advantages quite disproportionate to their size in the struggle for survival, especially in those instances when they confront such formidable adversaries as the Lion or the Elephant. Their world is one in which every creature must live by his or her wits or perish, and one in which all is fair in the pursuit of self-preservation. Accordingly, tricksters have time for scruples in their interactions with the world, their friends and neighbors, or even their own families. Friends and acquaintances who extend favors to them can expect no reciprocation; rather, they are more likely to receive betrayals that are often deadly as their reward. Family members are themselves little more than ready-at-hand sources of exploitable bodies. Apart from being ungrateful, unreliable, and dishonest cheats, they are also constitutionally averse to any form of physical exertion, instead scheming to gain their livelihood at the expense of others. These habits and traits ensure their widespread notoriety in their communities and beyond, but they somehow succeed in finding dupes on whom to practice their wiles.

Typically, the trickster tale begins by establishing a relationship (like friendship) between the trickster and another character. The two next embark on some joint venture, during which one or the other, usually the trickster, deliberately and premeditatedly betrays the other's trust. The conclusion is a termination, in one way or another, of the relationship that existed at the start. The tricksters' dupes (so designated because they often fall victim to the tricksters' duplicity) are characteristically much larger and more powerful than their nemeses, but their gullibility, slow-wittedness, or some appetitive weakness (like greed or excessive fondness for some particular food), makes them vulnerable to the tricksters' designs. For example, in a Yoruba tale Tortoise capitalizes on Elephant's addiction to honeyed bean fritters (*àkàrà*) and his vanity. He lures his victim to his death with the food and the assurance that the townspeople want him to succeed their dead king, whereas in fact the townspeople need an elephant to sacrifice.

The dupe's ill-advised, at times inadvertent, entanglement with the trickster does not always end in fatality. Often it results in no more than discomfiture and loss of face. The trickster repertoire of many cultures includes stories in which the trickster challenges his intended victim to a contest in which he vows to beat the latter at his forte. To stick with Tortoise and Elephant for the moment, the former challenges the latter to a tug-of-war, and secretly does the same with the Hippopotamus. At the agreed time he gets the two to pull against each other, each believing that Tortoise at the other end of the rope. The resulting stalemate results in a loss of face for the two powerful animals, and undeserved adulation for the trickster. In other examples the trickster challenges fleet-footed Hare to a race, and surreptitiously stations members of his family at intervals along the route. As Hare races towards the finish, a member of the trickster's family emerges from hiding just ahead of him, and he, incredulous that the trickster has thus far managed to get ahead of him, redoubles his effort, only to find the trickster already at the finish when he arrives there.

The trickster's success in his escapade is by no means assured. In quite a few instances he fails in his attempt to defraud others, himself falling victim instead to an adversary cleverer than he bargained for. In other cases, just as his dupes' weaknesses enable him to victimize them, so his own shortcomings land him in uncomfortable situation, sometimes resulting even in his death. The following Thonga tale of Hare (here the trickster) and Tortoise is an example.

Hare talks a reluctant Tortoise into joining him in stealing some sweet potatoes from a farm. When he is satisfied that they have gathered a large enough pile of potatoes, he asks Tortoise to go and check the entrances to the farm, so as to be sure that they will not be surprised by the farmer. Tortoise, correctly suspecting that Hare intends to trick him out of his share of the potatoes, suggests that they both go scouting, each in a different direction. No sooner is Hare out of sight than Tortoise scurries back to the potato pile and crawls into Hare's sack. Hare also sneaks back to the pile, quickly throws the potatoes into the sack, and hurries homeward with it. Along the way, tired and hungry, he stops for a meal of sweet potatoes, and is astonished to find Tortoise in the sack. What is more, he has devoured the better part of the stolen harvest. Tortoise quickly exits the scene before his devious friend recovers from his shock.

Incidentally, the foregoing story pits two animals with trickster qualifications against each other, although in this particular culture the trickster is Hare. Since each culture has but one acknowledged trickster, Tortoise appears here not in a trickster role, even though his accomplishment would qualify him as such. The story, thus, is not of dueling tricksters, but one in which an animal that functions as a trickster in one culture plays the dupe (or intended dupe) in another.

In some instances the repercussion for the trickster's miscalculation, or his yielding to his weakness, is some sort of permanent physical deformity. Anansi the Spider's dangerously thin waist is a case in point. He once learned that two feasts were set to take place on a certain day, and he resolved to attend both and gorge himself. Unfortunately for him, the two feasts were to take place at the same time, and at opposite ends of town, but his nimble wit obligingly suggested a solution to his dilemma. On the feast day, he tied two strings to his waist and gave one to one of his children, with instructions to proceed to one of the feasts. On the appearance of the feast, the child was to pull at the string, giving him his cue to hurry there and eat his fill. He gave the other string to another child and dispatched him to the other feast, with the same instructions. Unfortunately for Anansi, the food appeared at precisely the same moment in both places, and the children's pulling at the strings almost bisected Anansi at the waist before he succeeded in extricating himself. Similar etiological tales explain why the tortoise's shell is a mosaic of small panels.

In fairness to the trickster, one must concede that in some situations he is not the mischief maker but an aggrieved innocent, who wins the observers' sympathy when he eventually triumphs. The Hottentot tale involving Elephant and Tortoise is a good example. At a time of intense drought, Elephant prevails on Crow to use his magical powers to cause rain, after which he resolves to keep all the available water to himself. When he goes foraging, he leaves Tortoise to guard his pond and keep all other animals away. Tortoise succeeds with keeping all comers away except Lion, who gives him a thorough beating before helping himself to the water. Elephant is so angry on his return that he swallows Tortoise whole, a foolish move, because Tortoise eats his innards and escapes when Elephant dies. Tortoise is a sympathetic figure in this tale, which contains a criticism of Elephant's antisocial behavior in scheming to deprive other animals of water in an environment that rather mandates the sharing of that scarce resource.

In some tales the trickster's character and behavior are indeterminate, that is, neither edifying nor culpable. A Bakongo story provides an illustration. Gazelle and Leopard undertake to cultivate a farm, but Leopard finds excuses to be absent on the first two days of work. Thereafter, Gazelle excuses himself from the farm, leaving Leopard to do the rest of the clearing and planting by himself. When the harvest is ready, Gazelle invites his friends, without Leopard's knowledge, to feast on it. On discovering the depletion of the harvest, Leopard sets a trap for the thieves and catches Antelope, whom he kills for food. In retaliation, Gazelle and his friends entice Leopard into an ambush and kill him. They share his meat among themselves, and maliciously send the skinned head to Leopard's wife as her share. Ignorant of the sort of meat she has received, she eats it, and when, later, Gazelle taunts her with having eaten her husband, she deflects the blame to Gazelle because *he* committed the murder.

The anthropomorphic nature of the trickster is quite deliberate. The trickster is, by design, a human being in disguise, whose exploits may be highly entertaining to the human members of his culture, but, more importantly, constitute discourses on acceptable behavior. Whether he acts in conformity with societal mores or in violation of them, he provides the moralizer with material to makes his case. Besides, since the world of the trickster tales postulates an ethos of expediency, one might argue that for the most part, that is, with the exemption of instances of gratuitous contrariness, we should see the trickster's behavior as exemplary. The logic is, if survival and ease are the ultimate human goals, whatever expedient conduces to them is "good." Thus, even deceit that leads to survival and ease must be "good."

Studies that assign the role of the trickster in some cultures to a god, like Joan Westcott's 1962 study of Yoruba Èsù and Fon Legba, and, the Robert Pelton's 1982 essay, which it inspired, are misconceived because of the human focus of the trickster phenomenon. For the same reason, instances in which the trickster has occasional commerce with gods, as Anansi does with Nyankopon, are exceptions rather than the rule.

References

Evans-Pritchard, E. E., ed. 1967. *The Zande Trickster*. Oxford: Clarendon Press.
Pelton, Robert D. 1980. *The Trickster in West Africa: A Study of Mythic Irony and Sacred Delight*. Berkeley: University of California Press.
Owomoyela, Oyekan. 1989. Tortoise Tales and Yoruba Ethos. *Research in African Literatures* 20:165–80.
———. 1990. The Trickster in Contemporary African Folklore. *The World and I* 5:625–32.
———. 1997. *Yoruba Trickster Tales*. Lincoln and London: University of Nebraska Press.
Sekoni, Ropo. 1994. *Folk Poetics: A Semiotic Study of Yoruba Trickster Tales*. Westport, Conn.: Greenwood.
Westcott, Joan. 1962. The Structure and Myths of Eshu-Elegba, the Yoruba Trickster: Definition and Interpretation in Yoruba / Iconography, *Africa* 32:336–54.

OYEKAN OWOMOYELA

See also **Animals African Folklore; Evans-Pritchard, E. E.; Folktales; Tricksters: Eshu, The Yoruba Trickster**

TRICKSTERS: ESHU, THE YORUBA TRICKSTER

Eshu is one of the major *orisa* (deities) for the Yoruba of western Nigeria. Initially, foreign scholars equated Eshu with Satan in Christianity and with Shaitan in Islam. Christian missionaries who came to Yorubaland and translated the Bible into Yoruba used Eshu for Satan. In the eyes of the early missionaries, Eshu was a devil and, therefore, an embodiment of evil. However, trying to understand Eshu from the perspective of Christian religion or Islamic religion invariably leads to an inaccurate conception of the deity

It is very difficult for a casual observer of Yoruba religion to understand Eshu and his place in Yoruba beliefs. Eshu is not the personification of evil like Satan or Shaitan. Nor does Eshu stand in direct opposition to Olodumare (Almighty God). In Yoruba religion, there are not diametrically opposed embodiments of pure good and pure evil. Rather, Eshu is positioned as one of the functionaries of Olodumare in His theocratic world. In Yoruba tradition, it is believed that Eshu maintains relationships with both the spirit and physical realms. Eshu is the bearer of sacrifices made by human beings to Olodumare and the *orisha*. Because he acts as a messenger or go-between for divinity and humankind, he demands a portion of the sacrifices for himself. If this is not done, Eshu will make sure that the sacrifices are of no effect and will instead cause more confusion and trouble for all. Therefore, whenever other *orisa* receive sacrifices, Eshu's portion is first set aside and offered to him. Apart from conveying messages, part of the function of Eshu is to report human deeds to Olodumare.

Eshu can also be seen as a police chief–type figure. He is ubiquitous, with shrines in marketplaces, at road junctions, and at the thresholds of cities or houses. Eshu is ambivalent and amoral in his actions. He is the essence of unformed and undirected potentiality; he is regarded as the Yoruba trickster god. He is seen as that part of the divine that tests people. Even though he tempts people, that does not mean he hates humans or that he only does harm. He does not discriminate in carrying out errands whether for good or evil. Eshu is used by the wicked people to cause problems and tribulations for others; he can also be used as an instrument of retaliation. He can create enmity between parents and children, or close friends, or cause a person to misbehave or to act abnormally. At the same time, he can give children to the barren and make the market women to record good sales and good business deals. Some people also employ him to collect debts from chronic debtors. That is why the Yoruba say of him "Ke see sa fun, ko se e duro de" (One you can neither flee from nor wait for). In essence, Eshu is seen as the divine enforcer, punishing those who do not offer prescribed sacrifices and also rewarding those who offer appropriate sacrifices. Without Eshu, the dynamics of Yoruba ritual would not exist. If he is not appropriately appeased, he will retaliate by blocking the way of blessings and opening up the way of hardship. Therefore, many people, especially herbalists, priests, and priestesses, maintain a shrine for Eshu to help them ward off evil and bring peace and prosperity.

Eshu is represented in several ways. He may represented as mud that has been shaped into human form, with horns on his head and a knife or club in his hand. Small carved wooden staffs covered with cowrie shells represent Eshu, with a "horn" projecting from the back of his head. He may be represented by a rock stuck into the ground, or a clay pot turned upside down with a hole in the middle. Black or maroon is Eshu's color.

His favorite foods are grains of maize or beans, black roosters, male goats, and dogs. Dogs act as a stand-ins for Eshu during sacrifice rituals, eating the sacrifices laid at his shrine. This ex-

plains the popular Yoruba saying, "Ohun ti aga maa je, Eus a see" (What the dog will eat, Eshu would provide it). Eshu's favorite sacrificial item is red palm oil (*epo pupa*). On every service day, red palm oil must be poured on the emblem or image representing Eshu. The belief is that if Eshu is "dry," there will be outbreak of trouble (such as a fight, fire, or epidemic).

The Yoruba see Eshu as a nuanced representative of both good and evil; the attention paid to him by th Yoruba illustrates their belief in, and acknowledgment of, the presence and coexistence of good and evil forces in the world.

KAYODE FANILOLA

See also **Verbal Arts: African American; Diaspora; Tricksters in African Folklore**

TRICKSTERS: TURE OF THE AZANDE

The Azande, who number some 300,000 persons, live in central Africa, across the modern countries of the Central African Republic, the Republic of the Congo, and the Sudan. By the turn of the present century, the Azande became members of an ethnically diverse confederacy under the political control of a single dominant clan, from which princes and kings were selected for leadership. Numerous travelers and explorers traversed Azande country from the mid-1850s through the turn of the last century, but it is the late E. E. Evans-Pritchard who is still regarded as the leading anthropological authority on these peoples. He first lived among the Azande of the Sudan in 1926, and went on to carry out about twenty-two months of fieldwork by 1930. In addition to his classic monograph, *Witchcraft, Oracles, and Magic among the Azande* (1937), he contributed a major collection of Azande folkore, *The Zande Trickster* (1967) as well as a unique work shortly before his death, *Man and Woman among the Azande* (1974).

These folklore studies are especially interesting because Evans-Pritchard himself collected only a few of the many texts included. The majority of texts were recorded by Azande students at the University of Khartoum, or Azande individuals who worked with Evans-Pritchard as assistants during his field work. In this light, *The Zande Trickster* can be reasonably compared to some of the work by Franz Boas, and his collaboration with George Hunt among the indigenous peoples of the northwest coast of North America.

According to Evans-Pritchard, Azande are clever and calculating in conversation: they recognize the power of words and therefore use them with caution and intention. This is illustrated by what is known as *sanza*, or "double talk." Evans-Pritchard characterized *sanza* as a circumlocutory form of speech in which words and gestures have hidden meanings different from their manifest meanings, generally of a malicious intention. As Evans-Pritchard (1962, 351) wrote, "Azande are under no illusions about human nature. They know very well how spiteful, resentful, jealous, envious, etc. men may be, and they are also well aware of what psychologists today call projection, that those a man thinks hate him are often those whom he hates." He continues (1962, 353), an Azande is "always on the defensive. He peers out of his shell, like a snail, and then withdraws, and he sees that all the other snails do the same." And, hence, from the Azande point of view, there is the fraility of human relationships: can one look into a person as one looks into an open-woven basket?

These comments provide a background to understanding the central figure of Azande folklore, Ture, who is an animated and incarnate medium of *sanza*. Ture is, in the Azande idiom, a half-animal, half-human being: a creature that is a typical character on the social scene, but one that is always and ultimately amoral. Ture is the dark side of the Azande side of human nature. Evans-Pritchard suggests that what Azande (and by extension, all human beings) see in Ture is the obverse of the appearance we like to present. People are, like Ture, really animals behind the masks social conventions force us to wear.

In addition to *The Zande Trickster*, Evans-Pritchard privately published an extensive inventory of Azande folklore and texts. These works are fully listed in *An Introduction to Evans-Pritchard* (Burton 1992).

References

Burton, John W. 1992. *An Introduction to Evans-Pritchard*. Fribourg: University Press of Switzerland.
Evans-Pritchard, E. E. 1962. *Sanza*: A Characteristic Feature of Zande Thought and Language. In *Social Anthropology and Other Essays*. New York: Free Press.
———. 1967. *The Zande Trickster*. Oxford: Clarendon Press.

JOHN W. BURTON

See also **Tricksters**

TSONGA

See **Southern Africa; Southern African Oral Traditions**

TSWANA

See **Southern Africa; Southern African Oral Traditions**

TUNISIA

The smallest of the North African countries, Tunisia is framed to the north and east by the Mediterranean, with Libya to the east, and Algeria to the south and west. One of the Mediterranean's most famous ancient cities, Carthage, which was destroyed by the Romans in 149 BCE, was here. The Berber Hafsids, a powerful Berber dynasty, ruled from 1207 to 1574. Along with most of North Africa, Tunisia was next controlled by the Ottoman Empire from the end of the sixteenth century, until the French gained control in the late nineteenth century. In 1883, Tunisia became a French protectorate, and while the 1930s saw much anti-French activity, full independence was not granted until 1956. Habib Bourguiba became prime minister, then president a year later. Although named "president for life," Bourguiba was overthrown in 1987. Although democratic reforms were introduced, a long struggle with Islamic fundamentalists has resulted in occasional violence and restriction of political freedoms, as has been the case in neighboring Algeria.

In terms of language, Tunisia reflects the same tripartite division found throughout the Maghrib: Berber is spoken by the minority (1 percent of the population) of original inhabitants, the dominant population speaks Arabic as the official language, and French is the language of business and government reflecting the later European influence. Nearly two-thirds of the population is urban, with most living in the capitol of Tunis. Tunisia enjoys a high rate of literacy—79 percent among males—and education is free through the university level. There are more constitutional rights for women than in much of North Africa. Of an estimated population of 9.5 million, nearly 8.4 million are Sunni Moslems. There are about 20,000 Roman Catholics.

While crude oil is Tunisia's biggest export, refined oil is its largest import. Agricultural products comprise 15 percent of its exports, primarily in olive oil, citrus fruits, and grains. The country also exports a variety of minerals. The tiny country has the fewest natural resources of any North African country. The recent economic cooperation treaty with Mauritania, Morocco, Algeria, and Libya may improve its economic status. Tourism, as elsewhere in the Maghrib, is growing. Ceramics are among the crafts for which Tunisia is well known.

PHILIP M. PEEK

TUTSI

See **Central African Folklore; Rwanda**

TWA

See **Central African Folklore; Rwanda**

TYPOLOGY AND PERFORMANCE IN THE STUDY OF PROSE NARRATIVES IN AFRICA

In the area of folk narrative research, two basic classificatory devices have proven their usefulness. These are the concepts of the tale-type and the motif. A tale-type is a complete recurrent tale typically found cross-culturally. Stith Thompson defined it as "a traditional tale that has an independent existence. It may be told as a complete narrative and it does not depend for its meaning on any other tale" (1946, 415). A motif is the smallest narrative unit recurrent in oral literature; motifs are perceived as "those details out of which full-fledged narratives are composed" (Thompson 1955–1958, I:10).

Some early attempts were made toward developing a "logical" classificatory system for tales found cross-culturally. One schema sought to order folktales according to their affinity with Greek myths. Others tried indexing the materials according to the similarities between a tale and its presumed counterpart in the Grimm Brothers tale collection. Meanwhile a more widespread approach used recurrent tale titles, salient phrases and themes (comparable to the current concept of motifs) to accomplish the task. Such unsystematic approaches have proven ineffective, and often misleading.

Furthermore, during the latter part of the nineteenth century and the early decades of the twentieth century, the European intellectual milieu was fraught with conflicting hypotheses and notions concerning the origin and development of lore in general and folktales in particular. Folklorists' circles were also charged with a keen sense of nationalism, romantic and otherwise, coupled with a sense of pride in lore as a national heritage and the moral right that justifies claims to national ownership of that heritage; consequently, the creation of certain genres of folktales was accredited to privileged "races," or national groups (which did not include any of the peoples of Africa). Such theories attributed the origins of the materials concerned to common heritage from a parent Indo-European language, to India, to early man's attempts to understand the behavior of heavenly bodies, to the power of these materials to survive the evolutionary stages of "Savagery" and "Barbarism," to the disintegration of an exclusive ritualistic liturgy of a priestly class, among other suppositions (Dorson 1972). Proponents of these and other hypotheses were able to display numerous examples that seemed to validate their claims. Yet, the facility with which examples supporting one interpretive viewpoint or claim could be cited, was readily matched by the ease with which similar examples were marshaled by exponents to discredit that claim. No "theory" was able to prevail on the merits of being irrefutable. It is against these impressionistic generalizations that the "Historic-Geographic Method" (also known as the Finnish School and as the comparative approach) was developed. The concept of tale-type was its basic tool and the international tale-type—in all its available variants—was its basic unit of inquiry. The ordering and classifying of the folktales shared throughout the world was the first step towards a scientific method.

Recently, there have been attempts to use morphological patterns as criteria for indexing and classifying tales. However, the proposed structural systems seem to be impractical for that purpose.

The overriding concerns of the Finnish School (and its historic-geographic method) were the questions as to when (the historic) and where (the geographic) did these remarkable cultural expressions originate, what was their exact nature at the time and place of their first emergence, and why did they assume their present characteristics (among other directly related questions). This interest led to emphasizing questions of origins and attempts to reconstruct the original text in which a tale was first told: the Ur form (or Archetype). Due to numerous factors, Africa and African tales were assigned marginal roles in these attempts. This goal of establishing a tale's original form, however, has not been attained, and, consequently, the school's importance has diminished considerably.

Identification of Tale-Types

Rarely does the process of identifying the tale-type to which a narrative belongs prove to be simple. Usually it is only within the context of evident variants, potential variants, and texts with some similarities, that the typology of a tale can be established. Similar but independent tale-types frequently overlap and share certain motifs or episodes. Textual variations generated by characteristic differences in the sociocultural milieu and the natural environment (i.e., a narrator's worldview) must be taken in account. Also, the contents of a tale-type may differ from one narrator to another, particularly along lines of gender differences, and from region to region; they also change within the same

community over time due to social and cultural changes. The process of type identification is constrained further by the nature of the *Tale-Type Index*. Naturally, Aarne's original Index was oriented toward Western European materials, and it became the de facto yardstick with which tales from various cultures are reckoned.

Applying the Aarne-Thompson typology to non-European materials for the purpose of identifying international tales produced uneven results in various parts of the globe. For many countries, or cultures, particularly northern Africa, the index proved to have only partial relevance. In some other parts, especially in culture areas designated as sub-Saharan Africa, the type-index proved to be of even less usefulness. Thus, the system fell short of its intended objective of universality. It may be argued here that much of that deficiency is due mainly to shortcomings in the editorial aspects of the index itself (El-Shamy 1980, 237–38). Nonetheless, the need for another system of classification emerged. Thompson wrote: "if any attempt is made to reduce the traditional narrative material of the whole earth to order (as, for example, the scientists have done with the worldwide phenomena of biology), it must be by means of classification of single motifs" (Thompson 1955–1958, I:10).

The *Motif Index of Folk Literature* was introduced in 1932 to meet this need for an inclusive universal coverage. However, if applied as the primary criterion and independently of the tale-type, the motif proves too fragmentary to be an effective and meaningful means by which entire repertoires are to be classified (Clark 1957).

As of yet, no satisfactory classificatory tool other than the concept of the tale-type has been devised. Nevertheless, Aarne-Thompson's *The Types of the Folktale*, as it stands now, is of limited applicability to African tales, south as well as north of the Sahara.

Morphological Patterns as Bases for Classification

In his innovative study on the morphology of the "Wonder-tale," published in Russian in 1928, Vladimir Propp (1984) introduced a completely different concept for the classification of the "wonder-tale," typically referred to as *Märchen* or fairy tale. He designated thirty-one sequence patterns (functions) which he argued constituted the characteristic structure for that genre of folk narration. Propp clarified that not all of these functions are necessarily found in every tale, but those which are present will occur in the same sequence (Propp 1984, 23–4). Functions (i.e., syntagmatic structures) are not determined by actors nor by action—as is the case with Aarne-Thompson tale-types—but rather according to the sequence or role of the action (Propp 1984, 67).

The potential for applying the new structural model for classificatory use generated considerable interest. With reference to East African tales, E. O. Arewa expressed his desire to develop a "typology based on structural and morphological criteria." He, however, concluded that he "found this approach to be an impossible assignment (1980, 6).

Another morphological pattern emerged. In lieu of Propp's thirty-one possible linear sequences of events (which he opted to label functions), Denise Paulme (1976) proposed seven structural models, according to a set of traits on a circular compass.

In terms of the nature of action/plot the patterns designated are: (1) ascendant; (2) descendant; (3) cyclical; (4) spiral; (5) mirror; (6) hourglass; and (7) complex. This model was adopted, in part, for classification of Malagasy tales.

In this respect, these morphological patterns, while very significant in revealing universal patterns of thought, have limited relevance in the task of indexing or archiving and providing researchers with variants of specific texts. Grouping thousands of texts in a collection (archival or printed) in thirty-one, or in seven morphological patterns—which are not always stable cross-culturally—would be of little practical use.

In spite of the fact that as classificatory devices, the tale-type and motif have come under severe criticism and a number of substitutes—such as morphological/taxonomic schemas—were proposed, they still remain the most viable work tools in the area of identification, classification, archiving, and retrieving narrative lore—the first step in a truly objective and scientific inquiry. The availability of a representative sample of the renditions of a single tale-type is the minimum prerequisite for any objective study, regardless of that study's theoretical orientation.

Currently there is no comprehensive tale-type index for narrative folk traditions of Africa and adjacent Middle Eastern countries. The available indexes only partly meet research needs. The two indexes which deal with more than a single culture area in Africa (Klipple's 1992; Aarne-Thompson's 1961), though valuable, are incomplete and outdated. An index that treats Arabic tales includes the northernmost tier of Africa (Nowak 1969), but excludes what is narrowly perceived as non-Arabic including "African" data (El-Shamy 1988, 154).

Due to the shortcomings and difficulties inherent in the process of identifying and classifying multiple cultures according to a single classificatory system, scholars opted for regional (or culture area) or national indexes. With reference to the African folktale, of the four major indexes, three address only "black" Africa, while the other treats partly "Arab" Africa. All four have maintained the concepts of tale-type and motif as the basic classificatory devices. One index (Haring's) adopted a different theoretical stance with morphological patterns as the primary criterion for classification; yet, the tale-type and motif were also used as the actual classificatory devices.

Antti Aarne and Stith Thompson's *The Types of the Folktale* (1961) attempts a global coverage and is the most comprehensive work available on folk narratives, but its presentation of the African materials is derived almost totally from May Augusta Klipple's work. Major deficiencies limit the usefulness of the Aarne-Thompson index. First, only a fragment of the published collections from Africa and the Middle East were included. Second, only a fraction of the tales which comply with the designated contents of the Aarne-Thompson tale types in the collections it treated were recognized; for example, of the approximately twenty-five tale-types clearly identifiable in Littmann's collection from the Tigré of Ethiopia (1910), only one (AT 1262, "Roasting the Meat") is cited in the *Type Index* (El-Shamy 1980, 237).

May Augusta Klipple's *African Folktales with Foreign Analogues* (1992) (written in 1938) constitutes the main source for African materials in Thompson's second revision and expansion of the type-index. It treats only "black" African narratives but allows for few black groups that are typically viewed as part of northern Africa such as Nubians (Egypt and Sudan) and inhabitants of Kordofan (Sudan). Klipple's index is based on the 1928 edition of the type-index and, therefore, it represents an earlier stage of the Aarne-Thompson classificatory system. Several "new" tale-types were added to the later edition (1961) of the Aarne-Thompson index. Furthermore, it treats only narratives with "international" typological qualities (mostly found outside Africa); such tales constitute only a portion of African narrative lore.

Also, no attempt was made in Klipple's published edition (1992) to update her list of tale-types. Numerous texts she identified only by key motifs are actually tale-types. These include the following motifs: "Magic Speaking Reed (Tree) Betrays Secret"; "Man Marries Girl Who Guesses His Riddles"; "The Pot Has a Child and Dies"; "The Ass Without a Heart"; "Reward for Accomplishment of Task Deceptively Withheld"; and "Reductio ad Absurdum: The Decision about the Colt."

Erastus Ojo Arewa's *A Classification of Folktales of the Northern East African Cattle Area by Types* (1980) is concerned with only one of Africa's culture areas. In congruence with Aarne-Thompson index, Arewa applied a "combination of both the thematic approach and the formal approach; the formal, being used only to classify formula tales" (Arewa 1980, 6). The formula, in this situation, is not synonymous with morphological (in the Proppian sense or that of Lévi-Strauss); rather, it designates a category of tales in which the form dominates over the narrative contents. The system Arewa actually adopted is "based on arranging the African materials into thematic groups with reference to the Motif Index" (Arewa 1980, 7) that offers more classificatory categories (chapters) than does the type index (El-Shamy 1995, I:xiv–xvi). He designated 4350 types (1–4350); the actual number of tale-types designated is far less, since a considerable number of the tale-type slots were left as blanks for future additions (a practice begun in Aarne-Thompson's tale-type index).

Arewa matched sixty-one of the East African tales he treated with their counterparts in the Aarne-Thompson index. Yet, scores of other texts with obvious Aarne-Thompson typological qualities were not identified. These happen to be tale-types which occur frequently in North African countries and the southern Arabian Peninsula. Thus, it may be concluded that the shared narrative traditions between that East African culture area and the rest of the world is greater than current academic literature indicates. This is also the case with other culture areas throughout the continent.

Examples of texts that clearly correspond to the Aarne-Thompson tale-type system include the following: Arewa's type 3248 corresponds to AT 136A* "Confession of Animals" (El-Shamy 1980 No. 51); Arewa's 3974 corresponds to AT 315A "The Faithless Sister" (El-Shamy 1980, 242–244); Arewa's 3492 corresponds to AT 872*, "Brother and Sister" (El-Shamy 1999, No. 46); and Arewa's 3346 corresponds to AT 313E*, "Girl Flees from Brother who Wants to Marry Her" and an adaptation of a tale similar to the ancient Egyptian tale of the "Two Brothers," designated as a new tale type: 318B§, "Murdered Person (Lover, Husband, Brother) Brought Back to Life through Repeated Reincarnations (Transformations)" (El-Shamy 1999 Nos. 46 and 25 respectively).

Winifred Lambrecht's, *A Tale Type Index for Central Africa* (1967) follows in the footsteps of Arewa's work. The author pointed out some inconsistency in Arewa's divisions of "animal tales" and "ordinary tales," and the role accorded the "dramatic persona in assigning a tale to one category or the other" (1967, 4). Her divisions (1–4550) correspond to Arewa's system except for one new chapter (nos. 4251–4450), which she labeled "Personality Traits and Customs"; the rest of Lambrecht's divisions, from number 1 to number 4350, duplicate Arewa's classificatory schema. These "personality traits and customs" are not character motivation. Lambrecht specified (1967, 58) that stories classified under this rubric "are merely description or statements, and, as such do not represent cause-effect relationships or the presence of lack and the resolution of that lack," as per A. Dundes's morphological schema (1967, 6).

Lee Haring's *Malagasy Tale Index* (1982) presents a synthesis of Aarne-Thompson's themes and Paulme-Propp's morphological patterns. Haring classified some 850 Malagasy texts (published in European languages) into seven morphological categories. However, from a utilitarian standpoint, classification in the Haring schema is actually achieved through utilizing a combination of tale-type and motif, rather than the structural attributes. Some of the tale-type identification seem to be based on superficial similarities with the tale-type. Such is the case, for instance, with the Malagasy tale in which a youth seeks "trouble" or to learn "what poverty is" which Haring identifies as belonging to AT 326, "The Youth Who Wanted to Learn What Fear Is" ("1.7.326"—Haring 1982, 227–30, 482).

Conclusions

A universal tale-type index or a motif-index, though theoretically possible to develop, has proven impossible to achieve from a practical perspective. Consequently, the need for indices addressing more manageable amounts of data pertaining to less diverse groups led to the development of regional indices. In all instances, the key concept of a tale-type has been maintained. These regional indices offer much more data than a universal tale-type index does. Unfortunately, all followed in the footsteps of the original index of dealing with undifferentiated "national," "ethnic," or "culture" groups: the individual narrator and his or her social affiliations are still not accounted for (El-Shamy 1988, 1988a). As such, these useful indices were merely reflecting the general view in folklore scholarship that culture differences exist among various national, ethnic, or racial groups, rather than among specific social categories within folk communities.

It is also evident that the typological qualities of an international tale-type in Africa can be effectively identified not solely through comparisons with its European parallels as designated in the Aarne-Thompson index, but rather within the context of other African counterparts. The developing of an inclusive and comprehensive "Tale-Type Index for Folk Narratives in Africa,"

which would build on that which has been accomplished, is needed. The new index(es) should also provide vital data about the narrators (e.g., gender, age, religious affiliation, social status, and so on). Such a work would provide scholars with an essential tool for approaching the complex and varied questions they pose about culture, society, personality, literary genres, world views, oral history and more significantly, the tales themselves and their meanings.

References

Aarne, Antti, and Stith Thompson. 1961. *The Types of the Folktale*. Helsinki: Academia Scientiarum Fennica.

Arewa, E. Ojo. 1980. *A Classification of Folktales of the Northern East African Cattle Area by Types*. New York, Arno Press.

Clark, Kenneth W. 1957. A Motif Index of the Folktales of Culture Area V: West Africa. M.A. thesis, Indiana University, Bloomington.

Dorson, Richard M. 1972. Concepts of Folklore and Folklife Studies. In *Folklore and Folklife: an Introduction*, ed. R. M. Dorson. Chicago: University of Chicago Press.

Haring, Lee. 1982. *Malagasy Tale Index*. Helsinki. Academia Scientiarum Fennica.

Klipple, May Augusta. 1992. *African Folktales with Foreign Analogues*. New York and London: Garland.

Lambrecht, Winifred. 1967. A Tale Type Index for Central Africa. Ph. D. dissertation, University of California, Berkeley.

Littmann, Enno. 1910. *Tales, Customs, Names, and Dirges of the Tigré Tribes*. Leiden: Brill.

Nowak, Ursula. 1969. Beiträge zur Typologie des arabischen Volksmärchen. Ph.D. dissertation, Freiburg im Breisgau.

Propp, Vladimir, 1984. *Morphology of the Folktale*, ed. Svantava P. Jakobson, trans. Lawrence Scott. Farmington, Ind.

Shamy (El-), Hasan M. 1980. *Folktales of Egypt: Collected, Translated and Edited with Middle Eastern and [sub- Saharan] African Parallels*. Chicago: University of Chicago Press.

———. 1988. Towards A Demographically Oriented Type Index for Tales of the Arab World. In *Cahiers de Littérature Orale; La tradition au présent (monde arabe)* 23, ed. Praline Gay-Para: Paris: Publication Langues O.

———. 1988a. A Type Index for Tales of the Arab World. *Fabula* 29, nos. 1–2:150–63.

———. 1995. *Folk Traditions of the Arab World: a Guide to motif Classification*, 2 vols. Bloomington: Indiana University Press.

———. 1999. *Tales Arab Women Tell: And the Behavioral Patterns they Portray*. Collected, translated, edited, and interpreted. Bloomington: Indiana University Press.

Thompson, Stith. 1946. *The Folktale*. New York: Holt.

———. 1955–1958. *Motif-Index of Folk Literature*. 6 vols. Bloomington, Indiana University Press.

HASAN M. EL-SHAMY

See also **Dilemma Tales; Folktales; Initiation; Old Man and Old Woman; Orphan Motif**

U

UGANDA (REPUBLIC OF UGANDA)

The East African country of Uganda is surrounded by Tanzania, Rwanda, the Democratic Republic of the Congo, Sudan, Kenya, and Lake Victoria, with a climate that ranges from tropical to semiarid. Its population of 22.21 million include the Bantu, Nilotic, Nilo-Hematic, and Sudanic ethnic groups. Major languages spoken in the country are English, Kiswahili, Luganda, Iteso, Soga, Acholi, Lugbara, Nyakole, and Nyoro. Sixty-six percent of the nation is Christian, 18 percent practice traditional indigenous religions, and 16 percent are Muslim. Kampala, the nation's capital and largest city, is home to 773,000 people.

On October 9, 1962, Uganda gained its independence from Britain after sixty-nine years of colonial rule. When the British first administered a protectorate over the nation in 1893, they used the popular colonial tactic of "divide and conquer" to rule the nation. Uganda's territory includes two distinct geographic zones, the northeastern plains and the southern highlands. Beginning in the sixteenth century, both areas were inhabited by several African kingdoms. Upon seizing the nation, Britain implemented a program of "indirect rule" through which the ruling class of the southern highlands were chosen to assist the colonial government. With this long history of a segregated nation, inter-ethnic tensions and violence troubled the nation even after independence. Uganda's precarious situation was worsened by the oppressive rule of several dictators culminating in Idi Amin's regime in 1971. Under these repressive governments, hundreds of thousands of Ugandans were murdered by the state. In 1972, Asians were expelled and Amin's rule became increasingly brutal. A force comprised of the Tanzanian army and Ugandan exiles drove Amin out in 1979. President Yoweri Museveni was elected in 1986 (after Obote's second government was overthrown in 1985) and recent years have seen a return to peace.

Uganda's economy has subsequently improved. Exported natural resources include copper and other minerals, timber, and fish, while the agricultural sector produces coffee, tea, and cotton. Principle industries include processed agricultural goods, cement, shoes, fertilizer, steel, and beverages. Unfortunately, Uganda was one of the first African nations struck by the HIV/AIDS epidemic. Many thousands of Ugandans have died of the disease, though the situation may be improving.

A number of Ugandan peoples are well-known due to extensive ethnological studies. A number of these ancient peoples, such as the Buganda, Lugbara and Bunyoro, have persisted and continue to practice their traditional arts.

JENNIFER JOYCE

URBAN FOLKLORE: A SUDANESE EXAMPLE

For a long time, studies of folklore in the Sudan have been biased against urban folk groups. This can best be demonstrated by the complete absence of urban folklore studies in the publications issued by the Department of Folklore of the Institute of African and Asian Studies at the University of Khartoum. An excellent site for the study of urban folklore forms is the Sudan Textile Factory, located in Khartoum, with tens of thousands of workers who come from different parts of the Sudan. Workers at the Sudan Textile Factory qualify as a folk group because they share a number of factors, such as their jobs at the factory, as well as their ethnic associations and the neighborhoods in which they live.

Most definitions of folklore are inadequate for such folk groups in an urban setting. In a context as dynamic as the urban situation of Khartoum, it is very difficult, and even impractical, to delimit genres. To solve this problem, a performance-oriented definition needs to adopted. This entry uses the definition given by Roger Abrahams, who believes that the term *folklore* applies to "those traditional items of knowledge which arise in recurring performance" (1970, 195). Therefore, folklore in this discussion is meant to indicate a cultural behavior and a communicative process. A genre might consist of words, such as nicknames, games, or physical objects. What qualifies a certain item for a genre is the way it is accepted, adopted, and transmitted among the workers. In any case, a genre is transmitted and performed through a communicative process.

Jocular Genres

Jokes and jocular anecdotes are widely used by the workers at Sudan Textile Factory, mainly when they get together in their free time. Though most of the workers have a rich repertoire of jokes, not every worker is a good joke teller. Since telling jokes needs a degree of specialization, only a few workers are accepted as successful. Those recognized joke tellers do not only narrate jokes; they also invent jokes about the people and the machines of the factory.

Generally, the joke is thought to be a playful judgment of something or someone presented in a humorous expression. The meaning of this expression is a code that is not recognized by everybody, but is easily understood by the members of the same folk group—that is, the workers. Ideally, jokes are new for the audience; so the joke tellers among the workers do not perform the same joke repeatedly.

Jokes inside the factory, as in every other place, tend to be in a series: religious jokes, political jokes, and so forth. These series are usually performed in joke sessions. Sometimes a joke might be narrated while all the workers are having a cup of tea during a break, or possibly in the bus on the way home from work.

Most of the jokes collected from the workers were told in joke sessions. In most of these jokes, the dramatic personae are considered abnormal figures, such as a man with an exceptionally large penis, a homosexual youth, or a dogmatic religious figure. But in the anecdotes, the dramatic personae are usually depicted as real persons, such as a certain colleague or a foreman. Prominent figures, primarily the president of the country, are often made dramatic personae for a good number of the jokes and anecdotes. In fact, this is not only a characteristic of jokes in the factory society, but it is widely observed in the Sudanese community at large.

Moreover, foremen and the heads of departments are central characters for a considerable number of jokes and jocular anecdotes. Ethnic jokes are also widely spread inside the factory. In these jokes the punch line or the main theme usually aims at making fun of other ethnic groups by illustrating the superiority of the narrator's ethnic group. For instance, there is a joke about a newcomer on his first visit to the factory that ridicules his naive and unsophisticated reactions, primarily his reaction to the whistle that indicates timing in the factory. This joke has been narrated in at least three versions. In these versions, the dramatic personae are individuals from various ethnic groups, such as Shaiygi, Dinka, and Mahassi.

Each ethnic group focuses on a specific individual from other ethnic groups. Such jokes might be taken as ethnic slurs. Inside the factory, each ethnic group has its own jocular figure who is usually a good joke teller; sometimes he is the dramatic personae of several narratives. For instance, the westerners have Abu Digne and the Shaiygi have Al Sanjak as the main characters. Here are a few examples of such ethnic jokes:

Al Sanjak's wife annoyed her husband by continually requesting him to bring her a pair of slippers. At last he promised her to do so. She reminded him to take the size of the slippers. He retorted: "I know it by heart since your foot is on my shoulders every day!"

A Westerner, seeing the River Nile for the first time in his life, exclaimed: "What a Fula!" (large water ditch).

An "Arab" on his first visit to the cinema was astonished to see film stars fighting and he shouted to the audience,

"Oh, men, this is shameful! Why don't we go and settle these disputes?" [This joke is told by someone from southern Sudan].

Jocular figures usually perform the humorous narratives in a sort of minishow. These informal performances often occur during breaks from work or after meals. In one of these minidramas, Zakaria, who worked in the dyeing section, performed a funny narrative, the subject of which was a clash between Zakaria and his foreman. Zakaria dramatized the whole episode and the audience participated in the show, which depicted how cowardly and snobbish the foreman was. In another performance, a Nubian worker acted out a humorous narrative in which he dramatized how he saved himself by escaping from a bar which had been raided by the police. Most of these minishows are repeatedly performed, so the workers are usually acquainted with the repertoire of the performer. In some cases, the performer might be asked to present a specific episode. In such cases, whenever the narrator happens to forget any detail, members of the audience are usually anxious to remind him. These performances, moreover, contain some elements of folk dramas, such as an actor and an audience. But they lack other elements, such as costumes or decorations. These minishows could be incorporated into folk dramas, but the fact that they are usually performed by humorous figures relates them to the jocular narratives.

Graffiti

A subgenre, graffiti, is one of those peripheral genres of folklore which are usually found in a recorded visual form. Graffiti is usually found on posters and drawings on walls, sometimes on doors or windows. Any suitable surface can be used. In the Sudan Textile Factory, this subgenre is widely observed in the dyeing section, and to a lesser degree in the weaving department, but it is hardly ever observed in the embroidery department. In the dyeing section the availability of the material to write with (i.e., the dyes) allows the workers to express themselves in graffiti. In the embroidery section, however, general cleanliness is strictly observed (another relevant factor is that there are more women than men in the latter section). Graffiti is perceived as shouting or boasting, actions traditionally encouraged among men but discouraged among women. Related to the graffiti are the posters that are widely used throughout the city of Khartoum. These posters are fixed on cars, walls, doors, and any other suitable surfaces. The major theme of the posters is the fear of the Evil Eye, and sometimes an eye is drawn on a poster. One of these posters was fixed on a newly installed electric machine, certainly in an effort to protect the machine from the Evil Eye. Sometimes, a wall might be decorated with posters that carry an advertisement, such as "My Toyota is Fantastic."

Women's Folklore

Several factors constrain observing and collecting the expressive behavior of the female workers inside, as well as outside, the factory. The percentage of the females in the factory is very small, not exceeding 1 percent. The majority are found in the embroidery department. In fact, this department is dominated by females, in sharp contrast to other departments.

Some folkloric genres might be considered a part of women's folklore specifically, such as folk dress. It is easily observed inside the factory that women are keen to adopt exotic fashions, especially Egyptian. At the beginning of the twenty-first century, it is difficult to find a woman in the urban setting who has *mushat* (the classic Sudanese hairstyle). On the other hand, inside the factory, the *tobe* (traditional Sudanese folk dress), still dominates among women.

In brief, women's folklore inside the factory is slightly different from that which is performed outside the factory, although in both locations their behavior and dress are clearly linked to their gender. Many note that the behavior of the women generally reflects the impact of the mass media, particularly television. This can be observed primarily in their hairstyles and the wearing of earrings. These fashions are mainly Egyptian. Egyptian soap operas and television shows are especially popular, and Egyptian television stars serve as models for the workers.

Both new and traditional forms of folklore are continually employed by the factory workers of Khartoum. Urban men and women of various ethnic groups continue to express themselves through folklore, just like their rural counterparts.

References

Abrahams, Roger D. 1970. Complex Relations of Genre. *Genre* 2.
———. 1976. The Complex Relations of Single Forms. In *Folklore Genres*, ed. D. Ben-Amos. Austin: University of Texas Press.
Ben-Amos, Dan. 1975. *Folklore Genres.* Austin: University of Texas Press.
Degh, Linda. 1972. Folk Narratives. In *Folklore and Folklife*, ed. Richard M. Dorson. Bloomington: Indiana University Press.
Farer, Clair R. 1978. Women and Folklore: Images and Genres. *Journal of American Folklore* 88.
Galal-el-Din, Mohamed El Awad. 1974. The Factors Influencing Migration to the Three Towns of the Sudan. *Journal of Economic and Social Studies* 1.
Gelman, Susan. 1978. Towards the Study of Postal Graffiti: Text and Context in an Adolescent Girls' Genre. *Western Folklore* 37.
Jansen, William Hugh. 1978. Purposes and Functions in Modern Local Legends of Kentucky. In *Varia Folklorika*, ed. Alan Dundes. Paris: Mouton.
Mahjoub, Asia. 1977. Tradition and Urbanization in an African Metropolitan Area. Unpublished M.A. thesis, Institute of African and Asian Studies, University of Khartoum.
Paredes, Americo, and Ellen J. Stekert, eds. 1971. *The Urban Experience and the Folk Tradition.* Austin: University of Texas Press.

MOHAMED EL-MAHDI BUSHRA

See also **Gender Representation in African Folkore; Northeastern Africa (The Horn); Popular Culture**

URBAN FOLKLORE: THE SWAHILI OF ZANZIBAR

Three factors have contributed significantly to Zanzibar's development into a cosmopolitan city. The first is its geographic location. Lying close to the East African coast, on the Indian Ocean, Zanzibar is well placed for contact with countries across the seas. The monsoon winds traditionally facilitated trade with the Middle East, and trade was also conducted with mainland Africa and India.

The second factor is migration. As early as the second century BCE, an anonymous Greek traveler notes (in *The Periplus of the Erythrean Sea*) the mixture of peoples existing on the coast. Through settlement and marriage over several centuries, a group emerged speaking the same language, Swahili, and sharing a culture that was influenced as much by the customs of Africa as by Muslim values from the Middle East.

The third factor is foreign rule. After 1498, when Vasco da Gama found his way to India via the Cape of Good Hope, the Portuguese, the French, the German, and the British joined the Arabs in ruling intermittently over East African territories. In their wake came missionaries and settlers. The Roman Catholic and Anglican Churches had a strong presence in Zanzibar by the end of the nineteenth century, just as Muslim clerics had in previous years (and continued to have). By the mid-1950s—less than a decade before the Zanzibar Revolution of 1964—European, Arab, and Asian communities lived in the Zanzibar Old Town. The Swahili however, lived in *ng'ambo*—literally, the "other side" of town.

A social hierarchy developed during the colonial period. Europeans were at the top, followed by the Indians, the Arabs, and lastly, the Africans, including the Swahili. Each of these communities brought to the island their stories and folklore. The British, as rulers since 1895, introduced stories from Europe into the country-wide school curriculum. Children learned the stories of Cinderella, Goldilocks, Little Red Riding Hood, Dick Whittington, Hansel and Gretel, William Tell, and Jack and the Beanstalk. The Indians and the Arabs also introduced stories in the classroom, but only in their own schools. Indian stories included the tales of the Moghuls, the love story of Nur Jehan and Shah Jehan, the building of the Taj Mahal, and legends from the *Ramayana* and the *Mahabharata*.

It is worth noting that Swahili perceptions of Europeans and Indians are reflected in their language, Swahili. Europeans (*wazungu*) have two types of fruits named after them: *embe ya kizungu* (a European mango), which is smaller than the typical variety and tastes different, and *ndizi ya kizungu* (a European banana), which is larger and sweeter than the other types common to the region. Until recently, one way of telling time was also spoken of as "European" or "zonal" so as to distinguish it from "the time of the mosque" used for marking Muslim prayer times. Europeans, as rulers, were also associated with military might. Quite a few dance societies emerged in East Africa, including Zanzibar, which imitated the organizational structure of a colonial regiment, especially the British model, with ranks, titles, drills, and other activities (Ranger 1975).

Indians were considered shrewd businessmen, with an innate talent for accumulating wealth. Swahili novels evoke two Indian stereotypes: the small shopkeeper who sets up his business in remote villages, and the successful urban businessman who employs the Swahili. The word for an Indian is *mhindi*, derived from Hind (India); the Swahili employ the term *mahindi* for maize as well. The commercial link with India is reflected in a proverb quoted in a well-known anthology by the renowned missionary William Taylor (d. 1927), who had worked in Mombasa. The proverb conveys the sense that, whatever their economic condition may be in East Africa, they are like any other people in their own country: "Hindi ndiko kwenyi nguo, na wendao tupu wapo" (India, that is the country of clothes [place possessing clothes]: and yet there are those who go naked) (Taylor 1891, 19).

Another proverb common among the Swahili concerns the Baniyani, a term that refers to a member of a Hindu community. The Baniyani were craftsmen, shopkeepers, employees in the civil service, or teachers. As Hindus, they cremate their dead, a fact captured in a simile by the Swahili: "Umeadimika kama kaburi la Baniyani" (you are rare like the grave of a Baniyani), which is usually told to someone whom one has not seen in a long time.

Although the Arabs were placed third in the colonial hierarchy, their status was considered to be much higher by the Swahili. Centuries of contact between these two groups had generated a closeness reflected in shared Muslim values, literature, song, music and other cultural traditions. It is perhaps not surprising that the Swahili word for civilization is *ustaarabu* (to be like an Arab). Interestingly, the word for culture in current use is *utamaduni*, an Arabic derivative related to the concept of urbanism. Arab urbanism finds ample expression in Swahili tales and stories. In 1870, Bishop Steere of Zanzibar had published volume titled *Swahili Tales, As Told by Natives of Zanzibar*. In his introduction, Steere speaks of the tales as falling into three categories, one of which is "a court dialect whose style is more Arabic in its forms and vocabulary than the rest, and is characteristically represented by a strict translation of an Arab story" (1870, ix).

Arab stories were more prevalent among the Swahili than were Indian or even European ones. Any average Swahili individual was familiar with Arab tribal lore. Particularly well known were the tragic love stories of Antar and Abla and of Layla and Majnun. Most popular of all were the stories of the wily Abunuwasi, a character from the court of the Abbasid Caliph Harun al-Rashid in Baghdad (d. 809). The poet Abu Nuwas (d. 815) was famous for his love and erotic poetry and his witty lyrics (he composed several poems in praise of wine). Abu Nuwas appears as a folklore character in *The Thousand and One Nights*. It is possible that the character Abunuwasi of Swahili tales is based on the character in the *Nights*, for he is now transformed into a clever and wily person who lives by his wits and is always willing to help the poor. The text, *Hekaya za Abunuwasi* [The Wiles of Abunuwasi], has run in many editions and is still popular. The following is a brief example:

Abunuwasi borrows a saucepan from his neighbour. He keeps it for some time and then returns it together with a smaller one of similar make. Abunuwasi explains to his puzzled neighbour that, during the period that the saucepan was with Abunuwas, it had given birth. Abunuwasi insists that the neighbour should keep the baby saucepan as it is rightfully his. Just to humour Abunuwasi, the neighbour keeps the little saucepan. Abunuwasi again borrows the bigger saucepan but, this time, he keeps it for months. One day, the neighbour asks for it, only to be told by Abunuwasi that, during its stay with him, the saucepan died. The neighbour is furious: "How can a saucepan die?" Abunuwasi replies: "I am afraid it did. You know that it gave birth. You have the baby at home, don't you? You know that, naturally, whatever gives birth is sure to die someday. And it did."

Abunuwasi's cunning is matched in Swahili lore by the ubiquitous hare, who appears in several stories shared with the peoples of the mainland. Another common theme is that of spirits and the healers (*waganga*) who control them. Thus, over centuries, the folklore of the Swahili, like that of many other peoples, has developed an inclusive, accommodating characteristic. The urban environment has provided a useful, and perhaps necessary, setting for this syncretic trend.

References

Knappert, Jan. 1970. *Myths and Legends of the Swahili*. London: Heinemann.

Ranger, T.O. 1975. *Dance and Society in Eastern Africa, 1890–1970: The Beni Ngoma*. London: Heinemann.

Steere, Edward. 1870. *Swahili Tales As Told by Natives of Zanzibar*. London: Bell and Daldy.

Taylor, W.E. 1891. *African Aphorisms, or Saws from Swahili-Land*. London: Society for Promoting Christian Knowledge.

Huntingford, G.W.B., tr. and ed. (1980). *The Periplus of the Erythrean Sea*. London: The Hakluyt Society.

FAROUK TOPAN

See also **Identity and Folklore: The Kunda; Indian Ocean Islands; Languages**

V

VERBAL ARTS: AFRICAN AMERICAN

Artistic verbal behavior among African Americans includes a wide range of expressive forms that folklorists have identified and examined. Some of the most pervasive forms are trickster tales, toasts, rap, the dozens, sermons, proverbs, and urban legends, as well as blues, riddles, and chants.

Black English dialect that shapes these forms varies from Standard English in terms of a distinct grammar (e.g., dropping the /s/ in verbs), pronunciation (e.g., substituting /b/ for a medial /v/ in "heaven"), and vocabulary. An early example of dialect in print based on a folklorist's research is Zora Neale Hurston's *Mules and Men* (1935), in which Hurston documents folktales from Florida in the 1930s, offering readers a sense of the natural contexts of storytelling events, including turpentine camp employees who traded barbs, told jokes, and performed a range of verbal arts, all in dialect.

The folktales in Hurston's collection, and in other more recent folktale collections (Dance 2002), are common throughout the American South, and include examples of explanatory tales ("Why Negroes are Black," "Why the Black Man's Hair is Nappy," "Why the Rabbit Has a Short Tale," and "How the 'Gator Got His Mouth"); tales in which the protagonist (animal or human, such as slave John) either outwits his stronger foe ("The Coon in the Box," "Tar Baby," "Buh Lion and Buh Goat,") or falls victim ("The Signifying Monkey"); religious tales ("Upon This Rock," "How the Church Came to Be Split Up," and "Why The Guardian Angel Lets the Brazos Bottom Negroes Sleep"); tales of the supernatural and conjuration ("The Mojo" and "How Hoodoo Lost His Hand"); and other folk narratives that appear in collections of motifs and folktale indices specific to African American culture.

The Source of Dialect Tales

In contrast to collections that were based on folklore fieldwork, "Dialect" tales that appear in Joel Chandler Harris' *Nights with Uncle Remus* (1883) also make use of a black community's way of speaking, but the stories in this collection are those that the fictional black servant Uncle Remus tells the plantation owner's son. They are also the ones Harris (a white man) heard from blacks while growing up in the South. His intentions, literary in nature, attempted to convey to white readers the sound and richness of folk wisdom that characterized the stories and songs he heard. This, and subsequent publications by Harris, sparked a scholarly debate questioning the sources of New World black folktales, attracting the attention of folklorist Richard Dorson and Africanist William Bascom in the 1970s, a debate that John Minton and David Evans examine in their consideration of "The Coon in the Box" (2001).

Arguments favoring European origins attempt to dissuade opponents who forcefully demonstrate the African origins of numerous African American folktales. Drawing from an enormous number of folktale collections in both the old and new worlds, Bascom's comparative analyses substantiates the strong connection between African and New World folktales, soundly refuting Dorson's claims that most African American folktales are of European origin (1975). Revisiting the debate and its implications, Minton and Evans take "The Coon in the Box" as their subject matter, a version of which Dorson collected from black narrator John Blackamore. Blackamore's story places the servant Jack's life in danger when the servant's boss wagers with his peers that Jack possesses an uncanny ability to know everything (a "know-it-all"), unaware that Jack simply investigates facts before appearing to "know" them. Although the contents of a box containing a raccoon has not been revealed to Jack when the moment of truth arrives, the perplexed servant employs an old expression when he admits "You got that old coon at last," correctly "guessing" the box's content and assuring his boss's substantial gain in money and status (Dance 2002, 47).

Among the recurrent themes in these master–slave tales is that of ridicule of white authority figures who institutionalized and encouraged a corrupt political system that justified treating African slaves as human chattel. Indeed, those who advocate European origins of many African American folktales are convinced that the trauma of the Middle Passage between the old and new worlds, and subsequent slavery experiences, produced among black plantation workers cultural amnesia and a general inability to retain African traditions, oral or otherwise. Certainly the style of delivery in a storytelling performance has distinct African characteristics, including aesthetic dimensions that underscore the importance of the spoken word in African traditional societies, while enduring in different forms in the New World.

Whether they are telling a story in a southern rural community, engaging in verbal dueling (the "dozens"), or telling tall tales, black narrators constitute part of a rich cultural heritage that includes African griots—orators who share cultural knowledge and history with community members, and who thereby give the spoken word an extremely important place within traditional African societies. Among such a community of voices are performers who might employ gestures (cut eye and suck teeth), the African hare tricksters, Black English, the ubiquitous call-and-response in all expressive forms, as well as the verbal agility and imagination that are criteria in "signifying," toasts, and the dozens.

Signifying and Toasts

Many stories describe how slaves outwit their masters (purposely or otherwise), while some trickster tales pit characters against each other. In some versions of the "Signifying Monkey," the monkey ridicules a lion while laughing and jumping up and down a tree limb until he slips and falls to the ground, whereupon he begs the lion to let him up to live another day and they can be friends. Once freed, however, the monkey scurries back up the tree and continues his signifying, enraging the lion further until the outrageous monkey finally slips and meets his well-deserved end. In the folktale "Tar Baby," Brer Rabbit signifies on Brer Fox, when the physically weaker animal begs the other not to throw him in the briar patch, and later ridicules Fox's ignorance that the briar patch serves as Rabbit's refuge. A way of indirectly insulting somebody without the individual realizing he or she has been insulted, "signifying" carries many connotations within black oral traditions. Brer Rabbit is signifying when he tells Brer Wolf to hit Brer Possum in the mouth for stealing his cabbage, while Brer Rabbit goes home with the cabbage, infuriating Brer Wolf. After Rabbit escapes from Wolf's subsequent capture, he taunts him: " 'Why didn't you catch me when you had me?' " (quoted in Dance 2002, 26). Accordingly, a salient feature throughout African American verbal art forms, signifying is especially prevalent in the toast and playing the dozens, as well as much of rap music.

Toasts, like "The Signifying Monkey," are poetic forms of prose narratives, recitations that typically describe a situation or tell a story. They contain rhymed couplets and they come from several sources. Despite the popular idea among North Americans that a toast is something you say when you raise drink in hand, the toast can also appear in places such as in prisons, where alcohol is illegal. Not streetcorners or bars, but east Texas maximum security state prison farms, were the social settings in which Bruce Jackson heard many of the toasts he published in his collection *"Get Your Ass in the Water and Swim Like Me": Narrative Poetry from Black Oral Tradition* (1974). The contest toasts, such as "The Signifying Monkey," appear in Jackson's collection, as do several "badman" toasts, whose main character acts with total pathological abandon, and whose violent nature and superhuman strength enables him to overpower all others. Even after Billy Lyon murders Stagolee during a barroom brawl, sending him to hell, Stagolee exerts his dominance in a confrontation and defeats the Devil, sexually assaulting the Devil's wife. "Stagolee," also the subject of blues songs, is a transformation of both the Slave John figure and the relatively weaker trickster figure. His protest against authority is more overt than that of

previous folktale heroes. Moreover, the badman not only reverses the social roles, he typically displays characteristics that derive from stereotypical images whites have of blacks. After the third time the sinking *Titanic*'s captain commanded Shine to go back below and shovel more coal, Shine responded:

"Well, that seems damned funny, it may be damned
      fine,
but I'm gonna try to save this black ass of mine."
So Shine jumped overboard and begin to swim,
and all the people were standin' on deck watchin' him.

In subsequent verses of the "*Titanic*," rich women stand against the ship's railing and raise their dresses, offering sexual and monetary rewards to Shine if he will swim back and save them, but Shine rejects their offers, outswims a shark, and is back on dry land drinking whiskey in a bar before the ship sinks. The toast probably emerged soon after the 1912 tragedy and may well have gained in its popularity in part due to the ship's reported denial of passage of black passengers, including heavyweight championship boxer Jack Johnson. According to oral tradition, the only blacks aboard the *Titanic* were servants, and Shine occupied the lowliest of such jobs. The toast's concern with institutionalized inequalities between races, and its hero's display of hypervirility and superhuman strength must have contributed to the narrative's rise in popularity, and seeing rich white people drown as a lowly black servant swims to safety must have been irresistible.

These themes, common to so many badman toasts that John Roberts and other folklorists have explored, are ones that also emerge in other kinds of African American verbal art, such as rap, which is an aspect of hip-hop culture. In their examination of rap music and their identification of its possible sources and its relationships to other African American expressive forms, Cheryl Keyes (2002) and Tricia Rose (1994) have demonstrated rap music's affinities with badman toasts in general. In his *From Trickster to Badman* (1990), Roberts traces the transformations of the African American trickster in black oral tradition and conceptions of the badman as outlaw hero. The importance of technology's role and other aspects of hip-hop culture have produced an expressive form whose lyrics frequently demonstrate its affinities to this badman tradition within black oral culture. Perhaps the most important feature that links rap to the toast is signifying.

Rap and Hip-Hop

Rap is a musical form that grew out of hip-hop culture and incorporates dance, graffiti, and the manipulation of technology in its exploration of poverty, urban blight, and violence (although increasingly, a significant portion of rap details the so-called bling-bling lifestyle of fine cars, Cristal champagne, wealth, and good living). As economic development has transformed certain urban landscapes, such as that of the Bronx in New York, black adolescents have responded with a style that embraces expressive forms that include the artistic verbal arts informing rap music. As a verb, the word *rap* in black culture might refer to a style of speaking called *rapping*, and it is loosely related to *joning, capping, snapping, sounding,* and *woofing*—terms often synonymous with playing the dozens. But since its emergence during the last decades of the twentieth century, rap now refers to "a musical form that makes use of rhyme, rhythmic speech, and street vernacular, which is recited or loosely chanted over a musical soundtrack" (Keyes 2002, 1). Like toasts, rap includes stories told in rhyme, such as the long narrative poetic toast.

Keyes's discussion of aesthetics of style of rap music reminds one of its reliance on black dialect, characterizing it as black street speech that uses *bad* to mean *good*, while rappers have replaced the word *bad* with *def*, *dope*, and *phat* to describe that which is exceptionally good (2002, 123). Like other expressive forms, rap includes signifying terms like *cut*, *bite*, and *chill*, which have meanings that differ from their dictionary definitions and appear in rap lyrics to invert, for example, a stereotypically negative meaning to a positive one (Keyes 2002, 134). Men who call one another "bitch" or "ho" in the rap community, may simply be playfully "sounding" on one another, a common characteristic found in the dozens.

The Dozens

The dozens, also a feature of toasts, is predominantly black male verbal dueling, the object of which is to artistically insult one's opponent, usually targeting his relative, typically his mother, whereupon the opponent entertains an attentive audience with a clever rejoinder. Rewarding verbal agility and imagination (which may or may not include obscenity) are essential to this activity. In his collection of essays, *Mother Wit from the Laughing Barrel* (1990), Alan Dundes devotes a substantial section to verbal art and provides a number of essays written by scholars who focus on signifying, the dozens, and toasts that employ several stylistic devices, such as metaphor, repetition, rhyme, and other qualities that such performances might involve. Typically, those engaged in playing the dozens rely heavily upon formulaic patterns that often contain rhyme. In Dundes' book, William Labov provides the following example: "I went to your house to ask for a piece of cheese. The rat jumped up and say 'Heggies ("dibbs" or halfsies"), please'" (Dundes 1990, 276–283). Many sounding situations might develop into such opening phrases: "Yo mamma so ugly that she . . ." And the listener would respond accordingly, building on what was said before. Consequently, these expressive forms may be seen as ritual insults that entertain while also teaching the importance of thinking quickly under pressure and developing verbal skills. But by the 1990s, hip-hop had influenced such verbal art forms, and rhymed couplets of earlier dozens often emerged as one-liners: "Your mother is so stupid, she thought Boyz II Men was a day-care center," and "Your mother is so dumb, she couldn't pass a blood test."

Proverbs

One may also demonstrate verbal artistry in traditional proverbs that have developed in the New World, but proverbs, like all folklore, cannot be understood without taking into consideration the contexts in which they occur and the ways in which they have been used. "Different strokes for different folks" has been used in rhetoric and propaganda, but meanings are always context-sensitive. "An idle mind is the devil's workshop," a proverb coming from an African American Texas community, may be addressing the issue of young girls engaging in sex and becoming pregnant, or it could be used to criticize someone who is already pregnant, depending on who is performing the proverb and who is the intended audience (perhaps the parent of a daughter who has become unintentionally pregnant) (Prahlad 1996, 28). As in other verbal art forms, indirection, metaphorical speech, and other elements of poetry characterize these short statements that seem to express timeless wisdom. Swami Anand Prahlad has written a very interesting book that explores these and other dimensions, applying them to data he collected (primarily) in Oakland, California. His primary interest is in the ways in which proverbs emerge in their natural contexts. It is dangerous, Prahlad argues, to assume that a proverb somehow reflects a given set of issues specific to African Americans—a worldview characteristic of an entire group. Indeed, they may well reflect competing worldviews in the same situation, as the proverb above demonstrates. Others have argued that a defining characteristic of proverbs is that they propose an attitude or specific action in response to a recurring social situation. A structural definition identifies the proverb's topic, which is an object spoken about, and a comment or what is said about the topic, such as "two clean sheets don't smut." Proverbs may be descriptions that are made up of two or more elements that conform to two parts of a balanced structure, parts that are frequently tied together by a verb of equivalence or of causation, as in "Ask me no questions, I'll tell you no lies" (Dance 2002, 460) or "The higher monkey climb, the more you see his behind" (Dance 2002, 462).

Preaching

One of the most highly developed forms of African American verbal art is the subject of Gerald L. Davis's study of the African American sermon. Like Davis, Daryl Dance also provides texts of sermons from such notable preachers as the Reverend C. L. Franklin (the father of the vocalist Aretha Franklin) in *From My People*, along with a discussion of famous black speeches, demonstrating that both narrative forms—sermons and speeches—share similar poetic structures. Characterized by improvisation, formulaic expressions, metaphor, repetition, rhyme, and other poetic devices, as well as vocal color, a successful sermon on any Sunday within a black Southern Baptist church contains most of these elements (including a pattern of call-and-response) so common to other black expressive forms, such as the blues. Indeed, some scholars have pointed out the remarkable similarities in style between black folk preachers and traditional blues performers. It is no coincidence that the appeal of Jesse Jackson's oratorical style lies in his background as a minister. Moreover, an educated preacher will speak a language relevant to the congregation's, drawing from the Bible and from spirituals. He or she also accompanies the sermon with such paralinguistic features as body movements, clapping, jumping up and down, waving hands, moving the congregation to respond with a well-timed "amen!" and "hallelujah!" interspersed throughout the sermon. The end of a sermon will invite nonmembers to join the church, and the ritual may sometimes lead to conversions. Indeed, conversion-experience narratives attest to the power of sermons that inspire lost souls who seek the Holy Spirit.

Urban Legends

Finally, urban legends that circulated in black oral traditions are also an important part of black American cultures. An urban legend is a story that a narrator typically reports he or she heard from a friend of a friend of a friend, providing the narrator with a disclaimer to the story's veracity. Conspiracy legends emerged following the Atlanta child murders committed from 1979 until 1981, and rumors that the FBI was somehow culpable for the case's slow progress and subsequent arrest of a suspect whom many argue is innocent. According to the rumor mill, the murder was part of a Ku Klux Klan plot to destroy young blacks, and stories abound about the KKK's role in this and other so-called plots, such as contaminating various fast-food products (e.g., Church's Fried Chicken) in order to make black men sterile.

The line between rumor and legend is not always clear, but the themes that shape their content respond to everyday anxieties and fears that continue into the twenty-first century. Patricia A. Turner (1986) explores the relationship between rumor and legend among black Americans, as well as some of these themes, while Dance includes a section in *From My People* that focuses on what she calls "techlore," or the folklore that technology helps disseminate through E-mails, discussion groups, listserves, and chat rooms (2002, 647–699).

As the scholarship on African American folklore attests, a performance's stylistic linguistic dimensions and an understanding of the nature of specific folklore genres is necessary when surveying the kinds of verbal art enjoyed among African Americans. There are many other expressive forms of verbal art specific to children, such as rhymes and riddles (Lomax, Elder, and Hawes 1997), that have also attracted the attention of folklorists, but most scholarly attention has been given to the forms discussed here.

References

Abrahams, Roger D. 1985. *Afro-American Folktales*. New York: Pantheon Books.

Bascom, William. 1992. *African Folktales in the New World*. Bloomington: Indiana University Press.

Dance, Daryl Cucumber. 2002. *From My People: 400 Years of African American Folklore*. New York: Norton.

Davis, Gerald L. 1985. *I Got the Word in Me, and I Can Sing It, You Know: A Study of the Performed African-American Sermon*. Philadelphia: University of Pensylvania Press.

Dorson, Richard M. 1975. African and Afro-American Folklore: A Reply to Bascom and other Misguided Critics. *Journal of American Folklore* 88, no. 348:151–164.

Dundes, Alan. [1981] 1990. *Mother Wit from the Laughing Barrel: Readings in the Interpretation of Afro-American Folklore*. Jackson: University Press of Mississippi.

Hurston, Zora Neale. [1935] 1990. *Mules and Men*. New York: Harper and Row.

Jackson, Bruce. 1974. *"Get Your Ass in the Water and Swim Like Me": Narrative Poetry from Black Oral Tradition*. Cambridge, Mass.: Harvard University Press.

Keyes, Cheryl L. 2002. *Rap Music and Street Consciousness*. Urbana: University of Illinois Press.

Lomax, Alan, J. D. Elder, and Bess Lomax Hawes. 1997. *Brown Girl in the Ring: An Anthology of Song Games from the Eastern Caribbean*. New York: Pantheon.

Minton, John, and David Evans. 2001. *"The Coon in the Box": A Global Folktale in African-American Context*. Folklore Fellows Communication 277. Helsinki: Suomalainen Tiedeakatemia (Academia Scientiarum Fennica).

Percelay, James, Stephen Dweck, and Monteria Ivey. 1995. *Double Snaps*. New York: William Morrow.

Prahlad, Sw. Anand. 1996. *African-American Proverbs in Context*. Jackson: University Press of Mississippi.

Roberts, John W. 1990. *From Trickster to Badman: The Black Folk Hero in Slavery and Freedom*. Philadelphia: University of Pennsylvania Press.

Robinson, Beverly J. 1990. Africanisms and the Study of Folklore. In *Africanisms in American Culture*. Ed. Joseph E. Holloway. Bloomington: Indiana University Press.

Rose, Tricia. 1994. *Black Noise: Rap Music and Black Culture in Contemporary America*. Hanover, N.H.: University Press of New England.

Turner, Patricia A. 1993. *I Heard It Through the Grapevine: Rumor in African-American Culture*. Berkeley: University of California Press.

RICHARD ALLEN BURNS

See also **Caribbean Verbal Arts; Insults and Ribald Language; Tricksters in African Folklore**

VERBAL ARTS: THE IBIBIO OF SOUTHEASTERN NIGERIA

The Ibibio are the fourth largest ethnic group in Nigeria. According to P. Amaury Talbot, an anthropologist and colonial administrator during the early twentieth century, the Ibibio are one of the most ancient peoples in Nigeria. Among the prominent phases in the migration to their present home in Akwa Ibom State, historians include their sojourn from the Cameroon Highlands to the Central Benue Valley and Ibom in Arochukwu before they settled in southeastern Nigeria, where they have lived for thousands of years. They are bordered by the Ijo to the west, the Igbo to the northwest, the Ekoi to the northeast, and the Atlantic Ocean to the south.

In Ibibio country, the rainforest stretches northward from the mangrove swamp forest belt along the coastline. The land is generally flat, with rivers and abundant rain. The Ibibio are farmers, fishermen, hunters, traders, and craftsmen. Ibibio traditional religion holds Abasi Ibom to be the Supreme Being. They also worship *Ndem* (lesser deities) and serve their ancestors as necessary intermediaries between the Creator and men. In addition to the ritual experts, sacred sites, and ceremonies similar to all religions, the Ibibio mark certain animals, trees and locations, and days as sacred. They are widely known for their secret societies and extravagant masquerade performances.

Reflecting their antiquity, migratory influences, local geography, and religion, folklore among the Ibibio is bountiful, varied, colorful, and profound. (Folklore is defined here as the verbal and nonverbal lore of the people.) Nonverbal folklore includes arts, dances, carvings, games, ritual beliefs, customs, musical instruments, costumes, cults, and cookery. Of all the cultures east of the Niger, only the Ibibio create sculptures and masks with movable jointed limbs or jaws. Besides masks and sculpted works of wood and raffia, funerary houses (*nwomo*) and cement funerary statues abound in Ibibio land. The people also produce ritual objects, toys, dolls, and puppets. They are highly skilled in bamboo and cane furniture, mat making, basketry, raffia craft, pottery, weaving, metal art and body decoration.

Songs and Poetry

Oral poetry abounds in Ibibio culture. Its composition and performance are not limited to any particular group or event. It is prominent in sacred initiation rites and features in various activities of daily life. These compositions can be recited or chanted. One popular poem is associated with women's initiation rituals, which were widely practiced in the past among the Ibibio and involve confinement and grooming of the candidate:

Adiaha umo Nkoriko
Etie ke ufok oduk inam
Oduk inam enye ikponke kpon
Etie ke ufok adia

Adia nkpo eyen ufok nwed
Ayak nwed ikwo ono
Mme nkpe tetie
Mme nkpe nana
Kunana kam dada

Mme nkpedia nkpon ke ntokon
Ntokon ayayat owo
Adiaha adaha isan
Enye umik umik
Atuak ada unek

Afiak adaha isan
Enye umik umik
Afiak adaha isan
Enye umik umik

Translation:

Adiaha Umo Nkoriko (name of the candidate)
Stayed at home for *inam* initiation
Went into *inam* but did not grow fat
Stayed in the house to eat

A student that eats and eats
Surrenders her song book
Should I be sitting down
Should I be lying down
Don't lie down but keep standing

Should I eat cocoyam with pepper
Pepper is hot-tasting
Adiaha begins to walk
She walks *umiik umiik* (ideophone for the gait of
    someone who is very lean)
She stops and dances

She begins to walk again
She begins to walk again
She walks *umiik umiik*

Ibibio Prose Narratives

Ibibio prose narratives treat a variety of topics, but they do not have distinct genre categories similar to the European tradition of separating myth, legend, and folktale. The content of prose narratives represents communities where noble values always prevail over the indices of evil. Performance of the different genres of oral literature is a verbal feast whose poetry, fantasy, music, and dramatization refresh and revitalize traditional societies in their frequent battle against adversities.

All prose narrative performances involve the audience as an active element, along with the narrator, as all join in the singing and hand clapping, some even beating drums. The favorite time for storytelling is the evening, after the day's labor, when moonlight or the cloak of darkness enhance the aura of mystery as the stories unfold. The place is usually the veranda or the open space in the compound where the large family and their neighbors congregate for the session.

Among the most popular characters in these narratives are the tortoise, whose role is that of the trickster, ghosts, and various spirits and deities. The latter reflect the intermingling of universes, (the real with the supernatural). In addition to the tortoise, other animal characters, such as leopards, elephants, monkeys, hares, serpents, birds, and fishes abound in Ibibio stories.

For all prose narratives, both the narrator and the audience participate in the opening formula.

Narrator: Ekon nke-e
Audience: Nke-e ekon
Narrator and Audience: Ekon aka
                Ekon onyon
                Ekon isimaha udim

The literal translation of this formula is: *Ekon* (war), *nke-e* (tale or proverb), *Nke-e* (tale or proverb), *ekon* (war), *Ekon* (war), *aka* (goes), *Ekon* (war), *onyon* (returns), *Ekon* (war), *isimaha* (never exterminates), *udim* (a crowd or multitude). According to this expression, while there will always be war, with its devastation, it never results in annihilation. Thus, the various prose narratives, while evoking the vicissitudes of life, nevertheless still celebrate triumph and *udim* (the social group), and reflect these in both the content and actualization of the tradition.

Space does not permit an illustration of the full breadth of Ibibio prose narratives, but the two following examples give some idea of the vitality of these traditions.

Akpan, the Corpse and the Goddess
Ekong Nkee!
Nke Ekong

Once, there lived a man. He had four children. But two of them died. He wept bitterly because he had only two children left. His first son, Akpan, was a hunter and used to spend several days, deep in the forest, hunting. The other brother had no occupation and used to stay at home. One day, this junior brother fell ill. All efforts to cure him proved abortive. He was carried to several native doctors, but they all declared that he would die. In that community the custom was that when a person died, the body was placed in a coffin and carried to the river bank where it was deposited at midnight. When the river rose, the goddess of the river would come and carry away the corpse for her meal. The arrival of the goddess was usually preceded by a huge flame that made for the shore from the middle of the river. Then, the flame would be followed by a storm which swept up the coffin and, accompanied by the fire, returned to the depths of the river. After Akpan left for hunting, Udo's illness became worse. As he walked in the forest, Akpan was thinking of his brother. They were the only two left and loved each other very much. Akpan swore that the goddess would not feed on his brother's corpse. By the time he finally returned home, Udo was dead. That night the body was to be carried to the river. Akpan left the house that evening and went to the spot where the body would be abandoned. Dressed in black and armed with a gun, he climbed a tree. The family looked for him but did not know his whereabouts. In agony, his father concluded that the son had committed suicide. At last the corpse was carried to the river and the family went back. Akpan kept his position. The moment came: a powerful wind announced the arrival of the goddess. Akpan had carried palm wine with him. A native doctor had given him a substance he introduced into the liquor so that after drinking it his eyes were opened. The wind subsided. The thick darkness prevailed. Thunder began to growl and explode while lightning rent the air. Fire kept breaking into the tree, surrounding where Akpan was hiding. He was tense and immobile. Then he drank the palm wine again. The wind ceased. An enormous flame started advancing from far down the river. When the goddess came to the coffin, she halted, having sensed the presence of a human being. The light spread in a flash. Akpan pretended to be dead. The goddess stood on the tree. She felt Akpan's body. It was lifeless because of the effect of another juju that the native doctor had given to Akpan which made him appear dead, although he was aware of what was happening around him. The goddess left the body. It was dark again. With the coffin in the storm, she cascaded towards the river. Akpan fired at her. She collapsed on the ground, dead. The fire retreated rapidly into the river. There was tumult in the world. All the gods and goddess, wherever they were, rose in lamentation. Akpan broke the coffin and removed the corpse. The goddess ordered the villagers to remain indoors until she had proclaimed her message. Akpan carried the corpse to the native doctor who restored it to life. The two brothers did not return to the village until after the death of their father. At dawn, the voice of the goddess was heard. She announced that a member of the village had disgraced her and exposed her nakedness. She warned that from that day onward no corpse should be brought to the river but should be buried in the earth.

Ekong Nkee!
Nke Ekong.

Thus, Akpan combats and triumphs over supernatural forces. His victory transforms his status in the society and wins for his community, if not for humanity, the right to bury the dead. Also, the three phases—departure, trials, and triumph—can be identified in the tale.

In addition to providing explanations for cultural traditions, such stories also dramatize the full range of human attributes. These attributes include craftiness, wisdom, stupidity, indolence, intelligence, avarice, gluttony, and trickery. Often, two principal characters, each incarnating one of these attributes, are set in opposition. In the ensuing confrontation one attribute vanquishes the other. In "The Hare and the Tortoise," humility triumphs over arrogance.

The Hare and the Tortoise

Ekong Nkee!
Nke Ekong

The tortoise and the hare used to be intimate friends. There was no doubt in their minds as to which of them could run faster than the other. But the hare was fond of boasting about his speed and used to ridicule the sluggishness of his friend. One day, the tortoise was so incensed by this derision that he challenged the hare to a running contest. This only made the hare laugh the more. At last, however, both of them went for the race. As soon as they started, the hare darted forward and sped out of sight. Far, far behind the tortoise was sorting his steps.

The hare loves to sleep. After having covered more than half the distance, he said to himself: "Now, I can relax and take a nap. Before the tortoise comes this far, I shall have had enough rest. Even if he overtakes me while I'm asleep, I can always finish the race before him without having to strain myself. The tortoise competing against me in a race? What an idea! Ha! ha! ha!" The hare lay down, relaxed his limbs and fell asleep. For a long time he slumbered; the tortoise came abreast of his friend and pushed past the spot as stealthily as he could for fear of rousing the opponent snoring under the shade of a tree. On and on struggled the tortoise until he finished the race. The hare was still sleeping. Late in the evening, the latter opened his eyes and sprang to his feet. He ran his fastest and came to the finishing line, only to be booed by a large crowd that had declared the tortoise the winner in the race. The hare was thus silenced.

Ekon Nkee!
Nke Ekon

In many Ibibio fables, seemingly negative traits often overcome laudable human qualities. This is particularly true of the cycle of trickster stories, which frequently feature the tortoise.

Ibibio Proverbs

Before turning to proverbs, it should be remembered that riddles often serve similar functions of training children's speech abilities and memories. Sometimes riddles play off sounds (alliteration and assonance) or tones of words for their answers, rather than strict logic. Riddles can bring forth the wisdom of the group, though in a humorous and indirect fashion. One quick example:

Question: What is it that without hands and without feet can throw a person on the ground?
Answer: Slippery soil.

Proverbs are a favorite genre among the Ibibio. Old and young, male and female, everybody enjoys and appreciates the intervention of proverbs in a discourse. Though some are more skilled in the art than others, most people will try to use proverbs. Those who are most versed in proverbs and employ them most frequently and effectively are the aged. One explanation for this is that proverbs embody wisdom, which is associated with old age. Thus, Ibibio elders are renowned for the expertise and facility with which they embellish, deepen, and energize their speech through the use of proverbs.

It is always best to present the full context of the use of proverbs, but the following list gives some the character and flavor of Ibibio wisdom.

Ifiok iyokoke (One never knows enough).
Eyo ikimme inua (It's never nightfall for the mouth).

Eyo akeim, usen ikwereke (Sunset after sunset, but days never end).

Ofum ase akpeep eto unek (It is the wind that teaches trees how to dance).

Mmion afon se Obon anyai (The chief can pass effluvium with impunity).

Mmon akpene ke inua aforo etap (When water lingers in the mouth, it becomes saliva).

Adia nkpo aduma abene enyin enyon (Who appropriates thunder's substances keeps glancing into the sky).

Conclusion

Ibibio folklore is a rich, comprehensive phenomenon because of the coming together in one culture of elements from three major spheres; pastoral, fishing, and agricultural communities. These, coupled with their antiquity, the long migrations, and their religion, have engendered among the Ibibio a folklore that boasts great variety, vivacity, and charm. Unfortunately, much of the folklore has gone into oblivion, and what is left is threatened with extinction due to certain factors, including a rural exodus, neglect and rejection of the tradition through the influence of contemporary globalism, the passing away of the older generations who were the archives of the system, and the paucity of research and field work for documentation and presentation of the materials. While Ibibio folklore in general, and verbal arts in particular, share many features with similar manifestations in other cultures all over the world, they have also remained a unique facet in the global cultural gem.

References

Akpabot, S. E., 1975. *Ibibio Music in Nigerian Culture*. East Lausing: Michigan State University Press.

Esen, A. J. A. 1982. *Ibibio Profile: A Psycho-Literary Projection*. Lagos: Paico Press.

Essien, O. E. A. 1990. *A Grammar of the Ibibio Language*. Ibadan, Nigeria: University Press.

Forde, C. Daryll, and G. I. Jones. 1950. *The Ibo and Ibibio-Speaking Peoples of SouthEastern Nigeria*. Oxford: Oxford University Press.

Messenger, John C. 1959. The Role of Proverbs in a Nigerian Judicial System. *Southwestern Journal of Anthropology* 15:64–78.

———. 1960. Anang Proverb Riddles. *Journal of American Folklore* 73:225–235.

———. 1962. Anang Art, Drama, and Social Control. *African Studies Review* 5, no. 2:29–35.

Noah, I. A. 1991. Ibibio Oral Literature. In *The Ibibio*, ed. M. Abasiattai. Calabar, Nigeria: Akpan.

———. 1994. Literature and Folklore. In *Akwa Ibom State: The Land of Promise*, ed. S. W. Peters, E. Iwok, and O. E. Una, Lagos: Gabumo.

Udo, Edet A. *Who Are the Ibibio?* Onitsha, Nigeria: Africana Publishers.

IMEYEN A. NOAH

See also **Oral Narrative; Proverbs; West African Folklore: Overview**

VISUAL AND PERFORMANCE ARTS: THE SONGYE

Songye is the ethnic label for a cluster of linguistically and culturally related groups in the Democratic Republic of the Congo (formerly Zaire), located mainly in the eastern Kasai province, with additional groups located in the in Kivu and Shaba provinces. The main groups include Kalebwe, Eki, Ilande, Lembwe, Bala, Chibenji, Chofwe, Budia, Sanga and the small chiefdoms east of the Lomami River, who are the only ones to actually use the name Songye. Despite significant variations, the Songye complex as a whole is particularly known for its healing and divining cults (based on beliefs in ancestral and wandering spirits) and for their masquerades, which exploit the ideology of witchcraft and sorcery. Chieftancy, whether a hereditary and absolute rule, such as among the Kalebwe, or electoral and rotary, as among the eastern Songye, is ritually attributed with sacral powers, echoing traditions of the neighboring Luba, and related symbolically to life-enhancing culture heroes such as the blacksmith, hunter, and *nganga* (magic or ritual expert) (Hersak 1985, 12–22).

Craft of the Songye

The essential transformative role of these and other specialists, who use natural resources for the benefit of the community, is not only evident in myths, tales, and proverbs, but also in various forms of secular and ritual material culture. Metalworkers of the Songye were once renowned in the region, as Wissman observed in the 1880s (Van Overbergh 1908, 223). They produced a variety of utilitarian and ceremonial tools, such as knives and elaborate axes, which they traded with their southern Luba neighbors for essential commodities (Reefe 1981, 98). Pottery was produced by women well into the second half of the twentieth century. The large-scale water coolers with intricate geometric patterns, which were still in use in the 1970s, are very similar to examples documented by Leo Frobenius during his 1905–1906 voyage through the Kasai (1990, 97; Hersak 1985, 4). As among the Kuba, men wove raffia cloth that was used for items of dress, such as the floor-length ceremonial skirts of chiefs and dignitaries (Hersak 1985, 19, 21). When fashioned into squares and rectangles, it served as an important means of exchange (*ediba/madiba*). The value attributed to weaving can be seen in the sculptural elaborations of shuttles, as noted by Frobenius. Plaiting of mats and baskets, widely practiced by women at the turn of the century and distinguished by certain local design preferences, developed into a major commercial activity in the postindependence period (Merriam 1973, 251–252).

Among the various secular arts, perhaps the least-known expressive form is wall painting. Being noncollectable and ephemeral (given the use of natural pigments), little documentation was gathered by travelers and researchers. Frobenius provides evidence of a highly worked house facade covered with geometric patterns, including an unusual X-ray depiction of an expectant *mballa* antelope (1990, 116). In the 1930s, Maurice-Louis Bevel observed paintings in white and black pigments on beige or reddish mud walls. The geometric elements on these houses were done by women, whereas men were responsible for figurative images, such as those of the hunter with various animals, hammock carriers, or the smith, all shown in profile and often with unnaturally long arms. Depictions of colonial presence and power also appeared: the steam boat, the railway, soldiers energizing, the Western lady, the missionary, and even the ritual

Members of a *bwadi bwa kifwebe* society with two maskers: elder (foreground) and youth. Village Kikomo, Kiloshi Chiefdom, Eastern Songye.
Photo © D. Hersak, 1978.

aperitif hour of Europeans in Africa were all part of the repertoire.

Carving, especially in wood, is undoubtedly the activity for which the Songye are best known. Their production of a vast variety of utilitarian, prestige, and ritual objects such as bowls, ladles, musical instruments, headrests, stools, staffs, shields, figures, and masks figure among the most popular icons of Central African art. The skill of talented carvers was certainly recognized, though not always acknowledged or attributed with particular prestige or status. This is especially evident with certain types of artifacts whose context of use demanded secrecy, such as initiatory procedures and mediation with spirit forces. Figural carvings with magical ingredients (*mankishi, nkishi* [sing.]) implanted in the stomach cavity or in a hole or horn on top of the head were seen as creations of the *nganga*, as it was he who selected the symbolically significant mineral, vegetal, and animal substances (*bishimba*) that engendered a reaction with the spirit realm. These objects were used in healing, divining, and general betterment of individual and communal circumstances. As such, they possessed an ambivalent aspect: they would of necessity attack the evildoer in order to deliver the victim from the malediction. The variations in form, style, quality of workmanship, and content of the multitude of personal examples of these carvings, found throughout European and American museums, attest to an extensive and rich popular tradition of folk medicine in the broadest sense. In contrast, the village *mankishi* (figures about 50 cm–1 m in size), which recall figures of authority and culture heroes in dress and other external paraphernalia, served as historical time markers as they were remembered by name and associated to passing generations and events (Hersak 1985, 118–137).

Performance Arts

Music, dance, and performance arts constitute another category that has attracted significant interest. Torday and Joyce, in their 1922 ethnographic report on the Songye, were particularly taken by musical ensembles and instruments, especially those of the

chief, and they included more photographs of this activity than any other (1922, 17, 19). They drew particular attention to the cylindrical, single-note flutes, played in hocketing style, something like the ocarinas (*epudi*) described by Alan Merriam that were used either as signaling devices by hunters (noise producing) or as musical accompaniment for hunters' songs (1962, 177). While some instruments fell into disuse, in the 1970s Merriam analyzed the importance among the Bala of ideophones, skin-headed drums, xylophones, rattles, double metal gongs, and wooden slit gongs. Of these, the latter three were central to all music activity, although the trapezoidal slit drum (*lunkufi*) was accorded the highest status and considered the instrument that distinguished professional expertise. Like the metal gong, the *lunkufi* drum was village property, sometimes kept by the guardian of the community power figure. It was used as a signaling device and was indispensable in funerals, new moon rites, and in eastern Songye masquerades (Hersak, 1985).

Masquerades

Instrumental and vocal music, dance, proverbial lore, plastic arts, and essential magico-religious beliefs all converge in the masking context. While secular masquerades (*lumachecha*) existed among Songye youth and adult groups (*kalengula*), the best-known cult is that of the *bwadi bwa kifwebe* society (Merriam 1982, 29; Hersak 1985, 42). Unlike the gourd-constructed *lumachecha* or the raffia-fiber *kalengula* helmet, the *kifwebe* is a wooden mask with grooved or painted striations that bears the stylistic imprint of the Songye, although it probably evolved in a southern region of Songye/Luba convergence. *Kifwebe* appearances were a serious matter, maskers were agents of the ruling elite and exercised social and political control through the use of powerful magic; that is, the acquired techniques of sorcery (*masende*) and the inherited powers of witchcraft (*buchi*). Certain visual indicators, as well as performance roles, distinguished the gender and power of maskers. Male *bifwebe* among the eastern Songye in the late 1970s were characterized by red, white, and black striations and nose and forehead extensions, while the female masks were predominantly white and devoid of crests. Male masks carried out punitive and policing activities and exhibited erratic and spectac-

Village celebration, Lubao, Eastern Songye.
Photo © D. Hersak, 1977.

ular behavior based on their accumulation of *masende* and *buchi*, while female masks engaged in dance, thus animating benevolent spirit forces and detecting the malevolent ones. Symbolically, a single conceptualization of the supernatural *kifwebe* creature existed, based on the male model, in which all parts of the mask and costume were identified with references to nature, culture, and cosmology. The creature was also named in an esoteric terminology, taught during initiation into the society (Hersak 1985, 37–40).

Kifwebe masking provides a particularly poignant example of an ongoing and dynamic adaptation of folk traditions. Among the Luba, *kifwebe* masks of the 1970s, most of which resemble those of the white Songye female type, were used in entirely opposing contexts, that is, as agents of healers and antisorcerers (Mutimanwa 1974, 30–34; Hersak 1993, 156). At about the same time, on the eastern fringe of the Kalebwe, a workshop was producing a particularly powerful *kifwebe* model, which was used concurrently in *bwadi* practices, in popular dance performances, and as an article of commerce (Hersak 1985). For skeptics concerned with Western notions of authenticity and singular development patterns, the reality of such phenomena is difficult to reconcile.

Though Songye proverbial lore largely emphasizes conservatism, moderation and adherence to traditional values and lifestyles, the currents of change are recognized, even if reluctantly. Two proverbs summarize this as follows:

Ngoma lubilu, maja lubibu
(The "tempo" of the dance must follow that of the
    drum)
                    (author's translation; Samain 1923, 147).

Bipwa byalulukanga, bakashi baamena myefu
(The years change, women are growing beards)
                                  (Lumeka 1967, 42).

References

Bevel, Maurice-Louis. 1937. L'art de la décoration chez les Basonge. *Le Conseiller Congolais* 10, no. 1.
Hersak, Dunja. 1985. *Songye Masks and Figure Sculpture*. London: Ethnographica.
———. 1993. The Kifwebe Masking Phenomenon. In *Face of the Spirits: Masks from the Zaire Basin*, eds. Frank Herreman and Constantijn Petridis. Antwerp: Ethnographic Museum.
———. 1995. Colours, Stripes and Projections: Revelations on Fieldwork Findings and Museum Enigmas. In *Objects Signs of Africa*, ed. Luc de Heusch. Tervuren, Belgium: Annales du Musée Royal de l'Afrique Centrale.
Frobenius, Leo. 1990. *Ethnographiche Notizen aus den Jahren 1905 und 1906*. Vol. IV, *Kanyok, Luba, Tetela, Songo Meno/Nkutu*, ed. Hildegard Klein. Stuttgart: Franz Steiner Verlag.
Lumeka, P. R. 1967. Proverbes des Songye. In *Africana Linguistica III*. Tervuren Belgium: Annales du Musee Royal de L'Afrique Centrale.
Merriam, Alan P. 1962. *The Epudi—A Basongye Ocarina*. *Ethnomusicology* 6:175–80.
———. 1974a. *An African World, The Basongye Village of Lupapa Ngye*. Bloomington: Indiana University Press.
———. 1974b. Change in Religion and the Arts in a Zairian Village. *African Arts* 7.
———. 1982. Kifwebe and Other Cult Groups among the Bala (Basongye). In *African Religious Groups and Beliefs*, ed. Simon Ottenberg. Meerut, India: Folklore Institute.
Mutimanwa, Wenga-Mulayi. 1974. Etude socio-morphologique des masques blancs luba ou "*bifwebe*". Unpublished M.A. dissertation. Université Nationale du Zaire, Lubumbashi.
Reefe, Thomas Q. 1981. *The Rainbow and the Kings: A History of the Luba Empire to c. 1891*. Berkeley: University of California Press.
Samain, R. D. 1923. *La langue Kisongye: Grammaire-vocabulaire-proverbs*. Brussels: Goemaere.
Torday, Emil, and T. A. Joyce. 1922. *Notes ethnographiques sur des populations habitant les bassin du Kasai et du Kwango Oriental*. Brussels: Annales du Musée du Congo Belge.
Van Overbergh, Cyr. 1908. *Les Basonge*. Collection de Monographies Ethnographiques III. Brussels: Albert De Wit.

DUNJA HERSAK

See also **Central African Folklore; Masks and Masquerades; Performance in African**

VISUAL ARTS: ULI PAINTING OF THE IGBO

Uli is an Igbo word, in the Onitsha dialect, for a variety of trees and shrubs that bear pods or fruits, from which juice is squeezed to be used in body decoration. The same patterns that were historically drawn on the body also appear in murals executed in local pigments on earthen compound walls. In the early part of the twentieth century, these painting traditions were important women's art forms in the Igbo-speaking region of southeastern Nigeria. The typology of art forms and practice differ within and between Igbo-speaking subgroups, though village groups and groups on the periphery have some art practices in common with their neighbors (Jones 1984, 132–133). Body and wall paintings manifested differences in motifs, style, and the formal arrangement of designs, which were correlated to subgroups and village groups within the region.

In the pre- and early colonial periods, body and wall paintings, like other Igbo arts, celebrated ideals of individual and communal achievement (Cole and Aniakor 1986, 7), but uli paintings were also done on less auspicious occasions, motivated by impulses that were aesthetic and personal, including women wanting to look their best for market day. Body decoration drew attention to the wearer and complemented other forms of personal adornment and dress. According to Jeffreys, it was the artist's business "to weave into a unity of design the mosaic of patterns selected by her client" (1957, 221). Male title-takers and titleholders, wrestlers, and members of certain age-specific associations were also decorated with uli patterns by women. Uli dye is colorless, and the artist often added charcoal so she could see the trace of the designs as she worked. A range of drawing tools were used. In the Nri-Awka area, in the northwest of the region, designers used a small, blunt, fine-tipped uli knife (made by Awka blacksmiths) which was capable of producing fine tapering lines. In other places thin slivers of palm frond, or feathers, were used. In Umuahia, in the southeast of the region, women made body stamps by carving designs into the cross-section of a piece of bamboo. The uli dye oxidized overnight, and the next day the designs appeared in a deep blue-black color. They would last up to eight days before they began to fade. Body decoration was therefore suited to the regular cycle of four- and eight-day markets, which were also the setting for communal and personal celebrations including title-taking, marriage celebrations, the presentation of newborn babies, and obituaries. Uli body and wall paintings framed those events.

There were established design conventions within a subgroup or village group. In Achalla, in the northwest of the Igbo-speaking area, in the 1930s, body-painting styles could roughly be divided into two types. In one, thin lines crossed the body between groups of dots, concentric circles, and spirals. In the other, more common among male youths, the patterns were arranged more symmetrically and often included wide lines, circles, and ovals filled in with uli dye (Murray 1931–1935, 7). The artist was free to borrow or adapt designs from other villages, or to invent new ones, and the individual's way of drawing (her personal style) could introduce subtle modifications to the appearance of a popular motif. Some women gained reputations as talented designers and were in demand because of their artistic skills or their sureness of hand.

The sun and moon, plants and animals, everyday objects (from combs and hairpins to cooking pots and knives), and activities such as weaving, plaiting, and peeling were translated by uli designers in a highly schematic style. Within the same village a motif or design could have a number of interpretations depending on a person's knowledge of ritual matters and the context in which the design was seen.

There is evidence—in the similarity between the appearance of uli designs in the Nri-Awka area and the patterns on carved wooden doors and side panels executed by male carvers from the same area—of a relationship between the design vocabulary used by male and female artists. A comparison between uli designs by women from Arochukwu in the southeast of the Igbo-speaking area and the iconography of the all-male Ekpe secret society provides further evidence of this relationship. Ekpe had its origins in the non-Igbo Ekoi (or Ejagham) club, located east of the Cross River and named after the leopard, whose emblem is the repeated triangular pattern called *agu*, meaning "leopard's paw." Uli designs from Arochukwu include variations of repeated triangles (*agu*), checkerboard patterns, and four-sided shapes, and these motifs and their arrangements resemble the patterns that are found in the distinctive indigo blue and white *ukara* cloth worn by male members of the Ekpe society (Willis 1997, 118).

In the colonial and postindependence periods, changing social, economic, and ritual circumstances led to the irrelevance of uli to such an extent that the social traditions of which this painting was a part were themselves changing. Body and wall painting declined in direct relation to the increased use of Western cosmetics, wrappers, and modern fashions—and of concrete blocks in place of "traditional" building materials. Mural decoration of earthen walls was a women's art, but in general women have not adapted their legacy of artistic skills in order to be able to decorate modern compounds. Although the contexts and motivations for its appearance have changed, the traditions of uli design have been continued to the present day. Men have been more receptive to new media, and something of the uli idiom can be seen in the metal gates and low-relief plaster frieze work that are popular contemporary forms of decoration for entrance gates and compound walls. Moreover, uli became the focus of the Nsukka group of contemporary, art-school-trained artists (whose most preeminent members are also male). Based at the University of Nigeria, Nsukka, since the 1970s, the Nsukka group, under the leadership of Uche Okeke, has incorporated uli motifs and design arrangements in their paintings, textiles, ceramics, and sculpture (Ottenberg 1997, 77).

References

Cole, H. M., and Aniakor, C. C. 1984. *Igbo Arts, Community, and Cosmos.* Los Angeles: Museum of Cultural History, University of California.

Jeffreys, M. D. W. 1957. Negro Abstract Art or Ibo Body Patterns. *South African Museums Association Bulletin* 6, no. 9.

Jones, G. I. 1984. *The Art of Eastern Nigeria.* Cambridge, England: Cambridge University Press.

Murray, K. C. 1931–1935. Unpublished field notes on body and wall painting. Lagos: K. C. Murray Archives at the Federal Ministry of Antiquities, National Museum.

Ottenberg, S. 1997. *New Traditions from Nigeria: Seven Artists of the Nsukka Group.* Washington, D.C.: Smithsonian Institution Press.

Willis, E. A. 1997. *Uli Painting and Identity: Twentieth-Century Developments in the Art of the Igbo-Speaking Region of Nigeria.* Ph.D. thesis. University of London.

E. A. PÉRI-WILLIS

See also **Body Arts; Gender Representations in African Folklore; Popular Culture**

Uli drawing, southeast Nigeria, collected by K. C. Murray, c. 1930. Ink on imperial size paper, 23 × 32 in.
Photo © KC Murray Archive, National Museum of Nigeria, Lagos.

VODOU

Vodou (the preferred spelling, following a shift in Haitian Creole orthography) is an African-based religion born on the island of St. Domingue (now Hispaniola) during one of the wealthiest and most violent chapters in the history of chattel slavery. The

A *wanga* made for a woman whose husband was unfaithful.
Photo © Martha Cooper.

Haitian end of the island, currently shared with the Dominican Republic, is roughly the size of the state of Maryland, yet during the latter part of the eighteenth century this relatively small French colony produced the majority of the sugar consumed in Europe. Life on the plantations of Haiti was hard, and the life span of a field slave in the late eighteenth century was short. In 1791 discontent among slaves, free blacks, and mulattoes exploded into a long and difficult twelve-year revolution. On January 1, 1804, when Jean-Jacques Dessalines finally declared liberty for the first black republic in the Western hemisphere, two-thirds of the slaves who survived to celebrate their freedom had been born in Africa. For nearly a century after independence, Haiti was effectively cut off from Europe and the Americas. African-born blacks remaining in Haiti helped to re-create a culture of peasant farming. In the early days of the Republic, the great majority of the population in independent Haiti was rural. Only two cities, Port-au-Prince and what is now known as Cap Haitian, could claim a genuinely urban economy and lifestyle.

Vodou's Beginnings

Scholars in Haitian studies tend to agree that the years immediately following Haiti's slave revolution were crucial in shaping Haitian Vodou. African attitudes toward the land increased the retention of traditional religious practices. Unlike Cuban Santeria, which took shape primarily in urban contexts, Vodou emerged as a set of spiritual practices shaped largely by the ecological, social, and spiritual accommodations of peasant farmers. This history accounts for the importance of the land, sometimes literally of dirt or earth, in Haitian Vodou practices. A pinch of earth from a cemetery or a crossroads is a common ingredient in many kinds of *wanga*, a generic term for charms and talismans that are routinely used in Vodou *maji* (magic) and healing rites.

Cemeteries in rural Haiti are spiritual centers for the family. The graves of the oldest male and female buried in these cemeteries are spiritually empowered places, where members of the family can seek help from the ancestors and the Vodou spirits. Even some public cemeteries routinely function as churches or temples, places of communal Vodou ritualizing. This spiritual venue

includes the dead in the ongoing ritual life of the extended Vodou family.

Important Vodou rituals are carried out *pye pa tè-a* (with feet on the earth). People who "serve the spirits" need to be connected to the earth. As a result of this alliance, the land itself becomes a text, open for interpretation. For example, the fertility of the land (or the lack thereof) is understood as a sign of the mood of the spirits and ancestors.

Vodou and the Catholic Church

Immediately following Haiti's declaration of independence, the Catholic Church severed all ties with the struggling republic. This also influenced the direction in which Vodou developed. For half a century there were no real Catholic priests in Haiti, in spite of the fact that Catholicism had been the official religion of the colony for more than a century. Defrocked Catholic priests, and some ne'er-do-well types pretending to be priests, worked the heated social climate of postrevolutionary Haiti in search of money, sex, and power. In this period, there was also a lively competitive market for so-called magic, particularly love, health, and money charms. Faux Catholic priests competed with Vodou healers, claiming their charms and talismans to be superior to those of the *oungan* (Vodou priests) (See Greene 1993).

This was an age of Vodou expansion, when even the upper class turned to the *lwa* (Vodou spirits). Catholicism and the service of Vodou spirits were already understood to go together when the church withdrew from the island. Then, parishoners who could read prayer books or pray in French or Latin stepped into the role of Catholic priest. These self-appointed Vodou-Catholic leaders came to be known as *prêt-savan-yo* (bush priests). It is hard to know exactly what they did in the early nineteenth century, but quite a bit is known about the role of the bush priest today. They are now called to participate in such Vodou events as spirit marriages and the blessing of new temples. For important rituals, they are paid to open the ceremony with traditional Catholic prayers in French and Latin addressed to God, Mary, Jesus, and the saints. A *prêt-savan*, usually equipped with a dog-eared prayer book (he may or may not be able to

Wanga suspended from the ceiling of a Vodou altar room in New York City.
Photo © Martha Cooper.

read) and a bottle of holy water, is routinely called on to bless the bountiful tables of food laid out for Vodou spirits.

African Culture in Haiti

Haiti's sometimes chaotic transition into independence may also have increased the chances of African culture thriving in a Haitian context. The strongest African influences detectable in contemporary Haiti are those of the Fon people (formerly Dahomeans) and the peoples surrounding the ancient Kingdom of Dahomey—groups such as the Mahi, Evhe, and Adja, as well as the Nago or Yoruba.

These influences were already in place in the last decades of slavery in St. Domingue, when large numbers of slaves from central Africa came pouring in to maintain the labor force needed to sustain Haiti's feverish agricultural production. The number of Kongo slaves was far larger than any other group in Haiti's slave population, but their arrival was late, and thus their influence was somewhat muted. Songs and proverbs currently in use in Haiti hint that these late arrivals, known as *moun Kongo* (Kongo people), were treated like an underclass by slaves born on the island. It was well known, however, that Kongo people had the strongest "medicines." The Kongo region in central Africa is known for a religion that focuses on powerful medicines rather than deities or spirits, such as the Dahomean Vodun (see Herskovits 1967; Blier 1995).

Traditional art forms from the various African homelands of the people who worked Haiti's plantations were only indirectly preserved. Drums, for example, rarely made it across the Atlantic, and the few that did make it to Haiti were burned in the antisuperstition campaigns led alternately by the Catholic church and the Haitian government. These violent campaigns justified themselves by arguing that Vodou tarnished Haiti's image in the eyes of the larger world. Ironically, the reverse was more accurate: Vodou was being demonized by Europe and America in order to keep Haiti, and what it stood for, under control. The only art objects that seem to have survived the Atlantic crossing with some frequency were the small pouches of earth from the homeland that some slaves wore around their necks.

Caribbean Art Forms

Transitory and performative religious art forms did develop in the slave colonies of the Caribbean, but it is important to remember that all religious practices, except those of the colonials, were discouraged in such settings, which is not to say they did not persist anyway. One example of transitory art is the elaborate Vodou *veve*, traced in fragile cornmeal on temple floors, only to be destroyed before the end of the ceremony. Possession became more elaborate and more extemporaneous in Haiti than it was in the African homelands. The possession performances of those Vodou practitioners "ridden" by the spirits are not only evidence of religious practices enduring in the New World, they are a testament to the creative adaptation of old ritual techniques to new social environments.

Wanga represent another kind of art form. *Wanga* are a form of "treatment" in the healing repertoire of the average Vodou priest (*oungan*) or priestess (*manbo*). Although *wanga* may not be beautiful these homely, practical Vodou constructs (e.g., good luck charms and healing magic) are perhaps the most complex and the most aesthetically rich of Haiti's material art forms. *Wanga* are eclectic blends of similar objects produced in West and Central Africa (such as *bocio* and *minkisi*) with elements drawn from eighteenth-century French Catholicism and its saints, miracles, relics, and talismans.

The Kongo *minkisi*, sometimes little more than tied and sutured bundles filled with articulate discursive materials (seeds, bark, animal parts, bones, resin, rocks, leaves of all kinds, bits of chalk, and so forth) were models for Vodou ritual objects called *pake Kongo*. *Pake* are common on Vodou altars. These *pake* are manufactured in the process of Vodou initiation and are associated with cleansing and healing powers. The most common type of Vodou *pake* starts from a bundle of herbs and other materials pounded and flattened into a thick disk. The herbal mass is then enveloped in brightly colored cloth. Ribbons in contrasting colors bind the *pake* into a tight bundle. These same ribbons also bind the excess cloth at the top of the *pake*, thus creating an extended "neck." The neck rises straight up from the herbal base and is decorated with feathers, horns, and sometimes a crucifix. All of these objects further specify the spirits to whom the *pake* are dedicated, and therefore the person who has that *lwa* as a central spirit. *Pake*, like many Kongo *minkisi*, can be strikingly anthropomorphic. For example, some have "arms" sprouting from the ribbon-bound neck that make the *pake* look like a woman with her arms akimbo. Vodou *pake Kongo* also share with Kongo *minkisi* a tendency to blur the distinction between the sacerdote (priest) and the source of his or her power.

Fon *bocio* (a term translated as "empowered cadaver") are strong, expressive wooden figures manufactured through related traditions of tying and binding. Applying psychological theory to these figures, Suzanne Blier argues that they function to externalize strong feelings, fears, and memories. She calls them shocking figures because they append to the outer surface of the body emotions and desires usually retained within the person. In other words, *Bocio* have the inside on the outside. Furthermore, the ropes that are bound tightly around these images, as well the hunks of cloth, animal skulls, cowrie shells, bones, small calabashes, and knotted raffia that cover these body surfaces are designed not only to express fear but also to produce it. Thus, the *bocio*, often planted in the ground, become guardians of land, keepers of vows, and enforcers of law. To encounter the *bocio* is to be shocked, and that shock is ultimately meant to mobilize power.

West and Central African traditions of tying and binding charms and talismans are older than the trans-Atlantic slave trade. Slave chains nevertheless become profoundly articulate when they later appear in these expressive traditions. During the 1970s, the Haitian Bureau d'Ethnologie in Port-au-Prince had a small exhibition case devoted to eighteenth-century and early-nineteenth-century *wanga*. An especially noteworthy *wanga* in the exhibition was simple and powerful. It was made from a clear glass bottle, bound with two lengths of rusty, hand-forged slave chains. It is impossible to know what the person who made that *wanga* was trying to accomplish with it, yet it seems likely that this bit of *maji* was somehow addressed to the troubled relationships between slave and master. It also seems likely that this *wanga* might be an attempt to appropriate the power of the chains and to use that power to transform instruments of oppression and torture into tools of survival and empowerment (Brown 2003).

Ritual Healing

A fundamental contrast runs through Vodou, one between things that are bound, blocked, or tied (*bloke, mare*) and things that have been opened (*ouvri*), let go (*lage*), or allowed to flow (*koule*). In Vodou, people are seen as enmeshed in relationships—relationships with the living, the dead, and the *lwa*. A Vodou ethic recognizes no essential good or evil. In fact, the *lwa* are characters with both constructive and destructive dimensions, and they therefore work against stark ethical contrasts. Problems with family, friends, ancestors, or spirits are understood to be the result of relational knots or blockage, meaning the problem is located between the parties, not in either one. Vodou priests and priestesses think of their healing arts as focused on clearing these blocks. Ritual healing opens the conduits of relationship, to untie (*demare*) or loosen (*lage*) what blocks the flow of reciprocity, the central dynamic of all relationships. In order to get things flowing among persons (and between persons and spirits) gates have to be opened, knots untied, pathways cleared, blockages removed, and chains broken.

A statue of a maroon (a fugitive slave) with his arms held up in triumph, a broken chain dangling from each wrist, is a visual trope for Haiti's successful revolution. This figure is deep in the Haitian psyche and is part of the emotional context of the *wanga* with slave chains in the Bureau d'Ethnologie. The maroon who has broken his chains often shows up in political murals that appear throughout Haiti, like graffiti, at important times in the nation's history.

Wanga may also be classified as models or reifications of problematic relationships (Brown 1995). Objectifications of emotional knots expose a person's pain and vulnerability, and thus they share the dynamic of the *bocio*. They expose the private, turning things inside out, and such exposure becomes the first step of the cure. Because there is a certain deliberate confusion of the model of the troubled relationship with the actual troubled people, the *wanga* also share the dynamic of Kongo medicine bundles. An example drawn from the Haitian diaspora community in New York City illustrates these dynamics.

When a person whose husband was sexually involved with another woman turned to Mama Lola, a Haitian *manbo* and noted healer practicing in Brooklyn, Lola made a *wanga* for her. First, Lola took a small piece of cloth cut from an article of the husband's clothing. With this, she made a male doll with a small bundle of cloth rolled tightly and stitched to its crotch to represent his penis. Herbs and powders, plus the name of the wife written several times on white paper, were placed inside the doll, which then was tied into a small wooden chair with a length of copper wire. The wire, in turn, was secured with a padlock. (The wife was instructed to throw away the key to that lock.) Thus immobilized, the image of her husband was placed facing a wall on which a fragment of mirror hung, a visual trope for the sea. While gazing on the mirror-calm surface of the sea, those who serve the *lwa* are supposed to see reflections of ancestors and spirits who dwell beneath the water. An image of Santa Clara was tucked behind the mirror "to clear the man's eyes."

Making the *wanga*, an act in which the client often shares the labor, is not enough, however. It is also necessary to "work

the *wanga*." "Working" such a charm can mean something as simple as keeping a candle lighted in front of it, or it can involve long-term spiritual discipline. The troubled wife was told to keep an oil lamp burning, day and night, in the space between the seated doll and the fragment of mirror on the wall. Mama Lola then explained that, if she followed the instructions, her husband would "keep his head down," the way Santa Clara bows her head, and, all other women would disappear from his view.

The Vodou practice of making *wanga* resonates with its West and Central African predecessors. Yet there is one dimension of this ritual technology that Africans will not experience in the same way Haitians do, namely, the capacity of *wanga* to articulate the experience of slavery. The songs and stories that cluster around Haitian Vodou are mysteriously silent about slavery. There are few songs that even hint at things connected to slavery. What is said is indirect and disguised. There is, for example, one song that voices resistance to unnamed forces and also complains of insupportable suffering, yet the blame for that suffering is ultimately displaced onto the innocent heat of the sun.

This raises questions as to how ritual technologies interact with memory and history, especially those dimensions of ritual that are channeled through the body rather than the brain. Slave history apparently remains kinesthetically alive for Mama Lola. When she is binding and tying *wanga*, her body engages a dense tangle of affect, a kinesthetic sense of the control and confinement of enslavement. Every time Mama Lola makes *wanga* with yards of string, rope, or wire, her body rehearses the dialectic of binding and loosing central to the service of the Vodou spirits. So the practices passed on to her by generations of healers in her family may, in this way, also function to preserve the story of slavery in her family's history.

References

Brown, Karen McCarthy. 1987. The Power to Heal: Reflections on Women, Religion and Medicine. *Shaping New Vision: Gender and Values in American Culture*, eds. C. Atkinson, C. Buchanan, and M. Miles. Ann Arbor: UMI Research Press.
———. 1989. Systematic Remembering, Systematic Forgetting: Ogou in Haiti. *Africa's Ogun: Old World and New*, ed. Sandra T. Barnes. Bloomington: University of Indiana Press
———. 1999. Telling a Life: Race, Memory, and Historical Consciousness. *Anthropology and Humanism* 24, no. 2.
———. 2001. *Mama Lola: A Vodou Priestess in Brooklyn.* (1991). Berkeley and Los Angeles: University of California Press.
Blier, Suzanne. 1995. *African Vodun: Art, Psychology and Power.* Chicago: University of Chicago Press.
Dayan, Joan. 1995. *Haiti, History and the Gods.* Berkeley and Los Angeles: University of California Press.
Green Ann. 1993. *The Catholic Church in Haiti: Political and Social Change.* East Lansing: Michigan State University Press.
Leyburn, James G. 1996. *The Haitian People.* (1941). New Haven: Yale University Press.

KAREN MCCARTHY BROWN

See also **Diaspora; Orisha; Religion; Textiles: African American**

VOICE DISGUISERS

Voice disguisers are generally lightweight and relatively simple instruments that are employed to alter the sound of, and therefore disguise, an individual's voice. They are often used by masquerade "beings," generally considered emissaries from some aspect of the spirit world. They allow these beings to speak as part of their appearance in the mundane world.

A voice-disguise instrument widely used in West and Central Africa closely resembles a modern Western toy instrument, the kazoo. Referred to in many descriptions as a *mirliton* (from the French word for a toy reed or pipe), the instrument in its simplest form consists of a hollow tube open at one end and closed at the other end by a thin, flexible membrane. The membrane is set in motion by the user's voice spoken into the open end, creating a "buzzing," sympathetic sound. In Africa, *mirliton* tubes have been made in many forms and from a wide variety of materials, including wood, grass reed, hollow bone, gourd, animal horn, or cast metal. More recent examples have employed imported materials, such as the long metal drainpipe that Colin Turnbull reported being used among the Mbuti in the Democratic Republic of the Congo (1962, 24–25).

Materials used to create the *mirliton's* vibrating membrane include lizards skin, bats wing, and cellophane; however, a preferred material throughout most of the region is the membrane of a spider's egg sac. Voice disguisers of this kind are often used by masqueraders who sing or speak as part of their public appearance. In addition to having their voice disguised, masqueraders will often speak in archaic or nonlocal languages, further denying simple comprehension of the spirit by noninitiated members of the community. In most cases, this then requires that the masquerader be translated by a "speaker" or interpreter, an individual who translates for the public and is typically part of the masquerade entourage.

In some instances, voice-disguise instruments do not actually disguise a human voice, but instead are themselves employed to create sounds which are meant to be perceived as deriving from a nonhuman (e.g., spiritual) source. In other words, the voice disguise literally *is* the masquerade.

Generally used at night or hidden from sight, these devices include ceramic pot resonators (sometimes used in conjunction with *mirliton* instruments, or themselves serving as large spherical *mirlitons*), the ubiquitous bull-roarer (a rhomb attached to a long cord which is swung in a circle above the user's head), and various combinations of whistles, bells, and flutes used singly or in combination. More esoteric and complex "earth friction" and "water" drums (pots of water or small pits in the earth covered with large leaves) employ different resonators to create high-pitched, "unearthly" sounds emitted from tautly stretched lengths of moistened sinew or vine. Such spirit manifestations, which present only aural phenomena, have been termed "acoustic masks" (Lifschitz 1988, 223).

The spirit being manifested in this instance has no visual form and is perceived only by the sounds it makes. To reinforce and ensure this spirit's invisibility, noninitiated individuals (including women, children, and nonlocals) are forced to remain inside tightly shuttered houses. Reports from the Dan in Liberia (Zemp 1968) and the Mbuti in the Democratic Republic of the Congo (Turnbull 1962, 91) describe how teams of men strategically deployed around a village at night would create identical "spirit voices" to suggest that the spirit is everywhere all at once, or, utilizing consecutive sound emanations, that the spirit can "fly" from one part of a village to another.

Recent investigations into the nature and use of sound within African cultures suggests broad associations of altered, divergent, or "special" sounds with spiritual dimensions of human social interaction (Peek 1994). Voice-disguise instruments that are used to give "voice" to the spirit world may be but a single facet of an African propensity for utilizing sound to designate and to distinguish the spiritual from the mundane.

References

Lifschitz, Edward. 1988. Hearing is Believing: Acoustic Aspects of Masking in Africa. In *West African Masks and Cultural Systems*, ed. S. L. Kasfir. Tervuren, Belgium: Musee Royal de L'Afrique Centrale.

Peek, Philip M. 1994. The Sounds of Silence: Cross-World Communication and the Auditory Arts in African Societies. *American Ethnologist* 21, no. 3:474–494.

Turnbull, Colin. 1961. *The Forest People*. New York: Doubleday/Anchor.

Zemp, Hugo. 1968. *The Music of the Dan*. UNESCO Collection—An Anthology of African Music. Vol. 1. Kassel, Germany: Barenreiter Musicaphon.

EDWARD LIFSCHITZ

See also **Masks and Masquerades; Performance in Africa; Silence in Expressive Behavior; Speaking and Nonspeaking Power Objects of the Senufo**

WARI

Wari is a West African board game. This game is a variation of *mancala*, a group of board games particularly popular in Africa, but also in Asia and the Americas. It is played by two players on a board, or in the sand with two rows of six holes and forty-eight counters, such as seeds, beans, shells, or stones. The purpose of the game is to capture the majority of the counters on the board. *Wari* is the best-known African variation of mancala; apart from West Africa, where it is thought to have originated, it is popular in the Caribbean and South America and reached North America and Europe through various commercial introductions.

Wari is known under different names, including *warri*, *awélé*, *oware*, and *ayo*. Other *mancala* variations have been recorded which use the same names or the same board and counters but which apply different playing rules. In some studies *wari* has become a generic name for a large group of *mancala* variations. The same particularly popular variation is common in both the Caribbean and West Africa. This game is defined by the following playing rules: The game starts with four counters in each hole of the twelve playing holes. Players can take up the contents of a hole on their side or row of the board and spread the counters in counter clockwise direction one by one and in consecutive holes. Once the contents have been distributed, the move ends. If the last counter in hand ends up in a hole on the opponent's side and makes a total of two or three counters, these are captured by the player and taken from the board. If one or more holes directly preceding the captured hole also contain two or three counters, these are also captured. Such a multiple capture occurs as long as the captured holes are on the opponent's row and in an uninterrupted sequence. A hole that contains more than eleven counters completes a full round on the board when its contents are distributed. Such a move will always omit the hole it started from, leaving the starting hole empty.

If one player does not have any occupied hole left, then the opposing player is required to play a move that distributes counters to this player's row. For this reason, a player is not allowed to make a multiple capture that takes all counters on the opponent's side without leaving the opponent a move to play. If the player is not able to give counters or still plays such a multiple capture, then rules tend to vary when it comes to the solution to such a problem. The remaining counters may be divided or added to only one player's captured total, and the multiple capture may not capture or may capture only the contents of a few instead of all holes on the row. The player who captured the majority of the counters wins the game. *Wari* games, like *bao* and other *mancala* games, are often played in a series. These series usually consist of three games, in which only three consecutive wins count as a victory.

These *wari* rules have been described in detail in the 1890s and perhaps earlier. The close resemblance of West African and Caribbean *wari* rules indicate that at least since the end of the West African slave trade these rules have largely remained the same. This resemblance is perhaps partly explained by the players' organizations that can be found in parts of the Caribbean and West Africa. These organizations often oversee clubs and recognize master players. Masters or champions have been known for at least a century in this game. The relatively simple rules and the possibility of playing the game in the sand have made *wari* popular outside players' clubs as well. Although this widespread popularity is evident today, the literature cannot support the claim that these particular *wari* rules were popular or even known prior to the nineteenth century. *Wari* boards have been acquired by museums since the late nineteenth century, although it is not always clear which variation or variations of rules were supposed to be used in play. Stone boards may date from an earlier time but an accurate dating, and rules adhered to on these boards, are largely unknown.

Wari boards in West Africa have attracted attention for their sculptured shapes. They often include a stand or a base which may be decorated with incisions or which may be sculptured in three-dimensional motifs such as animals, people, a stool, or a boat. Some stands provide a storage space for counters for which separate closing pegs may be designed. Optional end holes are sometimes extended in a horn shape from the base to the rows of cup-shaped holes. Sculptured, colored, and iron or brass boards in museum collections may originally have been prestige objects rather than popular playing boards. Although *wari* is the most popular *mancala* game in West Africa, *wari* is one of many *mancala* variations played in the region. Most of these variations can be played on a board of two rows and six holes. Only in the Caribbean and South America do these variations seem to be limited to two or three, but in these regions sculptured boards have not yet been recorded in any significant number.

Two masters in Barbados playing *wari*.
Photo © Alex de Voogt.

In the twentieth century, a number of commercial introductions took place in Europe and North America. Sometimes different game rules were offered on the same playing board, and the name of *wari* would not always be used or mentioned. The popularity of *wari* in Africa and the Caribbean, together with these limited but regular commercial introductions, have made wari available for various studies conducted by Western scholars. The simple playing rules made *wari* suitable for experiments in education and developmental psychology. The strategic possibilities and the existence of master players allowed studies on expertise from a cognitive psychological perspective and studies on artificial intelligence, with the help of computer programs.

Wari remains a popular West African *mancala* game and one of the few African games that has gained popularity outside Africa. The sculptured boards and simple but challenging playing rules illustrate the different interests that *wari* has served. Although its origins appear West African, the history of the game prior to the nineteenth century still remains unclear.

References

Béart, C. 1955. *Jeux et jouets de l'Ouest Africain*. Dakar: IFAN.

Deledicq, A., and A. Popova. 1977. *Wari et solo. Le jeu de calcul Africain*. Paris: Cedic.

Herskovits, M. J. 1932. Wari in the New World. *Journal of the Royal Anthropological Institute* 32: 23–27.

Retschitzki, J. 1990. *Stratégies des joueurs d'awélé*. Paris: L'Harmattan.

Walker, R. A. 1990. Sculptured Mankala Gameboards of Sub-Saharan Africa. Ph.D. dissertation, Indiana University.

ALEX DE VOOGT

See also **Bao, Mancala**

WATER ETHOS: THE IJO OF THE NIGER DELTA

The several million Ijo-speaking peoples, who inhabit the Niger Delta, differ markedly from one side of the region to the other. The Eastern Ijo, who occupy a largely saltwater zone, have long traded inland for agricultural produce and later played a prominent role in the overseas trade; their reliance on trade led them to form a number of city-states. In contrast, many Central and Western Ijo live in freshwater regions and combine fishing with farming; largely cut off from the overseas trade by Eastern Ijo and Itsekiri middlemen, they have remained stateless.

Beliefs and art forms also differ: for example, the Kalabari Ijo, an eastern delta group, honor village heroes and commemorate leaders of trading concerns with elaborate sculptures called *nduen fobara*; the Ijo living to the west of the Nun River neither acknowledge village heroes nor commemorate the dead with sculptures. Nevertheless, all share what we might term a *water ethos*, which is apparent in shrines, masquerades, and rituals, as well as in aquatic exhibitions and performances on land that incorporate canoes and/or paddling displays.

Ijo living throughout the region acknowledge a female creator and credit nature spirits with introducing much of their art, including songs, dances, and funeral rites. They express beliefs in water spirits, who occupy the delta's myriad waterways, and use masks, carvings, and objects found in the water to represent them. People claim that these capricious but largely benevolent beings bring them prosperity, especially in the form of children and money. Because they associate water spirits with wealth acquired through trade, manufactured items like dolls and tableware often serve as their emblems, but paddles and fishing spears can also serve this function. Although the Central and Western Ijo produce figure carvings to satisfy the demands of the more volatile "bush" spirits for earthly embodiment, Adumu appears to be the only major water spirit to be depicted in this manner. Many, like Binipere, Lord of the Water, prefer to remain inside the rivers and do not request shrines or images.

Virtually all Ijo masks represent water spirits, but they can take a variety of forms: wooden masks depict them as composite monsters with a mix of human and aquatic features, as anthropomorphic figures, or as animals, particularly reptiles and marine animals. Fabric and raffia masks are also common. Although most masks do not incarnate powerful spirits, the Ijo generally believe that their performances promote health and prosperity. In the Eastern Ijo region, masking takes place under the auspices

Shrine for the water spirit Adumu. Azuzama, Bassan clan, central Ijo, 1978.
Photo © Martha G. Anderson.

of dancing societies known as Sekiapu or Ekine; to the west, where masking is less formal, individuals, families, or groups of friends may own masquerades. Performances in both areas typically include narratives that portray events in the lives of water spirits.

Most Ijo stories revolve around the antics of water spirits. Narrators typically present the tales they spin as true, no matter how incredible, and end by naming a particular person as the source of the story in order to bolster the appearance of veracity. Many set their yarns in Ado (Benin) or Beke-ama (overseas), much as Westerners introduce fairy tales by saying "Once upon a time" or "Long ago and far away." Plots often involve people who go into the water to look for lost articles, meet water spirits like Binipere and Adumu, then return home to report their marvelous adventures. The Ijo tell stories primarily to entertain, but many deliver moral lessons by illustrating the consequences of human foibles like greed and duplicity. Because storytelling involves multiples and repetitions, most tales take an hour or more to tell (Leis 1962, 153–154).

Oki (sawfish) masquerade and Oki dancing. Akedei, Oiyakiri clan, western Ijo, 1992. The sawfish's wicked-looking rostrum and enormous size make Oki a popular character in masquerades throughout the Niger Delta.
Photo © Martha G. Anderson.

Many of the proverbs the Ijo liberally employ to enliven their speech use animals to provide lessons for humanity, and many involve reptiles and aquatic animals. Proverbs tend to have two parts: the first part of an animal proverb usually names the creature; the second makes a statement about the animal or draws a moral, as in "A dead crab can no longer get into its hole," meaning "There can be no going back" or "The tilapia said: 'Until my bones are dumped on the rubbish heap, do not weep for me,' " meaning, "Do not accept defeat until every possible avenue of escape has been explored." Others draw on experience, for example: "A fish trapper does not set his trap once" reminds people that someone who wants something must persevere (Alagoa 1986).

The Ijo love to sing and have many types of songs, including paddling songs. Performances usually include multiple repetitions of both lyrics and songs. Some songs evoke the lapping of waves on the riverbanks or the rhythmic splash of paddles, like a song Central Ijo women sing while commuting to and from their farms by canoe:

> Paddle, paddle
> Oh! Paddle
> The carp was paddling
> A canoe underwater
> But the paddle
> Broke in his hand
> Paddle, paddle
> Oh! Paddle

> (Anderson and Peek 2002, 133)

Songs, like tales and proverbs, often refer to the environment or the spirits who live in the water and bush. A song for a water spirit reflects beliefs that spirits from this realm bring good fortune, such as this unpublished song collected by the author in Azuzama from the Bussan clan in 1979:

> A spirit-stick was floating in the water
> The rich man didn't see it
> The poor man picked it up
> Adumu has come to the poor man's house

In contrast, bush spirits offer support in war, hunting, and wrestling, as reflected in their songs and images. Most shrines feature a central male figure holding weapons and wearing bullet-proofing medicines. Feathers and body paint signify that he holds a title granted by the clan war god to proven warriors. He may be larger than life-size and have multiple heads, in keeping with the prevailing image of bush spirits as gargantuan, grotesque, and dangerous beings who roam the forest and command superhuman powers. Although the song sung for Benaaghe, a bush spirit from Azama in Apoi clan, is a war song, it, too, refers to the watery environment:

> I'have prepared my fishing basket and taken it to the
>   lake
> Benaaghe my father
> I've prepared my fishing basket and taken it to the lake
> Anyone who doesn't fish is afraid of the lake

> (Anderson and Peek 2002, 144)

In the nearly roadless region the Ijo occupy, the canoe plays a prominent role in both daily and ritual life. Not only does early every traditional occupation requires canoe travel, funeral rites, offerings for water spirits, and various other performances often incorporate real or conceptual canoes. In addition, dancers frequently employ paddling motions and mimic the way canoes move in the water. The Ijo distinguish between three types of canoe: the most common serves as everything from an essential mode of transportation to a convenient bathroom to a whimsical prop for masquerades. The war canoe, a larger version, nowadays appears on ceremonial occasions; the sacrificial canoe serves as a spiritual war canoe by warding off evil spirits and combating epidemic disease. Sacrificial canoes range from about one to seven or more feet long. After parading them through town to the accompaniment of drums and songs, the Ijo either mount them at the waterside or float them downstream.

The arts frequently incorporate references to both watercraft and fish. Fishing implements appear alongside canoes and paddles in shrines for water spirits, and wooden fish occasionally join paddles as props for dancing. Masquerades sometimes reenact fishing expeditions on land and maskers may arrive at their venues by canoe. The Kalabari, who continue to make masquerade headdresses in the form of ocean liners, once built grand houses using trading vessels as their models.

References

Alagoa. 1986. *Noin nengia, bere nengia: Nembe n'akabu. (More Days, More Wisdom: Nembe Proverbs)*. Delta Series No. 5. Port Harcourt, Nigeria: University of Port Harcourt Press.

Anderson, Martha G. 1996. Ijo. *In The Dictionary of Art*. London: Macmillan, vol. 15.

———. 1997. The Delta. In *Arts du Nigeria*. Paris: Réunion musées nationaux.

Anderson, Martha G., and Philip M. Peek, eds. 2002. *Ways of the Rivers: Arts and Environment of the Niger Delta*. Los Angeles: UCLA Museum of Cultural History.

Clark, J. P. 1977. *The Ozidi Saga*. Ibadan: Ibadan University Press and Oxford University Press Nigeria.

Eicher, Joanne B., and Tonye V. Erekosima. 1987. Kalabari Funerals: Celebration and Display. *African Arts* no. 1:38–45, 87.

Horton, Robin. 1965. *Kalabari Sculpture*. Lagos: Department of Antiquities, Federal Republic of Nigeria.

Leis, Philip M. 1962. Enculturation and Cultural Change in an Ijaw Community. Ph.D. dissertation, Northwestern University.

Okara, Gabriel. 1958. Ogboinba: The Ijaw Creation Myth. *Black Orpheus* 2:9–18.

MARTHA G. ANDERSON

WEST AFRICAN FOLKLORE: OVERVIEW

West Africa is generally understood to comprise the countries and cultures between the Atlantic Ocean and the southern edge of the Sahara, from Mauritania across to Lake Chad, and southwest to the Atlantic Ocean along the southern border of Cameroon. This area incorporates the territory of the once great kingdoms of the Western Sudan (old Ghana, Songhai, and Mali) as well as the formerly powerful kingdoms of the forests, such as the Ashanti Federation, the Yoruba city-states, and the Benin Kingdom. In large part due to the trans-Saharan trade between North Africa (and, by extension, Europe and the Middle East)

and the forests of West Africa, these kingdoms experienced large populations and great wealth long before Europeans reached the coast in the early fifteenth century. Trade routes shifted, and trade goods changed, after European contact. Soon the cruel traffic in African slaves dominated commerce, and the great cities of the Sahel, such as Timbuctu, Gao, Kong, and Kano, diminished in importance. As European powers consolidated their gains, capital cities developed along the West African coast. Broadly speaking, a north–south divide (too often a poorer–richer, Muslim–Christian divide as well) continues to plague the countries of West Africa, as all attempt to adjust to a new age of exploitation.

Although academic activities were seldom part of the early European colonial process, by the end of the nineteenth century Europeans were focusing more on the verbal arts and traditional cultures of the people. Missionaries sought language examples in folktales for Bible translations, colonial administrators studied local legal customs in order to administer their territories, and traders learned the objects of local value in order to make more money. By the early part of the twentieth century a number of individuals were making extraordinary collections of local tales and customs. Interestingly, each major European nation had a few key scholars; for example, Leo Frobenius was reporting to a German audience, R. S. Rattray collected traditional lore in both the Gold Coast (later Ghana) and Nigeria, and Francois-Victor Equilbecq recorded customs in the areas of French West Africa. Although some were seeking evidence for grand theories (such as Frobenius about Atlantis), most were satisfied with learning more about the people being colonized, for to know them better was to rule them better as was often asserted by the English.

It was not until around the time of World War II that rigorous academic research was conducted in West Africa (Griaule began his life's work with the Dogon in 1931 and Bascom first worked among the Yoruba in 1938). The earlier collections of folktales and proverbs are of some interest today, but their scholarly use is severely limited without cultural context. Occasionally, the earlier scholarship was still tainted with prejudiced notions of West African peoples. In the second half of the twentieth century, increasingly sophisticated and sensitive studies were made not only of traditional folklore topics, but of "emerging" areas, such as popular culture, electronic media, and tourism.

Most recently, there has been a significant growth in the number of African scholars interested in their own traditions. In a sense, once the racist and paternalistic terminology of European and American folklorists and anthropologists changed, more Africans felt comfortable studying their own traditions. Throughout West Africa, university-based institutes of African studies, once staffed only by foreigners, now boast rosters of African scholars. Although these institutes came to be negatively viewed by some Africans, the fact remains that they have produced an extraordinary body of scholarship by promoting research in West Africa, as with IFAN for Francophone countries and the university institutes in Anglophone countries, and by promoting publication in Europe, as with the International African Institute in London and the Centre National de la Recherche Scientifique, among others, in Paris. There is also a notable increased use of traditional themes, motifs, and materials by African artists and writers. This has also assisted in the "validation" of traditional folklore and art forms. All are benefiting from this renewed interest, although virtually all West African countries continue to suffer from little or no funding for higher education and research scholarship.

Nigeria provides many examples of the literary interest in verbal arts and oral traditions. One might first cite *Nigeria Magazine*, a quasi-government publication that always included articles on traditional arts and ceremonies as well as poetry. Uli Beier's efforts in founding, with other colleagues, the literary and arts journals *Black Orpheus* and *Odu*, at the University of Ibadan, provided great impetus for the dissemination of folklore. Among the Yoruba of western Nigeria, not only did a number of indigenous writers and playwrights, such as Duro Ladipo, publish and produce major work in Yoruba, but several writers became famous for their idiosyncratic use of English, such as Amos Tutola. Igbo novelist Chinua Achebe's early novels are virtual ethnographies, due to their detailed portrayal of Igbo village life, and use of proverbs. Nobel prizewinner Wole Soyinka also employs traditional Yoruba motifs and traditions in his plays, as does poet and playwright J. P. Clark. The vibrant city life of Lagos was captured by Cyprian Ekwensi. This use of local life, lore, and language has continued, as with novelist and television writer Ken Saro-Wiwa, who was killed by the last military government for his environmentalist activism in the Niger Delta.

The wealth of expressive forms in West Africa is too great to be easily summarized here. Although the courts of West Africa no longer have the power they once did, their art forms continue to be practiced. In the courts of the Asantehene of the Ashanti and the Oba of Benin City, there has been a serious revival of court arts and ancient ritual practices recently. Among the descendents of the Western Sudanese kingdoms, griots still perform the epics of Sundjata and the other great kings. In the Cameroons, the fabulous architecture of the royal villages still stands. Historical records are still found in the bronze plaques of the Benin kingdom, the Odu verses of Ifa divination among the Yoruba, and the applique flags of Dahomey in the Republic of Benin.

The sheer diversity of folklore forms is striking. Puppet theaters still perform among the Tiv and Ogoni of Nigeria and in Mali. Masquerades continue to develop and adapt new characters in the rural areas and to find revitalized expressions among urban populations. Synthetic raffia, enamel paints, plastic parts, whatever: all can be used. The increasing use of Theater for Development has revitalized traditional drama forms, from masquerades to folktale sessions among, for example, the Bamana of Mali and Tiv of Nigeria. Narratives filled with the exploits of tricksters and heroes entertain and advise their audiences.

Traditional ceremonies still mark life's passage from birth to death and are validated and embellished with verbal arts, music and dance, historical narratives, and appropriate food and dress. Local healing traditions, ancient divination practices, and all forms of traditional wisdom continue to guide people. No other area reflects the continuity and creativity of tradition better than textiles. In Cote d'Ivoire, new factory-printed textiles arrive daily in the markets and are absorbed into local cultures by being linked to proverbs and the esthetic preferences of the area. Ivoirian dyers and weavers continue to produce textiles in ancient colors and patterns, while simultaneously experimenting with contemporary motifs and dyes.

West African music is known throughout the world. Once typified by "highlife," West African musicians, often influenced by local, traditional music and instruments, perform a wide range of music. Many musicians have a worldwide audience and travel extensively, but still return to perform at home regularly. Islamic and Christian religious musical traditions have also influenced West African music, starting centuries ago and continuing through contemporary religious movements.

The "traditional" topics of folklore scholarship—major prose narrative forms such as myths, folktales, and legends, as well as riddles and proverbs—continue to be used by the people as well as scholars. Entertainment in villages and cities is still found in folktale sessions as well as more unique forms of verbal arts such as the tone riddles and tongue-twisters, which respectively use shifting phonemic tones and repeated consonants, of the Yoruba. The use of traditional verbal art and speech forms by contemporary West African writers, and the increased sophistication of folklore scholarship (both literary and anthropological) have further revealed the enormous value of these forms for understanding cultural values and creativity. We should appreciate not only the scholarly study and indigenous performance of these forms, but the insightful popular cultural use as well. While "Onitsha literature" and concert parties were once considered awkward idiosyncratic transitional practices, we now understand how much they have to tell us.

Tourism has had an impact as well. At one level, tourists' interests, though differing from the native peoples' interests, nevertheless provide income for artists. Sometimes, forgotten arts are revived for a distant market. Sometimes the artists create overseas. Malian and Senegalese musicians record in Paris and New York for expatriate as well as world music audiences. Some academic institutions in the United States invite traditional carvers and potters to their schools. Folkloric touring groups perform in the smallest cities of the United States and Europe; they also provide entertainment for national functions in their own countries.

Television and radio continue to record and broadcast traditional folktales as well as modern-day adaptations. Cote d'Ivoire has a regular evening program of folktales told in local languages, followed by videotaped footage of dances from the same area. Both Ghana and Nigeria have a busy industry of local video dramas many of which are sold in London and elsewhere overseas. And in the villages, local audiences now record their own celebrations on camcorders.

Another important area of continuity that we are learning more about is the degree to which West African folklore persists in the Americas. A majority of the Africans forced into slavery and taken to the Americas were from West Africa. As is seen elsewhere in this volume, one easily finds evidence of the African heritage throughout the Americas in religion, verbal arts, food, dance, daily speech, and celebrations. Ifá divination of the Yoruba is still practiced in Cuba; Western Sudanese musicians continue to influence musicians in the United State; religious practices from the Congo still protect people in Haiti. And, now that an African heritage is a matter of pride not shame, many African Americans travel to West Africa and return with arts and lore.

Despite the vitality of folklore in West Africa today, this area has seen its share of tragedy as well. Although not suffering from the HIV/AIDS epidemic to the horrific extent of southern

Africa, nor the genocide of Rwanda, West Africa still has areas of great suffering. Both Liberia and Sierra Leone have experienced prolonged civil wars. Nigeria had its civil war in the late 1960s, while Cote d'Ivoire is currently experiencing such a breakdown. Each country has had its share of military coups, corrupt governments, and ecological disasters. Nevertheless, creation and performance of folklore forms in all media continue to provide self-identity, spiritual aid, entertainment, and practical instruction for the people.

References

Abimbola, Wande. 1976. *Ifa: An Exposition of Ifa Literary Corpus.* Ibadan: Oxford University Press.

Barber, Karin. 1991. *I Could Speak Until Tomorrow: Oriki, Women, and the Past in a Yoruba Town.* Washington, D.C.: Smithsonian Institution Press.

Beier, Ulli. 1970. *Yoruba Poetry.* Cambridge: Cambridge University Press.

Calame-Griaule, Genevieve. 1986. *Words and the Dogon World* (1965), trans. D. La Pin. Philadelphia: Institute for the Study of Human Issues.

Cosentino, D. 1982. *Defiant Maids and Stubborn Farmers: Tradition and Invention in Mende Story Performance.* Cambridge: Cambridge University Press.

Derive, Jean. 1987. *Le fonctionnement sociologique de la litterature orale: L'exemple des Dioula de Kong.* Paris: Institut d'Ethnologie, Archives Sonores.

Finnegan, Ruth. 1967. *Limba Stories and Storytelling.* Oxford: Clarendon Press.

Furniss, Graham. 1996. *Poetry, Prose, and Popular Culture in Hausa.* Edinburgh: Edinburgh University Press.

Gorog-Karady, Veronika, and G. Meyer. 1985. *Contes bambara (Bamana and French Texts).* Paris: Conseil International de la Langue francaise.

Griaule, M., and G. Dieterlen. 1986. *The Pale Fox* (1965). Trans S.C. Infantino, China Valley, AZ: Continuum Foundation.

Hale, Thomas. 1998. *Griots and Griottes: Masters of Words and Music.* Bloomington: Indiana University Press.

Herskovits, Melville J. and Frances. 1957 *Dahomean Narrative.* Northwestern University Press.

Jackson, Michael. 1982. *Allegories of the Wilderness: Ethics and Ambiguity in Kuranko Narratives.* Bloomington: Indiana University Press.

Johnson, John W. 1986. *The Epic of Son-Jara: A West African Tradition.* Bloomington: Indiana University Press.

Okpweho, Isidore. 1992. *African Oral Literature: Backgrounds, Character, and Continuity.* Bloomington: Indiana University Press.

Olatunji, Olatunde. 1984. *Features of Yoruba Oral Poetry.* Ibadan: Ibadan University Press.

Seydou, Christiane, ed. and trans. 1976. *La geste de Ham-Bodedio au Hama le Rouge.* Classiques africains 18. Paris: Les Belles Lettres, and Armand Colin.

Yankah, Kwesi. 1995. *Speaking for the Chief: Okyeame and the Politics of Royal Oratory.* Bloomington: Indiana University Press.

PHILIP M. PEEK

See also **French Study of African Folklore; German Study of African Folklore; Institutional Study of African Folklore**

WESTERN SAHARA

Although the Western Sahara is not exactly an independent nation, there is cause to present it as such. After a complex history, it has been claimed by (and occupied by) Morocco since 1976; but this is in defiance of the Organization of African Unity and the United Nations. Of its 103,000 square miles (larger than England, Scotland, and Wales combined), Morocco controls two-thirds, while the Polisaro (those fighting for the country's independence) controls one-third.

The indigenous peoples of the area, the Saharawis, have ancient roots here. We know that Arabs reached the territory in their seventh-century sweep across northern Africa; but "modern" history usually begins in 1884 when the Spanish took control, establishing Rio de Oro in 1885 and Spanish Sahara in 1910. Spain did little with the area until the mid-1960s, as most of African began regaining its independence from European powers. The UN asked Spain to organize a referendum vote by the people in 1966. In 1967, liberation movements began, although they were violently repressed by the Spanish.

By the 1970s, Morocco claimed that, historically, it had controlled this area. Despite an International Court of Justice decision to the contrary, Morocco pursued its claim by allowing thousands of Moroccan troops to enter Western Sahara. A secret agreement was signed in 1975 by which Spain granted the country to Morocco and Mauritania. Therefore, in 1976, when Spain formally left the area, Morocco was already an occupying force in opposition to the claims of real independence by the Polisaro, who declared the region the nation of the Saharwi Arab Democratic Republic.

After several Polisaro attacks, Mauritania signed a peace agreement in 1979 and relinquished its claim to any territory. Nevertheless, armed conflicts continue. In 1997, it was estimated that there were 200,000 Moroccan settlers, 120,000 Moroccan soldiers, and 65,000 Saharawis in the occupied area. This area is separated from the Polisaro-controlled area by a huge fortified wall that Morocco built. This has been an extraordinarily expensive war for Morocco, costing it nearly one million dollars a day.

In 1985, the OAU recognized the Saharawi Arab Democratic Republic. This caused Morocco to leave the organization. Although sixty-seven countries recognized the republic, Morocco continued to deny it. In 1990, the United Nations put forward a peace plan. Although the ceasefire took effect in 1991, Morocco has yet to accept the call for a referendum by the people.

Among the area's riches are phosphates. Their exploitation by Morocco increases its status as the world's largest exporter of phosphates. Western Sahara's Atlantic fishing grounds are among the richest in the world.

PHILIP M. PEEK

WESTERN SUDANESE KINGDOMS

See **Epics; Griots and Griottes; West African Folklore: Overview**

WITCHCRAFT, MAGIC, AND SORCERY

The student of African folklore must be careful when encountering the terms *witchcraft, magic,* and *sorcery* to ascertain exactly what is meant. They have wide ranges of meaning, and may be used interchangeably and pejoratively. All three are frequently categorized under the pidgin English term *juju*—roughly equivalent to today's concept of *occult*. They are often regarded as embarrassing aspects of a superstitious, "primitive" past; and they may be omitted or given only brief mention in modern discussions of traditional African culture. Systematic recording of African cultural traditions began in the colonial era; European administrative agencies, and Christian missionaries, regarded magic, sorcery, and witchcraft—and, of course, much of African ritual and belief—as dangerous, evil, or even satanic. Often, indeed, the use of these terms may reveal more about the beliefs and biases of their users than about the phenomena under consideration. But in fact the concepts are important in both traditional and modern African societies. Understanding them yields insight into cosmological ideas and the workings of society; moreover, they are not uniquely African but are expressions of universal human ways of thinking.

A common meaning of any of these terms involves dealing with spirits, by means of possession, mediumship, or command. All African peoples recognize that spiritual beings: gods, ancestors, ghosts, and good or evil spirits in nature, can affect things in the material world; and that such beings can be influenced and even commanded by people. This is spirit invocation and it is dangerous, because most spirits are sentient beings with wills of their own. Magic, sorcery and witchcraft operate according to quite different premises. The most useful meanings are found in anthropologists' use of these terms (see Stevens 1996).

Magic

Magic involves the human use of symbols to harness and control power, and affect things without spiritual assistance. There are at least four fundamental and pan-human beliefs underlying the operation of magic: (1) all things in the world are invisibly ("mystically") interconnected past, present, and future; (2) all things have some degree of communicable power; (3) symbols—actions, objects, words, or thoughts—which in any way resemble, embody meaning of, or have been in contact with the thing to be affected, have an active connection with that thing in the classic principles of sympathetic magic; (4) symbols take on the power of the things they represent. A good discussion of the concept of mystical power and its role in magic, sorcery, and witchcraft in African belief systems is provided by Mbiti (1989, 189–98).

Magic requires no special skill or innate gift; it can be learned by anyone. Magic may be performed openly and routinely by individuals to enhance their own physical efforts, or for general good fortune, for themselves or for the good of the community. Verbal blessing is the most common example of individual beneficial magic. Magic may also be intertwined with religious ritual, as people may directly supplicate supernatural beings, while symbolically trying to influence nature. The symbolic use of colors in magical ways is common in ritual: white represents holiness and spiritual purity, but it is also the color of milk and semen, and hence it may be associated with growth and fertility respectively; red is blood, hence vitality, energy and life itself, but it is also anger or fire, and can be negative and dangerous; black is darkness and negativity (see Turner 1967).

Farmers may employ a variety of "rain charms," such as devices that when shaken imitate the sound of falling rain, or drums that imitate thunder. Whenever the king of Bachama (of northern Nigeria) ventures out of his palace, from the end of the dry season through the rainy season, he wears dark (dunge, "black") indigo dyed robes, in sympathy with the expected dark rain clouds; but towards the end of the rainy season and throughout the dry season, he wears pale blue robes to encourage the natural forces that bring about clear blue skies. Much of people's social activities reflect the belief that human actions or words can affect nature. No matter how adverse conditions may be, people are reluctant to speak or even think pessimistically. The widely popular sport of wrestling may also have magical implications; bouts between strong young men may be connected to agricultural rituals at the beginning of the cultivating and planting season. Similarly, orgies of sexual activity associated with such rituals were reported by early colonial chroniclers, before such activities were halted by Europeans with different ideas of morality.

The principles of magic may be evident in rituals of divination, most clearly those activated by words alone, like the famous Zande oracles discussed by E. E. Evans-Pritchard (1937), as opposed to instances in which the revelation is believed to be given directly by a spiritual agency. Taboo may be regarded as the avoidance of establishing a magical connection; a pregnant woman must never carry a water pot, engage in weaving or tying, or cut with sharp instruments. Some strong powers should not come into contact with others; menstruating women or people who have not washed after sexual intercourse should not handle food or come near small children. Magical methods are widely used in healing as well. Muslim healers often inscribe a verse from the Koran in soluble ink, rinse it off with water and give the solution to the patient to drink.

Magical power may be harnessed for protection against the spells of sorcerers or the activities of evil spirits and witches. Krige (1947) reported that the coastal Lovedu (in South Africa) placed magical "medicines" of whale oil, sea sand, and other products of the sea at strategic points around the village so that the night-flying witches would see only water and become disoriented. Children and the sick are believed especially vulnerable to evil forces and therefore may wear necklaces or waistbands of magical beads and various powerful items. Eggs, horns, and representations of the female genitals are powerful magical symbols often used for protection. Cowries are magically powerful, because of their resemblance to the vulva. Priests dealing routinely with spirits are especially vulnerable to any forms of supernatural evil when in states of possession. They employ a wide variety of magical protections, as do hunters, who spend long periods in the "bush" (a term used for any area outside human settlement) where various evil agents are known to dwell. Such people with dangerous professions often wear special shirts with leather pouches containing magical materials sewn into the fabric, or with dangling cowries or tiny horns. Collectors of African art and material culture have noted the variety of apotropaic devices used by householders and shrine-keepers. Words are powerful in Africa; the written word gives the word's meaning an awesome permanence and is used magically throughout the continent.

Magic for good fortune, protection and defense, and in offense as sorcery, is used today by athletes, including traditional wrestlers and boxers as well as participants in soccer and other modern sports; by soldiers and rebels, members of gangs and protest movements in encounters with civil authorities—indeed, by any persons in direct competition or conflict with others. Newspaper reports of armed conflicts routinely record "dangerous charms" in their inventories of weapons used.

Each culture has its own inventory of magical items, which may include particular minerals, insects, parts of specific plants or animals, and artifacts whose symbolic meanings might be intelligible only within that culture's tradition and language. Since the basic principles of magic are absolutely universal, they seem to illustrate fundamental human ways of thinking.

Sorcery

The natural order of things is inherently good. Magic enhances nature. Sorcery is negative magic that encourages natural forces to act in abnormal ways. This is dangerous as it disrupts the natural program. Any act of magic motivated by a desire to do harm to another person or to enrich oneself at the expense of another is sorcery. Sorcery is antisocial and illegal, and is therefore secretive, performed clandestinely and difficult to document. Fears of sorcery are ubiquitous. However, careful study may indicate that the actual practice is uncommon.

Materials for magic and hence for sorcery, are openly sold in public markets as *juju* items. They are usually displayed in stalls set apart from areas where foodstuffs and domestic items are sold. Sorcery, as Krige (1947) put it, involves "lawful means put to unlawful ends." Stevens (1988) records the case of a Yoruba boy, eleven years old, who performed sorcery openly against the opponents of his school's table tennis team. The boy had purchased a *juju* padlock at the local market, specifically a European metal padlock wrapped in hyena fur (the hyena is a common familiar animal of witches) with a red silk ribbon tied onto it, which is then attached to a large iron staple. When the staple is thrust into the ground, a spell is spoken and the padlock is locked around it; whatever is spoken will also be "locked" into place. The boy, naive about the dangers in what he was doing, had performed this little rite just outside the games hall where an important table tennis match was under way. The boy had to run for his life from an enraged mob of students from both schools, who were terrified about whatever powers he may have unleashed.

Similar cases involving adults are probably rare. A curse, a verbal expression of ill will toward another, is the most commonly recorded example of sorcery. Most often curses are made in the heat of argument or in drunkenness; and an apology, a retraction of the harmful words, is the minimal remedy. Court records throughout Africa contain many cases brought by people against alleged cursers.

People have fairly clear ideas of how sorcery can be done. The belief that one can hurt another by damaging or speaking a curse to a physical representation of the target person is common, in the universal fear of harmful "image magic." People everywhere take care to dispose of bodily leavings or soiled clothing, lest they be used by sorcerers. Such fears also account for the custom of not giving a baby a name until several days after its birth, and in many societies, never revealing the most intimate personal name given to a child. The name of a thing embodies the essence of the thing itself, and is a vital element in magic and sorcery.

It is presumed that herbalists and healers who have occult knowledge may be skilled at sorcery, and that people with social grievances can hire them, or purchase sorcery materials from them. Men are suspected of sorcery more often than women, but anyone can learn it; therefore the fear of it tempers people's social interactions. This is the classic "social control function" of sorcery beliefs and of witchcraft, as we shall see below.

African terms for *magic* and *sorcery* are often variants of each other; both may fall under the English word *medicine*, meaning any natural or supernatural substance or ritual activity that can affects one's health. The negative side of medicine may be expressed as *bad medicine* or *poison*. Poison often refers to negative mystical power as to a toxic substance. Furthermore, most African peoples distinguish linguistically between at least two forms of the human projection of supernatural evil, as Sir Edward Evans-Pritchard carefully noted for the Azande in his famous 1937 study. Among the Bachama of Nigeria human supernatural evil is *mwito*; sorcery is *mwito fore* or *mwito by day*, referring to the fact that, theoretically, anyone can learn and practice it. Sorcery by cursing is *mwito kwame*, *mwito* by mouth or speech.

Witchcraft

Another Bachama concept, *mwito surato* or original *mwito* is best translated as "witchcraft." Following Evans-Pritchard's pioneering work, it was realized that most sub-Saharan peoples differentiate between sorcery, learned evil magic, and witchcraft, which is an innate inherited ability. Sometimes, as in the Zande *mangu*, Tiv *tsav*, or pythons in the bellies of Nyakyusa witches, witchcraft power is vested in a real, tangible substance in the body, which can be mystically removed by a "witchdoctor" or discovered through autopsy. Witchcraft is a corrupted form of the personal power, sometimes equated with personality or the "soul" inherent in everyone, such as the Akan *sunsum*, Yoruba *ashe*, or Bachama *fwato*. Witchcraft power may operate independently of its bearer's will or even knowledge. When active, the power of witchcraft is always evil.

Activated by any negative emotion, the power has twelve attributes similar to witchcraft beliefs elsewhere in the world, of which a few seem to be uniquely African variants. Scholars have noted the similarities between African and medieval European witch beliefs. The following is a list of the twelve attributes: (1) The power renders the witch antisocial, dedicated to the subversion of the social order. (2) The witch is mostly nocturnal. (3) The power enables the witch to transform itself, into any other form, or to become invisible and to (4) fly through the air, often at great speed. (5) The witch has an alter-ego, usually an animal with which it shares the power and send out on its mission of evil; the "familiar" of European folklore. Killing or injuring the animal will kill or incapacitate the witch. (6) The witches of a community meet together periodically to collectively enhance their powers and to plot new evil against society. (7) Witches spread disease. A first task of AIDS workers today is to assure people that this disease is not spread by witchcraft. (8) Witches steal (the souls of) children, providing one explanation of infant mortality. (9) At their gatherings, witches engage in incest or other forms of illicit sexual behavior and (10) ritual murder of their kidnapped human victims, and the ritual use of body parts. (11) Witches eat the flesh and drink the blood of their victims. Whether or not any form of cannibalism ever actually occurred is a matter of ongoing debate in African and world ethnology; but it certainly is among the most abhorrent of human imaginings, and it is often the defining feature of African witches. Any long debilitating illness will most likely be attributed to a witch slowly "eating" the life-force of the sufferer. And (12) witches are invariably associated with death in three ways: they cause death, their gatherings are held in cemeteries, and myths say that a society's original witches were granted powers by a dark deity or other terrible supernatural being associated with human mortality.

In these ways, African witches are like witches elsewhere in the world, and have attributes with cultural elaborations on fundamental human fears. For example, in a classic 1951 article, Monica Hunter Wilson called witchcraft "the standardized nightmare of a group." There are also some witchcraft attributes shared only with a few others, or which may be uniquely African. Universally, women are suspected of being witches more often than men; but in a few regions, including Africa, it is generally believed that only women can pass on the trait to their offspring, or to other women who wish to acquire it. Among the Yoruba for example, it is believed that young girls may gather around a dying old witch, hoping she will vomit up the witchcraft substance and allow them to catch it and swallow it. When flying about at night African witches often emit visible light, conceived as fire shooting out from the anus or the armpits. African witches and sorcerers are suspected of enchanting and enslaving people, either as living victims or corpses (the origin of the Haitian *zombi*). Similar to the related phenomenon of Evil Eye in North Africa and elsewhere, the fact that witchcraft power may operate without its bearer's knowledge has important social implications in Africa. If general social opinion (usually confirmed by divination) identifies an individual as a witch and holds him or her responsible for some misfortune, the accused may make a credible claim of ignorance, an apology, or some recompense to the victim, and the issue is usually settled. An interesting aspect of African witchcraft is the belief that the corrupted power is evil and punishable only when active; when dormant it is benign and may be regarded as a distinctive marker of societal membership. Each society regards its own form of personal power as unique, and as evidence of direct lineal descent from the culture founders. The people of Bachama know that there are witches and cannibals in other societies, but only a Bachama person may have *mwito*. In some cases of disputed descent or rights to inheritance reference to this unique form of supernatural evil is made. For example, a person of original Bachama descent is referred to as *jibato ka mwito*, of the patrilineage with the potential for witchcraft. A person whose ancestors were adopted into Bachama society after its establishment is *jibato a mwito*, of the patrilineage but without this unique Bachama marker, and possibly ineligible for some important right or social position.

Magical defenses against witchcraft have been mentioned above; people also enlist a wide variety of spiritual aids, including masquerades like the Gelede of the Yoruba, aimed at placating the "mothers;" and the Nupe Ndako-Gboya, a large cloth cylinder containing a wild bush spirit that sweeps witches from the village. Some peoples have organizations, often called "secret societies," of witch finders and demon exorcisers, who identify witches through various mystical means, and with special devices and weapons can injure or drive out witches and malign spirits. Members of such a group among the Bachama have a special "sight" (*diya*), mystical eyes at the center of the forehead and at the occiput, which enable them to "see" witches, and to distinguish evil spirits from benign ones.

The Social Psychology of Sorcery and Witchcraft

Sorcery is malicious and dreaded, but witchcraft is a standard fact of African social life. The literature on African sorcery and witchcraft is tremendous, and many social, psychological, and cosmological explanations have been offered. They are favorite topics for analysis by the British structural school of anthropology, and most of the major African journals have devoted special issues to the topics (most recently Ciekawy and Geschiere 1998), and have many references to specific studies in their indices. (For a good summary of the ethnography of African witchcraft, see Mair 1969; a notable collection of studies focusing on East African cases is Middleton and Winter 1963; some of the more important early African studies are found in Marwick 1982.) There are also many monographs on specific societies.

All scholars agree on certain positive functions of sorcery and witchcraft beliefs. For example, they explain misfortune in nature and in society, promote responsible social behavior, and in times of stress, satisfy the human psychological need for a scapegoat. The scapegoating function of witchcraft beliefs is its most common explanation in Africa and elsewhere, and is strengthened by the observation that beliefs in witchcraft are absent in mobile societies. These include hunter-gatherers and pastoralists, in which social tensions can be resolved by people moving away from one another. The scapegoating function is clearest in the close correlation between witchcraft accusations and social anxiety and frustration, such as accompanies rapid social change.

Some scholars consider a linguistic or conceptual distinction between sorcery and witchcraft to be irrelevant, because both are allegedly performed for similar reasons, by persons in similar relationships to the victim, both achieve similar ends, and both are dreaded. In the context of collective social stress, the distinction becomes less important and may even be confused; what is important is who is causing the evil that spreads in society. It is in such contexts that traditional patterns of suspicion, accusation and methods of identification and punishment of witches may break down, social frustration may explode, and a society-wide witch-hunt may occur, which aims to drive out the perceived causes of social misfortune.

Witch-hunts were conducted by organized groups during the colonial times, such as the Bamucapi movement among Bemba in 1934 (Richards 1935); the Atinga witch-finding movement among the Yoruba in the early 1950s (Morton-Williams 1956); and the Kamcape movement among the Fipa in the early 1960s (Willis 1968).

With independence there have been new problems, new expectations, new political alliances, new disappointments, and new responses within the traditional idiom of sorcery and witchcraft beliefs. Sorcery and witchcraft suspicions are ever-present in the poverty and near-hopelessness of life for many in Africa's cities. Sexual proficiency, marked by fertility and sexual potency, may take on great importance such as a mark of personal achievement, making it a more frequent target for sorcery. In Lagos, Nigeria, in 1990, a wave of "penis-snatching" fears terrified the male population. An encounter with a stranger could result in an immediate shrinking of the penis and total disappearance of the entire genitals. Many deaths were caused by beatings of accused individuals by enraged mobs.

In 1980 and 1981 some ritual *muti* (occult, *juju*) murders, and rumors of many more, caused considerable social unrest in Swaziland. In the years following the dismantling of apartheid in South Africa in the early 1990s, many hundreds of people have been seized by mobs and burned as witches. In Tanzania between 1998 and 1999 allegations of ritual murders and dealings in human body parts led to hundreds, some reported as thousands, of lynchings and burnings of alleged sorcerers by mobs. Women with red eyes (a traditional distinguishing mark of a witch) were particularly suspect—often in the close unventilated atmosphere of urban slum quarters, where cooking smoke often reddened women's eyes. In August 1999, a mob in Port Harcourt, a large city in Nigeria's troubled Niger Delta region, attacked a homeless man who was reported by a small boy to have turned himself into a vulture and back again. Rumors of ritual murders spread in Lagos in the late 1990s after the discovery of a demented street person who killed people and dismembered their bodies. In South Africa in 1998 hospitals' organ donation and transplantation programs were disrupted because of similar fears.

Such cases can be seen to have occurred in social-psychological contexts of confused and unrealistic political/economic expectations (see Ciekawy and Geschiere 1999). Witchcraft and sorcery suspicions and accusations have long been recognized as associated with economic change, as Ardener (1970) reported for the Bakweri of Cameroon in the 1960s. Today's new and often baffling economic forces caused by multiculturalism and globalization have generated new fears of zombie labor and "occult economies" (Comaroff and Comaroff 1999, and Sharp 2001). Traditionally, children were considered pure and innocent and incapable of witchcraft. Brain (1970) reported fears of childwitches emerging in Bangwa, Cameroon, as early as the 1950s. Today the social image of children has changed radically, as poverty, AIDS, brutal civil rebellions, and rapid and massive migrations have created large numbers of child slaves, child soldiers, homeless urban street children, and increased fears of child-witches (see De Boeck, in press).

Magic, sorcery, and witchcraft beliefs persist in modern Africa, as they do in many other developing areas of the world for a variety of apparent reasons. Selective and incomplete education is only part of the answer. Magical thinking is reduced, but not eradicated, through modern science and technology. Sorcery and witchcraft beliefs were integral to traditional African cultures, as were remedies for them. Foreign agents attempted to change only parts of African cultures; the rest were left intact, through indifference or ignorance. The policies of European colonial governments involved either dismissal as superstition, or repression sanctioned by the same sorts of antisorcery laws that existed in their home countries. Christianity's attitude was unequivocal condemnation; it offered no sympathy toward nor accommodation for sorcery and witchcraft beliefs. It should be noted that Christianity did not replace traditional beliefs; rather, it supplemented them. For converts, most traditional beliefs remained intact. And in African thinking, nothing is random or fortuitous, everything has a reason for happening. For both traditional and modern systems, sorcery and witchcraft answer questions that cannot otherwise be answered: e.g., "Why me?" and "Why just then?" While it is recognized that sorcery and witchcraft are

social problems activated by the negative emotions that inevitably arise in situations of social stress, their persistence in modern times is better understood.

References

Ardener, Edwin. 1970. Witchcraft, Economics, and the Continuity of Belief. In *Witchcraft Confessions and Accusations*, ed. Mary Douglas. London: Tavistock.

Brain, Robert. 1970. Child-witches. In *Witchcraft Confessions and Accusations*, ed. Mary Douglas. London: Tavistock.

Ciekawy, Diane, and Peter Geschiere, eds. 1998. Containing Witchcraft: Conflicting Scenarios in Postcolonial Africa. *African Studies Review* 41, no. 3.

Comaroff, Jean and John L. Comaroff. 1999. Occult Economics and the Violence of Abstraction: Notes from the South African Postcolony. *American Ethnologist* 26, 2:279–303.

De Boeck, Filip. In press. The Second World: Children and Witchcraft in D.R. Congo. In *Makers and Breakers: Children and Youth as Emerging Categories in Postcolonial Africa*, eds. A Honwana and F. De Boeck. London: James Currey.

Evans-Pritchard, E. E. 1937. *Witchcraft, Oracles, and Magic among the Azande*. Oxford: Clarendon Press.

Krige, J. D. 1947. The Social Function of Witchcraft. *Theorisa* 1:3–21.

Mair, Lucy. 1969. *Witchcraft*. New York: McGraw-Hill.

Marwick, Max, ed. 1982. *Witchcraft and Sorcery: Selected Readings*. 2nd ed. Harmondsworth, England: Penguin Books.

Mbiti, John S. 1989. *African Religions and Philosophy*. 2nd. ed. Oxford: Heinemann.

Middleton, John F. M., and E. H. Winter, eds. 1963. *Witchcraft and Sorcery in East Africa*. London: Routledge and Kegan Paul.

Morton-Williams, Peter. 1956. The Atinga Cult among the Southwestern Yoruba: A Sociological Analysis of a Witch-Finding Movement. *Bulletin IFAN* 18:3–4, 315–34.

Richards, Audrey. 1935. A Modern Movement of Witch-Finders. *Africa* 8, no. 4. 448–61.

Turner, Victor. 1967. *The Forest of Symbols: Aspects of Ndembu Ritual*. Ithaca: Cornell University Press.

Sharp, Lesley A. 2001. Wayward Pastoral Ghosts and Regional Xenophobia in a Northern Madagascar Town. *Africa* 71, 1:38–81.

Stevens, Philips, Jr. 1988. Table Tennis and Sorcery in West Africa. *Play and Culture* 1, no. 2:138–45.

———. 1996. "Magic" and "Sorcery and Witchcraft." *Encyclopedia of Cultural Anthropology*, ed. by David Levinson and Melvin Ember. New York: Holt.

Wilson, Monica Hunter. 1951. Witch Beliefs and Social Structure. *American Journal of Sociology* 56:307–13.

Willis, R. G. 1968. Kamcape: An Anti-Sorcery Movement in Southwestern Tanzania. *Africa* 38:1–15.

PHILLIPS STEVENS JR.

See also **Ancestors; Divination; Evil Eye; Gender Representation in African Folklore; Gossip and Rumor**

WOMEN'S EXPRESSIVE CULTURE IN AFRICA

An African person belongs to different types of groupings, each of which gives the individual a particular identity. The most important of these is the family or lineage, which imparts an identity that lasts long after death and is carried in praise poems, dirges, genealogical songs, and epics. The second category that an African person is classified by is gender. Many activities in the social and working lives of traditional African persons are undertaken exclusively by males or females, either as individuals or in groups. These groups may be permanent or may come together only for a particular purpose and then dissolve. Naturally, such activities and organizations have developed a rich array of particular expressive cultures. This entry sweeps through a wide panorama of expressive culture associated specifically with Africa women's groups, activities, and perceptions of life.

The individual woman may compose a poem in praise of herself as Tonga (Zambia) women do with the Impango. She could also be a solo artist, such as a female Ijala singer among the Yoruba, who might be seen undertaking ritual begging of alms with her toothless python around her neck. Several types of dyads of women may be found based on the bonds of friendship occupation and kinship. The sharing of axioms among friends based on shared experiences with either the full phrase repeated or a call-and-response format may be cited. Other characteristic traditions include the wearing of identical attire: women affiliated by such as kinship or politics can be identified by their use of the same cloth.

Women have been recognized as custodians of oral traditions and fictional narratives. In Ghana, the Asantehemaa, or queen mother of Asante, has a court of her own and is consulted on historical facts crucial for the conduct of matters of state. The concept of "old lady" as the wise one to be consulted when matters get complicated is a pervasive one in many African cultures. Women, particularly elderly women, are also credited with the talent for telling folktales of various types. Thus some cultures, such as the Fulani of northern Cameroon, seem to relegate storytelling to a lower status than the cycle of epics, for example, performed by men. In other cultures, such as the Bulsa of northern Ghana, there are narrative forms that are marked by the nonparticipation of male adults.

Women performers of the folktale have, however, been recognized in scholarship. One of the most famous of these is Mrs. Zenani, a highly gifted Xhosa story teller from South Africa, whose prowess has been brought to the fore by Harold Scheub (1975). There is no denying that the conceptions of woman as nurturer and first teacher are confirmed by her association with this art form, which captures morality, fantasy, wit, and creative communication.

Activities concerning major life transitions of birth, puberty, marriage, and death are in many parts of Africa the prerogative of women. These are undergoing rapid transformation and are becoming modified, sometimes radically. However, in the conduct of ceremonies, women have developed the verbal and symbolic discourse that defines the nature of these ceremonies. This may go from the ululation at the birth of a child to the conduct of puberty schools, such as those managed by the Sande association in Sierra Leone. Throughout North Africa and among Akan-speakers in Ghana, women engage in the dramatic negotiation of marriage contracts. The Gas of Ghana have developed professional spokespersons who have impressive oratorical skills and a repertoire of songs and jokes. They may be hired to lead a family in these negotiations. Other well-known instances of women's vocal skills are those of the preparation of the dead for burial and the public mourning of the death particularly through the funeral dirges which in most African societies are the exclusive prerogative of women.

During festivals, women may act as jesters and may even wear male clothing and overtly take strong public roles, as has been seen above.

Certain occupations predominantly undertaken by women generate poetry. Pounding and grinding songs and chants are composed and sung to reduce the drudgery of the occupation. Some of these may accompany such solitary work as grinding in the Kamba and Basotho societies of southern Africa. Pounding songs, however, are of a different type, for these have to be done to the complex rhythm of the pounding and involve at least two women. These are found in many parts of the continent, particularly where processing of grain is undertaken by pounding. Throughout West Africa in every village and city one hears women accompanying themselves with song as they pound yams or cassavas in huge wooden mortars.

The folklore associated with occupations is not only verbal. For example, women have the responsibility of finishing, repairing, and decorating the walls of houses. The traditional communities of the Frafra of Ghana and the Basotho of South Africa may be cited as societies where an aesthetic canon of symbols and decorative patterns applied to house and compound walls has been developed.

One interesting type of occupational folklore is the duplication of formal governance systems from the political system of the traditional state to the guild. One of these is the position of chief. Thus the leader of tomato sellers in a given Akan market would be called Tomatoes-hemma. These associations also have the position of spokesperson or Okyeame. They often manifest their pride in their vocation at funerals where they arrive in an official delegation and often enact aspects of the work-life they shared with their fallen colleague.

Certain groupings of women may be said to be based on religions or parareligious imperatives. The Mende of Sierra Leone come in for mention once again as Sande is an esoteric grouping of women conveying the female essence. Others may involve the cult of female gods. One of the most famous is surely the cult of the Osun River goddess of the Yoruba pantheon in Nigeria who represents the essence and power of femininity and, therefore, has generated a paradigm of femaleness in all aspects of the conduct of activities related to this cult. It is important to draw attention to a large corpus of praise poetry especially dedicated to the goddess and what she represents, which forms an important classic of the Yoruba literary cannon.

Women have characteristic modes of expression, which take on particularly interesting dimensions because of their relative restriction to the domestic and emotional spheres of life. The culture of self-adornment is a vastly intriguing area, which involves the sculpturing of the body by the massage of the head and buttocks as among the Asante as well as scarification and application of intricate patterns through tattooing as found in southern Nigeria. Muslim communities in many parts of the continent, particularly the Sahelian and North African areas, tattoo the hands and feet of brides. More temporary but equally intriguing is body painting effected with natural substances such as various hues of clay and chalk often undertaken for ceremonial purposes or as a makeup for performance. The Surma and Karo women of Ethiopia are well-known for such decoration. Women Klama priests of the Dangbe area of southeastern Ghana as well as graduates from the puberty school known as Dipo from the same area also display fine examples of this form of body art.

The making and wearing of jewelery also constitute an area replete with creativity, symbolism, and dynamic tradition. The legendary bead cultures of Maasai and Zulu women turn out shoulder-length necklaces covering the neck and part of the shoulders. In the Zulu tradition, distinctive bead aprons are made as well as bead "letters," whose colors send messages to lovers. Beads form a part of the earliest traditions of self-adornment by Ghanaian women from various ethnic groups. As with many other African women, beads are worn around the neck, wrist, waist, forearms, knees, and ankles. They may be as large as a small hen's egg or just large enough to string, and may be made out of materials ranging from stone to glass and plastic. A saying in Akan goes, "Sophisticated beads do not jingle."

One manifestation of the embodiment of the culture of women's self-adornment is the institution of Neggafa, or beautician, in Morocco. These accomplished artists embellish the Moroccan woman's life at all stages, in both body and soul. One of the most vivid presentations of this exclusively female institution is the film *Pour le plaisir des yeux* written and directed by Morrocan filmmaker Izza Genini.

Groups of women often wear the same cloth sewn into several identical outfits for group identification and assertion. Clothes may be named according to axioms, topical events and names of (in)famous persons in many parts of West Africa. The famous East African Kanga cloths are named in Swahili and often have axioms written on them. They are frequently used in situations of polygyny by Swahili women to conduct quarrels. In Ghana, designs of wax prints typically worn by women are often named in Twi based on the same themes and sources mentioned above. For example, "If marriage was like peanuts in a pod, I would have cracked it." Cloths can be worn to express the emotional condition or social status of the individual.

This symbolism becomes very interesting when deployed antagonistically in actual or potential conflicts between affinal relations. It is not only the design of the fabric, but the manner of wearing that conveys the message. For example, a headtie worn in a specific way means, "Gyae me how" (Stop bothering me). The manner of tying the cloth may also have a meaning. For example, a cloth worn with the free edge behind the body denotes that "There is a fool walking behind me." Women may use items or clothing as significant props for performance or as part of ceremonial acts. This includes the presence or absence of clothing as well as the process of dressing or undressing. For example, in hailing persons whom they value highly for family or political reasons, women from all ethnic groups in Ghana will take off the second cloth which is part of the attire of a mature woman, and either fan a procession or lay it down for persons in a procession to walk on. This act is often accompanied by priase and histrionics. Such an act may take place during a traditional festival with the arrival of a chief, or during a wedding ceremony, for example.

On the other hand, a woman in mourning may throw off her headtie and attempt to take off other items of clothing while wailing for the dead. In addition to this, a historical rite that is rarely evoked today is the historical *Mmomome* rites of the Akan. Women awaiting the return of men from the battlefield used to parade through the streets naked and singing songs to invoke victory in battle. These are only performed in dire circumstances.

The Litolobonya performance session of Basotho women excludes men. Women taking part in this ceremony, which celebrates the birth of a child, are scantily dressed and dance till morning, making movements suggestive of sexual relations.

There is an entire area of women's knowledge and culture that is restricted by its nature. This may appear as the sub-text in the process of preparation for marriage. Or it may, form the overt content of quarrels, and exclusive sessions for women's recreation. Young Hausa brides, for example, are taught how to use douches and aphrodisiac preparations by trusted aunts. During women-only recreational performances by women they openly express their basic difficulties with relationships and express the frustration, stress, and joy of their private existence in the domestic domain, thus offering an alternative discourse to the public paradigm, which is controlled mostly by men. Somali women restricted from addressing their husbands directly may compose songs about a difficulty in their relationships, which they will sing in the presence of their husbands, expecting modified behavior in response.

None of this is to suggest that popular woman artists are not to be found in Africa. As the famous bardic tradition of Sahelian West Africa undergoes a transformation today, women stars who specialize in shorter lyrical pieces have emerged. The Jelimousow of Mali have increased in popularity and have taken their place among the great griots of the region.

Hausa women singers have an ambivalent position, due to a tendency to link classicism with Islamic written verse, while orally transmitted song are seen as a lesser, popular, and ephemeral art. The royal courts of northern Nigeria often have a woman poet, or Marokia Zabiya. Some Zabiya have gained great respectability and become independent popular stars, such as Maimuna Coge.

As may be seen from this brief survey, the rich variety of women's activities has generated, and continues to generate, a deep and multifaceted expressive culture.

References

Badejo, D. 1996. *Osun Segesi: The Elegant Deity of Wealth and Femininity*. Trenton, N.J.: African World Press.

Finnegan, R. 1970. *Oral Literature in Africa*. London: Oxford University Press.

Finnegan, R. 1970. *Oral Poetry. Its Name, Significance, and Social Context*. Cambridge: Cambridge University Press.

Furniss, G., and L. Gunner, eds. 1995. *Marginality and African Oral Literature*. Cambridge: Cambridge University Press.

Moitse, S. 1994. *The Ethnomusicology of the Basotho*. Rome: ISAS.

Nketia, K. 1955. *Funeral Dirges of the Akan People*.

Scheub, H. 1975. *The Xhosa Ntsomi*. Oxford: Clarendon Press.

ESI SUTHERLAND-ADDY

See also **Gender Representation in African Folklore; Performance in Africa**

WOMEN'S FOLKLORE: ERITREA

Eritrean women comprise approximately 50 percent of the total population. Before independence, the society was quite different from what it is now economically, politically and socioculturally. These changes started to appear before independence in 1991, as the area liberated during the war was already changing in many ways, due to the inability of the enemy to interfere in these areas. The status of women and their rights in the society was a prominent change. The main reason for this is that the Eritrean women fought alongside the men for independence.

Before independence, Eritrean women were victims of cultural and colonial oppression. The Italian, the British and Ethiopian colonial powers deprived them of their rights in their own country. The only option offered to women was to serve the colonizers as housemaids. The native patriarchal system of Eritrea also deprived them of equal rights with men in political, social, cultural and economic life. Women could not receive inheritances in a fashion equal to men, nor were they allowed to participate equally in political affairs. They were considered socially and culturally inferior to men.

Today in post-independence Eritrea, women participate in many areas of society once reserved exclusively for men. Eritrean women have made significant accomplishments through their participation in the independence war, yet, equality with men at all levels of the society calls for a continuous fight against oppressive institutions, such as arranged and underage marriages and female genital operations.

Eritrean folklore affords an opportunity to examine the lives of Eritrean woman before independence was gained, and patriarchal oppression was eased. Girls were not allowed to choose their mate; parents arranged marriages. Women's frustration at this state of affairs is reflected in the songs girls traditionally sang when they saw off a friend after her wedding day, as she moved to her husband's house. One such song contains the lyrics:

My friends are we like this?
Why do they give us away?
Like a goat's baby,
Which is dragged away.

Another song, also sung by the bride's friends, advise her to be wise and observant of what the in-laws, might do to her:

Go with them,
But smile while at the same time
Observing what they do to you.

Women taking part in a ritual of transition from summer to winter, praying for a good rainy reason and a good harvest in the coming season.
Photo © Senait Bahta.

Women learning to read and write, as part of the policy to eliminate illiteracy by 2004.
Photo © Senait Bahta.

These songs were sung by young women between the ages of fifteen and seventeen, who were aware that their fate would also be that of the bride given over in a marriage arranged by her parents. The songs symbolize women's opposition to cultural tradition.

Interestingly, now that the law prohibits child betrothal, underage marriage, female genital mutilation, and other institutions that serve to keep women inferior, contemporary songs now reflect how women have become equal with men and participate in all spheres of society. The young women sing to herald that it is high time for women to say goodbye to the kitchen, previously the females' domain, and to be full participants in national activities with males. One song goes:

Goodbye kitchen,
I have broken your prison,
To see the world
I am now in shorts
Fighting on my brothers side
For independence and equal rights.

It was not until 1979 that Eritrean women were organized at a national level. Before then, the colonial governments would not allow them to organize politically. However, there are stories that tell that Eritrean women, although not organized, were fighting against oppression in various ways.

Eritrean folklore holds that, during the Italian colonial period, women used to spray hot pepper powder in the fascists' eyes when they attempted to rape the women. Others defended themselves with sharp metal needles called *mesfe*, which they used for making baskets. Eritrean women have a history of forming new villages in an attempt to escape wife beating.

One interesting tale is that of Shuma, a woman from Barka in western Eritrea from the Beja ethnic group. Shuma had a cruel abusive husband whom she loathed. To escape from him, Shuma left home, taking her sister with her to the eastern lowlands of Eritrea. While living there, a wealthy man met, fell in love with, and married her. He took her with him to his village and provided for her sister, as well. Descendants of Shuma now live in that village, which is called Adi Shuma (the village/home of Shuma).

Another story about the role of Eritrean women in settling disputes or conflicts between people centers on Asmara, the capital city of Eritrea. According to one source, in the past, the place now called Asmara was covered with dense forest, where four villages were located. It was a dangerous place to live and the villagers suffered, since they were ambushed by bandits who took their property, killed men walking home from work, and kidnapped children. Although night guards were placed in each of the villages, this did not solve the problem. One day, the women from these four villages met in a church to discuss the problem. They agreed to ask their husbands to unite the small villages, thus creating a safe, defendable home for all. The women also decided that if the men will not comply with their request, they would not prepare food for them when they came home from work. The men in the village agreed to the women's request; the four villages were combined and named Asmara, which comes from the Tigrina word for unity.

References

Bahta, S. 2002. *The Impact of Modern Warfare on Rural Communities and the Environment in Eritrea.* PH. D. dissertation, unpublished.

Connel, D. 1999. Strategies for Change: Women and Politics in Eritrea and South Africa. *Reviews of African Political Economy* 76: 189–206.

Nadel, S. F. 1944. *Races and Tribes of Eritrea.* British Military Administration. Asmara, Eritrea.

Wilson, A. 1991. *The Challenge Road: Women and the Eritrean Revolution.* London: Earthscan.

Yosief, I. 1993. *Zanta ketema Asmera.* Addis Ababa, Ethiopia: Negdi Printing Press.

SENAIT BAHTA

See also **Gender Representations; Songs for ceremonies; Songs of the Dyula; Women's Expressive Culture**

WOMEN'S FOLKLORE: GHANA

Ghana is estimated to have forty-four languages and the women of each of these diverse linguistic groups have their own folklore forms. Consequently, a comprehensive survey of women's folklore is a difficult task. What follows is only a sketch of some of the genres that have been documented.

Many of the artistic verbal expressions of Ghanaian women are associated with transition rites, a reflection of their traditional role as child-bearers and caregivers. In many communities, birth, puberty, and marriage provide occasion for women to rejoice. For example, *bragoro* "puberty rites" of the Akan (Sarpong 1977), *dipo* of the Krobo, *otufo* of the Ga (Lartey 1971), *gbotoha* of the northern Ewe (Asamoah 1967), *narika yiila* of the Bulsa, all combine music, song, and dance. In these areas of Ghana, these multifunctional rites are still crucial in social control and in the education of young women. Also, during marriage ceremonies among the Ga, two women representing the bride's and the bridegroom's parties, engage in an artistic, innocuous verbal dueling. Although one eloquently applauds the bride's fine upbringing, parentage, beauty, and, nowadays, formal school education, the other expresses the man's attributes in matching poetic language.

Another major women's folklore form related to the life cycle is the funeral dirge. *Nsui* among the Akan (Nketia 1955) and *aviha* or *kpetavi* of the northern Ewe (Asamoah 1967) provide the women the opportunity to praise and express gratitude to departed relatives and loved ones as well as lament their own misfortunes such as barrenness, childlessness, loss of benefactor, illness, destitution, maltreatment in marriage. While it might seem that the dirge is a genre of the oppressed and the marginalized, Akan women use it as a powerful weapon against the uncharitable, self-seeking, and the vain by refusing to perform at their funeral, or by singing uncomplimentary lyrics that condemn their behavior. In this manner, women chastise the living and inculcate socially approved values into the young ones.

In spite of the burdensome responsibilities that their multiple roles as wives, mothers, caregivers, farmers, traders, and more place on them, Ghanaian women still find time for leisure. Consequently, there are a variety of social musical forms that are composed and performed exclusively or predominantly from. For example, *nnwonkoro* found in some Akan communities (Nketia 1963; Anyidoho 1994, 1995); *ayabomo* or "maiden songs" performed by Nzema women (Agovi, 1989) are recreational musical types. Women use these avenues to express joy, romance, sorrow, pain, praise, and thanksgiving as well as protest, warning, insinuation, and abuse. The label *recreational* is clearly a misnomer because it belies the serious nature of these activities; as they entertain themselves, women express their views on important social, cultural, and political issues.

There are other female verbal art forms that are not subsumed by the rubrics of "life cycle" and the "recreational." For example, through *tuima* and *nanzak yiila*, or "work songs" performed by Bulsa women while planting, harvesting, decorating walls, or milling corn, they communicate indirectly to their husbands, cowives and difficult in-laws about various problems. Also, *mmobomme* songs provide interesting insights into the role Akan women played in such crisis (Kwakwa 1994). On the contrary, *ose* or the "song of jubilation/victory" are still performed on joyous occasions such as when a chief is installed, when a member of the community wins a major court case, or when someone is rescued from a perilous situation. Furthermore, in Abibidwom (African music) women use biblical texts in songs performed recitatively in the call-and-response style in Christian worship. This relatively new form is an example of the many syncretic folklore forms attributable to external contact.

It should be noted that almost all the verbal activities and genres discussed in the preceding paragraphs are performed by groups of women, indicating their cooperative and supportive roles rather than competition.

Some of the areas where nonverbal artistic expressions of women are located include the textile (Nelson 1978), pottery, and bead making (Kumekpor 1995) industries. For example, the retailing of African wax prints (cherished by Ghanaian women) is dominated by females, who also name new textile designs. Often, the names are proverbs and pithy statements that comment on certain social, cultural, political, or religious situations, and women buy these designs because of the messages they convey. Consequently, a woman may choose to wear a particular design on a certain occasion in order to communicate in silence to her spouse, lover, cowives, enemy or society. Also, the styles that women wear speak eloquently to the knowledgeable in those matters.

Within the broad definition of folklore, other areas controlled by Ghanaian women include tie-dyeing, batik making, hair braiding and plaiting, hair design, body painting, engraving on calabashes, wall designing, mat making, cotton spinning, and funerary terra-cotta making (Freedman 1979). Although some of these artifacts are used for adornment and utilitarian purposes, others serve social, religious and magical functions.

References

Agovi, Kofi E. 1989. Sharing Creativity: Oral and Literary Linkages. *The Literary Grist* 1, no. 2: 1–43.

Aning, Ben A. 1964. Adenkum: a Study of Akan Female Bands. Legon: Institute of African Studies, University of Ghana, Unpublished Essay.

Anyidoho, Akosua. 1994. Tradition and Innovation in Nnwonkoro, An/Akan Female Verbal Genre. *Research in African Literature* 25, no. 3: 142–59.

———. 1995. Stylistic Features of Nnwonkoro: An Akan Female verbal Genre. *Text: An Interdisciplinary Journal for the Study of Discourse* 15, no. 2: 317–36.

Asamoah, Festus. 1967. Mourning Songs of Northern Eweland: a Study of the music of northern Ewe women. Legon: Institute of African Studies, University of Ghana, Legon. Unpublished essay.

Freedman, Gladys. 1979. Women as Artists and Artisans in West Africa: Special Reference to the Akan. Ph. D. dissertation, Union Graduate School, Center for Minority Studies.

Kumekpor, Maxine I., Yaw Bredwa-Mensah, and J.E.J.M. van Landewijk. 1995. *Ghanaian Dead Tradition*. Ghana Bead Society.

Kwakwa, Patience Abena. 1994. Dance and African Women. *Sage* 8, no. 2:10–15.

Lartey, Francis. 1971. Otufo: a Study of Music and Dance of the Ga-Mashie (Accra) Puberty Rite. Legon: Institute of African Studies, University of Ghana. Unpublished essay.

Nketia, J. H. K. 1955. *Funeral Dirges of the Akan People*. New York: Negro University Press.

———. (1963). *Folk Songs of Ghana*. Legon: University of Ghana Press.

Nelson, Joanna Alfretina. 1978. The Philosophy and Psychology behind the Naming of Textiles in Ghana. Kumasi: University of Science and Technology. Unpublished essay.

Sarpong, Peter. 1977. *Girl's Nubility Rites in Ashanti*. Tema: Ghana Publishing Corporation.

AKOSUA ANYIDOHO

See also **Dirges; Gender Representation in African Folklore; Queen Mothers; Textile Arts and Communication**

WOMEN POP SINGERS AND BROADCAST MEDIA IN MALI

In Africa, musical and oral performances have long been a favorite medium for women's verbal expression. Singing seems to be a particularly way for women to express popular feelings or wishes that they cannot express publicly, such as subtle criticism, the longing for a friend, and despair (Diawara 1990; cf. Wright 1993). Songs, proverbs, stories, and folktales are a favorite medium for women when they want to entertain themselves and others during social events.

In Mali, the central role of women in the oral and musical arts has led to a recent and remarkable development. Women have become pop stars of national, sometimes even international acclaim, as a result of the increased availability of radio (since 1957), audiocassettes, television, and music videos (since the 1980s). One important reason for the stunning success of women singers in the media market is that the new technologies of visualization accompanying aural recording move the voice quality and visible dimensions of women's performance to the foreground. Electronic media has triggered a significant shift in the conventions, contents, and economics of musical performances. National television, especially, provides a new platform for the conspicuous display of prestige and power by wealthy and influential individuals for a nationwide audience of consumers.

Almost all of the Malian pop stars come from the southern triangle of Mali, the heartland of the Mande people who speak two closely related languages, Bamanankan and Maninkakan. It is the musical repertoire, languages, and historical traditions of their home communities that the women pop stars draw upon in their performances. Over the past fifteen years, these women singers have become the pop icons of a national Malian culture, because television offers them a stage on which to present their regional musical styles as a "national" Malian music to national and international audiences.

This dominance of southern languages and traditions in the national Malian arena goes back to the colonial period, when peoples from the south were more easily integrated into colonial administration and the schooling system. The unequal representation of Malian local cultures has been supported by the fact that for more than twenty years, international popular press and scholarly publications focused on musicians from the south and their musical traditions (Ali Farka Touré and Boubakar Traoré being two notable exceptions). Approximately 80 percent of the audience that attends pop concerts and watches music videos are woman. The fans of the pop stars clearly distinguish between the singers according to their singing skills, their costumes, demeanors, and their knowledge of different local musical styles, songs, and historical traditions.

Most of the pop singers are from families of professional musicians and orators. The Bamana and Maninka in southern Mali call these orators *jeliw* and *Jaliw* (singular *jeli/jali*) respectively and consider them a special category of people distinct from "free-born" people (singular *hòròn*) and descendants of serfs (singular *jon*). Until French colonial occupation of the area in the nineteenth century, *jeli* families lived together with the most wealthy and powerful "free born" families of a rural community and passed down their patron family's traditions and histories in exchange for material support. On festive events that were of importance to the entire local community, jeli women were expected to praise their patron family's prestigious genealogy and heroic origins, and thus to enhance its reputation. Patron families compensated their jeli women's musical performances by giving them occasional gifts in the form of grain, cattle, and captives. To heighten the public renown of their patron families through musical performances and historical recitations was only one the jeliw's tasks. Other important functions were the resolution of conflicts and the restoring of social order and harmony to the local community. In compensation, wealthy patron families provided food and shelter for their jeli clients.

Over the past eighty years, these former affiliations between jeliw and their free-born patron families have been increasingly eroded as a consequence of altered sociopolitical hierarchies under colonial rule and the introduction of money as general mode of payment. As the social and political context changed within which jeli women performed their songs, the significance, contents and conventions of their performances were also transformed.

These changes are most apparent in urban areas, where jeliw can no longer call upon a patron to provide food and housing. People who are born into a jeli family pursue various kinds of income-generating activities. They teach, work in the state administration or have other jobs in the formal sector of the economy. Others live from occasional conflict resolutions or musical performances on behalf of various "patrons." Those who are solicited to intervene in conflicts or negotiations, or to sing a patron's praise, are generally paid in money (Schulz 1999). In remote rural settings of contemporary Mali, jeli families continue to live with and work for their patron families, but they depend less on their patrons' material support than before. Like their patrons, jeliw own land and are primarily agriculturalists. Jeli women sing for their patrons at family events and on other occasions of public importance and they receive gifts from their patrons in form of grain, cattle, or money.

Cultural conventions assign different oral and musical performance genres to men and women, but this division is not absolute (Duran 1995, 2001). The instruments on which men accompany women's songs or their own recitations very from region to region: the *kora* (a twenty-one-string harp-lute), the *n'goni* (a three to five string guitar), the *bala* (xylophone), or various kinds of drums. Women only play the *karanyan*, a slit iron tube on which they play the rhythm with a stick. Men generally recite epics and family genealogies and recount the deeds of historical personalities, legendary heroes, and other historical events that are relevant to the identity of the family and its clan name. Songs, in contrast, are the favorite genre of jeli women. People distinguish between different kinds of songs according to their function and the occasion of their performance. Women's songs cover a broad range of topics, and all girls and women may sing them, for themselves or in groups, during their work or leisure time. But only women of jeli origin should perform them on events of public importance.

In private settings, any woman may express in her songs, albeit in a subtle and indirect fashion, her dissenting views, feelings and wishes that should not be spoken of publicly. Other songs recount the stories of women or men who have excelled by outstanding deeds or attitudes. These songs, highly appreciated because of their educational value, are referred to as songs that "give a moral lesson" (*ladili*). In private settings, members of a free-born family may call upon a jeli woman whom they like and trust to come and "make the time pass more easily" by singing for their friends.

In contrast, the primary function of jeli women's songs that are performed before a public audience is to enhance the renown of a patron and to laud his prestigious family name or particular accomplishments (*fasadali*). Praise songs are composed of various textual elements; praise (*fasa*), benedictions, proverbs as well as formulaic expressions and honorific terms that are attributed to particular clan identities. The contents and musical arrangement of a song are left to the intuition of the artist. Praise songs, too, may include passages in which an individual may be presented as an example of moral excellence. Depending on the occasion of

the public gathering, a jeli woman will focus more on moralizing reflections or on praise. On festive occasions, such as weddings and baptisms, her performance will glorify her host family and remind the audience of the eminent deeds that her patron accomplished on behalf of the community. As a reward, the jeli woman can expect a generous gift—in kind or money—from her patron. For a free-born woman, in contrast, it would be unthinkable to publicly raise her voice in praise of another person and even less so, to receive a compensation for it.

A jeli woman's attractiveness and the visual aesthetics of her performance play an important role in her evaluation by the audience. In contrast to a woman of free birth who should dress modestly, jeli women dress in a spectacularly extravagant and conspicuous way and dance with elaborate and sometimes erotically evocative steps, slow and sustained gestures and body movements. It is thus easier for jeli women to attract the spectators' attention than it is for jeli musicians who are simply sitting and recounting a story or accompanying the singer's performance.

An important change brought about by the new electronic media is that it enhances the public nature of women's musical performances and transforms the patterns of interaction between audience, singer, and the orchestra. Television and video technologies support a process of commercialization, in the course of which praise performances have become a commodity: praise is no longer a client service, but has become a good that anybody can purchase. Because some wealthy individuals pay large sums for their public praise, there is a growing number of women who are not of jeli origin but do earn money by publicly flattering individuals in the jeli praise style (Schulz 1999). Another effect of broadcasting is, therefore, that it has turned public flattery into a very lucrative occupation, while rendering the social origin of the performance less important. With the mass mediation of praise songs and songs "that give a moral lesson," the social significance of the songs has also changed. Whereas the songs were performed at special events in the past, they have now become a background entertainment that accompanies everyday work and conversations.

Broadcast media seem to provide a new and particularly advantageous medium for women artists. The multilayered visual and musical performances broadcast on television bring dimensions to the foreground in which women excel over male artists. Certainly, some jeli men, historians, and musicians are still venerated emblems of a prestigious "Malian" past and of authentic traditions and knowledge. But male musicians in general seem to have lost ground in the popular music market to women. One reason for these changes might be that video and television allow women to move into the prominent positions during broadcast performances and to visually display fashion, elegance, and performance skills. The women performers, with their carefully designed and staged womanly demeanor, body movements, dresses, accessories, and background scenery, combine elements of Western consumer culture with emblems of a Malian cultural authenticity. This authenticity is evoked through visual allusions to the singer's geographic location in an idyllic, traditional, rural setting. The pop stars, such as Kandia Kouyaté, Tata Bambo Kouyaté, and Ami Koita, thus set new standards for women's identity constructions, because they fashion images of womanhood that draw on conventional stereotypes of an ideal women and on emblems of Western consumer orientation. In this way, women singers, in their visual enactment of new dancing styles and experimental body movements and postures, become not only trendsetters for new and daring dresses and demeanor, but also literally embody new consumer orientations (Schulz 2001).

References

Diawara, M. 1989. Women, Servitude and History: the Oral Historical Traditions of Women of Servile Condition in the Kingdom of Jaara (Mali) from the Fifteenth to the Mid-Nineteenth Century. In *Discourse and Its Disguises*, eds. K. Barber and P. F. de Moraes Farias. Birmingham: Centre of West African Studies, University of Birmingham.

Duran, L. 1995. Jelimusow: the Superwomen of Mali. In *Power, Marginality, and African Oral Literature*, eds. G. Furniss and L. Gunner. Cambridge University Press.

Schulz, D. 1999. Pricey Publicity, Refutable Reputations: Jeliw and the Economics of Honour in Mali. *Paideuma* 45: 275–292. (Frankfurt)

———. 2001. Music Videos and the Effeminate Vices of Urban Culture in Mali. *Africa* 71(3): 345–372.

Wright, M. 1993. *Strategies of Slaves and Women: Life Stories from East/Central Africa*. London: Currey.

DOROTHEA E. SCHULZ

See also **Electronic Media; Griots and Griottes; Performance; Women's Expressive Culture in Africa**

WORDS AND THE DOGON

With a population currently estimated at 450,000, the Dogon inhabit the mountainous region of the cliffs of Bandiagara, in the Great Bend of the Niger River in Mali. They also occupy an important place in the anthropological literature of African peoples, especially because of the work of Marcel Griaule and his colleagues. In this spectacular but difficult terrain, these ingenious and hardworking agricultural people have developed a remarkable civilization as witnessed by the beauty of their architectural constructions, the wealth of their artistic productions, and the vitality of their rites and ceremonies.

The traditional religion is still vibrant despite the advance of Islam. Dogon religion is characterized by the belief in a single creator god (the other mythical beings are his creation) and ancestor cults. Their society is organized as a gerontocracy; the oldest man of a region is the religious leader and the council of elders runs the affairs of the village. Filiation is patrilineal and residence is patrilocal.

One of the most original conceptions of Dogon thought is that of the "word" and speaking, the importance of which in myth and cosmogony was revealed to Marcel Griaule in 1946 by the old wise man Ogotemmêli. On the basis of his ideas, subsequent studies have analyzed in greater depth the function of "speaking" as it relates to society and the person. We now know that we are not dealing with an isolated system of thought and that similar ideas are also found in many other African societies.

The Origin of the Word

According to the myth, the creator god, Amma, shaped and fertilized by his word a placenta or "egg of the world" in which he placed the seeds of the first creatures, two androgynous twins. This placenta would become the Earth. The twins are key characters of Dogon mythology. One is a figure of a rebel, the Pale Fox (*Vulpes pallida*), whose criminal acts (theft of the word and the primordial seeds from Amma; incest with his mother the Earth) introduce disorder and impurity into the world. The other twin is Nommo, a perfect being whose sacrifice and resurrection purified the universe. Nommo descended onto earth in an ark carrying humanity's first ancestors as well as the fauna and flora destined to populate the world. He revealed language and civilizing techniques to man. Nommo represents order, fertility, life; his element is water. His action is opposed to that of the Fox, who is associated with sterility, aridness, and death.

The first human beings could only express themselves through screams and grunts, like infants or deaf-mutes. Nommo, in the primordial pond, expectorated threads of cotton and wove them together using his forked tongue like a shuttle. His word, incorporated into the interstices of the cloth, was heard by one of the ancestors (the first totemic priest) whose drum echoed it back and communicated it to the others. The first word, therefore, was also the first woven strip and the first musical rhythm. Society was organized and the ancestors, up to then gatherers, became cultivators and learned how to build houses.

This myth describes the birth of a human being, who evolves from the fetal state, where he is like a fish deprived of the word and bathing in the waters of the womb, to that of the newborn who, through the appropriate rites, receives the word upon his arrival into the world. This passage also describes the childhood of humanity that begins to organize itself with rudimentary means and gradually arrives at an evolved technical stage. In this evolution, the word plays a crucial role, for it is the foundation of social exchanges.

As the work of a thinking creator god, the universe is replete with meaning. Each parcel of matter contains a message that man must decode by interpreting, for example, the morphological features or the properties of a plant or an animal. It is the "word of the world," an expression we can translate by "symbol," and that is at the basis of a complex system of taxonomies and correspondences that express Dogon worldview.

The Word and the Human

The word is born in the human body; where it is "fabricated" from substances that it finds therein. The four elements, present in the human body as they are in the entire universe, provide it with life (water), meaning (earth), warmth (fire), and breath (air). The dosage of these elements, just as in the preparation of food, determines the nature of different words: too much fire produces words of anger, too much air, inconsistent words. Other symbolic ingredients come into play in its composition: oil which comes from the blood and confers charm and beauty upon the word; bile, bitter but purifying; salt; honey, and so forth. Like the human being, the word also has seeds, representing the vital principles; its delivery is comparable to germination. A word "without seeds" is empty of meaning and sterile.

The word as an act begins in the brain through an intellectual process (thought); it is fabricated in the viscera, through a mechanism akin to a forge: The liver, the seat of emotions, is a piece of pottery in which the water of the word, warmed by the heart (hearth), begins to boil; the lungs (bellows) expel the steam thus produced. It is woven at the level of the larynx and the mouth: the tongue represents the shuttle, the teeth are the comb through which pass the threads of the chain, and the uvula is the pulley of the loom. The steam emitted in the depths of the body resounds and, like a strip of cotton, speech takes on shape, color, design. These concepts shed light on the origin myth of the word.

Once emitted, the word, sonorous matter carried by steam, moves in the air in a spiraling line and enters into the ear of the listener. It is condensed, becomes liquid again and irrigates the listener's body. Depending on the elements composing it, it produces various effects: a word of fire "burns" and provokes an unpleasant answer; a gentle word, filled with water and oil, is beneficial, and so on.

The character of an individual is judged by the timber of his voice, even before one hears what he had to say. A sharp and strident feminine voice repels the suitors, for it betrays a quarrelsome temperament. The nose being the seat of vital breath, any word charged with nasal resonance evokes the last breath and the word of the dead, carried by the wind, wandering, aimless, and without answer. From a certain point of view, it can be said that, for the Dogon, death is characterized by the absence of words and speaking. The dead no longer communicate with the living, except when, through rituals (such as sacrifices or libations), the latter give them back a little humidity, therefore, words and life.

The Word in Social Life

Any word requires an answer; an elementary aspect of social life is dialogue. The soliloquy is a sign of madness and provokes uneasiness. The absence of an answer to a question, call, or salutation is a serious insult.

This dialogue upon which social life rests takes on special importance in the amorous exchanges between men and women. Sexual relations in themselves are a kind of "speech." The fertility of the couple (and thus the continuation of the group) depends upon a successful relationship. Woman is fertilized by the word of man but only when their exchanges are harmonious; jokes and gentle irony, which relieve tensions and conflicts, are the best kind of speech acts. However, according to a widespread notion, women's words are replete with ambivalence. At times, they are "good"—gentle, maternal, musical—at other times, they are "bad"—quarrelsome, jealous, generating conflicts and threatening social equilibrium. The ornaments a girl receives in early childhood (specifically, ear, nose, and lower lip rings) are intended to prevent her from listening to and uttering "bad words."

Verbal exchanges are the object of precautions, for quarrels destroy the social order and the harmony of the universe. Rules of etiquette, prohibitions, euphemisms, norms governing the circulation of words between age-groups, and so on facilitate communication. The use of individual names, bearers of the spiritual principles of the person, is regulated. The correct exchange of salutations promotes communication, punctuates the flow of time, and helps it proceed in the proper direction. Mockery, insult, normally the cause of quarrels, can play a cathartic role when they are used in the institutional framework of a "joking relationship." Rites of purification are performed to repair "bad words" when conflict could not be avoided.

Aesthetics of the Word

The Dogon make a distinction between "ordinary words" (common communication) and "beautiful words," which betray an aesthetic choice and which contain more "oil," the component that confers charm and beauty upon them. It is especially in the verbal arts that stylistic techniques are used to produce "beautiful words."

A generic term covers all the prose stories presenting a fictional aspect, including those comprising parts. Mythic tales are not part of these stories, for they are the object of belief and are thus considered as "true"; they are called "ancient words." This term is also applied to the historical, legendary tales concerning the ancestors, the foundation of villages, and so on.

The stylistic aspect of narrative prose concerns the lexicon (the choice of expressive terms, ideophones, the frequency of imagery, and the nuances of action) but also the structure of the sentence, the linkages, the liveliness of the dialogues, the play of intonations, and the art of gestures. The good storyteller has "a mouth as sweet as salt." He must neither make a mistake nor interrupt himself, for the continuity of the "weaving" of words is essential in verbal art.

We find among the Dogon, as we do elsewhere, animal, facetious, and marvelous tales. At one level, these stories give obvious lessons of social ethics; but their deeper meaning is more complex. Thus do the Dogon associate stories of animals with the great mythical themes, the struggle of antagonistic characters (for example, the Hare and the Hyena) represents the cosmic struggle of the principles of order and disorder governing the universe. Numerous tales deal, in symbolic form, with conflicts manifest in family relationships (generational conflicts, marriage issues, and incest) or with the initiation process that transforms the young individual into an adult. The elements (plants, animals, objects) mentioned in a tale are chosen not randomly but for symbolic reasons in relation to Dogon worldview. The tales play an important pedagogic role in the transmission of knowledge and cultural models. Their telling is governed by rules and prohibitions concerning the time (tales are told only at night), the site (married women tell stories indoors; young bachelors, outside), and the audience (no storytelling occurs between parents and children of the opposite sex when the young are nubile). These rules testify to the symbolic relationship between oral literature and fertility.

Among the poetic genres, reciting the motto or praise name, provokes the exaltation of the listener's personality; it brings into play all the stylistic techniques of oral poetry: play of sounds (assonance, alliteration), terms selected for their symbolic value, rhythmic structures, flexible syntax and bold constructions, a preference for imagery and enigmatic form. Many different songs figure in all sorts of circumstances, but musical performance take on the greatest importance in funeral ceremonies because music is a symbolic marriage, and the union of male and female rhythms promotes the birth of children who will replace the dead.

The concept of the "word" among the Dogon is connected to that of "survival" and "continuity." It is irreversible and its flow occurs in the direction of time. A vehicle of tradition, it must be transmitted from one generation to the next like a strip of cloth that has never been cut. It is a factor of social cohesion and relieves tensions.

If the ability to speak an articulated language endowed with meaning is peculiar to man and has been conferred upon him by a divine gift, he must show himself deserving and make good use of it. Mastery of the word, the wise use of effective words or, conversely, silence, discretion, and a respect for secret are the most valued social qualities. They constitute a real ethics of the word. The one who masters it proves that he holds knowledge and that, through divine delegation, he rules over the created world.

References

Calame-Griaule, Geneviève. 1965. *Ethnologie et Langage, La Parole chez les Dogon*. Paris, Gallimard, Rééd. 1987. Paris, Institut d'Ethnologie. English translation by Deirdre La Pin, 1986. *Words and the Dogon World*. Philadelphia: Institute for the Study of Human Issues.

———. 1987. *Des Cauris au marché: Essais sur des contes africains*. Paris: Société des Africanistes.

——— ed. 1987. Les Voix de la Parole. *Journal des Africanistes* 57, nos. 1–2.

———, and Blaise Calame. 1957. Introduction à l'étude de la musique africaine. In *La Revue musicale*, "Carnets critiques". Paris: Richard Masse.

Griaule, Marcel. 1948. *Dieu d'eau. Entretiens avec Ogotemmêli*. Paris: Editions du Chêne. Dernière rééd. 1966. Paris, Fayard. English translation, 1965. *Conversations with Ogotemmeli, An Introduction to Dogon religious Ideas*. Published for the International African Institute by Oxford University Press.

———, and Germaine Dieterlen. 1965. *Le Renard pâle*. Paris: Institut d'Ethnologie. Rééd. 1991. English translation, 1986. *The Pale Fox*. Chino Valley, Arizona: Continuum Foundation.

Guédou, Georges. 1985. *Xo et gbè. Langage et culture chez les Fon (Bénin)*. Paris: SELAF (Société d'Etudes Linguistiques et Anthropologiques de France).

Zahan, Dominique. 1963. *La Dialectique du Verbe chez les Bambara*. Paris-La Haye: Mouton.

GENEVIÈVE CALAME-GRIAULE

See also **Aesthetics; Cosmology; Languages; West African Folklore: Overview**

WORK SONGS

The child listens to work songs. The singers are farmers, fishermen, hunters, herdsmen, porters, camel drivers, soldiers, or coffee sifters. When brush cutters clear a field for planting rice, musicians entertain and encourage them by playing small slit drums. An agricultural song provides rhythm for work in the fields. Porters carrying African chiefs or Europeans in sedan chairs on long journeys through the bush or forest walked to the rhythm of their singing. In Equatorial Africa, boatmen and fishermen sing boat songs and paddling songs. Herd-boys play flutes as they watch the cattle. In desert areas there is even a song to make the camels drink. Soldiers sing to set the rhythm for their matching. Hunters celebrate a successful hunt with singing and dancing . . . A call-and-response form is common to many of these songs. A leader starts the song, the group answers, the leader sings again and is answered by the group, and so on. . . . At a gold mine near Johannesburg South Africa, a Bantu drummer . . . plays a homemade drum for his fellow gold miners. . . .

(Dietz 1965, 2)

These observations aptly describe the extensive use of song as an accompaniment to work activities throughout Africa. Such music serves a multitude of functions, including inspiration, motivation, celebration, coordination, and relaxation. Style and subject matter varies tremendously throughout the continent and cannot be easily classified, although the same stylistic commonalties found in all African music do exist. Topics may address the work being accomplished or may take the laborer's mind away from tedium by focusing on another topic entirely. Some work songs impart critical information about specialized tasks, while others manipulate nonsense syllables in rhythmic and linguistic play. The one feature African work songs do share is the desire to increase productivity while minimizing fatigue and discontent.

An understanding of work songs in Africa today must also take into consideration the dramatic social changes ushered in during the colonial and postcolonial eras. Colonialism in particular had a dramatic impact on the nature of work (and therefore work songs) all over the continent, reorganizing such activities to reflect European-based approaches to mass labor. For those displaced due to the Atlantic slave trade, labor songs became a defining feature in the construction of new, diasporic African identities, especially as the enslavement of Africans was specifically geared toward forced work. Within the continent, migration in search of work as well as enterprises requiring massive amounts of manpower (such as mining and plantation style agriculture) brought together people from disparate backgrounds, often for the first time. The result, coupled with the introduction of new instrumentation and tuning systems, generated great experimentation with new styles, many of which grew into regionally popular forms.

African music plays a central role in the facilitation of social action and as such, a great amount of African music can be considered work music. That is to say, the primary function of such performance activities is to accomplish the "work" of society (not only in meeting the basic needs of food, clothing, and shelter, but also in generating and maintaining group cohesion at the family, clan, and community levels). For the purposes of this article, discussion will center on three general categories as they relate to labor-oriented musical expression: music to prepare for work (songs of mobilization), music to accompany work (songs of labor), and music to assist in relaxation and renewal after work is completed (music of rejuvenation).

Songs of Mobilization

All over the continent, music, song, and dance are used as a vehicle through which to call people to work, focus their energies, and prepare them mentally and emotionally for specific types of labor. Thus, Kikuyu women's work groups in Kenya (rural work cooperatives and associations that help women participate in the economy as subsistence farmers) use song to call participants for work in the fields, moving as a group from compound to compound before heading off for work with an assembled team.

For the Dinka, cattle keepers living in what is today southern Sudan, sung poetry rich with oxen metaphors is a common feature of cattle-camps. In the morning, when girls wake up

A Ba Aka grandmother sings a hunting song into the rope she is weaving for a net used in net hunting.
Photo © Hal Noss, www.halnoss.com.

early to churn their milk for butter, they sing their favorite songs to the rhythm of their shaking gourds as a prelude to the days' work.

In situations of conflict and battle, particularly in precolonial Africa (warrior status being a primary "job" of unmarried young men in a great many societies), mental and emotional preparation was a critical element of successful engagement. The Maasai and the Nandi communities of Kenya had a habit of preparing for war before they went out to actually fight by staging a formal rehearsal. Among the Maasai, warriors created an imaginary enemy whom they had to fight and defeat in advance, projecting their intentions in practice before going to the battlefield. Similarly, the Ngoni of Malawi recognize two specific categories of war songs: *imigubo* that are performed before battle and *imihubo* that are performed upon the warriors' return.

Songs of Labor

Almost all work related activities may be accompanied by music in Africa. Such performances coordinate energies, pass time for repetitive and/or tedious activities, increase endurance, and make work more pleasurable. On one end of the economic scale, a lone Sotho woman in South Africa accompanies her cooking by singing alone about her absent husband who has gone to work in the mines. She uses the repetitive nature of her work as a tool through which to explore philosophical themes of love and marriage. Similarly, young Basoga boys in eastern Uganda sing comical songs as they beat out rhythms to chase termites (a significant source of protein supplement during key periods in the growing season) from their underground dwellings.

In more complex forms of organized labor, one finds songs that accompany and coordinate large groups of people in more formal ways. Such coordination is common in farming communities and contemporary industrial settings in which massive labor may be required. Concrete examples include farming songs of the Limba of Sierra Leone in which "companies," each with a designated drummer, coordinate the efforts of seed scatters and hoers working in groups of fifty or more. Even mundane activities that do not necessarily require group coordination but place large numbers of people to work on the same enterprise may use music to stem fatigue and stimulate mental acuity. In Accra, Ghana postal workers stamping outgoing mail whistle popular tunes in unison and generate complex polyrhythmic structures as they perform their work.

As with all forms of music, the nature of a community's economic enterprise also has an impact on their working music. Farming requires large groups of people and often employs a call-and-response motif (in which a lead singer initiates song lines collectively responded to by a group chorus). Cattle keeping, by contrast, involves long hours away from home in small groups (usually of young men and boys). In these settings, extended and complex narratives are emphasized to pass the time and take the mind away from the tedium of work. Individually recited poetry in praise of prized oxen or valor on the battlefield are more common than group performance and the flute is a favored instrument, owing to its light weight and small size.

For communities in which food collection and hunting predominated (such groups being increasingly rare today), work music was collective, but necessitated smaller groups than farming. Instrumentation was typically minimal owing to a highly mobile lifestyle, while vocal embellishments were greatly exploited. Hunting songs of the Mbuti of the Congo, for example, incorporate whistles, yodels, and vocal trills to communicate to others about animal movements in the thick forest context.

Within any society, there are members that perform special tasks or trades and these types of work may also have special songs. In some case, as with metalworking, healing, or other enterprises that build on specialized knowledge and training, work songs may serve a mnemonic devices to guide apprentices through the proper procedures of their vocation. The poetic utterances of diviners of the *ifá* system found among the Yoruba of Nigeria, for example, provide a framework within which readers of oracles may interpret the complex mathematical permutations of their divination system.

Songs of Rejuvenation

Work is a tiring activity and requires that the worker rejuvenate his energy daily. Furthermore, in the African context, fatigue may be perceived not simply as physical, but also as mental and emotional in nature. Entertainment is a key mechanism through which renewal is achieved. In the precolonial era, Africans had their own types of entertainment that took the form of sports, music, and dance, or what can be generally referred to as the performing arts. Music in African communities played a particularly key entertainment role. Entertainment is crucial to the worker, as it relaxes his/her muscles not only during work, but also for the next day's labor demands. Such rejuvenating activities provide increased and sustained productivity, especially in long-range enterprises. Thus, one finds a great wealth of music designed to relax and rejuvenate workers of all types, some of which is accompanied by dance as a way to ease stress and stimulate the body after a long day of repetitive tasks. Song content may reflect on the importance of the work accomplished, discreetly criticize authority figures (this is especially true of colonial and postcolonial systems of labor, which differ dramatically from earlier forms of African work), or nostalgically invoke themes entirely unrelated to work such as love or comedy.

Among the Itesot of eastern Uganda, the thumb piano continues to be a favorite accompaniment to postwork celebration. The history of the instrument in this community dates to plantation work undertaken in the early part of the nineteenth century by the British. Migrating long distances to sugar plantations where they remained encamped for weeks and sometimes months at a time, Itesot laborers interacted with workers from what was then the Congo. Through this exchange, the Itesot adopted the thumb piano which they dubbed *a-Kongo* or *from the Congo*, eventually drifting to the current *akogo*. Akogo music was used then for relaxation, and especially to accompany the long walking journey home (which could take several days). Even today, a great deal of akogo music is performed to a 60 to 80 beat per minute pulse—a standard marching beat that reflects its roots as migrational accompaniment.

Similarly, early in the 1900s, South African dock workers adapted a rural dance form called *is'catulo* (shoe) to develop what has come to be called gumboot dancing. Slapping, stomping, and adorning their rubber work boots with bottle caps as rattles, this form of dancing became popular among many labor groups, particularly those in South Africa's mining industry. A favorite of Sunday dance team competitions, dance styles borrowed heavily from diverse regional cultural groups, all which worked in the mines under extremely challenging conditions all the way through apartheid (many miners migrated from as far away as Zambia and Zimbabwe). Gumboot dancing is still performed today and songs are also often accompanied by guitar, illustrating the more cosmopolitan nature of styles that accompany urban, industrial ventures.

Labor and Work Songs in Colonial and Post-colonial Africa

Africa's contact with the outside world transformed work both in definition as well as in place and time. Work was one of the elements that colonial administrations sought to change and reorganize. Colonial economies sought male labor as opposed to female labor and changed the place of work for many Africans, stimulating great movements of people (particularly men) to plantations, mining districts, and urban centers. Africans were taught, sometimes forced, to work for the market as opposed to laboring locally for subsistence, subsequently adopting cash crop

agriculture and engaging in industrial labor. In this way, Africans were confronted with new work experiences to which they had to conform. Changes in the organization of work also affected work songs and stimulated an accelerated development of new forms and regional styles that have greatly impacted musical expression around the continent. As workers were often migrants who traveled great distances, they spent many days and nights together without returning to their homes, a development that has had far reaching impacts in many areas of contemporary society.

The emergence of specific guitar styles shared across vast distances in Africa has largely been traced to mining operations such as those in southern and central Africa. Such operations attracted individuals from cultural groups that did not typically interact and the development of new forms of musical expression helped unite them as a specialized cultural unit. The Congolese sound (also often called *soukous*, Lingala, rumba, or simply *la musique moderne*) that came to define the contemporary music of Zaire at independence, emerged as cultural groups from diverse areas interacted and exchanged ideas in the context of mining enterprises. By the mid-1960s, local variations on this form could be heard throughout Zaire and on into Uganda, Kenya, and parts of Tanzania. Today, this style retains a significant influence on the region's popular musical development.

In southern Africa, the emergence of township *jive*, and later *mbaqanga* music, resulted from the fusing of local guitar innovations with local clowning traditions and even martial arts movements gleaned from exposure to foreign films. Such music largely served a displaced, urban, industrial workforce anxious for a balance of local sounds and cosmopolitan sensibility. The massive displacement witnessed in South Africa in particular served as a dramatic catalyst for music that helped solidify emerging group identities in urban centers.

These and many other contemporary regional forms trace their roots to labor settings, particularly those first instituted during the colonial period. These new labor patterns effectively moved work enterprises from a setting in which economic enterprise, local culture and group identity were intimately linked into more urbanized and cosmopolitan contexts where new identities were configured through the medium of performance.

Ba Aka women sing songs in the forest before they hunt.
Photo © Hal Noss, www.halnoss.com.

References

Abimbola, W. 1965. The Odù of Ifá, *African Notes* [Ibadan] 1, no. 3.

Brakeley, T. C. 1949. Work Song. In *Standard Dictionary of Folklore, Mythology, and Legend*, ed. M. Leach. New York.

Brandel, R. 1961. *The Music of Central Africa: an Ethnomusicological Study. Former French Equatorial Africa, the Former Belgian Congo, Ruanda-Urundi, Uganda, Tanganyika.* The Hague.

Coplan, D. 1996. South Africa: Descriptive Notes. In *The JVC/ Smithsonian Folkways Video Anthology of Music and Dance of Africa*, Book 3, eds. Nketia and Greenberg. Washington D.C.: Victor Company of Japan.

Deng, F. M. 1972. *The Dinka of the Sudan* (1923). New York: Holt, Rinehart and Winston, Marguerite, 1923.

Dietz, Betty Warner, and Michael Babatunde Olatunji. 1965. *Musical Instruments of Africa: Their Nature, Use, and Place in the Life of Deeply Musical People.* New York.

Finnegan, R. 1967. *Limba Stories and Story-telling.* Oxford: OLAL.

———. 1970. *Oral Literature in Africa.* Nairobi: Oxford University Press.

Kidney, E. 1921. Native Songs from Nyasaland. *African Affairs* 20.

Opondo, P. 1996. Kenya: Descriptive Notes. In *The JVC/ Smithsonian Folkways Video Anthology of Music and Dance of Africa*, Book 3, eds. Nketia and Greenberg. Washington D.C.: Victor Company of Japan.

Orlean, S. 2002. The Congo Sound. *The New Yorker* October 14 and 21.

Read, M. 1937. Songs of the Ngoni People *Bantu Studies* 11.

Tracey, H. T. 1954. The Social Role of African Music. *African Affairs* 53.

———. 1958. African Music within its Social Setting. *African Music* 2, no. 1.

ALFRED ANANGWE
WADE PATTERSON

See also **Music; Performance in Africa.**

WRITING SYSTEMS

See **Nsibidi: An Infigenous Writing System**

Y

YARDS AND GARDENS, AFRICAN AMERICAN TRADITIONS

In 1969, Eldredge Cleaver stated that slavery had caused African Americans "to hate the land and to measure their own value according to the number of degrees they were away from the soil" (Kellert 1984, 219). At the beginning of the twenty-first century, most African Americans live in cities. However, a significant number of African Americans live in the rural South—the ancestors of many had managed to acquire some land and survive the hard times that forced fieldhands and sharecroppers to leave. The older families that remain, and continue to work small farms or large gardens, espouse agrarian values that are common to all who work the land. Not surprisingly, home ownership is a primary goal, and hard work, resourcefulness, and self-reliance are much admired. Many gardeners grow far more than their family can eat. This is partly because few gardeners irrigate and have a high tolerance of crop failure, but most express great pleasure in having produce to give away. The garden is a symbol of commitment to family and community.

One of the characteristics of African American yards (especially in the South Carolina Low Country, Alabama's "Black Belt," and the Georgia Piedmont) that recalls African traditions is the importance of maintaining a clean, well-swept area. Until very recently, most kitchen tasks were done in the "kitchen yard." In fact, except in foul weather, most family life was spent outside in the yard or on the porch. The kitchen stove was an open fire, and the laundry was generally boiled in the same cast-iron pots that were used for cooking. The kitchen sink was the wellhead. Permanent workstations were set up around the yard, sited so as to be shaded when the task was normally performed. In many yards, a tub in which hogs were scaled before being scraped to remove the bristle, a hoist on which hogs were hung when being scraped, and a cutting table on which they were butchered were still a common sight. Given that this area was subject to heavy use, and a fire was often burning, keeping it clean and bare was a matter of practicality and safety.

The practice of sweeping the yard extends to the flower yard as well. Shade trees are important and are sometimes surrounded by protective borders. This practice can also be traced to African traditions. For example, family compounds in southern Nigeria have trees that are marked in special ways for certain family members or for specific uses. Throughout West Africa, compounds are swept continually. This tradition is so strongly maintained in the United States that the overall impression of starkness—even barrenness—in African American yards is striking.

Even in the 1930s, flower gardens were common. These appear to have been almost defiant gestures of commitment to aesthetic beauty in spite of desperately hard lives. But decorating the yard with flowers was not an African tradition (although it was vigorously adopted by Christian converts among southern Nigerians). This thesis is supported by Jack Goody in his book *The Culture of Flowers* (1993). An examination of the photographic collections and the accounts of pre- and early-colonial-era travelers in Africa held in the Commonwealth Library in London do not show or suggest that flowers were grown for ornament around African dwellings. Despite the absence of an African tradition, the use of flowers in African American rural yards has evolved distinctive characteristics. Plants are always treated and admired as individual aesthetic objects, and they are never massed for effect or used as "structural" materials, ground covers, or foundation or background plantings (and rarely as hedges). Plants are selected mainly for their colorful flowers, but there are no constantly recurring color combinations or deliberate attempts to clash color, as was observed by Robert Farris Thompson in some African textiles (1988, 13). The actual design of decorative yards seems to have much in common with African American quilt design. Quilting is an art that is associated with a rigid geometry for European Americans, but African Americans do not hesitate to bend the discipline, and so their work has a rhythmic quality that nevertheless includes surprising or unexpected choices and patterns.

Yards are also decorated with found objects and treasured family items. In one Georgia yard for instance, a sewing machine is painted silver and set in front of the soft gray foliage of angle's trumpet and bright pink phlox. Color, form, reflectivity, and movement are all appreciated in the choice of objects, which are usually highlighted with plants. In addition, bottle trees decorate some African American yards. Empty glass bottles, usually of different colors, are stuck on bare branches or hung from them. Whether this continues similar traditions observed in Central Africa or is derived from German Easter-egg trees, it is clear that such trends are not common among European Americans.

In African American rural gardens and yards, aesthetic and ritual objects of individual choice and meaning, as well as the surrounding flowers and trees, are continually arranged and rearranged according to both traditional practices and artistic innovation. As John Michael Vlach put it, African American artistic expression "is marked by constant, individuating change, and improvisation is the touchstone of creativity" (1979, 3).

References

Goody, Jack. 1993. *The Culture of Flowers*. Cambridge, England: Cambridge University Press.

Kellert, Stephen R. 1984. Urban American Perceptions of Animals and the Natural Environment. *Urban Ecology* 8:209–228.

Thompson, Robert Farris. 1983. *Flash of the Spirit: African and Afro-American Art and Philosophy*. New York: Random House.

Vlach, John Michael. 1978. *The Afro-American Tradition in Decorative Arts*. Cleveland: Cleveland Museum of Art.

Westmacott, Richard. 1992. *African American Gardens and Yards in the Rural South*. Knoxville: University of Tennessee Press.

RICHARD WESTMACOTT

See also **Diaspora; Housing: African American Traditions**

YORUBA

See **Architecture; Diaspora; Ifa; Orisha; Religion; Surrogate Languages; Theater; Tongue Twisters**

Z

ZAMBIA (REPUBLIC OF ZAMBIA)

Zambia (Republic of Zambia) is a tropical to subtropical country in southern Africa that is landlocked and surrounded by Tanzania, Malawi, Mozambique, Zimbabwe, Namibia, Angola, Botswana, and the Democratic Republic of the Congo. Slightly larger than Texas, Zambia has a population of nearly 10,400,000. The country's capital is Lusaka, a city that is home to 982,000 people. Zambia's population is predominantly Bantu-speaking, although English is the official language. There are more than seventy different ethnic groups, among whom the Bemba (34%), Nyanja (14%), Tonga (16%), and Lozi (9%) are the most numerous. Half of Zambia's population is Christian, while 48 percent practice traditional religions. The remaining 2 percent is composed of Hindus, Muslims, and other smaller religious traditions.

After many years under the control of the British South African Company, the territory became Northern Rhodesia in 1911. On October 24, 1964, Zambia gained its independence from Britain. After many years of single-party rule, political upheaval forced the government to accept reforms leading to the creation of a multiparty republic in 1990. Nevertheless, years of political and economic corruption have left the country in a state of turmoil and underdevelopment.

Copper, zinc, cobalt, gemstones, tobacco, cotton, and textiles have been the main sources of the country's revenue. Until 1975, Zambia was one of the most prosperous African nations, primarily due to its status as the world's fourth-largest producer of copper and fifth-largest of cobalt; 80 percent of its export income came from copper. But the decreased international price of copper, internal political problems, and the decline of agricultural production all contributed to a weakening of Zambia's economy. In addition to reduced revenue, the Anglo-American Corporation, the nation's largest mining company, has refused to pay for a cleanup of the environment.

As in so many African countries, HIV/AIDS has taken a horrific toll in Zambia, where it was estimated in 2001 that over 20 percent of all adults are HIV positive.

JENNIFER JOYCE

ZAR: SPIRIT POSSESSION IN THE SUDAN

Zar (also called Dastur or Rih *Ahmar*) is a phenomenon associated mostly with women. It is a type of spirit possession that occurs primarily in Eritrea, Ethiopia, Egypt, Somalia, and as far west as Nigeria. Among scholars, the definition of Zar is agreed to be spirit possession by *jin* (spirits). In the Sudan, the Zar spirits are referred to by the name Al-Rih *Al-Ahmar*, which used to be considered a separate category of *jin*.

The word Zar is presumably borrowed from Amharic (spoken in Ethiopia), where the word is thought to be related to the ancient Agau religion, in which their sky god was called Zar. Among the Arabic-speaking people, the word is thought to be derived from the Arabic verb *Zara* which means "visited." Brenda Seligman (1914, 300) does not accept this view, however, and Samia Al Hadi Al-Nagar has recorded several other sources of the name. It might come from Zara, a town in northern Iran, or from Zar, an Arab village, east of Yemen, or from northern Nigeria (Al-Nagar 1975). Enrico Cerulli (1934) mentions the possibility of a derivation from Adjar, the name of the supreme deity of the Kushites of Ethiopia. Most scholars now agree that the name originated in Ethiopia and diffused to other areas of northern Africa.

In the Sudan, Zar is exclusively a woman's phenomenon. Men are only slightly involved in it, though elsewhere the situation may be different as there have been reports of possessed males. Another exception was recorded by Seligman who had been informed that, among the Fallahin of Egypt, men are frequently possessed by Zar spirits (1914, 305). In his study of Zar among the Nubians, John Kennedy notes that the leadership and musician roles in Zar ceremonies are filled by men (1967, 187). There are other accounts of male leaders at Zar ceremonies, as well. Therefore, while women are still the main practitioners of Zar, various roles are played by men.

As for the practitioners of Zar, the terms *Shaikha* (for women) and *Shaikh* (for men) are the most commonly used. In the Sinnar region, the female practitioner is called *Ommiva*, and they never use the term *Shaikha* there. Elsewhere, the terms *Usta* and *Kudiya* are also used interchangeably with *Ommiya* and the more common terms of *Shaikha* and *Shaikh* (Al-Nagar 1975).

The first procedure in Zar healing is called *Fath-al-ilba*. This refers to the opening (*fath*) of a tin box containing incense, which is related to several categories of spirits. The second step is to identify the spirit which possesses the victim, and hence activate the process by which the spirits can be controlled by the *Haflat al-zar* (Zar party). Frankincense is burned and drums are played to accompany the ritual Zar songs. The music and ritual songs continue until the patient becomes ecstatic and goes into a spirit trance. When the patient is absorbed by the spirit, an expert woman, acting as a mediator, calms the spirit by uttering some phrases, such as *Dasturkum Ya Asiad*, and promising to meet the spirits' demands. Then the victim, on behalf of the spirit (as the spirit speaks through the possessed individual), expresses his or her needs, which are often for new clothes, perfumes, and gold jewelry.

There are three different Zar ceremonies, of varying lengths. The longest lasts for seven days and is referred to as *Nasbal al-Aursi*. The shortest lasts for three days. At the end of either of these ceremonies, the patient has to make a sacrifice of an animal, because blood is essential in concluding a Zar ceremony.

The Shaikha herself makes a ceremony, once every year during the month of Rajab, called *Al-Rajaligya*. The *Shaikha*'s party marks the closing ceremony of the year that has passed, and no Zar is practiced during the months of Shaaban and Ramadan.

There are many different types of Zar characters or spirits, both male and female, although the majority are male. There are three main types:

1. Those with specific names, such as Shaikh Abdel Gadir Al-aylani or Luliyya al-Habashiyya.
2. Those of certain nationalities, such as Al-Habashi, Al-Khawaja.
3. Those of different occupations, such as Al-Diktur or Al-Basha.

The commonly known types of Zar are:

1. *Zar Habashi* (Ethiopian) which is represented by Bashir and Luliyya.
2. *Zar Khawaja* (European) which is characterized by a European name or habit (smoking, drinking, etc).
3. *Zar al-Darawish* (Dervish).
4. *Zar al-Arabi* (Arabic).
5. *Zar al-Fallatiyya* (Nigerian).
6. *Zar al-Zuruk* (Black people).
7. *Zar al-Niyamniyam* (cannibal).

The functions of Zar relate, directly or indirectly, to the particular social situation of the individual possessed. The following explanations reflect some of the possible social relationships that Zar possession affects. Most commonly, scholars note that, in Zar possession, women find an escape from the world dominated by men. It is true that the woman is able, through Zar, to do things she cannot in ordinary life; for example, she can disperse her husband's money, lessening his chance for another marriage. A woman who is normally accustomed to being ordered around and threatened is able, through being possessed, to order others and threaten them. The frequent demands for valuables can be seen as a kind of insurance against a possible divorce. But this appears to be a very weak function, because sometimes valuable objects can be borrowed and returned directly after the occasion.

The possessed person can escape certain social customs imposed upon women by society, such as Hadad (mourning), and she can avoid religious and socially prohibited behavior such as smoking and drinking alcohol. There is also a chance for more social interaction through the Zar ceremony, because in the Sudanese community women generally have a limited chance to interact with others.

Zar possession seems to have a positive effect on psychosomatic and physical illnesses, so it is a useful curative practice in some cases. For its audience, the Zar clearly serves psychological and social needs beyond the therapeutic. Most significantly, it is primarily an adult female activity reflecting Nubian social conditions of sex separation, low female status, restriction of women from religious participation, an unbalanced sex ratio, marital insecurity, and relative isolation.

Zar is of relevance to folklore, psychology, anthropology, and medicine, and a study of Zar in conjunction with any of these disciplines would prove useful.

References

Al-Nagar, Samia Al Hadi. 1975. Spirit Possession and Social Change in Omdurman. M.Sc. thesis, University of Khartoum.

Boddy, Janice. 1989. *Wombs and Alien Spirits: Women, Men, and the Zar Cult in Northern Sudan*. Madison: University of Wisconsin Press.

Cerulli, Enrico. 1934. Somali/Somalia/Somaliland: Ethography. In *Encyclopedia of Islam*, ed. M. Th. Houstma, et al. Leiden: Brill.

Kennedy, John G. 1967. Nubian Zar Ceremonies as Psychotherapy. *Human Organization* 26, no.4:186–94.

Seligman, Brenda Z. 1914. On the Origin of Egyptian Zar. *Folklore* 25: 300–323.

FARAH EISA MOHAMED

See also **Gender Representation in African Folklore; Healing; Spirit Possession**

ZIMBABWE (REPUBLIC OF ZIMBABWE)

Located in southern Africa, Zimbabwe is a subtropical country surrounded by Zambia, Mozambique, South Africa, and Botswana. Zimbabwe's population of approximately 12,390,000 people is predominantly comprised of the Shona group (71 percent), while 16 percent are Ndebele and 13 percent consist of other smaller ethnic groups. The major languages spoken in the country are English, (Chi)Shona, and (Si)Ndebele. Half of the population practice syncretic religions (a combination of both Christian and indigenous beliefs), 25 percent are Christian, 24 percent practice traditional indigenous religions, and 1 percent are Muslim. Harare, a city of 1,200,000, is the nation's capital and largest city.

On April 18, 1980, Zimbabwe (formerly a British colony called Southern Rhodesia) gained its formal independence. Zimbabwe was named after "Great Zimbabwe," the extraordinary sites of stone buildings created by the precolonial civilization that controlled the area and traded gold and other wealth with coastal peoples and others visiting the East African coast (including the Chinese). In 1890, these civilizations were invaded by the Rhode's British South Africa Company (BSACO) and, despite their efforts, the indigenous people were not able to resist the foreign invaders. In 1924 the self-governing British colony of Southern Rhodesia was formed, and local governing powers were placed in the hands of the white settlers. In 1953, Southern Rhodesia became federated with the other British colonies of Northern Rhodesia (Zambia) and Nyasaland (Malawi) in a plan to make the area a "multi-racial" federation of Central Africa. Power, however, remained in the hands of the white minority. Due to resistance by the indigenous populations, the federation ended in 1963. The independent nations of Malawi and Zambia were subsequently formed by black nationalists, while Southern Rhodesia remained under the domain of the white minority, despite the advances of black nationalists who desired independence.

In 1965, the Rhodesia Front (RF) government, led by Ian Smith, declared its independence from Britain in hopes of continuing white supremacy. While both Britain and the United Nations refused to recognize Smith's government, neither took strong measures to end it. Plans to overthrow the RF were carried out by black nationalists who, in 1966, began underground movements and an armed struggle for independence. The advances of these nationalists forced many of the white settlers into exile and the RF was eventually forced into negotiations. An election in 1980 allowed the black nationalists to take over the government, and Robert Mugabe subsequently became the first prime minister of independent Zimbabwe. Although once seen as a great leader of independent Africa, Mugabe now stands accused of political corruption and destroying the Zimbabwe economy with an ill-conceived and brutally managed land-resettlement plan.

The social conditions of most of Zimbabwe's people greatly improved immediately after independence, but now they have lost nearly all of the foreign-exchange income they were earning for agricultural products. Tobacco was a major crop, but most of the farms have been destroyed, as white landowners and their workers have been driven away. Recently the International Monetary Fund and the World Bank severed their relationships with the country due to nonpayment of loans. Yet another sobering note is the impact of HIV/AIDS—life expectancy dropped to forty-three years in 1990, and in 2000, one in five individuals was infected with HIV.

Harare, the capital, has become southern Africa's center for arts and communications. Many of the city's filmmakers, musicians, writers, and artists are internationally renowned for their work. Malachite carvings by Zimbabwean sculptors are also internationally valued and renowned.

JENNIFER JOYCE

ZULU

See **Beadwork**

APPENDIX:
African Studies Centers and Libraries in the USA and Africa

See entry: **Libraries**

African Centers and Libraries

- *Centre Regional de Documentation (CRDT)* was established in Niamey, Niger, as a joint venture between the government of Niger and UNESCO in 1968. One of the goals of the center was to collect data in sixteen West African countries.
- *The Swaziland Oral History Project*, based in the National Archives of Lobamba, established in 1985, has the goal to introduce an archive of Swazi oral history and publish select transcripts from the archive.
- *The Oral Traditions Association of Zimbabwe (OTAZI)*, formed in 1988, an organization that is closely linked with the Oral Traditions Association of Southern Africa (OTASA) aims at promoting Zimbabwe's oral history and at improving the methodology of working with oral data.
- *The East African Centre for Research on Oral Traditions and African National Languages (EACROTANAL)* is based in Zanzibar and founded in 1977 by Tanzania, Madagascar, Sudan, Ethiopia, and Burundi, with Somalia, Mozambique and the Comoros joining later. One of the center's goals is to promote regional research on oral traditions. The center has also published *Studies and Documents (Etudes et documents)* between 1980 and 1987.
- *The Institute of African Studies Documentation Centre (University of Ghana)* opened in 1990 and has as its goals to gather and disseminate oral data, serve as an information center for researchers, and to be a regional center for the collection of oral data.
- *The George Padmore Research Library on African Affairs in Ghana* opened in 1961. In the early 1980s, the library conducted a series of oral documentation that consisted of interviews of prominent Ghanaians and Africanists
- *The Cultural Archives of Senegal*, which is connected to Senegal's Ministry of Culture, has as its goal "the world-wide collecting and archival management of the various forms of expression of Negro-African civilization in order that elements of their original structure may be conserved" (Saliou Mbaye, "Oral Records in Senegal," 568).
- *The Center for the Study of Civilizations in Senegal* (also connected to the Ministry of Culture) opened in 1972 and has as its mission the "study of the interrelationship between language and culture, the development and goals of the humanities in Africa, the study of the imaginary world, and the promotion of cultural life among the people." (Ibid., 569) It collects oral literature and studies modes of traditional expression based on the spoken word.
- *The Primary Institute of Black Africa (IFAN Cheikh Anta Diop)* was established in 1966. Within the institute, the Department of Literature and Civilization and the Department of Islamic Studies collect oral records.
- *The University of Zambia's* oral history project was launched in 1979 and had as its goals to record oral data and to compile a two-volume bibliography of oral history projects in Zambia. The first volume, *Taped and Transcribed Projects*, came out in 1981; the second volume was delayed.

US-based Centers and Libraries

- *Indiana University's (IU) Main Library* has a separate Folklore Collection that is considered one of the finest working collections of folklore in the United States. It includes collections of folklore materials as well as reference works and has large holdings on Africa. Indiana University is also the home of the Archives of Traditional Music, which contains one of the largest collections of phonorecordings of African music and oral data in the world.
- *The Archive of Folk Culture of the American Folklife Center* (Thomas Jefferson Building, Room G152, Washington

D.C.), includes sources for the study of folk music, folklore, folklife, and oral history. It contains copies of original recordings, a reference collection, and several important collections of field recordings (Laura Boulton collection; The Arthur S. Alberts collection; Paul Bowles collection; James Rosellini and Kathleen Johnson collection; Halim El-Dabh collection; Darius Thieme collection; Helen R. Roberts collection).

- *The Schomburg Center for Research in Black Culture, New York Public Library* is among the world's largest collections of records "documenting the experiences of peoples of African origin and descent."
- *The Melville J. Herskovits Library of African Studies at Northwestern University* holds one of the world's largest Africana collections that includes sound recordings and several special collections.
- *Columbia University's Center for Studies in Ethnomusicology* has Africa-related recordings (field and commercial) and its collections includes the Laura Boulton collection, the Sviatoslav Podstavsk collection on the Argungu of northern Nigeria; the Barbara Hampton collection on the Ga of Accra, Ghana; and the Salwa El-Shawan collection on Egypt.
- *The Traditional Music Documentation Project* (Washington, D.C.) "is an independent non-profit organization which seeks to identify and document extant examples of traditional African music." It includes over eight thousand recorded items (field and commercial recordings).

APPENDIX:
Field and Broadcast Sound Recording Collections at the Indiana University Archives of Traditional Music (ATM)

See entry: **Archives of Traditional Music**

Guide to the Appendix

The following appendix was prepared by (ATM) staff members Ronda Sewald and Meredith Vaughn, with librarian Suzanne Mudge, archivist Marilyn Graf, and former associate director Mary Bucknum, who provided critical assistance and guidance. This appendix includes the entire holdings of field and broadcast collections of African music and oral data at the ATM; it does not include commercial releases. One can use this appendix to find collections of interest and then continue the search using the electronic catalog accessible on the website, *http://www.indiana.edu/%7elibarchml/*, which contains far more detail than do the entries below. Asterisks indicate that a collection is not yet cataloged; however, information on such collections can still be obtained by contacting ATM staff at *atmusic@indiana.edu*. Each entry is organized in the same manner, as are our original cataloging records, which typically include the following information:

1. Location (country/countries, and city/region where available, where recordings were made). Although organizing this list by country privileges a colonial perspective and organizational model, this arrangement has been chosen for two reasons. First, this will ease the use of this appendix by researchers, given that the titles of collections, as found in our catalog records, are organized this way. Second, some collections have no ethnic specification (e.g., a lecture on South African politics), which would have made problematic an organizational hierarchy that placed ethnicity at the top level.
2. Ethnic group(s)
3. Date(s) of recording
4. Collector(s)

5. Physical description of collection
6. Keywords
7. ATM Accession number

The following example shows how these categories appear in an actual entry. Boldface numbers indicate the categories above: **1.** Belgian Congo, Province du Kasai. **2.** Basongye. **3.** 1959–1960. **4.** Merriam, Alan P.; Merriam, Barbara W. **5.** 11 sound tape reels. **6.** Congo. funeral rites. Singing games. Praise songs. Children's songs. **7.** 66–128–F.

This appendix identifies the country where the recording was made, and not necessarily the performers' country of origin. For example, recordings of Africans and Africanist lecturers made in the United States are listed under the heading United States (N.B.: this appendix does not include recordings of African Americans or other African diaspora peoples). For purposes of historical accuracy, the country name that was current when each recording was made is listed; thus in some cases researchers must search the current country name and all historical country names to find materials from a single location (for example, researchers interested in Malawi must search both Malawi and Nyasaland). Collections are listed only once. If a collection features recordings from multiple countries, but materials from one country predominate, the collection is listed under that one country; if there is an even spread of materials from many parts of Africa, or if the country where a recording was made is unknown, then the collection is listed under the category Various and Unknown Locations.

Algeria

Algeria and Niger, Sahara region, Tuareg, 1958. Holiday, Geoffrey; Holiday, Finola. 1 sound tape reel. Folk music. Hunting songs. Love songs. 58–008–F.
Algeria and Niger, Tuaregs, 1978. Card, Caroline. 2 sound tape reels. Music. Folk music. Nigerians. 78–022–F.

531

Algeria, Tamarasset; Niger, Niamey, Tuareg, 1976–1977. Card, Caroline. 30 sound tape reels. Rites. Ceremonies. Fulute music. 78–017–F.

Algeria, Tuareg, 1935. Fodermayr, Franz; Zohrer, Ludwig G.A. 1 sound tape reel. Songs. 78–018–F.*

Algeria, Tuaregs, 1972. Wendt, Caroline Card. 1 sound tape reel. Folk songs. Imzad music. Tamacheq. 73–056–F.

Angola

Angola and South Africa, 1947. Camp, Charles M.; Boulton, Laura. 12 sound tape reels. Kimbundu. Ovambo. San. Zulu. Hottentot. 54–170–F.

Angola and Zaire, Ovimbundu, 1929–1930. Hambly, Wilfrid Dyson. 40 cylinders. Prayers. Singing games. Work songs. Linguistics. 54–007–F.

Angola, Chitau, Dondi, Lobito Bay, Vihela, 1931. Boulton, Laura. 5 sound tape reels. Folk songs. Mbundu. Chokwe. Work songs. Mbira music. 92–319–F.

Angola, Napika, Angolans, 1969. Boulton, Laura. 1 sound tape reel. Music. Songs. Dance music. 92–397–F.

Angola, South Africa, Namibia, Swaziland, 1947–1948. Boulton, Laura. 19 sound tape reels. Rites. Ceremonies. Work songs. Children's songs. Hymns. Puberty rites. Musical bow music. Mbira music. 92–317–F.

Angola; Dondi, Galangue, Kamatundo; Ovimbundu, Vachokwe, Gangela, Kuanyama, Humbe, Baluba; 1971 Boulton, Laura. 16 sound tape reels. Songs. Dance music. Puberty rites. Initiation rites. Circumcision rites. Mbira music. Xylophone music. 92–402–F.

Belgian Congo

Belgian Congo and Ruanda-Urundi, 1951–1952. Merriam, Alan P.; Merriam, Barbara W. 76 sound tape reels. Congo. Wedding songs. Work songs. Children's songs. Drinking songs. 66–127–F.

Belgian Congo: Kivu, Katanga, and Leopoldville Provinces, 1952–1954. Alberts, Arthur S. 9 sound tape reels. Congo. Children's Songs. Speeches. Highlife. Rites. Church music. 68–059–F.

Belgian Congo, Province du Kasai, Basongye, 1959–1960. Merriam, Alan P.; Merriam, Barbara W. 11 sound tape reels. Congo. Funeral rites. Singing games. Praise songs. Children's songs. 66–128–F.

Belgian Congo, Tumba, Bakongo, 1908. Laman, K. E. 7 cylinders. Congo. Folk songs. Work songs. 54–210–F.

Benin

Benin, Gun and Fon, 1981–1983. Chaabane, Rhonda. 2 sound cassettes. Songs. Music. 86–159–F.

Biafra, Republic of

Republic of Biafra, 1967. Irwin, Graham W. 1 sound tape reel. Nigeria. Speech. History. Civil war. 69–132–F.

Botswana

Botswana, c. 1970. Tlou, Thomas. 7 sound tape reels. Oral history. Interviews. Yei. Tawana. Kwena. Rolong. 73–001–F.

Botswana, N'gamiland, 1967. Lambrecht, Frank; Lambrecht, Dora. 4 sound tape reels. !Kung. Dance music. Mbira. Children's songs. 68–209–F.

Burkina Faso

Burkina Faso, Ouagadougou, 1983–1987. Sankara, Thomas. 18 sound cassettes. Burkina Faso. Politics. Government. 92–077–F/B.

Burundi

Burundi, Independence Day celebration, 1962. Cox, William L. 1 sound tape reel. Speeches. 74–002–F.

Cameroon

Cameroon, 1967. Quersin, Benoit. 24 sound tape reels. Bulu. Ngangte. Eton. Bamileke. Fefe. Tikar. Bafia. Bamun. 72–233–F.

Cameroon, Central Cameroon, Gbaya, 1966–1967. Noss, Philip A. 12 sound tape reels. Oral tradition. Proverbs. Parables. Riddles. 71–003–F.

Cameroon, Nso, 1977. Fanso, Verkijika G. 7 sound tape reels. Oral history. 77–072–F.

Cameroon, Yaounde, 1980. Keim, Karen Ruth King. 39 sound cassettes. Interviews. Popular music. Folklore. Literature. 85–290–F.

Chad

Chad and Central African Republic, 1974. Cordell, Dennis. 24 sound cassettes. Folklore. History. Interviews. 77–064–F.

Chad, Tarangara, 1965. Schultz, William L. 1 sound tape reel. Folk songs. Dance music. Instrumental music. Ndoka. 77–033–F.

Comoros

Comoros, Sirazi, 1981. Ottenheimer, Martin. Ottenheimer, Harriet. 33 sound tape reels. Shinzwani. Hingazija. Weddings. Legends. Rites. Ceremonies. Oral history. 81–098–F.

Congo

Congo, Bakuba, Baluba, and Bobangi, 1906. Starr, Frederick. 18 cylinders. Ocarina music. Bow music. Whistle music. Songs. 69–015–F.

Congo, c. 1940–1960 (?). Boulton, Laura. 3 sound tape reels. Amazon river region. Sahara. Egypt. Music. 92–534–F.

Congo, France, United States, 1986–1989. Martin, Phyllis M. 24 sound cassettes. Interviews. Leisure. Society. Brazzaville. Customs. Social life. 97–114–F.

Congo, Gandajika, Luba, 1968–1969. Callebaut, Jeroom. 1 sound tape reel. Children's songs. Ballada. Lullabies. 91–210–F.

Congo, Katanga Province, Luba-Shankadi and Balaba, 1970. Gansemans, Jos 29 sound tape reels. Folk music. Drum language. Rites. Ceremonies. Birth songs. 71–408–F.

Congo, Kinshasa, Luba, 1945–1967. Pruitt, William Franklin. 1 wire recording. Interviews. Oral history. School songs. Speeches. 74–101–F.

Congo, Lake McDonald, Basongye, 1973. Merriam, Alan. 2 sound cassettes. Folk songs. Folk music. Wedding music. 73–054–F.

Congo, Pool, Brazzaville, Teke, Bangala, Libangi, Kongo, 1986. Ngole, Jean-Pierre. 20 sound cassettes. Songs. Work songs. Women. Markets. 88–105–F.

Dahomey

Dahomey and Brazil, 1942–1950. Azevedo, Luiz Heitor Corrêa. 3 sound tape reels. Benin. Children's songs. Work songs. Rites. Cults. 68–064–F.

*Uncatalogued

Dahomey, Various culture groups, 1955. Agbo, Marius. 1 sound tape reel. Benin. Yoruba. Fon. Dendi. Mahi. Dompago. Funeral music. 67–165–F.

Egypt

Egypt, 1968–1971. El-Shamy, Hasan M. 7 sound tape reels. Egyptian folktales. Folk music. Legends. Marriage customs. 71–303–F.

Egypt, Copts, 1931–1977. Boulton, Laura. 144 sound tape reels. Coptic church. Music. Hymns. Church music. 93–161–B/C/F.

Egypt, Turkish, Arabic, c. 1960–1970. Roy, Martha. 74 sound tape reels. 6 sound cassettes. Folk songs. Ceremonial songs. Ramadan. Mawwal. Taqsim. 93–198–F/C.*

England

England, London, West Africans, 1943. Unknown. 7 sound discs. Igbo. Ewe. Yoruba. Music. Songs. 76–167–F.

Ethiopia

Ethiopia, 1947. Leslau, Wolf. 38 sound discs. Church music. Wedding music. Folk music. Children's songs. 54–002–F.

Ethiopia, 1966. Boulton, Laura. 26 sound tape reels. Folk music. Coptic church. Amhara. Sudanese. Oromo. Somalis. Masenqo. Washint. 92–309–F.

Ethiopia, Addis Ababa, 1970. Lemma, Tesfaye. 2 sound tape reels. Folk music. Work songs. Wedding music. Minstrels. 72–085–F.

Ethiopia, Addis Ababa, Ethiopians, 1966. Boulton, Laura. 1 sound tape reel. Music. Arabic. Tigrinya. Oromo. Amhara.Walamo. 92–330–F.

Ethiopia, Addis Ababa, Harrar and Jigiga, 1972. Kimberlin, Cynthia. 97 sound tape reels. Folk music. Popular music. Rock music. 76–178–F.

Ethiopia, Aduwa, Copts, 1968. Davis, Gordon A. 1 sound tape reel. Baptism. Churches. Church music. 71–180–F.

Ethiopia, Ethiopians, 1966–1967. Boulton, Laura. 1 sound tape reel. Music. Folk music. Sacred music. 92–421–F.

Ethiopia, Falasha and Amhara, 1973. Shelemay, Kay. 35 sound tape reels. Jewish chants. Jews. Interviews. 74–031–F.

Ethiopia, Falasha, 1940. Unknown. 5 sound discs. Cushitic. Folk music. 87–128–F.

Ethiopia, Falashas, c. 1945. Leslau, Wolf. 2 sound discs. Chants. Prayers. 54–214–F.

Ethiopia, Kaffa, Me'en (Teshenna), 1964–1965. Muldrow, William; Muldrow, Elizabeth. 2 sound tape reels. Funeral music. Harvest music. Work songs. 74–072–F.

Ethiopia, Tigre and Eritrea, 1942–1943. Courlander, Harold. 10 sound discs. Folk music. Work songs. Linguistics. Praise songs. 54–001–F.

France

France, Paris, Colonial Exhibition, 1931. Musée de la Parole. 2 sound tape reels. Tunisians. Moroccans. Fon. Lao. Benin. Congo. War songs. Work songs. Funeral music. 61–052–F.

French Equatorial Africa

French Equatorial Africa, Bateke, 1911. Laman, K. E. 21 cylinders. French Guyana. Folk songs. 54–211–F.

French Equatorial Africa, Lambarene, 1956. Boulton, Laura. 1 sound tape reel. Gabon. Music. Songs. Dance music. 92–393–F.

Gabon

Gabon and Río Muni, Fang, 1959–1960. Fernandez, James W. 20 sound tape reels. Linguistics. Drum language. Prayers. Lullabies. 71–255–F.

Gambia

Gambia and Senegal, Wolof, 1951. Ames, David W. 9 sound tape reels. Islam. Rites. Wedding music. Children's music. Work songs. 66–205–F.

Gambia, Senegal, Mandinka, Fula, and others, 1970. Knight, Roderic. 287 sound tape reels. Mandingo. Folk music. Drum music. Griots. 77–073–F.

Gambia, Senegal, Wolof, 1973–1974. Magel, Emil. 32 sound tape reels. Stories. Narratives. 76–001–F.

Ghana

Ghana and Nigeria, 1973. Hanley, Sister Mary Ann, C.S.J. 17 sound tape reels. Church music. 74–095–F.

Ghana and Upper Volta, 1972. Hanley, Sister Mary Ann, C.S.J. 19 sound tape reels. Burkina Faso. Band music. Mass music. Church music. Wedding music. 74–094–F.

Ghana, 1966. Boulton, Laura. 3 sound tape reels. Music. Folk music. Folk songs. Dance music. 92–310–F.

Ghana, Accra, Ga, 1972. Robertson, Claire. 38 sound tape reels. Interviews. Women. History. Oral history. 74–098–F.

Ghana, Akan, Ewe, and Ga, 1987–1988. 8 sound cassettes. Drumming. Ceremonies. Prayers. Interviews.*

Ghana, Ashanti, c. 1955. Prempeh, Kofi. 1 sound tape reel. Folk music. Folk songs. 73–058–F.

Ghana, Ashanti, Ewe, Krobo, 1974. Coplan, David B., Thomason, Lee. 7 sound tape reels. Funeral music. Drum music. Highlife music. Stool ceremony. 74–103–F.

Ghana, Brong and Ashanti, 1970–1972. Owen, Wilfred 40 sound cassettes. Festivals. Libations. Oral history. Praise songs. Tales. 72–237–F.

Ghana, Brong-Ahafo, Bono-Akan, 1969–1971. Warren, Dennis M. 44 sound tape reels. Oral history. Folklore. Cults. Children's songs. Rites. Praise songs. 72–249–F.

Ghana, Ga, Twi, Ewe, 1970–1972. Coplan, David. B. 5 sound tape reels. Folk music. Highlife music. 85–519–F.

Ghana, Juaben, Ashanti, 1966. Akyea, Ofori E. 2 sound tape reels. Ashanti. Folk songs. Funeral music. Percussion. 67–215–F.

Ghana, Kasena, 1973–1977. Robertson-DeCarbo, Carol. 5 sound tape reels. Kasem. Rites. Ceremonies. Drum music. 80–181–F.

Ghana, Navrongo and Tamale, 1960. Sarkisian, Leo. 2 sound tape reels. Praise songs. Work songs. Funeral music. Children's songs. 61–053–F.

Ghana, Northern Region, Lobi and Wala, 1975. Hagaman, Barbara L. 5 sound cassettes. Rites. Folk music. Work songs. Mbira. Drum music. 81–099–F.

Ghana, Northern Territories, 1950. Unknown collector. 2 sound tape reels. Instrumental music. 73–057–F.

Ghana, Togo and Benin, Ewe, 1968–1971. Aduamah, E. Y. 8 sound tape reels. Love songs. Cults. Processions. Prayers. Funerals. War songs. Puberty rites. Singing games. 73–096–F.

Ghana, University of Ghana, 1972. Kealiinohomoku, Joann. 3 sound tape reels. Lecture. Dance music. 74–050–F.

Ghana, Upper Region, Wala, 1966–1967. Fikry, Mona. 126 sound tape reels. Wa. Oral history. Folk music. Customs. Folklore. 69–129–F.

Ghana; United States, New York, Ewe, 1968–1978. Pantaleoni, Hewitt. 100 sound tape reels. Uganda. Drum music. Children's songs. Ga. Highlife. 96–239–F.

Guinea

Guinea, 1984–1993. Geysbeek, Tim 61 sound cassettes. Oral histories. Epic poetry. Interviews. Folk rituals. 98–379–F.*

Guinea-Conakry, Maninka, 1970s–1992. Conrad, David; Geysbeek, Tim. 12 sound cassettes. Mandingo. Epic poetry. Oral tradition. Music. 99–020–F.

Ivory Coast

Ivory Coast, Dan (Yacouba), Mahou, Kognawe, Djomande Mahou, 1997. Reed, Daniel B. 79 sound cassettes. 24 DAT. 28 Hi8 video cassettes. 3 VHS video cassettes. Ceremonial masks. Mask performances. Interviews. Drum music. 98–005–F.*

Ivory Coast and Upper Volta, Dyula, 1979–1980. Green, Kathryn. 37 sound cassettes. Burkina Faso. Cote d'Ivoire. Kong. History. 82–413–F.

Ivory Coast and Upper Volta, Mau, 1973–1974. Ellovich, Risa S. 5 sound tape reels. Cote d'Ivoire. Weddings. Oral history. Dyula. Folk music. 75–029–F.

Ivory Coast, 1963–1965. Tourgara, Adam. 14 sound tape reels. Cote d'Ivoire. Dyula. Mandingo. Bambara. 66–197–C.

Ivory Coast, Senufo, 1969–1970. Glaze, Anita J. 36 sound cassettes. Oral history. Folk music. Rites. Cults. Praise songs. 71–307–F.

Kenya

Kenya and South Africa, 1961. Morgenthau, Henry. 6 sound tape reels. Interviews. Jomo Kenyatta. Tom Mboya. 71–018–F/B.

Kenya, Didinga, 1974–1978. Moore, Robert O. 2 sound cassettes. Didinga language. Linguistics. Word lists. 89–073–F.

Kenya, Eastern Province and Ethiopia, Borana Province and Wollega Province, c. 1957–1985. Andrzejewski, Bogumi Witalis 16 sound cassettes. 11 sound tape reels. Oromo. Folk literature. Music. Boran. Qottu. Shoa. Orma. Gabra. Wollega. Tales. Proverbs. 94–205–F/B.

Kenya, Kalenjin, 1974–78. Moore, Robert O. 40 sound cassettes. Kalenjin language. Linguistics. Bok. Bongomet. Kony. Sabaot. Sebei. Endo. Geyo. Marakwet. Pakot. Tugen. Tenik. Sogoo. 89–072–F.

Kenya, Kisii District, Nyaribari Location, Gusii, 1966. Dobrin, Arthur. 1 sound tape reel. Rites. Ceremonies. Circumcision. Birth songs. 67–039–F.

Kenya, Lamu, Waswahili, 1976–1977. Boyd, Alan W. 77 sound cassettes, 47 sound tape reels. 77–091–F.

Kenya, Masai, 1975–1976. Berntsen, John Lawrence. 18 sound tape reels. Religion. Politics. 78–030–F.

Kenya, Mijikenda, Kamba and Wasta, 1971. Spear, Thomas. 18 sound tape reels. Interviews. History. 80–038–F.

Kenya, North Nyanza Bantu, Tanzania. Moore, Robert O. Manuscript. Vocabulary. Bugusu. Sanawe. 89–074–MS.*

Kenya, Nyanaza Province, Gusii, 1966. Dobrin, Arthur. 1 sound tape reel. Harvest songs. Funeral music. War songs. Children's songs. 66–148–F.

Kenya, Siyu, Mombasa, Nairobi, Swahili, 1981–1984. Brown, W. Howard. 13 sound cassettes. Swahili poetry. Oral history. Interviews. Swahili language. 85–282–F.

Kenya, Swahili and Masai, 1980. Schoenbrun, Lewis. 2 sound cassettes. Folk music. Children's songs. Swahili language. 80–228–F.

Kenya, Tabaka Mission, Kisii, 1975. Dobrin, Arthur. 5 sound cassettes. Rites. Ceremonies. Gusii. Songs. 85–346–F.

Kenya, Western Province, Busia District, Iteso, 1970. Karp, Ivan. 3 sound tape reels. Teso. Folk music. Funeral tires. Drinking songs. 84–492–F.

Liberia

Liberia and Sierra Leone, Gbande, Loma, Mandingo, 1935. Morey, Robert H. 16 cylinders. War songs. Folk music. Love songs. 54–003–F.

Liberia, Afro-Americans, 1973–1975. Shick, Tom W. 18 sound cassettes. Interviews. Oral history. 77–078–F.

Liberia, Bassa, Kru, Loma, and others, 1973–1976. Siegmann, William. 38 sound cassettes. Interviews. Oral histories. 78–158–F.

Liberia, Bong County, Kpelle, 1970. Stone, Ruth M.; Stone, Verlon L. 24 sound tape reels. Folk music. Drum music. Work music. Drum language. Rites. 73–052–F.

Liberia, Bong County, Kpelle, 1971–1973. Gay, Judith S. 30 sound tape reels. Oral history. Folklore. Folk tales. Epic songs. Jokes. 74–063–F.

Liberia, Bong County, Kpelle, 1975–1976. Stone, Ruth M., Stone, Verlon L. 72 sound tape reels. Language. Rites. Songs. Poetry. 82–434–F.

Liberia, Dei, Gbande, Gola, Kpelle, Mandingo, Vai, 1985–1986. Holsoe, Svend E. 115 sound tape reels and 75 sound cassettes. Broadcasts. Languages. Oral history. Tales. Recitations. 76–049–F.

Liberia, Kpelle, Mandingo, Kru, and other groups, c. 1942. Okie, Packard L. 24 sound tape reels. Work songs. Church music. Puberty rites. Ramadan hymns. 57–001–F.

Liberia, Kru, 1971–1972. Massing, Andreas. 5 sound tape reels. Linguistics. Church music. Folk songs. Christmas music. 72–079–F.

Liberia, Monrovia, 1949. Alberts, Lois; Alberts, Arthur S. 2 sound tape reels. Popular music. Songs. 68–060–F.

Liberia, Nimba County, Sanniquellie, 1970. Hawthorne, Richard. 2 sound tape reels. Traditional medicine. Healers. 70–149–F.

Liberia, Nimiah, Djabo, 1930–1931. Herzog, George. 236 cylinders. War music. Folk songs. Linguistics. Drumming. Xylophone. 54–223–F.

Liberia, Robertsport and Cape Mount, 1942. Okie, Packard L. 2 sound tape reels. Vai. Buzi. Bassa. Gola. Mende. Gbandi. Kissi. 54–004–F.

Liberia, Sinoe County, 1975–1976. Sullivan, Jo Mary. 58 sound cassettes. History. Church music. Oral history. Folk music. 76–177–F.

Libya

Libya, Cyrenaica, 1974, 1978–1979. Behnke, Barbara. 12 sound cassettes. Wedding music. Songs. Rites. Marriage customs. 80–115–F/C.

Libya, Cyrenaica, 1978–79. Behnke, Roy. 3 sound cassettes. Work songs. Arabic. 80–116–F.

Malawi

Malawi, Asena and Likuba, 1982–84. Strumpf, Mitchel. 4 sound cassettes. Folk music. Children's songs. Drums. 85–494–F.

Malawi, Blantyre, Cewa and Yao, 1988. Strumpf, Mitchel. 2 videocassettes. Interviews. Musicians. Music festivals. 88–087–F.

Malawi, Zomba, Chancellor College, 1991. 1 videocassette. Choral music. 91–343–F.

Mali

Mali, 1973–1974. Johnson, John William. 12 sound tape reels. Bambara. Epic poetry. Interviews. Sundiata. Sunjata. 76–131–F.

Mali, Bamako, Malinke, 1978. Massing, Andreas. 3 sound cassettes. Epic poetry. Mandingo. Folk music. Oral tradition. 78–104–F.

Mali, Bamako, Maninka, 1961. Bird, Charles S. 4 sound tape reels. Mandingo. Oral tradition. Epic poetry. 76–033–F.

Mali, Bamako, Maninka, 1967–1968. Bird, Charles S. 8 sound tape reels. Folk music. Griots. Praise songs. Kora music. 71–124–F.

Mali, Bamako, Maninka, 1968. Bird, Charles S. 5 sound tape reels. Oral tradition. Epic poetry. Hunting songs. 71–259–F.

Mali, Bamako, Maninka, 1972. Bird, Charles S. 2 sound tape reels. Mandingo. Oral tradition. Epic poetry. 76–035–F.

Mali, Bamako, Maninka, 1975. Bird, Charles S. 4 sound tape reels. Mandingo. Hunting songs. Epic poetry. Oral tradition. 75–190–F.

Mali, Bamako, North Americans, 1975. Johnson, John William. 1 sound tape reel. Tales. Festivals. Social customs. 85–266–F.

Mali, Bamana, Maninka, and Khassonke, 1975–1976. Conrad, David. 35 sound cassettes. Hunting songs. History. Ballads. Tales. 88–061–F.

Mali, Bambara (Jula), Minianka, 1989–1991. Maxwell, Heather A. (Adou) 8 sound cassettes. Music pedagogy. Folk music. Balafen. Dance music. 96–263–F.*

Mali, Dogon, 1989. Siegmann, William. 1 sound tape reel. Music. Folk music. 89–199–F.

Mali, Keyla, Mandinka, 1972. Bird, Charles S. 4 sound tape reels. Folk songs. Folk music. Wedding music. 72–230–F.

Mali, Keyla, Maninka, 1968. Bird, Charles S. 2 sound tape reels. Mandingo. Epic poetry. Oral tradition. 76–036–F.

Mali, Kita, Maninka, 1968. Bird, Charles S.; Diabate, Massa M. 3 sound tape reels. Oral tradition.Griots. Historical songs. 71–260–F.

Mali, Kita, Maninka, 1968. Diabate, Massa M.; Bird, Charles S. 3 sound tape reels. Mandingo. History. Praise songs. Oral tradition. 76–034–F.

Mali, Kolokani, Bamana, 1974–1976. Mahy, Judith. 28 sound tape reels. Bambara. Weddings. Rites. Ceremonies. Dance music. 76–127–F.

Mali, Kolokani, Bamana, 1975–1976. Brink, James. 12 sound cassettes. Songs. Bambara. 76–126–F.

Mali, Kondo, Bamako, Bamana, Fula, Dogon, 1984–1987. Lucas, Peter. 4 sound cassettes. Songs. Griots. Oral tradition. Lute music. 88–107–F.

Mali, Mandingo, 1980–1981. Courlander, Howard. 18 sound cassettes. Bambara. Soninke. Tales. Customs. Interviews. 83–736–F.

Mali, Maninka, 1968–1972. Diabate, Massa M.; Bird, Charles S. 51 sound tape reels. Epic poetry. Folk songs. Praise songs. Oral tradition. Kora music. 73–005–F.

Mali, Marka, 1972–1977. Roberts, Richard L. 35 sound cassettes. Oral history. Oral tradition. 77–063–F.

Morocco

Morocco, 1963, 1969. Wanklyn, Christopher. 5 sound tape reels. Festivals. Sufism. Weddings. Instrumental music. 74–119–F.

Morocco, ca. 1959. Bowles, Paul; Wanklyn, Christopher. 1 sound tape reel. Folk music. Rites and ceremonies. Islam. Ramadan. 62–017–F.

Morocco, Salé, ca. 1960. Cherki, Salah. 9 sound tape reels. Arabic. Folk music. Art music. Songs. 69–023–F.

Mozambique

Mozambique, 1965. Morgenthau, Henry. 3 sound tape reels. Politics. Government. Social conditions. Interviews. 69–204–F.

Mozambique, 1969. Boulton, Laura. 1 sound tape reel. Music. Mozambique. Popular music. 92–529–F.

Mozambique, 1969–1971. Boulton, Laura. 27 sound tape reels. Dance music. Chopi. Makua. Sena. Zezuru. Panpipes music. Lullabies. Xylophone music. 92–363–F.

Mozambique, Zambezi, 1968–1969. Isaacman, Allen. 29 sound tape reels. Oral history. Tawara. Chewa. Chopi. Slavery. 81–032–F.

Niger

Niger and Algeria, Niamey and Tamanrasset, Nigerians and Tuareg, c. 1970–1978. Card, Caroline. 2 sound tape reels. Music. 78–022–F.

Niger, Hausa, 1972–1973. Baier, Stephen. 26 sound cassettes. Interviews. Finance. History. 73–053–F.

Niger, Maradi, 1988–1990. Cooper, Barbara. 49 sound cassettes. Interviews. Hausa. Fula. Kanuri. Women. 93–237–F.

Niger, Mirria, Hausa, 1973–1975. Saunders, Margaret Overholt; Saunders, Stewart. 20 sound cassettes. Koran. Wedding music. Church music. Oral history. 75–186–F.

Niger, Songhay, and Zarma, 1980–1981. Hale, Thomas. 35 sound tape reels. Chants. Epic poetry. Griots. Music. 88–104–F.

Niger, Tanout, Diffa, Hausa, 1981. Beik, Janet. 19 sound tape reels. Theater. Drama. Praise songs. 88–062–F.

Nigeria

Nigeria and Dahomey, Yorubans, 1974. LaPin, Deirdre Ann. 78 sound tape reels. Songs. Proverbs. Stories. Jokes. Narratives. 75–034–F.

Nigeria, 1972. Armstrong, Robert G. 2 sound tape reels. Opera. 72–240–F.

Nigeria, Benin City, Bini, 1966. Ben-Amos, Dan. 85 sound tape reels. Mbira. Oral tradition. Praise songs. Singing games. 70–092–F.

Nigeria, Benue Plateau, Idoma, Agila, 1963. Armstrong, Robert G. 2 sound tape reels. Oral tradition. Masks. Tales. Folk songs. 72–244–F.

Nigeria, Benue Plateau, Oturkpo, 1963. Armstrong, Robert G. 2 sound tape reels. Children's songs. Idoma. 72–242–F.

Nigeria, Benue Plateau, Western State, 1960–1969. Unoogwu, Patrick; Wittig, Curt; Armstrong, Robert G. 6 sound tape reels. Folk music. Masks. Oral tradition. War songs. Ifa. 72–245–F.

Nigeria, Benue Province, Various groups, 1964–1965. Rubin, Barbara; Rubin, Arnold. 14 sound tape reels. Jukun. Chamba. Yergum. Kutep. Rites. Ceremonies. 67–122–F.

Nigeria, Bornu province, Maiduguri, Kanuri, 1956. Cohen, Ronald. 1 sound tape reel. Folk songs. Harvest festivals. Praise songs. 60–035–F.

Nigeria, Cameroon, Yoruba and Babinga, 1939. Unknown. 1 sound disc. Folk songs. Folk music. 87–163–F.

Nigeria, Dahomey and Togoland, Ashanti, Yoruba, and Fon, 1931. Herskovits, Melville J.; Herskovits, Frances S. 242 cylinders. War songs. Praise songs. Proverbs. Lullabies. Work songs. 67–152–F.

Nigeria, East Central and Benue Plateau State, 1973–1975. Lambrecht, Frank; Lambrecht, Dora. 4 sound cassettes. Xylophone music. Dance music. Rites and ceremonies. 75–191–B/F

Nigeria, Ibadan, 1971. Armstrong, Robert G. 1 sound tape reel. Folk music. Folk songs. 72–247–F.

Nigeria, Ibadan, Yoruba, 1967–1969. Peek, Philip M. 1 sound tape reel. Folk songs. Cult music. Popular music. Cults. 72–080–F.

Nigeria, Ibadan, Yoruba, 1970. Armstrong, Robert G. 2 sound tape reels. Theater. Title "Love of Money." Musical performance. 72–238–F.

Nigeria, Ife, c. 1960. Armstrong, Robert G. 3 sound tape reels. Chants. Divination. 72–243–F.

Nigeria, Igbo and Yoruba, 1943. Northwestern University. 14 sound discs. Igbo. Yoruba. Nigeria. Songs. Funeral music. 76–169–F/C.

Nigeria, Igbo, 1939. Unknown. 5 sound discs. Songs. War songs. War dance. 87–162–F.

Nigeria, Igbo, 1963–1964. Ames, David W. 18 sound tape reels. Praise songs. Funeral music. Hymns. Highlife. 68–245–F.

Nigeria, Igbo, 1975–1976. Ames, David; Eze, Samuel. 23 sound tape reels. Rites. Ceremonies. Funerals. Hymns. Highlife. 78–165–F.

Nigeria, Imo State, Igbo and Ijaw, 1977–1978. Aronson, Lisa. 12 sound cassettes. Oral tradition. Music. Rites. Funeral tires. Cults. 80–008–F.

Nigeria, Imo, Ohafia, Ebem, Akanu, Igbo, 1989. McCall, John. 8 sound cassettes. Burial ceremonies. Funerals. Rites. Rituals. Ceremonies. 90–228–F.

Nigeria, Jos Plateau, Birom, Challa, Chip, Hausa, Mushere, Ngas, Pyem, Rumada, 1975–1976. Tambo, David C. 104 sound cassettes. Oral history. Iron workers. Interviews. 77–079–F.

Nigeria, Kano, 1974. Rhodes, Willard. 43 sound tape reels. Songs. Fula. Hausa. Yoruba. Tuaregs. Tiv. 75–020–F.

Nigeria, Kano, Fulani and Hausa, 1975. Armer, Michael. 2 sound cassettes. Oral history. Fula. Folk songs. Folk music. 76–180–F.

Nigeria, Kano, Hausa Muslims, 1968–1970. Besmer, Fremont E. 79 sound tape reels. Court music. Festivals. Ramadan. Praise songs. 70–091–F.

Nigeria, Kano, Hausa, 1965–1980. Mack, Beverly. 50 sound tape reels. Women. Wedding music. Ramadan. Songs. Rites. Poetry. 81–100–F/B.

Nigeria, Kano, Hausa, Fulani, 1992–1994. Hutson, Alaine S. 57 sound cassettes. Islamic religious rituals. Education of women. Interviews. 92–262–F/B.

Nigeria, Katsina and Zaria, Hausa, 1963–1964. Ames, David W.; King, Anthony V. 92 sound tape reels. Fula. Yoruba. Epic poetry. Folk songs. Work songs. 71–258–F.

Nigeria, Madagali District, Gulak Village, Margi and Vengo, 1960. Vaughan, James Herbert. 1 sound tape reel. Interview. Songs. Folk music. 75–056–F.

Nigeria, Madagali District, Gulak Village, Margi, 1960. Vaughan, James Herbert. 1 sound tape reel. Funerals. Rites. Ceremonies. 75–053–F.

Nigeria, Madagali District, Gulak Village, Margi, 1960. Vaughan, James Herbert. 3 sound tape reels. Folk songs. Oral history. 75–054–F.

Nigeria, Madagali District, Gulak Village, Margi, 1960. Vaughan, James Herbert. 3 sound tape reels. Marriage rites. Puberty rites. Linguistics. Oral history. 75–055–F.

Nigeria, Ningi Town, Various culture groups, 1972–1974. Patton, Adell. 29 sound cassettes. Fula. Hausa. War songs. Oral history. Harvest songs. 75–175–F.

Nigeria, Ole, Isoko, 1970–1971. Peek, Philip M. 71 sound cassettes. Interviews, oral histories, religious services, music, festivals, musicians, carvers and diviners.

Nigeria, Oshgbo, Yoruba, 1966. Speed, Frank. 5 sound tape reels. Chants. Rites. Divination. Ifa. 72–241–F.

Nigeria, Oshogbo, Yoruba, 1970. Gleason, Judith Illsley. 8 sound tape reels. Ifa. Cults. 73–002–F.

Nigeria, Oyo province, Yoruba, 1971. Ambimbola, Wande. 2 sound tape reels. Hunters. Chants. Praise songs. Gods. 71–302–F.

Nigeria, Sierra Leone, Togo, various, 1952–1960. Turner, Lorenzo Dow. 267 sound discs. Work songs. Lullabies. Praise songs. Love songs. Slavery. Rites. Poetry. Proverbs. Tales. Riddles. Prayers. 86–110a/b–F.

Nigeria, Tiv and Yorubas, c. 1955. Sowande, Fela. 3 sound tape reels. Folk music. Proverbs. Praise songs. Drum language. 57–033–F.

Nigeria, various provinces, various languages, 1953. Wolff, Hans. 1 sound tape reel. Niger Delta languages. Anthropological Linguistics. 85–703–F.

Nigeria, Western region, Yoruba, 1966. Speed, Francis; Thieme, Darius L. 1 sound tape reel. Drum language. Proverbs. 66–226–F.

Nigeria, Western State, Oyo, Yoruba, 1972 and 1975. Ajuwon, Bade. 5 sound tape reels. Hunters. Folklore. Dirges. Funerals. 76–159–F.

Nigeria, Western State, Yoruba, 1965. Armstrong, Robert G. 2 sound tape reels. Operas. Oral tradition. Masks. 72–246–F.

Nigeria, Western State, Yoruba, 1967. Armstrong, Robert G. 3 sound tape reels. Funeral rites. Dirges. Praise songs. Chants. 72–239–F.

Nigeria, Wurno, Takai, Dambatta, Hausa and Fulani, 1985. Philips, John E. 24 sound cassettes. Occupations. Poetry. Cities. 94–006–F.

Nigeria, Yoruba, 1939. Unknown. 1 sound disc. Linguistics. Yoruba. 87–159–F.

Nigeria, Yoruba, 1952. Waterman, Richard. 1 sound disc. Yoruba. Language. Linguistics. 87–133–F.

Nigeria, Yoruba, 1974–1975. Wolff, Norma Hackleman. 31 sound tape reels. Medicine. Healing. Drum music. Shango. 75–178–F.

Nigeria, Yoruba, Sango, 1970–1971. Welch, David B. 38 sound tape reels. Rites and ceremonies. Epic poetry. Shango. Praise songs. 74–003–F.

Nigeria, Zaria and Niger Provinces, Hausa, 1963–1964. Ames, David W. 9 sound tape reels. Singing games. Children's songs. Folk music. War songs. 72–232–F.

Nigeria, Zaria Province, Hausa, 1963–1964. Ames, David W. 4 sound tape reels. Work songs. Wedding music. Singing games. Children's songs. 66–052–F.

Nigeria, Zaria, Bornu and Delta Provinces, 1953–1954. Wolff, Hans. 7 sound tape reels. Funeral rites. Hymns. Praise songs. 59–015–F.

Nigeria, Zaria, Hausa, 1966. Ben-Amos, Dan. 3 sound tape reels. Folklore. Riddles. Proverbs. Tales. 70–105–F.

Nyasaland

Nyasaland, 1929. Boulton, Laura. 1 sound tape reel. Malawi. Ngoni. Bhaca. Folk songs. Folk music. 92–311–F.

Rhodesia

Rhodesia and South Africa, 1948. Tracey, Hugh; Camp, Charles M. 20 sound tape reels. Zimbabwe. Folk tales. Songs. Hymns. Mbira. 54–171–F.

Rhodesia, Shona, Korekore and Zezuru, 1972–1973. Kaemmer, John E. 64 sound tape reels. Zimbabwe. Mbira music. Songs. Rites. Ceremonies. Folklore. 74–061–F.

Senegal

Senegal and Gambia, Mandinka, Serer and Fula, 1974–1975. Wright, Donald R. 40 sound cassettes. Oral history. Folk music. History. 75–185–F.

Senegal, 1971. Tolley, Dayna. 1 sound tape reel. Folklore. Love songs. Tales. Praise songs. 77–145–F.

Senegal, Baila, Diola, 1990. Gero, Glen. 2 sound cassettes. Linguistics. Songs. Diola-Fogny. 91–302–F.

Senegal, Bondu Province, Soninke, Mandingo, Fula, and Dyula, 1966. Curtin, Philip D. 37 sound tape reels. Genealogies. Children's songs. Chants. Fables. 67–096–F.

Senegal, Cap Vert, Louga, and St. Louis Provinces, 1992–1993. McNee, Lisa. 25 sound cassettes. Wolof. Islamic poetry. Baptism. Sufi poetry. Interviews. Women. Wolof poetry. 94–004–F.

Senegal, Eastern Senegal, 1966. Curtin, Philip D. 23 sound tape reels. Toucouleur. Soninke. Oral history. Folk music. 68–228–F.

Senegal, Futa Toro and Dakar, Fulahs, 1968–1969. Robinson, David Wallace. 83 sound cassettes. Oral history. History. Customs. 70–094–F.

Senegal, Kajor, Wolof, 1969 Colvin, Lucie. 2 sound tape reels. Oral tradition. Interviews. History. 86–104–F.

Senegal, Kaolack, 1963. Klein, Martin. 6 sound tape reels. Oral histories. Interviews. Broadcasts. Radio. 74–099–B/F.

Senegal, Linguere, Wolof, 1970–1971. Charles, Eunice. 12 sound tape reels. Oral history. Interviews. History. 73–004–F.

Senegal, Lower Casamance Region, Diola-Fogny, 1960–1965. Sapir, J. David 71 sound tape reels. Folk songs. Work songs. Children's songs. Rites. Oral history. 70–103–F.

Senegal, Lower Casamance Region, Diola-Kasa, 1966. Sapir, J. David 6 sound tape reels. Folk music. Funeral rites. Ceremonies. Folklore. 70–104–F.

Senegal, Sine-Saloum, Wolofs, Fulbe and Tukolor, 1974–1975. Klein, Martin. 37 sound cassettes. Fula. Toucouleur. Oral history. Family. Villages. 75–058–F.

Senegal, Wolofs, 1963–1964. Coifman, Victoria Bomba 9 sound tape reels. Oral tradition. Songs. History. 71–413–F.

Sierra Leone

Sierra Leone, 1964–1967. Oven, Cootje van. 6 sound tape reels. Fula. Mende. Mandingo. Temne. Limba. 68–215–F.

Sierra Leone, Bombali District, Lima, Creoles, and Temne, 1971. Bahman, Gary. 6 sound cassettes. Funeral rites. Children's songs. Work songs. Folk music. 72–231–F.

Sierra Leone, c. 1950 Allen, Leonard E. 1 sound tape reel. Folk tales. Folklore. Pidgin English. 73–059–F.

Sierra Leone, Eastern Province, Kenema, Mende, 1988. Conner, Diane. 1 sound cassette. Dance music. Songs. Rites. Ceremonies. 88–084–F.

Sierra Leone, Freetown, 1950–1969. Ware, Naomi. 74 sound tape reels. Yoruba. Fanti. Bambara. Igbo. Bassa. Creoles. Fula. Kissi. Limba. Mandingo. Temne. Vai. Gola. 70–041–F/C.

Sierra Leone, Freetown, 1969. Ware, Naomi. 6 sound tape reels. Jazz. Popular Music. Music festivals. 70–045–F.

Sierra Leone, Freetown, 1969. Edwards, Betty. 2 sound tape reels. Creoles. Church music. Nursery Rhymes. Songs. 70–046–F.

Sierra Leone, Freetown, Creoles, 1973–1974. Broderick, Sundiata Modupe. 6 sound tape reels. Creoles. Songs. Oral tradition. Tales. 85–488–F.

Sierra Leone, Freetown, Mende and Temne, 1967–1968. Johnson, Gerald T. 62 sound tape reels. Children's songs. Folk tales. Folk songs. Oral history. 73–055–F.

Sierra Leone, Mende, 1949. Williams, Charles. 1 sound disc. Mende. Language.Linguistics. Dictionaries. 87–134–F.

Sierra Leone, Mende, 1988. Harris, Laura. 3 sound cassettes. Folk music. Work songs. Death songs. Tales. 88–071–F/C.

Sierra Leone, Northern Province, Kabala, Mandingo, 1986. Harris, Laura. 3 sound cassettes. Children's songs. Oral tradition. Praise songs. 86–160–F.

Sierra Leone, Northern Province, Koinadugu district, Maninka, 1987–88. Harris, Laura. 55 sound cassettes. Praise songs. Work songs. Dance music. Interviews. 88–072–F.

Sierra Leone, Southern Province, Mende, 1973–1974. Cosentino, Donald. 24 sound tape reels. Tales. Oral narratives. 82–526–F.

Sierra Leone, Temne, 1966–1967. Geoffrion, Charles A. 2 sound tape reels. Chants. Tales. Ramadan. Rites. Ceremonies. 70–150–F.

Somalia

Somali Republic, Mogadiscio, Baijuni, 1962. Williams, Chester S. 1 sound tape reel. Somalia. Swahili. Songs. 65–136–F.

Somalia, 1966–1969. Johnson, John William. 78 sound tape reels. Love poetry. Political poetry. Wiglos. Hees. 70–151–F.

Somalia, 1976–1980. Abdillahi Deria Guled 21 sound cassettes. Folk songs. Politics. Poetry. 81–053–F.

Somalia, 1980. Johnson, John William. 20 sound tape reels. Folk music. Language. Poets. 81–050–F.

Somalia, 1980. Abdillahi Deria Guled 10 sound cassettes. Oral tradition. Folk songs. Praise poetry. Tales. 81–054–F/B.

Somalia, 1983. Johnson, John William. 1 sound tape reel. African poetry. Modern poetry. Heellos. 84–277–F.

Somalia, 1989. Ali Abokor, Ahmad; Johnson, John 4 sound cassettes. Poetry. 89–097–F.*

Somalia, Mogadishu, 1989. Johnson, John William. 8 sound cassettes. Poetry. 89–096–F.

Somalia, Mogadishu, Afgooye, 1987. Johnson, John William. 102 sound cassettes. Somali. Poetry. 89–058–F.

Somalia, Somalis, 1958–1991. Andrzejewski, Bogumi Witalis. 152 sound tape reels. Islam. Theater. Literacy. Proverbs. Tales. Music. Language. Poetry. Songs. Koran. Interviews. History. Politics. Social customs. 92–184–F/B.

Somalia, Somalis, 1980. Johnson, John William. 14 sound cassettes. Poetry. Festivals. Gubu. Gabays. Oral tradition. Interviews. 80–205–F/C.

Somalis, 1964–1994. BBC Somali Service. 207 sound cassettes. Interviews. History. Politics. Government. Poetry. Stories. 95.387–001B through 95–387.207B. The BBC Somalia Speech Archive consists primarily of poetry and interviews with historical personalities from a wide range of social and occupational backgrounds. The collection also contains stories, histories, linguistic materials, discussions of literature, and biographical and cultural information. The BBC used these materials for many of its broadcasts, and the tapes themselves, along with the tapes of the BBC Somali Music Archive (see next entry) comprise perhaps the largest collection of Somali materials in the world. While all the tapes are of Somali poets and personalities, the recordings were made in a variety of locations, including Somalia, Kenya, England, Yemen, Ethiopia, Dijibouti, and others.

Somalia, Hargeisa and Mogadishu; Dijibouti; Ethiopia, Somalis. 1947–1991. BBC Somali Service. 194 sound cassettes. Songs. Oral poetry. 94–228.001–B through 94–228.194–B. The BBC Somali Music Archive consists of oral poetry and a variety of musical genres created by various performers, composers, and lyricists.

South Africa

South Africa, 1964–1974. Carter, Gwendolen Margaret. 9 sound tape reels. Speeches. Politics. Race relations. Interviews. 76–027–B/F

South Africa, Cape Town, Xhosa, 1965. Versfeld, Barbara. 3 sound tape reels. Tales. Folk songs. 66–237–F.

South Africa, Johannesburg and other locations, 1960–1965. Carter, Gwendolen Margaret. 26 sound tape reels. African National Congress. History. Nationalism. Politics. Government. 92–045–F.

South Africa, Kwa Zulu, Zulus, 1982. Erlmann, Veit. 1 sound tape reel. Songs. Folk music. Musical bow music. 85–524–F.

South Africa, Natal, Nongoma, Kwazulu, Zulu, 1983. Impey, Angela. 9 sound cassettes. Guitar music. Musicians. Interviews. Bow music. 88–106–F.

South Africa, Tswana, 1966–67. Watkins, Mark Hanna. 8 sound tape reels. Tswana language. 89–092–F.

South Africa, various cultures, 1970. Boulton, Laura. 1 sound tape reel. Interviews. Description. Travel. 92–522–F.

South Africa, Zulu, 1940. Unknown. 1 sound disc. Linguistics. Interview. Zulu language. 87–153–F.

South Africa, Zulu, 1954. Unknown. 1 sound disc. Zulu. Language. Linguistics. 87–131–F.

South Africa, Ovamboland, Mbundu, 1955. Boulton, Laura. 1 sound tape reel. Angola. Customs. Social life. 92–360–F.

Sudan

Sudan, Gaaliin, 1970–1971. Hurreiz, Sayed Hamid A. 9 sound tape reels. Arabs. Epic poetry. Muslim saints. Storytelling. 71–012–F.

Sudan, Nilotic region, Dinka, 1962–1972. Deng, Francis Mading. 24 sound tape reels. War songs. Hunting songs. Hymns. Folk songs. Praise songs. 73–051–F.

Sudan, Republic of

Republic of Sudan, 1963. Carlisle, Roxane. 1 sound tape reel. Sudan. War songs. Rites. Wedding music. Epic songs. 66–185–D.

Tanzania

Tanzania, 1965. Morgenthau, Henry. 15 sound tape reels. Lectures. Speeches. Politics. Government. 71–017–F.

Tanzania, Mbulu and Muray, Iraqw, 1975–1976. Thornton, Robert. 1 sound tape reel. Prayers. Oral tradition. Poetry. 81–009–F.

Tanzania, Ukerewe Island, Kerebe, 1968–1969. Hartwig, Gerald W. 7 sound tape reels. Singing games. Children's songs. National songs. Bow music. 69–017–F.

Togo

Togo, Southern Togo, Ewe, 1965–1967. Agudze-Vioka, Bernard. 4 sound tape reels. Drum language. Folk songs. War songs. 68–248–F.

Uganda

Uganda, Buganda, Ganda, 1964–1968. Cooke, Peter. 1 sound tape reel. Flute music. Folk songs. Court music. 71–256–F.

Uganda, Bugembe, various groups, 1965–1968. Cooke, Peter. 16 sound cassettes. Work songs. Mbira music. Court music. Healers. Spirituals. Protest songs. Christmas music. Flute music. 92–007–F.

Uganda, Busoga, Kawete, Bunhyiro, 1988. Cooke, Peter. 14 sound tape reels. Songs. Rites. Ceremonies. Healing. Spirit possession. Wrestling. 91–246–F.

Uganda, Kampala, Ganda, Soga, Nyankore, 1987. Cooke, Peter. 16 sound tape reels. Instrumental music. Songs. Choral music. Hymns. Children's songs. 86–106–F.

Uganda, Kampala, Iru, Ganda, Soga, 1990. Cooke, Peter. 4 sound tape reels. Songs. Recitations. Instrumental music. 91–209–F.

Uganda, Karamojong, 1967. Coleman, Milton. 1 sound tape reel. Folk songs. 68–290–F.

United States

United States, 1977. Tejeda, Felipe. 5 sound tape reels. Gambia. Senegal. Mandingo. Folk songs. 78–007–F.

United States, California, Berkeley, 1969. Dalby, David. 1 sound tape reel. Lectures. "The role of the linguist in the reconstruction of African prehistory." Historical linguistics. Africa history. 69–019–F.

United States, California, Davis, Zairians. Crowley, Daniel J. 1 sound tape reel. Congo. Folktales. Interview. Kinshasa. 73–069–F.

United States, California, Igbo, 1968. Peek, Philip M. 1 sound tape reel. Interview. Folklore. Tales. Oral tradition. 69–195–F.

United States, Columbia University, 1969. Boulton, Laura. 2 sound tape reels. Lecture. Ethiopia. Christmas music. 92–442–F.

United States, Connecticut, New Haven, 1934. Herzog, George. 1 sound disc. Zulu. Language. Linguistics. 87–098–F.

United States, Illinois, Chicago, 1933–1934. Boulton, Laura. 2 sound tape reels. Hastings Kamazu Banda. Congo. Malawi. Nigeria. Chokwe. Hausa. Ngoni. Music. 92–315–F.

United States, Illinois, Chicago, Chewa, c. 1940 Andrade, Manuel Jose; Herzog, George. 3 sound discs. Hastings Kamazu Banda. Puberty rites. Funeral music. Folk songs. Lullabies. 54–233–F.

United States, Illinois, Chicago, Gweabo, 1929. Herzog, George. 16 cylinders. Jabo. Linguistics. Songs. Proverbs. 83–918–F.

United States, Illinois, Chicago, Jabo, 1929. Herzog, George. 1 cylinder. Folk songs. Prayers. 54–224–F.

United States, Illinois, Chicago, Jabo, 1931. Herzog, George; Andrade, Manuel. 10 sound discs. Jabo. Linguistics. 85–546–F.

United States, Illinois, Evanston, Ibo, 1943. Okala, J. 4 sound discs. Songs. Proverbs. Tales. 87–132–F.

United States, Indiana University, 1987. Seeger, Anthony. 1 sound cassette. Lecture. Performance. Alain Barker. 87–046–F.

United States, Indiana University, 1987. Richardson, Susan. 1 sound cassette. Nigeria. Performance. Folk songs. Highlife. 87–102–F.

United States, Indiana, Bloomington, Lukas, Scott. 1 sound cassette. Nigeria. Songs. Efik. Hausa. Yoruba. Nigeria. 89–208–F.

United States, Indiana, Bloomington, 1960. Voegelin, F.M. 6 sound tape reels. Afrikaans. Linguistics. 85–665–F.

United States, Indiana, Bloomington, 1965–1970. Unknown. 11 sound tape reels. Ethiopia. Sudan. Linguistics. 85–697–F.

United States, Indiana, Bloomington, 1969. Dalby, David. 1 sound tape reel. Mandingo. Lectures. 69–012–F.

United States, Indiana, Bloomington, 1969. Archives of Traditional Music. 1 sound tape reel. Lecture. Series: "Focus on Black America." Yoruba. Race identity. 69–328–F.

United States, Indiana, Bloomington, 1969. Barrett, David B. 2 sound tape reels. Lectures. "New religious movements in Africa and African responses to Christianity." Religions. Christianity. 69–331–F.

United States, Indiana, Bloomington, 1971. Gillis, Frank. 1 sound tape reel. Lecture. Hugh Tracy. International Library of African Music. 71–308–F.

United States, Indiana, Bloomington, 1975. Keim, Karen Ruth King. 1 sound tape reel. Lecture. Dr. Charles Bird. "The Hero in Mande Epic." 75–043–F.

United States, Indiana, Bloomington, 1975. Gordon, Meryl. 1 sound cassette. Lecture. Judith Hannah. "Stereotypes and realities of African dance." 75–045–F.

United States, Indiana, Bloomington, 1975. Gillis, Frank. 1 sound cassette. Interview. James H. Vaughan Jr. Nigeria. 75–052–F.

United States, Indiana, Bloomington, 1975. Arom, Simha. 2 sound cassettes. Lecture: "Emic and Etic Analysis Using Polyphonic Recording Techniques." 76–124–F.

United States, Indiana, Bloomington, 1978. Indiana University News Bureau 2 sound cassettes. Malawi. Speech. Press conference. Dr. Hastings Kamuzu Banda. 86–068–F.

United States, Indiana, Bloomington, 1988. Archives of Traditional Music. 1 sound cassette. Concert. West Africa. Percussion. 88–026–F.

United States, Indiana, Bloomington, 1989. Harris, Laura. 1 sound cassette. Ibo. Mandinka. Folk songs. 89–021–F.

United States, Indiana, Bloomington, 1989. Chernoff, John. 2 sound cassettes. Workshop. Lecture. Drumming. 89–037–F.

United States, Indiana, Bloomington, 1989. Lukas, Scott. 1 sound cassette. Zimbabwe. Mbira music. Tales. 89–202–F.

United States, Indiana, Bloomington, 1990. Lukas, Scott. 1 sound cassette. Folk songs. 91–371–F.

United States, Indiana, Bloomington, 1991. Stonefelt, Kay. 1 sound cassette. Buganda. Music. Xylophone. 91–369–F.

United States, Indiana, Bloomington, 1991. O'Meara, Patrick. 7 sound cassettes. Africa. Politics. Civilization. Conference. 92–065–F.

United States, Indiana, Bloomington, 1992. Barnes, Dr. Sandra. 2 sound cassettes. Lecture. Series: "Women and Power in Africa." Women. Politics. Benin. Nigeria. 92–041–F.

United States, Indiana, Bloomington, 1992. Feeley-Harnik, Gillian 2 sound cassettes. Lecture. Series: "Women and Power in Africa." Madagascar. Women. Politics. 92–042–F.

United States, Indiana, Bloomington, 1992. Thompson, Bob. 1 sound cassette. Concert. Igbo. Mandingo. Popular music. 92–076–F.

United States, Indiana, Bloomington, 1992. Manuh, Takyiwa. 2 sound cassettes. Lecture. Series: "Women and Power in Africa." 92–079–F.

United States, Indiana, Bloomington, 1992. Suzman, Helen. 1 sound cassette. Interview. Politics. South Africa. Progressive Party. 92–083–F.

United States, Indiana, Bloomington, 1992. Irvine, Dr. Judith 2 sound cassettes. Lecture Series: "Women and Power in Africa." Title: "Language, Ritual, and Power: A Wolof Wedding Ceremony." 92–101–F.

United States, Indiana, Bloomington, 1992. Yiadomi, Nana. 1 sound cassette. Lecture Series: "Women and Power in Africa." Title: "A Queen Mother at the U.N." 92–109–F.

United States, Indiana, Bloomington, 1992. Kalumbu, Isaac. 1 sound cassette. Zimbabwe. Reggae music. 92–185–F.

United States, Indiana, Bloomington, 1992. Smith, Chris; Stonefelt, Kay. 1 sound cassette. Taarab. Popular music. 92–193–F.

United States, Indiana, Bloomington, 1996. Asiama, Dr. Simeon. 1 sound cassette. Ghana. Music. Highlife. Popular music. Church music. 96–381–F.

United States, Indiana, Bloomington, Bantu, 1958–1962. Redden, James; Simpson, Al. 10 sound tape reels. Lingala. Bulu. Luhya. Linguistics. 85–710–F.

United States, Indiana, Bloomington, Grebo, 1958. Maring, Joel. 6 sound tape reels. Grebo. Linguistics. 85–705–F.

United States, Indiana, Bloomington, Hausa, 1950–1970. Wurm, S.A. 1 sound tape reel. Hausa. Linguistics. 85–699–F.

United States, Indiana, Bloomington, Ibo, 1950–1951. Nettl, Bruno; Raben, Joseph. 3 sound tape reels. Children's Songs. War songs. Folk songs. 54–182–F.

United States, Indiana, Bloomington, Kikamba, 1957–58. Madigan, Robert. 19 sound tape reels. Kikamba. Linguistics. 85–711–F.

United States, Indiana, Bloomington, Kikuyu, 1951–1961. Redden, James. 8 sound tape reels. Kikuyu. Linguistics. 85–712–F.

United States, Indiana, Bloomington, Kwa, 1956–1964. Redden, James; Brown, Herbert; West, Lamont; Hopkins, Jerry; Black, Paul. 12 sound tape reels. Kwa. Linguistics. 85–706–F.

United States, Indiana, Bloomington, Luo, 1959. Redden, James; Fraenkel, Gerd; Hung, Beverly. 8 sound tape reels. Luo. Linguistics. 85–700–F.

United States, Indiana, Bloomington, Malawian, 1989. Lukas, Scott. 1 sound cassette. Lecture. Recital. Folk music. 89–093–F.

United States, Indiana, Bloomington, Malian, 1990. Lukas, Scott. 1 sound cassette. Mali. Griots. 91–172–F.

United States, Indiana, Bloomington, Ndebele and Zulu, 1957–1958. Leuschel, Don. 6 sound tape reels. Ndebele. Zulu. Linguistics. 85–715–F.

United States, Indiana, Bloomington, Nigerians, 1967. Dorson, Richard Mercer. 1 sound tape reel. Interviews. Ballads. Proverbs. Oral history. 67–220–F.

United States, Indiana, Bloomington, Nigerians, 1989. Harris, Laura. 1 sound cassette. Ibo. Hausa. Efik. Yoruba. Edo. Songs. 89–023–F.

United States, Indiana, Bloomington, Shona, 1989. Mujuru, Ephat. 6 VHS cassettes. Lecture. Workshop. Mbira. Mbira music. 89–094–F.

United States, Indiana, Bloomington, Somali, 1959. Maring, Joel. 4 sound tape reels. Somali. Linguistics. 85–698–F.

United States, Indiana, Bloomington, Tonga/Bantu, 1959–1960. Redden, James. 7 sound tape reels. Tonga. Bantu. Linguistics. 85–714–F.

United States, Indiana, Bloomington, Twi, 1960–1967. Redden, James; Reibel, David; Blair, Robert; Stevick, Earl; Warren, Dennis. 75 sound tape reels Twi. Linguistics. Akim. Ashanti. Akwapem. 85–704–F.

United States, Indiana, Bloomington, Yoruba, 1949. Riggs, Venda. 2 sound tape reels. Yoruba. Linguistics. 85–707–F.

United States, Indiana, Bloomington, Zambians, 1970. Gillis, Frank. 2 sound cassettes. Lectures. "Music of Zambia." Folk music. Folk songs. 70–087–F.

United States, Indiana, Bloomington. Gillis, Frank J., Spear, Louise S. 2 sound cassettes. Nigeria. Traditional music. Akin Euba (lecture) 79–112–F.*

United States, Indiana, Bloomington. 1954. Hickerson, Nancy; Hymes, Virginia; Keller, James. 17 sound tape reels. Tigrinya. Linguistics. 85–694–F.

United States, Indiana, Bloomington. 1997. Archives of Traditional Music. 4 sound cassettes. Ghana. Oral heritage. Archives. Libraries. 97–226–F.*

United States, Indiana, Nashville, 1991. O'Meara, Patrick. 8 sound cassettes. Conference. Title: "Political Reform and Democratization in South Africa." 92–066–F.

United States, Mende, 1979. Sengova, Joko. 6 sound tape reels. Oral tradition. Proverbs. Hunting stories. Marriage. 85–483–F.

United States, Michigan, Yoruba, 1960–1964. Wolff, Hans. 4 sound tape reels. Folk tales. Folklore. 72–236–F.

United States, New Jersey, Camden, c. 1930. Boas, Franz. 3 sound tape reels. Bollum. Kru. Twi. Linguistics. Stories. 85–548–F.

United States, New York, Catskill Mountains, Nigerians, 1960. Cazden, Norman. 1 sound tape reel. Nigeria. Folk music. Folk dance music. 64–015–F.

United States, New York, New York City, 1959. Boulton, Laura. 4 sound tape reels. Nigeria. Gabon. Marimba music. Mbira music. 92–308–F.

United States, New York, New York City, 1963. LeMaster, Edwin. 1 sound tape reel. Spirituals. Choruses. Hymns. 76–064–F.

United States, New York, New York City, 1963. Boulton, Laura. 3 sound tape reels. Interviews. Laura Boulton. Angola. Nigeria. Mozambique. Mbira music. 92–528–F.

United States, New York, New York City, 1966. Boulton, Laura. 3 sound tape reels. Lecture. Ethiopia. Byzantine music. 92–524–F.

United States, New York, New York City, 1967. Boulton, Laura. 1 sound tape reel. Ethiopia. Music. Folk music. Amhara. 92–312–F.

United States, New York, New York City, 1968. Boulton, Laura. 5 sound tape reels. Musical instruments. Mbira music. 92–485–F.

United States, New York, New York City, 1968. Boulton, Laura. 3 sound tape reels. Lecture. Ethiopia. Music. Krar. Washint. Masenqo. 92–542–F.

United States, New York, New York City, 1969. Boulton, Laura. 2 sound tape reels. Sudan. Musical instruments. Interviews. 92–486–F.

United States, New York, New York City, 1972. Boulton, Laura. 1 sound tape reel. East Africa. Lectures. Songs. Dance music. 92–423–F.

United States, New York, New York City, Angolans, Mbundu, 1965. Boulton, Laura. 4 sound tape reels. Interview. Laura Boulton. Angola. 92–361–F.

United States, New York, New York City, Nigerians, 1964. Boulton, Laura. 1 sound tape reel. Folk songs. Folk music. Music. 92–318–F.

United States, New York, New York City, various cultures, 1958–1963. Boulton, Laura. 3 sound tape reels. Lecture. Music. Mbira music. Xylophone music. Swaziland. Mozambique. 92–523–F.

United States, New York, Yoruba, 1933. Boas, Franz. 3 sound discs. Folk songs. Folk tales. 54–085–F.

United States, New York, Zulus, 1935. Henry, Jules. 2 sound discs. Folk songs. 54–008–F.

United States, New York?, Mende, 1933. Aginsky, Ethel G. 5 sound discs. Dwight Sumner. Sierra Leone. Folk songs. 54–006–F.

United States, Office of Education, Gio, 1960. Griffes, Kenneth; Welmers, William. 10 sound tape reels. Gio. Linguistics. 85–701–F.

United States, Ohio, Columbus; Indiana, Bloomington, 1958–1971. Hale, Kenneth; Redden, James; Sapon, Stanley. 11 sound tape reels. Arabic. Linguistics. 85–694–F.

United States, Pennsylvania, Pittsburgh, Dahomeans, 1970. Smoley, Robert A. 2 sound tape reels. Folk dance music. Folk music. Rites. Ceremonies. 70–127–F.

United States, various cultures, 1978. Boulton, Laura. 2 sound tape reels. Interviews. Angola. Music. Puberty rites. Ceremonies. Customs. 92–532–F.

United States, Virginia, Zulus, and Vandau, c. 1915–1918. Natalie Curtis Burlin. 16 cylinders. Songs. Laments. Puberty rites. Slaves. Rain songs. Love songs. 54–065–F.

United States, Washington D.C.; Ohio, Columbus; Mande, 1957–1962. Redden, James; Sapon, Stanley. 6 sound tape reels. Bambara. Susu. Yalunka. Linguistics. 85–702–F.

United States, Wisonsin, Madison, 1966. Snyder, Emile. 1 sound tape reel. South Africa. Lectures. Politics. Apartheid. Poets. Race relations. 71–015–F.

Various and Unknown Locations

Unknown location, 1960. Boulton, Laura. 8 sound tape reels. Book. "The Abixi (Masked) from Northeast Angola." Masks. Angola. 92–316–F.

Unknown location, 1962. Boulton, Laura. 2 sound tape reels. Benin. Music. Worship. 92–428–F.

Unknown location, African people, 1940–1980. Boulton, Laura. 1 sound tape reel. Interviews. Lampblack. Customs. Social life. 92–362–F.

Unknown location, African, 1969. Boulton, Laura. 1 sound tape reel. Angola. Flute music. Mbira music. 92–438–F.

Unknown location, Angolans, 1969. Boulton, Laura. 3 sound tape reels. Angola. Mozambique. Music. 92–437–F.

Unknown location, Kuanyama Ambo, 1948–1960. Boulton, Laura. 5 sound tape reels. Rites. Ceremonies. Angola. Namibia. Puberty rites. 92–479–F.

Unknown location, Ovimbundu, unknown date. Boulton, Laura. 2 sound tape reels. Songs. Angola. Tales. Music. 92–359–F.

Unknown location, various cultures, 1950–1980. Boulton, Laura. 1 sound tape reel. Mozambique. Music. Warn horn calls. 92–537–F.

Unknown location, various cultures, 1960–1972. Boulton, Laura. 5 sound tape reels. Mozambique. Xylophone music. Mbira music. War horn calls. Kora music. 92–519–F.

Unknown location, various cultures, 1960–1980. Boulton, Laura. 1 sound tape reel. Music. Africa. Ethiopia. Harp music. Mbira music. Flute music. Musical bow music. 92–516–F.

Unknown location, various cultures, 1964. Boulton, Laura. 1 sound tape reel. Music. Swaziland. Angola. Mbira music. Nigeria. Xylophone music. 92–466–F.

Unknown location, Zulu, 1950–1959. Harley, George. 1 sound tape reel. Zulu. Linguistics. 85–713–F.

Unknown, Ethiopians, 1960 (?) Boulton, Laura. 4 sound tape reels. Music. Songs. Dance music. 92–398–F.

Unknown, Ethiopians, 1960 (?) Boulton, Laura. 1 sound tape reel. Music. World music. 92–434–F.

Unknown, Ethiopians, 1960 (?) Boulton, Laura. 1 sound tape reel. Music. Africa. 92–450–F.

Unknown, Ethiopians, 1960 (?) Boulton, Laura. 1 sound tape reel. World music. Ethiopia. Mbira music. Musical bow music. Angola. Flute music. War horn calls. Harp music. 92–516–F.

Unknown, Ethiopians, 1960 (?) Boulton, Laura. 1 sound tape reel. World music. Ethiopia. Mozambique. Xylophone music. 92–518–F.

Unknown, Gwa, 1970–1971. Unknown. 13 sound tape reels. Gwa. Linguistics. 85–709–F.

Unknown locations, Sahara Desert, Tuareg, no date. Card, Caroline. 2 sound tape reels. Tuaregs. Music. Sahara. Folklore. 78–019–F.

Unknown locations, Sahara Desert, Tuaregs, 1970–1978? Card, Caroline. 1 sound tape reel. Tuaregs. Music. Sahara. 78–020–F.

Unknown African locations, 1972. Boulton, Laura. 1 sound tape reel. Musical bow music. War horn calls. Mbira. Drum music. 92–517–F.

Various locations, various ethnic groups, 1972. Boulton, Laura. 1 sound tape reel. Fiddle music. Kora music. Mbira music. Drum music. War horn calls. Musical bow music. 92–465–F.

Various, Berlin Phonogramm Archiv Demonstration Collection, 1900–1913. Von Hornbostel, Erich. 120 cylinders. Music. Africa. Tunisia. Cameroon. Congo. Sudan. 83–899–F.

Various, c. 1955. Bush, Ed. 11 sound tape reels. Folk songs. Zulu. Drum language. 57–016–B/C/F.

Various locations, various ethnic groups, c. 1950–1967. Lloyd, A. L. 2 sound tape reels. Folk songs. International folk music. 68–207–F.

Various locations, various ethnic groups. 1973–1978. Nichols, Lee. 175 sound tape reels. Interviews with African writers. 96–284.1–B through 96–284.83–F/B. The Lee Nichols collection consists of a series of interviews with 83 African writers. The tapes were broadcast on Voice of America and selected interviews were published in *Conversations with African Writers* (Washington, D.C.: Voice of America 1981) and *African Writers at the Microphone* (Washington, D.C.: Three Continents Press 1984). The collection also includes photographs, transcripts, correspondence with the writers, and biographical information. Interviews focus on the authors and discussions of various literary topics related to their prose and poetry. The collections represent the following countries: Botswana, Cameroon, Ethiopia, Gambia, Ghana, Ivory Coast, Kenya, Lesotho, Liberia, Malawi, Nigeria, Sierra Leone, Somalia, South Africa, Sudan, Swaziland, Tanzania, Uganda, Zambia, and Zimbabwe.

Various locations, Africans African Americans, 1962–1970. Duerden, Dennis. 198 sound tape reels. Interviews. Lectures. Music. Poetry. Literature. 74–120a–F through 74–120z–F. The Dennis Duerden collection consists primarily of interviews with African and African American writers and musicians on topics including music, politics, law, literature, poetry, drama, and other aspects of African culture. The countries covered by the collection include Cameroon, Gambia, Ghana, Guinea, Guyana, Kenya, Malawi, Nigeria, South Africa, and Sierra Leone. The collection also includes lectures presented in the United Kingdom and the United States.

West Africa, c. 1960–1970 Snyder, Emile. 26 sound tape reels. Ivory Coast. Senegal. Ghana. Guinea. Cameroon. West Africa. Fula. Drum music. 85–486–F/B.

West Africa, French Sudan, and British Cameroons, 1934. Boulton, Laura. 21 sound tape reels. Senegal. Mali. Niger. Dahomey. Liberia. Nigeria. Cameroon. Folk music. Folk songs. Wolof. Mandingo. Bambara. Dogon. Fula. Songhai. Tuaregs. Toucouleur. Zarma. Hausa. Kru. Tiv. Igbo. Kwiri. Bini. Yoruba. 92–313–F.

West Africa, Guinea Coast, 1949. Northwestern University. 21 sound tape reels. Folk music. Drums. Bambara. Baule. Ewe. Fante. Ga. Igbo. Kissi. Mandingo. Mano. Mossi. Twi. Ashanti. Liberia. Buzi. 68–214–F.

West Africa, West Africans, 1934. Boulton, Laura. 1 sound tape reel. Music. Hourglass drum music. Riti music. 92–364–F.

Upper Volta

Upper Volta and Niger, Liptako and Tera, 1971–1976. Irwin, Paul. 21 sound tape reels. Oral history. Burkina Faso. Oral tradition. 79–085–F.

Upper Volta, Bissa, Gourmantch, Kwo, 1973–1974. Merriam, Valerie. 57 sound tape reels. Burkina Faso. Ceremonies. Oral history. Instrumental music. 74–069–F.

Upper Volta, Koupela, Mossi; Noura, Marka, and Fuebe, 1973. Merriam, Valerie; Rossellini, James. 4 sound tape reels. Burkina Faso. Instrumental music. Rites. Ceremonies. 74–068–F.

Upper Volta, Ouagadougou, 1962. Redden, James. 16 sound tape reels. Mlore. Linguistics. 85–708–F.

Zaire

Zaire, 1976–1981. Smith, Robert L. 21 sound tape reels. Oral history. Congo. 82–592–F.

Zaire, Bahemba, 1975–1979. Blakely, Thomas; Blakely, Pamela. 1 sound tape reel. Congo. Funeral music. Rites. Work songs. 80–201–D.

Zaire, Bandundu, Suku, 1986. Smith, Robert E. 6 sound cassettes. Oral history. Kituba. History. 88–005–F.

Zaire, Batwa and Ekonda, 1971. Quersin, Benoit. 24 sound tape reels. Rites. Folk music. Children's songs. Death songs. 72–235–F.

Zaire, Bobangi, 1976. Harms, Robert W. 54 sound cassettes. Oral history. Language. Rites. Funeral ceremonies. 79–027–F.

Zaire, Kivu Region, Bashi, 1970–1973. Sigwalt, Richard.; Sigwalt, Elinor. 51 sound cassettes. Congo. Folk songs. Weddings. Oral history. 76–091–F.

Zaire, Luba, 1972. Studstill, John D. 8 sound tape reels. Epic poetry. Congo. Folklore. Oral tradition. 73–003–F.

Zaire, Luba, 1972–1973. Reefe, Thomas Q. 12 sound tape reels. Congo. Oral history. Songs. Luba. 77–147–F.

Zaire, Mangbetu-Budu, 1973, 1976–1977. Keim, Curtis A.; Keim, Karen R. 114 sound cassettes. Interviews. Women. History. Folk music. Dance music. 79–092–F.

Zaire, Mongo and Ekonda, 1970. Quersin, Benoit. 11 sound tape reels. Batwa. Rites. Ceremonies. Mourning customs. Bobongo music. 72–254–F.

Zaire, Musanda, 1939. Unknown. 4 sound discs. Linguistics. Folk songs. 87–166–F.

Zaire, Rwanda, Cyangugu Prefecture, 1970–1971. Newbury, Catharine; Newbury, David S. 44 sound cassettes. Oral history. Songs. Instrumental music. 75–197–F.

Zaire, Tshilenge, Kabeya-Kamwanga, Baluba, 1974. Faik-Nzuji, C.; Feyes, P. Albert. 4 sound tape reels. Congo. Luba. Songs. Rites. Ceremonies. 85–317–F.

Zaire. Keim, Curtis A.; Keim, Karen R. 3 sound cassettes. Radio broadcasts. 79–093–B.*

Zambia

Zambia, Northern Province, Bemba, 1975. Frost, Mary. 37 sound tape reels. Tales. 76–047–F.

Zanzibar

Zanzibar, c. 1958. Farsy, Muhammad Saleh Abdulla. 1 sound tape reel. Tanzania. Folk music. Wedding music. Puberty rites. Initiation rites. 59–106–F.

Zanzibar. Allen, J.W.T.; Farsi, Abdullah Salih 10 sound tape reels. Tanzania. 88–073–F.*

Zimbabwe

Zimbabwe, c. 1978. Unknown. 2 sound tape reels. Shona. History. Ballads. Songs. Folk poetry. 85–489–F.

Zimbabwe, Chichijunda, Shona, Ndebele, Xhosa, 1989–1991. Impey, Angela. 39 sound cassettes. Women musicians. Popular music. Mbira music. Interviews. 97–011–F.*

Zimbabwe, Harare, Chikomba, Sadza, Shona, 1992–1993. Klassen, Doreen. 38 sound cassettes. 27 8mm video cassettes. Ngano. Storytelling. Marriage customs. Music. Education. 93–199–F.*

Zimbabwe, Harare, Shona, 1988–1990. Njoku, J. Akuma-Kalu 51 sound cassettes. Church music. Masses. Interviews. 90–324–F.

Zimbabwe, Harare, Shona, 1990. Stephens, Robert. 2 cassettes. 1 VHS video cassette. Religious music. Church music. Choral music. 90–241–F.*

Zimbabwe, Mashonaland, Masvingo, and Manicaland, Shona, 1960–1963. Kauffman, Robert. 29 sound tape reels. Folk tales. Dance music. Work songs. Lullabies. Rituals. 89–209–F.

Zimbabwe, Shona, Njanja, 1984–1988. Dewey, William J. 1 video cassette. Iron smelting. Ceremonial weapons. Ranga families. Interviews. 90–370–F.*

Zimbabwe, various locations, 1982. Kaemmer, John. 35 sound tape reels. Mbira music. Religious songs. Secular songs. 02–030–F.

APPENDIX: Filmography

See entry: **Documentary Films and African Folklore**

Abraham and the odd jobs (Abraham et les Petits Metiers). Director(s): Ahmed Diop (Sénégal). Senegal, 1996. 28 min. Prod.: Diop Système International. Diff: MMFF 96 / Bilan 1996.

Adama, the Fula Magician (Adama, le magicien Peul). Director : Jim Rosselini (USA). 22 min. 16 mm. Diff: Blue Ribbon Award, Am. Film Fest.

Africa I Remember: A Musical. 1995. Director: Paul Balmer. 30 min. MMFF 1996.

African Carving: a Dogon Kanaga Mask. Director: Eliot Elisofon, Mali, 1975, 19 min. Prod: Film Study Center of Harvard University.

African King (The). Director: Nigels Evans (G–B). 1991. 40 min. 16 mm. Prod and Dist: Nigels Evans. Diff: Bilan 1992.

African religions and ritual dances. 1971. 18 min. Prod. WCAU-TV – University Museum, Philadelphia – Olatunji Center of African Culture. Tell it like it was (Television program) IMPRINT: New York: Carousel Films.

Africans (The). Narrator: Mazrui, Ali AlAmin. 1988. Prod. WETA-TV and BBC. *I. Nature of a continent. II. Legacy of lifestyles. III. New gods. IV. Tools of exploitation. V. New conflicts. VI. In search of stability. VII. Garden of Eden in decay. VIII. Clash of cultures. IX. Global Africa.* 1986. 9 X 60 min. IMPRINT: Santa Barbara, CA: Intellimation. LOCATION: Meyer Media Center ZVC 2054 SERIES: The Annenberg/CPB Collection. WETA-TV (Television station: Washington, D.C.). British Broadcasting Corporation. Television Service. Annenberg/CPB Project.

Akum. Dir: Daniel Kamwa (Cameroon). Cameroon, 1978. 25 min. 16 mm. Prod: Daniel kamwa. Dist. Audecam.

Alter Ego: Letters from a Doctor in Africa. Director(s): Hillie Molenaar and Joop Van Wijk (Hol). 43 min. 1986.

Ambara Dama. Director: Jean Rouch. Mali 1974, 60 min. Distr. CNRS (France). 16 mm.

Angano. Angano: Nouvelles de Madagascar (Tales from Madagascar). Dir. Marie-Clémence and César Paes (Brazil). Madagascar, 1989. 64 min. Prod. Laterit (Fr) Dist: San Francisco, CA: California Newsreel.

A nous la rue. Director: Mustapha Dao (Burk. Faso). Burkina, 1987. 13 min. 16 mm. Prod: Diproci, Burkina Faso. Dist. Audecam (Paris). Diff. Bilan 1988, MMFF 1988, Fespaco 1988.

Appunti per un'Orestiade Africana / scritto e diretto da Pier Paolo Pasolini; regia di Pier Paolo Pasolini. Notes for an African Orestes. IMPRINT: [Rome?]: IDI Cinematografica, c1989 (Montauk, NY: Mystic Fire Video) 75 min. B&W.

Asante Market Women. Dir: Claudia Milne (G–B). Ghana, 1982,. Anthrop: Charlotte Boaitey. Ghana, 1982,. 52 min. Prod: Granada TV.

Assignment Africa. David Royle. 58 min. Distr. Jane Balfour, London..

Baabu Banza Réal: Mariana Hima (Niger). Niger 1984 – 20min Distrib /Prod : M. Hima/ORTN (office de Radio et Télévision du Niger)

Bagré (The). Director: Georges Savonnet. Images et sons de la recherche. CNRS, 29.

Bangusa Timbila. Director: Ron Hallis. Mozambique 1982. 30 min.Dist. Icarus, G–B, London– 30 min.

Baobab play. Dir: John Marshall. 8 min. 16 mm. Dist: DER. Tournage 1957–58; sortie : 1974

Baoulé Dir: H.Himmelheber (Germ). Ivory Coast, 1970, 13', 16 mm B&W.

Bambara of Mali (The). Dir: Dan Shafer and Tom O'Toole (USA). Mali, 1970. 10 min. silent. Dist. MINN.

Baraka. Dir: Jean-Paul Colleyn (Bel). Anthr: Victoria Ebin (USA). Senegal, 1999. Collaboration of Abib Seck. 54 min. video digital betacam. Prod: Lapsus-RTBF-Arte (Fr-Bel).

Batteries dogon. (Dogon Drums). Dir: Jean Rouch and Gilbert Rouget. Mali, 1966. 26 min. 16 mm. Prod. CNRS – EPHE, lab. Audiovisuel – CFE (Fr).

Batteurs de calebasses.(Calabash Drummers) Dir. Bernard Surugue (Fr). Niger, 1967. 30 min. 16 mm B&W. Prod. ORTSOM – CFE (Fr).

Bend in the Niger (The). Series: African Heritage (00858). Mali, Niger Nigeria, 1971. 50 min. 16 mm. Prod: Elisofon. Dist: EDUPAC (02947.

Bichorai. Burundi, 1994. Director(s): Philippe de Pierpont. Video 58 min.

Bikutsi, water blues. Dir: Jean-Marie Teno (Cameroon) prod : J.-M. TENO Dist : Les films du raphia. 93 min.

Biotope et geste de travail vezo: Technique de communication. Dir. And anthr: Bernard Koechlin.(Fr), Madagascar; 1975; 1 H 30. 16 mm. Prod :CNRS AV. Diff. Bilan 88.

Bitter Melons. Dir. John Marshall (USA), 1966. Prod:.L. and J. Marshall/DER. Dist. D.E.R.

Black Majesty. Prod. Télé ciné Ltd. Distributeur : Inter Ciné Tv.

Black Music in South Africa. (Musiques noires en Afrique du Sud). Dir: Claude Fléouter (Fr). South Africa, 1989. Video. Prod. Telescope/Fr3/La Sept (Fr). Dist. Telmondis.

Blanche-Neige en Afrique. Dir: Benoît Quersin (Bel). Zaïre, 1993. 30 min. video. Prod: Yumi-LA SEPT-ARTE (France). Dist. Yumi Productions.

Bois sacré. Dir: Edmond Agabra (Madagascar). Ivory Coast, 1975. 27 min. 16 mm. Prod: INA. Dist. Audecam.

Bongo. Les Funérailles du vieil Anaï. Mali, 1972. J. Rouch et G. Dieterlen (Fr), 45 min.

Bono Medicines. J.S. Dodds, T.J.Wallace and D.D. Ohl. Anth. D. Michael Warren. Ghana, 1981. 72 min. Distr. In U.S.A.: White Pine Films. Rev. AA. 86, 3, sept. 1984, 802.

Boran. Directors: David Mc Dougall, Ames Bue, Norman Miller. Kenya 1974.

Boran Herdsmen. Director: David MacDougall. 1974. 17 min. 16 mm. AUFS 21817,16

Boran Women. Director(s): David MacDougall. 1974. 18 min. 16 mm. AUFS 21918,16 1.

Born musicians: traditional music from the Gambia. Series Repercussions. Dir: Geoffrey Haydon and Dennis Marks (G–B). Gambia, 1984. Prod. Third Eye Production for RM Arts and Channel Four. Dist: Chicago, Ill.: Home Vision.

Borom xam xam (la route du savoir). Dir: Maurice Dorès.(France). Senegal, 1975, 62 min. 16 mm.Prod. Les films Esdès, SNC, M. Dores..

Bouche deliée (La). Olivier de Sardan. Images et sons de la recherche. CNRS.

Cameroon Brass Casting. Dir: Paul Gebauer. Cameroon, 1950. Dist. University of Pittsburgh, U.S.A.

Carnaval of Guinea Bissau (The). Dir: Tobias Engel. Anthr. Louis-Vincent Thomas. Guinea Bissau, 1982. 16 mm. 27 mn. Dist/ Prod: CNRS AV.

Chasse au lion à l'arc (La). (The Lion Hunters). Dir. Jean Rouch (Fr). Niger, 1970; 68 min; 16mm. Prod: CNRS/Films de la Pléiade. Dist. MGHT 70017,16 R

Chef de Dore (Le). Igor de Garine. Images et sons de la recherche. CNRS.

Children of the Chameleon, The (Les enfants du caméléon). Dir: Robert Gessain and Monique Gessain (Fr). Senegal, 1969. 13 minutes.Prod: Musée de l'Homme, LA 49, Paris.

Children of the River (The). Dir. Robert Gessain and Monique Gessain. Senegal, 1963. 13 min. Prod: Musée l'Homme, LA 49, Paris.

Chopi music of Mozambique; Banguza Timbila. Dir: Ron Hallis. Produced by Ron and Ophera Hallis. Mozambique 1989.56 min. Distr: El Cerito, Calif.: Flower Films & Video. Color, with B&W sequences.

Choreometrics. Dir: Alan Lomax. 1974; 40 min.

Chuck Davis, dancing through West Africa. Director(s): Gorham Kindem. Prod. Gorham Kindem and Jane Desmond. IMPRINT: New York, NY: Filmakers Library; NY: dist. by Modern Educational Video Network, 1992, ca.1986. 28 min.

Cocorico, Monsieur Poulet. Dir: Jean Rouch (Fr). 1974. 90 min.16 mm With Damoure Zika, Lam Ibrahim Dia, Tallou Mouzourane. Prod. CNRS – Centre Nigérien de Recherche en Sciences Humains (C.N.R.S.H.) – C.F.E.

Dance of the Queens in Porto Novo. (Danses des reines à Porto Novo). Dir: Gilbert Rouget. Camera: Jean Rouch. Dahomey (Bénin), 1969. 30 min. 16 mm. Prod. CNRS ER 165 – UNESCO – C.F.E.(Fr).

Dance of the spirits (The): mask styles and performances in the Upper Volta. Dir. Christopher Roy (U.S.A.). Upper Volta (Burkina Faso), 1988. 28 min. Prod. University of Iowa Video Center. Dist. University of Iowa, Video Center.

Danses Nande. Dir: Cecilia Pennacini (It). Zaire, 1989. 30 min. 16 mm. Coop. 28 decembre/University of Turino. Diff: Bilan 90.

Day of Rest. Dir and anthr: Peter Fry (G–B). Rhodesia (Zambia), 1957. B&W. 30 min Voir catalogue Royal Anthropological Institute.

Deep Hearts. Dir: Robert Gardner. Niger 1978. 53 min. Dist. Phoenix Films. Rev. American Anthropologist 82: 224–225, 1980; Weinberger, in Lucien Taylor, 21.

Discovering the Music of Africa. USA, 1967. 22 min; 16 mm Phenix 20818,16 R.

Dances of the Tshokwe in Northeastern Angola. Dir: Baumann, H. (Germ). Angola, 1930. 7 min. B&W. silent. Prod. and dist. RWU/IWF Gottingen.

Dialogue avec le sacré, les amants de l'au-delà. Dir: Stephane Kurc (Fr). Côte d'Ivoire, 1982. 26 min. 16 mm. Prod. Les Films du Sabre (Fr). Diff. Bilan 1984.

Diary of a Dry Season I: The Tyi-wara. Chronique d'une saison sèche: I.Le Tyi-wara. Dir: Jean-Paul Colleyn. Mali, 1987. 16mm, 40 min. Prod. ACME-RTBF (Bel). Diff: MMFF. 1987.

Diary of a Dry season II. Minyanka Funerals (Chronique d'une saison sèche: II. La qualité de la mort). Dir: Jean-Paul Colleyn. Mali, 1987. 16mm, 46 min. Prod. ACME-RTBF (Bel).Diff.

Diary of a Dry Season.III. Three Celebrations. (Chronique d'une saison sèche: III. Jours de fête). Dir: Jean-Paul Colleyn. Mali, 1987. 16mm, 40 min. Prod. ACME-RTBF (Bel).Diff: MMFF.

Diary of a Dry season IV. Possession (Chronique d'une saison sèche: IV. Possession). Dir: Jean-Paul Colleyn. Mali, 1987. 16mm, 54 min. Prod. ACME-RTBF (Bel).Diff: MMFF.

Dipri Festival in Gomon (Fête de Dipri à Gomon). Dir: Fernand Lafargue (Fr). Ivory Coast, 1968. 20 min. CFE (Fr). Dist. CNRS. 16 mm. Diff. Populi 69.

Disumba. Dir. Pierre Salée (Fr). Gabon, 1969. 52 min. 16 mm. B& W. Prod. ORSTOM – Musée des arts et des traditions du Gabon; topics: Gabon – Mitsogho – masks.

Djembefola Guinea. Dir: Laurent Chevallier (Fr). Guinea, 1991. 67 min. Prod: Rhéa fimls / La Sept. Diff: MMFF 1992.

Dodos (The). Dir: Sanou Kollo (Burk. Faso). Burkina Faso, 1980. 19 min. Prod: Sanou KOLLO. Dist: Audecam (Fr).

Duo has killed (Duo a tué). Dir: Guy Le Moal (fr). Upper Volta (Burkina Faso), 1970. 23 min. 16 mm. Prod. LA 221 (Fr).

Djembefola. Guinea 1991. Director(s): Laurent Chevallier. 67 min.

Dogon, Chronicle of a Passion. Director(s): Guy Seligman. 1997.

Dogon – Oracle. D. Luz (Germany). 1966. IWF.

Les enfants de la danse (= The Children of the Dance). Director(s): Genevieve Dourbon Taurelle. Author: Simha Arom. Prod. ER 165, Paris and Comité du film ethnographique. Central African Republic 1966. 11 min. film col.

Enterrement (L') du Hogon (The Burial of the Hogon). Jean Rouch, Mali 1973, 15 min. Distr. CNRS (France). 16 mm.

Faces of culture. 1994, 26 X 30 min. Producers, Ira R. Abrams, John Bishop; prod. Coast Community College District – Harcourt, Brace College Publishers [et al.]. IMPRINT: Fountain Valley, Calif.: Coast Telecourses.

From the Village of the Living People to the Village of the Dead. (Du village des vivants au village des morts). Dir: Annen, Liliane (Swiss). Anthr. Deluz, Ariane. Ivory Coast, 1983. 60 min. 16 mm. Prod. and Dist: RTSR.

Funerals in Bongo – Anai Dolo 1848–1970. Dir. Jean Rouch (Fr). Mali, 1972. 16 mm. Dist. CNRS AV.

Future Remembrance. Dir. Tobias Wendl and Nancy du Plessis (Germ).

Gelede: A Yoruba Masquerade. Dir: Peggy Harper. Nigeria, 1970, 24 min. Dist: SMI.

*Gens de la parole (Les).*Dir: Jean-Francois Schiano (Fr). Mali, 1980. 59 min. 16 mm. Prod. Films du village. Dist: Audecam (Fr).

God Gave Her a Mercedes-Benz. Dir: Katia Forbert Petersen (Can). Togo, 1992. 48 min. Prod: Sfinx Film/TV, National Film of Canada. Concept: Ingrid Nystrèom; narrator: Kossi Apkovi. Dist. N.Y.: Filmakers Library.

Gods-objects (The). From *To Live with the Gods* series. Dir: Jean-Paul Colleyn and Catherine De Clippel. Anthr: Marc Augé and Jean Pierre Dozon (Fr). Togo, 1989. 16 mm couleur. 51 min. Prod. ACME RTBF SEPT ORSTOM. Diff. Fr3, Arte, RTBF, RTSR.

Goumbé des jeunes noceurs (La). Dir. Jean Rouch (Fr.) 1965. 30 min. 16 mm et 35mm. Prod. CNRS Les films de la Pleiade. Dist. CNRS A-V.; MAE.

Grand Magal à Touba. Dir. Blaise Senghor (Senegal). Senegal, 1962. Prod: Service du cinema of Senegal. 35 mm.

Le grand masque Molo (The great Molo Mask). Director(s): Guy Le Moal. Upper Volta, 1968. 20 min. 16 mm col. Prod. L.A. 221, Paris and Comité du film ethnographique.

Griot Badye (The). (*Le griot Badye*). Dir: Jean Rouch (Fr) and Inoussa Ousseini (Niger). Niger, 1977. 15 min. 16 mm. Prod. CNRS, L.A. 221 (Fr) – INRSH (Niger).

Griot in the Circle, The (Griot dans le cercle, Le). Série Des arts et des Hommes. Dir: Ribadeau-Dumas (Fr). Senegal, 1975. 26 min. 16 mm col. Dist. Audecam.

Griots Today (The). (*Les griots d'aujourd'hui*). Séries: Des arts et des hommes. Dir: Colette Castagno (Fr). 1975. 19 min. 16 mm. Dist. Audecam.

Griottes of the Sahel : Female Keepers of the Songhay Oral Tradition in Niger. Dir. Marie Hornbein. Writer: Thomas A. Hale (USA). Niger, 1991. 12 min. Prod. Center for Instructional Design and Integrated Technologies and College of the Liberal Arts, Pennsylvania State University; WPSX-TV; dist: University Park, Penn.: PennState Audio-visual Services.

Hamar Herdsman and His Song. Dir. And anthr. Yvo Strecker (Germ). Ethiopia, 1987. 46 min. 16 mm.

Hamar Trilogy. I. Women Who Smile (The). Dir. Joanna Head. (G–B) Anthr: Jean Lydall (G–B). 50 min. 16 mm. Ethiopia, 1990. *II. Two Girls Go Hunting.* Ethiopia, 1991. 58 min.16 mm. *III. Our Way of Loving.* Ethiopia, 1994. 58 min. 16 mm.

Hampi. Dir. Jean Rouch (Fr). Niger, 1965. 25 min. 16 mm. Prod. CNRS L.A. 221 – C.F.E. (Fr).

Heal the Whole Man. Dir. Paul Robinson. Anthr. Jean Comaroff. 50 min. Dist: Chigfield Ldt. London. Rev. Heider, 1995, 121.

Hivernage a Kouroumani. Dir: Guy Le Moal (Fr). Burkina Faso, 1977. 50 min. 16 mm. Prod. and dist. CNRS A-V; Audecam.

Horendi. Dir. Jean Rouch (Fr). Niger, 1972. 90 min. 16 mm. Prod. L.A. 221, Paris. Dist. CNRS.

Hunters (The). Director(s): John Marshall. 1989. Prod. Film Study Center of the Peabody Museum of Harvard University. IMPRINT: Chicago, Ill.: Films Inc. 72 min. col.

Images of the Yacuba Country (Images du pays yacouba). Dir. Y. Colmar et C. Glise (Fr). 1963. 11 min. 16 mm. Dist. Audecam.

In Africa for a Spell. Dir. Ilan Flamer. Cameroon, 1986, 60 min. MMFF 1987.

In and out of Africa. Dir: Gabai Baaré, Ilisa Barbash, Christopher Steiner, Lucien Taylor. 1992. 59 min. Prod: Center for Visual Anthropology, University of Southern California.

Initiation. Dir: Jean Rouch. Niger, 1975. 45 min. 16 mm. Prod: CNRS, L.A. 221 (Fr).

Initiation to the dance of possession (Initiation à la danse des possédés). Dir. Jean Rouch. Niger, 1948. 25 min. 16 mm Prod. CNRS, L.A. 221 and C.F.E. Dist. Audecam; CNRS AV.

In Praise of Language. Prod. Kerygma Media International; filmed in cooperation with the Ministry of Information and Culture, the Ministry of Higher Education and Scientific Research, Yaoundé, Cameroon. IMPRINT: Dallas, TX: Summer Institute of Linguistics, [1989?].

Jaguar. Dir: Jean Rouch (Fr). Niger, 1954/67. 110 min. Prod: Films de la Pleiade. Diff. MMFF 77. Dist. DER.

Jungle Gods. Rituals in Gabon. Dir: Susumu Noro (Jap). Gabon, 1973. 52 min. 16 mm. Prod. NAV. Man TV series.

Kasarmuce. Director(s): Saddik Balewa; prod. Matthew Rose. This land is ours IMPRINT: [Los Angeles, CA]: Inter Image Video, 1991. 86 min.

Kin Kiesse. Dir: Ngangura Mweze (Congo). Zaïre, 1982. 28 min. PROD. : France 2/ Ministère des Affaires étrangères / OZRT (Office Zaïrois de Télévision) Dist. Audecam.

Kings of the Water. Director(s): Philip Haas. Prod. Fernando Trueba and the Centre Georges Pompidou. IMPRINT: New York, NY: Milestone Film & Video, c. 1991. 57 min.

Konkombe : Nigerian music. Dir. Jeremy Marre (G–B). Nigeria, 1988. 50 min. Prod. Harcourt Films. Dist: Newton, N.J.: Shanachie.

Koumen. Dir: Ludovic Segarra (Fr). Mali, 1977. 52 min. 16 mm. Prod: Ludovic Segarra Prod. Dist. Audecam. Diff. La Sept/Arte.

!Kung San: Traditional Life (The). Director(s): John Marshall. 1987. 26 min. Distr. Documentary Educational Resources (02195).

The Land of the Prophets. (Prophètes en leur pays). (Series: *To Live with the Gods*). Dir: Colleyn, Jean-Paul and Catherine De Clippel. Anthr: Marc Augé (EHESS) and Jean Pierre Dozon (ORSTOM). 16 mm couleur. 54'. Prod. ACME RTBF La SEPT, with the support of the Swiss TV and FR3. Ivory Coast.

Lassa fever / BBC-TV, WGBH; by John Foster; producer Ruth Caleb; directed by Roger Bamford. Nova (Television program). IMPRINT: New York, N.Y.: Time-Life Video: Ambrose Video Publishing Inc. [distributor], c. 1983. 57 min.

Leap across the Cattle (The). Ivo Stecker, Allemagne. Ethiopie, 1976. 43 min.

Left Handed Man of Madagascar (The). Dir. Jeremy Marre (GB), anthr. John Mack (GB). Madagascar, 1990. 50 min. 35 mm. Prod. Harcourt Films. Diff. MMFF 1990.

Living Africa, a Village Experience. Director(s): Jean Lefebvre. 1983. 34 min. Prod. Indiana University. IMPRINT: Bloomington, Ind.: Indiana University Audio-Visual Center. Study guide.

Lorang's Way. Director(s): David and Judith MacDougall. Kenya, 1977, 69 min. IMPRINT: Berkeley, Calif.: University of California Extension Media Center.

Lumumba, la mort du prophète (Lumumba, Death of a Prophet). Director(s): Raoul Peck. 1992, 69 min. Prod: Velvet Film GmbH, Berlin; Cinemamma GmbH, Zurick; IMPRINT: San Francisco, CA: California Newsreel. col. with b& w sequences.

Maasaï Manhood. Kenya 1975. 53 min. Chris Curling et Melissa Llewelyn-Davies (England). Granada TV.

Maasaï Women. Kenya 1974. 52 min. Chris Curling et Melissa Llewelyn-Davies (England). Granada TV.

Magiciens de Wanzerbee (Les). (The Wanzerbe Magicians). Director(s): Jean Rouch. Niger 1948. 33 min. 16 mm B&W. Prod. CNRS, L.A. 221 and Ministère de la Coopération.

Maîtres fous (Les). Ghana 1953 or 55, Jean Rouch (Fr) 1955. 30 min. 16 mm. Dist. DER; 33637,16.

Makumukas. Dir: Rui Duarte (Angola). Angola, 1977. 30 min. B&W. série Tempo Mumuila. Dist: Gemini Films (Fr).

Malles (Les). Samba Felix NDIAYE(Sénégal), Sénégal, 1989. 14 min; Prod : Almadies Films; Dist : Audecam

Mama Tsembu Oracle (L'oracle de Mama Tsembu). Dir: Dirk Dumon. Anthr: Renaat Devische. (BEL.), Zaïre, 1992; 50 min; Prod: BRTN

Mami Wata. The Spirit of the White Woman. Dir: Tobias Wendl and Daniela Weise. (Germ) Togo, 1988. 45 min. 16 mm. Prod: T. Wendl and D. Weise (Germ) Diff. Bilan 1989.

Mamy Water: In Search of the Water Spirits in Nigeria. Dir: Sabine Jell-Bahlsen (Germ). Nigeria, 1991(J'ai 1989 sur ma fiche). 59 min. Prod :. Sabine Jell-Bahlsen. Dist. Univ. of Calif. Ext.

Mary Akatsa, Stool of Jesus. Dir: Heike Berhend (Germ). Kenya, 1990. 55 min. 16 mm. Prod. H. Berhend. Dist: University of Bereuth (Germ). Diff. MMFF 1990. Bilan 1992.

Masks Made with Leaves (Masques de feuilles). Dir: Guy Le Moal (Fr). Upper Volta (Burkina Faso), 1961. 37 min. 16 mm. Prod. L.A. 221. CFE, Ministère de la Coopération (Fr).

Matsam. Director(s): Bernard Juillerat. Cameroon, 1969. Prod. RCP 587, Paris, Comité du film ethnographique. 30 min. 16 mm col. Distr. CNRS.

Mbira dza Vadzimu: Dambatsoko, an Old Cult Center with Muchatera and Ephrat Mujuru. Dir: Gei Zantzinger and Andrew Tracey. Rhodesia, 1978. 51 min. 16 mm. Prod: PSUPCR.

Mbira dza Vadzimu: Religion at the Family Level with Gwanzura Gwenzi. Rhodesia, 1978. 66 min. 16 mm. PSUPCR, 60286,16 S.

Mbira dza Vadzimu: Urban and Rural Ceremonies with Hakurotwi Mudhe. Rhodesia, 1978; 45 min. 16mm. Prod: PSUPCR 40310,16 S.

Memories and Dreams. Dir: Melissa Llewelyn-Davis (G–B). Kenya, 1992. 92 min.16 mm. Diff. MMFF 93, RTBF, Arte.

Memory of the Black People (The). (La mémoire du peuple noir). Dir : Claude Fléouter, Bernard Bouthier, Robert Manthoulis (FR). USA; 1979; 52 min; 16 mm; Prod: Téléscope Dist: Telmondis; Diff: Festival dei Popoli 1979.

Mille et une églises (Les). Dir: Secco Suardo Lanfranco (Italy). Ghana,1986. 47 min. Prod. Spectre-Asadin (Italia).

Mizike Mama. Dir: De Villiers, Violaine (Bel). Belgium, 1992. 52 min. 16 mm. Prod. Images Productions. Diff. RTBF; Bilan 1993.

Moi, un Noir. (I, a Black).Dir: jean Rouch (Fr) Ivory Coast, 1957. First prize Louis Delluc in 1959. Released in 1960. 80 min. 16 mm. Prod: Films de la Pléiade (Fr).

Monday's Girls. Ngozi Omwurah. Color; Sound. 1993. 49 min. Distr : CALIFORNIA NEWSREEL (03410)Series Library of African Cinema (01235).

Moon of Bogodi (The). (La Lune de Bogodi).Dir: Igor de Garine (Fr). Chad, 1965. 32 min. 16 mm. Prod. CFE. Dist. CFE/ CNRS-AV. Diff. Populi 1968.

Mukissi. Dir: Herbert Risz (Switzerland). Congo, 1974. 24 min. 16 mm. Distr. (Fr): Audecam.

Mursi (The). Dir: Woodlhead Leslie. Anthr. David Turton (G–B). Ethiopia, 1974. 58 min. 16 mm. Prod. Granada TV (Disappearing Worlds), Manchester, Great Britain.

Music of Guinea.(Série Musiques de Guinée). Dir: Yves Billon and Robert Minangoy (Fr). Guinée 1987. 55 min. 16 mm. Prod. Les films du village. Dist. Audecam. Diff. Bilan 1987.

N!ai, The Story of a !Kung Woman. Director(s): John Marshall. Botswana, 1980. 59 min. Prod. Documentary Educational Resources, inc. and Public Broadcasting Associates, inc. IMPRINT: Watertown, Mass.: Documentary Educational Resources. Study guide (56 p.)

Nawi. Uganda 1968, David and Judith MacDougall (USA). 22 min. 16 mm.

Naked spaces: Living is Round. Director(s): Trinh, T. Minh-Ha (1952-). Prod. Jean-Paul Bourdier. 1985. IMPRINT: New York: Women Make Movies. 2 hrs., 15 min.

N'doep (The). Dir: Michel Meignant (Fr). Senegal, 1972. 45 min. 16 mm. Prod. Office de documentation par le film. Dist. Audecam. Diff. Populi 1968.

N!owa T'ama: The Melon Tossing. Dir. John Marshall. 1966; 15 min.16 mm DER 21590,16.

N!um Tchai: The Ceremonial Dance of the !Kung Bushmen. Dir. John Marshall (USA). 1966; 20 min. 16 mm B&W. Prod. and dist. DER 21594,16 R.

Nitha. Dir. Leslie Woodhead. Anthr: David Turton (GB). Ethiopia, 1991. 51 min. 16 mm. Prod: Granada TV, Disappearing World Series (G–B). Diff. Bilan 1993. Rev. AA 94, 199, 1027–1028.

Noces de feu (Wedding of Fire). Director(s): Nicole echard. Niger, 1967. Prod. RCP 322, Paris et Comité du film ethnographique. 32 min. 16 mm col.

Nomades du soleil (Les). H.Brandt. Suisse, Niger, 1956. Location: Comité du film ethnographique.

Nsuyri lam (In Praise of Language). Kerygma Media International; [presented by] The Summer Institute of Linguistics. IMPRINT: Dallas, TX: Dallas Center Media, [198-?] 23 min.

Nuer (The). Dir: Hilary Harris and George Breidenbach (USA). Sudan, 1970; 74 min. 16 mm. MGHT: 70044,16 R

Nyangatoms (Les) 16 mm coul. Réal: Jean Arlaud et Philippe Sénéchal. Prod. Serddav-CNRS. Awa Film. South Western Ethiopia.

Old Woman and the Rain (The). (La vieille et la pluie). Dir. Jean-Pierre Olivier de Sardan. Niger 1972 (other sources say 74). 58 min. 16 mm col. Prod. ER 225-Sardan. Dist. CNRS AV.

Ouagadougou, Portraits of Gods (Ouagadougou, Portraits de Dieux). Dir: Benoit Lamy (Bel). Burkina faso, 1992, 50 min. prod: Lamy Film – RTBF.

Our Way of Loving. Director(s): Joanna Head, anthr.Jean Lydall. Ethiopia, 1994. 58 min.

Owu: Chidi Joins the Okoroshi Secret Society. (Owu, Geheim Initiazion). Dir. Sabine Jell-Bahlsen (Germ). Nigeria, 1994. 55 min. MMFF 1994.

Pageant of the Spirits: Mmanwu Festival '88. Anambra State Ministry of Information and Culture; producer Ikenna Ekwenugo; script writer, Lawrence Emeka. IMPRINT: Enugu: The Ministry, c. 1988. 104 min.

Pangols : the Spirit of West Africa in Music, Song and Dance. Le Ballet National du Senegal; director general, Pathe Gueye; production director, Jean Pierre Leurs; artistic director, Bouly Sonko. Spirit of West Africa in music, song and dance IMPRINT: New York, N.Y.: Columbia Artists Management, Inc., c. 1995. 50 min.

Pam Kuso Kar : Breaking Pam's Vases (Briser les poteries de Pam). Dir: jean Rouch (Fr). Niger, 1974 – 10 min. 16 mm. Systèmes de pensée en Afrique Noire, LA 221 – C.F.E. (Fr).

Pangols: The Spirit of West Africa in Music, Song and Dance Dir: Pathe Gueye. Senegal, 1995. 50 min. Dist: New York, N.Y.: Columbia Artists Management.

Papa Wemba, chef Coutumier de la rumba-rock. Dir Yvan Guypan, Michel Delire (Bel). Zaïre (Congo), 1986. 50 min. 16 mm. Prod. My films (Belgium).

Playing with the Scorpions. Dir: John Marshall. Dist: DER.; Prod: John Marshall. Tournage: 1957/58, issued in 1972.

Prince Charmant (Le). Dir: Michèle Fieloux et Jacques Lombard (Fr). Madagascar, 1991. 49 min. Beta SP. Prod. Orstom.

Profession féticheur. Dir: Georges Adou (Fr). Ivory Coast, 1981. 30 min. 16 mm. Prod. : Les Films du Sabre Distr. Audecam.

Profession revendeuse. Dir. Danielle Tessier (Fr). 1981. 55 min. 16 mm. Prod. INA. Dist. Ina, Audecam.

Reality (Réalité). Dir. Tidiane A. W. Cheikh (Sen). Senegal, 1969. 35 mm N/B. Distr: Audecam (Paris).

Reassemblage: from the firelight to the screen. Director(s): Trinh T. Minh-ha. 1982, 40 min. IMPRINT: Berkeley. Women Make Movies (Firm).

Rhythm of resistance: The Black music of South Africa. Dir: Chris Austin and Jeremy Marre. South Africa, 1988. Prod. Harcourt Films Production. Dist. Newton, NJ: Shanachie, Newton, N.J.

Rite of passage. Director(s): Laurence K. Marshall. IMPRINT: [Cambridge, Mass.]: Centre for Documentary Anthropology, 1966. 16 min.

Rouch in reverse. Director(s): Manthia Diawara; 1995?, A Formation Films production for ZDF/ARTE. IMPRINT: San Francisco, Calif.: California Newsreel.

Sacrifice and Divination in Hamar (Der Herr der Ziegen). Dir: Ivo Strecker. Ethiopia, 1984. 45 min. 16 mm. Prod: Inst. Fur Ethnologie – Mainz. Diff. Bilan 1985, MMFF 1985..

Sakoma Kuye, funerals (funérailles). Dir: Alphonse Kodini Sanou (Burkina). Burkina Faso, 1997, 26 min. Prod. and Dist. Diproci.

Sakpata. Dir. Jean Rouch and Gilbert Rouget. Dahomey (Benin), 1963. 25 min. 16 mm.

School of the Masks in the Dogon Country (The). (L'école des masques en pays dogon). François de Dieu (Fr.) 1959. 13 min. 16 mm.col and B&W. Prod: F. de DIEU. Dist: Audecam.

Senufo, The (West Africa, Upper Volta). Forging Iron. Dir: Kunz Dittmer (Germ). Upper Volta (Burkina Faso), 1955. 6:30 min. Prod. and dist. I.W.F. Göttingen.

Seven Nights and Seven Days. Dir: maurice Dorès.(Fr); 1982; 48 min. 16 mm. Dist: Filmakers Library, New York. Video.

Seven-up in South Africa. Prod. Granada Television. IMPRINT: Newton, N.J.: Shanachie Entertainment Corp., 1993. 83 mins.

Shan Kubewa. Dir: Marc Henri Piault (Fr). Nigeria, 1971. 12 min. 16 mm. Prod. CNRS, Sociétés d'Afrique occidentale et politiques de développement, ER 225, Sardan – C.F.E.

Sigui 1967 — L'enclume de Yougo. (The Anvil of Yougo). Dir: Jean Rouch. Anthr: Germaine Dieterlen (Fr). Mali, 1967. 50 min. 16 mm.

Sigui 1968: Les Danseurs de Tyougou (The Dancers of Tyougou). Dir: jean Rouch. Anthr: Germaine Dieterlen (Fr). Mali, 1968. 50 min. 16 mm. Prod: CNRS-CFE (Fr).

Sigui 1969 — La Caverne de Bongo (The Bongo Cave). Dir. Jean Rouch. Anthr. Germaine Dieterlen (Fr). Mali, 1969. 40 min. Prod. CNRS, Systèmes de pensée en Afrique Noire, L.A. 221 – CFE. (Fr).

Sigui 1970 — Les Clameurs d'Amani. (The Clamour of Amami) Dir. Jean Rouch. Anthr: Germaine Dieterlen (Fr). Mali, 1970. 35 min. Prod. CNRS, Systèmes de pensée en Afrique Noire, L.A. 221 – CFE (Fr).

Sigui 1972 — Les pagnes de Iame (The Pagnes of Iame). Dir. Jean Rouch. Anthr: Germaine Dieterlen (Fr). Mali, 1972. 50 min. 16 mm. Prod. CNRS, Systèmes de pensée en Afrique Noire, L.A 221 – C.F.E (Fr).

Sigui 1973 – 1974: L'auvent de la circoncision (The Circumcision Shelter). Dir: Jean Rouch. Anthr: Germaine Dieterlen (Fr). Mali, 1974. 15 min. 16 mm. Prod: CNRS – CFE.(Fr).

Sigui année zero.(Sigui, the Year Before). Dir. Jean Rouch Anthr: Germaine Dieterlen (Fr). Mali, 1966. 50 min. 16 mm. Prod. CNRS, L.A. 221 – C.F.E (Fr).

Sigui Synthèse (The Sixty Year Cycle of Sigui Ceremonies). Dir: Jean Rouch. Anthr. Germaine Dieterlen (Fr). 90 min. 16 mm. Prod: CNRS – CFE. (Fr).

Six Pence a Door. Black Art in South Africa. Dir. Mbele Sibiuso (South Africa).

Songs of the Adventurers. Dir. Gei Zantzinger. Lesotho, 1987. 57 min. Prod. Constant Springs Productions. Dist. USA.

Songs of the Badius. Gei Zantzinger, Cabo Verde, 1986; 30 mins. Prod:Constant Spring Production. Diff. MMFF 86.

Soro (The). Dir: Inoussa Ousseini (Niger). Série Fêtes et Traditions populaires du Niger. Niger, 1980. 18 min. 16 mm. Prod. : Inoussa OUSSEINI Dist. Audecam.

Spite. (Nkpiti, la rancune et le prophète) Dir: Jean-Paul Colleyn and Manu Bonmariage. Anthr. Marc Augé. Ivory Coast, 1984. 53 min. Prod: Acmé-Rtbf (Bel). Diff.MMFF 1984. Dist. (USA): Filmakers Library.

Spirits of Defiance. Dir: Jeremy Marre (G–B). Zaire, 1989. 49 min. 16 mm. Prod. BBC. Under the Sun (television program, Great Britain). Diff. :MMFF 89.

A Spirit Here Today. Director(s): Gei Zantzinger., 1994.

Statues also Die (The). (Statues meurent aussi [Les]). Dir: Alain Resnais and Chris Marker. France, 1953.

Strange Beliefs. Written and presented by Bruce Dakowski. IMPRINT: Princeton, N.J.: Films for the Humanities, 1990. 52 min.

Studies of Nigerian Dance No. 2. Dir. Francis Speed and Peggy Harper (USA). 1966. 16 mm. B&W. Dist: SMI.

Sur les traces du renard pâle (On the Tracks of the Pale Fox). Dir. Luc de Heusch (Bel). Anthr: L. de Heusch, G. Dieterlen, J. Rouch. Mali, 1983. 48 min. 16 mm. CBA-RTBF-FOBRA-CNRS (Bel).

Tanda Singui. Dir. Jean Rouch (Fr). Niger, 1972. 30 min. 16 mm. Prod. CNRS AV.

Tanz in der Savanne (Ox dance). Ivo Stecker, RFA, Ethiopie 1984. Ethnie: Hamar.

Théatre noir francophone videorecording / I.C.A.F. Espace francophone (Television program). IMPRINT: Iowa City, IA: PICS/The University of Iowa, [1992?]

Three tales from Senegal. Fary l'anesse, Franc, Picc mi. IMPRINT: San Francisco, Calif.: California Newsreel, [1994].

To Live with Herds. David. and Judith. MacDougall (USA). Uganda, 1972. 70 min. 16 mm. Prod. David. and Judith. MacDougall UCLA; Dist : SMI.

Togu na and cheko : Change and Continuity in the Art of Mali. Mali 1989. Prod. Staniski Media Resources for the National Museum of African Art (USA). Dist. Washington, D.C.: National Museum of African Art, Smithsonian Institution.

Tree of Iron. Directed by Peter O'Neill and Frank Muhly Jr.; Foundation for African Prehistory and Archaeology. IMPRINT: Watertown, Mass.: Documentary Educational Resources, c. 1988. 57 min.

Tribal Dances of West Africa. Dir. R. A. Piper. Ghana, 1969. 28 min. Prod. Piper 31542,16 R.

Tsé-tsé (France). Mame N'gor Faye, Papa Gora Seck, Badara Sissokho (Sénégal). 1986, 20 min. col. Prod. Varan. Bilan 87 (Pas vu).

Tug of War (The). Dir: John Marshall (USA). Dist: DER.

Turkana Conversations. Dir: David and Judith MacDougall (U.S.A.).I. Wedding Camels (The). Kenya, 1976. 109 min. 16 mm. University of California Extension Media Center 90116,16 R. II. Lorang's way. Kenya, 1977, 69 min. Prod. and Dist: UCEMC.

Turu and Bitti (Tourou et Bitti). Dir. Jean Rouch (Fr). Niger, 1967. Prod. L.A. 221 and C.E.F. (Fr) 8 min. 16 mm.

Un dieu au bord de la route. Dir. Stéphane Breton (Fr). Nigeria 1993. 52 min. Prod: LA SEPT-ARTE, Les Films d'Ici, Channel 4, CNC, FAVI (Fr). Dist: Les Films d'ici.

Under the African Skies. I. Mali. Dir. Marc Kiedel (GB). 16 mm. Prod. BBC. II. Zaire. Dir: Mike Macintyre (GB). 1989. 60 min. 16 mm. III. Zimbabwe.

Under the Black Masks (Sous les masques noirs). Dir. Marcel Griaule (Fr). 1938. 8 min. 35 mm B&W. Dist. CFE (Fr).

Under a Crescent Moon. Nigeria 1987. Phil Grasbky (Gr-B).

Under the Men's Tree. Dir: David and Judith MacDougall (USA). Uganda 1968–1974. 15 min. 16 mm. Dist. SMI.

Une pierre seule ne cale pas le chaudron. (One Single Stone Does Not Fix the Pot). Series: *Tempo Mumuila.* Dir. Rui Duarte (Angola). 1978. 40 min. 16 mm. B&W. Dist. (Fr) Gemini films.

Vieille et la pluie (La). Director(s): Jean-Pierre Olivier de Sardan. Niger, 1972. 58 min. 16 mm col. Prod. ER 225-Sardan. Distr. CNRS.

Vimbuza chilopa. Dir. Rupert Poschl & Ulrike Poschl. Malawi, 1991.55 min. 16 mm. Prod. Universitat Gottingen. Distr (USA): University Park, PA: Audio-Visual Services, The Pennsylvania State University.

Voices of the Gods. Director(s): Alfred Santana. Prod. Akuaba Production; IMPRINT: New York, N.Y.: Third World Newsreel, [1993?] 60 min. col.

Voices of the Spirits – Lobi Music from Burkina. (La Voix des génies; – Musiques Lobi du Burkina. Dir: Christophe Cognet and Stephane Jourdain (Fr). Burkina Faso, 1992. 52 min. 16 mm. Prod. La huit.Diff. Bilan 1993.

Voudouns – Die Kunst mit den geisten zu leben. Dir. Marianne Dötzer and Ursula Yanarocak (Germany). Benin, 1995. 43 min. Prod: Iris Film (Germany).

Voodoo's Daughters (Les filles du vaudou). Dir: Jean-Paul Colleyn and Catherine De Clippel (Bel). Anthr: Marc Augé and Jean Pierre Dozon (Fr). Togo, 1990. 27:11 min. 16 mm Production: Acmé RTBF La SEPT-ORSTOM.

The Ways of Nya Are Many (Les Chemins de Nya). Dir: Jean-Paul Colleyn and Jean-Jacques Péché. Mali, 1983. 16 mm couleur, 54 min. Prod. ACME RTBF CBA (Bel). Diff: MMFF 1983.

Wanzerbe. Dir. Jean Rouch (Fr). Niger, 1968. 20 min. 16mm. Prod. CNRS, L.A. 221 – C.F.E. (Fr)/

Ways of Nya Are Many (The). (Les Chemins de Nya). Jean-Paul Colleyn and Jean-Jacques Péché, Belgium, Mali 1983, 56 min. Prod. Acmé

We Jive Like This. 1992. 52 min. Dist. Filmakers Library. (New York). Diff. MMFF 1992.

Witchcraft Among the Azande. Director(s): Andre Singer. Prod. Granada television. Series Disappearing World. IMPRINT: New York, N.Y.: [Distributed by] Filmmakers Library, c1982. 52 min.

Wodaabe (The). Granada. Produced and directed by Leslie Woodhead. IMPRINT: Chicago, Ill.: Films Incorporated Video, c1990. 51 min.

Wodaabe, Herdsmen of the Sun. (Chroniques nomades. Les bergers du soleil). Director(s): Werner Herzog. 1992, 54 min. Interama. Prod: Patrick Sandrin; IMPRINT: New York, N.Y.: Interama Video Classics.

Women of Manga. Films for the Humanities and Sciences, Inc. Women of Manga (Niger). IMPRINT: Princeton, N.J.: Films for the Humanities, c. 1992. 12 min. col.

Women's Olamal. Dir. Melissa Llewelyn Davies and Chris Curling (G–B) 1984. 120 min. Kenya. Screenings. BBC, RTBF, MMFF 85.

Yaaba Soore : the Path of the Ancestors. Dir: Christopher Roy (USA). Upper Volta (Burkina faso, 1986). Prod. University of Iowa Video Center. Dist: Iowa City: University of Iowa, Video Center.

Yangba Bolo. Dir: Léonie Zowe (RCA). RCA 1985. 21 min. 16 mm. Prod. Léonie ZOWE Distr: Audecam.

Yenendi of Boukoki. Dir. Jean Rouch (Fr). Niger, 1973. 10 min. 16 mm. Prod. CNRS, L.A. 221 – C.F.E. (Fr).

Yenendi: The Men who Make Rain. (Les Hommes qui font la pluie). Dir. Jean Rouch (Fr). Niger, 1950. 35 min. 16 mm. Prod. CNRS. L.A. 221 – CFE – IFAN (Fr).

Zar (The). Dir: Ali Abdel GAYOUM (Soudan). Sudan. 1982. 25 min. 16 mm Ditr. Troy, MI: International Book Centre: Audecam.

Zulei. Director(s): Pèaivi Takala and Kristina Tuura. Prod. Proppu 1000, Finland 1990; producer Kristina Tuura. IMPRINT: Princeton, N.J.: Films for the Humanities and Sciences, c. 1992.

APPENDIX:
Sample of Earlier Dissertations and Theses on African Folklore At U.S. Institutions

See entry: **Institutional Study of African Folklore**

Indiana University

Doctoral Dissertations
Mary Klipple, *African Folktales with Foreign Analogues*, 1938.

Kenneth Clarke, *A Motif-Index of the Folktales of Culture Area V. West Africa*, 1957.

Hasan el-Shamy, *Folkloric Behavior: A Theory for the Study of the Dynamics of Traditional Culture*, 1967.

Mona Fikry, *Wa: A Case Study of Social Values and Social Tensions as Reflected in the Oral Tradition of The Wala of Norther Ghana*, 1969.

Sayid Hurreiz, *Ja' aliyyn Folktales: An Interplay of Africa, Arabian and Islamic Elements*, 1972.

Dandatti Abdulkadir, *The Role of the Oral singer in Hausa/Fulani Society: A Case Study of Namman Shata*, 1975.

John M. Vlach, *Sources of the Shotgun House: African and Carribean Antecedents for Afro-American Architecture*, 1975

Philip M. Peek, *An Ethnohistorical Study of Isoko Religious Traditions*, 1976.

Bade Ajuwon, *The Yoruba Hunters' Funeral Dirges*, 1977.

Mary Twining, *An Examination of African Retentions in the Folk Culture of the South Carolina and George Sea Islands*, 1977.

John W. Johnson, *The Epic of Sunjata: An Attempt to Define the Model for African Epic Poetry*, 1978.

Ayodele Ogundipe, *Esu Elegbara the Yoruba God of Chance and Uncertainty: A Study in Yoruba Mythology*, 1978.

Ruth M. Stone, *Communication and Interaction Processes in Music Events among the Kpelle of Liberia*, 1978.

Brunhilde Biebuyck, *Nkundo Mongo Tales: Analysis of Form and Content*, 1980.

Caroline Card, *Tuareg Music and Social Identity*, 1982.

Sharafelding Abdelsalam, *A Study of Contemporary Sudanese Muslim Saints' Legends in Socio-Cultural Contexts*, 1983.

K. Owusu Brempong, *Akan Highlife in Ghana: Songs of Cultural Transition*, 1984.

Dan Ben-Amos, *Communicative Forms and Techniques in Bini Oral Tradition*, 1966 (Postdoctoral).

Master's Theses
Hortense E. Braden, *A Classification of Incidents in Certain Collections of African Folktales*, 1926.

Ayodele Ogundipe, *An Annotated Collection of Folktales from African (Nigerian) Students in the United States*, 1966.

Hasan El-Shamy, *An Annotated Collection of Egyptian Folktales Collected from Egyptian Sailors in Brooklyn, New York*, 1964.

Agnes Nebo Bon Ballmos, *The Role of Folksongs in Liberian Society*, 1975.

Patricia O'Connell, *Bandi Oral Narratives*, 1976.

K. Owusu Brempong, *Attacking Deviations from the Norm: Insults in Bono-Ghana*, 1978.

Abdu Yahya Bichi, *An Annotated Collection of Hausa Folktales from Nigeria*, 1978.

Pamela Blakely, *Material Culture in a Hemba Village*, 1978.

Kofi Anyidoho, *Death and Burial of the Dead: Ewe Funeral Folklore*, 1983

Titus Odunlade Abodunde, *The Narrative Arts of Two Yoruba Raconteurs*, 1984

University of Wisconsin at Madison

Doctoral Dissertations
Harold Scheub, *The Ntsomi: A Xhosa Performing Arts*, 1969.

Clifford A. Hill, *A Study of Ellipsis within Karin Magana: A Hausa Tradition of Oral Arts*, 1972.

Donald J. Consetino, *Patterns in "Domesia": The Dialectics of Mende Narrative Performance*, 1976.

Sundiata Modupe Broderick, *The "Tori": Structure, Aesthetics, and Time in Krio Oral Narrative Performance*, 1977.

Mary Frost, *Inshimbi and Imilumber: Structural Expectations in Oral Imaginative Performance*, 1977.

Deidre A. La Pin, *Story, Medium, and Masque: The Idea and Art of Yoruba Storytelling*, 1977.

Emil A. Magel, *Hare and Hyena: Symbols of Honor and Shame in the Oral Narratives of the Wolof of the Senegambia*, 1977.

Ahmad A. Nasr, *Maiwurno of the Blue Nile: A Study of an Oral Biography*, 1977.

Okpure Obuke, *Isoko Narratives*, 1977.

Ernest Wendland, *Stylistic Form and Communicative Function in the Nyanja Radio Narratives of Julius Chongo*, 1979.

Kalunga S. Lutato, *The Influences of Oral Narrative Traditions on the Novels of Stephen Mpashi*, 1980.

Agnes Mukabi, *Kobebe the Oral Artist "Bury my Bones but Keep my Words,"* 1980.

Ronald Rassner, *Narrative Rhythms of Giryama Ngano*, 1980.

Obediah Mazombwe, *Umuntu: Worldview in the Structure and Theme of Nsenga Narrative Performance*, 1981.

Robert Cancel, *"Inshimi" Structure and theme: The Tabwa Oral Narrative Tradition*, 1981.

Beverly Blow Mack, *"Wakokin Mata": Hausa Women's Oral Poetry*, 1981.

Zinta Konrad, *Aspects of Trickster: Form, Style, and Meaning in Ewe Oral Narrative Performance*, 1983.

Master's Theses

Abrienna C. Schmelling, *Myth as a Reflection of Ruanda and Rundi Deism and Ethos*, 1969.

Abdulkadir Dandatti, *Modern Hausa Poetry by Sa'ad Zungur*, 1971.

Wandile Kuse, *The Traditional Praise Poetry of the Xhosa: Iziduko and Izibongo*, 1973.

David Westley, *Some Interpretations of the Significance of Variants in the Study of Oral Narrative Performances*, 1975.

University of California/Berkeley

Doctoral Dissertations

E. Ojo Arewa, *A Classification of Folktales of the Northern East African Cattle Area by Types*, 1966.

Winifred Lambrecht, *A Tale Type Index for Central Africa*, 1967.

University of Pennsylvania

Doctoral Dissertations

Peter Seitel, *Proverb and the Structure of Metaphor among the Haya of Tanzania*, 1972.

Rema N. Umeasiegbu, *Folklore in Anglophone West African Literature*, 1975.

INDEX

Note: Main encyclopedia entries are indicated by **bold** type. Figures are indicated by *italicized* type.